UNITED STATES ARMY IN WORLD WAR II

The European Theater of Operations

THE SIEGFRIED LINE CAMPAIGN

by

Charles B. MacDonald

MILITARY INSTRVCTION

CENTER OF MILITARY HISTORY

UNITED STATES ARMY

WASHINGTON, D.C., 1993

Library of Congress Catalog Card Number: 62–60001

First Printed 1963—CMH Pub 7–7–1

For sale by the Superintendent of Documents, U.S. Government Printing Office
Washington, D.C. 20402

THE SIEGFRIED LINE
CAMPAIGN

UNITED STATES ARMY IN WORLD WAR II

Stetson Conn, General Editor

Office of the Chief of Military History

Brig. Gen. James A. Norell, Chief of Military History

. . . to Those Who Served

Foreword

To many an Allied soldier and officer and to countless armchair strategists, World War II in Europe appeared near an end when in late summer of 1944 Allied armies raced across northern France, Belgium, and Luxembourg to the very gates of Germany. That this was not, in fact, the case was a painful lesson that the months of September, October, November, and December would make clear with stark emphasis.

The story of the sweep from Normandy to the German frontier has been told in the already published *Breakout and Pursuit*. The present volume relates the experiences of the First and Ninth U.S. Armies, the First Allied Airborne Army, and those American units which fought under British and Canadian command, on the northern flank of the battle front that stretched across the face of Europe from the Netherlands to the Mediterranean. The operations of the Third U.S. Army in the center, from mid-September through mid-December, have been recounted in *The Lorraine Campaign;* those of the Seventh U.S. Army on the south will be told in *The Riviera to the Rhine,* a volume in preparation.

Unlike the grand sweep of the pursuit, the breaching of the West Wall called for the most grueling kind of fighting. Huge armies waged the campaign described in this book, but the individual soldier, pitting his courage and stamina against harsh elements as well as a stubborn enemy, emerges as the moving spirit of these armies. In the agony of the Huertgen Forest, the frustration of MARKET-GARDEN, the savagery of the struggle for Aachen, the valor of the American soldier and his gallant comrades proved the indispensable ingredient of eventual victory.

Washington, D.C.
24 May 1961

JAMES A. NORELL
Brigadier General, USA
Chief of Military History

The Author

Charles B. MacDonald, a graduate of Presbyterian College, is the author of *Company Commander,*[1] an account of his experiences as an officer of the 2d Infantry Division in the European theater during World War II. He is coauthor and compiler of *Three Battles: Arnaville, Altuzzo, and Schmidt* and a contributor to *Command Decisions.* Since 1953 he has supervised the preparation of other volumes in the European and Mediterranean theater subseries of UNITED STATES ARMY IN WORLD WAR II and is currently writing another volume in the European theater subseries. In 1957 he received a Secretary of the Army Research and Study Fellowship and spent a year studying the relationship of terrain, weapons, and tactics on European battlefields. A lieutenant colonel in the Army Reserve, he holds the Purple Heart and the Silver Star.

---

[1] Washington, 1947.

Preface

Some who have written of World War II in Europe have dismissed the period between 11 September and 16 December 1944 with a paragraph or two. This has been their way of gaining space to tell of the whirlwind advances and more spectacular command decisions of other months. The fighting during September, October, November, and early December belonged to the small units and individual soldiers, the kind of warfare which is no less difficult and essential no matter how seldom it reaches the spectacular.

It is always an enriching experience to write about the American soldier—in adversity no less than in glittering triumph. Glitter and dash were conspicuously absent in most of the Siegfried Line fighting. But whatever the period may lack in sweeping accomplishment it makes up in human drama and variety of combat actions. Here is more than fighting within a fortified line. Here is the Huertgen Forest, the Roer plain, Aachen, and the largest airborne attack of the war. The period also eventually may be regarded as one of the most instructive of the entire war in Europe. A company, battalion, or regiment fighting alone and often unaided was more the rule than the exception. In nuclear war or in so-called limited war in underdeveloped areas, of which we hear so much today, this may well be the form the fighting will assume.

As befits the nature of the fighting, this volume is focused upon tactical operations at army level and below. The story of command and decision in higher headquarters is told only when it had direct bearing on the conduct of operations in those sectors under consideration. The logistics of the campaign likewise has been subordinated to the tactical narrative. It is a ground story in the sense that air operations have been included only where they had direct influence upon the ground action. It is also an American story. Although considerable attention has been paid British and Canadian operations where U.S. units were involved, this is designed only to place U.S. operations in proper perspective.

In the fullest sense of the term, this volume represents a co-operative enterprise. Reference in the footnotes and the bibliographical note can give only partial credit to the scores of officers and men who furnished information or unraveled questions of fact. Nearly every officer who held the post of division commander or above during the campaign has read the manuscript of this volume, and at least one ranking officer from each division, corps, and army headquarters has read and commented upon the manuscript.

To list all present and former officials of the Office of the Chief of Military History who by their advice and support helped make the work possible would be prohibitively lengthy. Those of my colleagues whose invaluable contributions to this co-operative enterprise can be precisely noted are as follows:

The historian who performed most of the original research in German materials and by his monographs on German actions provided in effect a companion manuscript to the author's American story was Lucian Heichler. The editor was Miss Ruth Stout, who accomplished her task with high professional skill and commendable tact and understanding. Copy editing was done by Mrs. Marion P. Grimes. The maps, which serve not only to illustrate the narrative but also to tie diverse actions together, are the work of Charles V. P. von Luttichau. Miss Ruth Phillips selected the photographs. Mrs. Lois Aldridge of the World War II Records Division, National Archives and Records Service, displayed remarkable patience in assisting the author's exploration of mountains of records from the European theater.

The contributions of Dr. Kent Roberts Greenfield, chief historian at the time this volume was prepared, cannot be so precisely stated, yet no individual contributed more. It was he who first brought the author into the field of military history and patiently and astutely guided his early efforts.

Any credit for this volume should be divided among all those who helped make it possible. On the other hand, the author alone is responsible for interpretations made and conclusions drawn, as well as for any errors of omission or commission which may appear.

Washington, D.C.   CHARLES B. MacDONALD
15 May 1961

Contents

PART ONE

Breaching the Siegfried Line

Chapter   *Page*

  I. THE ROAD TO GERMANY 3

      Allied Strategy 6

      The Shadow of Logistics 10

      The Germans in the West 14

  II. THE FIRST U.S. ARMY 20

      Weapons and Equipment 25

      The Terrain and the West Wall 28

      A Pause at the Border 36

  III. V CORPS HITS THE WEST WALL 39

      The Race for the West Wall 41

      Into Germany 43

      Battle of the Schnee Eifel 49

      Bridgehead at Wallendorf 56

      Defense of the Bridgehead 63

  IV. VII CORPS PENETRATES THE LINE 66

      German Developments 69

      The Battle of the Stolberg Corridor 71

      The Drive on the Second Band 75

      A Wall About Aachen 80

      Battle of the Monschau Corridor 82

      The Germans Strike Back 86

      The Onset of Position Warfare 90

      The First Fight in the Forest 92

Chapter		Page

V. ACTION ON THE NORTH WING 96
  Defense of the Albert 98
  From the Albert to the Border 101
  Delay in the Assault 112

PART TWO

An Airborne Carpet in the North

VI. OPERATION MARKET-GARDEN 119
  The Germans in the Netherlands 123
  Seven Days for Planning 127
  What Did the Germans Know? 134
  The Flight to the Corridor 136

VII. INVASION FROM THE SKY 140
  "a remarkably beautiful late summer day" 140
  Hell's Highway 143
  Six Bridges and a Ridge 154
  Taking the Objectives 160
  The Red Devils at Arnhem 170

VIII. DECISION ON THE GROUND 174
  Developments on D Plus 2 (19 September) 174
  The Fight for the Nijmegen Bridges 179
  First Attempts To Drive on Arnhem 184
  Keeping the Corridor Open 186
  The Outcome at Arnhem 195
  The Achievements and the Cost 198
  Release of the U.S. Divisions 201

IX. THE APPROACHES TO ANTWERP 207
  The Controversy About Antwerp 209
  The Battle of the Schelde 215
  Baptism of Fire 222
  South Beveland and Walcheren 227
  Something Beastly in Antwerp 229

X. THE PEEL MARSHES 231
  First Army Draws the Assignment 231
  The British Attempt 241
  A Spoiling Attack 242

PART THREE

The Battle of Aachen

Chapter		Page
XI.	A SET ATTACK AGAINST THE WEST WALL	251
	First Army Readjusts the Front	251
	Planning the West Wall Assault	252
	"Those infantrymen have guts!"	260
	Commitment of CCB	269
XII.	CLOSING THE CIRCLE	281
	The 18th Infantry Drives North	287
	The 30th Division Strikes South	293
	Sealing the Gap	304
XIII.	ASSAULT ON THE CITY	307
	The Assault Begins	309
	Holding the Last Link	313
	The Final Blow	314
	What Aachen Cost	317

PART FOUR

The Roer River Dams

Chapter		Page
XIV.	THE FIRST ATTACK ON SCHMIDT	323
	The Neglected Objective	324
	Objective: Schmidt	328
	To the First Clearing	331
	Toward Raffelsbrand and Vossenack	334
	Regiment Wegelein	337
XV.	THE SECOND ATTACK ON SCHMIDT	341
	Planning the Thrust	343
	Objective: Schmidt	348
	The Germans React	352
	Events Along the Trail	359
	Catastrophe in Vossenack	364
	The Kall Gorge	366
	Climax at Kommerscheidt	368
	Withdrawal Across the Kall	369
	New Missions	372

PART FIVE

The Huertgen Forest

Chapter		Page
XVI.	THE BIG PICTURE IN OCTOBER	377
	Air Support	381
	An Enigma Named Logistics	382
XVII.	NEW PLANS TO DRIVE TO THE RHINE	390
	German Resurgence and Deception	392
	First Army Plans	397
	Ninth Army Plans	400
	Operation QUEEN	403
	The Roer River Dams and the Weather	406
XVIII.	VII CORPS MAKES THE MAIN EFFORT	408
	The State of the LXXXI Corps	409
	Preliminary Bombardment	411
	The Push Northeast From Schevenhuette	415
	Armor in the Stolberg Corridor	421
	The Second Battle of the Donnerberg	424
	Another Victim of the Huertgen Forest	428
XIX.	V CORPS JOINS THE OFFENSIVE	440
	A Fourth Fight on the Bloody Plateau	440
	The Fight for Huertgen	447
	An Armored Drive on Kleinhau	448
	Broadening the Effort	451
	Bergstein and Castle Hill	457
XX.	THE FINAL FIGHT TO BREAK OUT OF THE FOREST	464
	The Fruits of Deception	464
	A Handful of Old Men	470
	Resuming the Corps Main Effort	474
	Towns, Woods, Hills, and Castles	479
	German Reinforcements	487
	Debacle at Merode	490

PART SIX

Battle of the Roer Plain

Chapter *Page*

XXI. CLEARING THE INNER WINGS OF THE ARMIES . . . 497
  The Fight North of the Boundary 499
  The Fight South of the Boundary 503
  The Push to the Inde 506
  Taking the High Ground 510

XXII. THE ROER RIVER OFFENSIVE 516
  Planning Period 516
  D Day on the Roer Plain 522
  Armor Attracts Armor 530
  Finding the Formula 534
  The Push to Gereonsweiler 540

XXIII. THE GEILENKIRCHEN SALIENT 545
  Operation CLIPPER 546
  The Jump-off 550
  An Exercise in Frustration 554

XXIV. NINTH ARMY'S FINAL PUSH TO THE ROER 558
  ". . . in effect we are there . . ." 560
  A Hundred Men of the XIII Corps 566
  A Shift in the Main Effort 571
  Gut Hasenfeld and the Sportplatz 574

PART SEVEN

Conclusion

XXV. THE APPROACHES TO DUEREN 581
  On the Plain 583
  In the Forest 587
  To the River 590

Chapter   *Page*

XXVI. OBJECTIVE: THE ROER RIVER DAMS   596
      The Neglected Objective   596
      The Second Battle of the Monschau Corridor   602
      Heartbreak Crossroads   606
      Something in the Air   611
      The VIII Corps in the Ardennes–Eifel   612

XXVII. THE END OF THE CAMPAIGN   616

Appendix

  A. TABLE OF EQUIVALENT RANKS   623

  B. RECIPIENTS OF THE DISTINGUISHED SERVICE CROSS .   624

  C. FIRST ARMY STAFF ROSTER AS OF 11 SEPTEMBER 1944 .   627

  D. NINTH ARMY STAFF ROSTER AS OF 4 OCTOBER 1944 . .   628

BIBLIOGRAPHICAL NOTE   629

GLOSSARY   633

CODE NAMES   636

BASIC MILITARY MAP SYMBOLS   637

INDEX   641

Maps

1. Drive From the Albert Canal to the West Wall, XIX Corps, 10–19
    September 1944   97
2. The Battle of the Schelde, 2 October–8 November 1944   216
3. Operations in the Peel Marshes, 29 September–3 December 1944 . . .   234
4. Encirclement of Aachen, 7–20 October 1944   282
5. The Roer River Dams   324
6. The First Attack on Schmidt, 9th Division, 6–16 October 1944 . . .   329
7. The Second Attack on Schmidt, 28th Division, 2–9 November 1944 . .   344
8. Tanks Along the Kall Trail   345
9. Objective: the Roer River Dams, V Corps, 13–15 December 1944 . .   599

Maps I–IX are in accompanying map envelope

Page

   I.   Pursuit to the Border, 26 August–11 September 1944

  II.   V Corps Hits the West Wall, 11–19 September 1944

 III.   Breaching the West Wall South of Aachen, VII Corps, 12–29 September 1944

 IV.   Invasion from the Sky, Operation MARKET-GARDEN, 17–26 September 1944

   V.   XIX Corps Breaks Through the West Wall, 2–7 October 1944

 VI.   The Huertgen Forest, 16 November–9 December 1944

 VII.   Drive to the Roer, 16 November–9 December 1944

VIII.   The Approaches to Dueren, 10–16 December 1944

 IX.   The Siegfried Line Campaign, 11 September–15 December 1944

Illustrations

The Siegfried Line . . . . Frontispiece

The Our River . . . . Facing   1

Field Marshal Sir Bernard L. Montgomery and General Dwight D. Eisenhower 9

Generalfeldmarschall Walter Model 17

Generalfeldmarschall Gerd von Rundstedt 17

Lt. Gen. Courtney H. Hodges 21

Thirteen Commanders of the Western Front 22

Captured Panzerfaust 26

Captured Nebelwerfer 28

Plan of Typical German Pillbox 32

Interior of German Pillbox 33

Maj. Gen. Leonard T. Gerow 41

Dragon's Teeth 51

Wallendorf 58

Maj. Gen. J. Lawton Collins 67

General der Panzertruppen Erich Brandenberger 69

Task Force Lovelady 73

Remains of a Pillbox 79

Maj. Gen. Charles H. Corlett 98

Fort Eben Emael 104

The Albert Canal 105

MARKET-GARDEN 117

Lt. Gen. Lewis H. Brereton 128

Generaloberst Kurt Student 141

Maj. Gen. Maxwell D. Taylor 143

		Page
101st Airborne Division Landings		144
506th Parachute Infantry		149
Maj. Gen. James M. Gavin and Lt. Gen. Sir Miles C. Dempsey		155
82d Airborne Division Drop		159
Dutch Farmer Near Zon		183
Hell's Highway		194
Nijmegen Highway Bridge		202
General der Infanterie Gustav von Zangen		218
Troops of the 104th Division		225
The Peel Marshes Area		239
Aachen	Facing	249
Practicing Flame Thrower Technique		256
Abandoned Crossing at the Wurm River		265
Rimburg Castle		268
Slag Pile and Tower Used for Observation		271
A German Boy		300
Civilian Refugees Leave Aachen		308
Rifleman in Burning Aachen		311
Col. Gerhard Wilck		317
Aachen Munster		318
View of Ruined Aachen		319
Urft Dam	Facing	321
Schwammenauel Dam		325
Kall Trail		354 and 356
Weasel		370
The Huertgen Forest	Facing	375
Lt. Gen. William H. Simpson		380
A Winter Overcoat Reaches the Front Line		387
Lt. Gen. Omar N. Bradley and Generals Eisenhower and Gerow		391
General der Panzertruppen Hasso von Manteuffel		394
A Rest Period Behind the Lines		398
155-mm. Self-Propelled Gun		415
American Tank Burning Outside Hamich		423
Struggling up a Wooded Hillside		435
V Corps Rocket Launchers		443
Engineers Repair a Road		447
A Tank Moves Through Huertgen		449
A Sea of Mud in the Huertgen Forest		456
Veterans of the Huertgen Forest		458
Medics Aid a Wounded Soldier		468
Infantry and Tanks Near Huecheln		483
The Frenzerburg		486
The Roer Plain		495
Maj. Gen. Raymond S. McLain		499

	Page
Devastated Duerwiss	504
Maj. Gen. Alvan C. Gillem, Jr.	517
Captured German Tiger Tank	531
British Flail Tank	549
British Churchill Tanks	552
British Flame-Throwing Crocodile	553
Gut Hasenfeld	575
Entrance to Swimming Pool Near *Sportplatz*	578
Winter Battlefield . . . . Facing	579
Men of the 331st Infantry Advance on Gey	588
2d Division Troops	605
Maj. Gen. Troy H. Middleton	613

Illustrations are from Department of Defense files.

The U.S. Army Center of Military History

The Center of Military History prepares and publishes histories as required by the U.S. Army. It coordinates Army historical matters, including historical properties, and supervises the Army museum system. It also maintains liaison with public and private agencies and individuals to stimulate interest and study in the field of military history. The Center is located at 1099 14th Street, N.W., Washington, D.C. 20005–3402.

Our River

PART ONE

BREACHING THE SIEGFRIED LINE

CHAPTER I

The Road to Germany

The shadows were growing long as five men from the Second Platoon, Troop B, 85th Cavalry Reconnaissance Squadron, 5th U.S. Armored Division, reached the west bank of the Our River. To cross and claim credit as the first patrol on German soil, their commander had told them, they would have to hurry.

Though the bridge over the Our had been demolished, the water was shallow enough for the men to wade across. On the far bank they climbed a hill to a cluster of farm buildings. Nearby they could see some nineteen or twenty concrete pillboxes. Around one somebody had built a shed for chickens.

The men made only a hasty inspection before starting back. An hour later the report of their crossing was on the way up the chain of command. At 1805 on 11 September 1944, the report read, a patrol led by S. Sgt. Warner W. Holzinger crossed into Germany near the village of Stalzemburg, a few miles northeast of Vianden, Luxembourg.[1]

Sergeant Holzinger's patrol preceded others only by a matter of hours. In early evening, a reinforced company of the 109th Infantry, 28th Division, crossed the

Our on a bridge between Weiswampach, in the northern tip of Luxembourg, and the German village of Sevenig. Almost coincidentally, southeast of St. Vith, Belgium, a patrol from the 22d Infantry, 4th Division, also crossed the Our near the village of Hemmeres. Men of this patrol spoke to civilians and, to provide proof of their crossing, procured a German cap, some currency, and a packet of soil.[2]

The armored and infantry divisions which furnished these patrols were units of the V Corps of the First U.S. Army. Their presence along the German border marked the start of a new phase in the execution of a directive that the Combined Chiefs of Staff of the Allied Powers had given earlier in World War II to General Dwight D. Eisenhower, Supreme Allied Commander in Europe. General Eisenhower was to "undertake operations aimed at the heart of Germany and the destruction of her armed forces."[3]

As the First Army's patrols crossed the border, three Allied army groups and seven armies were deployed in a grand arc stretching from the North Sea to Switzerland. On the Allied left wing was the 21 Army Group under Field Marshal Sir

---

[1] Other members of the patrol: Cpl. Ralph F. Diven, T/5 Coy T. Locke, Pfc. George F. McNeal, and a French interpreter, a Lieutenant DeLille. V Corps G–3 Jnl, 11 Sep 44; Combat Interv with Lt. L. L. Vipond, Ex O, Troop B, 85th Rcn Sq.

[2] 28th Div G–3 Jnl, 11 Sep 44; 4th Div AAR, Sep 44. A patrol from the 28th Division's 110th Infantry crossed a short while later near the village of Harspelt.

[3] For details, see Forrest C. Pogue, *The Supreme Command*, UNITED STATES ARMY IN WORLD WAR II (Washington, 1954), pp. 49–55.

Bernard L. Montgomery, consisting of the First Canadian and Second British Armies. (*Map I*)* In the center was the 12th Army Group under Lt. Gen. Omar N. Bradley, with the First and Third U.S. Armies and the new Ninth U.S. Army, which had become operational on 5 September and was reducing the Breton coastal fortress of Brest, far behind the current front lines. On the right wing were the 1st French and Seventh U.S. Armies, destined to become on 15 September the 6th Army Group under Lt. Gen. Jacob L. Devers.[4]

The crossing of the German border on 11 September was another strong draught contributing to a heady optimism with which Allied troops and their commanders were reeling. Operating along the Channel coast, the Canadians already had captured Dieppe and the 1st British Corps of the First Canadian Army was putting the finishing touches to conquest of Le Havre. The Second British Army had overrun Brussels and Antwerp, the latter with its deepwater port facilities almost intact.[5] The First Army had taken Liège and the city of Luxembourg. The Third Army in northeastern France was building up along the Moselle River and already had a bridgehead near the Lorraine city of

Metz.[6] Having successfully landed in southern France on 15 August, the two armies in the south soon would become part of a single western front. During 11 September a patrol from the Third Army made contact with French units from the south near Dijon.

Most of the fighting immediately preceding the crossing of the German border had been pursuit warfare. The Germans were on the run. Except for the Third Army, which had been handicapped for five days while bearing the brunt of a general transportation shortage and gasoline drought, the Allied drive had reached its zenith during the period 1–11 September. During these eleven days the British had traveled approximately 250 miles, from the Seine River to the Belgian-Dutch border. The First U.S. Army had taken time out near Mons, Belgium, to bag about 25,000 Germans in a giant pocket and make an abrupt change in direction, but still had covered approximately 200 miles. By 11 September the Allies had reached a general line which pre-D-Day planners had expected would be gained about D plus 330 (2 May 1945). The advance thus was far ahead of schedule, some 233 days.[7]

A most encouraging feature of Allied success was that casualties had been lighter than expected. Exclusive of the forces in southern France, Allied casualties from 6 June to 11 September were 39,961 killed, 164,466 wounded, and 20,142

---

* Maps numbered in Roman are placed in inverse order inside the back cover.

[4] For the story of the creation of the 6th Army Group, see Robert Ross Smith, The Riviera to the Rhine, a volume in preparation for the series UNITED STATES ARMY IN WORLD WAR II.

[5] Accounts of British and Canadian operations may be found in: Field Marshal the Viscount Montgomery of Alamein, *Normandy to the Baltic* (Boston: Houghton Mifflin Company, 1948); Charles P. Stacey, *The Canadian Army, 1939–1945* (Ottawa: E. Cloutier, King's Printer, 1948); and Maj. Gen. Sir Francis de Guingand, *Operation Victory* (New York: Charles Scribner's Sons, 1947).

[6] For Third Army operations in Lorraine, see H. M. Cole, *The Lorraine Campaign,* UNITED STATES ARMY IN WORLD WAR II (Washington, 1950).

[7] Maps in Post NEPTUNE Planning Forecast 1. 27 May 44, SHAEF SGS 381 Post OVERLORD Planning, I. The planners expected the surrender about D plus 360.

missing, a total of 224,569, or a little more than 10 percent of the total strength committed.[8] Since the landings in Normandy, the Germans had lost approximately 300,000 men, while another 200,000 were penned in various redoubts.

Despite an acute shortage of ports, Allied build-up in men and matériel had been swift. By the afternoon of 11 September a cumulative total of 2,168,307 men and 460,745 vehicles had landed in Normandy.[9] General Eisenhower, who had assumed direct operational command in the field on 1 September, controlled on the Continent 26 infantry divisions (including 1 airborne division) and 13 armored divisions (not including a number of cavalry groups and separate tank battalions). Of this total the British and Canadians had furnished 16 divisions (including 1 Polish armored division), while the Americans had provided 23 (including 1 French armored division).[10] As soon as General Eisenhower assumed direct command of the forces in southern France, he would gain 3 American infantry divisions (not including an airborne task force of approximately divisional size), 5 French infantry divisions, and 2 French armored divisions. The total for the Western Front would then be 35 infantry and 14 armored divisions. In addition, 2 U.S. and 2 British airborne divisions, 1 Polish airborne brigade, and a British airportable infantry division were in Supreme Headquarters reserve.

General Eisenhower's 49 divisions were opposed, theoretically, by about 48 infantry and 15 panzer-type divisions, plus several panzer brigades. As noted by Generalfeldmarschall Gerd von Rundstedt,

who on 5 September began a second tour as *Oberbefehlshaber West* (Commander in Chief West), these forces actually existed only on paper.[11] While Allied units were close to full strength, hardly a German division was. Most had incurred severe losses in both men and equipment, and many were badly demoralized from constant defeat in the field. The equivalent of five divisions had been corralled in the Channel Islands and the coastal "fortresses." Rundstedt estimated that his forces were equivalent to about half the number of Allied divisions. Allied superiority in guns was at least 2½ to 1 and in tanks approximately 20 to 1.[12]

The disparity between forces was less striking on the ground than in the air. The Allies had three tactical air forces: the IX and XIX Tactical Air Commands (both under the Ninth Air Force) and the 2d Tactical Air Force (British). Operating from bases in the United Kingdom and France were 5,059 American bombers, 3,728 American fighters, 5,104 combat aircraft of the Royal Air Force, and additional hundreds of miscellaneous types for reconnaissance, liaison, and transport.[13]

---

[8] SHAEF G–3 War Room Summary 102.
[9] SHAEF G–3 War Room Summary 99.
[10] *Ibid.*

[11] The German term *Oberbefehlshaber West* means either the Commander in Chief West or his headquarters. In this volume, the term Commander in Chief West will be used to refer to the person holding the title *Oberbefehlshaber West*, while the abbreviated form *OB WEST* will refer to his headquarters.
[12] *OB WEST*, A Study in Command, pp. 176, 180. This manuscript, by Generalleutnant Bodo Zimmermann (G–3, *OB WEST*) and others, was written under the auspices of the Department of the Army Historical Division in 1946 and is filed in OCMH. Matériel estimates are from Cole, *The Lorraine Campaign*, p. 3.
[13] AAF Staff Control Aircraft Inventory, Combined Allied vs. Axis Air Strength Rpts, 1 Sep 44. All U.S. air records used in this volume are located at the Air University Library, Maxwell Air Force Base, Montgomery, Ala.

The enemy's one tactical air force in the West, the *Third Air Force* (*Luftflotte 3*), had only 573 serviceable aircraft of all types. In the entire Luftwaffe the Germans had only 4,507 serviceable planes, and most of these had to be retained within Germany to contest Allied strategic bombers.[14]

The ground front was too fluid during the early days of September for Field Marshal von Rundstedt to accomplish much toward forming one of the new lines which Adolf Hitler designated with febrile frequency. Nevertheless, by 11 September Rundstedt and his subordinates were making honest efforts to conform to the latest decree, to man a new line that was to be held "under any conditions." The line ran from the Belgian coast, including the banks of the Schelde estuary—which might be employed to deny use of Antwerp even though the port had been lost— southeastward along the Dutch-Belgian border to the West Wall (the Siegfried Line) and along the West Wall to the western boundaries of Lorraine and Alsace.[15]

For all the catastrophic nature of the retreat from France, Rundstedt's order of battle at army and army group levels looked on 11 September much as it had before the Allied invasion. On the right wing, along the Dutch border and within the northern half of the West Wall opposite the 21 Army Group and the First U.S. Army, was *Army Group B* under Generalfeldmarschall Walter Model. Model, whom Rundstedt had replaced as Commander in Chief West, controlled the

Fifteenth, First Parachute, and *Seventh Armies.* On the left wing was *Army Group G* (Generaloberst Johannes Blaskowitz), composed of the *First Army,* which confronted the Third U.S. Army, and the *Nineteenth Army,* which faced what was to become the 6th Army Group. What was left of the *Fifth Panzer Army* was assembling behind the German border. The Germans had a sound framework upon which to hang reinforcements—*if* reinforcements could be found.[16]

Allied Strategy

Allied strategy, as expressed in pre-D-Day planning at Supreme Headquarters, Allied Expeditionary Force (SHAEF), looked toward the ultimate objective of Berlin; but on the way the Allies wanted an economic objective, which, if captured, "would rapidly starve Germany of the means to continue the war." This was the Ruhr industrial area, the loss of which, together with Belgium and Holland, would deprive Germany of 65 percent of its production of crude steel and 56 percent of its coal.[17]

The widespread deployment of the Allied armies on 11 September reflected General Eisenhower's pre-D-Day decision to go after the Ruhr and Berlin on a broad front. Later to become known as the "broad front policy," this concept was not appreciably different from the time-tested military strategy of multiple parallel columns.

---

[14] German figures furnished from Luftwaffe records by the British Historical Section, as cited by Cole, *The Lorraine Campaign,* p. 4.

[15] *OB WEST,* A Study in Command, pp. 175–78.

[16] Opns Maps (1 : 1,000,000) dtd 11 Sep 44, *Operationskarte West.* See also *OB WEST,* A Study in Command, p. 177.

[17] SHAEF Planning Staff draft of Post NEPTUNE Courses of Action After Capture of the Lodgment Area, Main Objectives and Axis of Advance, I, 3 May 44, SHAEF SGS 381, I. An exhaustive study of Allied strategy may be found in Pogue, *The Supreme Command.*

In considering which routes of advance were best, SHAEF planners had seriously studied four: (1) the plain of Flanders; (2) the Maubeuge–Liège–Aachen axis north of the Ardennes; (3) the Ardennes; and (4) the Metz–Kaiserslautern gap.[18] After deliberation, they had ruled out Flanders, because of too many water obstacles, and the Ardennes, because of rugged terrain and limited communications. The other two avenues merited greater attention.[19]

The northern route via Maubeuge–Liège–Aachen (the Aachen Gap) obviously leads more directly to the Ruhr. The terrain is relatively open, particularly beyond Aachen on the Cologne plain. Although an advance via Metz–Kaiserslautern leads also to another industrial prize, the Saar Basin with its mines and smelters, the terrain in both Lorraine and the Saar is broken. Advance to the Ruhr after reaching the Rhine along this route is canalized up the narrow Rhine valley. Although both avenues had exercised attraction in modern and earlier wars, the northern route had commanded almost obligatory attention since the northward shift of German industry about 1870 and since the neutrality of Belgium and the Netherlands ceased to command respect. In terms peculiar to the war at hand, the northern route offered promising intermediate objectives: a chance to meet and conquer major German forces expected to be concentrated in defense of the Ruhr; elimination of the enemy's strategic reserve; access to the best air-

fields between the Seine and Germany; a secure left flank resting on the coast; proximity to air bases in England; and access to the Channel ports, including Antwerp, lack of which would severely limit the forces that could be maintained.[20]

Before the invasion, General Eisenhower had concurred in the planners' recommendation that the main advance be directed toward the northeast "with the object of striking directly at the Ruhr by the route north of the Ardennes." He also had agreed that a "subsidiary axis" be maintained south of the Ardennes to provide a threat to Metz and the Saar. This was understood to mean an "advance on a broad front North and South of the Ardennes," which would avoid committing the Allied forces irretrievably to one or the other of the comparatively narrow gaps.[21] General Eisenhower looked to Field Marshal Montgomery's 21 Army Group to make the main thrust in the north; the Americans under General Bradley, the subsidiary effort in the south.

When the breakout from the Normandy beachhead had turned into wholesale pursuit, Allied commanders had been confronted with glittering opportunities at every turn. Yet the whirlwind advance also introduced logistical complications of a distressing complexity. Though supplies already ashore were for the moment adequate, the explosive advance so stretched lines of communication that a transportation system geared for slower, more methodical moves proved totally unequal to the prodigious tasks suddenly thrust upon it. Having neither the strength nor the transport to exploit all the tempting possibilities, the Supreme

---

[18] Two others, the Belfort and Saverne gaps, were too far south to afford any appreciable threat to the Ruhr or Berlin.

[19] SHAEF Planning Staff draft, 3 May 44; see also SHAEF Planning Staff draft, 30 May 44. Both in SHAEF SGS 381, I.

[20] Ibid.

[21] Ibid.

Commander had to face the fact that some kind of deviation from the original concept of a broad front advance had to be made. Out of this undeniable reality emerged decisions which were to affect the conduct of operations in the fall of 1944 throughout the course of the Siegfried Line Campaign.

Meeting with Bradley and Montgomery on 23 August, General Eisenhower remarked the likelihood that the logistical situation soon might crimp Allied operations severely. The crux of the problem, as General Eisenhower saw it, was in the ports. To provide a solid base for sustained operations, an invasion force must have ports; yet the Allies at this point had only the Normandy beaches and Cherbourg. Perhaps it would be best, while the momentum of the advance continued, to forego some of the glamorous tactical opportunities in favor of more utilitarian objectives.

Between the Seine River and the Pas de Calais, on a direct route north toward the Channel ports and Antwerp, sat the enemy's *Fifteenth Army,* the only sizable reserve the Germans still possessed in northern France. Were the 21 Army Group to attack northward through the plain of Flanders, this reserve might be eliminated even as the Channel ports were captured, whereupon, with a firm base assured, Montgomery might reorient his drive more specifically in keeping with the direction SHAEF planners had intended. In the process, the other intermediate objectives along the northern route, like the airfields and the flying bomb launching sites, also might be attained. In the meantime, the Americans might be establishing their own firm base by opening the Brittany ports and might be preparing to continue their subsidiary thrust.

Though Field Marshal Montgomery proved receptive to General Eisenhower's plan, he insisted on having an entire American army moving along his right flank. Since General Eisenhower already intended reinforcing the British with the airborne troops at his disposal, he thought Montgomery overcautious; but in order to assure success, he acceded to the request. The location of the First U.S. Army dictated its selection for the supporting role, while the Third Army was to clear the Brittany ports and amass supplies for an advance eastward through Metz.[22]

As developed in detail by Field Marshal Montgomery, the First Army's mission was to support the British advance by establishing forces in the area of Brussels–Maastricht–Liège–Namur–Charleroi. At the suggestion of General Bradley the boundary between the two army groups was adjusted so that Brussels was allotted to the British, the boundary then swinging distinctly northeast at Brussels. This adjustment would eliminate the possibility that the British might be pinched out at Antwerp.[23]

In essence, the decision emerging from the 23 August meeting resulted in a temporary shift of the main effort from the Maubeuge–Liège–Aachen axis to the plain of Flanders, a route that preinvasion planners had blackballed as a primary axis into Germany. Yet the shift was more

[22] Eisenhower to Gen George C. Marshall, CPA 90235, 22 Aug 44, SHAEF cable log; Ltr, Eisenhower to Montgomery, 24 Aug 44, SHAEF SGS 381, I; Eisenhower to Marshall, 5 Sep 44, Pogue files.
[23] Montgomery to army comdrs, M–520, 26 Aug 44, SHAEF SGS 381, I; 12th A Gp Ltr of Instrs 6, 25 Aug 44, 12th A Gp Rpt of Opns, V, 85–87; Ltr, Bradley to Montgomery, 26 Aug 44, 12th A Gp 371.3 Military Objectives, I; Montgomery, *Normandy to the Baltic,* p. 200.

FIELD MARSHAL MONTGOMERY AND GENERAL EISENHOWER *during an informal discussion at Montgomery's headquarters in France early in September 1944.*

tactical than strategic in that it was made for the purpose of gaining intermediate objectives vital to a final offensive along the lines of the original strategic concept. It could be argued that it involved no real shift of any kind because of the broad interpretation that had come to be accorded the route "north of the Ardennes."

The most salient change from original planning was the new location of the First Army. General Eisenhower had intended to employ both the First and Third Armies south of the Ardennes. Though both Eisenhower and Bradley were to try to get at least parts of the two armies moving together again, the fact was that through the course of the Siegfried Line Campaign the First and Third Armies were to be separated by the barrier of the Ardennes. The First Army—not the British—was to attack through the preferred Aachen Gap and eventually was to be designated the Allied main effort.

More than the shift of the First Army, the fact emerging from the August discussions which upset General Bradley was that the priority assigned the northern thrust meant severe restrictions on supplies for the Third Army. Both Bradley and the commander of the Third Army, Lt. Gen. George S. Patton, Jr., reacted to the decision as if Montgomery had stolen their birthrights.[24] General Bradley wanted instead a "modified double thrust," one that would achieve the goals in the north with the help of only one American corps, while the rest of the First Army joined the Third on the southern route.[25] Patton, for his part, thought his army by itself could get across the German border in record time if properly supplied. Even after General Patton had felt the stringent logistical pinch which held him immobile for five days along the Meuse, he still had visions of one thrust taking the Third Army across the Rhine River.[26]

General Eisenhower had no intention of abandoning the subsidiary thrust. Revelation of this fact prompted Field Marshal Montgomery to voice an objection as

[24] Omar N. Bradley, *A Soldier's Story* (New York: Henry Holt and Company, 1951), pp. 400–403; George S. Patton, Jr., *War As I Knew It* (Boston: Houghton Mifflin Company, 1947), pp. 114, 117, 132.

[25] Bradley, *A Soldier's Story*, p. 399.

[26] Patton, *War As I Knew It*, pp. 114, 117, 132. As late as 19 October, General Patton felt that, given proper maintenance and supplies, he could reach the Siegfried Line in two days and "stand a high probability of penetrating it and thus be in position to make a rapid advance to the Rhine." Patton to Bradley, 19 Oct 44, 12th A Gp 371.3 Military Objectives, II.

strong or stronger than those registered by Bradley and Patton. The crux of Montgomery's argument was that the thrust toward Antwerp should not be looked upon as a limited objective operation but should be broadened into "one powerful full-blooded thrust across the Rhine and into the heart of Germany, backed by the whole of the resources of the Allied Armies . . . ." This would involve relegating some sectors of the Allied front to a "purely static role." [27]

Both Montgomery's and Patton's "one-thrust" theories probably will attract polemic disciples through the years, despite the damage done these theories by German tenacity in later stages of the war. Yet even as Montgomery and Patton promoted their ideas, planners at SHAEF labeled them castles of theory built upon sand. A drive by General Patton's army alone was logistically and tactically feasible, the planners noted, only so far as the Rhine and thus was unlikely to force any decisive result. One thrust in the north, the planners admitted, might succeed in capturing the Ruhr and even in reaching Berlin; but it was neither tactically nor logistically feasible unless certain conditions were met. One was that by September all Allied armies would have reached the Rhine; another, that by the same date Antwerp would have been receiving at least 1,500 tons of supply per day. Neither premise had shown any immediate signs of becoming a reality.[28]

As an army commander, General Patton had few channels for making his voice heard on the subject after the first refusal. Not so Field Marshal Montgomery, who was both an army group commander and the top military representative in the theater of one of the major Allies. In one form or another, Montgomery was to raise the issue repeatedly, though the Siegfried Line Campaign was to open in an atmosphere of accord because of a temporary settlement reached on 10 September. Meeting Montgomery at Brussels, General Eisenhower refused to accept the view that the field marshal's priority should prevail to the exclusion of all other operations. Nevertheless, he agreed to a temporary delay in clearing the seaward approaches to Antwerp, a project which he felt should have chief emphasis, while Montgomery extended his northern thrust to gain a bridgehead across the Neder Rijn (Lower Rhine) in the Netherlands. Although Montgomery had failed to gain unqualified support for his northern thrust, his army group still retained the role of Allied main effort.[29]

The Shadow of Logistics

The fervor with which Allied commanders contended for supplies stemmed directly from the critical nature of the logistical situation. Perhaps the most dramatic and widely publicized result of the supply crisis was the enforced halt of the entire Third Army when it ran out of fuel along the Meuse River from 1 to 6 September. Yet the units in the north

---

[27] Montgomery, *Normandy to the Baltic*, pp. 193, 196; see also Ltr, Montgomery to Eisenhower, M-160, 4 Sep 44, SHAEF SGS 381, I.

[28] An exhaustive discussion of the subject is found in Roland G. Ruppenthal, *Logistical Support of the Armies,* Vol. II, UNITED STATES ARMY IN WORLD WAR II (Washington, 1959).

[29] Notes on mtg at Brussels, 10 Sep 44, by Air Chief Marshal Sir Arthur W. Tedder, OCMH; Dwight D. Eisenhower, *Crusade in Europe* (New York: Doubleday and Company, 1948), pp. 306–07.

had their problems as well, despite the priority assigned the northern thrust. A corps of the Second British Army, for example, was halted for two weeks west of the Seine so that its transport could help supply the rest of the army. A corps of the First Army also had to halt for four days in Belgium for want of gasoline.

It was not shortage of supplies on the Continent that plagued the Allies. Build-up of supplies in Normandy had exceeded expectations. It was shortage of trans-portation, a problem created and intensi-fied mainly by the sporadic and explosive nature of the tactical advance.[30]

For all the lack of deepwater port facilities and a steady, orderly advance, supply echelons could have built a sound logistical structure had they been afforded a reasonable pause after the breakout from the confined Normandy beachhead. That was how the invasion had been planned: a pause at the Seine River for regrouping and amassing supplies. But the planners had not foreseen the nature of the German defeat in France. Every path strewn with gems of tactical oppor-tunity, Allied field commanders had felt compelled to urge their armies to go faster, faster. They had leaped the Seine briskly and kept going.

While the timetable prepared by pre-invasion planners was admittedly con-jectural, it was nevertheless the only basis upon which those charged with delivering supplies could estimate the men, matériel, and transport needed. In gaining the D plus 330 line by D plus 97 (11 Septem-ber), the armies had covered almost the

entire distance in the last 48 days. The kind of logistical system that planners had expected would be developed over 233 days obviously could not be created in 48. Furthermore, the preinvasion planners had stipulated that in early September twelve U.S. divisions could be supported as far east as the Seine; in actuality, sixteen U.S. divisions were more than 200 miles beyond the Seine in early September and several others were fighting in Brittany. The fact that these divisions could be maintained in any fashion under these circumstances came under the heading of a near miracle, for the exploitation of the tactical situa-tion had produced a ruthless disregard for an orderly development of a sound com-munications zone.

During the period of confinement in Normandy, the inadequacy of the Norman rail net had not been felt too keenly. Distances were short and trucking proved equal to the demands placed upon it. When the armies spurted eastward, they uncovered a more extensive rail network, but it had been damaged severely by Allied bombing and French sabotage. Trucking companies had to carry their loads farther and farther forward. Despite extensive improvisation and emergency supply, de-liveries to the armies during the last few days of August dwindled to a few thou-sand tons.

At the end of August the First Army estimated its daily average tonnage re-quirement as 5,500 tons. Even after General Eisenhower vested supply priority in the First Army and halted the Third Army, only 2,225 tons daily reached the First Army.[31] In addition to immobiliz-ing an entire corps for four days for want

---

[30] Unless otherwise noted, this study of supply is based upon Roland G. Ruppenthal, *Logistical Support of the Armies,* Vol. I, UNITED STATES ARMY IN WORLD WAR II (Wash-ington, 1953), and Vol. II.

[31] By using its own transportation, the army raised this to 3,000 tons.

of gasoline, the First Army had to halt the armored divisions of the two advancing corps for periods as long as twenty-four hours.[32] When recorded receipts took a turn for the better on 5 September to reach 7,000 tons, General Bradley altered the previous allocation to split the available tonnage equally between his two armies, providing each with 3,500 tons. That was how the Third Army got moving again.

The day the new allocation went into effect the First Army claimed that the Communications Zone had failed by 1,900 tons to meet the 3,500 figure. This kind of thing was all the more serious because the army's meager reserves had long since been exhausted. By the end of August 90 to 95 percent of all supplies on the Continent lay in depots near the beaches.

There were two solutions: (1) Pause while the Communications Zone moved depots forward. Doing this would upset the momentum of a victorious advance and afford the enemy additional time to put the West Wall into shape. (2) Get new ports closer to the front. This Hitler himself had circumvented, over the objections of his generals, by designating the ports as "fortresses" and directing that they be held to the last, even though valuable troops would be sacrificed in the process.

The alternative to these solutions was a variation of the first. The 12th Army Group stated it as early as 27 August. "It is contemplated," the army group noted, "that the Armies will go as far as practicable and then wait until the supply system in rear will permit further advance."[33] The pursuit would come to

no dramatic end. It would sputter out.

In an effort to keep the armies moving, commanders from divisional units all the way back to the Communications Zone took extraordinary measures. That the advance carried as far as it did was attributable in no small part to these improvisations.

Though rail reconstruction was pushed with vigor, it hardly could have been expected to keep pace with the violent spurts of the combat formations. Nevertheless, by 30 August, railroad engineers and French civilians working round the clock had pushed two main routes as far as Paris. The network beyond the Seine was less severely crippled; but to get supplies through the damaged yards of Paris and beyond the destroyed rail bridges of the Seine, they had to be unloaded and trucked through the city. In the First Army area, reconstruction crews quickly opened a line from Paris northeast through Soissons and by 18 September were to push it to a point just west of Liège.[34]

For all the accomplishments under this program, motor transport had to assume the principal burden, even though production difficulties in the United States had imposed limitations on trucks long before D-Day. When confronted with the engulfing demands of the pursuit, available motor transport could not deliver even daily maintenance, much less provide stocks for intermediate or advance depots. To make the most of available facilities, commanders decided on 23 August to establish a special truck route, the Red Ball Express. By closing off civilian traffic on two parallel routes to points

---

[32] FUSA AAR, Sep 44.

[33] 12th A Gp Admin Instrs 13, 27 Aug 44, FUSA AAR, Sep 44.

[34] FUSA Rpt of Opns, 1 Aug 44–22 Feb 45, p. 62.

southwest of Paris and by pushing the trucks and their drivers to the limit, they delivered 89,939 tons in eight days between 25 August and 6 September. Beginning on 25 August with 67 truck companies, the Red Ball attained peak capacity on 29 August when 132 companies, using 5,939 trucks, moved 12,342 tons of supplies. The Red Ball was to continue operation for another eleven weeks and was to serve as the prototype for several less ambitious express services.

The armies themselves took over much of the hauling. On 22 August General Bradley told both his armies to leave their heavy artillery west of the Seine and use the artillery trucks for transporting supplies. Because Communications Zone depots were far in the rear, trucks of the First Army often had to make round trips totaling 300 miles or more. On a few occasions truck companies searched for supplies all the way back to the invasion beaches. The First Army quartermaster scouted for advancing gasoline trains from a cub airplane. The First Army had 43 Quartermaster truck companies, which were supplemented by 10 to 20 provisional companies made up from artillery and antiaircraft units. The infantry divisions advanced either on foot or by shuttling in trucks borrowed from their organic artillery and attached antiaircraft.[35]

Though emergency air supply proved highly valuable, tonnage delivered by this method fell short of 1,000 tons per day. Most of this went to the Third Army. The vagaries of weather, lack of serviceable Continental airfields, and the need to withhold planes for their primary mission of training for and executing tactical airborne operations imposed severe restrictions on the airlift program. Another restriction developed when the city of Paris was liberated far ahead of schedule. Responsible for providing 1,500 tons of supplies daily for civil relief in the capital, the 12th Army Group had to obtain 500 tons of this from the airlift.

Major efforts were made to speed construction of fuel pipelines, but this task was inherently slow and was retarded further by the limitations on moving pipe imposed by the transportation shortage. While construction sometimes reached a record 30 to 40 miles a day, the combat troops were going even faster. During the early days of September the terminus of the pipeline was some 170 miles southwest of Paris.

Combat commanders urged strictest supply economy.[36] All units rationed gasoline. Food was of emergency types, mostly C and K rations, supplemented in the First Army by approximately 75,000 captured rations that added a new monotony of canned fish to the diet. The Third Army captured huge quantities of German beef, not to mention the exciting acquisition of great stores of champagne. Cigarettes became so scarce in the First Army that the soldiers accepted even the mostly ersatz German cigarettes with relish.

Gasoline was the main problem, not because enough had not reached the Continent but because it could not be moved forward overnight and because worn-out vehicles used inordinate amounts. Ammunition presented no great problem during the mobile warfare of the pursuit, but it would, should a pitched battle develop at the gates of the West Wall. With all available transport used for daily

---

[35] FUSA AAR, Sep 44.

[36] See, for example, FUSA AAR, Sep 44.

maintenance and none for reserve stocks, what would happen should the armies run into intense fighting? How to equip the men with heavier clothing now that winter was coming on? How to replace the worn-out items of signal, quartermaster, medical, engineer, and ordnance equipment?

Had the effects of the logistical crisis disappeared with the close of the pursuit, the costly, miserable fighting that came to characterize the Siegfried Line Campaign might never have occurred. Yet the fact was that the pursuit ended because of the effects of the logistical crisis. The imprint of a weakened logistical system on the conduct of operations was to be marked for at least two more months. As many an Allied commander was to discover during the fall of 1944, a logistical headache is a persistent illness.

The Germans in the West

For all the implications of the logistical crisis, sober appreciations of the situation were none too common during late summer 1944. The German army was "no longer a cohesive force but a number of fugitive battle groups, disorganized and even demoralized, short of equipment and arms."[37] This was the Allied view. Political upheaval within Germany or insurrection within the Wehrmacht was likely to hasten the end.[38] The First Army G–2 believed that the enemy was concentrating all he had left opposite Metz and along the Lower Rhine, "leaving a gap from Trier to Maastricht which he is

attempting to fill with everything on which he can lay his hands." This, the G–2 declared, "had proved his undoing."[39]

This kind of optimism reflected no fleeting impression. In mid-September, when a corps commander took temporary leave of his troops for a short assignment elsewhere, he declared it "probable" that the war with Germany would be over before he could return.[40] On 15 September the First Army was almost sanguine over the possibility of enemy collapse in the Rhineland and the "enormous" strategic opportunity of seizing the Rhine bridges intact.[41] As late as the last week in September, the First Army commander believed that, given two weeks of good weather, Allied air and ground forces could "bring the enemy to their knees."[42] Although a few dissenting voices tried to make themselves heard, caution was not the fashion during the late summer season of 1944.

In many respects the true German situation nurtured optimism. In five years of war the German armed forces had lost 114,215 officers and 3,630,274 men, not including wounded who had returned to duty. The bulk of these had been Army losses. Many had been incurred during the recent months of June, July, and August, which had brought the Germans their most disastrous defeats in both East

---

[37] SHAEF Weekly Intel Summary 23, week ending 2 Sep 44.

[38] FUSA G–2 Estimate 24, 3 Sep 44, FUSA Rpt of Opns; TUSA G–2 Estimate 9, 28 Aug 44, TUSA AAR, Vol. II.

[39] FUSA G–2 Estimate 26, 11 Sep 44.

[40] Memo, Maj Gen Leonard T. Gerow for O's and EM of V Corps, 17 Sep 44, V Corps Operations in the ETO, 6 Jan 42–9 May 45, p. 256.

[41] FUSA G–2 Estimate 28, 15 Sep 44.

[42] Personal Diary of Maj William C. Sylvan, former aide to the First Army Commander, Lt Gen Courtney H. Hodges. Entry of 24 Sep 44. Major Sylvan kept his diary, dealing primarily with General Hodges' activities, with the approval of General Hodges. A copy is on file in OCMH through courtesy of Major Sylvan.

and West. During these three months the Army alone had suffered losses in dead, wounded, and missing of 1,210,600, approximately two thirds of which had been incurred in the East where both sides employed larger masses of men. Losses in transport and equipment also were tremendous; during August alone, for example, a total of 254,225 horses were lost.[43]

Not counting "paper units," which had headquarters but no troops, the Third Reich in early September possessed some 252 divisions and 15 to 20 brigades, greatly varied as to strength and capabilities. They were deployed in five theaters. In Finland, the East, and the Balkans they were supplemented by approximately 55 allied divisions (Finnish, Hungarian, and Bulgarian), for which the Germans had little respect. Most of the total of some 7,500,000 men were in the Field Army (Feldheer), the Replacement Army (Ersatzheer), or the services of supply. About 207,000 were in the Waffen-SS, a mechanized Army-type force originally made up of volunteers from Nazi-party organizations.

Of the 48 infantry and 15 panzer or panzer-type divisions which Field Marshal von Rundstedt controlled in the West, two represented a new class of 18 divisions which had been in process of formation since early July. These 18 divisions—15 of which went to the East and 1 to Scandinavia—were the first of the "volks grenadier" divisions, an honorific selected to appeal to the national and military pride of the German people (das Volk). The troops were hospital returnees, con-

verted naval and Luftwaffe personnel, previously exempt industrial workers, and youths just reaching military age.

When Hitler in late August began to consider how to stop the headlong retreat in the West, he settled upon a plan to increase the number of volks grenadier divisions. On 2 September—already seriously planning a large-scale operation designed to regain the initiative—he directed creation of an "operational reserve" of twenty-five new volks grenadier divisions. They were to become available in the West between 1 October and 1 December.

Organization and equipment of the new divisions reflected a tendency, current in the German Army since 1943, to reduce manpower while increasing fire power. Early in 1944 the standard infantry division had been formally reduced from about 17,000 men to 12,500.[44] By cutting each of the conventional three infantry regiments to two rifle battalions apiece and by thinning the organic service troops, the volks grenadier divisions were further reduced to about 10,000 men. Attempts were made to arm two platoons in each company with the 1944 model machine pistol (known to Americans as the burp gun), increase the amount of field artillery, and provide a larger complement of antitank weapons and assault guns (self-propelled tank destroyers). Approximately three fourths of the divisional transportation was horse drawn, while one unit, the Fuesilier battalion, had bicycles.

To supplement divisional artillery and antitank guns, Hitler ordered formation

---

[43] A detailed annotated account of German strength, losses, and organization may be found in Cole, The Lorraine Campaign, pp. 29–43.

[44] The 1944-type division and other divisional organizations are discussed in Gordon A. Harrison, Cross-Channel Attack, UNITED STATES ARMY IN WORLD WAR II (Washington, 1951), pp. 236–41.

of a number of general headquarters (*Heeres*) units; 12 motorized artillery brigades (about 1,000 guns), 10 *Werfer* (rocket projector) brigades, 10 assault gun battalions, and 12 20-mm. machine gun battalions. These were to be ready along with the last of the 25 volks grenadier divisions. In addition, Hitler on 4 September assigned the West priority on all new artillery and assault guns.

Two other steps were of a more immediate nature. As the month of September opened, 10 panzer brigades were either just arriving at the front or were being formed. These were built around a panzer battalion equipped with about forty Mark V (Panther) tanks. On the theory that the Mark V was tactically superior to the U.S. Sherman tank, the panzer brigades were expected to make up temporarily for Allied numerical superiority in armor.

The other step was to commit to battle approximately a hundred "fortress" infantry battalions made up of the older military classes and heretofore used only in rear areas. About four fifths of these were to be assigned to the West. Calling the battalions a "hidden reserve," the First U.S. Army later was to credit them with much of the German tenacity in the West Wall.[45]

Had Allied commanders been aware of the enemy's necessity to resort to expedients like these, it probably would have fed their optimism. Neither could they have been impressed by the command situation as it had developed at the top level. After the reverses on the Eastern Front during 1941–42, Hitler had assumed more and more the role of supreme military leader, so that by the fall of 1944 the concept of

maneuver had been all but stultified by a complete centralization of command. Hardly anybody could do anything without first consulting Hitler. After the unsuccessful attempt on his life in July, he looked upon almost every proposal from a field commander with unalloyed suspicion.

To reach the supreme military leader, field commanders in the West had to go through a central headquarters in Berlin, the *Oberkommando der Wehrmacht* (OKW), which was charged with operations in all theaters except the East. (*Oberkommando des Heeres*—OKH— watched over the Eastern Front.) Hitler's impression of the situation thus stemmed directly from a staff far removed from the scene of action.

OB WEST, the headquarters in the West that was comparable to *SHAEF*, was a supreme headquarters in theory only, for the ties imposed by OKW were stringent. The jealousies that played among the Army, the Luftwaffe, the Navy, the *Waffen-SS*, and Nazi party political appointees also limited *OB WEST*'s independence.

Hitler's order for early September to hold "under any conditions" a line from the Schelde estuary along the face of the West Wall and the western borders of Lorraine and Alsace had shown little appreciation of the difficulties facing *OB WEST*. This was despite the fact that Field Marshal Model, who had preceded Rundstedt as Commander in Chief West, had done his best to convey some sense of the crisis by sending report after report couched in dire terms. The retreating troops, Model had warned, possessed few heavy weapons and little else except carbines and rifles. Few of the eleven panzer divisions had more than five to ten tanks in working order. Artillery in both in-

---

[45] FUSA AAR, Oct. 44.

FIELD MARSHAL MODEL

FIELD MARSHAL VON RUNDSTEDT

fantry and panzer divisions was almost a thing of the past. The troops were depressed by Allied superiority in planes and tanks and by the contrast between their own horse-drawn transport and the motors of their enemy. In Alsace a wide gap had developed between the two groups of armies that could not be filled with less than three fresh infantry divisions. Hardly had Model reported this gap than he wrote it off as no longer of primary concern. The entire Western Front, he pleaded, needed propping up lest it give way completely.[46]

On 4 September Model had given a detailed appraisal of the front of *Army Group B,* which Model himself com-

manded in addition to his major post as Commander in Chief West. His army group alone, Model had said, needed a minimum of 25 fresh infantry divisions and 5 or 6 panzer divisions.[47]

To this plea Model received not even the courtesy of a reply. It was at this point that he was replaced in the top half of his dual command responsibility by Rundstedt.

Field Marshal von Rundstedt's return to his former command on 5 September came on the heels of personal indoctrination from Hitler. The Allies, Hitler had told him, were outrunning their supplies and soon would have to halt, at which time counterattacks could cut off the "armored spearheads" and stabilize the

[46] *Heeresgruppe B* (hereafter cited as A Gp B), *Lagebeurteilungen, Ia.*

[47] *Ibid.*

front. The West Wall, Hitler insisted, had all the elements of impregnability and would afford the much-needed respite. Hitler's final instructions were much like the earlier order to hold "under any conditions." Rundstedt was to stop the Allies as far to the west as possible, then was to counterattack along the boundary between the two army groups into the south flank of the Third U.S. Army.[48]

After assuming command in the main OB WEST command post near Koblenz, Rundstedt's most urgent problem was the restoration of a collective strategy for the whole of the Western Front, something to which Model, in his preoccupation with Army Group B, had paid scant attention. Rundstedt correctly held out little hope for the counterattack; for continued advances by the Third Army denied mounting one in any appreciable strength. Yet the very fact that any troops were on hand to counterattack lessened this particular threat. He could see no solution for two other threats: one against the Ruhr, particularly via Aachen, and another in uncommitted Allied airborne forces, which he expected might attack either in rear of the West Wall or east of the Rhine.

Rundstedt's first estimate of the situation, forwarded to OKW on 7 September, echoed Model's pessimistic reports. After emphasizing the overwhelming Allied superiority in divisions and in armor, Rundstedt insisted on the immediate need of at least five, "and better ten," infantry divisions. He needed tanks and tank destroyers desperately, he said, to counter the threat at Aachen. At the moment the only reserves of any description were a "weak" 9th Panzer Division, a "weak" Sturm panzer battalion, and two assault gun brigades. All of these already were on the way to Aachen.[49]

The answer from Berlin must have been as frustrating to Rundstedt as earlier responses had been to Model. Spike down the front as far to the west as possible. Pull out the shattered divisions for reconstitution. Counterattack into the flank of the Third U.S. Army. No promise of any immediate assistance. As the American First Army noted, "The moment called for a real soldier."[50]

Subsequent events might prove that in Field Marshal von Rundstedt the moment had found the soldier it called for. The German situation in the West was bad, even desperate. Yet it was a situation that a strong leader still might make something of.

The true German situation was perhaps most aptly described by one of the few voices of caution raised on the Allied side during the halcyon days of pursuit. On 28 August the Third Army G–2 had put it this way:

Despite the crippling factors of shattered communications, disorganization and tremendous losses in personnel and equipment, the enemy nevertheless has been able to maintain a sufficiently cohesive front to exercise an overall control of his tactical situation. His withdrawal, though continuing, has not been a rout or mass collapse. Numerous new identifications in contact in

[48] MS # T–122, Geschichte des "Oberbefehlshaber West," edited by Generalleutnant Bodo Zimmermann (G–3, OB WEST), hereafter cited as MS # T–122 (Zimmermann et al.), Part II, Kampf in Belgien und Holland von Mitte September–Mitte December 1944. MSS # T–121, 122, and 123—History of OB WEST—make up a million-word manuscript prepared in part by Zimmermann, in part by generals and general staff officers associated with OB WEST, OKW, OKH, OKL, OKM, and various subordinate commands. No page numbers are cited because the manuscripts exist in several differently paginated versions.

[49] A Gp B, Lagebeurteilungen, Ia.
[50] FUSA AAR, Sep 44.

recent days have demonstrated clearly that, despite the enormous difficulties under which he is operating, the enemy is still capable of bringing new elements into the battle area and transferring some from other fronts . . . .

It is clear from all indications that the fixed determination of the Nazis is to wage a last-ditch struggle in the field at all costs. It must be constantly kept in mind that fundamentally the enemy is playing for time. Weather will soon be one of his most potent Allies as well as terrain, as we move east to narrowing corridors . . . .[51]

The fact was that the German penchant and respect for organization and discipline had preserved organization at the headquarters levels basically intact. Though some top commanders and many staff officers had been lost, the Germans still had enough capable senior officers to replace them. Nor had the Germans as a nation resorted to total mobilization before the fall of 1944.[52]

This is not to say, the Germans had not full justification for alarm as the first patrols crossed their border. The situation still was chaotic, but the ingredients for stabilization were present. In the north, for example, opposite the British and the First U.S. Army, though the *Seventh* and *Fifteenth Armies* were skeletons, the army and corps staffs still functioned and each army had at least ten division staffs capable of attempting to execute tactical assignments. Upon news of the fall of Antwerp, Hitler had rushed to the Netherlands headquarters of a training command, the *First Parachute Army*, to fill a gap between the *Seventh* and *Fifteenth Armies*. Though the *First Parachute Army* brought with it little more than its own headquarters, it was able in a matter of days to borrow, confiscate from the retreating masses, or otherwise obtain functioning staffs of one corps and several divisions. Winning a war with a setup like this might be impossible, but it could be effective in stopping an overextended attacker long enough to permit creation of something better.

---

[51] TUSA G–2 Estimate 9, 28 Aug 44, TUSA AAR, Vol. II.
[52] See Charles V. P. von Luttichau, The Ardennes Offensive, Germany's Situation in the Fall of 1944, Part III, The Strategic Situation, MS in OCMH.

CHAPTER II

The First U.S. Army

In crossing the German border, the First U.S. Army had added another justification for its numerical name to that already earned in establishing the first American foothold in Normandy. After the landings, the First Army had forged the gap through which the more flamboyant Third Army had poured from the beachhead. Not to be outdone, the First Army also had taken up the pursuit, with less fanfare than its sister army, perhaps, but with equally concrete results. In less than a month and a half the First Army had driven from St. Lô to Paris, thence northward to Mons, thence eastward to the German border, a distance of approximately 750 miles. (*See Map I.*) This it had accomplished against the bulk of the German forces, including German armor, still opposing an American army in northern France.

At the beginning of September the First Army numbered 256,351 officers and men. It had 3 corps made up of 5 infantry divisions, 3 armored divisions, and 3 mechanized cavalry groups. The 8 combat divisions were almost at full strength: 109,517 officers and men. Also a part of the army were 9 separate tank battalions (7 medium, 2 light), 12 tank destroyer battalions, 31 antiaircraft battalions (including automatic weapons and gun battalions), 3 field artillery observation battalions, 46 separate field artillery battalions, 3 chemical (mortar) battalions, and a number of engineer, signal, quartermaster, and other service units.[1]

Though the First Army's strength in medium tanks was a theoretical 1,010, only some 85 percent was actually on hand. Many of even these were badly in need of maintenance following the rapid dash across France and Belgium. The 3d Armored Division, for example, reported on 18 September that of an authorized medium tank strength of 232, only 70 to 75 were in condition for front-line duty.[2]

The commander of the First Army was a calm, dependable, painstaking tactician, Lt. Gen. Courtney H. Hodges. After the manner of his predecessor in command of the First Army, General Bradley, General Hodges was a "soldier's soldier," a title to which no other American army commander and few corps commanders in action in Europe at the time could lay more just claim. No other was more sincere and sympathetic toward his troops and none except Hodges and one corps commander had risen from the ranks.[3] Though General Hodges had sought a commission at West Point, he had flunked

---

[1] 12th A Gp and FUSA G–1 Daily Summaries, 12 Sep 44; FUSA, Order of Battle, Combat Units, 20 Sep 44, FUSA G–2 TAC Misc file, Sep 44. *Cf.* Third Army strength as found in Cole, *The Lorraine Campaign,* p. 18.

[2] 3d Armd Div AAR, Sep 44, and Combat Interv with 3d Armd Div G–4.

[3] Maj Gen Troy H. Middleton, VIII Corps.

out in geometry during his first year. A man of determination, as he was to demonstrate often during the fall of 1944, he had enlisted in the Army as an infantry private and had gained his commission only a year later than his former classmates at the Military Academy. He served in the expedition against Pancho Villa in Mexico and was one of a small fraternity of top American commanders in World War II who had seen combat before at a line company level, in the Meuse-Argonne campaign of World War I.

Upon completion of a stint of occupation duty after World War I, General Hodges had served the usual tours of troop duty in the United States and attended the Army schools. During additional service in the Philippines his path crossed that of the future Supreme Commander in Europe. Later he served successively as assistant commandant and commandant of The Infantry School. In 1941 General George C. Marshall, Chief of Staff, who had first been impressed with Hodges while he himself was assistant commandant of The Infantry School, brought Hodges to Washington as Chief of Infantry. His performance as an administrator already proved, General Hodges showed his ability as a field commander while directing the Third Army during the 1943 Louisiana maneuvers.

In early 1944 General Hodges had left for England to become deputy commander of General Bradley's First Army and to direct the training and co-ordination of the various corps and divisions readying for D-Day. It was a foregone conclusion that Hodges would take over when Bradley moved upstairs. On 1 August he had become commanding general of the First Army.

GENERAL HODGES

General Hodges was fifty-seven years old at the start of the Siegfried Line Campaign. Tall, erect, his moustache closely clipped, he was an impressive-looking soldier. Averse to tumult and glitter, he preferred restrained behavior to publicity-provoking eccentricities. Discipline, General Hodges maintained, could be achieved without shouting.

A close friend of the Third Army's General Patton, Hodges shared Patton's enthusiasm for what machines and big guns could do for his infantrymen. The First Army almost always had more medium tanks than did the Third Army, despite the myth that the Third was "top-heavy with armor." That Hodges knew how to use tanks had been demonstrated amply during the pursuit. He was also alert to what artillery could do. General Hodges worked no more closely with nor

THIRTEEN COMMANDERS OF THE WESTERN FRONT *photographed in Belgium, 10 October 1944. Front row, left to right: General Patton, General Bradley, General Eisenhower, General Hodges, Lt. Gen. William H. Simpson. Second row: Maj. Gen. William B. Kean, Maj. Gen. Charles E. Corlett, Maj. Gen. J. Lawton Collins, Maj. Gen. Leonard P. Gerow, Maj. Gen. Elwood R. Quesada. Third row: Maj. Gen. Leven C. Allen, Brig. Gen. Charles C. Hart, Brig. Gen. Truman C. Thorson.*

depended more on the advice of any man on his staff than his chief of artillery, Brig. Gen. Charles E. Hart.[4]

The First Army headquarters under General Hodges was vitally concerned with precision and detailed planning. "When you did a situation report for the

Third Army," said a former corps G–3, "you showed the positions of the regiments. When you did one for the First Army, you had to show platoons." [5] The army's concern for detail was clearly reflected in the presence within the office of the Assistant G–3 for Plans and Operations alone of sixteen liaison officers

---

[4] Interv with Maj Gen Truman C. Thorson, former G–3, FUSA, 12 Sep 56; Sylvan Diary, *passim.*

[5] Interv with Brig Gen John G. Hill, former G–3, V Corps, 15 Oct 54.

equipped with jeep and radio.[6] "A good army headquarters," General Hodges' G–3 believed, "is always right on top of the corps and divisions, else you cannot carry out the orders and wishes of the commander." [7]

The staff which General Hodges inherited from General Bradley was basically intact at the start of September. Possibly reflecting the primary interest of both Bradley and Hodges, it was strong in infantry officers.

The chief of staff was a specialist in the role, a forty-seven-year-old infantryman, Maj. Gen. William B. Kean. General Bradley had brought General Kean along from earlier service as chief of staff of an infantry division to fill the same role, first with the II Corps in Tunisia and Sicily, and later with the First Army. Kean became "very close" to General Hodges as adviser and confidant and "a leading light" in the First Army headquarters. "It was Kean," one of his associates recalled, "who would crack the whip. We called him 'Old Sam Bly.' " [8] Both the G–2, Col. Benjamin A. Dickson, and the G–3, Brig. Gen. Truman C. Thorson, also were infantrymen.[9]

Like almost all American units in action at this stage, the corps and divisions under the First Army's command were thoroughly seasoned. Two of the 3 corps and 6 of the 8 divisions would provide the nucleus of the First Army through almost all of the Siegfried Line Campaign.

Weakest numerically of the three corps was the XIX Corps under Maj. Gen.

Charles H. Corlett, an infantryman who had gained combat experience earlier in World War II as a commander of the 7th Division in the Pacific. Under General Corlett the XIX Corps had become operational on 14 June. The corps had helped pave the way for the breakout of the original beachhead, fend off the enemy's desperate counterattack at Mortain, and close both the Argentan–Falaise and Mons pockets. On 11 September the XIX Corps had but two divisions—the 30th Infantry and 2d Armored, plus the 113th Cavalry Group and supporting troops. Unfortunately, General Corlett was not physically at his best during the summer and fall of 1944.

The VII Corps, which had assaulted UTAH Beach on D-Day and captured Cherbourg, was under Maj. Gen. J. Lawton Collins. Collins was an infantryman who had gained battle experience and a nickname—Lightning Joe—as an infantry division commander on Guadalcanal and New Georgia. Like the Third Army's General Patton, Collins was a dynamic, driving personality whose opinions often exerted more than the normal influence at the next higher level of command. At the time of the drive into Germany, the major units of the VII Corps were the 4th Cavalry Group, the 1st and 9th Infantry Divisions, and the 3d Armored Division.

Completing the triangle of corps was the V Corps under Maj. Gen. Leonard T. Gerow. Like the other corps commanders, General Gerow was a veteran infantryman. He had spent the early days of the war with the War Plans Division of the War Department General Staff and as commander of an infantry division in the United States. Two of the more notable accomplishments of the V Corps were the D-Day landing on OMAHA

---

[6] Interv with Col R. F. Akers, former Asst G–3, FUSA, 11 Jun 56.
[7] Interv with Thorson.
[8] *Ibid.*
[9] The G–1 was Col. Joseph J. O'Hare; the G–4, Col. Robert W. Wilson; the G–5, Col. Damon M. Gunn.

Beach and the liberation of Paris. On 11 September the corps controlled the 102d Cavalry Group, the 4th and 28th Infantry Divisions, and the 5th Armored Division.

Though almost all the infantry and armored divisions of the First Army were at or near full strength in mid-September, the army faced a handicap both at the start and all the way through the Siegfried Line Campaign in a lack of a reserve combat force. On occasion, a separate infantry battalion or a combat command of armor occupying a secondary defensive line would be called a reserve, but no one could accept these designations as other than nominal.

It could be said that the First Army had a fourth corps in an old ally, the IX Tactical Air Command, a component of the Ninth Air Force. Commanded by Maj. Gen. Elwood R. (Pete) Quesada, the IX TAC was the oldest unit of its kind in the theater and long ago had established with the First Army "an indissoluble operational partnership." [10] When General Hodges' headquarters settled down for the fall campaign in the Belgian town of Spa, General Quesada moved in next door. Air officers attended First Army briefings, and vice versa. For all the difficulties of weather that were to plague the airmen during the Siegfried Line Campaign, ground commanders were to continue to pay tribute to the close and effective co-operation they received from the IX TAC. [11]

Like divisions attached to ground corps and armies, the fighter-bomber groups assigned to tactical air commands often

varied. On occasion, the IX TAC controlled as many as eighteen groups, but usually the number averaged about six. [12] A group normally had three squadrons of twenty-five planes each, P-38's (Lightnings), P-47's (Thunderbolts), or P-51's (Mustangs), except in the case of night fighter groups, which had P-61's (Black Widows).

Requests for air support usually were forwarded from the air support officers at division through the air support officer and G-3 Air Section at corps to the G-3 Air at army for transmission to the IX TAC. The air headquarters ruled on the feasibility of the mission and assigned the proper number of aircraft to it. Since air targets could not always be anticipated, most divisions came to prefer a system of "armed reconnaissance flights" in which a group was assigned to the division or corps for the day and checked in by radio directly with the appropriate air support officer. Thus the planes could be called in as soon as a target appeared without the delay involved in forwarding a request through channels. [13]

Available also for direct support of the ground troops were the eleven groups of medium bombers of the IX Bombardment Division (Maj. Gen. Samuel E. Anderson), another component of the Ninth Air Force. Each of these groups normally employed thirty-six planes, either B-26's (Marauders) or A-20's (Havocs), which

---

[10] The Ninth Air Force and Its Principal Commands in the ETO, Vol. II, Pt. I.

[11] See, for example, testimony in Operational History of the Ninth Air Force, Book V, Ground Forces Annexes.

[12] As of 30 September, the IX TAC commanded the 368th, 370th, 404th, and 474th Fighter-Bomber Groups and the 67th Tactical Reconnaissance Group.

[13] Ninth Air Force, Vol. I, Ch. VII. For a detailed study of air-ground liaison, see Kent Roberts Greenfield, Army Ground Forces and the Air-Ground Battle Team Including Organic Light Aviation, Army Ground Forces Study No. 35, Historical Section, Army Ground Forces, 1948. Copy in OCMH.

bombed from altitudes of 10,000 to 12,000 feet.[14] Though the mediums sometimes made valuable contributions to direct support, they were used for the purpose somewhat infrequently, both because it was hard to find targets large enough to be easily spotted yet small enough to assure a good concentration of bombs and because the request for medium support had to be approved by the 12th Army Group G–3 Air Section and took from forty-eight to seventy-two hours to come through.[15]

Weapons and Equipment

The weapons and equipment with which the American soldier was to fight the Siegfried Line Campaign might have needed repair and in some cases replacement after the ravages of Normandy and the pursuit, but in general the soldier's armament and equipment were the envy of his adversary. Indeed, the theory which German officers and soldiers were to perpetuate to explain their defeat in World War II, in much the same way they blamed lack of perserverance on the home front for the outcome of World War I, was the superiority of American and Allied matériel.[16]

It is axiomatic that the American soldier in World War II was the best-paid and best-fed soldier of any army up to that time. He clearly was among the best-

clothed as well, even though controversy would rage later about the adequacy of his winter clothing.[17] In the matter of armament also American research and production had done exceedingly well by him. On the other hand, his adversary likewise possessed, qualitatively, at least, an impressive arsenal.

The basic shoulder weapon in the U.S. Army during the Siegfried Line Campaign was the .30-caliber M1 (Garand) rifle, a semiautomatic piece much admired by its users. Though the Germans possessed a few similar models, their basic individual piece was a 7.92-mm. (Mauser) bolt-action rifle not greatly different from the U.S. M1903. Two favorite weapons of the American soldier were outgrowths of World War I, the .30-caliber Browning Automatic Rifle (BAR) and the .30-caliber Browning machine gun in both light (air-cooled) and heavy (water-cooled) models. The most effective close-range antitank weapons were, on the German side, a one-shot, shaped-charge piece called a panzerfaust, and, on the American side, a 2.36-inch rocket launcher, the bazooka. The most widely used artillery pieces of both combatants were light and medium howitzers, German and American models of which were roughly comparable in caliber and performance.[18]

---

[14] IX Bomb Div, Medium Bombardment—Its Use in Ground Support, copy in History, IX Bomb Div, Nov–Dec 44.

[15] Ninth Air Force, Vol. I, Ch. VII. Though the masses of Allied heavy bombers were used on one occasion during the Siegfried Line Campaign for direct support of the ground troops, their role was primarily strategic and the effects on the ground fighting difficult to specify.

[16] Wartime prisoner of war interrogations and postwar manuscripts by German officers provide ample evidence of German belief in this theory.

[17] See Ruppenthal, Logistical Support of the Armies, Vol. II, pp. 218–35.

[18] This account is based primarily on Research and Development Service, Office of the Chief of Ordnance, Comparison of American, German, and Japanese Ordnance, 6 May 1945, Vols. I and II. A comprehensive study and comparison of American and German weapons and equipment will be included in Ordnance Overseas, a volume in preparation in the Ordnance subseries of THE UNITED STATES ARMY IN WORLD WAR II. The German infantry division, like the American, had four artillery battalions—three

CAPTURED PANZERFAUST

German artillery doctrine and organization for the control and delivery of fire differed materially from the American only in that the German organic divisional artillery was less well equipped for communication. The excellent American facilities of communication down to battery level, and the effective operation of the American fire direction centers on many occasions permitted more accurate fire and greater concentration in a shorter time. But the shortcomings of the enemy in the matter of effective concentrations during this campaign were largely attributable to the effects of war—loss of air observation,

shortages of ammunition and equipment, damage done to the artillery system, high casualties among skilled artillerists, and the disruption of smooth teamwork—rather than to deficiences of doctrine and organization.[19]

Both sides had the same excellent 1/25,000 metric scale maps of the area, reproduced from those originally made by the French Army, showing roads, railroads, contour lines, towns, and forests. To offset superior knowledge of the terrain that the Germans enjoyed, the Americans, controlling the air, had the advantage of aerial photographs, and they could use their artillery spotter planes while the

---

light and one medium. The German pieces were gun-howitzers (105-mm. light, and 150-mm. medium); the American pieces were howitzers (105-mm. and 155-mm.).

---

[19] Charles V. P. von Luttichau, Notes on German and U.S. Artillery, copy in OCMH.

Germans could not. The simple little monoplane that the Americans used for artillery observation appeared, in relation to contemporary fighters and bombers, to be an example of retarded development, a throwback to the aircraft of World War I. It was the L–4 (in some cases, L–5), variously called a Piper Cub, cub, liaison plane, grasshopper, or observation plane. Though its most significant role was as the eyes of the field artillery, it performed various other tasks, such as courier and liaison service, visual and photographic observation, emergency supply, and emergency evacuation of wounded. Not only the artilleryman but the infantryman and armored soldier as well swore by it, while the Germans swore at it. The very presence of one of the little planes aloft often silenced the German artillery. American air superiority permitted their consistent use, and also gave the Americans the benefit of air photographs made almost daily behind the German lines from the faster planes of the Army Air Forces. The photographs were made available to American artillerymen to identify pillboxes and other defensive installations of the enemy.[20]

In the matter of tanks the Americans possessed no such advantage. Their standard tank, the M4 Sherman, a 33-ton medium, was relatively obsolescent. Although a few Shermans equipped with a high-velocity 76-mm. gun in place of the usual short-barreled 75 were to become available during the Siegfried Line Campaign, most medium tanks still mounted the 75. They plainly were outgunned,

not only by the enemy's heaviest tank, the 63-ton Mark VI (Tiger), but also by the 50-ton Mark V (Panther).[21] The Tiger, the Panther, and the medium Mark IV all had thicker armor than the Sherman. Equipped with wider tracks than the Sherman, the enemy tanks likewise possessed greater flotation and thus on occasion might vitiate a superiority in mobility which U.S. tanks possessed when on firm ground. The only advantages left to the Sherman were superiority in numbers, comparatively easy maintenance, and greater flexibility and rapidity of fire as a result of a gyrostabilizer and power traverse.[22]

Some equalization in the matter of tank and antitank gunnery was to be provided in November when a considerable number of U.S. self-propelled tank destroyer battalions were to receive new vehicles. In place of the M10 destroyer with its 3-inch gun, the units were to receive M36 vehicles mounting a high-velocity 90-mm. piece. Though the 90-mm. had long been a standard antiaircraft weapon, its presence on the actual firing line was in the nature of an innovation.

Other than tanks, the German weapons which would most impress the American soldier in the campaign were the burp gun, the *Nebelwerfer*, and the 88. Two of these—the burp gun and the 88—he had met before and had long since accorded a ubiquitousness neither deserved. The burp gun—so-called because of a distinctive emetic b-r-r-r-p sound attributable to a higher cyclic rate of fire than

---

[20] For a detailed study of the liaison plane, see Kent Roberts Greenfield, Army Ground Forces and the Air-Ground Battle Team, AGF Study No. 35; I. B. Holley, Evolution of the Liaison Type Airplane, 1917–1944, USAF Historical Studies 1946.

[21] An American heavy tank did not reach the theater until 1945 and then in relatively insignificant numbers.

[22] Cole, in *The Lorraine Campaign*, pages 603–04, compares characteristics of German and American tanks during the fall of 1944.

CAPTURED NEBELWERFER

American automatic weapons—was an individual piece, a machine pistol, similar to the U.S. Thompson submachine gun. Because the standard German machine gun made a similar emetic sound, it seemed to the American soldier that burp guns were all over the place. The 88—an 88-mm., high-velocity, dual-purpose anti-aircraft and antitank piece—had been accorded the respect of the American soldier since North Africa. A standard field piece in the German army and the standard weapon of the Mark VI Tiger tank, the 88 was nevertheless not nearly so plentiful as reports from the American side would indicate. A shell from almost any high-velocity German weapon the American attributed to the 88.

The *Nebelwerfer* was a newer weapon, one which had seen some service in Normandy but which came into general use only at the start of the Siegfried Line campaign as the Germans called upon it to supplement their depleted artillery. It was a multiple-barrel, 150-mm. mortar, mounted on wheels and fired electrically. The screeching sound of its projectiles in flight earned for it the nickname, Screaming Meemie. The U.S. equivalent, a 4.5-inch rocket launcher, was not used widely until later in the war.

The Terrain and the West Wall

In less than a fortnight the forces in the north—the First Army and the 21 Army Group—had driven the enemy almost entirely from two countries: the kingdom of Belgium, approximately the size of the state of Maryland, and the grand duchy of Luxembourg, somewhat smaller than Rhode Island. In the process they had jumped a number of major obstacles, like the Escaut and Meuse Rivers and the Belgian and Luxembourgian Ardennes; but the path ahead was far from smooth.

The strategic goal of the forces in the north, the Ruhr industrial area, lay about seventy-five miles away. Germany's most important concentrated mining and industrial region, the Ruhr had grown up east of the Rhine largely after 1870. It embraces major cities like Essen, Dortmund, and Duesseldorf. An elliptical-shaped basin, it measures some fifty miles at its base along the Rhine and about seventy miles in depth.

The terrain next to be encountered on the march to the Ruhr can be divided into four geographical sectors: (1) Opposite the left wing of the 21 Army Group, the Dutch islands and the Dutch littoral, most of it land reclaimed from the sea and at this stage studded with fortifications denying seaward access to the prize of Antwerp. (2) In front of the 21 Army Group's right wing, the flatlands of the Netherlands, crisscrossed by waterways, including three major rivers, the Maas (Dutch equivalent of the Meuse), the Waal (a downstream branch of the Rhine), and the Neder Rijn (Lower Rhine). (3) Facing the left wing of the First U.S. Army, the Aachen Gap, guarded by the sentinel city of Aachen but affording access to an open plain leading all the way to the Rhine. (4) Opposite the right wing of the First Army, the Eifel, forested highlands whose division from the Ardennes is political rather than geographical.

Of the four sectors, the Dutch islands and the Dutch littoral, for all their importance to the use of Antwerp, offered little toward an advance on the Ruhr. Despite some major obstacles, the other three regions had greater possibilities.

The waterways of the Netherlands, like those which earlier had prompted Allied planners to rule out the plain of Flanders as a major route, might forestall a normal military advance; but the British already had proved in Flanders that in pursuit warfare waterways may not be a serious deterrent. As with Flanders, the rewards of success were tempting. The great Dutch ports of Amsterdam and Rotterdam might fall, the West Wall might be outflanked, the Rhine left behind, and the British positioned for envelopment of the Ruhr from the north via the North German Plain. On the other hand, defense of the east-west waterways was facilitated by a shortage of major roads and railroads leading north and northeast.

To the southeast, the Aachen Gap is a historic gateway into Germany dating from early Christendom. It was a major east-west route during the height of the Roman Empire when the old Roman highway ran slightly north of Aachen on a line Brussels–Maastricht–Cologne. Birthplace and reputed burial place of the Emperor Charlemagne and capital of the Carolingian Empire, Aachen had a prewar population of 165,710. Its military value lies in the roads that spread out from the city in all directions. In 1944 the city had an added military significance as a key to the second most heavily fortified portion of the West Wall.

The only troops in the Aachen region still to cross the major obstacle of the Meuse River were the divisions of the XIX Corps, which were approaching the city of Maastricht in the province of Limburg, which the Americans called "the Dutch Panhandle." At the border of Germany, the XIX Corps would have to cross a minor stream, the Wurm River, which German engineers had exploited as an antitank barrier for the West Wall. But once past the Wurm, the terrain is open plain studded by mining and farming villages and broken only by the lines of the Roer and Erft Rivers. Weakest of the First Army's three corps and the only one forced to undergo a handicap because of the gasoline drought, the XIX Corps was the unit most directly oriented along the route of the old Roman highway north of Aachen, the route which represents the most literal interpretation of the term *Aachen Gap.*

South of the XIX Corps, the VII Corps was headed directly for Aachen and for a narrow corridor of rolling hills between Aachen and the northern reaches of the Eifel. For convenience this corridor may be called, after an industrial town within it, the Stolberg Corridor. It leads onto the Roer plain near the town of Dueren (population: 45,441), nineteen miles east of Aachen. The fringe of the Eifel is clothed in a dense jungle of pines, a major obstacle that could seriously canalize an advance along this route. Communications through the forest are virtually nonexistent. Within the forest a few miles to the south lie two dams of importance in control of the waters of the Roer River, the Schwammenauel and the Urft.

Some of the hardest fighting of the Siegfried Line Campaign was to occur in the region toward which the XIX and VII Corps were heading. It is a fan-shaped sector with a radius of twenty-two miles based on the city of Aachen. The span is the contour of the Roer River, winding northeast, north, and northwest from headwaters near Monschau to a confluence with the Wurm River near Heinsberg.

Southeast of the VII Corps zone lay the heartland of the Eifel, heavily forested terrain, sharply compartmentalized by numerous streams draining into the Moselle, the Meuse, and the Rhine and traversed by a limited road and rail net. This was the region where the first patrols had crossed the German border. Not including the forested fringes between Aachen and Monschau, the Eifel extends some seventy air-line miles from Monschau to the vicinity of Trier. It is divided into two sectors: the High Eifel, generally along the border, and the Volcanic Eifel, farther east where the ground begins to slope downward toward the Rhine. One of the most prominent features within the High Eifel is a ridge—2,286 feet high, running along the border a few miles east of St. Vith, Belgium—the Schnee Eifel. Entrance to the Eifel from Belgium and Luxembourg is blocked by the escarpment of the Schnee Eifel, by a continuous river

line formed by the Our, Sauer, and Moselle Rivers, and by a high, marshy, windswept moor near Monschau called the Hohe Venn. Yet for all the difficulties of the terrain, German armies had turned the Eifel and the adjacent Ardennes to military advantage in both 1914 and 1940 and were to utilize it again in December 1944.

During the late summer of 1944 Allied vision had stretched across the obstacles of terrain to gaze upon the Rhine; but few eyes could ignore a man-made obstacle which denied ready access to the river. This was the fortified belt extending along the western borders of Germany from the vicinity of Kleve on the Dutch frontier to Lorrach near Basle on the Swiss border. Americans knew it as the Siegfried Line. The nation that built it called it the West Wall.[23]

Construction of a West Wall first had begun in 1936 after Hitler had sent German troops back into a demilitarized Rhineland. It was originally to have been a short stretch of fortifications along the

----

[23] The name Siegfried Line, or *Siegfriedstellung,* originated in World War I. It was a German code name given to a rear defensive position established in 1916 behind the central portion of the western front, from the vicinity of Arras to a point just east of Soissons. The position played an important role as the front line fluctuated during the last two years of the war. The Germans fell back on this line in early spring of 1917 and from it launched their last great offensive in March 1918. Unless otherwise noted, information on the West Wall is from the following: SHAEF Weekly Intel Summary 25 for week ending 9 Sep 44; 12th A Gp Weekly Intel Summaries 4 and 7 for weeks ending 26 Aug and 23 Sep 44, respectively; *OB WEST,* A Study in Command; German maps in OCMH; FUSA Rpt of Opns, pp. 51–54; VII Corps, Office of the Engineer, Initial Breaching of the Siegfried Line; Sidney Bradshaw Fay, West Wall, *The Encyclopaedia Britannica* (University of Chicago, 1948 edition), Vol. 10, p. 243c.

Saar River, opposite the French Maginot Line. Unlike the French position, it was to be no thin line of *gros ouvrages*—elaborate, self-contained forts—but a band of many small, mutually supporting pillboxes.

Work on the West Wall had begun in earnest in May 1938, after Czechoslovakia had taken a somewhat defiant attitude toward German indications of aggression. The task went to Dr. Fritz Todt, an able engineer who had supervised construction of the nation's superhighways, the *Reichs-autobahnen*. By the end of September 1938 more than 500,000 men were working on the West Wall. Approximately a third of Germany's total annual production of cement went into the works. The new West Wall was to extend from a point north of Aachen all along the border south and southeast to the Rhine, thence along the German bank of the Rhine to the Swiss border. More than 3,000 concrete pillboxes, bunkers, and observation posts were constructed.

As much because of propaganda as anything else the West Wall came to be considered impregnable. It contributed to Hitler's success in bluffing France and England at Munich. In 1939, when Hitler's designs on Danzig strained German-Polish relations, Hitler ordered a film of the West Wall to be shown in all German cinemas to bolster home-front conviction that Germany was inviolate from the west.

Although some additional work was done on the West Wall between 1938 and 1940, Germany's quick victory in France and the need to shift the defenses of the Third Reich to the Atlantic and the Channel brought construction to a virtual halt. Not until 20 August 1944, when Hitler issued an eleventh-hour decree for

a levy of "people's" labor, was any new effort made to strengthen the line.

When the first American patrols probed the border, Allied intelligence on the West Wall was sketchy. Most reports on it dated back to 1940. Because four years of neglect had given the works a realistic camouflage, aerial reconnaissance failed to pick up many of the positions.

The West Wall's value as a fortress had been vastly exaggerated by Hitler's propagandists, particularly as it stood in September 1944, after four years of neglect. In 1944 it was something of a Potemkin village. Dr. Todt and the German Army had never intended the line to halt an attack, merely to delay it until counterattacks by mobile reserves could eliminate any penetration. In early fall of 1944 no strong reserves existed.

In 1939–40 any threatened sector of the line was to have been manned by an infantry division for every five miles of front. Adequate artillery had been available. Although few of the pillboxes could accommodate guns of larger caliber than the 37-mm. antitank gun, this piece was standard and effective against the armor of the period. In 1944 the situation was different. The most glaring deficiency was lack of troops either to man the line or to counterattack effectively. Artillery was severely limited. Even the 75-mm. antitank gun, which could be mounted in a few of the pillboxes, was basically inadequate to cope with the new, heavier armor. The smaller works could not accommodate the standard 1942 model machine gun because embrasures had been constructed for the 1934 model. Expecting to find a strong defensive position in being, the troops falling back on the West Wall from France and Belgium saw only a five-year old derelict. There were

CONSTRUCTION OF PILLBOXES
SIEGFRIED LINE

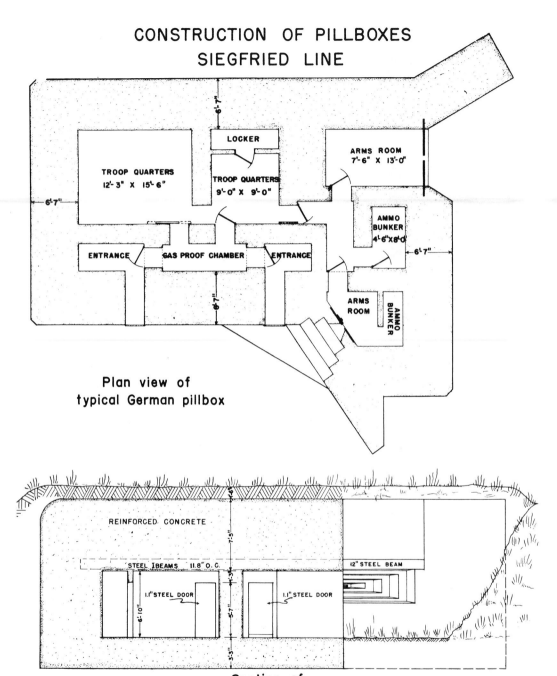

Plan view of
typical German pillbox

Section of
typical German pillbox

Typical Pillbox. *Above (left) exterior, showing door with firing embrasure. Interior of firing embrasure at right. Below (left) bunk area, and (right) ventilation device.*

no mines, no barbed wire, few communications lines, and few fortress weapons. Field fortifications had been begun only at the last minute by well-intentioned but un-co-ordinated civilians. The West Wall in September 1944 was formidable primarily on the basis of an old, unearned reputation.

The strongest portion of the line was the segment constructed in 1936 along the Saar River between the Moselle and the Rhine. Lying mainly in the zone of the Third U.S. Army, this portion would be spared until December because of the fighting in Lorraine. The next strongest portion was a double band of defenses protecting the Aachen Gap. Here the First U.S. Army already had reached the very gates.

The extreme northern segment of the West Wall—from Geilenkirchen, about fifteen miles north of Aachen, to Kleve— consisted only of a thin, single belt of scattered pillboxes backing up natural obstacles. South of Geilenkirchen, the pillboxes began to appear in a definite pattern of clusters on a forward line backed up by occasional clusters a few hundred yards to the rear. At a point about halfway between Geilenkirchen and Aachen, the density of the pillboxes increased markedly and the line split into two bands about five miles apart. Aachen lay between the two. Though two bands still were in evidence in the forest south and southeast of Aachen, the pillboxes were in less density. At a point near the northern end of the Schnee Eifel, the two bands merged, to continue all the way south to Trier as a single line with pillboxes in medium to heavy density. The greatest concentration in the Eifel was near the southern end of the Schnee

Eifel where the terrain is relatively open.

In many places the West Wall depended for passive antitank protection upon natural obstacles like rivers, lakes, railroad cuts and fills, sharp defiles, and forest. In other places, the German engineers had constructed chains of "dragon's teeth," curious objects that looked like canted headstones in a strange cemetery. In some cases the dragon's teeth were no more than heavy posts or steel beams embedded in the ground, but usually they were pyramid-shaped reinforced concrete projections. There were five rows of projections, poured monolithic with a concrete foundation and increasing in height from two and a half feet in front to almost five feet in rear. The concrete foundation, which extended two and a half feet above the ground on the approach side, formed an additional obstacle.

Roads leading through the dragon's teeth were denied usually by a double set of obstacles, one a gate and another three rows of steel beams embedded diagonally in a concrete foundation. The gate consisted of two 12-inch H-beams welded together and hinged at one end to a reinforced concrete pillar. The beams could be swung into place horizontally and bolted to another concrete pillar on the opposite side of the road. The second obstacle consisted of three rows of 12-inch H-beams offset like theater seats. Embedded in the concrete foundation at an angle of about 45 degrees, the beams were attached at their base by a flange connection which hooked over an iron rod in the bottom of the recess. Though this and other obstacles conceivably could be removed or demolished by an attacking force, it presumably would prove difficult under fire from nearby pillboxes.

Pillboxes in general were 20 to 30 feet in width, 40 to 50 feet in depth, and 20 to 25 feet in height. At least half of the pillbox was underground. The walls and roofs were 3 to 8 feet thick, of concrete reinforced by wire mesh and small steel rods and at times by heavy steel beams. Each pillbox had living quarters for its normal complement, usually about seven men per firing embrasure. Few had more than two firing embrasures, one specifically sited to cover the entrance. Although fields of fire were limited, generally not exceeding an arc of 50 degrees, pillboxes were mutually supporting.

Bunkers usually were designed to house local reserves and command posts and had no firing embrasures except small rifle ports to cover the entrance. Bunkers used as observation posts usually were topped by a steel cupola.

Most pillboxes and bunkers had several rooms, one or more for troop quarters and one or more either for ammunition storage or for firing. All were gasproof and equipped with hand-operated ventilation devices. Only a few installations had escape hatches. Heat might come from a small fireplace equipped with a tin chimney, both of which might be closed off by a heavy steel door. Each entrance usually had a double set of case-hardened steel doors separated by a gasproof vestibule. Bunks were of the type found on troop ships, oblong metal frames covered with rope netting and suspended in tiers from the ceiling. Sanitary facilities were rarely provided. Though both electric and telephone wires had been installed underground, it is doubtful that these were functioning well in September 1944. Some installations were camouflaged to resemble houses and barns. Except in the sparse sector north of Geilenkirchen, pillbox density averaged approximately ten per mile. Most pillboxes were on forward slopes, usually 200 to 400 yards behind the antitank obstacles.

Without question, these fortifications added to the defensive potentiality of the terrain along the German border; but their disrepair and the caliber of the defending troops had vitiated much of the line's formidability. It could in no sense be considered impregnable. Nevertheless, as American troops were to discover, steel and concrete can lend backbone to a defense, even if the fortifications are outmoded and even if the defenders are old men and cripples.

The climate in the region of the West Wall is characterized during autumn and winter by long periods of light rain and snow. Although less rain falls then than during summer, there are more days of precipitation likely to curtail air activity and maintain saturation of the fine textured soils found in the region. Even in winter temperatures are usually above freezing except during seven to eight days a month when snow covers the ground.[24]

These were the climatic conditions which Allied planners might expect. In reality, the fall and winter of 1944 were to produce weather of near record severity. Rainfall was to be far above average, and snow and freezing temperatures were to come early and stay for long periods. It wasn't very good weather for fighting a motorized, mechanized war or, as cold, rain-soaked infantrymen would attest, for fighting a foxhole war.

---

[24] More on climate may be found in: The Climate of the Rhine Valley, Germany, XIX Corps AAR Oct 44; The Climate of Central and Western Germany, Annex 1 to FUSA G-2 Per Rpt 92, 10 Sep, FUSA G-2 file, Sep 44.

A Pause at the Border

On 11 September the seemingly vagrant path which the Allied armies had followed through North Africa, Sicily, Italy, France, and Belgium at last was heading for its destination. The First Army was preparing to invade Germany.

The First Army's greatest concentration lay well to the north of the center of the army zone near Liège. Here General Collins had kept the three divisions of his VII Corps close to his left boundary in a relatively compact formation covering about fifteen miles. The 1st Division was astride the main Liège–Aachen highway less than ten miles from Aachen. (*Map III*) The 3d Armored Division had captured the city of Eupen in the borderland ceded to Belgium after World War I. The 9th Division was moving into assembly areas near Verviers, a textile and communications center about halfway between Liège and the German frontier. The 4th Cavalry Group, perhaps spurred by the nature of its objective, had occupied the beer-producing town of Malmédy. The cavalry was responsible for screening a twenty-five mile gap extending southward to the boundary with the V Corps.

General Gerow had tried to keep the main force of his V Corps near his northern boundary in order to be as close as possible to the main concentration of the VII Corps. The 4th Division was in assembly areas near St. Vith, about six miles from the German border. (*Map II*) The 28th Division was assembling in the northern tip of Luxembourg, its easternmost disposition not over four miles from Germany. To cover a front of approximately thirty miles from the infantry divisions south to the boundary with the Third Army, the 5th Armored

Division was assembling on three sides of the city of Luxembourg.

On the First Army's north wing, General Corlett's XIX Corps still had some twenty to thirty miles to go before reaching the German border. The XIX Corps still had to cross the Meuse River and clear the Dutch Panhandle around Maastricht. The 2d Armored Division was on the left, near the boundary with the 21 Army Group; the 30th Division and the 113th Cavalry Group were on the right. (*See Map 1, below.*)

Though the general location of the First Army was the result of the high-level decisions of 23 August, the specific orientation of the three corps had emerged from a meeting between General Eisenhower and his top commanders on 2 September at Chartres. Indeed, it was the tentative directive emerging from this meeting, plus amplifications on 4 and 14 September, that was to govern First Army operations through the remainder of the month and into October.[25]

Meeting at Chartres with Bradley, Hodges, and Patton, Eisenhower had directed that two corps of the First Army drive northeast alongside the British to help secure the Ruhr industrial area. The remaining corps was to be prepared to accept a handicap while accumulating enough gasoline and other supplies to permit a drive eastward in conjunction with the Third Army. It was at this meeting that General Eisenhower granted approval for the Third Army to resume its attack.

---

[25] Memo for Record, 2 Sep 44, Notes on Meeting of Supreme Commander and Commanders; FWD 13765, 4 Sep 44, and FWD 14764, 14 Sep 44, Eisenhower to Comdrs, all in 12th A Gp 371.3 Military Objectives, I.

As finally determined by General Bradley, the First Army was to get over the Rhine at Koblenz, Bonn, and Cologne, while the Third Army was to cross at Mainz and Mannheim.[26] Within the First Army, the V Corps was to drive toward Koblenz, the VII Corps toward Bonn, and the XIX Corps toward Cologne.

General Hodges, in turn, had ordered what might appear at first glance to have been a contradiction of General Eisenhower's assignment of priority to the two corps alongside the British. Instead of the V Corps on the right wing, the corps which he had halted for want of gasoline was the XIX Corps on the left wing, closest to the British. In reality, General Hodges had made the alteration in order to utilize the modicum of gasoline available at the moment to close a yawning gap that had developed between the First and Third Armies and to get at least two corps across the Meuse River, the only logical defensive line to be crossed in this sector short of the West Wall. He apparently had chosen the V and VII Corps because they had been closest to the Meuse.[27] General Hodges' reaction later in the month after the V Corps had entered the West Wall would demonstrate his basic obedience to the assignment of priority.[28]

Having crossed the Meuse, General Hodges on 11 September faced the second big step in the drive to the Rhine. Before him lay the prospect of two of his corps assaulting the vaunted West Wall. Gasoline suddenly dropped from the highest position of priority in the supply picture in favor of ammunition. Facing a heavily fortified line, General Hodges could not ignore the possibility that a period of intense fighting might ensue. Though the First Army had received a thousand tons of ammunition on 11 September, time would be required to move it forward from the railhead. Not until 15 September, the logistics experts estimated, would sufficient stocks of ammunition be available for five days of intensive fighting.[29]

Loath to upset the impetus of his victorious troops, General Hodges nevertheless deemed it imperative to order a pause of at least two days. He attempted to bridge the period by directing extensive reconnaissance and development of enemy strength and dispositions. Both the V and VII Corps then were to launch co-ordinated attacks not earlier than the morning of 14 September.

The VII Corps commander, General Collins, chafed under even this much delay. In the afternoon of 11 September, General Collins asked permission to make a reconnaissance in force the next day to advance as far as possible through the border defenses. If progress proved "easy," he wanted to make a limited penetration beyond the West Wall before pausing for supplies.

General Hodges was torn by a dilemma of time versus power. A hastily mounted attack might quickly bog down, yet every day of delay would aid the enemy's efforts to man the West Wall. Making his decision on the side of speed, General Hodges approved Collins' request. He also authorized General Gerow to make a similar reconnaissance in force with the V Corps. Should the maneuvers encounter solid opposition and fail to achieve quick

---

[26] 12th A Gp Ltrs of Instrs 8, 10 Sep 44, 12th A Gp Rpt of Opns, V, 91–92.

[27] This is the author's analysis of material found in FUSA AAR, Sep 44. See also Interv with Gen Bradley, 7 Jun 56.

[28] See below, Ch. III.

[29] Sylvan Diary, entry of 10 Sep 44.

penetrations, General Hodges directed, the corps were to hold in place to await supplies before launching major attacks.[30]

General Hodges obviously based these eleventh-hour authorizations on a hope that resistance still would be disorganized and spotty. The assault formation alone would indicate that pursuit still was the order of the day. Here were two corps, widely separated and without support on either flank. To the south, the closest concentration of the Third Army was more than eighty miles away from the main concentration of the V Corps. To the northeast, the First Army's XIX Corps had gained sufficient gasoline on 11 September to resume the northeastward drive, but it would be several days before the XIX Corps would be in a position to protect the exposed left flank of the VII Corps.

The first thrust toward the West Wall and the Rhine thus devolved upon the V and VII Corps, both widely extended, virtually devoid of hope for early reinforcement, and dangerously short of supplies. Still there was reason to believe that the reconnaissance in force might succeed.

Though resistance against both corps had been stiffening perceptibly as the troops neared the border, it was not strong enough to disperse the heady optimism of the period. Hardly anyone believed that the West Wall would be surrendered without a fight, yet the troops available to defend it probably would be too few and too disorganized to make much of a stand. The V Corps estimated that on its immediate front the enemy had only 6,000 troops. Not a single German unit of divisional size, the V Corps G–2 noted, had been encountered for at least a week. The VII Corps expected to encounter only about 7,700 Germans.[31]

The over-all First Army view was that the Germans would defend the West Wall "for reasons of prestige," but that they hardly could hope to hold for long. Even the increased resistance becoming manifest at the moment in Lorraine and the Netherlands, the First Army took to be a good omen. Since the enemy had concentrated elsewhere, he had nothing left for defending either the Eifel region or the Aachen Gap.[32]

---

[30] See Ltr, Hodges to Gerow, 11 Sep 44, V Corps G–3 file, 11 Sep 44.

[31] V Corps G–2 Estimate 11, 10 Sep 44; Order of Battle, Incl 2 to VII Corps G–2 Per Rpt 97.

[32] FUSA G–2 Estimate 26, 11 Sep 44.

CHAPTER III

V Corps Hits the West Wall

It was almost dark on 11 September when General Gerow, the V Corps commander, received General Hodges' authorization for a reconnaissance in force to penetrate the West Wall.[1] Thus General Gerow hardly could have expected to begin by the next morning a reconnaissance on the scale contemplated by General Collins and the neighboring VII Corps. He directed, in effect, little more than movement to assembly areas closer to the German border in preparation for the co-ordinated attack to be launched on 14 September.

Interpreting the order to mean sending only reinforced patrols against the West Wall for the moment, the infantry division commanders obviously anticipated no immediate breakthrough of the fortified line. The corps armor, in turn, was merely to reconnoiter the West Wall with patrols and provide a demonstration by fire "to conceal our real intention to make the main effort in the north half of [the] Corps zone."[2]

The plan which General Gerow had in mind for the co-ordinated attack on 14 September had been worked out several days earlier before General Hodges had indicated the necessity of a pause at the border.[3] It reflected in some measure a basic incongruity in corps objective and mission as transmitted down the chain of command from the meeting of top American commanders at Chartres. In driving toward Koblenz, the V Corps was to attack "in conjunction with Third Army."[4] Yet if the corps tried to stick close to the Third Army, this would mean attacking up the valley of the Moselle River, a narrow compartmentalized route of advance far removed from the rest of the First Army upon which the V Corps depended for supply and for assistance in event of trouble.

Having attempted to resolve the conflict by stationing the infantry divisions near the northern corps boundary, General Gerow then had to depend upon his armored division to cover the great gap between the infantry and the Third Army. Thus he in effect had demoted his armor to the role of a cavalry group, which meant that the weight of the armor would be lost to him in at least the initial stages of his attack. Meeting with his three division commanders on 10 September, General Gerow revealed his desire to get the armor into the fight if possible. He directed the 5th Armored Division to demonstrate to its front and be prepared to assault the West Wall on order, all the while holding out one combat command

---

[1] Ltr, Hodges to Gerow, 11 Sep 44, FUSA G-3 file, 9-23 Sep 44.

[2] Dir, Gerow to CO, 5th Armd Div, 11 Sep, FUSA G-3 file, 9-23 Sep 44.

[3] V Corps FO 26, 9 Sep 44, V Corps G-3 file, 9 Sep 44.

[4] Memo for Record, 2 Sep 44, Notes on Meeting of Supreme Commander with Subordinate Commanders.

prepared on short notice to exploit any breakthrough achieved by the infantry.[5]

Perhaps the incongruity between corps objective and mission was basically insoluble. The difficulty, for example, was clearly reflected on 11 September at First Army headquarters where General Gerow and the army commander, General Hodges, engaged in "an occasionally rather tempestuous discussion" over the V Corps plan. Aware of "the importance that General Bradley [12th Army Group commander] placed on the strength of the right flank," Hodges insisted that an infantry regimental combat team be attached to the armor on the right. General Gerow gave the role to the 28th Division's 112th Infantry. Possibly also as a result of General Hodges' views, Gerow on 11 September enlarged the armored division's assignment by ordering that if the armor found the West Wall in its zone lightly held, it was to attack to seize objectives in the south that would protect and promote the main advance in the north while at the same time lessening the gap between the First and Third Armies.[6]

No one had any illusions at this stage about the terrain over which the V Corps was to attack. Already familiar were the sharp ridges, deeply incised ravines, numerous streams, dense forests, and restricted road net of the Ardennes. Attacking through the Eifel meant more of the same but with the added obstacle of the West Wall.

All along the V Corps front the West Wall was a single belt of fortifications in

greatest density along a possible avenue of approach southwest of the Schnee Eifel, the high wooded ridge just across the Our River and the German border. (*See Map II.*) Along the Schnee Eifel itself the Germans had depended so much upon the rugged terrain that they had built fewer fortifications than at any point from Aachen south and southeast to the Rhine.

The objectives assigned the divisions of the V Corps were based upon three distinct elevations lying astride the route of advance. The first was the Schnee Eifel, extending unbroken for about fifteen miles from Ormont to the vicinity of the village of Brandscheid where it develops into a high, relatively open plateau. The 4th Division was to seize the crest of the Schnee Eifel to facilitate advance of the 28th Division across the plateau. Farther south the plateau is blocked by dense woods and sharp, clifflike slopes to a point between Vianden and Echternach. Here exists a suggestion of a corridor through which the 5th Armored Division was to advance upon order to take high ground about the village of Mettendorf.

The second elevation, taking the form of a high north-south plateau, lies beyond the Pruem River. At the western edge of the plateau lie the towns of Pruem and Bitburg. Though these towns have a population of only a few thousand, they are among the largest in the Eifel and are important communications centers. The infantry in the north was to take Pruem; the armor in the south, to secure Bitburg.

Beyond the second elevation lies the little Kyll River, barring access to a third, high mountainlike plateau which slopes, grooved and broken, to the Rhine. Across this plateau the divisions were to make the final advance on Koblenz, some fifty miles inside the German border.

---

[5] V Corps Memo for Record, 10 Sep 44, V Corps G–3 file, 11 Sep 44.

[6] Sylvan Diary, entry of 11 Sep 44; Memo, Gerow to CGs, 4th and 28th Divs, 11 Sep 44, FUSA G–3 file, 9–23 Sep 44.

Located opposite the Schnee Eifel near St. Vith, the 4th Division was about four miles south of the boundary with the VII Corps but some twenty miles from the main concentration of the VII Corps. To cover the gap, the 102d Cavalry Group was to screen and maintain contact with cavalry of the VII Corps and was to be prepared to advance eastward along the upper reaches of the Kyll through what is known as the Losheim Gap.

The location of the 28th Division (minus one regimental combat team) near the right flank of the 4th Division served to effect a concentration of five regiments on a frontage of approximately fourteen miles. South of this limited concentration, the 5th Armored Division and the 28th Division's 112th Infantry were to cover the rest of the corps front of about thirty miles.

As General Gerow was aware, he had achieved, for all his efforts, no genuine concentration for the attack. Yet the very fact that the corps had been assigned a rugged route of advance like the Eifel meant that American commanders still were thinking in terms of pursuit warfare. If pursuit remained the order of the day, the spread formation was acceptable, even in front of a fortified line like the West Wall.

Available intelligence gave no reason for concern. The V Corps G–2, Col. Thomas J. Ford, predicted that the corps would meet only battered remnants of the three divisions which had fled before the corps across Belgium and Luxembourg. These were the *5th Parachute, Panzer Lehr,* and *2d Panzer Divisions.* It was possible, Colonel Ford added, that the corps might meet parts of the *2d SS Panzer Division,* known to have been operating along the corps north boundary.

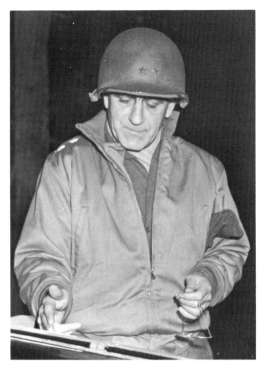

GENERAL GEROW

"There seems no doubt," Colonel Ford concluded, "that the enemy will defend [the Siegfried Line] with all of the forces that he can gather." But, he intimated, what he could gather was open to question.[7]

The Race for the West Wall

The true German situation in the Eifel was fully as dismal as the V Corps G–2 pictured it. The corps which controlled the sector roughly coterminous to that of the V Corps was the *I SS Panzer Corps* under General der Waffen-SS Georg Keppler. Of four divisions nominally under General Keppler's command, two had been so depleted that Keppler had merged them with another, the *2d SS Panzer Division.* This division was to

[7] V Corps G–2 Estimate 11, 10 Sep 44.

defend the Schnee Eifel. The remaining division, the 2d *Panzer*, was to guard the West Wall south of the Schnee Eifel.

Between them the 2d *Panzer* and 2d *SS Panzer Divisions* could muster no more than 3 nominal panzer grenadier regiments, none with greater strength than a reinforced battalion; 2 engineer battalions; 2 signal battalions; 17 assault guns; 26 105-mm. and 3 150-mm. howitzers; plus no more than 6 tanks, 3 in each division. To this force might be added the nondescript garrison troops actually in position in the West Wall in this sector, but these were so few that they could have manned no more than every fifth position.[8]

General Keppler's *I SS Panzer Corps* formed the southern (left) wing of the *Seventh Army*, commanded by General der Panzertruppen Erich Brandenberger. The *Seventh Army* in turn formed the left wing of Field Marshal Model's *Army Group B*. The corps, army, and army group boundaries ran through the southern part of the V Corps zone along a line Diekirch–Bitburg. Below this line was the *LXXX Corps*, which was the northern (right) wing of the *First Army* (General der Panzertruppen Otto von Knobelsdorff) in Lorraine, which was in turn the right wing of *Army Group G*.

Because the German unit boundaries did not correspond to the one between the First and Third U.S. Armies, the V Corps attack was to strike the inner wings of both German army groups. Thus, northernmost contingents of the *LXXX Corps* also would be involved. Commanded by

General der Infanterie Dr. Franz Beyer, the *LXXX Corps* had only one unit in this sector bearing a division label. This was the *5th Parachute Division*, which, like some of General Keppler's units, had little left except a name. To a nucleus of the division headquarters and a company of the reconnaissance battalion, General Beyer had attached a security regiment, a motorized infantry regiment, and a few miscellaneous units of company size. The division had neither armor nor artillery.

Although the *LXXX Corps* controlled a *Kampfgruppe* of the once-proud *Panzer Lehr Division*, the *Kampfgruppe* was a far cry from a division. It consisted only of a panzer grenadier battalion of company strength, an engineer company, six 105-mm. howitzers, five tanks, a reconnaissance platoon, and an *Alarmbataillon* (emergency alert battalion) of about 200 men recruited from stragglers and soldiers on furlough in Trier. Although the corps was destined on 14 September to receive a regiment and a light battery of a division newly committed in Lorraine, the addition hardly would make up for the over-all deficiencies in the command. The *First Army* put the matter succinctly in a report on 13 September: "At the present time, *LXXX Corps* cannot hold a defense line with these forces . . . ."[9]

---

[8] MS # C–048 (Kraemer). Generalmajor der Waffen-SS Fritz Kraemer was chief of staff of the *I SS Panzer Corps*. Greater detail and fuller documentation on the German side may be found in Lucian Heichler, The Germans Facing V Corps, MS prepared to complement this study, OCMH.

[9] Order, *A Gp B* to Armies, 10 Sep 44, *A Gp B KTB Anlagen, Operationsbefehle*, 1.IX.–30.IX. 44 (hereafter cited as *A Gp B KTB, Operationsbefehle*); Entries of 10 and 13 Sep 44, *A Gp G KTB 2*, 1.VII.–30.IX.44 (hereafter cited as *A Gp G KTB (Text)*); MSS # B–081 (Beyer) and # B–214 (Col Willy Mantey, CofS *First Army*); *Gen. St. d. H.* sit maps, *Lage Frankreich*, 10–14 Sep 44; Rpt, *A Gp G* to *OB WEST*, 13 Sep 44, *A Gp G KTB 2, Anlagen*, 1.IX.–30.IX.44 (hereafter cited as *A Gp G KTB, Anlagen*). Quotation is from entry of 13 Sep 44, *A Gp G KTB (Text)*.

In the feeble hands of units like these had rested German hopes of holding the Allies beyond the West Wall long enough for the fortifications to be put into shape. As the Commander in Chief West had recognized, this was a big assignment. As late as 10 September Field Marshal von Rundstedt had warned that he needed another five to six weeks to restore the West Wall. That very day he had been so perturbed by a gap which had developed between the *First* and *Seventh Armies* that he had authorized General Beyer's *LXXX Corps* to leave only rear guards behind in Luxembourg and to fall back on the West Wall. This move obviously foreshadowed a quick end to any hope that Keppler's *I SS Panzer Corps* might continue to hold beyond the West Wall; for it had left General Keppler without even a guise of a southern neighbor.[10]

On 11 September *Army Group B* summed up the gloomy story in a few words: "Continued reduction in combat strength and lack of ammunition have the direst effects on the course of defense action." That was understatement. On 11 September, for example, the *2d SS Panzer Division* possessed no ammunition for either its 75-mm. antitank guns, its 210-mm. mortars, or its light and medium howitzers. That evening General Keppler told the *2d Panzer Division* to fall back on the West Wall and the next day repeated the order to the *2d SS Panzer Division*.[11]

The fear behind these withdrawals was that American columns might exploit one of the yawning gaps in the line to spurt forward and gain a hold on an undefended West Wall while German units dangled impotently farther west. Reports reaching *Seventh Army* headquarters the night of 11 September to the effect that the *2d Panzer Division* had found the Americans already in possession of a number of West Wall bunkers for a while confirmed the Germans' worst apprehensions. German commanders breathed only slightly more easily when a new report the next day revealed the penetration to be the work of reconnaissance patrols.[12]

On 14 September, the day the V corps was to attack, the *I SS Panzer Corps* officially halted its retreat and began to occupy the West Wall along a forty-mile front stretching from the northern extremity of the Schnee Eifel to the vicinity of the little river village of Wallendorf, a few miles southeast of Vianden. General Keppler split the front between his two divisions, the *2d Panzer* and the *2d SS Panzer*.[13] Already the *LXXX Corps* had begun to occupy the bunkers farther south.

The race for the West Wall was over. Technically, the Germans had won it; but so soon were the Americans upon them that the end results looked much like a dead heat.

Into Germany

As the divisions of the V Corps began moving toward the German border early on 12 September, it was obvious that

---

[10] Entries of 10 Sep 44, *OB WEST KTB, 1.IX.–30.IX.44* (hereafter cited as *OB WEST KTB (Text)*), and *A Gp G KTB (Text)*.

[11] Quotation from Evng Sitrep, 11 Sep 44, *A Gp B, Ia Letzte Meldung, 10.VIII–30.IX.44* (hereafter cited as *A Gp B KTB, Letzte Meldung*); Rpt by Model (CG *A Gp B*) 11 Sep 44, *A Gp B KTB, Operationsbefehle;* MSS # B–730 (Brandenberger) and #B–623 (Keppler).

[12] MS # B–730 (Brandenberger).

[13] Sitrep, 13 Sep 44, *A Gp B KTB, Anlage, Tagesmeldungen, 6.VI.–15.X.44* (hereafter cited as *A Gp B KTB, Tagesmeldungen*).

General Gerow's plan of piercing the West Wall on a broad front with limited means could work as a genuine corps maneuver only if attended by considerable success. Because the various divisional attacks were to occur at relatively isolated points, only after attainment of unequivocal breakthrough could the divisions unite in concerted, mutually supporting maneuver. The V Corps attack thus began as three separate operations: the 4th Division on the Schnee Eifel, the 28th Division on the plateau southwest of the Schnee Eifel, and the 5th Armored Division far to the south.

The first of the three divisions to come full against the West Wall was the 28th in the center, both because the fortifications in the 28th Division's sector extended farther to the west and because the division commander gave a relatively broad interpretation to the authorization to make a reconnaissance in force.[14]

Even before receiving the authorization, the division commander, Brig. Gen. Norman D. Cota, [15] had issued a field order directing, in essence, a minor reconnaissance in force. His two regiments (the

third was attached to the 5th Armored Division) were to "attack" during daylight by sending strong patrols to feel the way and by closing up before dark to hold gains made by the patrols. In deference to the twelve- to fifteen-mile width of the division zone and to the unknown caliber of the enemy, neither regiment was to commit to action more than one reinforced battalion.[16]

The first objective was the crest of the high plateau a few miles beyond the German border in the vicinity of the West Wall village of Uettfeld. The route of approach was the closest thing to a natural corridor leading into Germany in this sector, even though it consisted of steep, broken terrain served by a limited road net. Though the pillboxes here were in but one band, they were dense and fronted by an almost continuous line of dragon's teeth antitank obstacles.

On the right wing, the 109th Infantry (Col. William L. Blanton) moved toward the village of Roscheid, which rested in a bend in the West Wall. Through Roscheid the regiment was to converge with the 110th Infantry (Col. Theodore A. Seely) on high ground around Uettfeld. By nightfall of 12 September a battalion had crossed a bridge over the Our River secured earlier by a patrol and had advanced unopposed through outpost pillboxes to the village of Sevenig, separated from Roscheid by the muddy course of the little Irsen creek.

To the north, the 110th Infantry also sent a battalion across the border to take up positions for the night west of Grosskampenberg, a village about 600 yards short of the dragon's teeth on a road

---

[14] The 28th Division had received its baptism of fire with the XIX Corps in the closing days of the Normandy hedgerow battles and had joined the V Corps on 28 August. By staging a liberation parade up the Champs Elysées on the way to the front, the division got its picture on a U.S. postage stamp. A nickname, The Bloody Bucket, probably was derived from a red keystone shoulder patch denoting the division's Pennsylvania National Guard origin. The division's story is based upon official records and combat interviews. The interview file contains a particularly valuable and detailed narrative on the 110th Infantry action, entitled Into Germany, by Capt. John S. Howe.

[15] Promoted to major general, 26 September 1944. General Cota assumed command on 14 August, after relief of one commander and the battle death one day later of his successor.

[16] 28th Div FO 17, 11 Sep 44, 28th Div G-3 file 11 Sep 44.

leading through Kesfeld to Uettfeld. The objective of Uettfeld lay about two miles beyond the dragon's teeth.

It was the report of the *2d Panzer Division*'s encounter with 28th Division reconnaissance patrols which disturbed the febrile *Seventh Army* headquarters into belief that the Americans had won the race for the West Wall. Even the clarification of the matter later on 12 September could have afforded little relief to the panzer division commander, General der Panzertruppen Heinrich Freiherr von Luettwitz. Although the line remained inviolate, the Americans had camped on the threshhold. Luettwitz' hope of stopping a thrust the next day, 13 September, rested mainly with three tanks and eight assault guns.[17]

General von Luettwitz might have breathed more easily had he known the true situation in the American camp. Moving directly from the scramble of pursuit warfare, the 28th Division was not ready for an attack on a fortified line. Neither of the two regiments had received special equipment needed in pillbox assault, such as flame throwers and explosive charges. Attached tank and self-propelled tank destroyer units still were repairing their pursuit-damaged vehicles and had yet to come forward. The infantry would face the West Wall with direct fire support only from organic 57-mm. antitank guns and a few platoons of towed tank destroyers, both highly vulnerable to return fire. Few units of the division had more than a basic load of ammunition, enough perhaps for a meeting engagement but not for sustained fighting. So concerned about the

ammunition shortage was the division commander, General Cota, that he forbade unobserved artillery fires except previously registered concentrations and others specifically approved by his headquarters. In addition, both regiments of the 28th Division would be restricted for still another day to committing but one battalion to action.

For all these problems, a battalion each of the 109th and 110th Infantry Regiments attacked the West Wall early on 13 September. Trying to cross the Irsen creek to gain a foothold among the pillboxes on high ground west of Roscheid, a battalion of the 109th Infantry failed even to reach the creek. Rifle and automatic weapons fire from the pillboxes brought the attackers up sharply more than 700 yards away from the West Wall. A battalion of the 110th Infantry met a similar fate halfway between Grosskampenberg and the line of dragon's teeth. Pinned to the ground by small arms fire from the pillboxes, the men were ready prey for German mortar and artillery fire. Though both attacking battalions tried to use towed antitank guns for direct fire support, enemy gunners endowed with superior observation made sudden death of the efforts. Indirect artillery fire did little damage to the pillboxes other than to "dust off the camouflage." [18]

When the next day, 14 September, brought removal of the restriction on committing more than one battalion, both regiments attacked frontally with one battalion while sending another around to a flank. Along with a company of tanks, the 109th Infantry was plagued all day by antitank fire and mines and by a natural tank trap in the muddy Irsen creek bot-

---

[17] MSS # B-730 (Brandenberger) and B-623 (Keppler).

[18] Howe, Into Germany.

tomland. At heavy cost the regiment finally seized a strip of forward pillboxes more than a mile wide but fell short of taking Roscheid.

Two miles to the north, the 110th Infantry renewed the attack toward Kesfeld while sending a battalion around to the north through the village of Heckhuscheid to move southeast on Hill 553, a West Wall strongpoint along the Heckhuscheid–Uettfeld highway. Once again the regiment found that without direct fire support the infantry could make no headway against the pillboxes. The battalion southeast of Heckhuscheid found the way barred by dragon's teeth and a roadblock at the base of Hill 553 and could get no farther. Though the battalion near Kesfeld had tried during the night to bring up explosives to blast a path through the dragon's teeth for tanks, the explosives had blown up unexplainably and killed the men who were carrying them. Arriving in midmorning, the tanks could provide little assistance because they could not get past the dragon's teeth and because poor visibility restricted fire against distant targets. Advance might have been stymied indefinitely had not 2d Lt. Joseph H. Dew maneuvered his tank to within a few feet of the dragon's teeth and methodically blasted a path with his 75-mm. gun.[19] Accompanied by the tanks, the infantry managed to seize a tiny foothold within the forward band of pillboxes, but at severe cost in casualties.

From prisoners, both regiments learned something of the desperation with which the Germans had tried to man the West Wall. Many pillboxes, prisoners revealed, still were unmanned, and others contained only two or three men armed with rifles and an occasional machine gun or panzerfaust. Gathered from almost every conceivable source, many of the men had arrived in the line only the night before. Complaining bitterly about having to fight, a forty-year-old cook said he was captured little more than two hours after reaching the front.

These revelations must have galled those American troops who had fought so hard to effect even these two small punctures in the German line. Maj. James C. Ford, the 110th Infantry S–3, spoke for them when he said: "It doesn't much matter what training a man may have when he is placed inside such protection as was afforded by the pillboxes. Even if he merely stuck his weapons through the aperture and fired occasionally, it kept our men from moving ahead freely." [20]

Though the 28th Division's gains were meager, they looked different when viewed against the backdrop of the situation along the entire corps front. Seeing the first punctures of the line as the hardest, the V Corps commander, General Gerow, ordered the 5th Armored Division to send an officer that night to advise the 28th Division on use of armor in event of a breakthrough the next day. The 5th Armored Division's Combat Command B, located northwest of Diekirch, was ready to move through if the infantry forged a gap.

When the next day came, General Gerow saw his hopes quickly dashed. Even before the 109th Infantry could get an attack going on 15 September, a small counterattack forced two platoons to relinquish some ground. For the next two days the 109th Infantry was to fight in

---

[19] Lieutenant Dew was awarded the Distinguished Service Cross.

[20] Howe, Into Germany.

vain to get past Roscheid and secure a hill that provided damaging observation off the regiment's right flank. In the process, the enemy's *2d Panzer Division* gradually chewed the regiment to pieces. Battered by German shelling, the American riflemen could not be trusted to hold the positions already gained. In at least two instances they fell back in panic before limited objective counterattacks. So poor was the showing that General Cota subsequently relieved the regimental commander.

Through most of 15 September the situation in the 110th Infantry's sector appeared equally discouraging. The 1st Battalion, commanded by Lt. Col. Floid A. Davison, was to try again to take Hill 553; but the late arrival of tanks and of engineers equipped with explosives to blow the troublesome roadblock precluded early success. Not until 1700 did the engineers arrive. The plan at this point was for the engineers to advance to the roadblock under cover of fire from the tanks and a platoon of towed tank destroyers. Blowing of the roadblock was to signal the start of an attack by infantry and tanks.

Ten unarmed engineers, each carrying a 50-pound load of TNT, began to creep slowly, carefully toward the roadblock. Though the day was foggy, the engineers felt naked. As they inched forward, tension mounted, passing almost electrically to the waiting infantrymen and tankers.

Reaching the objective at last, the engineers found that the roadblock consisted of six steel I-beams emplaced in concrete caissons on either side of the road. Large portable iron tetrahedrons reinforced the whole. Working swiftly, they placed their charges.

Shortly after 1830, an hour and a half after start of the tedious journey, the engineers completed their work. Activating the charges, they jumped to their feet. In the words of their lieutenant, they "went like hell to the rear." The roadblock disintegrated with a roar.

Acting on cue, the tanks fired point-blank at the pillboxes. The infantry went forward on the run. In about forty-five minutes the battalion had stormed the objective, Hill 553. It yielded seventeen pillboxes and fifty-eight prisoners. After almost three days of mounting casualties and frustrations, the 110th Infantry in a quick, co-ordinated assault at last had gained a significant objective within the West Wall.

The regimental commander, Colonel Seely, planned for his two committed battalions to converge the next day upon the regimental objective of Kemper Steimerich Hill (Hill 560), key to the commanding ground around Uettfeld. In order to better the jump-off position and to narrow a gap between the two battalions, the fatigued battalion west of Kesfeld sent a company in late afternoon to clear a nest of pillboxes in the direction of Hill 553. As darkness came, Company F under Capt. Robert H. Schultz completed the mission. Sending back more than fifty prisoners, the men began to settle down for the night in and about the pillboxes they had captured.

The first sign of an impending counterattack came about half an hour after midnight. The men could hear tracked vehicles moving through the darkness toward Company F's positions. On guard at the time at a pillbox occupied by the company's rear command group, Pvt. Roy O. Fleming said later, "Suddenly everything became quiet. I could hear the clank of these vehicles . . . . I saw the flame thrower start and heard the sounds of a helluva scrap up around Captain Schultz's position.. . . ." [21]

A few minutes after the firing began, another company intercepted a frantic radio message: "KING SUGAR to anybody. KING SUGAR to anybody. Help. We are having a counterattack—tanks, infantry, flame throwers."

What could anybody do to help? By the time the messages could be exchanged and artillery brought to bear, the action had subsided. Company F's radio apparently was defective, capable of sending but not of receiving. The situation thus was so obscure that Colonel Seely dared not risk immediate commitment of his reserve.

What happened remained a mystery difficult to piece together from the fragments of information provided by the few men who escaped. The Germans apparently had attacked with about seventy to eighty men reinforced by two flame-throwing vehicles. A prisoner captured some days later said the vehicles were improvised flame throwers constructed from *Schuetzenpanzerwagen* (armored half-tracks). As late as two days after the event, Company F could muster no more than forty-four men, including cooks and supply personnel.

The news of Company F's disaster dealt a heavy blow to the optimism engendered by the success of the preceding afternoon. Only a few hours before the Germans hit Company F, General Cota had expressed "high hopes" about the division's prospects.[22] He could have been thinking only of the 110th Infantry,

which now would have to use its reserve battalion to retake the pillboxes Company F had lost.

Delayed again by the late arrival of supporting tanks and unassisted by the rest of the regiment, Colonel Davison's 1st Battalion nevertheless attacked again in midmorning of 16 September. Assisted by effective counterbattery artillery fires, the battalion quickly seized Losenseifen Hill (Hill 568), adjacent to Hill 553 and one of the highest points in the 28th Division's sector. Leaving a company to hold the hill, the 1st Battalion continued to attack and stopped for the night only after capturing Spielmannsholz Hill (Hill 559), less than a thousand yards short of the regimental objective overlooking Uettfeld.

In a day of rapid, determined advance, Colonel Davison's men had progressed a mile and a half past the dragon's teeth and had captured some of the most commanding ground for miles around. Beyond them lay only scattered West Wall fortifications. Though the penetration was narrow and pencillike, the 28th Division had for all practical purposes broken through the West Wall.

It was ironic that even as Colonel Davison's men were achieving this feat, General Gerow was visiting the division command post with orders to call off the offensive. Having incurred almost 1,500 casualties, the two regiments of the 28th Division were in no condition to expand or exploit the 110th Infantry's narrow penetration.[23] Neither was the situation elsewhere in the V Corps encouraging enough to justify

---

[21] *Ibid.*

[22] 28th Div G–3 Jnl, 15 Sep 44.

[23] Though the casualty figures are for the entire month of September, the only heavy fighting occurred during these five days. See 28th Div AAR, Sep 44.

bringing troops from some other part of the front.

During the next few days, the 109th and 110th Infantry Regiments jockeyed for position, while the Germans registered their protest with small counterattacks and continued shelling.[24] The attempt to get across the high plateau into the rugged Eifel was over.

Battle of the Schnee Eifel

A few miles to the north, the 4th Division in the meantime had been more conservative in interpreting the authority to reconnoiter in force but had experienced more encouraging initial success. The action took place on the imposing ridge line east of St. Vith, the Schnee Eifel.

Preceded by combat patrols, the 4th Division had resumed eastward march on 12 September. By nightfall the next day two regiments had crossed the border and moved into assembly areas in the shadow of the Schnee Eifel. On the north wing, the 12th Infantry (Col. James S. Luckett) assembled at the village of Radscheid; the 22d Infantry (Col. Charles T. Lanham) nearby at Bleialf. Impressed by a lack of opposition, the division commander, Maj. Gen. Raymond O. Barton, ordered both regiments to push reconnaissance patrols forward; but he reserved any real attempt to move into the West Wall for the next day, 14 September, the day General

Gerow had designated for the V Corps attack.[25]

Patrols probing the woods line of the Pruem State Forest, which crowns the Schnee Eifel, learned little except that some Germans—number and capabilities undetermined—were in the pillboxes. This information did nothing to alter General Barton's anticipation that only a crust of resistance stood between the 4th Division and a breakthrough operation.[26]

General Barton ordered the 12th and 22d Infantry Regiments to attack abreast at 1000 on 14 September to seize an ambitious objective, commanding ground on the crest of the central plateau beyond the Pruem River, more than 10 miles away.[27] The 8th Infantry (Col. James S. Rodwell) was to remain in division reserve. Commanders of the two forward regiments designated initial objectives astride a lateral highway that follows the crest of the Schnee Eifel. These regiments also were to protect the division's exposed flanks, for to the southwest, closest units of the 28th Division were more than four miles away, and to the northwest, the closest friendly troops, except for a thin veil of cavalry, were twenty-five miles away.

The attack on 14 September was, at the start, more a reconnaissance in force than anything the division had attempted dur-

---

[24] During one counterattack, a squad leader in Company K, 109th Infantry, T. Sgt. Francis J. Clark, assumed command of two leaderless platoons. Moving among the men without regard for enemy fire, he encouraged them to hold. Later, though wounded, he refused evacuation. These were but two of a series of heroic actions over the period 12–17 September for which Sergeant Clark received the Medal of Honor.

[25] The 4th Division story is based on combat interviews and official records of the division and attached units. Veteran of the D-Day assault on UTAH Beach, the 4th Division also participated in the capture of Cherbourg and the battles to break out of the Norman hedgerows. The division joined the V Corps for the pursuit and shared in the liberation of Paris. The division's nickname, Ivy, comes from the Roman numerals, IV.

[26] See Ltr, Barton to OCMH, 5 Oct 53, OCMH.

[27] 4th Div FO 37, 13 Sep 44, 4th Div G-3 file, 13 Sep 44.

ing the two preceding days. Although the regiments had intended to attack together, the 22d Infantry was delayed until noon while awaiting arrival of an attached company of tanks and then used, according to plan, but one infantry battalion. The 12th Infantry intended to employ two battalions, but one took a wrong trail upon entering the forest and contributed little to the day's action. Thus the 4th Division attacked on 14 September in no greater strength at first than the 28th Division had employed the day before.

Screened by a drizzling rain, the 12th Infantry on the left advanced virtually unimpeded up the steep western slopes of the Schnee Eifel. The only battalion to make actual contact with the West Wall found the pillboxes undefended. Cutting the Schnee Eifel highway without difficulty, the battalion turned northeast along the highway toward the wooded high ground of Bogeyman Hill (Hill 697, the *Schwarzer Mann*). Only here did the battalion encounter a defended pillbox. Accompanied by tanks, the infantry moved along firebreaks and trails to outflank and carry the position. The men dug in for the night on Bogeyman Hill, all the way through the fabled West Wall. Resistance had been so light that the infantry had called only once for supporting artillery fire.

A mile to the south, the leading battalion of the 22d Infantry had been nearing the woods line east of Bleialf when a round from an 88-mm. gun ripped into one of the accompanying tanks. As the crewmen piled from the tank, the other tanks maneuvered about on the open hill. Thinking the tanks were withdrawing, the riflemen began to fall back in a panic. The attack might have floundered on this discreditable note had not unit com-

manders acted aggressively to bring the men under control.[28]   Then, as if to atone for their earlier hesitancy, the men charged forward at a run. In about twenty minutes their charge carried not only to the woods line but past a row of pillboxes all the way to the crest of the ridge. Like the 12th Infantry, the 22d Infantry had achieved an astonishingly quick penetration of this thin sector of the West Wall.

To enlarge the penetration, the regimental commander, Colonel Lanham, quickly committed his other two battalions. One continued the drive to the east to gain the woods line on the eastern slope of the ridge while the other joined the assault battalion in fanning out to right and left to roll up the line of pillboxes. Some of the fortifications turned out to be undefended, and the enemy had manned the others predominantly with middle-aged men and youths who had little unit organization and less conception of tactics. One or two rifle shots against embrasures often proved persuasion enough to disgorge the defenders, hands high. Only to the southwest at a crossroads settlement on the Bleialf–Pruem highway did the Germans fight with determination, and here close-in fire from self-propelled tank destroyers had a telling effect. By the end of the day the 22d Infantry held a breach in the West Wall about two miles wide. One battalion had reached a position on the eastern slopes of the Schnee Eifel overlooking the village of Hontheim, a mile and a quarter past the forward pillboxes.

On the German side, the *2d SS Panzer Division* either had waited a day too long before falling back on the West Wall or

---

[28] For their roles in rallying the troops, the regimental commander, Colonel Lanham, and the S–2, Capt. Howard C. Blazzard, received the DSC.

DRAGON'S TEETH *near Brandscheid. The wooded section at upper left is the edge of the Schnee Eifel.*

had concentrated first on manning the fortifications along more logical routes of advance than the rugged Schnee Eifel. The division commander, SS-Brigade-fuehrer und Generalmajor der Waffen-SS Heinz Lammerding, set out immediately to try to contain the penetration; but the strength available to him still was unimpressive, even though he had received a few new attachments upon withdrawal behind the border. He had about 750 men in four organic battalions and 1,900 in nine attached battalions, a total of about 2,650. To support them, he had 14 75-mm. antitank guns, about 37 artillery pieces, 1 assault gun, and 1 Mark V Panther tank. Two other tanks were in the repair shop.[29]

To the American commander, General Barton, the successes on 14 September confirmed his belief that the West Wall would be only a minor obstruction in the path of the pursuit. The corps commander, General Gerow, apparently shared this view, for it was during the night of 14 September that he directed an officer of

---

[29] TWX, *A Gp B* to *OB WEST*, 22 Sep 44 (based on weekly strength rpt of 16 Sep 44), *A Gp B KTB, Operationsbefehle;* MS # C–048 (Kraemer).

the 5th Armored Division to advise the 28th Division on the use of armor in event of a breakthrough. Though the greatest success had been in the 4th Division's sector, the terrain along the Schnee Eifel discouraged use of armor there.

Having virtually walked through the West Wall, General Barton acted on 15 September both to broaden his effort and speed the eastward advance. He committed his reserve, the 8th Infantry, in a motorized advance along the best axial highway in his zone to skirt the northern end of the Schnee Eifel along the narrow corridor afforded by the valley of the upper Kyll, the Losheim Gap. The regiment was to occupy a march objective on the north bank of the Kyll six miles inside Germany. The 12th Infantry meanwhile was to sweep northeastward along the Schnee Eifel for several miles in order to uncover roads leading east. The 22d Infantry was to turn southwest to take Brandscheid, a village within the West Wall at the southern end of the Schnee Eifel. These objectives accomplished, the 12th and 22d Infantry Regiments were to renew the eastward drive to seize march objectives fourteen miles away on the Kyll.[30]

With the 8th Infantry on 15 September rode General Barton's main hope for a breakthrough. If the 8th Infantry could push rapidly, the Schnee Eifel could be outflanked and the West Wall left far behind.

Starting early from the border village of Schoenberg, the 8th Infantry ran into **blown bridges and roadblocks almost from** the beginning. A heavy mist also slowed the column and for the second straight day denied tactical air support. At the

border near the village of Losheim the column hit definite resistance. Sideslipping to the south along a secondary highway, the regiment encountered a relatively stout outpost position near the village of Roth. By late afternoon the leading battalion had pushed the outpost back to the West Wall. But the 8th Infantry commander, Colonel Rodwell, saw no hope of readying a co-ordinated attack against the fortifications before the next morning.[31]

Colonel Rodwell's anticipation of delay was attributable more to organization problems than to any real concern about the enemy. One of his battalions, for example, reported finding German reconnaissance parties just moving into the pillboxes. Yet in the pressure of events, this information escaped the division commander, General Barton. Not having realized the rapid thrust he had anticipated and somewhat perturbed by the turn of events during the day on the Schnee Eifel, General Barton told Colonel Rodwell to abandon the maneuver.[32]

In the wet foxholes astride the Schnee Eifel, the infantrymen of the 4th Division's other two regiments had noted a distinct change in the situation early on 15 September. German mortar and artillery fire markedly increased and began to have telling effect from tree bursts in the thick forest. About 300 Germans counterattacked the most forward battalion of the 22d Infantry near Hontheim. A battalion scheduled to take Brandscheid spent the morning rounding up Germans who had

---

[30] 4th Div FO 38, 14 Sep 44, 4th Div G-3 file, 14 Sep 44; Ltr, Barton to OCMH.

[31] 8th Inf AAR, Sep 44, and S-3 Jnl, 15 Sep 44.

[32] *Ibid.*; Ltr, Barton to OCMH; Ltr, Maj Gen H. W. Blakely (former 4th Div Arty commander and later commander of the 4th Div) to OCMH, 26 Jun 56.

infiltrated behind the battalion during the night. Few pillboxes now were undefended. A battalion of the 12th Infantry spent several hours routing about sixty Germans from a nest of pillboxes at a crossroads, the Kettenkreuz (Hill 655). Two other fortified positions centering on crossroads occupied the 12th Infantry for the rest of the day, so that by nightfall roads leading east still were out of reach.

Though all advances by the 12th and 22d on 15 September were labored, they nevertheless had covered sufficient ground in diametrically divergent directions to create a gap between regiments of more than two and a half miles. Disappointed in the outcome of the 8th Infantry's maneuver farther north, General Barton saw a chance to secure the gap on the Schnee Eifel while at the same time exploiting it as a possible point of breakthrough. He told Colonel Rodwell to move his regiment to the Schnee Eifel and drive through the middle of the other two regiments. The flank regiments would open adequate roads to him later. Hope that a breakthrough still might be accomplished was nurtured by promising developments reported during the day to the south in the zone of the 5th Armored Division.[33]

Unfortunately for the 4th Division, it takes only a few defenders to hold up an attacker in cruel terrain like the Schnee Eifel. Though the Germans had no reserves to commit in this sector, they were able gradually to build up the *2d SS Panzer Division* with replacements and odd attachments while the original few were fighting effective delaying action. By 16 September, for example, the Germans had established a fairly strong blocking position

across the Schnee Eifel to deny the 12th Infantry the coveted road leading east. The 12th Infantry's casualties soared in exchange for almost no further advance. Several days later, on 19 September, the Germans had obtained two companies of infantry and three Mark IV tanks with which to counterattack. They would have recovered some ground had it not been for the courage and resourcefulness of an American company commander, 1st Lt. Phillip W. Wittkopf, who called down artillery fire almost atop his own position.[34]

The difficulties of terrain were nowhere more evident than in the center of the 4th Division's formation where the 8th Infantry began to drive down the wooded eastern slopes of the Schnee Eifel early on 16 September. By nightfall the next day parts of the regiment were near the eastern edge of the forest; but behind them lay hundreds of yards of dense woods crossed only by muddy, poorly charted firebreaks and trails subject to constant enemy infiltration.

On the division's south wing, the 22d Infantry could attribute a lack of success against the village of Brandscheid to the backbone which West Wall pillboxes put into the German defense. The only bright development on this part of the front came in the afternoon of 16 September when the 1st Battalion pushed out of the Pruem State Forest to seize a hill that commanded the Bleialf–Pruem highway a few hundred yards west of the German-held village of Sellerich. Even this achievement was marred by the loss from German shelling of some thirty-five men wounded and eight killed, including the battalion commander, Lt. Col. John Dowdy.

Encouraged by the 1st Battalion's ad-

---

[33] See Msg, Gerow to CGs 4th and 28th Divs, 15 Sep 44, 4th Div G–3 file, 14 Sep 44.

[34] Lieutenant Wittkopf received the DSC.

vance, the 22d Infantry commander, Colonel Lanham, ordered continuation of the attack the next day to pass beyond Sellerich and seize high ground east of the Mon creek on the road to Pruem. Commanded now by Maj. Robert B. Latimer, the 1st Battalion faced terrain that tended to funnel its attack dangerously. In front of the battalion were three villages: Hontheim, on high ground to the northeast; Herscheid, on high ground to the southeast; and Sellerich, along the main highway in a depression exposed to the dominating ground on either flank. Because Major Latimer deemed his strength insufficient for taking the high ground, he saw no alternative to attacking directly down the valley. Recognizing the danger in this approach, he requested artillery fire to blanket the high ground and directed only one company to move at first to the objective. Company A was to take the objective, Company B was to follow soon after with attached tank destroyers and tanks to help hold the objective, and Company C was to maintain the jump-off positions west of Sellerich.

Even before the attack began, adversity overtook the 1st Battalion. Into the morning of 17 September enemy shelling so unnerved several officers, including the commander of the attached tank platoon, that they had to be evacuated for combat exhaustion. About 0830, as Company A moved to the line of departure, another severe shelling so upset the company commander that he too had to be evacuated. 1st Lt. Warren E. Marcum assumed command of the company.

Still under German shellfire, Lieutenant Marcum and Company A moved quickly down the highway into Sellerich. They found not a single German in the village

and continued unopposed across the Mon creek. By 1100 they had occupied the crest of the objective, Hill 520.

When Company B and the tanks and tank destroyers started to follow, one of the tank destroyers hit a mine in the deeply incised ravine of the creek. Almost immediately the Germans came to life. Opening fire with antitank weapons from both north and south, they drove the armor to cover in Sellerich. With interlocking fires from machine guns and light caliber antiaircraft weapons, they sealed off the route of retreat. Mortar and artillery fire rained upon the trapped troops. East of the creek, about a hundred Germans began to counterattack Company A from two directions. Try as they would, Company B and the tanks could not cross the ravine to Lieutenant Marcum's aid.

Fearful of losing the hill west of Sellerich, Major Latimer was reluctant to commit his remaining company. To make it available, Colonel Lanham called off an attack at Brandscheid to send tanks and a rifle company to hold the hill; but by the time this force could disengage, the situation at Sellerich and beyond the creek had so deteriorated that reinforcement appeared futile.

Only minutes before Lieutenant Marcum was wounded, he requested permission to withdraw. Then his radio ceased to function. By the time Major Latimer got a decision from the regimental commander authorizing withdrawal, he had no communications with Company A. Although he sent two messengers forward, he could see no evidence that they reached the company. When the battalion S-3 tried to get forward, he was wounded five times.

Whether Company A ever received the withdrawal authority became incidental; for when Lieutenant Marcum was wounded, the other officers apparently lost all control. Men began to get back individually and in small groups. A few made it out with Company B, but most who survived the action beyond the creek did not reach the 1st Battalion's lines until after dark. A count showed later that but two officers and sixty-six men had escaped, a loss of more than 50 percent.

The disaster east of the Mon creek for all practical purposes ended the battle of the Schnee Eifel. That night the assistant division commander, Brig. Gen. George A. Taylor, went to the corps command post to give details on the division's situation. He emphasized the damage the 22d Infantry had incurred from shelling and counterattack, the inadequacy of roads and trails through the Pruem State Forest, and the effect of the woods and adverse weather on American advantage in air, artillery, and armor. He noted also how vulnerable the division was to counterattack on both flanks.[35]

General Taylor actually had no major selling job to do at V Corps headquarters. Already General Gerow had called off the attack of the 28th Division. When the 4th Division commander, General Barton, issued a new field order, he worded it in accord with confidential information that the First Army intended to call off the V Corps attack that night.[36]

For the next few days all three regiments of the 4th Division were to engage in local attacks to adjust their lines for defense, but they registered no major gains. The battle was over. Neither Germans nor Americans possessed either the strength or inclination to push all out for a decision. In four days of combat ranging from light to intense, the 4th Division had torn a gap almost six miles wide in the West Wall but at a point offering no axial roads and few objectives, short of the Rhine, attractive enough to warrant a major effort to secure them. The breach had cost the division about 800 casualties.

Four major factors had worked against both the 4th and 28th Divisions in making the V Corps main effort. First, the cruel terrain and the West Wall had enabled a few Germans to do the work of many. Second, rain and generally poor visibility had denied air support, restricted observation for tank and artillery fires, and produced poor footing for tanks. Third, a shortage of artillery ammunition, which in the case of the 28th Division had limited artillery units to twenty-five rounds per gun per day, had denied the infantry large-scale fire support and had afforded German guns an immunity that otherwise would not have existed. Fourth, an inability to concentrate had prevented either division from employing overwhelming weight at any critical point. The last factor had affected the 28th Division particularly, for General Cota had possessed no reserve regiment.

Had either General Gerow or the division commanders interpreted the authorization for a reconnaissance in force more broadly, they might have beaten the Germans into the West Wall. On the other hand, General Hodges, the

---

[35] Rpt, Gen Taylor to V Corps Comdr, 4th Div G–3 file, 17 Sep 44. Note that when the Germans launched their counteroffensive in this region in December, they cut off American troops on the Schnee Eifel by driving around both ends of the ridge.

[36] Ltr, Barton to OCMH; 4th Div FO 41, 17 Sep 44, in 4th Div G–3 file, 17 Sep 44.

First Army commander, had been distinctly conservative in his authorization. Hodges, for example, had insisted that "all troops should stay tightly 'buttoned up,'" and Gerow had received a "definite impression" that the army commander would not sanction the corps becoming "involved" in the West Wall before 14 September.[37] Even had the infantry divisions achieved a *coup de main,* might they not in exploiting it have encountered similar difficulties? Indeed, in view of the ammunition shortage and the dispersion of units, they might have had trouble even holding a major breach of the West Wall.

Bridgehead at Wallendorf

From the viewpoint of both the V Corps and the Germans, the main effort by the infantry divisions actually had shown less promise of far-reaching results than had another attack in the south of the V Corps zone. Here an anticipated secondary effort by the 5th Armored Division had developed into a genuine opportunity for a breakthrough which showed promise of welding the three separate division actions into a cohesive corps maneuver.

Withheld from immediate commitment against the West Wall, the 5th Armored Division in the interim had drawn a variety of responsibilities. Not the least of these was securing approximately thirty miles of the corps front. The division commander, Maj. Gen. Lunsford E. Oliver, assigned Combat Command A and the attached 112th Infantry to patrol the southern portion of the zone, maintain contact with Third Army cavalry far to the south, and protect the city of Luxembourg. He designated Combat Command

R to probe the West Wall with patrols along the central portion of the zone and be prepared upon order to attack the West Wall between Vianden and Echternach and seize the communications center of Bitburg on the Eifel's central plateau. He gave Combat Command B responsibility for the northern portion of the division zone and alerted it for commitment upon corps order to exploit any breakthrough achieved by the infantry divisions.[38]

Observers in posts along the Our and Sauer Rivers, which separate Luxembourg from Germany, and patrols that probed the West Wall brought back similar reports: In some places the pillboxes were not manned; in others the Germans were hurriedly moving in. Though the Americans did not know it, this was the sector of the great gap between the *I SS Panzer Corps* and the *LXXX Corps,* which was perturbing both enemy corps commanders, Generals Keppler and Beyer.

In the afternoon of 13 September, as the infantry divisions in the north closed to the West Wall, CCR conducted a reconnaissance by fire near the village of Wallendorf, about halfway between Echternach and Vianden. It failed to provoke a single return shot from the Germans.

Convinced that the West Wall opposite the armor was no more than weakly manned, General Gerow in early evening of 13 September ordered General Oliver to advance. With one combat command he

---

[37] Sylvan Diary, entry of 14 Sep 44; Ltr, Gerow to OCMH, 29 Aug 53, OCMH.

[38] The 5th Armored Division story is based on official records and combat interviews. Nicknamed Victory, the division entered combat with the Third Army on 2 August and joined the V Corps for the pursuit. Troops of the 5th Armored Division captured historic Sedan and the city of Luxembourg.

was to attack through Wallendorf to seize high ground near Mettendorf, about five miles inside Germany, and then drive to Bitburg, twelve miles beyond the border. The 1st Battalion, 112th Infantry, was to assist the attack.

In directing an attack between Vianden and Echternach, General Gerow had exercised a choice between two existing avenues of approach into Germany in this region. One extends northeast from the vicinity of Wallendorf, the other almost due north from an eastward bend in the German border east of Echternach. Though the Wallendorf corridor is more sharply compartmentalized and has fewer good roads, General Gerow chose it because it was somewhat closer to the infantry divisions (about fifteen miles).

General Oliver decided to attack from the southwestern corner of the Wallendorf corridor at the village of Wallendorf itself. Here his right flank might hug the Nussbaumer Hardt, a great forest barrier, leaving room for later broadening of the base of the penetration to the northwest and north. Though the ground rises so abruptly beyond Wallendorf that it reminded some men of the Palisades on the Hudson, similar heights bar the way all along the entrance to the corridor.

CCR knew little about the enemy situation across the border except what patrols and observers had discerned in the preceding three days. A number of patrols, including that of Sergeant Holzinger on 11 September at Stalzemburg, about eight miles northwest of Wallendorf, had encountered no opposition. Reports indicated that water seepage filled some pillboxes and that dust blanketed the inside of others; but on 12 and 13 September observers had noted a few German soldiers entering the pillboxes.

In light of the true German situation, the choice of the Wallendorf sector for an attack was fortunate. It was on the extreme right of the *LXXX Corps,* the weakest point in General Beyer's defenses. Not until the morning of 14 September, when the hastily recruited *Alarmbataillon* arrived from Trier, did any organized unit take over the sector. About two miles north of Wallendorf lay the boundary not only between the two enemy corps but also between the *First* and *Seventh Armies* and between *Army Groups B* and *G.* A certain element of divided responsibility was bound to exist.[39] As for the West Wall itself in this sector, it was markedly thin because German engineers had leaned heavily upon the rugged nature of the terrain. Although all bridges near Wallendorf had been demolished, the river is only about forty yards wide and at this time of year fordable at a number of points.

The status of supply in the 5th Armored Division was similar to that in the rest of the V Corps, although the logistical pinch might not be felt so severely since only one combat command was to see action. The three-day pause in Luxembourg had enabled the division to refill its fuel tanks and constitute a nominal gasoline reserve. Although artillery ammunition on hand was no more than adequate, a shortage of effective counterbattery fires in the coming offensive was to arise more from lack of sound and flash units and from poor visibility than from any deficiency in ammunition supply.

Shortly after noon on 14 September CCR began to cross the Sauer River into Germany at a ford below the confluence of the Our and the Sauer. When no antitank opposition developed, the com-

---

[39] MS # B-081 (Beyer).

WALLENDORF CIVILIANS *strive to save their belongings from the burning town after German troops have left.*

mander, Col. Glen H. Anderson, sent his armor and infantry across together. Although the enemy's *Alarmbataillon* had only small arms weapons, the troops defended with tenacity. Not until Wallendorf was wreathed in flame and smoke caused by artillery fire, tracer bullets, and infantry flame throwers was the enemy dislodged.[40]

---

[40] German propagandists cited the destruction of Wallendorf as evidence of "the Allies' will to destroy all Germans together with German culture and history." See Hq T Force, 12th A Gp, German Propaganda, Sunrise, 14 Oct 44, FUSA G–2 Tac file, 14–15 Oct 44.

The *Alarmbataillon* might have made an even better fight of it had not its artillery support, the *Alarmbatterie*, failed miserably. Court martial proceedings taken later against the battery commander revealed that (1) he was a reserve officer of Luftwaffe signal communication troops, (2) he knew nothing about artillery, (3) the battery had possessed little ammunition and almost no observation or optical equipment, and (4) among the entire enlisted personnel were only three trained artillerymen.[41]

---

[41] MS # B–081 (Beyer).

Continuing past Wallendorf, tanks and infantry of CCR knocked out lightly defended pillboxes to gain a firm foothold astride the first high ground, a promontory of clifflike terrain between the Sauer and the sharply incised Gay creek. As darkness came, the only exit the troops could find leading off the high bluff into the Gay gorge was blocked by a big crater. Awaiting results of further reconnaissance for another route, the tanks and armored infantry laagered for the night.

The armor temporarily stymied by the blocked road, Colonel Anderson ordered the attached 1st Battalion, 112th Infantry, commanded by Lt. Col. Ross C. Henbest, to take up the attack. Colonel Henbest's infantry was to seize Biesdorf, a village beyond the Gay creek, capture of which should facilitate CCR's efforts to get off the high bluff the next morning. Unfortunately, the infantry lost direction in the foggy darkness and wandered aimlessly through the night.

Having discovered another road leading north to span the Gay creek at Niedersgegen, the armor resumed the advance the next morning, 15 September. At the creek the combat command ran into an understrength company of Mark IV tanks supported by a scattering of infantry. In a noisy but brief engagement, the American gunners accounted for 3 enemy tanks and 6 half-tracks and sent 5 other tanks scurrying to the east. CCR's only loss came later when a wooden bridge over the Gay collapsed under the weight of a Sherman tank. The column crossed nearby at a spot that later came to be known by the dolorous name Deadman's Ford.

The enemy armor encountered at the creek probably was the major portion of the *Kampfgruppe* of the *Panzer Lehr Division*. Perturbed from the start about

this American thrust, the *First Army* commander, General von Knobelsdorff, had announced his intentions late the day before "to commit all forces which could possibly be spared" to the Wallendorf sector. In the meantime, the *Kampfgruppe* of the *Panzer Lehr* and the remnants of the *5th Parachute Division*, which held the line farther south near Echternach, were to do what they could to oppose the penetration.[42]

These two German units actually could do little more than harass CCR with a succession of small pinprick thrusts.[43] Pushing northeast and east from Niedersgegen, CCR moved virtually unopposed. In rapid succession the armor seized four villages and occupied Hill 407, the crest of the high ground near Mettendorf, the initial objective. Already CCR had left all West Wall fortifications in its wake. One column continued east and northeast and at dusk was nearing the village of Bettingen on the west bank of the Pruem River when German antitank guns suddenly opened fire. Forced back in confusion by the unexpected resistance, the column withdrew a few hundred yards into the villages of Halsdorf and Stockem to await daylight before coming to blows with the German gunners.

By nightfall of 15 September CCR had advanced through the West Wall and across the western plateau almost to the banks of the Pruem, some six miles inside Germany. Though the combat command actually controlled little more than the roads, the fact that a force could march practically uncontested through the enemy rear augured new life to hopes of a drive to the Rhine. With the armor apparently loose behind enemy lines, General Gerow

---

[42] *Ibid.*
[43] *Ibid.*

conceived an audacious scheme to assist his infantry divisions and reopen his front. He told General Oliver first to seize Bitburg, then to swing north on main roads to Pronsfeld and Pruem. This would place the armor squarely in rear of the enemy opposing the 28th Division and relieve the south flank of the 4th Division. The corps cavalry was to take over a portion of the 5th Armored Division's Luxembourg front to free another combat command, CCB, for the maneuver. The plan involved advances of from fifteen to thirty miles by two columns, parallel to, but deep behind, the enemy front.

For their part, the Germans had quickly recognized the portent of the situation. One enemy headquarters reported in alarm that American troops were only three miles from Bitburg. With no reserves to send, General von Knobelsdorff at *First Army* headquarters called for help. When *Army Group G* passed on the plea, Field Marshal von Rundstedt, the *OB WEST* commander, replied at first that responsibility for sealing off the penetration belonged to the army group, but he soon relented enough to order transfer to the *LXXX Corps* of two grenadier battalions and a flak regiment with eleven antiaircraft batteries.[44]

By shuffling troops in another corps, Knobelsdorff at *First Army* at last managed to put his hands on a reserve to send the *LXXX Corps*. He released a regimental combat team of the *19th Volks Grenadier Division*, which began moving north by truck during the night of 15 September. The rest of the division, minus one regiment, followed two days later. In yet another move, Knobelsdorff reduced the corps sector by ordering the adjacent corps to take over the southern wing of the *LXXX Corps* front.[45]

In the meantime, while the Germans had been making these frantic moves and while CCR had been recording its rapid advance, Colonel Henbest's 1st Battalion, 112th Infantry, had renewed the attack against Biesdorf. The battalion cleared the town by late afternoon of 15 September. On orders from the CCR commander, Colonel Anderson, the infantry then moved about two miles farther to assume positions protecting the southeast flank of the armor near the settlement of Stockigt.

Organic engineers at the same time were constructing a treadway bridge across the Sauer at Wallendorf. Late in the day the attached 254th Engineer Combat Battalion began construction of a wooden trestle bridge. Upon arrival of the engineer battalion, the organic engineers moved forward to begin demolition of captured pillboxes.

At dusk (16 September) an engineer reconnaissance party investigating the Gay creek crossing at Niedersgegen ran into enemy small arms fire near Deadman's Ford. Two engineers were killed. The experience presaged the fact that the Germans were going to do something about CCR's penetration, for this was the first example of what was to become a continuing difficulty with German infiltration into the undefended flanks of the penetration.

Among the first to feel the effect was the supporting artillery, which was leapfrogging forward in order to support the

[44] Entries of 15 and 16 Sep 44, *OB WEST KTB (Text)*; Entry of 15 Sep 44, *A Gp G KTB (Text)*; Evng Sitrep, 15 Sep 44, *A Gp G KTB, Anlagen.*

[45] MS # B-214 (Mantey); Entry of 16 Sep 44, *A Gp G KTB (Text)*; Sitrep, 17 Sep 44, *A Gp G KTB, Anlagen.*

next day's advance on Bitburg. When the 95th Armored Field Artillery Battalion tried to cross the Gay creek at Deadman's Ford, the column came under machine gun and mortar fire from the north. Though the CCR commander, Colonel Anderson, sent back a married platoon of infantry and tanks from Hill 407 to clean out the opposition, the force failed to reach the creek. On the way, about midnight, the lieutenant in charge came upon a portion of the combat command supply trains that had avoided the enemy fire by cutting cross-country south of Deadman's Ford. Because the lieutenant knew that the trains usually followed the artillery, he assumed that the artillery already had passed and that the ford was clear. As a result, the opposition was not eliminated until the next day, 16 September, and soon thereafter German tanks appeared to interdict the stream crossing. Not until late on 16 September did all the artillery get into firing positions east of the Gay creek.

The Germans hardly could have touched CCR at a more sensitive spot. Through most of 16 September Colonel Anderson held in place, wary of racing east with the armor until the artillery could get forward. By the time the big guns were ready to fire, a heavy fog had closed in and darkness was approaching. Enemy artillery had been moving up all day and had begun to shell CCR with disturbing accuracy. When the task force at Halsdorf and Stockem did launch an attack in late afternoon, the enemy near Bettingen proved to have lost none of his tenacity or fire power from the night before. The attack faltered almost immediately.

Infiltration at Deadman's Ford and a lieutenant's error thus had cost CCR any advance on a day when every effort should have been made to exploit the penetration. As it was, only Colonel Henbest's 1st Battalion, 112th Infantry, gained any ground on 16 September. The infantry moved from Stockigt through Stockem, eastward to the Pruem River at Wettlingen. Pushing quickly across the little river in the face of heavy shelling and small arms fire, the infantry by nightfall had seized high ground several hundred yards northeast of Wettlingen. Supported by a self-propelled tank destroyer platoon, Colonel Henbest's battalion had reached a point only five miles from Bitburg.

In midafternoon CCB, commanded by Col. John T. Cole, had begun to cross into the Wallendorf bridgehead and assumed responsibility for the troublesome north flank near Niedersgegen. Even though CCR had not moved during the day, the presence of CCB and the success of Colonel Henbest's infantry engendered optimism. At the end of the day the 5th Armored Division G–2 doubted that the enemy had sufficient strength "to do more than delay us temporarily." [46] While the Germans had countermeasures in the making, all they actually had accomplished was to fling a papier-mâché cordon about the penetration with every available man from the *LXXX Corps* and every man that could be spared from the adjacent *I SS Panzer Corps*, the latter to hold the north flank of the penetration with elements of the *2d Panzer Division*.

No matter what the G–2 estimate or the true enemy situation, General Gerow at 2040 on 16 September ordered General Oliver to call off the offensive. Consolidate your force, he said, and send strong

---

[46] 5th Armed Div G–2 Per Rpt, 16 Sep 44.

patrols to develop the enemy situation in the vicinity of Bitburg. The armor was also to "mop up" the West Wall north and northeast of Wallendorf but was to make no attack on Bitburg except on corps order. General Gerow's directive meant, in effect, that the 5th Armored Division was to assume the defensive. It must have come as a shock to both troops and commanders.

That the Germans had not stopped the V Corps armor was plain. The first real adversities to come in the Wallendorf sector hit after the issuance of this order. The explanation for the halt appeared to lie instead in the decisions that had emerged from the meeting of General Eisenhower and his top commanders on 2 September at Chartres and in a critical over-all logistical situation.

In commenting later on the reasons for calling off the 5th Armored Division's attack, General Gerow explained the halt of all three of his divisions.[47] The plan, General Gerow said, had been agreed upon by General Hodges and himself. It was to have been an "investigation" proceeding to the ambitious objectives if resistance proved "negligible." When defense actually proved "so stout," the First Army had instructed the V Corps "not to get too involved."

The fact was that the V Corps had been operating on borrowed time and borrowed supplies. The presence of the corps this far east was attributable only to the fact that General Hodges had deviated from the Chartres instructions, giving the V Corps some of the limited gasoline available rather than assigning all of it, as directed, to the other two corps next to

the British. Although Hodges had done this with an eye only to the limited objectives of closing the gap between the First and Third Armies and getting the V Corps across the obstacle of the Meuse River, he must have been reluctant to abandon without at least a trial the splendid opportunity which had developed to put the obstacle of the West Wall behind in the same jump. Under the circumstances he could have countenanced continued logistical priority for the V Corps only if far-reaching successes could have been had for the asking. Though the V Corps obviously could have continued the advance, it would have taken some fighting to achieve it, no matter how makeshift the units with which the Germans had shored up the West Wall in the Eifel.

Even had General Gerow not stopped the V Corps on 16 September, a halt within a few days probably still would have been imperative. The next day, for example, the 12th Army Group commander, General Bradley, brought to First Army headquarters a doleful picture of the over-all supply situation. "It is not improbable," noted General Hodges' aide-de-camp in his diary, "that we shall have to slow up, even altogether halt, our drive into Germany and this in the very near future." [48]

---

[47] Combat Interv with Gerow, filed with 5th Armd Div Intervs.

[48] Sylvan Diary, entry of 17 Sep 44. For a German viewpoint, see General Siegfried Westphal (chief of staff to Rundstedt), *The German Army in the West* (London: Cassel and Company Ltd., 1951). "If the enemy had thrown in more forces he would not only have broken through the German line of defences which were in process of being built up in the Eifel, but in the absence of any considerable reserves on the German side he must have effected the collapse of the whole West Front within a short time." (Page 174)

Defense of the Bridgehead

The most serious trouble in the Wallendorf bridgehead began after dark on 16 September, after General Gerow had called off the attack. Using air bursts from the antiaircraft guns of a newly arrived flak regiment with deadly effect, the enemy counterattacked the 1st Battalion, 112th Infantry, near Wettlingen. Although the infantry held in the face of almost overwhelming casualties, Colonel Anderson on 17 September ordered abandonment of the foothold beyond the Pruem.[49]

At dawn on 17 September German armor and infantry of the *Panzer Lehr* and *5th Parachute Divisions* struck several points along the eastern tip of the salient, while elements of the *2d Panzer Division* hit Hill 407. Although CCR knocked out eight of the German tanks, not until about 1000 could the combat command report the situation under control. The Germans captured one of the American tanks.[50]

Lamenting the basic failure of these countermeasures, the Commander in Chief West, Rundstedt, believed they might have succeeded had they been directed not at the tip of the salient but at the flanks close to the base at Wallendorf.[51] Though Rundstedt's criticism was largely justified, the Germans nevertheless had used much of their strength to prevent the newly arrived CCB from expanding the base of the salient appreciably. In many instances, after pillboxes were taken, the Germans had infiltrated back into them.

Unaware that the Americans had called off their attack, Rundstedt and the other German commanders saw the situation as extremely serious. Late on 17 September Rundstedt gave *Army Group B* a reserve panzer brigade, the *108th*, for employment under the *2d Panzer Division* against the north flank of the bridgehead. At the same time, General von Knobelsdorff at *First Army* laid plans to commit the *19th Volks Grenadier Division* in a counterattack against the south flank on 18 September.

Rundstedt also acted to remove the problem of divided responsibility occasioned by the location of the American strike along the army and army group boundaries. Extending the *Army Group B* and *Seventh Army* boundaries south to a line roughly the same as that between the First and Third U.S. Armies, he transferred the *LXXX Corps* to the *Seventh Army*. Responsibility for eliminating the Wallendorf salient passed entirely to Field Marshal Model's *Army Group B* and General Brandenberger's *Seventh Army*.[52]

Lack of time for preparation and a desperate shortage of ammunition and fuel forced postponement of the *19th Volks Grenadier Division*'s counterattack on 18 September. As it turned out, this meant a stronger counterattack in the end, for

---

[49] Infantrymen gave much of the credit for their stand to two officers of supporting units: the forward observer from the 400th Armored Field Artillery Battalion, 2d Lt. Roy E. Gehrke, who was mortally wounded, and the commander of the attached platoon of the 628th Tank Destroyer Battalion, 1st Lt. Leon A. Rennebaum. Both were subsequently awarded the DSC.

[50] German information from entries of 17 Sep 44, OB WEST KTB (*Text*); Daily Sitrep, 17 Sep 44, *A Gp B KTB, Tagesmeldungen;* Sitreps, First Army, 17 Sep 44, *A Gp G KTB, Anlagen.*

[51] Order, *OB WEST* to *A Gp G*, 17 Sep 44, *A Gp G KTB, Anlagen.*

[52] Entries of 17 Sep 44, *OB WEST KTB* (*Text*); Daily Sitrep, *Lageorientierung*, and Daily Sitrep *First Army*, 17 Sep 44, *A Gp G KTB, Anlagen;* Daily Sitrep, 18 Sep 44, *A Gp B KTB, Tagesmeldungen.*

during the day the *108th Panzer Brigade* arrived. Early on 19 September the panzer brigade, the *19th Volks Grenadier Division,* elements (probably a regiment) of the *36th Infantry Division,* and remnants of the *Panzer Lehr* were to launch an enveloping attack. In preparation, the *Seventh Army* issued two thirds of its entire fuel supply to the *108th Panzer Brigade,* a somewhat shocking commentary upon the state of the German fuel situation.[53]

The *LXXX Corps* commander, General Beyer, directed the *108th Panzer Brigade* to hit the main positions of CCR on Hill 407 from the north while the infantry units supported by the remnants of the *Panzer Lehr* attacked from the south. Unfortunately for the Germans, the Americans were ready, and a fortuitous break in the weather made possible the first major contribution by U.S. air since the crossing of the border.

Knocking out ten German tanks, CCR sent the enemy armor and infantry reeling back from Hill 407 in disorder. Adjusted from a light observation plane, American artillery followed the retreat. Taking quick advantage of the clearing weather, two squadrons of P-47 Thunderbolts of the 365th Group took up the fight. The air strike was so effective that the First Army subsequently sent the squadron leaders[54] a special commendation.

German artillery, which by this time had begun to fire on the bridgehead from almost every direction, eluded the pilots until the next day when the "enemy

caught hell." About fifty planes of the 365th Group participated on 20 September, primarily against German tanks and artillery. The artillery included a number of big railroad guns, of which the pilots claimed to have destroyed four. The armored troops rewarded the fliers with a laconic: "They sure do a fine job; thanks."

If the airmen were good on 19 and 20 September, they were superb the next day, 21 September. For the first time since the West Wall campaign began, the sky was cloudless, the ground perfectly devoid of haze. So helpful was the three-day air effort that the V Corps commander was moved to dispatch a letter of appreciation to the air commander, General Quesada.[55]

In the meantime, during the big German drive of 19 September, Colonel Henbest's infantry and the tanks of CCB had thrown back the bulk of the *19th Volks Grenadier Division* on the south flank of the bridgehead. Nevertheless, about noon, an enemy group infiltrating from the southeast reached the eastern end of the two tactical bridges across the Sauer at Wallendorf. For about an hour the issue of the bridges was in doubt until finally fire from the engineers and from antiaircraft guns west of the river drove the Germans back. The bridges still were intact.[56]

Though the 5th Armored Division had held at all points, General Oliver saw a chance to improve the positions by reducing the perimeter of the bridgehead. He ordered his battered CCR to withdraw. Defense of a reduced perimeter centering upon the high ground near Wallendorf

---

[53] Entry of 18 Sep 44, *OB WEST KTB (Text)*; Daily Sitrep, 18 Sep 44, *A Gp B KTB, Tagesmeldungen;* Forenoon and Noon Sitreps, 18 Sep 44, *A Gp B KTB, Letzte Meldung.*
[54] Maj William D. Ritchie and Maj John R. Murphy. IX Fighter Command and IX TAC, Unit History, Sep 44.

[55] *Ibid.*
[56] For courage in defending the bridges, 1st Lt. Stanford F. Hall, 254th Engineers, and Pvt. Sheldon D. Jennings, 461st Antiaircraft Artillery (AW) Battalion, were awarded the DSC.

was to pass to CCB and a fresh battalion of the 112th Infantry. The infantry and CCB were to hold the bridgehead "until corps permits withdrawal." Now that all hope of continuing the offensive was over, the 5th Armored Division plainly looked upon the Wallendorf assignment with distaste. Keenly aware of the shock role of armor, many officers in the division were none too happy about performing an infantry-type defensive role.[57]

Heavy shelling and ground pressure continued against the reduced bridgehead. Despite relentless attacks by the same German units that had opened the drive on 19 September, CCB gave no ground except according to plan. Then, in late afternoon of 21 September, the V Corps at last gave approval to abandonment of the bridgehead.

In pulling back across the Sauer before daylight on 22 September, CCB had to use the ford which the first troops to cross the river had employed eight days before. During the preceding night the Germans once again had penetrated to the Wallendorf bridges. In reporting the situation after having driven off this second infiltration, CCB had made a notable use of understatement. "Only change," the combat command had reported, "[is] both bridges blown."

Though the Wallendorf fight had ended in abandonment of the bridgehead, neither CCB nor CCR had incurred excessive losses in either personnel or equipment. For the month of September, for example, the entire 5th Armored Division, including

CCA, had incurred 792 casualties, of which 148 were killed or missing. Likewise for the entire month, the division's nonsalvageable vehicular losses included only 6 light tanks, 11 medium tanks, and 18 half-tracks. The 1st Battalion, 112th Infantry, incurred losses proportionately much heavier, more than 37 percent of the original command.[58]

At noon on 18 September, before withdrawal at Wallendorf, General Gerow relinquished command of the V Corps to Maj. Gen. Edward H. Brooks, formerly commander of the 2d Armored Division. Having been chief of the War Plans Division of the War Department at the time of the Japanese attack on Pearl Harbor, General Gerow had been called to Washington to testify in a Congressional investigation. In an optimistic farewell message to his command, he indicated that the opposition the Germans had mustered against his offensive had failed to impress him. "It is probable," General Gerow said, "the war with Germany will be over before I am released to return to the V Corps."[59]

Under General Brooks, the divisions of the V Corps rotated their battalions in the line while the corps staff worked on proposed plans for relief of the corps and a lateral shift to the north. In the meantime, the Ardennes–Eifel front lapsed into a relative quietness that was to prevail until December.

---

[57] This attitude is reflected clearly in combat intervs and in orders to CCR and CCB found in 5th Armd Div G-3 Jnl, 16–22 Sep 44. See also Ltr, General Oliver to OCMH, 4 Jul 56.

[58] The Germans said they took 52 prisoners, counted 531 American dead, and destroyed 10 half-tracks and 31 tanks. See Noon and Evng Sitreps, 22 Sep 44, *OB WEST KTB (Text)*; Daily Sitrep, 22 Sep 44, *A Gp B KTB, Tagesmeldungen;* Noon and Evng Sitreps, 22 Sep 44, *A Gp B KTB, Letzte Meldung.*

[59] V Corps Operations in the ETO, p. 256.

CHAPTER IV

VII Corps Penetrates the Line

Having engineered the authorization to reconnoiter the West Wall in force on 12 September, General Collins of the VII Corps expected to accomplish more by the maneuver than did General Gerow of the V Corps. General Collins had in mind a strong surprise attack which might breach the fortified line in one blow before the Germans could man it adequately. Even if he had to pause later for resupply, the West Wall would be behind him.

Though oriented generally toward the region known as the Aachen Gap, the VII Corps operated in a zone about thirty-five miles wide that encompassed only a narrow portion of the gap. This portion was the Stolberg Corridor, southeast and east of Aachen. The rest of the zone was denied by dense pine forests in sharply compartmented terrain. Stretching northeast from Verviers, Belgium, for about 30 miles almost to Dueren on the Roer River, the forest barrier averages 6 to 10 miles in width. (*See Map III.*) Within Belgium, it embraces the Hertogenwald; within Germany, the Roetgen, Wenau, and Huertgen Forests. Only one logical route for military advance runs through the forests, a semblance of a corridor extending from the German border near Monschau northeast across a village-studded plateau toward the Roer at Dueren. For convenience, this route may be called the Monschau Corridor.

It was obvious that the main effort of the VII Corps should be made in the north of the zone through the more open Stolberg Corridor. Yet even this route had some disadvantages. At one point it is less than six miles wide. At others it is obstructed by the sharp valleys of the Inde and Vicht Rivers and by a congested industrial district centering on Stolberg and the nearby town of Eschweiler.

General Collins entrusted the reconnaissance in force on 12 September to two combat commands of the 3d Armored Division and two regiments of the 1st Division. Each of the infantry regiments was to employ no more than a battalion at first. The infantry was to reconnoiter in the direction of Aachen, while the armor was to strike the face of the Stolberg Corridor. Should the West Wall be easily breached, the 1st Division was to capture Aachen, the 3d Armored Division was to push up the corridor to Eschweiler and thence to Dueren, and the 9th Division was to operate on the right wing to sweep the great forest barrier.[1]

In the event, the reconnaissance on 12 September failed to accomplish what General Collins had hoped for. Not through any great German strength did it fail, but because roadblocks, difficult terrain, and

---

[1] VII Corps Opns Memo 91, 11 Sep 44, VII Corps Opns Memos file, Sep 44; FO 11, 13 Sep 44, VII Corps G–3 FO's file, Sep 44.

occasional resistance held both armor and infantry outside the West Wall until too late in the day for an attempt to penetrate the line. Although a battalion of the 1st Division's 16th Infantry got well into the line south of Aachen in the Aachen Municipal Forest, where pillboxes were sparse, a counterattack by about eighty Germans discouraged farther advance for the evening. After losing three tanks to a nest of cleverly concealed antitank guns, the left combat command of the 3d Armored Division stopped for the night a thousand yards from the West Wall. The second combat command sent two task forces probing generally east from Eupen. Delayed by roadblocks and mines, one task force came up to the West Wall south of the village of Schmidthof too late to make an attack. Encountering similar obstacles, the other finally reached Roetgen, just short of the pillboxes, in late afternoon, only to find entry into the line barred by dragon's teeth on one side of the road, a precipice on the other, and a big crater in the road itself. The task force laagered for the night in Roetgen. The West Wall remained undented.

Still intent on pressing forward without delay, General Collins nevertheless interpreted the results of the reconnaissance as an indication that farther advance might not be gained merely by putting in an appearance. In these circumstances, capturing the city of Aachen at this stage would serve no real purpose. The open left flank of the VII Corps might be secured by seizing high ground overlooking Aachen rather than by occupying the city itself.[2] The decisive objective was the

second or main band of West Wall fortifications which ran east and southeast of Aachen.

Reflecting this interpretation, General Collins told the 1st Division to avoid the urban snare of Aachen and protect the left flank of the corps by seizing the high ground east of the city. When the XIX Corps came abreast on the north, Aachen then could be encircled. The 3d Armored

GENERAL COLLINS

Division was to proceed as before to penetrate both bands of the West Wall, capture Eschweiler, and turn east toward the Roer River; the 9th Division was to protect the right flank of the armor by penetrating the great forest barrier to seize road centers in the vicinity of Dueren. Though General Collins was not officially to label his advance an "attack" for another twenty-four hours, he was actually to launch a full-scale attack on 13 Septem-

_____

[2] Interv by the author with Gen Collins, Washington, 25 Jan 54; Ltr, Maj Gen Clarence R. Huebner (former CG 1st Div) to OCMH, 3 Sep 53, OCMH.

ber under the guise of continuing the reconnaissance in force.[3]

General Collins specified further that advance was to be limited for the moment to the west bank of the Roer River, a stipulation probably based upon the physical and logistical condition of the VII Corps. The troops, their equipment, and their vehicles had been taxed severely by the long drive across France and Belgium. Little more than a third of the 3d Armored Division's authorized medium tanks were in operational condition. Shortages in ammunition, particularly in 105-mm. ammunition, necessitated strict rationing. The divisions often had to send their own precious transportation far to the rear in search of army supply dumps that had fallen behind. Trucks of the 1st Division made two round trips of 700 miles each.[4]

For all these problems and more, the temptation to breach the West Wall before pausing was compelling. Even if the Germans had been able to man the line, there was some chance that they intended to fight no more than a delaying action within the fortifications, reserving the main battle for the Rhine River. "Militarily," the VII Corps G–2, Col. Leslie D. Carter, noted, "[the Rhine] affords the best line of defense." Yet, Colonel Carter conceded, "for political reasons, it is believed that the West Wall will be held in varying degrees of effectiveness." [5] Perhaps the most accurate indication of what the VII Corps expected came from the G–2 of the 9th Division. Vacillating for

a while between two theories, the 9th Division G–2 finally merged them in a prediction that the enemy intended to hold the West Wall but that he probably was capable only of delaying action.[6]

The first of the two bands of the West Wall facing the VII Corps was a thin single line closely following the border west and south of Aachen. This band the Germans called the Scharnhorst Line. About five miles behind the first, the second band was considerably thicker, particularly in the Stolberg Corridor. Called the Schill Line, the second band became thinner in the Wenau and Huertgen Forests before merging with the forward band at the north end of the Schnee Eifel. Dragon's teeth marked the West Wall in the Aachen sector along the forward band west of Aachen and across the faces of the Stolberg and Monschau Corridors.

Colonel Carter, the VII Corps G–2, expected the Germans to try to hold the two bands of the West Wall with the battered remnants of two divisions and a haphazard battle group composed primarily of survivors of the *105th Panzer Brigade* and the *116th Panzer Division*. All together, he predicted, these units could muster only some 7,000 men. Elements of two SS panzer corps, totaling no more than 18,000 men and 150 tanks, might be in reserve, while some or all of two panzer brigades and four infantry divisions—all makeshift units—might be brought from deep inside Germany. "However," the G–2 added, "transportation difficulties will add to the uncertainty of these units making their appearance along the VII Corps front." [7]

---

[3] VII Corps Opns Memo 92, 13 Sep 44, VII Corps Opns Memos file, Sep 44; VII Corps FO 11, 13 Sep 44.
[4] See 3d Armd, 1st, and 9th Div AARs, Sep 44.
[5] VII Corps, Annex 2 to FO 11, 13 Sep 44.

[6] 9th Div G–2 Per Rpts 58, 59, and 60, 12–14 Sep 44.
[7] VII Corps, Annex 2 to FO 11.

GENERAL BRANDENBERGER

German Developments

The German commander charged directly with defending the Aachen sector was the same who bore responsibility for the Eifel, the *Seventh Army*'s General Brandenberger. Not the Eifel but Aachen, General Brandenberger recognized, would be the main point of American concentration. Yet he had little more strength there than in the Eifel.

As was the *I SS Panzer Corps* for a time, the other two of General Brandenberger's three corps were trying to hold in front of the West Wall while workers whipped the fortifications into shape. On the north wing, sharing a common boundary with the *First Parachute Army* at a point approximately six miles northwest of Aachen, was the *LXXXI Corps* commanded by Generalleutnant Friedrich August Schack. General Schack's zone of responsibility extended south to Roetgen

and a boundary with the *LXXIV Corps* under General der Infanterie Erich Straube. General Straube's responsibility ran to the Schnee Eifel and a common boundary with General Keppler's *I SS Panzer Corps* near the Kyll River.[8]

Probably weakest of the *Seventh Army*'s three corps, Straube's *LXXIV Corps* was to be spared wholesale participation in the early West Wall fighting because of the direction of the U.S. thrusts. General Schack's *LXXXI Corps* was destined to fight the really decisive action.

General Schack had to base his hopes of blocking the Aachen Gap upon four badly mauled divisions. Northwest of Aachen, two of these were so occupied for the moment with the approach of the XIX U.S. Corps that neither was to figure until much later in the fight against the VII U.S. Corps. At Aachen itself General Schack had what was left of the *116th Panzer Division*, a unit whose panzer regiment had ceased to exist and whose two panzer grenadier regiments were woefully depleted. The fourth unit was the *9th Panzer Division*, earmarked to defend the face of the Stolberg Corridor.

The *9th Panzer Division* had been reorganizing in a rear assembly area when Field Marshal von Rundstedt had seized upon it as the only sizable reserve available on the entire Western Front for commitment at Aachen. Though traveling under urgent orders, only a company of engineers, three companies of panzer grenadiers, and two batteries of artillery had arrived at Aachen by 11 September. Desperate for some force to hold outside

---

[8] Greater detail on the Germans in the Aachen sector may be found in Lucian Heichler, The Germans Opposite VII Corps in September 1944, manuscript prepared to complement this volume, filed in OCMH.

the West Wall, General Schack had merged the early arrivals with remnants of the *105th Panzer Brigade*, which still had ten tanks. As might have been expected, this *Kampfgruppe 9th Panzer Division* was damaged severely in its first action west of the German border on 11 September. This was a harbinger of what was to come, for as other units of the *9th Panzer Division* reached the front General Schack would have to throw them piecemeal into the fighting and later shore them up with diverse reinforcements. The name "*9th Panzer Division*" thus was to become a collective term for a hodgepodge of armor, infantry, and artillery.[9]

Nominally, General Schack had a fifth unit, the *353d Infantry Division*, but about all that was left of it was the division headquarters. Schack assigned it a sector in the Schill Line, the second band of the West Wall, and put under it a conglomeration of five *Landesschuetzen* (local security) and Luftwaffe fortress battalions and an infantry replacement training regiment.[10]

The *LXXXI Corps* had in addition a few headquarters supporting units, of which some were as much a hindrance as a help. Overeager demolition engineers of one of these units in rear of the *116th Panzer Division* had destroyed bridges on 11 and 12 September before the panzer division had withdrawn. A battery of Luftwaffe antiaircraft artillery in position near Roetgen panicked upon hearing a rumor that the Americans were approach-

ing. Abandoning their three 20-mm. guns, the men fled.[11]

To General Schack's misfortune, he anticipated the VII Corps main effort against Aachen itself. Shoring up the *116th Panzer Division* at Aachen with three Luftwaffe fortress battalions and a few other miscellaneous units, he gave command of the city to the division commander, Generalleutnant Gerhard Graf von Schwerin. His limited corps artillery he put under direct control of Schwerin's artillery officer. For defense of the Stolberg Corridor, he subordinated all miscellaneous units between Aachen and Roetgen to the *9th Panzer Division*.[12]

Other than this General Schack could not do except to wish Godspeed for promised reinforcements. Most likely of these to arrive momentarily was the *394th Assault Gun Brigade*, which had six or seven assault guns. A firmer hope lay further in the future. During 12 September, Schack had learned that the first of three full-strength divisions scheduled

---

[9] MS # B-730 (Brandenberger).

[10] ETHINT-18 (Generalleutnant Gerhard Graf von Schwerin, comdr of the *116th Pz Div*); Order, *Seventh Army* to all corps, 9 Sep 44, *LXXXI Corps KTB, Anlagen, Befehle: Heeresgruppe, Armee, usw.*, 5.VIII.-21.X.44 (hereafter cited as *LXXXI Corps KTB, Befehle: Heeresgruppe, Armee, usw.*).

[11] TWX, *116th Pz Div* to *LXXXI Corps*, 0155, 12 Sep 44, *LXXXI Corps KTB, Anlagen, Meldungen der Divisionen* [Div Sitreps], 25. VIII.-1.X.44 (hereafter cited as *LXXXI Corps KTB, Meldungen der Div*); Tel Conv, *LXXXI Corps* with *116th Pz Div*, 0810, 12 Sep 44, *LXXXI Corps KTB, Anlagen, Kampfverlauf* [Operations], 2.VIII.-21.X.44 (hereafter cited as *LXXXI Corps KTB, Kampfverlauf*; Tel Conv, *Seventh Army* with *LXXXI Corps*, 0050, 22 Sep 44, *LXXXI Corps KTB, Anlagen, Befehle an Divisionen* [Orders to Divs], 3.VIII.-21.X.44 (hereafter cited as *LXXXI Corps KTB, Befehle an Div*).

[12] Order, *LXXXI Corps* to all divs, 2230, 12 Sep 44, *LXXXI Corps KTB, Befehle an Div*; TWX, *A Gp B* to *OB WEST*, 2350, 22 Sep 44, *A Gp B KTB, Operationsbefehle*; Daily Sitreps, *116th Pz Div*, 21 Sep 44, *LXXXI Corps KTB, Anlagen, Tagesmeldungen*, 6.VIII.-21.X.44 (hereafter cited as *LXXXI Corps KTB, Tagesmeldungen*); Tel Conv, *LXXXI Corps* with *9th Pz Div*, 1500, 15 Sep 44, *LXXXI Corps KTB, Kampfverlauf*.

to reinforce the Aachen sector in September would arrive in a few days. Hitler himself had ordered the *12th Infantry Division,* which was rehabilitating in East Prussia, to begin entraining for Aachen at 0001, 14 September.[13]

Though hope existed, an observer in Aachen the night of 12 September could not have discerned it. Aachen that night was Richmond with Grant in Petersburg. While General von Schwerin was regrouping his *116th Panzer Division* north of the city before moving into battle, only local defense forces remained between the Americans and the city itself. Through the peculiar intelligence network war-torn civilians appear to possess, this knowledge had penetrated to a civilian population already in a quandary over a Hitler order to evacuate the city. Entering Aachen, Schwerin found the population "in panic."[14]

Aware that the *116th Panzer Division* could not fight until regrouped and that local defense forces were no match for their opponents, Schwerin was convinced that the fall of the city was only hours away. This, the German commander thought privately, was the best solution for the old city. If Aachen was to be spared the scars of battle, why continue with the civilian evacuation? Schwerin decided to call it off. Though he may not have known that Hitler himself had ordered Nazi officials to evacuate the city, he must have recognized the gravity of his decision. He nevertheless sent his officers to the police to countermand the evacuation order, only to have the officers return with the shocking news that not only the

police but all government and Nazi party officials had fled. Not one police station was occupied.[15]

Not to be sidetracked by this development, General von Schwerin sent his officers into the streets to halt the evacuation themselves. By daylight of 13 September the city was almost calm again.

In the meantime, Schwerin searched through empty public buildings until at last he came upon one man still at his post, an official of the telephone service. To him Schwerin entrusted a letter, written in English, for transmission to the American commander whose forces should occupy Aachen:[16]

I stopped the absurd evacuation of this town; therefore, I am responsible for the fate of its inhabitants and I ask you, in the case of an occupation by your troops, to take care of the unfortunate population in a humane way. I am the last German Commanding Officer in the sector of Achen.

[signed] Schwerin.

Unfortunately for Schwerin, General Collins at almost the same moment was deciding to bypass Aachen. No matter if innocently done, Schwerin had countermanded an order from the pen of the Fuehrer himself. As proof of it, he had left behind an incriminating letter he would surely come to rue.

The Battle of the Stolberg Corridor

With the decision to bypass Aachen, the VII Corps scheme of maneuver became basically a frontal attack by the corps

---

[13] Order, *LXXXI Corps* to all divs, 2230, 12 Sep 44; Mng Sitrep, *A Gp B,* 12 Sep 44, *OB WEST KTB (Text).*

[14] ETHINT–18 (Schwerin).

[15] *Ibid.;* Rpt, Model to *OB WEST,* 2230, 15 Sep 44, *A GP B KTB, Operationsbefehle;* Ltr, General der Infanterie Franz Mattenklott (commander of *Wehrkreis VI,* the military district which included Aachen) to Reichsfuehrer SS Heinrich Himmler, 15 Sep 44, *LXXXI Corps KTB, Meldungen der Div.*

[16] Rpt, Model to *OB WEST,* 2330, 15 Sep 44, *A GP B KTB, Operationsbefehle.*

armor, protected on either flank by infantry, to penetrate the West Wall.[17] A corollary objective was the encirclement of Aachen in conjunction with the XIX Corps to the north. As events developed, because of terrain, the nature of resistance, and the delay imposed on the XIX Corps by the gasoline shortage, the battle actually took on the aspects of three distinct maneuvers. The least spectacular was to develop primarily as a defensive engagement involving the bulk of the 1st Division in containing Aachen. Another was to involve two regiments of the 9th Division in an attempt to break through the Monschau Corridor and secure the corps right flank in the forest barrier. The third and most critical was to be executed by the corps armor with an assist from a regiment of each of the two infantry divisions. This can be called the battle of the Stolberg Corridor.

Commanded by Maj. Gen. Maurice Rose, the 3d Armored Division was to pierce the West Wall with two combat commands abreast.[18] From Roetgen and

Schmidthof, Combat Command B was to drive northeast along the fringe of the Roetgen and Wenau Forests, on an axis marked by the villages of Rott, Zweifall, Vicht, and Gressenich. After crossing the Inde and Vicht Rivers, CCB was to attack over open ground east of Stolberg to come upon Eschweiler, some ten miles inside Germany, from the south. Assailing the face of the corridor near Ober Forstbach, about three miles north of Schmidthof, CCA was to pass through the villages of Kornelimuenster and Brand to hit Stolberg from the west, thence to turn northeast against Eschweiler.

The mission of the 1st Division having changed from capturing to isolating Aachen, the commander, Maj. Gen. Clarence R. Huebner, planned to send his 16th Infantry northeast along the left flank of the armor. After penetrating the Scharnhorst Line—the first band of pillboxes— the 16th Infantry was to secure hills that dominate Aachen from the east. The remainder of the 1st Division (minus a battalion attached to the armor) was to build up on high ground south and southeast of Aachen.[19]

Because the 9th Division still had to move forward from assembly areas near Verviers, the first participation by this division would come a day later. On 14 September one regiment was to move close along the right flank of the armor through the fringes of the Wenau Forest while another regiment attacked northeast through the Monschau Corridor.

The main attack began at dawn on 13 September when the 3d Armored Divi-

---

[17] Interv with Collins, 25 Jan 54.

[18] Like the 1st and 2d Armored Divisions, the 3d was activated before adoption of the organization of three combat commands. Instead of three separate tank and armored infantry battalions, these divisions had two tank regiments and an armored infantry regiment. Though usually holding out a portion of the three regiments as a reserve, the divisions had no "CCR" per se. The table of organization strength called for 3,822 more men than the later armored divisions. Nicknamed Spearhead, the 3d Armored entered combat with the XIX Corps in Normandy. The division joined the VII Corps for the breakout of the hedgerows, the Falaise gap operation, and the pursuit. At the instigation of General Rose, the division commander, combat commands in the 3d Armored Division were known by the names of their commanders. CCA, for example, was Combat Command Hickey. To avoid complications, the conventional CCA and CCB are used in this volume.

[19] The exploits of the Big Red One, the 1st Division, had become as renowned by this time as any in the American Army. The division's first combat in World War II was in the invasion of North Africa, followed by the invasion of Sicily and D Day at OMAHA Beach.

Task Force Lovelady *passes through the dragon's teeth near Roetgen, 15 September.*

sion's CCB under Brig. Gen. Truman E. Boudinot moved out in two columns. At Roetgen Task Force Lovelady (Lt. Col. William B. Lovelady) eventually had to blast a path through the dragon's teeth after dirt thrown in the big crater in the highway turned to muck. Not until late in the morning did the armor pass the dragon's teeth. As the task force proceeded cautiously northward along a forest-fringed highway leading to the village of Rott, the Germans in eight pillboxes and bunkers along the way turned and fled. In one quick blow Task Force Lovelady had penetrated the thin Scharnhorst Line.[20]

On the outskirts of Rott the picture changed suddenly when a Mark V tank and several antitank guns opened fire. In the opening minutes of a blazing fire fight, Task Force Lovelady lost four medium tanks and a half-track. For more than an hour the enemy held up the column until loss of his Mark V tank prompted withdrawal. Because a bridge across a stream north of Rott had been demolished, the task force coiled for the night.

At Schmidthof the second and smaller task force of CCB found the pillboxes in greater density and protected by a continuous row of dragon's teeth. From positions in and around the village, the Germans had superior observation. The task force commander, Lt. Col. Roswell H. King, recognized that to carry the position he needed more infantry than his

---

[20] The 3d Armored Division story is from official records, plus an authoritative unit history, *Spearhead in the West* (Frankfurt-am-Main: Franz Joseph Heurich, 1945).

single company of 60 men; but he nevertheless attempted an attack. German fire brought it to an abrupt halt, and night came before additional infantry arrived.

A few miles to the northwest, the other combat command, CCA, attacked at daylight against a nest of four or five pillboxes at a point south of Ober Forstbach. Supported by tanks and tank destroyers deployed along the edge of a woods, the infantry battalion of Task Force Doan (Col. Leander LaC. Doan) got across the dragon's teeth before machine gun fire from the pillboxes forced a halt. Because mortar fire prevented engineers from blowing a gap through the dragon's teeth, tanks could not join the infantry. Their fire from the edge of the dragon's teeth failed to silence the enemy gunners.

In midafternoon, when the attack appeared to have faltered irretrievably, someone made a fortuitous discovery a few hundred yards away along a secondary road. Here a fill of stone and earth built by local farmers provided a path across the dragon's teeth. Colonel Doan quickly ordered his tanks forward.

For fear the roadway might be mined, a Scorpion (flail) tank took the lead, only to founder in the soft earth and block the passage. Despite German fire, Sgt. Sverry Dahl and the crew of the Scorpion helped a tank platoon leader, Lt. John R. Hoffman, hitch two other tanks to pull out the Scorpion. Climbing back into the flail tank, Sergeant Dahl tried the roadway again. This time he rumbled across.

The other tanks soon were cruising among the pillboxes, but without infantry support. Pinned down and taking disconcerting losses, the infantry could not disengage from the first encounter. With panzerfausts the Germans knocked out

four of the unprotected tanks and accounted for others with three assault guns of the *394th Assault Gun Brigade*. Having detrained at Aachen at midday, these assault guns had been en route to oppose Task Force Lovelady at Rott when diverted to meet the new threat posed by Task Force Doan.[21] In an hour Colonel Doan lost half his tanks. Only ten remained.

To guarantee this foray beyond the dragon's teeth, the CCA commander, Brig. Gen. Doyle O. Hickey, called on two platoons of tanks from another task force, plus the attached 1st Battalion, 26th Infantry, provided from the division reserve. Together, Task Force Doan and the reinforcements were to push beyond the pillboxes to the village of Nuetheim, which affords command of roads leading deep into the Stolberg Corridor.

At first, these reinforcements merely provided more targets for the German gunners, but as the approach of darkness restricted enemy observation, both tanks and infantry began to move. Blanketing Nuetheim with artillery fire, the armor of Task Force Doan reached the western edge of the village in little more than an hour. Approaching over a different route, the fresh infantry battalion was not far behind. Because the hour was late, Task Force Doan stopped for the night, the first band of the West Wall left behind.

Slightly to the northwest, the 1st Division's 16th Infantry in the attempt to advance close along the north flank of the armor had run into one frustration after

---

[21] Daily Sitrep, *9th Pz Div*, 13 Sep 44, *LXXXI Corps KTB, Tagesmeldungen;* Tel Convs, *LXXXI Corps* with *9th Pz Div*, 1420 and 1830, 13 Sep 44, and *LXXXI Corps* with *116th Pz Div*, 1430, 13 Sep 44, *LXXXI Corps KTB, Kampfverlauf.*

another. The battalion which had entered the Aachen Municipal Forest the day before remained absorbed with small-scale counterattacks. Not until nightfall did the other two battalions fight their way past roadblocks and delaying detachments to approach the dragon's teeth not far from Ober Forstbach. A genuine attack against the West Wall by the 16th Infantry would await another day, after contingents of the 26th Infantry took over the 16th's left wing and the 18th Infantry moved up on the far left.

Despite the tribulations of the infantry regiment and of Colonel King's task force at Schmidthof, the "reconnaissance in force" on 13 September had achieved two ruptures of the Scharnhorst Line. That both were achieved along the face of the Stolberg Corridor rather than at Aachen went a long way toward convincing the German commander, General Schack, that he had erred in his estimate of American intentions.

General Schack had not been so sure when soon after noon he had ordered General von Schwerin at Aachen to counterattack immediately with the *116th Panzer Division* to wipe out the Americans in the Aachen Municipal Forest.[22] Reluctantly—for Aachen now would become a battleground—Schwerin had ordered his men to countermarch to the southern outskirts of the city. Augmented by a few replacements, which brought the panzer grenadier battalions to an average strength of about 300, and by half the six assault guns of the *394th Assault Gun Brigade*, the panzer division nevertheless succeeded only in driving back American patrols. Though the Germans claimed they had

"closed the gap" south of Aachen, the Americans in the forest remained.[23]

By nightfall of the 13th General Schack had fewer doubts. The main threat apparently was in the Stolberg Corridor. In response to pleas from the commander of the *9th Panzer Division*, Generalmajor Gerhard Mueller, Schack sent the only reserves he could muster—a Luftwaffe fortress battalion and a battery of artillery—to Kornelimuenster. The *LXXXI Corps* operations officer directed headquarters of the *353d Infantry Division* to alert its *Landesschuetzen* battalions to stand by for action because "the enemy will probably launch a drive bypassing Aachen . . . toward the second band of defenses." As the night wore on, engineers began to demolish all crossings of the Vicht River between the Wenau Forest and Stolberg in front of the Schill Line.[24]

The Drive on the Second Band

General Collins' plans for renewing the attack on 14 September were in effect a projection of the original effort. On the left wing, the 16th Infantry was to try again to get an attack moving against the Scharnhorst Line. At Nuetheim CCA's second task force coiled behind Task Force Doan in preparation for a two-pronged drive northeast on Kornelimuenster and

---

[22] Rad, *LXXXI Corps* to *116th Pz Div*, 1230, 13 Sep 44, *LXXXI Corps KTB, Kampfverlauf.*

[23] ETHINT–18 (Schwerin); Daily Sitrep, *116th Pz Div*, 13 Sep 44, *LXXXI Corps KTB, Kampfverlauf;* Rad, *116th Pz Div* to *LXXXI Corps*, 2235, 13 Sep 44, *LXXXI Corps KTB, Meldungen der Div;* Daily Sitrep, *A Gp B*, 0100, 14 Sep 44, *A Gp B KTB, Tagesmeldungen.*

[24] Tel Convs, Gen Mueller with *LXXXI Corps*, 1340, *LXXXI Corps* with *9th Pz Div*, 1730 and 2030, *LXXXI Corps* with *353d Div*, 2040, and *LXXXI Corps* with *116th Pz Div*, 2320, 13 Sep 44, *LXXXI Corps KTB, Kampfverlauf.*

Brand, thence into the second band of the West Wall near Stolberg. CCB prepared to continue from Rott into the Schill Line below Stolberg. While one regiment of the 9th Division began an attack in the Monschau Corridor, another, the 47th Infantry, was to move so closely along the right flank of the armor that it would become embroiled in the battle of the Stolberg Corridor.

German commanders, for their part, did not intend to fall back on the Schill Line without a fight. Yet to some American units, the German role as it developed appeared to be nothing more than a hastily executed withdrawal. Cratered roads, roadblocks, and what amounted to small delaying detachments were about all that got in the way.

As on the day before, CCB's Task Force Lovelady made the most spectacular advance on 14 September. Sweeping across more than four miles of rolling country, the task force approached the Vicht River southwest of Stolberg as night came. Though the bridge had been demolished, the armored infantry crossed the river, harassed only by an occasional mortar round and uneven small arms fire. Engineers began immediately to bridge the stream. On the east bank the infantry found a nest of 88-mm. guns well supplied with ammunition which could have caused serious trouble had the Germans used them. The infantrymen had to ferret the demoralized crews from their hiding places.

Though General Mueller's *9th Panzer Division* by this time had begun to move into the Schill Line, this particular sector was held by one of the *353d Division's Landesschuetzen* battalions. Before daylight the next morning, 15 September, the men of this battalion melted away in the darkness.[25] When the American armor crossed a newly constructed bridge about noon on 15 September, the pillboxes were silent. Winding up a road toward Mausbach, a village one mile north of a bend in the Vicht River on the planned route toward Eschweiler, the armor passed the last bunker of the Schill Line. Ahead lay open country. Task Force Lovelady was all the way through the West Wall.

CCB's other prong, Task Force Mills (formerly Task Force King but renamed after Colonel King was wounded and succeeded by Maj. Herbert N. Mills), matched Task Force Lovelady's success at first. Because Lovelady's advance had compromised the German positions in the Scharnhorst Line at Schmidthof, Task Force Mills had gone through the line with little enough difficulty. But by midmorning of 15 September, as Mills approached Buesbach, a suburb of Stolberg on the west bank of the Vicht River, the armor ran abruptly into four tanks of the *105th Panzer Brigade* and four organic assault guns of the *9th Panzer Division*, a force which General Mueller was sending to counterattack Task Force Lovelady.[26]

Confronted with the fire of Task Force Mills, the German tanks and assault guns fell back. Task Force Mills, in turn, abandoned its individual drive and tied in on the tail of CCB's larger task force.

Elsewhere on 14 and 15 September, General Hickey's CCA had begun to exploit the penetration of the Scharnhorst Line at Nuetheim. By nightfall of 14 September the combat command had advanced four miles to the fringes of Eilen-

---

[25] Rad, *9th Pz Div* to *LXXXI Corps,* 0353, 15 Sep 44, *LXXXI Corps KTB, Meldungen der Div.*
[26] Tel Convs, *LXXXI Corps* with *9th Pz Div,* 1740, 14 Sep, and 0015 and 1540, 15 Sep 44, *LXXXI Corps KTB, Kampfverlauf.*

dorf, a suburb of Aachen which marks the beginning of the high ground east of the city. Here CCA waited for the arrival of the 1st Division's 16th Infantry, which was to seize the high ground and protect CCA's left flank during the drive on Eschweiler.

The 16th Infantry, General Hickey knew, would be there soon. After days of frustration with outlying obstacles, this regiment at last had launched a genuine attack against the Scharnhorst Line on 14 September. The leading battalion found the pillboxes at the point of attack hardly worthy of the name of a fortified line. Though skirmishes with fringe elements of the Aachen defense forces prevented the infantry from reaching Eilendorf the first day, the regiment entered the town before noon on 15 September. Fanning out to the west, north, and northeast to seize the high ground, the 16th Infantry by nightfall of 15 September had accomplished its mission. The 1st Division now ringed Aachen on three sides.

Upon arrival of the 16th Infantry, CCA renewed the drive northeast toward Eschweiler. Nosing aside a roadblock of farm wagons on a main highway leading through the northern fringes of Stolberg, the armor headed for the Geisberg (Hill 228), an eminence within the Schill Line. As another unreliable *Landesschuetzen* battalion fled from the pillboxes, the going looked deceptively easy. Eight U.S. tanks had passed the roadblock when seven German assault guns opened fire from concealed positions. In rapid succession, they knocked out six of the tanks.[27]

For use in an event like this, General Hickey had obtained permission to supplement his armored infantry with a battalion of the 16th Infantry. He quickly committed this battalion to help his armor clear out the guns and the cluster of pillboxes about the Geisberg. The fighting that developed was some of the fiercest of the four-day old West Wall campaign, but by nightfall the tanks and infantry had penetrated almost a mile past the first pillboxes. Only a few scattered fortifications remained before CCA, like CCB, would be all the way through the West Wall.

From the German viewpoint, the advance of CCA and the 16th Infantry beyond Eilendorf was all the more distressing because it had severed contact between the *116th* and *9th Panzer Divisions*. Because the *116th Panzer Division* estimated that an entire U.S. infantry division was assembling south of Aachen and almost an entire armored division around Eilendorf, General Schack was reluctant to move the *116th Panzer Division* from Aachen into the Stolberg Corridor. Almost continuous pounding of Aachen by American artillery strengthened a belief that the city would be hit by an all-out assault on 16 September. Thus the German defense remained divided.[28]

In the meantime, the battle of the Stolberg Corridor had been broadened by commitment of the 9th Division's 47th Infantry close along the right flank of the 3d Armored Division. So that the regi-

[27] German material from Tel Conv, *LXXXI Corps* with *9th Pz Div*, 1540, 15 Sep 44, *LXXXI Corps KTB, Kampfverlauf;* Evng Sitrep, *LXXXI Corps,* 1700, 15 Sep 44, *LXXXI Corps KTB, Tagesmeldungen.*

[28] TWX, *LXXXI Corps* to *116 Pz Div,* 1718, 15 Sep 44, *LXXXI Corps KTB, Befehle an Div;* Daily Sitrep, *116th Pz Div,* 2100, 15 Sep 44, *LXXXI Corps KTB, Tagesmeldungen;* Tel Conv, *LXXXI Corps* with *116th Pz Div,* 0915, 15 Sep 44, and Rpt on Situation in Aachen Area, Gen Schack, 2145, 14 Sep 44, both in *LXXXI Corps KTB, Kampfverlauf.*

ment might be available, if needed, to assist the armor, General Collins had specified the route of attack. The regiment first was to roll up a portion of the Schill Line by outflanking from the east the towns of Zweifall and Vicht, both on the western edge of the Wenau Forest, then was to proceed along the fringe of the forest toward Dueren.[29]

Commanded by Col. George W. Smythe, the 47th Infantry began to move through Roetgen early on 14 September in the wake of Task Force Lovelady. Even after the route of the main column diverged from that of Task Force Lovelady, resistance was light. One battalion which moved into the Roetgen Forest to come upon Zweifall and Vicht from the east advanced rapidly, but the main column proceeding down a highway got to Zweifall first. While engineers began rebuilding bridges in Zweifall, a second battalion pushed into the forest to eliminate a line of pillboxes.[30]

On 15 September the situation in the forest near Zweifall and Vicht changed abruptly, not so much from German design as from the confusion of chance encounters with errant Germans of a poorly organized replacement training regiment. Before daylight enemy estimated at less than battalion strength blundered into the perimeter defense of one of the American battalions. One of the first to spot the Germans, Pfc. Luther Roush jumped upon a tank destroyer to fire its .50-caliber machine gun. Though knocked from his perch by an enemy bullet, he climbed up again. Eventually

the Germans melted in confusion into the forest. A mess sergeant on his way with food for one of the American companies bumped into a group of the fleeing enemy and captured six.

Another battalion attempting to move through the forest to envelop Vicht ran into a German platoon accompanied by a Mark V tank. Though an American Sherman knocked out the Mark V with its first round, the morning had passed before all these Germans were eliminated. Through the rest of the day both the battalions in the forest found that almost any movement brought encounters with disorganized German units. It was fact nonetheless that in their maneuvers within the forest the battalions actually had penetrated a portion of the Schill Line.

The fighting near Zweifall prompted the German corps commander, General Schack, to order General Mueller's *9th Panzer Division* for a third time to counterattack. "*9th Panzer Division* armor will attack the enemy," Schack directed, "and throw him back behind the West Wall. There is no time to lose!" [31] Although General Mueller tried to comply, his force could not advance in the face of heavy artillery, tank, and mortar fire.[32]

This was not to say that General Mueller could not cause trouble. Contingents of the *9th Panzer Division* demonstrated this fact in late afternoon of 15 September, after Task Force Lovelady had crossed the Vicht River and filed past the silent pillboxes of the Schill Line. The

---

[29] VII Corps FO 11, 13 Sep 44.

[30] The 9th Division combat interview file for September 1944 contains a detailed account of this action, Penetration of the Siegfried Line by the 47th Infantry Regiment.

[31] Tel Conv, *LXXXI Corps* with *9th Pz Div*, 0925, 15 Sep 44 *LXXXI Corps KTB, Kampfverlauf.*

[32] Tel Conv, *LXXXI Corps* with *9th Pz Div*, 1655, 15 Sep 44 *LXXXI Corps KTB, Kampfverlauf;* Daily Sitrep, *9th Pz Div*, 1910, 15 Sep 44, *LXXXI Corps KTB, Tagesmeldungen.*

REMAINS OF A PILLBOX, *showing massive construction.*

highway between the villages of Mausbach and Gressenich lies in a shallow valley bordered on the southeastern rise by the Wenau Forest and on the northwestern rise by the high ground of the Weissenberg (Hill 283). The expanse on either side of the highway is broad and open. As Task Force Lovelady reached a point not quite half the distance between the two villages, six or seven German tanks and self-propelled guns opened fire from the flanks. In quick succession they knocked out seven medium tanks, a tank destroyer, and an ambulance. Colonel Lovelady hastily pulled his task force back into Mausbach. Reporting that he had left only thirteen medium tanks, less than 40 percent of authorized strength, Colonel Lovelady asked a halt for the night.

Adroit use of a minimum of tanks and assault guns during the afternoon of 15 September thus had produced telling blows against both main columns of the 3d Armored Division—against CCB at Mausbach and CCA at the Geisberg. To the Germans, these events would have been encouraging even had the *LXXXI Corps* not been notified that night of the impending arrival of the *12th Infantry Division*. First contingents were scheduled to reach the Roer River towns of Dueren and Juelich during the night, and the entire division would arrive during the next thirty hours.[33]

Unaware of this development, the units of the VII Corps renewed their attacks the next day, 16 September. For the most part, the armored combat commands had a bad day of it, though no real cause for concern became evident. At the Geisberg the Germans mounted a local counterattack, but CCA's armored infantry soon disposed of it with concentrated machine gun fire. Nevertheless, when CCA tried to continue northeastward through the industrial suburbs of Stolberg, intense fire from commanding ground brought both armor and infantry up sharply. To the east, CCB shifted the direction of attack from Gressenich to the Weissenberg, only to be denied all but a factory building on the southwestern slope.

The 3d Armored Division's only real advance of the day came in late afternoon when the division commander, General Rose, acted to close a four-mile gap between his two combat commands. Scraping together a small force of tanks to join with the attached 1st Battalion, 26th Infantry, he sent them against high ground near Buesbach, within the Schill Line southeast of Stolberg. It was a hard fight, costly in both men and tanks, but the task force held the objective as night came.

The difficulties of the 3d Armored Division were offset by a spectacular advance achieved by the 9th Division's 47th Infantry. With the aid of a captured map, the 47th Infantry cleared Vicht and

mopped up nearby pillboxes during the morning. Thereupon, one battalion pressed on two and a half miles northeast through the fringe of the Wenau Forest to seize the village of Schevenhuette, east of Gressenich. This late-comer to the West Wall fighting thus had advanced deeper into Germany than any other Allied unit, approximately ten miles.

The 47th Infantry's deep thrust, which put a contingent of the VII Corps less than seven miles from the Roer at Dueren, augured well for a renewal of the attack the next day. On the other hand, indications began to appear during late afternoon and evening of possibly portentous stirrings on the enemy side of the line. In late afternoon, for example, a platoon of the 16th Infantry patrolling north from Eilendorf reported the enemy approaching the village of Verlautenheide in a column of twos "as far as the eye could see." That night almost every unit along the front noted the noise of heavy vehicular traffic, and the 47th Infantry at Schevenhuette captured a German colonel who had been reconnoitering, presumably for an attack. Even allowing for hyperbole in the patrol's report, these signs had disturbing connotations.

A Wall About Aachen

While events in the Stolberg Corridor gave some evidence of reaching a climax, other events transpiring on the left and right wings of the VII Corps exerted a measure of influence on the fight in the corridor. On the left wing, at Aachen, the most significant development was that two regiments of the 1st Division unintentionally maintained the myth that the city was marked for early reduction. Thus they prompted the Germans to con-

---

[33] Tel Conv, *Seventh Army* with *LXXXI Corps* 2015, 15 Sep 44, *LXXXI Corps KTB, Kampfverlauf.*

tinue to withhold the *116th Panzer Division* from the more critical fighting in the Stolberg Corridor.

In reality, the 1st Division commander, General Huebner, had no intention of becoming involved among the streets and bomb-gutted buildings of Aachen. He was trying to build a wall of infantry defenses on the southwest, south, southeast, and east of the city while awaiting arrival of the XIX Corps to assist in encircling the city. It was no easy assignment, for the 1st Division's left flank was dangling, and the defensive line eventually encompassed some eight miles of front.

As the 16th Infantry tried on 13 and 14 September to get through the Scharnhorst Line and advance alongside the 3d Armored Division, the 18th Infantry moved up west of the Liège–Aachen highway to push through the Aachen Municipal Forest southwest of Aachen. Before digging in on high ground in the forest, the 18th Infantry penetrated the Scharnhorst Line. A gap between the regiment's left flank and cavalry of the XIX Corps was patrolled by the 1st Division Reconnaissance Troop.

General Huebner's third regiment, the 26th Infantry, was minus a battalion attached to the 3d Armored Division. To the remaining battalions General Huebner gave the mission of·following in the wake of the 16th Infantry and filling in to confront Aachen from the south and southeast. By the evening of 15 September, the basic form of the wall about Aachen had set, a half-moon arc extending from the 18th Infantry's positions southwest of the city to the 16th Infantry's advanced hold at Eilendorf.

Stretched to the limit, the 18th and 26th Infantry Regiments patrolled actively toward the buildings and smoke-stacks of Aachen a mile and a half away and fought off enemy patrols and local counterattacks. It was no easy assignment, for the Aachen Municipal Forest was damp and cold and the enemy was always close.

The Germans, for their part, could not believe that the Americans would stop short of the city, particularly in light of the condition of the Aachen defenses. Charged with the defense, General von Schwerin's *116th Panzer Division* was only a shell. Schwerin had only five organic battalions with a "combat strength" [34] of roughly 1,600 men, plus two Luftwaffe fortress battalions and a grenadier training battalion. In armor and artillery, he had 2 Mark IV tanks, 1 Mark V, 1 organic assault gun, 4 assault guns of the *394th Assault Gun Brigade,* 9 75-mm. antitank guns, 3 105-mm. howitzers, and 15 150-mm. howitzers.[35]

To add to the problems of the German commander, the panic which had struck the population of Aachen the night of 12 September came back. Conditions on 14 September, Schwerin said, were "catastrophic." Because no police or civil authorities had returned, a committee of leading citizens begged Schwerin to form a provisional government with the city's former museum director at its head. On top of everything else came a special order from Hitler, this time through military channels rather than through the Nazi

---

[34] "Combat strength" is a translation of *Kampfstaerke,* which includes men actually engaged in the fighting or in immediate support forward of a battalion command post. See Gen Order Nr. *1/2000/44 g.,* 25 Apr 44, *OKH/Gen. St.d.H. Org Abt.*

[35] These strengths are as of 16 September 1944. For a detailed breakdown from contemporary sources, see Heichler, Germans Opposite VII Corps, pp. 41–42.

party, that Aachen was to be evacuated of civilians—if necessary, by force. Schwerin reluctantly agreed for the evacuation to begin.[36]

When police and Nazi officials returned to Aachen on 15 September, they found the civilian evacuation once more in full swing; but that wasn't enough to keep General von Schwerin out of trouble. Schwerin's compromising letter to the American commander had fallen into the hands of the Nazis. You are relieved of your command, they told Schwerin, to stand trial before Hitler's "People's Court."

The fractious Schwerin refused to comply. The men of his division, he believed, would protect him. While he took refuge in a farmhouse north of Aachen, a reconnaissance platoon from his division surrounded his hideout with machine guns. Confident that the battle of Aachen was about to begin, Schwerin determined to stick with his division to the bitter end.

As it gradually became evident that the Americans had no intention of fighting for Aachen immediately, Schwerin at last decided to present himself at *Seventh Army* headquarters to appear before a military court. Field Marshal von Rundstedt, the Commander in Chief West, apparently had interceded on Schwerin's behalf to get the trial shifted from a "People's Court" to a military tribunal. Rundstedt even proposed that Schwerin be reinstated as commander of the *116th Panzer Divi-*

sion. This last Hitler would not permit, though he agreed to no greater punishment than relegation to the OKH Officer Pool, which since the 20 July attempt on Hitler's life had become a kind of military doghouse. Surprisingly, Schwerin later emerged as commander of a panzer grenadier division and at the end of the war had risen to a corps command in Italy.[37]

Battle of the Monschau Corridor

At the southern end of the VII Corps front, the 9th Division in the meantime had launched an ambitious attack designed to clear the great forest barrier off the right flank of the Stolberg corridor. Though the 47th Infantry on the fringe of the forest was making the announced main effort of the 9th Division, the course of events had allied this regiment's attack more closely to that of the 3d Armored Division. The real weight of the 9th Division was concentrated farther south in the Monschau Corridor.[38]

In terms of ground to be cleared and variety of missions to be accomplished, the 9th Division had drawn a big assignment. The division's sector, for example, was more than seventeen miles wide. In sweeping the forest barrier, the division

---

[36] Tel Convs, *LXXXI Corps* with Schwerin, 0930, and with *116th Pz Div*, 2345, 14 Sep 44, *LXXXI Corps KTB, Kampfverlauf*; Rpt, *A Gp B* to *OB WEST*, 1200, 14 Sep 44, *OB WEST KTB* (*Text*); Rad, *116th Pz Div* to *LXXXI Corps*, 1310, 14 Sep 44, *LXXXI Corps KTB, Meldungen der Div*; ETHINT–18 (Schwerin); MS # B–058 (Generalmajor Heinrich Voightsberger, at this time commander of the *116th Pz Div*'s *60th Pz Gr Regt*).

[37] Rpt, Model to *OB WEST*, 2330, 15 Sep 44, *A Gp B KTB, Operationsbefehle*; Tel Convs, G–1 with G–3, *LXXXI Corps*, 1045, 16 Sep 44, and *Seventh Army* with *LXXXI Corps*, 1945, 17 Sep 44, *LXXXI Corps, KTB, Kampfverlauf*; 201 file on General von Schwerin, ETHINT–18 (Schwerin).

[38] Veteran of the invasions of North Africa and Sicily, the 9th Division had entered combat in Normandy on 14 June 1944. Its octofoil shoulder patch came out of the fifteenth century, a heraldic symbol denoting the ninth son. Official records of the division are supplemented by extensive combat interviews at battalion level.

would have to clear some seventy square miles of densely wooded, sharply compartmented terrain. Other responsibilities included seizing road centers near Dueren, protecting the right flank of the 3d Armored Division, and securing the right flank of the corps, which except for a thin cavalry screen was open for more than ten miles.

In other than a pursuit situation, the 9th Division's responsibilities clearly would have been out of keeping with the division's strength. Even as matters stood the only factor tending to license the scope of the assignment was the expectation that the enemy had no real strength in the forest.

To all appearances, this expectation was correct. On 14 September, that part of the forest lying in the zone of the enemy's *LXXXI Corps,* north of Roetgen, was virtually unoccupied while General Schack concentrated on holding Aachen and the Stolberg Corridor. South of Roetgen, the weakest of the *Seventh Army*'s three corps, General Straube's *LXXIV Corps,* had but two infantry divisions, the *347th* and the *89th.* Hardly any organic forces remained in either division.

The *347th Division,* which held the southern portion of the *LXXIV Corps* front and thus was to be spared direct involvement with the 9th Division, was perhaps the weaker. So understrength was the division that when a training regiment, a fortress battalion, and a "Stomach Battalion" [39] were attached, the

newcomers exceeded the organic personnel by more than ten to one.[40]

The other division, the *89th,* which held the Monschau Corridor, had few more organic forces left. Of two infantry regiments, one had been destroyed completely and the other had but 350 men. The commander, a Colonel Roesler, long ago had redesignated his artillerymen, engineers, and service troops as infantrymen. The only reinforcements upon arrival in the West Wall were a *Landesschuetzen* battalion, three Luftwaffe fortress battalions, 14 75-mm. antitank guns, about 450 Russian "volunteers" in a so-called *Ost-Batallion* (East Battalion), and a grenadier training regiment. The *Ost-Batallion* and the training regiment provided the *89th Division*'s only artillery. The former had four Russian 122-mm. howitzers; the latter, two pieces: a German 105-mm. howitzer and an Italian medium (about 150-mm.) howitzer. When the Italian piece ran out of ammunition after two days of firing, the Germans towed it about the front to give an impression of artillery strength.[41]

The American division commander, Maj. Gen. Louis A. Craig, assigned responsibility for pushing through the Monschau Corridor to the 39th Infantry. This regiment and the 47th Infantry, which was making the thrust alongside the 3d Armored Division, together were to clear the forest barrier and converge near Dueren. The remaining regiment, the

---

[39] Special units comprised of men with similar physical disabilities were not uncommon along the Western Front during the fall of 1944. All troops of the so-called Stomach Battalions had ailments of the digestive tract.

[40] Entry, 1320, 12 Sep 44, *LXXXI Corps KTB, Kampfverlauf;* TWX, *A Gp B* to *OB WEST,* 2350 and 2400, 22 Sep 44, *A Gp B KTB, Operationsbefehle;* MS # B–563 (Generalleutnant Wolf Trierenberg, comdr of the *347th Div*).

[41] TWX, *A Gp B* to *OB WEST,* 2350 and 2400, 22 Sep 44, *A Gp B KTB, Operationsbefehle;* MS # B–793 (Col Hasso Neitzel, CofS, *89th Div*).

60th Infantry, had to serve both as a division reserve and as security for the right flank of the corps. Deducing that the flank might be secured by seizing a high ridge line southeast of Monschau, crowned by the villages of Hoefen and Alzen, General Craig told the 60th Infantry to send a reinforced battalion to the ridge. Covered with West Wall pillboxes, this ridge represented in effect a fortified dagger pointed at the base of the Monschau Corridor and commanding the roads through Monschau.

Under Lt. Col. Lee W. Chatfield, the reinforced battalion of the 60th Infantry began operations a day ahead of the rest of the 9th Division by moving to Camp d'Elsenborn, a road center and former Belgian Army garrison ten miles south of Monschau. From here Colonel Chatfield turned north early on 14 September to come upon the Hoefen–Alzen ridge from the southwest. Pushing back a small delaying detachment at the German border, the battalion occupied the border village of Kalterherberg.

Though Colonel Chatfield attacked the Hoefen–Alzen ridge during the afternoon of 14 September, 350 men of the *1056th Regiment,* representing the hard core of veterans available to the *89th Division,* already had occupied the pillboxes.[42] When Chatfield's infantrymen crossed a deep ravine separating Kalterherberg from the ridge, they met the full force of small arms and machine gun fire from the pillboxes.

To make quick work of the ridge and get on with the main task of driving northeast up the Monschau Corridor, General Craig decided during the evening of 14 September to send the rest of the 60th

Infantry to help. Both remaining battalions were to move southeast from Eupen through the Hertogenwald to Monschau. Thereupon a battalion from Monschau and Colonel Chatfield's battalion at Kalterherberg were to press the ridge between them. The remaining battalion was to defend at Monschau; in effect, a reserve.

On 15 September Colonel Chatfield noted no slackening of fire from the pillboxes opposite Kalterherberg. Nor was the weight of the other battalions around Monschau felt appreciably, because the length of the journey from Eupen and demolished bridges at Monschau delayed any real participation by them. Only the advent of supporting tanks on 16 September had any real effect. With the help of the tanks, a battalion from Monschau drove into Hoefen on the 16th, but even then Colonel Chatfield could detect no break at the other end of the ridge. Indeed, the next day the Germans reacted actively with a counterattack which carried to the center of Hoefen before the Americans rallied. Not until 18 September, when Colonel Chatfield abandoned the attack from Kalterherberg and joined the other battalion in Hoefen, did the enemy relinquish his hold on Alzen and the rest of the ridge. By a tenacious defense, the *1056th Regiment* had tied up the entire 60th Infantry for five days at a time when the weight of the regiment might have been decisive elsewhere.

General Craig obviously could have used the regiment to advantage elsewhere, particularly in the Monschau Corridor. Here the 39th Infantry had been discovering how much backbone concrete fortifications can put into a weak defensive force.

That part of the Scharnhorst Line blocking the Monschau Corridor was one

---

[42] For distribution of German units, see MS # B–793 (Neitzel).

of the strongest in the forward band of the West Wall; for German engineers had recognized that the high, rolling plateau northeast of Monschau was a likely avenue for pushing through the forest barrier. Into the pillboxes the *89th Division* commander, Colonel Roesler, had thrust the 1,200–1,500 men of his attached grenadier training regiment. This regiment subsequently was to become an organic part of the division and be redesignated the *1055th Infantry*.[43]

Commanded by Lt. Col. Oscar H. Thompson, the 39th Infantry's 1st Battalion marched almost unopposed on 14 September across the German border into the village of Lammersdorf at the northern edge of the Monschau Corridor. Colonel Thompson then turned his men northward to strike the West Wall at a customhouse a mile away. The customhouse guarded a highway leading northeast through the Roetgen Forest in the direction of Dueren.

Hardly had the infantrymen emerged from Lammersdorf before small arms and mortar fire from pillboxes around the customhouse pinned them to the ground. Though Colonel Thompson sent two of his companies on separate flanking maneuvers, darkness came before any part of the battalion could get even as far as the dragon's teeth.

Soon after Colonel Thompson met his first fire, the 39th Infantry commander, Lt. Col. Van H. Bond, committed another battalion on Thompson's right. This battalion was to pass east through Lammersdorf, penetrate the Scharnhorst Line, and take the village of Rollesbroich, two miles away. Capture of Rollesbroich would open another road leading northeast

through the forest. But here again the Germans stopped the attackers short of the dragon's teeth, this time with antitank fire to supplement the small arms and mortars.

In a renewal of the two-pronged attack on 15 September, the 39th Infantry displayed close co-ordination between infantry and attached tanks and tank destroyers; but the fortifications in most cases proved impervious even to point-blank fire from the mobile guns. Sometimes the Germans inside the pillboxes were so dazed by this fire that the attacking infantry could slip up and toss hand grenades through firing apertures, but this was a slow process which brought reduction of only about seven pillboxes and by no means served to penetrate the entire band.

Attempting to open up the situation, Colonel Bond sent his remaining battalion far around to the north to pass through the Roetgen Forest in a wide envelopment of the customhouse position. By nightfall of 15 September this battalion had reached the rear of the enemy strongpoint, but not until after a full day of tedious, costly small unit fighting was the position reduced.

Three days of bitter fighting had brought a path only a mile and a half wide through the Scharnhorst Line and no advance beyond the line. Even this path could not be used, for strong West Wall positions stretching south to Monschau commanded almost all roads leading to Lammersdorf. By holding between Lammersdorf and Monschau, the Germans still kept a dagger pointed toward the 9th Division's flank and rear, thereby virtually negating the importance of the 60th Infantry's conquest of the Hoefen–Alzen ridge.

[43] MS # B–793 (Neitzel).

It had become apparent by this time that the 39th Infantry alone was insufficient for pushing through the Monschau Corridor. Separated by more than seven miles from the 47th Infantry at Schevenhuette and five miles from the 60th Infantry at Monschau, the regiment needed help. Not until 18 September, after the 60th Infantry at last eliminated the enemy on the Hoefen–Alzen ridge, would General Craig be able to provide it.

The Germans Strike Back

Looking beyond the troubles of the 39th Infantry to the situation of the entire VII Corps, the first five days of West Wall fighting had produced encouraging, if not spectacular, results. Though success probably was not commensurate with General Collins' early hopes, the corps nevertheless had pierced the forward band of the West Wall on a front of twelve miles and in the second belt had achieved a penetration almost five miles wide. The VII Corps clearly had laid the groundwork for a breakthrough that needed only exploitation.

On the other hand, was the VII Corps in a position to reap the rewards? The logistical situation, particularly in regard to 105-mm. howitzer ammunition, still was acute. Though supporting aircraft normally might have assumed some of the artillery missions, overcast skies, mists, drizzles, and ground haze had been the rule. Day after day since the start of the West Wall fighting the airmen had bowed to the weather: 13 September—"While we had cloudless skies, nevertheless, haze restricted operations . . . ." 14 September—"Weather again proved to be our most formidable obstacle . . . ." So it

had gone, and so it would continue to go: 17 September—". . . 77 sorties were abortive due to the weather." 18 September—"Only two missions were flown due to the weather." Although the weather often was good enough for long-range armed reconnaissance flights, these provided little direct assistance to the troops on the ground.[44]

Nor was the condition of the divisions of the VII Corps conducive to encouragement. The 3d Armored Division, for example, had only slightly more than half an authorized strength of 232 medium tanks, and as many as 50 percent of these were unfit for front-line duty.[45] By nightfall of 16 September, every unit of the VII Corps was in the line, stretched to the limit on an active front which rambled for almost thirty miles from Aachen to Eilendorf to Schevenhuette to the Hoefen–Alzen ridge. Great gaps existed on either flank of the corps and gaps of seven and five miles within the lines of the 9th Division.

The only genuine ground for optimism lay in the deplorable condition of the German units. The *89th Division* in the Monschau Corridor, for example, had re-

---

[44] IX FC and IX TAC, Unit History, Sep 44, and FUSA and IX TAC Daily Summaries, Sep 44. A compendious account of tactical air operations during the fall of 1944 may be found in Wesley Frank Craven and James Lea Cate, eds., *The Army Air Forces in World War II:* Vol. III, *Europe:* ARGUMENT *to V-E Day, January 1944 to May 1945* (Chicago: University of Chicago Press, 1951), pp. 600 and 614, (hereafter cited as Craven and Cate, eds., *Europe:* ARGUMENT *to V-E Day*).

[45] The 3d Armored Division on 18 September had 153 medium tanks, of which only 70 to 75 were actually available for use. See 3d Armd Div AAR, Sep 44, and Combat Interv with 3d Armd Div G–4.

ceived no major reinforcements since the start of the fighting and obviously was even more of a makeshift than before. The division still had to rely for artillery support upon antitank guns and mortars. In the sector of the *LXXXI Corps,* neither the *9th* nor *116th Panzer Division* had been shored up appreciably. Still facing the main weight of the VII Corps, the *9th Panzer Division* was in particularly bad shape. The division had less than 2,500 infantrymen, some 200 machine guns, 13 Mark V (Panther) tanks, 12 assault guns, 15 75-mm. antitank guns, 20 105- and 15 150-mm. howitzers, and 1 88-mm., 3 37-mm., and 3 20-mm. antiaircraft guns. As of nightfall, 16 September, the division lacked even a commander. Visiting the division command post, the *Seventh Army* commander, General Brandenberger, charged that General Mueller was unaware of the actual situation on his front. He relieved both Mueller and Mueller's chief of staff.[46]

To reduce the *9th Panzer Division*'s responsibility, the corps commander, General Schack, transferred a few hundred men to the headquarters of the almost-defunct *353d Infantry Division* and told that division to defend the Wenau, Huertgen, and Roetgen Forests from below Schevenhuette southward to the boundary with the *LXXIV Corps.* General Brandenberger, in turn, eased the responsibility of the *LXXXI Corps* by transferring the *353d Division* to General Straube's *LXXIV Corps* and altering the

boundary between the two corps to run just south of Schevenhuette.[47]

These adjustments obviously were feeble moves hardly worthy in themselves of any great expectations. Nevertheless, the Germans did possess a genuine hope in the impending arrival of a fresh division, something which the VII U.S. Corps could not duplicate. The first contingents of the *12th Infantry Division* arrived at detraining points along the Roer River early on 16 September. These and subsequent units of the division made a deep impression on a military and civilian population starved for the sight of young, healthy, well-trained soldiers.

Numbering 14,800 men, the *12th Division* was organized along the lines of the "Type-1944 Infantry Division." It had three regiments of two battalions each—the *27th Fusilier Regiment* and the *48th* and *89th Grenadier Regiments*—plus a separate infantry unit, the *12th Fusilier Battalion.* The division was fully equipped except for an authorized twenty assault guns, a defect which Field Marshal Model at *Army Group B* remedied by attachment of seventeen assault guns of the *102d Assault Gun Brigade.*[48] The *12th Artillery Regiment* had its authorized strength of nine batteries of 105-mm. howitzers and three batteries of 150-mm. howitzers. The division's antitank battalion had twelve 75-mm. guns. Thanks to priority growing out of specific orders from Hitler and Field Marshal von Rund-

---

[46] Rpt, Brandenberger to *A Gp B,* 16 Sep 44, *LXXXI Corps KTB, Befehle: Heeresgruppe, Armee, usw.* See Heichler, Germans Opposite VII Corps, pp. 42–44, for a detailed breakdown of *9th Panzer Division* strength as determined from contemporary German sources.

[47] Tel Convs, *LXXXI Corps* with *353d Inf Div,* 2310, 14 Sep, and 1510, 15 Sep 44, *LXXXI Corps KTB, Kampfverlauf;* Daily Sitrep, *LXXXI Corps,* 2100, 15 Sep 44, *LXXXI Corps KTB, Tagesmeldungen;* Order, *Seventh Army* to all corps, 16 Sep 44, *LXXXI Corps KTB, Befehle: Heeresgruppe, Armee, usw.*

[48] These assault guns were similar to the American tank destroyer. See above, p. 27.

stedt and of prevailing misty, rainy weather that had cloaked German trains from Allied aircraft, the *12th Division* was arriving in record time and in top condition.[49]

"*Seventh Army* will defend the positions . . . and the West Wall to the last man and the last bullet," General Brandenberger declared. "The penetrations achieved by the enemy will be wiped out. The forward line of bunkers will be regained . . . ."[50]

Cognizant of the dangers of piecemeal commitment, General Schack assured the *12th Division* commander, Col. Gerhard Engel, that he would try to wait until the entire division had arrived.[51] He kept the promise less than twenty-four hours. Straight from the railroad station at Juelich General Schack sent the first battalion of the *27th Fusilier Regiment* to Verlautenheide, north of Eilendorf, whence the battalion was to attack on 17 September to thwart the thrust of CCA, 3d Armored Division, toward Eschweiler. The second battalion of the *27th Fusiliers* moved to Stolberg. When the other two regiments and some of the organic artillery detrained before daylight on 17 September, General Schack ordered them to start immediately driving CCB from the vicinity of the Weissenberg (Hill 283) and Maus-

bach in order to restore the Schill Line southeast of Stolberg.[52]

Renewing the two-pronged thrust toward Eschweiler on 17 September, both combat commands of the 3d Armored Division bumped head on into the German reinforcements. On the left, while CCA was getting ready to attack shortly before dawn, the Germans began a heavy artillery barrage against both CCA and the 16th Infantry at Eilendorf. Plunging out of a woods between Verlautenheide and Stolberg, men of the *27th Fusilier Regiment* charged in well-disciplined waves with fixed bayonets. They made a perfect target for prepared artillery and mortar concentrations. Those who got through the curtain of shellfire were cut down close to American foxholes with small arms and machine gun fire. Though the fusiliers tried again in the afternoon and prevented CCA from attacking, they gained no ground. American casualties were surprisingly light. The hardest hit battalion of the 16th Infantry, for example, lost two men killed and twenty-one wounded.

Split into two task forces, CCB attacked at midday to take the Weissenberg. The task force on the left ran almost immediately into an attack by a battalion of the *89th Grenadier Regiment*, while the task force on the right encountered a thrust by a battalion of the *48th Grenadier Regiment* supported by three tanks. On the left, neither side could gain. On the right, the grenadiers shoved the armored task force back a thousand yards. Late

[49] Rpt, *A Gp B,* 1335, 14 Sep 44, *OB WEST KTB;* Tel Conv, Model to *Seventh Army,* 1350, 16 Sep 44, *LXXXI Corps KTB, Kampfverlauf;* TWX (Weekly Strength Report as of 1200, 16 Sep 44), *LXXXI Corps,* 22 Sep 44, *LXXXI Corps KTB, Befehle an Div;* Daily Sitrep, *A Gp B,* 0230, 17 Sep 44, *A Gp B KTB, Tagesmeldungen;* MS # A-971 (Col Gerhard Engel, comdr, *12th Inf Div*).

[50] Order, *Seventh Army* to all corps, 16 Sep 44, *LXXXI Corps KTB, Befehle: Heeresgruppe, Armee, usw.*

[51] Order, *LXXXI Corps* to *12th Div,* 2300, 15 Sep 44, *LXXXI Corps KTB, Befehle an Div.*

[52] Tel Convs, *LXXXI Corps* with *12th Div,* 0850 and 1800, and with *116th Pz Div,* 2130, 16 Sep 44; Tel Conv, *Seventh Army* with *LXXXI Corps,* 1150, 17 Sep 44; Order, *LXXXI Corps* to *12th Div,* 1015, 16 Sep 44; all in *LXXXI Corps KTB, Kampfverlauf,* MS # A-971 (Engel).

in the afternoon the enemy drive bogged down, but not before the situation had become so grave that the division commander, General Rose, had sent his reserve to CCB's aid. Though CCB noted the loss of only one light and one medium tank, the Germans claimed to have destroyed nine tanks and to have taken fifty-seven prisoners.[53]

The other battalion of the *48th Grenadier Regiment* intended to retake Schevenhuette. Here the 47th Infantry commander, Colonel Smythe, had decided to delay his attack in view of the indications of German build-up. In midmorning, a patrol under S. Sgt. Harold Hellerich spotted the Germans moving toward Schevenhuette from the village of Gressenich. Notifying his company commander, Sergeant Hellerich waited for the Germans to enter an open field, then pinned them to the ground with fire from his patrol. At this point gunners in the main positions of the 47th Infantry raked the field with machine gun, mortar, and artillery fire. Observers estimated that of at least 200 Germans who had entered the field no more than ten escaped.

Before daylight the next morning, 18 September, a reinforced company of the *48th Grenadier Regiment* sneaked through the darkness to surprise the defenders of a roadblock on the Gressenich–Schevenhuette road. Undetected until too late, the Germans pushed quickly into the village, only to encounter an American tank hidden among the buildings. Assisted by nearby riflemen and machine gunners, the

tank's fire virtually wiped out the enemy company. Not until four days later, on 22 September, did the *48th Grenadiers* desist in their attempts to retake Schevenhuette, and then only after a full battalion had failed in the face of "murderous" losses. Schevenhuette, the survivors reported, had been turned into a veritable fortress, fully secured by mine fields and barbed wire and tenaciously defended by 600–700 men.[54]

Even before this action at Schevenhuette, the very first day of active commitment of the *12th Division* had shown the division commander, Colonel Engel, how difficult—perhaps how insurmountable—was his task. On the night of 17 September, the Americans had begun to pound the fresh division with artillery fire of alarming proportions. In another few hours Colonel Engel was to report his units hard hit by casualties, particularly a battalion of the *89th Regiment* that was down to a hundred men, less than a fifth of original strength.[55] Somewhat disheartened by the outcome of the counterattacks and possibly more than a little displeased at the piecemeal commitment of his troops, Colonel Engel called off offensive action for most of the division the next day to permit regrouping.[56]

On the American side, General Collins had noted that the advent of a fresh German division had changed the situation materially. Though the Germans had gained ground in only isolated instances, he recognized that as long as his

---

[53] German sources are: Daily and Evng Sitreps, *LXXXI Corps,* 1620 and 2145, 17 Sep 44, *LXXXI Corps KTB, Tagesmeldungen;* Sitrep, *12th Div,* 1340, and Tel Conv, *LXXXI Corps* with *12th Div,* 1535 17 Sep 44, both in *LXXXI Corps KTB, Kampfverlauf;* MS # A–971 (Engel).

[54] Daily Sitrep, *12th Div,* 22 Sep 44, *LXXXI Corps KTB, Tagesmeldungen.*
[55] Evng Sitrep, *LXXXI Corps,* 1625, 18 Sep 44, *LXXXI Corps KTB, Tagesmeldungen.*
[56] MS # A–971 (Engel); Tel Convs, *LXXXI Corps* with *12th Div,* 0400 and 0425, 18 Sep 44, *LXXXI Corps KTB, Kampfverlauf.*

adversary had reserves and he had none further large-scale advances were impossible. Ordering the 1st Division, 3d Armored Division, and the 47th Infantry to consolidate, Collins directed the rest of the 9th Division to shorten the corps line by cleaning out the forest between Schevenhuette and Monschau.[57]

The Onset of Position Warfare

On the surface General Collins' order to consolidate looked like a sorely needed rest for most of the troops of the VII Corps. Yet the divisions were in the delicate situation of being through the West Wall in some places, being half through in others, and at some points not having penetrated at all. The line was full of extreme zigs and zags. From an offensive standpoint, the penetrations of the Schill Line were too narrow to serve effectively as springboards for further operations to the east; as a defensive position, the line was open to infiltration or counterattack through the great forest between Schevenhuette and Lammersdorf and through the daggerlike redan which the Germans held between Lammersdorf and Monschau. In addition, the positions within the Stolberg Corridor were subject to observation from high ground both east and west of Stolberg. To eliminate these flaws, the VII Corps was destined to attack on a limited scale for most of the rest of September.

The 9th Division drew what looked to be the major role. General Collins directed General Craig to drive through the Roetgen, Wenau, and Huertgen Forests to occupy a clearing near the villages of

Huertgen and Kleinhau, about six miles east of Zweifall. This would bring control of the only good road net between the forest barrier and the Roer River and also knit together the two forces in the Stolberg and Monschau Corridors. At the same time, the combat commands of the 3d Armored Division were to seize heights on either side of the Vicht River valley at Stolberg, both to eliminate superior enemy observation and to merge the two penetrations of the Schill Line. Only the 1st Division, in the half-moon arc about Aachen, was to stick strictly to the defense.[58]

As the fighting continued in the Stolberg Corridor, both German and American units wore themselves out. While the 3d Armored Division's CCA tried to take high ground about the industrial suburb of Muensterbusch, less than half a mile west of Stolberg, and CCB to occupy the high ground east of Stolberg, the enemy's *12th Division* and what was left of the *9th Panzer Division* continued their futile efforts to re-establish the Schill Line. The result was a miserable siege of deliberate, close-in fighting which brought few advantages to either side.

Attachment of the remnants of the *9th Panzer Division* to the *27th Fusilier Regiment* made CCA's task at Muensterbusch considerably more difficult.[59] Not until late on 19 September did troops of CCA gain a foothold in Muensterbusch from which to begin a costly, methodical mop-up lasting over the next two days.

For two days CCB fought in vain for

---

[57] VII Corps Opns Memo 94, 18 Sep 44, confirming oral orders issued the day before, VII Corps G-3 file, 18 Sep 44.

[58] The development of corps plans may be traced in VII Corps Opns Memos 94–97, 18–20 Sep 44.

[59] Tel Convs, *LXXXI Corps* with Engel, 2045, and with *12th Div,* 2230, 18 Sep 44, *LXXXI Corps KTB, Kampfverlauf.*

the Weissenberg (Hill 283) on the other side of Stolberg; then early on 20 September a task force under Lt. Col. Samuel M. Hogan employed a radical change in tactics. Instead of an artillery preparation and tank support, Colonel Hogan sent the attached battalion of the 26th Infantry forward alone under concealment of an early morning haze. Catching the Germans off guard, the infantry took the hill with hardly a shot fired.

CCB's remaining task was to occupy the Donnerberg (Hill 287), another major height overlooking Stolberg from the east. The assignment fell to Task Force Mills, which with but fourteen effective medium tanks still was stronger than Task Force Lovelady. Screened by smoke and protected on the east by fire of the combat command's tank destroyers, Task Force Mills dashed across a mile of open ground and took the height in one quick thrust.

Holding the Donnerberg was another matter. No sooner had the smoke dissipated than the Germans knocked out half of the tanks. Afraid that loss of the height would compromise a switch position under preparation in the center of Stolberg, the Germans on 22 September mustered a battalion of the *27th Fusilier Regiment* to counterattack.[60] In the meantime, CCB's Task Force Lovelady had moved up the hill to strengthen Task Force Mills. In danger of losing almost all the combat command at one blow, the division commander, General Rose, authorized withdrawal. Behind a smoke screen the two understrength task forces dashed down the slopes into Stolberg. Here they found sanctuary, for in bitter

fighting Task Force Hogan by this time had pushed the enemy back to the switch position across the center of the town.

This was about all either Germans or Americans could accomplish in the Stolberg Corridor. After 22 September the fighting died down. Despite grievous losses, the Germans actually ended up stronger than they had been since General Collins first opened his "reconnaissance in force"; for as the fighting died, reinforcements began to arrive. Unfortunately for the *LXXXI Corps* commander, General Schack, they came too late to benefit him. On 20 September, because of Schack's connection with the Schwerin affair in Aachen, General Brandenberger relieved him of command. General der Infanterie Friedrich J. M. Koechling took over.

The first major reinforcement to arrive was the *183d Volks Grenadier Division*, which had to be employed north of Aachen against the XIX U.S. Corps. Having shored up the line there, General Koechling pulled out the depleted *275th Infantry Division* and sent it southward to occupy a narrow sector around Schevenhuette between the *12th Division* and the *LXXIV Corps*. On 23 September a third full-strength division, the *246th Volks Grenadier*, entrained in Bohemia with a mission to relieve—at long last—the *9th* and *116th Panzer Divisions*. These two units were to pass into reserve for refitting and reorganization.[61]

---

[60] Mng Sitrep, *LXXXI Corps*, 0525, and Daily Sitreps, *LXXXI Corps* and *116th Pz Div*, 21 Sep 44, *LXXXI Corps KTB, Tagesmeldungen.*

[61] Tel Conv, *Seventh Army* with *LXXXI Corps*, 1130, 17 Sep 44, *LXXXI Corps KTB, Kampfverlauf;* Daily Sitrep, *LXXXI Corps*, 22 Sep 44, *LXXXI Corps KTB, Tagesmeldungen;* Order, *LXXXI Corps* to *275th Div*, 1730, 22 Sep 44, *LXXXI Corps KTB, Befehle an Div;* Order *A Gp B* to *Seventh Army*, 1315, 23 Sep 44, *A Gp B KTB, Operationsbefehle.*

The First Fight in the Forest

On the south wing of the VII Corps, General Collins' order to push through the forest barrier to the clearing around Huertgen and Kleinhau coincided roughly with completion of the 60th Infantry's conquest of the Hoefen–Alzen ridge on 18 September. Relinquishing responsibility for holding the ridge to the 4th Cavalry Group, the division commander, General Craig, left one battalion behind to back up the cavalry and moved the rest of the regiment northward for commitment in the forest. To make up for the battalion left behind, General Craig withdrew the 1st Battalion, 39th Infantry, from the fighting in the Monschau Corridor and attached it to the 60th Infantry.

The new drive through the forest in no way lessened the necessity for the 39th Infantry to enlarge the penetration of the West Wall in the Monschau Corridor. Given no respite, the two remaining battalions of the regiment were to fight doggedly for the rest of the month in quest of two dominating pieces of terrain which would secure the penetration. These were Hill 554, within the West Wall south of Lammersdorf, and an open ridge between Lammersdorf and Rollesbroich.

By this time the American battalions had developed closely co-ordinated patterns of maneuver with their attached tanks and tank destroyers, but at best reduction of the pillboxes was slow and costly. Late on 19 September success appeared imminent when tanks and infantry plunged through the line more than two miles toward Rollesbroich, but so fatigued and depleted were the companies that they had no energy left to exploit the gain. Having failed to reach Rolles-broich, the thrust provided no real control of an important road net leading northeast from the village. Hill 554 was finally secured on 29 September after two tenuous holds on it had given way.

In the meantime, the 60th Infantry's attempt to push through the forest and seize the road net around Huertgen and Kleinhau also had begun on 19 September. Something of the confusion the dense forest would promote was apparent on the first day when the lead battalion "attacked" up the main supply route leading to the 47th Infantry at Schevenhuette.

Embracing approximately seven miles, the 60th Infantry front in the forest corresponded roughly to the sector which the enemy's nondescript *353d Infantry Division* had assumed when transferred from the *LXXXI* to the *LXXIV Corps*. The 60th Infantry commander, Col. Jesse L. Gibney, planned to attack with two battalions moving directly through the center of the forest. This was tantamount to two separate operations; for as Colonel Gibney knew, secure flanks within a forested zone seven miles wide would become a fancy that one had read about long ago in the field manuals.

The attached 1st Battalion, 39th Infantry, commanded by Colonel Thompson, was to move almost due east from Zweifall to seize a complex of trails in the valley of the Weisser Weh Creek, about a mile from the woods line at Huertgen. Colonel Gibney intended later to send this battalion into Huertgen, thence northeast to the village of Kleinhau, only three miles from the flank of the 47th Infantry at Schevenhuette. On the right, a battalion of the 60th Infantry under Colonel Chatfield was to advance southeast from Zweifall, follow the trace of the second band of the West Wall, and occupy an initial objective astride a wooded ridge just north of Deadman's Moor (*Todten Bruch*), a stretch of marshy ground along the Lammersdorf–Huertgen highway. Colonel Chatfield's battalion then was to continue east through about two more miles of forest to cut the Lammersdorf–Huertgen highway at the village of Germeter.

Experiencing more difficulty from terrain than from the enemy, Colonel Thompson's 1st Battalion reached the valley of the Weisser Weh by nightfall of 20 September. Though Colonel Gibney ordered a push the next day into Huertgen, the enemy awoke at daylight to the battalion's presence. Colonel Thompson's men spent the entire day beating off diverse elements of the *353d Division* and trying to get tanks and tank destroyers forward over muddy firebreaks and trails to assist the attack on Huertgen.

Before the battalion could get going on 22 September, orders came to cancel the attack. Colonel Thompson was to move north to back up the 47th Infantry at Schevenhuette where the *12th Division's 48th Regiment* was threatening to push in that regiment's advanced position. The division commander, General Craig, also sent the 60th Infantry's reserve battalion northward to Schevenhuette.

Even though neither of these battalions had to be committed actively at Schevenhuette, concern over the situation there had served to erase the penetration through the forest to the valley of the Weisser Weh. By the time Colonel Thompson's battalion became available to return three days later, on 25 September, the Germans had moved into the Weisser Weh valley in strength. Not only that; now Colonel Thompson's men had to go

to the aid of Colonel Chatfield's battalion astride the wooded ridge near Deadman's Moor.

Colonel Chatfield's battalion of the 60th Infantry had found the opposition tough from the outset. Strengthened by the pillboxes in the Schill Line, the Germans clung like beggar lice to every position. Two days of fighting carried the battalion over a thousand yards to the western slopes of the objective, the ridge north of Deadman's Moor; but the next morning, 22 September, the Germans began to counterattack.

The counterattack resulted from direct intervention by the *Seventh Army* commander, General Brandenberger. Concerned about American advances in the forest on 20 September, Brandenberger had transferred an understrength assault gun brigade from the *LXXXI Corps* to the *353d Division*. About this brigade the *353d Division* had assembled a battalion each of infantry and engineers, an artillery battery, and five 75-mm. antitank guns.[62]

Though the counterattack on 22 September made no spectacular headway, close combat raged back and forth along the wooded ridge for the next three days. The fighting centered primarily on possession of a nest of three pillboxes that changed hands time after time. Having entered the forest with only about a hundred men per rifle company, Colonel Chatfield's battalion felt its casualties

---

[62] Tel Conv, *LXXXI Corps* with *353d Div*, 1720, 21 Sep 44, *LXXXI Corps KTB, Kampfverlauf;* Order, *Seventh Army* to *LXXXI Corps*, 1940 21 Sep 44, *LXXXI Corps KTB, Befehle: Heeresgruppe, Armee, usw.;* Evng Sitrep, *A Gp B*, 1840, 21 Sep 44, *A Gp B KTB, Letzte Meldung;* Daily Sitrep, *A Gp B*, 0110, 22 Sep 44, *A Gp B KTB, Tagesmeldungen.*

acutely. Though a few wide-eyed replacements arrived, the rate of attrition proved far greater than the build-up. At one point the Germans overran a pillbox and captured forty-five men, including all officers and the command group of one of the companies. Only thirty disorganized men remained in that company.

By 25 September losses had become so oppressive that the regimental commander, Colonel Gibney, saw no hope for the battalion's renewing the attack. Altering his plan of maneuver, he sent both his reserve battalion and Colonel Thompson's 1st Battalion, 39th Infantry, to take over the assault role. From the contested ridge, these two battalions were to drive south through Deadman's Moor, cut the Lammersdorf–Huertgen road, and make contact to the southwest with that part of the 39th Infantry which had pierced the forward band of the West Wall at the customhouse near Lammersdorf. If this could be accomplished, the 60th Infantry would have carved out a sizable salient into the forest and would have secured at least one of its flanks. Then the regiment conceivably might renew the drive northeast up the highway to the original objective of Huertgen.

Both battalions attacked early on 26 September. Five days later, by the end of the month, the 60th Infantry at last had cut the Lammersdorf–Huertgen highway near *Jaegerhaus,* a hunting lodge that marked a junction of the highway with a road leading northwest through the forest to Zweifall. But it had been a costly, frustrating procession of attack followed by counterattack, a weary, plodding fight that pitted individual against individual and afforded little opportunity for utilizing American superiority in artillery, air, and armor. Enemy patrols constantly infiltrated supply lines. Although units at night adopted the perimeter defense of jungle warfare, the perimeter still might have to be cleared of Germans before the new day's attack could begin. So heavy a toll did the fighting take that at the end of the month the 60th Infantry and the attached battalion from the 39th Infantry were in no condition to resume the attack toward Huertgen.

The Germans had effectively utilized terrain, the West Wall, and persistent small-unit maneuver to thwart the limited objective attack of the widespread 9th Division. As others had been discovering all along the First Army front, General Craig had found his frontage too great, his units too spent and depleted, and a combination of enemy and terrain too effective to enable the division to reach its objectives. In the specialized pillbox and forest warfare, "the cost of learning 'on the job' was high." [63]

As events were to develop, the 9th Division was the first of a steady procession of American units which in subsequent weeks were to find gloom, misery, and tragedy synonymous with the name Huertgen Forest. Technically, the Huertgen Forest lies along the middle eastern portion of the forest barrier, but the name was to catch on with American soldiers to the exclusion of the names Roetgen and Wenau. Few could distinguish one dank stretch of evergreens from another, one abrupt ridge from another. Even atop the ridges, the floor of the forest was a trap for heavy autumn rains. By the time both American and German artillery had done with the forest, the setting would

---

[63] Ltr, Craig to OCMH, 31 Aug 53.

look like a battlefield designed by the Archfiend himself.

The VII Corps was stopped. "A combination of things stopped us," General Collins recalled later. "We ran out of gas—that is to say, we weren't completely dry, but the effect was much the same; we ran out of ammunition; and we ran out of weather. The loss of our close tactical air support because of weather was a real blow." The exhausted condition of American units and the status of their equipment also had much to do with it. It was a combination of these things, plus "really beautiful" positions which the Germans held in the second band of the West Wall.[64]

General Collins had gone into the West Wall on the theory that "if we could break it, then we would be just that much to the good; if we didn't, then we would be none the worse." [65] Perhaps somewhere between these conditions lay the true measure of what the VII Corps had accomplished. The West Wall had been penetrated, but the breach was not secure enough nor the VII Corps strong enough for exploitation.

The fighting had cost the Germans dearly in casualties. In a single week from 16 to 23 September, for example, the *12th Division* had dropped from a "combat strength" of 3,800 men to 1,900, a position from which the division was not

to recover fully through the course of the autumn fighting. During a similar period, the *9th Panzer Division* had lost over a thousand men representing two thirds of its original combat strength. One unit, the *105th Panzer Grenadier Battalion*, had been reduced from 738 officers and men to 116. Only the *116th Panzer Division* in the relatively quiescent sector about Aachen had avoided appreciable losses.[66] On the other hand, the Germans had bought with those losses a priceless commodity. They had bought time.

As September came to an end, the VII Corps all along the line shifted to defense. Before General Collins could hope to renew the attack, he had somehow to shuffle the front to release some unit with which to attack.[67] The logical place to shuffle was in the defensive arc about Aachen; for the next fight lay not to the east or northeast but in conjunction with the XIX Corps against the city which General Collins had by-passed in favor of more critical factors like dominant terrain and the West Wall.

---

[64] Interv with Collins, 21 Jan 54.
[65] Interv with Collins, 25 Jan 54.

[66] For detailed figures and documentation on enemy strengths, see Heichler, Germans Opposite VII Corps, pp. 84–86.

[67] During this period a squad leader in the 18th Infantry, S. Sgt. Joseph E. Schaefer, earned the Medal of Honor. After helping thwart a local counterattack, Sergeant Schaefer went beyond his lines to overtake a group of withdrawing Germans and liberate an American squad captured earlier in the fighting. The sergeant personally killed between 15 to 20 Germans, wounded as many more, and took 10 prisoners.

CHAPTER V

Action on the North Wing

First Army's third major component, the XIX Corps under General Corlett, was out of the running in the race for the West Wall. Immobilized four days by the gasoline shortage and possessing but two divisions, the XIX Corps at the time the first patrols probed the German border still was west of the Meuse River. At the closest point, Germany still was fifteen miles away. The XIX Corps nevertheless had an integral role in the First Army's scheme of attack—to penetrate the West Wall north of Aachen and form the northern arm of a pincers enveloping the city.

In much of the XIX Corps sector, the Meuse River was strengthened by another obstacle, the Albert Canal. The Albert parallels the Meuse from Liège to the vicinity of Maastricht before swinging northwest toward Antwerp. (*Map 1*) Built before World War II with military utility in mind, the canal is no minor obstacle. In many places it cuts deep through the soft soils of the region. Its banks are great concrete-reinforced precipices, sometimes as high as 160 feet from the water line.

On the XIX Corps left wing, where the 2d Armored Division was approaching the canal and facing almost due north, the region beyond the canal is marshy and creased by numerous small streams. Here dug-in Germans reacted nervously and

apparently with some strength against XIX Corps patrols. On the corps right wing the 30th Division faced the dual obstacle of the Albert and the Meuse.

Near the center of the XIX Corps zone lay Maastricht, capital city of the province of Limburg, the Dutch Panhandle. A road hub through which the XIX Corps would have to funnel its supply lines, Maastricht was the logical pivot on which to base a wheeling movement through the Panhandle and thence east to the German border. The city lies on an island about seven miles long and two miles wide, formed by a complex of man-made waterways and by the Meuse (known in the Netherlands as the Maas). General Corlett was to clear the enemy from north of the Albert Canal and east of the Maas (Meuse) up to an operational boundary with the British. This boundary ran northeast from a point between Hasselt and Beeringen and passed about thirteen miles north of Maastricht.

Because the XIX Corps was running several days behind its neighbors on both left and right, General Corlett saw no necessity for assault crossings of the Albert and the Meuse. At Beeringen, northwest of Hasselt, the 30 British Corps already had forged a substantial bridgehead across the Albert, and at Liège the VII Corps had thrown a bridge across the Meuse. Since the Germans appeared ready to de-

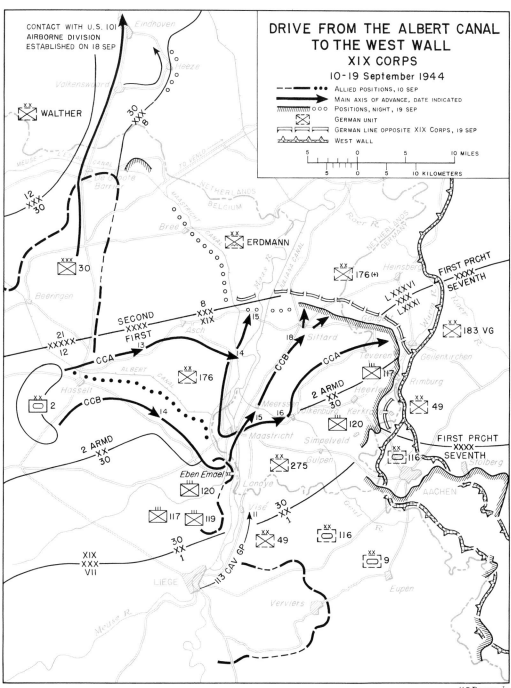

DRIVE FROM THE ALBERT CANAL
TO THE WEST WALL
XIX CORPS
10-19 September 1944

ALLIED POSITIONS, 10 SEP
MAIN AXIS OF ADVANCE, DATE INDICATED
POSITIONS, NIGHT, 19 SEP
GERMAN UNIT
GERMAN LINE OPPOSITE XIX CORPS, 19 SEP
WEST WALL

5   0   5   10 MILES
5 0   5   10 KILOMETERS

CONTACT WITH U.S. 101
AIRBORNE DIVISION
ESTABLISHED ON 18 SEP

MAP 1

H.C.Brewer, Jr.

GENERAL CORLETT

fend the obstacles, why not, General Corlett reasoned, utilize the crossings already
made?[1]

Defense of the Albert

As General Corlett suspected, the Germans were planning to defend the Albert
Canal. Also as General Corlett suspected,
they hadn't much to do the job with.

As the city of Maastricht marked
roughly the center of the XIX Corps zone,
so it represented a line of demarcation
between contingents of two German
armies. North of a line marked by the
Maastricht "island," Valkenburg, and
Stolberg, the defense was the responsibility of the *First Parachute Army,* a new-
comer in the line, most of whose troops

opposed the British. The other half of
the XIX Corps zone, that area between
Maastricht and Liège, was the responsibility of General Brandenberger's *Seventh
Army,* the same headquarters whose
troops faced the V and VII Corps.

As the northernmost portion of General
Brandenberger's zone, this sector came
under General Schack's *LXXXI Corps,*
that headquarters whose major responsibility was the defense of Aachen. An
extension of the boundary between the
XIX and VII Corps would run just north
of Aachen and thereby split General
Schack's zone almost in the center. The
two divisions on the *LXXXI Corps* south
wing (the *9th* and *116th Panzer Divisions*)
would oppose the VII Corps; the two on
the north wing could face the XIX Corps.[2]

These two divisions comprising General
Schack's northern wing were the *49th* and
275th Infantry Divisions. The strength
and caliber of neither could have afforded
the corps commander any genuine confidence.

Smashed in France, the *49th Division*
under the aegis of its commander, Generalleutnant Siegfried P. Macholz, had tried
to reorganize earlier in Hasselt; but only
about 1,500 men—mostly service troops—
had reached the assembly area. Of the
combat forces, hardly anything remained.
General Macholz had left but one regimental headquarters—that of the *148th
Infantry*—and no artillery or antitank
guns except one 112-mm. Russian howitzer. General Schack on 7 September had
ordered General Macholz to put a regiment of two battalions, created around

---

[1] Combat Interv with Corlett, filed with XIX
Corps Combat Intervs for Sep 44.

[2] For a detailed account of the German order
of battle and operations in this sector, see Lucian
Heichler, The Germans Opposite XIX Corps, a
study prepared to complement this volume; copy
in OCMH.

the headquarters of the *148th,* into the line along a seven-mile front on the east bank of the Meuse running north from an industrial suburb of Liège.

By 10 September the *49th Division* had been reinforced by a security regiment composed of older men, staffed by officers of World War I vintage, and equipped with small arms and a few machine guns but no heavy weapons. This unit General Macholz assigned to cover half his division front and was subsequently to redesignate to replace his defunct *149th Infantry Regiment.* Reinforcements were to continue to arrive in driblets so that by the time the battle was fully joined, General Macholz in one regiment had a strength of 1,188 officers and men and in the other, 858. Although both regiments gained a reasonable complement of machine guns, they had only two mortars and five 75-mm. antitank guns between them. The division still had no motor transport and no artillery.[3]

Sharing a common boundary with the *49th Division* in the vicinity of Visé, about halfway between Liège and Maastricht, was the *275th Division* under Generalleutnant Hans Schmidt. The *275th's* northern boundary coincided with that between the *First Parachute* and the *Seventh Armies,* which was in turn roughly comparable to the boundary between the U.S. 2d Armored and 30th Divisions. By 10 September, the day when patrols of the XIX Corps reached

the Albert Canal and the Meuse in force, General Schmidt had under his command approximately 5,000 men. Like General Macholz and the *49th Division,* he had only one regimental headquarters, the *984th Infantry;* but in comparison to the *49th,* General Schmidt was rich in artillery: he had a battery of four 105-mm. howitzers inherited from an SS division which had returned to Germany.[4]

The third German division opposing the XIX Corps held positions from Maastricht along the Albert Canal to the vicinity of Hasselt. This was the *176th Infantry Division* under the banner of the *First Parachute Army.*

The presence of the *First Parachute Army* in the line west of Maastricht was an exemplification of the kind of eleventh-hour improvisation to which the Germans had been forced by several factors: the haphazard nature of their retreat, the lengthening of their defensive front as they fell back on Germany and the Netherlands, and the virtual isolation of an army, the *Fifteenth,* when the British had captured Antwerp. Pinned against the Channel coast by the British *coup de main,* the *Fifteenth Army* had to employ all its resources in escaping across the Schelde estuary and in holding banks of the estuary in order to deny the Allies access to Antwerp from the sea.[5] This had left between the *Fifteenth Army* and the *Seventh Army's* westernmost position near Maastricht a vacuum of critical proportions, a gap along the Albert Canal of almost sixty miles. The "door to northwestern Germany stood open." [6]

---

[3] MS # B–792, *Die Kaempfe der 49. Inf Div von der Maas bis an den Westwall noerdlich Aachen* (2 Sep 44–18 Sep 44) *und die Kaempfe um den Westwall* (10 Sep 44–10 Nov 44) (Macholz); Rpt, *49th Div to LXXXI Corps,* 14 Sep 44, *LXXXI Corps KTB, Meldungen der Div;* TWX (Weekly Strength Rpt as of 16 Sep 44), *LXXXI Corps to Seventh Army,* 22 Sep 44, *LXXXI Corps KTB, Befehle an Div.*

[4] MS # B–372 (Schmidt).
[5] See below, Chs. VI and IX.
[6] *OKW/WFSt KTB, Ausarbeitung, der Westen 1.IV.–16.XII. 44,* MS # B–034 (Schramm).

When news of the fall of Antwerp had reached Berlin, the German headquarters OKW had acted quickly to do something about the great gap. Telephoning Generaloberst Kurt Student, commander of German parachute troops, OKW had ordered him to assume command of the *First Parachute Army*, a headquarters which previously had controlled units only in training. General Student and his new command, OKW directed, were then to come under the control of Field Marshal Model's *Army Group B* and defend the north bank of the Albert Canal from Maastricht west to the vicinity of Antwerp.[7]

Upon inspecting the Albert Canal on 5 September and getting an idea of the troops he would control, General Student could generate no enthusiasm for either. The initial organization of his new army he termed "an improvisation on the grandest scale."[8] Although Student's army was to increase rapidly in strength because his superiors considered this sector so important, the size of the army as the XIX Corps reached the Albert Canal left much to be desired. General Student had at this time but one corps headquarters, borrowed from the *Fifteenth Army*, with three infantry divisions and a parachute division, the latter little more deserving of the honorific "parachute" than was the army as a whole. These four divisions General Student had arrayed in a linear defense along the Albert Canal with the *176th Division* occupying the left sector between Maastricht and

Hasselt. Because of the northeasterly direction of the XIX Corps attack, the *176th Division* would be the only one of Student's divisions to be encountered by General Corlett's forces.

Commanded by Colonel Christian Landau, the *176th Division* was one of those replacement training units which the Germans had upgraded hurriedly to meet the crisis of the Allied march upon the homeland. Replacement trainees, convalescents, and semi-invalids in a total strength of approximately 7,000 made up the command. Only a few of these men were unconditionally fit for active fighting. Grouped for combat into three regimental teams, the division had a heterogeneous assortment of units: several infantry battalions formed from replacement training units, two Luftwaffe battalions made up of air force personnel, an "ear battalion," two engineer battalions, and a reconnaissance battalion made up of two bicycle companies.

Whereas Colonel Landau's infantry was about equal to that of the neighboring *275th* and *49th Divisions*, his artillery was stronger. He had two so-called light battalions with 6 105-mm. howitzers and 1 heavy battalion with 8 infantry cannon, 4 German, 2 Czech, and 2 Russian 150-mm. howitzers. Possessing 1 75-mm. gun, 20 20-mm. guns, and 5 88's, Colonel Landau also was better off than his neighbors in the antiaircraft and antitank departments. Like the other divisions, he had only limited signal equipment, almost no services, and no motor transport.[9]

When first committed, Colonel Landau had been impelled to put one battalion

---

[7] Entries of 3 and 4 Sep 44, *OB WEST KTB* (*Text*); MS # B–717, *Zusatz zum Bericht von Oberst i.G. Geyer* (concerning *First Prcht Army*) (Student).

[8] MS # B–717 (Student).

[9] Rpt on Trip to *176th Inf Div*, 1st Lt Klaus Liebrecht to Model, 7 Sep 44, *A Gp B KTB, Op.-Befehle;* MS # B–362, *176. Inf Div* (Landau).

forward of his main line on the opposite side of the Albert Canal in order to fulfill an order from Hitler to defend Fort Eben Emael, the most elaborate fort in what had once been a complex Belgian defensive system. Though conforming, General Student had protested the disposition because of numerous factors, not the least of which were that the main entrance to the fort was on the American side and that the firing embrasures were clogged with wrecked Belgian cannon from 1940 when German airborne troops had swooped down on the fort. Not until early on 10 September, a step ahead of the 30th U.S. Division, did Field Marshal Model's concurrence in Student's view permit the battalion of the *176th Division* to abandon Eben Emael and retire to the other side of the Albert.[10]

From the Albert to the Border

While the two German armies thus were concocting a defense on their inner wings, the American commander, General Corlett, was directing the maneuvers by which he hoped to turn the German flanks without the necessity of forcing bridgeheads across the Albert and the Meuse. Contacting the 30 British Corps and the VII Corps, he secured permission to utilize their bridges on either of his flanks at Beeringen and at Liège. Though Maj. Gen. Leland S. Hobbs,

commander of the 30th Division, wanted to put his entire division across the VII Corps bridge at Liège, General Corlett demurred. Tying up the bridge the length of time required to move an entire division he deemed an undue imposition on the VII Corps. Instead, Corlett ordered the 113th Cavalry Group (Col. William S. Biddle) to cross the Meuse at Liège and drive northward behind the dual obstacle of the canal and the river. As soon as the cavalry had cleared a portion of the east bank within the XIX Corps zone, the 30th Division then could cross unopposed in its own sector. The 2d Armored Division was to execute a similar maneuver with its own reconnaissance battalion at Beeringen.[11]

Delayed somewhat by mines, demolished bridges, and occasional defended roadblocks, Colonel Biddle's cavalry nevertheless made good progress. By late afternoon of 11 September, the cavalry had pushed north from Liège through all resistance General Macholz' feeble *49th Division* could offer and was engaging a part of General Schmidt's *275th Division* near Visé, well within the XIX Corps zone. In the meantime, reconnaissance patrols sent out by the 30th Division's 119th Infantry (Col. Edwin M. Sutherland) had discovered that a narrow strip of land between the canal and the Meuse was undefended. By the time the cavalry arrived opposite this point, Colonel Sutherland already had a footbridge across the canal and was ready with assault boats to cross the river. Disturbed only by an occasional round of artillery fire, the 119th Infantry reached the far bank and fanned out to the east and northeast. Before

---

[10] TWX, *A Gp B* to *OB WEST* (relaying and endorsing Msg, Student to *A Gp B*), 1400, 9 Sep 44, and Order, *A Gp B* to *First Prcht Army*, 2105, 9 Sep 44, both in *A Gp B KTB, Operationsbefehle*; MS # B-372, *Kaempfe [der 275. Inf Div] in Nordfrankreich* (Schmidt); and Noon Sitrep, *A Gp B,* 1345, 10 Sep 44, *A Gp B KTB, Letzte Meldung.*

[11] 113th Cav Gp and 2d Armd AARs, Sep 44.

daylight on 12 September, the 117th Infantry (Col. Walter M. Johnson) followed suit.[12]

While these crossings were in progress, the 30th Division's third regiment, the 120th Infantry, was holding the west bank of the canal farther north near the point where the canal swings northwest away from the Meuse. Commanded by Col. Hammond D. Birks, this was the regiment which on the day before (10 September) had occupied Fort Eben Emael.

Not content to sit idly while waiting for the other two regiments on the east bank to come abreast, Colonel Birks turned his attention to a lock on the canal near Fort Eben Emael. So long as the Germans held this lock, Colonel Birks believed, they might demolish it at any time to inundate some of the Dutch lowlands to the north and northwest.

Getting to the lock, Colonel Birks soon discovered, posed quite a problem. Located at the southeastern tip of the Maastricht island, the lock could be reached only from the island or from the narrow strip of flat terrain between the canal and the Meuse. At first glance, Colonel Birks and his engineer advisers could see no hope of crossing the canal at any point

close to the lock; for the concrete-faced west bank of the canal at this point is too high and steep for launching assault boats in any orthodox manner. The closest place where assault boats might be launched was opposite the village of Lanaye, a mile south of the lock, but the route from Lanaye to the objective was cruelly exposed to German fire from the east bank of the Meuse.

The problem of how to get to the lock remained until a local Belgian electrical engineer suggested a solution. Two tunnels, he pointed out, leading from deep in the bowels of Fort Eben Emael, emerge along the steep west bank of the canal a short distance from the lock. Large enough to permit passage of rubber assault boats, the upper tunnel emerges about halfway up the bank. More a drainage pipe than a passageway and so small a man would have to crawl to negotiate it, the lower tunnel opens directly below the upper tunnel right at the water line.

While engineers carried assault boats through the upper tunnel, a squad of infantry slithered 500 yards through the lower to gain the canal. When the engineers overhead lowered the rubber boats down the concrete face of the west bank, the infantry clambered in and quickly paddled across. Taking a small German party guarding the lock by surprise, the infantry made short work of the wires to the demolitions.

On the enemy side of the canal and the river, the outcome of fighting on 11 September had emphasized the patent impossibility of the *49th* and *275th Divisions'* holding even for a reasonable length of time along the east bank of the Meuse. As early as the day before, when the 113th Cavalry Group first had crossed the Liège bridge, the German generals

---

[12] For operations of the 113th Cavalry Group and the 30th Division, see official records of the group, division, and attached units. An unofficial history of the 30th Division by Robert L. Hewitt, entitled *Workhorse of the Western Front* (Washington: Infantry Journal Press, 1946), is comprehensive and apparently authoritative. Nicknamed "Old Hickory" in recognition of its Tennessee-Carolinas National Guard origin, the 30th Division entered combat on 10 June. At Mortain, in Normandy, the division held a flank of the American breakout at Avranches against the major German panzer counterattack to cut off Hodges' and Patton's armored spearheads. General Bradley, in *A Soldier's Story*, page 375, calls the 30th the "Rock of Mortain."

had recognized that fact.[13] Yet as night came on 11 September their corps commander, General Schack, reiterated their mission of preventing an attack on the West Wall before the fortifications could be readied. Form a new line, General Schack directed, facing south and running generally along the Dutch-Belgian border eastward from the Meuse in the vicinity of Lanaye. The *275th Division* was to stick close to the river while the *49th Division* held the line farther east and maintained contact with the *116th Panzer Division,* which was falling back on Aachen before the VII U.S. Corps. "The fight for time," General Schack warned, "is of paramount importance!" [14]

As General Schack must have realized, it would take more than platitudes to halt the onrush of American troops. On 12 September he appealed unsuccessfully to the *Seventh Army* commander, General Brandenberger, in hope of shortening his front by adjustment of the boundary with the *First Parachute Army.*[15]

On the American side, the 117th and 119th Infantry Regiments were handicapped through most of 12 September because lack of treadway bridges across the Albert and the Meuse prevented attached tank companies from crossing, but they continued to push steadily north and northeast. Driving northeast on the right flank of the infantry, Colonel Biddle's cavalry group also advanced steadily and

maintained contact with the 1st Division of the VII Corps. The 30th Division and the cavalry were shoving the Germans back as though forcing open a giant door hinged on Maastricht. In little more than two days after the cavalry had wedged a foot in the door near Liège, the gap was widening.

By nightfall of 12 September the infantry troops had gained as much as five miles to bring them abreast of Colonel Birks' 120th Infantry, which by this time had crossed the canal to take the village of Lanaye. In the process, the Americans hardly were aware that the Germans had attempted a new line along the Dutch-Belgian border. By nightfall they were almost a mile inside the Netherlands. Maastricht lay but four miles away.

The Germans made one feeble counterattack during the day, not for a tactical objective but in an attempt to rescue the driver and aide-de-camp of the *275th Division* commander, General Schmidt, and a dispatch case containing important papers. Traveling with his aide in a command car, General Schmidt earlier in the day had narrowly escaped capture when he came suddenly upon an American patrol. As the Americans opened fire, they killed both Schmidt's driver and his aide and wounded the general in the left hip. Unaware that his companions were dead, General Schmidt hobbled and crawled away from the scene and back to his own lines, whereupon he organized a counterattack in an attempt, he said, "to rescue my comrades." The German general might better have spared the effort. Both his aide and his driver were corpses by this time, and at 30th Division headquarters American officers already were poring over the papers from the dispatch case. 1st Lt. Elwood G. Daddow had

[13] Rad, *49th Div* to *LXXXI Corps,* 1440, 10 Sep 44, *LXXXI Corps KTB, Meldungen der Div;* MS # B-372 (Schmidt).

[14] Order, *LXXXI Corps* to *275th* and *49th Divs,* 2210 and 2215, 11 Sep 44, *LXXXI Corps KTB, Kampfverlauf;* Daily Sitrep, *LXXXI Corps* to *Seventh Army,* 2300, 11 Sep 44, *LXXXI Corps KTB, Tagesmeldungen.*

[15] Tel Convs, *Seventh Army* with *LXXXI Corps,* 1500 and 1600, 12 Sep 44, *LXXXI Corps KTB, Kampfverlauf.*

PORTION OF FORT EBEN EMAEL

spotted the case and dashed out under fire to get it.[16]

Intelligence officers of the 30th Division were elated to discover among the German papers documents indicating the strength and missions of many units under the *Seventh Army* and a situation map spotting the command posts of the *Seventh Army*, two corps, and twelve divisions. In light of the fluidity of German units at the time, the documents hardly could have been as valuable as either the Germans or the Americans indicated;

nevertheless, the incident had provided a cloak-and-dagger element often lacking in plodding infantry operations.

After a third day of fighting the *49th* and *275th Divisions* again had no alternative but to fall back and try to establish another line. Urging that the *275th Division* do everything possible to prevent a crossing onto the Maastricht island, General Schack authorized a withdrawal of about three miles.[17] Schack conceivably might have wished to withdraw the two divisions all the way back to the West Wall before the Americans could wipe them out completely; but *Army Group B*

---

[16] In MS # B-372, General Schmidt has provided a lucid if somewhat mock heroic account of this action. Records of American units also tell of it.

[17] Order, *LXXXI Corps* to all divs, 2230, 12 Sep 44, *LXXXI Corps KTB, Befehle an Div.*

The Albert Canal, *as seen from a machine gun emplacement in Fort Eben Emael.* (*Captured film.*)

thought otherwise. During the night of 12 September Field Marshal Model ordered specifically that the *LXXXI Corps* cling to the Maas River between Visé and Maastricht. Withdrawal from that front would require his special authorization, he said.[18]

Model probably did not know that Visé already had fallen at least twelve hours before and that his order was no longer relevant. Better informed about the true situation, General Schack paid scant at-

tention to the order. The *LXXXI Corps* commander told the *275th Division* to fall back on the Maastricht–Aachen highway but to hold a small sector alongside the Maas in order to keep U.S. forces away from Maastricht long enough to permit the garrison of the Maastricht island to withdraw eastward over the city's bridges.

For his part, the ailing *275th Division* commander, General Schmidt, had no faith in this plan. He apparently wanted to abandon Maastricht and fall back another four or five miles behind a minor but deep-cut stream, the Geul River. In the first place, he believed the Americans

[18] Rad, *Seventh Army* to *LXXXI Corps* (relaying order, *A Gp B*), 0300, 13 Sep 44, *LXXXI Corps KTB, Befehle: Heeresgruppe, Armee, usw.*

could break any line he might form other than one behind a difficult obstacle. In the second place, he saw no reason for trying to save the Maastricht bridges, because that part of the *First Parachute Army's 176th Division* on the Maastricht island surely would not withdraw eastward into another division's sector but northward into the division's own rear areas.[19]

Only one more day was necessary to prove General Schmidt right on both scores. Indeed, he had much less chance than before to hold the line; for during the night attached tanks and organic artillery had crossed the Meuse to join the 30th Division's infantry. The two assault regiments swept forward rapidly on 13 September. The commander of the *176th Division's* garrison of Maastricht and the island became convinced that the island positions were untenable. In withdrawing, the garrison turned, as General Schmidt had predicted, not to the east but to the north.

General Schmidt was not the first to discover that this American infantry-tank-artillery team was a difficult thing to stop. In the long march across northern France and Belgium, General Hobbs's troops and those of the other divisions had become masters of the art of pursuit warfare. They had attained an almost reflexive knowledge of how to fight this kind of war. The infantry-tank-artillery teams were close-knit families, into which had been adopted the fighter-bomber. At the first word to advance, the infantry would clamber to accustomed perches upon its attached tanks. Upon encountering opposition, the infantry would dismount and engage the enemy while forward ob-

servers for the artillery would bring down fire in a matter of minutes. Atop the tanks and trucks were brilliant fluorescent panels to serve as identification for the pilots of fighter-bombers flying column cover. Although weather often deterred air activity during these latter days of the pursuit, the pilots still were able to make the enemy's daytime movements a risky business.

Before dark on 13 September a battalion of the 117th Infantry entered Wijk, Maastricht's sprawling suburb lying east of the Maas, but discovered that the Germans had demolished the bridges between Wijk and the city on the island. Crossing the river in assault boats the next day (14 September), the men found the city empty of the enemy except for three Germans burning papers in the local Gestapo headquarters.

In the meantime, the other battalions of Colonel Johnson's regiment and those of the 119th Infantry were pushing northeast to gain the line of the Geul River. Not without some trepidation did the two regiments approach the Geul, for the valley of this little tributary of the Maas is a marked feature in a region where hills fuse with lowlands. From a captured document, XIX Corps intelligence had determined that the Germans planned to defend the line of the Geul as a switch position between Aachen and Maastricht, thereby tying in the West Wall at Aachen with the *First Parachute Army's* line along the Albert and Meuse–Escaut Canals,[20] in what had been designated as the *West Stellung*.

---

[19] MS # B–372 (Schmidt).

[20] See Defensive Line Between Maastricht and Aachen, notes on a captured document to be found in G–2 Sec, XIX Corps AAR, Sep 44; also *LXXXI Corps* Order for Preparation to Occupy West Wall, 10 Sep 44, V Corps G–2 file, 14 Sep 44.

The Germans did intend to defend the Geul, but the American advances on 13 September into Wijk and farther east along the boundary between the *49th* and *275th Divisions* near the town of Gulpen came close to compromising the position before it could be established. Registering particular concern about the gap at Gulpen, Field Marshal Model at *Army Group B* directed the *LXXXI Corps* to commit all available forces to restore a continuous front there. Though General Schack shifted a straggler battalion, a machine gun company, and two engineer companies of the *49th Division* into the gap, this was not enough.[21]

Early on 14 September a battalion of the 119th Infantry crossed the Geul at a ford a mile north of Gulpen without opposition. At the same time another battalion of the 119th Infantry crossed at Valkenburg, about seven miles east of Maastricht. Choice of the Valkenburg site for a crossing was unfortunate because of the proximity of the *275th Division's* artillery. With observation from atop a water tower, General Schmidt's lone original battery of 105-mm. howitzers plus three other newly attached batteries could readily adjust their fire on the crossing.[22] Though the Germans claimed to have reoccupied Valkenburg itself, the 119th Infantry still maintained a foothold beyond the Geul.

With Maastricht captured and bridgeheads having apparently compromised the Geul switch position, General Hobbs now was ready to wheel to the east in order to

assault the West Wall north of Aachen. The fact that he failed to do so immediately, the German commanders opposite him could attribute only to the possibility that he was busy regrouping and moving up reinforcements and supplies.[23]

Although General Hobbs did use the opportunity to move Colonel Birks' 120th Infantry forward, this was not his real reason for a pause. General Hobbs was, in reality, perturbed by the fact that any move to the east would leave his left flank dangling. On his right flank he had adequate protection from a screen raised by the 113th Cavalry Group along an eight-mile front in the direction of the VII Corps near Aachen; but on his left flank the 2d Armored Division still was straining to come abreast through the marshy flatlands west and northwest of Maastricht. General Hobbs told his regiments to put in bridges across the Geul and strengthen the bridgeheads, but the 30th Division would not drive eastward alone.

More dependent upon bridges than an infantry division, the 2d Armored Division under Maj. Gen. Ernest N. Harmon had been a day later than the 30th Division in beginning to advance beyond the Albert Canal.[24] Crossing the British bridge at

---

[21] Tel Convs, *Seventh Army* with *LXXXI Corps* (relaying order, Model to *Seventh Army*), 2050, 13 Sep 44 and *LXXXI Corps* with *275th Div*, 2345, 13 Sep 44, *LXXXI Corps KTB, Kampfverlauf*.

[22] MS # B-373, *Kaempfe in Rheinland der 75. Infanterie-Division* (Schmidt).

[23] MSS # B-372 (Schmidt) and # B-792 (Macholz).

[24] General Harmon formally assumed command on 12 September when General Brooks left in anticipation of assuming command of the V Corps (see above, Ch. III). The 2d Armored (Hell on Wheels) Division had the same organization as the 3d Armored Division of the VII Corps (see above, Ch. IV). Having campaigned previously in North Africa and Sicily, the division entered combat in Normandy on 10 June. Its after action reports for September are particularly detailed. The division has published a sketchy account of its operations, entitled, *A History of the Second United States Armored Division*, E. A. Trahan, ed. (Atlanta, Ga.: A. Love, 1947).

Beeringen at first light on 11 September, General Harmon's reconnaissance battalion had driven southeast to re-enter the XIX Corps zone before dark at a point north of Hasselt. A counterattack during the night by contingents of Colonel Landau's *176th Division* and occasionally stanch resistance the next day so delayed the battalion in clearing a stretch of the north bank of the Albert Canal that supporting engineers did not get a bridge completed until midnight of 12 September. Thereupon, CCA under Col. John H. Collier rumbled across, though not until daylight of 13 September would the left hook of General Corlett's double envelopment of the Albert Canal line really begin to roll.

With the reconnaissance battalion protecting the left flank, Colonel Collier's CCA drove eastward on 13 September toward the Maas. Resistance took the form of numerous roadblocks, reinforced by mines and occasional antitank guns and defended by tenacious knots of infantry. Though the marshy terrain forced the armor to stick to the roads and limited maneuver against the roadblocks, the enemy's *176th Division* was no more equal to holding an unyielding line than were the two divisions opposite the XIX Corps' other wing. On both 12 and 13 September, the enemy commander, Colonel Landau, had to fall back several miles and try to form a new line. Governed by the only main road even approximating the desired direction of advance, Colonel Collier's CCA had to take a somewhat circuitous route northeast toward the town of Asch, thence east and southeast to the Maastricht Canal north of Maastricht. Even so, the armor took only two days to cover the fifteen miles.

Before the 2d Armored Division could come fully abreast of the 30th Division, somebody had to clear the Maastricht island. General Harmon had intended that CCB (Brig. Gen. Isaac D. White) cross the Albert south of Maastricht, sweep the island, then pass through Maastricht and drive northeast along the east bank of the Juliana Canal, which parallels the Maas north of Maastricht. That would put CCB alongside the left flank of the 30th Division in a drive aimed at Sittard, a city that was to serve as a northern anchor when the assault turned eastward against the West Wall. But on 14 September a Bailey bridge General White's engineers were constructing across the Albert Canal to the Maastricht island buckled just before completion. CCB's attack had to wait another day.

Actually, little need remained for clearing the Maastricht island. The onrush of CCA driving eastward toward the Maastricht Canal and the entrance of a battalion of the 30th Division into Wijk, the eastern suburb of Maastricht, had convinced the *176th Division* commander, Colonel Landau, that any attempt to defend the island or the city could end only in destruction of the forces involved. Ordering all his units during the night of 13 September to fall back behind the Maastricht Canal north of Maastricht, Colonel Landau abandoned both the island and the city.

In approving this withdrawal, Field Marshal Model at *Army Group B* directed an adjustment of the boundary between the *First Parachute Army* and the *Seventh Army*. Heretofore, the *First Parachute Army*'s *176th Division* had operated only west of the Maas; now the division would be responsible for a sector on the east bank extending northeastward toward Sittard. The boundary would run from the vicinity of Meerssen, five miles northeast of Maastricht, northeastward in the direction of Geilenkirchen, a German border town twelve miles north of Aachen. The new enemy boundary would be roughly identical to that between the 2d Armored and 30th Divisions.[25]

Rather than sit idly on the west bank of the Maastricht Canal, Colonel Collier's CCA late on 14 September jumped the canal onto the Maastricht island, only a step behind Colonel Landau's withdrawing Germans. By the next day, when General White's CCB at last bridged the Albert south of Maastricht, Colonel Collier's combat command already had cleared all stragglers from the island. General White was free to move immediately east of the Maas and start the drive on Sittard. By nightfall of 15 September a task force of CCB had secured a tiny bridgehead under fire across the Geul northwest of Meerssen.

Now that the corps armor was coming abreast of the 30th Division, General Hobbs on 16 September renewed his attack eastward to reach the West Wall north of Aachen, though the promise of a protected north flank for the infantry still needed two days for fulfillment. Moving up assault guns, the *176th Division* delivered such intensive shellfire on CCB's little bridgehead near Meerssen that it took the armor all of 16 September to fill out the bridgehead. Although CAA utilized the 119th Infantry's bridge over the Geul at Valkenburg, Colonel Collier's combat command came under such heavy interdictory fires in the Valkenburg defile that it too needed an entire day to cross

the river. On 17 September the armor gradually expanded its two bridgeheads, each to a depth of about two miles, but not so much through sheer weight as through the enemy's fear of envelopment. Probings by the 2d Armored Division's reconnaissance battalion across the Maastricht Canal north of Maastricht had convinced Colonel Landau, the *176th Division* commander, that the Americans intended to drive from that direction to link with their forces from the Geul bridgeheads in a pincers movement. To escape envelopment, Colonel Landau began to withdraw in the direction of Sittard.[26]

On 18 September both CCA and CCB broke loose to cover the remaining six miles to Sittard. That set telephones to ringing high up the German chain of command. It was of "decisive importance," Field Marshal Model informed the *First Parachute Army's* General Student, that his forces hold the line at Sittard and keep the Americans out of the West Wall. *OB WEST* already had made available one infantry division (the *12th*), which was even then restoring the line against the VII U.S. Corps in the Stolberg Corridor southeast of Aachen; in a matter of days now General Brandenberger's *Seventh Army* was to get another fresh division, the *183d Volks Grenadier Division*, which General Brandenberger was to commit between Sittard and Aachen. Relief was on the way, the *Army Group B* commander said, in effect; hold out until then![27]

General Student might have reacted with more vigor to Model's appeal had he

[25] Noon Sitrep, *A Gp B,* 1530, 14 Sep 44, *A Gp B KTB, Letzte Meldung.*

[26] Mng Sitrep, *A Gp B,* 0730, 17 Sep 44, *A Gp B KTB, Letzte Meldung;* Daily Sitrep, *A Gp B,* 0400, 18 Sep 44, *A Gp B KTB, Tagesmeldungen.*
[27] Order, *A Gp B* to *First Prcht Army,* 2230, 18 Sep 44, *A Gp B KTB Operationsbefehle.*

not at this time had his hands full with as grave a threat as the Western Front had known since the Allies first neared the German border. Just the day before, deep in the rear areas of the *First Parachute Army* within the Netherlands, thousands of Allied parachutes had blossomed in an airborne operation awe-inspiring in scope.[28] General Student nevertheless spared a small *Kampfgruppe* from the *10th SS Panzer Division,* which had been refitting far behind the lines, to go to Sittard and counterattack on 19 September.[29]

As all concerned soon discovered, this *Kampfgruppe* might have served the German cause better had Student retained it to fight the Allied parachutists. The counterattack delayed the 2d Armored Division's CCB a day, but CCA continued to push northeastward toward Geilenkirchen to enter that portion of Germany which projects into Holland in the form of a cat's head and forequarters. The West Wall lay but a few miles to the east. The enemy commander, Colonel Landau, expected total disaster to overtake his division at any moment.[30]

In the meantime, General Hobb's 30th Division on the right wing of the XIX Corps had broken out of the Geul bridgeheads more readily than had the armor, despite the fact that the enemy had received several infantry battalions as reinforcements. By last light on 16 September the infantry columns and their supporting tanks and tank destroyers obviously were ready to roll across a

remaining eight or nine miles to the German border. Indeed, at the town of Simpelveld, some companies of the 120th Infantry already were no more than three miles from the border. Here Field Marshal Model directed a futile counterattack by an SS assault gun battalion that represented *Army Group B's* only remaining reserve for commitment in this sector.

All through the evening of 16 September, General Schmidt kept the *LXXXI Corps* switchboard busy with appeals to permit his *275th Division* to withdraw to a new line near the border. The American thrust to Simpelveld had sliced through on the boundary between his division and that of General Macholz' *49th Division.* Most of his units were north of that penetration, some still as far west as the Geul River near Meerssen, and all were in imminent danger of being taken from the rear should the Americans turn north from Simpelveld. Yet neither the *LXXXI Corps* commander, General Schack, nor the *Seventh Army* Chief of Staff, Col. Rudolf-Christoph Freiherr von Gersdorff, had any ear for General Schmidt's impassioned pleas. Except for a few scattered replacement units, the West Wall from Aachen northward, they knew, lay naked. No matter what happened, Generals Schmidt and Macholz must hold as far west of the West Wall as possible until the promised *183d Volks Grenadier Division* could arrive.[31]

---

[28] See below, Ch. VI.

[29] Daily Sitrep, *A Gp B,* 0230, 19 Sep 44, *A Gp B KTB Tagesmeldungen;* Mng Sitrep, *A Gp B,* 0900, 19 Sep 44, *A Gp B KTB, Letzte Meldung.*

[30] Tel Conv, *LXXXI Corps* with *176th Inf Div,* 2150, 19 Sep 44, *LXXXI Corps KTB, Kampfverlauf.*

---

[31] Tel Convs, *Seventh Army* with *LXXXI Corps,* 1910 and 2400, 16 Sep 44, and 0115, 17 Sep 44, Schack with G-3 *LXXXI Corps,* 2300, 16 Sep 44, and *LXXXI Corps* with *275th Div,* 0035 and 0110, 17 Sep 44, all in *LXXXI Corps KTB, Kampfverlauf;* Order, *LXXXI Corps* to all divs, 2000, 16 Sep 44, *LXXXI Corps KTB, Befehle an Div;* Daily Sitrep, *LXXXI Corps* to *Seventh Army,* 2140, 16 Sep 44, *LXXXI Corps KTB, Tagesmeldungen;* MS # B-373 (Schmidt).

Just as the *12th Division*'s race into the Stolberg Corridor to prevent a breakthrough southeast of Aachen must have left more than one German commander's hair on end, so the arrival of the *183d Volks Grenadier Division* in the West Wall north of Aachen was a matter of split-second timing. Under the command of Generalleutnant Wolfgang Lange, the *183d Division* had been refitted and rehabilitated in Austria. Like the *12th Division*, the *183d* was at full strength and completely equipped, except for its assault gun battalion. Its troops, however, were largely Austrian, inadequately trained, and inexperienced.[32]

On 17 September the inexorable push of General Hobbs's 30th Division continued. On the division's left wing, the 119th Infantry tore right through the middle of the *275th Division* to capture Heerlen, the last Dutch town of appreciable size in this sector. The 120th Infantry on the right actually crossed the German border east of Simpelveld but at a point where the West Wall lay more than a mile behind the border. The enemy still had time to get the *183d Division* into the pillboxes.

As was the American custom, the Germans noted, the U.S. troops during the night of 17 September "called off the war at midnight." As the front settled down, train upon train bearing arms and men of the *183d Volks Grenadier Division* rolled into blacked-out railheads along the Roer River. The entire division would require two more nights to arrive, but a strong vanguard was soon en route toward assembly areas near the front.[33]

Having won a third lap of the race for the West Wall, the Germans were in no haste to substitute the *183d Division* for those replacement units already in the pillboxes and for the withdrawing survivors of the *49th* and *275th Divisions*. Model instead withheld the fresh division close behind the pillboxes as a tactical reserve.[34]

Unaware that a frenzied race for the West Wall had been taking place, the Americans in the meantime had been pushing steadily forward. On 18 September General Hobbs committed the 117th Infantry to extend his left flank in the direction of the 2d Armored Division; by nightfall the 119th Infantry in the center of the 30th Division had reached positions overlooking the little Wurm River and the forward reaches of the West Wall. The 2d Armored Division, in turn, pushed into Gangelt on the corps north flank on 19 September. In the process the armor shoved what was left of Colonel Landau's *176th Division* back to the north and northeast and severed all contact between the *176th Division* and General Schmidt's *275th*.[35]

To Field Marshal Model the gap between the two armies appeared particularly dangerous, for it constituted an open route into Germany northwest of the West Wall strongpoint of Geilenkirchen by which the West Wall might be pierced in a sector where Model had virtually no troops at all. Drawing a new boundary between the *First Parachute* and *Seventh Armies*, Model gave part of the old *176th Division* sector to the *Seventh Army* and

---

[32] MS # B-753, *Die Kaempfe der 183. Volksgrenadier-Division im Raume Geilenkirchen von September 1944 bis Ende Januar 1945* (Lange).
[33] *Ibid.*

[34] Order, *A Gp B to Seventh Army*, 2230, 18 Sep 44, *A Gp B KTB, Operationsbefehle*.
[35] Tel Conv, *Seventh Army* with *LXXXI Corps*, 1115, 19 Sep 44, *LXXXI Corps KTB, Kampfverlauf*.

told General Lange to counterattack with a *Kampfgruppe* of his *183d Volks Grenadier Division,* re-establish contact between the *176th* and *275th Divisions,* and subsequently relieve the *275th Division* and northern elements of the *49th Division.* "I expect," said the *Army Group B* commander, not without some causticity, "that once [the] *183d Volks Grenadier Division* is committed, the withdrawal of the army's right wing will at last be brought to a halt." [36]

Unfortunately for the Germans, Field Marshal Model's information about the front was running several hours behind reality. In most of the sectors where he intended the *183d Division* to take over, either the 2d Armored or the 30th Division already had arrived. The 2d Armored Division, for example, reached the village of Teveren, a stone's throw from Geilenkirchen. In addition, the *LXXXI Corps* commander, General Schack, ran into difficulties at every turn in trying to assemble forces and arrange proper support for the *183d Division.* Delay after delay finally ended in ineffective improvisation. Though a *Kampfgruppe* eventually did attack into the north flank of the 2d Armored Division, it accomplished nothing other than to re-establish contact between the two German armies.

When this maneuver failed, the German commanders acted on the assumption that an immediate assault against the West Wall was inevitable. Relieving those troops of the *183d Division* that were west of the West Wall with heterogeneous forces, they thrust the entire division into the pillboxes. The division's responsibility extended from Geilenkirchen south to the area opposite Rimburg. From here the remains of the *49th Division,* holding a small bridgehead at the Dutch town of Kerkrade, tied in with the *116th Panzer Division* north of Aachen. The remnants of the *275th Division* were collected in the West Wall east of Geilenkirchen.[37]

An immediate assault was the American intention. As early as 18 September General Corlett alerted both the 2d Armored and 30th Divisions to prepare to hit the West Wall. The next day he ordered an attack on the following day, 20 September. The XIX Corps was to breach the West Wall, seize crossings over the Roer River nine miles beyond, and assist the VII Corps in encircling Aachen.[38]

Delay in the Assault

This was the intention. The event was different because of a factor beyond General Corlett's control.

This factor had seen its beginning during the first days of September when General Bradley had transferred one of Corlett's divisions to the Third Army. The loss added to Corlett's difficulty in solving the problem of an exposed left flank. Before the transfer, Field Marshal Montgomery had announced plans for commitment of part of his 21 Army Group close alongside the left flank of the First Army, and thus of the XIX Corps. Although Montgomery had stipulated that the main weight of the British drive was to be directed against the Lower Rhine

---

[36] *Ibid.;* Orders, *Seventh Army* to *LXXXI Corps* (relaying *A Gp B* orders intended for *183d VG Div*), 1050 and 1220, 19 Sep 44, *LXXXI Corps KTB, Befehle: Heeresgruppe, Armee, usw.*

[37] For fuller details and documentation on this period, see Heichler, Germans Opposite XIX Corps, pp. 54–63.

[38] XIX Corps FO 26, 19 Sep, XIX Corps G–3 file, 19 Sep 44.

between Wesel and Arnhem, he had stated that he intended to threaten frontally the western face of the Ruhr between Duesseldorf and Duisberg. Writing later, General Bradley maintained that Montgomery had told him he planned "to advance straight against the Ruhr as a feint, but after reaching the vicinity of the Rhine was then going to throw a force around to the north." [39] In either event, a feint against the Ruhr would have involved a British advance close alongside the First Army's left flank.

The trouble began when the threat against the face of the Ruhr did not develop. Instead, the Second British Army had begun to drive almost due north into the Netherlands at a point south of Eindhoven. Then Field Marshal Montgomery had suggested and General Eisenhower had authorized a special operation known as MARKET-GARDEN to be launched in the Netherlands on 17 September to extend the Second Army's axis of advance even farther to the north. When the First U.S. Army continued to drive northeastward, the result was a growing gap which left both British and Americans with exposed flanks. Neither had the troops at hand to fill the gap adequately.

To do what he could to fill the gap, Montgomery had committed the 8 British Corps to drive north and northeast on the right wing of the Second Army; but like the XIX Corps, the 8 Corps had only two divisions. Two divisions could not hope to eliminate a great right-angle gap which ran from the vicinity of Nijmegen to the

boundary with the XIX Corps near Sittard.

On 19 September, the date when General Corlett issued the order to attack the West Wall, the great gap already was a matter of primary concern. The front of the 8 Corps ran along the Maastricht Canal from a point near the army group boundary thirteen miles north of Maastricht northwest to Bree, thence to a bridgehead across the Meuse–Escaut Canal, eight miles beyond. The 30 Corps in the meantime had pushed north into Eindhoven, enabling patrols of the 8 Corps to get into Heeze, southeast of Eindhoven; thus the tip of the 8 Corps at Heeze was more than thirty-five miles from the main concentration of the 2d U.S. Armored Division at Sittard. A great triangular expanse of territory of more than 112 square miles lay open to the Germans. The northern flank of the XIX Corps already was exposed for more than nine miles. Continuing east through the West Wall would extend the flank proportionately.

No one could say that the XIX Corps had not kept its own house in order, for General Corlett had made special efforts to clear his zone right up to the boundary with the British. On 16 September, while the 2d Armored Division was attacking east of the Maas River to close up to the boundary around Sittard, a special task force had crossed the Maastricht Canal just north of Maastricht to attack north and clear a strip of land lying between the canal and the Maas as far north as the boundary with the British. Commanded by Lt. Col. William M. Stokes, Jr., the task force was composed of the separate 99th Infantry Battalion (Lt. Col. Robert G. Turner), a battalion of the 2d Armored Division's

---

[39] Ltr, Bradley to Eisenhower, 14 Sep 44, 12th A Gp 371.3, Military Objectives, I. Note also par. 6, 21 A Gp Gen Opnl Sit and Dir M–523, 3 Sep 44, same file.

tanks, plus increments of artillery, engineers, and medics. Either pushing back or annihilating parts of the *176th Division*, Task Force Stokes in three days had covered the nine miles north to the boundary. While the tanks returned to their parent division, the 99th Infantry Battalion stayed behind to defend the sector and maintain contact with the British to the northwest on the other side of the canal.[40]

On the other hand, clearing the entire zone was not sufficient to override the fact that the responsibility for protecting First Army's left flank belonged undeniably to the XIX Corps. First Army's General Hodges and the Second British Army's Lt. Gen. Miles C. Dempsey had discussed the problem on 15 September and reiterated that understanding.[41] For the moment, at least, the British had incurred no obligation to advance east of the Maas River. Even if the British cleared the west bank of the Maas, the XIX Corps still would be in danger, for most of the open flank lay east of the river.

For all the concern about the open flank, General Corlett intended to go through with the West Wall attack on 20 September before the Germans could get set in their fortifications. Assisted by a saturation air bombardment, the 30th Division was to assault the line near the village of Rimburg, between Geilenkirchen and Aachen, nine miles north of Aachen. The 2d Armored Division was to protect the corps north flank along the Sittard–Geilenkirchen highway and prepare to

send one combat command through the West Wall to exploit to the east the gains of the 30th Division. To assist the armor on the north flank, General Corlett told the 30th Division to take over the job of maintaining contact with the VII Corps west of Aachen; then he transferred the 113th Cavalry Group to the corps north flank on the left of the armor between Sittard and the Maas.[42]

As soon as the 30th Division could pierce the West Wall, General Hobbs was to turn his infantry southeast to make a junction seven miles away with the VII Corps northeast of Aachen. But by daylight of 20 September—D Day for the assault——both Hobbs and General Corlett were displaying mounting concern over the fact that once the 30th Division turned to make this junction, both the division's left and right flanks would be exposed, the latter toward enemy forces still remaining in Aachen. Although neither commander doubted that the infantry could pierce the West Wall itself, the experience of the VII Corps near Stolberg had shown that the Germans, for all their deficiencies, could muster reserves for commitment at critical points. Because the XIX Corps was drastically short on artillery ammunition, the fear of German reserves took on added weight. The ammunition shortage likewise increased the need for large-scale air support, and the weather forecast for 20 September was not at all promising. General Corlett insisted that he make no attack without adequate support from the air.

Because the weather failed to clear sufficiently either on 20 September or the day after, General Corlett postponed the

---

[40] For a detailed account of this operation, see Capt. Franklin Ferriss, Operation of Task Force "Stokes," 16–18 September, 1944 a preliminary manuscript in XIX Corps Combat Interv files.

[41] Memo to CG XIX Corps, 15 Sep 44, FUSA G–3 file, 9–23 Sep 44.

[42] XIX Corps FO 26, 19 Sep 44; 113th Cav Gp and 2d Armd Div AARs, Sep 44.

offensive both times. To the Germans, these two days meant an unexpected but welcome chance to improve their positions. To the Americans, they provided an opportunity to ponder those apprehensions generated by the exposed north flank, by the paucity of ammunition reserves, and by the possibility of violent enemy reaction whenever the 30th Division exposed both flanks to link up with the VII Corps. News about the German countermeasures against the V Corps bridgehead at Wallendorf did nothing to alleviate these fears. General Corlett must have noted that from the British front in the Netherlands all the way down to the Third Army's battleground at Metz, the enemy was rebounding almost miraculously.

Though not so obvious as cloudy skies or scant stocks of ammunition, this growing belief that, after all, the Germans had only been playing dead was perhaps the most important deterrent to launching the West Wall attack. Besides, the port of Brest had fallen; the commanders must have been aware that if they waited long enough, at least one of the divisions from Brittany might become available for the assault. In midmorning of 22 September, after all three of the First Army's corps commanders had conferred for two hours with the army commander, General Hodges authorized General Corlett to postpone the attack indefinitely.[43]

On this same day of 22 September, the VII Corps went on the defensive in the Stolberg Corridor and the V Corps withdrew the last troops from the ill-starred Wallendorf bridgehead. Thus, all of the First Army with the exception of two regiments of the 9th Division in the Huertgen Forest sector settled down to a period of readjustment of lines, replenishment of supplies, and general preparation for the day when General Hodges would direct a continuation of the drive toward the Rhine.

General Corlett's XIX Corps in ten days had pushed from the Albert Canal to the German border, a distance ranging from fifteen to thirty-three miles. The corps had cleared approximately 547 square miles of territory in Belgium, the Netherlands, and Germany and had pushed back parts of three German divisions. The Germans nevertheless had made noteworthy inroads on the speed of the American advance. When combined with the gasoline shortage and the reduction in strength which had cut the XIX Corps to two divisions, this resistance had provided sufficient time to enable a fresh German unit to reach the West Wall and to deny the XIX Corps a timely intervention in the neighboring battle of the Stolberg Corridor.

---

[43] 30th Div G–3 Jnl, 22 Sep 44. See also Tel Convs, Corlett with Hobbs, recorded in 30th Div G–3 Jnl file, 19–22 Sep 44; Memo, Corlett for Hodges, 21 Sep 44, XIX Corps G–3 file, 19–22 Sep 44; Sylvan Diary, entry of 22 Sep 44; Ltr, Corlett to OCMH, 2 Sep 53, OCMH.

PART TWO

AN AIRBORNE CARPET IN THE NORTH

CHAPTER VI

Operation Market-Garden

A maxim of war is that you reinforce success. In early September of 1944, the problem was not to find a success but to choose among many. The very nature of General Eisenhower's strategic reserve narrowed the choice. His reserve was not conventional but airborne.

In anticipation of an opportunity to use this latent strength, General Eisenhower as early as mid-July had solicited his planners to prepare an airborne plan marked by "imagination and daring." Spurred by this directive and the glittering successes of the breakout and pursuit, the planning staffs had begun almost to mass produce blueprints for airborne operations. By mid-August creation of a combined Allied airborne headquarters controlling most of the airborne troops and much of the troop carrier strength in the theater had implemented the planning. This headquarters was the First Allied Airborne Army.[1] General Eisenhower's desire for a suitable occasion to employ the army was heightened by the fact that the U.S. Chief of Staff, General Marshall, and General Henry H. Arnold, Commanding General, Army Air Forces, wanted to see what a large-scale airborne attack could accomplish deep in enemy territory.[2]

By the time the first Allied patrols neared the German border, eighteen sep- arate airborne plans had been considered. Five had reached the stage of detailed planning. Three had progressed almost to the point of launching. But none had matured. The fledgling plans embraced a variety of objectives: the city of Tournai, to block Germans retreating from the Channel coast; the vicinity of Liège, to get the First Army across the Meuse River; the Aachen-Maastricht gap, to get Allied troops through the West Wall. In most cases fast-moving ground troops were about to overrun the objectives before an airborne force could be thrown in.[3]

No matter that circumstances had denied an immediate commitment of SHAEF's strategic reserve; the maxim of reinforcing success was nonetheless valid. Indeed, each day of fading summer and continued advance heightened desire for early use of the airborne troops. The paratroopers and glidermen resting and training in England became, in effect, coins burning holes in SHAEF's pocket. This is not to say that SHAEF intended to spend the airborne troops rashly but that SHAEF had decided on the advisa-

---

[1] For details on formation of the FAAA, see James A. Huston, Airborne Operations, MS in OCMH.

[2] Pogue, *The Supreme Command,* p. 279 ff.

[3] The five major plans are discussed in detail in Hq, FAAA, History of Headquarters First Allied Airborne Army, 2 Aug 44–20 May 45 (hereafter cited as FAAA, History), SHAEF FAAA files. For a discussion of the methods by which planning was initiated see John C. Warren, *Airborne Operations in World War II, European Theater* (USAF Hist Studies: No. 97, USAF Hist Div, Research Studies Institute, Air University) (Maxwell, Ala.: Maxwell Air Force Base, September 1956), p. 82.

bility of buying an airborne product and was looking about for the right occasion. Even the Germans believed an airborne attack imminent, although they had no fixed idea where.[4]

The fact that a sensitive ear might have detected portentous sputterings as the Allied war machine neared the German border did little or nothing to lessen interest in an airborne operation. Except in the case of General Bradley, who was reluctant to relinquish the support of troop carrier aircraft flying supply missions, the signs that the pursuit might be nearing an end heightened the desire to use the airborne troops.[5] Both General Eisenhower and Field Marshal Montgomery began to look to the airborne forces for the extra push needed to get the Allies across the Rhine River before the logistical situation should force a halt and enable the Germans to recoup behind the Rhine.

Most of the airborne plans considered in the last days of August and in early September focused upon getting some part of the Allied armies across the Rhine. Among these was Operation COMET, a plan to seize river crossings in the Netherlands near Arnhem along the projected axis of the Second British Army. COMET still was on the drawing boards when concern mounted that the one and a half airborne divisions allotted for the job would be insufficient. On 10 September COMET was canceled.

Though canceled, COMET was not abandoned. On the day of cancellation, 10 September, Field Marshal Montgomery approached General Eisenhower with another proposal that was in effect a strengthening of COMET. After General Eisenhower had endorsed it, this plan looked like the real thing.

The new plan was labeled Operation MARKET. Three and a half airborne divisions were to drop in the vicinity of Grave, Nijmegen, and Arnhem to seize bridges over several canals and the Maas, Waal (Rhine), and Neder Rijn Rivers. They were to open a corridor more than fifty miles long leading from Eindhoven northward. As soon as an adequate landing field could be secured, an air portable division was to be flown in as reinforcement.

In a companion piece named Operation GARDEN, ground troops of the Second British Army were to push from the Dutch-Belgian border to the IJsselmeer (Zuider Zee), a total distance of ninety-nine miles. The main effort of the ground attack was to be made by the 30 Corps from a bridgehead across the Meuse–Escaut Canal a few miles south of Eindhoven on the Dutch-Belgian frontier. (See Map 1.) On either flank the 8 and 12 Corps were to launch supporting attacks.

Operation MARKET-GARDEN had two major objectives: to get Allied troops across the Rhine and to capture the Ruhr. Three major advantages were expected to accrue: (1) cutting the land exit of those Germans remaining in western Holland; (2) outflanking the West Wall, and (3) positioning British ground forces for a subsequent drive into Germany along the North German Plain.[6]

---

[4] See Lucian Heichler, Invasion From the Sky, MS prepared to complement this volume and filed in OCMH.

[5] General Bradley's views are expressed in *A Soldier's Story*, page 403.

[6] 21 A Gp General Operational Situation and Directive, M–525, 14 Sep 44, SHAEF SGS 381, I; FAAA, Operations in Holland, Sep–Nov 44, and Hq Br Abn Corps, Allied Airborne Operations in Holland (Sep–Oct 44), SHAEF FAAA files.

Although the proposed operation prompted some objections at 12th Army Group, at First Allied Airborne Army, and even among some members of Field Marshal Montgomery's staff, it conformed to General Arnold's recommendation for an operation some distance behind the enemy's forward positions and beyond the area where enemy reserves normally were located; it afforded an opportunity for using the long-idle airborne resources; it was in accord with Montgomery's desire for a thrust across the Rhine, while the enemy was disorganized; and it appeared to General Eisenhower to be the boldest and best move the Allies could make at the moment. At the least, General Eisenhower thought the operation would strengthen the 21 Army Group in its later fight to clear the Schelde estuary and open the port of Antwerp to Allied shipping. Field Marshal Montgomery examined the objections that the proposed route of advance "involved the additional obstacle of the Lower Rhine (Neder Rijn) as compared with more easterly approaches, and would carry us to an area relatively remote from the Ruhr." He considered these to be overridden by the fact that the operation would outflank the West Wall, would be on a line which the enemy would consider least likely for the Allies to use, and would be within easy range of Allied airborne forces located in England.[7]

Operation MARKET-GARDEN was nothing if not daring. It was particularly so in light of a logistical situation that, at best, was strained and in light of the unpredictable nature of the weather in northwestern Europe at this season. Set against these factors was the climate of

opinion that pervaded most Allied headquarters during early September. This was the same optimistic period when the First Army was preparing to dash through the West Wall in a quick drive to the Rhine. Not until the day Operation MARKET began was the First Army to experience any particular trouble in the West Wall; even then it would have been hard to convince most Allied commanders that this rugged countenance the Germans had begun to exhibit was anything more than a mask.

Fairly typical of the Allied point of view was SHAEF's estimate of the situation a week before the airborne attack. The SHAEF G–2 estimated enemy strength throughout the West at 48 divisions with a true equivalent of 20 infantry and 4 armored divisions. Four days before the airborne attack the 1st British Airborne Corps calculated that the Germans in the Netherlands had few infantry reserves and a total armored strength of not more than fifty to one hundred tanks. While numerous signs pointed to German reinforcements of river and canal lines near Arnhem and Nijmegen, the British believed the troops manning them were few and of a "low category." Thinking back after the operation was over, the 1st British Airborne Division recalled, "It was thought the enemy must still be disorganized after his long and hasty retreat from south of the River Seine and that though there might be numerous small bodies of enemy in the area, he would not be capable of organized resistance to any great extent."[8]

---

[7] Pogue, *The Supreme Command,* pp. 281–82.

[8] SHAEF Weekly Intel Summary 25, week ending 9 Sep 44; Hq Abn Troops Opnl Instr 1, 13 Sep 44, 1st Abn Div Rpt on Opn MARKET, Pts. 1–3, SHAEF FAAA files.

This is not to say that warning notes were not struck. By 10 September, the day when General Eisenhower approved the operation, the British had remarked that "Dutch Resistance sources report that battered panzer formations have been sent to Holland to refit, and mention Eindhoven and Nijmegen as the reception areas." [9] A few days later the SHAEF G–2 announced that these panzer formations were the *9th SS Panzer Division* and presumably the *10th SS Panzer Division*. They probably were to be re-equipped with new tanks from a depot reported "in the area of Cleves [Kleve]," a few miles across the German frontier from Nijmegen and Arnhem. [10]

News of these two German armored divisions near Arnhem caused particular concern to General Eisenhower's chief of staff, Lt. Gen. Walter B. Smith. Believing strongly that the Allies would have to employ not one but two airborne divisions at Arnhem if they were to counter the German armor, General Smith obtained the Supreme Commander's permission to go to Field Marshal Montgomery with a warning. Either they should "drop the equivalent of a second division in the Arnhem area" or change the plan and move one of the American divisions, scheduled to drop farther south, up to Arnhem. But, General Smith recalled after the war, "Montgomery "ridiculed

the idea" and "waved my objections airily aside." [11]

The likelihood of encountering enemy armor in the vicinity of the drop zones obviously was of serious concern to airborne commanders, particularly in view of the fifty-mile dispersion of the airborne drop. American commanders, whose troops possessed even less in the way of antitank weapons than did British airborne troops, were especially perturbed. [12] There were other disturbing signs. Stiffening resistance around the British bridgehead across the Meuse-Escaut Canal did not go unremarked. [13] The G–2 of the 82d U.S. Airborne Division noted further, "A captured document indicates that the degree of control exercised over the regrouping and collecting of the apparently scattered remnants of a beaten army [was] little short of remarkable. Furthermore, the fighting capacity of the new Battle Groups formed from the remnants of battered divisions seems unimpaired." [14]

Despite these warnings, the general view appeared to be as recounted after the operation by the British Airborne Corps. This was that "once the crust of resistance in the front line had been broken, the

---

[9] Chester Wilmot, *The Struggle for Europe* (New York: Harper & Brothers, 1952), p. 488. Though sparse in his annotation, Wilmot appears to speak with some authority on British sources not readily available to the American historian. In this instance he refers to an unspecified intelligence report of the Second Army.

[10] SHAEF Weekly Intel Summary 26, week ending 16 Sep 44.

[11] Interv by European theater historians with Gen Smith and Maj Gen Harold R. Bull (G–3, SHAEF), 14 Sep 45; Interv with Gen Smith by S. L. A. Marshall, 18 Apr 49, both in OCMH.

[12] Ltr, Lt Gen Anthony C McAuliffe (formerly CG, 101st Abn Div Arty) to OCMH, 8 Feb 54, and Ltr, Maj Gen James M. Gavin (formerly CG, 82d Abn Div) to OCMH, 17 Jan 54, OCMH.

[13] Wilmot, in *The Struggle for Europe*, notes that General Dempsey, commander of the Second Army, was so concerned about this and the reported panzer formations that he recommended a drop near Wesel, upstream from Arnhem, closer to the flank of the First U.S. Army.

[14] 82d Abn Div, Annex 1c to FO 11 (13 Sep 44), dtd 11 Sep 44, 82d Abn Div FO 11 file.

German Army would be unable to concentrate any other troops in sufficient strength to stop the breakthrough." Although the 30 British Corps would have to advance ninety-nine miles, leading units "might reach the Zuider Zee between 2–5 days after crossing the Belgian-Dutch frontier." [15]

The Germans in the Netherlands

Had MARKET-GARDEN been scheduled two weeks earlier than it was, the Allies would have found the German situation in the Netherlands much as they predicted. For not until 4 September, when news of the fall of Antwerp had jolted Hitler into dispatching General Student and headquarters of the *First Parachute Army* to the Dutch-Belgian border, was cohesion of any description introduced into German defenses along this "door to northwestern Germany." General Student had at first but one corps, the *LXXXVIII Corps* under General der Infanterie Hans Reinhard, and one division, the *719th Infantry Division* under Generalleutnant Karl Sievers. The corps headquarters General Student had borrowed from the neighboring *Fifteenth Army.* (*See Map I.*) The division was a "fortress" division that had been guarding the coast of the Netherlands since 1940.

Though at full strength, this one division was scarcely sufficient to cover the entire corps front, a fifty-mile stretch along the Albert Canal from Antwerp southeast to Hasselt. General Reinhard therefore concentrated the bulk of the *719th Division* in the west near Antwerp where he expected the main British attack. A drive north from Antwerp was

logical, for by continuing in this direction the British might seal off the island of Walcheren and the peninsula of South Beveland from the Dutch mainland. This appeared expedient; for even though seizure of Antwerp had trapped the German *Fifteenth Army* against the coast the bulk of that army yet might escape across the Schelde estuary to Walcheren and South Beveland and thence to the mainland. If the British corked up these two promontories, they might annihilate the *Fifteenth Army* at will and in so doing clear the seaward approaches to Antwerp, without which the port was useless.[16]

General Reinhard hardly could have anticipated that Field Marshal Montgomery was so intent on getting a bridgehead across the Rhine that he would turn his drive northeastward toward the left wing of the *LXXXVIII Corps* in the direction of Eindhoven. From a local viewpoint, the reorientation of the British drive meant that the *719th Division*'s Albert Canal line would be hit along its weak eastern extension.

Prospects for averting a major breakthrough across the Albert toward Eindhoven were dark, when from an unexpected source came assistance. It

---

[15] Hq Br Abn Corps, Allied Abn Opns in Holland.

[16] This account is based upon Heichler, Invasion From the Sky. Primary sources are: MS # B–717, *Zusatz zum Bericht von Oberst i.G. Geyer* (Student); MS # B–156, *Bericht ueber den Einsatz des General-Kommandos LXXXVIII. A.K. vom Albert Kanal bis zur unteren Maas, 5 Sept 44–21 Dez 44* (Reinhard); MS # B–004, *Bericht ueber de Einsatz der 719. Inf-Div im Raum Antwerpen-Breda Sep 44* (Sievers); MS # B–846, *Aufstellung und Einsatz der 85. Infanterie-Division im Westen (Feb–Nov 44)* (Lt Col Kurt Schuster, formerly G–3, 85th Inf Div); MS # C–001, *Kaempfe des Fallschirmjaeger-regiments 6 mit amerik. Fallschirmjaegern im Holland im Sept 44* (von der Heydte); 201 file of senior officers of the Wehrmacht; *Lage West* and *Lage Frankreich* sit maps for Sep 44.

emerged in the form of an audacious and prescient commander, Generalleutnant Kurt Chill. Retreating from the debacle in France with remnants of his own *85th Infantry Division* and two others, General Chill had received orders to assemble his survivors in the Rhineland. Soon thereafter, General Chill perceived the critical situation along the Albert Canal. Acting with independence and dispatch, he postponed his withdrawal in order to set up straggler rallying points along the canal. By nightfall of 4 September General Chill had caught in his net a conglomeration of Navy, Luftwaffe, and military government troops and men from almost every conceivable branch of the Wehrmacht. A crazy-quilt mob—but General Chill managed in a matter of hours to fashion a fairly presentable defense that was sufficient to repulse the first minor British probes toward the canal.

On 6 September General Chill reported to General Reinhard to subordinate his *Kampfgruppe Chill* to the *LXXXVIII Corps.* General Reinhard must have embraced the reinforcement with delight; for on this same day the British had penetrated the extended outposts of the *719th Division* to force a bridgehead over the Albert at Beeringen. (This was one of the bridgeheads subsequently employed by General Corlett's XIX U.S. Corps to get across the canal.) To General Chill fell the problem of containing the bridgehead.

For all the danger inherent in the Beeringen bridgehead, the *First Parachute Army* commander, General Student, could take satisfaction in the fact that tangible subordinate units now were controlling the bulk of his front from Antwerp to Hasselt. Only on the extreme eastern wing near Maastricht was there an out-and-out gap, and this he was to fill the

next day, 7 September, with the *176th Division* under Colonel Landau. (This was the division which subsequently opposed the left wing of General Corlett's XIX Corps.)

During the next fortnight, some of General Student's own parachute troops began to arrive in the army sector. Having been either rehabilitated or newly constituted, these units included five new parachute regiments, a new parachute antitank battalion, about 5,000 service troops, a battalion of the *2d Parachute Regiment,* and another formation with a noble record, the *6th Parachute Regiment.* Under command of Lt. Col. Friedrich-August Freiherr von der Heydte, the *6th Parachute Regiment* had acquitted itself admirably enough in Normandy to attain the prestige, if not the strength, of a division. The regiment had been reconstituted to a strength considerably in excess of a normal parachute regiment.[17]

General Student threw in the bulk of his parachute troops against the British bridgehead at Beeringen. First he committed one of the newly constituted parachute regiments, the battalion of the *2d Parachute Regiment,* and the entire *6th Parachute Regiment,* all organized into a *Kampfgruppe* that took its name from the commander, Colonel Walther.[18] Next General Student threw in three of his remaining new parachute regiments, organized into *Parachute Training Division*

---

[17] This regiment should not be confused with the *6th Parachute Division.*

[18] Few records pertaining to *Kampfgruppe Walther* survived the war. Composition of the *Kampfgruppe* apparently underwent constant change. Both the *6th Parachute Regiment* and the battalion of the *2d Parachute Regiment,* for example, subsequently were attached to *Kampfgruppe Chill,* while *Kampfgruppe Walther* took on new attachments.

Erdmann under Student's chief of staff, Generalleutnant Wolfgang Erdmann.[19]

These units were responsible for the stiffening German resistance noted along the Dutch-Belgian border. Yet the end result was merely to weaken the German paratroopers on the very eve of MARKET-GARDEN. By mid-September the British had defeated every effort to repulse them at Beeringen and had pressed forward an additional twenty miles to throw two bridgeheads across the Meuse–Escaut Canal. The main bridgehead was at De Groote Barrier on the road to Eindhoven. There the British paused to await their role in MARKET-GARDEN.

From west to east the *First Parachute Army* was lined up in this order of battle: From Antwerp to the juncture of the Albert and Meuse–Escaut Canals was General Sievers' *719th Division*. Opposing the two British bridgeheads beyond the Meuse–Escaut were *Kampfgruppe Chill* and *Kampfgruppe Walther*, the latter with at least two battalions of Colonel von der Heydte's *6th Parachute Regiment* still on hand. All these troops were under General Reinhard's *LXXXVIII Corps*. From the bridgehead on the Eindhoven highway east to the boundary with the *Seventh Army* near Maastricht were the two divisions under General Student's direct control, *Division Erdmann* and the *176th Division*.

In the meantime, the trapped *Fifteenth Army* under General der Infanterie Gustav von Zangen had been taking advantage of the reorientation of the British drive. Leaving some units to hold the south bank of the Schelde, Zangen began to ferry the bulk of his army across the estuary. Divisions released by this move-

ment he assembled behind the western wing of the *First Parachute Army*.

The first of these divisions was the *245th Infantry*, a collection of chaff that even a mild wind might blow away. On 16 September this division was transferred to the *First Parachute Army*'s *LXXXVIII Corps* and utilized by General Reinhard to back up the line in rear of *Kampfgruppe Chill*.

The second was the *59th Infantry Division* under Generalleutnant Walter Poppe, which was in transit to the *First Parachute Army*'s sector just as the Allied airborne landings occurred. General Poppe still had about a thousand good infantrymen and a few engineers, a field replacement battalion, eighteen antitank guns, and about thirty 105- and 150-mm. howitzers.[20]

Both the *First Parachute Army* and the *Fifteenth Army* were subordinate to Field Marshal Model's *Army Group B*, the same headquarters which controlled General Brandenberger's *Seventh Army* at Aachen. In addition, Field Marshal Model exercised tactical control over forces of the *Armed Forces Command Netherlands*, a headquarters not appreciably unlike that of a U.S. communications zone. Specifically, an armed forces commander was the highest military commander in occupied territories (like Norway or the Netherlands), which were governed by a civilian (Nazi party) Reich commissioner (*Reichskommissar*). His duties were to represent the interests of the Wehrmacht with the civilian administration, to safeguard the administration, to guard military installations such as railways, roads, and supply dumps, and to

---

[19] This unit later was redesignated the *7th Parachute Division.*

[20] MSS # B–156 (Reinhard) and # B–149, *Einsatz der 59. Infanterie-Division im Holland, 18 Sept–25 Nov 44* (Poppe).

co-ordinate the needs of individual branches of the Wehrmacht in his territory. In the Netherlands this post had been held since 1940 by the senior Luftwaffe officer, General der Flieger Friedrich Christiansen.[21]

Even though the *First Parachute Army* and part of the *Fifteenth Army* had moved into the Netherlands, General Christiansen's *Armed Forces Command Netherlands* on the eve of MARKET-GARDEN still was charged with considerable responsibility. Much as U.S. forces draw army rear boundaries delineating responsibility between the armies and the communications zone, the Germans had drawn a line across the rear of their two armies in the Netherlands. General Christiansen still was charged with defending all territory north of that line, which followed generally the Maas and Waal Rivers. Because MARKET-GARDEN involved a penetration deep into the enemy rear areas, Christiansen and his troops would be embroiled in the fighting much as would the field armies.

Through events culminating in departure of the *719th Division* for the Dutch-Belgian border, General Christiansen had lost to the active fighting commands all of three divisions which originally he had possessed for defense of the Netherlands. As mid-September approached, he had left only a miscellany of regional defense and housekeeping troops of all four services: Army, Navy, Luftwaffe, and *Waffen-SS*.[22]

Because the Allied landing zones at Nijmegen and Arnhem were but a few miles from the German border, troops and headquarters of another of the enemy's rear echelon formations also might become involved. This headquarters was *Wehrkreis VI*. Similar in some respects to the corps areas into which the United States was divided before the war, the German *Wehrkreise* were, in effect, military districts. The headquarters of these districts were administrative commands responsible for training replacements, organizing new units, and channeling matériel. Adjacent to the corridor the Allies planned to seize in the Netherlands, *Wehrkreis VI* embraced almost the whole of the province of Westphalia and parts of three other provinces. During the course of the war, *Wehrkreis VI* had activated numerous divisions and, as the war in the West had taken a turn for the worse, had relinquished as combat divisions even its replacement training units, the very framework about which the replacement system functioned. In mid-September the only major headquarters remaining in *Wehrkreis VI* was an administrative unit. This too had to go into the line to occupy the West Wall north of Aachen as the *406th (Landesschuetzen) Division*.

Upon reaching the front, the *406th Division* came under an *ad hoc* corps staff headed by General der Kavallerie Kurt Feldt, formerly Military Governor for Southwest France (*Militaerbefehlshaber Suedwestfrankreich*) until the inexorable

---

[21] *OKH/Op Abt (II), Befehlsbefugnisse,* NARS No. H 22/243; MS # T-101, *The German Armed Forces High Command* (Winter et al.), Pt. II, pp. 95–96. Heichler, Invasion From the Sky, Appendix A, provides a comprehensive essay upon the German command picture in the Netherlands.

[22] A complete list of all units and headquarters under *Armed Forces Commander Netherlands* may be found in TWX, *A Gp B to OB WEST,* 2355, 23 Sep 44, *A Gp B KTB, Operationsbefehle.*

march of events had dethroned him. In recognition of the provisional nature of the command, General Feldt's corps became known not by numerical designation but as *Corps Feldt*. Except for the *406th Division*, General Feldt had only a smattering of armored replacement units. Within his lone division the troops represented the very last reserve *Wehrkreis VI* possibly could muster: various *Alarmeinheiten* (emergency alert units), numerous "ear" and "stomach" battalions, and several Luftwaffe battalions formed from Luftwaffe noncommissioned officer training schools.

The Allied airborne attack under normal circumstances might have encountered only a portion of the *First Parachute Army*, those two divisions of the *Fifteenth Army* which by mid-September had escaped across the Schelde, and those scratch rear echelon formations of *Armed Forces Commander Netherlands* and *Wehrkreis VI*. But as luck would have it, Field Marshal Model late on 3 September had issued an order that was destined to alter markedly the German strength in the immediate vicinity of the Allied landing zones. On 3 September the *Army Group B* commander had directed that the *Fifth Panzer Army*, retreating in disorder from France, release the *9th* and *10th SS Panzer Divisions* to move to the vicinity of Arnhem for rehabilitation.[23]

Two days later Model ordered that headquarters of the *II SS Panzer Corps* under SS-Obergruppenfuehrer und General der Waffen-SS Willi Bittrich also move to the vicinity of Arnhem. General Bittrich was to direct rehabilitation of the *9th SS Panzer Division* and two panzer

divisions (the *2d* and *116th*), which were to move to the Netherlands whenever they could disengage from combat under General Brandenberger's *Seventh Army*.[24]

In failing to include the *10th SS Panzer Division* in the charge to General Bittrich, Model apparently had in mind another order which he issued formally four days later on 9 September. He instructed the *10th SS Panzer Division* to continue past Arnhem into Germany for rehabilitation presumably more thorough than could be accomplished near Arnhem. At the same time, Model altered General Bittrich's orders in regard to the *9th SS Panzer Division*. Seeing the threat to Aachen posed by continuing advance of the First U.S. Army, Model instructed the *9th SS Panzer* to prepare to move against this threat.[25]

Unfortunately for the Allies, only minor elements of either of these SS divisions had begun to move away when the first Allied parachutists landed unsuspectingly within half a day's march from their assembly areas. Field Marshal Model thus had a ready reserve with which to fight back.

Seven Days for Planning

On the Allied side, the planning and command for the airborne phase of MARKET-GARDEN became the responsibility of the First Allied Airborne Army. The army commander, Lt. Gen. Lewis H. Brereton, had been a top air commander

---

[23] Order, *A Gp B* to *Fifth Pz Army*, 2215, 3 Sep 44, *A Gp B KTB, Operationsbefehle*.

[24] Order, *A Gp B* to *II SS Pz Corps*, 1230, 5 Sep 44, *A Gp B KTB, Operationsbefehle*. See also MS # B–749, *Kurzschilderung der Kaempfe des II SS-Pz Korps in der Zeit vom 28 Aug–5 Sept 44* (Bittrich).

[25] Orders, *A Gp B* to *II SS Pz Corps*, 1345 and 1830, 9 Sep 44, *A Gp B KTB, Operationsbefehle*.

in the Pacific and the Middle East.[26] Having moved to England as commander of the Ninth Air Force for the air war against Germany, General Brereton had assumed command of the First Allied Airborne Army on 8 August 1944. He was given operational control of the following: headquarters of the XVIII U.S. Corps (Airborne), commanded by Maj. Gen. Matthew B. Ridgway; headquarters of the 1st British Airborne Corps, commanded by Lt. Gen. F. A. M. Browning, who served also as deputy commander of the First Allied Airborne Army; the IX U.S. Troop Carrier Command under Maj. Gen. Paul L. Williams; and two Royal Air Force troop carrier groups (38 and 46). American airborne troops under General Brereton's control were the veteran 82d and 101st Airborne Divisions and the untried 17th Airborne Division, the latter not scheduled to participate in MARKET. British troops at his disposal were the 1st Airborne Division and the 52 Lowland Division (Airportable), plus special air service troops and the 1st Polish Independent Parachute Brigade, the latter to serve in MARKET under command of the 1st Airborne Division.[27]

The first major planning conference on Operation MARKET convened in England late on 10 September, only a few hours after General Eisenhower in a meeting with Montgomery at Brussels had given his approval. The first conference dealt pri-

GENERAL BRERETON

marily with command and administration. As deputy commander of the First Allied Airborne Army, General Browning was to direct operations on the ground through headquarters of his British Airborne Corps. He and his headquarters were to fly in with the airborne divisions. The XVIII U.S. Corps was relegated to certain administrative functions and to general observation of the planning and conduct of the operation. Once the ground troops overran the airborne divisions, command was to pass to the 30 British Corps. Responsibility for the complex troop carrier role fell to the commander of the IX Troop Carrier Command, General Williams. The overall commander was General Brereton.[28]

Although planning proceeded swiftly, Operation MARKET did not mature with-

---

[26] In the Pacific as commander of the U.S. Far East Air Force and as deputy air commander in chief of the Allied Air Forces. In the Middle East as commander of the Middle East Air Force.

[27] For details see FAAA, History. The 6th British Airborne Division was not to participate in MARKET. Huston, Airborne Operations, discusses the location and training of airborne troops in England. A detailed discussion of the planning phase may be found in Warren, *Airborne Operations in World War II*, pp. 80–100.

[28] FAAA, Opns in Holland; XVIII Corps, Report of Airborne Phase, Operation MARKET, SHAEF FAAA files.

out acute growing pains. At the outset, lack of supply threatened to stunt or at least delay growth. On 11 September Field Marshal Montgomery protested to General Eisenhower that the Supreme Commander's failure to give priority to the northern thrust over other operations (that is, to the exclusion of other offensive operations) meant that the airborne attack could not be staged before 23 September, and possibly not before 26 September. "This delay," the British commander warned, "will give the enemy time to organise better defensive arrangements and we must expect heavier resistance and slower progress." [29]

General Eisenhower promptly sent his chief of staff, General Smith, to 21 Army Group headquarters to assure Montgomery that Allied planes and American trucks could deliver a thousand tons of supplies per day. Confirming this in writing, General Eisenhower promised this tonnage until about 1 October. At the same time, he said, the First U.S. Army would have sufficient supplies to continue its attack at Aachen.[30]

Except that Montgomery urged that emergency supply be continued a week past 1 October, by which time a through railway supporting the British should be in operation, he was thoroughly placated. "Most grateful to you personally and to Beetle," Montgomery wrote the Supreme Commander, "for all you are doing for me." Making the usual salaam to the vagaries of weather, he set forward the target date six days to 17 September.[31]

Field Marshal Montgomery's decision meant that the First Allied Airborne Army had but seven days for planning and preparation, a period strikingly short—even in view of the similarity to the defunct operation COMET—when contrasted with the long weeks and even months of planning and special training that had gone into most earlier airborne operations. Yet one of the cardinal reasons for executing MARKET at all was to take advantage of German disorganization: each day's delay lessened that advantage. With that in mind, Field Marshal Montgomery had made his decision on the side of speed. In approving, General Eisenhower noted that not only could advantage be expected from speedy exploitation of the enemy's condition but that an earlier release of the U.S. airborne divisions might be effected. This was desirable because of proposed operations to support General Bradley's 12th Army Group.[32]

One of the more crucial decisions facing General Brereton and the staff of the First Allied Airborne Army was that of daylight versus night attack. Moving by day, planes and gliders would be exposed to more accurate flak. This was a serious consideration, both because the C-47 (Skytrain) troop carrier planes were low-speed aircraft possessing neither armor nor self-sealing gasoline tanks and because marked increase had been noted recently in antiaircraft guns in the vicinity of the target area. On the other hand, moving by night invited greater danger from enemy aircraft. Although the enemy's daylight fighter force had been reduced almost to inconsequence, his night fighters

---

[29] Montgomery to Eisenhower, M–192, 11 Sep 44, SHAEF SGS 381, I.
[30] Eisenhower to Montgomery, FWD 14758, 13 Sep 44, SHAEF SGS 381, I.
[31] Montgomery to Eisenhower, M–205, 14 Sep 44, SHAEF SGS 381, I.

[32] Eisenhower to Montgomery, 13 Sep 44. Montgomery comments in *Normandy to the Baltic,* p. 229.

had retained some measure of potency. In regard to the actual drop, it went without saying that a daylight operation should provide a better drop pattern. To realize what could happen in the dark, one had but to recall the Normandy operation when drop sticks had scattered like windblown confetti.

A major factor governing selection of a night drop in Normandy had been a need to co-ordinate airborne and seaborne units. The plan for co-ordination of air and ground efforts in Operation MARKET-GARDEN imposed no restrictions. Neither had the Allies at the time of the Normandy drop possessed the unquestioned air supremacy they now had attained. It was an air supremacy that could be maintained through proximity of the target area to bases in England, France, and Belgium. Assured of a comprehensive antiflak program, General Brereton made his decision: by day.[33]

Another question was which of two routes to take to the target area. (*Map IV*) The more direct route from England passed over islands in the Schelde-Maas estuary. The aircraft would be subject to fire from flak barges and coastal flak positions and would have to fly some eighty miles over enemy-occupied territory. The alternative was a longer southern route. Over friendly Belgium most of the way, this route involved a maximum flight over enemy territory of sixty-five miles. On the other hand, flak was thick among the enemy front lines south of Eindhoven.

General Brereton and his planners considered that one long column would expose rear elements to an alerted enemy and that parallel columns along the same path

would provide too many flak gunners with optimum targets. With these points in mind, they found a solution in compromise. The two divisions scheduled to land farthest north were to take the northern route across the Dutch islands. The other division was to follow the southern route across Belgium to a point near Bourg-Leopold, thence north across the front lines into the Netherlands.[34]

A third task of selecting appropriate drop and landing zones was more complex. Factors like flak, terrain, assigned objectives, priority of objectives, direction of flight—these and countless others entered into the consideration, so that in the end the drop zones that were selected represented, as always, compromise in its least attractive connotation. The division scheduled to land farthest north, for example, wanted drop zones close to and on either side of the major objective of the Arnhem bridge across the Neder Rijn. Because of the buildings of the city, flak concentrations close to the city, and terrain south of the bridge deemed too boggy and too compartmented by dikes, this division settled for drop zones only on one side of the river and no closer to the bridge than six to eight miles. Whether flak and terrain might not have been less of a problem than distance from the objective hardly could have been answered unequivocally during the planning stage; indeed, the actual event may not always provide an unqualified answer.[35]

Terrain in the target area was unusual, a patchwork pattern of polder land, dikes,

---

[33] FAAA; Opns in Holland; XVIII Corps, Rpt of Abn Phase, comments by General Ridgway.

[34] FAAA, Opns in Holland.

[35] *Ibid.;* also Hq Br Abn Corps, Allied Abn Opns in Holland; Montgomery, *Normandy to the Baltic,* pp. 227–28; Ltr, Rev. Arie D. Bestebreurtje, formerly captain, commander of a Special Forces team attached to 82d Abn Div, to OCMH, 25 Oct 56, OCMH.

elevated roadways, and easily defended waterways. The biggest obstacles were the three major rivers, ranging in width from 200 to 400 yards, which provided the basic motive for airborne participation: the Maas (Meuse), the Waal (Rhine), and the Neder Rijn. The proposed corridor also encompassed two smaller rivers, the Dommel and the Aa, and three major canals: the Wilhelmina, the Willems, and the Maas-Waal.

Because of these waterways, the texture of the soil, and innumerable drainage ditches and dikes, a vehicular column would be road-bound almost all the way from Eindhoven to Arnhem. This was a harsh restriction. Although the cities of Eindhoven, Nijmegen, and Arnhem are communications centers, all with more than 100,000 population, only one main highway passes through them in the direction the ground troops in Operation GARDEN were to take. It runs from Eindhoven through St. Oedenrode, Veghel, Grave, and Nijmegen, thence to Arnhem. The planners had to consider that failure to secure any of the bridges along this route might spell serious delay and even defeat for the entire operation.

Between Eindhoven and Arnhem the highway passes through flat, open country with less than a 30-foot variation in altitude over a distance of fifty miles. The only major elevations in the vicinity of the road are two hill masses: one north of the Neder Rijn, northwest and north of Arnhem, rising to more than 300 feet; the other between the Maas and Waal Rivers, southeast of Nijmegen, rising to 300 feet. The two elevations represented some of the highest ground in the Netherlands.

Perhaps the most striking feature of the terrain is the extent and density of the vegetation. Almost every path and road is lined on either side by trees. Almost every field and every dike is topped by trees or large bushes. The result, during spring, summer, and early fall, is severe restriction of observation. Indeed, those who would fight in the Netherlands would encounter just as many problems of observation as did others in earlier wars in Flanders and the Po Valley of Italy. In terrain like this, it is difficult for the stronger force to bring its full power to bear at any one point, and the ability of the weaker, defending force may be considerably enhanced.

Either the bridges over the waterways or features necessary to ensure seizure and retention of the bridges made up the principal objectives assigned to the three airborne divisions. Dropping farthest south between Eindhoven and Veghel, the 101st Airborne Division was to secure approximately fifteen miles of the corridor, including the city of Eindhoven and bridges at Zon, St. Oedenrode, and Veghel. The 82d Airborne Division was to drop in the middle to capture bridges over the Maas at Grave, the Waal at Nijmegen, and the Maas–Waal Canal in between, plus the high ground southeast of Nijmegen. To the 1st British Airborne Division fell the role farthest from the start line of the ground troops, that of securing a bridge over the Neder Rijn at Arnhem and maintaining a bridgehead north of the river sufficiently large to enable the 30 Corps to pass through en route to the IJsselmeer.[36] The 1st Polish Parachute Brigade was to drop on D plus 2 to

---

[36] General McAuliffe recalls that in the original plan the 101st Airborne Division was to have dropped at Arnhem but that the 1st Airborne Division had requested a switch because its staff already had studied the Arnhem area for the defunct Operation COMET. Ltr to OCMH, 8 Feb 54.

strengthen the British at Arnhem, and the 52 Lowland Division (Airportable) was to be flown in north of Arnhem as soon as landing strips could be prepared. Reinforcing the British was in keeping with the fact that the 1st Airborne Division would be the last to be relieved by the ground columns.[37]

Operation MARKET was the largest airborne operation ever mounted and was destined to retain that distinction through the rest of World War II.[38] Nevertheless, the size of the initial drop was restricted by the number of troop carrier aircraft available in the theater. Only about half the troops of the three airborne divisions could be transported in one lift. Naturally anxious that all their strength arrive on D-Day, the division commanders asked that the planes fly more than one mission the first day. They pointed to the importance of bringing all troops into the corridor before the enemy could reinforce his antiaircraft defenses or launch an organized ground assault. For their part, the troop carrier commanders dissented. Flying more than one mission per aircraft, they said, would afford insufficient time between missions for spot maintenance, repair of battle damage, and rest for the

crews. High casualties among the airmen might be the result. If weather remained favorable, they pointed out, and if combat aircraft assumed some of the resupply missions, the troop carriers might fly but one mission daily and still transport three and a half divisions by D plus 2.

Although it meant taking a chance on enemy reaction and on the weather, General Brereton sided with the troop carrier commanders. He decided on one lift per day. Although subsequent planning indicated that it would in fact take four days to convey the divisions, General Brereton stuck by his decision.[39]

The D-Day lift would be sufficient for transporting the advance headquarters of the British Airborne Corps, the three parachute regiments of both the 82d and 101st Airborne Divisions, and three major increments of the 1st Airborne Division: a parachute brigade, an air landing brigade, and a regiment of air landing artillery. Enough space remained in the first lift to permit the division commanders a degree of flexibility in choosing small units of supporting troops to go in on D-Day. In the second lift, on D plus 1, the remainder of the British airborne division was to reach Arnhem, the 101st was to get its glider infantry regiment, the 82d its airborne artillery, and both American divisions another fraction of their supporting troops. On D plus 2, despite anticipated demands of resupply, the 1st Polish Parachute Brigade was to join the British at Arnhem, the 82d was to get its glider infantry, and the 101st was to

[37] XVIII Corps, Rpt of Abn Phase, 101st Abn Div, and A Graphic Account of the 82d Airborne Division; FAAA, Opns in Holland; Hq Br Abn Corps, Opn Instr 1 and 2, 13 and 14 Sep 44, Allied Abn Opns in Holland.

[38] In Operation VARSITY, launched in the spring of 1945, more planes, gliders, and troops were involved on D-Day than in Operation MARKET, but additional airborne troops flown in on subsequent days made MARKET the larger operation. For details on VARSITY, see The Last Offensive, a volume in preparation for the series UNITED STATES ARMY IN WORLD WAR II.

[39] FAAA, Opns in Holland; Hq Br Abn Corps, Allied Abn Opns in Holland; Montgomery, *Normandy to the Baltic,* p. 227; de Guingand, *Operation Victory,* p. 415.

receive its artillery. On the fourth day the tails of all divisions might arrive.[40]

For the D-Day lift the 101st Airborne Division was allotted 424 American parachute aircraft and 70 gliders and tugs, while the 82d Airborne Division was to employ 480 troop carriers and 50 gliders and tugs. The 1st Airborne Division was to have 145 American carriers, 354 British and 4 American gliders, and 358 British tugs. Variance in the number of parachute and glider craft assigned the British and American divisions stemmed primarily from organizational differences. The variations between the American divisions were attributable to differences in objectives and proposed tactical employment. The 101st, for example, was to use the second lift to build up infantry strength, while the 82d, in anticipation of a longer fight before contact with the ground column, was to concentrate on artillery. Some elements of all divisions not immediately needed were to travel by sea and thence overland in wake of the ground column.[41]

While the airborne planning proceeded in England, planning and preparation for the companion piece, Operation GARDEN, progressed on the Continent under General Dempsey's Second British Army. The 30 Corps under Lt. Gen. Brian G. Horrocks was to strike the first blow on the ground an hour after the first para-

chutists jumped. As soon as logistics and regrouping might permit, the 8 and 12 Corps were to attack along either flank of the 30 Corps and gradually were to assume responsibility for the flanks of the salient created by the main attack. The advance of these two corps obviously would be affected by the strained logistical situation, by belts of marshy terrain crossed by few improved roads leading northward, and by the weakness of the 8 Corps, on the right, which would possess at first only one division.

The start line for the main attack by the 30 Corps was the periphery of the bridgehead north of the Meuse–Escaut Canal beyond De Groote Barrier, thirteen miles below Eindhoven. By moving behind a heavy curtain of artillery fire and fighter bomber attacks, General Horrocks hoped to achieve a quick breakthrough with the Guards Armoured Division, supported by the 43d and 50th Infantry Divisions.

In his formal orders, General Horrocks assigned the armor a D-Day objective of the village of Valkenswaard, six miles short of Eindhoven, which was the designated point of contact with the 101st Airborne Division.[42] Yet General Horrocks said informally that he hoped to be in Eindhoven before nightfall on D-Day.[43] Certainly the corps commander's aside was more in keeping with Field Marshal Montgomery's directive that the ground thrust be "rapid and violent, and without regard to what is happening on the flanks." [44] In the same manner, a D-Day objective of Eindhoven rather than Valk-

---

[40] Montgomery, *Normandy to the Baltic,* p. 227; Leonard Rapport and Arthur Northwood, Jr., *Rendezvous With Destiny, A History of the 101st Airborne Division* (Washington: Combat Forces Press, 1948), pp. 256–57, one of the best of the division histories; XVIII Corps, A Graphic Account of the 82d Abn Div; Hq Br Abn Corps, Allied Abn Opns in Holland; 1st Abn Div Rpt on Opn MARKET, Pt. 1.

[41] FAAA, Opns in Holland; Hq Br Abn Corps, Opns Instrs 1 and 2, 13 and 14 Sep 44, Allied Abn Opns in Holland.

[42] See extracts from Guards Armd Div Opns Order 12, 21 A Gp, Opn MARKET-GARDEN, 17–26 Sep 44, SHAEF FAAA files.

[43] As quoted in Combat Interv with Col Curtis D. Renfro, Liaison Officer, 101st Abn Div.

[44] 21 A Gp Gen Opnl Sit and Dir, M-525, 14 Sep 44, SHAEF SGS 381, I.

enswaard was more realistic if General Horrocks was to succeed in expectations of reaching Arnhem "before the end of D plus 3" and of attaining the IJsselmeer, ninety-nine miles from his start line, in "six days or less." [45]

Directing that vehicles advance two abreast along the single highway through Eindhoven to Arnhem, General Horrocks prohibited southbound traffic. Over this highway to Arnhem, he told a briefing conference, he intended to pass 20,000 vehicles in sixty hours. Yet the British commander hardly could have been as sanguine as he appeared, judging from questions he asked later, in private. "How many days rations will they jump with? How long can they hold out? How many days will they be supplied by air?" [46]

What Did the Germans Know?

In hope of deceiving the Germans into believing that the Allied supply situation denied offensive action other than that already under way by the First and Third U.S. Armies, the British withdrew their advance patrols, in some cases as much as ten miles. They might have spared themselves the trouble. The Germans already had noted with apprehension a "constant stream" of reinforcements concentrating behind the right wing of the Second British Army. From 9 to 14 September the intelligence officer of Field Marshal

Model's *Army Group B* issued daily warnings of an imminent British offensive, probably to be launched in the direction of Nijmegen, Arnhem, and Wesel. The objective: the Ruhr.[47]

Projecting himself with facility into the position of the Allied high command, the *Army Group B* G-2 on 14 September put imaginary words into the mouth of General Eisenhower in the form of a mythical order:

. . . The Second British Army [he imagined the Supreme Allied Commander to say] will assemble its units at the Maas–Scheldt [Meuse–Escaut] and Albert Canals. On its right wing it will concentrate an attack force mainly composed of armored units, and, after forcing a Maas crossing (see order to First U.S. Army), will launch operations to break through to the Rhenish-Westphalian Industrial Area [Ruhr] with the main effort via Roermond. To cover the northern flank, the left wing of the [Second British] Army will close to the Waal at Nijmegen, and thus create the basic conditions necessary to cut off the German forces committed in the Dutch coastal areas [the *Fifteenth Army*].[48]

As far as the ground picture was concerned, this German intelligence officer should have been decorated for his perspicacity. The British actually had intended earlier to do as the German G-2 predicted, to strike close along the left flank of the First U.S. Army to cross the Rhine near Wesel. But the introduction of Operation MARKET had altered this concept drastically.

The German conception of what the Allies would do with their airborne reserve was far more daring than anything the

---

[45] Renfro Interv.

[46] *Ibid.* Other sources for British ground planning are: 21 A Gp, Gen Opnl Sit and Dir, M–525; Montgomery, *Normandy to the Baltic*, p. 229; Lt. Gen. Lewis H. Brereton, *The Brereton Diaries* (New York: William Morrow and Company, 1946); Hq Br Abn Corps, Allied Abn Opns in Holland, especially Instr No. 2, 14 Sep 44; 21 A Gp Opn MARKET-GARDEN.

[47] *A Gp B* G–2 Rpts, 9, 11, and 14 Sep 44, *A Gp B KTB, Anlagen, Ic/AO* [G–2], *1.VII.–31.XII.44* (hereafter cited as *A Gp B KTB, Ic/AO; OB WEST KTB (Text)*, 12 Sep 44.

[48] Assumed Eisenhower Order, *A Gp B* G–2 Rpt, 14 Sep 44, *A Gp B KTB, Ic/AO.*

Allies actually considered. Even though the Germans on the basis of purely strategic considerations expected an airborne operation about mid-September and even though they had a long-time paratrooper in command of the sector the Allies had chosen (*First Parachute Army*'s General Student), they could not see the southern part of the Netherlands as a likely spot. In putting words into the mouth of General Eisenhower, the *Army Group B* G-2, for example, predicted airborne operations in conjunction with the ground offensive which he outlined, but he looked far beyond the Netherlands to a spot fifty miles east of the Rhine.[49]

As incredible as an operation like this might have appeared to the Allies at the time, the Germans saw no fantasy in it. Indeed, a step higher up the ladder of German command, at *OB WEST*, Field Marshal von Rundstedt endorsed the view that the Allies would use their airborne troops east of the Rhine.[50] Even within Hitler's inner circle of advisers, none saw disparity between this prediction and reality. On the very eve of MARKET-GARDEN, the chief of the *Armed Forces Operations Staff*, Generaloberst Alfred Jodl, voiced his concern about possible airborne landings in the northern part of the Netherlands, northern Germany, and Denmark.[51]

Thinking independently of his G-2, the *Army Group B* commander, Field Marshal Model, strayed equally far from reality, but with results not unfavorable to the Germans. Having received a report on 11 September that the Allies were assembling landing craft in British ports, Model reasoned that this meant a seaborne invasion of the Netherlands.[52] Reports as late as the morning of 17 September, D-Day for Operation MARKET, of "conspicuously active" sea and air reconnaissance of the Wadden Islands off the Dutch coast fed both Model's and Rundstedt's apprehension.[53] Both believed that the Allies would drop airborne troops in conjunction with a seaborne invasion. Even as Allied paratroopers and glidermen were winging toward the Netherlands, Rundstedt was ordering a thorough study of the sea- and air-landing possibilities in northern Holland. The results were to be reported to Hitler.[54]

As for Field Marshal Model, he had gone Rundstedt one better. As early as 11 September, Model had alerted General Christiansen, the *Armed Forces Commander Netherlands*, and ordered him to defend the coast of the Netherlands with all forces at his disposal. Model went so far as to order that mobile interceptor units be formed from various forces, including elements of the *II SS Panzer*

---

[49] "In conjunction with [the Second British Army's attack]," the G-2 noted in his mythical order, "a large-scale airborne landing by the First Allied Airborne Army north of the Lippe River in the area south of Muenster is planned for an as yet indefinite date . . . ." *Ibid.* Eight days earlier this same G-2 had predicted, more conservatively, airborne operations near Aachen and in the Saar region. Summary Estimate of Allied Situation, 6 Sep 44, *A Gp B KTB, Ic/AO.*
[50] *OB WEST KTB (Text),* 15 Sep 44.
[51] MS # P-069, The Kreipe Diary (Generalleutnant Werner Kreipe).

[52] See Order, *A Gp B* to *Armed Forces Comdr Netherlands,* 0115, 11 Sep 44, *A Gp B KTB, Ic/AO.*
[53] Daily G-2 Rpt for 15 Sep 44, 0015, 16 Sep 44, *OB WEST KTB, Anlagen, Ic-Tagesmeldungen* [Daily G-2 Rpts], *1.VII.–30.–IX.44* (hereafter cited as *OB WEST KTB, Ic-Tagesmeldungen*); *OB WEST KTB (Text),* 17 Sep 44.
[54] *OB WEST KTB (Text),* 17 Sep 44.

Corps that had been sent to the Netherlands for rehabilitation.[55]

No indications existed to show that this order had any effect on the actual Allied attack. Another order, however, issued to provide *Army Group B* a reserve, did serve the Germans well. This was a directive from Model on 12 September transferring the *59th Division* (General Poppe) from the *Fifteenth Army* to the sector of the *First Parachute Army.*[56] As a result, the *59th Division* was in transit near Tilburg, seventeen miles northwest of Eindhoven, when the first Allied parachutists dropped. This good fortune—plus the chance presence of the *II SS Panzer Corps* near Arnhem—was all the more singular because not only Model but no other German commander, including Hitler, had so much as an inkling of the true nature, scope, or location of the impending Allied airborne operation.[57]

---

[55] Order, *A Gp B to Armed Forces Comdr Netherlands,* 11 Sep 44.

[56] *OB WEST KTB (Text),* 12 Sep 44.

[57] Oreste Pinto, *Spy Catcher* (New York: Harper & Brothers, 1952), maintains that presence of the SS divisions near Arnhem was the result of a betrayal of the MARKET-GARDEN plan before the event by a Dutch traitor. The theory has no basis in fact. It ignores German surprise at the landings as well as the fact that Model ordered the SS divisions to the Netherlands on 3 September, before the Allies even considered a plan like MARKET-GARDEN. The divisions were, in fact, ordered to Arnhem as the first step in later commitment of them in the Ardennes counteroffensive, an operation which Hitler had already decided upon. A retired Dutch army officer, Col. Th. A. Boeree, has prepared a point-by-point refutation of the betrayal story and has provided a copy of his findings, entitled The Truth About the Supposed Spy at Arnhem, for OCMH. A commission of inquiry of the Netherlands Lower House has reported its findings on the matter in the fourth volume of its proceedings (*Staten-Generaal Tweede Kamer Enquêtecommissie Regeringsbeleid 1940–1945,* Volume

The Flight to the Corridor

Back in England, troops not already on the airfields began to assemble on 15 September and were sealed in at daylight the next morning. At headquarters of General Browning's British Airborne Corps, the general belief, as recalled later, was "that the flight and landings would be hazardous, that the capture intact of the bridge objectives was more a matter of surprise and confusion than hard fighting, that the advance of the ground forces would be very swift if the airborne operations were successful, and that, in these circumstances, the considerable dispersion of the airborne forces was acceptable.[58]

The troops themselves underwent the inescapable apprehensions that precede almost any military operation. In spite of their status as veterans, their fears were in many instances magnified for Operation MARKET. Not only were they to drop far behind enemy lines; they were to fly for a half hour or more over enemy territory and land in the full light of day. Neither of these had they done before.[59]

Armed with forecasts for favorable weather, General Brereton at 1900 on 16

IV, 's-Gravenhage, 1950). Interrogated under oath by the commission, Mr. Pinto was unable to substantiate his conclusions. (*Enquêtecommissie* 4c, pp. 1581–91). See also C. T. de Jong, "La Pretendue trahison d'Arnhem," *Revue d'Histoire de la Deuxième Guerre Mondiale* (January 1955), pp. 110–12.

[58] Hq Br Abn Corps, Allied Abn Opns in Holland; FAAA, Opns in Holland. By dispersion, the British apparently referred to the extreme depth of the airborne penetration. American officers had found unacceptable an original plan that involved considerable dispersion of drop zones within division sectors and had insisted upon changes. See Ltrs, McAuliffe and Gavin to OCMH, 8 Feb and 17 Jan 54.

[59] This attitude is reflected clearly in the 505th Parachute Infantry AAR.

September made the final, irrevocable decision. D-Day was the next day, 17 September. H Hour was 1300.[60]

The campaign began that night when the Royal Air Force Bomber Command started a program to eliminate as much as possible of the enemy's antiaircraft defense while at the same time concealing the fact that anything unusual was in the offing. A force of 200 Lancasters and 23 Mosquitoes dropped some 890 tons of bombs on German airfields from which fighters might threaten gliders and C–47's. Another force of 59 planes struck by night at a flak position. In each case, the pilots reported good results. Particularly effective was a strike against an airfield where the enemy's new Messerschmitt 262 jet aircraft were based. So cratered were the runways after the RAF raid that no jets could take off on 17 September.[61]

Early on D-Day morning, 100 British bombers escorted by Spitfires renewed the assault by bombing three coastal defense batteries along the northern air route. As time pressed close for the coming of the troop carriers, 816 Flying Fortresses of the Eighth Air Force, escorted by P–51's, took up the fight. They dropped 3,139 tons of bombs on 117 flak positions along both the northern and southern routes. Six other B–17's hit an airfield at Eindhoven. Including escorts, 435 British and 983 American planes participated in the preliminary bombardment. Only 2 B–17's, 2 Lancasters, and 3 other British planes were lost.

To weave a protective screen about the two great trains of troop carriers, 1,131 Allied fighters took to the air. Along the northern route, a British command, Air Defense of Great Britain, provided 371 Tempests, Spitfires, and Mosquitoes. Along the southern route, the Eighth Air Force employed 548 P–47's, P–38's, and P–51's. Adding to the total, the Ninth Air Force employed 212 planes against flak positions near the front lines along the Dutch-Belgian border.

All flights got an invaluable assist from the weather. Overland fog at the airfields in England had cleared by 0900. Over the North Sea and the Continent the weather was fair with a slight haze. Visibility varied from four to six miles. Had the day been tailor-made it hardly could have been better for an airborne operation.

Beginning at 1025 on Sunday morning, 17 September, 12 British and 6 American transport planes flew into the east to drop Pathfinder teams on drop and landing zones 20 minutes before H-Hour. Close behind them, from the stationary aircraft carrier that England had become, swarmed the greatest armada of troop-carrying aircraft ever before assembled for one operation.[62]

A force of 1,545 transport planes and 478 gliders took off that day from 24 airfields in the vicinity of Swinden, Newbury, and Grantham.[63] Converging at rendezvous points near the British coast, the streams of aircraft split into two great trains to cross the North Sea. Along the

---

[60] FAAA, Opns in Holland.
[61] *OB WEST KTB (Text)*, 17 Sep 44. The air phase of Operation MARKET is covered in more detail in Craven and Cate, eds., *Europe:* ARGUMENT *to V-E Day*, pp. 598–611, and in Warren, *Airborne Operations in World War II, passim.*

[62] FAAA, Opns in Holland.
[63] American planes: 1,175; British planes: 370; American gliders: 124; British gliders: 354. For the air routes, see Craven and Cate, eds., *Europe:* ARGUMENT *to V-E Day*, map opposite p. 602.

northern route went the planes and gliders carrying the 1st and 82d Airborne Divisions and General Browning's corps headquarters. Along the southern route went the 101st Airborne Division. Beacons and searchlight cones marked both rendezvous points and points of departure from the coast, while two marker boats fixed the routes over the North Sea.[64]

A small percentage of planes and gliders aborted over England and the sea. To save personnel who ditched in the sea, the Air/Sea Rescue Service, a component of Air Defense of Great Britain, had placed a string of seventeen launches along the northern route and ten along the shorter southern route. In addition, planes of Air Defense of Great Britain, the British Coastal Command, and the Eighth Air Force flew as spotters for ditched planes and gliders. During the course of Operation MARKET, a total of 205 men were snatched from the sea.

The average time of flight from base to target area on D-Day was two and a half hours. From thirty to fifty minutes of this time was spent over enemy territory.

Once the planes and gliders on the northern route reached the Dutch coast, they attracted flak ranging from light to heavy; but few aircraft were hit. Many German batteries were silent, victims of the preliminary bombardment. Others gave in quickly to ubiquitous British escort craft.

Along the southern route the 101st Airborne Division encountered concentrated flak as soon as the planes headed across German lines. One of the Pathfinder planes was hit and crashed. Some of the lower-flying planes and gliders in the main waves drew small arms fire. Although some serials escaped the flak almost without losses, others incurred severe damage. Yet few crippled planes fell before reaching the targets and releasing their loads. The paratroopers had unqualified praise for pilots who held doggedly to their courses, sometimes with motors in flames or wings broken and often at the price of their own lives after passengers or gliders had been released. No instance of a pilot resorting to evasive action under the stress of antiaircraft fire came to light on D-Day.

Luftwaffe reaction was hesitant, almost nonexistent. Although Allied pilots spotted approximately 30 German planes, only one group of about 15 Focke-Wulf 190's dared to attack. These engaged a group of Eighth Air Force fighters over Wesel but quickly gave up after shooting down but 1 U.S. fighter, hardly fair exchange for the loss of 7 German planes.

The airmen executed two other missions on D-Day. Almost at H-Hour, 84 British planes of the 2d Tactical Air Force attacked German barracks at Nijmegen, Arnhem, and two nearby cities; and after nightfall the RAF Bomber Command executed two dummy parachute drops with 10 aircraft each at points several miles to both east and west of the actual drop zones.

Planning staffs for Operation MARKET had been prepared to accept losses in transport aircraft and gliders as high as 30 percent. In reality, losses were a phenomenally low 2.8 percent. The enemy shot down not one plane or glider carrying the British airborne division and knocked

---

[64] A comprehensive report on the intricate details of planning and operating the troop carrier units may be found in IX Troop Carrier Command, Air Invasion of Holland. Unless specifically cited, other sources for this section are FAAA, Opns in Holland, and Hq Br Abn Corps, Allied Abn Opns in Holland.

out only 35 American troop carriers and 13 gliders, most of them along the southern route. Of the escort, the British lost 2 planes, the Americans 18. Total losses in transports, gliders, and fighters were 68. Out of a total of 4,676 transports, gliders, fighters, and bombers that participated on D Day, only 75 craft failed to get through.

Almost exactly at H-Hour transports in the leading serials began to disgorge their loads in the beginning of what was to become the most successful drop any of the three airborne divisions ever had staged, either in combat or training. British landings were almost 100 percent on the correct drop and landing zones. The 82d Airborne Division's landings were "without exception" the best in the division's history. The 101st Airborne Division's operation was a "parade ground jump" that from any viewpoint was the most successful the division had ever had.[65]

A total of 331 British aircraft and 319 gliders and 1,150 American planes and 106 gliders got through. Within an hour and twenty minutes, approximately 20,000 American and British troops landed by parachute and glider in good order far behind enemy lines. The unparalleled success of the drops and landings made it clear early that the decision for a daylight operation had been, under the circumstances, a happy one. Up to this point, the Allies had staged an overwhelming success.

---

[65] Rapport and Northwood, *Rendezvous With Destiny,* pp. 260, 268; Ltr, Gavin to Maj Gen Paul L. Williams, reproduced in IX Troop Carrier Comd, Air Invasion of Holland; 1st Abn Div, Rpt on Opn MARKET, Pt. 1.

CHAPTER VII

Invasion From the Sky

Along a fifty-mile corridor extending from Eindhoven to Arnhem the sky in early afternoon of 17 September grew dark with a fecund cloud of planes and gliders. A minute or so after 1300, the cloud opened and seeded the sky.

"a remarkably beautiful late summer day"

Thousands of Dutch civilians craned to see the show. As many a soldier has come to know, civilians in a war zone possess a kind of sixth sense that tells them when to parade the streets and when to seek shelter. Those civilians paraded the streets. Most were strolling casually home from church. Others had sat down to Sunday dinners. Here and there, at once a part of the crowd and yet isolated, strolled German soldiers absorbing the sunshine and rest of a day away from their posts. Until the planes came, none knew 17 September as anything but another occupation Sunday.

From battalions on the scene to the Fuehrer's spartan command post in East Prussia, surprise in German headquarters was equally great. An SS battalion commander was entertaining an intimate lady friend. Upon first sight of the parachutes, the occupation "mayor" of Arnhem dashed out on a personal reconnaissance, only to take a British bullet for his troubles. The *Armed Forces Commander Netherlands,* General Christiansen, was dining leisurely with his chief of staff at a restaurant far from the scene near Amsterdam.[1]

The commander of the *First Parachute Army,* General Student, was at his desk in his command post in a cottage only nine miles west of one of the designated American drop zones. To Student the appearance of the Allied armada came as a "complete surprise."

The 17th of September, 1944 [General Student recalled later] was a Sunday, a remarkably beautiful late summer day. All was quiet at the front. Late in the morning the enemy air force suddenly became very active .... From my command post at Vught I was able to observe numerous enemy aircraft; I could hear the crash of bombs and fire from air craft armaments and anti-aircraft guns in my immediate vicinity .... At noon there came the endless stream of enemy transport and cargo planes, as far as the eye could see ....[2]

While Student had a front row seat, his superior, Field Marshal Model, sat virtually upon the stage. Model's headquarters of *Army Group B* was in a hotel at Oosterbeek on the western outskirts of Arnhem. Parachutists and gliders of the 1st British Airborne Division came to earth about two miles away. Unaware of this ripe chance to capture the commander

---

[1] Boeree, The Truth About the Supposed Spy at Arnhem, provides an informative, well-documented trip around various German headquarters at the time of the Allied strike.

[2] MS # B-717 (Student). German clock time was an hour behind the British Summer Time used by the Allies.

and entire staff of *Army Group B,* the British made no immediate move against the hotel. Model and his coterie folded their tents and stole away. They did not stop until they reached headquarters of the *II SS Panzer Corps* beyond the IJssel River about eighteen miles east of Arnhem.[3]

In East Prussia, first reports of the airborne landings threw Hitler's headquarters into a state of high excitement. Although report after report came in, the over-all picture remained obscure. Only highlights emerged.

Hitler's personal reaction could best be described as febrile. The narrow escape of Model and his staff from the British at Oosterbeek appeared to impress him most at first. "At any rate," Hitler raged, "the business is so dangerous that you must understand clearly, if such a mess happens here—here I sit with my whole supreme command; here sit the Reichsmarschall [Goering], the OKH, the Reichsfuehrer SS [Himmler], the Reich Foreign Minister [Ribbentrop]: Well, then, this is the most worthwhile catch, that's obvious. I would not hesitate to risk two parachute divisions here if with one blow I could get my hands on the whole German command." [4]

During the first hour or two, no German commander could begin to estimate the scope and strength of the Allied operation. Reports and rumors of landings at almost every conceivable spot in the Netherlands spread through every headquarters.[5] As late as the next day *OB WEST* still was excited enough to

GENERAL STUDENT

pass along the fantastic report that a U.S. airborne division had landed at Warsaw, Poland.[6]

By a stroke of luck for the enemy, this kind of delirium was not to last long at the lower headquarters. Someone in an American glider that was shot down near the *First Parachute Army*'s command post was carrying a copy of the Allied operational order. Two hours after the first parachute had blossomed, this order was on General Student's desk.[7]

Having the Allied objectives and dispositions at hand obviously facilitated

---

[3] MSS # T-121, T-122 (Zimmermann *et al.*).

[4] Minutes of Hitler Conferences, 17 Sep 44 (Fragment No. 42). Copy of transcribed notes in OCMH.

[5] MS # T-122 (Zimmermann *et al.*).

[6] Tel Conv, G-3 *OB WEST* to G-3 *A Gp B,* 1905, 18 Sep 44, in *A Gp B KTB (Text)* (Rommel Papers).

[7] MS # B-717 (Student). Though no confirmation of this event is to be found in American records, there appears no reason to question Student's recollection.

German reaction. Possibly as a result of the captured Allied order, Field Marshal Model divided the affected zone into three sectors corresponding roughly to the sectors of the three Allied divisions.

To General Student and the *First Parachute Army* Model gave the dual mission of containing the British ground offensive opposite the Meuse–Escaut bridgehead and of destroying the 101st Airborne Division in the vicinity of Eindhoven. (*See Map IV.*) Already committed along the Meuse–Escaut, *Kampfgruppe Chill* was to oppose the British ground troops. For fighting the Americans, Model gave Student the *59th Infantry Division*, so fortuitously in transit near Tilburg, and the *107th Panzer Brigade*.[8] Under command of Major Freiherr von Maltzahn, this panzer brigade had been en route to Aachen to engage the First U.S. Army.[9]

The job of contesting the 82d Airborne Division at Nijmegen fell to *Wehrkreis VI*, the rear echelon German headquarters which controlled *Corps Feldt* and the *406th (Landesschuetzen) Division*. These *Wehrkreis* units were ordered to destroy the airborne troops along the high ground southeast of Nijmegen, seize and hold the rail and road bridges across the Waal River at Nijmegen, and stand by for continued operations "in a southerly direction." Model must have recognized this as a pretty big assignment for a makeshift force like *Corps Feldt;* for he advised *Wehrkreis VI* that he intended shifting to Nijmegen corps troops and increments of parachute troops under General der Fallschirmtruppen Eugen Meindl, commander of the *II Parachute Corps.* Yet this help obviously could not arrive

immediately, for General Meindl's headquarters would have to move from Cologne.[10]

Whether from design or merely because the troops were at hand, Model sent stronger forces against the British at Arnhem. To General Christiansen as *Armed Forces Commander Netherlands* he gave a task of attacking toward Arnhem from the northwest and north. General Christiansen would have at his disposal *Division von Tettau*, a collection of regional defense and training battalions quickly thrown together under command of Generalleutnant Hans von Tettau, Christiansen's director of operations and training. In the meantime General Bittrich's *II SS Panzer Corps* with the *9th* and *10th SS Panzer Divisions* was to move toward Arnhem. After the bridge across the Neder Rijn at Arnhem was secure, the *10th SS Panzer Division* was to continue south to Nijmegen. The panzer corps was to be reinforced with a motorized infantry battalion commandeered from *Wehrkreis VI*, even though that headquarters could ill afford to part with anything.[11]

Bearing the proud names *Hohenstaufen* and *Frundsberg*, the two SS panzer divisions under Bittrich's command were drastically depleted. Badly mauled at Caen and in the Argentan-Falaise pocket, the two divisions apparently had the

---

[8] Order, *A Gp B* to *First Prcht Army*, 2315, 17 Sep 44, *A Gp B KTB, Operationsbefehle.*
[9] *OB WEST KTB (Text)*, 15 and 16 Sep 44.

[10] Order, *A Gp B* to *Wehrkreis VI*, 2315, 17 Sep 44, *A Gp B KTB, Operationsbefehle; OB WEST KTB (Text)*, 17 Sep 44.
[11] Orders, *A Gp* B to *Armed Forces Comdr Netherlands*, 2215, and *II SS Pz Corps*, 2315, 17 Sep 44, *A Gp B KTB, Operationsbefehle;* answers by Bittrich to questionnaire prepared by Colonel Boeree, 1955, copy in OCMH through courtesy of Colonel Boeree (hereafter cited as Bittrich Questionnaire). Bittrich notes that Model's orders to the *II SS Panzer Corps* were merely in confirmation of measures which he himself already had taken.

strength only of reinforced regiments. The
9th SS Panzer was the stronger with 1
armored infantry regiment, 1 artillery battalion, 2 assault gun batteries, 1 reconnaissance battalion, 1 company of Panther
(Mark V) tanks, and increments of
engineers and antiaircraft troops. The
10th SS Panzer probably had 1 armored
infantry regiment, 2 artillery battalions, 1
reconnaissance battalion, 1 engineer battalion, and 1 antiaircraft battalion.[12]

Confronted with a dearth of reserves all
along the Western Front, the Commander
in Chief West, Rundstedt, could do little
immediately to help. About all Rundstedt could contribute on the first day was
approval for rerouting from Aachen the
107th Panzer Brigade and another unit,
the *280th Assault Gun Brigade;* but these
obviously could not reach the threatened
sector for a day or two. As for Hitler,
he had to content himself for the moment
with somewhat empty orders to throw all
available Luftwaffe fighters into the fray
and with bemoaning the Luftwaffe's failure to set everything right. The entire
Luftwaffe was incompetent, cowardly, the
Fuehrer raged. The Luftwaffe had deserted him.[13]

GENERAL TAYLOR

Hell's Highway

On the Allied side, from the moment
men of the 101st Airborne Division came
to earth on 17 September, they began to
fight a battle for a road. Theirs was the
responsibility for a 15-mile segment of
narrow concrete and macadam ribbon
stretching northward and northeastward
from Eindhoven in the direction of Grave.
That segment men of the division were to
nickname Hell's Highway.[14]

---

[12] Strength of these two divisions on 17 September is a matter of some conjecture. Neither
of the usual sources (records of the
General Inspekteur der Panzertruppen and OKH,
Zustandberichte, SS-Verbaende—Strength Reports of SS units) is rewarding in this instance.
Figures given are based upon the Bittrich Questionnaire, copy in OCMH. Wilmot, *The Struggle for Europe,* page 532 and 532n, says the
divisions each had the "the strength of a brigade
plus some thirty tanks and assault guns." Although Wilmot provides no direct source for this
information, he notes that Rundstedt's chief of
staff (Westphal) "was as surprised as the Allies
to find that *II SS Panzer Corps* had so much
armor."
[13] MS # P–069 (Kreipe).

---

[14] The Screaming Eagles of the 101st Airborne
Division saw their first combat on D Day in
Normandy. Before Operation MARKET, the division's three organic parachute regiments had
been augmented by attachment of the 506th
Parachute Infantry. Unless otherwise noted,
this account is based on official unit records and
extensive combat interviews; on Rapport and
Northwood, *Rendezvous With Destiny;* and on
two preliminary manuscripts at a small unit level
prepared by Col S. L. A. Marshall, Parachute
Battalion in Holland and Parachute Infantry at
Best. Copies in OCMH.

101ST AIRBORNE DIVISION LANDINGS *near Zon.*

The objectives vital for subsequent passage of the British ground column were located at intervals along the entire 15-mile stretch of road. This meant that a lightly manned and armed airborne division would be widely extended in taking and defending the objectives. The division commander, Maj. Gen. Maxwell D. Taylor, later was to compare the situation to the early American West, where small garrisons had to contend with sudden Indian attacks at any point along great stretches of vital railroad.

The dispersion of the 101st Airborne Division's objectives made sense only in light of the expectation of early contact with the British ground column, probably within twenty-four hours after the jump. With this and the widely separated objectives in mind, General Taylor concentrated in his early lifts upon bringing in his infantry rather than his artillery. Centrally located artillery of the caliber available to airborne troops, he reasoned, could not reach targets on the extremities of his division. The number of objectives meant that the perimeter defenses about them would be so small that guns emplaced within the perimeters could render no more than limited service. Infantry and mortars were to do the work at first along Hell's Highway.

Recalling dispersion that had plagued the division in Normandy, General Taylor insisted upon drop zones fairly close together, no matter how scattered the objectives. Two regimental drop zones and the division landing zone were located near the center of the division sector, west of Hell's Highway in a triangle marked by the villages of Zon, St. Oedenrode, and Best. Dropping close to Zon, the 506th Parachute Infantry (Col. Robert F. Sink) was to secure a highway bridge over the Wilhelmina Canal a few hundred yards south of Zon, then was to march south on Eindhoven. Coming to earth just to the north, the 502d Parachute Infantry (Col.

John H. Michaelis) was to guard both drop zones in order to ensure their use as a glider landing zone and was to capture a road bridge over the Dommel River at St. Oedenrode. Because General Taylor believed his over-all position might be strengthened by possession of bridges over the Wilhelmina Canal south of Best, four miles from Zon off the west flank of Hell's Highway, Colonel Michaelis was to send a company to these bridges. The remaining parachute regiment, the 501st Parachute Infantry (Col. Howard R. Johnson), was to drop a few miles farther north near Veghel to seize rail and road bridges over the Willems Canal and the Aa River.

Despite flak and small arms fire, only 1 Pathfinder plane and 2 of the other 424 parachute aircraft of the 101st Airborne Division failed to reach the drop zones, although some planes went down after the paratroopers had jumped. Incurring casualties of less than 2 percent in personnel and 5 percent in equipment, 6,769 men made the jump. They did it in half an hour beginning three minutes after H-Hour, at 1303. Among the casualties was 1 man killed by antiaircraft fire as he poised in the open door of his plane. While floating earthward with parachutes open, 2 other men were cut to pieces by the propellers of a crashing C–47.

One of only two units of the division which were not delivered to the correct drop zone was the 1st Battalion (Lt. Col. Harry W. O. Kinnard, Jr.), 501st Parachute Infantry. Scheduled to drop just west of Veghel, between the Aa River and the Willems Canal, the battalion instead came to earth three miles to the northwest. The battalion nevertheless had a compact drop pattern and in less than an hour was on the move to seize the bridges over the Aa River at Veghel. An

officer and forty-six men, including eight jump casualties, stayed behind at a chateau (Kasteel) to care for the casualties and to collect equipment bundles.

While the bulk of Colonel Kinnard's battalion marched directly down a main road toward Veghel, an advance patrol occupied the railway bridge over the Aa without contest. Only as the battalion entered Veghel in quest of the highway bridge did any Germans fight back, and these offered only desultory, halfhearted fire.

Meanwhile the main force of this regiment had been landing southwest of Veghel on the other side of the Willems Canal. Unopposed in the drop and assembly, one battalion organized within forty-five minutes, quickly secured the nearby village of Eerde, and sent a detachment to throw a roadblock across Hell's Highway between Veghel and St. Oedenrode. The remaining battalion dispatched a small force to seize the railway bridge over the Willems Canal and then marched toward the highway bridge over the canal on the outskirts of Veghel. Inside Veghel, this battalion contacted Colonel Kinnard's men, who by this time had secured the road bridge over the Aa River. In approximately three hours, Colonel Johnson's 501st Parachute Infantry had seized all its D-Day objectives. Now the real problem was to organize a defense in spite of ecstatic Dutch civilians.

In late afternoon a message arrived that cast a shadow on the day's success. At the chateau (Kasteel) northwest of Veghel, a force of about fifty Germans supported by mortars had surprised the officer and forty-six men who had stayed behind to collect equipment bundles.

Mindful of the need to defend Veghel securely as darkness approached, the regimental commander, Colonel Johnson, could spare no more than a platoon for the relief of these men. A few hundred yards short of the chateau German fire forced this platoon to dig in for the night. The next morning it was obvious that the platoon either had to be reinforced or pulled back. Still apprehensive about the defense of Veghel, Colonel Johnson ordered the platoon withdrawn. That afternoon Colonel Kinnard sent a small patrol in another attempt to contact the bundle-collecting detail. "I am now at Kasteel," the patrol leader reported by radio, ". . . there are no signs of our men here but bloody bandages."

Other than Colonel Kinnard's battalion, the only unit of the 101st Airborne Division that was not delivered to the correct drop zone on D-Day was a battalion of Colonel Michaelis' 502d Parachute Infantry. The regiment was scheduled to drop on the northernmost of the two drop zones between Zon and St. Oedenrode; this battalion, commanded by Lt. Col. Patrick F. Cassidy, came down two miles away on the neighboring drop zone. Although delayed by this misadventure, Colonel Cassidy's battalion by nightfall had brought a persistent bunch of rear echelon Germans to heel in St. Oedenrode and thereby secured both a main highway and an alternate bridge over the Dommel River. Deploying to defend the village, Colonel Cassidy sent a patrol northeast along Hell's Highway to contact the 501st Parachute Infantry at Veghel.

Another battalion of the 502d Parachute Infantry deployed to protect the glider landing zone, while the bulk of the third battalion moved to an assembly area near Zon, ready to assist if need be the march of the neighboring regiment on Eindhoven. At the same time a com-

pany of this battalion proceeded upon a separate mission, to capture the rail and road bridges over the Wilhelmina Canal southeast of Best. Although these bridges were not assigned objectives for the 101st Airborne Division, General Taylor considered them valuable for three reasons: first, as an outpost protecting his glider landing zone and his main positions along Hell's Highway; again, as alternate crossings of the Wilhelmina Canal should the Germans destroy the bridges at Zon; and again, as control of a main highway (between Eindhoven and 's Hertogenbosch) by which the Germans otherwise might feed reinforcements to Eindhoven. To do the job, Colonel Michaelis sent Company H reinforced by a light machine gun section and a platoon of engineers.

En route to the bridges, the Company H commander, Capt. Robert E. Jones, lost his way in a thick woods, the Zonsche Forest. Emerging near a road junction east of Best, the company came under fire from a small group of Germans apparently rallied by some local commander. The Germans gained the upper hand when infantry reinforcements and several small cannon arrived by truck from the direction of 's Hertogenbosch. These could have been an advance detachment of General Poppe's *59th Infantry Division,* which was detraining at Tilburg under orders from the *First Parachute Army's* General Student to enter the fight.

Goaded by radio messages from his battalion commander to get somebody to the bridges over the Wilhelmina Canal, Captain Jones organized a reinforced patrol. A platoon leader, Lt. Edward L. Wierzbowski, was to take a rifle platoon and the attached engineers and machine gun section to the bridges.

Lieutenant Wierzbowski found in turn

that casualties and disorganization had left him with but eighteen riflemen and twenty-six engineers. The lieutenant and his little force still were picking their way through the Zonsche Forest toward the bridges when night came, and with the darkness, a cold, penetrating rain.

Back at regimental headquarters, Colonel Michaelis meanwhile had become perturbed about reports of Company H's encounter. He directed that the rest of the company's parent battalion go to Captain Jones's assistance. The commander, Lt. Col. Robert G. Cole, started with the battalion toward Best at 1800, but darkness fell before physical contact could be established with Captain Jones.

In the meantime, Lieutenant Wierzbowski and his men had crawled the last few yards on their bellies to reach the Wilhelmina Canal several hundred yards east of the highway bridge. Slithering along the dike, the men neared the bridge, apparently undetected. While the lieutenant and a scout crawled ahead to reconnoiter, the main body of the patrol slid down the embankment to await their return.

A barrage of "potato masher" hand grenades came suddenly from the darkness on the other side of the canal. Scared, a couple of men scrambled up the bank of the dike. Others followed. The night erupted with the fire of machine guns and rifles. Some of the men stampeded back toward the forest.

When he heard this firing, Lieutenant Wierzbowski had come within sight of the bridge, only to find it covered by German sentries. Scurrying back, he discovered he had left but 3 officers and 15 men, and 3 of these wounded. They had their individual weapons, plus a machine gun with 500 rounds of ammunition, a

mortar with 6 rounds, and a bazooka with 5 rockets. Here, as the cold rain fell, the men dug in for the night.

As these events had developed, the 101st Airborne Division's D-Day glider lift had begun to arrive. Although not as immune to mishap as the parachutists, a total of 53 out of 70 gliders landed successfully with 32 jeeps, 13 trailers, and 252 men. Of those that failed to make it, 1 fell in the Channel, 1 crash-landed on the landing zone, 2 collided in the air above the landing zone, 2 were unaccounted for, 4 landed in friendly territory, and 7 came down behind enemy lines.[15]

The part of the division headquarters that had not parachuted with General Taylor came in by glider. Also arriving by glider were reconnaissance, signal, and medical units. A radio net linked division headquarters with the three parachute regiments within minutes after the glider landings. By 1500 medics were treating casualties in a temporary hospital erected in a field and at 1700 began a major operation. An hour later the medics moved to a civilian hospital in Zon.

Before the gliders arrived, General Taylor's third regiment, the 506th Parachute Infantry, had assembled after a near-perfect drop on the southernmost division drop zone near Zon. Unhampered by opposition, a portion of one battalion assembled in less than forty-five minutes. Commanded by Maj. James L. LaPrade and accompanied by General Taylor, this battalion moved south to bypass Zon and come upon the highway bridge over the

---

[15] Another glider narrowly escaped a crash. When flak knocked out both pilot and copilot, Cpl. James L. Evans, a passenger unfamiliar with the controls and himself wounded by flak, steadied the ship until he could rouse the dazed pilot.

Wilhelmina Canal from the west flank. After capture of this bridge, the 506th Parachute Infantry was to continue south about six miles to Eindhoven.

As Major LaPrade and his men advanced, they came under deadly fire from an 88-mm. gun emplaced south of the Zonsche Forest. Hope for quick capture of the bridge from the flank began to fade.

As soon as the other two battalions of the 506th Parachute Infantry assembled, the regimental commander, Colonel Sink, directed them in a column of battalions to Hell's Highway, thence south through Zon toward the canal. In Zon the leading battalion also came under fire from an 88, but a platoon acting as a point deployed among the buildings and advanced undetected within fifty yards of the gun. A round from the bazooka of Pvt. Thomas G. Lindsey finished it off.

Evidently expecting that Major La-Prade's flanking battalion would have captured the highway bridge, these two battalions made no apparent haste in moving through Zon. They methodically cleared stray Germans from the houses, so that a full two hours had passed before they emerged from the village. Having at last overcome the enemy 88 south of the Zonsche Forest, Major LaPrade's battalion caught sight of the bridge at about the same time. Both forces were within fifty yards of the bridge when their objective went up with a roar. Debris from the explosion rained all about.

Rushing to the bank of the canal, Major LaPrade, a lieutenant, and a sergeant jumped into the water and swam across. Though Germans in a house on the south bank opened fire, other paratroopers found a rowboat and ferried a squad across. This advance party reduced the opposition. The little rowboat made trip after trip across the canal while a platoon of engineers improvised a shaky footbridge, but not until an hour before midnight was the entire regiment across.

Perturbed by civilian reports of a strong German garrison in Eindhoven, Colonel Sink was reluctant to enter the city by night. Aware that Eindhoven was a secondary objective on the division's timetable and that the British had been told the city might not be taken on D-Day, General Taylor approved a halt until daylight.

As matters stood, the British ground column was no closer to Eindhoven than were the paratroopers, so that this conservative approach worked no hardship. Yet it was a distinct risk, because General Taylor and Colonel Sink hardly could have known where the British were at the time. One of the gliders that failed to reach the 101st Airborne Division's landing zone had contained attached British signal personnel; without them, immediate contact with the 30 Corps proved impossible. Not until the next morning, when the 506th Parachute Infantry made radio contact with some American signalmen attached to the 30 Corps, could the Americans learn how far the British had advanced.

Behind an artillery barrage that began an hour after the first troop carrier aircraft passed over the British lines, the 30 Corps had attacked on schedule with tanks in the lead. Against five German battalions, including two SS battalions that 30 Corps intelligence had failed to detect, the spearhead Guards Armoured Division had made steady progress. In view of the fact that woods and marshy ground confined the attack to a front not much wider than the highway leading to Eindhoven, progress was remarkable,

THE DUTCH WELCOME *the 506th Parachute Infantry.*

though not sufficient to take the tanks to Eindhoven. As night came the British stopped in Valkenswaard, their "formal" objective. The objective of Eindhoven, which General Horrocks had indicated he hoped to reach on D-Day, lay six miles to the north.[16]

Against ineffective delaying actions by

small enemy groups, Colonel Sink's 506th Parachute Infantry pressed the advance on Eindhoven early on D plus 1, 18 September. By midmorning, the leading battalion had knocked out a nest of two 88-mm. guns and pushed deep into the heart of the city. Colonel Sink had expected to find at least a regiment of Germans in Eindhoven; he actually flushed no more than a company. Having taken four bridges over the Dommel River and a canal in the city by noon, the paratroopers spent the rest of the day

[16] The story of the ground attack is from Combat Interv with Renfro; Br Abn Corps, Allied Abn Opns in Holland; 21 A Gp, Opn MARKET GARDEN. Wilmot, *The Struggle for Europe,* provides a lucid account.

rounding up enemy stragglers and clearing the southern outskirts for entry of the Guards Armoured Division. As they performed these tasks, Eindhoven went on a binge. As if by magic the city blossomed with the national color. "The reception was terrific," said one American officer. "The air seemed to reek with hate for the Germans . . . ."

In the carnival atmosphere the paratroopers failed for a long time to hear the fretted clank of tanks they were listening for. At 1130 the first direct radio communication with the Guards Armoured Division had revealed that the armor still was five miles south of Eindhoven, engaged in a bitter fight. At 1230 hopes rose with the appearance of two British armored cars, but these had sneaked around the German flank to reach Eindhoven from the northwest. Shadows were falling when about 1900 the paratroopers at last spotted the head of the main British column.

The Guards Armoured Division pushed through Eindhoven without pause. At Zon, British engineers, who had been forewarned that the bridge over the Wilhelmina Canal was out, set to work. During the night they installed a Bailey bridge, so that at 0645 (D plus 2, 19 September) the armor rumbled across. The ground advance was proceeding swiftly, but was it swift enough? General Horrocks' 30 Corps was at least thirty-three hours behind schedule.

Though overshadowed by the events at Eindhoven, the side show that had developed near Best actually provided the 101st Airborne Division's stiffest fighting on D plus 1 and 2. Destruction of the bridge over the Wilhelmina Canal at Zon having lent exigency to the 502d Parachute Infantry's mission of securing al-

ternate bridges, Colonel Michaelis early on D plus 1, 18 September, committed a second battalion to the Best fight.

The answer to the situation at Best lay in General Poppe's *59th Division*. No sooner had this force detrained at Tilburg than the *First Parachute Army*'s General Student sent the bulk of the division to secure the bridges near Best. In the meantime, three companies reinforced by two replacement battalions and a police battalion were to cut Hell's Highway at St. Oedenrode.[17]

The Americans could be grateful that General Poppe's division faced an ammunition situation that was "nearly desperate," having had to leave behind most of its ammunition when ferried across the Schelde estuary as part of the *Fifteenth Army*.[18] As it was, the two American battalions had all they could do to hold their own. The fresh battalion, commanded by Lt. Col. Steve A. Chappuis, tried to drive to the bridges over the Wilhelmina Canal but had to fall back to a defense with Colonel Cole's battalion on the edge of the Zonsche Forest. A timely strike by a flight of P-47's held the Germans off. Colonel Cole himself fell, dead of a German bullet through the temple.

All through the day of D plus 1 the sound of firing had fanned hope of relief in the minds of Lieutenant Wierzbowski and his group of fifteen men along the dike near the highway bridge. Then, at 1100, the hundred-foot concrete span over the Wilhelmina Canal trembled and lifted with a violent explosion. The objective for which the 502d Parachute Infantry

---

[17] Mng, Noon, and Evng Sitreps, *A Gp B,* 1000, 1530, and 2000, 18 Sep 44, *A Gp B KTB, Letzte Meldung.*
[18] *Ibid.*

continued to fight the rest of the day was no longer worth fighting for.

The experiences of Lieutenant Wierzbowski and his little group were a testimonial to the kind of hardship small, isolated units sometimes are called upon to endure. In midafternoon their troubles increased when a small German force attacked. One man was killed outright. Seriously wounded in the base of the spine, another slowly died from loss of blood. Obsessed with a belief that enemy fire had torn off his testicles, one of the engineer officers pleaded with Lieutenant Wierzbowski to kill him. Wierzbowski finally convinced him his wounds were not that serious. Two German bullets hit the platoon's lead scout, Pfc. Joe E. Mann, who already had incurred two wounds; now both his arms hung useless. Though an engineer lieutenant and a sergeant tried to break through for aid, the lieutenant was captured and the sergeant wounded.

Hope stirred again during the late afternoon and early evening. First, a British armored car and a reconnaissance car appeared on the opposite bank of the canal. The British tried to raise headquarters of the 101st Airborne Division on their radio, but to no avail. They provided fire support until later in the evening when a platoon of paratroopers who had gotten lost stumbled onto Lieutenant Wierzbowski's position.

Although this platoon agreed to defend one of Lieutenant Wierzbowski's flanks, the men fell back during the night in the face of a small German attack. Again Wierzbowski and his little group were alone. Then a small patrol from Colonel Chappuis' battalion stumbled onto the position. Though the lieutenant sent word of his plight by this patrol, the report was not to reach Colonel Chappuis until the next morning. Distorted in transmission, the message said only that the bridge had been blown.

As a misty daylight began to break on D plus 2, 19 September, Lieutenant Wierzbowski spotted a small German force bearing down on his position. Though the lieutenant yelled an alarm, the Germans already were too close. Two German grenades rolled down among the wounded. Although the men tossed these out before they exploded, another hit the machine gun and blinded the gunner. A moment later another grenade rolled into this man's foxhole. One eye blown out entirely, the other blinded, the soldier groped wildly for the grenade. He found it and tossed it from his foxhole only a split second before it exploded.

Another grenade fell behind Private Mann, who was sitting in a trench with six other wounded. Mann saw the grenade come and felt it land behind him. Helpless, his arms bound and useless from the wounds incurred the day before, he yelled: "Grenade!" Then he lay back to take the explosion with his body.[19]

"Shall we surrender or fight?" the men had asked persistently. As the Germans made a final charge, Lieutenant Wierzbowski gave them a succinct answer: "OK. This is the time." Only three of his men had gone unscathed. They had virtually no ammunition. Their last grenade was gone. One man put a dirty handkerchief on a rifle and waved it.[20]

---

[19] Private Mann was posthumously awarded the Medal of Honor. The Dutch have erected a memorial in his honor in the Zonsche Forest.

[20] Cpl. Daniel L. Corman played dead by falling across what he thought was the corpse of his foxhole mate. Unmoving, Corman stayed there until late afternoon when other paratroopers at last arrived. Then he found that the man he had been lying on still had a breath of life in him.

In the meantime, a kind of stalemate had developed in the fighting along the edge of the Zonsche Forest. Though the two American battalions held their own, their regimental commander, Colonel Michaelis, could not reinforce them without neglecting defense of St. Oedenrode, which was one of his primary missions.

The solution came at last in the juncture with the British ground troops, whereby a squadron of British tanks and a modicum of artillery support became available. Arrival by glider in the afternoon of D plus 1 of two battalions of the 327th Glider Infantry under Col. Joseph H. Harper also helped.[21] Because of rain and mist along the southern air route, this glider lift had come in via the northern route and brought successful landing of 428 out of 450 gliders of the 101st Airborne Division. A total of 2,579 men, 146 jeeps, 109 trailers, 2 bulldozers, and some resupply had arrived.

General Taylor ordered his assistant division commander, Brig. Gen. Gerald J. Higgins, to take over-all command of the two battalions of the 502d Parachute Infantry near Best, contingents of the 327th Glider Infantry, a squadron of British tanks, and elements of British artillery and to reduce all enemy east of the highway between Eindhoven and 's Hertogenbosch and north of the Wilhelmina Canal. Though the destruction of the

Best highway bridge had eliminated the original purpose of the Best fighting, the job of protecting the west flank of the 101st Airborne Division remained.

The British tanks made the difference in an attack that began at 1400 on D plus 2. Within German ranks, a festering disintegration by late afternoon became a rout. "Send us all the MP's available," became the cry as hundreds of Germans began to give up. For almost three days a bitter, costly, and frustrating fight, the action at Best now became little more than a mop-up. By the end of D plus 2 the prisoners totaled more than 1,400, and the paratroopers actually counted more than 300 enemy dead. Some of the prisoners came in with Lieutenant Wierzbowski and the survivors of his little band. They had been taken to a German aid station and there had talked their captors into surrender.

Best itself remained in German hands, and much of the territory taken had to be abandoned as soon as the mop-up ended. Now the battle of Hell's Highway was developing into the Indian-type fighting General Taylor later was to call it, and these men from Best were needed at other points. The engagement near Best had been costly and had secured neither of the bridges over the Wilhelmina Canal, yet it had parried what could have become a serious blow by the *59th Division*. General Poppe now had scarcely a shell of a division.

While the fight raged at Best on D plus 1 and 2, the rest of the 101st Airborne Division was maintaining defensive positions at Eindhoven, Zon, St. Oedenrode, and Veghel. From Eindhoven, Colonel Sink's 506th Parachute Infantry sent a battalion to either flank to widen the base of the MARKET-GARDEN corridor, but in

---

[21] Like all glider regiments, the 327th Glider Infantry had but two organic rifle battalions. In informal reorganization between actions in Sicily and Normandy, the glider regiments of both the 82d and 101st Airborne Divisions had gained a third battalion by splitting between them another regiment, the 401st. Thus, the 1st Battalion, 401st Glider Infantry, while retaining formal status as an independent unit, normally functioned as the 3d Battalion, 327th Glider Infantry.

both cases Sink recalled the troops before they reached their objectives. On the west the battalion returned because the 12 British Corps had begun to advance along the left flank of the corridor and was expected soon to overrun the battalion's objective. The battalion on the east returned because Colonel Sink learned that a column of German armor was loose in the region and he wanted no part of a meeting engagement with armor.

Late in the afternoon of D plus 2 this German column struck toward Zon in an attempt to sever the thin lifeline over which the British ground column was pushing toward Nijmegen. It was Major von Maltzahn's *107th Panzer Brigade* that on D-Day had been rerouted from Aachen to the assistance of the *First Parachute Army.* Although General Student had ordered the panzer brigade and General Poppe's *59th Division* to make a concentric attack toward Zon, the *59th Division* at the time the brigade arrived was *hors de combat.*[22]

Even without the *59th Division* the German attack came close to succeeding. Only a scratch force that included General Taylor's headquarters troops was available at the time for defending the Bailey bridge over the Wilhelmina Canal at Zon. Darkness had fallen, a British truck struck by a round from a German tank was burning brightly atop the bridge, and a Panther was pumping round after round into a building housing the division command post when General Taylor himself arrived with reinforcements. He led part of a glider infantry battalion and a lone 57-mm. antitank gun. One of the first rounds from this gun knocked out a

German tank near the bridge. Bazooka fire disabled another. The Germans appeared to lose heart after this, and traffic gradually began to flow again along Hell's Highway.

Another German blow against Hell's Highway on D plus 2 came from the air, perhaps as a direct result of Hitler's exhortations that the Luftwaffe put his little world right again. About a hundred German twin-engine bombers came out of hiding after nightfall to bombard the central part of Eindhoven. Because most American units held positions outside the city, they incurred no damage; but more than a thousand civilians were killed or wounded, and British units were heavily hit. Whether from lack of planes, fuel, or trained crewmen, or because of all three, this was the only major strike by long-range German bombers during the course of the campaign in the West during the fall of 1944.[23]

At both Veghel and St. Oedenrode during these first days, Colonel Johnson's 501st Parachute Infantry and Colonel Cassidy's battalion of the 502d Parachute Infantry had held their positions about the canal and river bridges against persistent but small German attacks, most of which were in company strength. The strongest —by three companies of the *59th Division* reinforced by police and replacement units—struck Colonel Cassidy's battalion on D plus 2 on the road to Schijndel. Hard pressed at first, Colonel Cassidy's men gained assistance from Sgt. James M. (Paddy) McCrory, commander of a crippled tank that had dropped out of the

---

[22] Evng Sitrep, *A Gp B,* 19 Sep 44, *A Gp B KTB, Letzte Meldung.*

[23] Greater detail on this and other German air operations against Operation MARKET may be found in Hq, AAF, Airborne Assault on Holland, an Interim Report, Wings at War Series, No. 4, pp. 37–39.

British ground column. Although the tank could make no more than five miles per hour, McCrory plunged unhesitatingly into the fight. When the paratroopers tried to thank him, he brushed them off. "When in doubt," Sergeant McCrory said, "lash out." His words became a kind of unofficial motto of the battalion.

General Taylor had hoped to be in a stronger position by the end of D plus 2 with the addition of most of his airborne artillery. But the bugaboo that threatens all airborne operations had developed. The weather closed in. Though the flights on D plus 2 were postponed until late in the day on the chance the weather might clear, troops in the gliders still were to speak of a mist so thick they could see nothing but three feet of tow rope stretching out into nowhere. Because the glider pilots could not detect when their mother planes banked, many gliders turned over and had to cut loose prematurely. The Air/Sea Rescue Service worked overtime plucking ditched crewmen and passengers from the Channel. Many planes and gliders turned back. On the other hand, weather at German bases must have been better; for the Germans sent up more than 125 Messerschmitts and Focke-Wulfs. A total of 1,086 Allied troop carrier, tow, and resupply planes and 428 gliders took off on D plus 2. A large part of these returned to base, while 45 planes and 73 gliders were lost.[24]

Probably because the 101st Airborne Division's landing zone was relatively secure, General Brereton allotted General Taylor, at the expense of the 82d Airborne

Division, 384 gliders for the D plus 2 flight, more than twice the number originally planned. Only 212 of these arrived. After missing the landing zone and circling vainly, 82 tow planes returned to England. These were minus 31 of their gliders which cut loose behind friendly lines, 16 known to have crash-landed in enemy territory, and 26 not accounted for. Those glidermen who landed behind German lines and eventually rejoined their units brought with them harrowing tales of hairbreadth escapes punctuated with praise for the Dutch underground. Most of these men were artillerymen, for the flights bringing in the artillery units were particularly cut up. Of 66 artillery pieces and antitank guns that started the flight, only 36 arrived. None was larger than the 75-mm. pack howitzer; all planes towing gliders with 105-mm. howitzers had to turn back.

Difficulties imposed on the 101st Airborne Division by the adverse weather could not be ignored, and General Taylor's "Indian War" to keep open Hell's Highway would remain critical as long as men and supplies had to go north over the highway. Nevertheless, at the moment, a situation had developed farther north that overshadowed events along Hell's Highway. Moving on Grave and Nijmegen, the British ground column was hard pressed to cross the Maas and Waal Rivers and reach the British airborne troops at Arnhem. To ensure passage of the ground column, the 82 Airborne Division at Nijmegen was fighting against time.

Six Bridges and a Ridge

For the 82d Airborne Division, the mere possession of the towns, the bridges, and the highway in the division's assigned sec-

---

[24] FAAA, Opns in Holland. See also Rapport and Northwood, *Rendezvous With Destiny,* pp. 312–13.

GENERAL GAVIN *and General Dempsey (on left) confer during Operation MARKET-GARDEN.*

tor was not sufficient to ensure the passage of the 30 Corps ground column.[25]

[25] The 82d "All-American" Airborne Division made a first combat jump in Sicily, then reinforced the Fifth Army at Salerno. When the division returned to England, one regiment remained behind to fight at Anzio and missed the Normandy jump but later rejoined the division. Attachment of the 508th Parachute Infantry provided the division with a fourth infantry regiment. Unless otherwise noted, the story of the 82d in Operation MARKET is based upon official unit records and combat interviews. A unit history, *Saga of the All-American,* compiled and edited by W. Forrest Dawson (Atlanta, Albert Love Enterprises, 1946), is largely pictorial. As noted, because of sketchy records, considerable reliance has had to be placed upon postwar observations.

Even the bridges over two of the most formidable water obstacles along the entire path, the sprawling Maas and Waal Rivers, were overshadowed by another feature of terrain: the hill mass southeast of Nijmegen. This high ground is generally triangular in shape, but the most pronounced and highest elevations are mainly along the north and east, forming a wooded ridge line that extends southeast from Nijmegen past the resort hotel of Berg en Dal to the vicinity of the village of Wyler, thence south through Groesbeek to the village of Riethorst, close to the Maas River. Roughly 300 feet in height, the ridge line is about eight miles long. At the base of its eastern slope lies the Dutch-German border, where the ground rises again to the east into a big forest, the Reichswald.

In the eyes of the 82d Airborne Division commander, Brig. Gen. James M. Gavin,[26] possession of the ridge represented the key to success or failure. "With it in German hands," General Gavin was to note later, "physical possession of the bridges would be absolutely worthless, since it completely dominated the bridges and all the terrain around it." General Gavin believed that if he held this ridge, the British ground column ultimately could succeed, even if his airborne troops should be driven away from the bridges. The high ground also represented a ready airhead for later operations.[27]

An understanding of General Gavin's concern about this ridge involves going beyond consideration of the usual importance of high ground to success in almost any operation. The high ground in this instance was unusual in that almost all surrounding terrain was predominantly flat. Not only did the high ground dominate all the other objectives—the bridges over the Maas, the Maas–Waal Canal, and the Waal—it also represented the only real barrier to counterattack should the Germans strike from the east from the direction of the Reichswald. This last the 82d Airborne Division G–2, Lt. Col. Walter F. Winton, Jr., predicted might constitute the major reaction to the landings.[28] From the direction of the Reichswald the Germans would have two major routes, one leading from Kleve along the north edge of the forest east into Nijmegen, the other, from Venlo, passing along the south edge of the forest and thence northeast through the villages of Riethorst and Mook and generally alongside the Maas–Waal Canal into Nijmegen.

The possibility of counterattack from this direction took on added credence from the Dutch resistance reports of panzer formations assembling in the Netherlands. The 82d Airborne Division was led to believe that this armor was concentrating in the Reichswald. This information became "a major and pressing element in the predrop picture of German forces." [29]

The possibility of encountering German armor underscored, in General Gavin's mind, the importance of the defensive aspects of the 82d Airborne Division's assignment. Unlike the 101st Airborne Division, the 82d could anticipate contact with the ground column no sooner than D plus 1, at the earliest, and even this was highly conjectural. General Gavin believed it necessary to plan his fight "in such a manner as to be able to conduct a good fight, well in hand, for at least three days, and almost certainly well beyond this time, if need be." [30]

Had the entire strength of the 82d Airborne Division been available on D-Day, all assigned objectives might have been designated to be taken at once as a matter of course, despite the threat of the

---

[26] General Gavin was promoted to major general during the course of this operation.

[27] Ltr, Gavin to Capt John G. Westover, Hist Off, 25 Jul 45, in reply to questions submitted by Westover to CofS, 82d Abn Div, 82d Abn Div Combat Interv file.

[28] *Ibid.*, and Ltr, Gavin to OCMH, 17 Jan 54.

[29] Ltr, Winton to OCMH, 8 Mar 54, OCMH; Intelligence Trace No. 5 in Hq, Troop Carrier Forces FO No. 4, 13 Sep 44; 505th Prcht Inf AAR.

[30] Gavin, Ltr to OCMH.

Reichswald and delayed contact with the ground column. As it was, because of the limitations of the D-Day lift, the question of priority of objectives entered the picture. In anticipation of a heavy fight before the ground column could provide artillery and antitank support, General Gavin allotted a portion of his D-Day lift to a parachute artillery battalion. He also scheduled arrival of the rest of his artillery on D plus 1. This meant that the glider infantry regiment could not arrive until D plus 2, so that for the first two days the 82d would have but three regiments of infantry. If these three parachute infantry regiments tried to take all assigned objectives, they would be spread dangerously thin for holding the objectives in the event enemy armor materialized from the Reichswald.

Take only the bridges and you probably could not hold them without the high ground. Take only the high ground, the Waal bridge at Nijmegen, and the Maas–Waal Canal bridges, and the ground column could not get across the Maas either to use the other bridges or to relieve the airborne troops. With only so many troops at hand, General Gavin saw no solution at first other than to take first the high ground and the Maas and Maas–Waal Canal bridges—thereby ensuring juncture with the ground column—then Nijmegen.

General Gavin and his staff were not alone in this thinking. Indeed, the directive from the corps commander, General Browning, was "clear and emphatic" to the effect that the division was "not to attempt the seizure of the Nijmegen Bridge until all other missions had been successfully accomplished and the Groesbeek–Berg en Dal high ground was firmly

in our hands." [31] In his formal order General Browning stated: "The capture and retention of the high ground between Nijmegen and Groesbeek is imperative in order to accomplish the Division's task." [32]

On the other hand, the question of taking the magnificent 1,960-foot span across the Waal River at Nijmegen obviously was not dismissed summarily. The bridge in relation to strength available to take it on D-Day was the subject of continuing discussion, not only before D-Day but after the jump. As late as midafternoon of D plus 1 General Browning disapproved a projected plan for taking the Nijmegen bridge and directed instead that the 82d Airborne Division continue to concentrate for the time being upon defending the high ground and the bridges over the Maas and Maas–Waal. [33]

After "almost daily" discussions about the Nijmegen bridge in relation to the over-all plan, General Gavin and his staff

---

[31] Ibid.; Maj. Gen. James M. Gavin, Airborne Warfare (Washington: Infantry Journal Press, 1947), p. 75.

[32] Hq Br Abn Corps, Opn Instr No. 1, Allied Abn Opns in Holland. General Browning was to recall later: "I personally gave an order to Jim Gavin that, although every effort should be made to effect the capture of the Grave and Nijmegen Bridges as soon as possible, it was essential that he should capture the Groesbeek Ridge and hold it—for . . . painfully obvious reasons . . . . If this ground had been lost to the enemy the operations of the 2nd Army would have been dangerously prejudiced as its advance across the Waal and Neder Rhein would have been immediately outflanked. Even the initial advance of the Guards Armoured Division would have been prejudiced and on them the final outcome of the battle had to depend." Ltr, Browning to Maj Gen G. E. Prier-Palmer, British Joint Services Mission, Washington, D.C., 25 Jan 55, excerpt in OCMH.

[33] 82d Abn Div CofS Jnl, entry of 0700, 19 Sep 44, referring to conf, Gavin with Browning, 1530, 18 Sep 44. See also Gavin Ltr to OCMH.

finally decided, "About 48 hours prior to take-off, when the entire plan appeared to be shaping up well," that they could risk sending one battalion in a quick strike for the bridge. This was admittedly a minimum force, but if the Germans were not in strength at the bridge and if the expected counterattacks from the Reichswald could be held with a smaller force than originally deduced, the risk would be justified because of the nature of the prize. "I personally directed Colonel Roy E. Lindquist, commanding the 508th Parachute Infantry," General Gavin recalled later, "to commit his first battalion against the Nijmegen bridge without delay after landing but to keep a very close watch on it in the event he needed it to protect himself against the Reichswald." [34]

In the end, the 82d Airborne Division was to try to seize all its objectives on D-Day: bridges over the Maas at Grave; over the Maas–Waal Canal near Honinghutje,[35] Hatert, Malden, and Heumen; and over the Waal at Nijmegen; plus the high ground. The only exception was the railroad bridge at Nijmegen for which no force apparently was allotted.

The drop zone of the 508th Parachute Infantry (Colonel Lindquist) was on the high ground north of Groesbeek. In addition to the one-battalion assignment against the Nijmegen bridge, Colonel Lindquist drew responsibility for a major portion of the high ground from Nijmegen

---

[34] Gavin Ltr to Westover; Gavin Ltr to OCMH.

[35] The Honinghutje bridge was not mentioned in 82d Abn Div FO 11, 13 Sep 44, which listed assignments. General Gavin in his letter to OCMH says that the 504th and 508th Parachute Infantry Regiments together were to take the bridge. The task "was to depend upon the development of the fight once the landings were accomplished." Presumably the same was true of rail bridges over both the Maas and the Waal.

past the resort hotel of Berg en Dal to the village of Wyler, thence generally south to the vicinity of Groesbeek, a total distance of about six miles. The regiment also was to block enemy movement southward from Nijmegen and was to assist in taking the bridges over the Maas–Waal Canal at Hatert and Honinghutje, the last on the main Grave–Nijmegen highway. A final assignment involved securing the northernmost of two glider landing zones on the eastern slopes of the ridge line, south of Wyler.

The 505th Parachute Infantry (Col. William E. Ekman) was to drop south of Groesbeek. The regiment then was to take Groesbeek, high ground in the vicinity, the southern glider landing zone southeast of Groesbeek, and the ridge line extending south as far as the Kiekberg (Hill 77.2), a high point overlooking the village of Riethorst. Patrols from this regiment were to assist in taking the Maas–Waal bridges at Heumen and Malden.

The principal assignment of the remaining regiment, the 504th Parachute Infantry (Col. Reuben H. Tucker), was to take the 9-span, 1,800-foot bridge over the Maas River near Grave. In keeping with the theory that bridges are best taken by assault from both ends, one company was to drop south of the river. The rest of the regiment was to drop between the Maas and the Maas–Waal Canal. Other assignments included blocking enemy movement between the river and the canal from the west, assisting in taking the Honinghutje bridge, and capturing the Malden and Heumen bridges. Gaining at least one of the four bridges over the Maas–Waal Canal was vital, for the canal is a sizable waterway, in most places about 200 feet wide. The 504th also was to guard against counterattack from the west.

82D AIRBORNE DIVISION DROP *near Grave.*

The flight, drops, and landings of the 82d Airborne Division on D-Day, 17 September, proved even more phenomenally successful than did the 101st's. Employing the northern air route, the serials encountered only sporadic flak that was highly inaccurate even as it grew heavier near the drop zones. Only 1 of 482 planes and 2 of 50 gliders failed to reach the target area. Incurring only 2 percent casualties, 7,277 men made the jump. At least 2 were killed, 1 who was struck by a supply bundle and another whose parachute failed to open. Only 7 out of 209 men who arrived by glider were injured. Eight 75-mm. guns arrived without incident. The only miscalculation was the dropping of one battalion of the 508th Parachute Infantry a mile north of the assigned drop zone, but this had little effect on subsequent operations. Both General Gavin and the British Airborne Corps commander, General Browning, jumped with skeleton staffs.

Resistance to the drop and assembly was "negligible," although some individuals had to fight their way off the drop zones. The 508th Parachute Infantry met resistance from "a few widely scattered" antiaircraft crews and "some isolated labor troops," but the general picture was as summed up by the G-2: "Landed against almost no opposition." [36]

---

[36] Msg, G–2 to CO Base Echelon, 17 Sep, in 82d Abn Div G–2 Jnl, 17–21 Sep 44; 508th Prcht Inf AAR and other regtl AARs; Gavin Ltr to OCMH.

Taking the Objectives

The task of seizing the big highway span over the Maas River near Grave was easier because one stick of sixteen men failed to get the green light signal to jump until "a bit late."[37] When the signal came the officer in charge of this stick, Lt. John S. Thompson, noted that his plane was directly over a group of buildings. He decided "to wait a few seconds and jump on a field just southwest of the Grave Bridge."[38] The result was that he and his men came to earth only about 700 yards from the south end of the bridge, while the rest of the company of the 504th Parachute Infantry that jumped south of the Maas came down more than a mile away.

Lieutenant Thompson lost no time getting started toward the bridge. Despite occasional small arms fire, he and his men made their way through drainage ditches to the vicinity of a tower near the bridge. Two hits from a bazooka silenced a 20-mm. flak gun in the tower. In keeping with established practice, the men made every effort to prevent any Germans from moving about near the bridge, lest they set or activate demolitions. As the men reached the bridge, they cut all visible wires.

In the meantime, the main body of Lieutenant Thompson's parent battalion had been assembling on the other side of the Maas River. As the battalion reached the north end of the bridge, only a flak gun on river flats nearby offered any real problem. In less than three hours, the 504th Parachute Infantry was in firm control of the Maas bridge, one of the major prizes of the entire MARKET-GARDEN operation. That the Germans had failed to demolish the bridge could be explained either through the precautions Lieutenant Thompson and his men had taken or through prisoner revelations that the bridge was to have been blown only on order of the German corps commander, who was not present.[39]

The bulk of Lieutenant Thompson's parent company had been unable to reach the bridge from the drop zone west of Grave because of small arms fire from the town. Aware that a twelve-mile gap existed between the company and closest units of the 101st Airborne Division at Veghel, the company commander set up a roadblock across the main highway to forestall German reinforcements from the south. That night a patrol went into Grave to investigate strange noises emanating from the town. The patrol found civilians gathered in the town hall lustily singing the Dutch version of "Tipperary." The Germans had gone.

Of the other two battalions of Colonel Tucker's 504th Parachute Infantry, one swept stray Germans from between the Maas and the Maas-Waal Canal as far west as the main highway, while the second set out to take two bridges over the canal. Both bridges were near the southeast end of the canal where it joins the Maas River, one near the village of Malden, the other at Heumen. These bridges were important not only as possible routes north for the ground column but also as connections between the 504th Parachute Infantry and the other regiments on the high ground to the northeast.

---

[37] Combat Interv with personnel of Co E, 504th Prcht Inf.

[38] Gavin letter to OCMH, citing an account of the event written by Lieutenant Thompson.

[39] 82d Abn Div, Annex 3 to G–2 Rpt 91, Translation of Captured Document 15 Sep 44.

The battalion commander, Maj. Willard E. Harrison, sent a company to each objective. The men who charged the bridge at Malden saw their objective go up in smoke as they made a final dash toward it. At Heumen, small arms fire from an island in the canal a few yards north of the bridge stymied advance until at last 8 men infiltrated to a point near the bridge from which they could spray the island with machine gun fire. Covered by this fire, 2 officers, a corporal, and a radio operator ran for the bridge. Three of them made it. Before dark, another officer and 6 men rowed across the canal to join this trio.[40] Yet the presence of this little force on the east bank of the canal had no apparent effect upon the Germans who were covering the bridge from the island.

The American company commander, Capt. Thomas B. Helgeson, expected the bridge to be blown at any moment. As approaching darkness provided some concealment, Captain Helgeson sent the battalion demolition squad to search for and cut demolition wires. "The bridge had been prepared for demolition," men of the battalion recalled later, "and nobody knows why it was not blown." [41]

Darkness at last provided the antidote for the German fire from the island. Soon after nightfall, a strong patrol stormed across a footbridge and overran the German positions. Six hours after H Hour the Heumen bridge was safe. It subsequently was to serve as the main route across the Maas–Waal Canal for the British ground column.

---

[40] General Gavin recalls that the division Reconnaissance Platoon approached the east side of the bridge late in the afternoon. Gavin Ltr to OCMH.

[41] Combat Interv with personnel of 1st Bn, 504th Prcht Inf.

Of two other bridges over the Maas–Waal Canal—one near Hatert, northwest of Malden, the other on the main Grave–Nijmegen highway near Honinghutje—only the Hatert bridge was attacked on D-Day. To Hatert went elements of the 504th and a platoon of Colonel Lindquist's 508th Parachute Infantry, only to find the bridge demolished.

Before dawn the next morning, Colonel Lindquist sent a platoon to seize the bridge at Honinghutje. When German fire pinned this platoon to nearby drainage ditches, another platoon arrived to help. Together they stormed the bridge, but not before the Germans hurriedly set off demolitions. Though the explosion failed to demolish the bridge, it weakened it to the extent that the ground column subsequently avoided it in favor of a more circuitous route via the Heumen bridge.

Like Colonel Tucker's battalions, those of Colonel Lindquist's 508th Parachute Infantry and of Colonel Ekman's 505th Parachute Infantry had assembled within an hour after the D-Day drop. One battalion was moving toward its objective within twenty minutes after the drop.

With the assistance of the Dutch underground, one battalion of the 505th Parachute Infantry rounded up stragglers in Groesbeek. The battalion then occupied a peak (Hill 81.8) of the ridge line in woods west of the village, constituting a division reserve, and also sent patrols southwest toward Heumen where soon after dark they contacted the 504th Parachute Infantry at the Heumen bridge. Part of another battalion occupied the Nijmegen–Groesbeek ridge south of Groesbeek, including the Kiekberg (Hill 77.2), which overlooks the village of Riethorst and the highway leading from the Reichswald to Mook and Nijmegen. A company later in the day cleared Riethorst and set up roadblocks. Although patrols attempted to seize a railroad bridge over the Maas River near Mook, the Germans blew the bridge with moments to spare. Colonel Ekman's remaining battalion dug in along the ridge at Groesbeek and north of that village and sent a company-size patrol east to the Reichswald.

Because of the proximity of the 505th Parachute Infantry to the Reichswald, these men were particularly concerned about the report they had received in England that the Reichswald was a nest of German armor. They breathed more easily when the patrol returned with word that "no tanks could be seen." This was in keeping with information provided by Dutch civilians soon after the landings to the effect that "the report about the 1000 tanks in the Reichswald was false." [42]

Colonel Lindquist's 508th Parachute Infantry had begun work in the meantime on a variety of missions. One battalion moved west toward Hatert to assume defensive positions astride the Nijmegen–Mook highway, in order to block enemy movement southward from Nijmegen into the division's perimeter. This was the same battalion which sent a platoon on the unsuccessful quest of the Hatert bridge over the Maas–Waal Canal and the next morning sent two platoons to the Honinghutje bridge. Another battalion advanced north from the drop zone to occupy the northern prong of the wooded ridge line, a three-and-a-half-mile stretch extending from the southeastern fringe of Nijmegen past Hotel Berg en Dal. This the battalion had accomplished by nightfall of D Day "without serious resist-

ance." [43] Occupying the village of Beek at the foot of the ridge and thereby physically cutting the important Kleve–Nijmegen highway would have to await the next day.

In the hands of the remaining battalion of the 508th Parachute Infantry rested a special destiny. This battalion, the 1st, commanded by Lt. Col. Shields Warren, Jr., represented the 82d Airborne Division's best chance for a cheap and rapid capture of the highway bridge over the sprawling Waal River at Nijmegen.[44]

After receiving General Gavin's prejump orders in regard to the Nijmegen bridge, Colonel Lindquist had earmarked Colonel Warren's battalion as one of two battalions from which he intended to choose one to move to the bridge, depending upon the developing situation. General Gavin's understanding, as recalled later, was that Warren's battalion was to move "without delay after landing." [45] On the other hand, Colonel Lindquist's understanding, also as recalled later, was that no battalion was to go for the bridge

---

[42] 505th Prcht Inf AAR.

---

[43] 508th Prcht Inf AAR.

[44] Although extensive combat interviews were conducted with personnel of the 508th Parachute Infantry, they are inexplicably missing from Department of the Army files. The story has been reconstructed from unit records; Gavin's letters to Westover and OCMH; letters to OCMH from Colonel Warren, 5 July 1955, Colonel Lindquist, 9 September 1955, Col. Thomas J. B. Shanley formerly Executive Officer, 508th Parachute Infantry, 2 Sep 55, and Rev. Bestebreurtje, 25 Oct 56; a postwar interview with Colonel Lindquist by Westover, 14 Sep 45, copy in 82d Airborne Division Combat Interview file; and Westover, The American Divisions in Operation MARKET, a preliminary narrative written in the European theater shortly after the war, copy in OCMH. Captain Westover had access to all the combat interviews when writing his narrative.

[45] Gavin Ltr to Westover.

until the regiment had secured its other objectives, that is to say, not until he had established defenses protecting his assigned portion of the high ground and the northern part of the division glider landing zone.[46] Instead of moving immediately toward the Nijmegen bridge, Colonel Warren's battalion was to take an "assigned initial objective" in the vicinity of De Ploeg, a suburb of Nijmegen a mile and a quarter southeast of the city astride the Nijmegen–Groesbeek highway.[47] Colonel Warren was to organize this objective for defense, tying in with the battalion near Hatert and the other near Hotel Berg en Dal, and then was to "be prepared to go into Nijmegen later."[48]

The assembly and movement to De Ploeg took approximately three and a half hours. After organizing a defense of the objective, Colonel Warren about 1830 sent into Nijmegen a patrol consisting of a rifle platoon and the battalion intelligence section. This patrol was to make an aggressive reconnaissance, investigate reports from Dutch civilians that only eighteen Germans guarded the big bridge, and, if possible, capture the south end of the bridge. Unfortunately, the patrol's radio failed to function so that Colonel Warren was to get no word from the patrol until the next morning.[49]

As darkness approached, General Gavin ordered Colonel Lindquist "to delay not a second longer and get the bridge as quickly as possible with Warren's battalion."[50] Colonel Warren, in the mean-

time, had found a Dutch civilian who said he could lead the battalion to the bridge and en route check with resistance headquarters within the city for the latest developments on German strength at the bridge.[51] Colonel Warren directed Companies A and B to rendezvous at a point just south of Nijmegen at 1900 and move with the Dutch guide to the bridge. Company C, a platoon of which already had gone into the city as a patrol, was withheld in regimental reserve.

Although Company A reached the rendezvous point on time, Company B "got lost en route."[52] After waiting until about 2000, Colonel Warren left a guide for Company B and moved through the darkness with Company A toward the edge of the city. Some seven hours after H-Hour, the first real move against the Nijmegen bridge began.

At the edge of the city Company A halted again while a patrol searched the first buildings. Finding no Germans, the company continued for several blocks up a main thoroughfare, the dark, deserted Groesbeekscheweg. As the scouts neared a traffic circle surrounding a landscaped circular park near the center of Nijmegen, the Keizer Karel Plein, from which a mall-like park led northeast toward the Nijmegen bridge, a burst of automatic weapons fire came from the circle. The time was about two hours before midnight.

As Company A formed to attack, the men heard the noise of an approaching motor convoy emanating from a side street on the other side of the traffic circle. Enemy soldiers noisily dismounted.

---

[46] Lindquist Ltr to OCMH. See also letters from Shanley, Warren, and Bestebreurtje.
[47] 508th Prcht Inf AAR.
[48] Warren Ltr to OCMH.
[49] Ibid. See also Shanley Ltr to OCMH.
[50] Gavin Ltr to OCMH. See also letters from Lindquist and Shanley.

[51] Warren Ltr to OCMH.
[52] Msg, Harness Red to CO (no time signed, but sent to div hq at 2315, 17 Sep), 508th Prcht Inf Jnl file, 17 Sep–16 Oct 44.

No one could have said so with any finality at the time, but the chance for an easy, speedy capture of the Nijmegen bridge had passed. This was all the more lamentable because in Nijmegen during the afternoon the Germans had had nothing more than the same kind of "mostly low quality" [53] troops encountered at most other places on D Day.

Although the enemy commander, Field Marshal Model, had entrusted *Corps Feldt* under *Wehrkreis VI* with responsibility for Nijmegen, he apparently had recognized the dire necessity of getting a more mobile and effective force to the Nijmegen bridge immediately. Sometime during late afternoon or early evening of 17 September Model had dispatched an advance guard from the *9th SS Panzer Division's Reconnaissance Battalion* to defend the highway bridge. The commander of the *II SS Panzer Corps,* General Bittrich, in turn directed the entire *10th SS Panzer Division* to move to Nijmegen. The main effort of the *II SS Panzer Corps,* General Bittrich believed, should be directed toward thwarting the Americans at Nijmegen, whereupon the British at Arnhem might be defeated in detail. He directed the first arrivals of the *10th SS Panzer Division*—an infantry battalion and an engineer company—to relieve the *9th SS Panzer Division's Reconnaissance Battalion,* which presumably then was to return to Arnhem. [54]

The *9th SS Reconnaissance Battalion*

apparently had gotten across the Neder Rijn at Arnhem before British paratroopers reached the Arnhem bridge, but the men of the *10th SS Panzer Division* were too late. They subsequently crossed the Neder Rijn at a ferry near Huissen, southeast of Arnhem. Whether it was troops of the *9th* or of the *10th SS Panzer Division* which reached the Keizer Karel Plein was conjectural, though probably it was the former. What mattered was that they had arrived in time to stop the first American thrust toward the Nijmegen bridge. [55]

When Company A attacked at the traffic circle, the SS troops counterattacked. The men of Company A became so disorganized in the darkness that they might have had to withdraw altogether had not Company B arrived to help stabilize the situation.

While Colonel Warren reported news of the encounter to his regimental commander and asked reinforcement by Company C, the commander of Company A, Capt. Jonathan E. Adams, Jr., received a report from Dutch civilians that the control mechanism for demolishing the highway bridge was housed in the main post office, only a few blocks north of the Keizer Karel Plein. Captain Adams himself led a patrol of platoon size to destroy the mechanism. Though guards at the post office put up a fight, the paratroopers forced the building and destroyed what they took to be the control apparatus. Getting back to the traffic circle was another proposition. The Germans had closed in behind them. For three days these men and sympathetic civilians were to hold out at the post office until relief came.

---

[53] 82d Abn Div G-2 to Br Abn Corps G-2, 1810, 17 Sep 44, 82d Abn Div G-2 Jnl file, 17-21 Sep 44.

[54] Mng Sitrep, *A Gp B,* 0400, 18 Sep 44, *A Gp B KTB, Letzte Meldung;* Minutes of Hitler Conference, 17 Sep 44 (Fragment No. 42); Bittrich Questionnaire, OCMH.

[55] *Ibid.*

In the meantime Colonel Warren had tried to get a new attack moving toward the highway bridge; but this the Germans thwarted just before dawn with another sharp counterattack. While the counterattack was in progress, General Gavin arrived at the battalion command post. Noting that the companies had become "very heavily engaged in close quarters in city streets under very difficult circumstances," General Gavin directed that the battalion "withdraw from close proximity to the bridge and reorganize." [56] This was to mark the end of this particular attempt to take the Nijmegen bridge.

A new attack to gain the bridge grew out of an early morning conference between General Gavin and Colonel Lindquist. In considering alternate means of getting the bridge with the limited forces available, it appeared possible that one company still might succeed if the advance was made along the less constricted southeastern and eastern fringe of Nijmegen. The unit designated was Company G, part of the 3d Battalion, 508th, under Lt. Col. Louis G. Mendez, Jr., which was defending the three-and-a-half-mile stretch of high ground centered on Berg en Dal. Company G already had occupied Hill 64, little more than a mile from the south end of the highway bridge.[57]

At 0745 on 18 September, D plus 1, Company G under Capt. Frank J. Novak started toward the bridge. Civilians showered the paratroopers with fruit and flowers as the advance began; but closer to the bridge the crowds markedly thinned. The reason soon became apparent. From dug-in positions about a small traffic circle south of a common, the Hunner Park, which embraces the southern approaches to the bridge, the Germans lay in wait. The center of the defense was a historic observation tower, the Belvedere, and medieval walls surrounding it.

Company G was but two blocks from the Maria Plein when the Germans opened fire. With small arms and antiaircraft guns ranging from 20- to 88-mm., they searched the streets opening onto the circle.

Captain Novak quickly deployed his men and attacked. Storming into the teeth of the enemy fire, they gained a position only a block from the traffic circle. German artillery fire emanating from the north bank of the Waal reinforced the defense. The men of Company G could go no farther.

Reinforcement of Company G appeared inadvisable. The battalion commander, Colonel Mendez, could send no help without jeopardizing his defense of the high ground in the vicinity of Hotel Berg en Dal. The regimental commander, Colonel Lindquist, had only a company in reserve, and this company probably would be needed to clear one of the division's glider landing zones for a glider lift that was scheduled to arrive almost momentarily. Some consideration apparently was given at division headquarters to reinforcing the troops in Nijmegen with a portion of the 505th Parachute Infantry, one battalion of which was in division reserve in the woods west of Groesbeek, but it was not done.[58]

---

[56] Gavin Ltr to Westover.

[57] Gavin Ltr to OCMH. Colonel Mendez recalled after the war that he directed Company G's attack "on his own responsibility." Statement by CO, 3d Bn, 508th Prcht Inf, to Hist Off, 8 Sep 44, as cited by Westover, The American Divisions in Operation MARKET, Ch III, p. 38.

[58] 82d Abn Div G-3 to CO 508, 18 Sep (no time signed, but msg entered in jnl file at 1150), 508th Prcht Inf Jnl file, 17 Sep-16 Oct 44. See also Shanley Ltr to OCMH.

At 1400 on 18 September Colonel Mendez ordered Company G to withdraw from Nijmegen to Hill 64. Nijmegen and the highway bridge so vital to relief of the British airborne troops farther north at Arnhem remained in German hands.[59] Of three attempts to capture the bridge on D-Day and D plus 1, one of patrol size had failed because it was too weak and lacked communications; another of two-company size, because the Germans had had time to reinforce their garrison; and the third of company size, for the same reason. Though small, at least two of these attacks conceivably might have succeeded except for their timing. No attempt to seize the railway bridge over the Waal at Nijmegen had been made.[60]

The problem of the glider landing zones, which appeared to be one of the reasons why no stronger effort was made at Nijmegen, had grown out of two factors: the location of the landing zones and the 82d Airborne Division's shortage of infantry in relation to its numerous and widely dispersed objectives. The landing zones were situated near the bottom of the eastern slopes of the ridge between Groesbeek and the Reichswald. Though the landing zones had been fairly well cleared on D-Day, not enough infantry could be spared to hold them in strength. Beginning soon after daylight on D plus 1, the equivalent of two understrength Ger-

man battalions began to infiltrate from the Reichswald onto the landing zones. Some of this infiltration reached the proportions of strong local attacks, one of which encircled a company of the 508th Parachute Infantry near Wyler and others which exerted troublesome pressure against easternmost contingents of the 505th Parachute Infantry. The enemy troops probably were advance guards of *Corps Feldt's 406th (Landesschuetzen) Division*, only "line-of-communications" troops, as American intelligence soon fathomed, but supported by flak wagons mounting 20-mm. antiaircraft guns.[61]

Since Allied tow planes and gliders took off from England at 1000, their arrival soon after midday was almost a certainty. In preparation, Colonel Lindquist released the reserve company of Colonel Warren's battalion of the 508th Parachute Infantry to battalion control and directed that the company secure a line of departure overlooking the northern landing zone. After the other two companies had withdrawn from the Keizer Karel Plein in Nijmegen, they moved to assist in the clearing operation. The 505th Parachute Infantry scheduled one company to clear the other landing zone in an attack to begin at 1240.

As events developed, German pressure against the 505th Parachute Infantry was so strong that the designated company was not freed for its attack without some difficulty. Fortunately, resistance on the landing zone itself proved light and disorganized. The southern landing zone was cleared with a half hour to spare.

Opposition on the northern landing

---

[59] To anyone following progress of the fight for the bridge in the 82d Airborne Division G-2 Journal, withdrawal must have come as something of a surprise. Three separate entries in the journal early on 18 September—all erroneous—reported "patrols on Nijmegen bridge."

[60] Reconnaissance patrols were to move toward both bridges during the night of D plus 1. 82d Abn Div G-2 Jnl file, 19 Sep 44.

[61] Evng Sitrep, *A Gp B*, 2000, 18 Sep 44, *A Gp B KTB, Letzte Meldung;* 82d Abn Div G-2 Rpt 92 and Jnl, 18 Sep 44.

zone was stiffer. Beginning at 1300, after the troops had made a forced march of eight miles from Nijmegen, the attack by Colonel Warren's battalion might have stalled in the face of intense small arms and flak gun fire had not the paratroopers charged the defenders at a downhill run. At the last minute, the Germans panicked. It was a photo finish, a "movie-thriller sight of landing gliders on the LZ as the deployed paratroops chased the last of the Germans from their 16 20-mm. guns." [62] The enemy lost 50 men killed and 150 captured. Colonel Warren's battalion incurred but 11 casualties.

The gliders had been flown in via the northern air route over the Dutch islands. Totaling 450, they brought primarily the last of General Gavin's artillery, one parachute and two glider battalions. Following the gliders by about twenty minutes, a flight of 135 B–24 bombers dropped resupply south of Groesbeek. A good drop pattern resulted in an estimated recovery of about 80 percent.

Involving not only the 82d Airborne Division but the British and the 101st Airborne Division as well, these new landings on D plus 1 gave the Germans a jolt. This was in spite of the fact that the omniscient Hitler had predicted the course. "Tomorrow," the Fuehrer had noted at his D-Day conference, "they will surely come back; they are making such a fuss—appeal to the Dutch, and all that . . . ." [63] The possibility which disturbed the Germans on the scene was that the new landings might mean arrival of additional Allied divisions. Several hours passed before German intelligence determined the true nature of the reinforcement.

The gliders having arrived, the 82d Airborne Division by midafternoon of D plus 1 was in a position to focus attention upon gaining a bridge over the Waal at Nijmegen. Though enemy pressure from the Reichswald had been troublesome, it was more a "feeling out" than actual attack. "The intent was," noted the 82d Airborne Division G–2, Colonel Winton, "to apply pressure and gain information." [64] Noteworthy German counteraction had not developed elsewhere, except in the neighborhood of the 505th Parachute Infantry's reserve battalion west of Groesbeek where two somewhat bizarre incidents had occurred. After nightfall of D-Day, a German-operated railroad train had slipped out of Nijmegen and escaped through Groesbeek to the east. Before daylight on D plus 1, another train had tried it. This one the paratroopers knocked out with a bazooka and small arms fire. Though many of the Germans aboard escaped into the surrounding woods, they eventually were rounded up, sometimes only after hot little skirmishes.

A battalion each of the 505th and 508th Infantry Regiments had acted offensively during the day to improve the division's over-all position. A battalion of the 505th had cleared the village of Mook, southeast of Heumen, on the important Venlo–Nijmegen highway. Colonel Mendez' battalion of the 508th had secured Beek, at the foot of the ridge below Hotel Berg on Dal, and established roadblocks there astride the Kleve–Nijmegen highway.

If the few instances where casualties were recorded could be taken as indica-

---

[62] 508th Prcht Inf AAR.
[63] Minutes of Hitler Conference, 17 Sep 44 (Fragment No. 42).

[64] 82d Abn Div G–2 Rpt 92, 18 Sep 44.

tion, American losses had been-light. On D-Day, for example, one battalion of the 504th Parachute Infantry had incurred 19 casualties. On D plus 1 the entire 505th Parachute Infantry had lost 63 men. The battalion of the 508th Parachute Infantry which was defending near Hatert lost but 7 men wounded on D-Day. Enemy killed were an estimated 150; German prisoners, 885.[65]

The situation had been relatively quiet in the sector of the 504th Parachute Infantry between the Maas–Waal Canal and the Maas River and in the bridgehead south of the river, though some concern still existed that the enemy might move from the west against the 504th. Neither had the enemy been markedly troublesome in the sector of the battalion of the 508th Parachute Infantry, which was just across the canal near Hatert. Parts of both these units, General Gavin must have reasoned, might be used in a new attack against the Nijmegen highway bridge.

In response to a request from General Browning, the British Airborne Corps commander, General Gavin in midafternoon of 18 September outlined a plan for seizing the bridge that night. He intended using a battalion of the 504th Parachute Infantry "in conjunction with" the 508th Parachute Infantry to envelop the bridge from the east and west.[66]

General Browning at first approved this plan. Then, "on giving it more thought, [and] in view of the situation in the 30th Corps, he felt that the retention of the high ground S[outh] of Nijmegen was of

greater importance, and directed that the primary mission should be to hold the high gr[ound] and retain its position W[est] of the Maas–Waal Canal." General Gavin thereupon apparently called off the projected attack; for he "issued an order for the defence of the position."[67]

The "situation in the 30th Corps" to which General Browning referred certainly represented no incentive for urgency at Nijmegen. At this time, contact between the ground column and the 101st Airborne Division at Eindhoven still was two and a half hours away. It might be a long time before the ground column reached Nijmegen.

Whether the prospects of difficulty in holding the high ground in the 82d Airborne Division's sector justified delay in renewing the attack at Nijmegen, even in view of the "situation in the 30th Corps," was a matter for conjecture. Few concrete indications that the Reichswald was rife with German armor, or even infantry, had developed. Civilians had told men of the 505th Parachute Infantry on D-Day that the Germans had no armor in the Reichswald. Patrols from the 505th had found no armor. One patrol reported that the "high ground" in the Reichswald was unoccupied. "Towers are empty, woods are tank obstacles—too thick."[68] The 82d Airborne Division's G–2 estimated that the enemy had "probably two battalions of mixed L[ine] of C[ommunications] Troops" in the Reichswald, though he modified this low evaluation by listing first among enemy capabilities the likelihood of continuing piecemeal attacks, "but in increasing strength,"

[65] *Ibid.;* 504th and 505th Prcht Inf AARs; 508th Prcht Inf Jnl file, 17 Sep–16 Oct 44.
[66] 82d Abn Div CofS Jnl, 0700, 19 Sep 44, reporting a conf held at 1530, 18 Sep 44. See also Ltr, Gavin to OCMH, 8 Jul 55.

[67] *Ibid.*
[68] S–1 Jnl, 2040, 17 Sep, in 505th Prcht Inf AAR.

from the forest.[69] No tangible incidents of armor in action had developed; most vehicles reported as tanks turned out to be flak wagons.[70]

On the other hand, General Gavin recalled later that the "Dutch underground chief" told him during the morning of 18 September that "the Germans were in strength both with armor and infantry in the Reichswald area."[71] The division intelligence section noted early on 18 September that "civilians continue to report massing of German troops in the Reichswald Forest."[72] In late afternoon of the same day ninety-seven Spitfires and Mustangs of the British 2d Tactical Air Force bombed and strafed the Reichswald in response to a request from General Gavin.[73] The 82d's airborne artillery delivered harassing fire on the forest from time to time.[74]

No matter what the true situation in the Reichswald—which no one could have

known with any certainty at this point— General Gavin endorsed the corps commander's view that the best practice for the moment was to focus upon holding what he had. General Gavin's confidence in the ability of his paratroopers made the decision easier. "To those on the ground," he recalled later, "there was no doubt . . . that the bridge would be captured and it would be captured in time to relieve the Arnhem forces." General Gavin's earlier experience in airborne combat reinforced this view. He recalled later: "Experience indicated that we could expect a linkup in about two days and we felt quite sure of one in three. If, therefore, by the end of the third day the bridge were in my hands, and I had fought a good battle with whatever might develop in the remainder of the area, I felt that I would have been fortunate enough to have done a good job as planned."[75] On the basis of this theory, General Gavin had another full day in which to tackle the Germans at Nijmegen.

Perhaps the ultimate test of how urgent was the need for the bridge at Nijmegen lay not in the "situation in the 30th Corps" but in the status of the British airborne troops farther north at Arnhem. But this no one at Nijmegen—including both General Gavin and General Browning—knew much about. The only report that had been received on the fighting at Arnhem had arrived through the 505th Parachute Infantry at 1040 on 18 September. An intelligence unit of the Netherlands Interior Forces, located in this regiment's sector, had a telephone line to Arnhem. Because the telephone network was one connecting power stations and

---

[69] 82d Abn Div G–2 Rpt 92, 18 Sep 44.

[70] 82d Abn Div G–2 Jnl, 17–18 Sep 44.

[71] Ltr, Gavin to OCMH, 8 Jul 55. General Gavin's recollection is supported by Bestebreurtje, letter to OCMH, 25 October 1956.

[72] 82d Abn Div G–2 Jnl, entry dtd 0515, 18 Sep 44.

[73] A detailed analysis of tactical air support in Operation MARKET may be found in Weapons Systems Evaluation Group, A Historical Study of Some World War II Airborne Operations, WSEG Staff Study No. 3, pp. 160–64, copy in OCMH files. The incident on D plus 1 was one of the few instances, other than on D Day, when tactical air made any substantial contribution to direct support of U.S. troops on the ground in this operation. Adverse weather was partly responsible. Also, technical problems prevented aircraft of the 2d Tactical Air Force from operating while Eighth Air Force fighters were escorting the various lifts of airborne troops and supplies. The effect of these two factors resulted on occasion in a local German air superiority, a surprising paradox in view of Allied air superiority in the theater.

[74] See 504th Prcht Inf S–3 Jnl, 18 Sep 44.

[75] Ltr, Gavin to OCMH, 17 Jan 54.

waterworks and messages over it had to be disguised as technical messages concerning the operations of these public utilities, the message about the fighting at Arnhem was necessarily brief.

The 505th Parachute Infantry noted the message this way: "Dutch Report Germans Winning over British at Arnhem." [76]

The Red Devils at Arnhem

For all the lack of details, the message from the Dutch had not failed to state the situation as it actually existed with the 1st British Airborne Division at Arnhem. Having jumped into the quickest enemy build-up of any of the three Allied divisions, the paratroopers soon had found themselves in a bad way. The Germans *were* winning over the British at Arnhem.[77]

The British misfortunes had not begun with the D-Day landings. Like the two American divisions, men of the 1st Airborne Division—who called themselves Red Devils—experienced phenomenally successful flights, drops, and glider landings. Not an aircraft was lost as 331 planes and 319 gliders dropped or deposited their loads with almost 100-percent success on the correct drop and landing zones. Unlike the Americans, the British sent their gliders in first. They brought an air-landing brigade, which was to

protect the drop and landing zones, plus a light regiment of artillery and lesser anti-tank, medical, and reconnaissance units. Close behind the gliders came a parachute brigade with the primary mission of seizing the highway bridge over the Neder Rijn at Arnhem.

The difficulties the British soon began to encounter arose not from any failure to achieve surprise. They were attributable to chance presence of General Bittrich's *II SS Panzer Corps* in assembly areas beyond the IJssel River a few miles east of Arnhem and to location of the British drop zones a long way from the objectives at Arnhem. Bowing to reputed difficulties of terrain and flak concentrations close to the city, the planning staffs had selected drop zones six to eight miles away, northwest of the suburb of Oosterbeek. By the time the parachutists could assemble and approach the bridge, four invaluable hours had passed.

The location of the drop and landing zones imposed an added burden in that the troops defending these zones could take no part in the main action. They would be tied up for three days until the three successive lifts had arrived. This meant that on D-Day only a brigade would be available for seizing and holding the main objectives. These objectives included not only the bridge at Arnhem but, as in the case of the 82d Airborne Division, high ground. This was the high ground north of Arnhem, its capture essential to fulfilling one of the 1st Airborne Division's missions of providing a bridgehead of sufficient size to enable the 30 Corps to pass through.

The Red Devils had not long to wait to experience the difficulties emanating both from the dispersion of effort and the presence of the SS panzer troops east of

---

[76] 82d Abn Div G–2 Jnl, entry dtd 1040, 18 Sep 44; Ltr, Bestebreurtje to OCMH.

[77] This account is based primarily on 1st Abn Div, Rpt on Opn MARKET, Pt. 1. See also FAAA, Opns in Holland; Hq Br Abn Corps, Allied Abn Opns in Holland; Boeree, The Truth About the Supposed Spy at Arnhem; Boeree, correspondence with the author, in OCMH files; and a colorful account in *By Air to Battle, the Official Account of the British Airborne Divisions* (London: His Majesty's Stationery Office, 1945), pp. 93 ff.

Arnhem. Of three parachute battalions, two ran into serious difficulty almost at the outset. One heading northeast toward the high ground, the other moving east toward Arnhem, they both encountered armored reconnaissance patrols or advance guards of the *9th SS Panzer Division*. When darkness came on D-Day, the two British battalions still were held up, one near Wolfheze Station, about two miles northwest of Oosterbeek, the other on the western outskirts of Oosterbeek. This left but one British battalion moving toward the vital bridge over the Neder Rijn.

Commanded by Lt. Col. J. D. Frost, this battalion bypassed the Germans at Oosterbeek by taking a secondary road close to the river. En route toward Arnhem, one company detoured to capture the railroad bridge, only to see the Germans blow it. "It seemed," said one man, "to curl back on us . . . ."[78] Another company became involved in a fire fight in outlying buildings of Arnhem. This left but one company and the battalion headquarters to sneak through back streets toward the north end of the highway bridge. At 2030 this little band under Colonel Frost seized the north end. The bridge still was intact.

During the night another company also broke through to the bridge, but of the third, only remnants escaped from the fight in Arnhem. Colonel Frost's force at the highway bridge numbered at peak strength about 500.

Colonel Frost tried twice that night to capture the south end of the bridge, once by attacking across the bridge and again by sending a platoon across the river in rowboats. Both attempts failed. As day-light came of D plus 1, the men holed up in buildings about the north end to begin a dogged defense of their precarious grip on this vital prize.

Not long after daybreak (18 September) the enemy orders and preparations of the night before began to show effect. From the west, *Division von Tettau*, the haphazard collection of rear echelon and regional defense units belonging to the *Armed Forces Commander Netherlands*, attacked the air-landing brigade which was defending the drop and landing zones near Wolfheze Station. From the east, the bulk of the *9th SS Panzer Division*, and possibly some of the *10th SS*, by-passed Colonel Frost's little band at the highway bridge, pushed through Arnhem, and attacked westward, apparently in an attempt to link with *Division von Tettau*.[79]

The presence of the SS troops thwarted reinforcement of Colonel Frost at the bridge. Spurred by radio appeals for help, the two battalions of the British parachute brigade which had been held up on D-Day sideslipped to the south early on D plus 1 to try to reach the bridge. As they entered the western fringe of Arnhem, they ran head on into the attacking Germans. This rather than new airborne landings in reality stalled the German attack. Yet the meeting engagement brought high British casualties. Entire companies were cut off, and only shattered remnants survived.[80] In late afternoon the remaining men of one

[79] Daily Sitrep, *A Gp B*, 0200, 19 Sep 44, *A Gp B KTB, Tagesmeldungen.*

[80] With one encircled group was the brigade commander, Brig. G. W. Lathbury. Seriously wounded, he had to be left behind. Many days later, after having been treated for wounds at a German-controlled hospital, Brigadier Lathbury escaped and eventually led some 120 Red Devils through enemy lines to gain the south bank of the Neder Rijn. See *By Air to Battle*, pp. 130–131.

---

[78] *By Air to Battle*, p. 102.

battalion, numbering about 140, launched a last effort to reach the bridge. They could make no headway.

Despite *Division von Tettau*'s pressure against the air-landing brigade holding the drop and landing zones, the British commander, Maj. Gen. R. C. Urquhart, released an understrength battalion to go to the aid of the parachute brigade. The battalion could not penetrate a German cordon that had closed behind the paratroopers.

Delayed by the same soupy weather in England that had held up second lifts of the American divisions, the British lift on D plus 1 arrived about 1500. With this lift came the remainder of General Urquhart's division, including the other parachute brigade and last contingents of the air-landing brigade. Although this fresh parachute brigade was scheduled to capture high ground north of Arnhem, General Urquhart immediately diverted a battalion eastward to assist the hard-pressed men that were trying to reach Colonel Frost. Another battalion attempted the original mission, while General Urquhart withheld the third as a reserve.

The fresh paratroopers could make only slight inroads on the SS troops. Not until early the next morning (D plus 2, 19 September) did they reach the remnants of the other battalions in the edge of Arnhem. Even then the composite force could make no appreciable gains in the direction of the highway bridge. Eventually they had to give up. Those who remained, no more than 200 men out of three battalions of paratroopers and one battalion from the air-landing brigade, filtered back after nightfall on D plus 2 through the German cordon to the vicinity of the drop and landing zones.

Their inability to reach the highway bridge was all the more frustrating because General Urquhart still had radio communication with Colonel Frost and knew that the gallant little band at the north end of the bridge still held out.

The remainder of General Urquhart's division had been fighting in the meantime against increasing odds to hold the drop and landing zones. Under strafing from German planes, shelling by mortars and artillery, and intense ground attacks from both *Division von Tettau* and the *II SS Panzer Corps*, the perimeter began to shrink. The only hope for immediate relief lay in the scheduled arrival during the afternoon of D plus 2 of the 1st Polish Parachute Brigade. Even this hope failed as the weather closed in. Only a few gliders and no additional paratroopers arrived.

As evidenced by the lack of information about the British situation at General Browning's headquarters near Nijmegen, General Urquhart's communications to the outside had failed. His radios were not strong enough to transmit successfully from the wooded and urban districts in which the British had to fight. General Urquhart thus had no way of notifying British bases in England not to drop the day's resupply on those of the drop zones the Germans had by this time overrun. As a result of this and of the weather, virtually all the resupply panniers dropped on D plus 2 fell into German hands. Critical shortages in food and ammunition were quickly manifest.

Pinning his hopes on arrival the next day of the 1st Polish Parachute Brigade or on an early juncture with the 30 Corps ground column, General Urquhart disposed his depleted forces about his perimeter and in other positions designed to maintain a corridor to the Neder Rijn at the site of a ferry near Heveadorp, southwest of Oosterbeek. Perhaps either the Polish paratroopers or the ground column might push reinforcements across the river at the ferry site. Because of the failure of communications, General Urquhart had no way of knowing that early arrival of the ground column still depended upon getting a bridge at Nijmegen.

CHAPTER VIII

Decision on the Ground

Those Germans who were barring the way at Nijmegen and who subsequently might oppose the ground column between Nijmegen and Arnhem obviously held the key to the outcome of Operation MARKET-GARDEN. Should they continue to deny a crossing of the Waal, the Red Devils near Arnhem might be systematically annihilated.

Spearheading the 30 Corps ground column, reconnaissance troops of the Guards Armoured Division linked with Colonel Tucker's 504th Parachute Infantry at Grave at 0820 the morning of D plus 2, 19 September. (*See Map IV.*) Major formations of the British armor were not far behind. From that point priority of objectives within the sector of the 82d Airborne Division shifted unquestionably in the direction of the bridge at Nijmegen. Already at least thirty three hours behind schedule because of earlier delays south of Eindhoven and at Zon, the ground column had to have a way to get across the Waal.

Developments on D Plus 2 (*19 September*)

Holding the objectives the 82d Airborne Division already had taken would be facilitated by the artillery and antitank strength that arrived with the ground column. In keeping with this new situation, General Gavin adjusted his units. Part of the 504th Parachute Infantry

relieved the battalion of the 508th Parachute Infantry at Hatert and enabled this battalion to reinforce its parent regiment in defending the ridge line near Hotel Berg en Dal. Reducing defensive strength at the Maas bridge near Grave, General Gavin designated one battalion of the 504th as a new division reserve. The former reserve, the 2d Battalion, 505th Parachute Infantry, which had been located in the woods west of Groesbeek, was to drive for the Nijmegen highway bridge.

In early afternoon of D plus 2, 19 September, General Gavin met the commander of the British ground column, General Horrocks, and told him his plan to take the Nijmegen bridge. He intended immediately to commit the 2d Battalion, 505th Parachute Infantry, commanded by Lt. Col. B. H. Vandervoort, against the south end of the bridge and "as quickly as possible" to send another force across the Waal in boats to seize the north end. Since the paratroopers had not found any civilian boats to use, the British offered thirty-three canvas assault boats which were being carried in their engineer train and should be available early the next morning.[1]

---

[1] Ltr, Gavin to OCMH, 17 Jan 54. Gavin says twenty-eight boats, but most combat interviews say thirty-three. In addition to sources previously cited for the 82d Abn Div, see, for this period, 21 A Gp, Operation MARKET-GARDEN, 17–26 Sep 44.

In the meantime, the attack against the south end of the bridge was to begin. To assist the 2d Battalion, 505th, the British provided a company of infantry and a battalion of tanks of the Guards Armoured Division. Artillery of both the Guards Armoured and 82d Airborne Divisions lent support.

A small component of this force fought toward the south end of the railroad bridge over the Waal. Men of Company D, 505th Parachute Infantry, commanded by 1st Lt. Oliver B. Carr, Jr., climbed aboard five British tanks and five other armored vehicles and at 1500 struck direct for the bridge through the western fringe of Nijmegen. They moved unopposed until hit by sporadic rifle fire in railroad marshaling yards about a thousand yards south of the railroad bridge. Dismounting, Lieutenant Carr's men continued under cover of fire from the British guns until, at a point less than 500 yards short of the bridge, small arms and 20-mm. fire in serious proportions blazed from a common off the right flank between the station and the railroad bridge. Though the infantry and tanks tried together through the rest of the afternoon, they could make no progress. At last an enemy 88 knocked out the lead British tank. The first attempt to take the railroad bridge had failed.

The main attack against the south end of the highway bridge had begun concurrently. Following generally the same route through the eastern fringe of Nijmegen taken the day before by Captain Novak's Company G, the paratroopers, British infantry, and tanks met no resistance at first. Then the story became merely a variation on what had happened to Captain Novak and his men.

Approaching within 300 yards of the small traffic circle at the edge of Hunner Park, the force split. One American company and several British tanks veered to the left; the British infantry, the remaining American paratroopers, and the rest of the tanks to the right. At about the same time, the Germans at the traffic circle began to react. Each street radiating from the traffic circle became a deadly field of fire. Bullets and shells interlocked at street intersections.

On the left, Company F under Capt. Hubert S. Bass inched toward the park through incessant fire until at last stymied by a log barricade which the British tanks could not pass. On the right, the British infantry, the rest of the tanks, and Company E under 1st Lt. James J. Smith ploughed through deadly fire to come within a hundred yards of the circle. Here an antitank gun knocked out the lead tank. The fire grew more intense. When three more tanks were hit, the remaining armor and the infantry had to pull back. Though they tried other maneuvers through the afternoon—including blasting a path through buildings and advancing from rooftop to rooftop, the paratroopers could not negotiate the last few yards to the traffic circle.

Night came. Firing on both sides gradually died down. The fourth try for the south end of the highway bridge had failed.

The afternoon of fighting in Nijmegen prompted the 82d Airborne Division's intelligence section to revise upward earlier estimates of German strength in the city. The G–2 believed now that about 500 top-quality SS troops held the highway bridge alone. They had support, he estimated, from an 88-mm. gun on the traffic circle, a 37-mm. and four 47-mm. guns in Hunner Park, a number of mortars, and considerable artillery north of the Waal.[2]

Elsewhere in the 82d Airborne Division's sector, D plus 2 was "a quieter day."[3] Through most of the day the enemy had nothing in the Reichswald but *Corps Feldt's 406th (Landesschuetzen) Division* with but four battalions totaling about 500 men combat strength.[4] When concentrated against an isolated outpost or in defense of a strong natural position, these Germans nevertheless could make a stiff fight of it. To this men of Company A, 508th Parachute Infantry, could attest after fighting through the afternoon to secure an eminence called Devil's Hill. This was Hill 75.9, a high point east of Hotel Berg en Dal overlooking the Kleve–Nijmegen highway. In a determined charge covering 200 yards, Company A drove the Germans from the summit, but the enemy recovered on the slopes and counterattacked repeatedly with the support of eight machine guns. By nightfall Company A controlled the hill at a cost of seven wounded and ten killed, but so persistently did the Germans infiltrate during the night that another company had to flush the area the next morning.

In the meantime, Company B had less difficulty securing the village of Wyler, a mile and a half to the southeast. At the end of D plus 2, the 508th Parachute Infantry had firm control of the Kleve–Nijmegen highway at three points: Wyler, Devil's Hill, and Beek.[5]

Another event on D plus 2 that bore heavily upon the fighting was continued bad weather. So inclement was the weather that little resupply could be effected and the 325th Glider Infantry, scheduled to arrive on D plus 2, could not be flown in. This situation was to prevail for several days. Since General Gavin now was diverting much of his strength to Nijmegen, the lack of the glider regiment left an acute shortage of infantry that was heightened by the casualties the parachute battalions had incurred in three days of fighting. Company A, 508th, for example, in the attack on Devil's Hill had but 2 officers and 42 men. The commanders even moved 450 glider pilots into the line, a measure that to many of the paratroopers underscored the shortage of infantry.[6]

During the night General Gavin designated Colonel Tucker's 504th Parachute Infantry, less two companies defending bridges over the Maas and the Maas–Waal Canal, to make the amphibious assault across the Waal River upon which the main hope for getting a bridge at Nijmegen rested. Because the canvas assault boats were not expected to arrive before noon the next day, D plus 3, 20

---

[2] 82d Abn Div G–2 Sitrep, 19 Sep 44.
[3] 505th Prcht Inf AAR.
[4] Evg Sitrep, *A Gp B,* 19 Sep 44, *A Gp B KTB, Letzte Meldung.*
[5] 508th Prcht Inf AAR.

[6] Although quick to give credit to the glider pilots as pilots and to many as individual ground fighters, neither the 82d nor 101st Airborne Divisions had any real praise for the pilots acting collectively in tactical ground units. Rapport and Northwood, *Rendezvous With Destiny,* page 318, call glider pilots "the most uninhibited individualists in the Army." Much of the difficulty lay in that American pilots received only a minimum of ground training and had no tactical organization once they had delivered their loads. The subject is discussed in detail in Houston, Airborne Operations, Chapter VII, and in Warren, *Airborne Operations in World War II,* pages 152–53.

September, the crossing was set for 1400. In the meantime, in early morning of D plus 3, the 504th Parachute Infantry and two squadrons of tanks from the Guards Armoured Division set out to clear the south bank of the Waal in the vicinity of the designated crossing site. This was near the juncture of the Maas–Waal Canal and the Waal about a mile north-west of the Nijmegen railway bridge.

This maneuver was in process and Colonel Vandervoort's battalion had re-newed the attack toward the south end of the Nijmegen highway bridge when the Reichswald suddenly developed into some-thing of what it had been supposed to be. The fighting that ensued threatened for a time to upset the scheduled events at Nijmegen.

The change in the status of the Reichs-wald had begun during the preceding night with arrival of the first units of General Meindl's *II Parachute Corps,* which eventually was to assume control of the Nijmegen fighting from the German side. These first arrivals consisted of a Luftwaffe battalion and six battalions made up of heterogeneous elements banded together under the *II Parachute Corps,* plus a smattering of armor.[7] The strongest of these were two understrength battalions which had been training under the banner of the *6th Parachute Division.* Although American intelligence thought these two battalions the precursors of the entire *6th Parachute Division,* this division actually had been destroyed in Normandy and was not to be reconstituted until

October and would see no action until November.[8]

The addition of these hetereogeneous troops to those battalions operating under *Corps Feldt* nevertheless marked a sizable increase in German strength when meas-ured against the five understrength para-chute battalions responsible for holding almost twelve miles of front from Nijmegen to Wyler, thence southwest through Groesbeek to Riethorst and Mook. If concentrated adroitly, the Germans might attain a dangerous superiority in numbers, if not in fighting ability.

The German plan was to gain control of the high ground by means of two concentric attacks converging upon Groes-beek. Those battalions under *Corps Feldt* were to strike from the north and northeast against the ridge line near Hotel Berg en Dal and Wyler, while those under the *II Parachute Corps* attacked from the south and southeast in the vicinity of Mook and Riethorst.[9]

A barrage from 88's, *Nebelwerfer,* and mortars at about 1100 on 20 September signaled the start of the German attack at Riethorst and Mook. Because the 1st Battalion, 505th Parachute Infantry (Maj. Talton W. Long), was responsible for more than two miles of front in this vicinity, neither of these villages was de-fended by more than two platoons. By using one of the training battalions of the

---

[7] Mng and Evg Sitreps, *A Gp B,* 20 Sep 44, *A Gp B KTB, Letzte Meldung.* Mention of armor appears only in American accounts.

[8] MS # A–898, *Kampfhandlungen in Nord-frankreich 1944 der 6.Fallschirmjaeger-Division. II. Teil. Kaempfe an der Seine und Rueckzugs-bewegungen durch Nordfrankreich* (General-leutnant R. von Heyking, comdr, *6th Prcht Div*); MS # B–368, *Einsatz und Kampf der 6. Fallschirmjaeger-Division vom 19.11.1944 bis zur Kapitulation (10.5.1945)* (Generalmajor Rudolf Langhaeuser).

[9] Daily Sitrep, *A Gp B,* 0200, 21 Sep 44, *A Gp B KTB, Tagesmeldungen.*

6th Parachute Division at each village, the Germans attained a marked numerical superiority.

At Riethorst close support from ten 75-mm. pack howitzers enabled two platoons of Company B to stall the first German thrust. A second attack in mid-afternoon, featured by fire from a German tank that riddled American dugouts and machine gun positions, could not be repelled. Eventually the two platoons had to fall back on other positions on the high ground of the Kiekberg, north of the village. Here mortar fire and grenades rolled down the steep slopes helped to turn back every thrust.

At Mook the situation prompted more concern because of the proximity of the village to the bridge over the Maas–Waal Canal at Heumen, the bridge which was being used in the northward movement of the British ground column. By 1500 the Germans had overrun the outposts at Mook. When General Gavin arrived on the scene, he could detect little barring the way between Mook and the vital Heumen bridge. He hurriedly sent a messenger for help to the Guards Armoured Division's Coldstream Guards Group, a unit which had been designated as a reserve for the airborne division.[10] Apparently unknown to General Gavin, however, the battalion commander, Major Long, already had committed his battalion reserve, two platoons of infantry that even then were approaching Mook from the north. In late afternoon six British tanks joined these infantry platoons in a counterattack that gradually drove the Germans out of the village. By nightfall Mook again was in hand, and the Heumen bridge was safe. In the short-lived but intense ac-tion, Major Long's battalion had incurred casualties totaling 20 killed, 54 wounded, and 7 missing. A German withdrawal during the night and the next day facilitated re-establishment of roadblocks in Riethorst.[11]

The combat was none the less intense in the north where the Germans concentrated their efforts at Wyler and Beek. Despite close artillery support that broke up early strikes, two platoons of the 508th Parachute Infantry eventually had to abandon Wyler. This withdrawal posed no special concern, however, because of other positions on higher ground to the west. The point of real concern was at Beek where in early evening the Germans, in battalion strength, forced two platoons of parachute infantry to fall back up the hill toward Hotel Berg en Dal. General Gavin arrived here at the height of the crisis. "By shifting one platoon from one place to another, and disengaging it and shifting it again," General Gavin recalled later, "Colonel Mendez managed to contain the attack. If the Germans had had the wit to move even several hundred yards to the right they could have walked into the outskirts of Nijmegen almost unmolested . . . ."[12]

The fighting for Beek was to continue through most of the next day (D plus 4, 21 September) as the 508th Parachute Infantry sought to regain its positions. At times it looked as if the Germans might push beyond the village onto the high ground at Hotel Berg en Dal, but the paratroopers by nightfall had reoccupied Beek, not to relinquish it again.

---

[10] Ltr, Gavin to OCMH, 17 Jan 54.

[11] Combat Intervs with Long and personnel of Co B, 505th Prcht Inf.

[12] Ltr, Gavin to OCMH, 17 Jan 54.

The Fight for the Nijmegen Bridges

In stemming the counterattacks from the Reichswald, the paratroopers had been protecting a concurrent operation by their comrades in arms at Nijmegen that was one of the most daring and heroic in all the MARKET-GARDEN fighting. This was the 504th Parachute Infantry's assault crossing of the 400-yard width of the Waal River in order to get at the north ends of the rail and road bridges at Nijmegen.[13]

To provide more time for preparation, H Hour eventually was set back an hour to 1500 (D plus 3, 20 September). At this time the 504th's 3d Battalion under Maj. Julian A. Cook was to cross the river in thirty-three plywood and canvas assault boats from a point near a power plant a mile northwest of the Nijmegen railway bridge. Two squadrons of British tanks, a portion of another battalion of the 504th Parachute Infantry, and approximately 100 American and British artillery pieces were to provide fire support. The artillery was to lay down a fifteen-minute preparation, including a smoke screen on the north bank which was to be filled in where necessary by the tank guns firing white phosphorus. British planes were to bomb and strafe for thirty minutes before H-Hour. As soon as the 3d Battalion had crossed, the 1st Battalion under Major Harrison was to follow.

As assault crossing of the Waal would have been fraught with difficulties even had it not been so hastily contrived. Not only is the river wide, but the current is swift, running eight to ten miles an hour. The terrain on the south bank is flat, exposed to observation not only from the

opposite bank but from Nijmegen and towering girders of the railroad bridge. Though General Gavin had intended that the boats be loaded from a concealed position within the mouth of the Maas–Waal Canal, the current was so swift that boats launched at this point would have been carried too far downstream. The paratroopers would have to embark on the south bank of the river, east of the canal, in full view of the enemy.

Just what strength the Germans had on the north bank of the Waal, no one on the Allied side knew with any assurance. In reality, not long after General Gavin had ordered an assault crossing, Field Marshal Model had directed reinforcement of the SS troops in and north of Nijmegen with "additional forces and all available antitank weapons" sent south from Arnhem. This was to have been accomplished during the night of 19 September in time for a counterattack to be launched at dawn the next day, D plus 3.[14] The Germans en route to Nijmegen had to cross the Neder Rijn by the ferry near Huissen, because Colonel Frost's little band of British paratroopers still held the north end of the Arnhem bridge. Just how many "additional forces" arrived by this method was indefinite. In any event, the counterattack scheduled for dawn on D plus 3 never came off.

On the Allied side, tension rose as H-Hour for the assault crossing neared. The British boats were delayed. Not until twenty minutes before H-Hour, almost at the time the artillery preparation was to begin and even as rocket-firing Typhoons pummeled the north bank, did the paratroopers get their first look at the

---

[13] Combat interviews on this operation are available in considerable detail.

[14] Order, *A Gp B* to *Armed Forces Comdr Netherlands* and *II SS Pz Corps*, 2245, 19 Sep 44, *A Gp B KTB, Operationsbefehle.*

frail little craft. They were nineteen feet in length, of canvas with a reinforced plywood bottom. There were not thirty-three as expected; only twenty-six. To get all the men of the first-wave companies into the boats required dangerous overloading. Three engineers went along in each boat in order to paddle it back to the south bank for another load.

Fifteen minutes before H-Hour, the artillery began to pound the north bank. After ten minutes, the artillerymen changed from high explosive shells to white phosphorus, but an erratic wind generally denied an effective smoke screen. As the paratroopers struggled toward the water's edge with the assault craft on their shoulders, the launching site lay naked to German observation. German shellfire began to fall. Allied artillerymen shifted again to ten minutes of high explosive fire. The British tanks churned forward to blast the north bank with overhead fire. Mortars of the parachute regiment began to cough. The assault was on.

Almost from the start the crossing of the sprawling Waal was a nightmare. Because the water close to the south bank was shallow, the paratroopers had to wade far into the stream. Sometimes they climbed aboard where the water still was too shallow, then had to debark and push into deeper water. One boat pulled away, leaving a man standing behind, stuck in mud. As the man extricated himself, the current swept him into deep water. The commander of Company H, Capt. Carl W. Kappel, threw off his own heavy equipment, dived into the water to drag the man to safety, then regained his own boat.

Once the boats moved into deep water, the strong current seized them. Unfa-

miliar with the craft and buffeted by the current, the engineers and paratroopers could do little but point the boats toward the far shore and pray that the current would carry them across. At least one boat whirled crazily for a while in a dizzy circle. Any hope of maintaining unit organization upon touching the far shore was quickly dispelled.

All the while German fire rained upon the hapless craft. The bullets and shell fragments hitting the water reminded one man of "a school of mackerel on the feed." It was primarily fire from machine guns on the north bank and machine guns and 20-mm. antiaircraft guns on and near the railway bridge, but occasionally artillery fire from the north bank tormented the water. Bullets and shell fragments ripped the thin canvas on the assault boats. Some boats sank. One that was hit by mortar fire capsized only about twenty yards from the north bank, spilling its occupants into the water. Loaded down by an automatic rifle and heavy ammunition, Pvt. Joseph Jedlicka sank to the bottom in about eight feet of water. Holding his breath, he walked ashore without loss of equipment.

Almost incredibly, half of the boats made it. Exhausted, dizzy from the circumgyrations, some of the men were vomiting. They had gained the north bank, but only thirteen of the twenty-six boats remained to make the return trip for the next wave.

Virtually devoid of unit organization, the paratroopers rallied individually to the occasion. Killing more than fifty Germans near where the boats touched ground, the men dashed across an open field exposed to grazing fire to gain a diked road about 800 yards from the water's edge. Here they flushed Germans with bayonets, knocked out machine guns with hand grenades, and forged a temporary defensive line to await arrival of succeeding waves.

Still subject to German fire, engineers with the thirteen remaining assault boats started back to the south bank. Eleven boats made it. Through the course of the afternoon, engineers and paratroopers manning these eleven boats made six crossings of the Waal, bringing first the remainder of Major Cook's 3d Battalion and then Major Harrison's 1st Battalion.

The operations on the north bank developed in a series of courageous small-unit actions by squads and individuals belonging to different units. The companies had assigned objectives: Company H, for example, was to bypass an old Dutch fortress, Fort Hof van Holland, seize the juncture of the railroad and the Nijmegen–Arnhem highway, then drive southeast down the highway to take the north end of the highway bridge. Company I was to defend against enemy counteraction from the northwest and north and, if possible, take the north end of the railway bridge. Yet accomplishment of few of the missions could be attributed to one unit alone. The crossing of the Waal had been a hopper that had scrambled the men almost inextricably. The commander of Company G, for example, discovered in late afternoon that in addition to many of his own men he was commanding much of Company H, a platoon of Company I, and parts of the battalion communications and medical sections.

This handicap appeared to work little hardship on these veteran troops. The men saw jobs to be done and tried to do them. A platoon of Company H, scheduled to bypass Fort Hof van Holland, saw an opportunity to take the fort and silence machine guns and 20-mm. antiaircraft guns that were firing from its towers. Sgt. Leroy Richmond swam underwater to get across a moat surrounding the fort, then signalled his companions to follow across a narrow causeway. Small groups of both Companies H and I converged on the north end of the railway bridge where they set up BAR's to play fire on the bridge until reinforcements arrived from Company G and the 1st Battalion. Parts of Companies H and I also fought together toward the highway bridge. This vital prize still was intact.

In the meantime, in Nijmegen, Colonel Vandervoort's battalion of the 505th Parachute Infantry, augmented by British infantry and tanks, at last had begun to wear down the defenders of the south end of the highway bridge. A tank-infantry assault at 1620 by both British and Americans against the traffic circle south of Hunner Park finally began to produce results. Advancing through and on top of buildings and up fire-raked streets and alleys, the infantry charged. This time they made it. Bolstered by the British tanks, they plunged on almost without pause into Hunner Park. The fight neared an end.

The impending success in Nijmegen began to make trouble for the handful of Americans that were raking the north end of the railway bridge with fire, for the Germans began to retreat in wholesale numbers across the railway bridge. Not until the next day was it finally cleared of all enemy. Armament on this bridge alone totaled 34 machine guns, 2 20-mm. antiaircraft guns, and 1 88-mm. dual-purpose gun.

In Nijmegen, as the British tankers approached the south end of the highway bridge, they spotted an American flag floating atop what they took to be the north end of the bridge. This the British assumed to be an American signal that the tanks could cross. In reality, the paratroopers still were a few steps from the highway bridge; the flag was flying from the north end of the railroad span. Spraying shells and machine gun bullets into the girders, the British tankers nevertheless raced onto the bridge. Three tanks reached the far end. Three privates from Companies H and I, 504th Parachute Infantry, got on the north end of the bridge at almost the same moment. The time was 1910.

A lot of hard fighting remained before the toehold across the Waal could be deemed secure.[15] but as night fell on 20 September the fact was that the daring maneuver to gain the Waal bridges had succeeded. How and why in the light of all the obstacles could be explained only by the resourcefulness and courage of the men who did the job.

The cost had been high. During the afternoon, Major Cook's 3d Battalion alone lost 28 men killed, 1 missing, and 78 wounded. Total losses for the two battalions which crossed the Waal and Colonel Vandervoort's battalion in Nijmegen probably were about 200. Yet German losses must have been considerably more severe. On the railway bridge

alone the paratroopers subsequently counted 267 German dead.

Why the Germans failed to blow either the railway or highway bridge was a matter of some conjecture. Looking at it from the viewpoint of German commanders, the answer lay in German reluctance to admit until too late that these bridges—vital to taking effective countermeasures against the Allied landings—could not be held. Field Marshal Model himself had ordered that neither the bridges over the Waal nor those over the Neder Rijn were to be destroyed. Not until almost midnight on D plus 3, 20 September, after the Allies held the Nijmegen bridges, had Model relented. "It is necessary to hold, and if necessary to blow up the highway bridge at Nijmegen," Model's chief of staff notified General Bittrich, commander of the *II Panzer Corps*. General Bittrich replied that the word had come too late. For two hours, he said, he had heard nothing from the Nijmegen garrison and assumed that the German units there had been destroyed.

Despite this indication that the Allies were in control at Nijmegen, Model's chief of staff early the next morning, 21 September, again brought up the subject of the bridges. "The Waal bridges will be destroyed in the face of enemy pressure," he directed. This may have been a belated attempt to cover Model's tracks in the expectation that failure to destroy the bridges would bring repercussion from superiors. Indeed, only a few hours later, OKW began to press the matter. Model's chief of staff admitted that hindsight did reveal that "demolition would have been indicated. However," he said, "on account of the enemy attack from both sides on the [highway] bridge,

---

[15] On 21 September, near a Dutch fortress northeast of the highway bridge, a bazooka man from the 504th Parachute Infantry, Pvt. John R. Towle, rushed beyond his company's outposts to intercept a German attack that was supported by two tanks and a half-track. He was instrumental in breaking up the thrust before falling mortally wounded from enemy mortar fire. He was posthumously awarded the Medal of Honor.

DUTCH FARMER NEAR ZON *gives paratroopers a lift to their assembly area.*

the responsible commander was not able to blow up the bridge on his own authority." [16]

This coincided to a large degree with the opinion of the 82d Airborne Division commander, General Gavin. He later attributed German failure to demolish the highway bridge to three factors: (1) the assault from both ends, (2) destruction of the alleged demolition control mechanism

in the post office, and (3) the cooperation of the Dutch underground in keeping the bridge under fire so that the Germans could not work on the demolitions. "In my opinion, at this time," General Gavin wrote later, "the capture of the bridge intact, like the other bridges in the area, was the result of careful study and planning on the part of the parachutists of the 82d Airborne Division who were assigned the task, and the careful carrying out of those plans by everyone regardless of his grade or position who was associated with the task. The underground played a major part in getting this done and they deserve a lion's share of

---

[16] Tel Convs, CofS *A Gp B* to Gen Bittrich, 2330, 20 Sep 44; CofS *A Gp B* to CofS *II SS Pz Corps,* 0915, 21 Sep 44; CofS *OB WEST* to CofS *A Gp B,* 1355, 21 Sep 44; and CofS *A Gp B* to *OKW/WFSt,* 1440, 21 Sep 44. All in *A Gp B KTB* (Text).

the credit for saving the big bridge at Nijmegen." [17]

Regardless of who or what saved the Nijmegen bridge, the contributions of the Dutch underground not only to the operations of the 82d Airborne Division but to those of other Allied units as well cannot be ignored. Known officially as the Netherlands Interior Forces, the Dutch underground was one of the most highly organized and efficient resistance units in all Europe. Hardly any who fought in Holland were not affected in some manner by help from these intrepid, shadowy figures who moved by night. Dutch civilians were a constant source of intelligence on the enemy. Countless parachutists and glidermen who landed off the beaten track owed their safe return to the fearless assistance of the underground. Many times the Dutch assembled equipment and resupply bundles at central points where the soldiers could get at them easily. Many a Dutchman went hungry because he shared his meager rations with paratroopers whose resupply had been cut short by adverse weather. An officer who had visited frequently in the Netherlands before the war, Capt.

Arie D. Bestebreurtje, jumped with the 82d Airborne Division as commander of a three-man Special Forces team and coordinated the activities of the Netherlands Interior Forces at Nijmegen. In response to a Dutch request for weapons, General Gavin authorized Captain Bestebreurtje to dispense the weapons from American dead and wounded. General Gavin termed the conduct of the underground "exemplary." "Sleep, I have no time for sleep," a fatigued Dutch boy said when denied a request to fight in the line. "For four years I have been waiting for this. No, this is not the time for sleep." Some evidence indicates that at least one German commander was slow to move his troops in early stages of the airborne attack for fear of general Dutch uprisings. The Allied attack clearly benefited from the fact that it took place in a country where the population was unquestionably and often openly hostile to the enemy.[18]

First Attempts To Drive on Arnhem

Counting from the time of first contact between the British ground column and the 504th Parachute Infantry at Grave at 0820 on D plus 2, 19 September, until the Nijmegen bridge was taken at 1910 on D plus 3, 20 September, a case could be made to show that the ground column was delayed at Nijmegen for almost thirty-five hours. Yet this would be to ignore the facts that first arrivals of the ground column represented no more than a forward reconnaissance screen and that

---

[17] Ltr, Gavin to OCMH, 17 Jan 54. In 1949 an official board of inquiry reported to the Netherlands Government as a majority finding that it was likely a young Dutchman, Jan van Hoof, cut some detonator wires on the bridge, but the board did not say whether this act actually saved the bridge. See Letter to OCMH (24 Sep 56) from Dr. L. de Jong, Executive Director of the Netherlands State Institute for War Documentation. Though the story has attracted considerable notice in the Netherlands, only vague and inconclusive reference to it can be found in Allied records. See also Gilbert R. Martineau, ed., *Holland Travel Guide* (Paris: Nagel, 1951), p. 528; Ltrs in OCMH files from Col. A. L. van den Berge, Military Attaché, Embassy of the Netherlands, Washington, D.C.; and Ltr, Bestebreurtje to OCMH.

[18] Almost all after action reports and combat interviews contain references to Dutch assistance. See also Rapport and Northwood, *Rendezvous With Destiny, passim;* Ltr, Gavin to OCMH, 17 Jan 54; correspondence with Colonel Boeree; and Ltr, Bestebreurtje to OCMH.

several hours elapsed before sizable British units began to arrive. Indeed, almost another twenty-four hours would elapse after capture of the Nijmegen bridge before the British would renew the drive on Arnhem.

At nightfall on D plus 3, the British had at Nijmegen only the Guards Armoured Division. Because inclement weather continued to deny arrival of the 82d Airborne Division's glider infantry, the Guards Armoured's Coldstream Guards Group still was needed as a reserve for the airborne division. This left but two armored groups to go across the Waal. Even these did not make it until the next day (D plus 4, 21 September), primarily because of die-hard German defenders who had to be ferreted from the superstructure and underpinnings of the bridge. Once on the north bank, much of the British armor and infantry was used to help hold and improve the bridgehead that the two battalions of the 504th Parachute Infantry had forged.[19]

British commanders must have been aware of the necessity to get quickly to Arnhem. Although few details on the situation north of the Neder Rijn had emerged, some sketchy information had filtered back during the day through intermittent radio communication with General Urquhart's headquarters. Though garbled by distance and inadequate airborne radio sets, these fragmentary messages had basically confirmed the cursory Dutch communication of two days before. Yet the new details provided no occasion for despair. The report was that Colonel Frost and his little band still held the north end of the Arnhem bridge. Though under constant pressure, the rest of the Red Devils in the perimeter at Oosterbeek still controlled the north end of the Heveadorp ferry. If the ground column could break through quickly, the Red Devils—and possibly the entire MARKET-GARDEN operation—still might be saved.

For all the concern that must have existed about getting to Arnhem, only a small part of the British armor was freed late on D plus 4, 21 September, to start the northward drive. As the attack began, British commanders saw every apprehension confirmed. The ground off the main roads was low-lying, soggy bottomland, denying employment of tanks. A few determined enemy bolstered with antitank guns might delay even a large force. Contrary to the information that had been received, Colonel Frost and his men had been driven away from the north end of the Arnhem bridge the afternoon before, so that since the preceding night the bridge had been open to German traffic. At the village of Ressen, less than three miles north of Nijmegen, the Germans had erected an effective screen composed of an SS battalion reinforced with 11 tanks, another infantry battalion, 2 batteries of 88-mm. guns, 20 20-mm. antiaircraft guns, and survivors of earlier fighting at Nijmegen, all operating under General Bittrich's *II SS Panzer Corps*.[20] Arnhem lay seven miles north of this screen. The British could not pass.

Not until near nightfall on D plus 4 did another British division arrive at Nijmegen, the 43d Infantry Division. Because of severe traffic congestion on the

[19] For this account of British units, see FAAA, Opns in Holland; Hq Br Abn Corps, Allied Abn Opns in Holland; 1st Abn Div, Rpt on Opn MARKET, Pt. 1.

[20] Evg Sitrep, *A Gp B*, 1845, 21 Sep 44, *A Gp B KTB, Letzte Meldung*; Daily Sitrep, *A Gp B*, 0135, 23 Sep 44, *A Gp B KTB, Tagesmeldungen*; Bittrich Questionnaire, copy in OCMH.

lone highway extending from the Dutch-Belgian border to Nijmegen, it had taken three days for this division to travel sixty miles. The infantry would not attack until the next day, D plus 5, 22 September.[21]

Only one other possibility did the Allies have for helping the Red Devils at Arnhem on 21 September. By 1400 cloud above air bases in England at last had cleared sufficiently to enable parachutists of the 1st Polish Parachute Brigade to take to the air. Under a new plan, the Poles were to drop close to the village of Driel, near the southern terminus of the Heveadorp ferry. During the night they were to cross the river by ferry in order to strengthen the British perimeter on the north bank until the 30 Corps might break through.

Unfortunately, weather over the Continent had not cleared. Of 110 planes, only 53 dropped their loads. Those who jumped included the brigade commander, Maj. Gen. S. Sosabowski, and the equivalent of two weak battalions, a total of 750 men. After overcoming minor opposition on the drop zone, General Sosabowski made the disheartening discovery that but a short while earlier the Germans had driven the British from the north end of the ferry site and sunk the ferry boat. Although General Urquhart radioed that his Red Devils would attack immediately to regain the site, the theory that the weakened, closely confined British could recapture it was, no matter how admirable, wholly chimerical.

By now the Red Devils had been confined to a perimeter at Oosterbeek less than half a mile wide and a mile and a

---

[21] Wilmot, *The Struggle for Europe,* pages 514–16, vividly describes the traffic problems on the highway.

half deep. In that perimeter the day (21 September) had brought no brighter developments than it had outside. The Germans the day before had captured the British hospital; the plight of the wounded now was pitiful because of both a dearth of medical supplies and a lack of food and water. The inexorable pounding of enemy guns set the ammunition depot on fire. The only bright spot came in late afternoon when an artillery observation unit at last established firm radio contact with an artillery regiment of 30 Corps.

The news to be reported from Colonel Frost and his men at the Arnhem bridge was not good. By daylight of D plus 3, 20 September, the British paratroopers had retained control of only a few buildings near the bridge. During the afternoon of D plus 3 they had been driven by point-blank tank fire from the last of these. Some 140 able-bodied men still had refused to give up, but about 50 of these had fallen during the night. At dawn on D plus 4, 21 September, the order had been given to break into small parties and try to escape. None had made it.

Keeping the Corridor Open

For all the adversities north of the Neder Rijn, hope still existed as daylight came on D plus 5, 22 September, that the 43d Infantry Division might break through at Ressen, relieve the British paratroopers, and bring over-all success to Operation MARKET-GARDEN. The 30 Corps commander, General Horrocks, ordered the division "to take all risks to effect relief today."

Yet, almost coincident with this hope, another major threat to the success of the operation was developing to the south in the sector of General Taylor's 101st Airborne Division. Despite an aggressive defense designed to prevent the enemy from concentrating at any one crucial spot to cut Hell's Highway, General Taylor on 22 September was faced with report after report from Dutch sources of large-scale German movements against the narrow corridor from both east and west. At a time when the 30 Corps needed everything possible in order to break through to the Red Devils, severance of the vital lifeline could prove disastrous.

One reason the 101st Airborne Division still faced a major task in holding open the corridor was the slow progress of the attacks of the 8 and 12 British Corps on either flank of the corridor. West of the corridor, the 12 Corps, controlling three divisions, had begun to attack during the evening of D-Day, 17 September; but by D plus 5, when the reports of German concentration began to give General Taylor genuine concern, the 12 Corps still was several miles south and southwest of Best. East of the corridor, the numerically weaker 8 Corps had begun to attack before daylight on D plus 2, 19 September, but by D plus 5 still was southeast of Eindhoven. Both corps had run into stanch resistance and had found the marshy terrain an obstacle of major proportions. As Field Marshal Montgomery was to put it later, progress was "depressingly slow." [22]

The 101st Airborne Division commander, General Taylor, had recognized since late on D plus 2, 19 September, when his command post and the Bailey bridge over the Wilhelmina Canal at Zon had almost fallen to the first strike of the *107th Panzer Brigade,* that his division

had entered a second and more difficult phase of the fighting. The point was underscored in the morning mist of D plus 3, 20 September, when the *107th Panzer Brigade* struck again at the Zon bridge. Though a reinforced battalion of infantry had been disposed to guard the bridge, German tank guns soon controlled the bridge by fire. The bridge might have fallen to the Germans had not ten British tanks belatedly responded to an SOS dating from the crisis of the night before. Knocking out four German tanks, the British forced the enemy back.

Recognizing that he had not the strength to maintain a static defense along the 15-mile length of Hell's Highway, General Taylor on D plus 3 chose the alternative. He would keep the Germans surprised and off balance with limited offensive thrusts of his own.

Perhaps the most successful of these was a maneuver on D plus 3 by Colonel Kinnard's battalion of the 501st Parachute Infantry. Although Colonel Kinnard had a company outposting the village of Heeswijk, four and a half miles northwest of Veghel, the Germans had infiltrated in some strength along the Willems Canal between Heeswijk and Veghel. Using the bulk of his battalion, Colonel Kinnard drove northwest alongside the canal to sweep these Germans into Heeswijk, where the outpost company played the role of a dust pan. It was a classic maneuver, a little Cannae, which by the end of the day had accounted for about 500 Germans, including 418 prisoners.

On D plus 4, 21 September, a reconnaissance by a company of Colonel Michaelis' 502d Parachute Infantry encountered stiff resistance near the village of Schijndel, four and one half miles

---

[22] Montgomery, *Normandy to the Baltic,* pp. 230–43.

northwest of St. Oedenrode. This coincided with civilian reports that the Germans were concentrating south of Schijndel for a counterattack upon St. Oedenrode. Impressed by Colonel Kinnard's successful maneuver the day before, Michaelis and the commander of the 501st Parachute Infantry, Colonel Johnson, decided to press the Germans near Schijndel between them. Two battalions of Johnson's regiment were to take Schijndel from the north. Thereupon two of Michaelis' battalions were to attack northward against the German force that was south of the village.

In a swift move after dark on D plus 4, Colonel Johnson took Schijndel not long after midnight (21 September). Although a surprise counterattack against the village at dawn delayed start of the second phase of the planned maneuver, Colonel Michaelis' two battalions were able to begin their role by midmorning (D plus 5, 22 September). Progressing smoothly, the attack gave promise of bountiful success. Then, abruptly, at 1430, an urgent message from General Taylor forced a halt.

While these four battalions had fought near Schijndel, General Taylor had learned that the Germans were concentrating for a major blow to sever Hell's Highway. During the morning, a drive on Nuenen, southeast of Zon, had revealed that a German column contacted there the day before had gone elsewhere. This coincided with report after report from the Dutch of enemy movements both east and west of the Allied corridor. Indications were that the Germans intended a convergent attack in the vicinity of Veghel and Uden. Lying five miles northeast of Veghel astride Hell's Highway, Uden heretofore had been ignored by the Ger-

mans and unoccupied by the Americans.

General Taylor had ample reason for concern. A strong convergent attack upon Veghel was, in reality, the German plan. The plan had emerged from orders issued by Field Marshal Model the day before (D plus 4, 21 September).[23] While General Bittrich's *II SS Panzer Corps* and General Meindl's *II Parachute Corps* stepped up their operations against the British at Arnhem and the Americans at Nijmegen, General Student's *First Parachute Army* was to sever the Allied corridor farther south.

The spot Field Marshal Model chose was Veghel. Pushed back by the British ground attack on D-Day and by the subsequent drive of the 12 British Corps, General Reinhard's *LXXXVIII Corps* now was located west of Veghel and might mount an attack from that direction. On the east the attack was to be mounted by a headquarters new to the fighting, the *LXXXVI Corps* under General der Infanterie Hans von Obstfelder. This headquarters Model had moved up hurriedly on D plus 1 to assume control of *Division Erdmann* and the *176th Division* in order that General Student might give undivided attention to other units more directly involved against the Allied airborne operation.[24] General von Obstfelder now was to assume a more active role.

In the attack from the east, Obstfelder was to employ a force thrown together under Colonel Walther, who earlier had commanded a *Kampfgruppe* along the Meuse–Escaut Canal. The new *Kampfgruppe Walther* would control Major von

---

[23] Order, *A Gp B* to all subordinate commands, 1700, 21 Sep 44, *A Gp B KTB Operationsbefehle.*
[24] See Mng Sitrep, *A Gp B*, 1000, 18 Sep 44, *A Gp B KTB, Letzte Meldung.*

Maltzahn's *107th Panzer Brigade*, a small contingent of the *10th SS Panzer Division* (*Kampfgruppe Heinke*) that had earlier been used against the XIX U.S. Corps east of Maastricht, an artillery battalion with three howitzer batteries (105's and 150's), and an infantry battalion of the *180th Division*, the last an advance contingent of a replacement division which had been scraped together hurriedly by *Wehrkreis X*.

From the west, General Reinhard's *LXXXVIII Corps* was to employ a regimental combat team of the *59th Division* that had been shored up with replacements after a disastrous initial commitment at Best. Commanded by Major Huber, this force included three infantry battalions, a battalion of 105-mm. howitzers, a battery of 150-mm. howitzers, a battery of 20-mm. antiaircraft guns, seven antitank guns, and four Panther tanks. The axis of attack for *Kampfgruppe Huber* was from Schijndel through the villages of Wijbosch and Eerde to Veghel. *Kampfgruppe Walther* was to strike from Gemert through the village of Erp, three miles southeast of Veghel.[25]

On the American side, the maneuver near Schijndel during the morning of 22 September was occupying the bulk of Colonel Johnson's 501st Parachute Infantry, but one battalion of that regiment still was in defensive positions in Veghel. Yet not a man was in Uden, the other place which the Americans believed the Germans would strike. To Uden General Taylor turned his attention first.

The job of defending Uden General Taylor gave to Colonel Sink's 506th Parachute Infantry, which was becoming available as British ground troops took over farther south around Eindhoven and Zon. Upon first word of the threat, Colonel Sink hurriedly collected about 150 men from a rifle platoon and his regimental headquarters company and rushed them northward by truck. At 1100, 22 September, they reached Uden. Only a few minutes later the Germans appeared. For the remainder of D plus 5 and into the next day, the men of this little force dashed from house to house in Uden to spread their fire and give an impression of strength. They were fortunate that the Germans were concentrating instead upon Veghel.

In the main attack, *Kampfgruppe Walther* advanced through the village of Erp against Veghel shortly before noon. Commanded by Lt. Col. Robert A. Ballard, the lone American battalion in Veghel waited in houses and foxholes along the Erp road. In a stint of furious fighting, Colonel Ballard's men warded off the first German blow, but they could see part of the German column sideslip to the northwest. Unopposed in this direction, *Kampfgruppe Walther* with tanks of the *107th Panzer Brigade* in the lead readily cut Hell's Highway between Veghel and Uden. Then the tanks turned down the highway toward Veghel.[26]

Had it not been for the warnings of the Dutch underground, *Kampfgruppe Wal-*

---

[25] TWX, *A Gp B* to *OB WEST*, 0600, 22 Sep 44, *A Gp B KTB, Operationsbefehle*; MS # B–149 (Poppe); Noon Sitrep, *A Gp B*, 1330, 22 Sep 44, *A Gp B KTB, Letzte Meldung*.

[26] For the story of the defense of Veghel, the author is indebted to Rapport and Northwood, *Rendezvous With Destiny*, pp. 352 ff. The authors of this authoritative work conducted additional interviews and correspondence to supplement unit records and combat interviews. See also battalion histories of the 327th Glider Infantry in combat interview files of the 101st Airborne Division, plus unit journals and after action reports.

ther might have found in Veghel only Colonel Ballard's battalion and surprised British truck drivers who were trapped by the cutting of the highway. But upon receipt of Dutch warnings, General Taylor had acted swiftly. In addition to alerting Colonel Sink's 506th Parachute Infantry to move to Uden, he told the commander of the 327th Glider Infantry, Colonel Harper, to release a battalion from defense of the glider landing zone and send it to Veghel. Two battalions of infantry thus were advancing toward Veghel even as the German tanks turned toward the town.

Having come into Veghel during the morning to select a new division command post, the 101st Airborne Division's artillery commander, Brig. Gen. Anthony C. McAuliffe, was at hand to co-ordinate the defense. Spotting a 57-mm. antitank gun of the 81st Airborne Antiaircraft Battalion, General McAuliffe yelled to get the gun forward.

Divining the urgency of the situation, Colonel Harper meantime had intercepted his glider infantry battalion that was moving over back roads in deference to British priority on the main highway. He directed the battalion commander, Lt. Col. Ray C. Allen, to ignore the ban on travel on the main road. At the same time he told Colonel Allen's motorized antitank platoon to thread through traffic that was coagulating along the highway and race at full speed into Veghel.

Almost simultaneously, the 57-mm. antitank gun and the antitank platoon from the 327th Glider Infantry arrived at the northeastern fringe of Veghel. A dispute was to arise later between crews of these guns as to which fired the first shot, but what mattered at the moment was that the first round struck the leading Mark V

squarely and set it afire. Faced with what they could not recognize immediately as only a makeshift defense, the other German tankers backed away.

The delay thus imposed gave General McAuliffe time to get set. He directed the battalion of the 506th Parachute Infantry into position astride Hell's Highway in the northeast. Colonel Allen's battalion of the 327th Glider Infantry he ordered to defend in the north near a railroad bridge over the Aa River. General McAuliffe requested air support, but unfavorable weather denied any substantial assistance from that quarter.

Though the timely arrival of antitank guns had stymied *Kampfgruppe Walther* temporarily, this was but half of the German strength. *Kampfgruppe Huber* was even then striking toward Veghel from the west.

Because the Americans had taken Schijndel the night before, Major Huber had had to alter his plan of attack. Diverting an infantry battalion as a screen against Schijndel, he had advanced with the rest of his force along back roads and trails to Eerde, thence along a highway to Veghel.[27] About 1400 (22 September) Major Huber's tanks and artillery brought fire to bear upon the bridge over the Willems Canal at Veghel.

Once again General McAuliffe could thank the fortuitous arrival of fresh troops. General Taylor's order to the 506th Parachute Infantry to move to Uden was paying off, not in the defense of Uden but of Veghel. Even as the Germans took the bridge under fire, another battalion of the 506th Parachute Infantry arrived from the south in company with a squadron of British tanks. Discouraged, Major Huber's tanks and infantry recoiled.

---

[27] MS # B-149 (Poppe).

If he could not get to Veghel, Major Huber must have reasoned, still he might cut Hell's Highway. Rallying his men quickly, he sideslipped to the south. Advance elements actually had crossed the highway when once again American reinforcements arrived, this time the two remaining battalions of Colonel Harper's 327th Glider Infantry. Using marching fire, the glidermen quickly drove the Germans back.

It was Major Huber's attack at 1400 that had prompted the message to Colonel Johnson at Schijndel which in effect ended American attempts to eliminate the Germans south of that village. Although the message directed only that he release a squadron of attached British tanks to move to Veghel, Colonel Johnson did not stop there. Aware that defense of Veghel was his responsibility, he called off the maneuver at Schijndel and directed both his battalions to Veghel.

By the time these two battalions had fought through rear elements of *Kampfgruppe Huber* to reach the villages of Wijbosch and Eerde, General McAuliffe already had obtained sufficient strength for defending Veghel. Colonel Johnson therefore directed one battalion to defend at Wijbosch, the other at Eerde. These two battalions thus became the western segment of the Veghel defensive arc. In the process they in effect cut off *Kampfgruppe Huber*. Only a fraction of Major Huber's infantry escaped.[28]

Through the rest of the afternoon of 22 September, German artillery pounded Veghel, and *Kampfgruppe Walther* launched one strong attack and several probing thrusts. Yet the enemy would

have to show greater strength if he were to succeed at Veghel, for General McAuliffe now had in defense of the town a total of eight infantry battalions. These included two battalions of the 506th Parachute Infantry, all of the 501st Parachute Infantry, and all of the 327th Glider Infantry. Some guns of the airborne artillery, some British pieces gathered from the highway, and two squadrons of British tanks also had been included within the perimeter.

No matter how sanguine General McAuliffe might be about defending Veghel, the task was not so much holding the village as it was reopening Hell's Highway to the northeast in the direction of Uden. Already trucks, tanks, and supply vehicles so sorely needed at Nijmegen and Arnhem clogged the highway for miles, cruelly exposed to enemy attack along some other portion of the road.

General McAuliffe found his impending task eased by the fact that radio communications with the 30 Corps at Nijmegen had remained constant. The 30 Corps commander, General Horrocks, promised to send his 32d Guards Brigade to attack south the next day to assist in opening the road. General McAuliffe also received another assist from the British: during 22 September the 8 British Corps, which was advancing along the right flank of the corridor, had forced two crossings of the Willems Canal to the east of Eindhoven at Helmond and Asten. Even as *Kampfgruppe Walther* continued to fight, Colonel Walther had to keep one eye cocked to the southeast. A sudden spurt by the 8 Corps might sever his line of communications.

Early the next day, D plus 6, 23 September, *Kampfgruppe Walther* nevertheless resumed the attack against Veghel,

---

[28] Daily Sitrep, *A Gp B*, 0135, 23 Sep 44, *A Gp B KTB, Tagesmeldungen;* MS # B–149 (Poppe).

while General Reinhard's *LXXXVIII Corps* tried to co-operate with a complementary thrust from the west. Unlike Colonel Walther, General Reinhard had no real concern about British advances, for west of the corridor his troops had held the 12 British Corps in the vicinity of Best. Yet because *Kampfgruppe Huber* had been mauled severely, General Reinhard had to turn elsewhere to find troops with which to attack. During the night he had moved up Colonel von der Heydte's *6th Parachute Regiment,* which as a part of *Kampfgruppe Chill* had fought along the Meuse–Escaut Canal.

In order to co-ordinate with the renewed thrust of *Kampfgruppe Walther,* Colonel von der Heydte had to attack immediately after arrival, even though his troops were exhausted from two nights of marching. Moreover, one of the *6th Parachute Regiment*'s organic battalions had been left behind. In its stead von der Heydte had a battalion of the *2d Parachute Regiment,* "a rotten apple," an outfit poorly led and poorly disciplined. To add to the problems, the command situation left something to be desired, As a component of *Kampfgruppe Chill,* the *6th Parachute Regiment* received tactical orders from that source, but the regiment had to depend for supply upon the *59th Division.* Faced with these conditions, the colonel understandably had little faith in the prospects of his attack.

He was right. Scheduled to attack at 0700 (23 September), the *6th Parachute Regiment* did not get going until an hour and a half later. Striking toward Veghel along the same route taken the day before by *Kampfgruppe Huber,* von der Heydte's paratroopers ran into Colonel Johnson's parachute infantry at Wijbosch and Eerde. They could get nowhere. Soon after

noon von der Heydte told his men to defend the line they had reached.[29]

In the drive against Veghel from the east, *Kampfgruppe Walther* found the going equally tough. Apparently in recognition of the threat posed by continued advance of the 8 British Corps, *Kampfgruppe Walther* by noon had begun to fall back.

When at 1300 General McAuliffe seized the initiative to send two battalions of the 506th Parachute Infantry to break *Kampfgruppe Walther*'s stranglehold on Hell's Highway between Veghel and Uden, the paratroopers found only a shell of German defenders remaining. They advanced quickly more than a mile to a juncture with the British armor driving southwest from Uden. As soon as tanks and bulldozers could nose damaged vehicles aside, traffic once again rolled on Hell's Highway.

Even as fighting continued at Veghel, the 101st Airborne Division's last glider serial was arriving at the glider landing zone. Blessed by genuinely favorable weather for the first time since D Day, this lift on 23 September arrived almost without incident. Included was the 907th Glider Field Artillery Battalion, whose 105-mm. howitzers had been turned back by adverse weather on D plus 2. When the division's seaborne tail arrived during the night of D plus 5 and on D plus 6, General Taylor at last could count his entire division present.

The Germans were convinced that these new landings were designed primarily to alleviate German pressure at Veghel. Indeed, they in part attributed *Kampfgruppe Walther*'s failure to hold onto Hell's Highway to an erroneous belief that

---

[29] MS # C–001 (von der Heydte).

fresh Allied paratroopers had landed at Uden.[30]

The Germans were concerned even more about new Allied landings on this date at Nijmegen, where General Gavin at last received his 325th Glider Infantry.[31] Despite the reinforcement of *Corps Feldt* by seven battalions under the *II Parachute Corps*, the Germans had been thrown on the defensive in this sector after their short-lived successes at Mook, Riethorst, Wyler, and Beek on D plus 3, 20 September. To provide greater security for the Waal bridges at Nijmegen, General Gavin had ordered an attack to clear the flatlands between the ridge and the Waal as far as three miles east of Nijmegen. Parts of the 504th and 508th Parachute Regiments had begun to attack late on D plus 4, 21 September, as soon as Beek had been retaken. By nightfall of D plus 6, 23 September, the 82d Airborne Division's new line in this sector ran from the foot of Devil's Hill (Hill 75.9) northeast to the Waal near Erlekom. With the arrival of the 325th Glider Infantry (Lt. Col. Charles Billingslea) on 23 September the Germans at the southern end of the high ground also came under attack. Relieving the 505th Parachute Infantry, the glidermen began to clear a patch of woods on lower slopes of the Kiekberg (Hill 77.2).[32]

Perhaps as a corollary to the concern that grew from the new Allied landings, Field Marshal Model on 23 September reorganized his command in hope of a simpler and more effective arrangement. He in effect drew an imaginary line along the west boundary of the corridor the Allies had carved. All forces to the west of this line came under General von Zangen's *Fifteenth Army*. Relieving the *Armed Forces Commander Netherlands* and *Wehrkreis VI* of their unorthodox tactical responsibilities, Model assigned the *First Parachute Army* the following forces: General Bittrich's *II SS Panzer Corps* (plus *Division von Tettau*), General Meindl's *II Parachute Corps*, General von Obstfelder's *LXXXVI Corps, Corps Feldt*, and a new corps headquarters that was scheduled to arrive within a few days. With these forces, General Student was to execute the main effort against the Allied corridor.[33]

In the wake of this reorganization, a renewal of the attack by Colonel von der Heydte's *6th Parachute Regiment* near Veghel on 24 September was made under the auspices of the *Fifteenth Army* rather than the *First Parachute Army*. Yet the pattern of the action was much the same as the day before. This time the fighting occurred only at Eerde, where a battalion of the 501st Parachute Infantry under Colonel Cassidy fought a courageous, hand-to-hand engagement for possession of local observation advantage in a range of sand dunes near the village. As German success appeared imminent, another battalion under Lt. Col. Julian J. Ewell and a squadron of British tanks arrived. Thereupon Colonel Cassidy counterattacked to drive von der Heydte's paratroopers from the dunes.

The fight might have ended in unequivocal American success had not the Germans committed alongside von der

---

[30] Daily Sitrep, *A Gp B*, 0200, 24 Sep 44, *A Gp B KTB, Tagesmeldungen.*

[31] *Ibid.*

[32] See History of 325th Glider Infantry, 82d Abn Div Combat Interv file.

[33] Order, *A Gp B* to *First Prcht Army, Fifteenth Army, Armed Forces Comdr Netherlands, Wehrkreis VI*, 1200, 23 Sep 44, *A Gp B KTB, Operationsbefehle.*

HELL'S HIGHWAY. *Wrecked British supply trucks along the hotly contested route.*

Heydte's south flank a newly arrived unit, a *Battalion Jungwirth*. Advancing southeast down a secondary road, *Battalion Jungwirth* surprisingly found no Americans barring the way. As nightfall neared, the Germans approached the hamlet of Koevering, located astride Hell's Highway a little more than a third of the distance from St. Oedenrode to Veghel and heretofore unoccupied by the Americans.

When outposts reported this movement, the commander of the 502d Parachute Infantry at St. Oedenrode sent two companies racing toward Koevering. Arriving minutes ahead of the Germans, these companies denied the village; but they could not prevent *Battalion Jungwirth* from cutting Hell's Highway a few hun-

dred yards to the northeast. Scarcely more than twenty-four hours after the Allies had reopened the highway between Veghel and Uden, the Germans had cut it again.

Through the night airborne and British artillery pounded the point of German penetration in an attempt to prevent reinforcement. The 907th Glider Field Artillery Battalion in firing positions only 400 yards from the Germans laid the guns of one battery for direct fire, operated the others with skeleton crews, and put the rest of the artillerymen in foxholes as riflemen. Yet Colonel von der Heydte still managed to redeploy a portion of his *6th Parachute Regiment* to the point of penetration.

Marching during the night from Uden in a heavy rain, Colonel Sink's 506th Parachute Infantry attacked at 0830 the next morning (D plus 8, 25 September) to squeeze the Germans from the northeast. A regiment of the 50th British Infantry Division and a reinforced battalion of the 502d Parachute Infantry pressed at the same time from the direction of St. Oedenrode. As the day wore on, *Battalion Jungwirth* and reinforcements from the *6th Parachute Regiment* held firm. By nightfall the Allies had drawn a noose about the Germans on three sides, but a small segment of Hell's Highway still was in German hands.

During the night *Battalion Jungwirth* withdrew in apparent recognition of the tenuous nature of the position. The Germans nevertheless had held the penetration long enough to mine the highway extensively. Not until well into the day of D plus 9, 26 September, did engineers finally clear the road and open Hell's Highway again to traffic.

The elimination of this break near Koevering marked the stabilization of the 101st Airborne Division's front. Although the Germans struck time after time in varying strength at various positions along the road, never again were they to cut it. Actually, General Reinhard's *LXXXVIII Corps* to the west of the highway concentrated primarily upon interfering with Allied movements through artillery fire, and General von Obstfelder's *LXXXVI Corps* to the east was too concerned with advance of the 8 British Corps to pay much more attention to Hell's Highway.[34] Indeed, by nightfall of 25 September patrols of the 8 Corps had

contacted contingents of the 30 Corps at St. Antonis, south of Nijmegen, thereby presaging quick formation of a solid line along the east flank of the corridor. Both General Taylor's 101st Airborne Division and General Gavin's 82d Airborne Division now might hold basically in place while the British tried to make the best of what had been happening at Arnhem.

The Outcome at Arnhem

The day the Germans first cut Hell's Highway at Veghel, D plus 5, 22 September, a new attack by the British ground column to break through to the hardpressed paratroopers north of the Neder Rijn began auspiciously. Just after dawn, patrols in armored cars utilized a heavy mist to sneak past the west flank of the German line via Valburg. Taking circuitous back roads and trails, the patrols in a matter of a few hours reached General Sosabowski's Polish troops at Driel, across the river from the British perimeter at Oosterbeek.

When the main body of the 43d Infantry Division attacked, the story was different. During the night the Germans had reinforced their defensive screen with a headquarters infantry battalion and a company of Panther tanks.[35] After a minor advance to a point well southwest of Elst, still not halfway to Arnhem, the British infantry despaired of breaking through.

The British had one trick remaining. Mounting on tanks, a battalion of infantry traced the route of the armored cars over

---

[34] See Daily Sitreps, *A Gp B,* 27 Sep 44, and later dates, *A Gp B KTB, Tagesmeldungen.*

[35] Daily Sitrep, *A Gp B,* 0135, 23 Sep 44, *A Gp B KTB, Tagesmeldungen;* Bittrich Questionnaire, copy in OCMH.

back roads to the northwest and reached Driel before nightfall. The column included DUKW's loaded with ammunition and supplies for the Red Devils. During the night, the Polish paratroopers were to cross the Neder Rijn in these craft. The need for reinforcement and resupply north of the river grew more urgent by the hour, for on 22 September perhaps the worst weather of the operation had denied air resupply of any kind.

Unfortunately, the DUKW's could not make it. Mud along the south bank of the Neder Rijn was too deep. During the night of 22 September, only about fifty Poles riding makeshift rafts managed to cross.

The break in the weather on D plus 6, 23 September, permitted a degree of assistance for the Red Devils. Typhoons of the 2d Tactical Air Force and P–47's of the Eighth Air Force struck enemy positions all along the corridor, particularly around the perimeter at Oosterbeek. This was the day when the last serials of the 82d and 101st Airborne Divisions arrived. Upon order of General Browning, the remainder of the 1st Polish Parachute Brigade landed on the secure drop zone of the 82d Airborne Division near Grave instead of at Driel and became a reserve for the American division. Thereupon, the Coldstream Guards Group reverted to the Guards Armoured Division.

Now that the British had reached Driel, radio communication with the Red Devils at last was constant. As a consequence, General Horrocks and General Browning no longer anticipated recapture of the Arnhem bridge. At last the hard fact was evident that even should the ground column take the bridge, the Red Devils were too weak to help establish a bridgehead at Arnhem. The two commanders

agreed that the best chance of reinforcing or relieving the British airborne troops was through Driel. The 43d Infantry Division therefore concentrated upon strengthening the forces at Driel and upon clearing Elst, in order to open more direct secondary roads to Driel.

By nightfall of D plus 6, 23 September, a brigade had fought into the outskirts of Elst, while another brigade had built up about Driel. To Driel went a small number of assault boats for putting the rest of the Polish paratroopers across the river during the night; for General Horrocks still hoped to turn the British perimeter into a secure bridgehead. But the Germans continued to control the north bank of the river, so that during the night only a modicum of ammunition and supplies and some 150 Polish paratroopers got across.

This continued inability to reinforce the British at Oosterbeek brought the first formal recognition that Operation MARKET-GARDEN might have passed the point of saving. Even though the Allies controlled a grass landing field near Grave where planes could land the 52d Lowland Division (Airportable), the Second Army commander, General Dempsey, radioed during the evening of 23 September that this division was not to be flown in without his approval. He obviously was reluctant to throw additional airborne troops into the fray unless he could find more positive indication of eventual success. Apparently with the concurrence of General Brereton and Field Marshal Montgomery, he gave authority to withdraw the 1st British Airborne Division from north of the Neder Rijn, "if the position so warranted." [36]

[36] Hq Br Abn Corps, Allied Abn Opns in Holland.

For a time, however, General Horrocks refused to give up without at least one more attempt to establish a bridgehead beyond the Neder Rijn. He directed that during the night of D plus 7, 24 September, the rest of the Polish paratroopers be ferried across. Nearby, two companies of the 43d Division's Dorsetshire Regiment were to cross, a first step in projected eventual commitment of the entire 43d Division beyond the river.

Once again success hinged on whether sufficient troops could cross the river during the night. Using the limited number of assault boats available, the two companies of the Dorsetshire Regiment paddled over, but daylight came before the Poles could cross. Because of German fire, even the Dorsets failed to assemble in cohesive units on the north bank. Few of them reached the British perimeter. Only about seventy-five of 400 Dorsets to cross over made their way back to the south bank.

If judged against German expectations, General Horrocks' hope that even at this late stage he still might establish a secure bridgehead was not unreasonable. The German commander, Field Marshal Model, was convinced that the airborne landings the day before presaged a renewed Allied effort. In regard to the over-all situation, Model was pessimistic. "The situation of *Army Group B*'s northern wing," he reported on 24 September, "has continued to deteriorate . . . . In the bitter fighting of the past week we were able merely to delay the enemy in achieving his strategic objective . . . . The renewed large airborne operation of 23 September . . . is bound to result in highly critical developments . . . ." He needed, the *Army Group B* commander reported, "minimum reinforcements" of

one infantry and one panzer division, a panzer brigade, two assault gun brigades, increased supplies of artillery ammunition, and increased infantry replacements.[37]

For a few hours longer, General Horrocks' optimism continued to match Model's apparent pessimism. The British corps commander still wanted one more try at establishing a bridgehead before conceding defeat. Reasoning that he might force a bridgehead elsewhere while the Germans were occupied with the Red Devils at Oosterbeek, he directed the 43d Infantry Division to prepare to cross a few miles to the west at Renkum, where a British armored brigade, driving west and northwest from Valburg, had built up along the south bank of the river. Yet hardly had General Horrocks issued this order when he admitted his plan was illusory. A short while later he rescinded the order.

Operation MARKET-GARDEN was almost over. At 0930 on D plus 8, 25 September, General Horrocks and General Browning agreed to withdraw the survivors of the British airborne division from the north bank.

Hungry, thirsty, heavy-eyed, utterly fatigued, and reduced to a shell of a division after nine days of fighting, the Red Devils wrapped their muddy boots in rags to muffle the sound of their footsteps and began at 2145 on 25 September to run a gantlet of German patrols to the water's edge. The night was mercifully dark. A heavy rain fell. Thundering almost constantly, guns of the 30 Corps lowered a protective curtain about the periphery of the British position. In groups of fourteen to match capacity of

[37] TWX, Model to Rundstedt, 1300, 24 Sep 44, *A Gp B KTB, Anlagen, Lagebeurteilungen/ Wochenmeldungen, 15.V.–11.X.44.*

the boats, the men inched toward the river. They had to leave their wounded behind.

Patient despite nervousness, fatigue, and the cold rain, the men queued for an empty boat. As dawn approached and many remained to be ferried, all who could do so braved the current to swim across. Not all of them made it. As daylight called a halt to the withdrawal, some 300 men remained on the north bank. A few of these hid out to make their way south on subsequent nights, but most probably were captured.

Guides led the weary soldiers to a reception point south of Driel where friendly hands plied them with rum, hot food, and tea. The survivors included 1,741 officers and men of the 1st Airborne Division, 422 British glider pilots, 160 men of the 1st Polish Parachute Brigade, and 75 of the Dorsetshire Regiment, a total of 2,398. These were all that remained of approximately 9,000 who had fought on the north bank. Judging from German reports, these men who wore the jaunty red berets had inflicted upon their enemy approximately 3,300 casualties, including 1,100 dead.[38] Speaking for his troops, General Urquhart said: "We have no regrets." [39]

The Achievements and the Cost

Operation MARKET-GARDEN accomplished much of what it had been designed to accomplish. Nevertheless, by the merciless logic of war, MARKET-GARDEN was a failure. The Allies had trained

their sights on far-reaching objectives. These they had not attained.

On the credit side, MARKET-GARDEN had gained bridgeheads over five major water obstacles, including the formidable Maas and Waal Rivers. The bridgehead beyond the Maas was to prove a decided advantage in February 1945 when the 21 Army Group launched a drive to clear the west bank of the Rhine opposite the Ruhr. The bridgehead beyond the Waal was to pose a constant threat of an Allied thrust northward, through the Germans subsequently lessened the threat by a program of widespread inundation. Operation MARKET-GARDEN also had forged a salient sixty-five miles deep into enemy territory, had liberated many square miles of the Netherlands, and had gained some valuable airfields. It also had drawn some German formations from other sectors of the Western Front and had imposed upon these forces a high rate of attrition.

On the debit side, some might maintain that the cardinal point was the failure to precipitate a German collapse. Although the enemy's collapse was hardly a formal objective of the operation, few would deny that many Allied commanders had nurtured the hope. In regard to more immediate and clearly defined objectives, the operation had failed to secure a bridgehead beyond the Neder Rijn, had not effectively turned the north flank of the West Wall, had not cut off the enemy's *Fifteenth Army,* and had not positioned the 21 Army Group for a drive around the north flank of the Ruhr. The hope of attaining these objectives had prompted the ambition and daring that went into Operation MARKET-GARDEN. Not to have realized them could mean only that the operation had failed.

---

[38] German figures from Daily Sitrep, *A Gp B,* 0220, 27 Sep 44, *A Gp B KTB, Tagesmeldungen.* The Germans claimed approximately 8,000 British casualties, including 6,450 prisoners (1,700 of them wounded) and 1,500 dead.

[39] 1st Abn Div, Rpt on Opn MARKET, Pt. 1.

The cost was high. In what may be called the "airborne phase," lasting from D-Day until withdrawal from north of the Neder Rijn on 25 September, the British airborne troops, including glider pilots and headquarters of the British Airborne Corps, lost 7,212 men killed, wounded, and missing. The 82d Airborne Division lost 1,432; the 101st Airborne Division, 2,110. Casualties among the 1st Polish Parachute Brigade totaled 378; among American glider pilots, 122. British and American air transport units lost 596 pilots. Including airborne troops, glider pilots, and transport aircraft pilots, the airborne phase cost 11,850 casualties.[40]

To this total belong those casualties incurred by the 30 Corps, an estimated 1,480 through 25 September. In addition, the 30 Corps lost some 70 tanks, and together the Americans and British lost 144 transport aircraft.[41]

---

[40] Hq Br Abn Corps, Allied Abn Opns in Holland. A complete tabulations of losses through 25 September follows:

	Killed	Wounded	Missing	Total
Total	968	2,640	8,242	11,850
Hq Br Abn Corps and Sig Pers____	4	--------	8	12
1st Br Abn Div___	286	135	6,041	6,462
82d Abn Div_____	215	790	427	1,430
101st Abn Div____	315	1,248	547	2,118
1st Pol Prcht Brig_	47	158	173	378
Br Glider Pilots___	59	35	644	732
U.S. Glider Pilots_	12	36	74	122
38 Group RAF___	6	23	184	213
46 Group RAF___	8	11	62	81
IX U.S. Troop Carrier Command_____	16	204	82	302

[41] Casualty figures on British ground forces furnished by Cabinet Office Historical Section; others from Br Abn Corps, Allied Abn Opns in Holland. The 8 and 12 Corps for the same period (17–25 Sep) incurred 3,874 casualties and lost approximately 18 tanks.

Though MARKET-GARDEN failed in its more far-reaching ramifications, to condemn the entire plan as a mistake is to show no appreciation for imagination and daring in military planning and is to ignore the climate of Allied intelligence reports that existed at the time. While reasons advanced for the failure range from adverse weather (Field Marshal Montgomery) and delay of the British ground column south of Eindhoven (General Brereton) to faulty intelligence (the Germans),[42] few criticisms have been leveled at the plan itself. In light of Allied limitations in transport, supplies, and troops for supporting the thrust, in light of General Eisenhower's commitment to a broad-front policy, and in light of the true condition of the German army in the West, perhaps the only real fault of the plan was overambition.

Field Marshal Montgomery has written: "We had undertaken a difficult operation, attended by considerable risks. It was justified because, had good weather obtained, there was no doubt that we should have attained full success."[43] Whether one can ascribe everything to weather in this manner is problematical, for other delays and difficulties not attributable to adverse weather developed. Certainly the vagaries of weather played a major role. Weather delayed arrival of the 1st British Airborne Division's second lift on D plus 1 for five hours, thwarted all but a smattering of resupply north of the Neder Rijn, and delayed arrival of the 1st Polish Parachute Brigade for two days. Bad weather also delayed arrival of the 82d

---

[42] FAAA Memo, sub: German analysis of Arnhem, 18 Dec 44, in SHAEF FAAA files; Brereton, *The Brereton Diaries*, pp. 360–61; Montgomery, *Normandy to the Baltic*, pp. 242–43.

[43] Montgomery, *Normandy to the Baltic*, p. 242.

Airborne Division's glider infantry regiment and a battalion of the 101st Airborne Division's artillery for four days and helped deny any really substantial contribution after D-Day from tactical aircraft.

The major adversities attributable to unfavorable weather might have been avoided had sufficient aircraft been available to transport the entire airborne force on D-Day. Yet to have hoped for that many aircraft at this stage of the war would have been to presume the millenium. As it was, more transport aircraft were employed in Operation MARKET than in any other operation up to that time.

In the matter of intelligence, the Allies sinned markedly. In particular, they expected greatest opposition at those points closest to the German front line, that is, near Eindhoven, and failed to detect (or to make adjustments for) the presence of the *II SS Panzer Corps* near Arnhem, the *59th Division* in transit near Tilburg, two SS battalions in the line opposite the 30 Corps, and the proximity of Student's and Model's headquarters to the drop zones. The celerity of German reaction certainly owed much to the presence of Model and Student on the scene, as well as to the blunder of some American officer who went into battle with a copy of the operational order. Faulty intelligence indicating German armor in the Reichswald bore heavily upon General Gavin's disposition of his battalions. Allied intelligence also erred in estimates of the terrain and enemy flak near Arnhem, thereby prompting location of British drop and landing zones far from the primary objective of the Arnhem bridge.

Yet all these handicaps possibly could have been overcome had the British ground column been able to advance as rapidly as General Horrocks had hoped. Perhaps the real fault was dependence upon but one road. In any event, the ground troops were delayed for varying amounts of time south of Eindhoven, at the demolished bridge over the Wilhelmina Canal at Zon, and at the Waal bridge in Nijmegen. Had these delays been avoided, the Germans conceivably could not have seriously deterred the advance between the Waal and the Neder Rijn, for this would have put the ground column north of the Waal by D plus 2 at the latest. Not until the night of D plus 3 were the Germans able to use the Arnhem bridge to get tanks and other reinforcements south of the Neder Rijn in order to form the defensive screen that in the end constituted the greatest delay of all.

Perhaps the most portentous conclusion to be drawn from the failure of Operation MARKET-GARDEN was the fact that for some time to come there could be no major thrust into the heart of Germany. Combined with the kind of resistance the Americans had been experiencing at Metz and Aachen, MARKET-GARDEN proved that the Germans in the West might be down but they were not out.

To many commanders, the outcome meant that all efforts now must be turned toward opening Antwerp to shipping and toward building a reserve of supplies sufficient for supporting a major offensive. As for settling the great debate of broad front versus narrow front, the outcome of this operation proved nothing. To some partisans, it merely demonstrated that Field Marshal Montgomery had been wrong in insisting on his drive in the north. To others, it showed that General Eisenhower had erred in deciding to advance along a broad front, that when committing a strategic reserve a commander should be prepared to support it adequately.

Release of the U. S. Divisions

Before the two U.S. divisions jumped in Operation MARKET, General Eisenhower had approved their participation with the stipulation that they be released as soon as ground forces could pass the positions they had seized and occupied.[44] This had led to an expectation that at least one of the divisions might be released as early as forty-eight hours after the jump. Nevertheless, when the British Red Devils withdrew from north of the Neder Rijn to signal the end of the airborne phase, both American divisions still were in the line.

The Americans would be sorely needed; the Germans would see to that. The airborne phase might have ended, but the fighting had not. No lesser person than Hitler himself during the night of 24 September had commanded that the Allied corridor be wiped out with simultaneous attacks from Veghel northward. This was imperative, Hitler had warned, because the Allies had sufficient units to stage additional airborne landings in conjunction with seaborne landings in the western or northern parts of the Netherlands, "and perhaps even on German soil . . . ." Hitler had ordered that Student's *First Parachute Army* be given a fresh panzer brigade, an antitank battalion, a battalion of Tiger tanks, and

both the *9th* and *116th Panzer Divisions,* these last two as soon as they could be refitted after their fight with the First U.S. Army at Aachen.[45]

Even though the order came from Hitler, it was to encounter tough sledding from the start. Pointing to the "total exhaustion" of the forces immediately at his disposal, Field Marshal Model promptly notified his superior, Rundstedt, that "a simultaneous accomplishment of the missions ordered is unfortunately impossible . . . ." Noting that reinforcement by the *9th* and *116th Panzer Divisions* was but an empty gesture in light of the condition of these divisions, Model reiterated an earlier plea for genuine assistance. In particular, he pleaded for the *363d Volks Grenadier Division,* a fresh unit whose impending availability Model had watched covetously for some time.[46]

Although subsequently promised the *363d Volks Grenadier Division,* Model found his plans to carry out the Hitler order hamstrung by delays in troop movements. Not until 29 September could he see any chance of launching even a preliminary attack, which involved in effect no more than local efforts to gain desired lines of departure. In the long run, he did intend to carry out an ambitious plan. With the *9th* and *116th Panzer Divisions* attached, General Bittrich's *II SS Panzer Corps* was to make the main effort against Allied forces between the Waal and the Neder Rijn. A new corps headquarters, the *XII SS Corps* (Obergruppenfuehrer und General der Waffen-SS Curt von Gottberg) was slated to command the

---

[44] FWD 14764, Eisenhower to comdrs, 13 Sep 44, in SHAEF SGS 381, I.

[45] Copy of Hitler order, filed at 0500, 25 Sep 44, in *A Gp B KTB, Operationsbefehle.*
[46] TWX, *A Gp B* to *OB WEST,* 0100, 25 Sep 44, *A Gp B KTB, Operationsbefehle.*

NIJMEGEN HIGHWAY BRIDGE

363d Volks Grenadier Division in a supporting attack along General Bittrich's
west flank. At the same time General
Meindl's *II Parachute Corps* was to strike
from the Reichswald against the high
ground in the vicinity of Groesbeek,
while a relatively fresh infantry division of
the *Fifteenth Army* launched a supporting
attack from the west against Grave.[47]

It was, in fact, not until 1 October that
the *First Parachute Army* was able to
mount any kind of attack other than a few

local stabs. Even then General Student
had to attack without either the *9th* and
116th Panzer Divisions, which would require several days more to assemble, or
the fresh *363d Volks Grenadier Division*.
The latter would not become available
until the middle of October.[48]

This is not to say that German pressure
was not keenly felt by the British and
Americans who had to fight it. Indeed,
the Germans launched powerful but isolated attacks well into October. By this
time the 8 and 12 Corps had built up on
either flank of the Allied corridor in such

---

[47] TWX, *A Gp B* to *Fifteenth Army*, 1630, 26
Sep 44, and to *First Prcht Army*, 0030, 27 Sep
44, and 1330, 28 Sep 44, *A Gp B KTB*,
Operationsbefehle.

[48] Daily Sitreps, *A Gp B*, 0145, 2 Oct 44, and
0030, 3 Oct 44, *A Gp B KTB*, *Tagesmeldungen*.

strength that the 101st Airborne Division could be spared from the defense of Veghel to move north of the Waal River and reinforce the 30 Corps. Entering the line on 5 October in this sector, which the men called "the island," General Taylor's division was subjected to intense fighting and ever-mounting casualties; but in the process the *363d Volks Grenadier Division,* which Model had awaited so eagerly, merely smashed itself to pieces and gained no ground to show for it. Coincidentally, the 82d Airborne Division was successfully repulsing all attempts by the *II Parachute Corps* to take the high ground around Groesbeek.[49]

The only real success General Student could report occurred at the Nijmegen bridges over the Waal. On two separate days the Germans struck at the bridges from the air, once with approximately forty planes, and each time scored one hit on the highway bridge. Both hits damaged the bridge but failed to halt traffic. Before daylight on 29 September, German swimmers slipped through the darkness to place submarine charges against buttresses of both the rail and road bridges. For a day neither bridge could be used, though by 1 October engineers had repaired the road bridge to permit one-way traffic and restored it subsequently to full capacity.

On 9 October General Browning's British Airborne Corps headquarters took leave of its adopted American divisions to return to England. Already the 1st

British Airborne Division and the 1st Polish Parachute Brigade, both so severely battered that their value in the defensive battles was negligible, had left the combat zone. Also by this time headquarters of both the 12 and 30 Corps were in the vicinity of Nijmegen so that any need there for General Browning's command post had passed.

By this date, 9 October, the British had widened the waist of the corridor to about twenty-four miles. Thereupon, the 12 Corps assumed responsibility for the "island" between the Waal and the Neder Rijn in order to free the 30 Corps for a projected drive against the Ruhr. Field Marshal Montgomery intended to strike southeast from Nijmegen in order to clear the west bank of the Rhine and the western face of the Ruhr and converge with a renewal of First Army's push against Cologne.

Even as October drew to an end and enemy pressure against the MARKET-GARDEN salient diminished, no release came for the two U.S. divisions. Like the 101st Airborne Division, part of General Gavin's 82d moved northward onto the "island." Here the men huddled in shallow foxholes dug no more than three feet deep lest they fill with water seepage. In an attempt to deceive the Germans into believing the Allies planned another thrust northward, patrol after patrol probed the enemy lines. One patrol, composed of six men of the 101st Airborne Division under Lt. Hugo Sims, Jr., crossed the Neder Rijn and roamed several miles behind the German positions for longer than twenty-four hours. The patrol returned with thirty-two prisoners.[50]

---

[49] For the defensive phase of MARKET GARDEN, see Hq Br Abn Corps, Allied Abn Opns in Holland; FAAA, Operations in Holland; Montgomery, *Normandy to the Baltic,* pp. 240–41; Rapport and Northwood, *Rendezvous With Destiny,* pp. 374 ff; and unit journals and after action reports of the 82d and 101st Airborne Divisions.

[50] A colorful account of this action, entitled "The Incredible Patrol," by Cpl. Russ Engel appeared in *Life* Magazine, January 15, 1945.

This practice of keeping the two American divisions in the line long after they were to have been released became more and more a source of "grave concern" to the First Allied Airborne Army commander, General Brereton. "Keeping airborne soldiers in the front lines as infantry," General Brereton noted, "is a violation of the cardinal rules of airborne employment." [51] In protesting their continued employment to General Eisenhower, Brereton wrote that unless the divisions were withdrawn immediately, he could not meet a ready date for a proposed airborne operation to assist the 12th Army Group. "Further combat," he warned, "will deplete them of trained men beyond replacement capacity." [52]

Reminding Field Marshal Montgomery of the conditions under which use of the U.S. divisions had been granted, General Eisenhower pointed out that the maintenance of the divisions had been based on that plan and that he contemplated using the two divisions about the middle of November. "To enable this to be done," he said "at least one of these divisions should be released without delay, and the second one within a reasonably short time thereafter." [53]

This was on 2 October. Yet the days and the weeks and more artillery fire and more patrolling and more British rations and British cigarettes passed, and still the Americans stayed in the line. Even the British rum ration failed to act as a real palliative.

To condemn the British for failing to give up the divisions is to show no appreciation of the manpower problems that plagued the 21 Army Group at the time. The British recognized the "accepted principle" that, because of specialist training and equipment and the difficulty of replacing casualties, airborne troops should be relieved as soon as possible from normal ground operations. The British Airborne Corps noted, however, "It is also a fact that they cannot be released until the major tactical or strategical situation allows them to be spared or replaced by other troops." [54] The simple fact was that Field Marshal Montgomery had a lot of jobs to do in light of the number of men he had to do them with.

Even before creation of the MARKET-GARDEN salient, the 21 Army Group front had extended from near Ostend on the Channel coast to the boundary with the 12th Army Group near Hasselt, a distance of more than 150 miles. In addition, German garrisons in the Channel ports of Boulogne, Calais, and Dunkerque had to be either annihilated or contained. Upon creation of the MARKET-GARDEN salient, about 130 miles of front had been added to British responsibility, almost double the original length.

The need to hold the salient was obvious. It also was a big assignment that occupied most of the Second British Army.

Neither could the necessity to secure the seaward approaches to Antwerp be denied. To that task Field Marshal Montgomery assigned the First Canadian Army, but the Canadians had to assume two other major tasks as well: (1) cap-

[51] Brereton, *The Brereton Diaries*, pp. 361, 367–68.

[52] V–25550, Brereton to Eisenhower, 10 Oct 44, SHAEF SGS 381, II.

[53] FWD 16687 Eisenhower to Montgomery, 2 Oct 44, SHAEF SGS 381, II.

[54] Hq Br Abn Corps, Allied Abn Opns in Holland.

ture completely two of the Channel ports and contain a third, and (2) attack northward from the Meuse–Escaut Canal both to complement the drive to open Antwerp and to relieve the Second Army of long frontage on the west flank of the MARKET-GARDEN salient.[55]

Still remaining was a task that General Eisenhower had assigned jointly to the 21 Army Group and the First U.S. Army and had called "the main effort of the present phase of operations."[56] This was the conquest of the Ruhr. The First Army already was preparing to put another corps through the West Wall north of Aachen, seize Aachen, and renew the drive toward the Ruhr. The British shared responsibility for the drive on the Ruhr. To converge with the First Army along the west bank of the Rhine by driving southeast from Nijmegen became the "major task" of the Second British Army. The job would require at least two corps. Yet the emphasis on this task removed none of the Second Army's responsibility for holding the MARKET-GARDEN corridor. There could be no doubt about it: Field Marshal Montgomery needed men.

Despite the letter of 2 October urging quick release of the American airborne divisions, General Eisenhower was not unsympathetic to the British manpower problem. He knew that British Empire troops available in the United Kingdom had long since been absorbed and that only in reinforcement from the Mediterranean Theater, a long-range project, did the British have a hope of strengthening

themselves.[57] Even after Montgomery decided in early October that his commitments were too great and enemy strength too imposing to permit an immediate drive on the Ruhr, General Eisenhower did not press the issue of the airborne divisions. Though relieved temporarily of the Ruhr offensive, the British had to attack westward to help the Canadians open Antwerp. General Eisenhower had not underestimated the desirability of relieving the airborne troops; rather, he saw from his vantage point as Supreme Commander the more critical need of the 21 Army Group. At a conference with his top commanders on 18 October in Brussels, he gave tacit approval to the continued employment of the two U.S. divisions. They were to be released, he said, when the Second Army completed its part in clearing the approaches to Antwerp.[58]

As the fighting went on, figures in the day-by-day journal entries of the 82d and 101st Airborne Divisions continued to rise: D plus 30, D plus 40, D plus 50. Then, at last, on 11 November, D plus 55, the first units of the 82d Airborne Division began to move out of the line. Two days later, on D plus 57, the last of General Gavin's troops pulled back.

Still the ordeal did not end for the 101st Airborne Division. Not until 25 November, 69 days after the first parachutes had blossomed near Zon, did the first troops of General Taylor's division begin to withdraw. Two days later, on 27 November, D plus 71, the last American paratroopers pulled off the dreaded "island" north of the Waal.

[55] 21 A Gp Gen Opnl Sit and Dir, M–527, 27 Sep 44, and Ltr, de Guingand to Smith, 26 Sep 44, SHAEF SGS 381, II.

[56] FWD 16181, Eisenhower to CCS, 29 Sep 44, SHAEF SGS 381, II.

[57] Eisenhower, *Crusade in Europe,* p. 328.

[58] Report on Supreme Comdr's Conf, 18 Oct 44, dtd 22 Oct 44, SHAEF SGS 381, II.

The defensive phase had been rough. Casualty figures alone would show that. In the airborne phase, the 101st Airborne Division had lost 2,110 men killed, wounded, and missing. In the defensive phase, the division lost 1,682. The 82d had incurred 1,432 casualties in the first phase, 1,912 in the second. The cost of each of the two phases was approximately the same.[59]

In withdrawing after relief, the American divisions moved back by truck along the route of their landings. The Dutch

people turned out en masse. In Nijmegen, Grave, Veghel, St. Oedenrode, Zon, and Eindhoven, the Dutch set up a roar. "September 17!" the people shouted. "September 17!"

[59] Hq Br Abn Corps, Allied Abn Opns in Holland. Detailed figures follow:

	Killed	Wounded	Missing	Total
Total	685	2,703	206	3,594
82d Abn Div[a]	310	1,396	206	1,912
101st Abn Div	375	1,307	---------	1,682

[a] Figures for the 82d Airborne Division are not available for the last six days, past 5 November 1944.

CHAPTER IX

The Approaches to Antwerp

Legend has it that during the era of Roman transcendence in Europe, a regional lord by the name of Druon Antigon intercepted all ships plying the sixty miles of the Schelde estuary from the North Sea to the inland port of Antwerp. If the sailors refused or could not meet his demands for tribute, he cut off their right hands.

Whether true or not, the legend illustrates a fact that for centuries has influenced the use and growth of one of Europe's greatest ports. Whoever controls the banks of the Schelde estuary controls Antwerp. Plagued by Dutch jealousies that found expression in forts built along the Schelde, Antwerp did not begin until 1863 the modern growth that by the eve of World War II had transformed it into a metropolis of some 273,000 inhabitants.

Even before the landings in Normandy, the Allies had eyed Antwerp covetously. While noting that seizure of Le Havre would solve some of the problems of supplying Allied armies on the Continent, the pre-D-Day planners had predicted that "until after the development of Antwerp, the availability of port capacity will still limit the forces which can be maintained." [1] By the time the Allies had broken their confinement in Normandy to run footloose across northern France, the desire for Antwerp had grown so urgent that it had strongly influenced General Eisenhower in his decision to put the weight of the tottering logistical structure temporarily behind the thrust in the north. [2]

The decision paid dividends with capture of the city, its wharves and docks intact, by British armor on 4 September. (See Map 2.) Yet then it became apparent that the Germans intended to hold both banks of the Schelde along the sixty-mile course to the sea, to usurp the role of Druon Antigon. Antwerp was a jewel that could not be worn for want of a setting.

Had Field Marshal Mongomery immediately turned the Second British Army to clearing the banks of the estuary, the seaward approaches to the port well might have been opened speedily. But like the other Allies in those days of glittering triumphs, the British had their eyes focused to the east. Looking anxiously toward the possibility of having to fight a way across the Maas and the Rhine, the 21 Army Group commander wanted to force these barriers before the Germans could rally to defend them. "I considered it worth while," Montgomery wrote after the war, "to employ all our resources [to get across the Rhine], at the expense of any other undertaking." [3]

---

[1] SHAEF Planning Staff draft Post NEPTUNE Courses of Action After Capture of the Lodgment Area, II, 30 May 44, SHAEF SGS 381, I.

[2] *Report by the Supreme Commander to the Combined Chiefs of Staff* (Washington, 1946), p. 62.

[3] Montgomery, *Normandy to the Baltic*, p. 199.

Having captured Antwerp itself, General Dempsey's Second Army had made only a token attempt at opening the seaward approaches, an effort the Germans quickly discouraged with a series of small-scale counterattacks. Thereupon, one of the British corps resumed the chase northeastward toward Germany while another deployed about Antwerp in order to protect the left flank of the advancing corps. The Second Army's third corps had been left far behind, grounded in order to provide transport to move and supply the other two.[4]

Leaving Antwerp behind, the Second Army thus had embarked on a second part of its assigned mission, to "breach the sector of the Siegfried Line covering the Ruhr and then seize the Ruhr."[5] The task of clearing the banks of the Schelde eventually would fall to Lt. Gen. Henry D. G. Crerar's First Canadian Army, which was advancing along the Second Army's left flank under orders to clear the Channel ports.

Fanning out to the northeast, the Second Army had begun to encounter stiffening resistance along the line of the Albert Canal, not far from the Dutch-Belgian border. Nevertheless, by nightfall on 8 September, the British had two bridgeheads across the Albert and were driving toward the next barrier, the Meuse–Escaut Canal. It was on 11 September that the Guards Armoured Division seized the bridge over the Meuse–Escaut at De Groote Barrier, south of Eindhoven. Two days later other contingents of the Second Army crossed the canal fifteen miles to the west near Herenthals. Here, with supply lines

twanging, preparations necessary before the Second Army could participate in Operation MARKET-GARDEN made a pause imperative.[6]

In the meantime, the First Canadian Army had been investing the Channel ports, ridding the Pas de Calais of its launching sites for the deadly V-1 and V-2 bombs, and sweeping clear the left flank of the Second Army in the direction of Bruges and Ghent. On 1 September, the Canadians had seized Dieppe. On 9 September, they took Ostend and, on 12 September, Bruges, only to find that northeast of the two cities the Germans were preparing to defend the south bank of the Schelde estuary. The First Canadian Army's 1st British Corps[7] overcame all resistance at Le Havre on 12 September, but the port was so badly damaged that it was to handle no Allied tonnage until 9 October. Although Boulogne was the next port scheduled to be taken, the attack had to await special assault equipment used at Le Havre. Boulogne did not fall until 22 September. Of the two remaining ports, Dunkerque was masked, while Calais, attacked after seizure of Boulogne, fell on 1 October.[8]

Although capture of the Channel ports was expected to improve the Allied logis-

---

[4] *Ibid.*, p. 214.

[5] FWD 13765, Eisenhower to Comdrs, 4 Sep 44, SHAEF SGS 381, I.

[6] Montgomery, *Normandy to the Baltic,* pages 216-17, provides the tactical story for this period between 4 and 13 September.

[7] Most international of all Allied armies in the European theater, the First Canadian Army had two corps, one primarily Canadian, the other, during this phase of the war, primarily British. The army also included a Polish armored division, a Czechoslovakian armored brigade group, and at one time or another Dutch, Belgian, French, Norwegian, and American troops.

[8] Stacey, *The Canadian Army,* pp. 210-17; Charles P. Stacey, *The Victory Campaign,* vol. III of the official "History of the Canadian Army in the Second World War" (Ottawa: E. Cloutier, Queen's Printer, 1960), 323-425.

tical picture somewhat, none other than Le Havre could approach the tonnage potentiality of Antwerp. Le Havre itself was too far behind the front by the time of capture to affect the supply situation appreciably. Even with possession of the Channel ports, the importance of Antwerp to Allied plans could not be minimized.

While fighting to open the Channel ports, the Canadians had neither the strength nor supplies to do much about Antwerp. On 13 September one Canadian division had sought a bridgehead over two parallel canals northeast of Bruges (the Leopold Canal and the Canal de la Dérivation de la Lys) that marked the line which the Germans intended to hold on the Schelde's south bank, but German reaction was so violent and Canadian losses so heavy that the bridgehead had to be withdrawn the next day.

Beginning on 16 September the First Canadian Army assumed responsibility for Antwerp and its environs. Nevertheless, the supply demands of Operation MARKET-GARDEN and the battles for Boulogne and Calais continued to deny a large-scale offensive to open Antwerp. A lengthy stretch of the Schelde's south bank west and northwest of the city was clear as far west as a large inlet known as the Braakman, but it was from the Braakman to the sea that the Germans intended to hold the south bank. North of Antwerp the enemy remained perilously close to the city. During the night of 20 September contingents of the First Canadian Army began operations against the Albert and Antwerp–Turnhout Canals near the city to alleviate this situation somewhat. In the bridgehead finally established, the Canadians held temporarily to prepare for a contemplated advance northwest to seal off the isthmus

of South Beveland and thereby cut off the Germans holding this isthmus and the adjoining island of Walcheren.[9]

The Controversy About Antwerp

Because other responsibilities and the strained logistical situation would for some time deny unrestricted use of the First Canadian Army to open Antwerp, Allied plans for clearing the Schelde became inextricably tied up through September and well into October with Field Marshal Montgomery's determination to get a bridgehead beyond the Rhine. Though recognizing that use of Antwerp was "essential to sustain a powerful thrust deep into Germany,"[10] General Eisenhower had agreed at the conference with his commanders in Brussels on 10 September to defer the Antwerp operation while awaiting the outcome of Operation MARKET-GARDEN.[11] "The attractive possibility of quickly turning the German north flank led me to approve the temporary delay in freeing the vital port of Antwerp . . .," the Supreme Commander wrote later.[12]

Even after blessing MARKET-GARDEN, General Eisenhower continued to emphasize the importance of the Belgian port. "I consider the use of Antwerp so important to future operations," he wrote Field Marshal Montgomery on 13 September, "that we are prepared to go a long way in making the attack a success."[13] On the same day the Supreme Com-

---

[9] *Ibid.*, pp. 220–21.
[10] FWD 13889, Eisenhower to Montgomery, 5 Sep 44, Pogue files.
[11] Eisenhower, *Crusade in Europe,* pp. 306–07.
[12] *Report by the Supreme Commander to the Combined Chiefs of Staff*, p. 67.
[13] FWD 14758, Eisenhower to Montgomery, 13 Sep 44, SHAEF SGS 381, I.

mander issued a new directive in which he reiterated both his desire to have the Ruhr and his "previously expressed conviction that the early winning of deepwater ports and improved maintenance facilities in our rear are prerequisites to a final all-out assault on Germany proper." He continued, "Our port position today is such that any stretch of a week or ten days of bad Channel weather—a condition that grows increasingly probable with the receding summer—would paralyze our activities and make the maintenance of our forces even in defensive roles exceedingly difficult." [14]

For all the emphasis on the need for Antwerp, the Supreme Commander issued no dictum calling for a complete halt of the drive on the Ruhr in order to ensure opening the port. "The general plan . . .," he wrote, "is to push our forces forward to the Rhine, securing bridgeheads over the river, seize the Ruhr and concentrate our forces in preparation for a final non-stop drive into Germany." The 21 Army Group, which with the First U.S. Army was responsible for seizing the Ruhr, was "while this is going on . . ." to secure either Antwerp or Rotterdam as a port and forward base. [15]

In response to this directive, Montgomery quickly assured the Supreme Commander that he was "arranging to develop as early as possible operations designed to enable the port of Antwerp to be used." He explained that he was moving a British infantry division and headquarters of the First Canadian Army to Antwerp immediately. [16] On the same

day the Field Marshal issued a new directive to his army group. While stating that *"Our real objective . . . is the Ruhr,"* he said that "on the way" the Allies wanted Antwerp, plus Rotterdam. Clearance of the Schelde estuary to open Antwerp was to be "first priority" for the First Canadian Army. [17]

This matter of opening Antwerp became involved also with the continuing debate between General Eisenhower and Field Marshal Montgomery over the strategy of one thrust in the north as opposed to the Supreme Commander's "broad front" policy. The temporary accord that had come on this issue upon approval of MARKET-GARDEN at Brussels on 10 September had been short-lived. Five days later, on 15 September, General Eisenhower himself reopened the wound, perhaps with a view to healing it once and for all through a process of bloodletting. Looking beyond both Arnhem and Antwerp, he named Berlin as the ultimate Allied goal and said he desired to move on the German capital "by the most direct and expeditious route, with combined U.S.-British forces supported by other available forces moving through key centres and occupying strategic areas on the flanks, all in one co-ordinated, concerted operation." Writing this to his army group commanders, he virtually invited

---

[14] FWD 14764, Eisenhower to Comdrs, 13 Sep 44, SHAEF SGS 381, I.

[15] *Ibid.*

[16] Montgomery to Eisenhower, M–205, 14 Sep 44, SHAEF SGS 381, I.

[17] 21 A Gp Gen Opnl Sit and Dir, M–525, 14 Sep 44, SHAEF SGS 381, I. Italics in the original. Capture of Rotterdam was considered from time to time but primarily in the event Antwerp could not be opened. See SHAEF Planning Staff: Relative Priority of Operations for the Capture of Rotterdam and Antwerp, 16 Sep 44, Rapid Capture of Rotterdam, 18 Sep 44, and Rapid Capture of the Antwerp Area, dated only September 1944 but probably issued 18 September 1944, all in SHAEF SGS 381, I.

resumption of the strategy debate by asking them to give their reactions.[18]

Field Marshal Montgomery seized the opportunity to expound his view of one thrust in the north by the 21 Army Group plus the First U.S. Army. A cardinal principle of his theory was that men and supplies should be concentrated on the single operation, not frittered away in complementary drives.[19] General Bradley, for his part, returned to the pre-D-Day view that drives be made both north and south of the Ruhr. After seizure of the Ruhr, one main spearhead should be directed toward Berlin while the other armies supported it with simultaneous thrusts.[20]

In announcing his decision, General Eisenhower firmly rejected the idea of "one single knifelike drive toward Berlin" but denied he was considering an advance into Germany with all armies moving abreast. Instead, he intended, while placing his greatest support behind Montgomery and the First U.S. Army, that the Third Army advance in a supporting position to prevent concentration of German forces against the main drive and its flanks. At this time the Supreme Commander most concisely stated what has become known as his "broad front" policy:

What I do believe is that we must marshal our strength up along the western borders of Germany, to the Rhine if possible, insure adequate maintenance by getting Antwerp to working at full blast at the earliest pos-

sible moment and then carry out the drive you [Montgomery] suggest.[21]

This exchange of views, plus Field Marshal Montgomery's insistence on putting everything behind the drive in the north to the exclusion of the forces in the south, led General Eisenhower to conclude that he and his chief British subordinate were not talking about the same thing. Not one but two drives were under consideration: one for getting the Ruhr, one after getting the Ruhr. At a conference with his army group commanders and supply chiefs at Versailles on 22 September, he tried to clarify the matter.[22] He asked his commanders to make a clear distinction between the final drive on Berlin and present operations, which aimed at breaching the West Wall and seizing the Ruhr. For the second drive, he said, he required "general acceptance of the fact that the possession of an additional major deepwater port on our north flank was an indispensable prerequisite for the final drive deep into Germany. The envelopment of the Ruhr from the north by 21st Army Group, supported by 1st Army," he continued, "is the main effort of the present phase of operations." In addition, the 21 Army Group was to open Antwerp as a matter of urgency.[23]

As the meeting progressed on 22 September, General Eisenhower approved a plan whereby the 21 Army Group might utilize the gains of MARKET-GARDEN and the support of the First U.S. Army to

---

[18] Eisenhower to A Gp Comdrs, 15 Sep 44, SHAEF SGS 381, I.

[19] Montgomery to Eisenhower, 18 Sep 44; Montgomery to Eisenhower, M–223, 21 Sep 44, Pogue files.

[20] Bradley to Eisenhower, 21 Sep 44, Pogue files. A detailed discussion of the strategy debate during this period may be found in Pogue, *The Supreme Command,* Ch. XIV.

[21] Eisenhower to Montgomery, 20 Sep 44, Pogue files.

[22] Montgomery was not present because of operational duties connected with MARKET-GARDEN but was represented by his chief of staff, General de Guingand.

[23] Min, Mtg held at SHAEF Fwd, 22 Sep 44, SHAEF SGS 381, I.

envelop the Ruhr from the north. First Army support involved assuming responsibility for clearing the great gap which had developed west of the Maas River between the British right flank and the left flank of the XIX U.S. Corps, and, so far as current resources might permit, continuing a thrust toward Cologne and Bonn.[24] This plan General Eisenhower sanctioned despite a report from the 21 Army Group Chief of Staff, General de Guingand, that an attack on Walcheren Island, the most formidable German position guarding the mouth of the Schelde, could not be mounted before 7 October "at the earliest" and despite an estimate by the Allied naval commander, Admiral Sir Bertram H. Ramsey, that somewhere between one and three weeks would be required to remove the mines from the entrance to Antwerp. The port might not be usable until about 1 November.[25]

These decisions of 22 September were made at a time when hope still remained for the unqualified success of MARKET-GARDEN. Once the possibility of holding a bridgehead over the Neder Rijn at Arnhem and of outflanking the West Wall was gone, Field Marshal Montgomery had to turn to another plan for getting the Ruhr. While agreeing that the opening of Antwerp was "absolutely essential" to any deep advance into Germany, he proposed that he turn his attention for the moment to an existing opportunity to destroy the enemy forces barring the way to the Ruhr. He suggested that while the First Canadian Army cleared the approaches to Antwerp, the Second British Army operate from Nijmegen against the northwest

corner of the Ruhr in conjunction with a drive by the First U.S. Army toward Cologne. In effect, this was a return— after a deviation imposed by Operation MARKET-GARDEN—to Montgomery's long-advocated plan for capturing the Ruhr by a double envelopment.[26]

When General Eisenhower, at "first hasty glance," approved this plan,[27] Field Marshal Montgomery issued the necessary directive. For the Antwerp phase, he emphasized that "The Canadian Army will at once develop operations designed to enable us to have the free use of the port of Antwerp. The early completion of these operations is vital. . . ."[28]

Without augmentation of the First Canadian Army's ground strength and logistical support, this actually was little more than lip service to the Antwerp cause. Dutifully, the Canadians launched an operation on 2 October designed to push northwest from Antwerp to seal off the isthmus of South Beveland, thereby setting the stage for a subsequent drive to open the Schelde. At the same time they were expected to make another drive northward along the left flank of the MARKET-GARDEN salient to reach the south bank of the Maas River, in order to release British forces for the drive on the Ruhr. A few days later they set out to clear the south bank of the estuary. Judging from the fighting that developed the Canadians would need a long time to do the entire complex job of opening Antwerp plus clearing the MARKET-GARDEN left flank. Likewise, a prelim-

---

[24] *Ibid.* See also FWD 15510, Eisenhower to Bradley, 23 Sep 44, same file.
[25] Bradley to Patton, 23 Sep 44, in 12th A Gp 371.3, Military Objectives, I.

[26] De Guingand to Smith, 26 Sep 44, SHAEF SGS 381, II.
[27] Eisenhower to Montgomery, 27 Sep 44, SHAEF SGS 381, II.
[28] 21 A Gp· Gen Opnl Sit and Dir, M–527, 27 Sep 44, SHAEF SGS 381, II.

inary step necessary before the Second British Army could attack toward the Ruhr, that of eliminating the Germans from the British right and U.S. left flanks west of the Maas, failed when U.S. forces encountered unyielding resistance.[29]

Faced with four major tasks—opening Antwerp, maintaining the MARKET-GARDEN salient, conducting the Ruhr offensive, and committing British forces in the great gap west of the Maas—Montgomery reported to General Eisenhower at the end of the first week in October that his forces were insufficient. Much of the problem, he intimated, might be solved by a change in the existing command situation between the 21 Army Group and the First U.S. Army. This was a return to a long-standing tenet of the Field Marshal's that for purposes of co-ordination of the main thrust in the north, the First Army should be under British command.[30]

While admitting that the 21 Army Group's commitments were too heavy for its resources, General Eisenhower refused to agree that the problem had anything to do with command. He proposed either that U.S. forces relieve the British of some responsibility by pushing the 12th Army Group boundary northward or that General Bradley transfer two U.S. divisions to the British. He agreed that plans for a co-ordinated Ruhr offensive be post-

poned until more U.S. divisions could reach the front. Six of these, he noted, were marking time in staging areas on the Continent because of lack of transportation and supplies to maintain them up front.[31]

Of the two proposals for strengthening the 21 Army Group, Field Marshal Montgomery accepted the second. General Bradley thereupon transferred a U.S. armored division (the 7th) to British command to help clear the great gap between British and U.S. forces west of the Maas. He also alerted the 104th Infantry Division to move from a Normandy staging area to the vicinity of Brussels on 15 October to await any call for assistance in the Antwerp fight.[32]

Once the Ruhr offensive was postponed and two U.S. divisions became available, the way was clear for Montgomery to strengthen the First Canadian Army for the opening of Antwerp, or at least to remove the necessity for the Canadians to clear the left flank of the MARKET-GARDEN salient. But the British commander still thought the Canadians could handle both jobs. On 9 October in a directive he said: "The use of Antwerp is vital to the Allies in order that we can develop our full potential. Therefore the operations to open the port must have priority in regard to troops, ammunition, and so on." Yet once again, in the matter of an increase in troops, he offered no genuine assistance. Still looking ahead to the Ruhr offensive, Montgomery forewent strengthening the First Canadian Army substantially by chaining

<hr>

[29] For the First Canadian Army mission, see 21 A Gp, M–527. For the action west of the Maas, see below, Chapter X.

[30] Montgomery to Eisenhower, M–260, 6 Oct 44, and M–264, 7 Oct 44, both in Pogue files. General Eisenhower consistently refused this request. Because a command change did not occur during the period of the Siegfried Line Campaign and therefore did not affect First Army operations directly, the subject is not considered in detail in this volume. The command controversy is discussed at length in Pogue, *The Supreme Command.*

[31] Eisenhower to 21 A Gp for Bradley (msg undtd but apparently written 8 Oct 44), Pogue files.

[32] Bradley to Hodges, 8 Oct 44, in 12th A Gp 371.3, Military Objectives, I.

the Second British Army to two tasks he deemed prerequisite to a Ruhr offensive: (1) making "absolutely certain" the Nijmegen bridgehead was "firm and secure," and (2) clearing the Germans from the region west of the Maas.[33]

On the same day that Field Marshal Montgomery issued this directive, General Eisenhower received a report from the Royal Navy that stirred him to action. The report apparently climaxed an apprehension that had been growing in the Supreme Commander's mind for several days, a concern that the 21 Army Group could not open the Schelde estuary while at the same time pursuing its other objectives. Unless supplied immediately with adequate ammunition stocks, the report of the Royal Navy indicated, the First Canadian Army would be unable to move to open Antwerp until November.

General Eisenhower promptly placed all stress on clearing the banks of the Schelde. He warned Field Marshal Montgomery that unless Antwerp were opened by the middle of November, Allied operations would come to a standstill. He declared that "of all our operations on our entire front from Switzerland to the Channel, I consider Antwerp of first importance, and I believe that the operations designed to clear up the entrance require your personal attention." [34]

Apparently stung by the implication that he was not pushing the attack for Antwerp, the 21 Army Group commander promptly denied the Navy's "wild statements." The attack, he said, was already under way and going well. In passing, he reminded the Supreme Commander

that the Versailles conference of 22 September had listed the attack on the Ruhr as the main effort of the current phase of operations, and that General Eisenhower only the day before had declared that the first mission of both army groups was gaining the Rhine north of Bonn.[35]

In reply, General Eisenhower explicitly spelled out the priority of Antwerp. "Let me assure you," he declared in a message of 10 October, "that nothing I may ever say or write with regard to future plans in our advance eastward is meant to indicate any lessening of the need for Antwerp, which I have always held as vital, and which has grown more pressing as we enter the bad weather period." [36] Three days later, after Field Marshal Montgomery again had suggested changes in the command arrangement so that he might have greater flexibility in his operations, General Eisenhower acted to remove any doubts on both Antwerp and command. He declared that the question was not one of command but of taking Antwerp. He did not know the exact state of the Field Marshal's forces, he said, but he knew they were rich in supplies as compared with U.S. and French units. Because of logistical shortages, the need to put Antwerp quickly in workable condition was pressing. Field Marshal Sir Alan Brooke and General Marshall, British and U.S. Army chiefs, had emphasized on a recent visit to SHAEF that they shared this view. Despite the desire to open Antwerp, General Eisenhower said, he had approved MARKET-GARDEN. All recent experience, however, had pointed to the

---

[33] 21 A Gp Gen Opnl Sit and Dir, M–530, 9 Oct 44, SHAEF SGS 381, II.
[34] S–61466, Eisenhower to Montgomery, 9 Oct 44, Pogue files.

[35] M–268, Montgomery to Eisenhower, 9 Oct 44, Pogue files.
[36] Eisenhower to Montgomery, 10 Oct 44, Pogue files.

great need for opening of the Schelde estuary, and he was willing, "as always," to give additional U.S. troops and supplies to make that possible.

General Eisenhower added that the operation could involve no question of command, "Since everything that can be brought in to help, no matter of what nationality, belongs to you." Then he dealt at length with the subject of command. If, after receiving these views, Field Marshal Montgomery still classed them as "unsatisfactory," an issue would exist which would have to be settled by "higher authority." [37]

Even before this message reached the 21 Army Group commander, he apparently had concluded that the First U.S. Army could not reach the Rhine and thus that no reason existed for British forces to move alone toward the Ruhr. With the assertion that the Antwerp operations were to assume "complete priority . . ., without any qualification whatsoever," he had already dispatched "the whole of the available offensive power" of the Second British Army to help the Canadians speed the opening of the port.[38]

After receiving General Eisenhower's letter, the Field Marshal assured him that "you will hear no more on the subject of command from me." He added:

I have given you my views and you have given your answer. I and all of us will weigh in one hundred percent to do what you want and we will pull it through without a doubt. I have given Antwerp top

priority in all operations in 21 Army Group and all energies and efforts will now be devoted towards opening up the place. Your very devoted and loyal subordinate.[39]

The Battle of the Schelde

Much of the difficulty in clearing the approaches to Antwerp rested with terrain. This is the North Sea littoral, canal country, much of it below sea level and much of it at this time already inundated at the personal order of Hitler in hope of augmenting German defenses.[40] (*Map 2*) The Schelde actually is two huge mouths, known as the East Schelde and the West Schelde, the latter being of primary concern as the channel to Antwerp. On the West Schelde's south bank the enemy had withdrawn into a bastion lying west of the Braakman and extending along the south bank to a point opposite Zeebrugge on the Channel coast. This was to become known, after a minor port within the sector, as the Breskens Pocket. To protect this pocket on the landward side, the Germans had constructed their defensive line behind an almost continuous moat formed by the Braakman inlet and two canals, the Leopold and the Canal de la Dérivation de la Lys. The West Schelde's north bank is formed by South Beveland, a peninsula joined to the mainland by an isthmus carrying a road and a railway, and, farther to the west, by Walcheren Island. About ten miles wide and joined to South Beveland only by a narrow causeway, this island was heavily fortified. So formidable did the Allies consider the

[37] Eisenhower to Montgomery, 13 Oct 44, Pogue files. For a discussion of the command relationship between Eisenhower and Montgomery, see Pogue, *The Supreme Command*, pp. 289–90.

[38] 21 A Gp Gen Opnl Sit and Dir, M–532, 16 Oct 44, SHAEF SGS 381, II. See also M–77, Montgomery to Eisenhower, 14 Oct 44, Pogue files.

[39] M–281, Montgomery to Eisenhower, 16 Oct 44, Pogue files.

[40] TWX, *Army Group B* to *Fifteenth Army*, 1830, 7 Sep 44, *Army Group B, Operationsbefehle*.

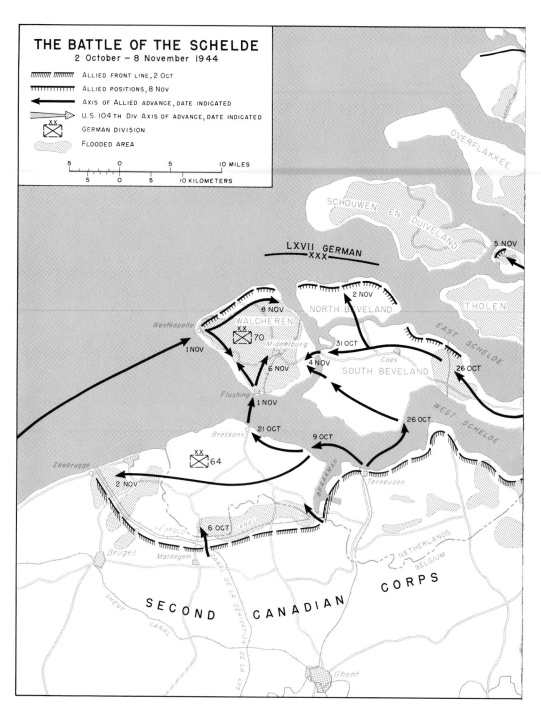

THE BATTLE OF THE SCHELDE
2 October – 8 November 1944

⫿⫿⫿⫿⫿⫿	ALLIED FRONT LINE, 2 OCT
⫿⫿⫿⫿⫿⫿	ALLIED POSITIONS, 8 NOV
◀━━━━	AXIS OF ALLIED ADVANCE, DATE INDICATED
▧▧▧▷	U.S. 104TH DIV AXIS OF ADVANCE, DATE INDICATED
⊠ XX	GERMAN DIVISION
░░░░░	FLOODED AREA

5   0   5   10 MILES

5   0   5   10 KILOMETERS

MAP 2

ROTTERDAM

ARMED
FORCES NETHERLANDS
XXXX
FIFTEENTH GERMAN

XX
346

XX
719

Waal R.

XX
85

XX
245

XX
711

LXVII XX LXXXVIII
GERMAN X GERMAN
X

XX
256

XX
59

Maas R.

HOLLANDSCHDIEP

Moerdijk

s'Hertogenbosch

6 NOV

Klundert

7 NOV

Raamsdonk

Steenbergen

5 NOV

Mark

30
OCT

Breda

XXX 12

4 NOV

Roosendaal

29 OCT

Tilburg

28 OCT
Rijsbergen

104 XX 1 Pol Armd

FIRST XX SECOND
CDN XXX BR

49 Br XX 104

Bergen op Zoom

22 OCT

Zundert

Baarle-
Nassau
3 OCT

Poppel

24 OCT Woensdrecht

16 OCT

27 OCT

LXVII XX LXXXVIII
GERMAN X GERMAN

346

30 OCT

US XX 104
22 OCT

Wuestwezel

St Leonard

ANTWERP

XX
711

XX
719

TURNHOUT   CANAL   Turnhout

TO EINDHOVEN

FIRST   BRITISH

CORPS

(FROM 23 SEP)

2 OCT

ANTWERP

Herenthals

ALBERT   CANAL

MEUSE - ESCAUT   CANAL

TO DE GROOTE
BARRIER

Scheide R.

E. DUNAY

defenses that, in the early stages of planning to open Antwerp, General Eisenhower had allotted the First Allied Airborne Army to taking Walcheren, though this was later canceled.[41]

Whoever set out to clear the banks of the West Schelde also had to face the fact that the enemy here was a strong, concentrated force. Here was a main part of the *Fifteenth Army*—once Hitler's "anti-invasion army," which had waited futilely for invasion along the Pas de Calais while the weaker *Seventh Army* had absorbed the actual blow in Normandy. Although some divisions and weapons had been detached for use in Normandy, much of the *Fifteenth Army* had continued to guard the coast against a feared second, and perhaps larger, Allied landing. By the time the Germans had hearkened to the steadily growing danger of Allied spearheads racing across northern France and Belgium, it was too late. The swift British armored thrust which captured Brussels and Antwerp during the first days of September had trapped the *Fifteenth Army* against the coast. When counterattacks failed to break the British cordon, the only way out for the Germans lay to the north across the waters of the Schelde.[42]

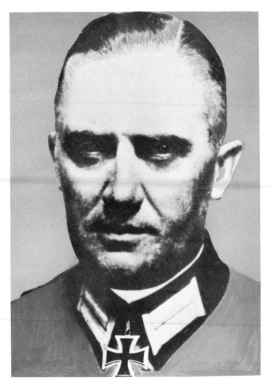

GENERAL VON ZANGEN

Having left contingents to hold the Channel ports, the *Fifteenth Army* commander, General von Zangen, had been withdrawing toward the south bank of the Schelde with the bulk of his forces when word had come from Hitler himself that Walcheren Island was to be held as a "fortress," after the manner of the Channel ports, and that a "permanent" bridgehead was to be maintained on the Schelde's south bank.[43] As finally formulated, the German plan called for General von Zangen to assume command of all of the southwestern part of the Netherlands in a sector adjacent to

---

[41] Cbl ADSEC (de Guingand) to TAC Hq EXFOR (Montgomery), 7 Sep 44, SHAEF SGS 381, I. Basing their judgment on terrain and types of targets, General Brereton, the airborne army commander, and Air Chief Marshal Sir Trafford Leigh-Mallory, chief of the Allied Expeditionary Air Force, recommended cancellation. General Eisenhower canceled the plan on 21 September 1944. See FWD 15384, Eisenhower to Montgomery, 21 Sep 44, same file.

[42] For additional details, see Lucian Heichler, German Defense of the Gateway to Antwerp, a study prepared to complement this volume and filed in OCMH.

[43] Rads, *A Gp B* to *Fifteenth Army*, 1530, 5 Sep, and 0100, 8 Sep 44, *A Gp B, Operationsbefehle.*

General Student's *First Parachute Army.* Leaving an infantry division (the *64th*) to defend the south bank of the Schelde, Zangen was to install another infantry division (the *70th*) on Walcheren Island and a third (the *245th*) on the peninsula of South Beveland. Because these positions were officially labeled "fortresses," the divisions operated through no corps headquarters but were directly subordinate to the *Fifteenth Army.* On the mainland, the *LXVII Corps* under General der Infanterie Otto Sponheimer was to be responsible for a sector north of Antwerp along the west flank of the *First Parachute Army.* General Sponheimer was to control three divisions, including the *719th Infantry Division,* which was in sad shape after having constituted the west wing of the *First Parachute Army* along the Albert Canal. Another division was to act as a *Fifteenth Army* reserve, while another, the *59th Infantry Division* (General Poppe), was to move to Tilburg as *Army Group B* reserve. As events developed, both the *59th Division* and the *245th Division* from South Beveland were to be shifted against the MARKET-GARDEN salient.[44]

By 17 September most of these arrangements had been either initiated or completed. In the meantime, General von Zangen had been conducting a withdrawal from the south bank of the Schelde to Walcheren Island. In the light of Allied air superiority, this withdrawal was one of the more noteworthy German accomplishments during this stage of the war. As early as four days after British armor had trapped the *Fifteenth Army* by seizing Antwerp, nearly ten thousand

Germans already had been ferried across the West Schelde from Breskens. By 11 September Allied air attacks had damaged Breskens so severely that daily shipping capacity had been cut by 40 percent and transport across the three-mile width of the estuary was impossible during daylight except under the foulest weather conditions. Nevertheless, by 22 September, German evacuation was complete. In two and a half weeks, the Germans had staged a little Dunkerque to the tune of more than 86,000 men, more than 600 artillery pieces, better than 6,000 vehicles, over 6,000 horses, and a wealth of miscellaneous matériel. For all the bombs and cannon of Allied aircraft, the Germans had saved a small army.[45]

Completion of the *Fifteenth Army*'s withdrawal across the West Schelde left the Breskens Pocket on the south bank a responsibility of the commander of the *64th Infantry Division,* Generalmajor Kurt Eberding. Possessing an infantry combat strength of roughly 2,350 men, General Eberding also had some 8,650 support and miscellaneous troops. The troops were well supplied with machine guns, mortars, and artillery.[46]

On the West Schelde's north bank, Generalleutnant Wilhelm Daser's *70th Infantry Division* had an infantry combat strength of nearly 7,500, plus some 300 engineers. These were organized into three regiments, two on the island and one on South Beveland, the latter after the *245th Division* was shifted eastward against the MARKET-GARDEN salient.

---

[44] Details and documentation of these developments may be found in Heichler, German Defense of the Gateway to Antwerp.

[45] Daily Sitreps, *A Gp B,* 0130, 9 Sep, 0215, 12 Sep, and 0135, 23 Sep 44, all in *A Gp B, Tagesmeldungen.* Strength figures from Navy Special Staff Knuth as furnished by Historical Section (GS), Canadian Army Headquarters.

[46] TWX, *A Gp B* to *OB WEST,* 1500, 23 Sep 44, *A Gp B, Operationsbefehle.*

Some German commanders later were to criticize commitment of the *70th Division* in a strategic spot like Walcheren, for the division represented a collection of men suffering from ailments of the digestive tract. Because of a special diet required, the division was nicknamed the White Bread Division.[47] As if to compensate for physical shortcomings of the troops, the *70th Division* controlled an unusual wealth of artillery, some 177 pieces, including 67 fixed naval guns.[48]

Two other German divisions were to figure prominently in the fighting about Antwerp. These were the *346th* and *711th Infantry Divisions* of General Sponheimer's *LXVII Corps* on the mainland north of Antwerp. Of the two, the *346th* (Generalleutnant Erich Diestel)[49] was the stronger with an infantry combat strength of somewhat better than 2,400 men, augmented by an artillery force of thirty-eight 105-mm. howitzers. The *711th Division* (Generalleutnant Josef Reichert) was considerably weaker, a "static" division which had been badly mauled during July and August. In mid-September, the *711th* had only three battalions of German infantry and another composed primarily of Armenians and remnants of an *Ost* battalion. The division had but nine artillery pieces of various calibers. Less prominent roles would be played by the *719th Infantry Division* on the *LXVII Corps* left wing and by contingents of the *LXXXVIII*

Corps, the latter after the left wing of the Second British Army got into the fight.

On the Allied side, the decisive phase of the Antwerp operation opened on 2 October, two weeks before Field Marshal Montgomery blessed it with unequivocal priority. Because the First Canadian Army commander, General Crerar, was absent on sick leave, his temporary replacement, Lt. Gen. G. G. Simonds, was in charge. General Simonds employed a plan previously formulated under General Crerar's direction and involving four main tasks: (1) to clear the region north of Antwerp and seal off the isthmus to South Beveland; (2) coincidentally, to reduce the Breskens Pocket south of the Schelde; then (3) to seize South Beveland; and finally (4) to reduce Walcheren Island. All these tasks were to be accomplished by the 2d Canadian Corps. When Field Marshal Montgomery assigned the additional task of clearing the region south of the Maas River between the Schelde and the MARKET-GARDEN salient, General Simonds gave the job to the 1st British Corps. With the new emphasis on Antwerp that came in mid-October, the 12 Corps of the Second British Army assumed part of the latter responsibility.[50]

From a bridgehead across the Antwerp–Turnhout Canal northeast of Antwerp, the 2d Canadian Division opened the decisive phase of the battle of the Schelde on 2 October. Against the enemy's *346th Division*, the Canadians attacked northwest to seal the isthmus to South Beveland. For the first few days the Canadian infantry made steady progress, but as the drive neared Woensdrecht the

---

[47] MS # B-274, 165. *Reserve Division und 70. Infanterie, Division 1944 Holland* (Daser).

[48] Strength figures for all but the *64th Div* are from TWX (Weekly Strength Rpt as of 16 Sep 44), *A Gp B to OB WEST,* 2400, 22 Sep 44, *A Gp B, Operationsbefehle.*

[49] After 11 October 1944 Generalmajor Walter Steinmueller.

[50] Unless otherwise noted, the story of the First Canadian Army operations is based upon Stacey, *The Canadian Army,* pp. 220–30, and Stacey, *The Victory Campaign.*

stalemate settling over the MARKET-GARDEN salient permitted the Germans to send reinforcements. At Woensdrecht they committed both Colonel von der Heydte's *6th Parachute Regiment* and a part of *Kampfgruppe Chill*.[51] Not until 16 October, two weeks after the start of the attack, did Woensdrecht fall.

In the meantime, on 6 October, the 2d Canadian Corps opened the drive on the Breskens Pocket with the 3d Canadian Division, moving behind massed flame throwers, forcing two crossings of the Leopold Canal. Here General Eberding's *64th Division* lay in wait. For three days the situation in the Canadian bridgeheads was perilous. On 9 October contingents of the 3d Canadian Division staged an amphibious end run from Terneuzen, but not until 14 October, after a few tanks got across the canal, did substantial progress begin. By mid-October, after nearly a fortnight's fighting, about half the Breskens Pocket remained in German hands.

This was the situation when on 16 October Field Marshal Montgomery accorded unqualified support to the battle of the Schelde. The net effect was that the 12 Corps of the Second British Army took over the eastern part of the Canadian line to launch a drive from the MARKET-GARDEN salient near s' Hertogenbosch to sweep the south bank of the Maas River. Their line thus shortened, the Canadians were to push their right wing forward to the Maas in that part of the zone remaining to them between Woensdrecht and the British.

The bitter fight to eliminate the Breskens Pocket continued. On 21 October Breskens finally fell. By the end of the month the Canadians had pushed General Eberding's remaining troops into a water-logged pocket near Zeebrugge and on 2 November captured the German general. All resistance in the Breskens Pocket ended the next day. After almost a month of the most costly kind of fighting, the south bank of the West Schelde was clear.

In fulfillment of Field Marshal Montgomery's directive of 16 October, a corps of the Second British Army on 22 October opened an offensive with four divisions to sweep the south bank of the Maas. At the same time, the 1st British Corps on the right wing of the First Canadian Army began to push northward toward the Maas. Its right flank thus protected, the 2d Canadian Corps was to accelerate operations to seize South Beveland and Walcheren, thereby to clear the West Schelde's north bank.[52]

Making labored but steady progress, the Second Army's drive resulted in capture of two main objectives, 's Hertogenbosch and Tilburg, two and six days, respectively, after the offensive opened. By the end of October Second Army patrols linked south of the Maas with the right flank of the First Canadian Army's 1st British Corps. By 5 November the Second Army had cleared its entire zone. Unfortunately, inclement weather during much of this period had enabled thousands of Germans to escape almost unhindered to the north bank of the Maas.

Commanded by Lt. Gen. Sir John T. Crocker, the First Canadian Army's 1st British Corps had been far from idle, even during the month between mid-September

---

[51] Daily Sitreps, *A Gp B*, 0045, 8 Oct, and 0115, 13 Oct 44, *A Gp B, Tagesmeldungen*.

[52] Unless otherwise noted, the account of the Second British Army's October offensive is based on Montgomery, *Normandy to the Baltic*, pp. 251–67.

and mid-October when this corps alone had faced the giant task of clearing the entire region between South Beveland and the MARKET-GARDEN corridor. Before the end of September General Crocker's troops had pushed north to occupy Turnhout and had established a sizable bridgehead beyond the Antwerp–Turnhout Canal. By the time the Second Army took over part of the zone and attacked on 22 October, the 1st British Corps had pushed north to the Dutch-Belgian border. As the Second Army joined the offensive, General Crocker's corps consisted of one British infantry division and two armored divisions, one Polish, one Canadian. On 23 October, the day after the big drive commenced, the corps assumed even more of an international complexion as the 104th U.S. Infantry Division began moving into the line to help in the drive northward to the Maas.

Baptism of Fire

Commanded by Maj. Gen. Terry de la Mesa Allen, who already had gained renown as commander of the 1st Division in North Africa and Sicily, the 104th (Timberwolf) Division which entered the line on 23 October had never experienced combat. Almost two months before, the 104th had sailed for Europe but had spent most of the interval in a Normandy staging area because the logistical situation precluded maintenance of additional units up front. The division became one of two—one British (the 49th Infantry), one American—with which Field Marshal Montgomery bolstered the First Canadian Army for the battle of the Schelde.[53]

Men of the Timberwolf Division assumed responsibility for a sector near the Dutch-Belgian frontier astride a main highway leading northeast from Antwerp to Breda, some twenty miles south of the Maas River and six miles southwest of a German strongpoint in the village of Zundert. Here, at the town of Wuestwezel, the troops scarcely had time to erase their awe of combat or to become familiar with their surroundings—flat, pine-studded, water-soaked terrain—before General Crocker ordered that they join the corps offensive northward. The initial division objective was Zundert.

The German situation in the sector of the 1st British Corps where the 104th Division was to operate obviously had become almost remediless. The day the Allied offensive began, the Commander in Chief West, Rundstedt, had admitted as much, though somewhat obliquely, in an appeal to the German high command. "On the occasion of my visit to *Fifteenth Army*," Rundstedt reported, "I was able personally to witness the exhaustion of the divisions fighting in the penetration area. For continuation of the operations there—which will decide the use of Antwerp harbor—immediate arrival of sufficient replacements is of decisive importance . . . ."[54] Four days later, in authorizing a withdrawal in front of the 1st British Corps, Rundstedt warned that this move was not to be interpreted "by

---

[53] The 104th Division story is based upon official unit records; a comprehensive unit history by Leo A. Hoegh and Howard J. Doyle, *Timberwolf Tracks* (Washington: Infantry Journal Press, 1946), pp. 43–102; and Lt Oliver J. Kline, Action North of Antwerp, in Ninth United States Army Operations, Vol. III, Combat in Holland, a mimeographed series prepared by the 4th Information and Historical Service and filed with official Ninth Army records.

[54] TWX, *OB WEST* to OKW, 1115, 22 Oct 44, *OB WEST, Befehle/Meldungen 21.X.–31.X. 44.*

any stretch of the imagination" as foreshadowing a general withdrawal. That, he said, "is, and will be out of the question." [55]

No amount of forceful language actually could conceal that this authorized withdrawal was, in fact, a first step in a general withdrawal behind the water barriers to the north. Two days later, Rundstedt noted in a report to the high command that the *Fifteenth Army* would fight forward of the Maas, "to the last. Nonetheless," he added, "it is my duty to report that, if the heavy enemy pressure continues, we must expect the gradual but total destruction of *Fifteenth Army*—unless its mission is changed." [56] When this report reached Hitler, the Fuehrer displayed—for him—a remarkably sympathetic acceptance of the facts. Though Hitler reiterated that the *Fifteenth Army* must hold well south of the Maas, he as much as sanctioned further withdrawals by adding, "If new and serious penetrations should result from continued enemy attacks, threatening to destroy elements of the army, *Fifteenth Army* will at least maintain large bridgeheads south of the Maas . . . ." [57]

Though unaware of these German conversations, General Crocker's intelligence staff nevertheless had divined that the Germans had no choice but to delay in successive positions. The last in the sector of the 1st British Corps no doubt would be based upon the little Mark River, which runs generally from east to west about five miles south of the Maas.

This was, in fact, the tack which the *Fifteenth Army* commander, General von Zangen, followed in interpreting Hitler's orders as sanction for withdrawing to bridgeheads south of the Maas. [58]

On a lower level the 104th Division, in assuming positions along the Antwerp–Breda highway, had occupied a line virtually astride the boundary between the enemy's *346th* and *711th Divisions*. The first of the delaying positions the 104th Division expected to encounter was southwest of Zundert almost exactly along the Dutch-Belgian border, a position manned by an estimated seven understrength infantry battalions.

Advancing due north with three regiments abreast, General Allen's Timberwolves received their baptism of fire on 25 October. By nightfall they had pushed back stubborn German patrols and outposts almost to the frontier. Continuing to advance in the darkness, the men made the first in a long procession of night attacks that were eventually to give the 104th Division something of a name in that department. The second day they forced the main delaying groups southwest of Zundert to withdraw and by daylight on 27 October were set to assault the village.

While two regiments maintained pressure west of the Antwerp–Breda highway, the 413th Infantry (Col. Welcome P. Waltz) moved close behind an artillery preparation to storm the objective. Supported by attached British Churchill tanks, the regiment seized Zundert before the end of the day. No longer did men of the 104th wonder at the swish of a shell

---

[55] Order, *OB WEST* to *A Gp B*, 2145, 26 Oct 44, *OB WEST, Befehle/Meldungen.*

[56] Rpt, Rundstedt to Jodl (OKW), 1330, 28 Oct 44, *OB WEST, Befehle/Meldungen.*

[57] Order, *OB WEST* to *A Gp B* (relaying Hitler order), 2355, 29 Oct 44, *OB WEST, Befehle/Meldungen.*

[58] Rpt, *A Gp B* to *OB WEST*, 29 Oct 44, *OB WEST, Befehle/Meldungen.* British intelligence estimates are reflected in 104th Div, Annex 2, Intel Annex to AAR, 23–31 Oct 44, dtd 5 Nov 44.

whether it was coming in or going out. They knew what it meant to kill men and to have their own killed. If a machine gun went "br-r-r-r-p," it was German; if it went "put-put-put," it was one of their own. The green division was fast becoming experienced.

The next day, 28 October, the 104th Division occupied Rijsbergen, about half-way from Zundert to Breda. That night the 415th Infantry (Col. John H. Cochran) launched the second night attack in the division's short combat history to break another delaying position covering the Roosendaal–Breda highway that ran diagonally across the division's front about seven miles north of Zundert. General Allen now was prepared to direct his troops either on Breda or to the north and northwest against the Mark River.

Even as Colonel Cochran's 415th Infantry was reaching the Roosendaal–Breda road, General Allen was receiving his orders. Along with the three other divisions of the corps, which had been advancing generally northward on either flank of the Americans, the 104th Division was to be reoriented to the northwest to force crossings of the Mark. Responsibility for Breda was to fall to the 1st Polish Armored Division on the 104th Division's right.

By 30 October, sixth day of the offensive, General Allen had concentrated his division along the Roosendaal–Breda highway. As the day opened, Colonel Cochran's 415th Infantry spearheaded a drive toward the Mark River in quest of a crossing near the village of Standdaarbuiten. The 414th Infantry (Col. Anthony J. Touart) subsequently was to cross and pursue the attack to seize Klundert, almost within sight of the south bank of the Maas.

As the 415th Infantry neared a bridge over the Mark at Standdaarbuiten, any doubt that this was to be the enemy's main position rapidly dissolved. Machine gun, mortar, and artillery fire showered across from the north bank. Even so, a sneak attack by one battalion almost succeeded in seizing the bridge intact; only at the last moment did the Germans blow it.

Neither the 49th British Infantry Division on the 104th's left flank nor the 1st Polish Armored Division on the right had yet reached the Mark. Perhaps counting on the surprise a quick thrust might achieve, the corps commander, General Crocker, told General Allen not to wait for the other divisions but to force a crossing of the river alone before daylight the next day. The 415th Infantry's 1st Battalion, commanded by Maj. Fred E. Needham, drew the assignment.

Crossing northeast of Standdaarbuiten just before dawn on 31 October, men of the leading company clung to the sides of their assault boats to avoid grazing machine gun fire that swept the crossing site. Once on the north bank, they stormed across an open meadow to gain protection along a dike from which they might cover the crossing of subsequent waves. By 0900 the entire battalion had made it and pushed more than a thousand yards beyond the river. But here the Germans forced a halt. The men could advance no farther, and German fire on the exposed crossing site denied reinforcement. Enemy shelling severely limited use of the battalion's 81-mm. mortars and frustrated all efforts to keep telephones working. A heavy mist not only precluded any use of air support but also restricted the effectiveness of counter-battery artillery fires.

MEN OF THE 104TH DIVISION *dig foxholes near Standdaarbuiten.*

Major Needham's men nevertheless successfully held their tiny bridgehead until late afternoon when the Germans stormed the position with infantry supported by six tanks. Firing into individual foxholes, the tanks soon encircled the position. As night came General Crocker gave approval to withdraw what was left of the battalion. A patrol led by Lt. William C. Tufts managed to cross the river and break through to the battalion to facilitate withdrawal of most of the men that were left. Two days later the division discovered that sixty-five officers and men, unable to withdraw, had hidden in buildings and foxholes, subsisted on raw beets and turnips, and withstood both American shelling and German patrols without the loss of a man.

For the next day and well into 2 November, the 104th Division held along the south bank of the Mark while General Allen and the other division commanders of the 1st British Corps planned with General Crocker for a co-ordinated attack. General Crocker's final order directed assaults on the river line by the British and Americans at 2100 on 2 November while the Poles launched a separate attack farther to the east, north of Breda. Colonel Waltz's 413th Infantry was to cross west of Standdaarbuiten with one battalion closely followed by the remainder of the regiment. Colonel

Cochran's 415th Infantry was to send a battalion across at Standdaarbuiten and another just east of the village. The 414th Infantry was to feign a crossing farther east and support the others by fire.

The 104th Division G–2, Lt. Col. Mark S. Plaisted, estimated that within the division's boundaries the Germans held the north bank with the remnants of nine infantry battalions totaling 1,200 to 1,300 men. Prisoners, he said, had told of the arrival of 200 replacements three days before and of German commanders who threatened their troops with force to fight to the last.

For an hour preceding the nighttime assault, guns all along the corps front ripped into the German line north of the river. Sprinkling their volleys liberally with lethal timed bursts, artillerymen of the 104th Division concentrated much of their fire on Standdaarbuiten, believed to be a German strongpoint.

In the left of the division sector, a battalion of the 413th Infantry commanded by Lt. Col. Collins Perry made the assault. Although the men were subjected to small arms fire even as they scrambled into their assault boats, they stuck to their task. Reaching the far shore, they found that only a few yards farther they faced a canal almost as wide as the Mark. Without hesitation, the men plunged into the chill water and waded across. Wet to their armpits and plagued in the darkness by persistent mortar and small arms fire, they nevertheless pushed steadily forward. The rest of the regiment followed and set about jamming a left hook around to the north of Standdaarbuiten.

A driving force in the advance of Colonel Perry's battalion was a weapons platoon leader, 1st Lt. Cecil H. Bolton.

Wounded while directing fire of his 60-mm. mortars on two German machine guns, Lieutenant Bolton nevertheless led a bazooka team against the positions. He charged the first machine gun alone to kill the crew with hand grenades. Then he led the bazooka team through intense fire toward the second gun. They killed the three Germans who manned it. Lieutenant Bolton later led the bazooka team against an enemy 88 and directed fire to knock out the gun. He subsequently received the Medal of Honor.

In the meantime, the battalion crossing at Standdaarbuiten found that the artillery preparation had taken an awesome toll of the village and the enemy positions. The men quickly swept through. A few hundred yards farther east, another battalion successfully hurdled the river, despite machine gun and rifle fire at the crossing site, and soon linked its bridgehead to the others. Shortly after midnight the Germans counterattacked with infantry supported by four tanks, but the men of the 415th Infantry were too well established. They dispatched the Germans with small arms fire and timely artillery support.

By 0115, 3 November, only slightly more than four hours after the infantry had begun to cross the Mark, 104th Division engineers had constructed a treadway bridge near Standdaarbuiten. As they began work on a Bailey bridge, disturbingly accurate German shellfire began to fall. Before daylight enemy shelling knocked out a section of the treadway bridge. Convinced that the Germans had an observer in the vicinity, the engineers after dawn conducted a thorough search. They found a German officer and a sergeant hidden beneath the abutment of the old bridge directing fire by radio.

By noon of 3 November a cohesive German line along the Mark River obviously had ceased to exist. Hostile artillery fire decreased as the Germans apparently withdrew their big guns toward their escape route at Moerdijk. Though countless strongpoints manned by diehard defenders remained to be cleared before the south bank of the Maas would be free, the British and the Poles had made comparable progress on either flank of the Americans, so that it could be only a question of time before the campaign south of the Maas would be over. Across the bleak and forbidding marshland and across canals and dikes swept by cold winds, the pursuit continued. At last the weather began to clear and British aircraft joined the battle. The Americans found close liaison between the British planes and air support teams attached to the infantry a rewarding experience.[59]

On 4 November the First U.S. Army directed that, as soon as released by the First Canadian Army, the 104th Division was to move to the vicinity of Aachen. The next day, when General Crocker assigned the division an additional mission of assisting the Polish armor to take Moerdijk, General Allen decided to give the task to his division reserve, the 414th Infantry, while withdrawing the rest of the division to prepare for the move to Aachen. On 6 November this move began.

Colonel Touart's 414th Infantry maintained pressure on the holdout position at Moerdijk until late on 7 November when relieved by a British regiment. The Poles and the British cleared the last Germans from the south bank of the Maas the next day, 8 November.

The campaign in the southwestern part of the Netherlands had cost the 104th Division in its first action almost 1,400 casualties.[60] The division made no estimate of enemy losses but recorded the capture of 658 prisoners. Though the fighting had been basically unspectacular, it had achieved the valuable end of establishing a firm and economical northern flank for the 21 Army Group along the south bank of the Maas.

South Beveland and Walcheren

By 24 October, only a day after the 104th Division first had moved into the line, earlier advances of General Crocker's 1st British Corps already had helped to provide a firm base near Woensdrecht for operations westward against South Beveland, while progress along the south bank of the West Schelde had removed any danger of German guns in the Breskens Pocket intervening in a fight on South Beveland. That same day the Canadians opened a drive to clear the estuary's north bank.

Despite the narrowness of the isthmus, a situation accentuated by flooded lowlands off the roads, the Canadians registered an advance of two and a half miles the first day. With the help of a British brigade that crossed the West Schelde in assault boats from the south bank on 26 October, they rapidly swept the peninsula. It was a hard fight; for the Germans had on the peninsula four battalions of infantry, two battalions of fortress troops, and ten batteries of artillery. But at last, in congruence with Hitler's expressed theory that "Defense of the Schelde Estuary is based on the heavy

---

[59] Kline, Action North of Antwerp.

[60] 179 killed, 856 wounded, 356 missing.

batteries on Walcheren Island," the *70th Division* commander, General Daser, withdrew the survivors from South Beveland for a last-ditch defense of Walcheren.[61] By the end of October, South Beveland was in Allied hands.

The worst obstacle to free use of the port of Antwerp remained: the island of Walcheren. The scene during the Napoleonic era of a disastrous British military failure, here a garrison of some 10,000 men formed around the *70th* (White Bread) *Division* awaited the inevitable final fight.[62]

Almost a month earlier the Allies had launched their first blow against the *70th Division* by invoking the wrath of the sea upon Walcheren Island. Because the island is shaped like a saucer and almost all the interior lies below sea level, the acting First Canadian Army commander, General Simonds, had believed that Allied bombs could breach the dikes and thereby flood most of the island. While German

movement would be restricted, the Allies might use their profusion of amphibious vehicles to turn the flood to advantage. Although some experts had been dubious, on 3 October the experiment had been tried. Striking the big Westkapelle dike along the western edge of the island, bombers of the RAF Bomber Command had sent the North Sea rolling through a breach eighty yards wide. The next day the bombers had returned to widen the gap by another hundred yards. Although the Germans had tried to stem the flood with emergency dikes, gravity and the sea had flouted their efforts.[63]

The greater portion of the island was flooded, but the fact remained that most German defenses were on higher ground. The main reliance for seizing Walcheren rested with seaborne assaults assisted by a drive across the causeway from South Beveland. During the night of 31 October the Canadians assailed the narrow causeway to gain a tenuous foothold on Walcheren, but they could not make it stick. On 1 November British commandos sailed across the West Schelde from Breskens to establish a beachhead against only moderate resistance near the island's southern port of Flushing. By nightfall much of Flushing was under British control. The same day a seaborne force mounted at Ostend launched a frontal assault on strong, undamaged fortifications near Westkapelle. Tidal conditions having dictated a daylight assault, the British craft were easy targets for the enemy's big coastal guns. Nevertheless, aided by a timely strike by RAF Typhoons, the commandos fought their way ashore. The fall of the bastion of

---

[61] Orders, *OB WEST* to *A Gp B,* 20 Oct, 2355, 29 Oct (relaying Hitler order), and 2215, 31 Oct 44, all in *OB WEST, Befehle/Meldungen.*

[62] In estimating German units on Walcheren, intelligence officers of the First Canadian Army drew a chuckle at their own expense. Having stated that one of the German battalions consisted of "Americans," the Canadians with tongue in cheek sought an explanation in their next intelligence summary. "The map has been inspected by a more experienced eye," the second summary stated, "and clearly indicates that '1/III/Armen/128' is the sub-unit in question. There are strong indications that this means 'Armenians.' That there may be elements of Americans operating to rearwards of almost any German force cannot be denied in the light of experience at Argentan and Elbeuf. But that they are an integral part of a German training division is considered on balance to be unlikely." See Incl 5 to VII Corps G-2 Per Rpt 115, 29 Oct 44, wherein the VII Corps follows the lead of SHAEF in reproducing the discussion "in the interests of Allied co-operation and North American unity."

[63] Daily Sitrep, *A Gp B,* 0115, 4 Oct 44, *A Gp B, Tagesmeldungen.*

Walcheren became only a question of hard fighting and time.

On the eastern side of the island, the Canadians at last had forced a bridgehead across the constricted causeway, but they could not expand it. British units took over with little more success until on the night of 2 November they moved in assault boats south of the causeway to gain another foothold on the island. Two days later troops in the two bridgeheads linked and started westward.

In the meantime, the British at Flushing and at Westkapelle had joined forces on 3 November. A systematic advance to clear all Germans from the island ensued. On 6 November the town of Middelburg fell and General Daser surrendered. On 8 November, eight days after the first attack, the British reported all organized resistance on Walcheren at an end. Meanwhile, on 2 November, North Beveland also had fallen.

The battle to clear the approaches to Antwerp was over. Only casualty figures could adequately bespeak the bitterness of a fight waged under appalling conditions of cold, rain, mud, and flood. Between 1 October and 8 November, the First Canadian Army—including Canadian, British, Polish, Czechoslovakian, French, and American troops—had incurred nearly 13,000 casualties. More than 6,000 of these were Canadians. The Germans had lost in prisoners alone more than 40,000 men.

Even as the commandos and infantry rooted the last resistance from Walcheren Island, mine sweeping began on the Schelde estuary. Some three weeks later, on 28 November, almost three months (eighty-five days) after British armor had seized Antwerp's wharves and docks intact, the first convoy of Allied ships dropped anchor in the port. Antwerp at long last was capable of producing for the Allied cause.

Something Beastly in Antwerp

Allied ships were free to enter the port, yet clearing the approaches to Antwerp failed to spell an end to troubles besetting the city itself. Indeed, as indicated by the date of 14 October on a terse announcement in the intelligence report of a British division, Antwerp's troubles overlapped. Noted the report: ". . . something beastly fell in Antwerp yesterday."[64]

That "something beastly" was a V–bomb, one of two types of long-range projectiles which the Germans introduced during 1944. Probably as counterpropaganda to Allied use of the letter V for Victory, German propagandists named these projectiles after the German *Vergeltung* for vengeance.[65] The first to be introduced was the V–1, a pilotless aircraft or flying bomb; the next was the V–2, a supersonic rocket. After London, Antwerp was the city most seriously affected by these weapons.[66]

From launching sites in the Netherlands and Germany, the Germans bombarded Antwerp with V–bombs and rockets all through the latter portion of the Siegfried Line Campaign and as late as 30 March 1945. At least 1,214 V–1's and V–2's, a conservative estimate, struck Antwerp,

---

[64] 7th Br Armd Div Intel Summary 124, 14 Oct 44, as cited in FUSA G–2 Per Rpt 130, 18 Oct 44, found in FUSA G–2 TAC Jnl file, 18–19 Oct 44.

[65] Harrison, *Cross-Channel Attack,* p. 140, n. 37.

[66] For a detailed study of the history and effect of the V–weapons upon Allied military operations, see Royce L. Thompson, Military Impact of the German V–weapons, 1943–1945, prepared in OCMH.

while another 2,500 exploded in the environs. Casualties were high. Some 2,900 Antwerp civilians were killed and another 5,433 seriously injured. Losses among Allied military personnel were 734 killed and 1,078 seriously wounded, a total of 1,812. The most disastrous single incident resulting from V–weapon attacks either in Antwerp or elsewhere on the Continent occurred in Antwerp on 16 December when a V–2 hit the Rex Cinema during a crowded matinee. In one blow, 296 soldiers were killed and 194 seriously injured.

In terms other than casualties, damage to military facilities in Antwerp and the port was slight, though civilian property loss was enormous. Major military losses were 2 or more warehouses, temporary damage to 1 lock, and slight damage to 20 berths. Perhaps the greatest advantage accruing to the Germans from the bombardment was a drain upon Allied manpower, ordnance, and equipment occasioned by intricate and heavily manned antiaircraft defenses employed about the city.[67] Although military authorities were concerned at times about unrest among dock workers and about civilian morale in general, the citizens of Antwerp rallied to the challenge much as did the people of London. In the end, Allied use of Antwerp as a port never was seriously impaired by the bombardment. At times the port handled an average of 25,000 tons of supplies per day.

The third primary target of the V–weapons was the Belgian industrial city of Liège. As the First U.S. Army turned Liège into a major supply center, the Germans as early as 14 September sited their bombs and rockets against the city. During the course of the war, Liège was hit about 1,086 times, while another thousand projectiles exploded nearby. Civilian casualties totaled 1,158, while 92 soldiers were killed and 336 wounded. The only major damage to military installations was the loss of a hospital and some 250,000 gallons of gasoline. As at Antwerp, the V–weapons, for all the terror of them, proved highly inaccurate and never interfered seriously with military operations at Liège.

---

[67] Labeled "Antwerp X," the antiaircraft defense of the city employed 18,000 troops and more than 500 antiaircraft guns.

CHAPTER X

The Peel Marshes

Culmination of the fight for Antwerp meant that with one exception the front of the 21 Army Group was economical and secure. Yet the exception was not minor. Until it could be taken care of, the British could not launch their long-delayed Ruhr offensive.

The problem lay in that region west of the Maas River between the MARKET-GARDEN salient and the 21 Army Group boundary with the XIX U.S. Corps eleven miles north of Maastricht. Situated between the British and Americans, this region had become a joint problem as early as mid-September when the Americans had driven northeastward via Aachen and the British had turned northward toward Eindhoven, two divergent thrusts creating a great gap which would remain a threat to the open flanks of both forces until somebody got around to closing it. As events developed, neither Americans nor British were to turn sufficient attention to the gap until the Germans had displayed their penchant for exploiting oversights and weaknesses of their adversaries.

First Army Draws the Assignment

On 22 September—the day when General Hodges authorized postponement of the West Wall assault of the XIX Corps, when Hodges' entire army went on the defensive, and when hope still existed that Operation MARKET-GARDEN might suc-

ceed—the great gap on the left flank of the XIX Corps became not only a threat and an annoyance to the First Army but also First Army's responsibility. This stemmed from the conference of 22 September at Versailles when General Eisenhower and his top commanders had noted the magnitude of the 21 Army Group's assignments and decided that the British needed help.[1]

To strengthen the British and thereby facilitate Field Marshal Montgomery's proposed new thrust against the Ruhr, the commanders agreed to adjust the boundary between the two army groups northward from the old boundary which ran eleven miles north of Maastricht. General Bradley's 12th Army Group— more specifically, the First Army and in turn the XIX Corps—was to assume responsibility for the major portion of the region west of the Maas that had been lying fallow in the British zone. At least two British divisions thus would be freed to move to the MARKET-GARDEN salient, the steppingstone for the projected Ruhr offensive. To become effective on 25 September, the new boundary ran northeast from Hasselt through the Belgian town of Bree and the Dutch towns of Weert, Deurne, and Venray to the Maas at Maashees (all-inclusive to the 12th Army Group). The detailed location of

---

[1] Min, Mtg held at SHAEF FWD, 22 Sep 44, 12th A Gp Military Objectives, 371.3, I; see also, Ltr, Bradley to Patton, 23 Sep 44, same file

the boundary was to be settled by direct negotiation between Montgomery and the First Army commander, General Hodges, while any extension of it beyond Maashees was to "depend upon the situation at a later date." [2]

The task of the First Army in the Ruhr offensive became, for the moment, to clear the region west of the Maas while preparing, as far as logistical considerations would permit, for a renewal of the push toward Cologne. To provide forces for the new area of responsibility, General Bradley ordered the Third Army to release the 7th Armored Division to the First Army and also gave General Hodges the 29th Division from the campaign recently concluded at Brest. These two divisions, Montgomery, Bradley, and Hodges agreed at a conference on 24 September, should be sufficient for clearing the region, whereupon one of the two might hold the west bank of the Maas while the other joined the main body of the First Army in the drive on Cologne. Because Montgomery intended that a British corps in a later stage of the Ruhr offensive would drive southeast between the Maas and the Rhine, the commanders foresaw no necessity for extending the new boundary east of the Maas beyond Maashees.[3]

Despite the expectation that the First Army would not have to go beyond the Maas in the new sector, General Hodges was unhappy with the arrangement. Without a firm guarantee that the new boundary would not be extended, he

could visualize a dispersion of his army's strength east of the river. Furthermore, he had been counting on the 29th Division to protect his own exposed flank, most of which lay east of the Maas; but use of the division for this mission now obviously would be delayed.[4]

General Hodges apparently took these concerns with him on 26 September when he conferred with Field Marshal Montgomery and the Second British Army commander, General Dempsey, for he emerged from the meeting with an arrangement that satisfied him. Instead of a plan using both the 7th Armored and 29th Divisions, a plan was approved whereby only the armor was to be employed, plus the 113th Cavalry Group and a unit of comparable size provided by the British, the 1st Belgian Brigade.[5] As for the boundary, the British had agreed on a line running from Maashees southeast, south, and southwest along the Maas back to the old boundary eleven miles north of Maastricht, thereby giving General Hodges the assurance he wanted against having to conduct operations

---

[2] Ltr, Bradley to Patton, 23 Sep 44; FWD 15510, Eisenhower to 12th A Gp for Bradley and 21 A Gp for Montgomery, 23 Sep 44; Min, Mtg at SHAEF FWD, 22 Sep 44. All in 12th A Gp 371.3, Military Objectives, I.

[3] Ltr, Bradley to Eisenhower, 25 Sep 44, 12th A Gp 371.3 Military Objectives, I.

[4] Sylvan Diary, entries of 24 and 26 Sep 44.

[5] Commanded by Colonel Piron, B. E. M., the 1st Belgian Brigade had three motorized infantry companies (325 men each), a field artillery battery, an engineer company, a squadron of armored cars, and headquarters, signal, supply, and medical personnel. Armed, equipped, and supplied by the British, the brigade fought with the British in Normandy and participated in the liberation of Brussels. Although the Kingdom of Belgium subsequently augmented Allied ranks with a number of units made up primarily of men from the Resistance, the troops of the 1st Belgian Brigade were Belgians who had escaped to England during and after 1940. See Narrative History by Colonel Mampuys, Directeur Superieur du Renseignment et de l'Historique, attached to Ltr, 6 Sep 51, Maj Count I. G. Du Monceau de Bergendal, Attaché Militaire et de l'Air, Embassy of Belgium, Washington, D.C., to OCMH.

east of the river.[6] The end result was that the First Army was assigned a giant, thumb-shaped corridor about sixteen miles wide, protruding almost forty miles into the British zone west of the Maas. The entire corridor encompassed more than 500 square miles.

That the basic objective in creation of the corridor, assisting the British in the Ruhr offensive, might have been handled with less complexity by attaching American forces to British command and leaving the boundary in its old position eleven miles north of Maastricht must have been considered. After the war, General Bradley noted three reasons for the unorthodox arrangement, all related to the matter of supply. First, U.S. supply lines led more directly into the region; second, putting U.S. troops under British command would have complicated the supply picture because of differences in calibers and types of weapons; and third, U.S. troops, General Bradley had remarked as far back as the Tunisian campaign, disliked British supplies, particularly British rations.[7]

The area which the First Army inherited is featured by the extensive lowlands of De Peel, or the Peel Marshes, a vast fen lying in the upper western part of the region. Covering some sixty square miles between the Maas and Eindhoven, the marshes are traversed only by a limited road net. They represent an obvious military obstacle of great tracts of swampland and countless canals. (*Map 3*) By 25 September, when the British relinquished control of the sector, the corridor was clear as far north as a canal several miles within the Netherlands, the Nederweert–Wessem Canal which runs diagonally across the corridor between the town of Nederweert at the southwestern edge of the Peel Marshes and a point on the Maas near Wessem, nine miles north of the old army group boundary.

In early planning, when it was expected that two U.S. divisions would be employed in the corridor, the XIX Corps commander, General Corlett, had intended to clear the base of the corridor as far north as the Peel Marshes with the two divisions, then to dispatch a highly mobile force along a narrow neck of comparatively high ground between the marshes and the Maas to link with the British at the north end of the corridor.[8] But General Hodges, after conferring with the British commanders on 26 September, had radically altered the plan. Hodges directed that the 7th Armored Division pass around through the British zone and make the main attack southward along the narrow neck of land between the marshes and the Maas. Coincidentally, the 1st Belgian Brigade and the 113th Cavalry Group were to launch a secondary thrust from the south. The 29th Division thus would be available immediately to hold the north flank of the XIX Corps east of the Maas, thereby freeing the entire 2d Armored and 30th Divisions to break through the West Wall north of Aachen and participate in the drive on Cologne.[9]

So optimistic was General Hodges that a combination of the XIX Corps West Wall offensive and a renewal of the attack

---

[6] Sylvan Diary, entry of 26 Sep 44.
[7] Interv with Bradley, 7 Jun 56; Bradley, *A Soldier's Story*, pp. 56–59.

[8] Memo, CG XIX Corps, to CG FUSA, 26 Sep 44, XIX Corps Combat Interv file.
[9] FUSA, Amendment 1, 27 Sep 44, to FUSA Ltr of Instrs, 25 Sep 44, FUSA G-2 Jnl file, 1–3 Oct 44; Sylvan Diary, entry of 26 Sep 44.

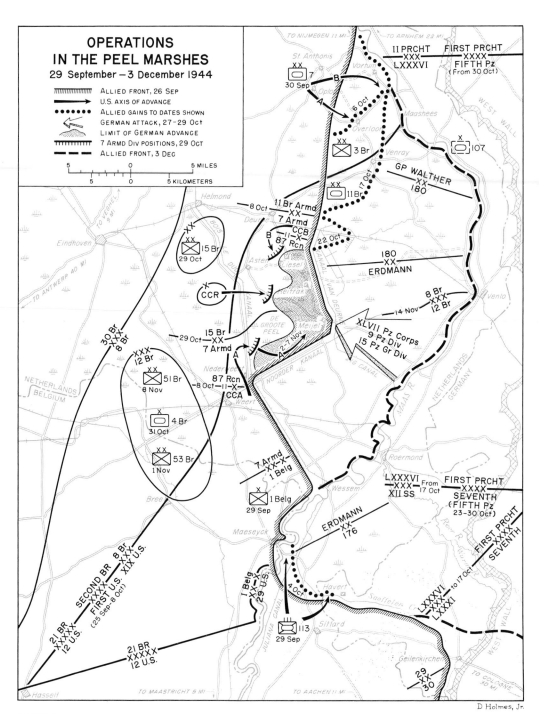

OPERATIONS
IN THE PEEL MARSHES
29 September – 3 December 1944

⊥⊥⊥⊥⊥	ALLIED FRONT, 26 SEP
→	U.S. AXIS OF ADVANCE
•••••	ALLIED GAINS TO DATES SHOWN
←	GERMAN ATTACK, 27–29 OCT
⬛	LIMIT OF GERMAN ADVANCE
⊥⊥⊥⊥⊥	7 ARMD DIV POSITIONS, 29 OCT
— —	ALLIED FRONT, 3 DEC

5   0   5 MILES
5   0   5 KILOMETERS

MAP 3

D Holmes, Jr.

by the VII Corps would produce a breakthrough toward the Rhine that he seriously considered the possibility that the 7th Armored Division's operation west of the Maas might prove . unnecessary. Not to be caught unawares should this develop, he directed that the 7th Armored Division be prepared to jump the Maas and drive eastward or southeastward to complement any breakthrough achieved by the bulk of the XIX Corps.[10]

Bowing to his superior's direction, General Corlett issued final orders for the Peel Marshes offensive on 28 September. The 7th Armored Division was to pass through the British zone to positions north of the Peel Marshes and attack southeast and south through Overloon and Venray to clear the west bank of the Maas. Because the British had not occupied all their zone within the new boundary, the **first five miles of the 7th Armored Division's** route of attack lay within the British zone. The 1st Belgian Brigade was to attack northeast across the Nederweert–Wessem Canal early on 29 September, eventually to link with the 7th Armored Division. The Belgians were to deny crossings of the Maas in the vicinity of Roermond, six miles northeast of Wessem, and were to regulate their advance with that of the 113th Cavalry Group attacking north toward Roermond from the vicinity of Sittard along the east bank of the Maas. This move by the cavalry would tend to soften the angle of a gap which still would remain on the left flank of the XIX Corps east of the Maas even after completion of the Peel Marshes offensive.[11]

To the detriment of the Peel Marshes operation, the plan to clear the thumb-shaped corridor from the north instead of from the south and with but one instead of two available divisions reflected an erroneous impression of the dispositions and strength of German forces in the corridor. Usually prescient in these matters, the XIX Corps G–2, Col. Washington Platt, had erred notably in this instance in his estimate of the enemy. Perhaps the error resulted from the fact that the XIX Corps had so recently taken over the corridor; perhaps the fact that the British who had heretofore borne responsibility for the corridor had had little enemy contact upon which to base accurate intelligence information. In any event, Colonel Platt estimated that within the corridor the Germans had only about 2,000 to 3,000 troops.[12]

In reality, the Germans occupying the thumb-shaped corridor were at least seven to eight times stronger than Colonel Platt estimated. Just as in the other sectors of the *First Parachute Army*, the enemy here had increased greatly in strength and ability since General Student first had assumed command of the army three weeks before. Within the corridor itself, General Student had the bulk of an entire corps, General von Obstfelder's *LXXXVI Corps.*

On 18 September the *LXXXVI Corps* had assumed command of Colonel

---

[10] FUSA Ltr of Instrs, 25 Sep 44; Ltr Corlett to OCMH, 20 May 56.

[11] XIX Corps FO 27, 28 Sep, and Ltr of Instrs, 29 Sep, XIX Corps G–3 file, 28–29 Sep 44.

[12] See XIX Corps G–2 Per Rpts for the period and Maj Franklin Ferriss, Notes on XIX Corps Opns, 28 Jul 44–13 Jan 45, in particular entries for 26 through 28 Sep 44. A combat historian attached to the XIX Corps, Major Ferriss kept a detailed record of XIX Corps operations, field orders, and the like, and of his own observations. Filed with XIX Corps Combat Intervs.

Landau's *176th Division* and *Parachute Training Division Erdmann,* the latter the division which General Student early in September had formed around a nucleus of three parachute regiments. After an initial commitment against the MARKET-GARDEN salient at Veghel, Obstfelder had gone on the defensive against the 8 British Corps, which had driven northward along the right flank of the MARKET-GARDEN corridor. As September drew to a close, the *LXXXVI Corps* still was defending along the east wing of the *First Parachute Army.* The *176th Division* was east of the Maas near Sittard but would be drawn into the battle of the corridor because of the 113th Cavalry Group's northward attack toward Roermond. Although the *176th Division* had been buffeted unmercifully in the 2d U.S. Armored Division's mid-September drive toward the German border, General von Obstfelder was able during the latter third of September to replenish the division with heterogeneous attachments. By the end of the month Colonel Landau was capable of a presentable defense against an attack in no greater strength than a cavalry group could muster.

Sharing a boundary with the *176th Division* near the Maas, the *Parachute Training Division Erdmann* held the widest division sector within the *LXXXVI Corps,* a front some twenty-two miles long extending along the Nederweert–Wessem Canal northwestward to include about half the Peel Marshes. Had the Americans followed their original plan of attacking northeastward across the Nederweert–Wessem Canal with two divisions, they would have encountered in *Division Erdmann* a unit of creditable strength and fighting ability but also a unit hardly capable in view of this elongated front of

holding the attack of two U.S. divisions.[13]

Had these been the only two German forces available, the choice of attacking along the narrow neck of land between the Peel Marshes and the Maas might have been a happy one. As it was, General von Obstfelder received two additional units only a few days before the Americans were to jump off. The first was an upgraded training division of doubtful ability, the *180th Replacement Training Division.* This division assumed responsibility for the northern half of the easily defensible Peel Marshes north of and adjacent to *Division Erdmann.* The second unit was *Kampfgruppe Walther,* the combat team of varying composition which first had opposed the British in the bridgehead over the Meuse–Escaut Canal and subsequently had cut the MARKET-GARDEN corridor north of Veghel. Having failed to maintain severance of the corridor, *Kampfgruppe Walther* had been pulled back into the *LXXXVI Corps* sector and reinforced with a strong complement of infantry from the *180th Division.* The major component still was the *107th Panzer Brigade,* which even after fighting against the MARKET-GARDEN salient had approximately seven Mark IV tanks and twenty Mark V's. Though *Kampfgruppe Walther* probably was no stronger than a reinforced U.S. regiment, it was a force to be reckoned with in constricted terrain.[14]

---

[13] Dispositions of German units are from TWX, *A Gp B* to *OB WEST,* 1330, 29 Sep 44, *A Gp B KTB, Operationsbefehle.* See Heichler, *The Germans Opposite XIX Corps.*

[14] Records of *Kampfgruppe Walther* are as sketchy for this as for earlier periods. The above is based on Strength Rpt, *107th Panzer Brigade,* 1 Oct 44, in records of *General Inspekteur der Panzertruppen, Strength Rpts of Panzer Divs, Sep–Oct 44;* TWX *A Gp B* to *OB WEST,* 1330,

Although the mission of the *LXXXVI Corps* was purely defensive, General von Obstfelder had specific orders to halt the Allies as far to the west as possible. That the point of decision in this defense might come at the exact spot the Americans had chosen for the main effort of their corridor campaign was indicated five days before the event by the *Army Group B* commander. "It is particularly important," Field Marshal Model said, "to hold the areas around Oploo and Deurne . . . ."[15] Deurne was but a few miles southwest of the spot chosen for the 7th Armored Division's attack. Oploo was to be the point of departure for the attack.

But these things the Americans did not know. Still under the impression that only about 3,000 Germans held the entire thumb-shaped corridor, the 7th Armored Division moved early on 29 September to pass through the British zone and reach jump-off positions near Oploo. At the same time, both the 1st Belgian Brigade and the 113th Cavalry Group began to attack along the south of the corridor toward Roermond.

Before crossing the Nederweert–Wessem Canal, the 1st Belgian Brigade had to reduce a triangular "bridgehead" which *Division Erdmann* had clung to about the town of Wessem near the juncture of the canal with the Maas. But even this the lightly manned, lightly armed Belgians could not accomplish. Although strengthened by attachment of a U.S. tank destroyer group, the Belgians could make little headway across flat terrain toward the canal. By 2 October revised estimates of enemy strength in Wessem and beyond

the canal were so discouraging that the attack was called off.[16]

The 113th Cavalry Group's coincident attack developed in a series of piecemeal commitments, primarily because one squadron was late in arriving after performing screening duties along the XIX Corps south flank. By 4 October, two days after operations of the adjacent Belgian brigade had bogged down, a special task force had cleared a strip of land lying between the Maas and the Juliana Canal to a point a few miles beyond the interarmy group boundary; an attached tank battalion (the 744th) had built up along a line running northwest from Sittard to the point on the Juliana reached by the special task force; and other contingents of the cavalry and the armor clung precariously to a scanty bridgehead across the Saeffeler Creek a few miles northeast of Sittard. Assisted by numerous small streams and drainage ditches, the enemy's *176th Division* had offered stout resistance all along the line, particularly in the bridgehead beyond the Saeffeler. The cavalry lost heavily in men and vehicles. Because the group had "exhausted the possibilities of successful offensive action" with the forces available, the commander, Colonel Biddle, asked to call off the attack. With its cessation, all hope that the main effort by the 7th Armored Division in the north might benefit from operations in the south came to an end.[17]

In the meantime, on 30 September, the 7th Armored Division under Maj. Gen.

---

29 Sep 44; and XIX Corps intel rpts for the period.

[15] Order, *A Gp B* to *First Prcht Army*, 1330, 24 Sep 44, *A Gp B KTB, Operationsbefehle.*

[16] For tactical information on the 1st Belgian Brigade, see XIX Corps G–3 Per Rpts 115 and 116, 29–30 Sep 44; XIX Corps G–3 Msg files, 29–30 Sep 44; XIX Corps AAR, Oct 44; and Mampuys, Narrative History.

[17] See 113th Cav Gp AARs, Sep and Oct 44, and 29th Div AAR, Oct 44.

Lindsay McD. Silvester had reached jump-off positions southeast of Oploo and was prepared to launch the main drive aimed at clearing the west bank of the Maas.[18] Having rushed north straight out of the battle line along the Moselle River near Metz, General Silvester had found little time in which to reorganize his troops and replace combat losses. Casualties in the Metz fighting, the division's first all-out engagement, had been heavy; and in seeking to get the best from his units, General Silvester had replaced a number of staff officers and subordinate commanders. Including officers killed or wounded as well as those summarily relieved, CCB now had its fourth commander in a month; CCR, its eighth.

Immediate objectives of the 7th Armored Division were the towns of Vortum, close along the Maas, and Overloon, near the northeastern edge of the Peel Marshes. Hoping to break the main crust of resistance at these points, General Silvester intended then to sweep quickly south and bypass expected centers of resistance like Venray and Venlo. At these two points and at Roermond, which was to be taken by the Belgians and 113th Cavalry, the Germans had concentrated the meager forces they had been able to muster for defense of the corridor. Or so General Silvester had been informed by those who predicted that the enemy had but two to three thousand troops in the corridor.

Attacking in midafternoon of 30 Sep-

---

[18] The 7th Armored Division first saw combat after the opening of the pursuit phase with Third Army's XX Corps. Just before assignment to the XIX Corps, the division had helped establish a hotly contested bridgehead across the Moselle River south of Metz. The story of the Peel Marshes offensive is based on: div AARs, Jnls, and Jnl files for Sep–Oct 44.

tember, the 7th Armored Division encountered terrain that was low, flat, open, sometimes swampy, and dotted with patches of scrub pines and oaks. Moving on Vortum, a town blocking access to a highway paralleling the Maas on the division's left wing, a task force of CCB (Brig. Gen. Robert W. Hasbrouck) ran almost immediately into a strong German line replete with antitank guns, mines, panzerfausts, and infantry firmly entrenched. Because drainage ditches and marshy ground confined the tanks to the roads and because the roads were thickly mined, the onus of the attack fell upon the dismounted armored infantry. Fortunately, the infantry could call upon an ally, the artillery. Although the 7th Armored Division had only one 4.5-inch gun battalion attached to reinforce the fires of its organic artillery, General Silvester could gain additional support from organic guns of a British armored division that was in the line farther north. Thus on 2 October seven British and American artillery battalions co-ordinated their fires to deliver 1,500 rounds in a sharp two-minute preparation that enabled the task force of CCB at last to push into Vortum. In the town itself, resistance was spotty; but as soon as the armor started southeast along the highway paralleling the Maas, once again the Germans stiffened.

In the meantime, General Silvester was making his main effort against the road center of Overloon, southwest of Vortum. Col. Dwight A. Rosebaum's CCA attacked the village along secondary roads from the north. After pushing back German outposts, the armor early on 1 October struck the main defenses. Here the main infantry components of *Kampfgruppe Walther* were bolstered by remnants of a parachute regiment which had

USING A DRAINAGE DITCH FOR COVER, *an infantryman carries a message forward in the Peel Marshes area.*

fought with the *Kampfgruppe* against the MARKET-GARDEN salient.[19] Employing the tanks of the *107th Panzer Brigade* primarily in antitank roles from concealed positions, the *Kampfgruppe* was able to cover its defensive mine fields with accurate fire that accounted for fourteen American tanks.[20] The American infantry nevertheless gained several hundred yards to approach the outskirts of Overloon; here small arms and mortar fire supplemented by artillery and *Nebelwerfer* fire forced a halt.

[19] 7th Armd Div G–2 Per Rpts, 1–2 Oct 44.
[20] Daily Sitrep, *A Gp B,* 0145, 2 Oct 44, *A Gp B KTB, Tagesmeldungen.*

Resuming the attack at daybreak on the third day (2 October) behind a preparation fired by seven battalions of artillery, the forces of the 7th Armored Division attempting to invest Overloon still could not advance. Although the first air support of the operation hit the objective in early afternoon and reportedly resulted in destruction of a German tank, this failed to lessen German obstinacy materially. An hour before dark, the enemy launched a counterattack, the first in a seemingly interminable series that must have left the American soldier in his foxhole or tank wondering just which side held the initiative. Fortunately none of the counterattacks was in strength greater than two companies so that with the aid of supporting artillery and fighter-bombers, the men of CCA and CCB beat them off—but not without appreciable losses, particularly in tanks.

Late on 3 October General Silvester relieved CCA with CCR (Col. John L. Ryan, Jr.). The counterattacks continued. In the intervals, the Americans measured their advance in yards. Even though the combined efforts of CCA and CCR eventually forged an arc about Overloon on three sides, the Germans did not yield.

By 5 October the 7th Armored Division had been stopped undeniably. For a total advance of less than two miles from the line of departure, the division had paid with the loss of 29 medium tanks, 6 light tanks, 43 other vehicles, and an estimated 452 men. These were not astronomical losses for an armored division in a six-day engagement, particularly in view of the kind of terrain over which the armor fought, yet they were, in light of the minor advances registered, a cause for concern. The 7th Armored Division in gaining little more than two miles failed even to get out of the British zone into the corridor it was supposed to clear.

As early as the afternoon of 2 October, the date of the first of the German counterattacks that eventually were to force acceptance of the distasteful fact that the 7th Armored Division alone could not clear the thumb-shaped corridor, General Corlett had irretrievably committed the main forces of the XIX Corps in an assault against the West Wall north of Aachen. Thus no reinforcements for the secondary effort in the north were available. On 6 October General Hodges told General Corlett to call off the 7th Armored Division's attack.[21]

The 7th Armored Division could point to no real achievement in terms of clearing of the corridor. Had the division's mission been instead to create consternation in German intelligence circles, General Silvester certainly could have claimed at least an assist. Indeed, had this been the purpose of the Allied commanders at Versailles in adopting a boundary creating such a cumbersome corridor, someone could have taken credit for a *coup de maître*. For the German G-2's just could not conceive of such an unorthodox arrangement.

The order of battle of the Second British and First U.S. Armies [the *Army Group B* G-2 wrote on 2 October] at present is obscure in one significant point: We have not yet definitely determined whether the presence of 7th U.S. Armored Division opposite the right wing of *LXXXVI Corps* indicates a shift of the British-American army group boundary to the area eight to ten miles south of Nijmegen. If this should be so . . . we would then have to expect that the enemy will stick to his original plan to launch the decisive thrust into the industrial area (the Ruhr) from the area north of the Waal and Neder-Rijn [i.e., a projection of the MARKET-GARDEN salient]; a new, major airborne landing must be expected in conjunction with such an operation.

In any event the enemy will continue his attacks to widen the present penetration area [the MARKET-GARDEN salient] in both directions . . . .

The assumption that the front of the American army group has been lengthened by 40–50 miles is a contradiction of intelligence reports concerning strong concentrations of forces at Aachen; it appears questionable whether the enemy forces [in the vicinity of Aachen] are strong enough that, in addition to this main effort concentra-

---

[21] FUSA Ltr of Instrs, 6 Oct, in FUSA G-2 file, 7–8 Oct 44; Sylvan Diary, entry of 6 Oct 44.

tion, they can also take over a sector heretofore occupied by the British . . . .

We must also consider the possibility that the intelligence reports concerning the intended offensive via Aachen toward Cologne were intentionally planted by the enemy, and that in contradiction to them, the Americans will shift their main effort to push northeastward from the Sittard sector, and to roll up the Maas defense from the south . . . .[22]

On the date the *Army Group B* intelligence officer wrote this remarkable treatise, he was wrong in almost every respect. The interarmy group boundary had seen no genuine shift northward; on this very day of 2 October, U.S. forces in the Aachen sector had begun a drive designed to put the XIX Corps through the West Wall, a preliminary to resuming a major thrust from Aachen toward Cologne; and the British commander, Field Marshal Montgomery, had abandoned his intention of extending the MARKET-GARDEN salient northward in favor of a drive from Nijmegen southeastward against the western face of the Ruhr.

A few days later Montgomery had to go a step further and forego all plans for an immediate drive on the Ruhr. Indications of enemy strength near Arnhem, British responsibilities in the opening of Antwerp, and the 7th Armored Division's experience with an unyielding enemy at Overloon—together these factors proved too overwhelming.[23] Except for operations to open Antwerp, about all Montgomery could do for the moment was to attempt to set the stage for a later drive on the Ruhr by eliminating once and for all this problem of German holdout west of the Maas.

In a conference on 8 October, the British commander and General Bradley agreed to readjust the army group boundary to its former position, thus returning the region of the Peel Marshes to the British. But the Americans still were to have a hand in clearing the sector. To General Dempsey's Second British Army General Bradley transferred the 7th Armored Division and the 1st Belgian Brigade, including American attachments. The complex situation whereby American units under American command had assumed responsibility for clearing a corridor running deep into the British zone was dissipated. Unfortunately, the problem of the Germans in this holdout position west of the Maas could be neither so readily nor so happily resolved.

The British Attempt

Upon transfer, General Silvester's 7th Armored Division came under the 8 British Corps, commanded by Lt. Gen. Sir Richard N. O'Connor. Relieving the armor in the Overloon sector with British units, General O'Connor directed General Silvester to take over an elongated, zigzag defensive sector within, west, and south of the Peel Marshes. The line ran from the vicinity of Deurne southeast along the Deurne Canal to Meijel, a town well within the confines of the Peel Marshes, then southwest along the Noorder Canal to Nederweert and southeast along the Nederweert–Wessem Canal to the Maas near Wessem. Though this front was some thirty miles long, defense would be facilitated by obstacles like the three canals and the limited routes of communication through the marshes. In addition, General Silvester had the 1st Belgian Brigade as an attachment to hold approxi-

---

[22] G-2 Rpt, *A Gp B,* 2 Oct 44, *A Gp B KTB, Anlagen, Ic/AO.*.

[23] Montgomery, *Normandy to the Baltic,* p. 257.

mately nine miles of the line along the Nederweert–Wessem Canal and the Maas River.

Seeing advance to the Maas as a prerequisite to renewing a British thrust on the Ruhr, Field Marshal Montgomery directed an early offensive by O'Connor's 8 Corps. Using an infantry division (the 3d), General O'Connor was to seize the elusive objective of Overloon and push on to Venray, the largest town the Germans held in this sector and the most important road center. Coincidentally, the 7th U.S. Armored Division was to feign an attack eastward through the Peel Marshes from the vicinity of Deurne. Upon seizing Venray, General O'Connor hoped to shake loose a British armored division (the 11th) to strike along the narrow neck between the marshes and the Maas southeastward to Venlo while as yet unidentified forces attacked northeastward to clear the southern part of the corridor from the vicinity of Nederweert. This offensive by the 8 Corps, Field Marshal Montgomery directed during the first week of October at a time before he had given unequivocal priority to the fight to open Antwerp.[24]

On 12 October infantry of General O'Connor's 8 Corps attacked Overloon and just before dark succeeded in entering the village. Renewing the attack the next day to cover three remaining miles to Venray, the British encountered dogged opposition like that the Americans had faced earlier: extensive mine fields, marshes, woods, antitank guns, *Nebel-*

werfer and artillery fire, and tanks cleverly employed in antitank roles. Not until five days later on 17 October did the British finally occupy Venray.

Any plans General O'Connor might have had for exploiting the capture of Venray had been negated even before his troops took the town. For on 16 October, a day before occupation of Venray, Field Marshal Montgomery had issued his directive shutting down all offensive operations in the Second Army other than those designed to assist the opening of Antwerp. Completion of the task of clearing the west bank of the Maas had to await termination of the battle of the Schelde.

A Spoiling Attack

For ten days following postponement of British plans to clear the corridor west of the Maas, activity throughout the sector was confined to patrol and artillery warfare, except for a small incursion by the 7th Armored Division's CCB during 19–22 October across the Deurne Canal along a railway running east from Deurne. Not until Field Marshal Montgomery could complete the onerous tasks on his left wing could he again turn attention to this annoying holdout position. In the meantime, the First U.S. Army became heavily engaged in reorganization around Aachen in preparation for a new attempt to reach the Rhine.

Where the Allies had to be content to file this region for future consideration, the Germans did not. Behind the façade of patrol clashes and artillery duels, German commanders hit upon a plan designed to exploit their holdout position to the fullest. In casting about for a way to assist the *Fifteenth Army,* which was

---

[24] For the British story during this period, see Montgomery, *Normandy to the Baltic,* pp. 258, 260–67, and 269–72. Unless otherwise noted, the 7th Armored Division story is based upon official unit records and Lt. Robert E. Merriam, Battle of the Canals, Ninth United States Army Operations, vol. III, Combat in Holland.

incurring Allied wrath along the Schelde and in southwestern Holland, the *Army Group B* commander, Field Marshal Model, suggested a powerful, raidlike armored attack from the Peel Marshes into the east flank of the MARKET-GARDEN salient. If strong enough, this kind of attack might force the British to call off their efforts in the southwestern part of the Netherlands.[25]

The forces required for this maneuver happened to be available. A week before Model broached his idea to the Commander in Chief West, Rundstedt, headquarters of the *XLVII Panzer Corps* under General von Luettwitz (former *2d Panzer Division* commander) had been disengaged from the front of *Army Group G*, whose forces sat astride the boundary between the 12th and 6th U.S. Army Groups. The corps had moved north to a position behind the left wing of the *First Parachute Army*, there to conduct training and rehabilitation of the *9th Panzer* and *15th Panzer Grenadier Divisions* and to constitute a reserve for *Army Group B*.[26]

By the latter part of October, strength of the two divisions under the *XLVII Panzer Corps* was not inconsiderable. Numbering about 11,000 men, the *9th Panzer Division* had at least 22 Panther tanks, 30 105-mm. and 150-mm. howitzers, and some 178 armored vehicles of various types, probably including self-propelled artillery. The *15th Panzer Grenadier Division* numbered close to 13,000 men and had at least 1 Mark II and 6 Mark IV tanks.[27]

Endorsing the *Army Group B* commander's plan, Rundstedt ordered that the *XLVII Panzer Corps* attack on 27 October with the *9th Panzer Division* and attachments from the *15th Panzer Grenadier Division*, whereupon the rest of the panzer grenadiers were to exploit early gains of the armor. The attack was to strike sparsely manned positions of the 7th U.S. Armored Division along the Deurne Canal and the Noorder Canal deep within the Peel Marshes west of Venlo. The center of the thrust was to be the town of Meijel, near the junction of the two canals. Only a limited objective was assigned: to carve a quadrilateral bulge into Allied lines six miles deep, encompassing about forty-five square miles. The deepest point of penetration was to be at Asten, northwest of Meijel alongside the Bois le Duc Canal.[28]

At 0615 on 27 October, after a week of bad weather that had reduced visibility almost to zero, the dormant sector within the Peel Marshes erupted in a forty-minute artillery preparation. The attack that followed came as a "complete surprise." As intelligence officers later were to note, the only prior evidence of German intentions had come the day before when

---

[25] Tel Conv, *OB WEST* to *A Gp B*, 1230, 24 Oct 44, *OB WEST KTB, Anlagen, Befehle und Meldungen, 21.X–31.X.44* (hereafter cited as *OB WEST KTB, Befehle und Meldungen*).

[26] MS # B–367, *Das XLVII Panzer-Korps im Rheinland*, 23 Oct–5 Dec 44 (Luettwitz).

[27] Establishing the strength of these divisions is difficult. Figures given are for 1 November 1944, after five days of combat in the Peel Marshes, and do not indicate either losses or reinforcements during that period. See Strength Rpt, *9th Pz Div*, 1 Nov 44, *General Inspekteur der Panzertruppen (OKH), Zustandsberichte–Panzerdivisionen, Nov–Dec 44*. Allied estimates of German tank strength in the spoiling attack ranged from thirty to fifty. See also Lucian Heichler, Surprise Attack in the Peel Marshes, a MS prepared to complement this volume and filed in OCMH.

[28] Rpt, *OB WEST* to *OKW/WFSt*, 2200, 25 Oct 44, *OB WEST KTB, Befehle und Meldungen*.

observers had detected about 200 infantry marching westward at a distance of several miles from the front and the night before when outposts had reported the noise of vehicles and a few tanks moving about.[29] Although no relationship between this attack and the enemy's December counteroffensive in the Ardennes could be claimed, the former when subjected to hindsight looked in many respects like a small-scale dress rehearsal for the Ardennes.

The commander of the *9th Panzer Division*, Generalmajor Harald Freiherr von Elverfeldt, made his first stab a two-pronged thrust at Meijel, held only by a troop of the 87th Cavalry Reconnaissance Squadron. Forced from their positions, the cavalrymen rallied and with the help of another troop of cavalry counterattacked. But to no avail.

A few miles to the north along the Meijel–Deurne highway at Heitrak another armored thrust across the Deurne Canal broke the position of another troop of cavalrymen. Reacting quickly the 7th Armored Division commander, General Silvester, got reinforcements of CCR onto the Meijel–Deurne highway to deny further advance for the moment in the direction of Deurne; but another highway leading northwest from Meijel out of the marshes to Asten still was open. Farther southwest, near Nederweert, another German push forced a slight withdrawal by another cavalry unit; but here commitment of tank, infantry, and tank destroyer reinforcements from CCA stabilized the situation by nightfall of the first day.

Seeking to bolster the 7th Armored

Division by shortening the division's elongated front, the British corps commander, General O'Connor, sent contingents of a British armored division to relieve CCB in the bridgehead the Americans had won earlier beyond the Deurne Canal along a railroad that traverses the marshes. This relief accomplished not long after nightfall on 27 October, General Silvester had a reserve for countering the German threat. He promptly ordered the CCB commander, General Hasbrouck, to counterattack the next morning.

Early on 28 October, General Silvester aimed two counterattacks at Meijel along the two highways leading to the town. A task force of CCR under Lt. Col. Richard D. Chappuis drove southeast along the Asten–Meijel road, while General Hasbrouck's CCB pushed southeast along the Deurne–Meijel highway. One column of CCB branched off to the east along a secondary road in an effort to recapture a bridge the Germans had used in their thrust across the Deurne Canal to Heitrak.

During the night, the Americans soon discovered, the *9th Panzer Division's Reconnaissance Battalion* had pushed several miles northwest from Meijel up the road toward Asten, and along the Deurne highway the Germans had consolidated their forces about Heitrak. At Heitrak, the *XLVII Panzer Corps* commander, Luettwitz, had thrown in the *15th Panzer Grenadier Division* while shifting the entire *9th Panzer Division* to the center and south of the zone of penetration near Nederweert and toward Asten.[30] In the face of these developments and marshy terrain that denied maneuver off the roads,

---

[29] See Annex 2 (Miscellaneous Information—Recent German Attacks) to XIII Corps G–2 Per Rpt, 16 Nov 44, citing XIX Corps, 13 Nov 44, found in XIII Corps G–3 Jnl file, 14–17 Nov 44.

[30] Rpt, *OB WEST* to OKW, 27 Oct 44, *OB WEST KTB, Befehle und Meldungen.*

none of the 7th Armored Division's counterthrusts made much headway.

Early on the third day, 29 October, the Germans renewed the attack. A strong thrust drove Colonel Chappuis' task force back almost half the distance to Asten before concentrated artillery fire forced the enemy to halt. Two other thrusts, one aimed northwest from Heitrak toward Deurne, the second along the secondary road from the east, forced both columns of General Hasbrouck's CCB to fall back about half the distance from Meijel to Deurne. Trying desperately to make a stand at the village of Liesel, the combat command eventually had to abandon that position as well. The loss of Liesel was particularly disturbing, for it opened two more roads to serve the Germans. One of these led west to Asten. If the Germans launched a quick thrust on Asten, they might cut off Colonel Chappuis' task force of CCR southeast of that village.

From the German viewpoint, capture of Liesel had another connotation. This village was the *15th Panzer Grenadier Division*'s farthest assigned objective along the Meijel–Deurne highway; its capture emphasized the rapid success the spoiling attack had attained. Perhaps equaling or surpassing Allied surprise upon the opening of the enemy's drive was German surprise at the speed and extent of their own gains. So impressed was Field Marshal Model that he saw visions of turning what had been conceived as a large-scale raid into something bigger. As early as 28 October, the second day of the attack, Model had asked Rundstedt at *OB WEST* to reinforce the *XLVII Panzer Corps* immediately with the *116th Panzer Division* and the *388th Volks Artillery Corps*.[31]

[31] *OB WEST KTB,* 28 Oct 44.

The latter was no minor force: it controlled six artillery battalions totaling 87 pieces ranging in caliber from 75-mm. guns to 210-mm. howitzers.[32]

This tract of marshland might have seen major German commitments had it not been for two related factors. First, neither the *116th Panzer Division* nor the *388th Volks Artillery Corps* was readily at hand. Second, before either could be committed, soberer heads than was Model's at this time had appraised the situation. On 28 October, they noted, the 7th Armored Division's counterattacks virtually had tied the Germans to their first day's gains while "droves" of Allied aircraft attacked delicate German communications lines through the Peel Marshes. On 29 October, for all the success at Liesel and along the Asten road, the Americans had resisted stubbornly. The Germans had lost up to thirty tanks. Furthermore, noted the *OB WEST G-2*, no indications existed to show that the attack had drawn any Allied strength from the attacks against the *Fifteenth Army* in the southwestern part of the Netherlands.[33]

Perceiving that gains thus far were ephemeral, Field Marshal von Rundstedt called a halt. "Continuation of the *XLVII Panzer Corps* attack no longer promises any results worth the employment of the forces committed," Rundstedt said. "On the contrary, there is great danger that *9th* and *15th Panzer Divisions* [*sic*] will suffer personnel and matériel losses which cannot be replaced in the near

[32] Rpt, *OB WEST* to *A Gp B,* 25 Oct 44, *OB WEST KTB, Befehle und Meldungen.*
[33] Annex 2 to XIII Corps G-2 Per Rpt, 16 Nov 44; *OB WEST KTB,* 28 Oct 44.

future. Hence the attack will be called off . . . ." [34]

Had Rundstedt waited a few more hours, he might have spotted an indication that the spoiling attack was accomplishing its purpose, that it was drawing Allied strength away from the *Fifteenth Army.* A British infantry division (the 15th) which had fought in southwestern Holland began relieving the 7th Armored Division's CCB at Liesel and CCR southeast of Asten during the night of 29 October. Noting the early identification of two fresh German divisions in the Peel Marshes, Field Marshal Montgomery himself had intervened to transfer this infantry division. Yet removal of the division from the southwestern part of the Netherlands was, in reality, no real loss there, for the division already had completed its role in the campaign south of the Maas.

Upon arrival of this relief, the 8 Corps commander, General O'Connor, directed General Silvester to concentrate his 7th Armored Division to the southwest about Nederweert and Weert. As soon as the situation at Meijel could be stabilized, the American armor was to attack northeast from Nederweert to restore the former line along the northwest bank of the Noorder Canal while British infantry swept the west bank of the Deurne Canal.

Arrival of British infantry to block the highways to Asten and Deurne and introduction of substantial British artillery reserves brought a sharp end to German advances from Meijel. For another day the Germans continued to try, for Field Marshal Model wrung a concession from Rundstedt to permit the attack to continue in order to gain a better defensive

line.[35] On two days the elusive Luftwaffe even attempted a minor comeback, but with little success. To strengthen the British position further, Field Marshal Montgomery shifted to the sector another British infantry division (the 53d) that had been pinched out of the battle south of the Maas. Though the German attack in the end had prompted transfer of two British divisions and artillery reinforcement, it had failed to result in any diminution of other operations on the 21 Army Group front. This the Germans failed to recognize when they belatedly—and wrongly—concluded that their attack had accomplished its original purpose.[36]

All three combat commands of General Silvester's American division were in the vicinity of Nederweert and Weert by nightfall of 30 October. The front had been stabilized both at Nederweert and near Meijel. The next day General O'Connor narrowed the 7th Armored Division's sector even more by bringing in a British armored brigade (the 4th) to strengthen the 1st Belgian Brigade along the Nederweert–Wessem Canal and by relieving the Belgians from attachment to the U.S. division. This left the 7th Armored Division responsible only for the Nederweert sector.

While this adjustment was in process, General Bradley on 30 October came to the 7th Armored Division's headquarters and relieved General Silvester of his command, replacing him with the CCB commander, General Hasbrouck. The relief, General Silvester believed, was based not on the Peel Marshes action but on personality conflicts and a misunderstand-

[34] Order, *OB WEST* to *A Gp B,* 1115, 29 Oct 44, *OB WEST KTB.*

[35] Entry of 29 Oct 44, *OB WEST KTB.*
[36] Daily Sitrep, *OB WEST* to OKW, 30 Oct 44, *OB WEST KTB.*

ing of the armored division's performance in earlier engagements in France. General Bradley wrote later that he had made the relief because he had "lost confidence in Silvester as a Division Commander." [37]

In the meantime, the Germans also were making adjustments. During the night of 30 October, the *15th Panzer Grenadier Division* withdrew to return to its earlier status as *Army Group B* reserve. The *9th Panzer Division* disengaged during the first week of November. Also on 30 October, headquarters of the *Fifth Panzer Army* (General der Panzertruppen Hasso von Manteuffel) assumed command of the *XLVII Panzer Corps*, General von Obstfelder's *LXXXVI Corps*, and *Corps Feldt*, the last the provisional corps that had opposed the 82d U.S. Airborne Division at Nijmegen. Thus the Germans carved a new army sector between the *First Parachute* and *Seventh Armies.* Command of the *Fifteenth* and *First Parachute Armies* was unified under *Army Group Student*, a provisional headquarters which subsequently was to be upgraded to a third full-fledged army group.[38]

On the Allied side, plans for a co-ordinated drive by the British and Americans to clear the Nederweert–Meijel sector were changed on the first day of November when Field Marshal Montgomery foresaw an end to his campaign in the southwestern part of the Netherlands and decided to introduce his entire 12 Corps on the right flank of the 7th Armored Division along the Nederweert–Wessem

Canal. The 12 Corps then was to drive northeast through the thick of the enemy's holdout position west of the Maas to Venlo, a first step in British co-operation with a new American offensive aimed at reaching the Rhine. The 7th Armored Division now was to attack alone to clear the northwest bank of the Noorder Canal. Not until the armor neared Meijel were the British to launch their part in the attack to take the town.

Though indications were that the 7th Armored Division would meet only about a battalion of Germans on the northwest bank of the Noorder Canal, it was obvious that even an undermanned defender could prove tenacious in this kind of terrain. The attack had to move through a corridor only about two miles wide, bounded on the southeast by the Noorder Canal and on the northwest by De Groote Peel, one of the more impenetrable portions of the Peel Marshes. The armored division's effective strength in medium tanks at this time was down to 65 percent, but in any case the burden of the fight in this terrain would fall on the armored infantry.

Directing a cautious advance at first, the new division commander, General Hasbrouck, changed to more aggressive tactics when resistance proved light. The principal difficulties came from boggy ground, mines, and German fire on the right flank from the eastern bank of the Noorder Canal. On 6 November, as the armored division neared its final objective just south of Meijel, the British north of that village began their attack southward. But the 7th Armored Division was not to be in on the kill. Late that day General Hasbrouck received orders for relief of his division and return to the 12th Army Group. The Americans had need of the

---

[37] Ltr, Bradley to Eisenhower, 2 Nov 44, copy in personal papers loaned by General Silvester; Ltr, Silvester to OCMH, 1 May 56; 7th Armd Div AAR, Oct–Nov 44. After the war an Army court of inquiry upheld General Bradley's action.

[38] See below, Ch. XVI.

division in a projected renewal of their offensive toward the Rhine. The relief occurred the next day, 7 November.

With this change, the British delayed the final assault on Meijel to await advance of the 12 Corps northeast from the Nederweert–Wessem Canal. The Germans subsequently abandoned Meijel on 16 November as the 12 Corps threatened their rear. The 8 Corps then drove southward from Venray while the 12 Corps continued northeastward on Venlo. Not until 3 December, more than two months after the first optimistic attempt to clear the enemy from west of the Maas with a lone American division, did these two full corps finally erase the embar-

rassment of the enemy's holdout. As the First U.S. Army had been discovering in the meantime in the Huertgen Forest southeast of Aachen, the Germans were great ones for wringing the utmost advantage from difficult terrain.

Elsewhere along the 21 Army Group front, the Canadians held their economical line along the south bank of the Maas and built up strength about Nijmegen, ready to help in Field Marshal Montgomery's Ruhr offensive. A British corps (the 30th) prepared to assist a new American offensive by limited operations along the American left flank. This general situation was to prevail on the 21 Army Group front until mid-December.

Lousberg   Hotel Quellenhoff   Farwick Park

Salvatorberg   Kurhaus

AACHEN

PART THREE

THE BATTLE OF AACHEN

CHAPTER XI

A Set Attack Against the West Wall

The day that had seen the start of American activity in the region of the Peel Marshes—the day of 22 September—was the same day when the First Army commander, General Hodges, had shut down almost all offensive operations on his front. The last troops withdrew from the Wallendorf bridgehead to mark the beginning of a lull in operations of the V Corps; except for a limited objective attack in the vicinity of the Monschau Corridor, the VII Corps quit trying to exploit the West Wall penetration southeast of Aachen; and the XIX Corps postponed its projected attack against the West Wall north of Aachen. A combination of German military renascence, American logistical problems, and a dispersion of forces had dictated a pause in First Army operations that was to last at least through the rest of September.

First Army Readjusts the Front

A major reason for the pause was the obvious fact that before renewing the drive to the Rhine the First Army had to gain greater concentration at critical points. Although few American commanders at this time had any genuine respect for the tissue-thin formations the Germans had thrown in their way, none could deny that a push to the Rhine would have to be a new operation, preceded by a penetration that could be vigorously exploited.

To help General Hodges concentrate, General Bradley sought to reduce the width of the First Army front. Into the line in the Ardennes-Eifel along the First Army's right wing he directed the Ninth Army under Lt. Gen. William H. Simpson, which had recently concluded the campaign at Brest.

Assuming responsibility for the old V Corps zone from the vicinity of St. Vith south to a new boundary with the Third Army near Echternach, the Ninth Army moved into the line during the days of transition from September to October. General Simpson had no alternative but to dig in and defend, for he was not strong enough either in men or supplies for an offensive. He had but one corps, Maj. Gen. Troy H. Middleton's VIII Corps, which had only two divisions.

When the Ninth Army arrived, General Hodges began to regroup. The point where he sought concentration was that upon which the army had focused since the start of the campaign, the Aachen Gap.

Having relinquished the bulk of the Ardennes-Eifel, General Hodges directed the V Corps to take over about fifteen miles of front from the south wing of the VII Corps in the Monschau-Elsenborn sector. He thereby reduced the VII Corps zone in the vicinity of Aachen from a width of about thirty-five miles to twenty. In the XIX Corps zone north of Aachen, Hodges made no change. Although the XIX Corps had incurred added responsibility in the thumb-shaped corridor west of the Maas, General Corlett's zone had been but sixteen miles wide originally, and he had received two new divisions (the 7th Armored and the 29th) to care for the added burden.

Although the First Army in the process of realignment had gained two divisions, the army's expanded north flank would absorb at least one of these for an indefinite period. Thus the net increase for renewing the drive to the Rhine was but one division. The more noteworthy gain was in reduction of the army front from about a hundred miles to sixty. In effecting this reduction, General Hodges had relinquished some mileage on his south wing and acquired a lesser amount on his north wing, so that the army had in effect shifted northward. For this reason Hodges now changed the corps objectives: the XIX Corps from Cologne to Duesseldorf, the VII Corps from Bonn to Cologne, and the V Corps from Koblenz to Bonn–Remagen.[1]

Even after realignment, General Hodges still was not ready to renew the offensive toward the Rhine. First he had to attend to four items of unfinished business.

On his right wing, to provide a secure right flank for the Rhine offensive, General Hodges had to take high ground in the vicinity of the Monschau Corridor, a task that involved clearing the German-infested Huertgen Forest. Because the northward shift of the V Corps had enabled the 9th Division of the VII Corps to concentrate opposite the forest, this job would fall for a second time to the 9th Division. Another task was to capture Aachen. This was closely tied up with a third problem, putting the XIX Corps

through the West Wall north of Aachen, for the XIX Corps had to get through the West Wall both to participate in a drive to the Rhine and to assist the VII Corps in encircling Aachen. The remaining responsibility was that of clearing the Peel Marshes.

The two most urgent tasks, clearing the thumb-shaped corridor and putting the XIX Corps through the West Wall, Hodges determined to undertake simultaneously as soon as the two new divisions reached the XIX Corps. While the incoming 7th Armored Division operated west of the Maas, the newly acquired 29th Division was to hold that portion of the exposed north flank lying east of the Maas. The 30th Division then could attack without further delay to penetrate the West Wall north of Aachen, while the entire 2d Armored Division stood by to exploit the penetration.

Planning the West Wall Assault

It was no news to the men of the 30th Division that they would make the first set attack against the West Wall. Through successive postponements since reaching the German border on 18 September, these men had known that eventually they must come to grips with the fortifications. From foxholes overlooking the little Wurm River, which marked the forward reaches of the enemy line in the sector between Aachen and Geilenkirchen, they had watched and waited.

The new target date for the 30th Division's assault was 1 October. Except that not one combat command but the entire 2d Armored Division was available for exploitation, plans for the attack varied little from the original conception. As soon as the infantry could pierce the

---

[1] FUSA Ltr of Instrs, 25 Sep, FUSA G–2 Jnl file, 1–3 Oct 44.

fortified line, the armor was to cross the Wurm, assume responsibility for holding the corps north flank east of the Wurm, and drive eastward to seize crossings of the Roer River, only nine miles away. The infantry, in the meantime, was to strike south to link with the VII Corps northeast of Aachen near the town of Wuerselen, thereby completing the encirclement of Aachen.

To assist the West Wall assault, the 29th Division was to make limited objective attacks along the corps north flank between Sittard and Geilenkirchen. At the same time the right wing regiment of the 30th Division, the 120th Infantry, was to be prepared to annihilate a re-entrant "bridgehead" the enemy had maintained outside the West Wall at Kerkrade and contain the enemy in the pillboxes and bunkers behind this "bridgehead." The other two regiments of the 30th Division were to make the assault upon the fortifications.[2]

The 30th Division commander, General Hobbs, had chosen to strike the West Wall on a narrow front little more than a mile wide along the Wurm nine miles north of Aachen and three miles southwest of Geilenkirchen near the villages of Marienberg and Rimburg. (*Map III*) Governing the choice was a desire to avoid stronger West Wall positions closer to Geilenkirchen and dense urban districts closer to Aachen. Whereas a rupture of the West Wall farther south might bring quicker juncture with the VII Corps, General Hobbs placed greater emphasis upon avoiding urban snares and upon picking a site served by good supply routes. That the enemy's fresh *183d Volks Grenadier Division* had entered the

line from Rimburg north toward Geilenkirchen apparently had no appreciable influence on General Hobbs's selection of an assault site, possibly because the XIX Corps G–2, Colonel Platt, deemed troops of this new division only "of a shade higher quality" than those of the *49th* and *275th Divisions*, which the XIX Corps had manhandled from the Albert Canal to the German border.[3]

In the period of slightly less than a fortnight between the original target date and 1 October, the 30th Division launched preparations with a keen appreciation of the importance and difficulties of this first set attack against the West Wall. Playing an integral role in the preparations was the infantry's sister arm, the artillery. On 26 September the artillery was to begin a systematic attempt to knock out all pillboxes along the 30th Division front, 75 percent of which had been plotted by air and ground observers. Fires were to increase in intensity until D-Day. An impressive total of 26 artillery battalions eventually was to participate, including artillery of the 2d Armored, 29th, and 30th Divisions, 4 artillery battalions attached to the 30th Division, 8 battalions of XIX Corps artillery, and 3 battalions of First Army artillery.

A few hours before the attack, the artillery was to execute "blackout" missions against enemy antiaircraft guns as protection for planes in a preliminary air bombardment. Then the artillery was to fire counterbattery and finally an intensive neutralization program in the specific

---

[2] XIX Corps FO 27, 28 Sep, XIX Corps G–3 file, 28–29 Sep 44.

[3] XIX Corps Special Rpt, Breaching the Siegfried Line, a narrative and convenient assimilation of relevant documents, filed with XIX Corps AAR, Oct 44; 30th Div G–2 Spot Estimate 11, 30 Sep, and G–2 Per Rpt, 1 Oct, 30th Div G–3 files, 1–2 Oct 44.

assault zone, including a rolling barrage in front of the attacking infantry.[4]

Expecting originally to have heavy bomber support, planners for the air phase grandiloquently announced that the air strike would include the greatest concentration of planes in close support of American ground troops since the "carpet" bombing along the St. Lô–Périers road in Normandy. That had involved more than 3,300 planes, including more than a thousand heavy bombers.[5]

Because the 30th Division had been hit on two separate occasions when Allied bombs fell short in Normandy, few old-timers in the division could have felt much regret when heavy bombers proved unavailable for the West Wall assault and participation by air forces proved less grandiose than originally conceived. As finally determined, the air bombardment was to approach the St. Lô bombing in neither bomb tonnage nor number of planes. Only 360 mediums (A–20 Havocs and B–26 Marauders) of the IX Bombardment Division and 72 fighter-bombers (P–38 Lightnings and P–47 Thunderbolts) of the IX Tactical Air Command were to participate.

Use of mediums rather than heavies nevertheless entailed minute planning by both air and ground units. Recalling with trepidation the holocaust along the St. Lô–Périers road, officers of the 30th Division were seriously concerned about safety precautions. Their concern grew vociferous after 22 September when a flight of P–38's that already had begun a bomb run before cancellation of the West

Wall attack on that day dropped four napalm bombs within 30th Division lines. The bombs destroyed an ammunition dump and six vehicles, injured four men, and killed two.[6]

General Hobbs and his staff wanted the bomb run made over enemy territory parallel to the Wurm River and the division front in order to ensure that inadvertent shorts would not strike friendly troops. Basing their judgment on prevailing wind conditions and a heavy belt of enemy flak, air officers wanted to make a perpendicular approach. As many men in the 30th Division remembered, insistence upon a perpendicular approach had contributed directly to the disaster in Normandy. One of three American divisions hit, the 30th Division had lost to American bombs seventy-five men killed and 505 wounded. For the West Wall operation, General Hobbs was protesting the perpendicular approach almost until the very moment the planes appeared in the sky above his command post.[7]

Most commanders in the 30th Division also wanted to mark target areas with smoke, but on the theory that smoke might obscure the targets, air officers refused. It is possible that the airmen were concerned lest wind blow the smoke back on friendly lines and thus precipitate another short bombing. As finally determined smoke was to be used only to mark targets for dive bombers.[8]

---

[4] Annex 1 to XIX Corps FO 27.

[5] For an account of this action, see Martin Blumenson, *Breakout and Pursuit,* UNITED STATES ARMY IN WORLD WAR II (Washington, 1961). See also Bradley, *A Soldier's Story,* pp. 337–41, 346–49.

[6] Msg, Hobbs to Corlett, 22 Sep, XIX Corps G–3 file, 22 Sep 44.

[7] Note telephone conversations recorded in 30th Div G–3 file, 1 Oct 44. A detailed explanation of the Air Force view in this instance may be found in Roswell King, Comments on the Medium Bombardment Effort to Support the 30th Division, OCMH files. King was an air officer participating in this operation.

[8] Note Msgs 5, 6, and 7, 30th Div G–3 Jnl, 1 Oct 44.

To initiate the attack, artillery units were to concentrate on antiaircraft blackout missions for twenty minutes before arrival of the first flights of medium bombers. The Havocs and Marauders were to saturate village road centers and logical locations for enemy command posts and reserves along the periphery of an arc approximately four miles beyond the Wurm. The next flights of mediums were to carpet an oblong sector, beginning a thousand yards east of the Wurm and extending east two miles, in which lay numerous pillboxes and bunkers, a German cantonment, several villages, and all the first objectives of the two assault regiments. About an hour after the start of the mediums' strike, fighter-bombers using napalm were to pinpoint specific targets among the pillboxes for half an hour before H-Hour. Artillery was to continue to fire during the saturation bombing but as a safety precaution for the low-flying fighters was to cease during the dive bombing. Shelling was to recommence at H-Hour as the foot troops crossed a line approximately a thousand yards west of the Wurm, a line representing both the line of departure and the no-advance line during the bombing.[9]

While plans progressed for supporting the attack with planes and artillery, infantry, tank, and engineer units prepared for the ground phase.

Patrols probing the front along the Wurm brought back information that materially affected planning. One patrol, for example, revealed that mapmakers had dignified the Wurm in calling it a river,

for in reality it is but 2 to 4 feet deep and 15 to 18 feet wide. This prompted acceptance of a plan to substitute duckboard footbridges for assault boats in the crossing. Another patrol discovered a concealed route of approach to the Wurm which a rifle company subsequently was to use to marked advantage. In at least two instances, patrols crept into the fortified belt to place demolitions in the firing apertures of pillboxes. These and other patrols determined that the Germans held no positions west of the Wurm other than outposts in Marienberg and Rimburg and that east of the Wurm the enemy's forward outposts were usually a few hundred yards back from the river along a railroad. This railroad, the men reported, was an effective antitank obstacle. Through the length of the attack zone it ran a course of either deep cuts or high fills.[10]

While awaiting D Day, the regiments rotated their battalions in the line, so that all might undergo refresher training in fundamental tactics, in assault of pillboxes, and in co-ordination with armor. No one could deny the need for this training: in one battalion, for example, only one man remained after four months of warfare who had any experience in operating a flame thrower. One regiment found a satisfactory training substitute for the Wurm in a stagnant stream; the other regiment had to call upon the power of imagination to create a river out of a rear-area road. Officers of the battalion which was to spearhead the 117th Infantry's assault improvised a sand table

[9] XIX Corps, Notes on Air Strike, 28 Sep, XIX Corps G–3 file, 28 Sep 44; 30th Div, Notes on Air Strike, 30th Div G–3 file, 28–30 Sep 44; 30th Div, Revised Air Plan, Annex 2 to FO 42, 29 Sep, XIX Corps G–3 file, 30 Sep 44.

[10] Extensive combat interviews supplement official records of the 30th Division and attached units for this period. See also XIX Corps Special Rpt, Breaching the Siegfried Line, and Ltr, Hobbs to OCMH, 26 Dec 53.

PRACTICING FLAME THROWER TECH-
NIQUE *for reducing pillboxes.*

and reconstructed the terrain to the regiment's front. From the sand table the two assault companies learned their respective roles in detail, while the reserve company memorized both roles in event of having to take over from either of the other companies. Tankers and engineers constructed expedient bridges out of metal culverts encased in logs, bound together, and placed on a sled which a tank might pull to the river and a tank dozer shove into the stream. In experiments conducted behind the lines, these expedients —which the men called "culverts"— worked satisfactorily. To supplement the culverts, the tankers planned to throw log mats into the stream to form a base for fords.

Faced with a dual obstacle like the Wurm and the West Wall, the regimental commanders tried to avoid any complexity

in their attack plans. Both chose a simple column-of-battalions formation. On the left (north), the 117th Infantry (Colonel Johnson) was to cross the Wurm just south of Marienberg to gain a foothold within a single band of pillboxes several hundred yards east of the railroad on the eastern slope of the Wurm valley. The line of pillboxes followed a road which runs from Palenberg, a coal-mining town just across the river from Marienberg, south and southwest to Rimburg Castle, lying east of the Wurm opposite Rimburg. Although other pillboxes in occasional clusters extended east to give the West Wall in this sector a depth of about a mile and a half, seizure of the forward band would mean a rupture in the outer crust of the fortified belt. The slopes beyond the Wurm are gentle like those west of the river, affording the enemy little advantage in observation except that inherent to a defender over an attacker and that provided by slag piles east of Palenberg.

With a foothold within the West Wall assured, the 117th Infantry was to fan out in two directions, northeast through the fringes of Palenberg to occupy high ground and anchor the northern flank of the bridgehead, and east through the town of Uebach to gently sloping high ground between Uebach and the village of Beggendorf. This eastward push was designed to sever a north–south highway that conceivably might serve the enemy as an artery of lateral communications.

The 119th Infantry (Colonel Sutherland) was in the meantime to have sent a battalion across the Wurm at Rimburg and through the first band of pillboxes to occupy a crossroads on the eastern crest of the valley just northwest of the village of Herbach. This would provide the regiment firm footing for subsequent attacks to expand the bridgehead toward the southeast in the direction the 30th Division eventually was to take in order to link with the VII Corps near Aachen.

Of the two regimental assault sectors, the 119th Infantry's would prove the more difficult. Between the river and the railroad, the 119th Infantry had to traverse a wider space of flatland before reaching the railroad embankment. At the northern edge of this flatland, the Rimburg Castle, encircled by a moat, afforded the enemy a strong outpost position. The pillboxes themselves were more difficult to locate in the 119th Infantry's sector, because a dense woods 300 to 500 yards deep concealed the defenses. To overcome these obstacles, the regimental commander, Colonel Sutherland, had to trust in the hope that the culverts tankers and engineers had developed would enable tanks to cross the river soon after the assault began. But concern that soft, muddy ground in the Wurm valley might stop the tanks grew as the sun failed to break through rain clouds for twelve days preceding the target date.

Few commanders failed to recognize the obvious fact that the delay in assaulting the West Wall afforded the Germans an opportunity to man their fortifications and procure reserves. On the other hand, the preparations by planes and artillery and the additional troops provided by availability of the entire 2d Armored Division might offset this advantage.

At the end of September General Corlett's G–2, Colonel Platt, estimated that from Geilenkirchen south to the corps boundary near Aachen, the Germans were manning the line with seven battalions of about 450 men each. From Geilenkirchen to Rimburg were two battalions

of the *183d Volks Grenadier Division's 330th Regiment*. South from Rimburg, five battalions, Colonel Platt calculated, were operating under the *49th* and *275th Divisions*. He estimated that the Germans had four battalions of light and medium artillery capable of firing into the 30th Division's zone, plus a battery of 210-mm. guns and one or two large caliber railroad guns. Observers had detected only an occasional tank in the vicinity. In the matter of reserves, Platt predicted the Germans would have at least one battalion from each of three regiments of the *183d Division* available for quick counterattacks, while the *116th Panzer Division* and contingents of an infantry division recently identified near Aachen might be backing up the line.[11]

Except in one instance, Colonel Platt was basically correct in his estimate of the enemy. That error was his failure to note that upon arrival of the *183d Volks Grenadier Division*, the new *LXXXI Corps* commander, General Koechling, who had replaced General Schack, had pulled the *275th Division* from the line and transferred it to the corps south wing in the Huertgen Forest.[12] Colonel Platt was particularly prescient in his estimate of enemy artillery, for between them the *49th* and *183d Divisions* had, as Platt predicted, four battalions. Two railroad guns, which the XIX Corps G–2 had noted might be present, were in the vicinity.[13]

From Rimburg south to a point three miles north of Aachen, the troops con-

---

[11] 30th Div G–2 Spot Estimate 11, 30 Sep 44, and G–2 Rpt, 1 Oct 44.

[12] Daily Sitrep, *LXXXI Corps,* 22 Sep 44, *LXXXI Corps KTB, Tagesmeldungen.*

[13] Details of enemy strength and organization may be found in Heichler, The Germans Opposite XIX Corps.

trolled by General Macholz's *49th Division* were organized around the same two regimental formations (*148th* and *149th Regiments*) which had fallen back before the XIX Corps from the Albert Canal to the border. In the interim, such changes had occurred among personnel that the division was hardly the same as the one that had breathed a sigh of relief upon gaining the West Wall. In a period of slightly more than a fortnight, General Macholz had absorbed 4,326 "replacements" in the form of a hodgepodge of miscellaneous units. A tabulation of the units this division assimilated during the period would indicate to a degree the problem General Macholz and other German commanders all along the Western Front faced in creating a cohesive fighting force. Among the miscellany General Macholz received were 2 *Landesschuetzen* battalions, 2 "straggler" battalions, 3 machine-gun battalions, 2 separate infantry battalions (probably replacement training units) 4 "security" battalions, and 1 *Alarm Company Aachen*.[14]

American commanders, for their part, entertained no illusions that intentions of the XIX Corps were secret. Without a doubt, General Hobbs and General Corlett believed, the Germans were expecting an attack on the first clear day. Yet little could be done to deceive the enemy even as to the site of the attack, for the blow obviously was going to fall somewhere between Aachen and Geilenkirchen. General Hobbs nevertheless attempted some deception by spreading pre-D-Day artillery fires along the entire front, with emphasis on the sector opposite the 120th Infantry on the division south wing, and

by concentrating artillery units in the southern part of the division zone. Also, once the offensive began, pressure by the 120th Infantry and the 29th Division on either flank might limit the forces the enemy could shift against the penetration.

The Americans actually need not have concerned themselves with this problem, for German intelligence officers could not see the forest for the trees. So concerned were they with fear of a major American offensive on a broad front southeast of Aachen, with the Roer River towns of Dueren, Juelich, and Linnich as first objectives, that they failed to accord any real importance to the preparations in the Geilenkirchen sector. The Germans even anticipated a possible large-scale Allied airborne operation between the Roer and the Rhine as a corollary of a new offensive.

With these ideas in mind, the new *LXXXI Corps* commander, General Koechling, wrongly assumed that the First U.S. Army would make a strong bid northeastward through the Stolberg Corridor during the very first days of October, with a possible diversion at Geilenkirchen. As a consequence, General Koechling and his staff spent the latter days of September in feverish preparations to strengthen the sectors of the *246th* and *12th Divisions* at Aachen and southeast of Aachen.[15]

Apparently the only commander to question Koechling's opinion was the *183d Division*'s General Lange; but he also guessed wrong. Cognizant of American armor opposite his division, Lange expected a major attack aginst his sector. Yet he could not believe that the Americans would try to push armor across the Wurm at the point they actually had

---

[14] Heichler, in The Germans Opposite XIX Corps, gives strength figures and date of arrival of each of these units.

[15] Rpt, *Seventh Army* to *A Gp B*, 30 Sep 44, *A Gp B KTB, Operationsbefehle;* MS # A-990 (Koechling); *OB WEST KTB*, 30 Sep 44.

chosen because there the eastern slopes of the Wurm valley are higher and afford more commanding positions for antitank guns than do the slopes a few miles to the north at Geilenkirchen. He expected the blow to fall at Geilenkirchen in the very center of his division sector.[16]

Even the one correct German prediction that the offensive would begin during the first days of October was to be discredited before the attack actually began. Noting on 29 September that American air activity had reached such a fortissimo that all daylight troop and supply movements in the *LXXXI Corps* had to be shut down, the Germans attached undue importance to virtual cessation of air attacks during the next two days. In reality, this could be attributed only to unfavorable weather; but when combined with lessening of American artillery fires, the Germans took it to mean that their earlier prediction had been wrong. Although General Koechling himself was not fooled, the fact that he expected the attack on his southern wing southeast of Aachen deprived his opinion of importance. The division commanders immediately concerned, Generals Lange and Macholz, were thoroughly lulled.[17]

Although part of the decrease in American artillery fires undoubtedly was caused by unfavorable weather limiting observation, it may have been more directly attributable to two other factors. First, earlier hopes that First Army's logistical situation might be showing marked improvement by this time had faded; General Corlett now found he could not afford the expenditure of artillery ammu-

nition he had planned. Indeed, on the very day of the West Wall attack General Bradley was to reinstitute rationing of artillery ammunition throughout the 12th Army Group. Second, both Corlett and General Hobbs had been disappointed with the effect of the elaborate pre-D-Day artillery program.

Other than to clear away camouflage, they discovered, most of the shelling had little effect on the pillboxes. Only self-propelled 155-mm. guns, often fired from exposed positions in order to engage the fortifications at close range, did any real damage, and then only after considerable expenditure of ammunition.[18] The firing did reveal some cleverly camouflaged pillboxes not previously located.[19] This in itself was an advantage but hardly what the planners had hoped for and hardly enough to justify an elaborate program. As the target date of 1 October approached, artillery units began to husband more and more ammunition for the assault.

At dawn on the target date, General Corlett, General Hobbs, and the men who were to make the West Wall assault looked with chagrin at a mournful sky which brought showers and visibility so limited that virtually no hope remained for a preattack aerial bombardment. Though reluctant to postpone the attack again, General Corlett was even more reluctant to move without aerial support. Eventually he bowed to the weather. A subsequent downpour brought more concern to tankers and engineers whose first

---

[16] MS # B-753 (Lange).

[17] *OB WEST KTB,* 29 Sep 44; *LXXXI Corps KTB, Tagesmeldungen,* 30 Sep and 1 Oct 44; MS # B-792 (Macholz).

[18] The 258th Field Artillery Battalion (SP 155's) claimed penetrations in all forty-three pillboxes engaged during a seven-day period. See Ltr, Lt Col Bradford A. Butler, Jr., comdg 258th FA Bn, to CG XIX Corps, 5 Oct 44, XIX Corps G-3 file, 5-6 Oct 44.

[19] One unit reported: "Fired at haystack with machine gun. Shots bounced off."

task was to get the tanks across the soft, muddy shoulders of the Wurm.

As night came a forecast of improved weather conditions for the next day put the offensive back in motion. After receiving an extra ration of cigarettes and chocolate during the night, few of the infantrymen had any doubt but that on 2 October the oft-postponed attack at last would begin. They joked about fattening pigs for the kill.

"Those infantrymen have guts!"

At 0900 on 2 October, under a scattered overcast, the air strike began. Although the planes made a perpendicular approach across 30th Division lines, they dropped no shorts. They also overshot the targets. Five groups of mediums missed the target areas altogether, and the remaining four groups dropped only a portion of their bombs accurately. An hour after the air strike began, the 117th Infantry commander, Colonel Johnson, reported that no bombs had fallen in front of his lines. Two of the groups of mediums were so late in arriving over the target that the low-flying dive bombers had to be cleared from the area to permit the mediums to drop their loads. One of these groups bombed on colored smoke markings which had been registered for the dive bombers in Palenberg and thereby produced the only results which ground observers could call "excellent." A note of tragedy entered the strike when one group of mediums bombed a town in Belgium, twenty-eight miles west of the assigned target, inflicting seventy-nine casualties upon Belgian civilians, including thirty-four killed.[20]

No one could blame the failure of the medium bombing on enemy action. The Luftwaffe showed no signs of renewed activity, and enemy flak was virtually nonexistent.

The fighter-bombers were more accurate in that they operated precisely over the target area, but they hit not one pillbox. "We had heard stories about thousands of planes that were supposed to have come and destroyed the pillboxes," said one private, "but we only saw a few of them and the damage was slight." Although this soldier obviously had been led to expect too much, even more conservative observers could discern no real benefit from the strike except that the bomb craters provided much-needed cover. Some napalm bombs hit field fortifications in the northern part of the zone, and others landed accurately in the woods east of Rimburg opposite the 119th Infantry, but since the woods were wet, the burning oil failed to achieve the desired effect. As determined later by prisoner interrogations, psychological effect on the Germans was negligible. Some prisoners said they slept through the bombardment. "What bombing?" one German wanted to know.[21]

---

[20] "This gross error," the IX Bombardment Division determined later, "was due to poor navigation, poor headwork, and misidentification of target." History, IX Bombardment Division (M) Sep–Oct 44, and attached copy of Teletype, Gen Anderson (CG IX Bomb Div) to Gp and Wing Comdrs; see also Craven and Cate, eds., *Europe: Argument to V-E Day*, p. 615.

[21] The air strike was called Operation Cisco. The story of the strike and the following attack is based upon observations in combat interviews; Hewitt, *Workhorse of the Western Front*, p. 112; Msg, 30th Div G–3 to XIX Corps CG, 2 Oct, in 30th Div G–3 file, 2 Oct 44; XIX Corps AAR, Oct 44; 30th Div G–3 Jnl, 2 Oct 44; History, IX Bombardment Division (M); Unit History, IX Fighter Comd and IX TAC, Oct 44; and Craven and Cate, eds., *Europe: Argument to V-E Day,* p. 615.

No matter what the shortcomings of the air strike, the XIX Corps now was irrevocably committed to the attack. There could be no turning back.

As the infantrymen climbed from their foxholes and cellars to move toward the line of departure, more than 400 tubes of American artillery and mortars fired thunderous salvos that searched out enemy batteries, assembly areas, and the forward line of pillboxes. Some VII Corps artillery joined the demonstration. Both 81-mm. and 60-mm. mortars participated. "Of course," said one platoon leader, "a 60-mm. mortar shell would bounce off a pillbox like a peanut, but they caused the personnel in the firing trenches to duck inside." Chemical mortars concentrated at first on chewing paths through tactical wire beyond the Wurm, then shifted to a rolling barrage which started at the crossing areas and led the infantry by several hundred yards. Direct support battalions of 105-mm. howitzers contributed to this shifting curtain of fire. To make up for deficiencies of the air strike, artillery commanders dug deep into ammunition stocks they had earmarked for use against counterattacks. Inadequately supported riflemen could not successfully attack an obstacle like the West Wall, General Corlett reasoned; he would take his chances on getting more ammunition later.[22] At the end of twelve hours twenty-six supporting artillery battalions had fired a total of 18,696 rounds.

At the line of departure, heavy machine gunners of the assault battalions delivered overhead fire against embrasures of the pillboxes. Because the machine gunners had to use tracer ammunition to regulate

their firing, the Germans quickly spotted the guns. Losses were swift and heavy. Five of eight machine guns of the 1st Battalion, 117th Infantry, for example, were knocked out.

Carrying the duckboards that were to provide dry paths across the river, the infantrymen raced down the west slope of the valley through soggy fields ridged with rows of stock beets and turnips. A moving target, their leaders had told them again and again, is less easily hit than a stationary one. They operated now on that theory.

At the river on the left of the crossing area, big 1st Lt. Don A. Borton of Company B, 117th Infantry, seized one of the duckboards, waded into the water, and slapped it into place. "There's your goddamned bridge!" he cried. Men of his platoon sped forward. Throwing high their hands, eleven Germans who had occupied foxholes close along the river bank jumped up to surrender. In a matter of minutes, the men of Company B had gained the protection of the railroad embankment. The forward platoons of this company had lost not a single man.

Although similarly impressed with the need for speed, the 117th Infantry's Company C was not so fortunate in crossing the open slopes to the river. A concentration of hostile shells hit squarely among one of the forward platoons, killing or wounding all but 6 men. By the time Company C reached the river, heavy shelling and casualties obviously had broken the company's momentum. In less than an hour Company C had lost 87 men, 7 of them killed.

Faced with the possibility that his entire attack might flounder because of the misfortunes of this company, the battalion commander, Lt. Col. Robert E.

[22] Ltrs, Corlett to OCMH, 2 Sep 53 and 20 May 56.

Frankland, quickly called on his reserve. Company A, he directed, was to cross the river on Company B's bridges and then assume the assault role of Company C. So thoroughly had the men of Company A learned the missions of the two assault companies that in less than half an hour they were building up along the railroad embankment beyond the river.

In the meantime, those men of Company B who had first reached the railroad fought a tendency to take cover behind the embankment. The alternative was none too pleasant, for open ground rising from the embankment to the line of pillboxes along the Palenberg–Rimburg road was devoid of cover and concealment other than that provided by the corpses of several cows. Under the prodding of a platoon leader, 1st Lt. Robert P. Cushman, the men nevertheless recognized that they had to act at once while the rolling barrage and overhead machine gun fire kept the enemy pinned inside his fortifications. Some later attributed Lieutenant Cushman's goading to the fact that ten minutes before the jump-off the lieutenant had received a telegram announcing the birth of a son. He was in a hurry, they said, to get the war over with.

The action that followed gave proof of the value of the refresher training Company B had undergone. As one part of each platoon took up support positions from which to fire into the embrasures of the pillboxes, specially organized assault detachments equipped with flame throwers and demolition charges pressed forward. Each man knew his job and did it.

The courage of a volunteer flame thrower, Pvt. Brent Youenes, featured the taking of the first two pillboxes by Lieutenant Cushman's platoon. Advancing

within ten yards of the first pillbox, Private Youenes squirted two bursts of flame into the front embrasure. The occupants must have been cowering inside, for they fired not a shot. As soon as the flame dissipated, Pvt. Willis Jenkins shoved a pole charge into the same embrasure. Still no fire came from the pillbox. When supporting riflemen stormed the position, five Germans filed out, shaking from their experience and muttering surrender. So co-ordinated and daring had been the performance that a member of Company B's weapons platoon, whose job was in itself so far forward that few soldiers envied it, could not suppress his admiration. "Those infantrymen have guts!" was the way he put it.

Turning to the other pillbox, Lieutenant Cushman and his assault detachment received machine gun fire from a trench outside the pillbox. Quick return fire killed one of two Germans manning the machine gun; the other retreated inside. Creeping around to a blind side of the pillbox, three riflemen tossed hand grenades through the embrasures and down a ventilator shaft. Arriving with his flame thrower, Private Youenes squirted an embrasure while another man placed a pole charge against the entrance to the pillbox. Soon after the explosion, a German officer dashed out, brandishing a pistol. When his first shot killed one man of the assault detachment, someone yelled, "He killed Smitty! The son of a bitch, he killed Smitty!" Every man in sight turned his weapon on the enemy officer. Six Germans who had remained in the pillbox then surrendered.

Turning to three other pillboxes, Lieutenant Cushman and his men found that concussion from mortars and artillery had so intimidated the occupants and that fire of the support detachment was so effective in keeping the enemy away from his firing embrasures that resistance came from none of them. The first pillbox fell to a pole charge placed once again by the intrepid Private Jenkins. Hand grenades thrown through firing slits brought surrender of the other two. In less than two hours after crossing the line of departure, Lieutenant Cushman's platoon had taken five pillboxes with the loss of but one man.

At the same time, Lieutenant Borton and his platoon were having similar experiences with two other pillboxes. Pvt. Harold Zeglien finished off the first with a pole charge set in an embrasure. The Germans in the second were not so easily subdued. Even after a pole charge had gone off against one of the embrasures, the enemy inside fired a machine gun to kill a bazooka man who was attempting to put a rocket through the entrance. Strangely, a change in tactics from force to intimidation at last did the trick. A prisoner captured earlier went inside the pillbox with word that if the Germans failed to surrender, they must face death from a flame thrower. Nine Germans filed out.

Another pillbox earmarked for reduction by Company B was the responsibility of the company's support platoon under T. Sgt. Howard Wolpert. Operating a flame thrower, Pvt. Henry E. Hansen had directed two blasts toward one embrasure and was moving to another side of the pillbox when he spotted a German lying in wait for him to appear from another direction. As the German whirled to face him, Private Hansen caught him full in the face with a blast from his flame thrower. When pole charges set by others of the platoon brought no response from inside the pillbox, Sergeant Wolpert

and his men began to reorganize, secure in the belief that they had taken their objective. The fight over, Private Hansen casually sprayed the embrasures of the pillbox again in order to empty his flame thrower and reduce its weight. Smoke began to seep from the embrasures, and small arms ammunition to explode inside the pillbox. A moment later ten Germans pushed open the door to surrender.

Even as Company B was breaching the first band of West Wall pillboxes with the loss of but two men in actual assaults on the fortifications, Company A was following to take over the assault mission of Company C. Like the platoon leaders of Company B, the officers of Company A found that the railroad embankment held an attraction for their men that could prove fatal. Already German mortar and artillerymen were turning the flatland between the river and the embankment into a maelstrom of bursting shells; in a matter of minutes the enemy's defensive fires might deny the route of approach from the embankment to the pillboxes. Using the theory that "you can't push a string, you gotta pull it," 1st Lt. Theodore Foote signaled men of his platoon to follow and clambered across the embankment. In a ragged skirmish line, the men charged across an open field toward a pillbox beyond the Palenberg–Rimburg road.

Directing his support detachment into position along the road, Lieutenant Foote and the assault detachment raced on toward the pillbox. Finding a bomb crater almost in front of the pillbox, the men took cover while Pfc. Gus Pantazopulos fired two rockets from a bazooka against the closest embrasure and Pvt. Martin Sirokin dashed forward to place a pole charge in the hole the rockets made. Cpl.

Russell Martin pegged hand grenades into the enlarged embrasure as the rest of the assault detachment charged from the crater. The charge carried both the pillbox and a series of field fortifications nearby where a nest of Germans had been lying low during the fracas. By the time the rest of Company A arrived, nothing remained but to organize defensive positions in the vicinity of the pillbox.

Only a few steps behind Colonel Frankland's 1st Battalion, the 117th Infantry commander, Colonel Johnson, sent a company of the 2d Battalion to clear enemy outposts from west of the river in the village of Marienberg. This done in less than two hours, despite delaying action by German riflemen and machine gunners, Colonel Johnson directed the company to cross the Wurm into the northern part of Palenberg while the remainder of the battalion crossed behind Colonel Frankland's battalion in order to approach Palenberg from the south.

Two pillboxes provided the crux of the opposition in Palenberg, but persistent small unit maneuver and daring use of bazookas and pole charges after the manner of Colonel Frankland's battalion eventually carried the strongpoints. By about 1600 the men had eliminated small arms fire from a permanent bridge site between Marienberg and Palenberg while others continued a house-to-house fight to eject the enemy from the rest of Palenberg. This fight often lapsed into hand grenade duels. One rifleman, Pvt. Harold G. Kiner, spotted an enemy grenade that landed between him and two fellow riflemen, threw himself upon it, and saved his companions at the cost of his own life. He was posthumously awarded the Medal of Honor.

Neither tanks nor tank destroyers be-

came available to the 117th Infantry during the day, not because the culverts designed for bridging the stream failed to work but because the banks of the Wurm were such a quagmire that the tank dozer which was to shave down the banks mired deep in the mud. Tanks brought up to pull out the tank dozer also bogged down. The tankers finally gave up to await construction of a treadway bridge.

Having worked under steady enemy shelling, the engineers at 1830 completed the treadway, but when the tanks crossed, the soil on the east bank proved too soft for maneuver. A short while later, when other engineers completed another treadway between Marienberg and Palenberg, the tanks found firmer footing. Yet now they were too late to assist in the first day's fighting.

Almost from the start, the 30th Division's other assault regiment, the 119th Infantry (Colonel Sutherland), had met with difficulties in the West Wall attack. Attempting to reach the Wurm south of Rimburg, to the right of the 117th Infantry's crossing area, the 119th's leading battalion came under German shellfire soon after crossing the line of departure. The two assault companies nevertheless reached the river and under light machine gun fire from the railroad embankment slapped their duckboard footbridges into place. One company then managed to build up along the railroad, but fire from three pillboxes located west of the railroad near the Rimburg Castle stymied the other. The Germans had expertly camouflaged one of the pillboxes as a house. All through the afternoon this company fought until at last a combination of small arms and bazooka fire reduced these three positions. Meanwhile, men of the other company found it impossible to

ABANDONED CROSSING *at the Wurm River.*

raise their heads above the railroad embankment. From positions hidden in the Rimburg woods, blistering fire frustrated every attempt to cross the embankment. Commitment of the battalion's reserve company served merely to pin more men along the railroad. Artillery and mortar fire against the enemy positions also had little effect. Limits on observation imposed by trees and bushes denied accurate adjustment, and as soon as supporting shellfire lifted to permit an assault, the Germans would rush from their pillboxes and renew their fire from field fortifications.

The 119th Infantry's plan of attack had leaned heavily upon the early availability of tanks to neutralize just such positions as these in the western edge of the woods. But the culvert that engineers had prepared for bridging the Wurm in this regiment's crossing area fell to pieces as the tankers towed it over rough ground to the river. Although the engineers rushed completion of a treadway bridge that enabled the tanks to cross in mid-afternoon, deep black mud halted every attempt to get the tanks up to the infantry positions.

In an attempt to open up the situation,

Colonel Sutherland early committed a second battalion of infantry on the left of the first. Delayed at the river because men responsible for bringing the duckboard footbridges had abandoned them en route, this battalion eventually crossed on bridges improvised from fence posts and doors. Once beyond the Wurm, the men came under intense fire from the Rimburg Castle. At last they drove the Germans from positions along the wall and moat of the castle and by nightfall had built up on three sides of this strong outpost position. Protected by medieval masonry, the Germans inside held out.

In late afternoon Colonel Sutherland committed his remaining battalion on his southern flank, but with no greater success. Once on the east bank, the men could advance no farther than the railroad. Like the others before them, they discovered it worth a man's life to poke his head above the level of the embankment.

When engineers at midnight completed a second treadway bridge at a permanent bridge site between Rimburg and the castle, the attached tanks at last had firm footing, but the arrival of the tanks had come too late to assist the 119th Infantry in getting beyond the railroad into the pillbox belt. The day's fighting had netted the regiment a shallow bridgehead a mile long and 300 yards deep, embracing only the flatland between the river and the railroad.

Anticipating immediate German reaction to the West Wall attack, General Hobbs and his regimental commanders waited apprehensively as night came for the first counterblow to fall. The bridgehead of the 119th Infantry was tenuous at best, and that regiment's inability to advance beyond the railroad had left the

117th Infantry with an exposed right flank. For those reasons, General Hobbs told his artillery commander to hammer through the night at likely enemy assembly areas and routes leading into the restricted bridgehead.

Unknown to General Hobbs, active German reaction to the West Wall assault had been delayed because the blow had achieved complete surprise. Deceived by diversionary attacks made during the day northwest of Geilenkirchen by the 29th Division and to the south at Kerkrade by the 30th Division's 120th Infantry, the commanders of the *49th* and *183d Divisions* had been unable to believe for several hours that this attack on the narrow Marienberg–Rimburg front was "it." [23] Even when they finally accepted this fact, General Macholz of the *49th Division* had virtually nothing to throw against the bridgehead and General Lange of the *183d Division* had only one battalion as an infantry reserve. This battalion General Lange ordered to counterattack soon after dark in company with an assault gun battalion. The counterattack could not be launched during the day because the Germans dared not move assault guns in this open terrain under the rapacious eyes of American planes and artillery. [24]

As night came, interdictory fires laid down by 30th Division and XIX Corps artillery were far more effective than any American commander could have dared to hope. "Murderous" artillery fires, the Germans said, delayed the counterattack

---

[23] MS # B–792 (Macholz).

[24] *183d VG Div* AAR; Evng and Daily Sitreps, *183d VG Div* to *LXXXI Corps,* 2 Oct 44, in *LXXXI Corps KTB, Tagesmeldungen;* Tel Convs, *LXXXI Corps* to *183d VG Div,* 1430, 1800, and 2120, 2 Oct 44, in *LXXXI Corps KTB, Kampfverlauf.*

by three hours.[25]   Not until midnight did the Germans strike and then only with a smattering of the original infantry force and but two assault guns.   The mobile guns American bazooka men and rifle grenadiers on the northeastern fringe of the bridgehead turned back quickly, but not until after a brisk fire fight did the German infantry retire, leaving behind seven dead.   The 117th Infantry lost three men, including Private Sirokin, one of those who had performed so courageously that afternoon in the taking of the pillboxes.   So discouraged by this feeble show was the German corps commander, General Koechling, that he ordered the *183d Division's* General Lange to confine his operations to "sealing off" the penetration until stronger forces could be assembled for more effective countermeasures.[26]

Though the 30th Division had made no phenomenal advances during the first day of the West Wall attack, this was no cause for discouragement.   The 119th Infantry had failed to move far enough even to clear the Rimburg crossing area of direct small arms fire; yet the 117th Infantry farther north had breached the forward line of pillboxes, had seized Palenberg and the high ground immediately south of it, and was ready to resume the advance along a main highway through Uebach.   The leading battalion of the 117th Infantry had incurred 146 casualties, including 12 killed, and the only other battalion to see major action had lost 70, including 12 killed.   Engineers had thrown sturdy bridges across the Wurm at both Marienberg and Rimburg.

Prospects for the next day were bright, even in the sector of the 119th Infantry where plans progressed during the night for outflanking the stubborn Germans in the Rimburg woods.

The diversionary attack northwest of Geilenkirchen which had fooled the German division commanders for several hours had been launched on the left flank of the 30th Division by two battalions of the 29th Division.   The purpose was to tie down enemy forces and prevent their use against the main attack.   From the first resistance was stanch.   Even on subsequent days when the 29th Division enlarged operations to include elements of two regiments, the Germans held firm.   This was not to say that the attack did not worry the Germans.   General von Obstfelder, whose corps of the *First Parachute Army* was adjacent to this sector and who was at the moment embroiled in a fight with the 7th U.S. Armored Division in the Peel Marshes, anxiously inquired on 3 October whether General Koechling's *LXXXI Corps* was going to take any countermeasures against the 29th Division's attack.   In view of the situation at Marienberg and Rimburg, General Koechling had to respond in the negative.[27]   The Germans nevertheless reacted sensitively to the 29th Division's attacks, and in one instance virtually annihilated a company of American infantry in a village named Schierwaldenrath.   A later raid on the village brought revenge, but as operations developed in the 30th Division sector, the 29th Division limited offensive action to reinforced

---

[25] *183d VG Div AAR;* Mng Sitrep, *LXXXI Corps* to *Seventh Army,* 0555, 3 Oct 44, in *LXXXI Corps KTB, Tagesmeldungen.*

[26] *Ibid.* See also American accounts in records of the 117th Infantry.

[27] Tel Conv, *LXXXVI Corps* to *LXXXI Corps,* 1920, 3 Oct 44, in *LXXXI Corps KTB, Kampfverlauf.*

RIMBURG CASTLE, *showing moat in the foreground.*

patrols. The Germans were content to let it go at that.[28]

In the meantime, along the railroad east of Rimburg, the 119th Infantry discovered early on the second day (3 October) of the West Wall attack that the passing of night had done little to lessen opposition in the Rimburg woods. The only progress at first was against the Rimburg Castle, and that because many of the

---

[28] See 29th Div AAR, Oct 44, and Joseph H. Ewing, *29 Let's Go! A History of the 29th Infantry Division in World War II* (Washington: Infantry Journal Press, 1948). This is among the better unit histories.

Germans who had made the castle such a fortress the afternoon before had sneaked out during the night.

No hope remaining for carrying the Rimburg woods in a frontal assault, the 119th Infantry commander, Colonel Sutherland, put into motion plans he had made during the night. He dispatched a task force under command of his executive officer, Lt. Col. Daniel W. Quinn, to cross the 117th Infantry's bridges at Marienberg, hit the Rimburg woods from the north, and cut off the German positions by moving behind the woods. Composed of two companies of infantry (both from the 2d Battalion) and a company each of tanks and self-propelled tank destroyers, Task Force Quinn quickly made its weight felt. A few rounds from the tank guns against the northern tip of the woods brought about a hundred Germans scurrying from two pillboxes and surrounding entrenchments to surrender. Relieving pressure on the 1st Battalion, 119th Infantry, the task force continued to work south. The only real difficulty came from intense enemy fire from the vicinity of the regimental objective, the crossroads atop the eastern slopes of the Wurm valley near Herbach.

This fire proved a harbinger of what was to greet the 1st Battalion when in late afternoon the men emerged from the Rimburg woods. Having cleared about a dozen pillboxes, the 119th Infantry had at last broken through the first band of fortifications, but Task Force Quinn's envelopment had not been deep enough to precipitate any substantial advance. Once again the Germans brought the regiment to an abrupt halt after a gain of only a few hundred yards. Casualties from this kind of close, confined fighting were becoming increasingly heavy: one rifle company, for example, had lost half of one platoon and all of another except the platoon sergeant. By the end of the second day of fighting, the depth of the 119th Infantry's bridgehead was still no more than a thousand yards.

For his part in renewing the attack on 3 October, the 117th Infantry's Colonel Johnson committed his reserve battalion (the 3d) to drive on Uebach, about a mile east of the Wurm, and then to cut the Geilenkirchen–Aachen highway and occupy high ground east of the highway between Uebach and Beggendorf. Almost immediately, tedious house-to-house

fighting developed. The Germans seemed determined to make of Uebach a point of decision. Round after round of mortar and artillery fire they poured into the little town. Some of the American infantry called it the heaviest German shelling since the battles at Mortain in Normandy. The commander of the regiment's supporting 118th Field Artillery Battalion hazarded a guess that the Germans had finally found a copy of the American field artillery manual telling how to mass their fires. The first few concentrations took a particularly heavy toll because the doors and windows of all houses except those actually defended were locked and barred. That made cover in the houses at first hard to get at.

Commitment of CCB

Into the maelstrom that Uebach had become rolled the tanks and half-tracks of the 2d Armored Division's Combat Command B. During the morning of 3 October, General Corlett had ordered the armor to start crossing the Marienberg bridges at noon. The 30th Division was to give priority to the armor's passage in order that the combat command might expand the bridgehead to the north and northeast and free the infantry for the push southward to link with the VII Corps. The rest of the 2d Armored Division was to follow CCB as soon as enough space for deployment could be gained.[29]

Committing a combat command with its wealth of vehicles in a confined bridgehead where an infantry regiment still was struggling to gain enough room for its own operations was a risky business.

---

[29] XIX Corps Ltr of Instrs 40, 3 Oct, XIX Corps Ltr of Instrs file, Oct 44.

None could have been more aware of this than General Corlett and the infantry commander, General Hobbs, for their memories would serve to remind them of a similar instance in Normandy where premature commitment of armor into a 30th Division bridgehead had brought a welter of confusion that had bogged down a promising attack.[30] Yet in the present situation Corlett was less concerned about likely confusion than about losing the little Wurm River bridgehead altogether. He wanted the weight of the armor on hand before the Germans could mount a sizable counterattack.[31]

For all the limitations of space, the commitment of the armor might have proceeded smoothly except for the intense German shelling. Although the infantry commanders adjusted their zones to give the armor free rein in the northern half of Uebach, the shelling intensified an inevitable intermingling of units in the winding streets of the town. A day of clouds and rain kept American planes from doing anything about the enemy's artillery. By nightfall (3 October) neither the armor nor the leading battalion of the 117th Infantry had advanced farther than the northern and eastern edges of Uebach, and not all buildings within the town, particularly in the southern portion, were yet in friendly hands. Lined up almost bumper to bumper back to the Marienberg bridges, CCB's vehicles provided any incentive the enemy might have needed to continue and even to increase his disturbing shellfires.

As General Corlett had feared, German commanders in the meantime had been rushing preparations for a concentric counterattack with main effort in the south (primarily against the 119th Infantry). To facilitate control in the attack, the enemy corps commander, General Koechling, put both *49th* and *183d Division* troops in the threatened sector under one commander, the *183d Division's* General Lange. Then Koechling ordered additional forces to the sector: two assault gun brigades, the *183d Division's* organic engineer battalion, two infantry battalions of the *49th Division*, and an infantry battalion of the *246th Division* from Aachen.[32]

To allow time for all these units to arrive, Koechling delayed the hour of attack until 0215 on 4 October.[33] Yet when that hour approached, nobody was ready except the engineer battalion. When the engineers attacked from the east, heavy concentrations of artillery fire assisted the 3d Battalion of the 117th Infantry in Uebach in beating off the assault, but not before the Germans had cut off about fifteen men in a house on the eastern edge of the town. These men played cat and mouse all day with German tanks and infantry and escaped only in late afternoon after artillery fire and advance of 2d Armored Division tanks scared off seven German tanks that were closing in.

Not until dawn on 4 October were the bulk of the German reinforcements ready to counterattack. Their main strike hit the center of the 119th Infantry. Supported by the two assault gun brigades, one battalion of the *49th Division* forced

---

[30] For this story, see Blumenson, *Breakout and Pursuit*, Ch. VI.

[31] Ltr, Gen Harmon to OCMH, 5 Jan 54.

[32] AAR, *183d VG Div;* Tel Conv, *LXXXI Corps* to *183d VG Div*, 1900, 3 Oct 44, in *LXXXI Corps KTB, Kampfverlauf.*

[33] *Ibid.*

SLAG PILE AND TOWER *used by Germans for observation in Uebach.*

an American company to fall back in confusion. Before the Germans could exploit the success, "shorts" from their own artillery threw the attackers into confusion. By the time they were able to renew the attack, the 119th Infantry was set.

The enemy was still much in evidence that afternoon when the 119th Infantry attempted to renew its drive from the Rimburg woods onto the eastern slopes of the Wurm valley. Knocking out two Sherman tanks, the Germans quickly broke the back of the push.

In the meantime, on the northeastern edge of Uebach, the third German blow had been doomed from the start. The German thrust ran head on into an attempt by the right task force (Task Force 1) of Combat Command B to emerge from Uebach. Only one German infantry battalion actually reached Uebach, there to be smashed completely and reduced to twenty-five men.

This force which had looked so impressive to German commanders on paper thus was reduced to impotency in a matter of hours. Yet the achievement had not come easy for the Americans. So severe were the casualties of the battalion of the 117th Infantry in Uebach that the commander, Lt. Col. Samuel T. McDowell, had difficulty reorganizing his men for resuming the offensive. Though not so hard hit by losses, the armor of CCB had similar difficulty in getting started, partly because of striking direct into one prong of the German counterattack.

Not until late afternoon of 4 October was any American advance of appreciable proportions achieved. At that time Task Force 2 of CCB under Col. Sidney R. Hinds attacked from Uebach to seize high ground about the settlement of Hoverhof, a mile north of Uebach, upon which to anchor the northern flank of the bridgehead. Delayed twice when two successive commanders of the armored infantry battalion fell victim to the blanketlike shelling in Uebach, the advance finally began about 1600. Even though the sector opposite the task force was studded with pillboxes, the armored infantry and supporting tanks moved forward quickly. Operating with well-executed co-ordination, a forward observer first brought down artillery upon the pillboxes to drive the defenders from field positions into the fortifications; then the tanks blasted apertures and entrances of the pillboxes with armor-piercing ammunition. Almost invariably, as soon as the tanks ceased fire and the infantry closed in, the Germans emerged docilely. By nightfall Task Force 2 held the high ground near Hoverhof. Eighty Germans surrendered, and the attackers sustained not a single casualty once the attack had gotten under way.[34]

In the meantime, Task Force 1 of CCB under Col. Paul A. Disney had been fighting its meeting engagement with one prong of the German counterattack northeast of Uebach. At one point Disney's task force dueled with a covey of seven

self-propelled guns and destroyed them all with the loss of but two of its own tanks. By the end of the day, Colonel Disney had gained positions about 800 yards beyond Uebach, only a few yards short of the Geilenkirchen–Aachen highway; but the task force had paid for the short advance with heavy personnel losses and eleven medium tanks.

Resuming the attack the next morning (5 October), CCB found the pattern of resistance unchanged. On the right wing, where the tanks and infantry faced German tanks and self-propelled guns, Colonel Disney's Task Force 1 gained only a few hundred yards. Though this was sufficient to cut the Geilenkirchen–Aachen highway, it fell short of the objective, the village of Beggendorf. In the north, men of Colonel Hinds's Task Force 2 repeated the tactics used so successfully the day before against the pillboxes and found the enemy thoroughly cowed. Discovering telephone communications intact in a captured pillbox, a noncommissioned officer, Sgt. Ezra Cook, notified the Germans in another pillbox, "We've just taken your comrades and now we're coming after you." From a nearby pillbox that Sergeant Cook and his companions had not detected, twenty-five Germans emerged with hands high. By nightfall the assault teams had cleared Zweibruggen, another river village farther north— Frelenberg—and had built up along a highway leading northeast out of Frelenberg.

Not until the next day, 6 October, did the Germans get tanks and antitank guns into position to meet this threat. They finally stopped Task Force 2 late on 6 October with dug-in infantry backed up by direct fire weapons along a spur railway less than a thousand yards short of

---

[34] Official records of the 2d Armored Division for this period are supplemented by one combat interview to be found in 30th Division Combat Interview files.

the West Wall strongpoint of Geilen-kirchen. On the same date, Task Force 1, its objective changed from Beggendorf to Waurichen, northeast of Uebach, followed closely behind a rolling artillery barrage to reach the edge of the village. An additional short advance the next day would carry the objective and forge the last segment of a firm arc along the northeastern flank of the bridgehead.

For all their inability to halt these armored thrusts on the third, fourth, and fifth days of the West Wall fight, German commanders were struggling to create another sizable reserve force capable of throwing back the American bridgehead. As early as 4 October, the day the first major counterattacks had failed, the Commander in Chief West, Field Marshal von Rundstedt, and the *Seventh Army* commander, General Brandenberger, had visited General Koechling's *LXXXI Corps* command post and come away with the impression that the forces locally available were insufficient. Directing General Koechling to send to the threatened sector every unit from the *LXXXI Corps* that possibly could be spared, General Brandenberger promised reinforcements from outside the corps.[35]

Before the day was through, General Koechling had ordered five more units to the Uebach sector: a *Landesschuetzen* battalion, an assault gun brigade, and a howitzer battalion, all from the sector of the *12th Division* southeast of Aachen, an antitank company with six 75-mm. antitank guns from the *246th Division* at Aachen, and a separate, so-called "tank company" equipped with relatively ineffi-cacious gimmicks called "remote-control robot assault guns." Believing that the addition of these forces to the miscellany already in the threatened sector would create a force too big for adequate control by one man, Koechling removed the single command he had invested in General Lange and restored the boundary between the *49th* and *183d Divisions* to run roughly from Beggendorf west to Uebach.[36]

For his part, the *Seventh Army* commander, General Brandenberger, lined up five units for transfer to the *LXXXI Corps*: Army NCO Training Schools Dueren and Juelich, which were to fight as infantry units; an infantry battalion from the *275th Division*, which was now with the *LXXIV Corps* in the Huertgen Forest; a fortress machine gun battalion; and an artillery brigade which had two batteries of 150-mm. howitzers and one battalion of very heavy howitzers.[37]

In the meantime, the corps commander, General Koechling, took further steps to gain a greater concentration of troops. Having already drawn upon the resources of the *246th Division* at Aachen, he nevertheless ordered that division to relinquish the entire *404th Grenadier Regiment*. At the same time he directed the two incoming NCO training schools to relieve the *183d Division*'s *343d Grenadier Regiment*

[35] *LXXXI Corps KTB, Kampfverlauf*, 4 Oct 44.

[36] Tel Convs, *LXXXI Corps* to *246th Div*, 1225, 4 Oct 44, *LXXXI Corps* to *12th Div*, 1230, 4 Oct 44, *LXXXI Corps* to *183d Div*, 1250 and 1535, 4 Oct 44, and *LXXXI Corps* to *49th Div*, 1530, 4 Oct 44, all in *LXXXI Corps KTB, Kampfverlauf;* Order, *LXXXI Corps* to *183d* and *49th Divs*, 1345, 4 Oct 44, *LXXXI Corps KTB, Befehle an Div;* AAR, *183d VG Div.*

[37] Order, Brandenberger to *LXXXI Corps*, 2035, 4 Oct 44, *LXXXI Corps KTB, Befehle: Heeresgruppe, Armee, usw.*

opposite the 29th U.S. Division northwest of Geilenkirchen in order that the *343d Regiment* also might be available for the counterattack. As for artillery, General Koechling now had 10 batteries of 105-mm. howitzers and 7 batteries of 150-mm. howitzers, a total of about 60 pieces. He expected to add another 27 150-mm. howitzers within a few days and to put 32 88-mm. antiaircraft guns opposite the threatened sector during the night of 6 October.[38]

Like the force assembled for the first major counterattacks on 4 October, the sum of these units was more impressive on paper than in reality. Nevertheless, if all could be assembled at once for a genuinely co-ordinated counterstroke, the possibilities were encouraging.

Unfortunately for the Germans, the projected troop movements took considerably more time than anticipated. For the second time in the West Wall fight, a lesson as often demonstrated as any other from German experience during the fall campaign was repeated: assembling units from various sections of the front in a minimum of time and hoping to execute a co-ordinated counterattack with such a multipartite force is an exacting assignment. Although General Koechling had intended to assemble all forces during the night of 4 October and strike the next day, almost every unit ran into difficulties. Moving from the sector of the *12th Division* southeast of Aachen, the *Landesschuetzen* battalion, for example, came under such heavy fire from artillery units of the VII Corps that the battalion had

to delay until dense morning mists concealed movement. The NCO trainees from Dueren and Juelich failed to arrive until just before daylight on 5 October, too late for relieving the *343d Regiment* northwest of Geilenkirchen, for that regiment could not disengage in daylight. The *246th Division's 404th Regiment* from Aachen did not reach a designated assembly area until noon on 5 October.[39]

Had the Americans been inactive in the meantime, the Germans might have been able to surmount the setbacks involved in these delays. As it was, the Americans were renewing their offensive. Having failed to strike early on 5 October, General Koechling had lost his chance. Now he might be forced to commit his units piecemeal according to the pattern of American attacks.

Early on 5 October, as CCB was taking the first steps toward forging a firm arc about the northeastern fringes of the West Wall bridgehead, the two regiments of the 30th Division renewed their drives—the one to break out of the Rimburg woods, the other to push southeastward from Uebach in the direction of Alsdorf, not quite three miles from Uebach and a major milestone on the road to juncture with the VII Corps northeast of Aachen.

The first objective of the latter thrust, to be made by Colonel McDowell's 3d Battalion, 117th Infantry, was a hamlet at a crossroads about halfway between Uebach and Alsdorf. Shortly after the jump-off, intense machine gun fire from the barracks of a cantonment on the eastern flank of the battalion's route of advance pinned McDowell's infantry to the ground. At the same time concealed

---

[38] AAR *183d VG Div;* Tel Convs, *Seventh Army* to *LXXXI Corps,* 2200, 2 Oct, and *LXXXI Corps* Arty O to aide, 2230, 4 Oct 44, *LXXXI Corps KTB, Kampfverlauf;* Order, *LXXXI Corps* to *183d* and *49th Divs,* 2040, 4 Oct 44, in *LXXXI Corps KTB, Befehle an Div.*

[39] AAR, *183d VG Div;* Tel Convs, *LXXXI Corps* to *183d Div,* 0145, 0600, 0640, and 1200, 5 Oct 44, in *LXXXI Corps KTB, Kampfverlauf.*

antitank guns knocked out five supporting tanks. Although the 117th Infantry commander, Colonel Johnson, quickly committed another battalion, this unit could make little headway. The Germans might have failed in their efforts to muster sizable force for counterattack, but what they did have was proving no pushover.

Meanwhile, the commander of the 119th Infantry, Colonel Sutherland, had decided to abandon his frontal assault out of the Rimburg woods against the cross-roads near Herbach. Instead, he planned to repeat the envelopment tactic he had used earlier in eliminating the Germans in the Rimburg woods, but this time the envelopment was to be deep enough to carve a sizable slice out of the German position. During the night of 4 October, Colonel Sutherland sent his 2d Battalion under Lt. Col. William C. Cox into the 117th Infantry's zone at Uebach to attack south across his regimental front along gently sloping ground a thousand yards behind the ridge which was his first objective. The maneuver got off to an auspicious start during the night when a patrol sneaked up on one of at least ten pillboxes lying in the battalion's path and captured fourteen occupants.

The real impetus to Colonel Cox's attack the next morning, 5 October, came from a platoon leader in Company E, T. Sgt. Harold L. Holycross, who adopted pillbox assault methods similar to those used north of Uebach by CCB's Task Force 2. Sergeant Holycross' methods may have been dictated by the fact that his company had neither flame throwers nor pole charges. While a platoon of self-propelled tank destroyers acted as over-watchers on the east flank, two platoons of tanks fired high explosive against the

pillboxes in order to drive the defenders from field fortifications into the pillboxes. Then the tankers switched to armor-piercing ammunition while Sergeant Holy-cross and an advance force of but four men pressed forward. When the five got within a hundred yards of the pillboxes, the tankers lifted their fire. Without exception, the enemy in each pillbox promptly raised a white flag. As one soldier put it, the infantry "just held the bag" while the Germans walked in.

By the end of the day Company E had pushed all the way down the ridge to a point east of Herbach, and another company had followed closely to occupy some of the fortifications. Only one pillbox remained to be taken at the southern tip of the high ground. Against the wishes of the company commander, 1st Lt. Warne R. Parker, Company E had to let this pillbox wait until the next day, because the supporting tanks were running low on ammunition.

As Lieutenant Parker had feared, failure to capture the last pillbox was a mistake. At daylight on 6 October, elements of two battalions of the *49th Division*'s *148th Regiment* used the pillbox as a forward base for counterattacking the other positions.[40] Under cover of fire from two tanks or assault guns, at least one of which sat in hull defilade behind the mound of the pillbox, German infantry moved forward with three other tanks or assault guns in support. As they approached, the American riflemen in the most forward pillboxes failed to heed the lesson demonstrated the day before by the

_____

[40] It presumably was a local counterattack of a type often launched for limited objectives but not always included in records of higher headquarters. German sources make no mention of this action.

ineffective German defense: pummeled by enemy fire, they retreated into the pillboxes. While some of the counterattacking infantry kept the apertures closed with small arms fire, other Germans assaulted. In this manner the enemy retook four pillboxes and captured at least a hundred men, including three officers.

Throughout the action, Colonel Cox and his company commanders called frantically for tank support, but both the tanks and tank destroyers had retired for maintenance and supply. Not for two hours did they return. Only the courage of the men in the next two pillboxes in the path of the German advance, plus heavy concentrations of mortar and artillery fire, saved the day. Despite the enemy fire, these men refused to budge from their foxholes and trenches outside the pillboxes. As the enemy lifted his shellfire to permit his infantry to close, they mowed the Germans down with rifles and machine guns. When American tanks at last arrived, one commanded by 1st Lt. Walter D. Macht knocked out three of the German vehicles. The other two withdrew. Using the same methods employed by both Sergeant Holycross and the Germans, a reserve company of the 119th Infantry subsequently retook the four pillboxes.

As on the day before, German artillery during the counterattack of 6 October continued to hammer the bridgehead with some of the heaviest concentrations many of the American troops had ever experienced. One man said it was "really big stuff—it came in like an express train." Obviously, the German corps commander, General Koechling, was making good instructions from his army commander to mass all *LXXXI Corps* artillery against the bridgehead, no matter how this might

deplete other sectors.[41] Ringed around the extended periphery of the bridgehead and protected by clouds and overcast denying large-scale Allied air operations and limiting sound and flash detections, the German artillery was difficult to neutralize with counterbattery fires. A telling shortage of artillery ammunition on the American side contributed to the problem. Unable to allot more than an average of twenty-four rounds per German battery, U.S. gunners could hope to do no more than silence the enemy guns temporarily. On 5 October XIX Corps artillery executed ninety-nine counterbattery missions, and still the Germans fired. Approximately 66 percent of all casualties incurred in the West Wall fight by the 2d Armored and 30th Divisions stemmed from artillery and mortar shell fragments.[42]

Even the elusive Luftwaffe tried to get into the bombardment act on 5 October. Taking advantage of cloudy skies that discouraged Allied airmen, German planes came over in high-flying groups of twenty and thirty with the objective of bombing Palenberg. Although German ground observers reported results as "very good," American units noted no appreciable damage. The enemy's *49th Division* requested that the planes strike American concentrations at Uebach next time, but there was no next time.[43]

Few could have recognized it as such at the time, but the German counterattack

---

[41] Order, Brandenberger to *LXXXI Corps,* 2035, 4 Oct 44.

[42] XIX Corps Special Rpt, Breaching the Siegfried Line, and comments on draft of this study by Col James R. Winn, FA, found in XIX Corps AAR, Oct 44.

[43] See Tel Convs, Air Ln O, *Seventh Army,* to *LXXXI Corps,* 1315, and *LXXXI Corps* to *49th Div,* 2140, 5 Oct 44, *LXXXI Corps KTB, Kampfverlauf.*

against Colonel Cox's men in the pillboxes east of the Rimburg woods on 6 October was the high-water mark of resistance to the XIX Corps bridgehead. Every unit that Koechling and Brandenberger had fixed upon for movement to the threatened sector had been absorbed by the un-remitting pressure of the 2d Armored Division's CCB and the two regiments of the 30th Division. Although the NCO training schools from Dueren and Juelich had at last relieved the *183d Division's 343d Regiment* northwest of Geilenkir-chen, that regiment was so disabled during the night of 5 October in piecemeal and inconsequential counterattacks south of Geilenkirchen against contingents of CCB that it was capable of little other than defensive missions. The *246th Di-vision's 404th Regiment* from Aachen had been thrown hurriedly into the defense against other units of CCB between Geilenkirchen and Beggendorf. At Beg-gendorf the *Landesschuetzen* battalion moved up from the *12th Division* sector was seriously depleted. Elsewhere about the bridgehead were the original con-tingents of the *49th* and *183d Divisions* and a few other miscellaneous units the German commanders had brought up, all severely damaged by the American assault. Sprinkled among the infantry were twenty-seven assault guns remaining in five assault-gun units.[44]

In early stages of the West Wall fight-ing, the Germans were denied use of at least one battalion of the *49th Division* because of holding the re-entrant "bridge-head" west of the Wurm at the town of Kerkrade. Even as two regiments of the 30th Division had struck at Marienberg and Rimburg, the third regiment, the 120th Infantry, had made a feint against the German position at Kerkrade. Then, on 4 October, the 120th Infantry had staged an actual attack. After fighting stubbornly and launching one futile coun-terattack, the Germans had withdrawn from the bridgehead during the night. This freed one battalion of the 120th Infantry to move the next day (5 Octo-ber) to cross the Wurm and fill a growing gap between the 117th and 119th Regi-ments southwest of Uebach. The re-mainder of the 120th Infantry would follow later.

During the afternoon of 6 October, the *Army Group B* commander, Field Marshal Model, went to the *LXXXI Corps* com-mand post to attempt to do what Generals Koechling and Brandenberger thus far had failed to accomplish: to assemble sufficient forces for making a decisive counterattack against the West Wall bridgehead.[45] But Field Marshal Model was too late. The Americans now were getting set to exploit their bridgehead; the Germans would have to go to ex-traordinary measures to assemble sufficient strength to push them back behind the Wurm. Although Field Marshal Model could not have known it at the time, any counterattack he might devise at this point would be directed more toward pre-venting a link between the XIX and VII U.S. Corps northeast of Aachen than toward eliminating the XIX Corps bridgehead.

Juncture with the VII Corps to en-

---

[44] AAR, *183d VG Div;* Table of Tank and Antitank Gun Situation as of 2100, 5 Oct 44, *LXXXI Corps KTB, Tagesmeldungen;* Table of independent units attached to *LXXXI Corps* divs as of 5 Oct 44, in *LXXXI Corps KTB, Befehle an Div.*

[45] Tel Conv, *Seventh Army* to *LXXXI Corps,* 1340, 6 Oct 44, in *LXXXI Corps KTB, Kampf-verlauf.*

circle Aachen now was uppermost in the minds of American commanders. Though General Corlett had hoped originally to use only the 30th Division for the link-up while the 2d Armored Division struck eastward for crossings over the Roer River, the army commander, General Hodges, made it clear that operations were to be confined to the West Wall until link-up was achieved.[46] In early afternoon of 6 October, General Corlett told the armor to hold in place along the northeastern and eastern fringes of the bridgehead while at the same time making a main effort southeastward to help the 30th Division link with the VII Corps.[47]

The stage had been set for this maneuver during the preceding afternoon when the 2d Armored Division commander, General Harmon, had brought his second combat command, CCA, across the Wurm bridges into Uebach. Once the armor had established a solid defensive line, General Harmon directed, CCB was to hold in place while CCA assisted the 30th Division. As finally constituted, CCB's defensive arc along the north, northeast, and east of the West Wall bridgehead would run from north of Frelenberg east along the spur railroad below Geilenkirchen, thence southeast through Waurichen almost to Beggendorf. The easternmost troops of CCB would be just over three miles beyond the Wurm River.

Even before General Corlett revealed his change of plan in the afternoon of 6 October, CCA had gone into action in conjunction with the 117th Infantry to expand the bridgehead. Early that day, as Colonel Cox's battalion of the 119th

[46] Corlett to OCMH, 20 May 56.
[47] XIX Corps Ltr of Instrs 4, 1400, 6 Oct, XIX Corps Ltr of Instrs file, Oct. 44.

Infantry was having trouble in the pill-boxes near Herbach, one column of CCA struck northeast to take Beggendorf and two other columns moved southeast. One headed in the direction of Baesweiler, southeast of Beggendorf; the other advanced close along the flank of the 117th Infantry in a renewal of the infantry's drive on the crossroads hamlet southeast of Uebach, where the 117th had been balked the day before. The weight of the armor and a clear day, which permitted six close-support missions by fighter-bombers of the IX Tactical Air Command, provided the margin of success. The crossroads hamlet fell and, in the process, the nearby cantonment which had bristled the day before with German guns. Beggendorf also fell, and CCA's center column pushed more than a mile to the east almost to the edge of the town of Baesweiler.

This success on 6 October and General Corlett's order in early afternoon clearly indicated that the fight for a West Wall bridgehead was nearing an end. Indeed, so successful were the day's operations that the necessity for any part of the 2d Armored Division to assist the 30th Division to link with the VII Corps became questionable. Nevertheless, CCA did continue to attack and by the end of 7 October had overrun Baesweiler and neared the neighboring town of Oidtweiler, thereby severing a main highway running northeast from Aachen to the Roer River town of Linnich. For the next few days the entire 2d Armored Division prepared an iron defensive arc about the eastern and northeastern rims of the bridgehead while the 30th Division continued the southward drive alone. A battalion of the 29th Division's 116th Infantry reinforced the armor, while the rest of the 116th Infantry relieved the two remaining battalions of the 120th Infantry at Kerkrade so that this third regiment might participate in the 30th Division's drive.

Although German commanders had anticipated in the first days of the West Wall fight that the XIX Corps might swing southward to link with the VII Corps, by the time the shift occurred, German strength was so depleted that there was little German commanders could do about it. Though they shifted the left regiment of the *49th Division* to control of the *246th Division* to place the defense of Aachen in the hands of one commander, the day of 7 October became a day of exploitation against a beaten and disorganized enemy. Approximately a thousand prisoners passed through the 30th Division's cage.

Led by tanks of the attached 743d Tank Battalion, the 117th Infantry charged two miles into the town of Alsdorf. Reduced now to one organic infantry regiment, the enemy's *49th Division* could do nothing about it. One unit overrun was an infantry battalion of the *12th Division* the Germans had hurriedly brought into the line the night before.[48] Once the Americans had broken a crust of resistance on the fringes of Alsdorf, they moved in easily. "Alsdorf was a ghost town . . .," one officer reported, "and it was so damned quiet it scared you."

Still assisted by a battalion of the 120th Infantry, Colonel Sutherland's 119th Infantry also surged southward. At the coal-mining town of Merkstein, one reason for speedy success was a well-directed

American air strike; another was the action of a one-man army, Pvt. Salvatore Pepe, a scout in one of the rifle platoons. Pepe refused to stay down when fire forced his platoon to cover. Firing his rifle and tossing hand grenades, he charged forward alone, wounded four Germans, and induced fifty-three others to surrender. He later received the Distinguished Service Cross.

At the end of the day the 119th Infantry was approaching the former 120th Infantry position around Kerkrade. The 30th Division was only about three miles away from Wuerselen, the planned point of contact with the VII Corps.

Late on 7 October the 30th Division commander, General Hobbs, reported to General Corlett that the XIX Corps battle of the West Wall was over. "We have a hole in this thing big enough to drive two divisions through," General Hobbs said. "I entertain no doubts that this line is cracked wide open." [49] The general's statement contained no excess exuberance, for the West Wall bridgehead now was almost six miles long and more than four and a half miles deep.

Executing this attack had cost the 30th Division and the 2d Armored Division more than 1,800 casualties in all categories, including about 200 killed.[50] The

---

[48] AAR on opns of 7 Oct 44, *49th Inf Div,* 10 Oct 44, *LXXXI Corps KTB, Meldungen der Div.*

[49] 30th Div Tel Jnl, 7 Oct, 30th Div G-3 file, 7-8 Oct 44.

[50] See 30th Div G-1 Jnl Supplements, Oct 44, Daily Cumulative Casualty Estimates, and CCB, 2d Armd Div, S-3 Per Rpt, 1-10 Oct 44, CCB AAR, Oct 44. See also 2d Armd Div AAR, Oct 44. Figures for CCA, 2d Armored Division, are available only for the entire month of October; the author has made a conservative estimate of CCA losses based on the total for the entire month and on CCB losses during a comparable period in the bridgehead battle. The 30th Division estimate includes the 120th Infantry but not attached units.

cost in medium tanks to CCB alone was fifty-two.[51] Although high, these losses were hardly disparate in relation to the importance of the task as a prerequisite to a renewal of First Army's drive to the Rhine. Not only had these two divisions ruptured the West Wall, they also had forced the Germans to take extraordinary steps and expend precious units and matériel. A capsule indication of the extent to which the enemy had gone to fight the penetration might be found in the number of big guns he had assembled against it. In their futile stand, the Germans had employed at least 2 railroad guns, a battalion of "very heavy" howitzers, 40 105-mm. howitzers, 47 150-mm. howitzers, 32 88-mm. guns, 40 antitank guns of 75-mm. caliber or larger, and approximately 50 assault guns of varying type and caliber.[52]

The first set attack against the West Wall was over. Though the 30th Division infantrymen and their supporting tankers might discern no break in the round-the-clock combat routine, the battle now was entering a new phase. The next step was to link with the VII Corps and encircle the city of Aachen.

---

[51] Compare losses of the entire 7th Armored Division in the unsuccessful Peel Marshes offensive. See Ch. X above.

[52] This estimate is based on Heichler, The Germans Opposite XIX Corps.

CHAPTER XII

Closing the Circle

Militarily, the city of Aachen in October 1944 had little to recommend it. Lying in a saucerlike depression surrounded by hills, Aachen is no natural fortress, nor was it an artificial fortress, even though it lay within the two bands of the West Wall. The city's roads were relatively unimportant, since American drives both north and south of Aachen already had uncovered adequate avenues leading toward the Rhine. Not for a long time would the city's railroads be of use to anyone, so shattered were they already from Allied bombs.[1]

But in regard to Aachen the Germans had more to work with than usual military considerations. Nor was Hitler's insistence upon a fanatical, house-by-house defense of the city simply a superficial propagandism of the first major German city to be threatened with capture. No shrine of National Socialism in the sense of Munich or Nuremberg, Aachen nevertheless embodied a heritage precious to National Socialist ideology. Aachen represented the Holy Roman Empire, the First Reich.

Hitler had no need to remind his followers of Aachen's proud history, how at one time Aachen was capital of the Holy Roman Empire. The Germans would know that here, where the Romans had built thermal baths amid an alien wilderness, a Carolingian king had established his residence in Aquisgranum in the 8th century A.D. That here his son Charles was born—Charlemagne, first emperor of the Holy Roman Empire. That from Aachen Charlemagne had reigned over an empire destined to last, in one form or another, more than a thousand years. That in Aachen, between the years 813 and 1531, thirty-two emperors and kings had been anointed.

Hitler and his disciples were aware further how Aachen and the Holy Roman Empire were tied to National Socialism. After Napoleon had smashed the legalistic shell to which by the year 1806 the political reality of the Empire had been reduced, the romantic element in German nationalism soon had forgotten the jibes leveled at the "Holy Roman Empire of the German Nation" and had identified itself with the ideological Empire, one of the eternal verities transcending temporal politics and nations, the secular counterpart of the universal Church. The romantic element in German nationalism in time had become the religion of National Socialism. Hitler himself often prophesied that his empire, like Charlemagne's, would last a thousand years.

To strike at Aachen was to strike at a symbol of Nazi faith.[2]

For all the importance of Aachen as a trademark of Nazi ideology, the Germans

---

[1] See 1st Lt Harry D. Condron, The Fall of Aachen, a preliminary MS in 1st Div Combat Interv files.

[2] For a similar view, see MS # A–991 (Koechling, comdr of the *LXXXI Corps*).

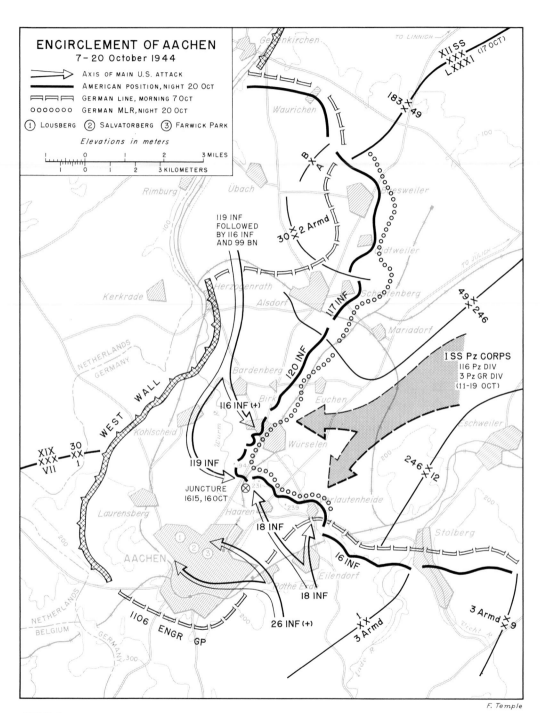

ENCIRCLEMENT OF AACHEN
7–20 October 1944

⟶ AXIS OF MAIN U.S. ATTACK
▬▬ AMERICAN POSITION, NIGHT 20 OCT
⊐⊐⊐ GERMAN LINE, MORNING 7 OCT
ooooooo GERMAN MLR, NIGHT 20 OCT
① LOUSBERG ② SALVATORBERG ③ FARWICK PARK

Elevations in meters

MAP 4

in early October were little better qualified to deny the city indefinitely than they
had been in September when the *116th
Panzer Division*'s General von Schwerin
had despaired of holding the city and
sought to spare it further fighting.
Schwerin long since had traveled the
ignominious path of military relief, and
his division had been withdrawn for refitting and reorganization; yet the higher
headquarters which earlier had borne
responsibility for the city still was on
hand. This was Koechling's *LXXXI
Corps* under Brandenberger's *Seventh
Army*. That the *LXXXI Corps* was no
leviathan already had been proved during
the early days of October by the West
Wall penetration of the XIX Corps.

On 7 October, as the XIX Corps
entered Alsdorf on the first step of what
looked like an easy move to encircle
Aachen, General Koechling's *LXXXI
Corps* comprised a nominal four divisions.
(*Map 4*)   North of Aachen were the *183d
Volks Grenadier* and *49th Infantry Di-
visions,* both severely hurt by the American West Wall breakthrough. Aachen
itself lay in the sector of the *246th Volks
Grenadier Division,* commanded by Col.
Gerhard Wilck, the division which in late
September had relieved the *116th Panzer
Division.*   Southeast of Aachen the south-
ern wing of the German corps was
defended by Colonel Engel's *12th Infantry
Division,* which had arrived in the nick of
time to thwart a breakthrough in the
Stolberg Corridor but which had drawn
a bloody nose in the process. The sum
total of organic infantry and artillery combat effectives in these four divisions on 7
October was about 18,000 men.[3]

The *LXXXI Corps* had increased considerably since mid-September in artillery
strength. Divisional and corps artillery
totaled 239 serviceable pieces: 140 light,
84 medium, and 15 heavy guns. An
antiaircraft regiment provided added
strength. Ammunition apparently was
adequate except for 14 Russian guns
which had neither ammunition nor transport. Moreover, four headquarters artillery battalions to serve under corps control
were en route to the sector on 7 October.[4]

Tank and antitank strength in the
LXXXI Corps was less impressive.
Among the divisional tank destroyer battalions were 12 serviceable assault guns
and 26 heavy antitank guns, while under
corps control were 2 assault gun brigades,
2 assault gun battalions, and a robot tank
company, with a combined total of only
36 serviceable pieces. The *506th Tank
Battalion* had only 4 Mark VI (Tiger)
tanks, while the *108th Panzer Brigade*
with 7 Mark V (Panther) tanks was

---

[3] *LXXXI Corps, KTB, Anlagen, Meldungen
der Div.* This figure takes no account of division staffs and organic service troops, corps

troops, or attached units. For the German story,
see Lucian Heichler, The Fall of Aachen, a
manuscript prepared to complement this volume,
in OCMH.

[4] *LXXXI Corps KTB, Anlagen, Kampf um
Aachen* (Corps AAR on Second Battle of
Aachen) (hereafter cited as *LXXXI Corps,
Kampf um Aachen*). For historical purposes,
the Germans divided the fighting around Aachen
into three phases or "battles": first, penetration
of the West Wall by the VII U.S. Corps in September; second, penetration of the West Wall
north of Aachen and encirclement and reduction
of the city; and third, operations east of Aachen
in November, referred to in this volume as the
"Battle of the Roer Plain." As a result of
preservation of *LXXXI Corps* records covering
the period of the "Second Battle of Aachen,"
plus many other types of sources, detailed information on almost every aspect of this engagement
from the German side is available. Only a small
portion could be used in this study. Additional
details may be derived from the original records
and from Heichler, The Fall of Aachen.

arriving in the sector on 7 October. Almost all these tanks and guns were clustered in the vicinity of Alsdorf where the XIX U.S. Corps was pressing southward in the direction of Wuerselen.[5]

In light of the condition and location of three of General Koechling's four divisions, the burden of the fighting at Aachen might fall upon the most recent arrival, the *246th Volks Grenadier Division*. Though this division had engaged in no major action in its own sector, Colonel Wilck's troops already had been decisively weakened. In the desperate efforts to stem the XIX Corps breakthrough, General Koechling had rifled his front, including four of Colonel Wilck's seven organic infantry battalions. The entire *404th Infantry Regiment* and a battalion each of the *352d* and *689th Infantry Regiments* had been attached to neighboring divisions.

From a local standpoint, the outlook for preserving Aachen as a citadel of Nazi ideology was bleak indeed. Yet General Koechling's superiors had not let him down completely. Their most immediate step was to try again to assemble an effective counterattacking force from diverse elements to strike this time at Alsdorf in hopes of thwarting encirclement of Aachen. The main component of this force was to be *Mobile (Schnelle) Regiment von Fritzschen*, which comprised three battalions of bicycle-mounted infantry and engineers. Major support was to come from the *108th Panzer Brigade* and a total of twenty-two assault guns from various units.[6]

Any genuine hope of denying Aachen for an extended time lay not with this small force but with a promise from Commander in Chief West von Rundstedt to commit his most important theater reserves. These were the *3d Panzer Grenadier* and *116th Panzer Divisions*. Attaching these to headquarters of the *I SS Panzer Corps* (General der Waffen SS Georg Keppler), Rundstedt directed major operations intended to restore the situation about Aachen. Since leaving Aachen in September, the *116th Panzer Division* had been built up to about 11,500 men and its tank regiment restored, but of 151 authorized Mark IV and Mark V tanks only 41 were on hand. Although the *3d Panzer Grenadier Division* was little more than a motorized infantry division, it numbered about 12,000 men and had 31 75-mm. antitank guns and 38 artillery pieces.[7]

Through 5, 6, and 7 October General Koechling had waited in vain for appearance of these reserves. They were on the way, but railroad disruptions from Allied air attacks had imposed serious delays. General Koechling feared catastrophe at Aachen before the reserves could be committed.[8]

From the American viewpoint, the timing of the operation to encircle and reduce Aachen depended upon the progress of the West Wall penetration north of the city. As soon as the XIX Corps drive to the vicinity of Wuerselen gave evidence of success, General Collins' VII Corps was to attack north from a jump-off base at Eilendorf, east of Aachen, seize Verlautenheide, a strongpoint in the second band of the West Wall, and meet

---

[5] *LXXXI Corps KTB, Tagesmeldungen.*

[6] Order, *49th Inf Div* to *Regt von Fritzschen,* 8 Oct 44, *LXXXI Corps KTB, Meldungen der Div.*

[7] See *General Inspekteur der Panzertruppen, Zustandsberichte Panzer-Divisionen,* Sep–Oct 44, and *Zustandsberichte Panzer Grenadier-Divisionen,* Oct 44–Jan 45.

[8] *OB WEST KTB,* 5, 7 Oct 44.

the XIX Corps near Wuerselen. With Aachen isolated, a part of the VII Corps might reduce the city at leisure while the XIX Corps and the rest of the VII Corps drove east and northeast to the Roer River.[9]

The broad outlines of this maneuver had been determined when the First Army first was approaching the German border. That various factors had delayed the XIX Corps outside the West Wall until October and that the Germans had halted the overextended VII Corps in the Stolberg Corridor had in no way decreased the necessity of occupying Aachen eventually. Indeed, the job had become more pressing. Containing the city was tying down the equivalent of a division, a precious commodity needed for more remunerative tasks. Besides, indications were that German propagandists were trying to make of Aachen a rallying point, a kind of German Stalingrad.

Events at Alsdorf on 7 October convinced commanders on the American side that the time to force the issue at Aachen was at hand. To the commander of the 30th Division, General Hobbs, the job of moving three more miles from Alsdorf south to the intercorps boundary and the link-up objective of Wuerselen appeared at worst no more than a two-day assignment. General Hobbs urged that the VII Corps waste no time in launching the other part of the encirclement maneuver.[10]

The 30th Division alone bore responsibility for the XIX Corps role in the encirclement. Except for the 30th Division and the 2d Armored Division, which was holding the eastern and northeastern

arcs of the West Wall bridgehead, the rest of General Corlett's corps still was occupied with the attenuated north flank west of the West Wall. Although Corlett on 6 October had stipulated that the armor help the 30th Division, he had grown wary of taking the armor away from defense of the West Wall bridgehead and left the task of link-up to the infantry alone.[11] He had strengthened the two regiments of the 30th Division in the West Wall by providing relief of the 120th Infantry, which had been containing Germans southwest of the West Wall penetration at Kerkrade. He then committed the 120th between the 117th and 119th Regiments.

By virtue of positions on an arc containing Aachen on the south and east, General Huebner's 1st Division was the logical choice to fulfill the role of the VII Corps. For more than a fortnight General Huebner had known his assignment; when General Hodges in late afternoon of 7 October endorsed the recommendation that the VII Corps begin to attack, the 1st Division needed little time for preparation. General Huebner announced a night attack to commence before dawn the next day, 8 October.[12]

General Huebner's primary concern in planning his part of the encirclement maneuver had been to reduce his long defensive frontage—more than twelve miles along a semicircle west, south, and east of Aachen—and thereby free at least one regiment to make the attack. Since the 9th Division was committed in the Huertgen Forest and the 3d Armored

---

[9] FUSA Dir, 29 Sep, as cited in FUSA and VII Corps AARs, Oct 44.

[10] 30th Div AAR and G-3 Jnl file, Oct 44; Hewitt, *Workhorse of the Western Front,* p. 126.

[11] XIX Corps Ltr of Instrs, 6 Oct, XIX Corps Ltrs of Instrs file, Oct 44; subsequent tel convs between Corlett and Hobbs, 30th Div G-3 Jnl file, Oct 44.

[12] VII Corps AAR, Oct 44.

Division at Stolberg, his corps commander, General Collins, had been unable to provide much help. He had exercised the only possibility, to put a corps engineer unit, the 1106th Engineer Combat Group (Col. Thomas DeF. Rogers), into the line south of Aachen, thus to release two battalions of the 18th Infantry to join the rest of the regiment for the first blow north against Verlautenheide. Another regiment, the 16th Infantry, could not participate in the offensive because of the necessity to defend the division's northeastern wing from a point near Eilendorf to a boundary with the 3d Armored Division at Stolberg. The third regiment, the 26th Infantry, also held a defensive line; yet the positions faced Aachen from the southeast so that the 26th Infantry might assault the city itself after the 18th Infantry had taken Verlautenheide and linked with the XIX Corps.

In terms of distance, the 18th Infantry's northward attack was no mammoth undertaking—only two and a half miles. On the other hand, terrain, pillboxes, and German determination to hold supply routes into Aachen posed a thorny problem. The first objective of Verlautenheide in the second band of the West Wall was on the forward slope of a sharp ridge, denied by a maze of pillboxes provided with excellent fields of fire across open ground. Crucifix Hill (Hill 239), a thousand yards northwest of Verlautenheide, was the next objective, another exposed crest similarly bristling with pillboxes. The third and final objective was equally exposed and fortified: Ravels Hill (the Ravelsberg, Hill 231).

Taking these hills was in itself no minor assignment, yet holding them afterward might prove even more difficult. This would absorb the regiment's three bat-

talions successively and leave them exposed in a thin salient to German blows from two sides. To send to the 18th Infantry's assistance, General Huebner had in reserve but one battalion of the 26th Infantry, plus a hope that some contingent of the 3d Armored Division might be released to his aid. One way he hoped to spare the 18th Infantry was to launch the drive against the city itself the minute encirclement was complete, thereby to tie down those Germans west of the 18th Infantry's salient.[13]

Perhaps because the 1st Division had faced the enemy at Aachen for several weeks, the G–2, Lt. Col. Robert F. Evans, had a fairly accurate impression of enemy strength and dispositions. Counting support and service troops, his figure of 12,000 Germans in Aachen and the immediate vicinity was fairly accurate, even though attempts to halt the American penetration north of Aachen had sapped considerable strength from the *246th Division*. Identifying this division and its neighbors correctly, Colonel Evans also ascertained most of the combat attachments to the *246th Division*. These included a weak infantry battalion that formerly had belonged to the *275th Division*, a battalion of Luftwaffe ground troops, a machine gun fortress battalion, and a *Landesschuetzen* battalion. The local or "fortress" commander of Aachen, Colonel Evans correctly identified as Lt. Col. Maximilian Leyherr. Neither Evans

---

[13] Unless otherwise noted, the 1st Division story is based on official unit records and combat interviews. The records include a special account, Report of Breaching the Siegfried Line and the Capture of Aachen, dated 7 November 1944. A division history, *Danger Forward* (Atlanta, 1947), is primarily a collection of impressions by war correspondents, of little value for this study.

nor intelligence officers of neighboring units knew of German plans to commit the *3d Panzer Grenadier* and *116th Panzer Divisions;* yet if events marched at the same pace as in recent days, the issue of Aachen might be settled before these reserves arrived.

The 18th Infantry Drives North

In preparing for the attack northward against Verlautenheide, the 18th Infantry commander, Col. George A. Smith, Jr., turned to the lessons he and his men had learned in their first encounter with the West Wall in September. Special pillbox assault teams were organized and equipped with flame throwers, Bangalore torpedoes, beehives, and pole and satchel demolition charges. A battery of 155-mm. guns and a company of tank destroyers, both self-propelled, were prepared to spew direct fire against the pillboxes on the slope about Verlautenheide. An air-ground liaison officer was to accompany each infantry battalion. Preceding the attack, eleven artillery battalions and a company of 4.2-inch chemical mortars were to fire an hour-long preparation. The division's other two regiments and the 1106th Engineers were to feign attack in their sectors. After daylight, a company of medium tanks was to join the infantry in the village.

Linked with a clever use of the cloak of night, Colonel Smith's elaborate preparations paid off, not only at Verlautenheide but against Crucifix Hill (Hill 239) and Ravels Hill (Hill 231) as well. Attacking before dawn on 8 October, a battalion commanded by Lt. Col. John Williams took full advantage of preliminary artillery fires and the darkness to gain Verlautenheide against defenders who for the most part cringed in their foxholes or pillboxes until too late. Other than minor disorganization inherent in a night attack, only one platoon, which stirred up a hornet's nest of machine gun fire along the Eilendorf–Verlautenheide road, met any real difficulty.

That afternoon a company of another battalion commanded by Lt. Col. Henry G. Leonard, Jr., followed preparation fires closely to overrun Crucifix Hill in an hour.[14] A giant crucifix atop the hill was demolished later in the afternoon, victim either of shellfire or of American infantrymen who thought the Germans had used it as an observation post. The next night, 9 October, two companies slipped through the darkness past the yawning apertures of enemy pillboxes to gain the crest of Ravels Hill without firing a shot. Even mop-up of eight pillboxes at dawn the next morning was accomplished without shooting. Unaware that the Americans had taken the hill, four Germans unwittingly arrived during the morning of 10 October with hot food for sixty-five men, a welcome change for the Americans from cold emergency rations.

This was not to say that the 18th Infantry did not encounter serious fighting during the forty-eight hours it took to occupy the three objectives. Indeed, small-scale but persistent German counterattacks began as early as dawn the first morning (8 October), then reached a zenith during the morning of 9 October.

---

[14] A driving force in the attack on Crucifix Hill was the company commander, Capt. Bobbie E. Brown. Though wounded three times, Captain Brown personally led the attack and knocked out three pillboxes himself. He subsequently received the Medal of Honor.

Since the enemy's *246th Division* was absorbing punishment on two fronts, both from the 18th Infantry's northward push and from southward attacks by the XIX Corps, the Germans had a real problem in releasing troops for counterattack. A solution was possible only because the Americans' northward thrust was on a limited front. Shifting the boundary between the *246th* and *12th Divisions* two miles to the west at Verlautenheide, General Koechling transferred responsibility for most of the sector threatened by the 18th Infantry to the *12th Division,* heretofore untouched by the American attack.[15]

More damaging than the local counterattacks was German shelling. Perhaps because both U.S. attacks to encircle Aachen were confined to a combined front measuring little more than five miles, the Germans could concentrate their artillery fire with deadly effectiveness. No sooner had Colonel Williams' infantry in Verlautenheide begun mop-up of pillboxes and buildings at daylight on the first morning than this shelling began. As riflemen left their foxholes to ferret the Germans from their hiding places, the shellfire took an inevitable toll. Shelling of open ground between Eilendorf and Verlautenheide prevented Colonel Leonard's battalion from reaching jump-off positions for the attack on Crucifix Hill until midafternoon of the first day. Neither were supporting tanks immune. Shying at the fire and maneuvering to avoid it, a company of tanks seeking to join the infantry in Verlautenheide lost six tanks to mines, panzerfausts, mud, and mechanical failure.

---

[15] *LXXXI Corps, Kampf um Aachen.* Unless otherwise noted, subsequent German material in this chapter is based upon the same source.

After capture of Crucifix and Ravels Hills, both these exposed heights were subjected to round after round of German fire. Captured pillboxes on the crests represented the only cover worthy of the name. When two tank destroyers tried to climb Ravels Hill, the enemy scored direct hits on both. In Verlautenheide Colonel Williams' infantrymen lived in cellars, popping out to man their foxholes only as shelling temporarily diminished and German assault appeared imminent. Because of thick morning mists that persisted in the form of ground haze for three days, neither American planes nor counterbattery artillery fires could deal effectively with the German guns.

Despite the shelling, the counterattacks, and the fact that the three battalions of the 18th Infantry were stretched thin, the regimental commander, Colonel Smith, succeeded in freeing two rifle companies to seize a fourth objective on 10 October. This was Haaren, a suburb of Aachen controlling the highway to Juelich between Crucifix and Ravels Hills. The division commander, General Huebner, wanted Haaren because capturing it would cut one of two major supply routes left to the Germans in Aachen. Just as in the 18th Infantry's three other attacks, the infantry found seizure of this objective relatively easy; mop-up and defense proved the harder tasks.

Occupation of Haaren underscored the success achieved during the preceding night against Ravels Hill. Because the position for making contact with the XIX Corps was at the base of Ravels Hill, the 18th Infantry's offensive role in encirclement of Aachen was over. Yet the regiment's defensive role might be stretched; for the 30th Division, which was making the XIX Corps attack, had encountered unexpected resistance during the last three days.

To General Huebner, a final sealing of the ring about Aachen nevertheless must have appeared little more than formality. On 10 October he ordered delivery of an ultimatum to the commander of the enemy garrison in Aachen. If the commander failed to capitulate unconditionally within twenty-four hours, the ultimatum warned, the Americans would pulverize the city with artillery and bombs, then seize the rubble by ground assault. Already troops of the 26th Infantry were jockeying for position in preparation for starting the attack against a jungle of factories lying between the city proper and Haaren.

Full meaning of the capture of Ravels Hill was no more lost upon German commanders than upon General Huebner. Appealing for replacements, Field Marshal Model reported in the trite phraseology of the day that "the situation around Aachen has grown more critical." Unless replacements arrived, Model noted, "continued reverses will be unavoidable." [16]

Though making no promise of individual replacements, the *OB WEST* commander, Rundstedt, took notice of the first arrivals of the *3d Panzer Grenadier* and *116th Panzer Divisions* in the Aachen sector on 10 October. On the same day he gave first official authorization for commitment of these two divisions under the *I SS Panzer Corps*. Yet several days still might elapse before the 18th Infantry or any part of the 1st Division encountered these reserves, for to his authorization Rundstedt attached a proviso that the reserve divisions must not be committed piecemeal but as closed units. In

---

[16] TWX, Rundstedt to Jodl, 1130, 11 Oct 44, relaying Msg, Model to Rundstedt, 1045, 10 Oct 44, *OB WEST KTB, Befehle und Meldungen*.

the light of this condition, the *Army Group B* commander, Field Marshal Model, saw no hope of a major counterattack before 12 October.

In the meantime, as these German reserves massed, as the ultimatum to the commander of Aachen expired, and as the 26th Infantry began to attack the city, the 18th Infantry continued to hold thinly stretched positions at Verlautenheide and Haaren and atop Crucifix and Ravels Hills. Long days and nights in the line began to tell on the infantrymen, sometimes with costly results. One night someone in a group laying antitank mines on Ravels Hill inadvertently set off one of the mines and precipitated a chain reaction that exploded twenty-two mines. Some thirty-three men were either killed or wounded. Another night a rifle company commander guided a relief platoon from a different company toward his own defensive positions from the enemy side. Confusion and casualties resulted before he could convince his own men of his identity. Setting out on two occasions to contact the 30th Division to the north, patrols made virtually no headway. Possibly no patrol could have accomplished the mission, and accidents like those with the mines and loss of direction are not uncommon; yet the fact remained that the men involved were nervous and tired. Even when not defending their foxholes or hugging the earth to escape shell fragments, they had to attack to clean out a multitude of pillboxes that dotted the landscape or man roadblocks on highways running on either side of Ravels Hill. Relieving these battalions for rest was out of the question in view of the impoverished state of General Huebner's reserve.

The Germans missed a chance for success when they failed to detect the true condition of the 18th Infantry's defenses. Here was a likely spot for counterattacking to enlarge the pathway into Aachen, yet the Germans in preparing a counterattack missed the spot by a few hundred yards.

That the Germans might be preparing a big blow became apparent to the 1st Division on 14 October upon receipt of an intelligence report noting that the *3d Panzer Grenadier Division* was moving to the Aachen sector. Through the early daylight hours of 15 October, both the 18th Infantry and its sister regiment, the 16th Infantry, which defended between Verlautenheide and Stolberg, reported build-up of German infantry and armor in the vicinity of Verlautenheide. By 0830, despite repeated shelling of enemy concentrations, reports indicating a pending attack persisted. An air strike by fighter-bombers at 0900 seemingly failed to deter German preparations. An hour later the Germans attacked.

To the Americans, the thrust which followed was a powerful, well-prepared attack that shattered nerves at more than one echelon of command. In reality, the thrust was a hasty compromise growing out of events that had begun as early as five days before on 10 October. On that day, in cognizance of indications that Aachen might be sealed off before the *3d Panzer Grenadier* and *116th Panzer Divisions* arrived in entirety, Field Marshal Model at *Army Group B* authorized piecemeal employment of first arrivals of the *116th Panzer Division.*[17] Although this measure was to be used only in event of dire emergency threatening loss of all access to Aachen, German commanders

on the ground had not far to look during these hectic days to find plenty of dire emergencies. Less than twenty-four hours after receipt of Model's authorization, the *Seventh Army*'s General Brandenberger directed commitment of a regiment of the panzer division against the XIX U.S. Corps.

This precedent established, Brandenberger had no real trouble convincing his superiors that another emergency existed at Verlautenheide, justifying commitment there of the *3d Panzer Grenadier Division*. A comprehensive plan for a co-ordinated counterattack thus became infected with the fungus of counterattack by installments that quickly ate away what could have been an effective reserve force. German counterattacks now had no genuine relationship other than a common goal of widening the corridor into Aachen.

Subordinated directly to the *Seventh Army* rather than the *LXXXI Corps,* the *3d Panzer Grenadier Division* concentrated upon a first objective of high ground south and southwest of Verlautenheide, lying generally between that village and Eilendorf. From there the division commander, Generalmajor Walter Denkert, intended to swing northwest against Crucifix Hill (Hill 239).[18]

General Denkert directed his *29th Panzer Grenadier Regiment* to make the main effort on the north from the skirt of a forest east of Verlautenheide. With a current strength of from ten to fifteen Tiger tanks, the bulk of the *506th Tank Battalion* was to support the main effort.

---

[17] TWX, *A Gp B* to *Seventh Army*, 1145, 10 Oct 44, *A Gp B, Operationsbefehle.*

[18] The German side of this action is based upon MS # A-979, *Die 3. Panzer-Grenadier-Division in der Schlacht von Aachen* (Denkert). Basic facts are corroborated by contemporary German records.

Anchoring a left (south) flank on the Aachen–Dueren railroad east of Eilendorf, the *8th Panzer Grenadier Regiment* was to launch a coincident subsidiary attack.

From the American viewpoint, the two German thrusts were to strike near the boundary between the 18th and 16th Regiments south of Verlautenheide. Here a 2,000-yard front covering the high ground between Verlautenheide and Eilendorf was held by a battalion of the 16th Infantry commanded by Lt. Col. Joe Dawson. The German thrusts were to converge not against the weakened 18th Infantry but against the extreme left wing of the 16th Infantry.

Upon leaving the woods line that represented the line of departure, both German columns had to cross a flat open meadow before reaching the base of the high ground held by Colonel Dawson's battalion. Forewarned by reports of enemy assembly, artillery of both the 1st Division and the VII Corps was ready. Using prearranged fires, six field artillery battalions were able to concentrate their fire within six minutes of the first warning. Watching the attack from the woods line, the German commander, General Denkert, was impressed with the volume of American shellfire. "It was obvious," General Denkert noted later, "that an advance through this fire was impossible. It was equally impossible to feed the attack from the rear, to move up reserves or ammunition."

General Denkert had no way of knowing that his attack actually was much closer to success than he believed. Though the defensive artillery fires stopped the bulk of his infantry, the Tiger tanks ploughed through to pour direct fire into American foxholes. The men said some of the tanks were captured Shermans and

that one still bore the unit markings of an American armored division.[19]

About noon, less than half an hour after the full fury of the attack hit, Colonel Dawson reported communications to his two left companies disrupted and the situation there "serious." The commander of one of the companies had called for artillery fire upon his own command post. "Put every gun you've got on it," he told his artillery observer. Only a short while later, a messenger arrived at Colonel Dawson's command post. The Germans, the messenger reported, were overrunning both companies.[20]

Possibly because he had so little concrete knowledge of what was going on, the regimental commander, Col. Frederick W. Gibb, delayed committing his reserve, which consisted only of tanks and tank destroyers. A section each of light tanks and tank destroyers in position in the threatened sector had managed to make but one kill. Instead, Colonel Gibb called for air support and for whatever assistance the 18th Infantry might provide. A report that the 18th Infantry's right wing company had been overrun already had prompted the 18th Infantry commander, Colonel Smith, to send a company from Haaren to set the matter right. Finding the report erroneous upon arrival at Verlautenheide in midafternoon, this company subsequently assumed defensive positions blocking a gap along the interregimental boundary. This was the only force Colonel Smith could spare.

General Huebner wasted no time alerting the division reserve, the battalion of the 26th Infantry, and requesting the

---

[19] The 5th; possibly captured at Wallendorf.
[20] 16th Inf S–3 Jnl, 15 Oct 44.

corps commander, General Collins, to alert anything the 3d Armored Division might spare. But like Colonel Gibb, General Huebner delayed committing the reserve until he could know more specifically the extent of the enemy attack.

In the meantime, both corps and division artillery continued to pound the German attack. Seven battalions, plus some of the 3d Armored Division's artillery, participated. Although the situation remained obscure on Colonel Dawson's left wing, the attack by the *8th Panzer Grenadier Regiment,* which hit a company on the right wing, definitely collapsed in the face of this fire and after loss of two out of three supporting tanks. The situation there never reached critical proportions.

Arrival of air support in time to save the day appeared doubtful until at 1340 the 30th Division announced release of a squadron which already had dispensed most of its bombs but which still had plenty of strafing ammunition. Ten minutes later P–47's of the 48th Group's 492d Squadron led by Capt. George W. Huling, Jr., were over the 16th Infantry's lines. Two 500-pound general-purpose bombs that the squadron still had the pilots dropped "in the midst" of a concentration of some thirty German vehicles. Then they strafed. "They came in about 25 feet from our front lines," an ecstatic 1st Division G–3 later reported, "and strafed the hell out of the enemy and came down so low they could tell the difference between the uniforms." It was a "beautiful job." So impressed by the performance was the corps commander, General Collins, that he sought the number of the squadron in order to commend the pilots.[21]

Though the air strike alone hardly

could be credited with stopping the *3d Panzer Grenadier Division*'s attack, it effectively crowned the achievements of the artillery. The fire fight went on at close quarters for the rest of the day, but no real penetration developed. As the situation cleared, General Huebner held on to his reserve. A battalion of tanks from the 3d Armored Division, made available at the height of the fighting, likewise remained uncommitted.

Lack of persistence certainly was no failing of the *3d Panzer Grenadier Division.* Despite the sound defeat during the afternoon of 15 October, the Germans came back before daylight the next morning. By the light of flares, Colonel Dawson's left unit, Company G, spotted a company of infantry and two tanks as they reached the very brink of the defensive position. Quickly overrunning two squads, the Germans poured through. Confusion reigned. "Nobody knew what the situation was," someone said later, "because the enemy was in front and on both sides of you." Soon thereafter another German company and three tanks struck the adjacent unit as well. This company commander resorted to the stratagem of calling down artillery fire on his own positions. His men later counted some forty enemy dead.

The main threat remained on the left in the sector of Company G. So concerned was General Huebner about the situation there that he released a company of his reserve battalion to back up the threatened sector and directed the rest of the reserve to move to an assembly area close behind the line.

Though the reserve stood by, it never

---

[21] See Msg, sub: Mission Y–21–1, FUSA G–3 file, Oct 44, and IX FC and IX TAC Unit History, Oct 44.

entered the fight. Aided by mortar and artillery support that was possible because communications remained constant, Colonel Dawson's infantry alone proved equal to the occasion. Though Germans were all among the foxholes and the enemy tanks perched little more than twenty-five yards away to pump fire into the holes, the men held their positions. Had it been daylight, the sight of some withdrawing might have infected others; as it was, the men stayed, basically unaware of what the over-all situation was. Out of little clumps of resistance and individual heroism they fashioned a sturdy phalanx.

Colonel Dawson tried to institute a fire plan whereby his men were to burrow deep in their holes while he called down a curtain of shellfire on and behind the enemy tanks. Coincidentally, a platoon of tank destroyers was to engage the Germans frontally. "The whole thing," Colonel Dawson said, "is to knock them out or make them fight." [22] Whether this did the job—indeed, whether the plan worked at all in the maelstrom of confusion—went unrecorded. What mattered was that soon after dawn the German tanks fell back under concealment of a heavy ground haze. The threatened rifle company soon thereafter cleared the last enemy from the positions.

At intervals throughout 16 October the *3d Panzer Grenadier Division* continued to probe this weakened sector but usually with small units of infantry supported by two or three tanks. The Germans had lost their chance to break through, thwarted by a rifle company that would not recognize when it was beaten.

The preponderance of losses incurred thus far by the 1st Division had occurred during the first two days while the 18th Infantry was pushing northward and during 15 and 16 October while the left wing of the 16th Infantry was repulsing these enemy thrusts. During the first two days the division incurred 360 casualties of all types; during the latter two, 178. Through 16 October the 1st Division had lost about 800 men, a relatively low figure that reflected the defensive nature of much of the fighting.[23]

On the German side, severe losses prompted abandonment of the *3d Panzer Grenadier Division*'s fruitless counterattack until the division could regroup.[24] In but two days of fighting, this division had lost about one third of its combat effectives.[25] Men of the 16th Infantry could attest to these losses; for in front of the left company alone they counted 250 dead, "a figure," the G–3 noted, "unprecedented in the division's history." That went a long way toward explaining why the *3d Panzer Grenadier Division* never again came close to breaking the 1st Division's defensive arc.

The 30th Division Strikes South

Thus had the 1st Division seized and then protected its assigned objectives during the first nine days of the operation to encircle Aachen. In the meantime, farther north, the 30th Division of the XIX Corps had been executing the other part of the joint maneuver.

Having turned southward from the West Wall penetration in high spirits on 7 October, the 30th Division commander, General Hobbs, had hoped by nightfall

---

[22] 16th Inf S–3 Jnl, 15–16 Oct 44.

[23] Casualty figures from VII Corps AAR, Oct 44.

[24] *OB WEST KTB*, 16 Oct 44.

[25] *LXXXI Corps KTB, Meldungen der Div.*

the next day to be sitting tight on his final objective, awaiting arrival of 1st Division troops. So optimistic was General Hobbs that early on 8 October he told his corps commander that "the job is finished as far as this division is concerned . . . ." He added that he hoped the First Army commander would appreciate "what this division has done." [26]

As General Hobbs was to learn to his chagrin, he had allowed the easy success of the day before, when his troops had plunged a third of the distance to the link-up objective of Wuerselen, to color his thinking. In the nine days that followed, the three-mile distance remaining before the job actually was completed was to become a route bathed in blood and frustration.

Unlike the 18th Infantry, the 30th Division had no problem at first with enemy pillboxes, for the bulk of the troops already were behind the West Wall. Only the right wing regiment in the west was to encounter pillboxes at the start, and these might be rolled up from a flank. Yet this did not mean that the route of advance was not replete with obstacles. This region to the north and northeast of Aachen is highly urbanized coal mining country, honeycombed with slag piles, mine shafts, and villages that might be adapted readily to defense.

General Hobbs could count on no direct assistance from other divisions of the XIX

Corps. Already occupied in protecting the elongated corps north flank west of the West Wall, the 29th Division had had to stretch its resources to send the 116th Infantry to contain Germans holding out northwest of Aachen in order to free the 30th Division's third regiment from that task to join the southward drive. This regiment, the 120th Infantry, commanded by Col. Branner P. Purdue,[27] General Hobbs thrust into the center of his sector to attack with his other two regiments on 8 October. The remaining division, the 2d Armored, still held the northern and eastern flanks of the West Wall bridgehead. General Corlett hesitated to weaken this defense, because German penetration of this bridgehead might cut off the 30th Division's southward drive at its base.

Although indications existed that the 30th Division already had neutralized all local German reserves, General Hobbs dared not concentrate on his southward drive to the exclusion of protecting a left (east) flank that would stretch steadily as his troops moved south. To shield his east flank, he directed the 117th Infantry (Colonel Johnson) to seize high ground in the vicinity of Mariadorf, about two miles southeast of Alsdorf, the town which the regiment had taken with ease on 7 October. In addition, he told the 120th Infantry (Colonel Purdue) to take the high ground northeast of Wuerselen.

General Hobbs also told Colonel Purdue to capture high ground east of Wuerselen, between that town and Broichweiden, in order to assure firm control of an arterial highway running diagonally across the 30th Division's zone

---

[26] 30th Div G–3 Jnl file, 7–9 Oct 44. The telephone journals in this file and others for this period are especially valuable. Unless otherwise noted, the 30th Division story is from these journals, from other official unit records of the division and the XIX Corps, from several noteworthy combat interviews, and from the division's unofficial unit history, Hewitt, *Workhorse of the Western Front.* The XIX Corps G–2 reports for this period are particularly well done.

[27] The previous commander, Colonel Birks, had left on 6 October to become assistant division commander of the 9th Division.

from Aachen northeast toward Juelich. This maneuver also was to set the stage for taking Wuerselen. The division's third regiment, the 119th Infantry (Colonel Sutherland), was to take North Wuerselen, little more than a mile (2,000 yards) from Ravels Hill, northernmost 1st Division objective, and protect the division's right (west) flank. Guarding the west flank appeared no major assignment, because the flank would rest on the Wurm River and Germans west of the Wurm seemed a sedentary lot.

Having dealt harshly with the enemy's *49th* and *183d Divisions,* General Hobbs expected now to encounter primarily portions of the *246th Division,* which was specifically responsible for defending Aachen. General Hobbs also might expect to meet diverse contingents of the *12th Division,* that might be spared from **defense about Stolberg and possibly a** panzer brigade which the XIX Corps G–2 persistently warned was in reserve a few miles to the east. Otherwise, the route to Wuerselen seemed clear, unless the enemy should rush in mobile reserves from other sectors or refitted units from deep behind the front. Should the Germans commit major reserves, the most likely spot was against the division's eastern and southeastern flanks.

The XIX Corps G–2, Colonel Platt, had displayed his usual prescience, for this was about the sum of things from the German viewpoint. Even as the 30th Division planned renewal of the southward drive, the panzer brigade which Colonel Platt had warned against, the *108th,* and a unit rushed from another sector, *Mobile Regiment von Fritzschen,* were preparing to strike into the 30th Division's east flank. Reserves from deep behind the front in the form of the *116th*

Panzer and *3d Panzer Grenadier Divisions* were on the way.

That the Germans soon might strike was not apparent on 8 October on the west and in the center of the 30th Division's sector. Closely following the valley of the Wurm, Colonel Sutherland's 119th Infantry picked a way through mined streets of a village on the east bank of the Wurm opposite Kerkrade, then pushed a mile and a half to another village. Advancing in the center toward objectives at Wuerselen and Broichweiden, Colonel Purdue's 120th Infantry soon secured two hamlets despite thick mine fields covered by small arms and antitank fire.

With Colonel Johnson's 117th Infantry on the east the situation at first was much the same. Moving southeast out of Alsdorf toward Mariadorf and the Aachen–Juelich highway, the regiment found advantage in a thick morning mist. The attack progressed steadily until about 0930 when leading platoons began to cross a railroad a few hundred yards west of Mariadorf. Germans from *Mobile Regiment von Fritzschen* suddenly emerged from Mariadorf behind a curtain of small arms and artillery fire. They quickly sliced off a leading platoon commanded by Lieutenant Borton, who had played a prominent role in the crossing of the Wurm at the start of the West Wall attack. Lieutenant Borton and twenty-six of his men were either killed or captured. German guns disabled three out of four supporting American tanks. Another platoon that tried to advance even after the Germans struck also was cut off; only six men ever made their way back. So costly was the fight that when one of the leading companies eventually retired west of the railroad, only thirty-three men were on hand.

Mobile Regiment von Fritzschen as it appeared against the 117th Infantry on 8 October was an effective force. In addition to two organic infantry battalions, the regiment possessed several attachments, including the eleven tanks available on this date in the *108th Panzer Brigade,* which included the *506th Tank Battalion,* twenty-two assault guns in three assault gun battalions, an engineer battalion, and a depleted battalion from the *246th Division.*[28] The mission of this force was to retake Alsdorf and thereby close a great gap in the line of the *49th Division* which the Americans had torn the day before in occupying Alsdorf.[29]

The German corps commander, General Koechling, had intended that *Regiment von Fritzschen* would attack before dawn on 8 October in order to cross an expanse of open ground between Mariadorf and Alsdorf before the Americans could bring observed artillery fires to bear. Instead, because of air attacks and fuel shortages, the regiment failed to reach Mariadorf until dawn. By the time the regiment was ready to attack the 117th Infantry's drive had reached the railroad west of Mariadorf. No matter how severe the casualties on the American side, German losses were greater. American artillery fire was particularly disturbing, because by the time the Germans struck, morning mists had begun to lift.

This charge west of Mariadorf was but half of *Regiment von Fritzschen*'s attack. At the same time a force of equal size

drove toward Alsdorf via the village of Schaufenberg. This attack, too, might have bogged down in the face of American shelling had not the buildings of Schaufenberg provided a partial oasis. From there, some of the tanks and infantry gradually fought their way into Alsdorf, a move that posed the possibility of trapping the bulk of the 117th Infantry southeast of the town.

In Alsdorf, men manning regimental and battalion command posts rallied to the defense. Though surrounded, men in a battalion observation post under the personal leadership of their battalion commander, Colonel McDowell, held off the Germans with carbines and pistols.

Roaming the winding streets of Alsdorf, attached tanks of the 743d Tank Battalion dealt the *coup de grâce* to *Regiment von Fritzschen*'s attack in less than an hour after the first Germans penetrated the town. The tankers knocked out three Mark IV's, while tank destroyers searched the streets the rest of the day for another which the crewmen christened The Reluctant Dragon. Weaker now by about 500 men, *Regiment von Fritzschen* shifted to defense.

The counterattack had blunted the 117th Infantry's offensive thrust effectively. Both the regimental commander, Colonel Johnson, and the division commander, General Hobbs, acted to reinforce the regiment at Alsdorf in event this was but an opening blow in a major German counteraction. Colonel Johnson authorized a withdrawal from the railroad to the fringe of Alsdorf, while General Hobbs moved a neighboring battalion of the 120th Infantry into a reinforcing position and solicited assistance from the nearest combat command of the 2d Armored Division. The combat command alerted a

---

[28] Order, *49th Div* to *Regt von Fritzschen,* 8 Oct 44, *LXXXI Corps KTB, Meldungen der Div.*

[29] AAR concerning opns of *Regt von Fritzschen* on 8 Oct 44, *49th Div* to *LXXXI Corps,* 10 Oct 44, *LXXXI Corps KTB, Meldungen der Div.* Details of this action on 8 October are available in Heichler, The Germans Opposite XIX Corps.

medium tank company for possible commitment at Alsdorf.

These measures taken, General Hobbs ordered resumption of the attack the next morning (9 October). This Colonel Johnson accomplished successfully at Schaufenberg, where a battalion routed remnants of *Regiment von Fritzschen*, but the bulk of the regiment could not advance across the open ground toward Mariadorf. Evidence existed to indicate that the 117th Infantry's long period of attack without rest—a total now of more than a week—had begun to tell. About noon General Hobbs approved a request from Colonel Johnson to defend the division's east flank from Schaufenberg and Alsdorf rather than from the original objective of Mariadorf.

Though the 117th Infantry made no major gains on 9 October, Colonel Johnson could note with relief that the Germans had not renewed their counterattack against his regiment. The fact was that opening of the VII Corps drive northward against Verlautenheide the day before had diverted German attention. Upon the instigation of Field Marshal Model, an infantry battalion, an engineer battalion and the *108th Panzer Brigade* (including the *506th Tank Battalion*) had been detached from *Regiment von Fritzschen* late on 8 October. This force, reinforced by the *404th Infantry Regiment*, now returned to its parent *246th Division*, was to launch a new thrust farther southwest in the direction of Bardenberg, northwest of Wuerselen, presumably to thwart what looked like impending juncture of the two American drives.[30]

As events developed, the *404th Regiment* and the *108th Panzer Brigade* had a hard time getting a thrust going on 9 October because every attempt ran into a prior American attack. Both at Euchen and Birk, two villages astride the route to Bardenberg, the Germans encountered battalions of the 120th Infantry which were driving toward that regiment's final objective, high ground near Wuerselen. Small-scale counterattacks and continuing pressure denied the Americans both Euchen and Birk, but the German timetable for the push to Bardenberg was seriously upset. Not until after dark did the Germans get started on the final leg of their journey.

In passing through Euchen and Birk, the *108th Panzer Brigade* had cut directly across the front of the 120th Infantry. In pushing on to Bardenberg, the brigade was to encounter the 30th Division's right wing regiment, the 119th Infantry. During the day of 9 October this regiment had been experiencing bountiful success in a drive aimed at North Wuerselen. Moving against halfhearted resistance from demoralized remnants of the *49th Division*, two battalions of Colonel Sutherland's regiment had occupied Bardenberg in late afternoon. With a last burst of energy before night set in, both battalions had charged southeast more than a mile into North Wuerselen. Here they stood little more than 2,000 yards short of the 18th Infantry's objective of Ravels Hill (Hill 231). Closing this gap looked like little more than a matter of mop-up and patrols.

Although the Germans had not known of this last advance when they had planned their thrust against Bardenberg, the chance timing of the attack made them appear Argus-eyed and omniscient.

[30] Tel Conv, *Seventh Army* to *LXXXI Corps*, 1100, 8 Oct 44, *LXXXI Corps KTB, Kampfverlauf*; Order, *LXXXI Corps* to all divs, 8 Oct 44, *LXXXI Corps KTB, Befehle an Div.*

By striking when and where they did, they made it hurt.

When the two battalions of the 119th Infantry moved into North Wuerselen, they left behind to protect their line of communications at Bardenberg an under-strength company commanded by Capt. Ross Y. Simmons. Captain Simmons put the bulk of his troops about a roadblock on the eastern edge of the village astride the highway leading east to Birk and Euchen. Not long after nightfall a covey of half-tracks spouting fire from 20-mm. antiaircraft guns struck this roadblock. No sooner had the Americans beaten back the half-tracks when a larger portion of the *108th Panzer Brigade* estimated at five tanks and 300 infantry attacked with fury. Captain Simmons and his men could not hold. The panzer brigade poured through into Bardenberg.

The portent of the German success at Bardenberg was not hard to see. Whether the enemy had strength enough to continue northward and cut off the XIX Corps West Wall penetration at its base was conjectural, but by taking Bardenberg he already had severed communications to the main body of the 119th Infantry in North Wuerselen.

The regimental commander, Colonel Sutherland, alerted his service company and regimental headquarters personnel for possible line duty and ordered his reserve battalion under Colonel Cox to retake Bardenberg from the north. Though one of Colonel Cox's companies got into action quickly, the Germans in Bardenberg were not to be pushed around. The advance carried no farther than a church in the northeastern part of the village.

Tension that prevailed through the night was relieved somewhat early the next morning, 10 October, by a report from the 120th Infantry. Having tried without success the day before to capture the Birk crossroads, a battalion of the 120th Infantry moved by stealth at 0530 and literally caught the Germans in Birk asleep at their posts. The battalion fired only one shot, that by accident. This lack of vigilance at a strategic point controlling the only road by which the enemy in Bardenberg might be supplied and reinforced helped convince General Hobbs and his regimental commanders that the *108th Panzer Brigade* had no real knowledge of what an advantageous *point d'appui* it held there. When the Germans virtually ignored the main body of the 119th Infantry in North Wuerselen until late in the day on 10 October, this belief was strengthened.

That capture of the Birk crossroads had imperiled the *108th Panzer Brigade* in Bardenberg hardly was apparent when Colonel Cox's battalion of the 119th Infantry renewed the attack to clear the village soon after daylight on 10 October. The Germans fought back intensely, their tanks hidden in gardens and behind houses, the cellars turned into imitation pillboxes. An estimated ten to twenty half-tracks mounting the pernicious multi-barrel 20-mm. antiaircraft gun formed a protective screen that thwarted all attempts at infiltration. As darkness approached, Colonel Cox could point to little ground gained; only in the knowledge that the attack was making inroads on enemy strength was there consolation. During the day, for example, at Bardenberg, North Wuerselen, and Birk, 30th Division troops and artillery had knocked out twelve German tanks. Ingenious soldiers of the 120th Infantry had destroyed one with a captured *Puppchen*, a two-wheeled bazooka.

At nightfall Colonel Sutherland reluctantly ordered withdrawal from Bardenberg to permit the artillery to pummel the enemy through the night without concern for friendly troops. In the meantime General Hobbs had become impatient to reopen the line of communications to the main body of the regiment at North Wuerselen so he could get on with the job of linking with the 1st Division. He decided to commit a fresh unit, the reserve battalion of the 120th Infantry.

Early on 11 October this battalion moved into Bardenberg against virtually no opposition. Not until reaching the southern half of the village did the battalion meet the grenadiers of the *108th Panzer Brigade* with their ubiquitous tanks and half-tracks. Here the battle was met, but the attrition of the preceding day and night and the commitment of a fresh American battalion had done the trick. The battalion commander himself, Maj. Howard Greer, made a sizable contribution in other than his command role by personally knocking out two tanks with a bazooka. The total bag of enemy armor was six tanks and sixteen half-tracks. Though wounded, a squad leader, S. Sgt. Jack J. Pendleton, ensured the advance of his company by deliberately drawing the fire of an enemy machine gun. He gave his life in the process.[31]

As the fight progressed in Bardenberg, expeditious use of artillery on other parts of the 30th Division front, the effect of the blocking position of the 120th Infantry at the Birk crossroads, and the action of four squadrons of IX Tactical Air Command fighter-bombers prevented the Germans from sending help. Clearing weather enabled planes to operate for the first time in three days. By last light on 11 October both Bardenberg and the route to North Wuerselen were clear.

Commitment of the 120th Infantry's reserve battalion in Bardenberg absorbed the last infantry unit available in the 30th Division. This worried the division commander, General Hobbs, for reports of continued German build-up with likelihood of a large-scale thrust from east or southeast continued to come in. A worrisome but ineffective visit by the Luftwaffe added to General Hobbs's concern; attention from the long-dormant Luftwaffe had been received with such increasing frequency of late that one hardly could miss the importance the Germans attached to this sector.[32] Furthermore, one of the reports General Hobbs received indicated that the *116th Panzer Division* might be arriving soon.

Under these conditions, Hobbs believed that to continue his attack eastward and southeastward into the teeth of what might develop into a major enemy blow had the makings of disaster. Since both the 117th Infantry near Alsdorf and the 120th Infantry near Euchen now occupied stanch defensive positions, he decided to forego further attempts to expand his left flank. He told these units to hold in place where they might be ready for any eventuality. Until German intentions were clear, he would confine offensive efforts to capture of Wuerselen in order to accomplish the primary mission of closing the gap in the circle about Aachen.

---

[31] Sergeant Pendleton was awarded the Medal of Honor posthumously. Major Greer received the Distinguished Service Cross.

[32] On 9 October Field Marshal von Rundstedt said the greatest danger to the entire Western Front was presently at Aachen. *OB WEST KTB,* 9 Oct 44.

GERMAN BOY *weeps over the few possessions saved from his home outside Aachen.*

Viewed from the German side, General Hobbs's concern was not without foundation, though urgency occasioned by continuing American successes might prompt dissipation of incoming German strength. Late on 11 October the first of the *116th Panzer Division*'s regimental combat teams, composed primarily of the *60th Panzer Grenadier Regiment*, had arrived. On the same day, the *LXXXI Corps* was reinforced further by arrival of a *Kampfgruppe Diefenthal*, a hybrid collection of survivors of two defunct *SS* panzer divisions[33] in strength of about two battalions. Also arriving on 11 October, headquarters of the *I SS Panzer Corps* (Keppler) at 2100 assumed command of the northern portion of the *LXXXI Corps* front.

Faced with the *108th Panzer Brigade's*

---

[33] *1st and 12th SS Pz Divisions.*

failure at Bardenberg and with loss of North Wuerselen, the *Seventh Army* commander, General Brandenberger, deemed this emergency serious enough to justify use of Field Marshal Model's recent authorization to employ the *116th Panzer Division* as it arrived. Reinforcing the *60th Panzer Grenadier Regiment* with the main body of *Kampfgruppe Diefenthal,* remnants of the *108th Panzer Brigade,* and two assault gun units possessing a total of thirty assault guns and howitzers, Brandenberger directed an attack early on 12 October. The mission was to push back the XIX Corps to a line Bardenberg–Euchen, that is, to widen and defend the corridor into Aachen.[34] This was a far cry from original German intentions of using the *116th Panzer* and *3d Panzer Grenadier Divisions* in a concerted counterattack to wipe out the entire West Wall penetration north of Aachen; indeed, commitment of the *60th Panzer Grenadier Regiment* was the precedent which four days later was to lead to similar piecemeal use of the *3d Panzer Grenadier Division* near Verlautenheide.

In line with the decision to maintain a static front except at Wuerselen, General Hobbs directed that the right wing of the 120th Infantry first was to seize high ground just northeast of the town. Thereupon, both the 119th and 120th Infantry Regiments were to reduce Wuerselen. This was the agenda for 12 October on the American side.

As events developed on 12 October, the 30th Division could not accomplish even the advance of little more than a mile from the Birk crossroads to the high ground northeast of Wuerselen. Every unit had to turn to the defensive, for at

---

[34] TWX, *Seventh Army* to *A Gp B,* 1315, 11 Oct 44, *A Gp B, Operationsbefehle.*

almost every point the front blazed. Apparently the Germans during the night had directed that the counterattack by the *60th Panzer Grenadier Regiment* be reinforced by local stabs all along the line.

The fight began just after dawn at Birk when a battalion of the *246th Division* counterattacked in conjunction with about ten tanks under the *506th Tank Battalion*. A three-hour fight ensued. At first, the battalion of the 120th Infantry at the crossroads had but one tank, that commanded by S. Sgt. Melvin H. Bieber. Engaging a brace of the German tanks simultaneously, Sergeant Bieber and his crew forced the enemy to abandon one tank and knocked out the other after twelve hits. As an early morning fog began to lift, other Shermans of Sergeant Bieber's company arrived. Together with supporting artillery, they accounted for five more of the enemy tanks.[35]

The situation appeared grim at one spot in the 120th Infantry's line when a rifle company lost all four attached 57-mm. antitank guns and when enemy shellfire knocked out the artillery observer and wounded another who tried to take his place. At last the battalion's artillery liaison officer, Capt. Michael S. Bouchlas, made his way forward. Up to this time friendly artillery had been firing spasmodically, sometimes even falling short. After Captain Bouchlas miraculously threaded his way through shellfire to the observation post, the picture changed. Within a half hour the threat was over. By 1030 the regimental commander, Colonel Purdue, could report the situation under control. "I never did see men going like these have been going," Colonel

Purdue reported ecstatically. "We are as strong as we can be . . . ."[36]

Another fight developed as a meeting engagement southeast of Bardenberg when Colonel Cox's battalion of the 119th Infantry moved to strengthen the bulk of that regiment in North Wuerselen. Aided by artillery fire, Colonel Cox quickly drove off the Germans, but identification of prisoners promoted anxiety. Colonel Cox had met a battalion of the *60th Panzer Grenadier Regiment*. General Hobbs's fears about arrival of the *116th Panzer Division* apparently had materialized. Another identification near nightfall of that division's *Panzer Reconnaissance Battalion* underscored the concern.

At North Wuerselen, about 200 infantry supported by eight tanks and a few assault guns struck the main body of the 119th Infantry. After destroying five tanks and an assault gun, the 119th Infantry beat off this attack with celerity; but here too identification of prisoners nurtured apprehension. Here the German infantry was *SS-Battalion Rink*, that part of *Kampfgruppe Diefenthal* which in happier days had belonged to the *1st SS Panzer Division* (*Leibstandarte Adolf Hitler*). To General Hobbs and his anxious staff, this posed the possibility that the entire *1st SS Panzer Division* either had arrived or was on the way.

Both General Hobbs and the XIX Corps commander, General Corlett, were frankly worried. They talked in terms of another Mortain and of commandeering antiaircraft, artillery, and service troops to back up the line. "If the *116th Panzer* and *Adolf Hitler* [*1st SS Panzer*] are in there," General Corlett said, "this is one of the decisive battles of the war."[37]

---

[35] Sergeant Bieber subsequently received the DSC.

[36] 30th Div G–3 Jnl, 12 Oct 44.
[37] *Ibid.*

While anxiety stimulated by these identifications remained, the 30th Division by noon of 12 October had contained every German thrust. The infantrymen were quick to transfer much of the credit to their supporting artillery and to fourteen squadrons of fighter-bombers that droned about the front all day like reckless but disciplined wasps. Sparkling weather gave both artillery and planes a clear field. At one time the planes attacked a concentration of a reported forty enemy tanks; they left eighteen of them, ground observers said, in flames. "The Germans are nibbling and pushing," General Hobbs reported in midafternoon, "but no general attack." [38] Everything was under control or—as General Hobbs put it—his men had "their tails over the dashboard."

The First Army commander, General Hodges, was less sanguine. Even should the 30th Division continue to defend successfully and even should the fight fail to develop in the proportions Generals Corlett and Hobbs feared, the persistent problem of closing the circle about Aachen still would remain. Less visibly perturbed about German potentialities than his two subordinates, General Hodges insisted that they get going again on this primary task. "We have to close that gap," he told General Corlett; "it will have to be done somehow." [39]

In turn, General Hobbs pleaded for assistance. After almost two weeks of fighting, including the first set attack against the West Wall, his men were worn out, their numbers depleted. Since the start of the West Wall attack on 2 October, the 30th Division had incurred 2,020 casualties, most of them hard-to-replace

riflemen. Yet the First Army could provide little help other than to place the separate 99th Infantry Battalion (Maj. Harold D. Hansen) in XIX Corps reserve and to assume control over a combat command from the relatively inactive V Corps front in order to create an Army reserve. If the 30th Division was to be reinforced, General Corlett would have to do it by shuffling his own units.

Though General Corlett hesitated to weaken the northeastern and eastern defensive arcs of the West Wall bridgehead, he nevertheless agreed to give General Hobbs a battalion of the 2d Armored Division's medium tanks. In addition, by assigning the 30th Division a battalion of corps engineers, he relieved the 119th Infantry of responsibility for protecting the division's right flank along the Wurm River. By putting another corps engineer unit, the 1104th Engineer Combat Group (Lt. Col. Hugh W. Cotton), into the line near Kerkrade to contain the enemy in those pillboxes lying west of the Wurm, he freed the regiment of the 29th Division that had been doing that job. This regiment, the 116th Infantry, minus one battalion already attached to the 2d Armored Division, Corlett awarded to Hobbs for continuing the link-up offensive.

These orders issued, General Corlett directed that the 30th Division attack early the next morning, 13 October. Though Corlett suggested a wide end run southeast from the vicinity of Alsdorf, both General Hobbs and his regimental commanders demurred. Again they were reluctant to abandon good defensive positions on the east and southeast lest the indicated German strength materialize. Another suggestion that the drive be directed south along the east bank of the Wurm also was abandoned for fear the

---

[38] *Ibid.*
[39] XIX Corps G–3 Jnl, 12 Oct 44.

rest of the *116th Panzer Division* had assembled there. An attack southward along the west bank of the Wurm was out, not only because that also might encounter the panzer division but also because it would involve either a river crossing or a frontal attack against pillboxes in the sector now held by the 1104th Engineers. Only one method of effecting the link-up appeared feasible: to advance on a narrow front through the streets and buildings of Wuerselen.

Assisted by attached tanks from the 2d Armored Division, the two fresh battalions of the 116th Infantry launched this attack on 13 October, but to no avail. Because the attack was on such a narrow front, the Germans were able to concentrate against it the fire of an estimated 6 to 7 battalions of light artillery, 1 or 2 medium battalions, and at least 2 batteries of heavy artillery. Co-ordination between the 116th Infantry and the tanks of the 2d Armored Division was slow to come.[40] Neither on 13 October nor on the next two days could the 116th Infantry make more than snaillike progress.

During these three days General Hobbs constantly exhorted the 116th Infantry commander, Col. Philip R. Dwyer, and even called on the commander of the regiment's parent division to help prod the unit forward. But more than this was needed to pry apart the German

defense of Wuerselen. Here was located the entire *60th Panzer Grenadier Regiment* supported by dug-in tanks and other armor cleverly concealed amid the houses and gardens of the town. Prisoner identifications also pointed to the presence of the *116th Panzer Division*'s engineer and reconnaissance battalions. Even three dive-bombing missions and an artillery TOT just before a third attack on 15 October failed to turn the trick.[41]

The First Army commander, General Hodges, was audibly perturbed at the slow pace. Indeed, both Generals Corlett and Hobbs considered they were "walking on eggs" in their relations with the army commander. "I always thought you ought to relieve Leland [Hobbs]," General Hodges told Corlett. "He hasn't moved an inch in four days." General Hobbs, Hodges observed, was always "either bragging or complaining." But General Corlett demurred. He could not believe that General Hodges or his staff realized how severe and constant had been the fighting to close the gap. On the other hand, Corlett was the first to admit that something had to be done to get the drive moving. By nightfall on 15 October he had become convinced that the 30th Division could not make it without broadening its effort. Ordering General Hobbs to make a general attack all along the line, General Corlett met every objection by repeating one sentence: "I want to close the (Aachen) gap."[42]

---

[40] A tank company commander, Capt. James M. Burt, did more than his share to alleviate the situation. Though he had two tanks shot from under him and was wounded at the outset on 13 October, Captain Burt personally directed artillery fire from exposed positions, reconnoitered into enemy territory, and rescued several wounded. "Captain Burt held the combined forces together," says his citation for the Medal of Honor, "dominating and controlling the critical situation through the sheer force of his heroic example."

[41] Details of the 116th Infantry attacks are available in regimental journals and AAR's for October 1944; see also Tel Convs in 30th Div G–3 Jnl for the period.

[42] 30th Div G–3 Jnl, 15 Oct 44; XIX Corps G–3 Tel Jnl, 14–16 Oct 44, loaned by General Corlett; Ltr, Corlett to OCMH 20 May 56; Sylvan Diary, entry of 14 Oct 44

General Hobbs nevertheless remained reluctant to order the troops on his east wing to leave prepared positions for exposed ground, capture of which would do little, Hobbs believed, toward closing the Aachen Gap except to provide diversion for the southward drive. Although no additional troops of the *1st SS Panzer Division* had been detected, General Hobbs was concerned about identification of the *3d Panzer Grenadier Division* opposite the VII Corps and about reports that at least another panzer grenadier regiment of the *116th Panzer Division* had arrived. In addition, the XIX Corps G–2 had been predicting cautiously that the *9th Panzer Division,* unidentified for some days on the British front, soon might be committed here. Hobbs insisted that the troops on his east wing should not debouch into the open to face these possibilities; they should make only diversionary demonstrations.

At last General Hobbs wore down his corps commander's objections. Born almost of desperation, a plan for a new link-up attack the next day, 16 October, took form.

Sealing the Gap

Concern on the American side about delay in forging the last arc of the circle about Aachen was matched if not exceeded by anxiety on the German side that the doom of Aachen was near at hand. Late on 15 October, for example, Field Marshal Model at *Army Group B* reiterated that "the situation in Aachen may be considered serious." [43]

43 Rpt, *OB WEST* to *OKW/WFSt* (relaying rpt, *A Gp B*), 1800, 15 Oct 44, *OB WEST KTB, Befehle und Meldungen.*

Among German commanders, the only hope of relieving Aachen rested with the counterattacks by the *3d Panzer Grenadier* and *116th Panzer Divisions.* In reality, this was a fairly vain hope, as demonstrated on 15 October when the *3d Panzer Grenadier Division* failed to break the lines of the 1st Division's 16th Infantry near Verlautenheide and Eilendorf. The Germans might have noted further that even though the entire *116th Panzer Division* had arrived by 15 October, that division had been able to accomplish nothing offensively except for the first commitment of the *60th Panzer Grenadier Regiment* four days earlier. So sure of their position were the Americans that they had delivered a surrender ultimatum to the commander of the Aachen garrison five days before on 10 October and the next day had begun assault against the city itself.

Though not so fatalistic, concern on the American side was just as genuine. General Hobbs had expected to reach the 1st Division and Ravels Hill on 8 October; now, seven days later, a gap of more than a mile still existed. In the last three days the 116th Infantry, in striking what was literally the stone wall of Wuerselen, had gained no more than a thousand yards. Obviously, if contact was to be made, the attackers would have to try some other maneuver.

No matter the earlier objections to driving south along the east bank of the Wurm or to crossing the Wurm and striking south along the west bank, these two routes appeared now to offer the only solutions. General Hobbs chose them both. He ordered Colonel Sutherland's 119th Infantry to send two battalions before daylight on 16 October across the Wurm into the village of Kohlscheid, thence south along the west bank. The remaining battalion was to launch the main effort close along the east bank to seize Hill 194, just across the Aachen–Wuerselen–Linnich highway, northwest of Ravels Hill (Hill 231). The 116th Infantry and a battalion of the 120th Infantry were to renew the frontal assault on Wuerselen, while the separate 99th Infantry Battalion moved from corps reserve to back up the line. General Hobbs's other two regiments, the 117th Infantry and 120th, were to stage diversionary attacks in company strength southeast from Alsdorf on the division's eastern flank. There could be no toleration of halfway measures. This was *it*.

Even as supporting engineers worked under mortar fire to bridge the Wurm, two battalions of Colonel Sutherland's 119th Infantry forded the river at 0500, 16 October. Within half an hour one of the battalions had reached the fringe of Kohlscheid; the other joined the mop-up an hour before daylight. By noon Kohlscheid was clear.

The main effort by Colonel Cox's 2d Battalion, 119th Infantry, along the east bank of the Wurm did not go so easily. Here *SS-Battalion Bucher* of *Kampfgruppe Diefenthal* and a relatively fresh home guard unit, the *2d Landesschuetzen Battalion,* had extended the line southwest from Wuerselen. Fire from pillboxes occupied by these units stalled Colonel Cox's leading platoons short of a hilltop lying about halfway between the line of departure and the objective of Hill 194. The situation was disturbing until a platoon under Sergeant Holycross, who early in the West Wall attack had become something of an expert at reducing pillboxes, managed to slip around to one

flank. Urging both his men and accompanying tanks forward through a driving rain, Sergeant Holycross once more demonstrated how pillboxes should be taken. Pinning the defenders in their shelters with tank fire, he worked his riflemen in close for the assault. Holycross and his men successively reduced seven pillboxes and captured about fifty prisoners.

As Colonel Cox tried to push through a fresh company to continue the drive to Hill 194 and link-up, the Germans took the intermediate hill under such deadly shellfire that hopes for success of the main effort fell. While seeking to avoid the fire, the tanks became stuck in the mud. Without them the infantry could not advance.

At about this same time the first of the diversionary efforts on the 30th Division's east wing began. Mortars and artillery in support of the 117th and 120th Infantry Regiments maintained a smoke screen across the regimental fronts for half an hour, then opened fire to simulate a preparatory barrage. The Germans bit. Enemy artillery shifted from Colonel Cox's battalion west of Wuerselen to pummel the two east wing regiments. The thunder of the German fires awed the most seasoned fighters.

The more guns the Germans turned against men of the 117th and 120th Infantry Regiments, who were relatively secure in foxholes, the less they had to use against the exposed troops of the 119th Infantry. Leaving one company on the intermediate hill as a base of fire, the rest of Colonel Cox's battalion once more shook loose to advance methodically southward toward Hill 194. Since one of the battalions on the west bank of the Wurm had come abreast, Colonel Cox was assisted by fire into the enemy's flank. Though the

116th Infantry's attack at Wuerselen was still a study in frustration in terms of ground gained, it assisted Colonel Cox by tying down that enemy strongpoint.

Lest the Germans fathom the deception on the east and again turn their full wrath against Colonel Cox's battalion, the two east wing regiments in early afternoon launched another diversion. This time a company of each regiment actually attacked along the common regimental boundary to occupy a limited objective. Two platoons of the 120th Infantry gained the objective, though they had to wade through withering fire to make it. Later in the afternoon, as they sought to withdraw, only well-planned covering fires permitted their escape.

The other diversionary attack by Company E, 117th Infantry, met insurmountable difficulties. First the company had to pass through 500 yards of woods, thick with enemy outposts, before reaching main German positions astride a slag pile and a railroad embankment. Here sat the second of the *116th Panzer Division's* panzer grenadier regiments, the *156th*.

Although devastating fire from automatic weapons drove back one of Company E's attacking platoons, the other struggled on almost to the railroad embankment. Then the panzer grenadiers emerged from a mine shaft in rear of the platoon. Only six of the Americans ever made their way back.

Reorganizing those of his men who had withdrawn, the company commander, Capt. George H. Sibbald, inched forward in an effort to rescue his surrounded platoon. For more than an hour he and his men fought doggedly through a hail of small arms and shellfire. They still were straining forward when word came that the diversionary thrust had done the job expected of it. Captain Sibbald made a last attempt to reach the surrounded platoon but failed. Reluctantly, he gave the order to withdraw.

Though Company E had lost about fifty men, the diversion had, indeed, helped accomplish the main objective. At 1544 on 16 October, the 1st Division's chief of staff had telephoned to say that men of his 18th Infantry on Ravels Hill could see American troops along the southwestern fringe of Wuerselen. They were men of Colonel Cox's 2d Battalion who had reached their objective, Hill 194. They were less than a thousand yards from the closest foxholes of the 18th Infantry.

Led by S. Sgt. Frank A. Karwell, a patrol left Hill 194 to make the actual physical contact, so long awaited. En route, German fire cut down Sergeant Karwell and prevented the main body of the patrol from crossing the Aachen–Wuerselen highway. Yet the two scouts, Pvts. Edward Krauss and Evan Whitis, continued. As they started up Ravels Hill, they made out figures in American uniforms.

"We're from K Company," the men on the hill shouted. "Come on up."

"We're from F Company," Whitis and Krauss replied. "Come on down."

The men from the 1st Division talked faster and more persuasively. Whitis and Krauss went up. At 1615, 16 October, they closed the Aachen Gap.

CHAPTER XIII

Assault on the City

When the Aachen encirclement maneuver began on 8 October, the city that was the ultimate objective was already a scarred shell. Less than 20,000 of Aachen's prewar population of some 165,000 had clung to their homes through the various vicissitudes of Nazi evacuation orders. As early as two months before D-Day in Normandy, the British had bombed the city; in late May British planes had struck again and again for three days at what was left. By 8 October much of Aachen already was a sterile sea of rubble. Long before American tanks first had poked their snouts over nearby hills in mid-September, Aachen had learned what war is like.[1]

Few in Aachen could have doubted that the end was near when on 10 October three Americans—1st Lt. Cedric A. Lafley, 1st Lt. William Boehme, and Pfc. Ken Kading—approached along the Trierer Strasse bearing a white flag and a surrender ultimatum. As most were to learn from listening to Radio Luxembourg or to American public address systems, or else from examining leaflets which American artillery shot into the ruins, the Americans were granting the commander of the Aachen military garrison twenty-four hours in which to surrender.

The city of Aachen [the ultimatum stated in part] is now completely surrounded by American forces . . . . If the city is not promptly and completely surrendered unconditionally, the American Army Ground and Air Forces will proceed ruthlessly with air and artillery bombardment to reduce it to submission.[2]

The military commander of Aachen at the time of delivery of the surrender ultimatum was Colonel Leyherr, one of the *246th Division*'s regimental commanders. Colonel Leyherr dutifully rejected the ultimatum in accord with "last stand" orders that had come from the Jovian pen of Hitler himself.

Two days later Colonel Leyherr was relieved in deference to the arrival of his division commander, Colonel Wilck (*246th Division*). Colonel Wilck established his headquarters in the Palast-Hotel Quellenhof, a luxurious *Kurhotel* in Farwick Park in the northern portion of the city. (*See Map 4.*)

For bringing Aachen to heel, the attack force available to General Huebner, the American commander, was numerically inferior to that Colonel Wilck had for defense. Forced to dispose the bulk of the 1st Division elsewhere on an elongated front and to husband one infantry battalion as a reserve, General Huebner had but two battalions of the 26th Infantry

---

[1] See U.S. Military Government files on Aachen and Condron, The Fall of Aachen. Unless otherwise noted, this chapter is based upon official records of the 1st Div (in particular, the 26th Inf), the VII Corps, and the 1106th Engr (C) Gp, plus 1st Div Combat Intervs and FUSA AAR, Oct 44.

[2] For a full text of the ultimatum and an account of the experiences of those who delivered it, see 1st Div G–3 Per Rpt, 10 Oct 44.

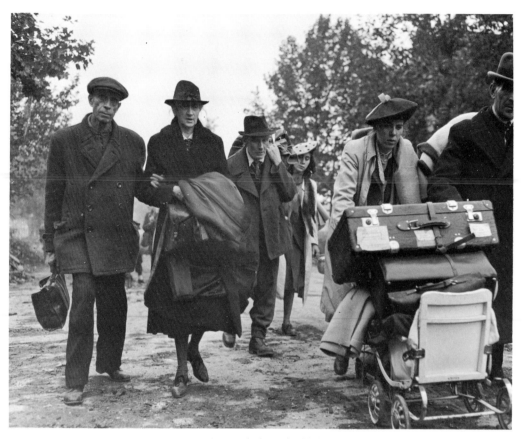

CIVILIAN REFUGEES LEAVE AACHEN

free to assault the city. Within the inner defenses of Aachen, Colonel Wilck had roughly 5,000 men. Most were from Wilck's own *246th Division,* though some represented nondescript fortress units and 125 were Aachen policemen thrust into the line under command of the chief of police. Some eighty policemen from Cologne were later to slip through the gap at Wuerselen to join the fight.

As Colonel Wilck must have known, the great American superiority was in armor, artillery, and planes. Although the Luftwaffe had begun to display recognition that a war still went on in the West, the German planes usually appeared only in small groups and at night when Allied aircraft were not around. As for armor, Colonel Wilck had no more than about five Mark IV tanks. As long as communications remained constant, Colonel Wilck might solicit substantial artillery support from outside the city; but at hand within the inner defenses were only 19 105-mm. howitzers, 8 75-mm. pieces, and 6 150-mm. guns.

On the American side, General Huebner naturally desired quick reduction of Aachen, yet he saw no point in a Pyrrhic victory. Even had he desired a bold thrust, he could permit only a cautious advance because the gap at Wuerselen still was open and from Stolberg to Ravels Hill his defenses were dangerously thin. He told the 26th Infantry commander, Col. John F. R. Seitz, not to get inextricably involved in Aachen. The regiment would have to attack, as the 26th Infantry S-3 put it, "with one eye cocked over their right shoulder." Yet in striking from the east defenses that until recently had been sited against assault from the west and south, the regiment held a distinct advantage.

During the two days when the 18th Infantry was driving north through Verlautenheide to Ravels Hill, the 26th Infantry had been eating away at Aachen's eastern suburb of Rothe Erde and otherwise getting into position for assault on the city. To reduce his frontage, Colonel Seitz put a provisional company into the line on his left wing to face Aachen from the southeast. This company tied in with defenses of the 1106th Engineers south of the city. Although the engineers were to pivot their right wing from time to time in order to maintain contact as the 26th Infantry advanced into the city, they were not equipped to make a full-blooded attack.

Colonel Seitz pressed his 2d Battalion under Lt. Col. Derrill M. Daniel up to the Aachen–Cologne railroad tracks at Rothe Erde and prepared to send the battalion westward through the heart of Aachen. His remaining battalion, the 3d, under Lt. Col. John T. Corley, moved to jump-off positions north of Rothe Erde (between Rothe Erde and Haaren). From there Colonel Corley was to strike northwestward against a wilderness of factories lying between Aachen proper and Haaren and thence westward to seize

three hills that dominate Aachen from the city's northern fringes.

The bulk of this hill mass, developed as a big public park, is known as the Lousberg. It rises to a height of 862 feet and casts a shadow over almost the entire city. The Americans were to know it as Observatory Hill after an observation tower on the crest. A lower knob on the southeastern slopes of the hill, crowned by a cathedral, is known as the Salvatorberg. Farther down the southeastern slopes in Farwick Park stands the elaborate Palast-Hotel Quellenhof and a municipal *Kurhaus* where, in happier days, patrons took the medicinal waters.

The Assault Begins

Soon after the surrender deadline expired on 11 October, four groups of IX Tactical Air Command P–38's and P–47's (about 300 planes) opened the assault. On targets primarily on the perimeter of the city, selected by the infantry and marked with red smoke by the artillery, the planes loosed more than sixty-two tons of bombs. In a deafening cacophony, twelve battalions of VII Corps and 1st Division artillery took up the bombardment. Division artillery hurled some 2,500 rounds into the city while corps artillery contributed 2,371 rounds, a total of 169 tons. Though both air and ground observers deemed the bombing and shelling accurate, patrols that tested the defenses in early evening found no appreciable lessening of German fire.[3]

_____

[3] In the light of cover available to the Germans in thick-walled building and cellars, seasoned observers hardly could have hoped for much more than a psychological effect from the bombardment. Airmen subsequently were to note "that the final capture of Aachen . . . was not materially speeded by bombing . . . ." See

After daylight the next morning, 12 October, three groups of fighter-bombers returned to drop ninety-nine tons of bombs. Thereafter Aachen became a secondary target. Except on the third day (13 October) when two groups dropped eleven and a half tons of bombs, airmen made no other sizable contribution to the assault. Artillery likewise resumed the attack on 12 October. Corps and division artillery expended 5,000 rounds on that date.[4]

Even as the air and artillery bombardment continued on 12 October, Colonel Corley's 3d Battalion, 26th Infantry, attacked to clear the factories lying between Aachen and Haaren, a preliminary to the main attack set to begin the next day. Despite the urban nature of the battlefield, the battalion methodically cleared the objective and by nightfall was poised for the main assault. Early on 13 October Colonel Corley's battalion was to push northwest toward Observatory Hill while Colonel Daniel's 2d Battalion began a painstaking sweep through the heart of the city.

In moving through the center of Aachen, Colonel Daniel's men not only

Hq, USAF in Europe, The Contribution of Air Power to the Defeat of Germany, Vol. 2, Western Front Campaign, p. 170.

[4] Not to be excluded from the bombardment, the 1106th Engineer Combat Group in defensive positions astride the heights south of Aachen rigged an ingenious device which the men dubbed the V–13. Towing an Aachen streetcar to the crest of a hill, they stacked the car with captured explosives set with a time fuse and sent it careening down the trolley tracks into the city. On the first try, the car exploded prematurely. A second ground to a halt at the wreckage of the first. After patrols had cleared the track, the engineers tried again. This time the car reached the city proper before it exploded. Whether it did any actual damage to German installations was irrelevant in view of the impish delight the engineers derived from it.

had to plow through the maze of rubble and damaged buildings in their path but also to maintain contact with Colonel Corley's main effort against the northern hills. His left (south) flank resting on the railroad, Colonel Daniel had an attack frontage of about 2,000 yards, no minor assignment in view of the density of the buildings. Of necessity, his advance would be slow and plodding.

The fighting in Colonel Daniel's sector quickly fell into a pattern. Dividing his resources into small assault teams, Colonel Daniel sent with each infantry platoon a tank or tank destroyer. These would keep each building under fire until the riflemen moved in to assault; thereupon, the armor would shift fire to the next house. Augmented by the battalion's light and heavy machine guns firing up the streets, this shelling usually drove the Germans into the cellars where the infantry stormed them behind a barrage of hand grenades. Whenever the enemy proved particularly tenacious, the riflemen used the other weapons at their disposal, including demolitions and flame throwers employed by two-man teams attached to each company headquarters. The men did not wait for actual targets to appear; each building, they assumed, was a nest of resistance until proved otherwise. Light artillery and mortar fire swept forward block by block several streets ahead of the infantry while heavier artillery pounded German communications farther to the rear.

To maintain contact between units, Colonel Daniel each day designated a series of check points based on street intersections and more prominent buildings. No unit advanced beyond a check point until after establishing contact with the adjacent unit. Each rifle company was

RIFLEMAN *in burning Aachen.*

assigned a specific zone of advance; company commanders in turn generally designated a street to each platoon.

After a few bitter experiences in which Germans bypassed in cellars or storm sewers emerged in rear of the attackers, the riflemen soon learned that speed was less important than pertinacity. The sewers posed a special problem; each manhole had to be located and thoroughly blocked and covered. Another special problem stemmed from glass and other litter that punctured tires on jeeps used for evacuating wounded. Medics found a solution in weasels (M–29), tracked, lightly armored cargo carriers.

In the other half of the attack, Colonel Corley's battalion, which was driving west toward the high ground marked by the Lousberg (Observatory Hill), the Salvatorberg, and Farwick Park, found the route blocked on the first day, 13 October, by stoutly defended apartment houses. The men measured their gains in buildings, floors, and even rooms. Someone said the fight was "from attic to attic and from sewer to sewer."

As riflemen of Company K advanced down Juelicher Strasse, 20-mm. cannon fire from a side street drove them back. Two accompanying tanks remained exposed to lethal panzerfausts. The Germans quickly knocked them out. One went up in flames. Disregarding enemy fire, a Company K squad leader, Sgt. Alvin R. Wise, rushed to the other tank to evacuate the wounded crew. The tank, he decided, might be recovered. Climbing inside, he began to spray adjacent German-held buildings with fire from the tank's machine guns. Under this covering fire, two privates from Sergeant Wise's squad joined him in the tank. Though none of the three ever had been inside a tank before, they somehow managed to start the motor, turn the tank around, and drive it down the street to safety.[5]

Having discovered on the first day that some apartment buildings and air-raid shelters could withstand the fire of tanks and tank destroyers, Colonel Corley called for a self-propelled 155-mm. rifle. Early the next morning the big weapon proved its worth in the first test when with one shot it practically leveled one of the sturdy buildings. Impressed, the regimental commander, Colonel Seitz, sent one of the big rifles to support his other battalion as well.[6]

By nightfall of the first day Colonel Corley's battalion had reached the base of the high ground. Early on 14 October, when two companies combined to overrun a strongpoint at St. Elizabeth's Church, the momentum of the attack carried one of the companies a few hundred yards past the church and into Farwick Park, the big park surrounding the *Kurhaus* and Palast-Hotel Quellenhof. Yet this company's hold was tenuous at best, for the rest of the battalion still was occupied in the buildings on the approaches to the

park. The Germans still held the buildings in Farwick Park: the hotel, the *Kurhaus,* a greenhouse (*Orangerie*), and several gardening buildings.

As early as 13 October, the drive toward the high ground had prompted the enemy commander, Colonel Wilck, to appeal for reinforcements. By nightfall, in response to this plea, the Germans on Observatory Hill were strengthened with about 150 men who were all that remained of Wilck's own *404th Regiment.* Although *Kampfgruppe Diefenthal's SS-Battalion Rink* also tried to reach the hill, that battalion was sidetracked by one of the 30th Division's attacks near Wuerselen. Colonel Wilck radioed his corps commander, in what was apparently a gross exaggeration, that American tanks had surrounded his command post in Hotel Quellenhof.

In response to this startling message, the corps commander, General Koechling, tried throughout 14 October to disengage *SS-Battalion Rink,* reinforce the SS troops with a convoy of assault guns, and send them to Wilck's relief. Eight assault guns made it by early evening of 14 October, but not until the next day was *SS-Battalion Rink* to arrive. In the meantime Colone Wilck apparently had moved his command post to some other structure less immediately threatened.[7]

For his part, Colonel Corley renewed the attack in Farwick Park early on 15 October with the assistance of close support from attached chemical mortars. By midday his men had wrested the gardening buildings, the greenhouse, and the *Kurhaus* from the Germans, but the enemy would not budge from behind the

---

[5] Sergeant Wise was awarded the DSC.
[6] These guns were from Btry C, 991st FA Bn.

[7] Unless otherwise noted, German material is from *LXXXI Corps, Kampf um Aachen.*

sturdy walls of Hotel Quellenhof. Colonel Corley was sending forward his 155-mm. rifle to blast the building and readying his reserve company to flank it when the Germans launched a sharp counterattack.

In strength of about one battalion, the counterattacking force apparently included remnants of both the *404th Regiment* and *SS-Battalion Rink*. For about an hour the American company on the north edge of Farwick Park parried the blows, but at last the company had to fall back. Supported by assault guns, the Germans swept southward to hit the next company. Although forced to relinquish the *Kurhaus*, the company held fast in the park surrounding it. Refusing to leave his post, a mortar observer called down shellfire on his own position. By 1700 the sting was gone from the German drive. Colonel Corley could report that his men not only would hold their own but soon would resume the advance.

The battalion did hold, but in light of the bludgeoning blows which the *3d Panzer Grenadier Division* had begun to direct against the 16th Infantry's linear defense near Eilendorf, General Huebner directed postponement of further offensive moves in Aachen. He told Colonel Seitz to hold in place until the situation along the division's east wing could be stabilized.

Only for a day was it necessary for the two battalions in Aachen to desist from attack. By 16 October the 16th Infantry had repulsed the best the *3d Panzer Grenadier Division* could offer. The long-awaited juncture between 1st and 30th Division troops to close the Wuerselen gap in the Aachen encirclement further allayed General Huebner's concern. Yet General Huebner still was to hold the

26th Infantry in check for another day while awaiting arrival of reinforcements promised for the final blow against Aachen by the corps commander, General Collins.

Holding the Last Link

In the meantime troops of both the 1st and 30th Divisions in the vicinity of Ravels Hill and Wuerselen fought to make a firm link from the tenuous patrol contact which Privates Whitis and Krauss had established between the two divisions late on 16 October. To prove their accomplishment no fluke, Whitis and Krauss led a patrol from the 18th Infantry to 30th Division positions on Hill 194 that night; yet German attempts to reopen a route into Aachen would deny genuine adhesion in the last link of the Aachen circle for several days. A company of the separate 99th Infantry Battalion (attached to the 116th Infantry) discovered this fact early when German forays during the night of 16 October seriously contested a roadblock which the infantry company established across the Aachen–Wuerselen highway.[8] It was obvious that so long as the enemy's *3d Panzer Grenadier* and *116th Panzer Divisions* remained in this sector, a major counterattack to break the encirclement was a logical expectation. The XIX Corps G–2 fed the apprehension by continuing to express concern over the whereabouts of the *9th Panzer Division*.

The Germans for their part recognized that unless the *3d Panzer Grenadier* and *116th Panzer Divisions* could break the encirclement soon, Aachen was lost. Cries of anguish from Colonel Wilck about the

---

[8] See 99th Inf Bn AAR, Oct 44; 30th Div Combat Intervs for the period.

weakness of his encircled forces heightened this concern. As commanders outside the city prepared a counterattack, the Commander in Chief West, Rundstedt, found it necessary to "remind the Commander of *246th Volks Grenadier Division* [Wilck] once more, and with the utmost emphasis, that [in accordance with Hitler's order] he will hold this venerable German city to the last man, and will, if necessary, allow himself to be buried under its ruins." [9]

This—or surrender—was the only fate left to Colonel Wilck. Attempts by the *3d Panzer Grenadier* and *116th Panzer Divisions* to break the encirclement on both 18 and 19 October again lacked co-ordination. Though some serious fighting occurred in the vicinity of Ravels Hill where the *3d Panzer Grenadier Division* struck the 18th Infantry, no genuine likelihood of a breakthrough developed.[10] An attempt by the Aachen garrison to complement these attacks from inside the circle got no place. By nightfall of 19 October the German commanders had decided to abandon the defenders of Aachen to their fate. Headquarters of the *I SS Panzer Corps* was relieved; the *3d Panzer Grenadier Division* (reduced to half its original combat strength) prepared to pull out; and the *LXXXI Corps* resumed command of the entire sector.[11]

---

[9] TWX, *OB WEST* to *Army Group B*, 2215, 18 Oct 44, *OB WEST KTB, Befehle und Meldungen.*

[10] During a counterattack against Ravels Hill on 18 October, an 18th Infantry sergeant, Max Thompson, played the role of a one-man army. Seeing that the Germans had overrun a neighboring platoon, Sergeant Thompson used successively a machine gun, bazooka, automatic rifle, and hand grenades to halt the attack. He received the Medal of Honor.

[11] *OB WEST KTB,* 20 Oct 44.

The Final Blow

From the time Privates Whitis and Krauss first closed the Aachen Gap late on 16 October, even the most fanatic of German defenders inside the city must have seen the end toward which they were headed. On that day Colonel Wilck had a total of 4,392 "combat effectives," plus 11 surgeons and 34 medics.[12]

As a result of a decision by the U.S. corps commander, General Collins, American strength in Aachen increased in a ratio greater than the decrease in German strength. General Collins had decided to reinforce the two battalions of the 26th Infantry with the two battalions of tanks and armored infantry of the 3d Armored Division that had been alerted to counterattack any penetration near Eilendorf but had not been needed there. Labeled Task Force Hogan, these two units were to join the fight on the north flank of Colonel Corley's battalion to fling a right hook against the Lousberg. The armor also was to occupy the village of Laurensberg, two miles northwest of Aachen, key to that part of the West Wall which remnants of the *49th Division* still held north and northwest of the city. As an additional reinforcement, General Collins, through the auspices of the First Army, attached to the 1st Division a battalion of the 110th Infantry, brought north from Camp d'Elsenborn in the V Corps sector where the 28th Division was holding a relatively inactive front. General Huebner was to use this battalion only in a defensive role, to cover a growing gap between Colonel Daniel's battalion of the 26th Infantry in Aachen and the 1106th

---

[12] For a detailed breakdown of units, see Heichler, The Fall of Aachen.

Engineers south of the city.[13] On 18 October as these new units moved into position, General Huebner authorized the 26th Infantry to renew the assault.

In Farwick Park, Colonel Corley's battalion set out to regain the ground lost there three days before, pass on to the Salvatorberg, and assist Task Force Hogan's drive on the Lousberg. One platoon rapidly recaptured the *Kurhaus*. While the enemy cowered in the basement of Hotel Quellenhof to escape American shelling, another platoon under 2d Lt. William D. Ratchford stormed into the hotel lobby. Hand grenade duels developed at every entrance to the basement. By the time Lieutenant Ratchford had procured machine guns to fire into the basement, the Germans had had enough. Twenty-five of the enemy had died in the fighting. A search of the hotel revealed large caches of food and ammunition and on the second floor a 20-mm. antiaircraft gun which the Germans had carted upstairs piece by piece, reassembled, and sited to fire into the park.

Farwick Park and its buildings firmly in hand and Colonel Daniel's battalion continuing a methodical advance through the center of Aachen, fall of the city now could be only a question of time. The next day (19 October) Colonel Corley's men seized the Salvatorberg against a modicum of resistance. At the same time Task Force Hogan was overrunning the awe-inspiring but ineffectively defended heights of the Lousberg. Because 30th Division troops already had occupied the village of Laurensberg, General Huebner changed the task force's second mission to cutting the Aachen–Laurens-

berg highway a short distance south of the village. By nightfall of 19 October, a part of the task force had occupied a chateau within 200 yards of this highway. In the chateau the men found stacks of ammunition of various types and, to their chagrin, whiskey bottles—all empty—scattered about the grounds.[14]

Reduction of the Salvatorberg and the Lousberg coincided with the enemy decision to abandon attempts to break the encirclement of Aachen. Within the city, Colonel Wilck during the afternoon of 19 October issued an order of the day:

The defenders of Aachen will prepare for their last battle. Constricted to the smallest possible space, we shall fight to the last man, the last shell, the last bullet, in accordance with the Fuehrer's orders.

In the face of the contemptible, despicable treason committed by certain individuals, I expect each and every defender of the venerable Imperial City of Aachen to do his duty to the end, in fulfillment of our Oath to the Flag. I expect courage and determination to hold out.

Long live the Fuehrer and our beloved Fatherland![15]

Exhortations actually would do little to forestall the end. On 19 and 20 October resistance rapidly crumbled. Even though the battalion of the 110th Infantry was committed officially only to a defensive role, that unit joined Colonel Daniel's battalion in eviscerating the city. Already Colonel Daniel's men had seized the main railroad station and were nearing a railway line leading north to Laurensberg and Geilenkirchen and separating the main part of Aachen from western resi-

---

[13] VII Corps Opns Memo 107, 18 Oct, VII Corps Opns Memo file, Oct 44. This confirms oral orders issued the day before.

[14] A detailed account of Task Force Hogan's role in the battle of Aachen may be found in 1st Division Combat Interview file, October 1944.

[15] TWX, *OB WEST* to *OKW/WFSt,* 1740, 20 Oct 44, *OB WEST KTB, Befehle und Meldungen.*

dential sectors. After collapse of a strong-point in the Technical University in the northwestern corner of the city, the battalion reached the western railroad tracks as night came on 20 October. The few Germans remaining were cor-ralled in the western and southwestern suburbs.

On 21 October, Colonel Corley's bat-talion approached a big air-raid bunker at the northern end of Lousberg Strasse. Colonel Corley called for his attached 155-mm. rifle. To the attackers, this was just another building that had to be reduced. They had no way of knowing that here was the cerebellum of the Aachen defense, the headquarters of Colo-nel Wilck.

From this bunker, Colonel Wilck and his staff had been exercising their pen-chant for the melodramatic. "All forces are committed in the final struggle!" "Confined to the smallest area, the last defenders of Aachen are embroiled in their final battle!" "The last defenders of Aachen, mindful of their beloved German homeland, with firm confidence in our final victory, donate Reichsmark 10,468.00 to the *Winterhilfswerk* [Winter Relief] Project. We shall fight on. Long live the Fuehrer!" Such was the tenor of Colonel Wilck's last messages to his su-periors on the outside.

As Colonel Corley called for his 155-mm. rifle, Colonel Wilck, despite his exhortations, was ready to end the fight. But how to surrender? Two Germans who had tried to leave the bunker under a white flag had been shot down in the confusion of the battle.

The solution appeared to lie among some thirty American prisoners the Ger-mans were holding. From the prisoners they solicited volunteers to arrange the surrender. Two men from the 1106th Engineers who had been captured early in the Aachen fighting responded. They were S. Sgt. Ewart M. Padgett and Pfc. James B. Haswell.

While Colonel Wilck by radio renewed his "unshakable faith in our right and our victory" and again paid obeisance to the Fuehrer, Haswell and Padgett stepped from the bunker. Small arms fire cracked about them. Bearing a white flag, the two men dashed into the middle of Lous-berg Strasse. As they waved the flag frantically, the firing died down. An American rifleman leaned from a nearby window to motion the two men forward. Sergeant Padgett beckoned to two Ger-man officers behind him to follow.

A company commander returned with Haswell, Padgett, and the Germans. Their luggage already packed, Colonel Wilck and his coterie were ready to depart. Before they left, Sergeant Pad-gett nabbed the prize souvenir of the occasion, the colonel's pistol.[16]

At Colonel Corley's headquarters, the assistant division commander, Brig. Gen. George A. Taylor, accepted the German surrender. At 1205 on 21 October, it was over.[17] Because Colonel Wilck's in-ternal communications had broken down, he had definite knowledge of the where-abouts of only some 500 of his soldiers. By nightfall, as American troops swept to every corner of the city, they had rounded up some 1,600 men, among them a bat-talion adjutant to whom Lieutenants

---

[16] Sergeant Padgett has provided a lucid account of his experiences. FUSA G–2 Per Rpt 154, 11 Nov 44, copy in 1st Div Combat Interv file.

[17] The German radio operator sent a final homespun message at 1238: "We now sign off, with regards to our buddies and the folks back home."

COLONEL WILCK *and his headquarters group after their surrender.*

Lafley and Boehme had delivered the surrender ultimatum eleven days earlier.

What Aachen Cost

The battle of Aachen was over. Though the Germans had failed to prevent encirclement and had held out within the city only five days after encirclement, the true measure of the battle from their standpoint was that they had imposed a telling, though costly, delay. The 30th Division listed 6,000 prisoners and the 1st Division another 5,637, including 3,473 taken within the city.[18] The way in which German units were squandered without major reward was indicated by the fact that an equivalent of twenty battalions had been used in counterattack roles against the 30th Division, yet in only one or two cases had any counterattack involved more than two reinforced infantry battalions. A never-ending compulsion to stave off recurring crises had sucked the enemy's units into the abyss of piecemeal commitment.

[18] The Germans admitted but 5,100 casualties of all types.

On the American side, the 30th Division and attached troops, since the start of the West Wall campaign on 2 October, had lost some 3,000 men. Indicative of 1st Division casualties was a figure of 498 incurred by the two battalions of the 26th Infantry. Of these, 75 were killed and 9 missing.[19]

A paradox of the battle, particularly in the sector of the 30th Division, was that it had involved primarily infantry units, yet it had assumed the complexion of an armored duel. Both sides had tank support, and few units, German or American, had experienced much success unless supporting tanks were on hand. By their own count, the Germans lost 45 tanks.[20] In one two-day period (9–10 October) the 30th Division claimed 20 German tanks: 12 destroyed by 105-mm. howitzers, 5 by supporting tanks and tank destroyers, and 3 by bazookas.

By way of an apologia for failure at Aachen, the Germans pointed to unchallenged American air superiority and to the ratio between American and German artillery in the Aachen sector. They estimated American batteries at 86 and reported opposing German batteries at 69. The average daily expenditure of rounds by U.S. artillery, they estimated, was 9,300; by German artillery, 4,500.[21]

AACHEN MUNSTER, *popularly known as the Charlemagne Cathedral.*

The estimate of American batteries was no more than a slight exaggeration. Counting regimental cannon companies, organic artillery of the 1st and 30th Divisions totaled 30 batteries. Exclusive of tank and tank destroyer pieces, the two divisions possessed 11 batteries of attached artillery. The two corps (VII and XIX) had at least 33 more batteries under direct corps control. Not counting artillery under control either of the First Army or of adjacent divisions, the Americans had a minimum of 74 batteries capable of firing upon Aachen and its environs.[22]

On 19 October the Germans fired leaflets into the 30th Division's zone. "The Ninth Army under General Simpson," the leaflets read, "[is] to relieve

---

[19] The Germans estimated total American losses at 13,320.

[20] The 30th Division alone claimed to have destroyed 70.

[21] *LXXXI Corps, Art.–Lage u. Art.–Gliederungen,* 11 Oct–18 Dec 44. On 17 October the Germans had narrowed the *LXXXI Corps* sector by inserting the *XII SS Corps* north of the *LXXXI Corps,* establishing the boundary between the *49th* and *183d Divisions* as the new corps boundary. Artillery in the *XII SS Corps* was not included in the estimate of batteries in the Aachen sector.

[22] Arty AARs of VII and XIX Corps, 1st and 30th Divs, Oct 44.

VIEW OF RUINED AACHEN

you on the 20th and 21st of October." The Germans were only one day off. At noon on 22 October, General Simpson's Ninth Army headquarters moved from Luxembourg to assume control of the XIX Corps. The boundary between the First and Ninth Armies was to follow the existing boundary between the VII and XIX Corps.

As the XIX Corps had fought its last fight under the aegis of the First Army, so had the corps commander, General Corlett, fought his last fight with the XIX Corps. His health already severely strained during previous combat service

in the Pacific, General Corlett had for the last few months found the rigor of his duties increasingly trying. On 18 October General Bradley relieved him of his command; shortly thereafter, General Corlett left for the United States on recuperation leave. He departed with the understanding that General Eisenhower wanted him to return to the theater when he was physically able.[23]

---

[23] Critics of General Corlett's West Wall campaign have intimated that he was relieved because General Hodges was dissatisfied with methods of the XIX Corps in sealing the Aachen Gap. See XIX Corps Combat Intervs, Oct 44.

General Corlett's successor was a former artillery commander of the 30th Division, Maj. Gen. Raymond S. McLain. General McLain had begun his army career when he enlisted in the Oklahoma National Guard. During the months preceding his assumption of command of the XIX Corps, he had made an enviable record as commander of the Third Army's 90th Division.[24]

If this was the case, it was diametrically opposite to General Eisenhower's view as expressed in a letter to the Chief of Staff, General Marshall, dated 20 October 1944. Eisenhower wrote that he was relieving Corlett to send him home for sixty days "for physical check-up and rest. He has performed most effectively throughout the campaign . . . . I should like for him to get a chance for real recreation and then return here sometime within the allotted period. I regard him as an outstanding corps commander." Eisenhower to Marshall, S–63258, Pogue files. See also, Corlett to OCMH, 2 Sep 53, and 20 May 56.

[24] In World War I, General McLain commanded a machine gun company in the Champagne and Meuse-Argonne Campaigns. In World War II, his early combat experience was as artillery commander with the 45th Division in Sicily. In July 1944, after the 90th Division had proved a disappointment in its first combat (see [Roland G. Ruppenthal] *Utah Beach to Cherbourg,* Washington, 1947, and Blumenson, *Breakout and Pursuit*), General McLain had assumed command of that division.

As the fighting died in Aachen, the German commander, Schwerin, who in September had tried to spare the city, would have been horrified to see that once-proud coronation capital. "The city is as dead as a Roman ruin," wrote an American observer, "but unlike a ruin it has none of the grace of gradual decay . . . . Burst sewers, broken gas mains and dead animals have raised an almost overpowering smell in many parts of the city. The streets are paved with shattered glass; telephone, electric light and trolley cables are dangling and netted together everywhere, and in many places wrecked cars, trucks, armored vehicles and guns litter the streets . . . ."[25]

The ironic truth of a prophecy which Hitler had made early in his career was nowhere more evident than on 21 October 1944 in Aachen, the first large German city lost in the war:

> *Give me five years and you will not recognize Germany again.*
>
> — ADOLF HITLER

[25] City of Aachen, Annex 3 to VII Corps G–2 Per Rpt 138, 21 Oct, VII Corps G–3 Jnl file, 21–22 Oct 44.

PART FOUR

The Roer River Dams

CHAPTER XIV

The First Attack on Schmidt

Looking east from the little German border villages southeast of Aachen, the Huertgen Forest is a seemingly impenetrable mass, a vast, undulating, blackish-green ocean stretching as far as the eye can see. Upon entering the forest, you want to drop things behind to mark your path, as Hansel and Gretel did with their bread crumbs.

By the end of September 1944 the 60th Infantry of General Craig's 9th Division already had tested the forest, encountered small but resolute German units, and drawn back bloodied. Seeking to pass directly through the woods to capture the Huertgen–Kleinhau road net along ridge-top clearings that characterize the eastern half of the forest, one regiment had proved no match for an enemy utilizing the defensive potentialities of the forest to advantage. Even an attempt to gain a compromise objective had failed. This was the try at turning south through Deadman's Moor (the *Todten Bruch*) to link with another regiment which had stalled half in, half out, of the West Wall in the Monschau Corridor. (*See Map III.*)

As October opened and First Army's General Hodges prepared to clear up unfinished business before renewing a general offensive, the Huertgen Forest still stood unconquered athwart the path to the Roer River of the right wing of General Collins' VII Corps. It could not be wished away. To General Collins, who

had served in the Meuse-Argonne campaign of World War I, the Huertgen Forest was a logical spot for concealed assembly and counterattack into the right flank of the VII Corps, much as the Argonne Forest had posed a threat to the American left flank twenty-six years before.[1] As had American commanders in the Argonne in October 1918, those in October 1944 believed they might neutralize the forest facing them by seizing heights along the eastern edge.

Beyond this negative factor of neutralizing the forest against enemy concentration, the prospect of conquering the forest posed several positive advantages. Most of these centered about the crossroads village of Schmidt, which sits astride one of the highest ridge tops west of the Roer in a clearing on the southeastern fringe of the forest. En route to Schmidt, an attacker might pave the way for subsequent capture of the Huertgen–Kleinhau road net leading northeast to Dueren by occupying the villages of Germeter and Vossenack. From Vossenack, a move two miles to the southeast across the deep gorge of the little Kall River leads to Schmidt. Occupying this crossroads village would expose from the rear the stubborn pillbox defenses in the Monschau Corridor that had halted the extreme right wing of the VII Corps in September. With both Schmidt and the Monschau

---

[1] See Interv with Collins, 25 Jan 54.

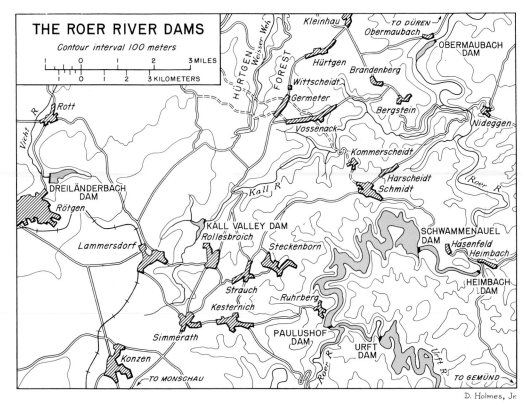

MAP 5

D. Holmes, Jr.

Corridor in hand, the VII Corps might peg its right flank firmly along the upper reaches of the Roer from Schmidt to the headwaters at Monschau. Another part of the front would have been put in order in preparation for the main drive across the Roer to the Rhine.

Having cut the 9th Division's frontage in half since the mid-September fighting, General Collins told General Craig to regroup the division for a stronger attempt to penetrate the forest. The objective he assigned was Schmidt.[2]

---

[2] VII Corps Opns Memo 101, 1 Oct, confirming oral orders of 30 Sep, VII Corps Opns Memo file, Oct 44.

The Neglected Objective

As the 9th Division in early October prepared to attack, few within the American command appeared to appreciate the critical importance of another objective which capture of Schmidt might expose. This was a multiple objective, a series of seven dams near the headwaters of the Roer. Though three of the seven are on tributaries of the Roer, all came to be known collectively as the Roer River Dams. (*Map 5*)

The two principal dams are the Urft and the Schwammenauel. Constructed just after the turn of the century on the Urft River between Gemuend and Ruhr-

SCHWAMMENAUEL DAM

berg, the Urft Dam is capable of im-
pounding approximately 42,000 acre-feet
of water. Built in the mid-thirties near
Hasenfeld, about two miles downhill from
Schmidt, the Schwammenauel Dam creates a reservoir encompassing about
81,000 acre-feet. The Schwammenauel is
of earth construction with a concrete
core. Both the principal dams were designed for controlling the Roer River and
providing hydroelectric power for Dueren
and other cities downstream to the north.[3]

Lesser dams downstream from the
Schwammenauel are at Heimbach and
Obermaubach. These were designed primarily to create equalizing basins in
accordance with industrial needs farther
downstream. Of the other three dams,
the Paulushof, near the confluence of the
Roer and the Urft at Ruhrberg, was
designed primarily to regulate water levels
at the headwaters of the Schwammenauel
reservoir; the Kall Valley Dam, on the
upper reaches of the Kall River near
Lammersdorf, has only a small capacity;
and the Dreilaenderbach Dam creates the
Hauptbecken Reservoir near Roetgen on
the headwaters of the Vicht River. The

[3] A theory prevalent among Americans that
the Schwammenauel Dam was constructed with
an eye toward augmenting the West Wall defenses cannot be supported.

Dreilaenderbach Dam was in American hands before the 9th Division's October attack.[4]

Value of the Roer River Dams to German defense was outlined several days before the 9th Division's October attack by the division G–2, Maj. Jack A. Houston. "Bank overflows and destructive flood waves," Major Houston concluded, "can be produced [on the Roer River] by regulating the discharge from the various dams. By demolition of some of them great destructive waves can be produced which would destroy everything in the populated industrial valley [of the Roer] as far as the Meuse [Maas] and into Holland."[5] The intimation was fairly obvious: should the Allies cross the Roer downstream from the dams, the Germans could release the impounded waters to produce a flood that would demolish tactical bridges and isolate any force east of the Roer. Allied troops beyond the river would be exposed to destruction in detail by German reserves.

Despite this hazard, the Roer River Dams were not a formal objective of the 9th Division's October attack.[6] Indeed, as the division prepared to attack, advisers to the First Army commander minimized the defensive value of any floods which might be produced. On 3 October, the day after the 9th Division's appraisal appeared, the First Army's intelligence section believed that if "all of the dams" in the entire First Army sector were blown, "they would cause at the most local floodings for about 5 days counted from the moment the dam was blown until all the water had receded."[7] Two days later the First Army engineer amended this view somewhat with the opinion that "widespread flooding" might result.[8] But not for a long time were American commanders to appreciate the true value of the dams to the Germans. One explanation might rest in the fact that during October all reservoirs in the system were "considerably drawn down, in amount estimated at 30–50 percent of total capacity."[9] Yet as late as 28 November, after water level in the reservoirs had risen as high as two thirds of capacity, the First Army G–2 still could express the theory that "the economic importance of the dams to life in the Rhenish cities

---

[4] One of the better contemporary studies of the Roer River Dams is to be found in Annex 2 to 5th Armd Div G–2 Per Rpt 85, 24 Oct, 5th Armd Div G–2 file, Oct 44. See also FUSA Rpt of Opns, Vol. 1, p. 95; VII Corps Engrs, Study of Possible Flooding of the Rur (Roer) River, 17 Nov, 1st Div G–2 Jnl file, 19–20 Nov 44.

[5] Annex 1 to 9th Div G–2 Per Rpt 78, 2 Oct, 9th Div G–2 file, Oct 44. The first recorded references to the dams were contained in reports by Belgian officers on 23 and 30 September. See Memo to Col Dickson (G–2 FUSA), 23 Sep, FUSA G–2 Tac Jnl file, Sep 44; Memo to CofS from 1st Div, 23 Sep, VII Corps G–3 file, Sep 44. FUSA repeated the report of 30 Sep in its G–2 Per Rpt 113, 1 Oct, FUSA G–2 Tac Jnl file, 1–3 Oct 44. Existence of the dams and reservoirs could have been no secret, for the 1:25,000 maps in use at the time showed most of them in detail. On 6 October a Belgian agent sent FUSA a report on the Urft Dam that was inexplicably labeled Secret, yet the agent's source was a French edition of Baedeker's *Rhineland*.

[6] See VII Corps and 9th Div FO's for this attack; also Notes for Chief of Staff, 22 and 23 Sep 44, in VII Corps G–3 file, 23 Sep 44, which relate plans and objectives of the 9th Division attack as discussed by Generals Collins and Craig. The dams are not mentioned. See also, Ltr, Craig to OCMH, 31 Aug 53.

[7] Record of tel conv between G–2, MASTER Command, and G–2 FUSA (Tac), 3 Oct, FUSA G–2 Tac Jnl file, 1–3 Oct 44.

[8] Msg, FUSA Engr to VII Corps Engr, 5 Oct, VII Corps G–3 file, 5 Oct 44. See also FUSA G–2 Estimate 31, 8 Oct, FUSA G–2 Tac file, 8–9 Oct 44.

[9] Ltr, FUSA to 12th A Gp, 29 Oct, FUSA G–3 Ltrs and Inds file, Oct 44.

could prevent the enemy blowing them up as part of a 'drowned earth' policy." [10]

Closer to reality was an early appraisal by the XIX Corps engineer. Aware that his corps eventually was to cross the Roer downstream from the dams near Juelich, where banks of the river are low, the XIX Corps engineer warned his corps commander on 8 October. "If one or all dams were blown," he estimated, "a flood would occur in the channel of the Roer River that would reach approximately 1,500 feet in width and 3 feet or more deep across the entire corps front . . . . The flood would probably last from one to three weeks." [11]

Unfortunately, the XIX Corps engineer went on to dismiss the subject because all the dams were in the VII Corps zone. The VII Corps, he noted, "could be requested to capture and prevent destruction although they can be presumed to do so as their area is affected also." [12] On the contrary, General Collins and the VII Corps at this time were engrossed in plans to subdue Aachen and to send the 9th Division through the Huertgen Forest. They paid scant attention to an objective like the dams that did not lie along the planned route to the Roer and the Rhine. [13]

General Eisenhower's headquarters, SHAEF, remained aloof from the subject of the dams until 20 October, several

days after the 9th Division's Huertgen Forest attack had ended. On that date the SHAEF G-2 repeated and enlarged upon information originally obtained by the V Corps from a German prisoner. In Dueren, the prisoner said, a persistent ringing of the city's church bells was to mean the dams had been blown. The people were to evacuate the city, because the flood there would reach a depth of almost twenty feet. Turning to photographic files, SHAEF noted that air cover of all dams except the Urft had existed since 10 September. Allied air officials, SHAEF remarked, were "prepared to study [the] question of [air] attack." [14]

Like the First Army, General Bradley's headquarters, the 12th Army Group, minimized the possible effects of a flood. Like SHAEF, the 12th Army Group in October looked upon the dams as "an Air Force matter." [15]

A realistic view toward the Roer River Dams was slow to come. All through October and November, the First Army and, in later stages, the Ninth Army were to fight to build up along the west bank of the Roer downstream from the dams without making any specific effort to capture the dams. Yet neither army could cross the Roer until the dams were either captured or destroyed.

Just how long it took the American command to adopt a realistic attitude toward the dams is apparent only from the denouement of First Army operations through October and November and into December. As one considers the unfold-

---

[10] FUSA G-2 Per Rpt 171, as cited in VII Corps G-2 Per Rpt 164, 28 Nov, FUSA G-2 Tac Jnl file, 29 Nov 44.
[11] Memo, XIX Corps Engr for XIX Corps G-3, 8 Oct, XIX Corps G-3 Jnl file, 12 Oct 44.
[12] Ibid.
[13] Planning for an offensive by the V Corps to complement a VII Corps push to the Rhine was in progress at this time, though it subsequently was canceled. Like the VII Corps, the V Corps made no plans to seize the dams. See V Corps Operations in the ETO, pp. 272-278.

[14] Msg, SHAEF (MAIN) to 12th A Gp, 20 Oct, FUSA G-2 Tac Jnl file, 20-21 Oct 44.
[15] 12th A Gp Weekly Intel Summaries 11 and 12 for weeks ending 21 and 28 Oct, dtd 22 and 29 Oct, respectively, 12th A Gp G-2 AAR, Oct 44.

ing of operations in the Huertgen Forest and farther north amid the villages of the Roer plain, it becomes increasingly evident what a predominant role these dams came to play in German thinking and how determined German defense of the region of the dams had to become before American commanders heeded the danger.[16]

What happened in February 1945 as troops of the First Army at last neared the dams and the Germans attempted in panic to blow them was a flood in the valley of the Roer lasting one day short of two weeks.[17] This the Germans accomplished with only partial destruction of but one dam, the Schwammenauel.

Objective: Schmidt

Had the Roer River Dams been an objective of the 9th Division's October attack, it is logical to assume that some extraordinary effort might have been made to reinforce the division. As it was, the division commander, General Craig, had a problem of concentrating enough strength to make a genuine difference between the projected attack and the one-regiment thrust which the 60th Infantry had launched without success in September.

Through September the 9th Division had operated on a front stretching from Schevenhuette, near Stolberg, south through the Huertgen Forest and the Monschau Corridor to the Hoefen–Alzen ridge, southeast of Monschau, a distance of almost twenty miles. Even after entry of the Ninth Army into the line in Luxembourg enabled the First Army to adjust its corps frontages, the 9th Division still covered a front of nine miles. One regiment, the 47th Infantry, had to remain on the defensive at Schevenhuette. (*Map 6*) This left but two regiments free to attack: the 39th Infantry, which had been relieved in the Monschau Corridor by the 4th Cavalry Group, and the 60th Infantry. Even this concentration would have been impossible had not an attached unit, the 298th Engineer Combat Battalion, held much of the Huertgen Forest front with roadblocks at intervals between Schevenhuette and Deadman's Moor (*Todten Bruch*).

Hope for success of the 9th Division's attack obviously rested less with American strength than an expectation of German weakness. For all the sacrifices the Huertgen Forest already had exacted from the 60th Infantry, no one yet had accorded any particular respect to the enemy units defending there. The division G–2, Major Houston, estimated that German strength opposite the entire nine-mile front totaled no more than 5,000 men representing some fourteen separate home guard and replacement battalions. These, Major Houston believed, possessed no definite regimental organization and probably were no more than loosely and ineffectively knit together under an ersatz division staff. Although German leadership was for the most part excellent, Major Houston remarked, morale was "characteristically low." [18]

---

[16] See Interv with Col Akers, 11 Jun 56.

[17] See The Last Offensive, a volume in preparation in the series UNITED STATES ARMY IN WORLD WAR II.

[18] Intel Annex to 9th Div FO 39, 3 Oct, 9th Div AAR, Oct 44. Unless otherwise noted, this account is based upon official unit records and a series of detailed combat interviews at company and battalion level. An accurate presentation at a small unit level is available in an unpublished manuscript by Maj. Henry P. Halsell, Huertgen Forest and the Roer River Dams, copy in OCMH files through courtesy of Major Halsell.

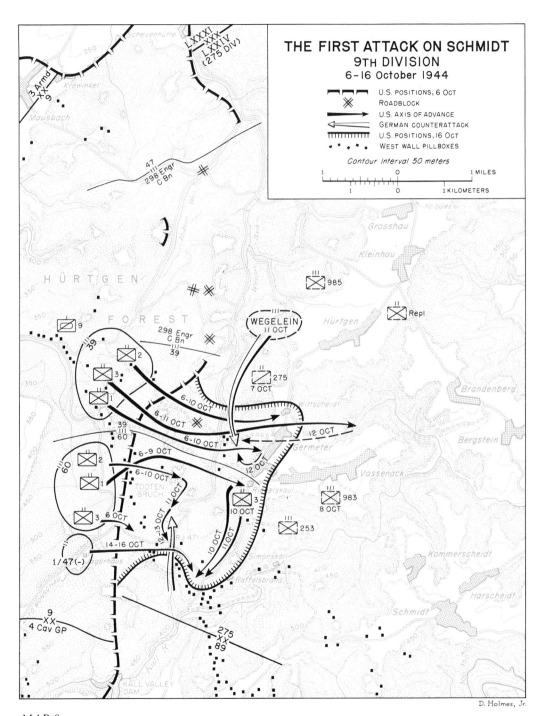

THE FIRST ATTACK ON SCHMIDT
9TH DIVISION
6-16 October 1944

U.S. POSITIONS, 6 OCT
ROADBLOCK
U.S. AXIS OF ADVANCE
GERMAN COUNTERATTACK
U.S. POSITIONS, 16 OCT
WEST WALL PILLBOXES

Contour Interval 50 meters

1   0   1 MILES

1   0   1 KILOMETERS

MAP 6

D. Holmes, Jr.

Basically, American intelligence estimates were correct. What they failed to remark was that in this kind of terrain high-level organization and even morale might not count for much.

Until the day after General Collins directed a new attack, German units opposite the 9th Division had represented two divisions, the 275th and 353d Infantry Divisions. During the battle of the Stolberg Corridor in mid-September, the 353d Division had been little more than a headquarters attached to the LXXXI Corps; but subsequently the division had been shifted into the Huertgen Forest, shored up with conglomerate units, and transferred to the neighboring LXXIV Corps (General Straube). In the meantime, the 275th Division had been falling back in front of the XIX U.S. Corps from Maastricht to the West Wall. After arrival of a new division to occupy the West Wall in front of the XIX Corps, the LXXXI Corps commander had transferred the remnants of the 275th Division into the forest near Schevenhuette. So that defense of the forest might not be weakened by a corps boundary, the Seventh Army commander, General Brandenberger, had transferred the 275th Division in place to the LXXIV Corps. During the latter days of September, both divisions had pursued the laborious task of rebuilding.

On 1 October, as the 9th Division began to prepare its attack, the commander of the 275th Division, General Schmidt, unexpectedly received orders to absorb into his division both the troops and the sector of the 353d Division. Headquarters and noncombatants of the 353d Division were disengaged. A man who bore the same name as the 9th Division's objective now became lord of the entire Huertgen Forest.[19]

The total of General Schmidt's infantry combat effectives when he first had moved into the Huertgen Forest was roughly 800. By 3 October, when absorption of the 353d Division was complete, he could point to a combat strength of 5,000, plus an additional 1,500 men in headquarters and service units. As the 9th Division G–2 had predicted, regimental organization was shaky; nevertheless, the front had been formally broken down into three regimental sectors. In the north was the 275th Division's organic 984th Regiment; in the center, a variety of units from the 353d Division which were to be designated the 985th Infantry Regiment; and in the south, where the 9th Division was to strike, a former component of the 353d Division labeled the 253d Regiment. This regiment commanded a colorful array of unrelated units composed of replacements, Landesschuetzen, a few combat veterans, and others.

In division reserve, General Schmidt had a replacement battalion numbering about 200 men and the 275th Fusilier Battalion with about 400 men. Also available but currently engaged in constructing defenses near Dueren were about 600 men under one of the division's organic regiments, the 983d.

For artillery support, General Schmidt had only 13 105-mm. howitzers, 1 210-mm. howitzer, and 6 assault guns. Other

---

[19] The basic source for the German side of this action is MS # B–810, Generalleutnant Hans Schmidt, Kaempfe im Rheinland 275. Infanterie Division. Additional details may be found in Lucian Heichler, The First Battle of the Huertgen Forest, a manuscript prepared to complement this volume and filed in OCMH.

than bazookas and panzerfausts, the assault guns were the only weapons available for antitank defense.

Other weapons were almost as diverse as the men who manned them. Though machine guns and mortars were of various types, they had enough of neither. Even rifles were of various types and makes, a fact which further complicated an ammunition supply situation already acute. All weapons, particularly artillery pieces, had to practice stringent ammunition economy, though presence in the division sector of an adequately supplied antiaircraft artillery regiment was to alleviate the artillery situation somewhat.

During the first week of October, the *275th Division* worked night and day on defensive positions. Mainly these were field fortifications—log bunkers, foxholes, connecting trenches, wire entanglements, mine fields, and roadblocks. The line followed generally the Rother Weh and Weisser Weh Creeks which bisect the approximate center of the forest, though some strong outposts were established west of the creek beds.

Like the Americans, General Schmidt at this stage apparently took no special cognizance of the Roer River Dams. His mission, as he interpreted it, was to repulse the Americans inside the Huertgen Forest in order to deny access to the high clearings near the Roer which overlook flatlands leading to the Rhine. If he considered any feature within his sector more important than the others, it was the Huertgen–Kleinhau road net which leads to Dueren. Paradoxically, neither adversary in the first big fight to occur in the vicinity of the Roer River Dams apparently was thinking in terms of this important objective.

To the First Clearing

The American commander, General Craig, directed attack from positions deep in the forest about a mile west of the Weisser Weh Creek. Ordering his two regiments to move abreast, he designated as first objectives the village of Germeter and settlements of Wittscheidt and Richelskaul, which lie north and south, respectively, of Germeter. Capture of these points would sever the main Monschau–Huertgen–Dueren highway and also provide egress from the forest into the first big clearing along the projected route to Schmidt.

Attacking toward Wittscheidt and Germeter, the 39th Infantry on the left wing also was to guard against counterattack from the north from the direction of Huertgen. After occupying the first objectives, the 39th Infantry was to push on to Vossenack and subsequently southeast across the Kall River gorge to Schmidt. Upon seizure of Richelskaul, the 60th Infantry on the right wing was to turn south to occupy high ground about two forest-cloaked road junctions. Control of these points would block enemy movement against the division's penetration from the direction of the Monschau Corridor and open the way for a subsequent advance into the flank of the corridor.

As demonstrated in later fighting over this same terrain, the weak point in General Craig's plan lay in an inability to protect the left (northern and northeastern) flank once the 39th Infantry left Germeter for Vossenack and subsequently for Schmidt. This flank would stretch eventually to at least six miles. To help protect it, General Craig would have at best but one battalion in division reserve. This probably would be a battalion of the 60th Infantry which on the first day was to feign attack eastward from a position near *Jaegerhaus,* a forester's lodge southwest of Deadman's Moor (*Todten Bruch*).

If General Craig found any consolation in regard to this situation, it would have been in an erroneous belief which the division G–2 expressed two days after the attack began. "It is felt," the G–2 said, "that should a major breakthrough occur, or should several penetrations occur, the enemy will begin a withdrawal to the Rhine River, abandoning his Siegfried Line." [20] It was late in the West Wall fighting for this kind of thinking to persist.

To initiate the attack on Schmidt, seven squadrons (eighty-four planes) of IX Tactical Air Command fighter-bombers were to hit three priority targets: first, a heavily forested plateau between the Weisser Weh and Germeter, where the enemy had located his main line of resistance; second, Germeter; and third, the forest-cloaked road junctions which were the 60th Infantry's final objectives. Supplemented by three battalions and two additional batteries of corps guns, 9th Division artillery was to follow the air strike with a sharp five-minute preparation.

Though the attack was scheduled for 5 October, low-hanging clouds which obscured targets from the fighter-bombers prompted successive postponements. At noon General Craig called off the attack until the next day. On 6 October, the weather cleared over the targets, but local fog over airfields in Belgium persisted. To the infantrymen, waiting with keyed nerves beneath the dark umbrella of fir

branches, it looked like another dry run. At last, shortly after 1000, a steady drone of planes drew near.

Against targets marked with red smoke by the artillery, the bombing began. Diving low, P–47 Thunderbolts of the 365th and 404th Groups struck with precision. Then outgoing shells from the throats of big artillery pieces stirred the tops of the tall firs. Three minutes of fire. Five minutes of silence. Two minutes of fire. At 1130, attack.

Men of both regiments discovered early that the first clearing in the Huertgen Forest was much farther away in terms of fighting and time than was indicated by the mile that showed on maps. Still 800 yards west of the Weisser Weh, the 2d Battalion, 60th Infantry, under Maj. Lawrence L. Decker, smacked against an outpost position that eventually would require almost a week to reduce. Though the 39th Infantry pushed back outposts in its sector, it was a gradual process crowned by even more rigid resistance from pillboxes along the east slope of the Weisser Weh. The Germans and the forest together were putting a high price on this little piece of real estate.

Some idea of the stiff asking price was apparent from the first. One company of the 2d Battalion, engaging the outpost west of the Weisser Weh, ended the first day with two officers and sixty men, little more than a platoon. Though not engaged during the day by small arms fire, another battalion lost a hundred men to shellbursts in the trees.

As reflected in casualty figures, advances were for the most part painfully slow. Because each regimental sector contained only one trail leading east and because these and the firebreaks were blocked with mines and felled trees, tanks

[20] 9th Div G–2 Per Rpt 84, 8 Oct, 9th Div AAR, Oct 44.

and other direct fire weapons could not assist. Fighting was reduced to the simple equation of man against man, rifle against rifle, machine gun against machine gun. Though supporting artillery averaged about 5,000 rounds a day along the division front and fighter-bombers were active most of the time, so closely were the combatants locked that little of this fire could be directed against those positions posing the immediate problems. Relatively impervious to shelling themselves, the Germans in their bunkers could direct mortar and artillery fire to burst in the treetops and spray deadly ricochet fragments upon the floor of the forest. On the American side, the fight amid the firs was a plodding exercise in unsupported infantry maneuver.

Two exceptions to the pedestrian pace developed, both on the second day, 7 October. While P–47's strafed and bombed Germeter, a company of the 39th Infantry slipped past German positions on the wooded plateau between the Weisser Weh and Germeter to gain the woods line overlooking the village. In the face of immediate reaction by fire from Germans in the buildings, the battalion commander, Colonel Thompson, hesitated to order the company from the concealment of the woods. Before risking his men in the open astride a main highway, Colonel Thompson wanted tanks or antitank guns and some means of supplying them other than by long hand-carry through the woods.

In the 60th Infantry's sector, a battalion under Colonel Chatfield faced much the same situation. Committed around a flank of the German outpost that had stymied the 2d Battalion west of the Weisser Weh, Colonel Chatfield's men by nightfall were overlooking the settlement of Richelskaul. Like Colonel Thompson, Colonel Chatfield was reluctant to debouch from the woods without armor or antitank support.

To grant passage for heavier weapons, engineers worked around the clock clearing firebreaks and trails. Because the Germans opposing Major Decker's 2d Battalion west of the Weisser Weh continued to hold out obstinately, the most direct route to the rear for the 60th Infantry was denied. Supply parties hand-carrying rations and ammunition incurred severe losses from shelling, antipersonnel mines, and roving patrols. Not until nightfall of the third day (8 October) did tanks and tank destroyers negotiate the tortuous terrain to gain the woods line.

From the German viewpoint, an American offensive in such "extensive, thick, and nearly trackless forest terrain" had come as a surprise.[21] The 275th Division commander, General Schmidt, nevertheless had marshaled his 275th Fusilier Battalion and committed it, as the Americans had anticipated, against the north flank of the 39th Infantry. That regiment took care of the thrust in short order. On 8 October the 275th Division engineers and 600 men of the 983d Regiment arrived from Dueren to strike Colonel Chatfield's battalion of the 60th Infantry near Richelskaul. In a case like this, the Germans instead of the Americans were prey to tree bursts and other confusions of the forest. They fell back in disorder.

By 8 October German shelling had increased. It stemmed from an order by the LXXIV Corps commander, General Straube, that more than doubled the 275th Division's original artillery strength. General Straube directed support from batteries of the neighboring 89th Division,

---

[21] MS # B–810 (Schmidt).

an antiaircraft artillery regiment, and a volks artillery corps.

The *Seventh Army* commander, General Brandenberger, provided meager assistance in the form of two fortress infantry battalions, but both battalions incurred forbidding losses on the first day of commitment. By the end of the third day the Germans still maintained a continuous line along the west edge of the first clearing at Wittscheidt, Germeter, and Richelskaul, but further counterattacks before additional reserves could arrive were out of the question. The impoverished state of German reserves was illustrated dramatically on 9 October when two companies of overage policemen from Dueren were thrust into the line near Wittscheidt.

The Germans in the Huertgen Forest were convinced that they faced an enemy with a well-nigh unlimited supply of topnotch, rested, and well-equipped combat troops specially trained and experienced in forest fighting. That the two regiments of the 9th Division could create an impression so different from the fact of a tired, overextended division, replete with inexperienced replacements, represents perhaps the highest tribute that can be paid them. The Germans were awed particularly by the efficiency of American communications as manifested by lightning shifts and adjustments in artillery fires.

After tanks and tank destroyers at last reached both American regiments late on 8 October, plans progressed to break out of the forest into the first clearing the next day. At Richelskaul, Colonel Chatfield's battalion attacked in a wedge formation behind a platoon of medium tanks. Their machine guns and cannon blazing, the tanks stormed so quickly from the forest that the Germans had

virtually no chance to fight back. When a lieutenant dared to rise from his foxhole to fire a panzerfaust, one of the tank gunners sliced him in half with a round from his 75. So demoralized were the other Germans that almost a hundred surrendered and others fled. A count revealed fifty German dead.

In the sector of the 39th Infantry, another day was needed before both attacking battalions could build up along the woods line. Only two platoons that occupied westernmost buildings of Wittscheidt emerged from the woods on 9 October. Before dawn the next morning, a local counterattack apparently staged by a conglomerate German force overran these platoons. Retaking the position with the aid of tanks was all that could be accomplished here during the rest of 10 October. Of the two platoons, which had totaled forty-eight men, only one body was found.

Wariness over this action on the regimental north wing forestalled any major offensive action by Colonel Thompson's battalion at Germeter until early afternoon when patrols reported that the Germans had withdrawn. Advancing cautiously into the village, the battalion found only enemy dead. After five days the 39th Infantry at last had gained one of its first objectives. From the line of departure west of the Weisser Weh to the first clearing, the forest fighting had cost the 9th Division's two regiments together almost a thousand men.

Toward Raffelsbrand and Vossenack

Having gained the first clearing a day ahead of the 39th Infantry, the 60th Infantry began the second leg of the attack on 10 October even as the other regiment was moving into Germeter. Shifting his reserve battalion to hold Richelskaul, the regimental commander, Col. John G. Van Houten, directed Colonel Chatfield to re-enter the woods to secure the first of the two road junctions which were the regiment's final objectives. The first was near Raffelsbrand, a forester's lodge about a mile southwest of Richelskaul.

As Colonel Chatfield's battalion attacked soon after noon on 10 October, the first impression was of dreary repetition of the pedestrian pace which had prevailed most of the time elsewhere in the forest. Then suddenly, as one company knocked out a pillbox near the road leading from Richelskaul to Raffelsbrand, the drive picked up momentum. Urging their men forward, the company commanders unhesitatingly bypassed enemy strongpoints. The Germans began to surrender in bunches. In less than three hours Colonel Chatfield's men seized the road junction and staked claim to the wooded high ground around it. They had taken more than a hundred prisoners.

Despite this creditable operation, as night fell Colonel Van Houten must have considered his regiment in an unenviable position. His reserve committed at Richelskaul, he had no force available to prevent the Germans cutting in behind Colonel Chatfield's advanced position. The 2d Battalion, commanded now by Maj. Quentin R. Hardage, still was engaged west of the Weisser Weh against the German outpost which since the opening day of the offensive had shown no signs of collapse. Continued attacks against the position had shrunk the battalion alarmingly.

Before daylight the next morning, 11 October, German action began to emphasize these concerns. A company-size

counterattack struck Colonel Chatfield's position at Raffelsbrand. Though beaten off, the enemy maintained pressure here the rest of the day and crowned it just before dark with a bayonet charge. Although tanks and tank destroyers passed the roadblocks to reach Raffelsbrand, their presence complicated the supply picture. As expected, German patrols and snipers made supply through the thick forest a hazardous task.

Taking the risk of defending Richelskaul with but one company, Colonel Van Houten sent the rest of his "reserve" battalion in midmorning to attack northwest from Raffelsbrand toward the regiment's remaining objective, Road Junction 471. This road junction lies not quite half the distance between the two forester's lodges of Raffelsbrand and *Jaegerhaus*.

Hope that this move might develop into a rapid thrust like Colonel Chatfield's was stymied, a direct result of the fact that Colonel Chatfield's battalion had advanced so quickly the day before. Of two companies which headed for Road Junction 471, one became fruitlessly embroiled with pillboxes which had not been cleared along the Richelskaul–Raffelsbrand road. The other became similarly engaged with a pillbox in rear of the Raffelsbrand position.

Events on 11 October might have proved thoroughly discouraging had not Major Hardage's 2d Battalion west of the Weisser Weh at last begun to detect signs of collapse in the outpost that had thwarted the battalion for five days. Driving southward against a flank of the outpost, the battalion began to make measured but steady progress. By the end of the day, the Germans had fallen back about 800 yards. While the weary riflemen probably could detect little difference between one forest-cloaked piece of terrain and another, the battalion's position at nightfall actually posed a threat to the remaining regimental objective, Road Junction 471.

Reports from prisoners that they had received no reinforcements and had not eaten for three days somewhat dimmed the luster of this advance; yet Major Hardage's battalion after five days of Huertgen Forest fighting was almost as depleted as the enemy unit. Any numerical advantage the Americans may have possessed lay only in bug-eyed replacements who had begun to arrive in small, frightened bunches.

Like the others of the two regiments when they first entered the Huertgen Forest, these replacements had to adjust themselves to the tricks of woods fighting. Protection against shells that burst in the treetops was the main thing. Foxholes, the men soon learned, meant little unless roofed with logs and sod. If caught by shelling while out of a foxhole, your best bet was not to fall flat but to stand or crouch close against the base of a tree so that the smallest possible body surface would be exposed to fragments from above. As anyone would tell you, moving about at night was tantamount to suicide. Adjusting artillery and mortar fire by sight was impossible, even with the aid of smoke shells. You had to rely on sound. If you had a map, you might determine your position in the forest by means of cement survey markers to be found at intersections of firebreaks. Numbers on these corresponded to numbered squares on the map. Without a map, you had to depend on a compass—if you had a compass. There was a lot to learn in the Huertgen Forest.

While the 60th Infantry re-entered the forest to seize the road junctions southwest of Richelskaul, the 39th Infantry attempted to move into the open, to advance across fields from Germeter to the regiment's second objective, the village of Vossenack. From Vossenack the 39th Infantry was to continue southeastward across the Kall gorge to Schmidt, the final objective.

In this instance, men of the 39th Infantry found that the thick forest which they hated actually might be employed to advantage. During 11 October several attempts by Colonel Thompson's battalion in Germeter to move across open ground to Vossenack accomplished nothing. Each time German assault guns in Vossenack exacted a prohibitive toll of Thompson's supporting tanks. Yet at the same time another battalion under Lt. Col. R. H. Stumpf advanced under the cloak of a wooded draw from Wittscheidt to a position north of Vossenack, only a few hundred yards from the objective.

Though delayed at first by a severe shelling, once Colonel Stumpf's battalion entered the woods east of Wittscheidt, the men found surprisingly light resistance. By late afternoon the battalion had advanced almost a mile apparently undetected, and was ready to emerge from the woods onto an open nose of the Vossenack ridge northeast of the village, where it could cut off the objective from the rear.

Despite the encouragement provided by this battalion's success, the 9th Division commander, General Craig, was cautious. To defeat Colonel Stumpf's move against Vossenack, all the Germans had to do was to hold fast in the village while striking with another force from the north into the rear of Stumpf's battalion. General Craig directed that Colonel Stumpf delay until the next day when Colonel Thompson's battalion in Germeter might hit Vossenack simultaneously from the west.

As night came on 11 October Colonel Stumpf's battalion was stretched in an elongated column of companies through the woods north of Vossenack. This put a maximum strain on still another battalion of the 39th Infantry that heretofore had not participated in offensive thrusts eastward, yet had been heavily engaged nevertheless. Commanded by Lt. Col. Frank L. Gunn, this battalion had been charged with protecting the regimental north flank against likely counterattacks from the direction of Huertgen. This was no minor task, as Colonel Gunn soon discovered. Though the 298th Engineers and the 9th Division's reconnaissance troop assumed responsibility for blocking the Weisser Weh draw, Colonel Gunn's companies still became overextended. After Colonel Stumpf's battalion had moved fingerlike into the woods north of Vossenack, Colonel Gunn not only had to defend Wittscheidt but also had to send a company east of the highway to maintain contact with the tail of Stumpf's battalion.

Plans for 12 October were for Major Hardage's 2d Battalion, 60th Infantry, to continue southward down the Weisser Weh to Road Junction 471 and for the 39th Infantry to launch a co-ordinated, two-battalion attack against Vossenack. Though no battalion of the two regiments could field more than 300 men and neither the regiments nor the division had other than a nominal reserve, prospects for success on 12 October were relatively bright. Both the preceding days had brought undeniable cracks in German defenses.

Regiment Wegelein

Though persisting in the belief that the enemy's over-all policy was withdrawal, the 9th Division G–2 noted that the enemy's more immediate concern was to re-establish a Huertgen Forest line similar to that which had existed before the 9th Division's attack. The most likely direction for a counterattack to take to accomplish this, the G–2 remarked, was from the northeast against the 39th Infantry, probably from Huertgen. In addition, the enemy might counterattack the 60th Infantry with a complementary drive from the south.

As to the enemy's immediate plans, the 9th Division G–2 hardly could have been more prescient, even had he known that on 10 October the enemy commander, General Schmidt, had been honored by visitors who had promised help. These were the army and corps commanders, Generals Brandenberger and Straube, who had informed Schmidt they would send him a regiment with which to counterattack on 12 October.

During the night of 11 October trucks carrying 2,000 men of *Regiment Wegelein* rolled north from former positions along the Luxembourg border. Commanded by a colonel from whom the regiment drew its name, the unit was well equipped with machine guns and heavy and medium mortars. The men were of good quality, about half of them officer candidates. General Schmidt had reason to expect big things from the counterattack on 12 October.

Behind a brief but concentrated artillery preparation, Colonel Wegelein launched his counterattack at 0700 due southward along the wooded plateau between the

Weisser Weh and the Germeter–Huertgen highway. The objective of Richelskaul appeared at first to be within easy reach. Quickly enveloping a part of Colonel Gunn's overextended battalion of the 39th Infantry, the Germans poured through to cut an east–west trail leading into Germeter, a trail which served as the 39th Infantry's main supply route.

The 39th Infantry commander, Colonel Bond, had virtually no reserve to throw against the penetration. Receiving an erroneous report that the engineer roadblock on the Weisser Weh road had been overrun, he requested the 298th Engineers to send their reserve there. He told Colonel Thompson, whose positions at Germeter were under pressure by fire, to release two platoons to Colonel Gunn's assistance. These two platoons actually had a strength no greater than one. Judging from the wording of this order, Colonel Bond believed Colonel Stumpf's battalion in the fingerlike formation north of Vossenack also to be under attack. In reality, Colonel Stumpf had experienced no enemy action and knew virtually nothing about what was going on to his rear.

For his part, General Craig alerted the division reserve—which consisted of a portion of the division reconnaissance troop and a platoon of light tanks. Acting on his own initiative, the reconnaissance troop commander actually committed the reserve to cover the 39th Infantry's exposed left flank. Though General Craig approved the move, it left him with no semblance of a division reserve. In early afternoon he sought to remedy the situation by directing that the 47th Infantry at Schevenhuette withdraw two companies to create a motorized reserve.[22]

For reasons that at the time appeared

<hr>

[22] See Ltr, Craig to OCMH, 20 Apr 56.

inexplicable, *Regiment Wegelein* failed to advance farther than the east–west trail leading into Germeter. The *275th Division* commander, General Schmidt, said later that the battalion commanders were to blame. Yet prisoners, including a loquacious adjutant, said the fault lay in inadequate communications. Colonel Wegelein had protested the communications arrangement before the attack, the prisoners said, but General Schmidt would not sanction a delay to set it right. American artillery fire had quickly dealt a death blow to a communications system that was shaky from the start.

Perhaps the genuine explanation lay in a combination of these two factors, plus the fact that confusion in the Huertgen Forest was not confined to the American side. Tenacious resistance by little knots of men in Colonel Gunn's battalion no doubt had contributed to the enemy's confusion. Although enveloped in early stages of the counterattack, Colonel Gunn's Ammunition and Pioneer Platoon and a platoon of Company G had held out in little islands of resistance while the Germans surged around them. Other groups also had continued to fight, though surrounded, including four men, three officers, and the crew of a heavy machine gun who represented Colonel Gunn's advance command group.

Unaware of the problem on the German side, Colonel Bond in midafternoon ordered Colonel Stumpf to withdraw from his salient in the woods north of Vossenack, leave one company east of the Huertgen highway to strengthen defense of Wittscheidt, and with the rest of his battalion attack the German penetration from the east. By nightfall Stumpf was poised for an attack the next morning, 13 October.

Though *Regiment Wegelein*'s counter-attack had struck before the 39th Infantry's planned attack against Vossenack had begun, the 60th Infantry already had started a new drive against Road Junction 471 before trouble developed. Pushing southward down the Weisser Weh toward the road junction, Major Hardage's battalion of the 60th Infantry ran into a force of about 300 men, which apparently was attempting to complement *Regiment Wegelein*'s attack. Because American units controlled the only roads in the vicinity of Road Junction 471, this complementary effort was doomed from the start. A stiff engagement developed, nevertheless. After beating off the counterattack, the U.S. battalion had to spend the rest of the day in reorganization.

Though General Schmidt intended that *Regiment Wegelein* renew the attack on 13 October, the plan was crossed up by an order from the *LXXIV Corps* that all officer candidates in the regiment be detached immediately. This cut the regiment's strength in half. Having lost 500 men in the first day's fighting, Colonel Wegelein had only a smattering of his original force remaining. Further offensive action was out of the question.

By midafternoon of 13 October, the 39th Infantry had established a fairly solid line containing *Regiment Wegelein*'s penetration. Then Colonel Bond set about to push the enemy back.

It took three days for the 39th Infantry to restore the original flank positions running from the engineer roadblock astride the Weisser Weh highway across the wooded plateau to Wittscheidt. In light of *Regiment Wegelein*'s depleted condition, this turtlelike pace obviously was attributable less to stout opposition than to the fact that the forest fighting had left

the 39th Infantry spent and groggy. One company commander had but two platoons left, one with twelve men, another with thirteen. One company lost two platoons in one fell swoop as they strayed into an ambush.[23] Nevertheless, by nightfall of 15 October, Colonel Bond could point to the fact that his men had restored the northern flank and still held on to Wittscheidt and Germeter. Despite depletion of his units, he had been able to constitute a reserve with two companies of Colonel Stumpf's battalion.

Among the victims of the elimination of the German penetration was the enemy commander, Colonel Wegelein. During the morning of 14 October, a noncommissioned officer of Company E saw an enemy soldier walking alone in front of his position and shot him. It was Colonel Wegelein.

During this time the 60th Infantry resumed its attack to capture Road Junction 471. By nightfall of 13 October, Major Hardage's 2d Battalion possessed the road junction, though the Germans held on to nearby pillboxes. Uncontested claim to the objective came the next day after General Craig committed to the sector the two-company reserve from the 47th Infantry. Reinforced by a medium tank company on loan from the 3d Armored Division, these two companies had moved in the day before behind the 60th Infantry.

By 16 October few could have expected the 9th Division under existing circumstances to renew the offensive. As more than one division was to learn later with grim emphasis, it was impossible to fight

---

[23] In another instance, Pvt. James E. Mathews earned the posthumous award of the DSC as he saved his company commander from ambush at the cost of his own life.

in the Huertgen Forest for ten days without ending up spent and depleted. Only in the matter of weather, which had been generally favorable, did the 9th Division have an easier time in the forest than those units which would come later.

Behind the scenes in the chain of command, plans progressed for the division's relief. The battle of Aachen was drawing to a close; thereupon, priority in the VII Corps was to go to the drive to the Roer. Although capture of Schmidt remained a prerequisite to the big drive, the VII Corps in providing a force to take Schmidt would have to siphon strength from the main effort. The First Army commander, General Hodges, erased this possibility by directing a temporary adjustment in the boundary between the V Corps and the VII Corps to give the V Corps responsibility for Schmidt. Running east–west just north of Huertgen, this boundary was to become effective on 25 October. The 9th Division, less the 47th Infantry at Schevenhuette, was to pass to the V Corps for relief and movement to the vicinity of Camp d'Elsenborn, while a fresh unit,

the 28th Division, renewed the attack on Schmidt.[24]

The two regiments of the 9th Division had fallen far short of the objective of Schmidt. Yet for some 3,000 yards in depth they had carved from the Huertgen Forest, they had paid dearly with more than one casualty per yard. The division had lost about 4,500 men. The drive had enveloped about 1,300 prisoners and inflicted on the enemy an additional estimated 1,500–2,000 casualties.[25] On the basis of these statistics, neither side could claim undisputed victory in the October fighting. The real winner appeared to be the vast, undulating, blackish-green sea that virtually negated American superiority in air, artillery, and armor to reduce warfare to its lowest common denominator. The victor thus far was the Huertgen Forest.

---

[24] See VII Corps Opns Memo 107, dtd 18 Oct, confirming oral orders issued 17–18 Oct, VII Corps Opns Memo file, Oct 44.

[25] Although both American and German losses are for the entire month of October, most occurred during the ten days of offensive action. In MS # B–810, General Schmidt estimates German losses through 12 October at 1,600 men, obviously conservative in light of confirmed prisoner statistics.

CHAPTER XV

The Second Attack on Schmidt

As October neared an end, General Hodges set a tentative target date of 5 November for renewal of the First Army's big push to the Roer and the Rhine. Additional divisions soon were to arrive to bolster the front. The Ninth Army was reorganizing hastily in the old XIX Corps zone, preparing to share responsibility for the coming offensive. The divisions near Aachen brought in replacements and readjusted their lines. The critical shortage of artillery ammunition was easing as stockpiles grew.[1]

As plans for the big push progressed, one deplorable fact persisted: you could not wish away the Huertgen Forest. General Hodges continued to believe that before launching his main effort, he needed a secure right flank along the headwaters of the Roer from Monschau to Schmidt and at least a line of departure behind the Huertgen Forest for early seizure of the Huertgen–Kleinhau road net beyond the forest. The key to all this was capture of Schmidt.

Two factors had influenced General Hodges in his decision to shift responsibility for Schmidt from the VII Corps to General Gerow's V Corps. First, because after more than a month since collapse of the Schnee Eifel–Luxembourg offensive, the V Corps was rested; second,

because he wanted to keep the VII Corps fresh for the main drive. Having transferred the Vossenack–Schmidt sector to the V Corps by means of a temporary corps boundary just north of Huertgen, General Hodges directed that General Gerow attack on 1 November to clear the Vossenack–Schmidt–Lammersdorf triangle down to the headwaters of the Roer. Since the main First Army drive was to follow on 5 November, Hodges stipulated that under no circumstances was the V Corps attack to be delayed beyond 2 November.

Though addition of the depleted 9th Division (minus one regimental combat team) gave General Gerow a nominal strength of four divisions to cover a front of some twenty-seven miles, he had in effect but three, because the 4th Division was earmarked to join the VII Corps for the main drive. In addition, Gerow had to husband some strength for his own attack toward the Rhine, which was to begin soon after the VII Corps had pierced the enemy's positions west of the Roer.

General Gerow at first directed attack on Schmidt by only one unit, the 28th Division. Upon further study, he amplified this plan to provide that after seizure of Vossenack and Schmidt, a combat command of the 5th Armored Division was to assist the 28th Division in clearing the Monschau Corridor. While the infantry turned southwest from Schmidt

---

[1] Tentative plans for renewing the offensive may be found in Operations Plan, VII Corps, 28 October 1944, dated 27 October, VII Corps G–3 FO file, Oct 44.

into the corridor, the armor was to drive northeast from the vicinity of Monschau. Thus the stubborn West Wall positions in the Monschau Corridor, which had defied the 9th Division in September, would be hit by a double assault, front and rear.[2]

Again as American commanders readied an attack on Schmidt, they made no specific plans for the objective which was in reality the ripest fruit that could be plucked as a corollary of an attack on Schmidt—the Roer River Dams. (*See Map 5.*) Even though the First Army drive which was to follow the preliminary thrust might be punished severely should the Germans make tactical use of the waters of the Roer reservoirs, neither the V Corps nor the First Army made any recorded plans for continuing the attack beyond Schmidt to gain the dams. The commander of the regiment that made the main effort of this second drive on Schmidt said later that the Roer River Dams "never entered the picture."[3]

This is not to say that the Americans were totally unaware of the importance of the dams. After the war, General Bradley noted, "It might not show in the record, but we did plenty of talking about the dams."[4] Earlier in the month of October the V Corps staff had studied the dams, and on 27 October the V Corps engineer had warned it would be "unwise" for American forces to become involved beyond the Roer at any point below the

Schwammenauel Dam before that dam was in American hands.[5] Nevertheless, not until 7 November, six days after start of the second attack on Schmidt, was the First Army to call for any plan to seize the dams. On that date, General Hodges' chief of staff, General Kean, told the V Corps to prepare plans for future operations, one of which would be "in the event First Army is ordered to capture and secure the [Schwammenauel] dam . . . ."[6]

Even as late as 7 November, General Hodges apparently had no intention of ordering an attack to the dams on his own initiative. All signs seemed to indicate that American commanders still did not appreciate fully the tremendous value of the dams to the enemy. As late as 6 November, for example, one of the divisions that would have to cross the Roer downstream from the dams assumed the Germans would not flood the Roer because it might hinder movement of their own forces.[7]

---

[2] V Corps FO 30, 21 Oct, and Ltrs of Instrs, 23 and 30 Oct 44, V Corps Operations in the ETO, pp. 282, 284, and 288.

[3] Interv with Col Carl L. Peterson (formerly CO, 112th Inf), Bradford, Pa., 21–22–23 Sep 48.

[4] Interv with Bradley, 7 Jun 56.

[5] V Corps Supplement No. 1 to Engr Intel Rpt 27, 27 Oct, V Corps G–3 file, 26–27 Oct 44; Interv with Gens Gerow and Hill (formerly G–3, V Corps), and Brig Gen Charles G. Helmick (formerly arty comdr, V Corps), 15 Oct 54.

[6] Memo, FUSA to V Corps, Plans for Future Operations, V Corps, dtd 7 Nov, in V Corps G–3 FO file, Nov. 44. The FUSA Report of Operations, Volume 1, says the 28th Division's Schmidt attack was "a preliminary phase of a plan by V Corps to seize the two large dams on the Roer River . . . ." Though General Hodges, in a letter to OCMH, 11 July 1956, calls attention to this entry, the author has rejected it in the absence of contemporary evidence. The VII Corps commander, General Collins, has noted that American commanders are open to criticism for their delay in facing the problem of the dams. See Interv with Collins, 25 Jan 54.

[7] 1st Div, Annex 2 (Intel) to FO 53, 6 Nov, 1st Div G–3 Opns Rpt, Nov 44.

Planning the Thrust

Though General Gerow seemingly had no plans in regard to the Roer River Dams, he chose nevertheless to reinforce the 28th Division strongly for the attack. Because at this time the cynosure of the V Corps—indeed, of the entire First Army—was one division, the 28th, supporting units were readily available. General Gerow attached to the division a chemical mortar battalion and the entire 1171st Engineer Combat Group with three combat battalions. A battalion of towed tank destroyers supplemented the usual attachment of a battalion each of medium tanks and self-propelled tank destroyers. In recognition of the thick forest and roller-coaster terrain, he gave the division 47 weasels (M29 Cargo Carriers) to ease supply and evacuation. In direct and general support he placed eight battalions and a separate battery of V and VII Corps artillery. Six battalions of VII Corps artillery were to participate in preparatory fires.[8] Using five fighter-bomber groups and a night fighter group, the IX Tactical Command was to direct its main effort toward air support of the division.[9]

The logical starting point for planning the V Corps attack was the experience of the 9th Division. The decision to crush the defenses of the Monschau Corridor in a vise, for example, no doubt was influenced by the 9th Division's difficulties in the corridor in mid-September. Be-

sides that, General Gerow had the secondary missions, dictated by First Army, of securing a line of departure overlooking the Huertgen–Kleinhau road net and of occupying Vossenack. (*Map 7*) These virtually ordained that the 28th Division's attack follow closely the planned route of the 9th Division's unsuccessful October thrust: Germeter, Vossenack, thence across the Kall River gorge to Kommerscheidt and Schmidt.

In passing his orders to the 28th Division, General Gerow specified employment of one regiment in securing the line of departure overlooking Huertgen and guarding against repetition of the kind of counterattack the late Colonel Wegelein had thrown against the north flank of the 9th Division. To alleviate an admittedly precarious supply route to Schmidt via Vossenack and Kommerscheidt and to pave the way for the subsequent assault on the Monschau Corridor, Gerow specified that another regiment break past the Raffelsbrand road junction southwest of Germeter and clear a road net leading into the corridor. Only one regiment remained for the main effort of seizing Schmidt. These dictates left the 28th Division commander, Maj. Gen. Norman D. Cota, with little initiative in the planning.[10]

---

[8] V Corps FO 30, 21 Oct, and Ltrs of Instrs, 23 and 30 Oct, V Corps Operations in the ETO, pp. 282, 284, and 288. See also VII Corps Annex 1 to Opns Memo 114, 1 Nov, VII Corps Opns Memo file, Oct 44.

[9] FUSA and IX TAC Summary of Air Opns, IX Fighter Command and IX TAC, Unit History, 1–30 Nov 44.

[10] As General Cota so stated in an interview filed with 28th Div Combat Intervs for Nov 44. More combat interviews were obtained on this operation than on any other specific ground action in the European Theater of Operations. Unless otherwise noted, these interviews and official records of the V Corps, the 28th Division, and attached units constituted the sources for this account. Of additional value was a factual study on almost every phase prepared soon after the operation by a board of V Corps officers appointed by General Gerow, filed with V Corps records. A detailed, thoroughly documented account of the action at a small unit level, entitled "Objective: Schmidt," is to be

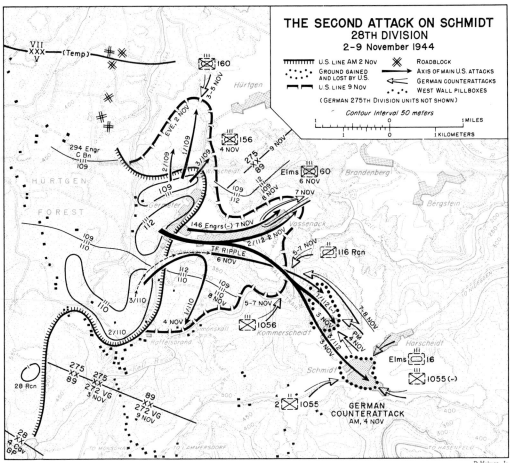

MAP 7

D. Holmes, Jr.

The problem facing General Cota was how best to use such limited freedom as was left him in trying to circumvent three obstacles which always exercise heavy influence on military operations but which promised to affect the attack on Schmidt to an even greater extent than usual. These were: terrain, weather, and enemy.

The overbearing factor about the ter-

found in Charles B. MacDonald and Sidney T. Mathews, *Three Battles: Arnaville, Altuzzo, and Schmidt,* UNITED STATES ARMY IN WORLD WAR II (Washington, 1952).

rain in this region is its startlingly assertive nature. Ridges, valleys, and gorges are sharply defined. The Roer and subsidiary stream lines, including the little Kall River, which cut a deep swath diagonally across the 28th Division's zone of attack, slice this sector into three distinct ridges. In the center is the Germeter–Vossenack ridge. On the northeast is the Brandenberg–Bergstein ridge, which gives the impression to the man on the ground of dominating the Vossenack ridge. Except for temporary periods of neutralization by artillery fire, the 28th Division would have to operate through the course of its attack under observation from the Brandenberg–Bergstein ridge. The third ridge line runs between the Kall and the Roer, from the Monschau Corridor through Schmidt to the Roer near Nideggen. A spur juts out northwestward from Schmidt to Kommerscheidt. Because this ridge represents the highest elevation west of the Roer, the 28th Division would be under dominant enemy observation all the way to Schmidt.

Though the 9th Division had pierced the Huertgen Forest to the Germeter–Vossenack clearing, the 28th Division still would be enmeshed among the thick firs and undergrowth. Both the regiment attacking north from Germeter to gain the woods line overlooking Huertgen and the regiment attacking south through Raffelsbrand would have to fight in the forest. The regiment making the main effort toward Schmidt would pass in and out of the woods. Along the route to be taken the trees hugged the lines of the streams for about 600 yards on either side, while the ridges were bald.

Along the bald high ground ran the roads. A dirt road linked Germeter and Vossenack. From Vossenack to the southeast, the map showed a narrow cart track dropping precipitously to the Kall River, then rising tortuously to Kommerscheidt and along the spur to Schmidt. Through Schmidt passes a highway linking the Monschau Corridor to Nideggen and another leading downhill to Hasenfeld and the Schwammenauel Dam. General Cota could only hope that the cart track across the Kall, which had to serve as a main supply route, would prove negotiable: on aerial photographs parts of the track did not show up. (*Map 8*) He also could do little but hope for the best

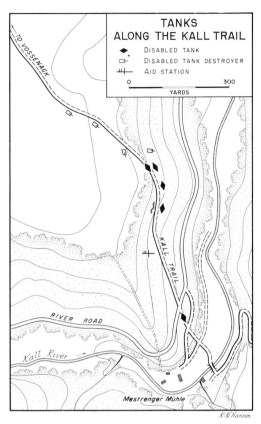

TANKS
ALONG THE KALL TRAIL
◆ DISABLED TANK
▭ DISABLED TANK DESTROYER
⊣⊢ AID STATION

0   300
YARDS

MAP 8

in regard to those places where the track crossed the exposed Vossenack ridge and the bald spur leading to Schmidt.

The factor of weather assumed tyrannical proportions, primarily because of the problem of getting tanks across the Kall gorge from Vossenack to Schmidt. Rain obviously would lessen chances of traversing the treacherous cart track across the Kall gorge, but more important still, rain would mean grounded aircraft. This might prove calamitous, for the planes had a big assignment. They were to isolate the battlefield to prevent the Germans from committing tanks and other reserves, particularly in the crucial zone beyond the Kall River where American tanks probably could not go.

Even assurance of fair weather would not have afforded peace of mind to the airmen. Few could cite an example where air power had been able to isolate such a small battlefield. In this instance, isolation would require destruction of bridges spanning the Roer, and bridges are difficult targets for planes. To compound the problem, the weather augury was anything but encouraging.

In considering the enemy, General Cota must have noted with some alarm that his would be the only U.S. attack along more than 170 miles of front, from the thumb-shaped corridor west of the Maas beyond Roermond all the way south to the Third Army near Metz. Whereas the 28th Division G–2 estimated the enemy had little more than 5,000 troops facing the division, these already had proved their mettle against the 9th Division. Although the same grab-bag assortment under General Schmidt's *275th Division* that had opposed the earlier attack still held the front, nothing in the 9th Division's experience showed that the slackness of the enemy's organization appreciably lessened the vigor of his defense. Indeed, the *275th Division*'s organization of the various *Kampfgruppen* under three regiments— the *983d*, *984th*, and *985th*—had been progressing steadily. The *275th Division* remained a part of General Straube's *LXXIV Corps* under General Brandenberger's *Seventh Army*.

Although intelligence officers long had known that the *89th Infantry Division* held the line farther south in the Monschau Corridor, they had not ascertained that a date for relief of the *89th* by a volks grenadier division was fast approaching. The *89th*'s relief might provide a reserve

close at hand to influence the battle for Schmidt.

As the 28th Division moved into the Huertgen Forest, the Germans knew an attack was imminent. They had identified the division, though they had failed to detect the shift in boundaries that had assigned this sector to the V Corps.

One thing the Germans recognized now without question: the importance of the Vossenack–Schmidt sector. Not only did it represent the key to the Roer River Dams; by holding its dominating ridges, the Germans also might forestall any threat to the road and communications center of Dueren while at the same time keeping the Americans bottled up in the Huertgen Forest. Those officers near the top of the German ladder of command recognized also that loss of Vossenack and Schmidt would pose a serious threat to plans already under way for a counter-offensive in the Ardennes.[11]

Unaware of the full value of Schmidt to the enemy, General Cota nevertheless did not like the idea of splitting his division in cruel terrain on three divergent missions. Moving with his men into the former 9th Division positions on 26 October did nothing to help matters. They found themselves in a dismal forest of the type immortalized in old German folk tales. All about them they saw emergency rations containers, artillery-stripped trees, loose mines along muddy firebreaks and trails, and shell and mine craters by the hundreds. The troops they relieved were tired, dirty, unshaven, and nervous.

---

[11] MSS # A–891 (Generalmajor Rudolph Freiherr von Gersdorff) and # A–905 (Generalmajor Siegfried von Waldenburg); ETHINT–53 (Gersdorff), ETHINT–56 (Gersdorff and Waldenburg), and ETHINT–57 (Gersdorff); and Relief Schedule, *Abloesungsplan*, 28 Oct 44, found in *OB WEST KTB, Anlage* 50, Vol. I.

Everywhere the forest scowled—wet, cold, and seemingly impenetrable.

By 29 October General Cota was ready to enunciate his plan. The attack was to open with a preliminary thrust northward by the 109th Infantry (Lt. Col. Daniel B. Strickler). Attacking through Wittscheidt and across the same wooded terrain that earlier had seen defeat of Colonel Wegelein's counterattack, the 109th Infantry was to advance about a mile to gain the woods line on either side of the Germeter–Huertgen highway overlooking Huertgen. From that point the regiment was to prevent any repetition of Colonel Wegelein's counterattack.

Meanwhile, a battalion of the 112th Infantry (Lt. Col. Carl L. Peterson) was to attack from Germeter through Vossenack to occupy the northeastern nose of the Vossenack ridge. From here this battalion was to help protect the division's north flank. Subsequently, at H plus three hours, the remainder of the 112th Infantry was to drive for the main objective. Passing through the road junction at Richelskaul, the bulk of Colonel Peterson's regiment was to move cross-country through the woods south of the Vossenack ridge, ford the Kall River, seize Kommerscheidt, then move on to Schmidt—a total advance of more than three miles.

Coincident with this main effort, the 110th Infantry (Colonel Seely) was to attack southward to take a nest of pillboxes at Raffelsbrand and be prepared to continue on order southward into the Monschau Corridor. Colonel Seely was to withhold one of his battalions from offensive assignment to provide the division commander a small infantry reserve.

Reflecting concern about counterattack from the direction of Huertgen, artillery units planned the bulk of their concentrations along the north flank. Except for one company of tanks to assist the 112th Infantry in the attack on Vossenack, attached tanks and self-propelled tank destroyers were to augment division artillery fires. Of the supporting engineers, one battalion was to assist the 112th Infantry by working on the precipitous cart track across the Kall gorge, another was to support the 110th Infantry in the woods south of Germeter, and the third was to work on supply trails in the forest west of Germeter. During the planning, General Cota charged the engineers specifically with providing security for the Kall River crossing. Because both ends of the gorge led into German-held territory and no infantry would be in a position to block the gorge, this was an important assignment. Nevertheless, as it appeared in the final engineer plan, the assignment was one of providing merely local security.[12]

North of the 28th Division, engineers of the 294th Engineer Combat Battalion had taken over the job of holding roadblocks in the Huertgen Forest generally along the Weisser Weh Creek. Southwest of the 28th Division's main positions, the division reconnaissance troop screened within the forest and patrolled to positions of the 4th Cavalry Group along the face of the Monschau Corridor.

After advancing the target date for the attack one day to 31 October, General Gerow had to postpone it because of rain, fog, and mist that showed no sign of abatement. This was a matter of serious concern in view of the vital role planned for air support in the 28th Division's attack; yet by the terms of the First

---

[12] See Engr Plan, 30 Oct, 28th Div G–3 Jnl file, Oct 44.

Army's original directive, the attack had to be made by 2 November, regardless of the weather. Much of the reason behind this stipulation—the hope that the 28th Division's attack might divert enemy reserves from the main First Army drive, scheduled to begin on 5 November—ceased to exist on 1 November when the main drive was postponed five days. Yet General Hodges, the army commander, apparently saw no reason to change the original directive. The 28th Division was to attack the next day, no matter what the state of the weather. H Hour was 0900, 2 November.[13]

Objective: Schmidt

The weather on 2 November was bad. As the big artillery pieces began to fire an hour before the jump-off, the morning was cold and misty. Even the most optimistic could not hope for planes before noon. The squadrons actually got into the fight no sooner than midafternoon, and then the weather forced cancellation of two out of five group missions and vectoring of two others far afield in search of targets of opportunity. Perhaps the most notable air action of the day was a mistaken bombing of an American artillery position in which seven were killed and seventeen wounded.

Though mist limited ground observation also, both V Corps and VII Corps artillery poured more than 4,000 rounds into the preliminary barrage. Fifteen minutes before the ground attack, direct support artillery shifted to targets in the immediate

---

[13] Sylvan Diary, entry of 31 Oct 44; Msg, Gerow to Cota, 28th Div G–3 Jnl, 31 Oct 44; Msg, CG FUSA to CG VII Corps, FUSA G–3 Jnl file, Nov 44. Though the latter message is undated, it obviously was sent on 1 November.

sector. By H Hour the 28th Division artillery had fired 7,313 rounds.

At 0900 men of the 109th Infantry clambered from their foxholes to launch the northward phase of the operation. Harassed more by problems of control in the thick forest than by resistance, the battalion west of the Germeter–Huertgen highway by early afternoon had reached the woods line overlooking Huertgen. Yet consolidation proved difficult. Everywhere the Germans were close, even in rear of the battalion where they infiltrated quickly to reoccupy their former positions. Advancing along the highway, another battalion had tougher going from the outset. After only a 300-yard advance, scarcely a stone's throw from Wittscheidt, the men encountered a dense antipersonnel mine field. Every effort to find a path through proved fruitless, while German machine guns and mortars drove attached engineers to cover each time they attempted to clear a way.

The next day, on 3 November, the battalion along the highway sought to flank the troublesome mine field. This was in progress when about 0730 the Germans struck twice with approximately 200 men each time at the battalion on the other side of the road. Though both counterattacks were driven off, they gave rise to a confusing situation on the American side. Misinterpreting a message from the regimental commander, the battalion near Wittscheidt sent two companies to assist in defeating the counterattacks. As these units became hopelessly enmeshed in the other battalion's fight and the depths of the forest, the day's attempt to outflank the mine field and occupy the other half of the 109th Infantry's woods line objective ended.

Though the regimental commander,

Colonel Strickler, still had a reserve, attempts to thwart enemy infiltration behind the front had virtually tied up this battalion already. By evening of 3 November, the mold of the 109th Infantry's position had almost set. The regiment had forged a narrow, mile-deep salient up the forested plateau between the Weisser Weh Creek and the Germeter–Huertgen highway. But along the creek bed the Germans still held to a comparable salient into American lines. For the next few days, while the men dug deep in frantic efforts to save themselves from incessant tree bursts, Colonel Strickler tried both to eliminate the Weisser Weh countersalient and to take the other half of his objective east of the highway; but to no avail. Every movement served only to increase already alarming casualties and to ensnare the companies and platoons more inextricably in the coils of the forest.

Coincident with the 109th Infantry's move north on 2 November, the 112th Infantry had attacked east from Germeter to gain Vossenack and the northeastern nose of the Vossenack ridge. The 2d Battalion under Lt. Col. Theodore S. Hatzfeld made the attack. The presence of a company of tanks with this battalion clearly demonstrated why the Germans wanted to keep the Americans bottled up in the Huertgen Forest. By early afternoon Colonel Hatzfeld's men had subdued Vossenack and were digging in almost at leisure on the northeastern nose of the ridge, though with the uncomfortable certainty that the enemy was watching from the Brandenberg–Bergstein ridge to the northeast and from Kommerscheidt and Schmidt.

The 28th Division's main effort began at noon on 2 November in the form of an attack by the two remaining battalions of Colonel Peterson's 112th Infantry. Heading east from Richelskaul to move cross-country through the woods south of Vossenack and cross the Kall gorge to Kommerscheidt and Schmidt, the lead battalion came immediately under intense small arms fire. For the rest of the day men of the foremost company hugged the ground, unable to advance. Though this was the divisional main effort, Colonel Peterson still did not commit the remainder of this battalion or his third battalion. Neither did he call for tank support nor make more than perfunctory use of supporting artillery. What must have occupied his mind was the ease with which his 2d Battalion had captured Vossenack. Why not follow that battalion, he must have reasoned, and strike for Kommerscheidt and Schmidt from the southeastern tip of Vossenack ridge? At any rate, that was the plan for the next day, 3 November.

Even as the 112th Infantry launched this irresolute main effort, Colonel Seely's 110th Infantry had begun a frustrating campaign in the forest farther south. One battalion was to take the pillboxes near Raffelsbrand while another drove through the woods to the east to the village of Simonskall alongside the Kall River. Seizure of these two points would dress the ground for advancing south along two roads into the Monschau Corridor, opening, in the process, a new supply route to Schmidt.

If any part of the 28th Division's battleground was gloomier than another, it was this. Except along the narrow ribbons of mud that were firebreaks and trails, only light diffused by dripping branches of fir trees could penetrate to the forest floor. Shelling already had made a debris-littered jungle of the floor and left naked yellow gashes on the trunks and branches of the trees. Here opposing lines were within hand grenade range. The Germans waited behind thick entanglements of concertina wire, alive with trip wires, mines, and booby traps. Where they had no pillboxes, they had constructed heavy log emplacements flush with the ground.

No sooner had troops of the two attacking battalions risen from their foxholes than a rain of machine gun and mortar fire brought them to earth. After several hours of painful, costly infiltration, one battalion reached the triple concertinas surrounding the pillboxes, but the enemy gave no sign of weakening. In midafternoon, the battalion reeled back, dazed and stricken, to the line of departure. With the other battalion, events went much the same. Platoons got lost; direct shell hits blew up some of the satchel charges and killed the men who were carrying them; and all communications failed except for spasmodic reception over little SCR–536's. The chatter of machine guns and crash of artillery and mortars kept frightened, forest-blind infantrymen close to the earth. In late afternoon, the decimated units slid back to the line of departure.

The 110th Infantry obviously needed direct fire support. Though the 9th Division's 60th Infantry had used tanks to advantage in the woods about Raffelsbrand, Colonel Seely bowed to the density of the woods, the dearth of negotiable roads, and the plethora of mines. Again on 3 November the infantry attacked alone. If anything, this second day's attack proved more costly and less rewarding than the first. One company fell back to the line of departure with but forty-two men remaining.

Failure of this second attack and more favorable developments in the 112th Infantry's main effort prompted General Cota in early evening of 3 November to release Colonel Seely's remaining battalion, the one he had earmarked as division reserve. Before daylight on 4 November, this battalion was to move to Vossenack and then drive due south into the woods to Simonskall. This might bring control of one of the 110th Infantry's assigned objectives while at the same time creating a threat to the rear of the pillboxes at Raffelsbrand. What had to be chanced in this decision was the possibility that after commitment of this reserve before dawn, something disastrous might happen elsewhere in the division zone—say, at daylight on 4 November, perhaps at Schmidt.

To the surprise of almost everyone concerned, the 112th Infantry by nightfall of 3 November possessed Schmidt. The regiment had done it by passing two battalions in column through Vossenack, thence southeast into the Kall gorge. While a company of tanks neutralized Kommerscheidt with fire from the Vossenack ridge, the leading battalion under Lt. Col. Albert Flood forded the cold, swift-flowing Kall and picked a way up the steep slope beyond. Pausing in Kommerscheidt only long enough to rout a handful of rear echelon Germans, Colonel Flood urged his men on toward Schmidt. By 1430 they were on the objective. Though persistent snipers delayed mop-up, Colonel Flood's men by nightfall had begun to organize the village for defense.

Because Schmidt sprawled spread-eagled across a bald ridge, defending it with only one infantry battalion was a question more of outposts than of a solid line. Neither tanks nor antitank guns had crossed the Kall gorge, and not until after midnight did the infantry have any antitank defense other than organic bazookas. At midnight a supply train of three weasels got forward with rations, ammunition, and sixty antitank mines. These mines the men placed on the three hard-surfaced roads leading into the village. Weary from the day's advance, the men made no effort either to dig in the mines or to camouflage them.

The other battalion of the 112th Infantry, commanded by Maj. Robert T. Hazlett, had in the meantime followed Colonel Flood's battalion as far as Komerscheidt. Because Major Hazlett had left one company to defend an original position far back at Richelskaul, he had but two companies and his heavy weapons support. These he split between Kommerscheidt and a support position at the woods line where the Kall trail emerges from the gorge. Major Hazlett's battalion was to have joined Colonel Flood's in Schmidt, but the regimental commander, Colonel Peterson, had decided instead to effect a defense in depth in deference to his regiment's exposed salient. General Cota must have approved, for he recorded no protest.[14]

Because inclement weather on 3 November again had denied all but a modicum of air support, the need of getting armor across the Kall gorge to Schmidt grew more urgent. The spotlight in the 28th Division's fight began to settle on the precipitous trail leading through the gorge.

An erroneous report prevalent in Vossenack during most of the day of 3 November that the bridge spanning the

Kall had been demolished served to discourage any real attempt to negotiate the trail until late in the afternoon. After two engineer officers reconnoitered and gave the lie to this report, a company of tanks of the 707th Tank Battalion under Capt. Bruce M. Hostrup made ready to try it. The trail, the engineer officers said, was a narrow shelf, limited abruptly on one side by a dirt wall studded with rock obstructions and on the other by a sheer drop. A weasel abandoned on the trail by a medical unit blocked passage, but once this was removed tanks might pass by hugging the dirt bank. At the Kall itself, a stone arch bridge was in good condition.

In gathering darkness, Captain Hostrup left the bulk of his tanks near the point where the Kall trail enters the woods, while he himself continued in his command tank to reconnoiter. About a quarter of the way from the woods line to the river, the trail became narrow and slippery. The left shoulder, which drops sharply toward the gorge, began to give way under weight of the tank. The rock obstructions in the dirt wall on the other side denied movement off to the right. The tank slipped and almost plunged off the left bank into the gorge.

Returning to the rest of his company, Captain Hostrup reported the trail still impassable. His battalion commander, Lt. Col. Richard W. Ripple, radioed that the engineers were to work on the trail through the night and that Captain Hostrup's tanks were to be ready to move through to Schmidt at dawn.

Under no apparent pressure except to get the trail open by daylight on 4 November, the 20th Engineer Combat Battalion, which was assigned to support the 112th Infantry, made a notably small outlay for

14 See 28th Div G-3 Jnl, 3 Nov 44, and interv with Col Peterson, 21-22-23 Sep 48.

a job of such importance. Only two platoons worked on the trail west of the river and but one on the east. Because no one during the original planning had believed that vehicles could get as far as the Kall, the engineers had with them only hand tools. Not until about 0230 in the morning did a bulldozer and an air compressor reach the work site. The bulldozer proved of little value; after about an hour's work, it broke a cable. The only vehicular traffic to cross the Kall during the night was the three-weasel supply train which carried the antitank mines to Schmidt.

Despite failure of tanks to cross the Kall and no evidence of clearing weather, the map in the 28th Division's war room on the night of 3 November showed that prospects were surprisingly good. While Colonel Strickler's 109th Infantry had attained only half its objective, the regiment nevertheless was in position to thwart counterattack from Huertgen. By commitment of the reserve battalion of the 110th Infantry before daylight to seize Simonskall, stalemate in the woods south of Germeter might be broken. Enemy units encountered were about what everyone had expected: the three regiments of the 275th Division, representing, in fact, consolidations of numerous Kampfgruppen. Albeit the weather had limited observation, no one yet had spotted any enemy armor. Most encouraging of all, the 28th Division had two battalions beyond the Kall, one in Kommerscheidt and the other astride the division objective in Schmidt. Capture of Schmidt meant that the main supply route to the German forts in the Monschau Corridor was cut. The Germans would have to strike hard and soon or the 28th Division would be in

shape to start a push into the corridor. Division and corps commanders all along the front had begun to telephone their congratulations to General Cota, so that despite his reservations he was beginning to feel like "a little Napoleon." [15]

The Germans React

Had General Cota and his staff considered two facts about the enemy, one of which they did have at hand, no one in the 28th Division could have slept that night, no matter what the elation over capture of Schmidt. First, the relief from the line in the Monschau Corridor of the *89th Infantry Division* by the *272d Volks Grenadier Division* had begun on 3 November. Indeed, when the first of Colonel Flood's troops had entered Schmidt, two battalions of the *89th Division's 1055th Regiment* had just passed through going northeast. They stopped for the night between Schmidt and the village of Harscheidt, less than a mile northeast of Schmidt. The remaining battalion of the *1055th Regiment* found upon nearing Schmidt after midnight that the Americans had cut the route of withdrawal. This battalion dug in astride the Schmidt–Lammersdorf road just west of Schmidt. A little patrolling by Colonel Flood's battalion might have revealed the presence of this enemy regiment deployed almost in a circle about Schmidt. Even without patrols, the 28th Division might have been alert to the likely presence of the *89th Division,* for during the day of 3 November other units of the V Corps had taken prisoners who reported the division's relief. This information had

---

[15] Interv with Gen Cota, 15 Sep 48.

reached the 28th Division during the day.[16]

The second fortuitous occurrence on the enemy side had as far-reaching effects for the Germans as the other. At almost the same moment that the 28th Division attacked at H-Hour on 2 November, staff officers and commanders of *Army Group B,* the *Fifth Panzer* and *Seventh Armies,* and several corps and divisions, including the *LXXIV Corps,* were convening in a castle near Cologne. There the *Army Group B* commander, Field Marshal Model, was to conduct a map exercise. The subject of the exercise was a theoretical American attack along the boundary of the *Fifth Panzer* and *Seventh Armies* in the vicinity of Huertgen. The meeting had been in session only a short time when a telephone call from the *LXXIV Corps* chief of staff told of the actual American attack. The situation, the chief of staff said, was critical: the *LXXIV Corps* had not enough men even to plug the gaps already opened; *Seventh Army* would have to send reserves.

Directing the *LXXIV Corps* commander, General Straube, to return to his post, Field Marshal Model told the other officers to continue the map exercise with the actual situation as subject. Continuing reports of further American advances then prompted a decision to send a small reserve to General Straube's assistance.

<hr>

[16] V Corps and 28th Div G–2 Jnl files, 3 Nov 44; sitreps 2–4 Nov 44, found in *OB WEST KTB, Befehle und Meldungen;* Order of the Day commemorating the battles of Kommerscheidt and Schmidt, entitled Division Review of the *89th Division* (hereafter cited as *89th Div* Order of the Day). This captured document is available only in translation by V Corps IPW Team 11, both in the 28th Div AAR, Oct 44, and as reproduced in Halsell, Huertgen Forest and the Roer River Dams.

A *Kampfgruppe* of the old warhorse, the *116th Panzer Division,* was to leave immediately to assist local reserves in a counterattack against the 109th Infantry's penetration north of Germeter. Like the counterattack Colonel Wegelein had tried against the 9th Division, this was designed to push through to Richelskaul and cut off that part of the 112th Infantry which had penetrated into Vossenack. Without a doubt, chance presence of the various major commanders at the map exercise facilitated German reaction against the 28th Division's attack.

Though the counterattack took place at dawn on 3 November, the 109th Infantry beat off what amounted to two thrusts without loss of ground. At the map exercise, which was still in progress on 3 November, news of the counterattack's failure prompted Field Marshal Model to send an entire regimental combat team of the *116th Panzer Division* to Huertgen. The remainder of the division was to follow that night and the night of 4 November. Since the pattern of American attack now indicated a thrust toward Schmidt, Model ordered the *1055th Regiment* of the *89th Division* to halt in its movement from the Monschau Corridor and be ready to strike back at Schmidt.

When the map exercise broke up, the *Seventh Army* commander, General Brandenberger, returned to his headquarters. There he learned in early evening of the 112th Infantry's conquest of Schmidt. Because he now controlled the *116th Panzer Division,* he was able to order the commander, Generalmajor Siegfried von Waldenburg, to reroute tanks of his *16th Panzer Regiment* from Huertgen to Harscheidt. At dawn on 4 November this tank regiment and the *89th*

KALL TRAIL, *looking toward Vossenack. Note thrown tank tracks.*

Division's 1055th Regiment were to counterattack at both Schmidt and Kommerscheidt. At the same time Waldenburg's *60th Panzer Grenadier Regiment,* en route to Huertgen, was to launch a new counterattack after the old plan against the 109th Infantry.

The pattern for German counteraction was taking shape rapidly. Because of terrain and mine fields, major tank participation was to be confined to Schmidt and Kommerscheidt. While the bulk of the *116th Panzer Division's* armor (some twenty to thirty tanks) operated there in conjunction with the *89th Division,* the panzer division's two panzer grenadier regiments were to strike at the 109th Infantry and at Vossenack. Having traveled at night, neither armor nor infantry had encountered American planes and were arriving in good shape.[17]

Before daylight on 4 November, two events were happening on the American side that were to bear heavily on the outcome of the day's action. First, General Cota was committing his only infantry reserve, a battalion of the 110th Infantry, to drive south from Vossenack through the woods to Simonskall in an effort to turn the stiff enemy line at Raffelsbrand. Launched before dawn, the attack met negligible resistance. By 0900 the battalion had seized Simonskall, a commendable success but one which failed to weaken resistance at Raffelsbrand and served to occupy the only infantry reserve which General Cota might have used as the day's events developed.

Second, after a somewhat feeble effort by attached engineers through most of the night to improve the Kall trail, tank crewmen under Captain Hostrup warmed their motors an hour or so before daylight for another try at crossing the Kall. The lead tank under 1st Lt. Raymond E. Fleig had just entered the woods along the slippery Kall trail when it struck a mine. A track disabled, the tank partially blocked the trail.

By using a winch, the tankers finally got four tanks past. Lieutenant Fleig then boarded the lead tank and by tortuous backing and turning finally reached the Kall to begin the toilsome last lap to Kommerscheidt just as day was breaking. Behind him Fleig left the shoulder of the

17 MSS # A-891 and A-892 (Gersdorff) and A-905 (Waldenburg); ETHINT-53 (Gersdorff) and ETHINT-56 (Gersdorff and Waldenburg); Sitreps, 2-4 Nov 44, found in *OB WEST KTB, Befehle und Meldungen; 89th Div* Order of the Day; 28th Div G-2 Jnl file, 3 Nov 44.

trail torn and crumbling. Only with the utmost difficulty and caution did the remaining three tanks of his platoon make their way. The tankers encountered a particular problem at one point where a giant outcropping of rock made it impossible to hug the right side of the trail. Near the bottom of the gorge, the last of the three tanks stuck in the mud and threw a track. Only two tanks now were following Lieutenant Fleig's toward Kommerscheidt.

Trying to maneuver the rest of the tank company across the Kall, Captain Hostrup first met difficulty at the tank which Lieutenant Fleig had abandoned after hitting a mine. Here one tank in attempting to pass plunged off the left shoulder of the trail. Using the wrecked tank as a buffer, two more tanks inched past; but near the rock outcropping both these slipped off the trail and threw their tracks. As battle noises from the direction of Schmidt began to penetrate to the gorge, three tanks under Lieutenant Fleig were beyond the river on the way to Kommerscheidt; but behind them, full on the vital trail, sat five disabled tanks. Not even the dexterous weasels could slip through.

In Schmidt, as daylight came about 0730 on 4 November, the crash of a German artillery barrage brought Colonel Flood's battalion of the 112th Infantry to the alert. About half an hour later the peripheral outposts shouted that German tanks and infantry were forming up in the fringe of Harscheidt. For some unexplained reason, American artillery was slow to respond; not until 0850 did the big guns begin to deliver really effective defensive fires. By that time the fight was on in earnest. Infantrymen from the battalion of the *1055th Regiment*

KALL TRAIL, *showing the Kommerscheidt side of the gorge in the background.*

that had found their route of withdrawal cut by American capture of Schmidt charged in from the west. The other two battalions of the regiment and at least ten tanks and assault guns of the *16th Panzer Regiment* struck from the direction of Harscheidt.[18]

As the German tanks clanked method-

ically onward in apparent disdain of the exposed mines strung across the hard-surfaced roads, the defenders opened fire with bazookas. At least one scored a hit, but the rocket bounced off. The German tanks came on, firing their big cannon and machine guns directly into foxholes and buildings. Reaching the antitank mines, the tanks merely swung off the roads in quick detours, then waddled on. Such seeming immunity to the bazookas and mines demoralized the men who saw it.

---

[18] Unlike most German regiments during this period, those of the *89th Division* had three instead of two battalions of infantry, but the division had only two regiments.

Confusion mounted. As rumor hummed about that orders had come to withdraw, individually and in small groups those American infantrymen still alive and uncrippled pulled out. The overwhelming impulse to get out of the path of the tanks sent the men streaming from the village in a *sauve qui peut*. About 200 fled into the woods southwest of Schmidt, there to find they actually were deeper in German territory. The others tore back toward Kommerscheidt. The dead lay unattended. Because the battalion's medical aid station had not advanced any farther than a log-walled dugout beside the Kall trail west of the river, the only comfort for the wounded was the presence of company aid men who volunteered to stay with them.

By 1100 most Americans who were to get out of Schmidt had done so. By 1230 the 28th Division headquarters apparently recognized the loss, for at that time the first air support mission of the day struck the village. For the third straight day fog and mist had denied large-scale air support. No more solid proof than the German attack on Schmidt was needed to show that the attempt to isolate the battlefield had failed.

In Kommerscheidt and at the Kall woods line several hundred yards north of Kommerscheidt, the men of Major Hazlett's understrength battalion of the 112th Infantry were exposed fully to the sounds of battle emanating from Schmidt. By midmorning small groups of frightened, disorganized men began to filter back with stories that "they're throwing everything they've got at us." By 1030 the numbers had reached the proportions of a demoralized mob, reluctant to respond to orders. Some men wandered back across the Kall to Vossenack and Germeter. Yet within the mass a few frantic efforts to stem the withdrawal had effect. When the enemy did not pursue his advantage immediately, groups of Colonel Flood's men began to reorganize and dig in with Major Hazlett's. About 200 joined the Kommerscheidt defenses.

Despite air attacks against Schmidt and round after round of artillery fire poured into the village, the reprieve from German tanks and infantry did not last long. In early afternoon a posse of at least five Mark IV and V tanks and about 150 infantry attacked. Imitating the tactics they had used at Schmidt, the enemy tankers stood out of effective bazooka range and pumped shells into foxholes and buildings.

The day might have been lost save for the fact that Major Hazlett had an ace which Colonel Flood had not had in Schmidt. He had Lieutenant Fleig's three tanks. From right to left of the position Fleig and his tanks maneuvered fearlessly. Spotting a Mark V Panther overrunning positions in an orchard on the eastern fringe of Kommerscheidt, Lieutenant Fleig directed his driver there. Although the lieutenant got in the first shots, his high-explosive ammunition bounced off the Panther's tough hide. All his armor-piercing rounds, Fleig discovered, were outside in the sponson rack. When Fleig turned his turret to get at these rounds, the Panther opened fire. The first shot missed. Working feverishly, the lieutenant and his crew thrust one of the armor-piercing rounds into the chamber. The first shot cut the barrel of the German gun. Three more in quick succession tore open the left side of the Panther's hull and set the tank afire.

By 1600 the Germans had begun to fall back, leaving behind the hulks of five tanks. A bomb from a P–47 had knocked out one, a bazooka had accounted for another, and Lieutenant Fleig and his tankers had gotten three. The presence of the lieutenant and his three tanks obviously provided a backbone to the defense at Kommerscheidt that earlier had been lacking at Schmidt.

In midafternoon General Cota ordered that the units in Kommerscheidt attack to retake Schmidt, but no one on the ground apparently entertained any illusions about immediate compliance. When the regimental commander, Colonel Peterson, and the assistant division commander, Brig. Gen. George A. Davis, arrived in late afternoon to survey the situation, they must have realized that the question was not of retaking Schmidt but of holding Kommerscheidt. As the men on the ground soon came to know, it was a difficult position to hold, situated as it was under direct observation from the higher part of the Schmidt–Kommerscheidt spur and from the Brandenberg–Bergstein ridge.

Not all the day's events brought on by entry of German reserves took place beyond the Kall. No one, for example, was more conscious of major additions to enemy artillery strength than the men of Colonel Hatzfeld's battalion of the 112th Infantry on the bald Vossenack ridge. Both *Army Group B* and *Seventh Army* had sent several artillery, assault gun, antitank, and mortar battalions to the sector, and General Straube committed a portion of the artillery and antitank guns of the three of his *LXXIV Corps* divisions not affected by the American attack.[19]

Subject as Colonel Hatzfeld's troops were to dominant observation from the Brandenberg–Bergstein ridge, they found it worth a man's life to move from his foxhole during daylight. Even if he stayed he might be entombed by shellfire. The companies began to bring as many men as possible into the houses during the day, leaving only a skeleton force on the ridge. Still casualties mounted. In the western end of Vossenack, troops carried on their duties while traffic continued to flow in and out of the village. Someone entering Vossenack for only a short time, perhaps during one of the inevitable lulls in the shelling, might not have considered the fire particularly effective. But the foot soldiers knew differently. To them in their exposed foxholes, a lull was only a time of apprehensive waiting for the next bursts. The cumulative effect began to tell.

The other center of German activity was against the 109th Infantry's salient on the wooded plateau north of Germeter. Even as Colonel Strickler sent his reserve battalion on a futile attempt to take the other half of the regimental objective east of the Germeter–Huertgen highway, the *116th Panzer Division's 60th Panzer Grenadier Regiment* counterattacked west of the highway. Either poorly organized or thrown awry by American defensive fires, the strike became less a counterattack than amorphous infiltration. Yet before desisting, the Germans infiltrated the rear of the northernmost battalion, surrounded the battalion command post, and captured or killed about fifteen men, including most of the battalion staff and the artillery liaison party.

Arrival during 4 November of two other units strengthened the German forces that now strongly penned the 28th

[19] MSS # C–016 (Straube) and # A–905 (Waldenburg); Sitreps, 2–4 Nov 44, *OB WEST KTB, Befehle und Meldungen.*

Division on three sides. In and south of the Monschau Corridor, continuing relief by the *272d Volks Grenadier Division* made available the *89th Division*'s second regiment, the *1056th.* The *89th Division* commander, Generalmajor Walter Bruns, ordered the *1056th Regiment* into the woods to hold a line between Simonskall and the *1055th Regiment,* which was attacking Kommerscheidt.[20] Also during the day of 4 November, the remaining regiment of the *116th Panzer Division,* the *156th Panzer Grenadier Regiment,* arrived at Huertgen. The division commander, General von Waldenburg, ordered the regiment into the woods north and northeast of Vossenack. He told attached engineers to build a road through the woods so that tanks might assist the panzer grenadiers in taking Vossenack, though eventually he had to abandon this venture.[21]

As ordered by the *Seventh Army* commander, General Brandenberger, German plans to restore the situation which had existed on the opening day of the American offensive now were definitely formulated. The *275th Division* was to ensure that the wings of the American salient were held against further widening. Renewing the attack against Kommerscheidt on 5 November, General Bruns's *89th Division* was to clear the east bank of the Kall with the assistance of the bulk of the *16th Panzer Regiment.* Continuing to punch at the 109th Infantry with one panzer grenadier regiment, General von Waldenburg was to maneuver the rest of the *116th Panzer Division* into position for a concentric attack on Vossenack. Both to gain a position from which to assist the attack on Vossenack from the south and also to cut off the Americans in Kommerscheidt, the *116th Panzer Division*'s *Reconnaissance Battalion* was to drive on 5 November down the Kall gorge from the northeast to effect a link with the *89th Division.* The Germans did not realize that the 28th Division had taken virtually no defensive measures in the Kall gorge.[22]

Events Along the Trail

Although the spotlight from the American side was focused on the Kall gorge, the 28th Division was concentrating not on defending the gorge but on getting the precarious Kall trail open so that armor might cross to Kommerscheidt. Only three weasels and three tanks had crossed the Kall, and five disabled tanks now blocked the way. Despite the urgency of opening the trail, only a company and a platoon of engineers worked there during 4 November. For fear of damaging the disabled tanks, the engineers hesitated to use explosives on the main obstacle, the giant outcropping of rock. Indeed, everybody appeared to treat the disabled tanks with the kind of warm-hearted affection an old-time cavalryman might lavish on his horse. Why not sacrifice the five disabled tanks by pushing them off the trail into the gorge? This tank company under Captain Hostrup still had six more tanks, and the 28th Division had two other companies of tanks and almost a battalion of self-propelled tank destroyers available to cross the Kall. Yet all

[20] MS # P-032a (Bruns); *89th Div* Order of the Day.
[21] MS # A-905 (Waldenburg).
[22] MSS # A-891 and # A-892 (Gersdorff), # A-105 (Waldenburg), # C-016 (Straube), and # P-032 (Bruns); ETHINT-56 (Gersdorff and Waldenburg); Sitreps, 2-4 Nov 44, *OB WEST KTB, Befehle und Meldungen; 89th Div* Order of the Day.

through the day of 4 November and far past midnight the tankers worked at the frustrating task of righting the tracks on the tanks, inching the vehicles forward a few paces, and watching the tracks jump off again.

Part reason for dalliance no doubt lay in the fact that General Cota all day long was ill informed about the condition of his vital main supply route across the Kall. Most reports reaching 28th Division headquarters repeatedly asserted that the trail was open. Neither the 112th Infantry nor General Cota had liaison officers on the spot. Not until approximately 1500 did General Cota intervene personally by ordering the 1171st Engineer Combat Group commander, Col. Edmund K. Daley, to send a "competent officer" to supervise work on the trail. After visiting the site himself, Colonel Daley ordered the commander of the 20th Engineer Combat Battalion, Lt. Col. J. E. Sonnefield, to take personal charge.

Not until approximately 0230, 5 November, did the tankers desist in their admirable but illogical struggle to save their tanks. At that time General Cota gave them a direct order either to have the trail clear by daybreak or to roll the immobilized tanks down the slope. As the engineers blew the troublesome rock outcropping, the tankers threw all their vehicles off the trail except the one stuck in the mud near the bottom of the gorge. That one might be bypassed, someone had discovered, by following a circuitous cutoff provided by two smaller trails.

The first vehicular traffic to cross the Kall after removal of the tanks was a convoy of 5 weasels carrying rations and ammunition. Later, soon after daylight on 5 November, 9 self-propelled M10 tank destroyers of the 893d Tank De-stroyer Battalion and the 6 remaining tanks of Captain Hostrup's company crossed the river. By noon of 5 November the Americans had 9 tanks and 9 tank destroyers east of the Kall.

They needed these and more. Even before the first of these reinforcements arrived, the Germans struck again at Kommerscheidt. Weak from cold, rain, and fatigue, the remnants of the two battalions of the 112th Infantry had no recourse but to huddle miserably in their foxholes, awaiting whatever the Germans might throw at them. Enemy observation from Schmidt was so damaging that men dared not emerge from their holes, even for sanitary reasons. As everywhere in the 28th Division sector, casualties from combat fatigue and trench foot were on the rise. The only real comfort the infantrymen had was the knowledge that their artillery was punishing the Germans with "terrific" fires.

Lieutenant Fleig and his three veteran tanks saved the day against the first German attack soon after dawn on 5 November. When they immobilized one of five enemy tanks, the others gradually withdrew. Although the Germans made several more strikes during the day, their tanks participated only by fire from covered positions in Schmidt. No doubt they hesitated to emerge because for the first time since the offensive had begun, American planes had good hunting. Clearing weather permitted the first planes to take to the air as early as 0835 and remain out all day. The pilots claimed at least 10 enemy armored vehicles destroyed, but only 2 or 3 of these at Schmidt.[23]

In the meantime, the Germans had taken up arms against another group of

---

[23] A not unlikely estimate in light of MS # A-905 (Waldenburg).

American infantrymen whose detailed story may never be told. These were the men, perhaps as many as 200, who had fled from Schmidt on 4 November into the woods southwest of that village. On 5 November the enemy's *1055th Regiment* noted the first prisoners from this group. Before dawn on 9 November three from the trapped group were to make their way to American lines but with the report that when they had left two days before to look for help, the remaining men had neither water nor rations. The three men doubted that on 9 November any still survived. They probably were right. The *89th Division* reported that on 8 November, after the Americans had held out for four days, the Germans captured 133. Presumably, these were the last.[24]

A definite pattern in the fighting now had emerged. The battlefields of the 112th Infantry at Kommerscheidt and Vossenack, while separated in locale by the fissure of the Kall gorge, were wedded in urgency. For even as the fight raged at Kommerscheidt, the inexorable pounding of the bald Vossenack ridge by the enemy's artillery went on. Not even presence overhead of American planes appeared to silence German guns. Casualties of all types soared. So shaky was the infantry that the assistant division commander, General Davis, ordered at least a platoon of tanks to stay in Vossenack at all times to bolster infantry morale.

Action on the other two battlefields, that of the 109th Infantry on the wooded plateau north of Germeter and of the 110th Infantry to the south at Simonskall and Raffelsbrand, ebbed and flowed with the fortunes of the center regiment. On 5 November the 109th Infantry held against continued counterattacks by the *60th Panzer Grenadier Regiment*. The 110th Infantry made virtually no progress in persistent attempts to close the pillbox-studded gap between the battalions at Simonskall and Raffelsbrand. Not for some days would the fact be acknowledged officially, but the 110th Infantry already was exhausted beyond the point of effectiveness as a unit.

As these events took place on 5 November, another act was about to begin along the Kall trail. When the assistant division commander, General Davis, had traversed the trail the afternoon before en route to Kommerscheidt, he had noted that the engineers had no one defending either the bridge or the trail itself. Encountering a company of the 20th Engineers, General Davis told the commander, Capt. Henry R. Doherty, to assume a defensive position where the trail enters the woods southeast of Vossenack. Captain Doherty was also, General Davis said, to "guard the road near the bridge."[25] At the bridge, the engineer officer stationed a security guard of three men under T/4 James A. Kreider, while the remainder of the engineer company dug in at the western woods line. Except for Kreider's small force, the defensive positions chosen were of little value, for a thick expanse of woods separated the engineers from the bridge and from the main part of the Kall trail.

The first indication that the Germans might accept the standing invitation to sever the 112th Infantry's main supply route came about midnight on 5 November. Bound for Kommerscheidt, an anti-tank squad towing a gun with a weasel

---

[24] German sources are an entry of 5 Nov 44 in *OB WEST KTB* and *89th Div* Order of the Day.

[25] Quotation from a combat interview with Doherty.

was attacked without warning near the bottom of the gorge. Even as this ambush occurred, engineers were working on the trail not far away, and two supply columns subsequently crossed the Kall safely.

A few hours later, at approximately 0230 on 6 November, two squads of engineers working on the trail near the bridge decided to dig in to protect themselves against German shelling. As they dug, these two squads and the four-man security guard at the bridge represented the only obstacle to uninterrupted German movement along the Kall gorge.

The engineers still were digging when a German appeared on the trail some fifteen yards away, blew two shrill blasts on a whistle, and set off a maze of small arms fire. Taken by surprise, the engineers had no chance. Those who survived did so by melting into the woods. At the Kall bridge, Sergeant Kreider and the men of his security guard saw the Germans but dared not fire at such a superior force.

Another group of Americans was in the Kall gorge at this time. They were medics and patients who occupied a log-walled dugout alongside the trail halfway up the western bank. The dugout was serving as an aid station for both American battalions in Kommerscheidt. About 0300 several Germans knocked at the door of the dugout. After satisfying themselves that the medics were unarmed, the Germans posted a guard and left. At intervals through the rest of the night, the medics could see the Germans mining the Kall trail.

At about 0530, as two jeeps left Vossenack with ammunition for Kommerscheidt, a platoon of Germans loomed out of the darkness on the open part of the trail southeast of Vossenack. Firing with machine guns and a panzerfaust, the Germans knocked out both jeeps. The lieutenant in one vehicle yelled to an enlisted man riding with him to fire the jeep's machine gun. "I can't, Lieutenant," the man shouted; "I'm dying right here!"

These events clearly demonstrated that local security, as enunciated in the engineer plan, was not enough to prevent German movement along the Kall gorge. Indeed, these incidents indicated that the 20th Engineers had an unusual conception of what constituted security. Except at the woods line where Captain Doherty's company held defensive positions, soldiers of the *116th Panzer Division's* *Reconnaissance Battalion* controlled almost every segment of the Kall trail west of the river.

Erroneous reports about the status of the supply route through the hours of darkness on the morning of 6 November forestalled any last-minute attempt to defend the trail. Not until about 0800 did the engineer group commander, Colonel Daley, get what was apparently accurate information. He immediately ordered the 20th Engineers to "Get every man you have in line fighting. Establish contact with the Infantry on right and left . . . ."

No one did anything to comply with the order. By this time another crucial situation arising in Vossenack had altered the picture.

The first step taken by the 28th Division to counteract the enemy's intrusion into the Kall gorge actually emerged as a corollary of a move made for another purpose. It had its beginning in late afternoon of 5 November when General Cota announced formation of a special task force under the 707th Tank Battalion commander, Colonel Ripple. Task Force Ripple was to cross the Kall and assist the remnants of the 112th Infantry to retake Schmidt. Thereupon, the task force was to open the second phase of the 28th Division's attack, the drive southwest into the Monschau Corridor.

Task Force Ripple looked impressive— on paper. Colonel Ripple was to have a battalion of the 110th Infantry, one of his own medium tank companies and his light tank company, plus a company and a platoon of self-propelled tank destroyers. Yet, in reality, Task Force Ripple was feeble. The stupefying fighting in the woods south of Germeter had reduced the infantry battalion to little more than 300 effectives, of which a third were heavy weapons men. The company of medium tanks was that of Captain Hostrup, already in Kommerscheidt but with only nine remaining tanks. The company of tank destroyers was that in Kommerscheidt, reduced now to seven guns. The other platoon of tank destroyers and the company of light tanks still had to cross the mined and blocked Kall trail. So discouraging were prospects of passage that no one ever got around to ordering the light tanks to attempt it.

The platoon of tank destroyers contributed to passage of Task Force Ripple across the Kall, though the destroyers themselves never made it. Moving along the open portion of the trail southeast of Vossenack, the destroyers dispersed the Germans who earlier had knocked out the two jeeps with machine guns and panzerfaust. When the depleted infantry battalion arrived at the entrance of the trail into the woods about 0600 on 6 November, the tank destroyer crewmen asked at least a platoon of infantry to accompany their guns down the Kall trail. Colonel Ripple refused. Considering his infantry force already too depleted, he intended to

avoid a fight along the trail by taking instead a firebreak paralleling the trail.

Almost from the moment the infantry entered the woods at the firebreak, they became embroiled in a small arms fight that lasted all the way to the river. Not until well after daylight did the infantry cross the Kall and not until several hours later did they join Colonel Peterson's troops at the woods line north of Kommerscheidt. In the crossing the battalion lost seventeen men. Yet in getting beyond the Kall, Colonel Ripple in effect had made a successful counterattack against the *116th Panzer Division's Reconnaissance Battalion.* The enemy had fallen back along the river to the northeast. Though the Americans did not know until later in the day, the Kall trail as early as 0900 on 6 November was temporarily clear of Germans.[26]

The scene that Task Force Ripple found upon arrival beyond the Kall was one of misery and desolation. Though one artillery concentration after another prevented German infantry from forming to attack, the enemy's tanks sat on their dominating perch in the edge of Schmidt and poured round after round into Kommerscheidt. Maneuvering on the lower ground about Kommerscheidt, the American tanks and tank destroyers were no match for the Mark IV's and V's.[27] By midday on 6 November, only 6 American tanks remained fully operational and only 3 of an original 9 destroyers. The clear weather of the day before had given

---

[26] See Sitreps, 6 Nov 44, *OB WEST KTB, Befehle und Meldungen.*

[27] For heroic action at Kommerscheidt during 4–6 November, one of the tank destroyer platoon leaders, 1st Lt. Turney W. Leonard, who was subsequently seriously wounded, was awarded the Medal of Honor.

way to mist and overcast so that the enemy tanks again had little concern about American planes.

After seeing Task Force Ripple's battered infantry battalion, the 112th Infantry commander, Colonel Peterson, could divine scant possibility of success in retaking Schmidt. He nevertheless fully intended to go through with the attack. But as the officers reconnoitered, one adversity followed another. In a matter of minutes the battalion of the 110th Infantry lost its commander, executive officer, S–2, and a company commander. Canceling the proposed attempt to retake Schmidt, Colonel Peterson told the men of the 110th Infantry to dig in along the woods line north of Kommerscheidt in order to strengthen his defense in depth.

The lonely despair of the men east of the Kall by this time must have deepened, for surely they must have heard that the main drive by the VII Corps had been postponed to 11 November and that even this target date was subject to the vagaries of weather. That higher commanders were concerned—as evidenced by visits to the 28th Division command post on 5 November by Generals Hodges, Gerow, and Collins—was scarcely sufficient balm for the bitter knowledge that theirs would remain for at least five more days the only attack from the Netherlands to Metz.

Catastrophe in Vossenack

Though dreadful to the men involved, the retreat from Schmidt and the trouble at Kommerscheidt had posed no real threat to the 28th Division's integrity. As dawn came on 6 November, at the same time Task Force Ripple was unwittingly clearing the Germans from the Kall gorge, another crisis was arising that

did spell a threat to the very existence of the division.

As day broke across the bald northeastern nose of the Vossenack ridge, events there were striding to a climax. Their men unnerved by three days and four nights of merciless shelling under the shadow of the Brandenberg–Bergstein ridge, the harassed company commanders of Colonel Hatzfeld's 2d Battalion, 112th Infantry, had been apprehensive of what the day of 6 November might bring. They had reported to Colonel Hatzfeld that their men's nerves were shattered, that they had to order some to eat, and that many cried unashamedly when told to remain in their foxholes. But nobody had done anything about it. The battalion commander himself sat in his basement command post, his head in his hands.

Few of the men on the Vossenack ridge could comprehend why the Germans failed to herald the dawn with their customary artillery concentrations. The unusual quiet bred misgivings. Then a burst of small arms fire sounded. Someone let go a piercing scream; then silence again. A half hour later, as daylight increased, the German guns spoke.

Already groggy to the point of insensibility, the men could stand no more. Panic-ridden, men of one company grabbed wildly at their equipment and broke for the rear. Seeing his position compromised by the flight of his neighbor, the commander of another company ordered his platoons to fall back on the battalion reserve. The impulse to run was contagious. Once the men got going, they would not stop. The reserve company too pulled out. Although no one professed to have seen any enemy soldiers, few doubted that the Germans were close on their heels. Pushing, shoving, strewing equipment, the men raced wild-eyed through Vossenack. Circumstances had evoked one of the most awful powers of war, the ability to cast brave men in the role of cowards.

Dashing from the battalion command post near the church in the center of Vossenack, the battalion staff tried frantically to stem the retreat. It was an impossible task. Most men thought only of some nebulous place of refuge called "the rear." By 1030 the officers nevertheless had established a semblance of a line running through the village at the church, but in the line were no more than seventy men.

Even as the retreat had begun, a platoon of tank destroyers and a platoon of tanks were in the northeastern edge of Vossenack. Although both stayed there more than a half hour after the infantry pulled out, crewmen of neither platoon saw any German infantry either attacking or attempting to occupy the former American positions. First reports of the flight brought four more platoons of tanks racing from Germeter into the village. Not until midmorning did the last of the tanks leave the eastern half of Vossenack to join the thin olive drab line near the church.

On the enemy side, General von Waldenburg's *116th Panzer Division* had planned an attack on Vossenack for 0400, 6 November. The *156th Panzer Grenadier Regiment* and some portions of the *60th Panzer Grenadiers* were to have struck from the woods north and northeast of the village. But something had happened to delay the attack; either the infantry or the supporting artillery was not ready on time. No positive identification of German troops in Vossenack before noon developed. It was safe to assume

that the rout of Colonel Hatzfeld's battalion had resulted not from actual ground attack but from fire and threat of attack.[28]

As the chaotic situation developed in Vossenack, the highest ranking officer on the scene, the assistant division commander, General Davis, found himself torn between two crises: that at Vossenack and that in the Kall gorge. He could not have known at this time that Task Force Ripple's advance through the gorge already had cleared the Germans from the Kall trail. His only hope for a reserve to influence either situation was the 1171st Engineer Combat Group.

Despite some contradictory orders and a lack of liaison between General Davis and the engineer commander, Colonel Daley, a pattern of commitment of the engineers as riflemen had emerged by midafternoon of 6 November. Into Vossenack went the 146th Engineer Combat Battalion (minus a company on detached service). To the Kall gorge went the remnants of the 20th Engineers and two companies of the 1340th Engineer Combat Battalion. A third company of the 1340th Engineers remained in support of the 110th Infantry.

In the Kall gorge the engineers happily discovered that the Germans had gone. By nightfall a company of the 1340th Engineers was digging in at the Kall bridge while another company and most of what was left of the 20th Engineers assumed Captain Doherty's old positions at the western entrance of the trail into the Kall woods.

---

[28] German sources on this point are vague. See MS # A–905 (Waldenburg) and # C–016 (Straube); ETHINT–56 (Gersdorff and Waldenburg); Sitreps 6 Nov 44, *OB WEST KTB, Befehle und Meldungen;* 28th Div G–2 and G–3 Jnls and files, 6 Nov 44.

In Vossenack the two companies of the 146th Engineers were committed so quickly that the men still wore hip boots they had been using on road repair work. They moved immediately to take responsibility for the thin infantry line near the church.[29]

The crisis in Vossenack had repercussions all the way back to headquarters of the V Corps. Upon first news of the catastrophe, General Gerow hurriedly alerted the 4th Division's 12th Infantry. Beginning that night, the 12th Infantry was to relieve Colonel Strickler's 109th Infantry on the wooded plateau north of Germeter. Upon relief, the 109th Infantry was to be employed only as approved by General Gerow. Even though this regiment had been mutilated in the fight in the woods, freeing it would decrease somewhat the apprehension over the recurring crises within the 28th Division. General Gerow must have recognized that should the Germans push on from Vossenack past Germeter, they would need only a shallow penetration to disrupt the First Army's plans for the main drive to the Roer by the VII Corps.

During the night of 6 November both the 146th Engineers and the *156th Panzer Grenadier Regiment* laid plans for driving the other out of Vossenack. Both attacks were to begin about 0800.[30] As daylight came the Americans started their preparatory artillery barrage first.

When the barrage had ended and the two engineer companies moved into the open to attack, German fire began. Although this shelling hit one of the companies severely, both charged forward, one on either side of the village's main street. They had beaten the Germans to the draw.

Despite relative unfamiliarity with an attack role and a lack of hand grenades, radios, and mortars, the engineers attacked with enthusiasm and energy.[31] Where particularly stubborn resistance formed, a tank platoon advancing along the southeastern fringe of the village went into action. By early evening the engineers in a superior demonstration had cleared the eastern end of Vossenack at a cost to the *116th Panzer Division* of at least 150 casualties. A battalion of the 109th Infantry that had been relieved in the woods north of Germeter took over from the engineers. This time the infantry heeded the lesson demonstrated at such a price by Colonel Hatzfeld's battalion and holed up in the village itself rather than on the exposed nose of the ridge. Though patrol clashes and heavy shelling continued, the tempo of fighting at Vossenack gradually slackened.

The Kall Gorge

The situation in the Kall gorge was neither so quickly nor so decisively set right. To be sure, events along the trail had taken a turn for the better on 6

---

[29] As the engineers neared the church, Pvt. Doyle W. McDaniel climbed atop a building to search for enemy riflemen who were impeding his company's advance. Later he repeated the action; but the second time the Germans spotted and killed him. He was awarded the DSC posthumously.

[30] For German plans, see Sitreps, 7 Nov 44, *OB WEST KTB, Befehle und Meldungen,* and ETHINT-56 (Gersdorff and Waldenburg).

[31] Though out of ammunition, Pfc. Henry J. Kalinowsky stormed across an open field in the face of fire from five Germans in a house, jumped through a window, and forced the Germans to surrender at the point of his empty rifle. He was awarded the DSC.

November when passage of Task Force Ripple had driven away the enemy's *116th Panzer Reconnaissance Battalion* and when the 1340th Engineers had moved one company to the Kall bridge and another to the western woods line. Yet even as the engineers dug in, the Germans were planning a new move in the Kall gorge.

Commanded by Capt. Ralph E. Lind, Jr., the engineer company at the Kall bridge had a strength of not quite a hundred men. Splitting his force, Captain Lind put one platoon east of the river and the remainder on the west. About a half hour before midnight on 6 November, the *Reconnaissance Battalion* began to move back into the gorge. Behind heavy shelling, about a platoon attacked that part of Captain Lind's company west of the river. Some of the engineers left their foxholes to retreat up the hill toward the other engineer positions at the woods line. For the rest of the night the Germans again roamed the Kall gorge almost at will.

Unaware of this development, a supply column carrying rations and ammunition to Kommerscheidt started from Vossenack about midnight. Once the men in the column thought they heard German voices, but no untoward incident occurred. On the return journey, the vehicles were loaded with wounded. Again the column crossed the river successfully but near the western woods line had to abandon two big trucks because of a tree that partially blocked the trail.

By daylight on 7 November, the situation along the Kall trail was something of a paradox. The Germans claimed that despite "considerable losses" the *116th Panzer Reconnaissance Battalion* again

had cut the trail and established contact with the *89th Division* in the woods to the south.[32] Yet an American supply column had crossed and recrossed the Kall during the night. The Americans thought their engineers controlled the trail, but by midmorning of 7 November, the only force in position to do so—that of Captain Lind—was down to the company commander and five men. The rest of the engineers had melted away into the woods.

Upon learning in early afternoon that the engineers had deserted the bridge, the battalion commander, Lt. Col. Truman H. Setliffe, ordered his third company that had been supporting the 110th Infantry to move to the bridge and "stay there." Commanded by Capt. Frank P. Bane, this company moved down the firebreak paralleling the Kall trail, left a platoon near the foot of the firebreak, and then moved to the bridge. Considering his force too small to justify positions on both sides of the river, Captain Bane remained on the west bank and echeloned his squads up the trail to the west. They made no effort to contact the infantry forces east of the Kall. Thus only a portion of the Kall trail west of the river was secure.

One more effort on 7 November to get a firm grip on the elusive Kall trail emerged as a corollary to another commendable but feeble plan to retake Schmidt. Banking on a battalion of the newly relieved 109th Infantry as the main component, General Cota ordered formation of another task force under the assistant division commander, General

---

[32] Sitreps, 7 Nov 44, *OB WEST KTB, Befehle und Meldungen.*

Davis, to recapture Schmidt. As had Task Force Ripple, Task Force Davis looked impressive on paper. In addition to the battalion of the 109th Infantry, General Davis was to have the 112th Infantry (minus Colonel Hatzfeld's destroyed battalion), the battalion of the 110th Infantry that had gone to Kommerscheidt as a part of Task Force Ripple, two companies of tanks, and two companies of self-propelled tank destroyers. Of this force only the battalion of the 109th Infantry in reality had any offensive potential, and that based primarily upon arrival of green replacements the night before. Half of the armor still would have to cross the perilous Kall trail. Four of the tank destroyers tried that in early afternoon of 7 November, only to wreck on the open ridge southeast of Vossenack while shying at enemy shellfire.

Both General Cota and General Davis nevertheless intended on 7 November to proceed with the attack on Schmidt by Task Force Davis. To ensure passage of the task force across the Kall, General Cota ordered another battalion of the 109th Infantry to go to the gorge and secure the bridge and the trail. An hour or so before dark on 7 November this battalion reported being in position, but the next morning General Cota was to learn that in reality the battalion had got lost in the forest and ended up a thousand yards southwest of Richelskaul in rear of the 110th Infantry.

By daylight of 8 November, General Cota still had issued no movement orders for Task Force Davis. At the task force command post a belief gained credence that the orders might never come. For by 8 November events at Kommerscheidt already had dictated a more realistic appraisal of the 28th Division's capabilities.

Climax at Kommerscheidt

During the evening of 6 November, while the issues at Vossenack and in the Kall gorge remained in doubt, the commander of the enemy's *89th Division,* General Bruns, had convened the leaders of his *1055th* and *1056th Regiments* and the attached *16th Panzer Regiment.* The inertia at Kommerscheidt, General Bruns said, must end. At dawn on 7 November the *89th Division* was to strike in full force.[33]

As daylight came, a cold winter rain turned foxholes and shellholes into miniature wells and lowered a gloomy backdrop for the climax of fighting at Kommerscheidt. A solid hour of the most intense artillery and mortar fire left the gutted buildings in flames and the fatigued remnants of Colonel Flood's and Major Hazlett's battalions of the 112th Infantry in a stupor. Through the rain from the direction of Schmidt rolled at least fifteen German tanks. With them came a force of infantry variously estimated at from one to two battalions.

In the pitched fight that followed, American tank destroyers knocked out five German tanks, while an infantry commander, Capt. Clifford T. Hackard, accounted for another with a bazooka.[34] Still the Germans came on. They knocked out three of the tank destroyers and two of the American tanks. By noon German tanks were cruising among the foxholes on the eastern edge of the village. Enemy infantrymen were shooting up buildings and systematically reducing each position. The Americans began to give. Individually and in small groups, the men

---

[33] *89th Div* Order of the Day.
[34] Captain Hackard subsequently received the DSC.

broke to race across the open field to the north in search of refuge in the reserve position along the Kall woods line.

Before the 112th Infantry commander, Colonel Peterson, could counterattack with a portion of his reserve from the woods line, a message arrived by radio directing him to report immediately to the division command post. Colonel Peterson did not question the message for two reasons: (1) he believed the situation at Kommerscheidt had been misrepresented to General Cota, and (2) he had heard a rumor that a colonel recently assigned to the division was to replace him as commander of the 112th Infantry. Designating Colonel Ripple to command the force east of the Kall, Colonel Peterson started the hazardous trip westward across the Kall gorge.

Wounded twice by German shellfire, Colonel Peterson was semicoherent when engineers digging along the firebreak west of the Kall came upon him in late afternoon. When medics carried him to the division command post, General Cota could not understand why the regimental commander had returned. Not until several days later did General Cota establish the fact that, by mistake, a message directing Colonel Peterson's return had been sent.

In the meantime, at Kommerscheidt, Colonel Ripple found the situation in the village irretrievable. Reduced now to but two tank destroyers and three tanks, the armored vehicles began to fall back on the woods line. The last of the infantry took this as a signal to pull out. In withdrawing, two of the tanks threw their tracks and had to be abandoned. Only two destroyers and one tank remained.

Aided immeasurably by steady artillery support, Colonel Ripple's battered force held through the afternoon at the woods line against renewed German attack. Yet few could hope to hold for long. Expecting capture, one man hammered out the H that indicated religion on his identification tags.

Withdrawal Across the Kall

Bearing the dolorous tidings that the Germans had ejected his forces from Kommerscheidt, General Cota talked by telephone during the afternoon of 7 November with General Gerow, the V corps commander. Cota recommended withdrawal of all troops from beyond the Kall. Concurring, General Gerow a short while later telephoned the tacit approval of the First Army commander, General Hodges.

The army commander had kept in close touch with the 28th Division's situation and was "extremely disappointed" over the division's showing.[35] On 8 November during a conference at the division command post attended not only by Hodges but by Generals Eisenhower, Bradley, and Gerow, General Hodges drew General Cota aside for a "short sharp conference." He particularly remarked on the fact that division headquarters appeared to have no precise knowledge of the location of its units and was doing nothing to obtain the information. Hodges later told General Gerow to examine the possibility of command changes within the division.[36]

Certain conditions went with General Hodges' approval of withdrawal from beyond the Kall. In effect, the conditions indicated that the army commander would settle for a right flank secured along the Kall River instead of the Roer.

---

[35] Sylvan Diary, entry of 8 Nov 44. See also entries of 1 through 7 November.
[36] Ibid.

WEASEL (*M29 Cargo Carrier*), *similar to those used for evacuating wounded, pulls jeep out of the mud.*

General Gerow ordered that the 28th Division continue to hold the Vossenack ridge and that part of the Kall gorge west of the river, assist the attached 12th Infantry of the 4th Division to secure a more efficacious line of departure overlooking Huertgen, continue to drive south into the Monschau Corridor, and be prepared to send a regiment to work with the 5th Armored Division in a frontal drive against the Monschau Corridor. As events were to prove, these were prodigious conditions for a division which had taken a physical and moral beating.

After locating the battalion of the 109th Infantry that had become lost en route to the Kall gorge, General Davis on 8 November directed the battalion to continue to the Kall. With the battalion went a new commander for the 112th Infantry, Col. Gustin M. Nelson, who was to join what was left of the regiment beyond the river and supervise withdrawal.[37]

Nearing the Kall bridge, the battalion of the 109th Infantry dug in along the

[37] Colonel Nelson's presence confirmed the fact that Colonel Peterson was to have been relieved, but not summarily, that is, not in the sense that his performance had been unsatisfactory. Interv with Cota.

firebreak paralleling the Kall trail. Why a position was not chosen which would include the medical aid station in the dugout alongside the trail went unexplained.

Assisted by a volunteer patrol of four men, Colonel Nelson continued across the river where in late afternoon he reached his new, drastically depleted command. Preparations for withdrawal already were in progress. Soon after nightfall, while supporting artillery fired upon Kommerscheidt to conceal noise of withdrawal, the men were to move in two columns westward to the river. In hope of consideration from the Germans, a column of wounded and volunteer litter bearers was to march openly down the Kall trail. The column of effectives was to proceed cross-country along the route Colonel Nelson and his patrol had taken.

The night was utterly black. Moving down the eastern portion of the Kall trail, the column of wounded at first encountered no Germans; but enemy shelling split the column, brought fresh wounds to some, and made patients out of some of the litter bearers. At the bridge the men found four German soldiers on guard. A medic talked them into letting the column pass.

With the effectives, Colonel Nelson found the cross-country route through the forest virtually impassable in the darkness. Like blind cattle the men thrashed through the underbrush. Any hope of maintaining formation was dispelled quickly by the blackness of the night and by German shelling. All through the night and into the next day, frightened, fatigued men made their way across the icy Kall in small irregular groups, or alone. More than 2,200 men had at one time or another crossed to the east bank of the Kall. A few already had returned as stragglers or on litters; little more than 300 came back in the formal withdrawal.

In the confusion of withdrawal, the litter bearers carried the wounded no farther than a temporary refuge at the log-walled aid station alongside the western portion of the Kall trail. Situated in a kind of no man's land between the Germans and the battalion of the 109th Infantry along the firebreak, the medics for several days had been able to evacuate only ambulatory patients. Their limited facilities already choked, the medics had to leave the new patients outside in the cold and rain.

After the Germans had turned back three attempts by weasels to reach the aid station, the medics decided early on 9 November to attempt their own evacuation. Along the Kall trail they found two abandoned trucks and a weasel. Though they loaded these with wounded, they found as they reached the western woods line that only the weasel could pass several disabled vehicles which partially blocked the trail. With instructions to send ambulances for the rest, the driver of the weasel and his load of wounded proceeded to Vossenack.

By the time the ambulances arrived, a German captain and a group of enemy enlisted men had appeared on the scene. They refused to allow evacuation of any but the seriously wounded and medics with bona fide Red Cross cards. The two American surgeons and two chaplains that were with the aid group also had to stay behind. For the next two days, these officers and the remaining wounded stayed in the aid station, virtual prisoners. Not until late on the second day, 11 November, when a German medical officer at the bottom of the gorge requested a local truce to collect German dead, did the American surgeons find an opportunity to bypass the enemy officer at the western woods line and evacuate their remaining patients.

New Missions

As early as 8 November the battered 110th Infantry at Raffelsbrand and the recently attached 12th Infantry on the wooded plateau north of Germeter set out to accomplish two of the missions assigned when General Gerow had approved withdrawal. The 110th Infantry tried to drive south into the Monschau Corridor while the 12th Infantry attempted to better the line of departure overlooking Huertgen.

The attempt by the 110th Infantry to continue to attack long after the regiment's offensive ability had reached a point of diminishing returns served little purpose other than to prolong an exercise in futility. For five more terrible days Colonel Seely's two mutilated battalions tried to reduce the pillboxes at Raffelsbrand. The lines at the end remained almost the same. Visiting the regiment on 13 November, the assistant division commander, General Davis, caught a glimpse of the depressing situation at first hand. What he discovered prompted him to call off all offensive action by the regiment. One battalion, for example, though strengthened at one point by ninety-five replacements, had but fifty-seven men left, little more than a platoon. In the rifle companies not one of the original officers remained and only two noncommissioned officers.

Though the attached 12th Infantry was near full strength at the start of attacks on 8 November, that regiment soon discovered what tremendous sacrifices this ogre called the Huertgen Forest demanded. In five days the 12th Infantry's casualties soared to more than 500. As rain and snow persisted, more than a fifth of these were trench foot and frostbite cases.

All about the salient the 12th Infantry had inherited on the wooded plateau north of Germeter, the Germans by this time had erected barbed wire obstacles, constructed log bunkers at ground level, and trimmed the woods with antipersonnel mines. To strengthen the regiment of the *275th Division* that had held so stubbornly here against the 109th Infantry, the Germans had moved in an assault engineer battalion and a fortress machine gun battalion. None of the 12th Infantry's attacks made any noteworthy gains.

One reason for the 12th Infantry's troubles was a shift in German plans brought about by the enemy's success at Kommerscheidt and his failure at Vossenack. On 9 November the Germans had decided to abandon their attempts to reduce Vossenack by frontal assault and returned to the original plan of driving south through the American salient north of Germeter to cut off Vossenack. The corps commander, General Straube, shifted the division boundaries to give the *89th Division* responsibility for Vossenack while the *116th Panzer Division* concentrated at Huertgen to counterattack down the wooded plateau through the 12th Infantry. By this time, however, the German units were about as disorganized as was the 28th Division. Expecting momentarily to have to face the main American drive, the *116th Panzer Division* hesitated to become deeply involved on the wooded plateau. Its counterattack amounted to little more than local thrusts that served to stymie the 12th Infantry's offensive moves but failed to achieve any significant penetration.[38]

The issue on the wooded plateau still was undecided when on 10 November the army commander, General Hodges, directed establishment of a new corps boundary between the V and VII Corps in preparation for the beginning of the main First Army drive. The 12th Infantry reverted to control of the 4th Division, which was moving into the Huertgen Forest to fight under the VII Corps in the coming offensive.[39]

Before the 12th Infantry passed to the VII Corps on 10 November, General Cota ordered an attack to assist the attached regiment in securing the other half of the proposed line of departure overlooking Huertgen. The attack was to be made by the 1st Battalion, 109th Infantry. Driving north from the Vossenack church into the wooded (Tiefen creek) draw separating the Vossenack and Brandenberg–Bergstein ridges, this battalion was to gain that part of the woods line which had remained inviolate to repeated American attacks from the salient north of Germeter.

This was a far different battalion from that which had moved toward Huertgen on 2 November. Even with some replacements the rifle companies now totaled only 62, 55, and 73 men, respectively. On 10 November a heavy German artillery concentration held up one company and another got lost in the woods, but the third reached the objective. There the company at first enjoyed magnificent solitude. Nobody knew where the company was. For three days the men remained undetected while Germans shuffled past them in the forest. Yet even without enemy action, the basic process of keeping alive began to assume awesome proportions. Aggravated by snow, sleet, and cold and the total impossibility of rehabilitation, trench foot swept through the ranks. Some men stood guard in muddy foxholes on their knees. By the time the Germans discovered the company on 14 November, food already was exhausted. As the enemy surrounded them, the men clung to their position without food, drinking water, or ammunition other than that in their belts. To the *89th Division* elimination of this position became a "point of honor." [40] Three days later a relief column finally broke through to halt the vendetta. Two days later the men fought their way back to Germeter. Only thirty-three were left.

That marked the end of the 28th Division's participation in the carnage around Vossenack and Schmidt. By 13 November General Hodges had recognized the patent impossibility of securing the right flank of the VII Corps with this battered division and ordered relief. The 8th Division from the VIII Corps was to exchange sectors with General Cota's regiments. By 19 November the relief was completed.

The second attack on Schmidt had developed into one of the most costly U.S. division actions in the whole of World War II. Hardest hit was the infantry regiment making the main effort, the 112th Infantry. This regiment lost 232 men captured, 431 missing, 719 wounded,

---

[38] MS # A–891 (Gersdorff); ETHINT–56 (Gersdorff and Waldenburg); Entries of 1–12 Nov 44, *OB WEST KTB,* Sitreps, 9–10 Nov 44, *OB WEST KTB, Befehle und Meldungen.*
[39] For this story and greater detail on the trials of the 12th Infantry, see below, Chapter XVIII.

[40] MS A–891 (Gersdorff).

167 killed, and 544 nonbattle casualties—a total of 2,093. Including these and the losses of attached units and of the rest of the 28th Division, the second attack on Schmidt had cost 6,184 casualties.

American matériel losses included 16 out of 24 M10 tank destroyers and 31 out of 50 medium tanks. Losses in trucks, weasels, antitank guns, machine guns, mortars, and individual weapons were tremendous. Some of this equipment the Germans transported to a training area for study and use less than a month later in the Ardennes counteroffensive.[41]

During the main phase of the battle for Schmidt, between 2 and 8 November, the 28th Division took 913 prisoners and inflicted an estimated 2,000 other casualties on the enemy. Although one American source claimed the Germans lost about

40 tanks, the enemy panzer commander, General von Waldenburg, put the losses at 15.[42]

Though the men of the 28th Division did not know it at the time, the end of their experience corresponded roughly with the first genuine Allied concern about the Roer River Dams. In mid-November, SHAEF became seriously concerned about the dams.[43] The First Army, nevertheless, was to continue to build up downstream from the dams before doing anything specific about them.

---

[41] Secret order of 8 Nov 44, found in *OB WEST KTB, Befehle und Meldungen.*

[42] V Corps Factual Study, V Corps records; MS# A–905 (Waldenburg).

[43] Statement by Maj Gen Harold R. Bull, SHAEF G–3, in conf with Gen Smith, SHAEF CofS, and Gen Bull by ETO Theater Historians, copy in OCMH files. This document is undated, but the conference was held in the European Theater of Operations in September 1945. Other than those instances mentioned in Chapter XIV, above, SHAEF files contain no reference to the Roer River Dams before mid-November.

PART FIVE

THE HUERTGEN FOREST

CHAPTER XVI

The Big Picture in October

During the early days of October, at the start of the bitter campaigning near Aachen and Schmidt, it had become obvious that the halcyon days of pursuit had ended. Yet because Allied commanders reckoned the enemy's resurgence more a product of transitory Allied logistical weakness than of any real German strength, they seem to have assumed that a lucky push at the right spot still might catapult the Allies to the Rhine.[1]

Not until October passed its mid-point, a fortnight before the start of the second attack on Schmidt, had the full portent of the hard fighting at Aachen, in the Huertgen Forest, along the Schelde estuary, in the Peel Marshes, and with the Third Army at Metz become apparent. The Germans had effected a remarkable reorganization. This made it imperative that General Eisenhower make a new decision. How best to pursue the war to advantage during the harsh, dreary days of poor campaigning weather that soon must set in?

As the Supreme Commander met with top officers at Brussels on 18 October to plan his decision, he faced the fact that in the period of slightly more than a month —since first patrols had crossed the German border—the most notable advance had been that of MARKET-GARDEN, which had fallen short of expectations. That was the story all along the line. Operations begun in an aura of great expectations usually had ended in bitter dogfights and plodding advances not unlike that in the Norman hedgerows.

In the far north, Field Marshal Montgomery's 21 Army Group, having failed with MARKET-GARDEN's bold thrust to turn the north flank of the West Wall and sweep to the IJesselmeer, at last had given consummate priority to clearing Antwerp's seaward approaches. This the British commander had done even though it meant postponement of his plans to clear the western face of the Ruhr by driving southeast from Nijmegen and to eliminate the enemy's bridgehead west of the Maas in the Peel Marshes. Bright prospects of opening Antwerp to Allied shipping had ensued. As the situation developed, the first cargo ship was not to drop anchor in the harbor until 28 November, but no one could have known in mid-October that the campaign along the Schelde would take so long.

On the northern wing of General Bradley's 12th Army Group next to the British, the First Army had registered

---

[1] For an example of this state of mind, see XIX Corps combat interviews for October 1944. In *A Soldier's Story,* page 426, General Bradley relates that on 28 September 1944, more than a week after the first drives into the West Wall had stalled, First Army sent him a bronze bust of Hitler with this inscription: "Found in Nazi Headquarters, Eupen, Germany [*sic*]. With seven units of fire and one additional division, First U.S. Army will deliver the original in thirty days."

several impressive achievements, including penetrations of the West Wall both north and south of Aachen. The fall of Aachen itself was only a few days off. Yet the sobering fact was that after more than a month of fighting, the First Army in no case had penetrated deeper than twelve miles inside Germany. The enemy had sealed off both West Wall breaches effectively and in the process had dealt the First Army almost 20,000 casualties.[2]

Though the hard-won gains about Aachen meant a good jump-off point for a renewal of the drive to the Rhine, the development in this sector auguring most for the future was not in the nature of an offensive thrust into the line but of a lateral shift in units behind the line. General Bradley had decided to introduce General Simpson's Ninth Army between the First Army and the British in the old XIX Corps zone north of Aachen. The 12th Army Group commander had made the decision as early as 9 October, only five days after General Simpson's army, then containing only one corps of two divisions, had arrived from the conquest of Brest and assumed responsibility for the old V Corps zone in Luxembourg.[3]

Though Ninth Army's commitment in Luxembourg thus was to be but a pause in transit, General Bradley had not intended it that way. He had hoped that the Ninth Army's defense of the lengthy but relatively inactive front in the Ardennes might permit his two more experienced armies—the First and Third—to achieve greater concentration for renewing

the drive to the Rhine.[4] But before the Ninth Army could be fleshed out with new divisions and accomplish much in this direction, Bradley made his decision to abandon this plan in favor of moving the Ninth Army to the north. General Bradley based his decision in part on a reluctance to put American troops under foreign command, in part on his knowledge of the working methods of the First and Ninth Army staffs. During these early days of October, while the Ninth Army was moving into Luxembourg, Bradley had come to believe that General Eisenhower would not long resist Field Marshal Montgomery's persistent request for an American army to strengthen the 21 Army Group. Bradley reasoned that unless he acted quickly to juxtapose another army next to the British, the army he would lose would be the First, his most experienced army, his former command for which he held much affection, and an army whose "know-it-all" headquarters staff was difficult to work with unless the higher commander understood fully the staff's idiosyncrasies. "You couldn't turn over a staff like that to Montgomery."[5] "Because Simpson's Army was still our greenest," General Bradley wrote after the war, "I reasoned that it could be the most easily spared. Thus rather than leave First Army within Monty's reach, I inserted the Ninth Army between them."[6]

[4] See 12th A Gp Ltr of Instrs 9, 25 Sep 44, 12th A Gp, Rpt of Opns, V, 93–95.

[5] Interv with Bradley, 7 Jun 56.

[6] Bradley, *A Soldier's Story*, pp. 435–37. General Bradley errs in pinning the date of his decision to 18 October after the Brussels conference. Moses Memo for Rcd, 9 Oct 44, and Sylvan Diary, entry of 10 Oct 44. The Ninth Army subsequently was to come under Montgomery's command during the Ardennes campaign (as was the First Army for a brief period)

[2] FUSA Rpt, Annex 1, Vol. 2, p. 7.

[3] Memo for Rcd, Brig Gen Raymond G. Moses (G–4, 12th A Gp), 9 Oct 44, in 12th A Gp Supplies, Misc, filed with SHAEF records, Folder 79, Drawer 392.

To decide five days after moving an army into the center of the line to transfer the same army to the north wing during the height of a transportation shortage might appear at first glance impractical if not actually capricious. Yet a closer examination would reveal that General Bradley never intended to make a physical transfer of more than the army headquarters and a few supporting troops. Beyond circumventing loss of the First Army to the British, the transfer would in effect further Allied concentration north of the Ardennes, which was in keeping with the Supreme Commander's long-expressed determination to put greatest strength there. In addition, to put the army that was the logical command for absorbing new corps and divisions into the line along the American north flank would serve to shore up what had been a chronic Allied weakness along the boundary between national forces.

To avoid the complicated physical transfer of large bodies of troops and supplies, Bradley ordered that the First Army take command of the Ninth Army's VIII Corps and its divisions, thereby reassuming responsibility for the Ardennes, while the Ninth Army took over the XIX Corps north of Aachen. By the time written orders for the exchange could be distributed, the VIII Corps had grown from two divisions to four, including the veteran 2d, 8th, and 83d Infantry Divisions and the untested 9th Armored Division. These were to pass to the First Army. Artillery was to be exchanged on a caliber-for-caliber basis. Supply stocks were to be either exchanged or adjusted on paper in future requisitions and allocations. The Ninth Army was to open a

new command post at Maastricht on 22 October, and at noon on that date the paper transfer of corps and supporting units was to take place.[7]

The commander of this youngest Allied army on the Continent was an infantryman with a fatherly devotion to his troops after the manner of Bradley and Hodges. Even without insignia of rank, Bill Simpson looked the part of a general. His rangy, six-foot-four frame would have commanded attention even had he not kept his head clean-shaven. Having had wide combat experience—against the Moros in the Philippines, Pancho Villa in Mexico, and the Germans in the Meuse-Argonne—General Simpson had a healthy respect for the assistance machines and big guns could give his riflemen.

Like their commander, most members of the Ninth Army general staff were infantrymen. The exception was the G–2, Col. Charles P. Bixel, a cavalryman who had transferred his affection to armor. Though the Ninth Army had been organized no earlier than 22 May 1944 and had become operational on the Brittany peninsula only on 5 September, the commander and staff had worked together for a longer period. Both had been drawn primarily from the Fourth Army in the United States, a training command General Simpson had held for seven months. The young Chief of Staff, Brig. Gen. James E. Moore, had even longer association with his commander, having come with General Simpson to the Fourth Army from a previous command. The important G–3 post was held by Col.

___

and to remain under the 21 Army Group to and beyond the Rhine.

___

[7] *Conquer—The Story of Ninth Army* (Washington: Infantry Journal Press, 1947), pp. 66–68; FUSA Rpt, Vol. 1, p. 65, and Annex 1, Vol. 2, p. 114.

GENERAL SIMPSON

Armistead D. Mead, Jr.[8] Under Simson's tutelage, the Ninth Army was to mature quickly and to draw from General Bradley the compliment that "unlike the noisy and bumptious Third and the temperamental First," the Ninth Army was "uncommonly normal."[9]

Even younger than the Ninth Army was the tactical air headquarters which was to work closely with General Simpson's command. This was the XXIX Tactical Air Command under Brig. Gen.

---

[8] Other staff members included: Col. George A. Millener, Deputy Chief of Staff; Col. Daniel H. Hundley, G–1; Col. Roy V. Rickard, G–4; and Col. Art B. Miller, Jr., Secretary of the General Staff.

[9] Bradley, A Soldier's Story, p. 422. For details on the birth of the Ninth Army, see Conquer—The Story of Ninth Army, pages 15–25.

Richard E. Nugent, which was created by taking a rib from the other two tactical commands in the theater. Activated on 14 September, the XXIX TAC, for want of assigned planes, pilots, and headquarters personnel, had operated through September more as a wing than as a separate command. The airmen nevertheless had gotten in a few licks at Brest, gaining a measure of experience for the support to be rendered the Ninth Army through the rest of the European campaign.[10]

Elsewhere on the American front during September and early October, German resurgence and American logistical limitations had restricted operations as much or more than in the northern sector. Though the logistical crisis had prompted General Eisenhower on 25 September to put the Third Army on the defensive, General Patton had refused to take the blow lying down. Under the guise of improving his positions, Patton had managed to concentrate enough ammunition and supplies to launch limited attacks in the vicinity of Metz. Yet neither General Patton's legerdemain in matters of supply nor his dexterity in interpreting orders from above had permitted a large-scale offensive. All of October was to pass before the Third Army could hope to push far beyond the Moselle.[11]

South of the Third Army, General Devers' 6th Army Group was more independent logistically by virtue of Mediterranean supply lines, yet this force too had ground to a halting pace. After crossing the upper Moselle in late September and

---

[10] Conquer—The Story of Ninth Army, pp. 29–30; Craven and Cate, eds., Europe: ARGUMENT to V-E Day, p. 597: The Ninth Air Force and Its Principal Commands in the ETO, Vol. IV, Ch. I.

[11] See Cole, The Lorraine Campaign.

entering the rugged Vosges Mountains, neither General Jean de Lattre de Tassigny's 1st French Army nor Lt. Gen. Alexander M. Patch's Seventh U.S. Army could make major gains.[12]

Air Support

A disturbing aspect of the over-all situation was the marked increase of unfavorable flying weather, which severely limited effectiveness of the tactical air arm. The IX Tactical Air Command, for example, was able to fly only two thirds as many missions in October as in September, and the prospects for November and the winter months were less than encouraging.[13] "There's lots of times," noted a platoon leader, "when we can't move an inch and then the P-47's come over and we just walk in almost without a shot."[14] When weather drastically curtailed the number of times the P-47's could come over, this obviously was a serious turn of events.

Weather had a particularly damaging effect as long as the crippled ground transport situation prevented the airmen from moving their bases close to the front lines. At the end of September most of the bases were far back in northern or northwestern France. Not only was time in flight wasted, but often the weather at the bases differed radically from that over the target area, forcing the pilots to return home prematurely. By the time transport became available to move the bases, heavy autumn rains had set in, making bogs of likely airfield sites and requiring increased outlay of time and equipment for airfield construction. By the end of October, most bases of the IX TAC had been moved into Belgium, with the greatest concentration in the vicinity of Charleroi and Liège; but airfields even closer to the front were needed, particularly after the move of the XXIX Tactical Air Command with the Ninth Army to Maastricht.[15]

The primary missions of the tactical aircraft continued as before: rail-track cutting designed to interfere with movement of German reserves; armed reconnaissance and column cover; and close support of the ground troops against targets like gun positions, troop concentrations, and defended villages. Medium bombers of the IX Bombardment Division concentrated primarily upon interdicting enemy communications by bombing precision targets like road junctions and bridges. Though the airmen protested that pillboxes were an unprofitable target for tactical aircraft, they continued to answer ground requests for support against the West Wall fortifications. In general, the results of the fighter-bomber strikes were less spectacular than during the days of pursuit; but the workmanlike, deliberate effort of the air forces still was rewarding. "We could not possibly have gotten as far as we did, as fast as we did, with as few casualties," said General Collins of the VII Corps, "without the wonderful air support that we have consistently had."[16]

---

[12] See Smith, The Riviera to the Rhine.
[13] IX FC and IX TAC, Unit History, Oct 44.
[14] XXIX TAC History, Operation Q.

[15] IX FC and IX TAC, Unit History, Oct 44; Hq AAF, Office of Asst Chief of Air Staff-3, Condensed Analysis of the Ninth Air Force in the ETO, p. 39.
[16] Operational History of the Ninth Air Force, Bk. V, Ground Force Annexes; The Ninth Air Force and Its Principal Commands in the ETO, Vol. II, Ch. II.

The differing duties and living conditions of air and ground troops sometimes led to misunderstanding, a problem intensified in the wake of short bombing or misdirected strafing.[17] For all this, the ground troops gradually developed confidence in their air support and a genuine appreciation of it. Troops who early in the campaign seldom asked for air strikes against targets closer than a thousand yards from the front lines later were naming targets as close as 300 yards. For their part, airmen came to appreciate the effective protection which artillery could provide against enemy flak.[18] To help promote mutual understanding, teams of pilots and ground officers were exchanged for several days at a time to share their opposites' living conditions and combat hazards.

A particular weakness of U.S. tactical air commands was a lack of night fighters. For a long time German troop movements after nightfall were virtually unopposed, and the Luftwaffe was free to operate with impunity. Noting during October that German night interceptor attacks against heavy bombers had decreased markedly, top air officers made available the two P-61 (Black Widow) night fighter squadrons in the theater to the IX and XIX (supporting the Third Army) Tactical Air Commands. Impressed by the accomplishments of the P-61's in this role, air officials lamented only that they had so few of them.[19]

In an effort to make the best of the unfavorable weather, the air commands turned more and more to special techniques of "blind bombing." The most widely used was the MEW (Mobile Early Warning) or SCR-584 radar system, whereby forward director posts equipped with radio and radar vectored the planes to the target area over the overcast, talked them into the proper approach, and took them down through the overcast directly over the target. At this point either the pilot himself made final adjustment for the attack or the forward director post specified the moment of bomb release. MEW also was used successfully in night control of aircraft. Despite the weather, the number of fighter-bomber missions, which dropped in October, was to rise again in November and December.[20]

An Enigma Named Logistics

Two of the reasons for only limited Allied territorial gains in late September and early October were the weather and German resurgence. But the real felon was the crippled logistical structure which still had a long way to go before recovering from the excesses of the pursuit. Although commanders all the way up to General Eisenhower had been willing to defer capture of ports in favor of promised lands farther east, the tactical revelers at last were being forced to penitence. No matter how optimistic the planners or how enthusiastic the executors, the logistical situation never failed to rear its ugly head. October was destined to be the worst month in matters of supply the

[17] See, for example, Incoming Msg, IX TAC Opns from 28th Div, 9 Nov, IX TAC Opns Orders, 9 Nov 44.

[18] The Ninth Air Force and Its Principal Commands in the ETO, Vol. II, Ch. II.

[19] Hq AAF, Condensed Analysis of the Ninth Air Force in the ETO.

[20] The Ninth Air Force and Its Principal Commands in the ETO, Vol. II, Ch. II, and IX TAC Memo 100–57, 12 Apr 45, included in annex thereto.

Allies were to experience during the campaign on the Continent.[21]

Though the bulk of American supplies still came in at only two points, Cherbourg and the Normandy beaches, the crux of the problem continued to lie less in shortage of ports than in limitations of transport. How to get supplies from Cherbourg and the beaches to a front that in the case of the First Army at Aachen was more than 500 road miles away? The answer obviously had two facets: improve the transportation system and/or get new ports closer to the fighting lines.

Through all of September and until Field Marshal Montgomery in mid-October gave unequivocal priority to opening Antwerp, hope of new ports was dim. Even capture of Le Havre on 12 September failed to help much, both because damage to the harbor was extensive and because by this time Le Havre was far behind the front. The only hope for the moment lay in improvement in the transport situation. That would be a long uphill struggle.

Railway repairmen, air transport pilots, truck drivers—all soon were performing near miracles. By 10 September sleepy-eyed truckers had completed an original mission of delivering 82,000 tons of supplies to a point southwest of Paris near Chartres and were hauling their loads on an extended Red Ball Express route beyond Paris. By the first of October repairs on the rail net east and northeast of Paris made it possible to transfer truck cargoes near Paris to the railways. Yet

not until 16 November was the Red Ball Express to halt operations. By that time, during a life of eighty-one days, the express service would have carried a total of 412,913 tons of supplies.

Many of the trucks borrowed during the pursuit from artillery and antiaircraft units had to be returned as the nature of the fighting again called for all tactical formations at the front. The armies themselves nevertheless continued to augment the trucking resources of the Communications Zone. Because army depots still were far behind the line, much army transportation went toward bridging the gap between the depots and the front. First Army, for example, transported supplies from army dumps at Hirson on the French-Belgian border until early October, when advancement of rail lines brought the dumps to Liège. To obtain winter clothing, the 5th Armored Division sent its organic trucks all the way to the beaches to pick up duffel bags containing long underwear and overcoats. To meet a crisis in 105-mm. ammunition, the First Army on 21 September sent six truck companies back to the beaches.[22]

Though transport aircraft had made major contributions to supply during the pursuit, they had been withdrawn from this task in order to participate in Operation MARKET-GARDEN. Despite vociferous cries for renewal of an airlift, the SHAEF Air Priorities Board ruled this means of transport too extravagant for large-scale supply movements. Airlift gradually came to be restricted to meeting emergency requirements, as originally intended.

In the last analysis, the railways were the workhorse of the transportation sys-

---

[21] Detailed information on logistical matters during this period is to be found in Ruppenthal, *Logistical Support of the Armies,* Vol. II. Unless otherwise noted, the logistical story herein is drawn from that source.

[22] FUSA Rpt, Annex 2, Vol. 2, pp. 110–13.

tem. Engineers, railway construction battalions, and French and Belgian laborers worked round the clock to repair lines running deep into the army zones. By mid-September, although the Allies had uncovered almost the entire rail system of France, Belgium, and Luxembourg, rail lines actually in use were few. In little more than a fortnight repairmen opened approximately 2,000 miles of single track and 2,775 miles of double track. Two routes accommodated the First Army, one extending as far northeast as Liège and another as far as Charleroi, there to connect with the other line to Liège.

For all the diligence of the truckers, the airmen, and the railway repairmen, no quick solution of the transport problem was likely. The minimum maintenance requirements for the 12th Army Group and supporting air forces already stood in mid-September at more than 13,000 tons per day and would rise with the commitment of new divisions. In addition, the armies needed between 150,000 and 180,000 tons of supplies for repair or replacement of equipment, replenishment of basic loads, rebuilding of reserves, and provision of winter clothing. Against these requirements, the Communications Zone in mid-September could deliver only about 11,000 tons per day. Some 4,000 tons of this had to be split among the Ninth Air Force and other special demands. Only 40,000 tons of reserves, representing but two days of supply, had been moved any farther forward than St. Lô. Temporarily, at least, U.S. forces could not be supported at desired scales. Tactical operations would have to be tailored to the limited means available. So tight was the supply situation that General Bradley saw no alternative but to continue the unpopular system of tonnage

allocations instituted at the height of the pursuit. On 21 September Bradley approved an allocation giving 3,500 tons of supplies to the Third Army, 700 tons to the Ninth Army (which was en route to Luxembourg), and the remainder to the First Army with the understanding that the First Army would receive a minimum of 5,000 tons. This was in keeping with General Eisenhower's desire to put his main weight in the north. A few days later, upon transfer of the 7th Armored Division from Metz to the Peel Marshes, an adjustment in tonnage gave the First Army 5,400 tons per day to the Third Army's 3,100. The new allocation took effect on 27 September, at a time when General Hodges had ten divisions to General Patton's eight.

By careful planning and conservation the two armies conceivably could execute their assigned missions with these allotments on a day-by-day basis. Yet the wildest imagination could not foresee accumulation of reserve stocks on this kind of diet. The fact that the First Army's operations during the latter days of September and through October developed more in a series of angry little jabs than in one sustained thrust thus had a ready explanation.

Under these circumstances, the armies had to confine their requisitions to absolute essentials, for every request without exception went against the allocation. Even mail ate into assigned tonnage. That friction between the armies and the Communications Zone would arise under these conditions could not have been unexpected. The armies were piqued particularly by a practice of the Communications Zone of substituting some other item, often a nonessential, when temporarily out of a requested item. This practice finally stopped after the Communications Zone adopted a First Army recommendation that, when it was out of a requisitioned item, tonnage in either rations or ammunition be substituted. Less easily remedied was a failure of the Communications Zone to deliver total amounts allocated. From 13 September to 20 October, for example, the First Army averaged daily receipts of 4,271 tons against an average daily allocation of 5,226.[23] Only time and over-all improvement in the logistical structure could remove this source of contention.

The Communications Zone, in turn, complained about an apparent paradox in the supply situation. During the latter days of October, supply chiefs noted that the armies were improving their reserve positions, even though deliveries had increased only slightly, to about 11,000 tons daily. By the end of October, though serious shortages existed in many items, stocks in the combat zone of the 12th Army Group totaled more than 155,000 tons.

That the armies could accumulate reserves at a time when deliveries averaged only 11,000 tons against stated requirements of 25,000–28,000 could be explained partially by the quiescent state of the front; but to the Communications Zone it bore out a suspicion that the armies were overzealous in their requisitioning. The supply and transport services hardly could have let pass without question the dire urgency of army demands which listed as "critically short" items like barber kits and handkerchiefs. The Communications Zone suspected the First Army in particular of having taken for granted the supply advantage it had enjoyed since before the Normandy landings. The Third Army appeared to accept the supply hardship more graciously, and the Ninth Army, having been born in poverty, usually could be counted on to limit requests to actual needs. Of the three, the First Army was the prima donna, a reputation seemingly borne out by the army's own admission that the six truck companies which returned to the beaches for critically needed 105-mm. ammunition used some of their cargo space for toilet paper and soap.[24] Even General Bradley, whose esteem for the army he formerly commanded was an accepted fact, later termed the First Army "temperamental" and deserving of a reputation for piracy in supply. "First Army contended," General Bradley wrote, "that chicanery was part of the business of supply just so long as Group [headquarters] did not detect it." [25]

Both the Communications Zone and the armies found another supply expedient in local procurement. Though the economy and industrial facilities of the liberated countries were in poor shape, they made important contributions to alleviating the logistical crisis. Local procurement provided the First Army particular assistance in relieving shortages in spare parts for tanks and other vehicles. During October alone, First Army ordnance officers negotiated for a total of fifty-nine different items (cylinder head gaskets, batteries, split rings, and the like).[26]

A factory in Paris overhauled radial tank engines. Liège manufactured tires and tubes and parts for small arms. The First Army quartermaster entered into

[23] Ibid.

[24] Ibid., p. 113.
[25] Bradley, A Soldier's Story, pp. 422 and 431.
[26] FUSA Rpt, Annex 2, Vol. 2, pp. 114–18.

contracts for such varied services as manufacturing BAR belts, assembling typewriters, and roasting coffee.[27]

No matter what the value of these expedients, the very necessity of turning to them was indicative of the fact that the logistical structure might be frail for a long time. In the first place, the shift from pursuit to close-in fighting had increased rather than decreased supply requirements. Though gasoline demands were lower, ammunition needs were higher. On 2 October, the day when the XIX Corps attacked to penetrate the West Wall north of Aachen, General Bradley instituted strict rationing of artillery ammunition. A few days later Bradley discovered that even at the rationed rate of expenditure the armies by 7 November would have exhausted every round of artillery and 81-mm. mortar ammunition on the Continent. He had no choice but to restrict the armies further. They were to use no more ammunition than that already in army depots, en route to the armies, or on shipping orders. Not until the first of November was artillery ammunition to pass out of the critical stage.[28]

Maintenance was a major problem. With the pause in the pursuit, commanders could assess the damage done to their vehicles during the lightninglike dashes when maintenance had been a hit-or-miss proposition. As autumn deepened, so did the mud to compound the maintenance problem. Depots often had to be moved to firmer ground. Continental roads, not built for the kind of traffic they now had to bear, rapidly deteriorated.

Sharp edges of C Ration tins strewn along the roads damaged tires. This and the deterioration caused by overloading and lack of preventive maintenance quickly exhausted theater tire reserves. Lack of spare parts put many a vehicle in deadline.

Through September the First Army operated with less than 85 percent of authorized strength in medium tanks. To achieve an equitable distribution of those available and to establish a small reserve, the army adopted a provisional Table of Organization and Equipment (T/O&E) reducing authorized strengths in medium tanks. The new T/O&E cut the authorized strengths for old-type armored divisions from 232 to 200, for new-type divisions from 168 to 150, and for separate tank battalions from 54 to 50. The Ninth Army later adopted the same expedient.

The needs of winterization added greatly to the logistical problem. Transporting sleeping bags, blankets, wool underwear, overshoes, and overcoats often had to be accomplished by emergency airlift. In one instance the First Army took advantage of transfer of three DUKW companies from the beaches to obtain wool underwear and blankets. First Army engineers turned to local sawmills for more than 19,000,000 board feet of lumber needed to meet winter housing requirements.[29] Not until well into November, after the winds had become chill and the rains were changing to sleet, was the bulk of the winterization program met. The 28th Division, for example, jumped off on 2 November in the cold and mud of the Huertgen Forest with only ten to fifteen men per infantry company equipped with overshoes. Through

---

[27] For a detailed study of this subject, see Royce L. Thompson, Local Procurement in the ETO, D Day to V-E Day, MS in OCMH.

[28] 12th A Gp Rpt of Opns, VI, 44. General Bradley gives a personal view of the situation in A Soldier's Story, pages 430–32.

[29] FUSA Rpt, Annex 2, Vol. 2, pp. 114–18.

A WINTER OVERCOAT *reaches the front lines.*

almost all of November antifreeze for vehicles was dangerously limited.

Further compounding the logistical problem was the continuing arrival of new units, both new divisions and smaller separate units. From the time the first patrols crossed into Germany on 11 September until General Eisenhower convened his commanders at Brussels on 18 October, 357,272 more men (exclusive of those arriving via southern France) set foot on the Continent. The cumulative total rose to 2,525,579.[30] In terms of divi-

sions, the Allied logistical structure at start of the Siegfried Line Campaign had to support 39 divisions. By 18 October General Eisenhower commanded 30 infantry, 15 armored, and 2 airborne divisions, an increase of 8 for a total of 47.[31]

Though the 6th Army Group was outside the orbit of the supply services

---

[30] SHAEF G–3 Daily Summary 137, 18 Oct 44.

[31] U.S. divisions: 21 infantry, 9 armored (including 1 French armored division), and 2 airborne, a total of 32. British and Canadian divisions: 9 infantry and 6 armored (including 1 Polish armored division), a total of 15. SHAEF G–3 Daily Summary 134.

operating from Normandy, General Eisenhower's assumption of command over that group had raised total Allied strength under SHAEF to 58 divisions.[32] This figure was to stand through the rest of October, though 83,206 more men, either members of small units or replacements, were to arrive. Two more U.S. divisions were scheduled to arrive through Normandy soon after the first of November.[33]

Tactical commanders naturally chafed to get the new divisions into the line; yet logistical planners on 11 October warned General Bradley that for some six to eight weeks to come their resources would permit support in active combat of no more than 20 divisions, the number already committed. The incoming divisions would have to stick close to the Normandy depots. Though General Bradley did not heed this warning, he had to commit the divisions one by one, so that their arrival failed to produce any immediate marked change in the tactical situation.

Of the new units, 1 infantry division went to the 6th Army Group, another to the Ninth Army, 1 armored and 2 infantry divisions to the Third Army, and 1 armored division to the First Army. The 2 other new units were the airborne divisions which were paying a second visit to the Continent via MARKET-GARDEN. Of 2 additional divisions which had been arriving just as the first patrols crossed into Germany, the 94th Division had come directly under the 12th Army Group for

containing bypassed Germans in the lesser Brittany ports, and the 104th Division had helped the Canadians open Antwerp and was soon to go to the First Army. Neither of these was included in the reckoning of 20 divisions supportable in the 12th Army Group. Two other infantry divisions which arrived soon after the first of November were split between the First and Ninth Armies. The net effect of these arrivals on the three armies of the 12th Army Group was to provide 3 additional divisions each for the First and Third Armies and 2 for the Ninth.

The new divisions represented only about one third of the new troops that had set foot on the Continent since early September. The others were in separate units—tank, tank destroyer, antiaircraft, and engineer battalions, line of communications units, and the like—or were replacements. Many were airmen. Most of these men and units had to be transported to the front, and all had to be supplied.

Replacements by this time had high priority, for during September and October casualties had risen by 75,542 to a cumulative total, exclusive of the 6th Army Group, of 300,111. Two thirds of these were U.S. losses.[34] Like ammunition at one time in October, replacements were a commodity in short supply on the Continent. On a series of inspection trips down to divisional level during October, General Eisenhower saw at first hand the need for replacements, particularly riflemen. He appealed to the War De-

[32] SHAEF G–3 Daily Summary 134. Two French armored, 5 French infantry, 3 U.S. infantry divisions, and 1 U.S. airborne task force of divisional size.

[33] SHAEF G–3 Daily Summary 150. The figure on new arrivals is exclusive of the 6th Army Group.

[34] SHAEF G–3 Daily Summaries 152 and 153. Including casualties of the 6th Army Group, the over-all Allied total at the end of October was roughly 332,000.

partment and also directed a rigid comb-out of men in the Communications Zone who might be converted into riflemen.[35]

Not the least of the logistical worries was the shift of the Ninth Army into an active campaigning role north of Aachen. Though General Bradley's "paper trans-fer" helped, the Ninth Army still had to amass reserve supplies before opening a major offensive. The logistical pie now had to be cut in three big slices. From the tonnage allocation of 14 October, for example, the Ninth Army drew almost 5,000 tons, an increase over 8 October of 3,200.[36]

Somewhat paradoxically, even as supply forecasts were gloomiest, the black cloud which had hung depressingly over the logistical horizon actually began to lift.

During the last few days of October and the first week of November, forward de-liveries fell short of the somewhat modest requirements set; nevertheless, the armies improved their reserve positions. The historian who tells the supply story for this period finds himself in the role of a novelist who leads his reader to believe one thing, then switches dramatically but incredibly to another. But in the autumn of 1944 that was how it was. This was clearly apparent from the fact that by the end of October, when stocks in the com-bat zone of the 12th Army Group totaled more than 155,000 tons, deliveries still were running far under the armies' stated requirements. By the end of the first week in November, army reserves were to reach 188,000 tons.

The fact was that a relatively quiescent front and the extraordinary efforts of the supply and transport services at last had begun to show effect. The logistical pa-tient had gained a new lease on life.

---

[35] See Pogue, *The Supreme Command,* pp. 306–07.

[36] 12th A Gp, Breakdown of Current Ton-nage Allocations, in 12th A Gp, Tonnage, Folder 89, filed with SHAEF records, Drawer 392.

CHAPTER XVII

New Plans To Drive to the Rhine

On 18 October, as General Eisenhower met his command chiefs at Brussels, he could only have speculated that the logistical situation even without Antwerp soon might permit resumption of the offensive. But as of 18 October, prospects for early use of Antwerp were bright, so bright that General Eisenhower's chief of intelligence saw November as the month Hitler dreaded most.[1] In any event, a commander failing to lay the groundwork for a new offensive purely on the basis of logistical question marks might one day find himself in the role of a foolish virgin with no oil in the lamp.

General Eisenhower and his advisers dutifully considered a theory that with winter coming on, the best policy might be to hold in place, then to launch a final victorious offensive in the early spring. Three factors tipped the scales against the theory: (1) The enemy's casualties were running about 4,000 per day, "or one 'division' on his new standard every day or two, through simple attrition in the line." (2) A winter sit-down would give the enemy's new divisions time for detailed training and combat blooding, would enable enemy industry to turn out new guns and tanks, and would provide time for building new concrete cordons about the rents in the West Wall. (3) A pause might enable the Germans to get their jet-fighter production into high gear and

possibly to discover the proximity fuze, with which they might blast Allied bombers from the skies. "We were certain," General Eisenhower wrote after the war, "that by continuing an unremitting offensive we would, in spite of hardship and privation," shorten the war and save "thousands" of Allied lives.[2]

This issue decided, the conferees at Brussels turned to the task of planning a new offensive.[3] In keeping with General Eisenhower's "broad front" strategy, the first phase was to be a build-up along the west bank of the Rhine. General Eisenhower directed that as soon as possible, probably between 1 and 5 November, the First Army undertake an offensive to gain a footing over the Rhine south of Cologne. Protecting First Army's left flank, the Ninth Army also was to drive to the Rhine, then turn northward to assist in clearing the region between the Rhine and the Maas along the western face of the Ruhr. Preoccupied with the vital objective of Antwerp, Field Marshal Montgomery's 21 Army Group was not to participate until about 10 November, when, upon expected termination of the

---

[1] Pogue, *The Supreme Command*, p. 306.

[2] Eisenhower, *Crusade in Europe,* p. 323; SHAEF G–2 Weekly Intel Summary, 15 Oct 44, copy in Pogue files; Bradley, *A Soldier's Story,* p. 434; Pogue, *The Supreme Command,* p. 306.

[3] Decisions at Brussels are drawn from Memo, sub: Decisions reached at Supreme Commander's Conf, 18 Oct 44, dtd 22 Oct 44, and SCAF 114, Eisenhower to comdrs, 28 Oct 44, both in SHAEF SGS 381, II.

Antwerp campaign, the Second British
Army was to drive southeast from
Nijmegen to meet the Ninth Army. Depending upon the logistical situation, the
Third Army was to drive northeastward
from the vicinity of Metz to protect the
First Army's right flank. In the south
the 6th Army Group was to resume its
advance to the Rhine at Strasbourg.

Upon gaining a foothold beyond the
Rhine, the 12th Army Group was to
assume responsibility for encircling the
Ruhr by sending the Ninth Army north of
and the First Army south of the Ruhr.
But this was planning for the long pull.
Despite some pressure from the home
front,[4] General Eisenhower could not look
upon the November drive as an end-the-
war offensive, rather as a modest first of
three phases in new plans to bring the
Germans to heel. Thinking of the need
for Antwerp, he could not see build-up
beyond the Rhine and advance deep into
Germany except as future operations dependent upon logistical improvements.
The November offensive was expected
neither to bring conquest of the Ruhr nor
to end the war but to attain the more
modest objective of clearing the Germans
from the relatively narrow sector remaining west of the Rhine.[5]

Three days after the Brussels conference—on 21 October, the day Aachen
fell—General Bradley outlined instructions to his three armies for the November
offensive. He set a target date for the
First and Ninth Armies of 5 November.
In anticipation of improvements in the
supply situation, he directed the Third

GENERALS BRADLEY, EISENHOWER,
AND GEROW *making a front-line inspection early in November.*

Army to attack about five days later on
10 November.[6]

As the target date for the First and
Ninth Armies approached, Field Marshal
Montgomery proposed a change in the
British role. He acted in deference to the
enemy's re-entrant bridgehead west of the
Maas, the strength of which was demonstrated by the spoiling attack in late
October in the Peel Marshes. Rather
than a delayed attack southeast from
Nijmegen that would involve risk to the
British flank and rear from the re-entrant
bridgehead, Montgomery suggested that
the Second Army begin immediately to
clear the Peel Marshes, then develop later
operations east of the Maas close along-

---

[4] See Pogue, *The Supreme Command,* pp.
307–09.
[5] This attitude is clear from SCAF 114, 28
Oct 44.

[6] 12th A Gp Ltr of Instrs 10, 21 Oct 44, with
amendments, 12th A Gp Rpt of Opns, V, 97–
102.

side the Ninth Army's left flank. This was the decision behind the British attack in the Peel Marshes which began on 14 November.[7]

In the meantime, it had become clear that neither the 104th Division from the Antwerp fight nor the 7th Armored Division from the Peel Marshes would be returned in time to meet the American target date of 5 November. Ostensibly because the First and Ninth Armies needed these two divisions before jump-off, but also because of the support a British drive close along the Ninth Army's left flank would provide, General Bradley set back the target date to 10 November. Even this date was subject to the weather; for Bradley intended to ensure success of the new drive with a saturation air bombardment.[8]

Still hopeful of getting at least a part of the drive going quickly, General Bradley turned on 2 November to the Third Army. Could the Third Army begin the offensive alone? General Patton answered with customary alacrity that he could attack on twenty-four-hour notice. The two commanders agreed that the Third Army should attack as soon as weather permitted the air forces to soften up the enemy, but in any event, not later than 8 November.[9] So it was that the Third Army, after waiting in vain three days for good weather, was to strike the first blow of the offensive on 8 November in a driving rain.

German Resurgence and Deception

The Allies hardly could have hoped to achieve strategic surprise with the November offensive; it was betrayed by its very logicality. After the fall of Aachen, the Germans were bound to know that the Allies soon would launch the offensive for which they had been setting the stage so meticulously for several weeks.[10]

Whether the Germans could be ready to meet the new offensive was another question. Certainly the Germans in November were better qualified to execute a steadfast defense than they had been, say, in mid-September when with little more than a *coup de main* the Americans might have taken Aachen. Nowhere had the Germans better demonstrated their resurgence than at Aachen itself in October.

This remarkable resurgence the Germans hailed as the "Miracle of the West," in remembrance of, and answer to, World War I's Miracle of the Marne. Much credit for it belonged to one able, energetic, and fanatical soldier: Generalfeldmarschall Walter Model; but the basic explanation for it rested in one simple truth: contrary to almost universal belief, Germany had not reached the peak of war production until the fall of 1944 and still retained a considerable pool of manpower.

For all the Allied bombs, Germany's war industry in the fall of 1944 felt critical shortages only in oil and communica-

---

[7] 21 A Gp Gen Opnl Sit and Dir, M–534, 2 Nov 44, 12th A Gp 371.3 Military Objectives, II.
[8] Memo by Brig Gen A. Franklin Kibler (12th A Gp G–3), sub: Change of Plans, 1 Nov 44, 12th A Gp 371.3, Military Objectives, II.
[9] TUSA Dairy, 2 and 5 Nov 44, as cited in Cole, *The Lorraine Campaign,* p. 301.

[10] This is obvious from almost all German records of the period. See in particular Entry of 4 Nov, *OKW/WFSt, KTB Ausarbeitung, der Westen 1.IV.–16.XII.44,* MS # B–034 (Schramm). For details on this period from the German side, see Lucian Heichler, The Third Battle of Aachen—The German Situation in Mid-November 1944, MS prepared in OCMH to complement this volume.

tions.[11] Low as manpower reserves were after five years of war, the Germans still were able to mobilize waves of new divisions. They filled them by replacing more men in factories and farms with women and foreign slave labor, by lowering physical standards, by systematically combing out the Navy, Luftwaffe, and rear echelon units, and by extending both ends of the induction spectrum. During the second half of 1944, the skeletons of some 35 burned out divisions were refitted and returned to the front as the new volks grenadier divisions. The Replacement Army furnished 15 more, so that by the end of the year 50 volks grenadier divisions had reached either the Eastern or Western Fronts.[12] Albeit the caliber and training of the replacements left something to be desired, the Germans were much like the giant Antaeus who regained his strength whenever he touched his mother earth.

The most remarkable facet of the resurgence was not that the Germans found men and guns to fill the line but that coincidentally they mobilized a separate force eminently stronger and capable of offensive action. For three months— from 16 September to 16 December 1944 —the Germans planned and prepared for the great counteroffensive to be launched in the Ardennes. While the fight raged about Aachen and on the approaches to the Roer River, some thirty divisions were massed behind the Roer and in the Eifel, ammunition and fuel were stockpiled, and new volks artillery corps and *Volks-werfer*

brigades were assembled. Of the titantic German mobilization and production effort for the West, the lion's share went to the build-up for the counteroffensive.

All forces and matériel set aside for the Ardennes were designated OKW Reserves. No one, not even the Commander in Chief West, had any power to employ them without Hitler's authorization, though as the target date approached a few of the volks grenadier divisions were to be used in a kind of round robin of temporary reliefs so that some units long in the line might be refitted. The only contingents which, by Hitler's permission, might be used for any extended period were some of the volks artillery corps and *Volks-werfer* brigades. Any analysis of the enemy's defensive achievement during the fall of 1944 must be made in the light of these facts.

While awaiting the Allied blow, the Germans cleverly utilized their foreknowledge that an Allied offensive was bound to come as a cover for their own preparations for the Ardennes counteroffensive. Lest the secret of the counteroffensive reach Allied ears, the Germans intended to conceal it from almost everyone on their own side below the rank of army group commander. Not even German army commanders were trusted with knowledge of the counteroffensive until late in the planning.

To justify to friend and foe alike the massing of men and matériel, the Germans pointed to the imminent Allied offensive. Almost all moves were justified in the first paragraph of the order by "the anticipated enemy offensive." Indeed, the historian often finds it difficult to determine which moves were bona fide measures against the Allied blow, which concerned only the Ardennes counteroffensive, and

---

[11] Charles V. P. von Luttichau, The Ardennes Offensive, Germany's Situation in the Fall of 1944, Part II, The Economic Situation, MS in OCMH.

[12] MS # P–065b, The Volks Grenadier Division and the Volkssturm (Generalmajor a.D. Hellmuth Reinhardt).

which concerned both. When the *Sixth Panzer Army*, for example, earmarked for the counteroffensive, was ordered to mass near Cologne, the following entry appeared in the *OB WEST* War Diary: ". . . there can be no doubt that the enemy will commit maximum strength and maximum matériel to force the breakthrough to the Rhine. Our own defensive measures must be attuned to this . . . . Hence the Commander-in-Chief WEST will order the transfer of *Sixth Panzer Army* to the *OB WEST* theater on 7 November. . . ." [13]

That the Ardennes counteroffensive remained a secret was to be demonstrated by American surprise when it began. As to the deception in regard to the *Sixth Panzer Army*, the Americans swallowed it wholeheartedly. While unaware at first of the existence of a panzer army per se, they perceived as early as 11 November that the Germans were resting and refitting a panzer reserve of at least five divisions. On the eve of the November offensive the 12th Army Group G–2 saw in the disposition of the panzer and panzer grenadier divisions "the key to the enemy's essential capabilities and intentions." Through November and until mid-December, both this intelligence officer and his opposite numbers at headquarters of the First and Ninth Armies expected the panzer reserve to be used to counterattack either west or east of the Roer. [14]

In another German move truth and deception walked hand in hand. This was a shift on 23 October of *Headquarters Fifth Panzer Army* (General von Manteuf-

GENERAL VON MANTEUFFEL

fel) from *Army Group G* to *Army Group B*. Like the Ninth U.S. Army, the *Fifth Panzer Army* brought no combat troops along and also moved to the vicinity of Aachen. The army entered the line between the *First Parachute* and *Seventh Armies* and assumed command of two corps already committed, the *XII SS Corps* and *LXXXI Corps*. Thus, two days after the fall of Aachen, General Brandenberger's *Seventh Army* ceased to be responsible for this sector and retained control only of the mountainous forest region of the Eifel. [15]

Adjustment of the *Seventh Army*'s front was overdue, for it had become too long and the number of corps and divisions too large for one army headquarters to control

---

[13] *OB WEST KTB,* 6 Nov 44.

[14] 12th A Gp Weekly Intel Summary 14 for week ending 11 Nov, dtd 13 Nov, 12th A Gp G–2 AAR, Nov 44; subsequent 12th A Gp rpts until mid-Dec. See also G–2 Estimates of the First and Ninth Armies for the period.

[15] Mng Sitrep, *OB WEST* to *OKW/WFSt,* 23 Oct 44, *OB WEST KTB, Anlagen, Befehle und Meldungen.*

efficiently. Also, a panzer army was needed in the Aachen sector to face the coming Allied blow. The *Fifth Panzer Army* did effective work in preparing the sector for defense, but paradoxically, because of the deception program for the Ardennes, the army fought against the November offensive in name only.

In a grand deception maneuver, *Headquarters Fifth Panzer Army* was disengaged secretly on 15 November. Equally secretly, *Headquarters Fifteenth Army* (General von Zangen) arrived from Holland to take over the sector, the troops, and even the name of its predecessor. The *Fifteenth Army*'s alias became *Gruppe von Manteuffel.* So that, in turn, the Allies in western Holland would not spot the absence of the *Fifteenth Army,* headquarters of the *Armed Forces Commander Netherlands* (General Christiansen), which took over the sector, called itself *Fifteenth Army.* To complete the deception game, *Headquarters Fifth Panzer Army,* after moving east of the Roer to prepare for the Ardennes fight, hid behind the innocuous name of *Military Police Command for Special Assignment (Feldjaegerkommando z.b.V.).*[16]

A parallel, though not so intricate, adjustment took place on the army group level. Bearing responsibility for most of the German front in the West—from Antwerp nearly to the Franco-German border—and controlling four armies— *Fifteenth, First Parachute, Fifth Panzer,*

and *Seventh*—Field Marshal Model's *Army Group B* also was to command the Ardennes counteroffensive. It was imperative that Model be relieved of some of his burdens. Hitler therefore decided to commit a third army group headquarters in the West. This was *Army Group H,* to be headed by General Student, commander of the *First Parachute Army.* On 10 November *Army Group H* assumed command of the *First Parachute* and *Fifteenth Armies.* In geographical terms, the lineup of army groups then was as follows: *Army Group H* under Student held Holland, *Army Group B* under Model defended those portions of Germany bordering on Belgium and Luxembourg, and *Army Group G* under General der Panzertruppen Hermann Balck continued to hold in Alsace and Lorraine.[17]

Model's *Army Group B* now commanded two armies: *Fifth Panzer* under Manteuffel and *Seventh* under Brandenberger. The army group's northern boundary ran south of Roermond, thus corresponding roughly to the boundary between the Americans and the British. The southern boundary remained unchanged, in effect a prolongation of the boundary between the First and Third U.S. Armies. Within *Army Group B,* the boundary between the *Fifth Panzer* and *Seventh Armies* cut through the northern edge of the Huertgen Forest. Thus the *Fifth Panzer Army* (later to be relieved by the *Fifteenth Army* under an assumed name) faced the Ninth U.S. Army and part of the VII Corps of the First U.S. Army. The *Seventh Army* confronted the rest of the VII Corps, plus

[16] *OB WEST KTB,* 15 Nov 44; *OB WEST KTB, Anlagen, Angriff H. Gr. "B". 16 Dez. 44, 24.X.–31.XII.44.* Vol. I, V (Planning Papers); MS # A–857, Questions for CG *Fifth Panzer Army,* Statement made by PW LD 918 Gen von Manteuffel (Manteuffel). Greater detail on this deception maneuver may be found in Charles V. P. von Luttichau, The Ardennes Offensive, Planning and Preparations, MS in OCMH.

[17] Order, *OB WEST* to all subordinate commands, 2 Nov 44, *OB WEST KTB, Anlagen, Befehle und Meldungen.*

the V and VIII Corps of the First U.S. Army.[18]

One trenchant fact about German improvement in the Aachen sector as the enemy awaited the November offensive stood out above all others. This was the intrinsic and potential strength of the *Fifth Panzer Army* in artillery. For once the Germans had reasonable complements of divisional artillery and "somewhat above average" amounts of ammunition. Artillery of the *3d Panzer Grenadier Division*, for example, was fully motorized. The division had 24 105-mm. and 13 150-mm. howitzers, 7 150-mm. rocket launchers, 2 100-mm. cannon, 2 command tanks, 11 88-mm. antiaircraft guns, and 35 assault guns. Although a portion of these weapons were in either short-term or long-term repair, the bulk was on hand, and almost all were to see service in some phase of the November fighting.[19]

Both corps of the *Fifth Panzer Army* had considerable forces of GHQ and corps artillery. The *LXXXI Corps*, for example, controlled an artillery regiment of varied but effective pieces: 2 240-mm. railway guns, 9 French 220-mm. howitzers, 2 240-mm. guns, 24 76.2-mm. fortress antitank guns, and a few fully motorized Russian 152-mm. howitzers. The same corps also controlled a battalion of 14 Russian 122-mm. howitzers. Both corps had one of the new volks artillery corps and one of the *Volks-werfer* brigades. The volks artillery corps consisted of from 50 to 100 pieces, including guns and howitzers ranging from 75-mm. to 210-mm., and were fully motorized. The *Volks-werfer* brigades had four firing battalions equipped in part with 150-mm. rocket projectors, in part with 210-mm. or 280-mm. projectors. Several tank and assault gun units were available under army control to supplement artillery of either or both corps.[20]

This was the artillery strength before the Allied offensive began. In comparison to the number of pieces which the Germans would be using at the height of the offensive, it was only a beginning. In late November the *Fifth Panzer Army* (known then as *Gruppe von Manteuffel*) would be employing an estimated 1,000 artillery pieces, including antiaircraft guns used against ground targets. The guns were well directed, their positions so well concealed that they incurred little damage from either counterbattery fires or air attacks. The ammunition situation was satisfactory. For once the Germans were capable of laying down really massive fires.[21]

Not only in artillery but also in frontline divisions the *Fifth Panzer Army* was to gain greater strength after the November offensive began. The biggest addition

---

[18] *OKH / Kriegswissenschaftliche Abteilung: Kampf um Aachen/Kampf um Metz:* a collection of dated situation maps (hereafter cited as *Kampf um Aachen:* Maps).

[19] Strength Rpts, 15 Nov 44, *LXXXI Corps, IIa/b KTB Anlagen, 20.X–30.XI.44; LXXXI Corps, Ia KTB Anlagen, Kriegsgliederungen, 22.X–31.XII.44; LXXXI Corps, Ia KTB Anlagen, Art.-Lage u. Art.-Gliederungen, 11.X.–18.XII.44* (hereafter cited as *LXXXI Corps KTB, Art.-Lage u. Art.-Gliederungen*); *LXXXI Corps Ia KTB Anlagen, Wochenmeldungen, 22.IX.–31.XII.44; LXXXI Corps Ia KTB Anlagen, Zustandsberichte, 10.X–17.XII.44; Kampf um Aachen:* Maps.

[20] *LXXXI Corps* Arty Sit as of 10 Nov 44, *LXXXI Corps KTB, Art.-Lage u. Art.-Gliederungen; LXXXI Corps KTB, Zustandsberichte; Kampf um Aachen:* Maps; MS # B–290, *Das XII. SS-Korps (7.bzw 15.Armee, Heeresgruppe B) westlich und an der Roer vom 20.X.1944–31.I.1945* (General der Infanterie Guenther Blumentritt): MS # P–065b (Reinhardt); and MS # A–994 (Koechling).

[21] See, in particular, MS # T–122 (Zimmerman *et al.*), III.5.

was the number one *OB WEST* reserve and fire brigade, the *XLVII Panzer Corps* (General von Luettwitz), which in late October had launched the spoiling attack in the Peel Marshes but which was to have pulled back by the time the Allied offensive began. The corps still contained the two divisions which fought in the Peel Marshes, the *15th Panzer Grenadier* and *9th Panzer Divisions*. Together these two divisions could muster 66 tanks, 41 assault guns, 65 105-mm. and 150-mm. howitzers, and numbers of other lesser armored vehicles.[22]

Of particular import for the November fighting was the value of the Aachen sector to the Germans in terms of their plans and preparations for a counteroffensive in the Ardennes. When first informed of Hitler's plans, the Commander in Chief West, Rundstedt, had lamented that in case the Allies launched large-scale attacks at Metz and Aachen, the counteroffensive would have to be called off. Hitler would entertain no such idea. On 9 November he instructed OB WEST to hold the line without committing a single unit earmarked for the Big Offensive, even if that meant losing some terrain. In subsequent discussions about which terrain might be relinquished with least impunity, it was decreed that holding in the Aachen sector was paramount. The Allies must not be allowed to cross the Roer River. In particular, the Germans were to maintain "at all cost" bridgeheads west of the Roer at Juelich and Dueren.[23]

---

[22] Strength Rpts, 1 Nov 44, *XLVII Pz Corps O. Qu., KTB Anlagen, Einzelbefehle, 17.X.–18.XI.44* (hereafter cited as *XLVII Pz Corps O. Qu. KTB Einzelbefehle*); *Kampf um Aachen: Maps.*

[23] Luttichau, The Strategic Situation, citing *OB WEST KTB* (Text) for Sep–Nov 44.

First Army Plans

On the Allied side, the army that was to carry the main burden of the new drive—General Hodges' First U.S. Army —also was stronger than before, though in no such ratio as displayed by the enemy. Two new divisions, the 99th and 104th, had been assigned to the V and VII Corps, respectively. This brought the army total within three corps (V, VII, and VIII) to three armored and nine infantry divisions. In addition, the army included a high number of nondivisional units, among them: 1 separate infantry battalion, 1 ranger infantry battalion, 30 antiaircraft artillery battalions, 10 tank battalions (9 medium, 1 light), 12 tank destroyer battalions, approximately 40 field artillery battalions, 6 cavalry reconnaissance squadrons, 4 engineer combat groups, 12 engineer combat battalions, and numbers of miscellaneous engineer and service units. As compared with a total strength in early September at the start of the Siegfried Line Campaign of 256,351 men, the First Army now had 318,422. Yet despite this gain, the First Army through the latter half of the Siegfried Line Campaign, as in the first half, would find its responsibilities too great to permit the luxury of more than a nominal army reserve.[24]

Except for men of the 28th Division, most troops of the First Army were basically rested. Although life in a front-line position was far from ideal under any conditions, the hardships of a relatively quiet period in no way compared with the

---

[24] 12th A Gp G–1 Daily Summary, 11 Nov, 12th A Gp G–1 Daily Summaries file, Nov 44; FUSA G–1 Daily Summaries, 12 Sep and 11 Nov 44; FUSA Rpt, Annexes 1, 5, 6, and 7, Vol. 2; FUSA AAR, Nov 44; V Corps Opns in the ETO, p. 326.

REST PERIOD BEHIND THE LINES

rigors of a sustained attack. Displaying sometimes amazing ingenuity, the men scrounged material and equipment from damaged buildings to provide a measure of creature comforts for the foxhole or dugout. A wooden door covered by a shelter half, for example, was infinitely preferable to no roof at all. Wherever possible, divisions rotated battalions in the line to give as many men as possible a night or two in a dry place a few hundred yards behind the front. Most regiments maintained shower points close to the front, run on the order of an assembly line, where a dirty man entered one end of a tent or converted building and came out the other end clean. Division, corps, and army rest centers in cities beyond normal artillery range, like Verviers, Liège, and Maastricht, in time managed to accommodate almost every forward soldier with a forty-eight-hour rest, complete with bath, bed, movies, USO shows, and doughnuts and coffee dispensed from a Red Cross Clubmobile. A lucky few got to Paris. Post exchange supplies and cigarettes—the latter issued free to combat troops—became more plentiful. Quartermaster bakeries increased the issue of fresh bread, and company kitchens in most cases found time and shelter for preparing the relatively palatable B Ration.

After almost two months of campaigning since the first patrol crossed the German border, the First Army's front line now ran from a point slightly northeast of Aachen near Wuerselen southeast through Stolberg to Schevenhuette, thence through the Huertgen Forest to Germeter and Vossenack, thence across the Monschau Corridor to Camp d'Elsenborn and on generally southward along the Schnee Eifel and the Luxembourg frontier to the Franco-Luxembourgian border. Though this front embraced approximately 120 miles, about 80 of it belonged to the newly arrived VIII Corps for which no immediate offensive was contemplated.[25] General Hodges had concentrated the bulk of his strength in the V and VII Corps zones from Camp d'Elsenborn to Wuerselen, a distance of about 40 miles.

The northernmost corps, General Collins' VII Corps, was General Hodges' choice for executing the army's main effort. The VII Corps was located in the foothills of the Eifel and along the fringe of the Roer plain with forward lines pointed along the most direct route northeast to Cologne. Hodges told Collins to plan a drive on Cologne. He also alerted General Gerow's V Corps and General Middleton's VIII Corps to be prepared to complement any VII Corps breakthrough by driving on Bonn and Koblenz, respectively.[26] The V Corps also was to execute the preliminary operation to assure a firm right flank for the main effort by establishing a line along the headwaters of the Roer River. This was the disastrous second attack on Schmidt by the 28th Division.

General Hodges issued his order directing the VII Corps to make the main effort at a time when the target date still stood at 5 November. Even at this time—late October—doubt existed about availability by the target date of the 104th Division.[27] General Hodges told the VII Corps to prepare two plans, one based on a target date of 5 November and a strength of but three divisions, another based on a target date between 10 and 15 November and the services of a fourth division, the 104th.

The two plans as developed by General Collins and his staff proved to be little different except in strength and in position of various divisions within the line. Both plans were predicated upon the objective of seizing crossings of the Roer—at the closest point, not quite seven miles away—whereupon supplemental orders were to be issued for renewing the drive across the Cologne plain to the Rhine. Both plans also named the same three initial objectives as prerequisites for breaking the German containment of the VII Corps West Wall penetration and reaching the Roer. (*Map VI*) These were: (1) the Eschweiler–Weisweiler industrial area northeast of Stolberg, capture of which would spell access to a more open portion of the Roer plain and firm contact with the Ninth Army on the north; (2) the Hamich ridge, one of the more prominent terrain features along a sixteen-mile corps front and one that denied egress from the Stolberg Corridor between the industrial complex and the Huertgen Forest (that is, the Wenau Forest); and (3) in the south of the corps zone, the long-sought Huertgen–Kleinhau–Gey road net, cap-

---

[25] On 8 November VIII Corps relinquished approximately twenty miles on its southern wing as the 83d Division passed to "operational control" of the Third Army, but the arrangement lasted only four days. See 83d Div AAR, Nov 44.
[26] FUSA Rpt, Vol. 1, p. 67.

[27] For a time, it looked as if the First Army would get the 84th Division instead of the 104th. The 84th eventually went to the Ninth Army.

ture of which would end the miserable confinement within the Huertgen Forest.[28]

After General Hodges heard from General Bradley on 1 November of the decision to postpone the offensive five days, he notified General Collins that he sanctioned the VII Corps Plan No. 2. This involved four instead of three divisions. The target date was 10 November with a deadline date of 15 November.[29] In the meantime, the 28th Division of the V Corps was getting set to launch the preliminary operation against Schmidt on 2 November, regardless of the weather.

In the days preceding the new target date of 10 November, while the 28th Division was fighting it out at Vossenack and Schmidt, General Collins regrouped his divisions. Inexperienced in combat except for brief commitment near Antwerp, the incoming 104th Division was to relieve the 1st Division on the corps left wing northwest of Stolberg. The veteran 1st Division then was to move to the center of the corps zone to carry the weight of the corps main effort. Discovering three days before the target date that the 104th Division would not arrive in time for this regrouping, the First Army G–3, General Thorson, recommended another postponement of twenty-four hours. General Hodges concurred. As finally determined, the First Army was to attack on 11 November or the first day thereafter that weather permitted large-scale air support. The deadline date was 16 November.[30]

Ninth Army Plans

The extent of the Ninth Army's participation in the early phase of the new offensive was inevitably tied up with the army's growing pains. When General Simpson received the assignment to attack to the Rhine along the First Army's north flank, his headquarters only recently had moved north to Maastricht. In addition to perplexing problems of supply, he faced a shortage of combat units. Though two corps headquarters and six divisions were assigned to the Ninth Army, only one corps (the XIX) and three divisions were available for operations. Recently arrived from a Normandy staging area, the XIII Corps under Maj. Gen. Alvan C. Gillem, Jr., had no troops.[31] Of three divisions technically assigned to the Ninth Army that might have been attached to the XIII Corps, the 104th Division was destined to go to the First Army, the 7th Armored Division still was with the British, and the 102d Division lacked organic transport and artillery. The only tangible force the Ninth Army could muster was General McLain's veteran XIX Corps, controlling the 113th Cavalry Group and the 2d Armored, 29th, and 30th Divisions.[32]

[28] Operation Plan VII Corps, 28 Oct 44, dtd 27 Oct, VII Corps G–3 FO file, Oct 44.

[29] Msg, CG FUSA to CG VII Corps, FUSA G–3 Jnl file, Nov 44. Though undated, this message obviously was sent on 1 November.

[30] Memo CG FUSA for Thorson, 7 Nov, FUSA G–3 Ltrs and Inds file, Nov 44.

[31] Like the commander of the Ninth Army's other corps, General Gillem had risen from the ranks. Between wars he attended the usual staff colleges, served as an instructor at Fort Benning, Ga., and commanded both infantry and armored units. After the start of World War II, his early important posts included command of the Desert Training Center in California and later the Armored Force at Fort Knox. He trained the XIII Corps after assuming command in December, 1943.

[32] Unless otherwise noted, the story of Ninth Army planning is based upon Ninth United States Army Operations, Vol. IV, Offensive in November, part of a mimeographed series prepared by the 4th Information and Historical

Though the Ninth Army's frontage in the projected direction of attack was only about eleven miles, General Simpson had inherited from the First Army the old conundrum of what to do about an exposed north flank stretching some seventeen miles from the Maas River to the West Wall at Geilenkirchen. Defending this flank was eating up the services of a cavalry group and a division. As the advance progressed northeastward, the length of the exposed flank would grow proportionately.

While the target date for the new offensive stood at 5 November, General Simpson's only hope for solving this problem was in obtaining at least one more division which he could put with his cavalry under the XIII Corps to defend the flank. But the chance of getting another division by 5 November looked slim. Hope of using either the 7th Armored, 104th, or 102d Division appeared doubtful, as did a possibility that a new unit earmarked for the Ninth Army, the 84th Division, might arrive in time.

Concerned with the exposed flank and the threat to it inherent in enemy strength in the region of the Peel Marshes west of the Maas, General Simpson well may have played a role in General Bradley's decision to postpone the offensive until 10 November. He was present at Eindhoven on 31 October when, in conference with Field Marshal Montgomery, Bradley made the decision.[33] The Ninth Army clearly stood to benefit by postponement. Should the British clear the Peel Marshes, their

first order of business, a definite threat to the Ninth Army's rear would be eliminated. Should the British then execute their second assignment, which was to "develop offensive operations" on their right wing "in conformity with the advance" of the Ninth Army,[34] the exposed left flank would be taken care of. Even should the British be delayed in attacking alongside the Ninth Army, Montgomery had promised that on or about 15 November he would assume responsibility for the seventeen-mile line east of the Maas. Another advantage to the Ninth Army in delaying the offensive was the time provided for the 7th Armored Division and the rear echelon of the 102d Division to arrive. The 84th Division also might make it.

Even a superficial glance at the terrain in front of the Ninth Army as opposed to that facing the First Army would raise the question of why the First instead of the Ninth drew the role of "main effort" in the November offensive. The answer, as recalled after the war by the army group commander, General Bradley, had two facets. "You don't," General Bradley said, "make your main effort with your 'exterior' force." Because the extent of British participation in the offensive was tied up with British problems of reorganization and manpower, it appeared doubtful that the British on the left could lend genuine assistance to the drive. The Ninth Army thus became in effect an "exterior" force. In addition, the First Army's staff and troops represented the more experienced American force. The Ninth Army, still involved during the early days of November in assembling sufficient

---

Service and filed with official Ninth Army records (hereafter cited as NUSA Opns, Vol. IV), and upon *Conquer—The Story of Ninth Army,* pp. 71–85. Another useful source is the Ferriss Notes, described in Ch. VI.

[33] NUSA Opns, IV, 2.

---

[34] 21 A Gp Gen Opnl Sit and Dir, M–534, 2 Nov 44.

divisions to make the attack, was "relatively untried." [35]

On 4 November General Simpson issued a caveat to his two corps. With the 113th Cavalry Group and the 102d Division, General Gillem's new XIII Corps was to occupy the seventeen-mile defensive line on the army's north flank until relieved by the British. Upon arrival, both the 7th Armored and 84th Divisions were to go to the XIII Corps. Upon relief by the British, the XIII Corps was to be prepared to drive northeast along the left of the XIX Corps to the Rhine. [36]

Making the Army's main effort, General McLain's XIX Corps was to prepare plans for seizing a bridgehead over the Roer River at Juelich. In line with the mission of protecting the First Army's left flank, General McLain was to make his main effort close alongside the First Army.

General Simpson's plans had an obvious bug in them from the start. What to do about the West Wall crossroads village of Geilenkirchen? Without this village—a logical base for enemy counterattack—Simpson would have to funnel his army and subsequently support it through a narrow gap little more than ten miles wide between Wuerselen and Geilenkirchen. (*Map VII*) Yet taking it involved a special problem, for when the British assumed control of the seventeen-mile line west of Geilenkirchen, the village would lie virtually astride a new boundary between national forces. The solution eventually was to be found in help from the British.

In planning for the main drive to the Roer, General Simpson and his corps

commanders focused their attention on the river at Juelich and a few miles downstream at Linnich. From the bridgehead through the West Wall—some nine miles wide and as much as six miles deep—the XIX Corps was to attack on D Day. After the British had relieved the XIII Corps and after the XIX Corps had uncovered sufficient ground along its left flank between Geilenkirchen and the Roer, the XIII Corps was to be committed along the left of the XIX Corps to seize a Roer bridgehead at Linnich.

With but one corps of either the Ninth or First Army scheduled to participate at the start of the new offensive, the force directly involved in the first phase thus was to be considerably less powerful than a superficial glance might indicate. Whereas two armies were involved, little more than a third of the combat strength of the two actually was to attack on D Day. Nevertheless, this was to be the biggest drive in the Aachen sector since position warfare had begun in September. In the south, the Third Army's attack on 8 November and a complementary drive by the 6th Army Group would contribute to the over-all effect, while in the Peel Marshes the British were to be engaged in a limited offensive.

By 8 November arrival of additional units had started to provide the Ninth Army more ready muscle for its part in the November offensive. Indeed, the narrow zone between the Maas and the West Wall became a hive of activity. More than one traffic control officer must have torn his hair as rain fell almost perpetually, roads began to break down, and still the troops and trucks churned about.

Controlling the 113th Cavalry Group and the complete 102d Division, General Gillem's XIII Corps on 8 November took

---

[35] Intervs with Gen Bradley, 7 Jun 56, and Gen Thorson, 12 Sep 56.

[36] NUSA Ltr of Instrs 7, 4 Nov 44.

over defense of the seventeen-mile line west of Geilenkirchen. The next day, 9 November, General Horrocks began moving his 30 Corps headquarters and a British infantry division into the area as prelude to relief of the XIII Corps. At least thirty-three field artillery battalions, not counting either divisional units or the British, sought firing positions. The bulk of the 84th Division began to close to await its baptism of fire. Having been released by the British after fighting in the Peel Marshes, the 7th Armored Division began to occupy a reserve position while resting and refitting. Supply trucks rolling to and from the front compounded traffic problems. To add a final touch, the 104th Division en route to the First Army from Antwerp was cutting across the Ninth Army's rear lines of communication.

Faced with this deluge of troops, the Ninth Army staff hardly could have been other than elated to learn of another postponement of twenty-four hours. General Simpson readily agreed to the new target date of 11 November.

Operation QUEEN

To ensure success of the new offensive —indeed, in the hope of creating a sea of sterile rubble through which the ground forces might effect a swift breakthrough to the Roer—General Bradley requested air support of unprecedented magnitude. All types of planes—heavies, mediums, and fighter-bombers, both American and British—were to participate.[37]

After close co-ordination in early planning, top air commanders and representatives of the ground forces met on 7 November at Ninth Air Force headquarters to discuss and approve a final plan. Out of this conference emerged a blueprint for Operation QUEEN, "the largest air-ground cooperative effort yet undertaken . . . ."[38]

Because weather at this season was the great imponderable, the conferees prepared three different plans: one for fighter-bombers in event only tactical aircraft could operate, another for fighters and mediums, and a third for all three— fighters, mediums, and heavies. Should adverse weather prevent any type of aircraft from operating between the target date of 11 November and the deadline date of 16 November, the attack would begin on 16 November without air support.

The alternate programs for fighters and for fighters and mediums were, in effect, but variations of the main plan for all three types of planes. Under this most comprehensive plan, the bulk of the air effort was to be centered in front of the First Army's VII Corps in keeping with the emphasis of the ground plan. Three divisions (more than 1,200 planes) of Eighth Air Force heavy bombers were to concentrate on destroying personnel and field installations in two major target areas: the Eschweiler–Weisweiler industrial complex and the Langerwehe–Juengersdorf area, an urban obstacle at the northeastern tip of the Wenau Forest

---

[37] Unless otherwise noted, the air plan is drawn from the following sources: Ninth Air Force, Summary of Air Plan, 7 Nov 44, NUSA G–3 Jnl file, 1–11 Nov 44; FUSA, Air Support, Annex 4 to FO 12, 8 Nov, VII Corps Admin

and FO file, Nov 44; FUSA Rpt, Vol. 1, pp. 73–74; Conquer—The Story of Ninth Army, pp. 80–81; NUSA Opns, IV, 34; and Craven and Cate, eds., Europe: ARGUMENT to V-E Day, pp. 631–32.

[38] Craven and Cate, eds., Europe: ARGUMENT to V-E Day, pp. 631–32.

lying squarely astride the projected route of the VII Corps main effort.

While this use of heavy bombers represented a radical departure from the norm, it had ample precedent in several missions flown earlier in support of British and Canadian ground troops and in the "carpet" bombing preceding American breakout from Normandy. The assault troops in Normandy had been only 1,200 yards behind the bomb line, whereas in Operation QUEEN the heavies were to drop their loads no closer to the forward troops than three times that distance. Though the setting of this interval was obviously due to the disaster that short bombing had produced in Normandy, some wondered whether the ground troops could advance across the two-mile interval quickly enough to capitalize on the shock effect of the bombs.

An equal number of heavy bombers (more than 1,200) from the Royal Air Force Bomber Command was to attack Dueren, Juelich, and Heinsberg, the latter a communications center north of the Ninth Army zone. In contrast to the American heavies, which were to employ fragmentation bombs for maximum effect against personnel and minimum cratering in areas through which the ground troops would have to pass early in the attack, the British bombers were to seek complete destruction of the three target cities in hope of blocking roads and intersections.

A portion of eleven groups (approximately 600 planes) of Ninth Air Force medium bombers drew a similar mission of devastating the towns of Linnich and Aldenhoven in the Ninth Army zone. The rest of the mediums were to concentrate on personnel and field installations in front of the First Army. The target areas were around three villages representing

likely sites for enemy command posts and local reserves: Luchem, Echtz, and Mariaweiler.

In general, the fighter-bombers were to operate on call from the ground troops upon targets of opportunity, although some squadrons were to perform normal tasks of column cover and reconnaissance. Employing four groups (about 300 planes), the XXIX Tactical Air Command was to support the Ninth Army. The First Army's old ally, the IX TAC, was to employ three groups (about 225 planes) in direct support of the VII Corps and three other groups on general missions throughout the First Army zone. Although most fighter-bombers would have no predesignated targets, those three groups in direct support of the VII Corps were to hit three specific target areas. These were: the Huertgen–Kleinhau sector on the VII Corps right wing; the southeastern end of the Hamich ridge near the village of Hamich; and a built-up area around the villages of Hastenrath and Scherpenseel in the center of the VII Corps zone.

The total fighter-bomber force numbered some 750 planes. In addition, 800 American and British fighters were to fly escort for the heavy bombers. Other Eighth Air Force fighters were to escort the mediums.

Thus, for Operation QUEEN, World War II's largest air attack in direct support of ground troops, the Allied air forces were to employ more than 4,500 planes, approximately half of them heavy bombers.[39] Though the bombing was

---

[39] The largest up to this time was Operation GOODWOOD, a strike by 1,676 heavies and 343 mediums and lights with 7,700 tons of bombs in support of the Second British Army near Caen on 18 July. The largest in support of American troops was along the St. Lô–Périers road in

not to be as concentrated as that in Normandy, both air and ground commanders expected it to disrupt enemy communications thoroughly and certainly to disorganize enemy front-line units and immediate reserves.

A major question facing the air-ground planners was who should be responsible for designating the specific D Day within the allotted target period of 11–16 November. With alternate though less attractive air plans available, they also had to consider what circumstances were to guide this commander in settling or not settling for one of the alternate plans, that is, for less effective air support. Early in the target period, for example, whoever was to make the decision might bow to a fear that better weather or weather even as good might not be forthcoming. Having settled, then, for a day permitting only limited support, he might see the ground attack bog down for want of heavier air support and a day or so later watch in vexation as the sun began to shine. On the other hand, should one pass up weather permitting minor support on the gamble that weather favoring a full-scale air effort might arrive by the deadline date? The ground attack had to go off on 16 November regardless of

the weather. Rain and fog on the last day would mean no air support at all.

In making their decision, the planners leaned toward compromise. During the first three days of the target period, responsibility for designating D Day fell to the top American airman in the European theater, Lt. Gen. Ira C. Eaker, who obviously understood fully the weather requirements of his big bombers. Thus, in effect, the planners were to gamble during half the target period on an all-or-nothing basis. During the last three days, if the attack had not begun, designation of D Day was to be up to the First Army's General Hodges. Thus the decision during the period of greatest gamble would rest with the ground commander who had most at stake.

In either event, decision would have to be made before 2200 the night before D Day in order that both air and ground commanders might get their complex machines into gear. H Hour was to depend upon the time required to execute the bombing program, but in order that ground troops might have sufficient daylight in which to exploit the bombing and then consolidate, H Hour was not to be later than 1400.

Recalling the catastrophe short bombing had wrought in Normandy, the planners developed an elaborate safety program in addition to designating a bomb line for the heavy bombers two miles in front of the troops. Two giant white panel markers were to be placed in rear of the First Army's lines to guide the pilots toward target areas. One panel was to be approximately nineteen miles in rear of the front line near Liège, the other about two miles behind the line near Aachen. At about the same distance from the front as the second panel, eleven

---

Normandy where 1,495 heavy bombers and 338 fighter-bombers dropped 4,790 tons of bombs. Another large-scale bombing was in support of the First Canadian Army the night of 7 August when 1,450 planes dropped 5,210 tons of bombs. See Air Chief Marshal Sir Trafford Leigh-Mallory, Air Commander in Chief, Allied Expeditionary Air Force, "Despatch, Air Operations by the Allied Expeditionary Air Force in N. W. Europe," Nov 44, found in *Fourth Supplement to The London Gazette* (December 31, 1946), dtd 2 Jan 47. The story of early uses of heavy bombers in this role in the European theater and of the Normandy bombing may be found in Blumenson, *Breakout and Pursuit.*

captive balloons borrowed from the British were to be flown in line parallel to the front at about 2,000 feet altitude. Five hundred yards in rear of forward ground positions, troops were to display a row of bright-hued panels, four per mile. Sixty-four 90-mm. antiaircraft guns within both the First and Ninth Armies were to fire red flak to mark the actual forward ground positions. The Eighth Air Force was to establish a series of beacons and buncher beacons close to the lines and a radio fan marker to transmit a thin vertical signal over the row of balloons. Bomb bays were to be opened and locked while over the English Channel to avoid damage should bombs be released accidentally in the process. To protect the bombers themselves, both First and Ninth Army artillery units were to fire a comprehensive counterflak program planned in close relation to incoming and outgoing flight routes. If elaborate precautions could do the trick, ground troops in Operation QUEEN need fear no repetition of the mishap in Normandy.

The Roer River Dams
and the Weather

Continuing a weather pattern that since the start of the second attack on Schmidt on 2 November had been plaguing the 28th Division, leaden skies on 11 November made it evident that the big November offensive would not begin that day. Already rain far in excess of normal had fallen. Roads had deteriorated, streams were approaching flood levels, and the ground was such a morass that grave doubts were arising about trafficability for armor. In long-range meteorological forecasts the commanders could find little of comfort.

Almost coincident with increasing concern over weather, another threat to the new offensive had festered and grown in the minds of American commanders so that by 11 November it could not be ignored. This was a growing realization of the defensive importance to the Germans of the Roer River Dams. On 29 October, before the 28th Division had jumped off for Schmidt, General Hodges had noted, "Present plans of this Army do not contemplate the immediate capture of these dams." [40] But on 7 November, after the violent German reaction to the 28th Division's attack, General Hodges had directed the V Corps commander to prepare a plan for use "in the event First Army is ordered to capture" the dams. [41] Four days later, faced with the hard facts that if all went well American troops soon might be east of the Roer River and subject to whatever plan the Germans might have for blowing the dams and flooding the Roer valley, the Americans adopted a more realistic attitude toward the dams. Apparently acting on orders from General Bradley, both General Hodges and Simpson on 11 November told their respective armies: "Troops will not—repeat—not advance beyond line of Roer (Rur) River except on Army order." [42]

This restriction did not foreshadow any major change of plan for the new offensive other than a possible pause at the Roer. As soon as weather permitted, the First

---

[40] Ltr, FUSA to 12th A Gp, 29 Oct, FUSA G-3 Ltrs and Inds file, Oct 44.

[41] Memo, FUSA for V Corps, Plans for Future Operations, V Corps, 7 Nov, V Corps G-3 FO file, Nov 44.

[42] Msg, Col Akers (G-3 Sec FUSA) to CGs V and VII Corps dtd 1237, 11 Nov, FUSA G-3 Jnl file, Nov 44: *Conquer—The Story of Ninth Army,* p. 85.

and Ninth Armies were to attack as scheduled, though in the end they might have to wait impotently downstream while someone made a belated attack to take the dams.

In regard to weather, the day of 11 November passed with no sign of a break. Again on 12 November, and the next day, and the next, the ground troops and their commanders anxiously scanned the skies. No perceptible change appeared in the overcast. By nightfall of 15 November they could hope only for something close to a miracle to break the weather pattern so that full burden of the attack would not fall on the ground forces. For on 16 November, the ground troops were to attack, air support or not.

CHAPTER XVIII

VII Corps Makes the Main Effort

Designating the VII Corps as the main effort of the First Army added fire support for the corps but did nothing to erase the difficult terrain which the corps would have to cross before reaching the open plain leading to the Roer. On the north wing lay the Eschweiler–Weisweiler industrial complex; in the center, the Hamich ridge; and on the south wing, a part of the Huertgen Forest which had been penetrated hardly at all.[1] (*See Map VI.*)

The forest and the industrial area—the latter a kind of obtuse triangle whose sides were the long-held front line from Wuerselen to Stolberg, the boundary with the Ninth Army, and the course of the little Inde River—clearly ruled out the ends of the line for making the main effort within the corps. To General Allen's 104th Division fell the task of clearing the triangle; to General Barton's 4th Division, which had been transferred from the V Corps, went the assignment within the forest. General Barton first had to push through the forest to the road net about the villages of Huertgen, Kleinhau, Grosshau, and Gey, then had to continue northeastward to the Roer at Dueren. Attached to the 4th Division to assist in taking Huertgen, key village of the four,

was the 5th Armored Division's CCR, also moved up from the V Corps.[2]

The only logical spot for the main effort thus was in the center of the corps zone opposite the Hamich ridge, even though the ridge line blocked the northeastern exit of the Stolberg Corridor from the edge of the industrial triangle at Nothberg to the forest at Hamich. The assignment fell to General Huebner's 1st Division. The division also would encounter the northernmost fringes of the Huertgen Forest, including the last vestiges of the Eifel heights, and the twin industrial towns of Langerwehe and Juengersdorf. Only after clearing these towns would the division gain the relatively open plain, whereupon its regiments were to spread northeastward all across the northern half of the corps zone and drive a few remaining miles to the Roer north of Dueren. If by this time the 104th Division had not finished clearing the Eschweiler–Weisweiler industrial triangle, the corps cavalry and a regiment of the 1st Division were to block off the triangle at its eastern extremity along the line of the Inde River.

To ensure success of the main effort in the early stages, General Collins gave General Huebner the 47th Infantry, which had remained at Schevenhuette when in October its parent 9th Division

---

[1] The planning story is based mainly on VII Corps FO 12, 8 Nov 44, VII Corps Admin and FO file, Nov 44.

[2] VII Corps Opns Memo 116, 10 Nov 44, VII Corps Opns Memo file.

had gone to the V Corps. The 47th Infantry first was to take Gressenich, thereby opening a road serving the 1st Division's attack, and then was to assist in reducing the Hamich ridge. Buttressing the 1st Division's attack further, a combat command of the 3d Armored Division was to finish clearing the Stolberg Corridor by driving to the little Omer River at the base of the Hamich ridge, taking four villages in the process—Werth, Koettenich, Scherpenseel, and Hastenrath. The combat command thus was to serve in opening stages of the attack as a bridge between the 1st and 104th Divisions. The 104th Division in turn also was to assist the corps main effort by making its divisional main effort at first on its right wing alongside the armor. This involved clearing a forested sector about two miles wide, the only major portion of the 104th Division zone that lay south of the Inde River.

A combination of General Collins' scheme of maneuver and of features of terrain, particularly the meandering course of the Inde, in effect dictated a geographical divorce between that part of the VII Corps north of the river and the bulk of the corps to the south. Most of the corps was to fight either within the Huertgen Forest or in that region between the forest and the Inde where the wooded highlands reluctantly give way to the Roer plain. Geographically speaking, those troops north of the Inde were more properly a part of the battle of the Roer plain. The unit to be divided by this divorce was the 104th Division. Indeed, the fact that a division on the inner wing of the Ninth Army also had an assignment of clearing an industrial triangle along the army boundary might mean that the 104th Division would be inclined to the

north tactically as well as geographically.

In any event, the force assembled under General Collins for the main effort of the November offensive was impressive. General Collins had 3 divisions and an extra regiment of infantry, 1 division and an extra combat command of armor, plus 1 cavalry group. On D Day 9 infantry regiments and 1 combat command were to attack. In support of the VII Corps attack alone were more than 300 tank and tank destroyer pieces and a total of 32 battalions of field artillery. The big guns were to commence fire an hour before jump-off. If the weather cleared, the greatest air armada ever assembled in direct support of a ground operation was to pave the way on a two-army front.

The three top American commanders most directly involved in the big push, Generals Collins, Hodges, and Bradley, were optimistic about it. For the ebullient Collins, this perhaps was not surprising, but the usually more restrained Hodges and Bradley were almost as enthusiastic. To at least one observer, General Bradley gave the impression that he believed this might be "the last big offensive necessary to bring Germany to her knees." [3]

The State of the LXXXI Corps

By this time the VII Corps G–2, Colonel Carter, had acquired a measure of respect for German resurgence and tended to temper his estimates of enemy weakness. Nevertheless, he could not conceal the fact that the enemy opposite the VII Corps was no Goliath. The ratio of attacker to defender was almost 5 to 1.

---

[3] Sylvan Diary, entry of 16 Nov 44. See also entries of 25 Oct and 9 Nov 44.

Only the possibility already expressed by the 12th Army Group that the Germans might employ part of the panzer reserve they were assembling west of the Rhine to counterattack gave the intelligence officer any real pause.[4]

Six weeks of holding a fairly static line had provided a reasonably accurate estimate of the enemy's order of battle at corps and division levels. General Koechling's *LXXXI Corps,* which controlled most of the front opposite the VII Corps, had three divisions. Farthest north, beyond the sector of the VII Corps, opposite the Ninth U.S. Army, was the *246th Volks Grenadier Division,* resurrected from the ruins of Aachen after the melodramatic surrender of Colonel Wilck. In the center, northwest of Stolberg, generally astride the U.S. interarmy boundary, was the *3d Panzer Grenadier Division,* which had intervened unsuccessfully at Aachen. In the Stolberg Corridor and the northern fringes of the Huertgen Forest was the *12th Volks Grenadier Division,* which had arrived in the nick of time during the West Wall breakthrough in September. The sector deep within the Huertgen Forest opposite the right wing of the VII Corps was held by the *Seventh Army*'s *275th Division.*

To have expected American intelligence before the November offensive to divine the intricate German deception maneuver practiced with the *Fifth Panzer* and *Fifteenth Armies* would have been asking too much; for the Germans made the move only on the eve of the American attack. As it was, the Americans before the jump-off had not even discovered that the *Fifth Panzer Army* had taken over the line between the *First Parachute* and *Seventh Armies.* They still thought the *XII SS* and *LXXXI Corps* to be under command of the *Seventh Army.*[5]

After arriving in the Aachen sector in mid-October, General von Manteuffel and his staff of the *Fifth Panzer Army* had organized a comprehensive digging program involving the troops, some men of the Organization Todt, boys of the Hitler Youth, and the civilian population. Extensive mine fields were sown, both in front of the main line and on approaches to second, third, and fourth lines of defense. Agreements were reached with the *Seventh Army* in regard to controlling the level of the Roer River by means of the Roer River Dams.[6] During the three weeks in which the *Fifth Panzer Army* commanded the Aachen sector, it organized an impressive battle position, complete with several lines of defense, co-ordinated artillery positions, barbed wire entanglements, mine fields, and antitank obstacles.

By the time Manteuffel relinquished command on 15 November to the *Fifteenth Army*'s General von Zangen, the sector had been accorded the army group reserve, the *XLVII Panzer Corps.* Thus, when Zangen assumed command under the alias of *Gruppe von Manteuffel,* he controlled two corps on line and an armored corps in reserve.

The divisions opposite the VII Corps in General Koechling's *LXXXI Corps* had been shored up with personnel and matériel replacements since the battle of Aachen. The *3d Panzer Grenadier Division* (General Denkert) had about 11,000 men and was assigned the combat rating of "suitable for unlimited defensive

---

[4] See Annex 2 to VII Corps FO 12, 8 Nov 44.

[5] FUSA G–2 Estimate 35, 12 Nov 44, copy found in 104th Div G–2 Jnl file, 14 Nov 44.

[6] MS # A–857 (Manteuffel).

missions." The *12th Volks Grenadier Division* (General Engel) had but 6,381 men but was rated higher because of morale and training. The *12th Division* was rated capable of limited offensive operations. The *246th Division*, which was opposite the Ninth Army, was rated lowest of the lot.

The *12th* and *246th Divisions* had, besides an artillery regiment, the usual three regiments of infantry with two battalions each and a tank destroyer and engineer battalion each. The *3d Panzer Grenadier* had two armored infantry regiments, an artillery regiment, and a tank battalion equipped primarily with assault guns.

The three artillery regiments possessed a total of 66 105-mm. and 31 150-mm. howitzers, plus 31 other pieces ranging from 75-mm. cannon to 122-mm. Russian howitzers. The three tank destroyer battalions, plus the so-called heavy tank battalion, had 54 assault guns, 11 88-mm. guns, and 45 other antitank pieces of lesser calibers.[7]

Having been chosen to participate in the Ardennes counteroffensive, the *12th Volks Grenadier Division* was earmarked for relief by a new unit, the *47th Volks Grenadier Division*. American intelligence had noted the impending arrival of this division but did not know its identification, role, or destination.[8]

Commanded by Generalleutnant Max Bork, the *47th Division* had drawn roughly half its men from the Luftwaffe

and the Navy, the other half from new levies of 17- and 18-year-olds sprinkled with a few veterans of the Russian front. Contrary to usual territorial organizational procedures, the *47th* was made up of men from all parts of Germany. Though weapons and matériel assigned to the division were new and modern, the crippled German transportation system had delayed their arrival at the division's training site. The artillerymen, for example, had but one week with their pieces before commitment near Aachen, and antitank weapons failed to arrive until the November offensive was well under way. The infantry had about six weeks' training.[9]

Preliminary Bombardment

To the American troops who pondered the skies, preparations for the November offensive had all the earmarks of breakout after the manner of Normandy. Yet spirits could not but fall as day after day dawned with rain and overcast. As night came on 15 November, all was in readiness except the weather. Farther south, the 28th Division was stumbling off the stage, having completed its tragic role in the drama of the Huertgen Forest. Now, air support or not, the main show was to go on. Shortly after midnight the First Army's General Hodges gave the word. D Day was 16 November. H Hour was 1245.

Dawn on 16 November brought slight encouragement. It looked like another day of ragged clouds, overcast, and mists;

---

[7] *LXXXI Corps* Arty Sit as of 10 Nov 44, *LXXXI Corps KTB, Art.-Lage u. Art.-Gliederungen; LXXXI Corps KTB, Zustandsberichte; Kampf um Aachen:* Maps; MSS # B–290 (Blumentritt), # P–065b (Reinhardt), and # A–994 (Koechling).

[8] See FUSA G–2 Per Rpt 157, 14 Nov, 1st Div G–2 file, 15–18 Nov 44.

[9] Order, *OB WEST* to *A Gp B,* 2245, 5 Nov 44, in *OB WEST KTB, Anlagen, Befehle und Meldungen;* MS # B–602, Generalleutnant Max Bork, *Die 47. VolksgrenadierDivision im Westen* (*V.G.D.*)

but by midmorning even the least optimistic among the sun worshipers of the First and Ninth Armies could hope for a miracle. The clouds were thinning. By 1100 a ceiling of broken clouds hovered about 1,000 to 1,500 feet over the target area. Above 8,000 feet visibility was from one to two miles in light fog.[10] Steadily the weather improved. The day was not one for lounging in the sun, but planes could operate. At 1130 the first of the big bombers in Operation QUEEN droned overhead.[11]

In contrast to the weather miracle over the target area, fog clung assiduously about some heavy bomber and fighter bases in England and about almost all medium and fighter-bomber bases on the Continent. Many planes could not take off. Nevertheless, 1,191 Eighth Air Force heavy bombers arrived and dropped 4,120 tons of fragmentation bombs within the Eschweiler–Weisweiler industrial triangle and on Langerwehe. A total of 1,188 heavies of the RAF Bomber Command unloaded 5,640 tons of bombs on Dueren, Juelich, and Heinsberg. Almost half this tonnage fell on Dueren. Only 80 medi-

um bombers of the Ninth Air Force reached the scene to drop 150 tons of bombs on Eschweiler and two small towns deeper in the VII Corps zone. Almost a thousand fighters flying escort flushed only four enemy aircraft, and these did not attack.

As with the medium bombers, fog at the bases severely crimped operations of both the IX and XXIX Tactical Air Commands. Throughout the day fighter-bombers of the XXIX TAC in support of the Ninth Army flew but 136 sorties and dropped but 46.5 tons of bombs. The IX TAC did somewhat better in the VII Corps zone with 8 missions, 212 sorties, and 140.5 tons of bombs. In addition to armed reconnaissance in support of the 1st and 104th Divisions, the fighter-bombers flew several missions at the request of ground control and struck two of the preplanned target areas, the Hamich ridge and the Huertgen–Gey sector.

Meager and generally ineffective anti-aircraft fire claimed 12 planes, 4 of them fighter-bombers, 8 heavy bombers. One other fighter-bomber cracked up in an accident.

If judged solely by the safety of the ground troops during the bombing, the elaborate precautions taken to ensure accuracy paid off. Yet the safety plan was not entirely foolproof. One man was killed and two wounded in a field artillery unit of the 3d Armored Division when four bombs apparently released by a faulty bomb release mechanism fell near a gun position. A P–38 later dive-bombed this same artillery unit but caused no casualties.[12] The 1st Division reported five instances of stray bombs falling near

---

[10] FUSA Rpt, Vol. 1, p. 74.

[11] Craven and Cate, eds., *Europe:* ARGUMENT *to V-E Day*, page 632, points out that statistical data on Operation QUEEN vary so widely in various operations reports and special studies "as to preclude reconciliation." The author has leaned heavily upon the conclusions in this source and on a contemporary ground report, Summary of Operations for 16 Nov 44, found in FUSA G-3 Tac file, 16–17 Nov 44. For results of the air strike, the historian has depended upon contemporary ground records, German sources, and three special reports: (1) FUSA, Effects of Our Air Attacks of November 16, 20–21 Nov 44; (2) NUSA, Operation "Q," A Study in Air Support, 23 Jan 45; and (3) Annex 2 to FUSA G-2 Per Rpt 165, 22 Nov 44, The Enemy's View of Our Air Support on 16 November. All in FUSA G-2 Tac file, 21–22 Nov 44.

[12] 391st Armd FA Bn, AAR, Nov 44; 3d Armd Div AAR, Nov 44.

its troops but noted only one casualty. One bomb exploded within 150 yards of the division artillery command post, and another knocked the wings off a liaison plane and destroyed the runway at the division artillery airfield.[13] Yet if these were the sole losses among friendly troops, the margin of error was indeed small for a fleet of 4,000 heavy and medium bombers, fighter-bombers, and escort fighters which unloaded a total of more than 10,000 tons of bombs through a mask of haze and cloud.

It was hard to say just how effective the bombing was. Since the bomb line was far in front of friendly troops, few of the enemy's forward units were hit hard, and most that were had been holding this front for so long that they had substantial cover close at hand. Prisoners from two forward regiments of the *12th Division*, for example, estimated casualties no higher than 1 to 3 percent. Another group of prisoners reported that only one bomb fell in Langerwehe, one of the principal targets, though areas near Langerwehe were damaged severely.[14] No indication developed of any overwhelming psychological impact like that in Normandy. "It should be noted," the First Army remarked later, "that the most forward of the enemy targets were 4,000 yards from our front line and that the target frontage in the zone of the First Army was approximately 9 miles wide. These facts prevent any comparison being made between this attack and the breakthrough at St. Lô." [15]

The effect upon enemy communications was another matter. The consensus of fifteen prisoners from the *12th Division* was that "communication with the command echelons to the rear was impossible." [16] "I tried to use the telephone," one German said, "but the line had been cut by the bombardment and it was obviously too late to send one of my messengers back." [17] Other prisoners reported lack of warm food for days because the bombardment had knocked out kitchens, supply vehicles, and horses.

American air commanders admitted that the bombing did not measure up to expectations. The airmen blamed clouds, haze, smoke, and snow that obscured many targets, plus reluctance of many bombardiers to bomb short. Nevertheless, the airmen said, the destruction wrought was "enormous." Juelich, they claimed, was "almost completely destroyed"; results in Dueren and Eschweiler were "similar." [18] Most air headquarters said the real trouble was the wide safety margin which enabled the Germans to recover before the ground attack reached them.[19]

Most ground echelons agreed that the bombing failed to soften German lines as much as expected, though the First Army noted that resistance at first was not so strong as it was several hours later. "Damage to his artillery installations must have been great," the First Army said,

---

[13] 1st Div G-3 Per Rpt 164, 16 Nov, 1st Div G-2 file, 15-18 Nov 44; 26th Inf S-3 Jnl, 16 Nov 44.

[14] 1st Div G-2 Per Rpt 152, 18 Nov, 1st Div G-2 file, 15-18 Nov 44.

[15] FUSA AAR, Nov 44.

[16] FUSA PWI Rpt, Incl 4 to VII Corps G-3 Per Rpt 167, 19 Nov, VII Corps G-3 Jnl file, 20 Nov 44.

[17] Annex 2 to FUSA G-2 Per Rpt 165, 22 Nov 44.

[18] Craven and Cate, eds., *Europe:* ARGUMENT *to V-E Day,* p. 632, citing 8th AF and IX and XXIX TAC summaries and opns rpts.

[19] See, for example, the Ninth Air Force and Its Principal Commands in the ETO, Vol. I, Ch. II.

"for throughout [the day of 16 November] comparatively light [artillery] fire was received."[20] About eight batteries plus some single weapons near Eschweiler reacted first, followed by fire from a few guns in the forested sector opposite the right wing of the VII Corps. "These fires . . .," the First Army noted, "totalled the enemy artillery opposition."[21]

The most dramatic and damaging single event of the bombardment was attributable to chance. Someone or something must have crossed the star of the *47th Volks Grenadier Division*, for even as Allied planes struck, some units of this division were detraining in the Roer towns and others were relieving parts of the *12th Division* in the line. A battalion of artillery caught at the railroad station in Juelich was all but annihilated. Signal and headquarters troops were hit at Dueren. In process of relieving part of the *12th Division*, a few companies of the *103d Regiment* had reached the front where cover was at hand, but others were caught immediately in rear of the line where the blow was hardest. It was in this region behind the front line that the only indication of psychological impact developed. "I never saw anything like it," said a German noncommissioned officer. "These kids . . . were still numb 45 minutes after the bombardment. It was our luck that your ground troops did not attack us until the next day. I could not have done anything with those boys of mine that day."[22]

In some ways as impressive as the bombing program was the artillery effort. On the First Army front alone, 694 guns in an hour-long preparation fired approximately 45,000 light rounds, almost 4,000 medium, and 2,600 heavy.[23] In addition, hundreds of tank guns, 81-mm. and 4.2-inch mortars, plus a battalion of 4.5-inch rocket projectors, contributed to the barrage. On the Ninth Army front, another 552 field artillery pieces participated, raising the total in the two armies to 1,246.[24]

The ill-starred *47th Volks Grenadier Division* came in for a share of this pounding, though just how many of this division's troubles stemmed from American shelling was difficult to judge. The division was a primary target; for in early morning of D Day a prisoner had revealed the enemy's plan of relieving the *12th Division* that day. Both 1st Division and VII Corps artillery then had taken all likely routes of approach under fire.[25]

In the final analysis, the only true measure of the effect of both air and artillery preparations was the amount of resistance to the ground attack. At 1245 on 16 November ground troops all along the line from the vicinity of Geilenkirchen to Huertgen initiated that test. The big November offensive was on.

---

[20] FUSA G–2 Per Rpt 160, 17 Nov, FUSA G–2 Tac file, 17–18 Nov 44.
[21] FUSA Arty Intel Rpt 156, 17 Nov, FUSA G–2 Tac Jnl, 18 Nov 44.
[22] Annex 2 to FUSA G–2 Per Rpt 165, 22 Nov 45; MS # B–602 (Bork); Annex 3 to

FUSA G–2 Per Rpt 166, 23 Nov, The Rise and Fall of the *47 V. G. Division,* FUSA G–2 Tac file, 21–22 Nov 44.
[23] FUSA AAR, Nov 44, Field Artillery Firing 16–23 November. The figures on number of rounds are estimates based upon FUSA's statistics of 450 light, 126 medium, and 108 heavy guns, and an expenditure of 1,087 tons of ammunition.
[24] Statistics on Ground Effort, found in Hq IX TAC, Operation Q.
[25] 1st Div Intel Activities, Nov 44, dtd ·1 Dec 44, found in 1st Div Combat Interv file, Nov 44.

155-MM. SELF-PROPELLED GUN *bombarding Gressenich.*

The Push Northeast
From Schevenhuette

The main effort within the First Army's VII Corps was to be launched from the village of Schevenhuette, the farthest point of penetration yet made by Allied troops into Germany. From Schevenhuette General Huebner's 1st Division was to attack northeast through the fringes of the Huertgen Forest to Langerwehe and Juengersdorf, not quite four miles away. From there the Roer lies but three miles distant across the open Roer plain.

Getting across the first four miles past obstacles like the forest and the Hamich ridge obviously posed the big problem. This the VII Corps planners had foreseen. In attaching the 47th Infantry to the 1st Division and in assigning the 3d Armored Division the left portion of the 1st Division's zone for the first stage of the attack, they had enabled General Huebner to concentrate his strength at Schevenhuette in a sector less than two miles wide. Only after the major obstacle of the Hamich ridge was in hand would General Huebner have to spread his troops across the entire width of his zone north to the Inde River.

To clear the fringes of the Huertgen Forest, then to seize Langerwehe and Juengersdorf, General Huebner directed the 26th Infantry on his right wing to attack through the forest on the right of the Weh Creek and the Schevenhuette–Langerwehe highway. Meanwhile the 16th Infantry was to take Hill 232, just to the northwest of the village of Hamich and key to the Hamich ridge. This hill was the enemy's primary observation point across the open spaces of the Stolberg Corridor. Seizure of it was prerequisite to occupying a series of hills along the left of the highway to Langerwehe and thus to opening the highway as a supply route. Following the valley of the little Weh Creek, this highway was needed by both the 16th and 26th Regiments, particularly by the 26th because of a dearth of roads in the forest.

In the meantime, the attached 47th Infantry was to capture Gressenich, thereby opening a road to Hamich. The 47th Infantry then was to complete the task of clearing the Hamich ridge north from Hill 232 to the boundary with the 104th Division along the Inde River. As the attached regiment completed this task, General Huebner planned to commit his reserve, the 18th Infantry, in order to secure a firm foothold on the Roer plain alongside the Inde. This accomplished, the 16th and 26th Regiments were to make the final thrust to the Roer.[26]

Perhaps the best spot for measuring the effect of the preliminary bombardment in front of the VII Corps was the sector

of the 16th Infantry at Hamich. Here were to be found all three major types of terrain confronting the corps: forest, open ground, and villages.

Commanded by Lt. Col. Edmund F. Driscoll, the 16th Infantry's 1st Battalion moved on D Day north from Schevenhuette into the woods toward Hamich, only to run immediately into determined resistance from the kind of log-covered emplacements typical of the defenses of the Huertgen Forest. Through clinging mud that two weeks of inclement weather had produced, a platoon of tanks inched forward to the woods line to take out the enemy's automatic weapons. Only then could the 1st Battalion move through the woods to the objective of Hamich, a mile away.

It began to look less and less as if the mammoth preliminary bombardment had precipitated a breakthrough. Certainly the men of the 16th Infantry could attest to the fact that even in the face of this bombardment, the enemy's resistance was tough. Only in artillery fires did they note any slackening, and from the infantryman's standpoint a prodigious enemy use of mortars more than made up for that deficiency.

Hand-carrying their weapons, men of Colonel Driscoll's 1st Battalion reached the edge of the woods overlooking Hamich just before dusk. From there full portent of the enemy's textbook observation post on Hill 232 became readily apparent. Not even a field mouse could get into Hamich without being seen. His first view of American troops at the edge of the woods prompted a hail of small arms fire from Hamich and artillery and mortar fire obviously adjusted from Hill 232. As night fell, the American battalion had to beat off persistent local

---

[26] 1st Div FO 53, 6 Nov, 1st Div G–3 Opns Rpt, Nov 44. The division's records for the period are superior and include detailed journal entries. A small number of combat interviews supplement the official records.

counterattacks by elements of the *12th Division*'s *48th Regiment*.

The 16th Infantry's best hope for getting armor to assist the attack on Hamich lay in taking Gressenich with the division's attached regiment, the 47th Infantry, thereby opening a road to Hamich for tanks. Attacking at H Hour on 16 November close behind the fire of five artillery battalions, a battalion of the 47th Infantry met initial success because the enemy in Gressenich had focused his attention on an attacking column of the 3d Armored Division. As the battalion of the 47th Infantry reached the first buildings, the Germans discovered their oversight and began a systematic house-to-house defense.

Not until the next morning (17 November) did hopes rise for clearing Gressenich and getting armor to Hamich. Advance of the 3d Armored Division north of Gressenich and of the 16th Infantry through the woods to Hamich had threatened encirclement of Gressenich. During the night the Germans had withdrawn.[27]

After daylight on 17 November a platoon of tanks from the attached 745th Tank Battalion moved to join Colonel Driscoll's infantry at Hamich, and in the afternoon tanks and infantry attacked. By this time, however, the processes of beating off the enemy during the night and of trying to get into Hamich without tank support had made serious inroads in the strength of Colonel Driscoll's companies. Having started the fight the day before with about 160 men per rifle company, one company was down to a hundred men and the other two down to 60 or 70 each. About 70 percent of the casualties, Colonel Driscoll estimated, were from enemy shellfire, the rest from small arms fire. Neither tanks nor infantry could get into Hamich.

The enemy's defensive success thus far at Hamich was attributable to men who had held the line from the first, for none other than local reserves yet had been committed. Soon after it had become evident that this was the big Allied attack, General von Zangen, new commander of the *Fifteenth Army* (alias *Gruppe von Manteuffel*), had canceled the impending relief of the *12th Division*.[28] Though Zangen had ordered artillery of the incoming *47th Volks Grenadier Division* to reinforce the fires of the *12th Division*'s artillery, he had directed that the *47th Division*'s other troops assemble as an *LXXXI Corps* reserve. A small combat team of the *116th Panzer Division*, moving north from Huertgen, was to strengthen the corps reserve. These were the only immediate German orders at an army level directly affecting the sector opposite the 1st Division.[29]

To reinforce the assault on Hamich on the third day, 18 November, the 16th Infantry used the unit originally intended for taking Hill 232, the 3d Battalion

---

[27] In addition to 47th Infantry and 1st Division official records, a combat interview with Lt. Col. James D. Allgood, 1st Battalion, 47th Infantry, provides details on the 47th Infantry action. See 1st Div Combat Interv file, Nov 44.

[28] Because Zangen and his staff of the *Fifteenth Army* had assumed command of *Gruppe von Manteuffel* only the day before the U.S. offensive, Manteuffel and his staff stayed on to assist until about 20 November. Orders apparently were prepared on a kind of informal "team" basis.

[29] Order, *Gruppe von Manteuffel to XII SS and LXXXI Corps*, 2225, 16 Nov 44, *LXXXI Corps KTB Anlagen, Befehle Heeresgruppe und Armee an Generalkommando, 24.X.–30.XI.44* (referred to hereafter as *LXXXI Corps KTB, Bef. H. Gr. u. Armee*).

under Lt. Col. Charles T. Horner, Jr. While Colonel Driscoll's depleted battalion maintained a base of fire and while artillery pummeled Hill 232, Colonel Horner's infantry with tank and tank destroyer support pressed the attack. Dashing through a steady thunder of German artillery fire, they gained the first houses. This signaled the start of a methodical house-by-house killing match against an enemy who had to be rooted from barricaded cellars that often were connected by communications trenches.[30] Five German tanks that started down the Hamich ridge toward the village might have turned the balance in favor of the enemy had not clearing weather on 18 November enabled planes to operate. P–47's of the IX Tactical Air Command with an assist from the artillery quickly turned the tanks back. By midafternoon Colonel Horner's infantry and armor had cleared all but a few houses on the northern edge of Hamich.

Seizing quickly upon his advantage, the 16th Infantry commander, Colonel Gibb, directed his remaining battalion under Colonel Dawson to strike immediately for Hill 232. Preceding the assault, fifteen battalions of field artillery laid an impressive TOT on the height. With no conspicuous struggle, Colonel Dawson's infantry took the hill. Dazed, bewildered survivors of the *12th Fusilier Battalion,* which had been sent to bolster the faltering *48th Regiment,* hardly knew what had hit them.

In the meantime, remnants of the *48th Regiment* had tried to get back into Hamich. In particular, they punched against Colonel Driscoll's 1st Battalion in the woods southeast of the village. Here the hero of the defense was a platoon leader, T. Sgt. Jake W. Lindsey, who refused to budge from his position even after casualties reduced his command to only six men. Despite a shell fragment in one knee, he personally accounted for two enemy machine gun crews, drove off two tanks with rifle grenades, and was credited officially with killing twenty of the enemy.[31]

Though these counterattacks were troublesome, the toughest was reserved for the night of 18 November. It grew out of an authorization by the Army Group B commander, Field Marshal Model, for active commitment of the *47th Volks Grenadier Division.* Reversing General von Zangen's earlier order, Model directed that the new division assume responsibility for the southern half of the *12th Division's* line. This meant that almost the entire line in front of the 1st Division was to be taken over by the new division.[32]

The Germans threw a green division into the thick of the fight not without considerable reluctance. They chose the line opposite the 1st Division as the lesser of two evils, for they considered that the

---

[30] For personally eliminating a machine gun and an antitank gun in the attack on Hamich, S. Sgt. Paul W. Robey, Jr., was awarded the DSC. For sweeping the road into Hamich with a mine detector in the face of intense enemy fire, an attached engineer, Cpl. Bertol C. Swanberg, also received the award.

[31] As the one-hundredth infantryman to be awarded the Medal of Honor, Sergeant Lindsey subsequently received the award from the hands of President Truman before a joint session of Congress. Other decorations for action in the Hamich sector included the posthumous award of the DSC to 1st Lt. Kenneth L. Johnson, Pfc. John W. Adams, Sgt. Alfred B. Nietzel, and S. Sgt. Robert D. Farmer.

[32] TWX, *Gruppe von Manteuffel* to *LXXXI Corps,* 1800, 17 Nov 44, relaying Order, *A Gp B* to *Gruppe von Manteuffel, LXXXI Corps KTB, Bef. H. Gr. u. Armee.*

U.S. main effort was not here but farther north along the boundary between the *XII SS* and *LXXXI Corps,* within the zone of the Ninth Army, where terrain was more negotiable. If committed opposite the main effort, the Germans reasoned, the *47th Division* surely would be chewed to pieces. If committed in the less threatened southern sector, the new division might survive while enabling the other divisions to shorten their zones and achieve greater concentration opposite the main effort.[33]

One of the first moves of the *47th Division* was to prepare a counterattack with the support of the combat team of the *116th Panzer Division* to retake Hamich and Hill 232. This combat team consisted of a battalion each of tanks and half-tracks, an artillery battery, and an engineer company. Half the combat team was to join each of two battalions of the *47th Division's 104th Regiment* after nightfall on 18 November in assembly areas near Hill 232. At 0530 the next morning, half the force was to retake Hill 232, the other half, Hamich.

To the detriment of the German plan, the always imponderable human equation worked for the Americans. Leading half the counterattack force of tanks, half-tracks, and engineers toward the assembly area, a German lieutenant lost his way in the darkness. Instead of taking a road which would have led to his assembly area near Hill 232, the lieutenant chose a route leading along the valley of the Weh Creek in the direction of Hamich. Southeast of Hamich, the enemy column blundered into positions held by Company C, 16th

Infantry. Reduced to but forty-five men, Company C might not have been able to hold had the German lieutenant not tried to rectify his mistake by withdrawing.[34]

Trying next a trail that led north into the woods, the German lieutenant unwittingly led his forces directly into Hamich. The errant group had barely reached the village when outposts of Colonel Horner's 3d Battalion called for artillery fire. While Horner's infantry took cover in houses and cellars, fifteen battalions of artillery blanketed the village with time fire.[35] Though the German engineers and half-tracks fell back, several of the tanks pushed on. An eager but unidentified American bazooka man sent a rocket through the turret of one of the tanks from a second floor window. Two other tanks blundered into bomb craters and could not get out. The remaining tanks escaped to the north, while the German lieutenant, still bewildered, became the sole prisoner of the engagement.

Alerted by this enemy blunder, the Americans in Hamich were ready a few hours later when a battalion of the *104th Regiment* went through with the scheduled counterattack against the village. Though seven or eight tanks supported the maneuver, this stronger force actually made less of an impression than had the enemy lieutenant's. By daylight the Germans had been stopped.

---

[33] Order, *Gruppe von Manteuffel* to *XII SS* and *LXXXI Corps,* 0130, 18 Nov 44, *LXXXI Corps KTB, Bef. H. Gr. u. Armee; LXXXI Corps Gefechtsbericht,* AAR of 18 Nov 44.

[34] This incident is based primarily on American sources, including 1st Div Intel Activities, Nov 44, and 1st Div G–2 Per Rpt 153, 19 Nov, in 1st Div G–2 file, 19–20 Nov 44. Identifying the German officer as a Lieutenant Bayer, the 1st Division G–2 may have been confused by the name of the combat team commander, Colonel Bayer, of the *16th Panzer Grenadier Regiment.*

[35] In this and earlier firing during 18 November at Hamich, American artillery expended 5,350 rounds, almost two thirds of normal daily German expenditure along the entire *LXXXI Corps* front.

Meanwhile, the other battalion of the *104th Regiment,* which was to have been supported against Hill 232 by the lieutenant's tanks, had waited in vain. Aided by interrogation of the lieutenant, American artillery took the enemy's assembly area under fire. Though the artillery scattered one company, the enemy commander decided to go ahead with the attack. At 0530 his two remaining companies charged up the north slope of Hill 232, only to be mowed down by the concentrated fire of Colonel Dawson's machine gunners and riflemen. Of one German company, only the commander survived. Even he was captured.

Elsewhere in the 1st Division's sector, an attack by the 26th Infantry on the division's right wing moved into an area which had been accorded little of the preliminary bombardment. Preparation fires had been limited in front of the regiment because trees and undergrowth restricted identification of targets, not because the 26th Infantry's attack was any the less important to accomplishment of the 1st Division's mission. No matter how successful the 16th Infantry's advance west of the Weh Creek and the vital Schevenhuette–Langerwehe highway, the road could not be used without control of four wooded hills within the Huertgen Forest along the right of the highway. After taking these hills, the 26th Infantry was to continue to Langerwehe and Juengersdorf.

Like many another unit which fought within the Huertgen Forest, the 26th Infantry engaged in an almost unalloyed infantry battle. Trees and undergrowth so limited observation that the effectiveness of artillery was reduced severely. Mud and a dearth of roads restricted armored support. The inevitable hazards of forest fighting—shellbursts in the trees and open flanks—plagued the regiment from the start. Though the lead battalion gained but a few hundred yards, it still was necessary as night came to commit another battalion to bolster the lead unit's flanks.

Inching forward on the second day, the 26th Infantry's lead battalion under Lt. Col. Derrill M. Daniel gained only a few hundred yards more. Two days of fighting had brought an advance of little more than a mile. Return of wet weather on 17 November had eliminated any hope of getting tanks or tank destroyers forward along the muddy forest trails.

A second battalion joined the attack early on the third day, 18 November. Still the enemy yielded his bunkers grudgingly. Early on the fourth day, 19 November, as the regimental commander, Colonel Seitz, prepared to commit his remaining battalion, the Germans struck back. The counterattack grew out of Field Marshal Model's directive of two days before by which the *47th Volks Grenadier Division* was thrust into the line along the interarmy boundary. A battalion of the *47th Division's 115th Infantry* made the counterattack.

Nowhere in the Huertgen Forest fighting was the stamina and determination of American infantry more clearly demonstrated than here as Colonel Daniel's fatigued, depleted battalion of the 26th Infantry beat off this fresh German force. Among numerous deeds of individual heroism, the acts of Pfc. Francis X. McGraw stood out. Manning a machine gun, McGraw fired until his ammunition gave out, then ran back for more. When artillery fire felled a tree and blocked his field of fire, he calmly rose from his foxhole, threw his weapon across a log, and continued to fire. Concussion from a shellburst tossed his gun into the air, but he retrieved it. His ammunition expended a second time, McGraw took up the fight with a carbine, killed one German and wounded another before a burst from a burp gun cut him down. He was posthumously awarded the Medal of Honor.

As demonstrated soon after the counterattack, the *47th Division*'s commitment had come a little late. No sooner had Colonel Daniel's men beaten off the enemy than the 26th Infantry's remaining fresh battalion under Colonel Corley pressed an attack that carried northward more than a mile. Not until they had reached an improved road less than 500 yards from a castle, the Laufenburg, did the men pause for the night. The castle marked the center of the four forested hills which were the 26th Infantry's objective.

No matter how commendable and how encouraging this thrust, the 26th Infantry would have to stretch a point to find room for elation in the four days of slow, plodding fight. The regiment still had no adequate supply route and no way to get supporting weapons forward. Before renewing the drive to seize the hills around the Laufenburg and conquer a remaining mile and a half of forest, Colonel Seitz deemed it imperative to clear that part of the Langerwehe highway leading to his forward position. The force he had to do this with was reduced now by some 450 men who had succumbed to the enemy's fire and the cold, wet weather. Though high by ordinary standards, this casualty figure was about par for four days of fighting in the Huertgen Forest.

Looking at the situation from a division standpoint, the 1st Division G–2 found occasion at nightfall on 19 November for some encouragement. "It is believed," Colonel Evans remarked hopefully, "that the units which have been identified . . . are not capable of preventing our further advance to the northeast. No reserve units of sufficient size to bolster up these forces are now believed to be available . . . west of the Roer River." [36]

Under ordinary circumstances, there might have been room for such cautious optimism as Colonel Evans expressed. Both the 16th and 26th Infantry Regiments had penetrated the enemy's forward line to a maximum depth of about two miles, even though the feat had required four days and over a thousand casualties to accomplish. But these were not ordinary circumstances. This was the sector of the main effort of the VII Corps where the 1st Division was to have followed closely on the heels of a historic preliminary bombardment to effect a rapid thrust to the Roer. General Hodges and General Collins had bargained for a spectacular breakthrough. After four days of fighting from 16 through 19 November, it looked as though they had bought a drab slugging match.

Armor in the Stolberg Corridor

Indications that this was the case were not confined to the vicinity of Schevenhuette and Hamich. Slightly to the west among the quartet of villages still remaining to the Germans in the Stolberg Corridor, even the added weight of tanks and tank destroyers of an armored combat command had not been enough to produce a rout.

---

[36] 1st Div G–2 Per Rpt 153, 19 Nov 44, in 1st Div G–2 file, 19–20 Nov 44.

This was the only portion of the VII Corps zone where armor might maneuver during the opening stages of the new offensive. Here General Boudinot's CCB of the 3d Armored Division was to attack at H Hour on 16 November through Weissenberg to bridge the space between the 1st and 104th Divisions. The armor was to seize four villages: Werth, Koettenich, Scherpenseel, and Hastenrath. Lying at the western base of the Hamich ridge, these villages were not more than two miles from the armor's existing front line. The projected advance of the 104th Division against the Eschweiler–Weisweiler industrial triangle and of the 47th Infantry from Hill 232 northwest along the Hamich ridge eventually would pinch out the armor and permit the combat command to return to its parent division in time to exploit any breakthrough achieved by the infantry divisions.[37]

Rejuvenated by replacements in both tanks and personnel since bogging down in the Stolberg Corridor almost two months before, General Boudinot's Task Forces Lovelady and Mills both participated in the opening attack. Of approximately equal strength, each task force had a battalion of tanks and a company of armored infantry. Task Force Lovelady on the right was to take Werth and Koettenich; Task Force Mills on the left, Scherpenseel and Hastenrath.

Though some dive bombing and heavy concentrations of artillery fell on the four villages during the preliminary bombardment, the armor's observers could not

[37] 3d Armd Div FO 16, 9 Nov 44. Though no copy of this order can be found, the contents are given in some detail in the CCB AAR, Nov 44. AARs of the 3d Armd Div, CCB, and subordinate units contain valuable material on this action.

determine in the hazy weather just what damage was done. It was equally difficut to judge the effects of the bombardment from the progress of the ground attack.

Task Force Lovelady on the right had little difficulty. In about two hours both Werth and Koettenich were in hand. Yet while mopping up and consolidating, the men of Task Force Lovelady became aware that the Germans on Hill 232 and other parts of the Hamich ridge were breathing down their necks. With unerringly accurate artillery and mortar fire, the enemy left no doubt for the next two days of his superior observation. A Panther tank firing from the ridge knocked out three of five tanks in Koettenich before one of the remaining Shermans could silence it.

Task Force Mills's troubles began at the start. The task force spent the first afternoon trying to get through mud and a mine field under the muzzles of antitank and dual-purpose antiaircraft guns located in the Eschweiler woods to the north within the 104th Division's zone. Incurring a loss of fifteen tanks, the task force fell several hundred yards short of Scherpenseel and Hastenrath.

The second day, 17 November, brought several disturbing developments. First, the adjacent regiment of the 104th Division had run into CCB's old problem of the Donnerberg (Hill 287), the strategic height east of Stolberg, and had failed to keep abreast of the armor. This meant that the armor on the relatively low, open ground of the Stolberg Corridor still was exposed to fire from the north as well as from the Hamich ridge. Second, though parts of Task Force Mills got into the fringes of both Hastenrath and Scherpenseel, the cost in armored infantry was

AMERICAN TANK BURNING *outside Hamich.*

alarming. Though General Boudinot ordered forward the bulk of his reserve, primarily another company of armored infantry, antipersonnel mines and shelling prevented the reserve from reaching the task force until darkness had restricted the enemy's observation. Third, after only a day and a half of action, the combat command was down to 50 percent of original strength in tanks. Task Force Mills at the main point of danger had left only seven light tanks and eight mediums. Not all were permanently lost—the mud had claimed some—but for the moment those in the mud were of no more use

than others that had succumbed to enemy fire. So perturbed was the 3d Armored Division commander, General Rose, that he alerted his division reserve to stand by for commitment upon an hour's notice.

The problem was not so much the nature of the enemy as the nature of his observation. Combat Command B's adversary was, as expected, its old antagonist from the days of the first battle of the Stolberg corridor, the *12th Division.* Here elements of the *89th Grenadier Regiment* held the line. Perhaps the enemy might have taken even greater advantage of his superior observation had not some of his heavier weapons already been displaced in preparation for the impending relief by the *47th Volks Grenadier· Division*.[38]

The day of 18 November opened inauspiciously when a shell fragment cut down the task force commander, Lt. Col. Herbert N. Mills.[39] Yet with the assistance of the infantry reserve, the task force went through with the planned attacks against Hastenrath and Scherpenseel. This time adroit co-operation between tanks and infantry did the trick, so that by midafternoon Task Force Mills had cleared both villages. At 1745 the task force called for a fifteen-minute concentration of time and impact artillery fire to thwart a two-company counterattack which struck between the villages.

With Hastenrath and Scherpenseel secured, CCB could turn to the defensive. The 1st Division's capture of Hill 232 during the afternoon of 18 November eased the problems of enemy observation to a degree; but until the 104th Division could clear the combat command's left flank and the 47th Infantry sweep the rest of the Hamich ridge across the combat command's front, damaging German fire still could be expected.

Though CCB had taken its four objectives in less than three days, the results would stand as a monument to the celerity with which an enemy endowed with advantages in observation and assisted by nature can seriously cripple an armored force. The armored infantry had incurred losses of about 50 percent. Of 64 medium tanks at the start of the attack, all but 22 had been eliminated. Including 7 light tanks, total tank losses

were 49. Panzerfausts had claimed 6; mistaken U.S. bombing, 1; artillery fire, 6; mine fields, 12; and antitank fire, 24.[40] These did not look much like statistics of a breakthrough operation.

The Second Battle of the Donnerberg

Much of the difficulty experienced by the armor might have been avoided had the 104th Division on the combat command's left flank been able to keep abreast. Here the problem again was dominant German observation, in this case from the Donnerberg (Hill 287), near Stolberg, the height which had defied the 3d Armored Division in September.

In clearing the Eschweiler–Weisweiler industrial triangle on the north wing of the VII Corps, the 104th Division was to operate basically astride the snakelike valley of the little Inde River. Because of the terrain, the division in early stages of the offensive would assist the VII Corps main effort directly only on the division's right wing. The assignment involved clearing a sector of about five square miles, made up basically of the Eschweiler woods lying between Stolberg and Eschweiler.

Having joined the VII Corps immediately after a baptism of fire with the Canadians near Antwerp, the 104th Division under General Allen had moved into the old positions of the 1st Division. These extended from the army boundary near Wuerselen southeast through Verlautenheide to the Inde River at Stolberg. On the eve of the attack one regiment of the 104th assumed control of a part of the

---

[38] CCB AAR, Nov 44.
[39] Colonel Mills was posthumously awarded the DSC.

[40] Detailed statistics may be found in CCB AAR, Nov 44.

3d Armored Division's sector east of Stolberg and south of the Eschweiler woods opposite the Donnerberg (Hill 287). Told by General Collins to put greatest strength on the right wing in order to support the corps main effort, General Allen had noted from the first how the Donnerberg dominated this part of the front. Without control of this eminence, there was obviously little hope either for a drive northward to clear the northern half of Stolberg or for a drive northeastward on Eschweiler through the Eschweiler woods.[41]

Given two distinct missions—one to assist the VII Corps main effort by sweeping the Eschweiler woods, the other to clear the industrial triangle—General Allen divided his operations into two distinct phases. He directed Colonel Touart's 414th Infantry on the right wing to make the divisional main effort northeast against the Donnerberg and the Eschweiler woods. In the meantime, the other two regiments were to be executing limited operations which General Allen described as "pressure attacks." After clearing the woods, thereby signaling the end of the first phase, Colonel Touart's 414th Infantry was to pause while the main effort shifted to the division's north wing.

The main effort of the second phase was to be launched by the 413th Infantry from the vicinity of Verlautenheide, north-

eastward along the southernmost reaches of the Roer plain to come upon Eschweiler from the north. This drive and a renewal of Colonel Touart's push would converge upon Eschweiler, the heart of the industrial triangle. In the process, the center regiment, which by this time would have cleared the northern half of Stolberg, would be pinched out. With Eschweiler in hand, the division was to continue northeast to clear the remainder of the industrial triangle lying between the army boundary and the Inde. For assistance in clearing the last of the triangle, General Allen had the promise of the 47th Infantry, which by that time should have completed its work with the 1st Division.

As in the sector of the VII Corps main effort, the Germans defending Stolberg, the Donnerberg, and the Eschweiler woods were a part of the *12th Division*. In the left of the 104th Division's zone, in that sector close alongside the Ninth Army where General Allen intended the main effort of his second phase, the enemy units belonged to the *3d Panzer Grenadier Division*. The 104th Division had fairly detailed intelligence information on these units, passed on when the 1st Division had relinquished this sector.

Though the Eschweiler–Weisweiler industrial triangle was high on the priority list for the saturation bombing on 16 November, most targets were so deep inside the triangle that the men of the 104th Division heard more of the bombing than they saw. None of the targets of the heavy bombers was closer than two miles from the division's forward lines. Somewhat inexplicably, 104th Division artillery played no large-scale role in the preliminary bombardment. Though reinforced by an attached battalion of

---

[41] For details of the attack plan, see 104th Div FO 10, 9 Nov, 104th Div G–3 file, 9 Nov 44. The only sources for this section are the official records of the division and attached units, and a letter from General Allen to OCMH, 26 Apr 56. Hoegh and Doyle, *Timberwolf Tracks*, provides only a sketchy account of the opening phase of the November offensive. See pages 111–24. Combat interviews with the 104th Division cover only later actions.

155-mm. guns, the division's artillery fired only 271 rounds all day. Even more surprising was the fact that the organic artillery battalion in direct support of the main effort by the 414th Infantry fired not at all.[42]

If surprise was the object of muzzling the artillery, the experience of the attacking infantry soon after crossing the line of departure on 16 November indicated that the stratagem was ill-advised. Only a drugged enemy could fail during daylight to spot attacking formations from an advantageous height like the Donnerberg.

Despite incessant attacks all through 16 and 17 November and into the next day, Colonel Touart's 414th Infantry made scarcely a dent in the enemy's hold on the Donnerberg. Possibly in an attempt at gaining surprise, one battalion attacked fifteen minutes before H Hour, but to no avail. Achieving a measure of cover and concealment among buildings, the right battalion of the 415th Infantry gained an insecure toehold in Birkengang, an industrial suburb of Stolberg located a few hundred yards northwest of the Donnerberg; but this was no real accomplishment toward the final end. Another battalion trying to bypass the Donnerberg and strike directly for the Eschweiler woods got nowhere.

So late into the evening of 16 November was the 414th Infantry attacking that General Allen set the hour for the next day's attack no earlier than noon. By that time he had worked out a detailed plan of artillery support and had the promise of fighter-bombers against both the Donnerberg and the Eschweiler woods. Still the infantry could make no marked progress. During long weeks of stationary defense in this sector, the enemy's *12th Division* had sown mines and strung barbed wire lavishly. On the Donnerberg itself three giant pillboxes provided stanch protection. Artillery directed from the Donnerberg and antitank guns in the Eschweiler woods punished not only the American infantry but supporting tanks as well.

By nightfall, optimists in the division could point out nevertheless that the advance of the battalion of the 415th Infantry into Birkengang, northwest of the Donnerberg, and limited success of a wide envelopment maneuver to the east through the zone of the 3d Armored Division had created an arc about the Donnerberg. In reality, so widespread were the segments of this arc that they offered little real hope for greater success the next day. As the assistant division commander, Brig. Gen. Bryant E. Moore, was to put it early on the third morning: "We must make some progress today. [It is] getting awful . . . ." The corps commander, General Collins, would agree. On 16 November he had told the 104th Division "in no uncertain terms to get moving and get moving fast."[43]

With just how much audacity the 414th Infantry had attacked during the first two days was difficult to determine. The only casualty figure the regiment had given, a record of 7 percent, or about fifty-four men, lost in the battalion that was attacking the Donnerberg frontally, revealed no fanatic determination. Never-

---

[42] See Arty Annex to 104th Div AAR, Nov 44, copy in 104th Div G-1 file, Nov 44. General Allen in his letter to OCMH, 26 April 1956, notes that a detailed program of division artillery fire was carried out.

[43] 104th Div G-3 Jnl, 18 Nov 44; Sylvan Diary, entry of 16 Nov 44.

theless, the 414th Infantry obviously was facing a formidable position which, except at Birkengang, had to be approached over terrain almost devoid of cover. The difficulty on 17 November did not lie with the volume of supporting fire, for the 104th Division's organic and attached artillery had expended 5,621 rounds, a marked change from the first day.

Because the enemy had failed to counterattack in any strength, Colonel Touart could hope that this meant the enemy had no reserves. In this event, continued attack eventually would wear down the resistance. Because all the 414th Infantry's strength already was committed, Colonel Touart actually had little alternative but to pursue the same pattern of attack he had followed unsuccessfully for the first two days. While two battalions on the east pressed toward the Eschweiler woods, another was to renew the frontal strike against the Donnerberg and the right battalion of the 415th Infantry was to mop up in Birkengang.

A lack of reserves was, in reality, the problem the enemy faced. The only reserves available to the *LXXXI Corps,* not released for commitment at all until late on 17 November, were those consigned to the Schevenhuette sector. Though movement of the reserves was designed to enable the *12th Division* and the other units of the corps to constrict their zones and thereby gain local reserves, this would take time. The admittedly cautious "pressure attacks" that the other two regiments of the 104th Division were conducting enabled the adjacent *3d Panzer Grenadier Division* to release some troops; these, however, the *LXXXI Corps* commander consigned not to the Donnerberg but to the north opposite the Ninth Army, where he believed the Americans had

pointed their main effort.[44] The fact was that the attrition which naturally accompanied warding off persistent attacks had rendered those Germans near Stolberg much less capable of defending themselves on 18 November than they had been earlier.

One factor the Germans on the Donnerberg, along with others on the *LXXXI Corps* front, would miss on 18 November was the kind of artillery support they had been receiving. Thanks in part to stockpiling and in part to a "one-time issue" of artillery ammunition from the *Fuehrer Reserve* (that is, ammunition stockpiled for the Ardennes offensive), the Germans in the *LXXXI Corps* sector had stepped up their artillery fire on 17 November to 13,200 rounds. This was abnormally high. On 18 November and for several days thereafter, they were to be restricted to 8,000 rounds. Even this figure was to decline, despite the fact that Rundstedt attributed any defensive successes achieved thus far "to a very large extent to our artillery operations . . . ."[45]

During the early part of the renewed attack against the Donnerberg on 18 November, Colonel Touart's 414th Infantry could detect little change in the situation. Again advances were measured in feet and yards. Then, about noon, the bottom suddenly fell out of the German defenses. This could have been the result of the execution of an earlier order from the *LXXXI Corps* for the *12th Division* to bend back its north wing

---

[44] Opns Order, *LXXXI Corps* to all divs, 1850, 16 Nov 44; Orders, *LXXXI Corps* to *12th Div,* 1845, and to *12th* and *47th VG Divs,* 1929, 17 Nov 44. All in *LXXXI Corps KTB, Befehle an Div.*

[45] *OB WEST KTB,* 17 Nov 44; *LXXXI Corps KTB, Art.-Lage u. Arty.-Gliederungen.*

to a second line of defense.[46] More likely it was attributable at this particular point to the fact that persistent small unit maneuver at last paid off for the attackers. Germans in two of the big pillboxes surrendered. Though the occupants of the third refused to come out even after encirclement, for all practical purposes the Donnerberg by night of the third day of attack was in American hands.

Having lost the fortified high ground, the enemy stood little chance of holding the Eschweiler woods. In late afternoon, despite a mistaken strafing by U.S. fighter-bombers, the enveloping force on the east broke into the southern edge of the woods. As night came, Colonel Touart directed the kind of attack for which General Allen had specially trained the division. In the darkness, one company slipped past the enemy to drive almost a thousand yards to a road junction atop high ground in the center of the woods. Colonel Touart wasted no time in reinforcing the advantage, so that by daylight on 19 November the task remaining to the 414th Infantry before completion of the first phase of the 104th Division's attack was mop-up and consolidation.

The news of the 414th Infantry's success prompted the division commander to direct an immediate step-up of operations by his other two regiments. The main effort for the second phase of the attack shifted to the left wing regiment in the north alongside the Ninth Army, as much a complement to Ninth Army's battle of the Roer plain as to the VII Corps fight in the fringes of the Huertgen Forest.

Another Victim of the Huertgen Forest

These attacks by armor and infantry on the north wing of the VII Corps were subsidiary attacks designed primarily to assist the corps main effort. The same was true in some respects of the coincident attack by General Barton's 4th Division on the corps south wing. Yet the 4th Division also had a long-range mission. After assisting the corps main effort by clearing the Huertgen Forest between Schevenhuette and Huertgen, the 4th Division was to continue to the Roer River south of Dueren.[47]

With the depressing results of the 28th Division's experience in the forest fresh in mind, General Barton must have been perturbed that even before the jump-off his division already had one strike against it. As the 4th Division had been moving from the V Corps to an assembly area behind the VII Corps lines the night of 6 November, word had reached the 12th Infantry to drop out of the column. To shore up the faltering 28th Division, this regiment was to relieve the 109th Infantry astride the wooded plateau between the Weisser Weh Creek and the Germeter–Huertgen highway. Danger from the recurring crises within the 28th Division left no time for prior reconnaissance. The 12th Infantry had to go into the line that night.

This urgency prevented the 12th Infantry commander, Col. James S. Luckett,

---

[46] Opns Order, *LXXXI Corps* to all divs, 1850, 16 Nov 44, *LXXXI Corps KTB, Befehle an Div.*

[47] Details of the attack plans may be found in 4th Div FO 53, 7 Nov, and FO 53 revised, 15 Nov, both in 4th Div FO file, Oct–Dec 44. The account of this period is based upon official unit records, combat interviews, and a narrative, Huertgen Forest Battle, written from the interviews by combat historians and found in 4th Div Combat Interv file, Nov 44.

from improving the dispositions which attack and counterattack had imposed upon the 109th Infantry. He had to relieve in place, unit for unit. Much of the effect of a fresh regiment entering the battle thus was dissipated at the start. In succeeding days, it was amply illustrated that while closely locked with the enemy a regiment has a hard time coordinating its battalions into a cohesive striking force. In the case of the 12th Infantry, divergent missions, made so remote by the dense forest that mutual support was impossible, quickly drained the battalions of offensive vitality.

While attached to the 28th Division, Colonel Luckett was to reduce the enemy's countersalient in the Weisser Weh valley and also improve and lengthen the line of departure overlooking Huertgen, which the 109th Infantry was to have secured. The 12th Infantry could accomplish neither. One reason was that the regiment could not operate as a whole. Another was the situation that by 9 November had enabled the Germans to shift strength from Kommerscheidt and Schmidt and counterattack southward from Huertgen against the 12th Infantry in an attempt at cutting off that part of the 28th Division still in Vossenack.

On 10 November—the day that the First Army established a new intercorps boundary and thereby returned the 12th Infantry to 4th Division control—the Germans launched their counterattack. Coincidentally, one of Colonel Luckett's battalions was attacking northward. The enemy quickly surrounded two of the American companies. Only by hastily contriving a line several hundred yards to the south was the 12th Infantry able to hold onto as much as a third of the plateau. Two days later, on 12 Novem-

ber, when two other companies of the 12th Infantry broke through to the encircled companies, the Germans closed in behind them. Then four companies instead of two were surrounded.

Not until 15 November, on the very eve of the November offensive, was Colonel Luckett able to extricate these four companies. Even then he had to settle for a final defensive line near the southern edge of the plateau. In nine days of bitter combat, the 12th Infantry had lost rather than gained ground. A thousand men had fallen victim either to enemy fire or to combat exhaustion, trench foot, or respiratory diseases. The way the battalions had to absorb replacements accurately depicted the condition of the regiment: new men entered the line wherever gaps existed. Then each surviving platoon leader assumed control of all men in a designated sector.

The contributions of Colonel Luckett's 12th Infantry to the main offensive obviously would be limited. Anticipating this fact, General Hodges had on 10 November attached to the VII Corps the 5th Armored Division's CCR. On 16 November Colonel Luckett was to renew his attack to regain the ground he had lost and secure control either of the Weisser Weh road or the Germeter–Huertgen highway so that the armor might debouch against Huertgen.

That this maneuver never developed could have come as no surprise to those who knew the true condition of the 12th Infantry. Only in the Weisser Weh valley was the regiment able to gain any ground, and there only a few hundred yards. Casualties continued to soar so that by the end of the action the 12th Infantry counted its battle and nonbattle losses at more than 1,600. On 21 November this dismal failure astride the bloody little plateau by a commander and a regiment heretofore possessing enviable reputations cost Colonel Luckett his command. It was apparent, however, that Luckett's superior, General Barton, recognized extenuating circumstances, for Colonel Luckett was given command of a regiment in another division.

Thus it was that the Germans already had called one strike on the 4th Division. General Barton had left but two regiments with which to attack on a four-mile front to penetrate three and a half miles of Huertgen jungle and then to push another three and a half miles to the Roer. In light of the involvement of the 12th Infantry in the V Corps zone, General Barton had requested reinforcement, but none was forthcoming. Though the shift in the corps boundary at midnight 10 November and the attachment of the armored combat command were designed to assist, the increased responsibilities entailed in these changes created in the long run more hindrance than help.

Because a primary part of the 4th Division's mission was to assist the advance of the 1st Division, General Barton had to direct one of his regiments to hug his north boundary close alongside the 1st Division's 26th Infantry. This assignment fell to the 8th Infantry (Col. Richard G. McKee). From a point just south of Schevenhuette, the 8th Infantry was to attack northeast two miles through the forest to high ground about Gut Schwarzenbroich, a forest manor on the grounds of a ruined monastery. This would put the regiment about two thirds of the way through the forest in position to continue northeast toward Dueren.

To cover a remaining three forested miles between this regiment's southern boundary and the positions of the 12th Infantry, General Barton had only one regiment, Colonel Lanham's 22d Infantry. Trying to maintain greatest strength in the north, in keeping with the requirement of assisting the 1st Division, while at the same time reducing the gap to the 12th Infantry, General Barton directed an attack on a two-battalion front in the center of the three-mile zone. He told Colonel Lanham to make his main effort on the left, hold his reserve on the left, and with the help of an attached squadron of cavalry keep the area north to the regimental boundary clear. The danger inherent in the regiment's dangling right flank would have to be risked in the hope that the 12th Infantry might be able to close the gap.

To the 22d Infantry General Barton gave initial objectives on the far fringe of the forest, the villages of Kleinhau and Grosshau. From these villages the regiment was to turn northeastward on Gey for eventual convergence with the 8th Infantry on the approaches to Dueren.

On the eve of the November offensive, the disturbing thing about the 4th Division's impending attack was not so much that the 4th Division must fight in the Huertgen Forest. That division after division might have to do this had been foreordained weeks before when the Americans had persisted in trying to push straight through the forest even after the first attempts had been set back rudely. This American fixation would remain a puzzle to more than one enemy commander. As one German officer was to put it later, the Germans hardly could have used the forest as a base for large-scale operations into the American flank at Aachen, both because "there were no forces available for this purpose and because tanks could not be employed in this territory." [48] The disturbing thing was that despite the hundreds of American dead who had fallen victim to the forest, the Americans had not altered their methods of attack. As early as mid-September the 9th Division had demonstrated that to send widely separated columns through such an obstacle was to invite disaster. Yet on a second occasion in October the 9th Division had tried the same thing and in early November the 28th Division had followed suit. Now the 4th Division was to pursue the same pattern.

The First Army commander, General Hodges, did not like the method of attack. On the day the 4th Division jumped off, Hodges came away from a visit to the division with the impression that "they are going about the attack in the wrong way—running down roads . . . instead of advancing through the woods tightly buttoned up yard by yard." [49] On the other hand, what was a division commander to do when faced with a frontage requiring regimental attack zones from one to three miles wide? A zone this wide was usually considered great even for open ground; the attacks of the 9th and 28th Divisions already had proved it distinctly too much for the Huertgen Forest. [50]

It is possible that by some untried legerdemain the First Army might have juggled its units to decrease divisional frontages in the forest. Yet the basic

fact was that, in view of available troops, the First Army had a lot of ground to cover. This fact was clearly apparent from General Hodges' inability to constitute other than a nominal army reserve. [51]

A superficial glance at the enemy opposite the 4th Division would not, of course, have inspired awe. The same nondescript *275th Infantry Division*, which earlier had opposed the 9th and 28th Divisions and which by this time had absorbed remnants of thirty-seven different units, held the line all the way from Schevenhuette to the forested plateau near Germeter. The controlling corps, General Straube's *LXXIV Corps*, was virtually without reserves. Except for the combat command sent north to strengthen the reserve of the *LXXXI Corps*, the depleted *116th Panzer Division* still was on hand; but higher headquarters was becoming increasingly insistent that this division be released for refitting before the Ardennes counteroffensive. As events developed, the panzer division was to be withdrawn on 21 November, along with most of the headquarters troops that had helped defeat the 28th Division's attack on Schmidt. The adjoining *89th Division*, fatigued and markedly understrength after the Schmidt fight, obviously could provide the *275th Division* little help. [52]

A closer analysis of the German situation would reveal that the *275th Division*

---

[48] MS # A–892 (Gersdorff). At least one U.S. commander, General Oliver of the 5th Armored Division, could not understand why the Huertgen Forest was not pinched out by attacks from north and south. See Ltr, Oliver to OCMH, 4 Jul 56, OCMH.

[49] Sylvan Diary, entry of 16 Nov 44.

[50] See War Department FM 7–40 (9 Feb 42), p. 173.

[51] Interv with Thorson, 12 Sept 56.

[52] MSS # C–016 (Straube) and # A–891 (Gersdorff). German sources on *Seventh Army* operations during the latter part of November and early December are limited. The postwar German manuscripts provide almost the only material, although high-level references in the *A Gp B* and *OB WEST KTB's* are pertinent. One of the postwar accounts is excellent: MS # B–810, Generalleutnant Hans Schmidt, *Kaempfe im Rheinland 275. Infanterie Division*, Part IV.

had demonstrated twice already that within the Huertgen Forest large, well-organized units composed of first class troops were not essential to a steadfast defense. Having thickly sown the limited network of firebreaks, trails, and roads with mines, a few poorly co-ordinated squads in well-prepared field fortifications might hold off a company or a battalion at heavy cost to the attackers. The ground under the closely planted trees so hoarded the late autumn rains that mud could deny routes of communication even when other means failed. Barbed wire, antipersonnel mines, log bunkers, and log-covered foxholes and machine gun emplacements honeycombed the forest. Meshed branches of trees hid them from view.

What is more, the *275th Division* had a strength in men and guns which was considerably more impressive than could have been deduced from the conglomeration of subordinate units involved. Two of the division's organic regiments were basically intact. Though the third was down to about 250 men and was held in reserve, a composite regiment created from various attached units had taken its place in the line. The division had some 6,500 men, 106 tubes of artillery, 21 assault guns, and 23 antitank guns of 75-mm. or above.[53]

Operating under strictest security while awaiting D Day, the 4th Division could learn little of the specific locations of the German positions. Because only small engineer units had held most of the line here with isolated roadblocks, intelligence information passed on to General Barton's G–2 was limited. In general, the division knew only that the enemy's main line of resistance ran in the extreme south behind the Weisser Weh Creek, except for a small salient extending toward the Rother Weh Creek. After confluence of the Rother Weh and the Weisser Weh, about two miles southeast of Schevenhuette, the two creeks continue as the Weh.

Of vital concern in the 4th Division's attack preparations was the limited road net. The key road was a lateral route that follows the course of the Weisser Weh and Weh. For purposes of identification, this was labeled Road W. From Road W other routes led both west and east like sparse branches on a grotesque tree. Those on the west afforded both regiments tortuous but adequate supply routes to their lines of departure. Attacking from the Weh Creek, the 8th Infantry would have one good road leading east as well, a route labeled Road U, which meandered northeast past Gut Schwarzenbroich all the way through the forest in the desired direction of Dueren. In the southern portion of the 8th Infantry's sector, another route called Road V also might serve the regiment during early stages of the attack.

It was the 22d Infantry that would feel most the effects of the limited roads. From this regiment's line of departure along the Rother Weh, a mile west of lateral Road W, no road existed within the regimental sector to provide access across Raven's Hedge ridge (*Rabenheck*), a mile-wide forested highland lying between the Rother Weh and the Weisser Weh. For getting supplies across Raven's Hedge ridge, the regimental commander, Colonel Lanham, had to bank upon improving a firebreak. Once past the Weisser Weh, however, the 22d Infantry would have one good route, Road X, leading east to the village of Grosshau,

---

[53] MS # B–810 (Schmidt).

which was one of the 22d Infantry's objectives. A branch of Road X, labeled Road Y, led to the other objective, Kleinhau, and a second branch, Road Z, to Huertgen.

Unlike most other units in the November offensive, the 4th Division could count on little direct assistance from preliminary bombardment. Indeed, even though the division was strengthened by the attachment of four artillery battalions, General Barton decided against an artillery preparation. Under the conditions prevailing in the forest, he deemed the chance of achieving surprise more promising. The only preliminary support scheduled in the 4th Division zone was by fighter bombers against the villages of Huertgen, Kleinhau, Grosshau, and Gey.

On the 4th Division's left wing, the 8th Infantry attempted penetration of the enemy's Weh Creek line at a firebreak several hundred yards south of axial Road U. The leading battalion under Lt. Col. Langdon A. Jackson, Jr., took a few casualties from 120-mm. mortar fire while climbing a precipitous wooded slope beyond the creek, but contined to advance until, at a junction of firebreaks, a well-organized German position came into view. Barring further advance was a pyramid of three concertinas of heavy wire, eight to ten feet high. The ground in front was thick with *Schuh* mines. A hail of machine gun fire met every attempt to move up to the obstacle.

Inching forward, daring men tried to slide a Bangalore torpedo beneath the concertinas. As German fire cut down one man, another would take his place. At last they had the explosive lodged beneath the wire. Anxiously, the rest of the battalion waited for the explosion to signal a rush through the wire. The cue never came. The Bangalore torpedo was wet. It would not go off.

That night the battalion's Ammunition and Pioneer Platoon at last blew a gap through the wire, but as daylight came on 17 November the enemy stymied every attempt to charge through. Three times Colonel Jackson's men tried it, only to falter each time as man after man fell before the enemy's fire. By noon this battalion had lost about 200 men, the most concentrated casualties any unit of the regiment was to incur in the costly forest fighting.

Even after a platoon leader, 1st Lt. Bernard J. Ray, had sacrificed his own life to blow another gap in the concertina obstacle, the men could not get through. Thrusting explosive caps in his pocket, wrapping a length of primer cord about his body, and carrying a Bangalore torpedo, Lieutenant Ray moved alone toward the wire. As he paused to prepare his demolition charge, an exploding mortar shell wounded him severely. Apparently aware that unless he completed his task in a matter of moments, he would fail, Lieutenant Ray hastily connected the explosive to the caps in his pockets and the primer cord about his body. Having turned himself into a human torpedo, he set off the explosion.[54]

In the meantime, deep in the forest several miles to the southwest, the 22d Infantry also had attacked at 1245 on 16 November. In driving toward Grosshau and Kleinhau, this regiment first had to cross the wooded Raven's Hedge ridge, lying between the line of departure at the Rother Weh and the Weisser Weh. Though the enemy line here was primarily a series of outposts, the going was far from

---

[54] Lieutenant Ray was posthumously awarded the Medal of Honor.

easy. By nightfall of D Day the leading battalion of the 22d Infantry still was some 300 yards short of the Weisser Weh.

This first day's advance across a mile of wooded, precipitous ground that had no axial road quickly demonstrated the supply problems the 22d Infantry would experience for days to come. So onerous was the task that the leading battalion could not be ready to resume the attack the next morning. Instead, the regimental commander, Colonel Lanham, directed another battalion to move on 17 November northeast up the ridge along a firebreak, which he hoped to develop as a supply route. Upon reaching a junction of several firebreaks, which the men called Five Points, this battalion was to turn east, cross the Weisser Weh, and drive on toward Grosshau along the north of Road X. As soon as the other battalion had been resupplied, it was to resume the attack eastward along the south of Road X.

The firebreak leading to Five Points became troublesome almost from the start. Hardly had the fresh battalion begun to advance when an aptly directed German shelling inflicted fifty casualties on the lead company, knocked out all communications, and killed the battalion commander. When Colonel Lanham risked commitment of a platoon of light tanks, the first two tanks struck mines and blocked passage of the others. Even when the advance reached Five Points, the firebreak remained a problem. The enemy had strewn it with both antitank and antipersonnel mines. Carrying parties had to dodge mines and shells while fighting running battles with German patrols. The enemy artillery scored another lucky hit late on 17 November when a concentration wiped out the commander

of the 22d Infantry's reserve battalion and most of his staff.

Despite the problems in the rear, the battalion at Five Points made a surprisingly swift advance on the third day, 18 November. By early afternoon its troops not only had crossed lateral Road W but had moved several hundred yards beyond to occupy a wooded hill lying in the northeast angle of the juncture of Roads X and W.

Coincidentally, the battalion on the south ran into myriad problems. Its south flank exposed, this battalion had to beat off a small counterattack before advance could begin. Thereupon the men encountered an extensive antipersonnel mine field. Trying to find a path around the mines, one company got lost and could not be located until late in the day. In the afternoon enemy fire claimed this battalion commander as well. The operations and communications officers and two company commanders also were wounded. When the battalion executive officer and a replacement S-3 moved forward to take over, the executive too was hit and the new S-3 killed. Not until the regimental S-2, Maj. Howard C. Blazzard, arrived in late afternoon to assume command was this battalion at last able to move. Darkness was falling as the depleted companies crossed Road W on the run, waded the icy Weisser Weh, and climbed the steep slope beyond.

With a battalion entrenched beyond Road W on either side of Road X, the 22d Infantry at last had registered an appreciable gain. But such a strain had the task been that Colonel Lanham appealed to General Barton for twenty-four hours in which to consolidate. In three days the regiment had incurred more than 300 battle casualties, including all three

STRUGGLING UP *a wooded hillside.*

battalion commanders, several key staff officers, about half the company commanders, and many key company officers and noncommissioned officers. As others had found out before, the close combat of the Huertgen Forest was rough on leaders. Colonel Lanham had not only an exposed south flank, where the 12th Infantry was two miles away, but an open north flank as well. The 8th Infantry to the north was a mile away, and a mile was an alarming distance in the forest. Even between the two forward battalions on either side of Road X a problem of contact existed, for both enemy mines and shelling decreed

that the troops give Road X a wide berth.

Behind the lines lay one of the biggest problems of all: how to get a supply route across Raven's Hedge ridge. Though engineers had gone to work quickly on the firebreak leading to Five Points, the task had proved more difficult than any could have imagined. Constant dripping from sodden trees had so permeated the ground that passage of even a few vehicles quickly transformed the firebreak into a sea of mud. The enemy in some instances had stacked one mine upon another like pancakes and often had fitted them with antilifting devices so that the engineers had to explode them in place and then fill the craters. Wheels of vehicles digging deep in the mud often exploded mines missed by the mine detectors.

Even had the firebreak been passable, another obstacle still existed at the juncture of Roads X and W. There the enemy had destroyed a bridge across the Weisser Weh. Uncanny accuracy of German shellfire on the site denied speed in rebuilding the bridge and set many to wondering if the enemy had not left an artillery observer hidden nearby in the forest.

Aside from the difficulty of getting supplies forward, the road problem also prevented getting tanks, tank destroyers, or antitank guns to the front. These were urgently needed, not only to support further infantry advance but also for defense in the event the enemy employed tanks either along Road X or against either of the undefended flanks along Road W.

In light of these conditions, General Barton hardly could have denied Colonel Lanham's request for a twenty-four hour respite. Yet in authorizing a day's postponement, Barton sought to implement a plan contemplated from the first for easing the 22d Infantry's supply problems. He told the 8th Infantry also to postpone any further eastward advance temporarily while turning instead to clear lateral Road W southeast to the interregimental boundary. The 22d Infantry in the meantime was to clear north to the boundary. Vehicles supporting the 22d Infantry then might proceed northeast along a road paralleling the Rother Weh into the 8th Infantry's sector to the confluence of the Rother Weh and the Weisser Weh, thence south along Road W back into the 22d Infantry's zone.

Despite the hold-up at the concertina obstacle during the first two days of the attack, Colonel McKee's 8th Infantry at last had begun to advance. On the third day, 18 November, while the 22d Infantry was trying to cross Road W, Colonel McKee had decided that no matter how discouraging the terrain for use of tanks, the close fire support of tanks was the only solution. Committing a fresh battalion of infantry, he sent along a platoon of light tanks, a platoon of mediums, and three tank destroyers.

As the armor hugged the trees along either side of the firebreak, the infantry used the path of the treads as protection against antipersonnel mines. Remarkably, the tanks struck no antitank mines before reaching the concertina wire. Blasting away with their 75-mm. guns, the mediums tore away the obstacle. The infantry quickly followed them through.

Not until the attack had carried a thousand yards to reach a clearing near the junction of Road U and the Renn Weg—the latter a trail leading southeastward in the direction of Gey, then turning sharply south toward Grosshau—did the infantry and tanks meet another nest of organized opposition. This was an elaborately prepared position within what was apparently a second line of defense, but the Germans had neglected to mine in front of it. While the medium tanks and tank destroyers provided a base of fire, the light tanks and a company of infantry threaded through the trees to come upon the enemy flank. A fortuitous assist from the pilot of a P–47, who flew low over the trees to diagnose the situation and then strafe the German position, aided the envelopment.

A battalion of the 8th Infantry now had penetrated more than a mile past

Road W and stood no more than a thousand yards from high ground in the vicinity of Gut Schwarzenbroich, the regiment's first objective. Yet the penetration was so slim and pencillike that it hardly could be exploited without a broader base. To alleviate this situation and at the same time fulfill General Barton's directive of clearing Road W as far as the interregimental boundary, Colonel McKee on 19 November sent a battalion southeastward parallel to Road W to seize high ground south of Road V. By nightfall this battalion was in place.

Despite this advance, a short stretch of Road W between the 8th and 22d Infantry Regiments still remained in enemy hands. Also, German shelling of the bridge site at the junction of Roads X and W again had prevented engineers from rebuilding the bridge. Thus no easing of the 22d Infantry's supply problems was discernible by nightfall of 19 November.

For all the American supply problems, it was obvious from the relative ease with which the 8th Infantry had advanced on 18 and 19 November and from the achievements of the 22d Infantry in crossing Road W on 18 November that the enemy's overextended 275th Division was incapable of denying further advance. That this situation would arise could not have been unanticipated by the German commanders. For days they had been engaged in an almost frantic search for troops to back up the 275th Division. Already they had used contingents of what was left of the 116th Panzer Division, but these were not enough.

By stretching defensive lines dangerously thin, the adjacent corps to the south at last managed to pinch out and release the 344th Infantry Division. A day later a volks grenadier division arrived in the Seventh Army's southernmost corps and eventually would relieve the 353d Infantry Division. Though the 344th and 353d Divisions "had little combat value in the unusually bitter fighting of the Huertgen Forest," the Germans rushed first the 344th, then the 353d, to the forest. During the night of 19 November and the next day, the 344th moved in behind the 275th Division.[55]

When both American regiments renewed their attacks to the east and northeast on 20 November, the effect of the German reinforcements was readily apparent. Colonel McKee's 8th Infantry cleared additional ground to the southeast in the direction of the interregimental boundary, but in the main effort toward Gut Schwarzenbroich, neither of two attacking battalions could gain. So close were the opposing forces in the forest that as night came, enemy fire prevented the men from cutting logs for overhead cover on their foxholes. As all had come to know, failure to provide overhead cover in the forest was an invitation to death.[56]

Resistance was stiff and local counterattacks severe as the 22d Infantry renewed its two-battalion attack toward Grosshau and Kleinhau. Counterattacks brought particularly heavy casualties along the open right flank of the regiment. As night came, the regiment could note ad-

---

[55] MS # A–891 (Gersdorff) and ETHINT 57 (Gersdorff).

[56] During the day, Maj. George L. Mabry, Jr., who had just assumed command of the 8th Infantry's center battalion, advanced alone to find a path through a mine field. He captured three of the enemy and had resorted to hand-to-hand combat with nine others when his own scouts came to his aid. He subsequently received the Medal of Honor.

vances of only a few hundred yards, though this meant that the battalion on the north of Road X had moved almost to the junction of Roads X and Y.

Going any farther than this in the face of determined resistance and without an adequate supply route obviously was a hazardous proposition. Although Colonel Lanham had but two battalions actually up front, his reserve already was tied up with diverse missions: protecting the regiment's exposed flanks, clearing Road W north to the 8th Infantry, and eliminating German infiltration and bypassed strongpoints, one of which had taken the regimental command post under fire. One company of the reserve was combing the woods near the Weisser Weh bridge site, trying to find the enemy artillery observer suspected of directing the uncannily accurate shellfire on the site. Casualties, even in the reserve, had been alarming. In addition, German tanks (or assault guns) had been spotted along Roads X and Y. Though these had operated singly in passive defensive roles, no one could say when they might change their tactics.

By constructing a bridge in sections within the woods away from the bridge site, the engineers at last got a firm crossing of the Weisser Weh in place during the night of 20 November. The next day they were to find the enemy's artillery observer hidden in the woods. Yet the 22d Infantry still had no supply route, for not until late on 21 November were patrols of Colonel Lanham's regiment to make contact along Road W with those of Colonel McKee's.

By nightfall of 20 November the awful price the 4th Division's two regiments had had to pay in the five-day attack that had brought no penetration deeper than a

mile and a half was readily apparent. Some rifle companies were down below fifty effectives. Several had only one or two officers left. Losses in battalion commanders had been strikingly severe, particularly in the 22d Infantry. Perhaps the hardest hit unit of either regiment was the south-wing battalion of the 22d Infantry, which had both to attack and defend the regiment's open southern flank. That battalion had been reduced to the size of a company. For the two regiments the toll in battle casualties alone was about 1,500. Several hundred more men had been evacuated with respiratory diseases, trench foot, and combat exhaustion. Although replacements had begun what was to become a daily trek to the front lines, they never were to equal the fallen men in numbers, and days and weeks would pass before they might approach the fallen in experience. The 4th Division obviously needed a pause for breath.

Out of a decision made at First Army level developed the opportunity for a pause. A day before, on 19 November, General Hodges had ordered the V Corps to join the offensive. The inability of the 12th Infantry to gain ground from which the attached combat command of the 5th Armored Division might take Huertgen had underscored the importance of that village. Transferring Huertgen to the V Corps sector would ensure its capture and at the same time help the 4th Division by decreasing its zone of responsibility.

General Hodges reckoned that by speeding the relief of the 28th Division in the Germeter–Vossenack area, the V Corps might attack as early as 21 November with a fresh infantry division. To assist this division, he gave the combat command to the V Corps. So that the new force might assist the 4th Division even more, General Hodges gave the V Corps responsibility not only for Huertgen but also for Kleinhau, the southernmost of the 22d Infantry's objectives.[57]

As soon as troops of the V Corps passed through the 12th Infantry in the attack on Huertgen, the 12th Infantry was to move north into 4th Division reserve. After shoring up the regiment with replacements, General Barton might use it to protect the south flank of the 22d Infantry. No doubt infinitely relieved by this turn of events, General Barton told Colonel McKee and Colonel Lanham to take another twenty-four-hour rest from the offensive. Use the time, he said, to consolidate gains and open adequate supply routes. The attack would be renewed on 22 November.[58]

On 21 November, fresh forces were to enter the November offensive. On the German side, the *344th Division* had replaced the *275th*. On the American side, the V Corps was to strike for Huertgen.

---

[57] See V Corps Ltr of Instrs, 19 Nov 44, V Corps Operations in the ETO, p. 310.

[58] 4th Div FO 54, 20 Nov, 4th Div FO file, Oct–Dec 44.

CHAPTER XIX

V Corps Joins the Offensive

Except for the preliminary operation by the 28th Division to capture Schmidt, General Hodges originally had not contemplated employing General Gerow's V Corps until after the VII Corps had achieved a penetration. At that point, General Gerow was to have launched a major drive close alongside the VII Corps in the direction of Bonn.[1] But by 19 November, three days after start of the offensive, it had become obvious that extra weight was needed if the VII Corps was to achieve a genuine pentration. Because advance had not been sufficient to enable commitment of additional forces within the zone of the main effort, the most likely hope for quick assistance appeared to lie with the adjacent V Corps. (*See Map VI.*)

Sharing a common boundary running just south of Huertgen with the 4th Division of the VII Corps, General Gerow by 19 November had almost completed relief of the exhausted 28th Division with the full-strength 8th Division. By establishing a temporary corps boundary north of Huertgen and Kleinhau, this fresh division might be employed to broaden the offensive. Thereby progress of the main effort might be facilitated while at the same time the bulk of the V Corps would be reserved for exploiting a breakthrough.

Commitment of the 8th Division surely could be expected to facilitate advance of the 4th Division through the Huertgen

Forest. Aside from reducing the width of the 4th Division's zone by over a mile and enabling unrestricted use of all three of General Barton's regiments, relieving the 4th Division of responsibility for a stanchly defended objective like Huertgen would be a big help. With Huertgen in hand, the V Corps would be in position for continuing the attack to the southeast to clear the Brandenberg–Bergstein ridge, which had proved such an embarrassment to earlier operations of the 28th Division.

General Hodges specified his decision late on 19 November. Laying on a new intercorps boundary, he directed that the V Corps take Huertgen and Kleinhau. To assist, he relieved the 5th Armored Division's CCR from attachment to the VII Corps and gave it back to General Gerow for attachment to the 8th Division. D Day for the attack was 21 November.[2]

A Fourth Fight on the Bloody Plateau

Despite the misfortunes that earlier had befallen three regiments of as many different divisions on the bloody, wooded plateau north of Germeter and astride the Germeter–Huertgen highway, this was the only place within the V Corps boundaries

---

[1] FUSA Rpt, Vol. 1, p. 67.

[2] Although no copy of Hodges' order as contained in FUSA Ltr of Instrs, 19 Nov 44, can be found, the essence is discernible from V Corps Ltr of Instrs, 2230, 19 Nov 44, as reproduced in V Corps Operations in the ETO, p. 310. See also FUSA Rpt, Vol. 1, p. 79.

that presented any real chance of success in attacking Huertgen. Indeed, a stipulation from General Hodges that the V Corps accomplish a rapid passage of the 12th Infantry's existing lines so that the 12th Infantry might move quickly to the zone of its parent division all but dictated that the first stage of the attack follow the old pattern.

Both because of the configuration of terrain along the wooded plateau and because of defensive responsibilities inherited from the 28th Division, the burden of the first stage of the 8th Division's attack was to fall upon one infantry regiment. The division commander, Maj. Gen. Donald A. Stroh, had little choice but to conform rigidly to the framework that had been devised for the earlier attack on Huertgen by the 12th Infantry. As soon as the infantry could secure the long-sought line of departure along the woods line overlooking Huertgen, the attached combat command of armor would debouch from the woods against the village.[3]

Because two of the 8th Division's regiments already had occupied defensive positions around Vossenack, the logical choice for making the attack was the regiment which had not yet arrived from the division's former zone in Luxembourg. This was the 121st Infantry, commanded by Col. John R. Jeter. Unfortunately, when General Stroh received the order to

attack, Colonel Jeter's 121st Infantry was 107 road miles away from what would be its line of departure. The regiment could not arrive in the Huertgen Forest until late on 20 November, only a few hours before H Hour at 0900, 21 November. The stage was set for the same kind of bruising tumble Colonel Luckett and the 12th Infantry had taken in this same sector little more than a fortnight before.

Though General Stroh ordered the 121st Infantry to begin moving north immediately, rain, fog, mud, and darkness so slowed the column that the last serial did not close in the detrucking area until just before dark on 20 November. The infantry then had a seven-mile foot march to assembly areas behind the 12th Infantry. Fatigued from the journey and the march, harassed by enemy shelling, and bewildered by the confusion of moving tactically into a strange woods at night, Colonel Jeter's troops at last lined up behind the 12th Infantry about three hours before daylight on D Day, 21 November.

Despite the dismal record of other units on the wooded plateau, some, including the army commander, General Hodges, believed that this fresh force had a strong chance for quick success. Indeed, by ordering originally that the attached armor pass through the 121st Infantry on the second day of attack, the corps commander had indicated an expectation that the infantry might reach the woods line on the first day.[4] Even though General Gerow subsequently acceded to a request from General Stroh to leave the date of commitment of the armor indefinite, the V Corps commander hardly

---

[3] See 8th Div FO 16, 20 Nov, 8th Div AAR, Nov 44. Unless otherwise noted, the story of this action is taken from official records of the 8th Division and CCR, 5th Armored Division, and from extensive combat interviews with officers and men of both units. Having entered combat with the First Army on 6 July 1944, the 8th (Pathfinder) Division subsequently had moved to Brest to fight under the Ninth Army until capture of Brest on 19 September. Since that time the division had been holding defensive positions with the VIII Corps in the Ardennes.

[4] Sylvan Diary, entry of 20 Nov 44; see also Combat Interv with Colonel Jeter.

could have felt any particular concern for the enemy set to oppose the fresh American regiment. Latest identifications had revealed that the same four understrength German battalions of the *275th Division* which had fought the 12th Infantry for more than ten days still held the area.

In the immediate sector of the wooded plateau this was pretty much the true German situation. Yet intelligence officers had failed to note the arrival in the last few hours of the *344th Infantry Division*, which German commanders had milked from adjacent corps farther south. Though these new troops might have "little combat value," as German commanders maintained, they still might give a good account of themselves in the constricted terrain of this region.[5]

An hour before the scheduled jump-off, V Corps artillery with an assist from some guns of the VII Corps began a preparation involving 4,500 rounds against known and suspected enemy gun positions. All were TOT missions with an average of five battalions of artillery on each target. Reinforced by guns of the 5th Armored Division's CCR and by two companies of chemical mortars, the 8th Division's organic artillery fired on the enemy's front lines and the villages beyond. By the end of the day 8th Division artillery was to have expended an impressive total of 9,289 rounds.[6] Just how effective these fires were was hard to say, for the woods and a thick, low overcast severely restricted observation. The weather also prevented any assistance from fighter-bombers. Though medium bombers got

through to drop thirty-two tons of bombs on Bergstein, their strike was too far in advance of the ground troops to have immediate value.[7]

With all three battalions on line, the 121st Infantry attacked at the scheduled hour, 0900, 21 November. One battalion headed north up the Weisser Weh valley, another moved astride the bloody plateau, and the third attacked along the Germeter–Huertgen highway.

Hardly had the artillery finished its bombardment before the pattern the ground fighting would take for the next four days emerged. On the first day, no unit made any appreciable advance except one company east of the Germeter–Huertgen highway, which gained a meager 500 yards.[8] The woods were as thick as ever with antipersonnel mines, with log bunkers bristling with automatic weapons, with barbed wire, and even more than ever with broken tree trunks and branches that obscured the soggy ground and turned any movement, even when not under enemy fire, into a test of endurance. Any hope that the enemy might not have much fight left was quickly dispelled. For all the good the American infantry could detect, the attempts by American artillery to silence the enemy's big guns and mortars might have been made with

---

[5] MSS # A-891 (Gersdorff), B-810 (Schmidt), and ETHINT-57 (Gersdorff).

[6] V Corps Operations in the ETO, p. 316; V Corps Arty Per Unit Rpt 164, 21–22 Nov, V Corps G-3 file, 21–23 Nov 44.

[7] FUSA Rpt, Vol. 1, p. 79, and V Corps Operations in the ETO, p. 316.

[8] The men of this company could attribute much of this success to a squad leader, S. Sgt. John W. Minick. Having picked his way through a mine field crisscrossed with barbed wire, Sergeant Minick personally dispatched a force of German defenders by killing twenty and capturing as many more. Later he knocked out a machine gun. As he tried to find a path through a second mine field, he stepped on a mine and was killed. Sergeant Minick was posthumously awarded the Medal of Honor.

V Corps Rocket Launchers *bombarding German positions.*

peashooters. Not until last light of the first day did Colonel Jeter's regiment complete even a passage of the 12th Infantry's lines.

For three more days the 121st Infantry plodded on, absorbing sometimes alarming casualties, enduring conditions that made men weep, and registering daily gains that varied from nothing to 600 yards. On the second day, 22 November, a cold, driving rain mixed at intervals with snow added to the other miseries. Visibility was so poor that no planes could operate, not even the brave little liaison planes from which observers registered artillery fires. Although 8th Division and V Corps artillery fired 12,500 rounds during the second day, many of them against suspected mortar positions, visibility was so restricted and sound and flash conditions so poor that no one could make any definite claim for these fires. On 23 and 24 November Colonel Jeter committed attached light tanks along the firebreaks, but they bogged helplessly in the mud. Other tanks trying to move up the Germeter–Huertgen highway fell quick prey to German guns in Huertgen.

German shelling prompted one American commander to remark that the enemy "threw back an equal amount of artillery." [9] As attested by a field artillery officer directly supporting the 121st Infantry, this was hardly the case, but the artillery officer did note that the Germans "fired unusually heavy concentrations for them." [10] The shelling probably took on added weight because the limited zone of operations permitted the Germans to concentrate their fires. For the first few days of the attack, German artillery and self-propelled guns estimated at from eight to ten battalions fired in excess of 3,500 rounds per day. At first, this fire was distributed equally between light and medium rounds, but by 23 and 24 November medium shells had come to predominate, indicating that the German light batteries might be displacing rearward. [11]

The first positive indication of success in the attack arose on 24 November on the 121st Infantry's left wing. Here the westernmost battalion was trying to drive up the Weisser Weh valley in order that the subsequent attack by armor might be made up the Weisser Weh road (Road W) instead of the cruelly exposed Germeter–Huertgen highway. In three days this battalion had registered only minor gains, but on 24 November the commitment of a company around the left flank resulted in an encouraging advance.

This news had scarcely reached the regimental command post when the bottom dropped out. The flanking company came suddenly under a heavy concentration of artillery fire, heightened as always

in the forest by deadly bursts in the trees and followed by a sharp local counterattack. The strain of the previous days of fighting apparently had unnerved both men and officers of this company. The men fell back. [12]

Colonel Jeter promptly relieved both the company and battalion commanders involved in this incident and a day later had to appoint a third company commander when artillery fire cut down the second. These were the first in a wave of summary reliefs touched off by the inconclusiveness of the regiment's advance. In four days a total of three company commanders lost their commands. In one company all officers either were relieved or broke under the strain. A second battalion commander also was replaced. One platoon leader who refused to order his men back into the line was placed under arrest. Unless the regiment could find some way to break the impasse, heads higher up also might roll. Two days before, for example, the army commander had "made it quite clear" to General Stroh that he expected better results. [13]

Justified or not, the reliefs took place under extenuating circumstances imposed by the misery and incredible difficulty of the forest fighting. It was attrition unrelieved. Overcoats soaked with moisture and caked with freezing mud became too heavy for the men to wear. Seeping rain turned radios into useless impedimenta. So choked with debris was the floor of the forest that men broke under the sheer physical strain of moving supplies forward and evacuating the wounded. The fighting was at such close quarters that hand

[9] Combat Interv with Maj Joseph D. Johnston, 1st Bn, 121st Inf.

[10] Combat Interv with Maj R. W. Wiltsie, Exec O, 56th FA Bn.

[11] Annex 3 to 8th Div AAR, Nov 44.

[12] See Combat Interv with S Sgt Anthony Rizzo, Co G.

[13] Sylvan Diary, entry of 23 Nov 44.

grenades often were the decisive weapon. The mine fields seemed endless. A platoon could spend hours probing, searching, determining the pattern, only to discover after breaching one mine field that another just as extensive lay twenty-five yards ahead. Unwary men who sought cover from shellfire in ditches or abandoned foxholes might trip lethal booby traps and turn the promised sanctuary into an open grave. When a diabolical enemy planted booby traps underneath one seriously wounded soldier, the man lay motionless for seventy-two hours, driven almost insane in his efforts to maintain consciousness in order to warn whoever might come to his rescue.[14]

Added to all the other miseries was a constant reminder of the toll this bloody little plateau already had exacted. Because concern for the living had from the first taken precedence over respect for the dead, the swollen bodies of the fallen of three other regiments still lay about in grotesque positions. At the end of the fourth day of fighting on 24 November, the 121st Infantry had deposited fifty known dead of its own on the ground and incurred a total of about 600 battle casualties. Almost as many more men had fallen prey to the elements or to combat exhaustion.

By nightfall of 24 November, the 121st Infantry still had not gained the objective along the edge of the woods overlooking Huertgen. Unless some method could be devised for relieving the infantry of some of the offensive burden, there seemed to

be no immediate hope of gaining the objective. Particularly disturbing was the fact that the regiment's left wing had failed to advance far enough up the Weisser Weh valley to enable the attached armor to use the Weisser Weh road in preference to the exposed Germeter–Huertgen highway.

Despite the patent impossibility of committing the armor anywhere but along the perilous highway, a conference at 8th Division headquarters during the day ended in a decision to use the armor the next day as the only real hope for breaking what was beginning to look like a stalemate. The 8th Division commander, General Stroh, told the 5th Armored Division's CCR to move up the Germeter–Huertgen highway before daylight the next day, 25 November, and to strike at 0730 for Huertgen.

For his part, the CCR commander, Colonel Anderson, noted that more than the enemy's long-range observation on the Germeter–Huertgen highway stood in the way of his combat command's successful debouchment against Huertgen. Although a company of the 121st Infantry had reached the woods line on the east of the highway, the Germans still controlled several hundred yards of forest bordering on the west of the road, a logical hiding place for antitank guns or panzerfausts. So long as the Germans held there, engineers could not sweep that portion of the highway for mines. Besides that, a big bomb crater near the southern edge of the woods would have to be bridged before the tanks could get into position for their jump-off.

As the night deepened, the 121st Infantry and the 8th Division's organic engineers set out to put these matters right. At 0055, 25 November, the 8th

[14] A vivid, moving account of the Huertgen Forest fighting may be found in Paul Boesch, *Road to Huertgen: Forest in Hell* (Houston: Gulf Publishing Co., 1962). The author assumed command of Company G, 121st Infantry, at the height of the battle.

Division's assistant G–3 acted upon reports from the 121st Infantry to assure Colonel Anderson that both sides of the highway were clear as far as the woods line and that the engineers had swept the road for mines. Although the 8th Division recorded no specific message to the effect that the engineers had bridged the bomb crater, several recorded messages gave that impression. In any event, the 8th Division engineer personally assured the combat command that by daylight either the crater would be bridged or a path around it cleared. CCR got set to move.[15]

Just as day was breaking on 25 November the lead tanks of CCR's 10th Tank Battalion reached the crater. They found neither a path around it nor a bridge. A great, yawning chasm, the crater blocked all vehicular passage.

The commander of the first tank, 1st Lt. J. A. Macaulay, was not easily discouraged. "I'm going to try to jump the damned thing," he called back on his radio. Gathering speed, his tank roared up the muddy road. At the last moment, the driver applied one final burst of speed. It wasn't enough. The tank slammed into the far wall of the crater, rolled to the left, and lay disabled on one side.

The Germans obviously would not ignore the sound of all this activity along the road. Aided by increasing daylight, they began to plaster the road with mortar and artillery fire. Even though the 121st Infantry had reported the woods along the highway clear, small arms fire from the woods inflicted serious losses on CCR's armored infantry. In less than an

hour one of the infantry companies took over sixty casualties, including all platoon sergeants and platoon leaders.

Through the rest of the day men and commanders worked to get the armor moving. In a constant search for the enemy guns that were pounding the exposed highway, supporting artillery and tank destroyers poured over 15,000 rounds into enemy lines. A temporary break in overcast skies enabled three squadrons of the IX TAC's 366th Group to bomb and strafe suspected tank and artillery positions near Huertgen and along the Brandenberg–Bergstein ridge. Chemical mortars laid down smoke so that the engineers might try to bridge the big crater.

Aided by a slight lessening of hostile shellfire, the engineers finally got a bridge across the crater in midmorning. First to cross was a tank commanded by Sgt. William Hurley. The tank had proceeded along the road only seventy-five yards when it struck a mine. Disabled, the tank blocked passage as effectively as had the crater. Though a tank retriever moved up and nosed Sergeant Hurley's tank aside, a round from an enemy tank or antitank gun ripped into the retriever. Again the highway was blocked.

Though the armored infantry tried later to advance alone, this was in effect the end of CCR's abortive attempt to reach Huertgen on 25 November. Having lost some 150 men in an unfortunate experience, the combat command withdrew.

In the meantime, that part of Colonel Jeter's 121st Infantry that was west of the highway had been renewing the attempts to penetrate the forest. Though the infantry began to make toilsome but encouraging progress during the after-

---

[15] See 8th Div G–3 Jnl, 24–25 Nov, 8th Div Jnl file for 23–27 Nov 44, and Combat Intervs with CCR personnel, particularly Interv with Capt Frank M. Pool, 10th Tank Bn.

ENGINEERS REPAIR A ROAD *in the Huertgen Forest, 25 November.*

noon, the advances came too late to save Colonel Jeter his command. In mid-afternoon General Stroh relieved him. The 8th Division's Chief of Staff, Coi. Thomas J. Cross, assumed command of the regiment.[16]

The Fight for Huertgen

To the fatigued men of the 121st Infantry, the failure to shake the armor loose on 25 November meant another prolongation of their trials. No doubt impressed by the facility with which German guns in Huertgen could deal with armor, General Stroh directed that the infantry alone take Huertgen. Only

---

[16] Like the 12th Infantry's Colonel Luckett, Colonel Jeter retained his rank and was given command of a regiment in another division.

then, with firm control of the Germeter–Huertgen highway assured, would CCR's armor be committed in quest of the remaining objective, the village of Kleinhau.

The prospects of the infantry reaching the woods line and then taking Huertgen were not so dismal as a cursory look at the first five arduous days of fighting might indicate. Whereas the 121st Infantry's advances had been laborious, the regiment nevertheless had prodded the enemy from the more readily defensible lines in the forest. To the north, fairly consistent progress by the 4th Division had outflanked those Germans still in the woods along the left flank of the 121st Infantry. By juggling troops on the defensive fronts held by the 8th Division's other two regiments, General Stroh had freed the 1st Battalion, 13th Infantry, to assist in renewing the attack. He gave this battalion to Colonel Cross, the new 121st Infantry commander, who told the battalion commander, Lt. Col. Morris J. Keesee, to circle around through the forest into the 4th Division's zone and on 27 November to strike for Huertgen along the left flank of the 121st Infantry from the woods line northwest of the village.

On 26 November, while Colonel Keesee's battalion was shifting position, the 121st Infantry tried again to clear the Huertgen woods line. Even the most optimistic hardly could have predicted the ease with which the battalions advanced. The Germans had withdrawn from the woods. Only mines, sporadic shelling, and a few stragglers barred the way. By 1100 the 121st Infantry overlooked Huertgen from the west and southwest.

The 121st Infantry commander, Colonel Cross, ordered an immediate attack on Huertgen. A report from the Intelligence

and Reconnaissance Platoon of a neighboring regiment to the effect that the
Germans had abandoned the village
spurred the preparations.

Unfortunately, as men of the 121st
Infantry and Colonel Keesee's battalion
of the 13th Infantry soon discovered, the
report of withdrawal from Huertgen was
unfounded. The village that for more
than two months had lain so near and yet
so far still was not to be had at a bargain
price.

On 27 November tank destroyers took
position along the woods line to spew
covering fire into the village, and a platoon
of Sherman tanks joined the leading
infantry battalion. Artillery took quick
advantage of improved observation and in
one instance knocked out a German tank
with five hits, not a unique but a nonetheless noteworthy accomplishment for
guns laid indirectly.[17] By nightfall the
Germans still held the bulk of Huertgen's
shell-shattered buildings; but Colonel Keesee's battalion had severed the Huertgen–
Kleinhau highway and gained a toehold in
the northeastern edge of the village, while
a battalion of the 121st Infantry under
Lt. Col. Henry B. Kunzig wriggled into a
few buildings in the western edge.[18]

Bolstered by the *31st Machine Gun
Battalion,* one of several small units General Brandenberger's *Seventh Army* had
solicited from the inactive front farther
south, the enemy would make a fight of it
in Huertgen for still another day. Even
when Colonel Keesee's battalion at daybreak on 28 November seized Hill 401, a
strategic height a thousand yards northeast of Huertgen, commanding the village,

the Germans held on in Huertgen. They
folded only in the afternoon after Colonel
Kunzig's reserve company, riding medium
tanks of the 709th Tank Battalion, edged
onto the main street. Over 200 prisoners
had been rounded up when Colonel Cross
was able to announce about 1800 on 28
November that Huertgen was in hand.
Scores of other Germans lay buried amid
the debris that long weeks of war had
inflicted upon this little agricultural com-
munity. For a long time the village
would bear the terrible stench of war.

An Armored Drive on Kleinhau

About the time Huertgen fell, the 8th
Division commander, General Stroh, was
departing the division on a leave of absence. A veteran of the fighting since the
North African campaign, General Stroh
had seen his son shot down and killed
while flying a fighter-bomber in support of
the 8th Division at Brest. Higher commanders had deemed it time General Stroh
had a rest, with the proviso that he return
later to command another division. A
former assistant commander of the 90th
Division, Brig. Gen. William G. Weaver,
assumed command of the 8th.[19]

As one of his first official acts in his
new post, General Weaver directed the
attached CCR, 5th Armored Division, to
move to Huertgen. CCR was to attack
at dawn the next day, 29 November,
toward the 8th Division's next objective a
mile north of Huertgen, the village of
Kleinhau.

---

[17] V Corps Operations in the ETO, p. 319.
[18] The trials of the latter battalion are vividly
depicted in Boesch, *Road to Huertgen.*

[19] 8th Div AAR, Nov 44; Ltr, Weaver to
OCMH, 9 Apr 56, OCMH; Interv with General
Cross, 23 Aug 56; Sylvan Diary, entry of 27 Nov
44. See also Maj. Gen. William G. Weaver,
Yankee Doodle Went to Town (privately
printed, 1959).

TANK ATTACHED TO THE 8TH DIVISION *moves through Huertgen.*

To soften up the objective, 8th Division and V Corps artillery and IX TAC fighter-bombers co-operated closely during the afternoon of 28 November in an attack by fire against Kleinhau. The artillery first laid down an antiflak barrage which the fliers subsequently termed "very effective." [20] As the planes appeared, the artillery switched to red smoke to mark the target. Coming in at treetop level, P–38's of the 474th Group dropped sixty-three napalm fire bombs, some as close as 300 yards to friendly infantry.

[20] See Daily Summaries in IX TAC, Unit History, Nov 44.

Pilots ecstatically reported the objective "practically destroyed by flames." More reserved in their comments, ground observers nevertheless praised the accuracy of the strike. This joint air-artillery operation was a model of its kind, one of the more spectacular examples of the type of co-operation between air and ground arms that became increasingly effective as the fall campaign wore on.

At 0730 the next day, 29 November, a task force from CCR composed of two companies each of medium tanks and armored infantry under Lt. Col. William A. Hamberg, commander of the 10th

Tank Battalion, moved forward. Because prisoners had reported an antitank mine field between Huertgen and Kleinhau, Colonel Hamberg attacked first with dismounted infantry; but when German fire forced the infantry to cover, he had little choice but to throw his tanks into the assault echelon.

If the Germans actually had a mine field protecting Kleinhau, they had neglected to mine the road itself. Following closely in the tracks of a lead tank commanded by Capt. Francis J. Baum, the tankers plunged into the village. By 0900, only minutes after entering the fight, the Shermans were cruising in the center of Kleinhau.

A lone Mark IV tank in Kleinhau knocked out one Sherman before the Americans could eliminate it, and an SP gun in the woods east of the village scored one hit. Enemy shelling also made it difficult for infantry to accompany the tanks in mopping up. Not until early afternoon when the weather cleared and American planes appeared did the shellfire abate. "The mere presence of the planes caused a noticeable decrease in enemy artillery . . . ."[21] By midafternoon some fifty-five prisoners from diverse units were en route to PW enclosures. Kleinhau was clear.

Task Force Hamberg continued to receive fire from the neighboring village of Grosshau to the north. This the armor could do little about, because the 4th Division was to have assaulted Grosshau at the same time CCR hit Kleinhau. During the morning the 4th Division's attack had been delayed, so that Colonel Hamburg had obtained permission to fire on the village to silence antitank guns;

but by midafternoon the 4th Division's attack was on again. Grosshau again was out of bounds to fire from CCR.

In late afternoon, Colonel Hamberg pushed a small force beyond Kleinhau to establish two roadblocks, one on either side of a commanding eminence, Hill 401.3. The armor did not occupy the hill itself because—Colonel Anderson, the CCR commander, said later—the crest was "as flat as a billiard table" and the tanks could control it by fire.[22] Colonel Keesee's battalion of the 13th Infantry during the night relieved Task Force Hamberg.

For all the speed of the attack on Kleinhau, it was not without appreciable cost. In armor, Task Force Hamberg had lost 8 tanks—2 to high-velocity fire and 6 to mines; 13 half-tracks, most of which were recovered; and 1 tank destroyer. In personnel, the task force lost approximately 60 men, most of them victims of German shellfire.

The nine-day fight for Huertgen and Kleinhau had cost the 121st Infantry and the attached CCR and 1st Battalion, 13th Infantry, a total of approximately 1,247 casualties.[23] This was an awesome price to pay for a limited advance, but all who fought in the Huertgen Forest came to know that this was the kind of price that had to be paid. German casualties were at least equal and probably greater in view of the fact that the enemy lost 882 in prisoners alone.

A question existed as to whether this limited attack had, as intended, materi-

---

[21] CCR, 5th Armd Div, AAR, Nov 44.

[22] Combat Interv with Colonel Anderson.

[23] CCR: approximately 210 casualties of all types; 121st Infantry: 63 killed, 899 others; 1st Battalion, 13th Infantry: approximately 75 of all types. The last figure is an estimate based on figures for the entire 13th Infantry.

ally assisted advance of the VII Corps; but, even if the answer was negative, the fact was that control of Huertgen and Kleinhau marked an important contribution to subsequent operations. In driving northeastward on the Roer at Dueren, the 4th Division now could flaunt its tail at Kleinhau, something which heretofore would have been perilous. Possession of the two villages spelled control of a sizable segment of the only good road network between the Huertgen Forest and the Roer and represented in effect a "bridgehead" upon the Brandenberg–Bergstein ridge, the most commanding terrain in the vicinity. Capture of the ridge would enable the V Corps to gain the Roer—a little more than two miles from Huertgen—and at last provide the long-sought secure right flank for the main drive of the VII Corps. The Brandenberg–Bergstein ridge also was important to any drive that subsequently might be aimed at the Roer River Dams. Anyone familiar with the 28th Division's tragic attack for Schmidt could attest to that.

Broadening the Effort

It hardly could have come as a surprise when General Hodges late on 28 November directed a continuation of the V Corps offensive to take the Brandenberg–Bergstein ridge. Indeed, so obvious was the assignment that even before consultation with General Hodges the corps commander had told the 8th Division's new commander, General Weaver, to get started. CCR of the 5th Armored Division remained attached for the operation.[24]

---

[24] V Corps Ltrs of Instrs, 28 and 29 Nov 44, V Corps Operations in ETO, p. 320; FUSA Ltr of Instrs, 28 Nov 44. Although no copy of the FUSA order has been found, FUSA Rpt, Vol 1, p. 83, contains an adequate summary.

Attacking the Brandenberg–Bergstein ridge from Huertgen and Kleinhau was infinitely preferable to the other route of approach across the heavily wooded draw from Vossenack, but the preferred route had drawbacks nonetheless. The Kleinhau–Brandenberg highway, running southeast along the spine of the ridge, marks a narrow corridor between two woods. On the southwest the enemy still controlled the Tiefen Creek woods between the ridge and Vossenack. He also still held a stretch of woodland embracing the northeastern slopes of the ridge. Advancing down the highway from Kleinhau to Brandenberg would be like attacking down a fairway while the enemy controlled the rough on either side.

With explicit detail quite typical of most of his orders during the fall campaign, the V Corps commander, General Gerow, told General Weaver how to overcome the obstacle.[25] Using part of the 28th Infantry Regiment from Vossenack and a battalion of the 121st Infantry, General Weaver was to clear the Tiefen Creek woods as far east as a dip in the ridge line about halfway between Hill 401, already held by the 121st Infantry, and Brandenberg. At this point the main effort might be launched southeast from Hill 401 via the Kleinhau–Brandenberg highway.

The obvious answer to the question of which unit should make the main effort was the attached combat command, the 5th Armored Division's CCR. Of the 8th Division's remaining infantry, two battalions of the 13th Infantry were to maintain defensive positions in the Huertgen Forest southwest of Vossenack;

---

[25] V Corps Ltrs of Instrs, 28 and 29 Nov 44. See also 8th Div Fragmentary Orders, 29 Nov and 1 Dec, 8th Div AARs, Nov and Dec 44.

Colonel Keesee's battalion of the 13th Infantry was to continue to hold the division's north flank at Kleinhau; and those two battalions of the 121st Infantry not engaged in clearing the Tiefen Creek woods were to assist the armored drive by clearing the edges of the woods north of the dip. This latter task First Army's General Hodges made easier administratively by shifting the V Corps boundary temporarily in order to permit the V Corps to operate through almost all of the woods north and east of Brandenberg.[26]

Perhaps because the premature commitment of CCR toward Huertgen was fresh in mind, General Weaver insisted upon a healthy margin of safety before sending the armor down the fairway to Brandenberg. Before committing the armor, he intended to hold not only the Tiefen Creek woods as far east as the dip in the ridge line but also a comparable position in the woods on the other side of the route of attack.

In executing these precautions, infantrymen of both the 121st and 28th Infantry Regiments found in these offshoots of the Huertgen Forest the familiar pattern of stubborn German defense behind mine fields, barbed wire, and log emplacements for automatic weapons. Not until nightfall of 1 December was the infantry able to occupy the desired line. Even then a pocket of small arms resistance held out in a wooded gully just southwest of the dip.

Having regrouped after capturing Kleinhau, CCR's Task Force Hamberg launched the main effort down the road to Brandenberg shortly after dawn on 2 December. At the start it must have

seemed to the tankers and armored infantry that somebody had slipped them the same old script CCR had used in the fiasco on the Germeter–Huertgen road. No sooner had the tanks reached the dip in the ridge line between Hill 401 and Brandenberg than one of the lead tanks struck a mine. "Things not going worth a damn," reported the tank company commander.[27] A few minutes later this officer had even greater cause for concern. Two more tanks struck mines. Small arms and mortar fire, much of it from the uncleared gully near the dip, stymied the armored infantry. Long-range, highvelocity fire from the Kommerscheidt–Schmidt ridge to the south greeted every movement the tankers tried to make. Ironically, it had been the Brandenberg–Bergstein ridge which had posed serious problems for the 28th Division in the earlier attack against Kommerscheidt and Schmidt; now the situation was reversed. "Having hell of a fight," was the way CCR's S–3 put it. Tank losses soon had risen to four.

Not much time elapsed before the 8th Division commander, General Weaver, became convinced that Task Force Hamberg could do nothing until the mine field in the dip had been cleared. Considering the enemy's observation, that could not be done until after dark. Assuring Colonel Hamberg that the infantry battalions would clear the small arms opposition during the rest of the day, General Weaver told the tankers to seek defilade and prepare to renew the attack the next morning.

That night, as artillery of CCR, the 8th Division, and the V Corps executed a determined program of interdictory fires,

---

[26] FUSA Ltr of Instrs, 28 Nov 44.

[27] CCR, 5th Armd Div, S–3 Jnl, 2 Dec 44.

men of CCR's 22d Armored Engineers probed carefully, perilously, through the darkness for mines. By daylight of 3 December they had removed from the road and adjacent fields in the vicinity of the dip some 250 mines. Few veterans in Task Force Hamberg could recall ever having encountered a mine field so intricately patterned nor one so effectively blocking all passage. Even after the engineers had lifted this impressive total of mines, the task force was destined to lose two more tanks in the same mine field.

At 0800 on 3 December, two battalions of the 121st Infantry in the woods north of Brandenberg, another battalion of the 121st Infantry and all of the 28th Infantry in the Tiefen Creek–Vossenack area, and CCR in the dip resumed their respective roles in the attack. Of the infantry units, the two battalions in the woods north of Brandenberg made the readiest progress. Patrols probing northeast reached the corps boundary, almost a mile inside the woods east of Hill 401. At one point they found mute testimony to the effectiveness of American artillery fire in "a mass" of dead enemy, dead horses, and abandoned vehicles.[28] In the meantime, progress in the Tiefen Creek woods was spotty. Aided by medium tanks of the 709th Tank Battalion that somehow negotiated the muddy trails and firebreaks, one battalion gained positions on a nose of the Brandenberg–Bergstein ridge southwest of Brandenberg, but other units could make scarcely any advance in the face of stubborn German strongpoints.

In the main effort by Task Force Hamberg along the spine of the Brandenberg–Bergstein ridge, the decision to

postpone the attack until 3 December proved a happy one. For the first time in several days, the weatherman smiled early and benignly. As supporting artillery completed a ten-minute preparation, P–47's of the 366th Group circled the area. A controller with a very high frequency (VHF) radio mounted in a tank at headquarters of Task Force Hamberg "talked" the pilots onto the target, the village of Brandenberg. "Keep the buzz boys up," was the reaction of the leading tank company commander, "they are doing a good job." Maintaining close contact with the planes through the ground controller, the task force with infantry mounted in half-tracks began to roll. Even after reaching the very threshold of the village, the leading company commander was loath to relinquish his air support. "Keep the buzz boys up," he cried again. "We are at a critical stage." Six minutes later (at 0926) the first tanks and infantry entered Brandenberg. As soon as tank guns had blasted the buildings, the infantry boiled down into the cellars with rifles, tommy guns, and hand grenades to root out a cowed enemy. At 1115 Colonel Hamberg could report the village in American hands.[29]

Apparently carried away by the momentum of the attack, a platoon leader in charge of three tanks, Lt. George Kleinsteiber, roared all the way past the objective across the less than half a mile into Bergstein. Quickly knocking out two antitank guns, Lieutenant Kleinsteiber and his companions might well have seized the entire village had not Colonel

---

[28] 121st Inf AAR, Dec 44.

[29] For direct quotations, see CCR, 5th Armd Div, S–3 Jnl, 3 Dec 44. The 366th Group erroneously reported its attack against Bergstein rather than Brandenberg. See IX TAC, Unit History, Dec 44.

Hamberg called them back. Although Colonel Hamberg himself originally had recommended that Brandenberg and Bergstein be taken in a single operation, he had come to recognize that his task force had not the strength to hold both villages. Task Force Hamberg was far understrength by this time, and all other elements of the 8th Division and attachments, including CCR's other task force, were occupied elsewhere. Not until some other unit could be freed to defend Bergstein was it wise to take that village.

As if to emphasize the capriciousness for which the weather had become noted during the Siegfried Line Campaign, the weatherman withdrew his support soon after Task Force Hamberg had taken Brandenberg. Though the weather remained favorable in the Huertgen Forest area, it began to close in at the air bases farther west in Belgium. The P-47's had to scurry home.

This situation gave rise to one of the few noteworthy interventions by the Luftwaffe since the ground campaign along the German border had begun. Starting in early afternoon, about sixty Messerschmitt 109's roared in over the V Corps sector. Strafing front-line troops and bombing and strafing artillery and rear-echelon installations as far back as the V Corps headquarters city of Eupen, the planes were active for more than an hour. It was a new experience for most of the American troops, for even the most seasoned rarely had seen more than one to three German planes at a time. "Send up some more .50-cal ammo," an officer of CCR radioed back from Brandenberg; "have knocked down 3 Me 109's and there are still plenty to shoot at." [30]

That appeared to be the spirit with which most V Corps troops accepted the Luftwaffe's venture. For the first time in months antiaircraft units got an opportunity to do what they were trained to do. The corps subsequently claimed 19 of the enemy aircraft destroyed and 10 others probably destroyed. The antiaircraft unit attached to the 8th Division claimed 8 of the definites. As for the effectiveness of the enemy strike, it was not the kind of thing to sell anybody on the value of air power. Hardly any matériel damage resulted, and not a single unit reported a man killed or wounded. [31]

The enemy's air strike over, Task Force Hamberg settled down for the defense of Brandenberg—somewhat unhappily, for Colonel Hamberg was perturbed both about his lack of strength and about dominant German observation on the village. At Bergstein and on the Kommerscheidt-Schmidt ridge the Germans were on higher ground; in particular Colonel Hamberg was conscious of enemy observation from Castle Hill (the *Burg-Berg*, Hill 400.5), a conical eminence a few hundred yards outside Bergstein that rises like a giant pimple at the eastern end of the Brandenberg-Bergstein ridge. Enemy shelling directed from some or all of these places pointed up the depleted condition of Colonel Hamberg's command and the need for additional troops before attacking Bergstein and Castle Hill. Although the attack on Brandenberg had not been particularly costly in itself, the cumulative losses since the armor's first action in this sector on 25 November had reduced the task force markedly. In Brandenberg

---

[30] CCR, 5th Armd Div, S-3 Jnl, 3 Dec 44.

[31] V Corps Operations in the ETO, p. 322; 8th Div AAR, Dec 44; IX TAC, Unit History, Dec 44.

were only eleven tanks, five tank destroyers, and 140 infantrymen.

Officers of the combat command chafed in their desire to get CCR's other task force into Brandenberg. Led by Lt. Col. Howard E. Boyer, commander of the 47th Armored Infantry Battalion, basic components of this second and smaller task force were a company each of tanks and armored infantry. The 8th Division commander, General Weaver, had attached Task Force Boyer to the 28th Infantry Regiment in Vossenack for a special operation. The armor was to eliminate a German strongpoint located amid the debris of the northeasternmost houses of Vossenack, a strongpoint that had withstood infantry attempts at reduction. The position had become known as the "rubble pile." It had fallen into German hands during latter stages of the 28th Division's Schmidt operation after the tragic experience of an infantry battalion exposed to guns on the Brandenberg–Bergstein ridge had prompted abandonment of the more exposed portion of the Vossenack ridge.

So expertly had the Germans organized the "rubble pile," so thickly had they fenced it with mines, and so deeply had they burrowed into the debris that Task Force Boyer fought all day on 3 December and well into the next day before overrunning the position. In the meantime, the 8th Division commander had no other unit to send to Brandenberg, either to strengthen Task Force Hamberg or to attack Bergstein. So concerned was General Weaver about his lack of a reserve that he petitioned General Gerow for use of the 2d Ranger Battalion, a special unit which had been backing up the line in this sector for about a week under V Corps control. General Gerow himself earlier

had noted the complete involvement of the 8th Division and had taken care to provide a corps reserve by moving an infantry regiment to back up the line a few miles to the south opposite the Monschau Corridor.[32] Although General Weaver might have used his organic engineer battalion as a reserve, he had become so perturbed over the depleted condition of some of his infantry battalions that he already had put the engineers into the line in the woods north of Brandenberg to bolster the infantry.

Having fought almost continuously for thirteen days since 21 November, the 121st Infantry was particularly feeble. Although this regiment had received several score of replacements, these men for all their individual courage hardly were equivalent to the veterans who had fallen. The conditions of cold, rain, and close contact with the enemy under which these men were introduced to front-line warfare made matters worse. "Our missing men were mostly replacements," the 121st Infantry's sergeant major commented later. "Some were captured before they could get into action." Heavy shellfire, this same noncommissioned officer remarked, caused some of the new men to "scatter and run." [33]

Trench foot and combat fatigue hit veteran and replacement alike. Because few men had a chance to dry out, little could be done to reduce instances of trench foot. Severe cases of combat fatigue had to be evacuated through regular medical channels, but others merely

---

[32] The 9th Division's 60th Infantry. See V Corps Directive, 30 Nov 44, V Corps Operations in the ETO, p. 320.

[33] Combat Interv with M Sgt Willard Bryan, 121st Inf.

A SEA OF MUD *in the Huertgen Forest.*

retired to a rest tent in Huertgen. There they were given "coffee, a shot of whiskey, and some sleeping pills. After a day or two of rest and warm food, they went back." For one of the few times in the history of the 121st Infantry, some men refused to stay in the line. "We have found," said the sergeant major, "that old men break down under this weather. When we see they are about to crack we bring a lot of them back to do overhead work and thus keep down court martial cases of this type and also crack-ups." [34]

_____
[34] *Ibid.*

Nevertheless, the regiment soon had eleven men awaiting trial.

This was how a regimental staff officer saw the plight of one battalion:

The men of this battalion are physically exhausted. The spirit and the will to fight are there; the physical ability to continue is gone. These men have been fighting without rest or sleep for four days and last night were forced to lie unprotected from the weather in an open field. In some instances men were forced to discard their overcoats because they lacked the strength to wear them. These men are shivering with cold and their hands are so numb that they have to help one another on with their equipment. I firmly believe that every man up there should be evacuated through medical channels.[35]

To men in this condition, there obviously was scant consolation in the knowledge that German troops were undergoing similar hardships. "Great losses were occasioned by numerous frostbites," one German officer recalled later. "In some cases, soldiers were found dead in their foxholes from sheer exhaustion." [36]

Bergstein and Castle Hill

Unable to reinforce Task Force Hamberg on 4 December, General Weaver delayed attacking Bergstein until the next day, when Task Force Boyer should be available after having cleared the "rubble pile." In the interval, he concentrated on pushing his infantry farther east and southeast through the woods on either side of the Brandenberg–Bergstein ridge in order to provide flank protection for the projected armored thrust.

Not all the infantry battalions were so bitterly fatigued or so woefully depleted as that described by the staff officer of the 121st Infantry, but they were a far cry from the formations which first had entered the Huertgen Forest a fortnight before. On 4 December a sleet storm that carried over from the preceding night added to the discomforts. By nightfall the infantry still had a long way to go before providing secure flanks for an armored drive on Bergstein.

In the woods north of Brandenberg, Colonel Keesee's 1st Battalion, 13th In-

fantry, moving east from Kleinhau, and a battalion of the 121st Infantry pushed deep into the forest to gain the corps boundary in the wake of patrols that had reached that line the day before. Another battalion of the 121st Infantry, trying to drive eastward to seal off Bergstein from the north by occupying wooded noses of high ground overlooking the Roer River, made virtually no progress. As night came this battalion still sat in the woods north of Brandenberg, in no spot to assist a drive on Bergstein and so perilously understrength that the regimental commander strove to ready another battalion to take its place.

In the Tiefen Creek woods between Vossenack and Brandenberg–Bergstein the going was equally slow. Nevertheless, by nightfall of 4 December, a battalion of the 28th Infantry had gained a road that winds from the Kall River gorge to Brandenberg from which fire could control an exposed nose southwest of Bergstein. Thus a measure of assistance could be provided from this quarter for the next day's armored drive.

No matter what the shortcomings on 4 December, General Weaver scarcely could afford to delay longer before assaulting Bergstein. Though he sanctioned a late attack hour (1400) in hope the weather might clear sufficiently to permit air support, he insisted that whether the skies cleared or not, CCR was to attack on 5 December. CCR would more than welcome air support; for, even with the addition of Task Force Boyer, the combat command had only twenty-two medium tanks and some 200 armored infantrymen.

Though the weather did improve, CCR failed to get the kind of closely coordinated air support which Task Force Hamberg had enjoyed during the attack

[35] Remarks of the 121st Inf S-3 as taken down by S Sgt Carlton R. Brown and recorded in Combat Interv with Brown. See also Personal Diary of Maj Gen Thomas J. Cross, pp. 154–56, loaned to OCMH by General Cross.
[36] MS # A-892 (Gersdorff).

Veterans of the Huertgen Forest

on Brandenberg. The difficulty appeared to lie in misunderstandings between CCR's controller and the air officer at 8th Division headquarters as to who was responsible for directing the strike.

"STANZA screwed it up," the CCR controller said at 1415, referring to the Air Force code name for the 8th Division.[37] "[He] told planes Bergstein [was] ours and sent them to Nideggen. [I] got them back and put them on wooded hill east of town and southeast part of town . . . ."[38]

Fifteen minutes later the CCR controller was thoroughly piqued. "FOXHUNT here," he said, referring to the 366th Fighter Group. "Hard to work [the] planes—STANZA constantly interferes . . . . Finally got FOXHUNT to bomb and strafe . . . southeast of Bergstein. Between weather, STANZA, and questions from turret, am tearing [my] hair."[39]

CCR evidently could thank a clever attack plan and an apparent breakdown in enemy communications for offsetting the deficiencies in air support. Having placed assault guns in defilade northeast of Brandenberg to provide covering fire, the combat command divided into three attacking forces, each composed of married companies of tanks and armored infantry. One delivered a long left hook against the northeastern fringe of Bergstein; another delivered a right hook against the southwestern fringe; and the third struck down the middle. In a matter of minutes the force in the middle had penetrated the edge of the village. Not until this force had reached the objective did German shellfire begin to fall and then apparently in response to a series of signal flares.

Again CCR's controller was in a state. "FOXHUNT bombing," he reported at 1437. "STANZA put them on [the] town while I was trying to tell them our troops [are] there. Finally got them off and back on the enemy." An hour later the controller had another scare. "Nearly frantic," he radioed. "STANZA nearly had Bergstein bombed."[40]

CCR's tankers and armored infantrymen in Bergstein hardly could have been aware of these near mix-ups, so occupied were they with their own problems. What the enemy's artillery fires lacked in timing, they made up in intensity. And the German infantry was not going to relinquish the objective without a fight. Not until nightfall was the bulk of Bergstein in hand. Even then snipers and small pockets of resistance held out.

As CCR prepared to defend the village, few considered the objective secure. Towering menacingly on the eastern fringe of the village, Castle Hill (Hill 400.5) in itself was enough to discourage a sense of security. In addition, Bergstein was exposed to counterattack from almost every side. Only at one point, where a battalion of the 28th Infantry was covering the exposed nose southwest of Bergstein, was there physical contact with friendly forces. To the north, where CCR had reason to expect protection, not even patrol contact existed. A battalion of the 121st Infantry, which was to have pushed through the woods to reach the Roer and seal off Bergstein from the north, had gained but 400 yards

---

[37] Air and ground headquarters had different code names for the same units. The ground force code name for the 8th Division, for example, was GRANITE.

[38] CCR, 5th Armd Div, S-3 Air Jnl, 5 Dec, S-3 Jnl file, Dec 44.

[39] Ibid.

[40] Ibid.

during the day. That was not nearly enough to do the job.

Although the enemy had been markedly parsimonious with his counterattacks up to this point, few could expect that he would let Bergstein and the Brandenberg–Bergstein ridge go without at least a token attempt to retake it. Not a man to endorse the use of armor in a defensive role under hardly any circumstances, the CCR commander, Colonel Anderson, looked with particular antipathy upon the situation in which he now found his command.[41] Not only was he concerned about the exposed nature of his position but also about the number of men and tanks he had to defend it with. By combing every source—including his organic engineers and reconnaissance platoon—he was able finally to assemble about 400 men, including crewmen of six remaining tank destroyers and sixteen tanks. For defending an exposed position, that left little margin for comfort.

Colonel Anderson may well have been concerned. German commanders considered CCR's penetration of "critical importance." Should the Americans reach and cross the Roer River at this point, they reasoned, it would "jeopardize the execution of the Ardennes offensive."[42]

On the basis of this thinking, the *Seventh Army's* General Brandenberger already had resorted to committing the remnants of the *47th Volks Grenadier Division* on 29 November in a switch position along the threatened Roer sector northeast of the Brandenberg–Bergstein ridge. He now turned to the only nearby

unit that had sufficient strength to afford any real promise of a successful counterattack. This was the *272d Volks Grenadier Division* (Col. Eugen Kossmala), holding a quiet sector in the Monschau Corridor while awaiting an assignment in the counteroffensive. Reluctantly, for all concerned shuddered with the realization that heavy casualties at this late date would seriously hamper the effectiveness of the division in the Ardennes, *OB WEST* gave permission, but with the proviso that the division be released in time to regroup for the Ardennes. Two-thirds of the *272d Volks Grenadier Division* started marching toward the threatened sector, while the remainder continued to hold the Monschau Corridor.[43]

At 0710 on the morning of 6 December first arrivals of the *272d Volks Grenadier Division* counterattacked at Bergstein. Supported by at least five tanks or assault guns—all the *Seventh Army* could provide—some 200 to 300 men of the *980th Regiment* took advantage of early morning haze and darkness to get almost upon the village before discovery.

The fight raged not on the approaches to Bergstein but amid the debris and the few remaining buildings. German infantry stalked the American tanks with Panzerfausts while CCR's gunners tried desperately to locate the German armor in the darkness. Even when they managed to pin their sights on the enemy vehicles, CCR's tankers had trouble. Most of the

---

[41] See CCR, 5th Armd Div, S–3 Jnl, 6 Dec 44, and Combat Interv with Anderson. An earlier indication of this attitude may be found in CCR and 5th Armored Division journals for the Wallendorf fight. See Ch. III, above.

[42] MS # A–891 (Gersdorff).

[43] *Ibid.* See also Charles V. P. von Luttichau, The Ardennes Offensive, Progressive Build-up and Operations, MS in OCMH; MSS # B–602, Generalleutnant Max Bork, *Die 47. Volksgrenadierdivision* (*V.G.D.*) *im Westen;* B–171, Generalmajor Eugen Koenig, *Kaempfe im Rheinland.* (This latter MS covers the battles of the *344th Volks Grenadier Division,* formerly the *91st Air Landing Division.* General Koenig later commanded the *272d Volks Grenadier Division.*)

remaining American tanks were armed with 75-mm. instead of 76-mm. guns; rounds from the 75's "bounced off." [44]

Fifteen more minutes of darkness, some participants ventured later, might have done the Americans in. [45] With the coming of daylight, those few American tanks equipped with the more powerful 76-mm. guns made quick work of the enemy armor. As the German infantry fell back, artillery fires requisitioned from both the 8th Division and the V Corps pummeled the retreat. By 0900 CCR again was in control of Bergstein.

Halting of this counterthrust meant no day of serenity in Bergstein. Possessed of observation from Castle Hill (400.5), the enemy's big guns chewed viciously at the village. Twice more during the day contingents of the *272d Volks Grenadier Division* came out of the woods and counterattacked. Fortunately, they made these sorties only in company strength. CCR beat them back.

As night approached on 6 December, CCR was without question too weak to defend Bergstein with any degree of assurance. In medium tanks, for example, the combat command was down to seven. Had the two adjacent infantry regiments made any real progress toward clearing the woods north and south of Bergstein, that might have compensated somewhat for the day's losses in men and armor. Yet neither regiment had gained substantially, although a battalion of the 121st Infantry after nightfall at last was to reach a point overlooking the Roer north of Bergstein and thereby provide some protection from that quarter.

To the V Corps, the 8th Division commander, General Weaver, appealed for aid. Again he had absolutely no unit with which to reinforce CCR, either for defending Bergstein or for seizing Castle Hill. He asked permission to use the 2d Ranger Battalion, that force which was present in the 8th Division's zone but which still was under V Corps control. Cognizant of the importance of Castle Hill both to defense of Bergstein and to accomplishment of the 8th Division's mission of reaching the Roer, both General Gerow and First Army's General Hodges approved the request. General Weaver promptly set about to commit the Rangers at Bergstein before daylight on 7 December.

The 2d Ranger Battalion was a special assault force, organized originally to perform especially hazardous and arduous tasks. The first of these had been to seize a dominating cliff on a flank of OMAHA Beach on D Day in Normandy. [46] Composed of about six companies of sixty-five men each, the battalion still had many of its original members. Its commander was Maj. George S. Williams. [47]

Probably no news short of rotation to the United States could have cheered the men of CCR more than did the word that the Rangers were coming. This was how three officers of the 47th Armored Infantry Battalion described it:

About midnight a guy came down the road, then two others, each one five yards

---

[44] Combat Interv with Maj W. M. Daniel, Exec O, 10th Tank Bn.

[45] Combat Interv with Lts Lewis, Stutsman, and Goldman, 47th Armd Inf Bn.

[46] See "Pointe du Hoe," in *Small Unit Actions,* AMERICAN FORCES IN ACTION (Washington, 1946).

[47] Even as the Rangers prepared to move to Bergstein, their original commander, Lt. Col. James E. Rudder, was relieved to assume command of a regiment in the 28th Division. The story of the 2d Ranger Bn in this action is from the unit AAR, Dec 44, and from a Combat Interv with Williams.

behind the other. They were three Ranger lieutenants. They asked for enemy positions and the road to take; said they were ready to go. We talked the situation over with the officers. They stepped out and said, 'Let's go men.' We heard the tommy guns click and, without a word, the Rangers moved out. Our morale went up in a hurry.[48]

In addition to seizing Castle Hill, Major Williams' Rangers were to strengthen the defense of Bergstein by establishing roadblocks on three noses of the ridge, southwest, south, and southeast of the village. Reinforced by two platoons of self-propelled guns from the 893d Tank Destroyer Battalion, three companies of the 2d Ranger Battalion had established these roadblocks two hours before daylight on 7 December. Because a battalion of the 121st Infantry by this time protected Bergstein on the north, this meant that the village was relatively secure on all sides except the east. In that direction lay Castle Hill.

Designating one company to support the attack by fire, Major Williams sent his two remaining companies charging up the height just as dawn was breaking. So swiftly did the Rangers move that the Germans were thoroughly cowed, even though these were respectable troops of the *272d Volks Grenadier Division*. By 0835 the two companies had taken twenty-eight prisoners and held the crest.

That was when the real fight began. Before the Rangers could dig in, a hail of enemy shellfire descended. Because the hill was predominantly wooded, bursts in the trees heightened effect of the fire. All morning the enemy kept up the shelling, so that by noon the two Ranger companies

were perilously depleted. They could muster only thirty-two men between them.

In the afternoon the Germans counterattacked twice, each time with about 150 men, and maintained constant pressure. By 1600 the Rangers had only twenty-five men left. Although Major Williams dispatched an urgent message to General Weaver for reinforcements, he must have known that his only real hope lay in those of his own men still in Bergstein. He scraped together a platoon and sent them scurrying up the hill. The help arrived at precisely the right moment. The Germans fell back.

The explanation for the seeming paradox of one platoon turning the tide against a superior enemy force lay, Major Williams said, in the artillery support he had received. The Rangers got that support primarily through one man, 1st Lt. Howard K. Kettlehut, a forward observer from CCR's 56th Armored Field Artillery Battalion. The Rangers said Lieutenant Kettlehut was "the best man they ever worked with." At one point this officer requested simultaneous support from almost every caliber of artillery in the American arsenal up to 8-inch and 240-mm. guns, a total of eighteen battalions. Lieutenant Kettlehut directed this fire not only to keep the Germans out of the hilltop positions but also to hem them in so that the infantry could destroy them with small arms and mortar fire. The key to his men's resistance, Major Williams said, was artillery.

So certain was General Weaver that the back of the opposition in this sector had been broken that he ordered the remnants of CCR to withdraw from Bergstein during the night of 7 December. In the meantime, the 28th Infantry had renewed attempts to clear the woods south of

---

[48] Combat Interv with Lewis, Stutsman, and Goldman.

Bergstein and had advanced almost to the southern exit of the village. No longer were the troops in Bergstein exposed to enemy fangs on any side.

By nightfall of 8 December, General Weaver had adjusted his lines in order to free a battalion of the 13th Infantry. This battalion went up Castle Hill, and the Rangers came down. The engagement had been but a two-day fight for the 2d Ranger Battalion, yet it had made up in intensity what it lacked in duration. The Rangers had lost more than a fourth of their original strength—107 men wounded, 19 killed, and 4 missing.

Anyone who stood atop Castle Hill and looked south could have predicted with a fair amount of certainty the direction of the next effort by troops of the V Corps. For from Castle Hill, one can see Schmidt, and beyond Schmidt, the waters of the Roer backed up behind the Roer River Dams. After a day or so of skirmishing the 8th Division would be overlooking the west bank of the Roer in the little angle formed by the Kall River and the Roer. Much farther to the north, troops of the Ninth Army earlier had closed to the river, and First Army's VII Corps could not be denied much longer. Unless those dams could be breached from the air, somebody would have to take them in a ground attack. That somebody obviously would be the V Corps.

"You can say," said one officer of the 8th Division, "that we got to the Roer River by sheer guts." [49] A look at the casualty figures would bear him out. Total losses for the 8th Division, the 5th Armored Division's CCR, and the 2d Ranger Battalion were nearly 4,000, including approximately 1,200 felled by exposure or combat exhaustion. The 8th Division (and its attachments) would go down in the book as another victim of the Huertgen Forest.

---

[49] Combat Interv with Johnston.

CHAPTER XX

The Final Fight To Break Out of the Forest

Take a "giant step," First Army's General Hodges had said in effect at the start of the November offensive. By 19 November, the day when Hodges directed commitment of the V Corps, results of the first four days of fighting had indicated that a giant step was not in the books. Certainly not for the moment. (*See Map VI.*)

A regiment of the 104th Division on the VII Corps north wing had had a whale of a fight to capture dominating heights of the Donnerberg and the Eschweiler woods east and northeast of Stolberg. At the same time a neighboring attack for a limited objective by a combat command of the 3d Armored Division had proved as costly as many a more ambitious armored attack. In the sector of the 1st Division, which was making the corps main effort, getting a toehold on the Hamich ridge and carving out a segment of the Huertgen Forest near Schevenhuette had been laborious tasks. On the corps south wing between the 1st Division at Schevenhuette and the V Corps near Huertgen, the 4th Division still was ensnared in the coils of the forest.

The 4th Division stood to benefit most directly from General Hodges' order to the V Corps to join the offensive. General Barton would gain both additional troops and a narrowed sector. The 12th Infantry, which had fought so long and so futilely on the bloody plateau near Germeter, at last was to join its parent division, and the shift northward of the intercorps boundary removed both Huertgen and Kleinhau from 4th Division responsibility.

No lengthy wait would be necessary before measuring the effects of the V Corps commitment upon the 4th Division's fight. Having paused to consolidate the limited gains of the first four days, General Barton had ordered renewal of the attack on 22 November, the day after the start of the V Corps offensive.[1]

The Fruits of Deception

Despite alarming casualties, neither assault regiment of the 4th Division before 22 November had penetrated much more than a mile beyond north-south Road W, which follows the Weisser Weh and Weh Creeks and marks the approximate center of the Huertgen Forest. On the north wing, Colonel McKee's 8th Infantry between axial routes U and V still was a thousand yards short of its first objective, forested high ground about the ruined monastery at Gut Schwarzenbroich. Troubled by a right flank dangling naked in the forest, Colonel Lanham's 22d Infantry had progressed little beyond the intersection of axial

[1] Unless otherwise noted, sources for the 4th Division action are as given in Chapter XVIII, above.

routes X and Y, still more than a mile away from the objective of Grosshau. To many, the final division objective of the Roer River at Dueren, not quite six miles to the northeast, must have seemed as far away as Berlin.

On the more positive side, a day or so of consolidation had temporarily eased two of the more serious problems the 4th Division faced. First, both regiments now had vehicular supply routes reaching within a few hundred yards of the front. Second, a gap more than a mile wide between the two regiments had been closed.

Had General Barton believed that these two problems would not recur and had he been fighting an inanimate enemy incapable of reinforcements or other countermeasures, he might even have entertained genuine optimism. As it was, mud, mines, enemy infiltration, and shelling again might compound the supply situation; and so long as the 22d Infantry drove east on Grosshau while the 8th Infantry moved northeast more directly toward Dueren, a gap between the two regiments would reappear and expand.

As for the enemy, it was true that the *275th Division* had incurred crippling losses, as had the *116th Panzer Division's 156th Panzer Grenadier Regiment,* a skeleton masquerading as the same regiment which had fought earlier near Germeter and Vossenack.[2] But by 21 November, the eve of the renewal of the American attack, the last contingents of the *344th Infantry Division* which the *Seventh Army* had summoned up from the south were arriving. As this division took over, the *116th Panzer Division* was pulled out for refitting, and the new division began absorbing nonorganic survivors of the

275th Division. Thus the Americans at this point faced a completely new German unit.[3]

The closeness of opposing lines and the density of the forest having denied unqualified use of air, armor, and artillery support, both commanders of the 4th Division's assault regiments in their attacks of 22 November turned to deception. Both Colonel McKee and Colonel Lanham directed one battalion to make a feint to the east with every weapon available, including smoke. At the same time, another battalion of each regiment was to make a genuine attack through the woods off a flank of each demonstrating battalion.

The Germans reacted exactly as desired. Upon the demonstrators, who were relatively secure in foxholes topped by logs and sod, they poured round after round of artillery and mortar fire. Against the battalions which were slipping through the woods, they fired hardly a shot.

On the north wing, the flanking battalion of the 8th Infantry swept through a thousand yards of forest to reach Gut Schwarzenbroich. Only there, in a cluster of buildings about the ruined monastery, did the Germans resist in strength. While this fight progressed, Colonel McKee poured his reserve battalion in behind the main enemy positions opposite his demonstrating battalion. Although the Germans soon deciphered this maneuver and opposed later stages of the advance, the fact that they had been lured from their prepared positions meant that the ruse had succeeded. As night came

---

[2] 4th Div Opns Rpt, Nov 44.

[3] MSS # A-891 (Gersdorff), # B-810 (Schmidt), and ETHINT-57 (Gersdorff). The 4th Division G-2 identified the *344th Division* by its old name, the *91st Air Landing Division.*

Colonel McKee's reserve battalion dug in securely about a triangle of roads at the intersection of Road U and the Renn Weg (Point 311.1). From here Colonel McKee might exploit both northeast along Road U and southeast along the Renn Weg.

In one respect the fruits of deception in the sector of Colonel Lanham's 22d Infantry west of Grosshau were even more rewarding. While a battalion on the regiment's north wing demonstrated, the battalion stealing around the enemy's flank met not a suggestion of opposition. Alongside a creek and then along firebreaks, the battalion slipped like a phantom through the thick forest. More than a mile the men marched without encountering a German and at nightfall dug in to cover the junction of Roads V and X near the edge of the forest no more than 700 yards west of Grosshau.

Colonel Lanham's reluctance to order this battalion alone and unsupported out of the woods into Grosshau may have stemmed from experience elsewhere in his sector. The enemy remained in strength astride the 22d Infantry's route of communications, as Colonel Lanham's right wing battalion had found while trying to protect the regimental southern flank. Only after incurring the kind of casualties that had come to be associated with fighting in the forest did this battalion succeed in gaining 900 yards to reach a junction of firebreaks between Roads X and Y, still a thousand yards short of the eastern fringe of the forest. The battalion was so understrength and so disorganized from losses among officers and noncommissioned officers that at one point Colonel Lanham had to plug a gap in the line with a composite company of 100 replacements.

The problems to be solved before Grosshau might be attacked were serious. Though the 12th Infantry had left the wooded plateau near Germeter on 22 November to begin an attack to secure the 22d Infantry's right flank, this depleted regiment would require several days to do the job. It took, in fact, four days, until 26 November. In the meantime, the 22d Infantry was open to a punishing blow from those Germans who at this point still held Huertgen and Kleinhau. Neither was there a quick solution to eliminating the enemy that had been by-passed in the swift advance or to sweeping Road X of mines and abatis so that an attack on Grosshau might be supported.

On 25 November, the day before the 12th Infantry reached the woods line to provide the 22d Infantry a secure flank, Colonel Lanham saw a chance to capitalize on the commitment that day of the 5th Armored Division's CCR against Huertgen. In conjunction with that attack, he ordered an immediate attempt to capture Grosshau.

Seeking surprise, Colonel Lanham maneuvered one battalion through the woods to hit the village from the northwest while another battalion converged on it from the southwest. The plan did not work. Delayed four hours while tanks and tank destroyers picked a way over muddy trails and firebreaks, the attack lost every vestige of surprise. When the jump-off actually came at noon, coordination with the armor failed. Only three tanks and a tank destroyer emerged from the woods with the infantry. Antitank gunners in Grosshau quickly picked off the tanks. At the same time violent concentrations of artillery fire drove the infantry back. Men who had yearned for so long to escape the stifling embrace of the forest now fell back on it for refuge.

The sad results of this attack prompted the division commander, General Barton, to approve another pause in the 22d Infantry's operations. Colonel Lanham was to consolidate his positions, bring up replacements, and make detailed plans for taking Grosshau. In particular, the regiment was to make maximum use of nine battalions of artillery which were either organic or attached to the division. Here on the edge of the forest the artillery for the first time might provide observed, close-in fires capable of influencing the fighting directly and decisively.

In the meantime, on the division's north wing, Colonel McKee's 8th Infantry on the second and third days of the renewed attack had come to know the true measure of the advantage the regiment had scored. The battalion which on 22 November had reached the junction of Road U and the Renn Weg drove northeast along Road U for more than a mile. Although subjected to considerable shelling, this battalion encountered only disorganized infantry resistance. On 24 November Colonel McKee sent this battalion northward to fill out the line between Road U and the division's north boundary and at the same time to cut behind those Germans who still were making a fight of it at Gut Schwarzenbroich. During the same two days, another battalion moved slowly against more determined resistance southeast along the Renn Weg and on 25 November surged to the regiment's south boundary. The total advance was more than a mile.

Colonel McKee's 8th Infantry stood on the brink of a breakthrough that could prove decisive. In four days, the regiment had more than doubled the distance gained during the first six days of the November offensive. The forward positions were almost two miles beyond the line of departure along Road W. Only just over a mile of forest remained to be conquered.

Yet how to achieve the last mile? The troops were exhausted. Because the leaders had to move about to encourage and look after their men, they had been among the first to fall. A constant stream of replacements had kept the battalions at a reasonable strength, but the new men had not the ability of those they replaced. For all the tireless efforts of engineers and mine sweepers, great stretches of the roads and trails still were infested with mines. Even routes declared clear might cause trouble. Along a reputedly cleared route, Company K on 23 November lost its Thanksgiving dinner when a kitchen jeep struck a mine. Every day since 20 November had brought some measure of sleet or rain to augment the mud on the floor of the forest. To get supplies forward and casualties rearward, men sludged at least a mile under constant threat from shells that burst unannounced in the treetops and from bypassed enemy troops who might materialize at any moment from the depths of the woods. Again a gap had grown between the 8th Infantry and the 22d Infantry. The gap was a mile and a quarter wide.

With the failure of the 22d Infantry at Grosshau on 25 November, the 4th Division commander, General Barton, had at hand an all too vivid reminder of the condition of his units. Much of the hope that entry of the V Corps into the fight might alter the situation had faded with the disastrous results of the unrewarding early efforts of that corps to capture Huertgen. The successes of the 8th and 22d Infantry Regiments in renewing the

MEDICS *aid a wounded soldier in the woods.*

attack on 22 November appeared attributable more to local maneuver than to any general pattern of enemy disintegration. General Barton reluctantly ordered both regiments to suspend major attacks and take two or three days to reorganize and consolidate.

Unable to strengthen the regiments other than with individual replacements, General Barton turned to a substitute for increased troops—decreased zones of action. Having reached the high ground about Gut Schwarzenbroich, the 8th Infantry now would derive some benefit from a boundary change made earlier by the VII Corps which transferred a belt of forest northeast of Gut Schwarzenbroich to the adjacent 1st Division.[4] This reduced the width of the 8th Infantry's zone by some 800 yards. To close the gap between the 8th and 22d Infantry Regiments and enable the 22d to concentrate on a thousand-yard front at Grosshau, General Barton directed that the 12th Infantry prepare to move northward into the center of the division zone. Once the 22d Infantry had taken Grosshau and turned northeastward along an improved

[4] VII Corps Opns Memo 119, 22 Nov, VII Corps Opns Memos file, Nov 44.

road net toward Dueren, the 12th Infantry might assist an attack on Gey, the last major village strongpoint that could bar egress from the forest onto the Roer plain.

For three days, 26 through 28 November, the 4th Division paused. Yet for only one regiment, the 8th Infantry, was there any real rest. Aside from the usual miseries of mud, shelling, cold, and emergency rations, the 8th Infantry engaged primarily in patrolling and in beating off platoon-sized German forays. These augured ill for the future, for indications were clear that the enemy had by 27 November begun to move in the *353d Division* to relieve the *344th*.[5]

Having cleared the 22d Infantry's right flank by nightfall of 26 November, the 12th Infantry the next day relinquished its positions to a battalion from the V Corps. Dropping off one battalion as a division reserve, a luxury General Barton had not enjoyed since the start of the November offensive, the 12th Infantry on 28 November attacked to sweep the gap between the 8th and 22d Infantry Regiments. Not until the next day was this task completed.

In the meantime, most men of the 22d Infantry were scarcely aware that the division had paused. For two of the three days, the regiment made limited attacks with first one company, then another, in order to straighten the line and get all units into position for a climactic attack on Grosshau. One of these attacks inspired an intrepid performance from an acting squad leader, Pfc. Marcario Garcia. Although painfully wounded, Garcia persistently refused evacuation until he had knocked out three machine gun emplacements and another enemy position to lead his company onto its objective.[6]

Undoubtedly aware that an attack on Grosshau was impending, the Germans concentrated their mortar and artillery fire against the 22d Infantry. In two days of admittedly limited operations, the 22d Infantry suffered over 250 casualties. Despite a smattering of replacements, two companies had less than fifty men each in the line.

The subject of replacements was a matter upon which the 4th Division by this time could speak with some authority, for during the month of November the division received as replacements 170 officers and 4,754 enlisted men. Most commanders agreed that the caliber of replacements was good.[7] "They *had* to be good quick," said one platoon leader, "or else they just weren't. They sometimes would take more chances than some of the older men, yet their presence often stimulated the veterans to take chances they otherwise would not have attempted."[8]

Integrating these new men into organizations riddled by losses among squad and platoon leaders was a trying proposition. "When I get new men in the heat of battle," one sergeant said, "all I have time to do is . . . impress them that they have to remember their platoon number, and tell them to get into the nearest hole and to move out when the rest of us move

---

[5] 4th Div Opns Rpt, Nov 44; MS # B–503, The 353d Division in the Rhineland (Gen Mahlmann); and contemporary German situation maps.

[6] He was awarded the Medal of Honor.

[7] Among those who dissented was Capt. Robert D. Moore, Company C, 8th Infantry. He said the replacements never had been taught the prime essentials that an infantryman must know, such as "the use of cover and concealment and the fire and movement principles," or else they were too frightened to use them. Combat Interv with Moore.

[8] Combat Interv with Lt. Bernasco, Co A, 22d Inf.

out." [9] That heavy casualties would strike men entering combat under conditions like these hardly could have been unexpected. Indeed, so unusual was it to get a packet of replacements into the line without incurring losses that companies noted with pride when they accomplished it. So short was the front-line stay of some men that when evacuated to aid stations they did not know what platoon, company, or even battalion and sometimes regiment they were in. Others might find themselves starting their first attack as riflemen and reaching the objective as acting squad leaders.

Most of the newcomers were reclassified cooks, clerks, drivers, and others combed from rear echelon units both in the theater and in the United States. Somewhat typical was Pvt. Morris Sussman:

From a Cook and Baker's School in the United States, Private Sussman had been transferred for 17 weeks' basic infantry training, then shipped overseas. Docking in Scotland in early November, he found himself in the Huertgen Forest by the middle of the month. At the Service Company of the 22d Infantry someone took away much of what was called "excess equipment." From there Sussman and several other men "walked about a mile to some dugouts." At the dugouts the men received company assignments, and their names and serial numbers were taken down. A guide then led them toward the front lines. On the way they were shelled and saw a number of "Jerry" and American dead scattered through the forest. Private Sussman said he was "horrified" at the sight of the dead, but not as much as he might have been "because everything appeared as if it were in a dream."

At a front line company, Sussman's company commander asked if he knew how to operate a radio. Sussman said no. Hand-

ing him a radio, the captain told him: "You're going to learn." Learning consisted of carrying the radio on his back and calling the captain whenever he heard the captain's name mentioned over the radio. For all his ignorance of radios, Sussman felt good. Being a radio operator meant he would stay with the captain and back in the States he had heard that captains stayed "in the rear." Subsequently, Private Sussman said, he "found out different." [10]

A Handful of Old Men

In the kind of slugging match that the Siegfried Line Campaign had become, little opportunity existed, once all units were committed, for division commanders to influence the battle in any grand, decisive manner. That was the situation General Barton had faced through much of the Huertgen Forest fighting. But as of 28 November, matters were somewhat different. Having narrowed his regimental zones of action, Barton had managed for the first time to achieve a compact formation within a zone of reasonable width. Looking at only this facet of the situation, one might have anticipated an early breakout from the forest.

Unfortunately, General Barton could not ignore another factor. By this time his three regiments were, in effect, masqueraders operating under the assumed names of the three veteran regiments which had come into the forest in early November. In thirteen days some companies had run through three and four company commanders. Staff sergeants and sergeants commanded most of the rifle platoons. The few officers still running platoons usually were either replace-

[9] Combat Interv with S Sgt Louis Pingatore, Co C, 22d Inf.

[10] From The Story of Private Morris Sussman, in 4th Div Combat Interv file.

ments or heavy weapons platoon leaders displaced forward. Most squad leaders were inexperienced privates or privates first class. One company had only twenty-five men, including replacements. Under circumstances like these, command organization hardly could be effective. Men and leaders made needless mistakes leading to more losses and thereby compounded the problem. This was hardly a division: this was a conglomeration. One man summed up the campaign and the situation in a few words: "Then they jump off again and soon there is only a handful of the old men left." [11]

This was how it was. Yet a job had to be done, and these were the men who had to do it. General Barton issued his orders. His subordinates passed them down the line. "Well, men," a sergeant said, "we can't do a ——— thing sitting still." [12] He got out of his hole, took a few steps, and started shooting. His men went with him. That was how this weary division resumed the attack.

The critical action was at Grosshau, for here was the ripest opportunity to break out of the forest and at last bring an end to these seemingly interminable platoon-sized actions. If Colonel Lanham's 22d Infantry could capture Grosshau, the division finally would be in a position to turn its full force northeastward on Dueren along a road net adequate for a divisional attack. Already commanders at corps and army level were making plans to strengthen the division for a final push. Except for CCR, which was fighting with the V Corps, the entire 5th Armored Division was transferred to the VII Corps

and CCA earmarked for attachment to the 4th Division. [13]

The 22d Infantry commander, Colonel Lanham, intended to attack early on 29 November at the same time the V Corps was striking the neighboring village of Kleinhau. For all their proximity, Grosshau and Kleinhau were different types of objectives. Kleinhau is on high ground, while Grosshau nestles on the forward slope of a hill whose crest rises 500 yards northeast of the village. Appreciating this difference and all too aware of the carnage that had resulted on 25 November when the regiment had tried to move directly from the woods into Grosshau, Colonel Lanham planned a wide flanking maneuver through the forest to the north in order to seize the dominating ridge. Thereupon the enemy in Grosshau might be induced to surrender without the necessity of another direct assault across open fields.

German shelling interrupted attack preparations early on 29 November, so that the 5th Armored Division's CCR under the V Corps already was clearing Kleinhau before Lanham's flanking force even began to maneuver. Perhaps because CCR was getting fire from Grosshau, the 4th Division's chief of staff, Col. Richard S. Marr, intervened just before noon in the name of the division commander to direct that Grosshau be taken that day. [14]

Because Colonel Lanham could not guarantee that his delayed flanking maneuver would bring the downfall of Grosshau immediately, Colonel Marr's instruction meant in effect that he had to launch a direct assault against the village.

[11] T/5 George Morgan, as quoted in Combat Interv with Capt Jennings Frye, 1st Bn, 22d Inf.
[12] Combat Interv with Pingatore.

[13] VII Corps Opns Memo 123, 30 Nov, VII Corps Opns Memo file, Nov 44.
[14] 22d Inf AAR, Nov 44.

Too late to recall his flanking force, he had only one battalion left. This was the 2d Battalion under Major Blazzard, which during the attack through the forest had borne responsibility for the regiment's exposed right flank and therefore had sustained correspondingly greater losses than the other battalions. Indeed, at this point, the 2d Battalion, 22d Infantry, was easily as weak as any battalion in the entire 4th Division. To make matters worse, Major Blazzard had only one company in a position to attack immediately.

Quickly scraping together two tanks and a tank destroyer to support this company, Blazzard ordered an attack on Grosshau down the main road from the west. Within an hour after receipt of the chief of staff's directive, the attack jumped off. Within fifteen more minutes, the infantry was pinned down in the open between the woods and the village and the two tanks had fallen prey to German assault guns.

Two hours later Major Blazzard assembled eight more tanks of the attached 70th Tank Battalion and sent them around the right flank of the infantry to hit the village from the southwest. Two of these tanks hit mines at the outset. The others could not get out of the woods because of mine fields and bog.

The sun was going down on an abject failure when two events altered the situation. In the face of persistent resistance, Colonel Lanham's flanking battalion finally cut the Grosshau–Gey highway in the woods north of Grosshau, and as night came one battalion emerged upon the open ridge northeast of Grosshau, virtually in rear of the Germans in the village. Almost coincidentally, a covey of tanks and tank destroyers took advantage of the gathering darkness to reach Major Blazzard's stymied infantry along the road into Grosshau from the west. Firing constantly, the big vehicles moved on toward the village. The infantry followed. In a matter of minutes, the resistance collapsed. By the light of burning buildings and a moon that shone for the first time since the 4th Division had entered the Huertgen Forest, Major Blazzard's infantry methodically mopped up the objective. More than a hundred Germans surrendered.

In a larger setting, Grosshau was only a clearing in the Huertgen Forest, the point at which the 22d Infantry at last might turn northeastward with the rest of the 4th Division to advance more directly toward the division objective of Dueren. During the night of 29 November, General Barton directed the shift. The first step was to sweep the remainder of the Grosshau clearing and to occupy a narrow, irregular stretch of woods lying between Grosshau and Gey. This accomplished, CCA of the 5th Armored Division might be committed to assist the final drive across the plain from Gey to Dueren and the Roer River.

To help prepare the way for CCA, General Barton attached the combat command's 46th Armored Infantry Battalion to the 22d Infantry. Colonel Lanham in turn directed the armored infantry to move the next day, 30 November, to Hill 401.3, an open height commanding the entire Grosshau clearing, whose lower slopes the 5th Armored Division's CCR had occupied temporarily in conjunction with the attack on Kleinhau. From Hill 401.3 the armored infantry was to attack into the woods east of the clearing in order to block the right flank of the 22d Infantry when that regiment turned northeast toward Gey.

Colonel Lanham held one battalion of his own infantry in reserve, directed another to attack alongside the Grosshau–Gey highway to gain the woods line overlooking Gey, and ordered Major Blazzard's unfortunate 2d Battalion to cross 800 yards of open ground east of Grosshau, enter the woods, and then turn northeastward along the right flank of the battalion that was moving on Gey.

The direct move through the narrow stretch of woods to Gey was blessed with success. Behind a bank of crossfire laid down by fourteen tanks and tank destroyers advancing on either flank of the infantry, a battalion of the 22d Infantry by nightfall on 30 November was entrenched firmly at the edge of the woods overlooking the village.

Things did not go as well for the rest of the regiment and the attached armored infantry. As men of the 46th Armored Infantry Battalion moved up Hill 401.3, German fire poured down the open slopes. All day long the armored infantry fought for the hill and as night came finally succeeded through sheer determination. Yet in one day this fresh battalion lost half its strength.[15]

Fire from this same hill and from the edge of the woods east of Grosshau made the attempted advance of Major Blazzard's 2d Battalion, 22d Infantry, just as difficult. The edge of the woods was to have been Blazzard's line of departure. In reality, the battalion fought all day to get to this line. Upon gaining it, the two companies that made the attack had

between them less than a hundred men.

That this little force could continue northeast through the woods to come abreast of the battalion which had gained the woods line overlooking Gey was a patent impossibility. Early the next day, 1 December, Colonel Lanham reluctantly relinquished his reserve to perform this task. Now that Hill 401.3 was in American hands, the job was easier. A favorable wind that blew a smoke screen across open ground leading from Grosshau to the woods also helped. By nightfall the reserve battalion had reached the woods line overlooking Gey, refused its flank, and dug in. At long last, sixteen days after the start of the November offensive, the 22d Infantry—or what was left of it—was all the way through the Huertgen Forest.

Success, yes; but how to maintain it? Every man of the rifle battalions was hugging a foxhole somewhere, yet the line was desperately thin. As a last resort, Colonel Lanham robbed his Antitank, Headquarters, and Service Companies of all men that possibly could be spared to form a reserve. He could not have been more prescient, for early the next morning, 2 December, the Germans counterattacked. In estimated company strength, the Germans struck southeast from Gey, quickly penetrated the line, surrounded a battalion command post, and gave every indication of rolling up the front. Only quick artillery support and commitment of the composite reserve saved the day.

Had events followed earlier planning, the 5th Armored Division's CCA now would have joined the 22d Infantry and the rest of the 4th Division for the push across the Roer plain to Dueren. But one look at the condition of the 22d Infantry would have been enough to

---

[15] Much of the eventual success against Hill 401.3 could be attributed to courageous and resourceful action by the battalion commander, Lt. Col. William H. Burton, Jr. He subsequently received the DSC. For heroic action during the same attack, S. Sgts. Robert M. Henley and Brady O. Kelley also received the DSC.

convince anyone that this regiment could contribute little if anything to a renewed push. And the sad fact was that the 22d Infantry was a microcosm of the entire 4th Division.

In the center of the division's zone, the 12th Infantry had been attacking in the woods west of Gey ever since first moving on 28 November to close the gap between the other two regiments. On 30 November the 12th Infantry had swept forward more than a thousand yards to gain the woods line west of Gey, whence the regiment was to make the main effort in an attack against that village. But the 12th Infantry had entered the Huertgen Forest fighting ten days ahead of the rest of the division; after twenty-six days of hell, artillery fire alone against the regiment's woods line position was enough to foster rampant disorganization.

On the 4th Division's north wing, the 8th Infantry had attacked on 29 November in conjunction with the general renewal of the offensive. The objective was a road center at the eastern edge of the forest about a settlement called Hof Hardt. One day's action was enough to confirm the worst apprehensions about the enemy's forming a new line during the three-day pause that had preceded the attack. Not until 1 December did Colonel McKee's regiment make a genuine penetration, and then the companies were too weak to exploit it. Company I, for example, was down to 21 men; Company C had but 44 men; and some other companies were almost as weak. Total gains in three days were less than a thousand yards, and the regiment had almost as far again to go before emerging from the forest.

Since 16 November the 4th Division had fought in the Huertgen Forest for a maximum advance of a little over three miles. Some 432 men were known dead and another 255 were missing. The division had suffered a total of 4,053 battle casualties, while another estimated 2,000 men had fallen to trench foot, respiratory diseases, and combat exhaustion. Thus the 4th Division could qualify for the dubious distinction of being second only to the 28th Division in casualties incurred in the forest.[16]

Late on 1 December General Barton spoke in detail to the VII Corps commander, General Collins, about the deplorable state of the division. The 22d Infantry, in particular, he reported, had been milked of all offensive ability. Replacements were courageous, but they did not know how to fight. Since all junior leadership had fallen by the way, no one remained to show the replacements how.

General Collins promptly ordered General Barton to halt his attack. As early as 28 November, both the VII Corps and the First Army had noted the 4th Division's condition and had laid plans for relief. On 3 December a regiment of the 83d Division brought north from the VIII Corps sector in Luxembourg was to begin relief of the 22d Infantry. In the course of the next eight days, the entire 4th Division was to move from the Huertgen Forest and arrive in Luxembourg just in time for the counteroffensive in the Ardennes.

Resuming the Corps Main Effort

Though the slowness of the advance through the Huertgen Forest was disappointing, it was to the north, in that

---

[16] The division took 1,757 prisoners. For detailed casualty figures, see 4th Div Opns Rpt, Nov 44.

region where the forested hills merge with the Roer plain, that the issue of whether the VII Corps had purchased a slugging match or a breakthrough would be decided. Here, in a sector no more than three and a half miles wide, extending from within the forest near Schevenhuette to the Inde River along the south boundary of the Eschweiler–Weisweiler industrial triangle, General Collins was making his main effort. Here he had concentrated an infantry division, the 1st, reinforced by a regiment, the 47th Infantry, and backed up by an armored division, the 3d.

After four days of severe fighting, by nightfall of 19 November, there were limited grounds for encouragement in this sector. Given one or two days of good weather, the corps commander believed, "the crust could be smashed." [17] On the 1st Division's left flank, the 104th Division had assisted the main effort by seizing high ground near Stolberg and now could start to clear the adjacent industrial triangle that lay between the 1st Division and the Ninth Army. A combat command of armor had cleared the last Germans from the Stolberg Corridor up to the base of the Hamich ridge, which stood astride the 1st Division's axis of advance. The 1st Division's 16th Infantry had taken the village of Hamich and a dominating foothold upon the Hamich ridge at Hill 232. In holding these gains, the 16th Infantry had decimated the fresh *47th Division's 104th Regiment,* which had rushed to the aid of the faltering *12th Division.* In the forest near Schevenhuette, the 26th Infantry now stood a stone's throw from the Laufenburg, the castle halfway through this portion of the Huertgen Forest.

17 Sylvan Diary, entry of 18 Nov 44.

So fierce had been the conflict to this point that the 1st Division commander, General Huebner, saw now that he could not afford the luxury of withholding reserves for exploitation upon the Roer plain. So obdurate were the Germans and so intractable the weather and terrain that he might need everything he had even to reach the plain. Huebner ordered his reserve regiment, the 18th Infantry, into the center of his line to make what was in effect a new divisional main effort. The fresh regiment was to attack northeastward astride the Weh Creek to clear the road net bordering the creek and seize the industrial town of Langerwehe, the last obstacle barring egress from the forest onto the plain.

Originally scheduled to take Langerwehe and the neighboring town of Juengersdorf, the 26th Infantry in the thick of the forest on the division's right wing now was to make a subsidiary effort. This regiment was to take Juengersdorf and a new objective, the village of Merode at the eastern edge of the forest near the boundary with the 4th Division. Having cleared Hamich and Hill 232, the remaining organic regiment, the 16th Infantry, was to advance close alongside the left flank of the newly committed 18th Infantry through broken terrain lying between the forest and the Eschweiler–Weisweiler industrial triangle. This would bring the 16th Infantry to the edge of the plain along the Weisweiler–Langerwehe highway close on the left of the center regiment.

A change in plan instituted by the corps commander also affected the 1st Division. Attached to the 1st Division, the 47th Infantry (9th Division) was to continue as originally directed to sweep the Hamich ridge extending northwest from Hill 232. Under the original plan, this regiment then was to have passed to control of the 104th Division for seizing a narrow strip of land just south of the Inde River, lying between two parallel rail lines and embracing the industrial towns of Huecheln and Wilhelmshoehe. Apparently in anticipation of communications problems because of the Inde, General Collins now decided to leave the 47th Infantry under control of the 1st Division until these towns had fallen. He shifted the interdivision boundary accordingly north to the Inde.[18]

This boundary change effected, the territory left to be cleared by the corps main effort before reaching the Roer plain took the form of a giant fan. The outer rim extended from Nothberg, at the northern tip of the Hamich ridge, a town still assigned to the 104th Division, northeastward through Huecheln to Wilhelmshoehe, thence east to Langerwehe and southeast to Juengersdorf and Merode. At the conclusion of the renewed attack, the 47th Infantry and the 1st Division's three organic regiments would be arrayed along the rim of the fan on the threshold of the plain.[19]

A battalion of the 18th Infantry gained a leg on the renewed offensive during the afternoon of 19 November by driving on the village of Wenau, less than a mile northeast of Hamich on the route to Langerwehe. Temporarily off balance in the wake of the defeats at Hamich and Hill 232, the Germans could not genuinely contest the move except with mortar and artillery fire. Although this was sufficient to deny occupation of Wenau until early on 20 November, the 18th Infantry then had a solid steppingstone for launching the divisional main effort toward Langerwehe.

Capture of Wenau also meant an assist to the 26th Infantry in clearing the Weh Creek highway and thereby gaining an adequate supply route to replace the muddy, meandering firebreaks and trails that had served this regiment during the first four days of attack. Assured of this supply route, the 26th Infantry commander, Colonel Seitz, renewed his drive on 20 November against the Laufenburg and the four wooded hills surrounding the castle. First the regiment had to beat off a counterattack by a battalion of the *47th Division's 115th Regiment,* sister battalion to that which had lost heavily in a similar maneuver the day before. In the end, this meant an easier conquest of the castle, for Colonel Seitz sent a battalion close on the enemy's heels before the defenders of the castle could get set. By nightfall Colonel Seitz had pushed a battalion beyond the castle along a forest trail leading east toward Merode.

For two more days, through 22 November, the 26th Infantry continued to push slowly eastward through the dank forest with two battalions and to refuse the regimental right flank with the other. The operation was monotonously the same. You attacked strongpoint after strongpoint built around log pillboxes, scattered mines, foxholes, and barbed wire. You longed for tank support but seldom got it. You watched your comrades cut down by shells bursting in the trees. Drenched by cold rain, you slipped and slithered in ankle-deep mud.

[18] VII Corps Opns Memo 118, 19 Nov, VII Corps Opns Memos file, Nov 44.
[19] 1st Division and 47th Infantry records for this period are detailed and are supported by adequate journal entries. Combat interviews exist for all units except the 18th Infantry.

Every advance brought its counterattack. When dusk approached you stopped early in order to dig in and thatch your foxhole with logs before night brought German infiltration and more shellfire.

The 26th Infantry nevertheless made steady progress. Indeed, by nightfall of 22 November, prospects were bright for sweeping a remaining mile of forest and emerging at last upon the Roer plain at Merode. Arrival of a contingent of the 4th Cavalry Reconnaissance Squadron on the regiment's right flank to refuse the flank and maintain contact with the 4th Division meant that Colonel Seitz would have the full weight of all three of his battalions for the final push.

Only from a regimental viewpoint, however, was the 26th Infantry ready to push out of the forest. In the division picture, General Huebner was concerned lest Colonel Seitz get too far beyond his neighbors. On the left, the 18th Infantry had become heavily engaged in the valley of the Weh Creek; and the 4th Division's 8th Infantry at Gut Schwarzenbroich still was a long way from the eastern skirt of the forest. General Huebner was perturbed particularly that the Germans might push through the 8th Infantry down Road U to Schevenhuette to cut off the entire 1st Division.[20] He directed that until further notice Colonel Seitz make only limited attacks, some designed to assist the 18th Infantry.

After a relatively painless conquest of Wenau, the 18th Infantry had stepped into hot water. "Shove off as fast as you can," General Huebner had told the 18th Infantry commander, Colonel Smith. "[If you] run into resistance, bypass it

and go around." [21] This might have worked except for two factors. First, the Germans during the night had hurriedly shored up the depleted *104th Regiment* with the *47th Division*'s *147th Engineer Battalion*. The second was the nature of the next objective, the village of Heistern, about 500 yards beyond Wenau. Like Wenau, Heistern is perched on the western slope of the Weh Creek valley. Bypassing it was next to impossible, for by little more than rolling grenades down the slope the Germans in the village could deny movement up the valley toward Langerwehe. From Heistern they enjoyed almost as great an advantage over the 16th Infantry's sector to the west. "We need Heistern," said one officer of the 16th Infantry, "before we can go anywhere . . . ." [22]

The fight for Heistern might have been as lengthy and as costly as the fight for Hamich except that here the Germans had no Hill 232 from which to pinpoint the slightest movement. Employing artillery and tank fire against fortifications on the fringe of the village, a battalion of the 18th Infantry by nightfall had reached a main road junction in the center of the village. Still the Germans clung like cockleburs to the northern half.

During the night, the commander of the enemy's *104th Regiment*, Col. Josef Kimbacher, personally led his training and regimental headquarters companies into Heistern to reinforce what was left of the German garrison. At 0330, 21 November, behind damaging concentrations of mortar and artillery fire, Colonel Kimbacher counterattacked. Not until short-

[20] This is reflected in 1st Div G–3 Jnl, 19–21 Nov 44.

[21] CG to 18th Inf, 0830, 20 Nov, 1st Div G–3 Jnl, 19–21 Nov 44.
[22] 16th Inf to G–3, 1500, 20 Nov, 1st Div G–3 Jnl, 19–21 Nov 44.

ly before daylight did the Americans beat off the enemy and spill over into the northern half of the village. They took about 120 prisoners, including Colonel Kimbacher, and subsequently counted 250 German dead. Taking both Wenau and Heistern cost the 18th Infantry 172 casualties. As often happened, the Germans in a swift and futile counterattack had wasted the very troops who in a stationary defense might have prolonged the fight considerably.[23]

Even before the attack for Heistern, the 18th Infantry had sent another battalion on 20 November to cross the Weh Creek and advance on Langerwehe along a wooded ridge marking the east slope of the valley. Having no Heistern to contend with, this battalion moved fast until on 21 November the leading company smacked into a real obstacle, Hill 207. Not quite a mile northeast of Heistern, wooded, and with an escarpment for a southern face, Hill 207 dominates the Weh Creek valley from the east as Heistern does from the west. Pounded by artillery fire in disturbing proportions and raked by small arms fire from atop the escarpment, the first company to test the hill fell back under severe losses. Eschewing another direct assault, the battalion commander the next day attempted to maneuver through the woods to take the hill from a flank. Maneuver in the Huertgen Forest, he soon discovered, was a complex and costly commission. Not for another twenty-four hours, 23 November, was this battalion able to get into position for a vigorous flanking attack that at last carried the hill.

---

[23] German material is from 1st Div Intel Activities, Nov 44, 1st Div Combat Interv file.

Having lost Hill 207, the Germans had no real anchor short of Langerwehe itself upon which to base a further defense along the east slope of the Weh Creek valley. Although they made a try a few hundred yards beyond Hill 207 at Schoenthal, they could hold onto this hamlet only through the night. On 24 November the battalion of the 18th Infantry pushed on northeastward parallel to the valley. Except for minor strongpoints, a wooded door to Langerwehe stood ajar.

Like the 26th Infantry deeper within the woods, the battalion of the 18th Infantry could not pursue its advantage. The most elementary caution would proscribe sending an understrength battalion into a town the size of Langerwehe unless a better supply route than muddy firebreaks was available. To the chagrin of the regimental commander, Colonel Smith, that was the supply situation this battalion had to face: the Weh Creek highway could not be used until both east and west slopes had been cleared. On the west slope, another battalion of the 18th Infantry had run into trouble.

This was Colonel Smith's reserve battalion, committed through Heistern at midday on 21 November to project the left prong of the regiment's double thrust on Langerwehe. Lying between the reserve battalion and the objective were two obstacles: a rectangular patch of woods covering the western slope of the valley and a dominating height at the northern end of the woods no more than half a mile from Langerwehe, Hill 203. Getting through the woods alone was bad enough. Hill 203 was worse.

The critical importance of Hill 203 obviously was not lost on the Germans. Topped by an observation tower and a religious shrine, the hill is bald once the rectangular patch of woods gives out on the southern slope. From the hill the enemy controlled both the Weh Creek highway and another road running from Heistern across the crest of the hill into Langerwehe. Without Hill 203, the Germans could not hope to hold onto Langerwehe. Without Hill 203, the 18th Infantry could not hope to take the town.

Admonished by General Huebner not to commit full strength against Hill 203 because "Langerwehe is where your big fight is," [24] Colonel Smith's reserve battalion at first sent only a company against the hill. No sooner had men of this company emerged from the trees toward the crest late on 23 November than small arms and artillery fire literally mowed them down. This was enough to convince Colonel Smith that he had a big fight here, no matter what he might run into later in Langerwehe. "The 1st Battalion," Colonel Smith reported, "will be unable to get to Hill 203 until we get armor." [25] Getting tanks forward over roads literally under the muzzles of German guns obviously would be toilsome.

Through the night of 23 November and most of the next day, attached tanks of the 745th Tank Battalion tried to reach Hill 203. Slowed by mud, at least two were picked off by antitank guns concealed on the hill. Not until too late in the afternoon to be of any real assistance on 24 November did the tanks gain the woods line. Neither could tactical aircraft help, for the weather was rainy and dismal. Even the contribution of the artillery was limited, because the fighting was at such close quarters. Though Colonel Smith called on the battalion of

the 18th Infantry on the other side of the valley to help, that battalion soon had its hands full with a counterattack by contingents of the *47th Division*'s *115th Regiment*.

Supported by two tanks, one company in midafternoon of the next day, 25 November, at last began to make some progress against Hill 203. Although the enemy knocked out one of the tanks, a rifle platoon managed to gain a position near the crest of the hill. All through the night and the next day this little band of men clung to the hillside. Yet for all their courage and pertinacity, these men scarcely represented any genuine conquest of Hill 203. It would take more than a platoon to carry this tactical prize.

Towns, Woods, Hills, and Castles

Concurrently with the fight in the forest and along the Weh Creek valley, the 16th Infantry and the attached 47th Infantry had been extending the 1st Division's battle line to the west and northwest. The 47th Infantry was to attack northwest along the Hamich ridge, thence northeast through Huecheln and toward Wilhelmshoehe in a scythelike pattern designed to place the attached regiment eventually on a line with the rest of its foster division. Attacking northeast from Hamich, the 16th Infantry was to serve as a bridge between this operation and the divisional main effort of the 18th Infantry up the Weh Creek valley. The 16th Infantry's first objective was high ground about a castle, the Roesslershof, at the edge of a patch of woods south of the Aachen–Dueren railroad.

The sector through which the 16th and 47th Infantry Regiments were to attack

---

[24] CG to 18th Inf, 0843, 23 Nov, 1st Div G–3 Jnl, 22–24 Nov 44.
[25] 1st Div G–3 Opns Rpt, Nov 44.

took the form of a parallelogram, bounded on the southwest by the Hamich ridge, on the northwest by the Inde River, on the northeast by the Weisweiler–Langerwehe highway, and on the southeast by the Weh Creek. The parallelogram embraced the purlieus of the Huertgen Forest. A nondescript collection of farms, villages, industrial towns, railroads, scrub-covered hills, and scattered but sometimes extensive patches of woods, this region would offer serious challenges to an attacker, particularly during the kind of cold, wet weather late November had brought. Indeed, these troops who would fight here where the Huertgen Forest reluctantly gives way to the Roer plain would experience many of the same miseries as did those who fought entirely inside the forest. Yet they might be spared the full measure of the forest's grimness. Sometimes they could spend a dry night in a damaged house, and most of the time they could see the sky.

Both regiments began to attack during the afternoon of 19 November after the 16th Infantry's decisive victory at Hamich and Hill 232. Like the 18th Infantry at Wenau, the 16th Infantry found that closely following up the defeat of the enemy's *104th Regiment* was a good stratagem. By the end of the day the regiment's leading battalion had reached the eastern part of the Bovenberger Wald, a patch of woods lying in the middle of the parallelogram. The next day the 16th Infantry would be ready to advance close alongside the 18th Infantry's left flank to cover the less than two miles to Roesslershof Castle.

Given flank protection by the advance of the 16th Infantry, a battalion of the 47th Infantry attacked northwest along the Hamich ridge from Hill 232 with an eye toward Hills 187 and 167, which mark the terminus of the ridge a few hundred yards short of Nothberg.

The Germans on Hill 187 were part of the *47th Division's 103d Regiment.* Having become embroiled earlier in the fight to keep the 3d U.S. Armored Division out of the villages southwest of Hill 187, the regiment had incurred serious losses. Yet when afforded advantageous terrain like Hill 187 and nearby Hill 167, even a small force was capable of a stiff fight.

This the 47th Infantry discovered early on 20 November. Commanded by Lt. Col. James D. Allgood, a battalion attacked Hill 187 repeatedly but without appreciable success. Hill 187, the Germans recognized, was worth defending, for from it they could look down upon three U.S. divisions—the 104th in the Eschweiler–Weisweiler industrial complex, the 3d Armored in the Stolberg Corridor, and that part of the 1st Division in the parallelogram.[26]

As the fighting stirred again on Hill 187 the next day, 21 November, the 47th Infantry commander, Colonel Smythe, sent another battalion through the Bovenberger Wald to the east of the hill. By taking the settlement of Bovenberg at the northern tip of the woods, this battalion would virtually encircle both Hills 187 and 167 in conjunction with a concurrent attack by a unit of the 104th Division on the town of Nothberg. At the same time, an advance on Bovenberg would pave the

---

[26] When a round from a German gun set afire a tank destroyer supporting the 47th Infantry, a platoon leader, S. Sgt. Herschel F. Briles, 899th Tank Destroyer Battalion, lowered himself into the burning turret to rescue the wounded crewmen inside. The next day he repeated the feat when another destroyer burst into flames. Sergeant Briles subsequently received the Medal of Honor.

way for executing the 47th Infantry's next mission of taking the industrial towns of Huecheln and Wilhelmshoehe, which lie north of Bovenberg.

The idea was good. But it would not work without first wresting from the Germans the dominating observation from Hills 187 and 167. Tanks trying to accompany the infantry along a road skirting the western edge of the trees found the going next to impossible because of felled trees and antitank fire from the hills. In the thin northern tip of the woods, the infantry too was exposed to punishing shellfire obviously directed from the heights. The leading company nevertheless prepared to debouch from the wood to strike a strongpoint in the main building of a dairy farm on the edge of Bovenberg.

Despite grazing small arms fire, one platoon actually reached the dairy, only to fall back in the face of hand grenades dropped from second story windows. Protected by thick brick walls, the Germans inside called down artillery fire on their own position. Another platoon which penetrated to a nearby copse could get no farther and could withdraw only by means of a smoke screen. Even then only 6 men emerged unscathed, though they brought with them 15 or 20 wounded. The company lost 35 men killed in a matter of a few hours. All officers except the company commander were either killed or wounded. The company had only 37 men left.

In the meantime, Colonel Allgood's battalion was having as much trouble as before with Hill 187. Despairing of taking the hill with usual tactics, the 1st Division commander, General Huebner, turned in midafternoon of 21 November to the same pattern he had used two days

before against Hill 232. As soon as Colonel Allgood's men could pull back a safe distance, 1st Division artillery was to fire a TOT.

Hearing of this plan, the corps commander intervened. Because he deemed the effort too modest, General Collins directed assistance by all VII Corps artillery and any divisional artillery within effective range. Within ten minutes after the 1st Division's organic 155-mm. howitzer battalion had zeroed in on the hill, the 1st Division's artillery headquarters had transmitted the adjustment to all other firing battalions. At 1615, an awesome total of twenty battalions, including a 240-mm. howitzer battalion and two 8-inch gun battalions, fired for three minutes upon a target area measuring approximately 300 by 500 yards. "It just literally made the ground bounce," said one observer.[27] Well it might have; for this ranked among the most concentrated artillery shoots during the course of the war in Europe.

For some unexplained reason, Colonel Allgood made no immediate effort to occupy the hill. Instead, the 47th Infantry's Cannon Company interdicted the target through the night. The next morning, 22 November, a patrol that crept up the hill found only enemy dead and about eighty survivors who still were too dazed to resist. Another patrol discovered that the enemy had abandoned Hill 167.

Rather than renew the drive on the dairy at Bovenberg and continue along that route to the next objectives of Huecheln and Wilhelmshoehe, the 47th Infantry commander, Colonel Smythe, asked permission to move into the 104th Division's zone at Nothberg and attack

---

[27] Combat Interv with Allgood.

from that direction. The 104th Division had occupied Nothberg during the morning of 22 November. Because the route via Bovenberg was more a trail than a road, the 47th Infantry's line of communications eventually would run through Nothberg anyway.[28]

Although granted this permission, Colonel Smythe was reluctant to leave intact a strongpoint like the dairy at Bovenberg. This time the attacking company took a leaf from the successful artillery bombardment of Hills 232 and 187. After an 8-inch gun battalion had scored at least twenty-six hits on the dairy, the riflemen attacked. The artillery alone, they discovered, had been enough. The Germans had fled.

To make the main drive between the parallel rail lines toward Huecheln, Colonel Smythe early on 23 November committed his reserve battalion under Lt. Col. Lewis E. Maness. Canalized by the railroads into an attack zone only 500 yards wide, Colonel Maness leaned heavily in his attack upon supporting fires. Artillery fired a ten-minute concentration upon the western edge of Huecheln, 81-mm. mortars laid a smoke screen, a platoon of tanks accompanied the infantry, and tank destroyers and machine guns spewed overhead fire from the eastern edge of Nothberg.

Unfortunately, Germans of the *12th Division's 27th Fusilier Regiment* had shunned the obvious defensive spot along the fringe of Huecheln in favor of open ground west of the town. Though they had dug an elaborate zigzag trench system protected by mines, not a stray clod of earth betrayed their positions. Dependent upon an observation post in Nothberg,

---

[28] 47th Inf to 1st Div G–3, 1448, 22 Nov, 1st Div G–3 Jnl, 19–21 Nov 44.

a mile away, Colonel Maness had not accurately determined the enemy's line. Most of the supporting fire was over. The enemy for his part had a towering observation post atop a slag pile in the 104th Division's zone north of the northern railroad. On 23 November Colonel Maness' battalion hardly got past the eastern edge of Nothberg. Renewing the attack the next morning, Maness could detect nothing in the passing of night to alter the picture.

Unknown to Colonel Maness, his superiors were concocting a formula which might prove just what this particular problem required. For several days the corps commander, General Collins, had been considering the idea of employing his armored reserve. Although Collins hardly could have entertained any illusions that a breakthrough calling for armored exploitation was near, he did see a possibility that an assist from armor might provide the extra push necessary to get onto the Roer plain. Impressed by unexpected celerity in the 104th Division's fight to clear the Eschweiler–Weisweiler industrial triangle, he had on 22 November increased that division's responsibility beyond the industrial triangle to the Roer. A byproduct of the change was an opportunity—almost a need—for a short, quick thrust by a small increment of armor.

In directing the 104th Division to continue to the Roer, General Collins had extended that division's boundary east from Weisweiler to include a crossing of the Inde River along the Aachen–Cologne autobahn. A quick jab by armor through Huecheln and Wilhelmshoehe to the Frenzerburg, a medieval castle crowning a gentle hill a mile beyond Wilhelmshoehe, would enable the armor to control the

INFANTRY AND TANKS *move through small truck farms near Huecheln.*

104th Division's Inde crossing site by fire.[29]

Shortly before noon on 24 November General Collins attached Colonel Maness' battalion of the 47th Infantry to the 3d Armored Division as the infantry component of a task force to make the thrust to the Frenzerburg. Other components of the task force were a medium tank battalion from the 3d Armored Division's CCA, an armored field artillery battalion, and increments of tank destroyers and armored engineers. All were under the command of Lt. Col. Walter B. Richardson.[30]

Task Force Richardson's first attack in midafternoon of 24 November ran into trouble at the start. Two medium tank companies in the lead blundered into a mine field. Attempts to find a path around the mines usually ended in tanks

---

[29] VII Corps Opns Memos 119 and 120, 22 and 24 Nov, VII Corps Opns Memos file, Nov 44.

[30] In addition to records of the 47th Inf and 1st Div, the story of Task Force Richardson is based on official records of the 3d Armd Div and Combat Interv filed with 1st Div Intervs. The force shows on Map VII as TF R.

bogging deep in mud. One tank actually sank so deep that mud came up on the hull.

As dusk approached, the armored engineers at last managed to clear a path. The enemy's observation severely restricted by gathering darkness, the attack began to roll. Tanks and infantry together stormed across the zigzag trenches into Huecheln. By 2100 (24 November) the town was clear. A hundred Germans were on their way to prisoner cages.

Neither Huecheln nor the next town of Wilhelmshoehe are on commanding ground, so that in renewing the attack on 25 November Task Force Richardson strove toward more dominating terrain along the Weisweiler–Langerwehe highway from which to attack the Frenzerburg. The Germans employed fire from self-propelled guns across the Inde at Weisweiler and from small arms and mortars among the houses and factories of Wilhelmshoehe. During the course of the day 200 Germans of the *12th Division's 27th Regiment* and the *47th Division's 103d Regiment* were captured. So long as tanks and infantry enjoyed the protection of buildings, American losses were moderate; but once in the open, casualties rose alarmingly. An attempt on the right to reach the highway stalled when the bulk of one tank company bogged in the mud. At one time eighteen tanks were immobilized. A thrust on the left ran into intense fire upon emerging from Wilhelmshoehe. German guns knocked out three tanks, and small arms and artillery fire virtually destroyed an infantry company. That company had but thirty-five men left. The infantry commander, Colonel Maness, appealed for reinforcement before striking into the open for the Frenzerburg.

The officers of Task Force Richardson had ample justification for concern about moving alone onto the Roer plain. On the left, the task force would have some protection from the Inde River, even though the 104th Division had not yet come abreast; but on the right, the task force would be exposed to counterattack from Langerwehe. Nothing existed at this time (25 November) to indicate that the 1st Division's 18th Infantry soon might push the enemy off Hill 203 and get into Langerwehe. Neither was there any hope that the 1st Division's 16th Infantry soon might come abreast along the Weisweiler–Langerwehe highway between the task force and the 18th Infantry, for on 25 November the 16th Infantry was having trouble holding onto terrain already taken. This was high ground about Roesslershof at the edge of a patch of woods southeast of Wilhelmshoehe.

After the paths of the 16th and 47th Regiments had diverged on 19 November in the Bovenberger Wald, the 16th Infantry had delayed its attack until the 18th Infantry had secured Heistern, the village alongside the Weh Creek valley which dominated the 16th Infantry's route of advance. Although able to make a genuine attack on 23 November, the regiment had been handicapped because General Huebner had withdrawn one battalion as a division reserve.

Not until near nightfall on 23 November had the 16th Infantry pushed back stubborn remnants of the *47th Division*, called *Kampfgruppe Eisenhuber*, and broken into Roesslershof. From that point the regiment had been involved in repulsing counterattacks and in clearing a patch of woods between the castle and Wilhelmshoehe. None other than a desultory effort had yet been made to cover about 750 yards remaining between

Roesslershof and the Weisweiler–Langer-wehe highway.[31]

In response to Colonel Maness' appeal for reinforcement before attacking the Frenzerburg, the 47th Infantry provided Company K, a unit seriously depleted but closer at hand than any other. The regimental commander, Colonel Smythe, also did something about the threat of counterattack from Langerwehe by send-ing another infantry battalion early on 26 November toward Langerwehe to occupy a rough-surfaced hill only 800 yards short of the town. Colonel Smythe hardly could have anticipated how handsomely his perspicacity in sending a battalion to this hill was to be repaid.

Task Force Richardson's plan of attack against the Frenzerburg on 26 November involved two simultaneous thrusts. In-fantrymen mounted on tanks were to hit the castle from the south, while the infan-try Company K was moving generally eastward alongside the Aachen–Juelich railroad.

Hardly had the tanks and infantry reached open, cultivated fields south of the castle when German fire from positions a mile to the east near the village of Luchem knocked out two of the tanks. Scattering quickly, the infantry miracu-lously escaped injury, but German fire continued in such intensity that Colonel Richardson ordered the composite force to fall back.

For all practical purposes, this marked dissolution of Task Force Richardson. The armor assumed a role of long-range

fire support, while the full burden of the attack fell upon Colonel Maness' 2d Bat-talion, 47th Infantry, and Company K.

When the Germans spotted the men of Company K sneaking along the Aachen–Juelich railroad, they smothered them with shelling. "It was the heaviest mortar and artillery fire since El Guettar," said 1st Lt. William L. McWaters, the company commander and a veteran of North Africa. Having started his attack with but eighty men, McWaters could ill afford the twenty he lost in this shelling.

To the east Lieutenant McWaters could see the towers of the Frenzerburg rising behind tall trees as if the castle stood in the middle of a wood. Wary of turning back over the open route he already had traversed, McWaters saw the concealment of the wood as his only hope. Once among the trees, however, he discovered with chagrin that the wood was no more than a copse. The castle stood full in the open, 300 yards beyond the last trees.

Down to sixty men, Lieutenant Mc-Waters hesitated before crossing this open ground to the castle. Yet only a mo-ment's reflection was enough to remind him that his route of withdrawal was even more exposed and that the copse would be a hard place to hold once the Germans discovered his presence. He would attack.

His radio destroyed in the earlier shell-ing, McWaters had no way to solicit supporting fire from other than his own machine guns. These he set up at the edge of the trees to form a base of fire. As the machine guns began to chatter, his riflemen dashed for the castle.

They made it. Not to the castle itself but to an open rectangle of outbuildings enclosing a courtyard in front of the entrance. One glance was enough to reveal that getting into the castle was

[31] Combat Interv with Capt. Fred W. Hall, Jr., S–3, 2d Bn, 16th Inf. The 16th Infantry's official records for this period are notably poor. Details to be found in Combat Intervs should be checked against the 1st Div G–3 Opns Rpt, Nov 44.

THE FRENZERBURG

another proposition altogether. Of modest proportions as medieval castles go, Frenzerburg was nonetheless a formidable bastion to an unsupported infantry force reduced now to some half a hundred men. Denied on all sides by a water-filled moat twenty feet wide, the castle was accessible only by means of a drawbridge guarded by a gatehouse tower built of heavy stone. Although the drawbridge was down, a heavy oak gate blocked passage. A stone wall no more than waist high, bordering the moat near the drawbridge, offered the only protection to a move against the entrance.

A lone bazookaman, Pfc. Carl V. Sheridan, dashed from the outbuildings toward the wall. Covered by two riflemen who pumped fire into windows of the gatehouse tower, Sheridan worked his way slowly toward the drawbridge. Unable to fire upon Sheridan because of the wall and the covering fire, Germans in the gatehouse tossed hand grenades from the windows. Somehow they missed. From the corner of the wall on the very threshold of the drawbridge, Sheridan loaded his bazooka, fired at the oak gate, calmly reloaded, and fired again. The heavy gate splintered but did not collapse.

Sheridan had one rocket left. Again he loaded the awkward weapon. Ignoring grenades and rifle fire that popped about him, he took careful aim at the hinges of the gate and fired. Jumping to his feet, he brandished his bazooka, called to the men in the outbuildings behind him to "Come on, let's get 'em!" and charged.

The Germans cut him down a few feet from the gate.[32]

Lieutenant McWaters had no time to capitalize on Private Sheridan's feat before the Germans counterattacked from the gatehouse. They overran a squad in one end of the rectangle of outbuildings, captured the squad, and rescued about forty Germans Company K earlier had captured. In the face of this display of force, Lieutenant McWaters became acutely conscious of his plight. He sent a volunteer, Sgt. Linus Vanderheid, in quest of help.

Sergeant Vanderheid had not far to go, for the 2d Battalion commander, Colonel Maness, had traced the route of Company K with four tanks and two rifle companies. This force already had reached the copse. Pointing up the anachronism of this twentieth century fight against a fifteenth century bastion, the tanks blasted the walls of the castle from the edge of the trees. As darkness came, Colonel Maness pushed his tanks and infantry across the open ground. Two tanks bogged down, an antitank gun in the castle set fire to another, and the one remaining blundered into the water-filled moat. Deprived of close support, Colonel Maness made no effort to assault the castle that night.

Three hours before daylight the next morning, 27 November, the Germans counterattacked. About sixty paratroopers from the *3d Parachute Division*, supported by six assault guns, struck the outbuildings. The Americans kept most of the assault guns at a respectable distance with artillery fire and bazookas, but one broke through into the courtyard.

---

[32] Sheridan was awarded the Medal of Honor posthumously. A combat interview with Maness and McWaters describes his deed.

Churning back and forth, the German vehicle systematically shot up the landscape. The outbuildings began to burn. Somehow a section of the castle caught fire. Only as daylight approached did bazookas and hand grenades force the assault gun to retire. The paratroopers also fell back.

All through the rest of 27 November American and German riflemen exchanged shots between the outbuildings and the castle, but not until early the next day did any break appear. During the night Colonel Maness brought up three tank destroyers. After the gunners had pummeled the gatehouse with 90-mm. projectiles for several hours, the infantry moved in. The assault itself was an anticlimax. As a final anomaly in this battle, the Germans had slipped away through an underground passage.

German Reinforcements

The presence of sixty German paratroopers in the counterattack at the Frenzerburg marked the first major change in the line-up opposite the VII Corps since the early introduction (18 November) of the *47th Volks Grenadier Division*. That no other help had been accorded this part of General Koechling's *LXXXI Corps* was attributable to the jealous hoarding of the admittedly limited reserves for the Ardennes counteroffensive and to continued German belief that the biggest threat was farther north opposite the Ninth U.S. Army. Indeed, the southern wing of the *LXXXI Corps* had even provided one small reinforcement for the northern front when on 21 November *Kampfgruppe Bayer*, which had fought at Hamich, was relieved from attachment to the *47th Division* and sent north. Only in artillery had there been any help provided; early on 22 November the partially motorized *403d Volks Artillery Corps* had been committed between Dueren and Juelich.[33]

The presence of the *3d Parachute Division* stemmed indirectly from another request made on 22 November for at least one division from the *Fuehrer Reserve*. While turning down the request flatly, OKW sugared the pill with word that the *3d Parachute Division* soon would be shifted from the relatively inactive Holland front. Two days later, when confirming this move, OKW insisted that the parachute division must relieve at least one and preferably two divisions which might be refitted for the Ardennes.[34]

One division or two made little difference to the *LXXXI Corps*, so depleted were its units. The *12th Volks Grenadier Division*, which had been fighting continuously since mid-September and which recently had been opposing the 104th U.S. Division and the 47th Infantry, finally was finished as a fighting force. The *27th Regiment*, for example, had but 120 combat effectives left; another regiment, but 60. After eight days of combat, the "new" *47th Division* also had been virtually wiped out. The *104th Regiment* had about 215 combat effectives left; the *103d Regiment*, 60; and the *115th Regiment*, 36.[35]

On 24 November *Fifteenth Army* (*Gruppe von Manteuffel*), the army head-

quarters superior to the *LXXXI Corps*, had directed that these two divisions be formed into a single *Kampfgruppe* under General Engel, commander of the *12th Division*. This was the unit, designated *Gruppe Engel*, which the *3d Parachute Division* eventually was to relieve.[36]

Submergence in a *Kampfgruppe* was an unhappy fate for a division which had acquitted itself as well as had the *47th*. Having walked into a body blow at the start of the November offensive, this division had fought back by throwing every available man into the front lines—headquarters clerks, artillerymen, green replacements, engineers, even veterinarians. Flagging morale and steadily decreasing resolution could have been expected under these circumstances, but somehow the *47th Division* had escaped these viruses. The 1st U.S. Division later was to call it "the most suicidally stubborn unit this Division has encountered . . . on the Continent." [37]

Composed for the most part of boys aged sixteen to nineteen, steeped in Nazi ideology but untested in combat, the *3d Parachute Division* began to move into the line the night of 26 November. The division inherited a front about five miles long extending from Merode northward almost to the boundary between the First and Ninth U.S. Armies.[38]

As the German commanders soon were to discover, they had waited a day or so too long to act. Staging a relief under fire is risky business even with veteran

---

[33] *OB WEST KTB*, 20 Nov 44; *LXXXI Corps Gefechtsbericht*, AAR of 21 Nov 44; Order, *Gruppe von Manteuffel* to *LXXXI Corps*, 0010, 22 Nov 44, *LXXXI Corps KTB, Befehle, H. Gr. u. Armee*.
[34] *OB WEST KTB*, 22 and 24 Nov 44.
[35] Notes of Inspection Trip by CG, *LXXXI Corps*, 24 Nov 44, in *LXXXI Corps KTB, Befehle an Div*.

[36] Order, *Gruppe von Manteuffel* to *LXXXI Corps*, 1435, 24 Nov 44, *LXXXI Corps KTB, Bef. H. Gru. u. Armee*.
[37] 1st Div Intel Activities, Nov 44.
[38] TWX, *Gruppe von Manteuffel* to *XII SS* and *LXXXI Corps*, 0050, 25 Nov 44, *LXXXI Corps KTB, Bef. H. Gru. u. Armee*; *LXXXI Corps Gefechtsbericht*, AAR for 26 Nov 44.

units. About the only claim the *3d Parachute Division* had to experience was the name of the division, but an honorific is hardly a substitute for experience.

The first of the young paratroopers to run into trouble were those scheduled to counterattack at the Frenzerburg. These included a company each of reconnaissance, engineer, and antitank troops attached temporarily to *Gruppe Engel* and reinforced by assault guns of the newly arrived *667th Assault Gun Brigade.*[39] The base for the attack was to be the hill along the Langerwehe–Weisweiler highway 800 yards west of Langerwehe which a battalion of the 47th Infantry had occupied in order to protect the attack on the castle. No one had told the paratroopers of the 47th Infantry's presence. As the Germans approached the hill, the Americans cut them down almost without effort. The German commander could reassemble only sixty men for the counterattack at the castle.

In the meantime, a battalion of paratroopers moved west from Langerwehe to occupy positions at a settlement named Gut Merberich, south of the Weisweiler–Langerwehe highway. Presumably this battalion was to thwart what looked like an impending attack by the 16th Infantry designed to assist a final drive by the 18th Infantry on Langerwehe. No sooner had these paratroopers reached Gut Merberich just after dawn on 27 November when artillery fire began to fall, a prelude to the 16th Infantry's attack. The Germans dived for the cellars. They were still there a few minutes later when the 16th Infantry moved in. This was a

prime example of what some of the few experienced noncommissioned officers in the parachute division meant when they said that under artillery fire, "the iron in the hearts of these kids turned to lead in their pants." [40]

To see two fresh battalions meet a fate like this must have convinced the Germans that they had a new enemy called Coincidence. This view must have been underscored an hour or so later on 27 November when the 18th Infantry renewed its attempt to take Hill 203, which for more than three days had stymied an advance into Langerwehe.

Relinquishing the crest of Hill 203, survivors of the *47th Division's 104th Regiment* still clung to another position on the reverse slope. To strengthen the new position and then retake the hill, the *3d Parachute Division* sent a battalion of the *9th Parachute Regiment.* The young paratroopers arrived just in time to catch the preparation fires of a renewal of the 18th Infantry's attack. Like those at Gut Merberich, these Germans had no taste for shellfire. They surrendered in bunches.

With Hill 203 out of the way, the industrial town of Langerwehe, gateway to the Roer plain, lay unshielded. Though the paratroopers and what was left of the *47th Division* fought persistently to soften the blow, the 18th Infantry and a battalion of the 16th Infantry had swept the last Germans from demolished buildings and cellars by nightfall of 28 November. At the same time the 26th Infantry was sending a battalion into the neighboring town of Juengersdorf. Despite counterattacks by the *5th Parachute*

---

[39] TWX *LXXXI Corps* to *12th Div* and *3d Prcht Div*, 2115, 26 Nov 44, *LXXXI Corps KTB, Befehle and Div.*

[40] Personnel and Equipment of *3d Prcht Div*, Incl 6 to VII Corps G–2 Per Rpt 177, 29 Nov, FUSA G–2 Tac file, 30 Nov 44.

Regiment, Juengersdorf too was secure by nightfall on 28 November. On this ignominious note, *Gruppe Engel* was officially relieved from the front and started rearward for refitting.[41]

Up to this point the debut of the *3d Parachute Division* had been something short of spectacular. In only two more instances were the paratroopers to have an opportunity to make amends. One of these came five days later at Luchem, a village north of Langerwehe which the VII Corps commander, General Collins, ordered the 1st Division to seize in order to form a straight line between Langerwehe and objectives of the 104th Division.[42] In a deft maneuver, a battalion of the 16th Infantry slipped into the village before dawn without artillery preparation, and at daylight tanks and tank destroyers raced forward to assist the mop-up. The paratroopers hadn't a chance.[43]

In the other instance, location of the objective was not so propitious for a swift, unsupported infantry attack. The objective was Merode, a village at the eastern edge of the Huertgen Forest southeast of Juengersdorf. At Merode the young German paratroopers had a chance to discover that war can be an exhilarating experience—when you win.

---

[41] *LXXXI Corps Gefechtsbericht,* AAR for 28 Nov 44.

[42] VII Corps Opns Memo 121, 26 Nov, VII Corps Opns Memos file, Nov 44.

[43] As revealed by the experience of a 16th Infantry rifleman, Pvt. Robert T. Henry, Luchem was not taken without serious fighting. His platoon held up by a nest of five German machine guns, Private Henry voluntarily charged across 150 yards of open ground toward the position. Struck by a burst of fire when but halfway to the German emplacement, he staggered on until he fell mortally wounded only a few yards short of his goal. The intrepid rifle-

Debacle at Merode

To the 26th Infantry, Merode was no ordinary objective. It was a promise of no more Huertgen Forest. To fulfill that promise, the 26th Infantry had but one battalion, already seriously weakened by thirteen brutal days in the forest. Another battalion was in Juengersdorf. The third had to hold the regiment's right flank in the woods because the adjacent 4th Division had not reached the eastern edge of the forest.

Merode lies on a slope slanting downward from the eastern woods line. Although numerous roads serve the village from the Roer plain, only a narrow cart track leads eastward from the forest. Astride this narrow trail across 300 yards of open ground the 26th Infantry had to move.

Behind a sharp artillery preparation, the attacking battalion commander, Colonel Daniel, sent two companies toward Merode shortly before noon on 29 November. Despite stubborn resistance from a battalion of the *5th Parachute Regiment* in a line of strongpoints along the western edge of the village, Colonel Daniel's men by late afternoon had gained the first houses. Yet no one believed for a moment that the Germans were ready to relinquish the village. Employing numbers of pieces that the 1st Division G–2 estimated to be equal to those of the Americans, German artillery wreaked particular havoc. Despite several strikes by tactical aircraft and several counter-battery TOT's by 1st Division artillery, the German pieces barked as full-throated and deadly as ever.

---

man was awarded the Medal of Honor posthumously.

The minute the riflemen gained the first houses, Colonel Daniel ordered a platoon of tanks to join them. Two got through, although one was knocked out almost immediately after gaining the village. Commanders of the other two tanks paused at the woods line, noted the "sharpness" of the enemy's shellfire, and directed their drivers to turn back.[44] As they backed up, a shell struck a track of the lead tank. The tank overturned. Because of deep cuts, high fills, and dense, stalwart trees on either side of the narrow trail, no vehicle could get into Merode past the damaged tank.

Various individuals tried in various ways through the early part of the night to get more tank and antitank support into Merode. They might have been dogs baying at the moon, so futile were their efforts. Someone called for a tank retriever to remove the damaged tank, but not until the next morning did one arrive. Then for some unexplained reason, the retriever could not remove the tank. Someone else called for engineers to build a bypass around the tank, but this would be at best a long, tedious process. A sergeant trying to borrow tanks attached to another battalion of the 26th Infantry met a rebuff from the regimental operations officer. "You keep your tanks," the S-3 told the battalion commander. "He can't have them unless we know the [full] story on [his tanks]."[45]

This was fiddling while Rome burned. The Germans even then were laying down a curtain of shellfire to prevent reinforcement of American troops in Merode. Soon after, they counterattacked. Because American radio batteries had been weakened by constant use, communications with the two companies in Merode failed. No one knew where to throw artillery fire to stop the German drive. Not until near midnight was there further word from the men in Merode. Then a plaintive message, barely audible, came over Colonel Daniel's radio set. "There's a Tiger tank coming down the street now, firing his gun into every house. He's three houses away now . . . still firing into every house . . . Here he comes . . . ."[46]

That was all anyone heard from the two companies in Merode until about three hours later when a sergeant and twelve men escaped from the village. Using these men as guides, a combat patrol tried to break through to any men who still might be holding out. Shellfire and burp guns forced the patrol back.

For all practical purposes, this marked the end of the 26th Infantry's fight for Merode. Though prisoner reports through the next day of 30 November and into 1 December continued to nourish hope that some of the two companies still survived, attempts to get help into the village grew more and more feeble.[47] Failure of every strong patrol that tried to get into the village convinced Colonel Daniel that only a full-strength battalion could do the job. The 26th Infantry commander, Colonel Seitz, dared not weaken the rest of his front by sending another of his battalions. Even when the 1st Division G-3 offered to send a battalion from another regiment, Colonel Seitz declined. "What is in town may be annihilated by now," Colonel Seitz's

---

[44] Combat Interv with Lt. Col. Wallace J. Nichols, CO, 745th Tank Bn, et al.
[45] 26th Inf Unit Jnl, 29 Nov 44.

[46] Combat Interv with Capt James Libby, S-3, 2d Bn, 26th Inf, et al.
[47] The 26th Infantry Unit Journal for this period makes stark reading.

S–3 told the G–3. "Moreover any attack on the town would have to be strictly an infantry attack. There is no road . . . ."[48]

Made to look like fools in their first fighting, the enemy's young paratroopers at last had found the right time and place to deal a punishing blow. The 26th Infantry listed 165 men missing on the day of the Merode engagement. For the Americans it was an ignominious end to the final fight to break out of the Huertgen Forest.

Had the VII Corps commander, General Collins, been unaware of the physical and even spiritual atrophy of the 26th Infantry and the entire 1st Division, the debacle at Merode certainly would have demonstrated the fact. On 2 December General Collins revealed that he would ask no more of the division than that it straighten the line and consolidate in preparation for relief by a fresh division. On 5 December the 9th Division began to arrive. The 47th Infantry was relieved from attachment to the 1st Division and went into 9th Division reserve. Both the 1st and 4th Divisions now were leaving the fight. The goal of the Roer River still was three miles away.

In fifteen days the 1st Division and the 47th Infantry, with an assist on two occasions by contingents of the 3d Armored Division, had registered a total advance of not quite four miles from Schevenhuette to Langerwehe. The division had cleared a rectangle of approximately eleven square miles embracing the northeastern extremities of the Huertgen Forest and a fringe of the Eschweiler–Weisweiler industrial triangle. In light of original plans for a quick breakthrough on the heels of an unprecedented preliminary

bombardment, that kind of progress was more than disappointing. The bombardment had not done all expected of it, and imponderables of German perseverance, adverse weather, and intractable terrain had entered the equation.

For all the damage inflicted on the enemy's *3d Parachute, 12th,* and *47th Divisions,* the 1st Division also had paid dearly. Indeed, with 3,993 battle casualties, including 641 in the attached 47th Infantry, the 1st Division would go down as one of the more severely hurt participants in the Huertgen Forest fighting. The 26th Infantry, which fought fully within the forest, lost more than any of the other regiments, 1,479 men, including 163 killed and 261 missing.[49] These did not include nonbattle losses attributable to combat exhaustion and the weather. For the 26th Infantry, at least, these must have been as severe as in regiments of other divisions which fought completely within the confines of the forest.

For all practical purposes, the dread battle of the Huertgen Forest was over. The 83d Division, which had relieved the 4th Division, and parts of the 5th Armored Division still would have to drive through a narrow belt of woodland before reaching the Roer; but the bulk of the forest at last was clear.

Since 14 September, when part of the 9th Division first had entered fringes of the forest near Roetgen, some American unit had been engaged continuously in the forest. A total of five American divisions,

---

[48] 26th Inf Unit Jnl, 30 Nov 44.

[49] Casualty figures are contained in annexes to 1st Division Combat Interviews. Losses for other regiments were as follows: 18th Infantry: 871, including 188 killed and 21 missing; 16th Infantry: 1,002 including 156 killed and 63 missing; Task Force Richardson (3d Armored Division): 101, including 14 killed and 6 missing.

plus a combat command of armor, an additional armored infantry battalion, and a Ranger battalion had fought there. One division, the 9th, had engaged in two separate fights in the forest, one in September, another in October, and one of its regiments, the 47th Infantry, had been involved a third time. The 28th Division in early November had lost more men in the forest than any other U.S. unit. The 1st, 4th, and 8th Divisions, the 2d Ranger Battalion, and the 5th Armored Division's 46th Armored Infantry Battalion and CCR completed the tragic roll.

To some at the time and to many after the event, the question occurred: why did the First Army keep feeding more and more units into the Huertgen Forest? Throughout the fighting, the army commander, General Hodges, was acutely conscious of the difficulties his troops were facing in the forest.[50] In early December, for example, on one of his tours of the front, he watched in admiration mixed with marked concern as a truck convoy passed carrying from the front the dirty, unshaven men of the 4th Division's 22d Infantry. Yet to General Hodges, his staff, and his corps commanders, there was no alternative. They admittedly might have bypassed the forest; but under the kind of conditions existing at the time, should an army with absolutely no reserve expose its flank to counterattack in this manner? Furthermore, when the First Army first entered the forest, nobody expected any real trouble. After the hard fighting de-

veloped, the Germans had to endure the same kind of hardships as the Americans did and were infinitely less capable of replacing battle-weary formations with rested units. The expectation was always present that one more fresh American division would turn the trick. As the First Army G–3, General Thorson, put it succinctly: "We had the bear by the tail, and we just couldn't turn loose."[51]

More than 8,000 men from the First Army fell prey in the forest to combat exhaustion and the elements. Another 23,000 were either wounded, missing, captured, or killed. That was an average of more than 5,000 casualties per division.

What had been gained at this cost? The Americans had battered at least six German divisions. They also had eliminated hundreds of individual replacements. They had conquered a formidable forest barrier by frontal assault. They also had forced the Germans to commit some of the forces intended to be held intact for the Ardennes counteroffensive. Beyond these, the fight in the forest had achieved little in the way of positive advantages—no German industry, limited roads. The basic truth was that the fight for the Huertgen Forest was predicated on the purely negative reason of denying the Germans use of the forest as a base for thwarting an American drive to the Rhine. In the process the fight thus far had failed to carry the only really critical objective the forest shielded—the Roer River Dams.

[50] Sylvan Diary, entry of 4 Dec 44.

[51] See Intervs with Thorson, 12 Sep 56; Collins, 25 Jan 54; and Akers, 11 Jun 56.

PART SIX

BATTLE OF THE ROER PLAIN

CHAPTER XXI

Clearing the Inner Wings of the Armies

Coincident with the First Army's push through the Stolberg Corridor and the Huertgen Forest, the November offensive of General Simpson's Ninth Army began at 1245 on 16 November. The drive started from the periphery of the West Wall bridgehead secured in October on the east bank of the Wurm River north of Aachen. (*See Map VI.*)

Except for the timing, the fighting on the Ninth Army front was as different from that on the First Army front as, say, Normandy was from Guadalcanal. While the First Army was engaged within a forest and its purlieus, the Ninth Army fought for possession of village strongpoints dotting a fertile plain.

This was the Roer plain, lying between the Wurm and the Roer. Although geographers seldom isolate the Roer plain from the broader Cologne plain that stretches to the Rhine, the fact that the Roer River was the objective of the first phase of the November offensive sharply delineated the region between the Wurm and the Roer in the minds of the men who fought there. Encompassing a maximum width of about twelve miles, the Roer plain is bounded by the irregular skirt of the Huertgen Forest, by the Roer itself, and by the meandering course of the Wurm, which rises near Aachen and empties into the Roer about twenty-two miles north of Aachen near Heinsberg. As defined by American troops, the plain

embodies approximately 200 square miles roughly in the form of a right-angle triangle marked at the corners by Aachen, Heinsberg, and Dueren.

Most of the terrain in this triangle is low and flat, providing long, unobstructed fields of fire and observation broken only occasionally by perceptible elevations. Scattered across the tableland are at least a hundred towns, villages, and settlements connected by an elaborate network of improved and secondary roads radiating like the strands of a spider's web. The villages seldom are more than one to three miles apart. Much of the ground in between is given over to agriculture. Only in the southwest and south near the base of the triangle is there a marked difference. Here deposits of coal along the upper valleys of the Wurm and the Inde account for a more urban district featured by mines, slag piles, factories, and densely populated towns and villages. Having inherited the bridgehead carved onto the plain in October, General Simpson's Ninth Army already possessed a portion of this urban district but still had to clear another portion along the interarmy boundary near the town of Wuerselen. An adjacent portion about the industrial town of Eschweiler was a responsibility of the First Army.

The Ninth Army's initial assault was to be a simple frontal attack to break out of the West Wall bridgehead and gain a crossing of the Roer in the southeastern corner of the army zone at Juelich. This was to be accomplished by the XIX Corps, commanded now by General McLain.

Like the First Army, the Ninth Army contemplated assistance from the preliminary bombardment by Allied planes, Operation QUEEN. Unlike the First Army, which wanted "carpet" bombing, the Ninth Army saw in the village strongpoints dotting the plain a need for "target" bombing. Air operations against the villages close to the army's forward positions would be confined to the four groups of fighter-bombers available in General Nugent's newly operational XXIX Tactical Air Command. Medium and heavy bombers were to concentrate upon communications centers some distance behind the line, like the village of Aldenhoven, three miles short of the Roer, and the Roer River towns of Juelich, Linnich, and Heinsberg.

A major consideration influencing General Simpson's plan was that General Bradley had ordered the Ninth Army to protect the First Army's north flank and make its main effort close alongside the First Army.[1] This General Simpson had fulfilled from an army standpoint by assigning his main effort to the south-wing XIX Corps. Yet from a corps standpoint, if General McLain followed instructions to the letter, the first step of the main effort would have to be made through the urban coal-mining district about Wuerselen in the southwest corner of the corps zone. Judging from the 30th Division's experience near Wuerselen in October, this might prove more difficult than a push through the rural regions a few miles to the north.[2]

His problem analogous to that posed to the First Army's VII Corps by the Eschweiler–Weisweiler industrial complex, General McLain chose a course similar to that pursued by General Collins. In the VII Corps, the 1st Division was to make the main effort near the center of the corps zone; then, once past the congested urban districts, was to expand northward to the army boundary. General McLain similarly directed his 29th Division to make the XIX Corps main effort in the center of the corps zone on a narrow front, then later to broaden the main effort southward to the army boundary. In each case, the corps main effort would bypass a triangular sector where German defense might benefit from urban congestion.

In effect, the clearing of these two triangles would mark a renewal of the joint fight which the VII and XIX Corps had staged in October in closing the gap about Aachen. The front lines were much the same as they had been upon conclusion of the fight in October. The only real changes that had occurred were the transfer of the XIX Corps to the Ninth Army and the assignment of the 104th Division to carry the banner of the VII Corps in place of the 1st Division. To renew the fight for the XIX Corps, General McLain had the same 30th Division which had participated in October.

Assigned missions so similar and in a sense separated from their parent corps by the nature of the missions, the 30th and 104th Divisions formed, in effect, a kind of *ad hoc* corps. So long as the missions remained as originally given, the separate

---

[1] 12th A Gp Ltr of Instrs 10, 21 Oct 44, with amendments, 12th A Gp Rpt of Opns, V, 97–102.

[2] XIX Corps AAR, Nov 44.

GENERAL McLAIN

fights to clear the two industrial triangles actually would represent a single, broader engagement to clear an industrial parallelogram along the inner wings of the two armies.

The Fight North of the Boundary

The interarmy boundary, which bisected this parallelogram, ran from the Ravelsberg (Hill 231) between Wuerselen and Verlautenheide—both of which had figured prominently in the October fighting—northeast between the villages of Kinzweiler, on the north, and Hehlrath, on the south, thence on to the northeast to cross the Inde River near Inden. South of the boundary, the 104th Division's triangular share of the parallelogram was described clearly by existing front lines running from Verlautenheide southeast to Stolberg and by the trace of

the Inde; while on the north, the triangle assigned to the 30th Division was less clearly defined without recourse to a map. One side was the existing front line, which ran from Alsdorf southwest to Wuerselen, the lower segment of the bridgehead arc the XIX Corps had forged in October. The second side was the boundary between the 29th and 30th Divisions. This ran southeast from a point near Alsdorf, past the villages of Hongen, Warden, and Luerken to the interarmy boundary. The sector embraced approximately twenty-four square miles.

To strengthen the 30th Division in clearing the urban sector, General Simpson directed attachment of a regiment of the newly arrived 84th Division to act as a reserve. This freed all three of the 30th Division's regiments for the attack.[3] The corps commander, General McLain, added additional strength by placing three battalions of corps artillery in general support.[4]

The Germans in this sector composed the northern wing of General Koechling's *LXXXI Corps.* In Wuerselen, five battalions of the *3d Panzer Grenadier Division,* which had denied the bulk of the town in October, still were around. The responsibility of this division, 11,000 strong, extended southeastward in the direction of Stolberg, including Verlautenheide, opposite the northern wing of the 104th U.S. Division. Northeast of Wuerselen from Euchen to include Mariadorf was the *246th Volks Grenadier Division's 404th Regiment,* while the rest

---

[3] XIX Corps Ltr of Instrs 64, 8 Nov, NUSA G-3 Jnl file, Nov 44.

[4] For details on attachments, see NUSA Opns, IV, 11. This account, plus Hewitt, *Workhorse of the Western Front,* and official records of the corps and division provide the basic sources for the 30th Division story.

of the *246th* held positions a little farther north opposite the center portion of the XIX Corps line. Of the three divisions in the *LXXXI Corps* at the start of the November offensive, the *246th* was rated the weakest, despite the fact that its personnel numbered the same as the *3d Panzer Grenadier Division*'s. After the debacle at Aachen, the *246th Division* had been fleshed out with replacements, including all survivors of the defunct *49th Division*. Part of the *404th Regiment* contained survivors of the old *Mobile Regiment von Fritzschen*, which had made a dramatic entry into the October fighting near this same spot.[5]

Perhaps because of earlier experience at Wuerselen, the 30th Division commander, General Hobbs, expected stiffest resistance among the rubble-strewn streets and battered buildings of that town. To eliminate this obstacle, Hobbs planned a maneuver not unlike the game of Crack the Whip. By means of a concentrated attack at Wuerselen, Colonel Sutherland's 119th Infantry was to act as the pivot or snapper, while the other two regiments in more extended formation were to swing southeastward in a broad arc to clear the remainder of the urban district. Although Colonel Johnson's 117th Infantry on the end of the whip would have to cover at least three times more ground than the 119th Infantry, this was in keeping with the belief that resistance would be weaker on the less congested outer rim.

Much as did the divisions of the VII Corps, the units of the XIX Corps learned before daylight on 16 November that after many postponements the big offensive at last was to begin. In keeping with the fact that 1944 was an election year, "The Democrats have won" were the code words General McLain telephoned to General Hobbs to indicate that the attack was on.[6]

Only three of the villages in the 30th Division's sector were hit in the aerial bombardment. Fighter-bombers of the XXIX Tactical Air Command struck both Mariadorf and Hongen in front of Colonel Purdue's 120th Infantry in the division center. Medium bombers attacked Luerken, at the extreme eastern end of the 30th Division's zone. None of these strikes was close enough to friendly positions to permit observation of the results.

In the ground attack, each of the 30th Division's three regiments struck with two battalions abreast. Having studied the terrain thoroughly both on the ground and on sand-table models, the troops experienced few surprises. What did impress them was a prolific use of mines. Particularly disturbing were extensive nests of nonmetallic antipersonnel *Schuh* mines and antitank *Topf* mines, neither of which responded to ordinary mine detection devices.[7] The first day's worst losses occurred when the 117th Infantry's Company F stumbled into an antipersonnel mine field on the western fringe of Mariadorf. German shelling forced abandonment of all attempts to extricate the company until after nightfall. The company lost sixty men.

So thick were antitank mines in Wuerselen that supporting tanks and tank destroyers were reduced to providing

[5] Strength Rpts, 15 Nov 44, *LXXXI Corps, IIa/b KTB Anlagen, 20.X.–30.XI.44; LXXXI Corps, Zustandsberichte; Kampf um Aachen:* Maps; MS # A–994 (Koechling).

[6] Tel Jnl in 30th Div G–3 Jnl file, 17–18 Nov 44.
[7] *Conquer—The Story of Ninth Army,* p. 90.

static fire support. At any turn amid the rubble of the town a man or a machine might set off an explosion. Pvt. Alexander Mastrobattista of the 119th Infantry's Company L had to lie in an exposed position for four hours with one leg blown off by a *Schuh* mine before a litter team preceded by probers and mine detectors could reach him.

For all the difficulty with mines, progress in the over-all division picture was encouraging. By nightfall four companies of the 117th Infantry had advanced more than a mile to establish firm control of Mariadorf. In the village of Euchen Colonel Purdue's 120th Infantry had caught the Germans cowering in their holes to escape shelling and machine gun fire which supporting weapons were firing over the heads of the attackers. Only in Wuerselen was there no major gain, but a plodding advance in this stronghold was understandable. Fighting in Wuerselen had developed into myriad small unit maneuvers as one squad or platoon after another tried to penetrate intricate cross fires laid down by well-positioned machine guns.[8] Despite the hard going at Wuerselen, the entire division on 16 November incurred only 137 casualties, almost half of them in the mine field at Mariadorf.

The penetration at Mariadorf disturbed the Germans particularly. As the 30th Division commander, General Hobbs, had hoped, the Germans saw this attack along the 30th Division's north wing as a first

step in a likely outflanking of Wuerselen. The *Fifteenth Army* headquarters (alias *Gruppe von Manteuffel*) authorized withdrawal to a second line of defense based on the next series of villages.[9]

At Broichweiden, a sprawling, loose confederation of four settlements a mile southeast of Euchen, the retiring troops of the *3d Panzer Grenadier Division* had little chance to get set before the 120th Infantry hit them a half hour before dawn on 17 November. The Americans literally charged into the northern half of Broichweiden. In the course of mopping up, Colonel Purdue's battalions took 326 prisoners, including virtually the entire strength of one panzer grenadier battalion. Buttressed by artillery, the Americans were too well set to be dislodged when at noon the Germans counterattacked with the support of seven tanks and assault guns.

In Wuerselen the effects of the night withdrawal were readily apparent, yet advance in the face of a stubborn rear guard and an unprecedented profusion of mines still was agonizingly slow. Although a marked map captured from German engineers helped considerably, not until late afternoon was the whole of Wuerselen occupied.

In the meantime, Colonel Johnson's 117th Infantry on the division's north wing had been keeping pace. One battalion moved in conjunction with the 120th Infantry's drive on Broichweiden to occupy a miners' housing development a mile southeast of Mariadorf. Another battalion met greater resistance in a drive northeast from Mariadorf against Hongen, but with the help of overhead fire from

---

[8] S. Sgt. Freeman V. Horner, Company K, 119th Infantry, charged alone across open ground into the teeth of fire from three machine guns hidden in a building. Armed with a submachine gun, he forced his way into the building, killed or captured seven of the enemy, and eliminated the enemy weapons. Sergeant Horner was awarded the Medal of Honor.

[9] Order, *Gruppe von Manteuffel* to *XII SS* and *LXXXI Corps*, 2225, 16 Nov 44, *LXXXI Corps KTB, Bef. H. Gr. u. Armee.*

supporting armor entered the village in midafternoon.

For all practical purposes, the 30th Division had broken the enemy's hold on the strictly urban portion of the triangle north of the interarmy boundary by the end of the second day. The part remaining to be cleared was more rural in nature.

On the third day, 18 November, at Warden, southeast of Mariadorf, an adroit use of machine guns and assault guns across flat, coverless fields enabled the enemy to repulse two attacks before succumbing to a third; but this was, in effect, no more than a delaying tactic preceding another shift to a new line of defense. During the evening of 18 November, the XIX Corps intercepted a German message designating a gentle ridge line a mile east of Warden as the new main line of resistance. A northeastward extension of high ground lying north of Stolberg, that part of the ridge opposite the 30th Division was little more than a ground swell on the Roer plain.

The commander of the *3d Panzer Grenadier Division,* General Denkert, could have entertained no more hope of holding this line than he had had of holding the two he had occupied earlier. As seen by the corps and army commanders, the focal point of danger was not here but farther north, in the sector of the *246th Division* and even farther north outside the zone of the *LXXXI Corps.* When General Koechling on 18 November had introduced the *47th Division* opposite the VII U.S. Corps and directed a general shift of division boundaries northward, he had done it in order that the *246th Division* might achieve greater concentration. The *3d Panzer Grenadier Division* thus became responsible for the

entire sector opposite the 30th U.S. Division and part of the 104th as well. At the same time the division was called upon to relinquish an infantry battalion for attachment to the *246th Division.*[10]

Despite this situation, General Denkert hardly could have anticipated the celerity with which the 30th Division might break his new line. Because the 30th Division was nearing the extremity of the triangle it had been assigned to clear, General Hobbs could concentrate almost unrestricted fire support against one short segment of the new line—at the villages of St. Joeris and Kinzweiler. Virtually all the divisional artillery, two companies of the 743d Tank Battalion, as many tank destroyers, and the heavy weapons of an adjacent regiment were available to support an attack by the 117th Infantry.

The Germans might have done better to raise a white flag. During the morning of 19 November, two battalions of the 117th Infantry struck the villages simultaneously on the heels of thunderous supporting fire. In forty-five minutes both villages were secure. Two battalion commanders and 221 other prisoners were headed west. In St. Joeris the 117th Infantry sustained but eight casualties; in Kinzweiler, only three.

Although some mop-up work remained in the southern half of Broichweiden, General Hobbs might say without reservation that his division's part in clearing the parallelogram was over. In four days, at a cost of sixty killed and 474 wounded, the 30th Division had erased a position which could have embarrassed the XIX Corps. Enemy losses included 1,595 prisoners, mostly from the *3d Panzer*

---

[10] Order, *Gruppe von Manteuffel* to *LXXXI Corps,* 2230, 18 Nov 44, *LXXXI Corps KTB, Bef. H. Gr. u. Armee.*

Grenadier Division. In achieving this goal, the 30th Division had realized little direct assistance from units on either flank, for not until 19 November did the 104th Division embark in earnest upon its part in clearing the inner wings of the armies, and not until the last two days had the 29th Division to the north, making the XIX Corps main effort, come abreast.

The fact was that the 30th Division's advance was one of the better gains made anywhere during the early days of the November offensive. Impressed by this development, the XIX Corps commander gave the division a new assignment. Redrawing his division boundaries, General McLain directed General Hobbs to renew his attack two days later. Along a front narrowing to a width of a mile and a half, the 30th Division was to cover a remaining six miles to the Roer.[11]

The Fight South of the Boundary

In view of the coup at St. Joeris and Kinzweiler on 19 November, the 104th Division could have chosen no more auspicious time to begin clearing that part of the parallelogram lying south of the interarmy boundary. Because of the proviso that the 104th Division make no major attack on its north wing until after capture of the Donnerberg (Hill 287), the height east of Stolberg, the two regiments which were scheduled to work alongside the 30th Division had been making only "pressure attacks," a kind of jockeying for position. But late on the day before, the Donnerberg had fallen. On 19 November the 104th Division was to attack with no holds barred.

Because the Germans had shifted their division boundaries slightly, the basic unit opposite two regiments of the 104th Division remained the same, the *12th Volks Grenadier Division* which the 414th Infantry had encountered at the Donnerberg. Opposite the 413th Infantry on the left were a few contingents of the *3d Panzer Grenadier Division.*

The division commander, General Allen, intended that once the Donnerberg had fallen the 414th Infantry was to continue northeast through the Eschweiler woods into Eschweiler and a nest of industrial suburbs southeast of that town. Coincidentally, the 413th Infantry on the division's north wing was to sweep northeast from Verlautenheide past the northern fringe of Eschweiler, or perhaps converge upon the town in the event the 414th Infantry ran into trouble. The third regiment, the 415th Infantry, was to clear the northern half of Stolberg and wooded high ground beyond. After serving briefly as a bridge between the other two regiments, the 415th Infantry under the original plan was to be pinched out short of Eschweiler.[12]

While the 414th Infantry consolidated gains made in the Eschweiler woods in a night attack, the other two regiments struck early on 19 November. Because of the enemy's general withdrawal to a new line marked in this sector by the towns of Roehe, a northwestern suburb of Eschweiler, and of Hehlrath, near St. Joeris and Kinzweiler, resistance was spotty. Nevertheless, harassed by *Schuh* mines, barbed wire, rubble, and congestion, the 415th Infantry (Colonel Cochran) took the entire day to clear Stolberg. Guiding on the Aachen–Cologne autobahn, the 413th Infantry (Colonel Waltz) pushed

---

[11] XIX Corps Ltr of Instrs 73, 19 Nov, NUSA G-3 Jnl file, 19–25 Nov 44.

[12] 104th Div FO 10, 9 Nov, in 104th Div G-3 Jnl file, 5–10 Nov 44.

DEVASTATED DUERWISS, *saturated by Allied bombs.*

the division's north wing forward more than three miles to the base of the gentle ridge line marked by Roehe and Hehlrath.

That the Germans intended to stand here was readily apparent early the next morning, 20 November. Not until late in the afternoon, after a TOT by VII Corps artillery using time fire, was one battalion able to gain a toehold in Roehe. Clearing the objective took another twenty-four hours. In the meantime, another battalion crossed the army boundary to Kinzweiler in order to use an approach to Hehlrath that afforded a measure of cover in houses and farmyards. Although this battalion and a platoon of supporting tanks got into Hehlrath before nightfall, they had to mop up from house to house in the darkness. As General Allen earlier

had informed a neighboring commander, men of his 104th Division "don't go to bed too early. In fact, they have insomnia." [13]

Roehe and Hehlrath were clear examples of the pattern which fighting on the Roer plain would assume. There was seldom any "high ground" in the usual sense of the term. Here the men fought instead for towns, villages, and settlements. For one thing, the upper stories of buildings and the spires of churches often provided the only genuine observation advantage; for another, the buildings represented the only cover worthy of the name and spelled relief from cold, rain, mud, and sometimes sleet and snow. Seldom, if ever, would the Germans re-

[13] Tel Jnl in 30th Div G–3 Jnl file, 17–18 Nov 44.

linquish a town or a village without a fight. If the buildings happened to occupy ground rising above the surrounding fields, then that made them correspondingly harder to get at.

Unlike the 413th Infantry, the 104th Division's other two regiments would serve a stint of street fighting before plunging fully into combat typical of the Roer plain. This was because of the industrial towns of Eschweiler and Weisweiler and their suburbs.

Under General Allen's original plan, the center regiment, the 415th Infantry, was to have been pinched out short of Eschweiler. But on 19 and 20 November, the 414th Infantry on the right wing became too embroiled in Eschweiler's southeastern suburbs to afford much promise of an early capture of the industrial town itself. In a belief that the Germans would abandon Eschweiler if advances north and south of it threatened encirclement, the VII Corps commander, General Collins, suggested that General Allen "let [Eschweiler] go." [14] General Allen for his part saw no reason to skip this objective—the largest town remaining to the Germans west of the Roer—so long as he had a ready force in the form of the 415th Infantry to take it. While the two flank regiments pushed their attacks on the north and south, Colonel Cochran was to take Eschweiler. Instead of converging at Eschweiler, the two flank regiments would converge a few miles farther east at Weisweiler.

When the 415th Infantry first probed the western outskirts of Eschweiler on 21 November, no evidence of German withdrawal was apparent. Yet on this day the 413th Infantry north of the city, in

renewing the fighting more typical of the Roer plain, pushed a mile beyond Hehlrath into Duerwiss. From the German viewpoint, Eschweiler was outflanked. *OB WEST* granted approval for withdrawal to a new line east of the town.[15] Four hours before dawn on 22 November, two companies of the 415th Infantry entered Eschweiler in a night attack to find no more than a feeble and sleepy rear guard remaining. Hot food and burning candles told how recent had been the withdrawal.

This matter of authorized withdrawals was a departure from Hitler-imposed tactics. Having always insisted upon standfast tactics in the West,[16] Hitler had allowed himself early in November to be reconciled to limited withdrawal in an attempt to avoid committing those forces which he had earmarked for the Ardennes counteroffensive. The Fuehrer nevertheless had stipulated that his reversal of policy not become known below the level of army headquarters.[17] *OB WEST* sanction of the withdrawals in this sector resulted partly from a hope of shortening the line and gaining some local reserves and partly from a recognition that, authorized or not, the withdrawals were inevitable.[18]

In the southeastern suburbs of Eschweiler, the 414th Infantry had begun to attack two days before the German withdrawal. Close to the boundary with

---

[14] Collins to Allen, 104th Div G-3 Jnl, 20 Nov 44.

[15] Order, *Gruppe von Manteuffel* to *XII SS* and *LXXXI Corps*, 2225, 21 Nov 44, *LXXXI Corps KTB, Bef. H. Gr. u. Armee; OB WEST KTB*, 21 Nov 44.
[16] See Harrison, *Cross-Channel Attack*, pp. 445 ff.
[17] TWX, Jodl to Westphal, 9 Nov 44, *OB WEST KTB, Anlage 50*, I, 114–15.
[18] *LXXXI Corps Gefechtsbericht*, AAR of 20 Nov 44.

the 1st Division, the 414th Infantry's objectives of Bergrath and Nothberg were subject to observation from Hills 187 and 167, which were holding out against the 1st Division's attached 47th Infantry. Here German mortars and artillery put backbone into an infantry defense amid houses and factories. Because of a five-day siege of inclement weather beginning on 20 November, fighter-bombers could not temper the curse of this fire. The 414th Infantry measured its advance to Bergrath in blood-stained yards until finally, late on 21 November, artillery supporting the adjacent regiment smothered Hill 187 with fire. The next morning the 414th Infantry moved into Nothberg against nothing more than rear guard opposition.

Early the same day, 22 November, the 413th Infantry encountered one of the few instances during the battle of the Roer plain where high ground other than that occupied by towns or villages figured prominently in the enemy's defense. The next objective facing the 413th Infantry was Puetzlohn, which occupies the western slope of a sharply discernible ridge line lying two miles west of the Inde River. Here the Germans would have to stand or else expose the entire valley of the Inde in the 104th Division's sector to damaging observation. To hold here, they counted not only upon defending Puetzlohn but upon denying a high point of the ridge south of Puetzlohn, Hill 154. To the south the new German line covered the western periphery of Weisweiler; to the north, the town of Lohn across the U.S. army boundary in the sector of the 30th Division.

Because the excavation of a strip mine blocked the direct route eastward from Duerwiss to Puetzlohn, the 413th Infantry

again had to enter the 30th Division's sector to reach its objective. Attacking early on 22 November, the regiment's leading battalion scarcely had re-entered its own sector when savage fire from tanks or assault guns in Puetzlohn and from artillery caught the men in open fields west of the village. By working forward slowly under cover of artillery concentrations, the infantry at last gained the westernmost buildings, but even this advance was wiped out partially in late afternoon when flanking fire from the 30th Division's sector forced a slight withdrawal. Puetzlohn and the high ground about it obviously were going to be hard to crack. Recognizing this as night came, the division commander, General Allen, prodded Colonel Touart's 414th Infantry to get a complementary drive under way. "Weisweiler is necessary," General Allen said, "to take the curse off Puetzlohn." [19]

The Push to the Inde

For all the difficulty at Puetzlohn, the 104th Division by nightfall of 22 November had cleared the bulk of its share of the industrial parallelogram along the inter-army boundary. Only Puetzlohn and Hill 154, both about two miles short of the Inde, plus Weisweiler and a trio of little towns hugging the west bank of the river, remained to be taken. Although the fighting at times had been severe, the 104th Division had incurred no more than moderate casualties. The 415th Infantry, for example, in a four-day fight from the northern reaches of Stolberg to the capture of Eschweiler had lost 37 men killed, 7 missing, and 118 wounded. The entire

---

[19] 104th Div G–3 Jnl, 22 Nov 44.

division took 600 prisoners. The Germans listed total casualties for the *12th Division*, part of which also had opposed the north wing of the 1st U.S. Division, at 1,845.[20]

The noteworthy aspect of the 104th Division's campaign to this point was that the attack had carried almost four times as far as had the 1st Division's in the VII Corps main effort, despite the urban nature of the battlefield. Because the 104th Division's start line had been farther west than had the 1st Division's, the two units by 22 November were approximately on line. The VII Corps commander, General Collins, saw in the situation an opportunity to revise his original plan. In the beginning he had directed that the 104th Division be pinched out at the Inde while the 1st Division was to assume responsibility for the entire northern half of the corps zone across the remaining five miles to the Roer. General Collins now redrew one of his boundaries, much as had General McLain of the XIX Corps three days before. The 104th Division now was to continue across the Inde all the way to and beyond the Roer.[21]

Upon the immediate employment of the 104th Division's regiments, General Collins' change in plan had no effect. Colonel Waltz's 413th Infantry on the north wing was to continue to attack Puetzlohn and Hill 154, then to take two of the three villages along the west bank of the Inde. Colonel Touart's 414th Infantry on the south wing was to occupy Weisweiler and the remaining village. Only upon reaching the Inde did General Allen intend to vary his formation by replacing the 414th Infantry with Colonel

Cochran's 415th Infantry. The latter regiment had gone into reserve after taking Eschweiler.

As the 104th Division renewed the attack before daylight on 23 November, another aspect of fighting upon the Roer plain was emphasized: many of the towns and villages were mutually supporting. Conquest of Puetzlohn was influenced by progress of the adjacent 30th Division against Lohn; capture of Weisweiler, by the degree of success in the 1st Division's sector against Huecheln and Wilhelmshoehe.

Turning once again to the stratagem of night attack, two companies of the 413th Infantry moved in the predawn darkness of 23 November, one against Puetzlohn, the other against Hill 154. Although the Germans at each place were awake to the attack, their artillery and assault guns now lacked the observation necessary to prevent advance. Company L got atop Hill 154, while Company K gained a tenuous hold on the southwestern fringe of Puetzlohn.

Soon after daybreak, the Germans counterattacked for the first time since the 104th Division had jumped off five days earlier. They used only an *Alarmbataillon* and six to eight tanks borrowed from a GHQ battalion operating farther north; yet even this force made for a disturbing day because the Americans had but two companies on the objectives and because in the daylight German fire on open fields around the objectives could deny reinforcement. As night came, the 413th Infantry still controlled both Puetzlohn and Hill 154, but at a cost to Companies K and L of 116 casualties, including 16 killed and 50 missing.

In the meantime, at Weisweiler, the 414th Infantry was encountering a more

[20] Chart of Losses up to 24 Nov 44, *LXXXI Corps IIa/b KTB, Anlagen, 20.X.–30.XI.44.*

[21] VII Corps Opns Memo 119, 22 Nov, VII Corps Opns Memos file, Nov 44.

passive defense, though it was none the less stubborn. On General Allen's theory that "The more they push under cover of darkness the better it is for 'em," [22] the 414th Infantry also tried a night attack, but by the time the men had threaded their way to the line of departure, the predawn darkness of 23 November had dissipated. The men were subject to a house-by-house German defense along the route of approach while at the same time drawing flanking fire from Huecheln on the south and a high, flat-topped slag pile almost a mile square on the north. Not until the next day, 24 November, after the slag pile had been cleared, was any substantial progress made. One battalion reached the southwestern fringe of Weisweiler, while a company from another made a daring night attack to carry a power plant a few hundred yards west of the town. Once inside the plant, the men became acutely aware that they had sneaked into a building that housed a host of Germans. When the enemy commander assembled his men in an adjacent courtyard preparatory to routing the intruders, the American commander, Capt. Charles Glotzbach, called for time fire from his supporting artillery. While his men took cover in the building, the Germans in the courtyard caught the full force of the fire.[23]

Although the 414th Infantry had gained a steppingstone leading to the conquest of Weisweiler, actions outside the regimental sector actually brought about the fall of the town. The first of these was capture of Puetzlohn and Hill

154 on 23 November, thereby affording observation upon Weisweiler from the north. The others occurred at nightfall of 24 November and in the morning of 25 November in the 1st Division's sector when Task Force Richardson took Huecheln and Wilhelmshoehe. By early afternoon of 25 November, German withdrawal from Weisweiler was clearly evident. Taking quick advantage of the first break in the weather in five days, fighter-bombers of the IX Tactical Air Command roared to the attack. Only the size of the withdrawing columns limited the scope of the kill.

Though the actual occupation of Weisweiler was easy, the condition of the battalion of the 414th Infantry which had borne the brunt of the attack on the town showed how creditable had been the early stages of the German defense. So spent and depleted was this battalion that Colonel Touart wanted to replace it before following the enemy's withdrawal. The battalion was particularly hard hit in rifle company commanders. On 24 November when all three had assembled with the artillery liaison officer and a lieutenant from the weapons company for a conference, the Germans had captured the entire group.

Now that the 104th Division possessed dominant observation upon the three villages along the floor of the shallow valley of the Inde, a German withdrawal to the east bank of the river would not have been unexpected. Yet this was not to be, probably because the villages made excellent outposts for the high ground on the east bank. Though the *12th Volks Grenadier Division* was so depleted— down to 800 combat effectives—that it soon would be lumped with the *47th Division* under the designation *Gruppe*

---

[22] 104th Div G-3 Jnl, 22 Nov 44.

[23] Hoegh and Doyle, *Timberwolf Tracks,* pages 141-44, contains a detailed description of this action by Al Newman, correspondent for *Newsweek* Magazine.

Engel, the division had some fight left and on 28 November would be replaced by the *3d Parachute Division.* Not until 2 December—a week after the fall of Weisweiler—were the last Germans to retire or be eliminated from the west bank of the Inde.

Employing automatic weapons and light mortars from trenches along the western periphery of the villages, the Germans halted the attacking infantry in flat, open fields leading to the villages. With antitank guns and a few tanks hidden among the buildings, they held off American tanks and destroyers. From eminences east of the river, almost as high as the Puetzlohn ridge, they had unrestricted observation upon the shallow valley for their artillery. Observers for the 104th Division plotted more than forty gun positions between the Inde and the Roer capable of firing into the valley of the Inde.

Perhaps because the Germans had little time to perfect this pattern before the first blow, Colonel Touart's 414th Infantry took the southernmost village of Frenz on 26 November without undue difficulty. At the other two villages, Lamersdorf and Inden, the enemy was ready. A first try by the 413th Infantry to roll up the line by striking first Lamersdorf and then Inden from the 414th Infantry's positions at Frenz was abandoned after only a half day's exposure to crippling fire from the big guns east of the Inde. The regimental commander, Colonel Waltz, next directed separate attacks on each of the two objectives.

Despite persistent efforts by tactical aircraft and divisional and corps artillery to silence the German batteries, and despite attempts to hide behind smoke, the attacks developed into costly slugging matches. Even the 104th Division's forte of night attack brought little advantage. Once when the battalion driving on Inden tried it, one company got lost and ended up assisting the 30th Division against the neighboring village of Altdorf.

Not until after three days of close combat at Lamersdorf did the Germans finally withdraw the last of the tanks and antitank guns from this village to the east bank. Demolishing the Inde bridges behind them, they left only a thin rear guard in the village. By midnight of 29 November, Lamersdorf was in hand.

Inden took longer. By nightfall of 28 November, a rifle company had gained a toehold in the village and had even grabbed a bridge intact and put a platoon onto the east bank of the river, but the hardest fighting began later. During the night, this village passed to the responsibility of the enemy's *3d Panzer Grenadier Division.* Using miscellaneous forces from this division, plus some troops provided for the occasion by the *LXXXI Corps,* the Germans counterattacked in strength. Not only did they drive the platoon from the east bank, they split the American company and denied coordination with another company which arrived during the night as reinforcement. Shortly before daylight on 29 November the Germans captured about a platoon of men from both companies who had become intermingled in a factory alongside the river.[24] Their bag included one of the company commanders. Two other men—S. Sgt. Paul Shesniek and Pvt. Ben J. Travis—eventually escaped by hiding under heavy sacks filled with nuts.

---

[24] The Germans claimed seventy-nine prisoners. *LXXXI Corps Gefechtsbericht,* AAR of 30 Nov 44.

Though cut to pieces, the bulk of these two companies fought on through the day of 29 November. By late afternoon Colonel Waltz was ready to relieve them by attacking with his reserve battalion and a company of the 750th Tank Battalion. Only three of the tanks escaped both German fire and paralyzing mud, but the infantry gained entry into the village. The next day the reserve battalion commander, Lt. Col. William M. Summers, took command of all five companies in Inden and began a methodical attempt to rid the village of Germans.

Despite pressure to complete the job so the 104th Division could mount a crossing of the river, Colonel Summers could find no ready formula for rapid reduction of Inden. Enemy artillery fire, "at times, reached fifty rounds per minute." [25] Infantry reinforcements arrived when the *246th Volks Grenadier Division,* recently pulled from the line for a quick, three-day rehabilitation, took over from the *3d Panzer Grenadier Division.*[26] Colonel Summers and the companies of the 413th Infantry nevertheless gradually increased their holdings. Late on the fifth day the Germans finally retired to the east bank. In the five-day fight, two American battalions had lost 319 men, 40 of them killed and 156 missing.[27] Inden was nothing but rubble.

Taking the High Ground

The last German position in the industrial triangle south of the interarmy boundary thus eliminated, the 104th

Division turned next to crossing the Inde. In keeping with the change in plan which the VII Corps commander had directed on 22 November, the division was to continue to the Roer alongside the corps main effort. That the main effort by 2 December was sputtering on the fringe of the Roer plain at Langerwehe and Merode did nothing to lessen the need for the 104th Division to get across the Inde in order to come abreast of the main effort and void the tactical divorce which the meandering Inde heretofore had imposed.

The obvious key to a successful crossing was the village of Lucherberg, which crowns the high ground a mile beyond the river. In comparison to other high ground on the Roer plain, the Lucherberg ridge line is almost clifflike. Though not quite so high as the Puetzlohn ridge, the Lucherberg ridge's western approaches are steep, gutted by strip mines with sheer walls, and further obstructed by a nest of factories. From the southwest and south, the village and the ridge are denied by the bed of the Weh Creek, a slag pile, and more strip mines, one of which had filled with water to form a lake. On the north, the approach is open as the ridge line slopes gently northward parallel to the Inde. Recognizing that possession of Lucherberg spelled control not only of the Inde valley but also of a remaining three miles of flatland east to the Roer, the Germans had crisscrossed the northern approach with deep trenches from which machine guns might spew grazing fire across open fields. The positions were currently occupied by the *3d Parachute Division*'s *8th Regiment.*[28]

---

[25] 413th Inf AAR, Dec 44.
[26] *LXXXI Corps Gefechtsbericht,* AAR of 30 Nov 44.
[27] Casualty Figures for the Battle of Inden, 104th Div Combat Interv file, Nov–Dec 44.

---

[28] *LXXXI Corps Gefechtsbericht,* AAR of 3 Dec 44.

Had the Inde River been more of an obstacle, the 104th Division commander, General Allen, might have asked to attack from the 1st Division's sector on the other side of the river, where troops of the 47th Infantry on 28 November had taken the Frenzerburg. But the Inde normally is little more than a winding creek, and even after abnormally heavy rainfall during the previous month was easily fordable by infantry at several points.

Before the 413th Infantry had become so involved in severe fighting at Inden, General Allen had intended that the 413th force a bridgehead opposite Inden while the reserve regiment, the 415th Infantry, crossed the river at Lamersdorf to seize Lucherberg. Faced with severe losses at Inden, General Allen directed instead that the 413th Infantry fall back as division reserve, Colonel Touart's 414th Infantry take over the assignment at Inden, and Colonel Cochran's 415th Infantry proceed as originally planned to accomplish the more critical task at Lucherberg.

Colonel Cochran had four days to plan and prepare for the river crossing before the final conquest of Inden gave a green light. Deciding early on his maneuver, he provided his officers and men an opportunity for detailed study of their roles and the terrain. Although aware of the obstacles to attacking Lucherberg from the west, Colonel Cochran was equally aware of the defenses the Germans had erected along the open northern approach. Confident of the ability of his men in night operations, he believed they might get past the strip mines, the factories, and the clifflike portion of the ridge into Lucherberg before the Germans awoke to their presence.

Colonel Cochran directed his 2d Battalion to send two companies across the river at Lamersdorf by fording—one to seize the nest of factories between the river and Lucherberg, the other to provide flank protection by taking a castle (Luetzelen) south of the factories. An hour after these companies began to move, the 3d Battalion was to send two companies across the river on the debris of a spur railroad bridge between Lamersdorf and Inden. These two companies were to skirt the north side of the factories and move directly into Lucherberg. Each company received a detailed map upon which the artillery had plotted concentrations by number at almost every conceivable point of trouble.[29]

For an hour before the attack, artillery of both the 104th Division and the VII Corps fired constant concentrations upon Lucherberg. These were to continue at intervals until the infantry requested a concentration of white phosphorus, a signal that friendly troops were entering the village.

At a point at Lamersdorf where the river was no more than knee deep, the two companies of the 2d Battalion waded across at 2300 the night of 2 December. Almost without enemy contact, one company raced southeast to Luetzelen Castle. In a matter of minutes, this objective on the south flank was secured. At the same time, the other company rushed through inky darkness into the factory buildings between Lamersdorf and Lucherberg. The Germans in the buildings were too surprised to offer more than desultory resistance. Under strict orders to use nothing but bayonets and hand grenades in the darkness, the Americans

---

[29] Combat interviews on the battle of Lucherberg are valuable and detailed and constitute the major source for this account.

knew that anyone who fired was a German. Within an hour after crossing the Inde, these men had a firm grip on the factories, though mop-up was a task that reached into the next day.

Having allowed an hour for these preliminary operations to get under way, the two companies of the 3d Battalion began to cross the Inde between Lamersdorf and Inden at midnight. Commanded by 1st Lt. John J. Olsen, Company I was first. The men crossed on the remains of a spur railroad bridge. They negotiated the gap in the bridge by holding onto one of the rails which still was in place and walking on the other, which had been blown to a twisted position underneath. Though this kind of tight-rope crossing enabled the men to reach the east bank with dry feet, it was a slow process. Not until 0100, 3 December, did all of Company I get across.

As Lieutenant Olsen and his men picked their way southeastward across marshy bottomland toward the nest of factories and Lucherberg, a three-quarter moon emerged. Occasional small arms fire began to search the column. Though the fire was inaccurate, it prompted some confusion. Company I's rear platoon became separated from the others. No doubt acutely conscious that success depended upon reaching Lucherberg before daylight, Lieutenant Olsen decided to continue with his two remaining platoons.

Unknown to Lieutenant Olsen, the Germans had begun to fire on the crossing site soon after Company I had reached the east bank. Company L could not follow. Through the rest of the night Company L was to wander errantly in search of another place to cross, while the onus of the attack fell upon Lieutenant Olsen and the forward platoons

of Company I. In light of reports gleaned from prisoners the afternoon before, this was a big assignment. Some 500 to 600 Germans and several tanks, prisoners had reported, garrisoned Lucherberg and the vicinity.

Just how big the assignment was soon became apparent. Preceded by a platoon leader, 1st Lt. David Sheridan, who reconnoitered in advance, then sent a messenger back for the platoons, the men stumbled past the factories and up the steep slope toward Lucherberg more in a "column of bunches" than in any orthodox military formation. In spite of persistent but wild fire from an alerted German tanker, the men pushed into the village to gain three houses near a road junction in the northern end. At this point, trouble started. Even as the Americans tried to expand their holdings, the Germans set out to dislodge them. The company commander, Lieutenant Olsen, was shot in the head. He died before daybreak.

In the meantime, the rear platoon, which had become separated from the others, also reached Lucherberg, but the leaders didn't know where to find the rest of the company. They holed up in what the men called a double house in the southwest part of the village. With this platoon were observers for both mortars and artillery, who had radio contact with the 3d Battalion headquarters. Unable to locate Lieutenant Olsen and the rest of Company I, they radioed the battalion commander for help. Though this request went out about 0400, no genuine assistance was to materialize until late in the day.

While this platoon held in the double house, one of those bizarre incidents that make war a logical haven for lunatics was developing near the road junction in the north edge of Lucherberg. There a German medical officer, a lieutenant colonel, asked for a fifteen-minute truce in order that both sides might care for their wounded. As the truce more or less informally developed, most of Company I's men leaned their weapons against walls of the houses and began to help with the wounded. Three German medics assisted in a vain attempt to sustain Lieutenant Olsen.

The truce still was in effect when another group of about thirty Germans arrived under command of a captain. Refusing to honor the truce, the German captain directed his men to collect the American weapons. The Americans, he insisted, were to surrender. The men of Company I gradually became aware that in the darkness the new arrivals had stealthily encircled them.

Reminding the German captain of the tradition of discipline in his army, an interpreter, Sgt. Leon Marokus, insisted that the ranking officer, the lieutenant colonel, have the say. The captain refused. The lieutenant colonel, he said, was only a medical officer.

In the end, the captain agreed to a compromise. Angrily, he announced that he would give the Americans fifteen minutes to get out of the village. Conscious of their encirclement, Sergeant Marokus and his companions had little choice. As they assembled to leave, they became aware that only about twenty men out of an original two platoons and a machine gun section remained. Because the German captain insisted upon holding Company I's sole remaining officer, Lieutenant Sheridan, as a hostage, Sergeant Marokus refused to part with the lieutenant colonel. Only as the fifteen-minute period expired were these two exchanged.

In the interim, the men of Company I's rear platoon in the southwestern edge of Lucherberg had made contact with the others. Fleeing the truce site, Sergeant Marokus and the twenty who had escaped fell back to the double house. Through most of the day of 3 December, the composite group fought from this position, an island of resistance sustained only through persistent and effective employment of mortar and artillery fire. Fortunately for the forty-five men who made up the defense, two were the observers from the 81-mm. mortars and the artillery, 1st Lts. John Shipley and Arthur A. Ulmer. Some idea of the kind of fire support provided might be discerned from the day's artillery statistics. During the twenty-four hour period, organic and attached artillery fired 370 missions and 18,950 rounds along the 104th Division's front, now only four miles wide.

Reinforcing Company I was a slow process. Company L, which was to have followed Company I across the Inde the preceding night, had been stymied by fire both at the crossing site used by Company I and at the Lamersdorf site employed by the companies of the 2d Battalion. Not until daylight on 3 December had the company found another crossing site at Frenz. Conscious of German observation, the men crawled and infiltrated in small groups to the nest of factories west of Lucherberg, whence they might make a concerted effort to reach the village. So slow was the process that the last men of Company L did not reach the factory buildings until noon.

In the meantime, the reserve company of the 2d Battalion, Company F, tried infiltrating across the river at Lamersdorf and reached the factories soon after Company L. Placing both companies under Capt. F. J. Hallahan, Company L commander, Colonel Cochran directed an attack on Lucherberg at 1500 that afternoon, 3 December. The infantry would have to attack alone, for German shelling had stultified efforts to bridge the Inde, and an alarming rise in the waters had prevented tanks from fording.

The ease and speed with which the attack progressed was hard to explain other than that an artillery preparation effectively pinned the enemy inside his foxholes and cellars. In a matter of only ten to fifteen minutes, both Companies F and L had broken into Lucherberg, and Company L had established contact with the forty-five men in the double house. Mop-up was slower, so that near midnight, when the men paused to strike a defense, some parts of the village remained in German hands.

Before the companies could renew their mop-up the next morning, 4 December, the Germans counterattacked with infantry supported by damaging concentrations of mortar fire. From upper stories of the buildings, the Americans turned the village into a shooting gallery. By noon, it was over. An hour or so later, engineers at last bridged the Inde at Lamersdorf, and a section of 57-mm. antitank guns reached Lucherberg. Before midnight, a platoon of tanks and a platoon of towed tank destroyers also arrived.

The enemy's major effort to retake Lucherberg began before daylight on 5 December. Employing some eight to ten tanks and assault guns and about 450 infantry from the *3d Parachute Division's 8th Regiment,* the Germans sneaked into the village through the early morning

darkness. For several hours the fighting raged at close quarters. Two of the American tanks and one of the 57-mm. antitank guns were knocked out early in the engagement. One of the towed tank destroyers accounted for two German assault guns which bogged in the mud on the fringe of the village. Firing upon a German rifleman who apparently was carrying explosives, a squad of American infantry watched in horror as the German literally disintegrated in a loud explosion. An enemy tank laid some direct hits into Company F's command post, killing several men, including the company commander and the artillery observer.

Like a storm that blows itself out, the fighting in Lucherberg the morning of 5 December was too intense to last for long. Again with a noteworthy assist from mortars and artillery,[30] the men of the 415th Infantry were in control of the situation by 0830. Leaving behind the hulks of two Tiger tanks, two Panther tanks, and two assault guns, the Germans began to withdraw to the northeast. By midafternoon the arrival of a fresh company to relieve what was left of Company I underscored the fact that the enemy's chance of retaking Lucherberg had passed. Through means of continued shelling and a minor counterattack on 6 December, the Germans showed somewhat reluctant acceptance of that fact; but it was fact nonetheless.[31]

In the three-day fight for Lucherberg, the Germans lost at least 204 men killed and 209 captured, plus an estimated 400 to 500 wounded. Despite the initial

---

[30] Within a period of two hours, 8,000 rounds of artillery were fired in the vicinity of Lucherberg. 104th Div Arty AAR, Dec 44.

[31] *LXXXI Corps Gefechtsbericht,* AAR of 5 Dec 44.

misfortunes of Company I, the 415th Infantry's losses were relatively small. Incomplete figures showed 25 killed, 21 missing, and about 60 wounded.[32]

In pushing beyond the Inde, the 104th Division had come abreast of the other divisions of the VII Corps. A smaller bridgehead which the 414th Infantry had been establishing at Inden even as the 415th Infantry took Lucherberg made the division's position more secure and pro-vided an adequate base for renewing the push across the remaining three miles to the Roer. The 104th Division might have begun the new push immediately had not the corps commander, General Collins, ordered a pause. Because the other divisions of the corps had spent themselves in fighting to the fringe of the Roer plain, he needed time to replace them with fresh troops. Thereupon, the entire VII Corps would join the battle of the Roer plain in a final push to the Roer in the general direction of Dueren.

---

[32] All casualty figures are from 104th Division combat interviews.

CHAPTER XXII

The Roer River Offensive

Among numerous considerations affecting the Ninth Army's role in the November offensive, one of the most telling was German possession of the West Wall strongpoint of Geilenkirchen. Located ten miles north of Aachen along the Ninth Army's northern boundary, Geilenkirchen in German hands severely restricted the frontage available for deployment at the start of the planned offensive. The solution to the problem posed by the town eventually was to alter a simple plan for a frontal attack into a complicated blueprint involving progressive shifts in corps and division boundaries. (*See Map VII.*)

Shifting the Ninth Army boundary northward was no solution, for any troops that attacked from northwest or north of Geilenkirchen eventually would have to cross the Wurm River, which could be a costly procedure. The situation was complicated further on the south wing because the congested urban district of Wuerselen was not desirable for early stages of the main attack. Once a sizable portion of the front at Wuerselen had been allotted to one division, the 30th, not quite six miles of frontage remained. The Ninth Army commander, General Simpson, had available for employment here the rest of the XIX Corps and all of General Gillem's newly operational XIII Corps. Thus developed perhaps the only instance during the Siegfried Line Campaign when a commander had more troops than he had space in which to use them.

Planning Period

In the final analysis, General Simpson found his solution in temporary boundaries.

First, the adjacent 30 British Corps was to encompass Geilenkirchen in its sector temporarily and reduce the town with the assistance of the 84th U.S. Division. This arrangement had the dual virtue of taking care of Geilenkirchen while at the same time permitting employment at the start of at least a portion of the troops of General Gillem's XIII Corps (the 84th Division). Beyond Geilenkirchen, the northeastward trace of the Wurm promised enlargement of the Ninth Army's sector, thus permitting the 84th Division to return to the XIII Corps and other units of the corps to enter the line.

Second, General Simpson directed that the 2d Armored Division, which as northernmost element of the XIX Corps was to attack northeastward toward the Roer at Linnich, was to halt a mile or so short of Linnich at the communications center of Gereonsweiler. After capture of Gereonsweiler, the XIX Corps north boundary was to be shifted to the south, further broadening the sector available to the XIII Corps. Upon shift of the boundary, the 2d Armored Division was to pull into an assembly area near Juelich and prepare to exploit a river crossing to be staged by infantry of the XIX Corps. The 2d Armored Division thus had the twofold mission of protecting the north flank of the XIX Corps during the drive on Juelich while at the same time developing maneuver space for commitment of the XIII Corps.

Third, after supply lines of the XIX Corps had been adjusted to the earlier temporary boundary, General Simpson planned another boundary adjustment, widening the XIII Corps sector by more than a mile and giving the XIII Corps more direct lines of communication leading to Linnich.[1]

As finally determined, the basic outline of the Ninth Army's role in the November offensive was as follows:

On the heels of the target bombing which represented the Ninth Army's share of Operation QUEEN, General McLain's XIX Corps with three divisions (the 2d Armored, 29th, and 30th) was to make the Ninth Army's main effort alongside the First Army's left flank to seize a crossing of the Roer at Juelich. As an attached component of the 30 British Corps, which on 12 November had assumed responsibility for the Ninth Army's troublesome seventeen-mile north flank running eastward from the Maas River, the 84th Division was to attack on D plus 1 to capture Geilenkirchen. Thereupon, General Gillem's XIII Corps with the 113th Cavalry Group, two active divisions (the 84th and 102d), and a reserve division (the 7th Armored, which was recuperating from fighting in the Peel

GENERAL GILLEM

Marshes) was to be committed on the Ninth Army's north wing to cross the Roer at Linnich. After jumping the Roer, both corps were to drive northeast to the Rhine at Duesseldorf. Detailed plans for both the Roer crossings and the drive to the Rhine were to await developments, particularly in regard to the dams on the upper Roer which the Germans might blow to isolate any force east of the river.

Most of the terrain in the XIX Corps zone was typical of the Roer plain: generally flat, averaging about 300 feet above sea level, dotted with villages ranging in population from one to two thousand, composed primarily of cultivated fields outlined by shallow ditches and sparse hedges. Having seized the eastern slopes of the Wurm River valley during the October penetration of the West Wall, the XIX Corps already possessed the highest ground in the sector. From four villages along the periphery of the West

---

[1] NUSA Ltr of Instrs 7, 4 Nov, and various other ltrs of instrs found in NUSA G-3 Jnl file, 1–16 Nov 44. See also NUSA Opns, IV, 1–9, and *Conquer—The Story of Ninth Army,* pp. 71–78, 81–83. Ninth Army journals for the planning period are of little value.

Wall "bridgehead"—Waurichen, Beggendorf, Baesweiler, and Oidtweiler—the ground slopes gently downward a remaining six miles to the Roer. The highest ground still in German hands was along the proposed route of advance of the 29th Division, from Baesweiler and Oidtweiler east through the road center of Aldenhoven to Juelich, and near the village of Setterich, northeast of Baesweiler, no more than a stone's throw from the projected line of departure. Two major highways, both originating at Aachen, traversed the plain in the direction the XIX Corps wanted to go. One would serve the 2d Armored Division in the direction of Linnich; the other, the 29th Division on the route through Aldenhoven to Juelich. Another major road cuts laterally across the plain from Geilenkirchen southeast through Aldenhoven in the direction of Dueren.

Not only the main roads but also the secondary roads, crisscrossing the plain from village to village, attracted special attention. This was because commanders feared the soil off the roads might be too moist and soft for cross-country maneuver of tanks. Already indications had developed that the month of November might produce some kind of record for incessant rainfall and cloudiness. Meteorologists later were to note that a trace of rain appeared on all but two days of November and that one and a half inches fell in excess of a normally high precipitation.[2]

In hope of increasing tank flotation, the Ninth Army, as did the First Army, called upon maintenance companies and battalions to set up special shops and adopt assembly line methods to equip

tanks with track connector extensions ("duck bills"). These were five-inch steel end connectors, a form of grouser. By D Day approximately three fourths of the medium tanks in both the 2d Armored Division and separate battalions supporting the infantry would have been modified.[3]

Still concerned, tankers lashed fascines to their vehicles to be used for increased traction should the tanks bog down. The 2d Armored Division commander, General Harmon, mounted a tank shortly before D Day for a personal test of the soil situation.[4]

General Harmon's preoccupation with mobility had somber overtones. As an armored commander, he must have recognized the maxim that "armor attracts armor;" and the Ninth Army G-2, Colonel Bixel, had warned that the enemy's *9th Panzer Division* occupied a reserve position only a few miles behind the front line. In the *15th Panzer Grenadier Division,* Colonel Bixel noted, the Germans had another force containing armor in a reserve location not much farther away.[5]

Colonel Bixel was referring quite accurately to the two divisions which made up the *OB WEST* reserve in this sector, General von Luettwitz' *XLVII Panzer Corps.* Only recently returned from the

---

[2] NUSA Opns, IV, 9, citing Rpt of Detachment "ZP," 21st Weather Sq, 4 Jan 45.

[3] NUSA Opns, IV, 7; *Conquer—The Story of Ninth Army,* p. 100; The Armored School, Hell on Wheels in the Drive to the Roer, App. VII. p. iii. The latter is a detailed study of the 2d Armored Division's part in the Roer offensive, prepared at Fort Knox in 1949. Copy in OCMH. Most track connector extensions were procured locally. See Thompson, Local Procurement in the ETO.

[4] NUSA Opns, IV, 58; *Conquer—The Story of Ninth Army,* pp. 85-86.

[5] NUSA Opns, IV, p. 6; XIX Corps AAR, Nov 44.

spoiling attack in the Peel Marshes, the *LXVII Panzer Corps* had assumed a reserve position straddling the boundary between the *XII SS* and *LXXXI Corps* in rear areas of the *Fifteenth Army* (alias *Gruppe von Manteuffel*). From this position the reserve might move to the assistance of either corps.[6] With their combined total of 66 tanks, 41 assault guns, and 65 105-mm. and 150-mm. howitzers, the two divisions of the *XLVII Panzer Corps* were capable of a telling contribution in the battle of the Roer plain.[7] The boundary between the enemy's *XII SS* and *LXXXI Corps* ran from the vicinity of Beggendorf and Loverich northeastward to Linnich.[8]

Other than the *3d Panzer Grenadier Division*, which held the urban district about Wuerselen, that part of the *LXXXI Corps* opposite the Ninth U.S. Army consisted only of the *246th Volks Grenadier Division*. Since Colonel Wilck's melodramatic surrender at Aachen, the division had been commanded by a Colonel Koerte. Though rated weakest of all *LXXXI Corps* units, the *246th Division* had 11,141 men organized into three infantry regiments, an artillery regiment with about 30 pieces of varying caliber, an engineer battalion, and additional units containing 13 assault guns, 7 88's, and 21 lesser pieces.[9]

Commanded temporarily by General der Infanterie Guenther Blumentritt, the *XII SS Corps* bore responsibility for al-

most twenty-two miles of front northwest of Loverich through Geilenkirchen all the way to the Maas River. This was a big assignment for a corps that had but two divisions, the *176th Infantry* (Colonel Landau) and the *183d Volks Grenadier* (General Lange). Having absorbed rough treatment at the hands of the XIX U.S. Corps in September, the *176th Division* since that time had undergone major reorganization. It now was capable of fairly creditable defensive action. Though numbering only about 8,000 men, the division had able troops and relatively high morale. The division's sector was opposite the British, from a point northwest of Geilenkirchen to the Maas River. The *183d Division*, which had been rushed into the West Wall at the end of September, controlled Geilenkirchen and the corps south wing.

The commander of the *XII SS Corps*, General Blumentritt, was less concerned about the American front east of the Wurm than about the British front west of the river. The position of the *176th Division*, General Blumentritt noted, invited a pincers attack from the west and from the south up the valley of the Wurm through Geilenkirchen to cut off the entire division. With this in mind, he directed the main weight of his defenses on either side of Geilenkirchen. His infantry reserve—a battalion from each division—was located in that vicinity and his artillery batteries were instructed to be ready to mass fire on Geilenkirchen. Having been promised the assistance of the new *388th Volks Artillery Corps*, General Blumentritt intended to commit it so that its fires also could be directed on the Geilenkirchen sector.

General Blumentritt also concentrated his antitank defenses around Geilenkir-

[6] See Heichler, The German Situation in Mid-November 1944.

[7] Strength Rpts, 1 Nov 44, *LXVII Pz Corps O. Qu., KTB Anlagen, Einzelbefehle, 17.X.–18.XI.44.*

[8] *Kampf um Aachen:* Maps.

[9] Strength Rpts, 15 Nov 44, *LXXXI Corps, IIa/b KTB Anlagen, 20.X–30.XI.44; Kampf um Aachen:* Maps.

chen. The backbone of the antitank screen was provided by 20 assault guns and the 75-mm. and 88-mm. pieces of both divisions. The *301st Tank Battalion* with 31 Tiger tanks and the *559th Assault Gun Battalion* with 21 assault guns were held in reserve.[10]

Neither General Blumentritt nor the commander of the *LXXXI Corps*, General Koechling, had any doubts that the Allies would resume their drive to the Roer and the Rhine in early November. Both expected the main effort to be directed toward Juelich and Dueren with a subsidiary effort toward Linnich. As indicated by concern about the *176th Division*, General Blumentritt believed the British would participate actively in the offensive, thereby extending the zone of attack as far as Roermond, at the juncture of the Maas and the Roer sixteen miles northwest of Geilenkirchen.[11]

On the American side, Colonel Bixel and the XIX Corps G–2, Colonel Platt, had discerned quite accurately the kind of defense to be expected on the Roer plain. Having taken a leaf from Russian defensive tactics, the Germans had transformed the numerous villages into mutually supporting strongpoints. Fire trenches, foxholes, communications trenches, and antitank ditches wreathed the villages. Antitank and antipersonnel mines liberally dotted roads and other likely avenues of approach. Self-propelled guns could furnish direct support from within the villages, where they might be hidden behind stalwart stone houses. If driven from the trenches, German infantry might retire into the villages to cellars remarkable in the strength of their construction.[12]

American intelligence also had divined that the Germans looked upon the villages west of the Roer as integral parts of concentric arcs of defense fanning out from Juelich and Linnich, after the manner of ripples that spread on a pond when a pebble is thrown in. Since Juelich was the more important of the two towns, the concentric arcs protecting it overlapped at some points with those protecting Linnich.

The outer, or westernmost, defensive arc was marked by a radius a little less than six miles from Juelich. Not quite four miles from the Roer was an intermediate arc. The inner arc ran not quite two miles from Juelich.[13]

Probably because aerial photographs had revealed the enemy's defensive pattern, most of the villages on the plain—plus Juelich, Linnich, and Heinsberg, the last a road center along the Wurm outside the Ninth Army's zone—were included in plans for the target bombing in Operation QUEEN. Along with Dueren in the First Army's zone, Juelich and Heinsberg were scheduled as targets for heavy bombers of the Royal Air Force Bomber Command. Mediums of the Ninth Air Force were to strike Linnich and Aldenhoven, while fighter-bombers of General Nugent's XXIX Tactical Air Command were to concen-

---

[10] *Kampf um Aachen:* Maps; MS # B–290, The *XII SS Corps,* 20 Oct 44–31 Jan 45 (Blumentritt).

[11] MS # B–290 (Blumentritt) and MS # A–994, untitled (Koechling).

[12] Although many Americans assumed that the solid cellars had been constructed with an eye toward support positions for the West Wall, this type of construction is characteristic of German cellars and no evidence supporting the thesis can be found.

[13] NUSA Opns, IV, 6; XIX Corps AAR, Nov 44. See also Intel Annex, dtd 10 Nov, to 29th Div FO 47, 7 Nov 44. German sources confirm this defensive arrangement.

trate upon the villages, including most of those comprising the outer defensive arc. Although target bombing as contrasted with carpet bombing to be executed for the First Army involved less danger to friendly troops, safety measures prescribed were basically the same.

In the matter of logistics, the Ninth Army on the eve of the Roer offensive was in a more delicate situation than was the First Army. Having moved to the sector north of Aachen only twenty days before the target date of 11 November, and having existed on a starvation diet for several weeks before the move, the Ninth Army had had little time to amass any sizable stockpiles or to alleviate shortages in several critical items. Artillery ammunition was of particular concern. Giving personal attention to this problem, General Simpson set up a strict rationing program by which he was able to build a small reserve before the attack began; nevertheless, certain types of ammunition were to remain on the ration list through the entire month. Mostly these were multipurpose high explosive shells for almost all calibers and white phosphorus for some artillery calibers and for 81-mm. mortars. Although the Ninth Army noted later that "Greater success would have been attained if more ammunition had been available," stocks accumulated through rationing were to prove basically adequate.[14]

Never during November was the Ninth Army able to keep its armored units supplied with medium tanks to fully authorized levels. This was true even

after adoption of the First Army's expedient table of organization and equipment reducing tank authorizations in units like the 2d Armored Division from 232 to 200 and separate tank battalions from 54 to 50. Because of slow replacement of combat losses and the fact that at least 10 percent of tank strength usually was in maintenance shops, both organic and attached tank battalions would operate during the Roer offensive at about 60 to 75 percent of authorized strength in medium tanks.[15]

One of the more serious problems confronting the Ninth Army's G-4 section grew out of a combination of the Army's narrow sector and its rapid increase in troop strength. Almost overnight, the Army had expanded from three to six divisions, plus a cavalry group and at least one tank, tank destroyer, and antiaircraft artillery battalion per infantry division. In addition, the Army had thirty-three nondivisional field artillery battalions, plus the numerous other units necessary for support: ordnance, signal, medical, quartermaster, and the like. Nowhere along the Western Front during the fall of 1944 were so many troops and installations jammed into such a narrow sector. Shelter against the cold and rain was at a premium. The solution to providing storage facilities with hard-road access lay only in stacking supplies along shoulders of main highways. An already difficult problem was compounded when the 30 British Corps on 12 November assumed responsibility for the sector from the Maas River to the area of Geilenkirchen. A limited number of bridges across the Albert Canal and the Maas providing access to the Army's rear areas also added to

---

[14] NUSA G-4 AAR, Nov 44. Details on many facets of the supply situation are conveniently available in *Conquer—The Story of Ninth Army*. See also XIX Corps AAR, Nov 44, and NUSA Opns, IV, 7, 8, and 37.

[15] XIX Corps AAR, Nov 44.

the logistical problems. Later in the month that aspect was to reach critical proportions as the Maas rose to flood stage and washed out British bridges downstream. Supplies for the 30 Corps then had to move across already overloaded and flood-strained American bridges at Maastricht.[16]

Encumbered with hundreds of vehicles, both in combat formations and supply trains, General Harmon's 2d Armored Division was particularly hard-pressed for space. An exchange between General Harmon and the XIX Corps G–3, Col. Gustavus W. West, illustrates the point:

Colonel West: G–4 told me that the 102d [Division] is trying to crowd you. They are getting pinched out and have to go someplace.

General Harmon: They can't disturb my supply installations; they will have to go someplace else . . . . I am not moving anything and I don't want any 2d Armored installations disturbed . . . . Keep those people off my back until I get some ground.[17]

For all these problems and more, the Ninth Army nevertheless was ready to attack by the target date of 11 November, little more than six weeks after leaving the Breton peninsula and not quite three weeks after departure from a temporary post in Luxembourg. Small wonder that the American press dubbed this a "phantom" army and hailed the rapid shift as a miracle of modern warfare. Even so, many a commander within the Ninth Army must have been gratified by the

additional opportunity for preparation provided by the five-day delay which bad weather imposed on the offensive.

On the eve of the attack, General Simpson and his subordinates were optimistic. In approving a policy of rest before the jump-off, the XIX Corps Commander, General McLain, told one of his division commanders he would need plenty of rest, because "when you go again it will be a long drive. Right into Berlin." [18] Though General McLain may have indulged in hyperbole, the commanders in general apparently shared "high hopes . . . that the enemy's stronghold could be breached and he be beaten down before the harsh winter . . . set in." [19] For his part, General Simpson warned against taking the enemy too lightly. Even second-rate troops, he noted, "can fight well from fortified areas like the towns of the Roer Valley." He put the matter succinctly when he told his staff, "I anticipate one hell of a fight." Nevertheless, the general view was that the XIX Corps could reach the Roer in five days.[20]

D Day on the Roer Plain

In transposing General Simpson's plans from army to corps level, the XIX Corps commander, General McLain, inherited the problem of narrow frontage. Having bowed to reputed pitfalls in the Wuerselen industrial district and given the 30th Division a special mission there, he already had used more than half of ten miles of front available at his line of departure. To split the remaining four and a half miles equally between the 2d Armored

[16] Conquer—The Story of Ninth Army provides lucid details on these problems.
[17] 2d Armd Div G–3 Jnl, 11 Nov 44.

[18] 29th Div G–2—G–3 Jnl, 4 Nov 44.
[19] NUSA Opns, IV, 2.
[20] Ibid., pp. 6, 8; Combat Interv with McLain.

and 29th Divisions was no ready solution, for the natural route of approach to the village of Setterich, which under this kind of arrangement would fall to the 2d Armored Division, would lie in the 29th Division's sector. Yet Setterich was important to the armor, because General Harmon needed to employ a main road leading from the Wurm River through Uebach, Baesweiler, and Setterich to the armored division's objective of Gereonsweiler. On the other hand, if Setterich and the natural route of approach to the village were given to the armor from the start, the 29th Division would be left with a zone hardly wide enough at the line of departure for even one regiment.

Much as had General Simpson, General McLain solved his problem by means of a temporary boundary. Setterich and that portion of the road running through the village were to be captured by the 29th Division. Thereupon, the interdivision boundary was to be shifted a mile to the south to give the village and the road to the armor.[21]

At divisional level, plans of the 2d Armored Division also were influenced by the narrow zone. The armor drew a sector a mere two miles wide at the line of departure, marked by the villages of Waurichen and Beggendorf. Probably with the limited zone in mind, General McLain directed that the 2d Armored

[21] XIX Corps FO 28, 5 Nov, XIX Corps FO and Ltrs of Instrs file, Nov 44. Unless otherwise noted, other sources for the XIX Corps story are as follows: *Conquer—The Story of Ninth Army,* pp. 89–93; NUSA Opns, IV, 1–89, 112–73; XIX Corps AAR, Nov 44; XIX Corps G–2 and G–3 Jnl files, Nov 44; Ferriss Notes (cited in Ch. X, above); and official records of the 2d Armd and 29th Divs. Both these divisions recorded a number of telephone messages which are valuable in reconstructing the story of their engagements.

Division commit at first no more than one combat command. Designating CCB for the role, General Harmon told the commander, General White, to drive directly northeast to the division objective of Gereonsweiler, three miles away. Attached to CCB, both to assist in protecting the left flank and later to hold the high ground about Gereonsweiler after the objective was relinquished to the XIII Corps, was the 102d Division's 406th Infantry, a part of the XIII Corps.

Once past the line of departure, the 2d Armored Division's sector funneled out to an ultimate width of about five miles, so that in later stages of the attack General Harmon would have room for the rest of his division, plus two attached battalions of the 30th Division's 119th Infantry. His maneuver space also would increase once the 29th Division captured Setterich. The second combat command, CCA, was to prepare to attack from Setterich almost due east along the division's right flank to occupy the assembly area northwest of Juelich where the division was to prepare for crossing the Roer.

Having drawn responsibility for Setterich, the 29th Division had a sector about a mile wider than that of the armor. Attack plans of the 29th Division thus were less strongly affected by space limitations. Instead, the division commander, Maj. Gen. Charles H. Gerhardt, gave his attention to a scheme of maneuver based upon an analysis of the enemy's defensive plan as interpreted through the 29th Division's earlier experience in Normandy. Noting that the Germans depended upon the villages as strongpoints, General Gerhardt prepared to exploit what he deemed the weak points, the open ground between the villages. He told his regiments to stick to the open terrain while isolating the villages; thereupon, company-size attacks should be sufficient to reduce each village.[22]

The 29th Division's line of departure was marked by the villages of Baesweiler and Oidtweiler. The first division objective was the road center of Aldenhoven, not quite four miles away; then the Roer at Juelich, three miles beyond Aldenhoven. As for the special mission of reducing Setterich, General Gerhardt intended to wait until his main drive opposite Baesweiler and Oidtweiler had uncovered the southern flank of Setterich. At that point he intended to commit a portion of his division reserve along the natural route of approach to the village, the Aachen–Linnich highway.

General Gerhardt's plan for taking Setterich reflected an air of basic optimism about the coming offensive. In view of the importance of Setterich to progress of the armor, Gerhardt hardly would have adopted a plan dependent upon his main drive turning the flank of the village had he anticipated that his main drive might be stopped or even slowed. In like manner, General McLain's attack order to the 2d Armored Division conveyed an air of optimism. After the initial attack by one combat command, General McLain directed, the rest of the armor "*assembles* on corps order northwest of Juelich . . . ."[23]

Only General Harmon appeared to express any real concern about the situation as reflected in the planning. For several days he tried in vain to solicit a limited objective attack by the 102d Division to secure a knoll close alongside his left flank. Neither was he happy about the arrange-

ment for taking Setterich. "I am quite concerned about that south end there," General Harmon told his CCB commander. "I am not so sure that it is going to work out so well."[24]

Certainly the American commanders had reasons for optimism, not the least of which was the strong American artillery arm. Counting both divisional and corps artillery, the XIX Corps had at hand 25 field artillery battalions. In organizing the artillery for the offensive, the XIX Corps artillery commander Brig. Gen. George D. Shea, allotted 3 of 13 corps battalions to general support of the 30th Division, 2 to the 29th Division, 3 to the 2d Armored Division, and the remaining 5 to general support throughout the corps zone as needed. To supplement this impressive strength, each infantry division had a battalion each of towed tank destroyers and medium tanks, the 2d Armored Division had its organic tanks and assault guns, and the bulk of the 92d Chemical Battalion's 4.2-inch mortars were apportioned throughout the corps. Furthermore, organic artillery of the 84th Division of the XIII Corps was to provide support as needed on D Day to the 2d Armored Division. In general, the XIX Corps plan for artillery support called for a preliminary counterflak preparation during the air strike, followed by concentrations for a half hour against the initial village objectives, intensive counterbattery preparations by corps guns, and subsequent on-call missions.[25]

Commanders and troops in the XIX

---

[22] NUSA Opns, IV, 34; Ewing, *29 Let's Go!*, p. 169; 29th Div and 175th Inf AARs, Nov 44.
[23] XIX Corps FO 28. Italics supplied.

[24] 2d Armd Div G-3 Jnl, 7 Nov 44, *passim*.
[25] No copy of the artillery annex to XIX Corps FO 28 can be found. This information is gleaned from the following sources: NUSA Opns, IV, 11; *Conquer—The Story of Ninth Army*, p. 71; 2d Armd Div AAR, Nov 44; and 29th Div FO 47, 7 Nov.

Corps no doubt watched the clearing skies on D Day, 16 November, with much the same jubilation as did their neighbors in the First Army. Soon after midnight assault units of both the 2d Armored and 29th Divisions had begun to move to the line of departure. Considering the bulk and noisiness of tanks and the muddy, slippery condition of the roads, secrecy during the moves was particularly difficult for the 2d Armored Division. Yet no untoward incidents occurred, and the enemy displayed no indication that he detected anything unusual. Several dry runs which the armor had conducted on previous nights may have accustomed the Germans to the noise of churning vehicles behind the lines.

Though the air strike began on schedule, it subsequently proved as difficult to measure the effect of the bombardment in support of the Ninth Army as of the saturation bombing in front of the First Army. Thus no worth-while comparison between the two types of air support could be made. That Juelich, Linnich, and Heinsberg incurred severe damage was readily apparent; [26] yet how serious were these blows to the enemy's war machine was open to question. A consensus of reports from prisoners was that the strikes on Linnich and Juelich "forced personnel to cover but did not cause excessive casualties or military damage. The bridge at Juelich was destroyed, effectively blocking movement through that town; however, German engineers quickly installed three ponton bridges capable of bearing more traffic than the original structure." [27]

The only major change in the original air plan was a last-minute cancellation of Aldenhoven as a target for the mediums. The change was requested by the 29th Division, which was reluctant to risk being blocked by rubble in the event an anticipated rapid thrust into Aldenhoven should materialize. Instead, the mediums hit the village of Luerken opposite the 30th Division.

In noting that the XXIX TAC's fighter-bombers "did the best job they have ever done for the XIX Corps," [28] the corps apparently was favoring quality over quantity; for despite the dramatic clearing of the skies at the last minute, the P-47's and P-38's still ran into visibility problems. They flew but 136 sorties, and dropped but 46.5 tons of bombs. [29] Yet to judge from initial reactions of the ground units, this limited program was effective. "Had excellent results," reported the 2d Armored Division. The air strike was effective, noted the 29th Division's 115th Infantry, "On Setterich particularly so." The other regiment in the line, the 175th Infantry, said the bombing was "fine." [30] Although German artillery fire subsequently proved "considerably less intense and effective than was expected," [31] it was ha.. to tell whether this was any more attributable to the air effort than to counterbattery fires or even to a possible G-2 overestimation of available German artillery.

Close behind the air strike, even as the

---

[26] OB WEST KTB, 16 Nov 44.
[27] NUSA Opns, IV, 39, citing Capt Carl Wheeldryer, PW interrogator, 2d Armd Div, to Maj Walter H. Mytinger, G-3 Air, 2d Armd Div.

[28] XIX Corps AAR, Nov 44.
[29] Specific figures vary; those given are an average from several sources.
[30] 2d Armd Div G-3 Jnl, 16 Nov 44; 29th Div G-2—G-3 Jnl, 16 Nov 44.
[31] XIX Corps AAR, Nov 44.

artillery concluded its own target preparation, tanks and infantry of the 2d Armored Division's CCB struck northeastward just at H hour—1245. General White employed three task forces. The strongest operated on the south wing, first to seize the village of Loverich, then Puffendorf. The latter was a major objective, a crossroads village astride both the enemy's main route of lateral communications and the highway leading northeast from Setterich to the division objective of Gereonsweiler. The second task force, in the center, first was to take Floverich, then Apweiler and a rise of ground between Apweiler and Puffendorf, not quite a mile from the final objective of Gereonsweiler. The third task force attacked from the vicinity of Waurichen toward Immendorf, there to defend the combat command's north boundary.

Moving at first behind a smoke screen laid upon the enemy's outpost line by chemical mortars, all three task forces found resistance weak and spotty. The Germans appeared awed by the horde of tanks descending upon them and often surrendered in bunches. In the absence of stanch resistance, the muddy ground offered few problems to the tanks. Soon the countryside was dotted with fascines which the tankers unceremoniously discarded when they did not need them for increased traction. As elsewhere in the XIX Corps zone, a major surprise was lack of accurate German shellfire. Much of the artillery fire the Germans belatedly expended landed well in rear of the attacking tanks and infantry. Early prisoners suggested the explanation that they had been surprised because American artillery had not employed the kind of heavy blanket preparation the Germans

had come to expect before an attack.[32]

Task Force 1, strongest of the three task forces, was commanded by Col. Paul A. Disney, commander of the 67th Armored Regiment. Possessing a battalion of armored infantry and two battalions (less one company) of tanks, Colonel Disney had strength enough to split his force into two components, one to take Loverich, the other to bypass that village and capture Puffendorf. Though the component moving on Loverich came under intense antitank fire from the south flank at Setterich, a lieutenant bearing the illustrious name of Robert E. Lee directed fire of the leading tank company upon Setterich and in a matter of minutes silenced the guns. Loverich was under control not twenty minutes later.

Moving past Loverich on Puffendorf, the largest portion of Task Force 1 lost four tanks to mud and six to mines. Nevertheless, by 1500, little more than two hours after the jump-off, leading tanks and armored infantry were entering the village. "Get that place tonight if you can," General Harmon admonished, "so the men will have some place to sleep.[33]

Colonel Disney did that and more. After taking Puffendorf, he sent the component which earlier had taken Loverich to occupy a hill 700 yards northeast of Puffendorf astride the highway to Gereonsweiler. Boggy ground and antitank fire from higher ground southeast of Gereonsweiler interfered with this attack. Two tanks mired, another was lost to mines, two were disabled by antitank fire, and another burned after a direct hit. Nevertheless, as night came, the American

[32] XIX Corps AAR, Nov 44; Ferriss Notes.
[33] 2d Armd Div G-3 Jnl, 16 Nov 44.

tanks commanded the hill along the Gereonsweiler road. Colonel Disney's task force had seized the first day's objectives and at the same time had gained a leg on the next day's journey to Gereonsweiler.

Both CCB's other task forces had similar experiences at first. Composed primarily of a battalion each of tanks and armored infantry, Task Force 2 in the center cleared Floverich in less than two hours. In the process the task force lost six tanks to mines, panzerfausts, mortar fire, and mechanical failure but received no fire from antitank guns, possibly because tank destroyers kept neighboring villages under fire. On CCB's north wing, Task Force X, with a battalion of the 406th Infantry supported by Company H, 67th Armored Regiment, moved against Immendorf. In the assault echelon, Task Force X used two companies of infantry rather than tanks, but otherwise the story was much the same as elsewhere. Although four tanks were lost to mines, the village was secured in less than two hours. Task Force X spent the rest of the afternoon digging in to hold this village as protection for CCB's left flank.

In the meantime, in the center of CCB's attack zone, the most portentous event of the day had developed. Having occupied Floverich, Task Force 2 in midafternoon continued northeast toward the next objective of Apweiler. Moving slowly in second gear because of the soggy ground, the tanks were unopposed until they reached a point about 300 yards from Apweiler. Unannounced, antitank guns that lay hidden in orchards and groves along the fringe of the village suddenly opened an intense and unrelenting fire. In less than two minutes the German gunners knocked out seven of the

U.S. tanks and scored glancing blows on a number of others. Three tanks burned.

Task Force 2 could not silence this fire. Every attempt to rush the defenses with infantry failed in the face of fire from automatic weapons also hidden among the trees. In the end, Task Force 2 fell back a few hundred yards to the Geilenkirchen–Aldenhoven highway and dug in for the night.[34]

The difficulty at Apweiler was strangely inconsonant in view of the relative ease with which CCB had conquered the other objectives. Yet any veteran tanker might point to numbers of instances where a few strategically placed antitank guns had dealt costly blows to an attacking combat command but had failed in the long run to alter the over-all picture. On the other hand, the defense at Apweiler might have broader implications. Many a tanker and infantryman in CCB must have pondered that thought during the night as one outpost after another reported the noise of track-laying vehicles moving behind German lines.

Meanwhile, to the south, in the zone of the 29th Division, events had been unfolding that were more in keeping with the difficulty at Apweiler than with CCB's successes. At 1245, at the same time CCB had crossed the line of departure, a battalion each of the 29th Division's 115th and 175th Infantry Regiments attacked. In line with General Gerhardt's scheme to reduce the village strongpoints by first penetrating the reputed weak spots in between, the first

[34] After nightfall, a freakish accident put another tank out of action. A sliver of metal from a German shellburst wedged a round so securely in the barrel of one of the tank guns that ordnance crews subsequently had to replace the piece.

objectives were high ground north and southeast of the village of Siersdorf and southeast of Bettendorf.

Lying behind open, gently rolling fields a mile and a half southeast of the regimental line of departure at Baesweiler, the 115th Infantry's objective was high ground about a coal mine 400 yards north of Siersdorf. It provided an acid test of General Gerhardt's plan.

Though screened at first by smoke, the two leading companies of the 115th Infantry's 1st Battalion came under small arms fire no more than 600 yards past the line of departure. The men still managed to advance by squad rushes. In the process, the commander of Company C on the left was killed, but the company nevertheless gained another 200 yards. Here a deadly cross fire struck both companies. From four directions it came—from Setterich off the left flank, from the settlement of Roetgen to the northeast, from Siersdorf to the southeast, and from a windmill a few hundred yards to the east. A platoon leader later called it "the most intense and accurate small arms fire . . . I have ever encountered." [35]

The men hit the ground. Hugging the earth between rows of beets, they gained a measure of protection from the small arms fire, only to be subjected to round after round of mortar and artillery fire. An automatic rifle man who had expended his ammunition tried to crawl through a beet row to reach the corpse of his ammunition bearer. "He was hit, tore off his pack and rolled over to get at his canteen and sulfa pills. The Germans saw him move and shot him again and again as he struggled." [36] Many men

threw away their combat packs because the Germans could spot them protruding across the tops of the beets. Forced to court the ground like the others, squad and platoon leaders could do little to reorganize their men. Here in all the terror and misery of it was a clear example of what infantrymen meant by a term that was common in their language. These men were "pinned down."

The bulk of Company B on the south wing succeeded in falling back behind a slight rise in the ground, but Company C could not follow. Through the afternoon the men of Company C lay there, cruelly exposed. The battalion commander committed his reserve company. Artillery pounded the German positions. Yet neither helped appreciably. Not until after nightfall were any men of Company C able to escape. Only about twenty of them made it.

Had it not been for a drainage ditch furrowing open ground between Oidtweiler and Bettendorf, the 29th Division's other attacking battalion from the 175th Infantry might have met the same fate. Otherwise the experiences were much the same. Small arms fire pinned the men to the ground. Shellfire pummeled them. The farthest advance was to the drainage ditch, not quite 400 yards west of Bettendorf. Every attempt to progress beyond the ditch brought unrelenting fire from Bettendorf and a railroad embankment to the southeast. As night came, the men clustered in the ditch for protection. Like the 115th Infantry, the 175th Infantry had moved no more than 600 yards past the line of departure.

The results on 16 November had revealed a fundamental misconception in General Gerhardt's scheme of attack. Unlike Normandy, the Roer plain is open

[35] NUSA Opns, IV, 41, quoting 1st Lt Joseph D. Blalock, Co C.
[36] Ibid.

country. Defensive positions could be mutually supporting, so that an attacker could not concentrate upon the weak spots to the exclusion of the strongpoints. Someone in the 175th Infantry later put it this way: "One objective (usually a town or village) must be made secure and used as an anchor before attacking the next objective. Because of this, towns which in reality are strong points cannot be bypassed." [37] It could have been added that infantry alone might find the difficulties of advancing across exposed ground like this almost insurmountable. Some special provision might be needed, like, for example, exploiting the shock value of tanks.

Only after darkness produced immunity from German observation did any contingent of the 29th Division make any real advance on D Day. Near midnight, the 115th Infantry commander, Col. Edward H. McDaniel, sent his depleted 1st Battalion to eliminate the closest of the positions which had held up the battalion that afternoon. This was the windmill about halfway between Baesweiler and Siersdorf. When the battalion got there, the Germans had gone.

For all the limited advance in the 29th Division's sector, the basic fact was that the division had fought only half a day and had committed but two battalions. Nevertheless, the neighboring 2d Armored Division was perturbed because of the effect the situation might have upon the taking of Setterich and thus upon continued progress of the armor. During the afternoon, General Harmon had reminded both General Gerhardt and the corps commander, General McLain, that he wanted to commit his second combat

command through Setterich the next morning.[38] Still, as night came, the 29th Division was yet to make a move against the village. "It's head-on stuff," General Gerhardt told General Harmon, "and just how we're going to work it out in the morning we don't know. Whether we can guarantee that town by noon [17 November] is debatable .... Until we can get some ground straight ahead, we don't want to start fooling with that flank thing ...." [39]

For his part, General McLain was inclined to be patient. Although both the armor and the 30th Division had far exceeded the 29th Division's gains during the day, the 29th Division was striking frontally against the outer defensive arc of Juelich, whereas the other two divisions were hitting glancing blows along the receding ends of the arc. General Gerhardt's job obviously was toughest. Committing more strength, General McLain told the 29th Division commander, "should loosen things up .... I think you'll bust on through there tomorrow." [40]

General McLain's patience was understandable, for from an over-all standpoint, progress of the XIX Corps on 16 November compared favorably with that of the VII Corps, where the First Army troops had run into trouble with the Donnerberg, the Hamich ridge, and the Huertgen Forest. In the Wuerselen industrial district, the 30th Division had gained a mile or more at two points and had sustained surprisingly light losses. The 2d Armored Division had made the most notable gains, more than two miles in one instance, and near Puffendorf had pierced the outer defensive arc of Juelich. For all the

[37] 175th Inf AAR, Nov 44.

[38] 2d Armd Div G-3 Jnl, 16 Nov 44.
[39] 29th Div G-2—G-3 Jnl, 16 Nov 44.
[40] Ibid.

difficulties encountered by the 29th Division, the average gain along the XIX Corps front was about a mile.

The XIX Corps also had dealt the enemy serious blows. The 2d Armored Division, for example, had virtually annihilated the *183d Volks Grenadier Division's 330th Regiment* and had taken 570 prisoners. The armor in turn had lost 196 men, 21 of them killed and 18 missing. Tank losses were 35, a somewhat disturbing figure except that many tanks were out of action only temporarily.[41] No German armor had been sighted; German artillery, though troublesome and even deadly in some instances, had not lived up to expectations. American artillery, on the other hand, had fired the impressive total of 20,758 rounds while remaining within rationing restrictions.

All things considered, General McLain had reason to be encouraged. There was time for things to open up later.

Armor Attracts Armor

In reality, the situation was more fraught with danger than General McLain estimated. Under normal circumstances, a commander could consider himself relatively immune from intervention by major enemy reserves for at least twenty-four hours after the start of an attack,

and often longer. This was not to be the case in the battle of the Roer plain.

In midafternoon of 16 November, officers at *OB WEST* had estimated that five Allied armored and seven infantry divisions were involved in the offensive against *Fifteenth Army (Gruppe von Manteuffel)*. Though they overestimated the number of divisions, they were correct in divining this as the Allied main effort. At 1715 Field Marshal von Rundstedt released his strongest reserve force to *Army Group B* for use in *Fifteenth Army's* sector. This was the *XLVII Panzer Corps* with the *15th Panzer Grenadier* and *9th Panzer Divisions,* already positioned close behind *Gruppe von Manteuffel's* front lines. Rundstedt also ordered two volks artillery corps and "all available GHQ combat forces" to move to the threatened sector.[42]

The most immediately dangerous threat obviously was the 2d U.S. Armored Division's penetration at Puffendorf in the open "tank country" of the Roer plain. *Fifteenth Army (Gruppe von Manteuffel)* ordered that the *9th Panzer Division* counterattack early the next morning, 17 November, to "wipe out" this penetration. The counterattack was to be supported by an attached headquarters unit, the *506th Heavy Tank Battalion,* which had thirty-six Mark VI (Tiger) tanks.[43]

The track-laying vehicles which outposts of the 2d Armored Division reported moving behind German lines during the night of 16 November were those of General Harald Freiherr von Elverfeldt's *9th Panzer Division.* Unaware of the full import of these reports,

---

[41] A German estimate of 18 U.S. tanks destroyed was conservative. See Order, *Gruppe von Manteuffel to XII SS and LXXXI Corps,* 2225, 16 Nov 44, *LXXXI Corps KTB, Bef. H. Gr. u. Armee.* A breakdown of CCB's tank losses on 16 November follows: to antitank guns—10; to mines—14; to panzerfausts—1; to mines and antitank guns—1; to mortar fire—1; to mud—6; to artillery fire—1; to mechanical failure—1. Total: 35. Of these, 2 tanks which mired were returned to action before the end of the day, and 8 lost to mud and mines were returned within twenty-four hours.

[42] *OB WEST KTB,* 16 Nov 44.

[43] Order, *Gruppe von Manteuffel to XII SS and LXXXI Corps,* 2225, 16 Nov 44, *LXXXI Corps KTB, Bef. H. Gr. u. Armee.*

CAPTURED GERMAN TIGER (MARK VI) TANK *with temporary U.S. markings. Note 88-mm. gun with flash hider.*

the 2d Armored Division's CCB prepared to renew the offensive at dawn on 17 November. One force was to take Apweiler, the village denied by the Germans the first afternoon, while another headed for the division objective of Gereonsweiler.

CCB's tanks were moving to their lines of departure when out of a heavy mist rolled the German armor. Preceded by round after round of artillery fire, two columns of Mark V's and VI's appeared, one from the direction of Gereonsweiler against Colonel Disney's Task Force 1 at Puffendorf, the other from Prummern, beyond the XIX Corps boundary, against Task Force X at Immendorf.

At Immendorf, the Germans employed a battalion of the *10th Panzer Grenadier Regiment* supported by tanks variously es-

timated at from three to ten. Soon after the fight began, General Harmon placed the commander of the 406th Infantry, Col. Bernard F. Hurless, in command of Task Force X and authorized him to use all his regiment, if necessary. As events developed, Colonel Hurless needed no more than the one infantry battalion and a company each of tanks and tank destroyers already in the village. Using mortar, artillery, and small arms fire with deadly effect, the task force threw back the Germans after a fight lasting most of the morning. Guns of the 771st Tank Destroyer Battalion knocked out three Panther tanks.

When the Germans came back at dusk with a battalion of infantry and eight tanks, Colonel Hurless did dip into his reserve. This time one of the Mark V's with a small escort of infantry broke into Immendorf. Calling up another of his infantry battalions, Colonel Hurless sent the men into action from their approach march formation to expel the German infantry, while a gunner from the 771st Tank Destroyer battalion knocked out the Panther at a range of thirty yards.

The heaviest of the counterstrokes hit Colonel Disney's Task Force 1 at Puffendorf. Using twenty to thirty Panthers and Tigers accompanied by a battalion from the *11th Panzer Grenadier Regiment,* the Germans caught Colonel Disney's tanks drawn up in attack formation on the open hill northeast of Puffendorf. Lacking depth of formation, caught by surprise in the open, and outmaneuvered on the soggy ground by wider-tracked German tanks, the Americans were hard put to stop the thrust. German shelling pinned down Task Force 1's infantry while American artillery stopped the panzer grenadiers. The fight developed as a purely armored engagement.

Some idea of the amount of U.S. artillery fire used at Puffendorf could be gained from the figure of 26,628 rounds expended during 17 November on the XIX Corps front, the largest volume of any day of the November offensive; yet the artillery could claim but one enemy tank destroyed. Fighter-bombers of the XXIX TAC braved unfavorable elements to maintain a semblance of air cover over the battlefield through most of the day, but mists and rain denied any real contribution against pinpoint targets like tanks.

After several hours of fighting, some tanks of Task Force 1 were down to three or four rounds of ammunition. Although at least 11 German tanks were knocked out, the Panthers and Tigers obviously had the better of the situation. In one of Colonel Disney's battalions, at least 2 light tanks and 7 mediums burned after direct hits. One company was down to 8 tanks, another to 4. Less directly engaged, the other tank battalion nevertheless came under fire from German support tanks near Gereonsweiler, perched out of range of U.S. 75-mm. and 76-mm. pieces. Long-range hits put the torch to at least 4 lights and 3 mediums. His tank afire, Sgt. Dennis D. French nevertheless managed to back into defilade and extinguish the blaze. Despite heroic actions like this, one of the companies of this battalion soon was down to 5 tanks, another down to 3. Colonel Disney decided to abandon the hill and fall back to the protection of the buildings in Puffendorf.

Task Force 1 was in no shape after the withdrawal to repel another strong German thrust. Fortunately, the Panthers and Tigers did not follow. As night came, the men of Task Force 1 worked without pause to replenish their ammunition over muddy, blacked-out secondary roads leading from distribution points far back near the Wurm River.

For all the strength of German thrusts on either wing of CCB's sector, the 2d Armored Division nevertheless made two offensive moves on 17 November. The first was in the center of CCB's sector at Apweiler, where the CCB commander, General White, directed that Task Force X send one of the newly acquired battalions of the 406th Infantry to assist Task Force 2. Both components were to attack from the south along parallel axes of advance from the Geilenkirchen–Aldenhoven highway near Floverich.

At 0800, even as the fight against the counterattacks raged, the two-pronged thrust against Apweiler began. It was a mistake. The Germans were as strong as before in Apweiler. In addition, the enemy tanks on the high ground near Gereonsweiler turned the approaches to Apweiler into a shooting gallery. They set one U.S. tank ablaze, knocked out another by a hit on the rear deck, and damaged the gun shield of a third. Another tank was disabled by a mine. In little more than an hour after the jump-off, both Task Force 2 and the battalion of the 406th Infantry were back at the Geilenkirchen–Aldenhoven highway. The Task Force 2 commander, Lt. Col. Harry L. Hillyard, notified General White that under existing circumstances, the nature of the ground precluded a successful attack by his force against Apweiler.

The second offensive move on 17 November involved a fresh force, a portion of CCA. Although General Harmon had counted upon committing CCA through Setterich, he had told the commander,

Colonel Collier, to prepare an alternate plan to bypass Setterich, move over secondary roads to Puffendorf, and drive northeast along CCB's right flank on the village of Ederen.[44] Whether to relieve pressure against CCB or merely in a general extension of the offensive, General Harmon ordered Colonel Collier to put the alternate plan into effect.

German shelling of the secondary roads leading to Puffendorf, a corollary of the counterattack, delayed a move by CCA until 1100. Even then, Task Force A, commanded by Col. Ira P. Swift and composed primarily of the headquarters and one battalion of the 66th Armored Regiment and a battalion of the 41st Armored Infantry, was subjected to brutal shelling while passing through Puffendorf.

Colonel Swift knew that between Puffendorf and Ederen he would encounter an antitank ditch of impressive proportions, about fifteen feet wide and ten feet deep. The ditch originated in the 29th Division's sector, paralleled the Aldenhoven–Geilenkirchen road to a point east of Puffendorf, then swung north along the highway to Gereonsweiler. Aware of the obstacle, the 2d Armored Division had devised two methods of crossing it, one to form a bridge by driving tanks into the ditch and bulldozing them over with earth, another to use a portable treadway bridge improvised by the 17th Armored Engineer Battalion and transported by a T2 tank retriever.

Unfortunately, Task Force A on 17 November had no opportunity to test either expedient. German antitank guns emplaced beyond the ditch near Ederen and the same tanks on high ground near Gereonsweiler that had spelled trouble elsewhere denied so much as egress from Puffendorf. In a matter of minutes, Task Force A lost four medium tanks and a tank destroyer.

By this time the division commander, General Harmon, had become convinced that his men and tanks could do little through the rest of the day and possibly into the next day but hold their own. "I've been up there to see what the thing is like," General Harmon telephoned his operations officer. "Pretty tough. These tanks are on the other side of the ditch. We will have to come up on the other side of the ditch to get any place . . . ." Later General Harmon repeated this view to the corps commander. "Not much luck today," he said. "We have that tank ditch in front of us and can't do much to the north [toward Gereonsweiler] unless we flank it . . . ."[45]

Though the 2d Armored Division had relinquished little ground during the first encounter with the *9th Panzer Division,* General Harmon obviously was concerned about what another day might bring. In the second day's fighting, CCB had lost 18 more medium tanks destroyed and 16 more damaged and out of action, plus 19 light tanks in similar categories. In a brief commitment, CCA had lost 4 mediums. Personnel casualties were double those of D Day: 56 killed, 281 wounded, 26 missing. "Sit tight the first thing tomorrow and see what develops," General Harmon told the CCB commander. "Have them alerted to be sharp as hell in the morning . . . . And for God's sake, get word to me as soon as you get

[44] See CCA, 2d Armd Div, Opns Plan, 7 Nov, CCA Rpts, Nov 44. General McLain authorized commitment of CCA late on 16 November. XIX Corps Ltr of Instrs 71, 16 Nov, XIII Corps G-3 Jnl file, 14–17 Nov 44.

[45] 2d Armd Div G-3 Jnl, 17 Nov 44.

attacked." He noted in conclusion, "I think you will have a holding mission tomorrow." [46]

Finding the Formula

General Harmon would have been much less concerned about renewing his attack in the face of the *9th Panzer Division* had he possessed Setterich and the main highway leading from Setterich to Puffendorf. Without Setterich, he had no road adequate for supporting two combat commands. "There's a question in my mind," General Harmon noted, "if by noon [18 November] I might make a try to cross that ditch with Swift [Task Force A]." On the other hand, he reflected, "I may have too much in Puffendorf. [I] was up that road . . . and it's terrible. This rain isn't [any] help . . . ." [47]

The 29th Division commander, General Gerhardt, had told General Harmon on D Day that he hoped to have Setterich by noon on 17 November, but he was not so optimistic after the new day dawned. "It looks more dubious now than it did," General Gerhardt telephoned. "I think I can say no." [48] As events developed, the 29th Division by noon had not even begun an attack against Setterich.

Discouraged, General Harmon told the commander of his reserve to reconnoiter a route of attack toward Setterich because the 2d Armored Division "might have to attack it tomorrow." Later, General Harmon asked the corps commander to put pressure on the 29th Division. Because the infantry was to secure a crossing of the antitank ditch northeast of Setterich

as well as take the village, a successful attack would afford the armor not only a good supply route but passage over the obstacle that was deterring Task Force A at Puffendorf. On this point, General Harmon himself discreetly pressured General Gerhardt. "We have that tank ditch in front of us," he said, "and it is giving us a lot of trouble. If you can get me a foothold across it, I will send a tank column across that will give them hell." [49]

For his part, the corps commander, General McLain displayed less patience than he had the night before. When General Gerhardt told him that his assault regiments had to reorganize and could not attack before late morning, General McLain objected. "That reorganization should have been done last night," he said. "It will slow us up another day." Later he specifically directed General Gerhardt to "push that left thing in front of the 2d Armored." Talking to a liaison officer from General Gerhardt's reserve regiment, General McLain emphasized that the operation at Setterich "is the most important thing we've got." [50]

For all the pressure, the 29th Division was slow getting started on the second day of the offensive. In the main eastward drive, this no doubt was attributable to major alterations in the plan of attack; in the push on Setterich, possibly to General Gerhardt's expressed reluctance to "start fooling with that flank thing" until he had secured "some ground straight ahead."

The plans for the main drive indicated recognition that the enemy strongpoints—the villages—had to be attacked directly. Yet the new plans revealed no appreciation of the fact that the shock value of

---

[46] *Ibid.;* NUSA Opns, IV, 74.
[47] 2d Armd Div G-3 Jnl, 17 Nov 44.
[48] 29th Div G-2—G-3 Jnl, 17 Nov 44.

[49] 2d Armd Div G-3 Jnl, 17 Nov 44.
[50] 29th Div G-2—G-3 Jnl, 17 Nov 44.

tanks was what had enabled the 2d Armored Division to advance. Again, neither of the 29th Division's regiments made any provision for tanks to accompany the infantry.

In the end, the eastward drive accomplished no more than on the preceding day. A company of the 175th Infantry striking directly for Bettendorf eventually had to return to the drainage ditch 400 yards short of the village where the men had taken cover the night before. A battalion each of the 115th and 175th Infantry Regiments attacked due east against Siersdorf but gained no more than a few hundred yards. Small arms fire from deep zigzag trenches pinned the men to the flat, exposed ground, whereupon German mortars and artillery worked them over. It was a lamentable repetition of what had happened on D Day to the 115th Infantry's Company C.

Not until near noon on the 17th did General Gerhardt waver from his theory that he had to gain ground to the east before attacking Setterich. Late the night before he had attached a battalion of his reserve regiment to the 115th Infantry to take Setterich, but not until he saw that his main drive would be delayed did he authorize the attack. At 1300 the 1st Battalion, 116th Infantry, commanded by Maj. James S. Morris, was to move on Setterich from the southwest astride the Baesweiler–Setterich highway.[51]

Major Morris' attack actually did not begin until more than an hour past the appointed time. Again none of the tanks attached to the division accompanied the infantry, and when small arms fire from trenches on the fringe of Setterich pinned

the men to the ground, little could be done about it. A process of fire and movement enabled a handful of men to gain a toehold in a series of zigzag trenches 150 yards short of the village as night fell, but this achievement represented no real break in the issue.

During the evening, General Gerhardt turned to General Harmon for assistance. Specifically, Gerhardt wanted to pass a battalion through the 2d Armored Division's sector to hit Setterich from the north and to obtain direct fire support from some of the armor. To this General Harmon agreed while reminding the 29th Division commander that he also wanted the infantry to get him a crossing of the antitank ditch northeast of Setterich. "If you could get me over that ditch," General Harmon said, "we'll put 75 tanks over there."[52]

Having decided to broaden the efforts at Setterich, General Gerhardt gave full responsibility for taking the village to the 116th Infantry commander, Lt. Col. Harold A. Cassell.[53] As finally determined, Major Morris was to continue to hit Setterich from the southwest while sending his reserve company to strike from the west. This attack was to begin before dawn the next day. In the meantime, another battalion of the 116th Infantry was to pass into the 2d Armored Division's sector and as soon as possible— probably about noon on 18 November —attack from Loverich. In both attacks, General Gerhardt was to abandon his prejudice against using tanks on this sea of mud. A platoon of the 2d Armored

---

[51] See 29th Div G-2—G-3 Jnl; 116th Inf Jnl, 16-17 Nov 44.

[52] 29th Div G-2—G-3 Jnl, 17 Nov 44.

[53] A few days before D Day, Gerhardt had relieved the former 116th Infantry commander, in a dispute over the handling of a subordinate. See 29th Div G-2—G-3 Jnl, 13 Nov 44.

Division's 66th Armored Regiment was to assist the attack from Loverich, while a platoon from the attached 747th Tank Battalion was to be split between the two components of Major Morris' battalion.

In the first instance, the 29th Division's reluctance to employ tanks appeared justified, though not because of mud. Of three tanks assigned to that part of Major Morris' battalion southwest of Setterich, one struck a mine before reaching the line of departure, another succumbed to a panzerfaust, and the third withdrew after a projectile stuck in the barrel of its 75-mm. gun.

On the other hand, the difference tanks might make was demonstrated west of Setterich where two tanks supported the 116th Infantry's Company A. When fire from a network of trenches in a sparse wood pinned down a platoon of riflemen, the tanks advanced to smother the trenches with both 75-mm. and machine gun fire. Another rifle platoon then found it relatively simple to swing around a flank of the first and charge the trenches. In much the same manner, the riflemen and their two tanks worked their way into the western fringe of Setterich and by nightfall had established a firm toehold.

Similarly, the platoon of tanks from the 2d Armored Division assisted the battalion of the 116th Infantry which attacked from Loverich. When the riflemen came upon an antipersonnel mine field, the tanks smashed a path through the mines. When the Germans opened fire with small arms from a trench system 150 yards short of the village, the tankers quickly silenced them. Some Germans threw up their hands without resistance. By midafternoon the infantry had reached the fringe of the village, while the tankers waited in the open to provide fire support without becoming involved among the streets and debris.

By nightfall of 18 November, third day of the offensive, the tide had turned at Setterich, though the 116th Infantry would require most of the next morning for mopping up and for gaining a crossing of the antitank ditch northeast of the village. The latter operation proved relatively simple because contingents of the 115th Infantry had come in behind the ditch farther south and sent a combat patrol northward along the east bank.

Not only at Setterich but also at Siersdorf and Bettendorf the 29th Division began to roll on 18 November. A clear day providing unobstructed observation for artillery and air support no doubt helped, but, much as it was at Setterich, the factor most directly affecting operations appeared to be the use of tanks.

On the south wing, a company attacking Bettendorf lost 2 of 5 tanks to mines and another to mud, but with the help of the other 2 gained the first buildings. Having expended their ammunition, the tanks withdrew; yet already they had accomplished their mission of helping the infantry across the open ground. By midafternoon of 18 November, Bettendorf was free of Germans. A battalion each of the 115th and 175th Infantry Regiments had support from the 747th Tank Battalion, both in reaching Siersdorf and in clearing the village. Of two platoons of tanks, only two were lost, both to fire from antitank guns.

At the coal mine north of Siersdorf, the impact of tank support was most markedly demonstrated. Here the 115th Infantry's 2d Battalion attacked in concert with a platoon of mediums. For all the exposed ground leading to the coal mine, the attack progressed satisfactorily until the tankers balked at German artillery fire and lost contact with the infantry. At this point the Germans began to spew small arms fire from trenches and foxholes near the mine. Just as were the earlier drives on the first two days of the offensive, this attack was stopped. Meanwhile, the 2d Battalion S–2, 1st Lt. James E. Ball, led the tanks into Siersdorf and directed an attack northward against the mine. As the tanks approached the enemy positions, Lieutenant Ball related, "They opened up with their 75-mm. guns and their .30-caliber machine guns. The enemy fire from the emplacements ceased and the enemy riflemen and machine gunners moved down deep in their holes." [54] The Germans were finished.

After two days of halting, almost negligible, advance, the 29th Division had found itself. The day of 18 November had brought the first application of what proved to be the correct technique for fighting the battle of the Roer plain: determined infantry accompanied by close tank support and covered by mortars and artillery.

General Gerhardt himself reflected a changed viewpoint. During the first two days he had been almost placid.[55] On 17 November, for example, he had cautioned the 175th Infantry commander against yielding to pressure "just to make us look good. Do it the way it ought to be," he said. "Don't want you pushing it before we are ready." But on 18 November and for several days thereafter, General Gerhardt turned the telephone lines to his subordinates into his personal whiplash. "You've been doing nothing

at all there now," General Gerhardt told the 175th Infantry commander in reference to Bettendorf. "We've got to do better . . . . We've got to quit fooling around." To another regimental commander he was equally insistent. "Corps 6 [General McLain] was just here and the general impression was, what's the matter with us . . . . We've got to plan to go today, tomorrow, and the day after." Later General Gerhardt upbraided the same regimental commander again. "There's been a tendency in your outfit to argue about things . . . . I think it's just a stall. What we want to do is get down there. Change the mental attitude there if it needs it . . . . So pull up our socks now and let's get at it."

No detail—from distribution of cigarettes to an unauthorized type of jacket worn by a company commander—was beyond General Gerhardt's province. He called an engineer commander to "give him the devil" for not getting engineers into one town. "I want to push patrolling," he told another officer. "There seems to be a tendency to alibi it on somebody else." "That Fisher did a good job," he commented in another case; "put him in for a ribbon." [56]

Something—whether General Gerhardt's remonstrance or, more likely, simply co-ordination of the various facilities available to the division—had an effect. By the end of 18 November, the 29th Division had broken the crust of the enemy's *246th Division* and in taking Siersdorf and Bettendorf had broken into the outer defensive arc of Juelich. On 19 November the division pushed into the next two villages, Duerboslar and Schleiden. Early on 20 November the

---

[54] NUSA Opns, IV, 86.
[55] See Ltr Gerhardt to OCMH, 31 May 56.

[56] 29th Div G–2—G–3 Jnl, 16–21 Nov 44.

next village of Niedermerz fell to a battalion of the 175th Infantry, whereupon the regimental commander, Col. William C. Purnell, directed a two-pronged attack against the major road center of Aldenhoven. By nightfall of 21 November, Aldenhoven too was in hand. This meant that the second, or intermediate, defensive arc of Juelich was cracked. In the meantime, a battalion of the 116th Infantry had been committed along the 29th Division's new boundary with the 2d Armored Division, which had come into effect after capture of Setterich. During three days, from 19 to 21 November, this battalion cleared three hamlets along the boundary and on 21 November seized the village of Engelsdorf, a mile northeast of Aldenhoven. This represented another break in the enemy's intermediate defensive arc and put the 29th Division within a mile and a half of the Roer River.

Of all these attacks, none was more typical of the successful application of the techniques developed for assaulting the village strongpoints than was the 175th Infantry's conquest of Schleiden on 19 November. Schleiden lies amid gently undulating fields less than a mile southeast of Siersdorf and a little more than a mile east of Bettendorf. Like most of the villages on the Roer plain, Schleiden is spread-eagled about a crossroads, a rambling, omnifarious collection of houses, barns, and shops made gray and grimy by the rain, mud, and dismal skies of November.

The 175th Infantry's 3d Battalion under Lt. Col. William O. Blanford made the attack. Until the advance masked their fires, all the regiment's heavy machine guns and 81-mm. mortars delivered support from nearby villages. A forward observer accompanying the leading in-

fantry companies maintained artillery concentrations on the objective until the troops were within 300 yards of the westernmost buildings. Until the artillery was lifted, not a bullet or a round of German fire struck the infantry.

The infantry advance began in a skirmish formation just at dawn on 19 November. At the same time a platoon of medium tanks from the 747th Tank Battalion paralleled the infantry some 350 yards to the north so that shelling attracted by the tanks would not fall upon the infantry. The tankers maintained constant machine gun fire into German trenches and foxholes on the periphery of Schleiden and occasionally fired their 75's into the village. When the forward observer lifted the supporting artillery, the tankers quickly shifted their 75-mm. fire to the trenches. It was only a question of time before the infantry gained the first houses and mop-up began. By 1430 Schleiden was clear of Germans.[57]

After the unexpected stand of the *246th Volks Grenadier Division* in Siersdorf, Bettendorf, and Setterich, the Germans in Schleiden and the other villages provided few surprises. The bulk of the defenders were still from the *246th Division,* though the efforts of the *LXXXI Corps* commander, General Koechling, to provide help resulted in commitment of a battalion each from the *3d Panzer Grenadier* and *12th Divisions.* At Niedermerz the appearance of a company of the *116th Panzer Division*'s *Reconnaissance Battal-*

---

[57] Although air support was available on 19 November, it was not used at Schleiden because "there was little need for it and it was too close for safety." NUSA Opns, IV, 120, citing 2d Lt William T. Callery, Co K.

ion alerted the 29th Division G–2 for the coming of the entire division, but in reality this was no more than a portion of *Panzer Group Bayer,* which Koechling had managed to release from attachment to the *47th Division* by shortening the front with staggered withdrawals.[58]

Though General von Zangen, the *Fifteenth Army* commander, frequently exhorted the *LXXXI Corps* to eliminate the 29th Division's penetrations, General Koechling of the *LXXXI Corps* had only inadequate resources with which to work. Basically, the only reserves available were hastily re-formed remnants of disorganized units. Bigger developments were reserved during this period for the sector of the *XII SS Corps* farther north. The *LXXXI Corps* had to be content with a glimmer of hope for the future in word that came late on 19 November. This was that a volks grenadier division earmarked for the Ardennes offensive was en route to the front and would be used to back up the *LXXXI Corps* as an *Army Group B* reserve.[59]

Only in two instances was the *LXXXI Corps* able to mount genuine counterattacks against the 29th Division. The first was at Duerboslar on 19 November where the Germans committed twelve assault guns. Although bazooka teams either disabled or frightened away four guns which penetrated the village, it remained for fighter-bombers of the XXIX TAC to force the bulk of the guns to retire from a nearby hill from which they were making a misery of the 115th Infan-

try's occupation of the village. The next day, after the 175th Infantry had moved into Niedermerz and Aldenhoven, a force of tanks variously estimated at from six to nine and accompanied by a hundred infantrymen counterattacked from the east. In this instance, credit for stopping the drive went to the artillery, which virtually annihilated the German infantry and prompted the tanks to wheel about in retreat.

After two days of disappointment, the 29th Division in four more days had reached the two-thirds mark in the drive to the Roer. In the process the division had incurred some 1,100 casualties, a figure that hardly could be considered disturbing in light of the fact that the Germans lost almost as many men as captives alone and in light of the kind of losses the divisions of the First Army's VII Corps were taking in the neighboring drive.

As General Gerhardt on 21 November directed his regiments to continue their attacks across the remaining mile and a half to the Roer, two major developments influenced his plans. First, the new boundary between the 29th and 30th Divisions had become effective, allotting a narrow portion on the southern part of General Gerhardt's former zone to the 30th Division. Second, various indications pointed to a possible German withdrawal behind the Roer. Get going, General Gerhardt told his regiments, get patrols down to the river. Unfortunately, as the 29th Division was to learn as early as the next day, 22 November, the mile and a half to the river would contain a brier patch or two. As night came on 22 November, the division's forward position would remain almost the same as the night before.

---

[58] *LXXXI Corps Gefechtsbericht,* AAR for 16–21 Nov 44.

[59] *Ibid.;* TWX, *Gruppe von Manteuffel* to *LXXXI Corps,* 2345, 19 Nov 44, *LXXXI Corps KTB, Bef. H. Gr. u. Armee.*

The Push to Gereonsweiler

While the 29th Division on the third day of the offensive had been concocting a formula for overcoming the village strongpoints, General Harmon's 2d Armored Division still had been concerned with the *9th Panzer Division.* Although CCB had stopped the first thrusts by this major reserve on 17 November, General Harmon expected the panzers to come back in strength the next day.

This was, in fact, what the Germans did. During the night of 17 November, *Army Group B* strengthened the armor by shifting the other component of the *XLVII Panzer Corps,* the *15th Panzer Grenadier Division,* to a position backing up the *9th Panzer Division.*[60]

Even so, the counterattacks on 18 November were feeble in comparison to those on the preceding day. The most sizable thrust was a minor company-size counterattack against Task Force X on the 2d Armored Division's north wing at Immendorf. A rare day of good flying weather may have kept the Germans under cover; for the XXIX TAC's fighter-bombers roamed far and wide. The planes knocked out at least two German tanks, while tank destroyers accounted for three more, and the 2d Armored Division's 92d Armored Field Artillery Battalion took credit for another.

For all the feebleness of the German strikes, General Harmon still needed a day of rest; first, to care for the wounds the panzers had inflicted; and second, to await access to Setterich in order to gain a main supply route and a crossing of the antitank ditch which was deterring commitment of a second combat command. What General Harmon did during 18

[60] *OB WEST KTB,* 18 Nov 44.

November was to conceal his tank weaknesses and his desire for a day's respite by darting a swift jab toward a limited objective that had given trouble for two days— the village of Apweiler near the division's northern boundary.

Because of long-range fire from German tanks and self-propelled guns, the formula of attacking the Roer villages with closely co-ordinated tanks and infantry had not worked in this case. On 18 November, the CCB commander, General White, proposed a variation. He gave the task to Colonel Hurless, commander of the attached 406th Infantry, who was doubling in brass as commander of Task Force X. Colonel Hurless was to use an infantry battalion without tank support along a new route of approach to Apweiler from the west, from the direction of Immendorf. At the same time, a company of the 67th Armored Regiment was to utilize a newly discovered draw to gain an open knoll southeast of Apweiler. The rest of CCB's armor was to silence long-range German fire.

At 1400 Colonel Hurless sent his 3d Battalion, 406th Infantry, toward Apweiler under cover of an artillery preparation that began five minutes earlier. Crowding the artillery dangerously, the infantry was upon the German defenders before they could recover from the barrage. Not until the leading companies had gained an orchard on the western fringe of the village did the artillery lift. By 1445 Task Force X held Apweiler.

Though General Harmon might have put his entire division on the offensive the next day, 19 November, he played it safe.[61] First he wanted to assure a firm

[61] The 2d Armored Division still had considerable tank strength. On 19 November the division had 154 medium and 119 light tanks.

right flank for the main drive on Gereons-weiler by committing Colonel Collier's CCA to seize a spur of high ground between the villages of Ederen and Freialdenhoven, east of Puffendorf. Both of Colonel Collier's task forces were to attack: Task Force A from Puffendorf to traverse a newly discovered gap in the antitank ditch, Task Force B through Setterich to cross the ditch by means of the bridgehead established by the troops of the 29th Division.

Before CCA could strike on 19 November, CCB got another taste of German reserves sufficient to justify General Harmon's foresight. Before daylight, a contingent of seven tanks and a battalion of infantry of the *15th Panzer Grenadier Division* struck that part of Task Force X which was occupying Apweiler. Sgt. Stanley Herrin and the crew of his tank of Company I, 67th Armored Regiment, were largely instrumental in stopping one prong of the counterattack. Spotting the foremost German tank, Sergeant Herrin knocked off its track with his first round. A tank destroyer finished the job by blowing off the turret. Sergeant Herrin and his crew then accounted for two tanks which followed.

Infantry alone took care of two other prongs of the German thrust. At one point, bazooka gunners knocked out three tanks, while an unidentified infantryman climbed atop the rear deck of a fourth and silenced the Germans inside by dropping hand grenades into the turret. At the other point, the Germans were without tank support and were stopped by a withering fusilade of small arms fire delivered at close range.

Rpt of Liaison Office in 102d Div G-3 Jnl, 1215, 19 Nov 44.

When CCA's Task Force A attacked during the afternoon eastward from Puffendorf toward the gap in the antitank ditch, the Germans counterattacked again, this time against what they must have taken to be Task Force A's exposed left flank. Using about a hundred infantry supported by four tanks, they seemingly forgot that CCB's Task Force 1 still held Puffendorf. Catching the Germans in the flank, CCB's tank destroyers knocked out two of the tanks, while a Sherman mounting a 76-mm. piece caught a Panther broadside. The Panther went up in flames. That ended the threat.

For all the help from Task Force 1, CCA's Task Force A made only limited gains on 19 November. Enjoying excellent observation from Ederen, the Germans first stopped Task Force A's infantry, then the tanks, and subjected both to round after round of accurate shellfire. When darkness provided relief, engineers hurried forward with bulldozers to shave the banks of the antitank ditch so that the tanks might cross the next morning on a broader front.

In the meantime, CCA's Task Force B, composed basically of a battalion of the 66th Armored Regiment and an attached battalion of the 119th Infantry, attacked at 1245 from the bridgehead across the antitank ditch northeast of Setterich. In the face of the tanks, the German infantry fell back. Task Force B in less than an hour gained the Geilenkirchen-Aldenhoven highway only a few hundred yards short of Freialdenhoven. Here the attack stalled. Every attempt to advance ran into German mines which formed a barrier extending several hundred yards in either direction. Both the high ground about Freialdenhoven and the village itself were denied until engineers might breach the mine field after night fell.

Having recuperated for two days, CCB on 20 November was ready to resume the main drive to cover a remaining mile to Gereonsweiler. In ordering the attack, General Harmon directed also that CCA renew the push on Ederen and Freialdenhoven and assist CCB's attack, if need be. After a deluge of rain that began during the night and continued into the day of 20 November, some wondered if at last November's erratic weather had not erased all hope of trafficability. For his part, CCB's General White was more perturbed that his tankers couldn't see. "The sights will get wet and fogged up," he said. Yet General Harmon was reluctant to face postponement. "Don't want to call if off if possible as the corps commander is anxious to get it started," General Harmon said. This drive was the pay-off to the four days of hard fighting that had preceded it. With Gereonsweiler in hand, the 2d Armored Division might award this sector to the XIII Corps and move to an assembly area behind the 29th Division to prepare for crossing the Roer.

They did not call it off. After delaying several hours in a vain hope of improved visibility, both CCA and CCB attacked in a driving rain.

Moving first about midmorning, CCA quickly resolved the question of trafficability. Despite the mud, the tanks in Colonel Swift's Task Force A moving on Ederen soon outdistanced the infantry.

In the attack on Ederen, Task Force A lost a tank destroyer and six tanks to antitank guns emplaced on the fringe of the village before good fortune gave an unexpected assist. Ignited by tracer bullets, four haystacks along the line of march erupted in great swirls of smoke. A providential wind blowing perpendicular to the axis of attack turned the smoke into a first-rate screen. Advancing unseen, the tanks and infantry pounced upon the Germans in trenches near the skirt of the village and sent them streaming to the rear in captive bunches.

At Freialdenhoven, CCA's Task Force B ran into the same mine field that had thwarted the attack on the village the day before. Until 1400, the commander, Colonel Hinds, delayed while engineers probed the field. At last he decided to commit his infantry and four attached British tanks, while withholding his organic tanks. The British tanks were from a squadron of the 1st Fife and Forfar Yeomanry, a unit equipped with flamethrowing Churchill tanks called Crocodiles.

The four Crocodiles and the infantry were almost through the mine field and into the village before three of the tanks struck mines and the fourth bogged down. But already the Crocodiles had done what was expected of them. They had helped the infantry across the open field. Only the mop-up process remained in Freialdenhoven, and by late afternoon (20 November) the village was clear.

In the main drive against Gereonsweiler, General White's CCB concentrated the power of all three of its task forces in contemplation that here the Germans would make their most determined stand. Paradoxically, Gereonsweiler turned out to be one of the easier targets on the Roer plain.

At 1100 on 20 November, General White sent three columns toward Gereonsweiler: Task Force 1 to move from Puffendorf to take the high ground astride the road to Gereonsweiler that had been relinquished four days earlier to the *9th*

Panzer Division, thence east to high ground between Ederen and Gereonsweiler; Task Force 2 in the center to seize the southern part of Gereonsweiler; and Task Force X attacking from Apweiler to capture the northern half of Gereonsweiler. Two troops of Crocodiles were attached to Task Force X.

Artillery officers prepared a detailed artillery fire plan, including heavy concentrations designed to isolate the village after capture. Beginning ten minutes before jump-off, six artillery battalions fired five rounds per gun into the western fringe of the village. During the next quarter hour, corps guns pounded commanding ground around the objective. Thereupon, the fire by the six battalions shifted from the fringe of the village to a rolling barrage that swept the entire objective.

Without the loss of a man or a tank, Task Force 1 took the high ground along the Puffendorf–Gereonsweiler highway. Because Task Force 2 on more exposed ground ran into trouble from machine gun emplacements and long-range tank fire, General White directed Task Force 1 to abandon its next objective and swing instead against Gereonsweiler. The maneuver worked. Within forty-five minutes after the start of the attack, some contingents of both task forces were entering the village.

In the meantime, Task Force X had been deterred by fire from self-propelled guns outside the corps sector to the north. When problems arose in getting clearance for artillery fire against the guns because of the reputed presence of troops of the XIII Corps, the task force commander, Colonel Hurless, turned a company of his tank destroyers against them. Though this cost the destroyers heavily, it was successful in diverting the German fire. Preceded by the British Crocodiles, which put the torch to everything in their path, the infantry of Task Force X moved rapidly into Gereonsweiler.

Not until the next day, 21 November, after CCB had pushed out to higher ground outside Gereonsweiler, did the Germans muster a counterattack. They concentrated against a particularly vulnerable infantry company of Task Force X—Company A, 406th Infantry—which was holding with exposed flanks on a rise a thousand yards north of Gereonsweiler. The first strike by a company of infantry in late afternoon was repulsed, but as darkness fell, three companies of the *11th Panzer Grenadier Regiment* dealt a cruel blow. Two platoons of Company A were almost obliterated as the company fell back some 300 yards to gain defilade against small arms fire. There, with the aid of another company rushed up to one flank, Company A held. When Colonel Hurless rushed tanks and tank destroyers to help, the infantry and armor together pushed back to the crest of the rise and restored the line.

In the meantime, both task forces of CCA had been pushing eastward from Ederen and Freialdenhoven so that by nightfall of 21 November they held a line just outside Ederen and at least a thousand yards beyond Freialdenhoven. The Roer was plainly visible little more than a mile and a half to the east. Here and on the hills at Gereonsweiler the 2d Armored Division was destined to hold for several days while the XIII Corps effected relief at Gereonsweiler.

In six days, from 16 through 21 November, the 2d Armored Division had moved approximately six miles in a limited objective attack through a strongly defended zone. This was a kind of attack far less attractive to armor than is exploitation but a legitimate function of armor nevertheless.

A notable feature of the attack was General Harmon's employment not only of his division but of major attachments, including a regiment of the 102d Division, the 406th Infantry, and one of two battalions of the 119th Infantry; this in spite of a markedly narrow sector. Thereby General Harmon had upped the ratio of infantry to tanks in his division and had demonstrated that, in this instance, at least, a more balanced ratio was desirable.

In six days the 2d Armored Division had sustained some 1,300 personnel casualties, including approximately 600 in the attached 406th Infantry. Of the divisions of the XIX Corps, the armor had been the only one to meet major German reserves, yet the casualty figures were roughly similar to those of the infantry divisions. As reflected by a figure of 2,385 prisoners of war captured by the armored division during the entire month of November, German losses were considerably higher. Judging from subsequent activities of the *9th Panzer Division,* that unit had been hard hit, and the *15th Panzer Grenadier Division* also had been stopped. German tank losses the 2d Armored Division estimated at 86 for the entire month. Tank losses for the U.S. division might be estimated from figures provided for CCB. That combat command reported 18 medium tanks destroyed but noted that approximately 32 mediums were damaged and temporarily out of action for varying periods during the month.[62] The entire 2d Armored Division to the end of the month probably incurred destruction or temporary damage to from 70 to 80 tanks, most of them in the first six days at Puffendorf, Apweiler, Immendorf, Ederen, Freialdenhoven, and Gereonsweiler.

Like the 29th Division, the 2d Armored had only a short distance to go to the Roer. Indeed, with the arrival of the XIII Corps and adjustment of the corps boundary on 24 November, the armor would have only two more villages to occupy. Yet, like the 29th Division, the armor might discover that this short distance was not to be taken for granted.

As of 22 November, the XIX Corps entered upon the final phase of the drive to the Roer. Already the 30th Division had completed clearing the Wuerselen industrial district and had pushed on abreast of the rest of the corps. Now all three divisions were to continue eastward side by side. Their mission was to penetrate the last defensive arc about Juelich.

---

[62] CCB S–3 Per Rpt, Nov 44.

CHAPTER XXIII

The Geilenkirchen Salient

The town of Geilenkirchen on the Ninth Army's extreme left wing was more than a block severely restricting maneuver space at the line of departure for the November offensive. It also was the hard tip of a German salient—or re-entrant—created and exaggerated by the advance of the XIX Corps northeastward toward Gereonsweiler. Following generally the course of the Wurm River as it winds northeastward between Geilenkirchen and the Roer, the salient formed a wedge between the Second British Army's 30 Corps west of the Wurm and the XIX Corps between the Wurm and the Roer. (*See Map VII.*)

In devising the plan and securing British approval for the 30 Corps to take Geilenkirchen, the Ninth Army commander, General Simpson, had been motivated by the need for a two-pronged thrust against the town and by the problems which might have developed had headquarters of different nationalities tried to control the attack. Temporary attachment of the 84th U.S. Division to the 30 Corps had solved the problem. Knowledge that the British in November had greater stocks of artillery ammunition than had the Ninth Army also had influenced the arrangement.[1]

Scheduled originally for D plus 1, the attack was postponed a day in the hope that additional time might drain some German strength from the salient to the front of the XIX Corps. As events developed, the delay prompted no shift of German troops actually in the line, but it did encourage the movement of part of the *Army Group B* reserve, the *15th Panzer Grenadier Division*, to a point from which it might engage the XIX Corps.[2] This did not negate use of the panzer grenadiers in the vicinity of Geilenkirchen, though it did delay their employment there.

Flanked by clusters of West Wall pillboxes, Geilenkirchen sits astride the Wurm River, which is the only terrain feature distinguishing this sector from other portions of the Roer plain. In the valley of the Wurm and on undulating slopes on either side are to be found the same drab farming and mining villages and the same endless rows of stock beets and cabbages that characterize the greater part of the plain. An occasional patch of woods may be found in the valley. "At best," wrote one who was there through the dismal weather of November, 1944, "the Geilenkirchen area was not one of Germany's more attractive places."[3]

Two main highways in the salient laterally bisected the planned northeasterly direction of attack. Though secondary roads connecting the villages were muddy, they were adequate for normal tactical purposes. The Aachen–Geilen-

[1] *Conquer—The Story of Ninth Army*, p. 83.

[2] *OB WEST KTB*, 18 Nov 44.
[3] Theodore Draper, *The 84th Division in the Battle of Germany* (New York: The Viking Press, 1946), a reliable unit history.

kirchen–Muenchen-Gladbach railroad follows the valley for several miles past Geilenkirchen before veering eastward at the village of Wuerm.

Having assumed control of the seventeen-mile sector from the Maas River to the vicinity of Geilenkirchen, General Horrocks' 30 British Corps had positioned the 43d Infantry Division northwest of Geilenkirchen. South and southeast of the town, between Geilenkirchen and the left flank of the XIX Corps, a regiment of the 102d Division, the 405th Infantry, held a narrow sector which at this time was the only front-line responsibility of the XIII U.S. Corps.

Operation CLIPPER

Labeled Operation CLIPPER, the fight to eliminate the Geilenkirchen salient was to develop in four phases. Attached for operations to the British but still tied for other purposes to the XIII Corps, the 84th Division was to make the main effort by passing through the 102d Division's narrow sector in early morning of the first day, 18 November, two days after the start of the Roer River offensive. Using but one regiment at first, the 84th Division was to take high ground east of Geilenkirchen and about Prummern, two miles to the northeast.

A second phase was to begin about noon on the first day when the 43d British Division was to attack to gain high ground in the vicinity of Bauchem and Tripsrath, villages west and north of Geilenkirchen. In conjunction with the 84th Division's first attack, this drive was designed to promote virtual encirclement of Geilenkirchen, whereupon the 84th Division was to launch a third phase by moving into the town and continuing a

mile and a half northward to Sueggerath in the valley of the Wurm. In the fourth phase, the 43d Division was to continue to clear the west bank of the Wurm as far as Hoven, three miles to the north of Geilenkirchen, while the 84th Division pushed beyond Sueggerath and Prummern to a trio of villages located near the point where the railroad veers away from the Wurm River. These villages—Muellendorf, Wuerm, and Beeck—are approximately three miles northeast of Geilenkirchen.[4]

Taking all these objectives would eliminate the German wedge between the British and Americans. The front line then would describe a broad arc from the Maas River near Maasbracht, southwest of Roermond, to the Wurm River at the trio villages, thence southeast to Gereonsweiler. The final boundary between the XIII and the 30 Corps (and thus between Second British and Ninth U.S. Armies and the 12th and 21 Army Groups) was to follow generally the course of the Wurm to the villages, thence northeastward along the Aachen–Muenchen-Gladbach railroad.

---

[4] Unless otherwise noted, this chapter is based upon official records of the 84th and 102d Divisions and of the XIII Corps. See also *Conquer—The Story of Ninth Army,* pp. 55–94; Draper, *The 84th Division in the Battle of Germany;* NUSA Opns, IV. The British story is based upon British documents found in American files (e.g., 30 Corps intelligence summaries), plus liaison reports between the 30 Corps and XIII U.S. Corps. Advance of the 84th Division beyond Sueggerath and Prummern apparently was not directed until the eve of the attack. See Memo, XIII Corps G–3 Sec, 17 Nov, sub: Time Schedule (Result of Conference of Commanders Concerned in Linnich Operation); Amendment 1 to XIII Corps FO 1, dtd 17 Nov. Both in XIII Corps G–3 Jnl file, 17–20 Nov 44.

A successful Operation CLIPPER combined with the 2d Armored Division's capture of Gereonsweiler would broaden the Ninth Army's maneuver space by some five to six miles. As this space became available, General Gillem's XIII Corps was to assume control of operations in the new sector. After relief of the 2d Armored Division at Gereonsweiler, General Gillem intended to send the 102d Division across a remaining two and a half miles to the Roer at Linnich, there to force a crossing. In the meantime, a special force, named Task Force Biddle and composed of the 113th Cavalry Group strongly reinforced with additional tanks and artillery, was to protect the corps north flank. Task Force Biddle was to occupy the sector along the railroad between the trio of Wurm villages and the Roer. Later, the 84th Division and the recuperated 7th Armored Division were to join the 102d Division in the Roer bridgehead at Linnich to make the final push to the Rhine.[5]

No immediate British participation, once Operation CLIPPER had been concluded, was planned, though the 30 Corps did contemplate a later local advance along the west bank of the Wurm to high ground overlooking Heinsberg, seven miles north of Geilenkirchen near the confluence of the Wurm and the Roer. The British intended eventually to drive either southeast from Nijmegen or northward from Nijmegen, but extensive preparation and reorganization were necessary before the drive could be undertaken. Other than Operation CLIPPER, the only British offensive action coincident with the November offensive was the continuing drive to clear the Peel Marshes west of the Maas River. As events developed, the fact that no large-scale offensive was launched by the British—not even a large-scale feint—worked to the detriment of the November offensive. It enabled the Germans to shift divisions from the front of the 21 Army Group to oppose the First and Ninth U.S. Armies.

Since virtually all German reserves in the West had been marked "untouchable" in preparation for the Ardennes counteroffensive, the Commander in Chief West could obtain reserves only by denuding fronts not considered immediately threatened. Hardly had Field Marshal von Rundstedt received the reports on 16 November of the multiple strikes in the vicinity of Aachen before he divined the extent of the Allied offensive. He immediately ordered the shift of the *10th SS Panzer Division* from the Holland front to the extreme south wing of *Army Group H* where it could be committed quickly in support of *Army Group B*. He also took steps to prepare a volks grenadier and two infantry divisions for movement from Holland to the same sector.[6]

On 17 November Rundstedt found justification for these moves in the intelligence that the 104th U.S. Division, identified earlier in the Antwerp fight, had been moved to participate in the new offensive.[7] By 18 November Rundstedt had gained even greater confidence in his situation estimate and his decisions:

. . . To date [*OB WEST* noted] there are no indications for an equally strong British attack against the Maas front [in Holland], coordinated with the present offensive. The

---

[5] XIII Corps FO 1, 13 Nov, XIII Corps G-2 file, 14–16 Nov 44; Amendment 1 to XIII Corps FO 1.

[6] *OB WEST KTB,* 16 Nov 44.

[7] *OB WEST KTB,* 17 Nov 44. Though the Germans named this division as the 184th, they obviously meant the 104th.

relatively feeble attacks against the Venlo Bridgehead [*i.e.*, the Peel Marshes] even speaks against such a possibility. Hence . . . *OB WEST* orders the immediate transfer of *10th SS Panzer Division* to *Army Group B*.[8]

Subsequent events were to demonstrate even more clearly that the offensive was confined primarily to the American part of the front. During the course of the fighting west of the Roer, the Germans were to move from Holland to active participation against the U.S. armies not only the *10th SS Panzer Division* but also the *3d Parachute Division* and an infantry and a volks grenadier division.

As to the immediate situation at Geilenkirchen on the eve of the 30 Corps attack, the German line-up was the same as it had been two days before when the November offensive began. Both Colonel Landau's *176th Division*, northwest of Geilenkirchen, and General Lange's *183d Volks Grenadier Division*, in and southeast of the town, had concentrated their greatest strength about Geilenkirchen. Here also General Blumentritt, commander of the *XII SS Corps*, had emplaced the bulk of his artillery.

Attacking two days behind the main forces in the November offensive, the 30 Corps could count upon little direct assistance from the big air bombardment of Operation QUEEN, though Linnich and Heinsberg were scheduled to be hit. The 30 Corps counted instead upon a steady softening process by fighter-bombers which began as early as 8 November with a napalm strike against Geilenkirchen. Assistance was to be provided by both the Second British Tactical Air Force and the Ninth Army's usual ally, the XXIX TAC. At least two groups of XXIX TAC

fighter-bombers were to operate on 18 November, D Day for Operation CLIPPER.[9]

In addition to artillery support to be expected from the 30 Corps, the 84th Division was reinforced by two U.S. battalions attached from the XIII Corps. Because position areas in the congested sector between the Maas and the Wurm were at a premium, four other artillery battalions available in XIII Corps were not to participate.

In its first combat experience, the 84th Division had two handicaps: inexperience and only two instead of its usual three regiments. (The third was attached to the 30th Division of the XIX Corps at Wuerselen.) In the first step of the attack, the division was to be reinforced by a special British unit named Drewforce, which included two troops of flail tanks, and by a troop of the 357th Searchlight Battery, Royal Artillery, manning four giant beacons. A flail tank had a rotor in front to which were attached heavy chains that flailed the ground as the rotor was driven by the tank engine. The searchlight provided "artificial moonlight" on dark nights by bouncing light off low-hanging clouds.[10] By light of the searchlights, the flail tanks before dawn on 18 November were to clear two paths through a thick mine field which the 84th Division had to cross. The mine field was southeast of Geilenkirchen, south of a spur railroad running from Geilenkirchen into the sector of the XIX Corps at Immendorf and Puffendorf and on to Juelich. Because the number of flail

[8] *OB WEST KTB*, 18 Nov 44.

[9] XIII Corps AAR, Nov 44, and Mtg on Air Support Plan with XXIX TAC, 15 Nov, XIII Corps G–3 Jnl file, 14–17 Nov 44.

[10] For a detailed description of flail tanks, see NUSA Opns, IV, 103–04. Details on use of searchlights may be found in Searchlights in Battle, NUSA Opns, III.

BRITISH FLAIL TANK *beating the road to explode mines.*

tanks for piercing the mine field was limited, the division commander, Brig. Gen. Alexander R. Bolling, decided to use only one regiment at first. The 334th Infantry under Col. John S. Roosma was to capture high ground east of Geilenkirchen and at Prummern, whereupon on the second day, the 333d Infantry was to attack Geilenkirchen and proceed up the Wurm valley to Sueggerath. Both regiments presumably would combine for the final push into the trio of Wurm villages, Muellendorf, Wuerm, and Beeck.

As D Day for Operation CLIPPER approached, the atmosphere as influenced by progress of the main forces in the November offensive was conducive neither to elation nor to discouragement. Early success of the adjacent 2d Armored Division, for example, had been tempered by arrival of the *9th Panzer Division.* During the evening of 17 November, reports of tank concentrations near Geilenkirchen convinced the staff of the 84th Division that a prompt counterattack from the direction of Geilenkirchen was "very probable"; but the news failed to deter General Bolling from proceeding as scheduled. He might, he said, "beat the Germans to the punch." [11]

---

[11] Ln Rpt at 2040 in 102d Div Jnl, 17 Nov 44; Ltr, Bolling to OCMH, n.d., but written early in 1956.

The Jump-off

As British searchlights provided hazy illumination across the fields between Geilenkirchen and Immendorf, the flail tanks of Drewforce at 0600 on 18 November churned toward the German mine field. Because mud gummed the flail chains and lessened their effectiveness, engineers checked behind the tanks with mine detectors. Only desultory German fire interfered.

An hour later, after a sharp five-minute artillery preparation, two battalions of the 334th Infantry began moving through the two gaps in the mine field. Concealed by the fading darkness, neither unit encountered accurate fire while passing through the gaps. On the west, attached British tanks could not accompany the advance at first because of deep mud, but the 2d Battalion nevertheless plodded ahead through use of marching fire and small unit maneuver. By midmorning the battalion had gained the high ground east of Geilenkirchen. On the regiment's right wing, the 1st Battalion was held up for a while along the spur railroad by a cluster of ten pillboxes, an intermediate objective en route to Prummern. The battalion commander, Lt. Col. Lloyd H. Gomes, moved among his platoon leaders encouraging them to urge their men forward. Once the men had overcome the temptation to court the protection of the railroad embankment, they used marching fire to advantage. When they had driven the Germans from trenches into the pillboxes, they discovered as had others before them that this was three fourths of the battle.

Still concerned lest the Germans counterattack from Geilenkirchen, the regimental commander, Colonel Roosma, delayed the final push to Prummern until he could send his reserve battalion to hold the high ground east of Geilenkirchen. Though an expected counterblow by the *9th Panzer Division* had failed to develop, Colonel Roosma had another reason for concern. In midmorning, artillery observers of the 30 Corps had reported a force of 4,500 men in a column of tanks and vehicles stretching for three and a half miles en route south from Heinsberg in the direction of Geilenkirchen. These observers probably were correct in assuming this to be part of the *15th Panzer Grenadier Division*. That division was moving, however, not to Geilenkirchen but, in compliance with orders issued the night before, to back up the *9th Panzer Division* opposite the XIX U.S. Corps.[12]

To relieve the 84th Division of some concern, the XIII Corps commander, General Gillem, alerted two regiments of the 102d Division for possible commitment in event of a German blow.[13] When by midday the Germans had not struck, the 334th Infantry resumed the attack in the direction of Prummern. The 2d Battalion on the right aimed at the village, while the 1st Battalion moved toward Hill 101, west of the village.

Routes to both these objectives were across exposed ground, and the Germans by this time obviously were alert. Working with attached British Sherman tanks, both battalions nevertheless made steady progress. By late afternoon the 334th Infantry could report both Hill 101 and Prummern in hand, though some re-

---

[12] Fragmentary Order, CG XIII Corps, 1030, 18 Nov, XIII Corps G-3 Jnl file, 17–20 Nov 44; various messages in XIII Corps G-2 Jnl file for the same period; *OB WEST KTB*, 18 Nov 44.

[13] Fragmentary Order, 1030, 18 Nov.

sistance still had to be eliminated in the village. The defenders of Prummern represented both the *183d Division* and the *9th Panzer Division's 10th Panzer Grenadier Regiment*. In a commendable operation, the novice 334th Infantry had taken its D-Day objectives, bagged 330 prisoners, and reached a point almost on line with Task Force X of the 2d Armored Division, which during the day had occupied Apweiler, a mile and a half southeast of Prummern. American losses had been moderate: 10 killed and 180 wounded.[14]

On the opposite side of Geilenkirchen and the Wurm River, the 43d British Division had attacked about noon on 18 November. By the end of the day the British controlled Tripsrath and most of Bauchem, north and west of Geilenkirchen. The day's advances on both banks of the Wurm obviously had taken the starch out of the hard tip of the Geilenkirchen salient. Allied forces now looked down upon the town from three sides.

Having learned much during their first day's combat, men of the 334th Infantry had another lesson in store as dusk approached. What is listed as a day's final objective, they were to discover, sometimes can change to an intermediate objective with surprising abruptness. Even as the 1st and 2d Battalions were fighting for Hill 101 and Prummern, the division commander, General Bolling, directed that they continue past these objectives before stopping for the night. On the left, the 1st Battalion was to push a company northwest along a nose of Hill 101 to gain a position dominating Sueg-

gerath and the Wurm valley, while the 2d Battalion was to seize high ground northeast of Prummern in the direction of Beeck, an objective known by the code name given it as Mahogany Hill (Hill 92.5).[15]

Out of context, this order must have been hard to understand; for as night approached, both battalions had incurred the disorganization inherent in a day of fighting, and the men were cold, muddy, and hungry. Yet, in the over-all pattern, taking advantage of the momentum of the day's advance to get these additional objectives before pausing made sense. The 30 Corps commander, General Horrocks, had directed during the afternoon that the 84th Division the next day combine the third and fourth phases of Operation CLIPPER. On 19 November the 84th Division was to take Geilenkirchen and Sueggerath and, on the same day, the trio of villages Muellendorf, Wuerm, and Beeck.[16] Holding the tip of Hill 101 overlooking Sueggerath obviously would facilitate advance of the 333d Infantry into Sueggerath and beyond against Muellendorf and Wuerm. Occupying Mahogany Hill would provide the 334th Infantry high ground between Prummern and Beeck that would improve the defense of Prummern and at the same time assist materially an attack upon Beeck.

As night fell on 18 November, the attached British searchlight battery moved forward. The attack continued.

A company of the 1st Battalion made the move along the nose of Hill 101 with little real difficulty, but in Prummern the

---

[14] Casualty figures from Msg, 30 Corps to XIII Corps, 1800, 18 Nov, XIII Corps G–3 Jnl file, 17–20 Nov 44.

[15] 84th Div. G–3 Jnl, 18 Nov 44.
[16] Operation CLIPPER Tasks for 19 Nov, XIII Corps G–3 Jnl file, 17–20 Nov 44; NUSA Opns, IV, 105.

COLUMN OF BRITISH CHURCHILL TANKS *on a road near Geilenkirchen.*

2d Battalion could not get an attack started against Mahogany Hill. Men of Colonel Gomes' battalion were too involved still with eliminating points of resistance within the village.

Only a reconnaissance patrol moved toward Mahogany Hill during the night. Returning two hours after midnight, the patrol brought back disturbing news. The men had spotted six German tanks moving against Prummern from the north.

The blow that followed was delivered by an estimated two companies of the *9th Panzer Division's 10th Panzer Grenadier Regiment,* plus six tanks.[17]

---

[17] Draper, *The 84th Division in the Battle of Germany,* p. 30.

Though the situation never reached critical proportions, the men in Prummern had their hands full the rest of the night and into the next day.

The result was that no attack could be mounted against Mahogany Hill until an hour before noon the next day, 19 November, when Colonel Roosma committed his reserve battalion to the task. Fire from three pillboxes atop the hill, from two pillboxes at a crossroads in the northeastern fringe of Prummern, and from field fortifications on the eastern edge of the village stymied this attack. For another day Mahogany Hill remained somewhat aloof from the fighting while the Americans tried to eliminate the last resistance from the fringes of Prummern.

BRITISH FLAME-THROWING CROCODILE (MK-7) TANKS *in action.*

This they finally accomplished late on 20 November with the help of flame-throwing British Crocodile tanks, used against the pillboxes at the crossroads. Mahogany Hill itself was to fall two days later after only a token engagement as a company caught the Germans atop the hill by surprise.

The nature of resistance at Prummern emphasized to the 84th Division commander, General Bolling, a concern which had begun to grow during the first day of Operation CLIPPER.[18] Instead of the division's west flank opposite Geilen-

kirchen, the danger spot fast was beginning to look like the east flank between Prummern and the closest positions of the 2d Armored Division a mile and a half to the southeast at Apweiler. "Our flank is sort of out in the breeze now," was the way General Bolling put it on 19 November after his second regiment had begun to attack up the Wurm valley. "Our chief concern . . . is our right flank. The 2d Armored Division has advanced only to Immendorf–Apweiler. I have pushed a salient up the river valley and they [the armor] haven't advanced." [19]

Though certainly aware of why the 2d Armored Division had not advanced—

---

[18] Note Records of Important Telephone Conversations, 1130 and 1140, 18 Nov, NUSA G–3 Jnl file, 12–13 Nov 44.

[19] NUSA Opns, IV, 111.

because of the *9th Panzer Division*'s counterattacks and because a main supply route through Setterich still was not open—General Bolling's superiors apparently shared his concern. Early on 19 November they provided help in the form of the 102d Division's 405th Infantry. The regiment was attached to the 84th Division with the proviso that it be committed "only in case of emergency." [20]

An Exercise in Frustration

As this precaution was taken, the initiative remained with the Allies except for the local counterattack at Prummern and one or two minor forays out of the Wurm valley against the British. Expected commitment of the *15th Panzer Grenadier Division* against the XIII Corps still had not developed.

On 19 November the 84th Division's second regiment, the 333d Infantry, launched another phase of Operation CLIPPER at Geilenkirchen amid an aura of success. Advancing up the Wurm valley to seize successively Geilenkirchen, Sueggerath, Muellendorf, and Wuerm, the 333d Infantry discovered early on 19 November that Geilenkirchen was not the Gibraltar it was supposed to be. Already encompassed on three sides, the Germans in the town provided little more than a stiff delaying action.

The biggest problem in the attack, explained the leading battalion commander, Lt. Col. Thomas R. Woodyard, was lack of artillery support. "After the artillery preparation for the jump off," Colonel Woodyard said later, "we received no artillery support because it was con-

sidered that our own troops, on the flanks, were too close . . . for safety in firing." [21] Though two attached troops of tanks from the British Sherwood Rangers Yeomanry provided close support, they could not make up entirely for lack of artillery.

While another battalion mopped up in Geilenkirchen, Colonel Woodyard's battalion continued northeast on either bank of the Wurm toward Sueggerath. Marked by increased shelling, resistance stiffened, but the battalion plodded ahead. Flame-throwing Crocodiles were a big help, especially against two pillboxes guarding the road into Sueggerath. "A few squirts from the flame-throwers," related an infantry company commander, Capt. James W. Mitchell, "and the Germans poured out . . . . The bastards are afraid of those flame-throwers and won't be caught inside a pillbox . . . ." [22]

Within Sueggerath, the Germans were not so easily cowed. Though one company pushed quickly through the village, bypassed strongpoints continued to hold out. As night came, Colonel Woodyard's battalion still was heavily engaged in Sueggerath. Because the village sits in a depression, Colonel Woodyard wanted to continue to high ground a few hundred yards to the northeast; yet he was concerned that the day's losses and disorganization had so weakened his battalion that he could not reach that objective alone. Not until near midnight was the regimental commander, Col. Timothy A. Pedley, Jr., able to get another battalion forward to help. An attack by both battalions in the darkness did the job.

At the conclusion of this attack, the 333d Infantry still was more than a mile short of the final objective of Wuerm.

---

[20] Msg, 84th Div to XIII Corps, 0850, 19 Nov, XIII Corps G-3 file, 17-20 Nov 44.

[21] NUSA Opns, IV, 106.
[22] *Ibid.*, p. 158.

Nevertheless, the bulk of the Geilenkirchen salient had been eliminated. If the regiment could adjust its positions to tie in with the British to the northwest and with the 334th Infantry to the southeast, the 30 Corps could present a solid and fairly straight front line. Still concerned lest the *15th Panzer Grenadier Division* materialize against the 84th Division's southeastern flank, General Bolling told Colonel Pedley to take precautions against this possibility during the third day, 20 November. In the meantime, the 334th Infantry was to clear the last dogged resistance from Prummern. Both regiments then might renew the attack on the fourth day against Muellendorf, Wuerm, and Beeck.

On this fourth day, 21 November, an exercise in frustration began. Through the preceding day and night, rain had fallen intermittently. Early on 21 November it became a downpour that turned the loamy soil of the Wurm valley into a virtual quagmire. Because the road from Sueggerath toward Muellendorf and Wuerm obviously was mined, British tanks supporting the 333d Infantry would have to wade through the mud. Though the tankers tried to use an alternate road along the railroad, debris at a demolished underpass in Sueggerath blocked movement in that direction.

The immediate problem facing Colonel Pedley's infantry was a nest of pillboxes on a gentle forward slope where the Germans could employ grazing fire with devastating effect. Attacking alone time after time through mud and rain, the infantry could get no place. "Christ!" exclaimed the battalion commander, Lt. Col. William S. Barrett; "I wish I could get some help . . . . Tell Colonel Pedley that these men are fighting and dying up

here. No one is lying down. But we gotta have power to do this thing." [23]

That night engineers tackled the underpass in Sueggerath with explosives while artillery officers worked out an elaborate fire plan. To protect infantry and tanks, whose movement in the mud would be snaillike at best, artillery of the 84th Division and the 30 Corps was to lay down a rolling barrage. The barrage was to begin even before the tanks left Sueggerath, because the tankers had several hundred yards of exposed ground to cross before reaching the infantry positions.

Sometimes the best-laid battle plans can go awry for the want of a single piece of equipment. That happened on 22 November when a bulldozer failed to arrive to complete the task of clearing the underpass in Sueggerath so that the tanks might move. Not until midafternoon, after the infantry already had jumped off and run into much the same frustration as on the day before, did the tanks get forward.

To the relief of all concerned, the tanks were all that was needed. As flame throwers on the Crocodiles went into action, the Germans emerged from the nest of pillboxes that had barred the way, hands high. Three pillboxes fell in rapid succession.

This success was encouraging, but the objective of Muellendorf still was 500 yards away. Because the heavy fuel wagons which the Crocodiles had to pull were bogging in the mud, the tank commander refused to go farther. When the riflemen tried to move alone into the village, they encountered the same kind of

---

[23] *Ibid.,* p. 155, citing notes taken by Capt John O'Grady in Comd Post, 3d Bn, 333d Inf, 21–23 Nov 44.

intense grazing fire that earlier had denied the pillboxes. As night came, one platoon broke into the village, only to be engulfed without trace in the darkness. At last the infantry dug in about the pillboxes, still a half mile short of Muellendorf.

The change from half-hearted to stanch resistance was not confined to the Muellendorf sector alone. On both 21 and 22 November the 43d British Division also encountered opposition which denied the division's final objectives on the other side of the Wurm River northwest of Muellendorf. Likewise, in the sector of the 334th Infantry, frustration again was the keynote. A one-battalion attack from Prummern against Beeck was repulsed by the same sharp resistance and the same appalling conditions of mud.

Though frustrating, the attacks as early as 21 November did reveal an illuminating bit of intelligence information. Prisoner identifications all along the front of the 30 Corps left no doubt that the iron which the Germans had added to their resistance was the *15th Panzer Grenadier Division*. Having first employed the panzer grenadiers in counterattack against the XIX Corps, the Germans then had committed most of the division to fixed defense in front of the 84th Division.

Concern about the 84th Division's southeastern flank alleviated by this identification, General Bolling sought permission to reinforce his attack with the regiment of the 102d Division which had been provided three days before for use in event of emergency. General Bolling wanted to send two battalions of this regiment to flank the village of Beeck by seizing high ground on the east and north, while the remaining battalion struck frontally and two battalions of the 84th Division provided fire support.

Approval gained, the 102d Division's 405th Infantry attacked toward Beeck on 22 November, only to discover as had the other regiments that a combination of mud and exposed ground was too much. The fight swung up and down the open slopes between Prummern and Beeck. Though several pillboxes were eliminated and forty Germans captured, no major gain could be registered.

Before the attacks at Muellendorf and Beeck could be renewed, an organizational change took place. As early as 20 November, the two Allied divisions under the 30 Corps had cleared the major portion of the Geilenkirchen salient, even though the final objectives still were denied. Coincidentally, the armor of the XIX Corps had captured Gereonsweiler. Thus the two requisites for providing a zone of action for the XIII Corps had been fulfilled. As of 23 November, the 84th Division and its attachments reverted to control of General Gillem's XIII Corps.[24]

The 84th Division's attack at Muellendorf and Beeck continued through 23 November, but to no avail. At the end of the day, General Gillem directed the 84th to go over to the defensive. For five more days the 84th Division was to hold here while the 113th Cavalry Group gradually took over to maintain contact with the British and while General Gillem prepared his XIII Corps for participation in the final phase of the drive to the Roer. In early plans, the XIII Corps was to have begun to attack on 23 November, but that obviously was illusory in the light of the hard fight experienced by the 84th Division and of the scattered position of the regiments of the 102d Division.

---

[24] XIII Corps Ltr of Instrs 4, 22 Nov, XIII Corps G-3 Jnl file, 20–24 Nov 44.

In clearing the Geilenkirchen salient, the two regiments of the 84th Division together had incurred approximately 2,000 battle casualties, including 169 killed and 752 missing. Nonbattle losses, primarily from trench foot, raised the total by another 500.[25]

[25] 12th A Gp, G–1 Daily Summary, 26 Nov 44.

As a kind of temporary stalemate settled over this part of the Roer plain, the battlefield was a dreary spectacle. The sun seldom shone. A damp, grayish mist predominated. Sodden by rain, gashed by shells and tank tracks, the beet and cabbage fields were dismal and ugly. Drab enough at the start of the fighting, the villages now were desolate.

CHAPTER XXIV

Ninth Army's Final Push to the Roer

In contrast to the frustration that by 21 November had begun to mark the 84th Division's attack in Operation CLIPPER, optimism was the keynote with the other attacking force of the Ninth Army, General McLain's XIX Corps. After an arduous six days of fighting, the XIX Corps now appeared ready for a quick and easy final push to the Roer River. (*See Map VII.*)

By nightfall of 21 November, the 2d Armored Division's CCB held Gereonsweiler. As soon as high ground nearby was secure, the town was to be turned over to the XIII Corps. CCA had pushed to Ederen and beyond Freialdenhoven to within a mile and a half of the Roer, so that only two villages remained to be taken in the narrow zone that would be left the armor after adjustment of the corps boundary. Having seized Engelsdorf, the adjacent 29th Division was farther east, though equidistant from the Roer. After having relinquished a sector about two miles wide on the south wing of the corps to the 30th Division, the 29th had only three villages west of the Roer still to take.

Having been scheduled at first only to clear the Ninth Army's inner wing near the original line of departure, the 30th Division at dark on 21 November was about a mile and a half short of the easternmost of its neighbors. Yet the division might catch up quickly if a performance executed on 21 November could

be repeated. In rapid succession, the 120th Infantry and attached 743d Tank Battalion had overrun five villages.[1] As night came, the 120th Infantry's most advanced position encompassed Fronhoven, four miles from the Roer.

The optimism that marked the beginning of operations the next day, 22 November, was based primarily upon expectation of German withdrawal behind the river. "If they have pulled back . . .," the 29th Division's General Gerhardt had remarked, "we want to develop it."[2] The 2d Armored Division had noted various indications of withdrawal. The 30th Division the day before had encountered only remnants and rear echelon troops of the same units which had been falling back steadily since the start of the November offensive. Even if the enemy planned no formal withdrawal, he hardly could make much of a fight of it with troops like these before a concentration of three American divisions on a front less than seven miles wide.

It did not take long on 22 November for events to prove this kind of thinking wishful. Even if German commanders wanted to pull back behind the Roer,

---

[1] So impressed by this performance was the Ninth Army commander, General Simpson, that he later had it staged as an orientation demonstration for officers newly arrived at the front. Hewitt, *Workhorse of the Western Front*, p. 162.

[2] 29th Div G-2—G-3 Jnl, 21 Nov 44. Unless otherwise noted, sources for this chapter are the same as for Chapter XXI.

they had to hold on as long as possible because of the coming counteroffensive in the Ardennes. Almost coincidentally with the renewal of the American drive, one of the steps the Germans had been taking in response to appeals for help from the *Fifteenth Army (Gruppe von Manteuffel)* began to produce results.

Originally scheduled to participate in the Ardennes, the *340th Volks Grenadier Division* had been directed on 17 November to move to the Roer sector. On 19 November *Fifteenth Army* had ordered the division to assume a position near Dueren from which to back up the *LXXXI Corps*. The next day, when the threat to Linnich and Juelich became immediate, the army commander, General von Zangen, changed the order. He directed that two regiments move west of the Roer, one to Linnich, the other to Juelich. The third regiment was to assemble east of the river between the two towns as a reserve. The division was to assume responsibility for holding bridgeheads at Linnich and Juelich.[3]

Using the *340th Division* in active combat before the Ardennes counteroffensive would appear at first glance to have been a violation of Hitler's strict order about the OKW Reserve. In reality, it conformed to a compromise which Hitler had been forced to accept because of a shortage of forces for the counteroffensive. Two or three of the new divisions created especially for the Ardennes would have to be used temporarily to relieve old divisions also earmarked for the Ardennes so that

the old divisions might be rehabilitated.[4]

The first regiment of the *340th Volks Grenadier Division* reached Juelich during the morning of 21 November and that night began to relieve the *246th Division*. It was high time the *246th* got some rest. Two of its regiments were down to about 350 men each, another to 120.

To supplement the fresh regiment, General von Zangen committed to the Juelich–Linnich area two newly released volks artillery corps.[5] He also inserted into the Juelich defensive arc a fresh infantry replacement battalion, 300 men strong, and a battalion of *Jagdpanther* assault guns.[6]

The Americans smacked into these reinforcements early on 22 November. On the XIX Corps south wing, the 30th Division's 120th Infantry took and held the village of Erberich, but two companies which gained the village of Lohn had to withdraw by infiltration after German guns denied passage for the tanks and tank destroyers needed to clear the objective.

In the center of the XIX Corps, two platoons of the 29th Division's 175th Infantry which had slipped into Bourheim during the night were ejected unceremoniously before daylight by fresh troops of the *340th Division*. Though two battalions tried during the course of the day (22 November) to regain Bourheim, they could not force entry through

---

[3] *OB WEST KTB*, 17 Nov 44; TWX, *Gruppe von Manteuffel* to *LXXXI Corps* 2345, 19 Nov 44, *LXXXI Corps KTB, Bef. H. G. u. Armee;* Order *LXXXI Corps* to *340th Div*, 2030, 20 Nov 44, *LXXXI Corps KTB, Befehle an Div.*

[4] Charles V. P. von Luttichau, The Ardennes Offensive, Planning and Preparations, Chapter I: The Preliminary Planning, p. 24, MS in OCMH.

[5] Order, *Gruppe von Manteuffel* to *LXXXI Corps*, 0010, 22 Nov 44, *LXXXI Corps KTB, Bef. H. Gr. u. Armee.*

[6] These identifications are from American sources. The *Jagdpanther* was a hybrid vehicle, a Mark V tank chassis mounting an 88-mm. gun.

small arms and mortar fire emanating from extensive field fortifications about the village. At Koslar, a mile to the north, the story was the same. Here the 116th Infantry fought all day to no avail. The 29th Division's positions at the end of 22 November remained virtually the same as on the day before.

Koslar, Bourheim, and another village, Kirchberg, represented the final or inner defensive arc protecting Juelich. When the 29th Division's General Gerhardt heard that the Germans had thrown fresh troops into these villages, he admitted that an enemy withdrawal appeared unlikely. "Your boy Mansfield," said Gerhardt to a neighboring commander, "wants to know when we're going to move. It won't be soon. We have a war on again." [7]

In the zone of the 2d Armored Division, German reinforcements had not yet arrived, but the armor had to deal with contingents of the *246th Division* led by a capable battalion commander, the same man who earlier had denied Setterich for so long. The going looked easy at first as a task force composed of a battalion of the 66th Armored Regiment, an attached battalion of the 119th Infantry, and two Churchill and three Crocodile tanks made a two-pronged attack against the village of Merzenhausen. First sight of the flame-throwing Crocodiles produced white flags in abundance. Then German tanks knocked out the Crocodiles. From that point, the going was rough.

As darkness approached, the task force at last gained entrance to Merzenhausen. "Think we lost 8 tanks in exchange for 6 tanks," reported the CCA commander, Colonel Collier, "which is a fair swap

because their tanks are the big babies." [8] But that was hardly the whole story. A few minutes later two more German tanks emerged from hiding in the northeastern part of the village. Accompanied by men of the *246th Division,* the tanks counterattacked a company of the 119th Infantry that was proceeding up the main street. Unaware in the deepening darkness of the proximity of other units, the infantry company fell back all the way to a crossroads on the southwestern fringe of the village. Though CCA sent a battalion of the 41st Armored Infantry to bolster a line formed at the crossroads, no resumption of the attack could be mounted before the next morning. Merzenhausen remained in German hands. Like the 29th Division, the 2d Armored at the end of 22 November could point to no new gains. [9]

. . . in effect we are there . . ."

Abandoning the hope of enemy withdrawal, the XIX Corps on 23 November adopted a cautious, almost leisurely pattern of operations. "[Merzenhausen] will have to be taken eventually," the corps commander told the 2d Armored Division, "as it's in line with the way you're going. [But I] would wait 'till you get ready to take Barmen too. Then you can make one big effort in that direction." [10] General Gerhardt told his regiments to "wait until the 30th Division gets up." He said, "Omar [General Bradley, 12th Group commander] was in this morning and was very pleased. . . . Omar says in effect we are there, there's no

---

[7] 29th Div G-2—G-3 Jnl, 22 Nov 44.

[8] 2d Armd Div G-3 Jnl, 22 Nov 44.
[9] *LXXXI Corps Gefechtsbericht,* AAR for 23 Nov 44.
[10] 2d Armd Div G-3 Jnl, 23 Nov 44.

sense pushing at it until the other people get up there." [11]

The "other people" were the First Army's V and VII Corps. Committed on 21 November, the V Corps two days later still had not penetrated the forested approaches to Huertgen. Part of the VII Corps also was bogged down in the Huertgen Forest with no immediate hope of breaking out.

Despite close support from a company of tanks, a battalion of the 41st Armored Infantry was able on 23 November to gain only about half of Merzenhausen. Thereupon, the division commander, General Harmon, ordered consolidation. In keeping with the new boundary between the XIII and XIX Corps that would become effective on 24 November, the 2d Armored Division had begun to regroup. Not for several days would the division attempt to cover the remaining distance to the Roer.

The 30th Division adopted a similar pattern: one day of attack followed by consolidation. Despite shellfire that inflicted thirty-five casualties on one company alone, a battalion of the 120th Infantry in little more than an hour fought back into Lohn. In the face of two counterattacks the battalion held.

Deception played a role in the capture of Pattern, a mile northeast of Lohn. While a battalion of the 119th Infantry moved into the 29th Division's zone to strike southeast against Pattern from Aldenhoven, a battalion of the 120th Infantry in Erberich opened fire. Their attention diverted to the apparent threat from Erberich, the Germans in Pattern were unprepared for attack from another quarter. A TOT by eleven battalions of artillery preceded the attack. Within less than an hour the men of the 119th Infantry had seized the village without a casualty.

Only Altdorf in the valley of the Inde River remained to be taken in the 30th Division's sector. Because exposed approaches and a clifflike drop in the ground near the village would complicate this task, the division commander, General Hobbs, asked a delay. He wanted to wait until neighboring divisions on north and south had taken adjacent objectives of Kirchberg and Inden. The corps commander, General McLain, approved. Not for another four days would the 30th Division attack.

Unlike the other two units of the XIX Corps, the 29th Division found no pause. The explanation lay in the enemy's *340th Volks Grenadier Division.* During 23 November a second regiment of this division moved into the Juelich bridgehead.[12]

After another grueling day of generally fruitless attacks across muddy, exposed ground about Bourheim, one of two attacking battalions of the 175th Infantry at last broke into the village late on 23 November. If Bourheim was hard to take, it was even more difficult to hold. Beginning just after midnight, a severe fifteen-minute concentration of artillery and mortar fire heralded the first of what was to develop as a three-day siege of counterattacks. Almost all the enemy thrusts were preceded by intense shelling. In between, German guns on high ground beyond the Roer pounded the village. On 24 November, for example, the enemy fired an estimated 2,000 rounds into Bourheim.

---

[11] 29th Div G-2—G-3 Jnl, 23 Nov 44.

[12] *LXXXI Corps Gefechtsbericht,* AAR for 23 Nov 44.

On the American side, artillery also played a basic role. Infantrymen were quick to credit the artillery with dispersing German infantry and in some cases German tanks.[13] Though hampered by ammunition shortages that in heavier calibers was acute, the artillery also conducted a program of interdictory and harassing fires to discourage further German build-up west of the Roer. On 26 November XIX Corps artillery doubled its normal counterbattery program; 191 counterbattery missions were fired that day. This was accomplished in spite of ammunition restrictions that "placed a severe burden on artillery commanders, as it was necessary to carefully weigh all missions . . . before deciding whether . . . to fire them." [14]

The widespread use of artillery by both sides at Bourheim was in keeping with the general pattern everywhere during the November offensive. In many respects, the battle of the Roer plain was an artillery show. Opposite the *LXXXI Corps* alone the Germans estimated the average daily ammunition expenditure of American artillery at 27,500 rounds, a not unlikely figure. Artillery of the *LXXXI Corps* fired an average 13,410 rounds daily, an unusually large amount for the Germans.[15]

The village of Koslar came in for a share of the pounding. Just before daylight on 25 November, two companies of the 116th Infantry broke into Koslar in a determined bayonet charge. "We moved out at a rapid run in waves with fixed bayonets, one following behind the other,"

related a company commander, Capt. Daniel E. Kayes. "We jumped over the third row of trenches and in less than 10 minutes were inside Koslar . . . . It was still dark and my greatest difficulty was in slowing down the company. The men scattered all over town." [16]

The strongest counterattacks at both Koslar and Bourheim came soon after dawn on 26 November. The commander of the *LXXXI Corps,* General Koechling, planned counterattacks on both villages as a co-ordinated major effort to re-establish the inner defensive arc about Juelich.[17] Both the regiments of the *340th Division* that were in the Juelich bridgehead participated. They had the support of fourteen battalions of artillery and twenty-eight armored vehicles (the *301st Tiger Tank Battalion,* the *341st Assault Gun Brigade,* and four assault guns borrowed from the *3d Panzer Grenadier Division*).

Though the Germans lamented that their artillery was hamstrung by drastic ammunition shortages and that their tanks could not provide proper support in the narrow streets of the villages, few on the American side could have detected that the enemy had his problems. The Germans plowed through every American artillery concentration. Fighting moved into the streets of the villages.

Hampered by a mounting shortage of ammunition, the two battalions of the 175th Infantry in Bourheim appealed for help. The regimental commander rushed a company from his reserve into the village. Jeeps loaded with ammunition raced forward along a road blanketed

---

[13] See, for example, NUSA Opns, IV, 214, 218–19.

[14] XIX Corps Arty AAR, Nov 44.

[15] *LXXXI Corps KTB, Arty.-Lage u. Art.-Gliederungen.*

[16] NUSA Opns, IV, 220, citing Combat Interv with Kayes.

[17] *LXXXI Corps Gefechtsbericht,* AAR for 25 and 26 Nov 44.

by German shellfire. At 1030 fighter-bombers only recently unleashed by improvement in the weather arrived. Not until noon was the situation brought under control.

The Germans isolated the two companies of the 116th Infantry in Koslar. They were not surrounded, insisted General Gerhardt; they were merely in close contact, "right up against the Krauts." [18] In any event, patrols from other units of the 116th Infantry could not reach them. During 26 November pilots of the 29th Division's artillery observation planes flew eleven missions over Koslar to drop sorely needed food, ammunition, and medical supplies. Out of eleven bundles, eight were recovered. Despite intense small arms fire, not a plane was lost.

Before daylight on 27 November the 116th Infantry sent a battalion to break through to the two companies. Though this battalion became involved in arduous house-to-house fighting, contact was made by late afternoon. When the rest of the 116th Infantry entered the village the next morning, the enemy had gone.

As this fight had developed, General Gerhardt had committed his third regiment to subdue Kirchberg, last of the three villages comprising the inner defensive arc about Juelich. Kirchberg lies near the confluence of the Inde and the Roer. On the assumption that the Germans would be alert to attack from the direction of Bourheim, where the conflict had waxed so hot for days, the regimental commander chose to strike instead from the vicinity of Pattern. The situation at this village in the 30th Division's zone had been static for several days.

While a battalion in Bourheim made a feint by fire, another moved from Pattern

during the morning of 27 November without artillery preparation but behind a smoke screen. By this stratagem the 115th Infantry achieved almost complete surprise. By late afternoon, Kirchberg was secure. For all practical purposes, the 29th Division had closed up to the Roer. Only two strongpoints in a small part of Juelich on the west bank of the river remained to be cleared. The enemy's *340th Division* withdrew its two regiments to the east bank, leaving only a rear guard in the two strongpoints. Take your time in closing to the river, the American corps commander said.

Though the American commander, General McLain, had sanctioned pauses in the attacks of the 2d Armored and 30th Divisions, he had directed on 26 November that the final push to the Roer be resumed all along the corps front. In conjunction with the 29th Division's attack on Kirchberg, the 2d Armored Division was to complete capture of Merzenhausen and push on to Barmen. The 30th Division was to take Altdorf.

Though both the regimental and division commanders favored a night attack on Altdorf, they bowed to General McLain's desire to co-ordinate with the 29th Division's push on Kirchberg and a new attempt by the First Army's 104th Division to take Inden. In midmorning of 27 November, a battalion of the 119th Infantry, attached to Colonel Purdue's 120th Infantry, struck for Altdorf. As feared from information developed earlier by patrols, fire from at least twelve machine guns emplaced in a reverse slope defense 800 yards west of Altdorf forced the men of this battalion to the ground. Here the exposed plateau lying between Pattern and Altdorf drops off sharply; any force that somehow got this far

---
[18] 29th Div G-2—G-3 Jnl, 26 Nov 44.

without detection no longer had a chance to escape observation. Deprived of tank support because of muddy ground, a dearth of roads, and the sharp grade near the village, men of this battalion had nothing readily at hand capable of eliminating the German machine guns. They had no recourse but to dig in.

The regimental commander, Colonel Purdue, decided at length that a night attack was the only solution. Having desired a night attack from the first, he had a plan ready. Before daylight the next morning, he sent a battalion under Lt. Col. Ellis V. Williamson to move by stealth through the positions reached by the attached battalion of the 119th Infantry.

As luck would have it, artillery of the 104th Division began to shoot timed fire on the neighboring village of Inden soon after Colonel Williamson's battalion crossed the line of departure. Only momentarily, but long enough to alert the German gunners, the air bursts illuminated the men of the 120th Infantry. For a moment the attack appeared doomed. Then a special attack formation Colonel Williamson had adopted paid dividends. He had positioned four squads in a line of skirmishers formation in front of the main body of his force. Each man in the skirmish line had a rifle grenade at the ready. As a German machine gun opened fire, some part of the skirmish line would silence it quickly with grenades.

Having gained entrance to Altdorf by this method, Colonel Williamson's men faced a two-hour fight before they could label the village secure. The main difficulty came from seven enemy tanks which roamed the village in search of escape. Hasty mine fields that Colonel William-

son's men placed at every exit soon after gaining entry had turned the village into a cage. Two of the tanks eventually were destroyed—one by a white phosphorus grenade after the tank had blundered into a building, another by a bazooka. After one hair-raising cat-and-mouse episode after another, the others eventually escaped by breaking through a roadblock the Americans had established on a bridge across the Inde River.

Except for a minor assignment of clearing a narrow triangle of land between the Inde and the Roer, which would be accomplished later without incident, the 30th Division by 28 November had completed its role in the drive to the Roer. The division could feel relieved that its casualty list, for nearly two weeks of fighting, was comparatively small: 160 men killed, 1,058 wounded.

On the opposite wing of the XIX Corps, the 2d Armored Division in renewing the attack on Merzenhausen on 27 November turned to a three-pronged attack. Discerning the key to Merzenhausen to be the elevations—Hills 100.3 to the northwest and 98.1 to the east—the CCA commander, Colonel Collier, assigned a battalion of infantry to each. Coincidentally, another battalion of infantry was to take the remaining half of the village.

In this sector, the regiment of the *340th Volks Grenadier Division* that was designated to hold a bridgehead about Linnich, a few miles to the north, had relieved the remnants of the *246th Division* in and about Merzenhausen. Thereupon, the village had become the southern anchor for the Linnich bridgehead.[19]

[19] *LXXXI Corps Gefechtsbericht*, AARs for 22–27 Nov 44.

On Hill 98.1 a battalion of the 41st Armored Infantry, attacking on 27 November over soggy ground without tank support, ran into heavy fire near the crest. A counterattack followed. By utilizing trenches earlier cleared of Germans, the men managed to hold, but they could not push to the crest.

Within Merzenhausen, the attached 2d Battalion, 119th Infantry, resumed tedious house-to-house fighting. Though a brace of tanks and tank destroyers tried to assist, mines and panzerfausts discouraged their use. It took the infantry all day to do the job alone, but they ended the assignment in a blaze of success with capture of the enemy commander and his entire staff. A driving force in the attack was 2d Lt. Harold L. Holycross, who as a sergeant had played a leading role in the 30th Division's West Wall assault in October.

Of the three assignments, Colonel Collier considered that tanks were needed most against Hill 100.3. Yet because of various obstacles, including an escarpment, a small stream, and an antitank ditch, he saw no way to employ them. In the end, he committed the attached 1st Battalion, 119th Infantry, alone to the task, though he told the commander, Lt. Col. Robert H. Herlong, that if he found a defiladed route with reasonably good traction, tanks would join him.

Concealed by early morning mists, Colonel Herlong's infantry got within 400 yards of the crest of Hill 100.3 before discovery. To counteract intense small arms fire that followed, Colonel Herlong called for a rolling artillery barrage to precede a final assault. Though seemingly accurate, the artillery failed to silence the German fire. In a matter of minutes the battalion lost five killed and fifteen wounded and gained but fifty yards.

In the meantime, someone had discovered a route along a railroad embankment whence tanks might proceed up a narrow draw onto the hill. Advised of this development, Colonel Collier immediately designated a company of the 66th Armored Regiment. An hour and a half later, the tanks reached the infantry positions.

Effect on the enemy was marked. As the tanks advanced with infantry following at from 100 to 200 yards, German fire slackened, then ceased altogether. At least forty Germans were killed or wounded and an equal number captured. By late afternoon, Hill 100.3 was secure.

To make the day a complete success, Colonel Collier soon after dark committed a second battalion of the 41st Armored Infantry to the attack on Hill 98.1. A position that in daylight had failed to crack now dissolved rapidly. By midnight CCA held all three of the day's objectives. A tank-supported counterattack against Merzenhausen got no place in the face of accurate defensive artillery fires. Because the two hills near Merzenhausen overlooked the remaining objective of Barmen, capturing that village and pushing patrols another few hundred yards to the Roer was a routine task. It progressed without incident the next day, 28 November.

Except for two German positions on the west bank of the Roer near Juelich in the zone of the 29th Division, the XIX Corps by 28 November had reached the river. Since no one considered capture of the two remaining points either particularly difficult or pressing, the 29th Division was not to begin the task for several days. In the meantime, General McLain, his staff, and his divisions turned to planning for crossing the river, though the shadow of the dams on the upper reaches of the Roer still loomed over all preparations.[20]

A Hundred Men of the XIII Corps

Not until the day after the XIX Corps reached the Roer did the Ninth Army's other component, General Gillem's XIII Corps, commence the push to the river. By nightfall of 24 November, General Gillem had assumed responsibility for about six miles of front from the Wurm River at Muellendorf to the new boundary with the XIX Corps below Ederen. Nevertheless, the hard fighting experienced by the 84th Division in Operation CLIPPER and the dispersion of the 102d Division's regiments made it impossible for the XIII Corps to be ready to attack until 29 November. At least one commander, the 102d Division's Maj. Gen. Frank A. Keating, thought even this was rushing things; not until twenty-four hours before the jump-off did the last of his regiments return to the fold. Though General Keating had yet to command his division as an entity in offensive combat, one regiment already had engaged in heavy fighting while attached to the 84th Division and another which had fought as the infantry component of the 2d Armored Division's Task Force X was markedly fatigued.

The six-mile line which the XIII Corps held ran southeast from the Wurm near Muellendorf to a point about midway between Prummern and Beeck, thence east to a highway leading north from Gereonsweiler to the village of Lindern, thence southeast in an arc extending a thousand yards east of Gereonsweiler to a point of contact with the 2d Armored Division southeast of Ederen. The 84th Division held the left half of the line, the 102d Division the right, while the 7th Armored Division still recuperated in corps reserve from the earlier fight in the Peel Marshes.

High ground in the north along an extension of the XIII Corps boundary with the 30 British Corps was a primary consideration in attack planning. In a broad sense, the corps zone sloped gradually upward to this high ground, which is marked by the Aachen–Geilenkirchen–Muenchen-Gladbach railroad and by the villages of Wuerm, Leiffarth, and Lindern. Even beyond a normal precaution of protecting the rear of a subsequent Roer crossing, General Gillem considered possession of this terrain vital. He was concerned lest the Germans commit the *Sixth Panzer Army,* which they reputedly were mustering between the Roer and the Rhine, in a counteroffensive against the corps north flank.[21]

Before Operation CLIPPER had revealed how determined the Germans were to hold this high ground, General Gillem had intended taking the bulk of it with Task Force Biddle, composed of the 113th Cavalry Group reinforced by increments of medium tanks and artillery. Thereupon, the 102d Division was to have captured Linnich on the Roer and to have prepared to cross the river. The 7th Armored and 84th Divisions were to have been available to exploit a bridgehead.

In the revised plan, General Gillem

---

[20] Note various messages of concern about the dams in corps and division journals during this period.

[21] On 22 November, for example, the corps artillery commander, Brig. Gen. R. P. Shugg, had recommended that two additional tank destroyer battalions be attached to the corps to protect the north flank. XIII Corps Arty AAR, Nov 44.

displayed full appreciation of how hard it might be to take the high ground. Dissolving Task Force Biddle, he attached the 113th Cavalry to the 84th Division, in order that the cavalry might hold some of the 84th Division's front opposite Muellendorf and Wuerm, and directed the 84th Division to make the corps main effort. Not Linnich but the high ground along the north boundary was to be the objective. Meanwhile the 102d Division was to stage limited objective attacks to protect the 84th Division's right flank and eventually was to reduce three villages near the corps south boundary, capture Linnich, and occupy high ground north of Linnich overlooking German supply routes through the Roer village of Brachelen.[22]

The decision to send greater strength against the high ground stemmed in part from the contemporary intelligence picture. In addition to survivors of the *9th Panzer*, *15th Panzer Grenadier*, and *183d Volks Grenadier Divisions*, which had opposed earlier attacks in this sector, American intelligence officers anticipated meeting the *10th SS Panzer Division*, veteran of the MARKET-GARDEN fighting in Holland.[23] Some took this as evidence that other SS divisions from the *Sixth Panzer Army* would be sent to this sector.[24]

German artillery, noted those who plotted the fires, was grouped in the north behind the high ground and to the northeast beyond Linnich and the Roer. It was "a potentially destructive weapon."

As for tanks, the Germans were expected to employ only small groups, despite addition of the *10th SS Panzer Division*. Fortifications included pillboxes of the West Wall in the northwest near Muellendorf, Wuerm, and Beeck and elsewhere the usual extensive field fortifications that had come to typify the Roer plain. An antitank ditch extending more than a mile and a half from Beeck northeast to a point beyond Lindern was of particular note.

Except that the projected Ardennes counteroffensive made the *Sixth Panzer Army* untouchable, the true enemy picture was much as American G–2's divined it. After the unsuccessful commitment of the *9th Panzer* and *15th Panzer Grenadier Divisions* in counterattacks controlled by the *XLVII Panzer Corps*, these divisions had passed to the *XII SS Corps*. Thus General Blumentritt and the *XII SS Corps* again bore responsibility for the entire sector from the Maas River to the Roer near Flossdorf. The *XLVII Panzer Corps* apparently stood by as a headquarters temporarily without troops.

The *10th SS Panzer Division* was the first unit to be alerted for movement early in the fighting when Field Marshal von Rundstedt had determined that the Allies intended no complementary attack in Holland. The division had begun to move southeastward on 20 November and three days later had started relieving the *9th Panzer Division*, which was to be rehabilitated for the Ardennes.[25] The front was strengthened by commitment of the *407th Volks Artillery Corps* near Linnich, and a volks grenadier division earmarked for the Ardennes was moved to

---

[22] NUSA Ltr of Instrs 8, 25 Nov, and XIII Corps FO 2, 27 Nov, both in XIII Corps G–3 Jnl file, 24–28 Nov 44.

[23] Annex 1 to 84th Div G–2 Per Rpt 8, 25 Nov, and XIII Corps G–2 Per Rpt 17, 25 Nov, both in XIII Corps G–2 Jnl file, 25–26 Nov 44.

[24] See, for example, XIX Corps G–2 Estimate, 26 Nov, XIII Corps G–2 Jnl file, 27 Nov 44.

[25] Order, *Gruppe von Manteuffel to XII SS and LXXXI Corps*, 2045 19 Nov 44, and TWX, *Gruppe von Manteuffel to LXXXI Corps*, 2225, 23 Nov, both in *LXXXI Corps KTB, Bef. H. Gr. u. Armee.*

a position east of the Roer from which it might back up the *XII SS Corps*.[26]

While the Germans made these moves, the XIII U.S. Corps was spending five days in reorganization and attack preparations. Both the 84th and 102d Divisions were strengthened with attachments, and the corps artillery was fleshed out with units transferred from the XIX Corps. Three battalions of XIX Corps artillery reverted to Ninth Army control, in order to facilitate their use in support of both corps; while eight battalions of the XIX Corps artillery passed directly to the XIII Corps. This increased General Gillem's corps artillery to thirteen battalions, of which two and a battery of self-propelled 155-mm. guns were attached to the 84th Division. The bulk of artillery remaining under corps control was to give priority to the main effort of the 84th Division. In addition the British were capable of firing into the 84th's sector with a field regiment of 25-pounders, a battery of 4.5-inch guns, and a regiment of 5.5-inch guns. Both the 84th and 102d Divisions received separate self-propelled tank destroyer battalions, the 102d a separate tank battalion, and the 84th a tank battalion attached from the 7th Armored Division.[27]

To achieve the assigned mission, the 84th Division needed to take five villages —Muellendorf, Wuerm, Beeck, Leiffarth, and Lindern—and an elevation northeast of Beeck which bore the code name, Toad Hill (87.9). Having attacked frontally and without success against three of these villages for three days in Opera-

tion CLIPPER, the 84th Division commander, General Bolling, had no taste for a repeat performance. Flanking action to the right, he noted, "would not force attacking troops directly against pillboxes and villages that are of no particular tactical value." Instead of assaulting as before from the southwest against Muellendorf, Wuerm, and Beeck, he wanted to strike from the southeast and south to take first Toad Hill and Lindern, the latter because it occupies an elevation comparable to Toad Hill. These two points in hand, the division then might turn west and southwest to hit the other four villages from the rear.[28]

To take both Toad Hill and Lindern, General Bolling designated the 335th Infantry, which had missed Operation CLIPPER because of a stint as an uncommitted reserve with the XIX Corps. The 333d Infantry was to support the attack by fire and, together with the 113th Cavalry, to stage a frontal demonstration against Beeck.

Because routes of attack toward both Toad Hill and Lindern were devoid of concealment, the 335th Infantry commander, Col. Hugh C. Parker, elected a night attack. From a line of departure in open fields southeast of Beeck, the 2d Battalion under Maj. Robert S. Kennedy was to move toward Toad Hill while the 3d Battalion under Maj. Robert W. Wallace guided on the Gereonsweiler–Lindern highway to take Lindern. The attacks were to begin without artillery preparation at 0630 on 29 November. Colonel Parker hoped that systematic artillery and fighter-bomber attacks for several days preceding 29 November would suffice as

---

[26] TWX, *Gruppe von Manteuffel* to *XII SS* and *LXXXI Corps,* 0050, 25 Nov 44, *LXXXI Corps KTB, Bef. H. Gr. u. Armee.*

[27] XII and XIX Corps Arty AARs, Nov 44, and Annex 3 to XIII Corps FO 2, 27 Nov, XIII Corps G–3 Jnl file, 24–28 Nov 44.

[28] Memo to CG XIII Corps, 24 Nov, and 84th Div FO 7, 28 Nov, both in XIII Corps G–3 Jnl file, 24–28 Nov 44.

preparation fires. A company of the 40th Tank Battalion was attached to each infantry battalion for close support.[29]

An hour before dawn on 29 November there began an odyssey involving finally about a hundred men of Major Wallace's 3d Battalion that was to have marked effect upon the push to the Roer. At that hour, Companies I and K moved northward through the darkness along either side of the Gereonsweiler–Lindern road. Stripped down to gas masks and essentials—rifle belts, two bandoleers of ammunition, and three bars of chocolate D ration per man—these companies were imbued with one idea: speed. Get across the mile of open ground to Lindern before daylight.

German fire at first was hesitant. A flare here, a burp gun there, a mortar shell or two. Yet sometimes even one bullet can be fateful. That was the case when a stray bullet cut the aerial of Company K's SCR–300. Though the radio operator fell back to the end of the column to pick up a spare, no one saw him again. That incident was to assume more and more importance as the attack progressed.

At the antitank ditch which stretched from Beeck to Lindern, two leading platoons of Company K and one of Company I ran, jumped, fell, crawled, and slithered across. Don't hold up in the ditch, their leaders had told them time after time; German mortars and artillery could ruin you there.

These three platoons made it. Their companies did not. No sooner had the leading platoons slipped through than the Germans in a main line of resistance centered on the antitank ditch came to life. With artillery, mortars, machine guns, and rifles, they drove back the remainder of Company K and inflicted serious losses on Company I.

Accompanying the two platoons of Company K that crossed the antitank ditch was the company commander, 1st Lt. Leonard R. Carpenter. Though Lieutenant Carpenter knew that half his company had failed to get across, he hoped that Company I had fared better. The leader of the one platoon of Company I which actually had succeeded, 1st Lt. Creswell Garlington, Jr., trusted that Company K was intact. Neither force had any form of communication with the battalion commander. Company I's radios were with the company headquarters; Company K's radio operator had taken that company's SCR–300 to the rear after German fire had snapped the aerial. Though Lieutenant Carpenter had another radio, an SCR–509, it did not work.

Deluded in the darkness about their combined strength, the three platoons pressed on toward Lindern. They reached the fringe of the village as day was breaking. Though uncertain at first whether they had come to the right objective, they nevertheless attacked. They had been told to avoid trouble, if possible; to leave mop-up to those who came behind. Racing through back yards and orchards, the men tossed an occasional grenade whenever some lone sentry opened fire. But for the most part, Lindern slept.

At 0745 the three platoons were digging in beyond the railroad enbankment a few hundred yards north of Lindern. Only then did Lieutenants Carpenter and Garlington discover that together they had

---

[29] Unless otherwise noted, the account of the 84th Division action is based upon official division and corps records; Draper, *The 84th Division,* pp. 50–74; and NUSA Opns, Vol. IV. The last contains rich combat interview material.

only about a hundred men. This little band had reached one of the 84th Division's primary objectives, yet nobody else on the American side knew about it.

The Germans knew. In less than a quarter-hour three Tiger tanks approached the position. Someone fired a bazooka. The tanks retreated to the vicinity of two pillboxes not over 400 yards away. Later, several truckloads of German infantry dismounted at the pillboxes. Still the Germans did not attack. Apparently they did not recognize how small the American force was. The two lieutenants had chosen to dig in on a gentle reverse slope where they were partially screened by a rise to the north and by the railroad enbankment at their backs.

Though the situation was obviously precarious, the Americans were not too concerned at first. They expected relief momentarily. Yet the hours passed, and no relief came. At length, Lieutenant Carpenter sent volunteers back to the railroad where he had abandoned the SCR–509 after having despaired of getting it to function. After two hours of tinkering, they finally picked up faint voices emanating from radios of American tanks, but they could not transmit. As a last resort, four men volunteered to go back on foot in search of help. No one saw them again.

The situation actually was more obscure than even Lieutenants Carpenter and Garlington realized. At the antitank ditch south of Lindern, the battalion commander had lost contact not only with the leading platoons but also with the rest of Companies I and K. Though the regimental commander, Colonel Parker, had committed his reserve battalion in midmorning to outflank Lindern from the

west, communications to that unit too had failed. A company of the 40th Tank Battalion, which was to have followed the infantry to Lindern, waited in Gereonsweiler with no word that there was any infantry to follow.

Perhaps because they had no other hope, the little band of men north of Lindern continued to tinker with the SCR–509. About an hour past noon, someone suggested they tape an aerial from a little, short-range SCR–536 to a high fence and run a telephone wire from the fence to the SCR–509. The expedient worked. Somewhere a radio operator in an American tank picked magic words out of the air: "We made a touchdown at 0745." [30]

The commander of the 40th Tank Battalion, Lt. Col. John C. Brown, acted without hesitation. He ordered a company of tanks to Lindern. Behind a smoke screen fired by artillery, six Shermans made it. "It was about 1430 when we saw those six General Shermans," someone recalled later. "Boy! We figured the whole German army couldn't drive us out of there." [31]

As dusk fell, the rest of the company of tanks reached Lindern along with the reserve company of the 335th Infantry's 3d Battalion, Company L. Soon thereafter, Colonel Brown ordered another tank company into the village. There the tankers fretted for an hour or so for lack of infantry protection, until at last the 335th Infantry's reserve battalion arrived. Having been committed in midmorning, this battalion had swung in a wide arc to come upon the village from the west; but fire along the antitank ditch and from pillboxes had imposed telling delays.

[30] Draper, *The 84th Division*, p. 58.
[31] NUSA Opns, IV, 265.

The Germans had dallied too long in attempting to eliminate the two lieutenants and their hundred men. During the night of 29 November and through the next two days, they tried to remedy the situation, first with contingents of the *10th SS Panzer Division* and later with a *Kampfgruppe* recruited from the *9th Panzer Division* and the *506th Tank Battalion.* This *Kampfgruppe* was an *Army Group B* reserve controlled by the *XLVII Panzer Corps.*[32] For several days the Americans had to supply their troops in Lindern along a route the tankers christened the "Blue Ball Express." But for all the violence of their reaction, the Germans were too late. They had lost Lindern to a little band of intrepid infantrymen who had gone where they had been told to go and had stayed there. The entire German position in this sector had been weakened materially.

Why the Germans were slow at Lindern was hard to explain. Possibly they had been wary of the size of the American force. Perhaps more likely, they were occupied at many other points in this sector all through 29 November. About a mile southwest of Lindern, a regiment of the 84th Division and parts of the 113th Cavalry had demonstrated with fire at Beeck, while another battalion of the 335th Infantry had attacked Toad Hill, northeast of Beeck. Though this battalion had tried a sneak night attack, the Germans had met them at daylight along the antitank ditch with fire from tanks emplaced in hull-down positions.

To the southeast, in the zone of the 102d Division, a regimental attack had been directed at high ground along the Lindern-Linnich highway near Crossroads 87 in order to protect the 84th Division's right flank. Here too the Germans had fought stubbornly, though the American commander, Col. Laurin L. Williams, maintained that he might have advanced farther had he not been concerned about tenuous contact with the 84th Division's 335th Infantry.[33] The breakdown of communications within the 335th Infantry may have been responsible. Even farther to the southeast, on the right wing of the 102d Division, the Germans had to contend with another attack, a successful limited objective maneuver by another regiment of the 102d Division to seize an efficacious line of departure for subsequent moves.

A Shift in the Main Effort

Late on 28 November, even before the 84th Division had marched on Lindern, the XIII Corps Commander, General Gillem, had altered his corps plan. He directed that on the second day of the attack the main effort be shifted from the 84th to the 102d Division, perhaps with an eye toward gaining quick control of bridge sites over the Roer to deny them to German reinforcements.[34] The 102d Division's missions were to reach the Roer in the southeastern part of the corps sector at the villages of Roerdorf and Flossdorf, to secure the high ground along the Lindern–Linnich highway near Crossroads 87, and to occupy Linnich. By accomplishing these missions, the 102d

---

[32] Opns Order for 30 Nov 44, *Gruppe von Manteuffel* to *XII SS* and *LXXXI Corps,* 2250, 29 Nov 44, and Opns Order for 2 Dec 44, *Gruppe von Manteuffel* to *XII SS, XLVII Pz,* and *LXXXI Corps,* 0040, 2 Dec 44, both in *LXXXI Corps KTB, Bef. H. Gr. u. Armee.*

[33] NUSA Opns, IV, 278.
[34] XIII Corps Ltr of Instrs 5, 28 Nov, XIII Corps G-3 Jnl file, 24–28 Nov 44.

Division would in the process protect the 84th Division's right flank and thereby help to guarantee retention of Lindern.

Even before the 102d Division's assignment to make the main effort became effective, the division commander, General Keating, decided that two regiments were insufficient to seize all his objectives.[35] Having intended originally to withhold his 406th Infantry, because that regiment already had fought hard as an attachment to the 2d Armored Division, General Keating late on 29 November decided to use the 406th to take Linnich. The 405th Infantry was to continue toward the high ground near Crossroads 87 between Lindern and Linnich, while the 407th Infantry on the right was to take a preliminary objective, the village of Welz, then Roerdorf and Flossdorf.[36]

The Germans in the 102d Division's sector represented both the *10th SS Panzer Division*, near Crossroads 87, and the regiment of the *340th Volks Grenadier Division* which had been given responsibility for holding a bridgehead at Linnich. The terrain and weather in this sector were little different than elsewhere on the Roer plain: gradually sloping, exposed fields that could be raked with fire from automatic weapons and dug-in tanks; villages encompassed by a labyrinth of interconnected trenches and other field

fortifications; dismal rain, mud, and bone-chilling cold. Nor did the fight go much differently. As elsewhere, the Germans fought stubbornly for each village. "We are in Welz doing a lot of plain and fancy mopping up and there are a lot of things to take out," reported General Keating in midafternoon of 30 November. "We are partially in Flossdorf and there are a lot of things to take out there." [37]

There were a lot of things to take out everywhere. Not the least of the problems was German artillery fire from the east bank of the Roer, much the same difficulty encountered earlier by the XIX Corps. Forewarned by the experience of the XIX Corps, both divisional and corps artillery had readied a detailed program of counterbattery fires that on occasion raised the day's total of rounds expended above the 20,000 mark. Supplementing this program were numerous strikes by XXIX TAC fighter-bombers [38] and prodigious use of smoke shells fired both by artillery and by attached chemical mortars. Nevertheless, shelling remained a real problem for several days until German batteries could be plotted accurately. In Welz and Linnich, particularly, German artillery turned what might have been routine mop-up tasks into costly and time-consuming projects.

Welz was the first of the 102d Division's objectives to fall. This little village, a mile short of the Roer, was in the hands of the 407th Infantry at the end of 30 November, with some opposition remain-

---

[35] The corps commander apparently thought the same. If the 102d Division had not captured Linnich by 2 December, he directed, the 7th Armored Division was to be called upon. *Ibid.*

[36] 102d Div FO 4, 29 Nov, XIII Corps G–3 Jnl file, 29–30 Nov 44. Official records of the 102d Division are supplemented by Ninth U.S. Army Operations, Vol. IV, several combat interviews, and a good unit history, Allan H. Mick, *With the 102d Infantry Division Through Germany* (Washington: Infantry Journal Press, 1947), pp. 73–84.

[37] 102d Div G–3 Jnl, 30 Nov 44.

[38] On 2 December, for example, the XXIX TAC flew 143 sorties and dropped ninety-seven tons of bombs, mostly on villages and artillery positions beyond the Roer. On other days, bad weather and proximity of American troops to the river limited close support missions.

ing to be eliminated the next day. Although Flossdorf on the bank of the Roer was next on the 407th Infantry's agenda, German guns beyond the river knocked out six of eight supporting tanks to bring the attackers up sharply. A co-ordinated attack against both Roerdorf and Flossdorf on 2 December brought success at Roerdorf, but Flossdorf held out until the next day.

In the center of the 102d Division's sector, the 406th Infantry made more rapid initial gains against Linnich. Though advance during the afternoon of 30 November came in erratic spurts, a battalion had reached the fringe of the town by nightfall. The rest of the regiment built up against the town after dark, but the regimental commander, Colonel Hurless, decided to wait until morning before risking involvement in house-to-house fighting. Linnich fell on 1 December, but into the next day the Germans maintained a path through the northeastern fringe to make matters unpleasant and enable some of the enemy to escape across a damaged bridge to the east bank of the Roer. Tanks attached from the 7th Armored Division at last managed to cross a drainage ditch south of Linnich, gain access to the town, and block this passage.

The regiment of the *340th Division* which had borne responsibility for Linnich fell back behind the Roer. Having been battered severely in the fighting for the Linnich and Juelich bridgeheads, this division was in process of relief by another unit moved down from Holland, the *363d Volks Grenadier Division*, which in October had battered itself against the 101st U.S. Airborne Division north of Nijmegen. Since Linnich had gone by the board, the regiment scheduled to relieve at Linnich was instead attached to the *10th SS Panzer Division*.[39]

Entry into Linnich no doubt was eased by the 405th Infantry's conquest of the high ground near Crossroads 87. After two days of bitter and frustrating fighting on exposed ground where men and machines were naked to German fire, the regiment used a double-envelopment maneuver on 1 December to carry the objective.

Their right flank partially protected by the 102d Division's attack, troops of the 84th Division in the meantime held onto Lindern and continued to fight for remaining objectives. Though General Bolling had intended taking the high ground of Toad Hill (87.9) before the adjacent village of Beeck, the *10th SS Panzer Division's 22d SS Panzer Grenadier Regiment* made such a fight of it on Toad Hill that General Bolling ordered a simultaneous attack on Beeck. The village occupies a shallow hollow, but the Germans fought for it as if it were an elevation dominating the countryside. A battalion of the 335th Infantry fought all day before gaining the village at nightfall on 30 November.

Two days later resistance suddenly collapsed, both on Toad Hill and on high ground southeast of Lindern, where the 334th Infantry had taken up the fight to make Lindern more secure. Presumably the collapse stemmed from an attempt to spare the SS troops pending relief by a swiftly rehabilitated *340th Volks Grenadier Division*, a move scheduled for 8 December.[40] Also on 2 December, a

[39] *LXXXI Corps Gefechtsbericht*, AAR for 2 Dec 44; Opns Order for 6 Dec 44, *Gruppe von Manteuffel* to *LXXXI Corps*, 2100, 5 Dec 44, *LXXXI Corps KTB, Bef. H. Gr. u. Armee*.

[40] Opns Order for 6 Dec. 44, *Gruppe von Manteuffel* to *LXXXI Corps*, 2100, 5 Dec 44.

battalion of the 334th Infantry followed preparation fires closely and marched into Leiffarth, northwest of Toad Hill. Within half an hour after crossing the line of departure, the 334th Infantry had Leiffarth.

The 84th Division was nearing the end of its part in the final push to the Roer. German reinforcements in the form of the *59th Infantry Division* (General Poppe), leaving Holland on 2 December, would arrive too late to do much good in this sector.[41] Of the 84th Division's original objectives, only Muellendorf and Wuerm remained to be taken. Because no crossing of the Roer appeared likely until the Roer River Dams were taken or neutralized, no one was in any particular rush in regard to these last two villages. Not until more than two weeks later, on 18 December, would the 84th Division attack them. At this time there would be no more than a hint of the kind of resistance that had denied the villages during Operation CLIPPER. By midday on 18 December, both Wuerm and Muellendorf would be secure.

Except for these two villages, all assignments of the XIII Corps in the drive to the Roer were completed by 4 December. In four days two infantry divisions had advanced about a mile and a half each. Yet this was hardly the whole story of XIII Corps participation in the battle of the Roer plain, for the role of the 84th Division and a regiment of the 102d Division in Operation CLIPPER and that of another regiment of the 102d in the push to Gereonsweiler were rightfully part of the broader performance. During the four days when the two divisions fought under the aegis of the XIII Corps, they

each incurred about a thousand battle casualties, including 176 killed in the 84th Division and 142 in the 102d. The 84th listed 209 missing; the 102d, 104. Together the two divisions lost the services of another thousand men to combat fatigue and exposure. Indeed, for all the determination of German resistance on the Roer plain, the one aspect most men who fought there probably would recall most vividly was the abominable weather and the mud that went with it.

Gut Hasenfeld and the Sportplatz

Like the 84th Division at Muellendorf and Wuerm, the 29th Division of the XIX Corps had two more assignments before the battle of the Roer plain could be termed at an end. These were to reduce two German outposts alongside the Roer opposite and northwest of Juelich, one a group of farm buildings called Gut Hasenfeld, the other a *Sportplatz* consisting of an elliptical concrete stadium and a covered swimming pool nearby.

Before the event, reduction of these outposts looked like a minor assignment. Because delay in mounting a Roer crossing removed any real urgency in regard to the outposts and because the 29th Division commander wanted to maintain the bulk of his division intact for the crossing, only one regiment, the 116th Infantry, was to do the job.

Night had not fallen on the first day of attack (1 December) before some measure of the difficulties that would be involved had become apparent. The ground about both Gut Hasenfeld and the *Sportplatz* was flat, cruelly exposed to observation from higher ground a few hundred yards away on the east bank of the Roer. No concealment was available

---

[41] *OB WEST KTB,* 2 Dec 44.

GUT HASENFELD

near either objective except for a patch of woods south of the *Sportplatz*. These woods, it developed, were literally abloom with antipersonnel mines. Nor did the Germans stint on the troops manning the defenses. Only the night before the first American attack the Germans had begun to relieve the fatigued remnants of the *340th Division* with fresh troops of the *363d Volks Grenadier Division*, one of the units moved from Holland.[42]

A dismal pattern that would prevail for six days was set on the first day. Concealed either by darkness or by elaborate smoke screens maintained by 4.2-inch mortars of the 92d Chemical Battalion, troops of the 116th Infantry would get within a few hundred yards of the objectives. Then they would run into mines. "A man would hit a trip wire and there would be a click, then the mine would spring out of the ground and explode five or six feet in the air, spraying metal splinters."[43]   At first sound of exploding mines, the Germans would lay down final protective fires with machine guns, mortars, and artillery. If the men fell to earth to escape this fire, they might

[42] *LXXXI Corps Gefechtsbericht,* AAR for 1 Dec 44.

[43] NUSA Opns, IV, 328, citing combat interv with 2d Lt Sears G. Sutton, Co I, 116th Inf.

detonate more mines. Some elected to remain erect through intense shellfire rather than risk falling upon a mine.[44] "Nothing was more feared than mines. They were insidious, treacherous things hiding in the deep grass and in the earth."[45]

On occasion, some companies approached as close as a hundred yards to one or the other of the objectives before being repulsed. Yet no genuine threat to either Gut Hasenfeld or the *Sportplatz* could be developed. One of the more promising attacks during the night of 2 December was thwarted when a bright moon suddenly emerged to bathe the flat ground in light and trigger the enemy's protective fires.

Artillery and air support bombarded both objectives and the town of Juelich across the river but with no telling effect on the enemy's will to resist. Because this was the lone offensive action on the entire XIX Corps front, the corps artillery was free to concentrate its fires, including round after round from 8-inch howitzers. Later inspection was to reveal that these shells had done considerable damage; yet the Germans in both places had underground shelters which spared them major losses and, presumably, they reinforced the garrisons at night by ferrying troops across the Roer. On at least two occasions, fighter-bombers of the XXIX TAC pounded the objectives for fifteen minutes before attacks; yet as the infantry tried to close, German fire remained thick. Observation from across the Roer and mud deterred use of tanks. On one occasion, when three tanks of the 747th Tank Battalion tried to reinforce an infantry company near Gut Hasenfeld, German artillery quickly sent one up in smoke. The others scurried back to cover among the buildings of Koslar.

On 3 December General Gerhardt replaced the 116th Infantry commander with one of the battalion commanders, Lt. Col. Sidney V. Bingham, Jr. Still the pattern of events remained unchanged.

In early morning of 7 December, Colonel Bingham reported that further attacks by his regiment would be of no avail. In six days the 116th Infantry had lost 250 men, including 15 killed and 64 missing. That was only part of the story: cold, rainy weather also had taken an inevitable toll, and the regiment had been far from full strength when the operation started. His men, Colonel Bingham reported, were too exhausted to continue with any real chance of success.[46]

Gone was the hope of keeping the bulk of the 29th Division fresh for crossing the Roer. Later that day General Gerhardt replaced Bingham's regiment with the 115th Infantry. By midnight of 7 December a fresh battalion was in position to attack both Gut Hasenfeld and the *Sportplatz*.

The success that crowned the 115th Infantry's first efforts was attributable in part to fresh troops. Yet to a large extent it was based upon the 116th Infantry's six days of futility, which had worn down the German defenders. In one instance, the 115th Infantry extracted distinct advantage from the other regiment's experience: an analysis of the enemy's fires against the 116th Infantry revealed a zone northwest of Gut Hasenfeld where no defensive shellfire had fallen; acting on the theory that the

---

[44] *Ibid.*, p. 331, citing combat interv with 1st Lt Elmer C. Reagor, Co K, 116th Inf.

[45] Ewing, *29 Let's Go!*, p. 195.

[46] 29th Div G-2—G-3 Jnl, 7 Dec 44.

Germans had planned no final protective concentrations there, one infantry company took that route. It paid off. Because the 92d Chemical Battalion maintained a dense smoke screen about Gut Hasenfeld, the Germans had to depend upon their "blind" final protective fires. The company that approached Gut Hasenfeld from the northwest went through almost unscathed.

It was not easy, however, either at Gut Hasenfeld or at the *Sportplatz*. Attacking in early morning darkness, some companies ran into mine fields, much as had the men of the 116th Infantry, inadvertently awakened German fire, and got confused and lost.

In the end, it was small unit maneuver that did the job. Eighteen men of Company I plunged through the smoke screen northwest of Gut Hasenfeld, found a hole in a wall about the farm, and caught the Germans inside cellars where they were awaiting end of a preparatory barrage. "All right, you sons of bitches, come on out!" [47] These eighteen men had broken the back of German defense at Gut Hasenfeld by the time greater strength arrived. Prisoners numbered eighty-five.

Somewhat inexplicably, two platoons of Company B got through to the *Sportplatz* without setting off a single mine and without drawing any fire. Starting with a series of dressing rooms at the west side of the stadium, the men of Company B began methodically to eliminate enemy machine guns. By midmorning they had gained all but one corner of the arena, where two or three machine guns could be approached only across the open

playing field in the center of the stadium. Two noncommissioned officers, S. Sgt. Floyd Haviland and Sgt. Noah Carter, at last demolished this opposition by moving with daring into the open to take the enemy under fire with rifle grenades. By 1500 resistance has ceased at the stadium.

At the swimming pool several platoons had approached the position, but none could traverse the last few yards to open ground. The swimming pool was, in effect, a giant covered concrete foxhole. In midafternoon two 105-mm. assault howitzers dared dominant German observation to join the infantry. While the Germans cowered before fire from these guns, S. Sgt. Daniel Menkovitz led his platoon in an assault. When cornered, the Germans surrendered docilely.

As night came, patrols pushed to the river bank. By dawn of 9 December the entire west bank of the Roer in the zone of the Ninth Army had been cleared.

After twenty-three days of slow, plodding advance, the Ninth Army had reached the Roer—not the Rhine which had been the original objective, but a flood-threatened stream only six to twelve miles from the original line of departure. German defense never had cracked, despite Allied air and artillery superiority. The XXIX Tactical Air Command alone had dropped 1,500 tons of general-purpose bombs and 22,200 gallons of napalm during November. Artillery of the XIX Corps during only the first four days of the offensive had expended 56,000 rounds of light ammunition and 34,000 rounds of medium. Yet the Germans had held with a patchwork assortment of divisions. They had inflicted upon the Ninth Army more than ten thousand battle casualties: 1,133 killed, 6,864 wounded, and 2,059 missing. German

---

[47] Ewing, *29 Let's Go!*, p. 198.

ENTRANCE TO SWIMMING POOL *adjacent to the Sportplatz.*

prisoners totaled 8,321; the Ninth Army actually buried 1,264 enemy dead and estimated that the Germans lost another 5,000 killed. The Ninth Army lost eighty-four medium and fifteen light tanks destroyed, plus numerous others that were out of action for varying periods.

Except for a small sector in the zone of the First Army, the battle of the Roer plain was over. It had been a lengthy and costly attempt to eliminate a checkerboard of villages that extensive field fortifications and inclement weather had strengthened.

PART SEVEN

CONCLUSION

CHAPTER XXV

The Approaches to Dueren

By the end of the first week of December, three of the four attacking corps of the First and Ninth Armies had planted their standards on the west bank of the Roer River. The corps still with some distance to go was General Collins' VII Corps, which originally had been labeled "main effort." In this case, "main effort" was no empty term; the VII Corps had been provided greater strength than the others—an extra division and an extra regimental combat team, plus preference in artillery support. The corps also had been furnished a preponderance of tonnage in the air bombardment preceding the offensive. Under these circumstances, the VII Corps might have been expected to be among the first at the river. Yet labeling the corps attack the "main effort" had done nothing to eliminate the difficult and constricted terrain in front of it, particularly the Huertgen Forest. (*Map VIII*)

By 28 November, when the neighboring XIX Corps had staked the first claim to the Roer's west bank, indications already were developing that at least one of Collins' four divisions might have to be replaced before the corps could reach the river. This was the 4th Division, reduced to near impotence by losses in the Huertgen Forest. By 3 December, when the XIII Corps gained the Roer, events at the village of Merode on the fringe of the forest had provided pointed evidence that the 1st Division also needed replacement.

By 7 December, when the V Corps for all practical purposes reached the river at the eastern end of the Brandenberg–Bergstein ridge, Collins had halted all offensive operations within the VII Corps and was involved in a detailed realignment of troops. The VII Corps still had a little more than three miles to go to the Roer.

On General Collins' north wing, the 104th Division remained in the line, tired from clearing the Eschweiler–Weisweiler industrial complex and establishing bridgeheads across the Inde River at Inden and Lucherberg, but nevertheless capable of continuing to attack. Having seen but limited commitment, the 3d Armored Division also stayed with the corps. In the center, the veteran 9th Division replaced the 1st Division in a line running from the Aachen–Cologne autobahn at Luchem, southward through Langerwehe and Juengersdorf into the Huertgen Forest to a point south of Merode. Where the 4th Division had stalled at the western skirt of the forest opposite the settlement of Hof Hardt and the village of Gey, the 83d Division took over. This too was a veteran replacement which had seen action in Normandy and Brittany and for more than a month had rested with the VIII Corps in Luxembourg. To reinforce the corps right wing much as the 3d Armored Division strengthened the left, General Collins obtained the 5th Armored Division, minus one combat command which had fought with the V Corps on the Brandenberg–Bergstein ridge.

General Collins ordered the attack to be resumed on 10 December.[1] On the left, the 104th Division was to clear a three-mile stretch of the Roer plain between the Inde and the Roer where three villages represent the only breaks in monotonously flat terrain. In the center, the 9th Division and a combat command of the 3d Armored Division were to operate "in close conjunction" in a zone less than four miles wide that technically was assigned to the 9th Division. The two units were to clear the northwestern and western approaches to Dueren, the Roer town which had been the VII Corps objective since September. On the right, the 83d Division was to sweep the southwestern approaches to Dueren. After gaining additional roads on the fringe of the Huertgen Forest, the 83d Division was to relinquish the extreme right of the corps zone to the 5th Armored Division so that the armor might bridge a gap between the infantry's objectives near Dueren and the point on the Brandenberg–Bergstein ridge where the V Corps had reached the river.

To supplement divisional artillery, General Collins had available considerably less corps artillery strength than in earlier stages of the drive to the Roer, yet a substantial force nevertheless: fourteen battalions ranging from 105-mm. howitzers to 8-inch howitzers and 4.5-inch guns, plus a separate battery of 155-mm. self-propelled guns.[2] Five battalions also were self-propelled. To each of his divisions Collins attached one battalion, leaving nine battalions under corps control. The separate battery he split between the 9th and 104th Divisions.

Having seen ample evidence of the enemy's pertinacity in this sector, the VII Corps G-2, Colonel Carter, expressed no expectation that the successes of the adjacent corps might prompt German withdrawal. In effect, the Germans were maintaining a re-entrant bridgehead on the west bank of the Roer along the approaches to Dueren. The question, Colonel Carter noted, was not the intent to hold the bridgehead but "how long can the enemy continue his defense in the face of his present rate of losses and the new demand for troops in the south [to counter successes achieved by the Third U.S. Army]." [3] Colonel Carter correctly divined that the enemy's main strength was in his artillery arm. He estimated 20 light artillery battalions, 5 medium battalions, and 15 to 20 self-propelled guns, plus some 10 tanks and likely assistance from the guns of the SS divisions, which presumably were in reserve between the Roer and the Rhine.

The enemy's order of battle had undergone several changes while the VII Corps was regrouping. Immediately north of a new corps boundary, which was adjusted to give full responsibility for Dueren to General Koechling's *LXXXI Corps*, was

---

[1] VII Corps FO 13, 8 Dec, VII Corps FO file, Dec 44. Unless otherwise noted, sources for this account include official corps and division records, unofficial unit histories as cited in previous chapters, and several valuable combat interviews with personnel of the 9th and 83d Divisions. Records of telephone messages in 83d Div G-2— G-3 Jnl are particularly valuable. An 83d Division history, *Thunderbolt Across Europe* (Munich, Germany: 1945), is sketchy and of little historical value.

[2] On 28 November the 32d Field Artillery Brigade had reverted to First Army control. The brigade at this time controlled three 240-mm. howitzer battalions and two 8-inch gun battalions.
[3] Annex 2 to VII Corps FO 13.

the *3d Parachute Division,* which had arrived in late November to relieve *Gruppe Engel* (remnants of the *12th* and *47th Volks Grenadier Divisions*). Brought almost to full strength by replacements, the parachute division was directed to provide two battalions for the specific task of defending Dueren.[4] North of the parachutists stood the *246th Volks Grenadier Division.* Removed from the line in late November for rehabilitation, the *246th* had been sent back only a few days later. It was not much of a rehabilitation. Not one of the eight infantry battalions could muster as many as a hundred men.[5]

Still opposing the southern wing of the VII U.S. Corps was General Straube's *LXXIV Corps.* For so long a component of the *Seventh Army,* the *LXXIV Corps* on the day the Americans resumed the offensive was to pass to control of the *Fifteenth Army (Gruppe von Manteuffel)* while *Seventh Army* headquarters moved south for its role in the Ardennes counteroffensive.[6]

That part of the *LXXIV Corps* front which would be involved at first in the renewed fighting belonged to the *353d Infantry Division,* which had come up from the Luxembourg front in mid-November. A few remnants of the *344th Infantry Division,* which like the

353d had been rushed into the Huertgen Forest in mid-November, still were around, but these were destined to be pulled out in a few days so that the division might be rehabilitated for the counteroffensive. South of the *353d,* opposite the Brandenberg–Bergstein ridge, contingents of the *272d Volks Grenadier Division* also were destined for relief in a few days for return to the Monschau Corridor. The relieving unit was to be the *85th Infantry Division,* brought down from Holland. This division also was to relieve the *89th Infantry Division,* south of the *272d;* but in the merry-go-round of reliefs preceding the counteroffensive, the *89th* was to be recommitted on the extreme south of the *Fifteenth Army* on 15 December.[7]

Because of the configuration of terrain, the fighting in the final push to the Roer was to fall into two categories—one akin to the battle of the Roer plain, the other to the battle of the Huertgen Forest. In general, the dividing line between the two followed the boundary between the 9th and 83d Divisions. It ran from within the Huertgen Forest between Merode and Hof Hardt northeast to the Roer at Dueren. Almost from the outset, the engagements on either side of this line became replicas in miniature of the earlier campaigning on the plain and in the forest.

On the Plain

The script for the fighting north of the dividing line had been written and tested

---

[4] Opns Order for 1 Dec 44, *Fifteenth Army* (*Gruppe von Manteuffel*) to *Corps Group Blumentritt* and *LXXXI Corps,* 0115, 1 Dec 44, *LXXXI Corps KTB, Befehle Heeresgruppe und Armee an Gen. Kdo., 1.–31.XII.44.*

[5] *LXXXI Corps Gefechtsbericht,* AAR for 30 Nov–1 Dec 44; Weekly Strength Rpt, *LXXXI Corps to Gruppe von Manteuffel,* 0001, 26 Nov 44, *LXXXI Corps Ia KTB, Wochenmeldungen, 22.IX.–31.XII.44.*

[6] Luttichau, Planning and Preparations, MS in OCMH.

[7] Shifts and countershifts of German divisions in these last few days before the counteroffensive were common. The moves may be traced in detail in Luttichau, Progressive Build-up and Operations, MS in OCMH.

by the Ninth Army's XIII and XIX Corps. In adopting it, the 3d Armored, 9th, and 104th Divisions made only minor revisions.

As might have been expected, the 104th Division continued to exploit its proficiency in night attacks. Though used directly against but one of three villages still to be taken in the 104th Division's sector, night attack was the key that opened all three.

The drive began conventionally early on 10 December as a battalion of the 414th Infantry attacked from the Inde bridgehead east of Inden toward each of the two northernmost villages, Schophoven and Pier. As elsewhere on the Roer plain, the enemy (*246th Division*) had dug elaborate entrenchments about the villages. Fire from the fortifications at Schophoven pinned down one battalion. Behind a rolling artillery barrage, the other battalion penetrated the defenses at Pier, only to be forced out after nightfall by a counterattack supported by three self-propelled guns. Through the next day of 11 December, the Germans continued to hold both Pier and Schophoven.

Against the third village of Merken, which lies along the Roer near the Aachen–Cologne autobahn southeast of Schophoven and Pier, a battalion of the 415th Infantry turned to the device of night attack. Moving before dawn on 11 December, the men guarded surprise by advancing with empty rifles. Employing a carefully detailed plan developed in close liaison with the infantry, artillery boxed in the route of advance. As the infantry neared a hamlet several hundred yards northwest of Merken, artillery fired a white phosphorus marker. Thereupon, a platoon dropped off to clear the hamlet while the main body effected an abrupt

change of direction in the darkness to move southeast on Merken. Again the artillery fired white phosphorus to guide the way. Both Merken and the hamlet succumbed quickly to surprise assaults.[8]

In advancing to Merken, the 415th Infantry had passed south of Pier, thereby opening a route for a flanking force to hit that village from the south. Early the next day, 12 December, while the bulk of a battalion continued to strike Pier from the west, a company of infantry supported by tanks approached from the south. Actually, the maneuver was anticlimactic; the Germans had begun to withdraw. Artillery of the 104th Division wreaked havoc on enemy infantry scrambling across the Roer on a bridge east of Pier.

At Schophoven, the Germans proved more tenacious, but a flanking maneuver over the newly opened avenue from the south proved their undoing.[9] By mid-afternoon of 13 December, four days after renewal of the offensive, the 104th Division had reached the Roer on a four-mile front.

Elsewhere north of the dividing line between the plain and the forest, the 3d Armored and 9th Divisions developed a variation upon an old theme, close coordination between infantry and armor. A combat command first was to stage a limited objective attack into the left half

---

[8] In the process of reducing Merken, an artillery observer, 2d Lt. Paul H. Schafer, executed an unusual assignment. Spotting seventeen Americans marching across a field as prisoners of two German guards, he adjusted time fire beyond the group so that the guards had no choice but to turn back the column toward American positions. See 104th Div Arty AAR, Dec 44.

[9] An unusual aspect of this maneuver was a smoke screen laid down by tank guns. See VII Corps AAR, Dec 44.

of the infantry division's zone, perhaps with a view to breaking any hard crust of resistance which might have formed while the VII Corps had been regrouping. Advancing two thirds of the distance to the Roer northwest of Dueren, the armor was to take three villages, Geich, Obergeich, and Echtz. After capture of Echtz, the 9th Division's 60th Infantry was to relieve the combat command, presumably as a prelude to taking two remaining villages close along the west bank of the river, though General Collins did not at first spell out a definite plan for these last objectives. In the right half of the 9th Division's zone, infantry alone was to attack but not until advance of the armor into Obergeich had bared one of the enemy's flanks.

The difference between this tank-infantry attack and the usual was that neither command was subordinated to the other. Presumably, General Collins placed the onus of responsibility for co-ordination upon the infantry when he directed that the 9th Division attack "in close conjunction with" the armor.[10] Yet in comparison with the usual method of attaching one unit to another, this was a somewhat loose command arrangement.

As events developed, the feature of the drive to the Roer in this sector was the close co-ordination achieved by these separate units of infantry and armor without formal and distinct command curbs. Perhaps the explanation lay in acceptance from the first by the infantry commander, General Craig, that the drive on Geich, Obergeich, and Echtz was not a separate assignment for the armor but a joint responsibility.[11]

On the first morning, 10 December, after the armor had run into trouble from a combination of mines and mud, General Craig sent a battalion of his 60th Infantry to assist. Together this battalion and a contingent of the 33d Armored Infantry Regiment pushed into the first objective of Obergeich. The same infantry battalion assisted the tanks and armored infantry in subduing the next village of Geich while General Craig sent another battalion of infantry to help a second contingent of armor take Echtz. By nightfall of the first day, all three initial objectives had fallen.

On 11 December, as General Collins decided on a definite plan for taking the two remaining villages west of the Roer, he varied from his arrangement of command by co-ordination to attach a battalion of the 60th Infantry to CCR (Col. Robert L. Howze, Jr.). The combined force was to take Hoven, northernmost of the two villages. The rest of the 60th Infantry was to take the other village of Mariaweiler.[12]

As troops of the XIII and XIX Corps earlier had discovered, pinning the enemy to a small toehold west of the Roer was no guarantee of his collapse. During the night of 11 December, for example, the Germans reinforced their garrisons in Hoven and Mariaweiler with two refitted companies of the *47th Volks Grenadier Division*. The troops of the VII Corps also learned, as had others before them, that German observation from higher ground east of the Roer could be deadly. A first attack against Hoven on 11 December recoiled in the face of German artillery fire that reduced the attacking infantry by a third. On 12 December a

---

[10] VII Corps FO 13.

[11] See 9th Div FO 45, 8 Dec 44, 9th Div AAR, Dec 44.

[12] VII Corps Opns Memo 129, 11 Dec, VII Corps Opns Memo file, Dec 44.

battalion of the 60th Infantry moving on Mariaweiler took more than a hundred casualties from shellfire before gaining protection of the first buildings. On the same day a smoke screen enabled the armor and infantry to make good on a second try at taking Hoven.

By nightfall of 12 December, despite a sharp counterattack supported by self-propelled guns at Mariaweiler, CCR and the 60th Infantry could claim control of most of the west bank of the Roer northwest and west of Dueren. A few tenacious outposts remained, but these the infantry alone could deal with almost at leisure. The last, a factory between Mariaweiler and Dueren, would fall on 14 December.

In the meantime, while armor and infantry had been co-ordinating in the main push, the 39th Infantry had been attacking alone to clear three villages in the southern portion of the 9th Division's zone. These were Schlich, Derichsweiler, and Merode, the last the site where troops of the 1st Division had plunged out of the Huertgen Forest only to be annihilated by counterattack because they lacked a route for reinforcements. Perhaps in cognizance of this incident, the 39th Infantry commander, Colonel Bond, directed his battalions to delay until capture of Obergeich had bared the German north flank and provided good roads into all three objectives, including Merode. Colonel Bond also hoped by striking from the north to trap any Germans who remained in a promontory of the Huertgen Forest southwest of Merode.[13]

From the first the wisdom of Colonel Bond's decision was apparent. In late

afternoon of the first day of the renewed offensive, 10 December, a battalion advanced southeast from Obergeich to take a hamlet from which to stage the big push the next day. The hamlet fell readily. A hundred Germans surrendered, members of the same *3d Parachute Division* which had dealt the cruel blow to the 1st Division in Merode.

After systematic fighting aided by an effective dive-bombing mission by P-38's of the 368th Group, both Schlich and Merode were cleared by nightfall of 11 December. From this point, the going was relatively easy, for during the night the Germans had begun to replace the *3d Parachute Division* with the hurriedly and inadequately rehabilitated *47th Volks Grenadier Division*.[14]

In the afternoon of 12 December, the 39th Infantry established a firm grip on part of Derichsweiler and on 13 December completed the job. Because the 83d Division, attacking northeast out of the Huertgen Forest, would pinch out the regiment by passing diagonally across its front en route to the Roer at Dueren, the 39th Infantry was not to continue to the river. Except for some assistance to be given the 83d Division, the regiment had completed its assignment.

As elsewhere north of the dividing line between the Huertgen Forest and the Roer plain, the final push had taken most of four days. A dirty fight, lacking in both glamour and surprise, it had cost the 3d Armored, 9th, and 104th Divisions 1,074 casualties, of which 179 were killed and 75 missing.[15]

---

[13] Combat Interv with Bond, 9th Div Combat Interv file, Dec 44.

[14] *LXXXI Corps Gefechtsbericht,* AAR for 12 Dec 44.

[15] Figures compiled from VII Corps FO and Battle Casualties file, Dec 44.

In the Forest

South of the dividing line between the 9th and 83d Divisions lay both forest and plain. As in the sector east of Stolberg through which part of the VII Corps earlier had attacked, densely wooded hills reluctantly give way to larger and more frequent clearings. Within a mile of Dueren the highlands merge with the flatlands of the plain. In approaching the settlement of Hof Hardt, in occupying Grosshau, and in gaining positions overlooking Gey, the 4th Division technically had reached the edge of the Huertgen Forest before casualties had prompted replacement. Yet in many aspects, including some of terrain, the fighting to be experienced by the two units renewing the drive would be markedly similar to that which had occurred deep within the forest.

The principal similarity had to do with a struggle for adequate roads. On the left wing of a four-mile zone which the 83d Division inherited initially, one regiment, which was to take Hof Hardt and drive northeast alongside and eventually pinch out the 9th Division's 39th Infantry, had a good road, an extension of axial Route U which the 4th Division had used. But in the center and on the right wing, routes of communication were more potential than actual. Though the V Corps at Huertgen and Kleinhau and the 4th Division at Grosshau had made down payment on a good road net, another big installment would be required before clear title could be claimed.

The road net problem facing the 83d Division centered about the two villages of Gey and Strass, both northeast of Grosshau. These villages gather in several roads and trails from the Huertgen Forest, subject them to a minor multiplication process, then release them to the northeast, east, and southeast toward the Roer. To travel from Grosshau northeast toward Dueren, it is necessary to pass through Gey; to move east and southeast to the river, control of Strass is needed. The 83d Division commander, Maj. Gen. Robert C. Macon, assigned one regiment to each village, the 330th Infantry on the right to Strass, the 331st Infantry to Gey. The third regiment, the 329th Infantry, was to pursue the somewhat separate assignment of driving northeast along axial Route U on the division's left wing.

After capture of Strass and Gey, the 330th Infantry presumably was to revert to reserve and the 331st Infantry to continue northeast from Gey toward Dueren. At this point, both villages were to serve as jump-off bases for the 5th Armored Division (less CCR) in a sweep east and southeast to the Roer to clear the southeastern corner of the VII Corps zone. One combat command was to move through Gey, thence east to an elevation overlooking the Roer, Hill 211. The other was to advance southeast from the vicinity of Strass to another height on the west bank of the Roer, the Hemgen Berg (Hill 253).[16]

The key to early success in this miniature battle of the Huertgen Forest obviously lay in quick seizure of Gey and Strass. That explained General Macon's decision to put a regiment on each objective. It also explained why the enemy's

---

[16] Both combat commands originally were to move through Strass. Subsequent complications at Strass prompted the change. See 1st Lt George M. Tuttle, Seizure of Gey and Strass, 83d Div Combat Interv file.

353d Division made the villages keystones of their defense.

General Macon expected to take Gey and Strass in one swift stroke; indeed, the 5th Armored Division was scheduled to join the operation before nightfall of D Day, 10 December.[17]   Each regiment was to employ a battalion just before dawn, one to advance astride a dirt road leading from the west into Gey, the other along another unimproved road winding northeast through a patch of woods, past the settlement of Schafberg, thence to Strass. Each regiment would have to depend at first upon a narrow, muddy supply route closely embraced at some points by woods. Veterans of earlier fighting at Merode, at Huertgen, and at Schmidt might have looked upon the prospect with some degree of alarm.

Conscious of the need to get into Gey and Strass before daylight provided the enemy observation on open fields near the villages, the two attacking infantry battalions moved swiftly. On the left, troops of the 331st Infantry picked their way over deeply buried antitank mines, skirted unoccupied but booby-trapped trenches, and reached Gey shortly after dawn. The battalion of the 330th Infantry moved with equal success through the woods toward Schafberg, bypassed that settlement, and continued to Strass.

Both battalions got into the villages. In Gey the Germans fought tenaciously from house to house so that reduction of the village became a slow, systematic proposition. In Strass, the occupants gave up more readily, but an hour later they counterattacked with about a company of infantry supported by tanks or assault guns.

[17] See messages in 83d Div G–2—G–3 Jnl, 10 Dec 44.

Men of the 331st Infantry *advance on Gey.*

In both Gey and Strass, the Americans needed tanks—in Gey to tip the balance between infantry forces of about equal size, in Strass to halt the counterattack. Complexity and vexation entered the 83d Division's operation when in midmorning of 10 December attached tanks of the 744th Tank Battalion first tried to get forward.

On the dirt road to Gey three tanks soon lost tracks in the antitank mine field through which the infantry had passed safely. They blocked the road. Through this day and the next engineers attempted to clear both this road and a main highway leading northeast from Grosshau into Gey. Observed German fire severely hampered the work. The dirt road was so full of shell fragments that mine detectors were of little use. On both roads the engineers might deem a mine field cleared, only to watch in consternation as the lead tank would strike an undiscovered mine. The Germans in the meantime strengthened their garrison in Gey with infantry reinforcements. On 11 December, the 331st Infantry commander, Col. Robert H. York, also sent infantry reinforcements. The result was a stalemate.

First efforts to get tanks to Strass proved more successful. An entire tank company began the trip, but one platoon apparently took a wrong turn, ventured into enemy territory, and was annihilated. The rest made it. Yet in passing, the tank tracks cut deeply into the muddy dirt road so that many doubted if other vehicles would be able to follow.

As night came on 10 December, Strass was secure, though the Germans remained in close contact at some points, particularly along a half-mile stretch between Strass and Gey where they denied any liaison between the Americans in the two villages. Because of "traffic problems," presumably in moving through the Huertgen Forest to Grosshau and Kleinhau, the 5th Armored Division commander, General Oliver, decided to wait until the next day before joining the push.

After darkness, the Germans resorted to an old Huertgen Forest trick of infiltration. Along the wooded portion of the supply route to Strass, near Schafberg, they emplaced several antitank guns. Into Schafberg, which had not been cleared of Germans even though American tanks had passed through, they thrust infantry reinforcements. The American battalion in Strass was, in effect, cut off.

The 83d Division commander, General Macon, insisted nevertheless that armor could move over the road to Strass on 11

December. "The road is about as open as we can get it," he told General Oliver. "We can't keep out the snipers." [18] A commander like General Oliver, who less than three weeks before along the Germeter–Huertgen highway had seen what premature commitment could do to one of his combat commands, could be excused a measure of trepidation about a situation that appeared to be shaping up the same way. He discussed the matter with the corps commander, General Collins. Having checked with General Macon, Collins assured the armored commander that the road was open. "I told General Oliver," the corps commander said, "to go on ahead."

By daylight of 11 December, however, General Macon had decided, "We may have more to do than we anticipated." A new counterattack had hit Strass just before dawn; though contained, it made for intense fighting through much of the morning. More accurate reports of enemy strength along the road through Schafberg had prompted the 330th Infantry commander, Col. Robert T. Foster, to commit a fresh battalion to clear the road. The armored commander, General Oliver, decided nevertheless to proceed as planned. "Our going down there," he told General Macon, "ought to at least complicate their job of going in against you very severely [at Strass]."

Since no one even presumed that either a road to or a path through Gey was clear, no plans were made for immediate commitment of any but one combat command. This was CCB (Colonel Cole). The armor was to pass beyond Schafberg to a wooded knoll a mile to the east

---

[18] This and subsequent direct quotes are from 83d Div G–2—G–3 Jnl, 10–11 Dec 44. See also Ltr, Macon to OCMH, 10 Aug 56.

(Hill 266), then to turn northeast against the village of Bergheim, and finally to occupy the Hemgen Berg (Hill 253) on the west bank of the Roer. The column actually was not to pass through Strass, though movement east from Schafberg obviously would be impossible if the enemy still held Strass.

In recognition of the fluid situation along the route to Schafberg, mounted armored infantry led the column. The infantry still was several hundred yards short of Schafberg when small arms fire and contact with the battalion of the 330th Infantry, which was attempting to clear the road, prompted an order to dismount. Though CCB's infantry joined an attack toward Schafberg, the Germans when night came still were holding the settlement and effectively blocking the road. The fight had cost CCB 150 casualties.

Meanwhile, in Strass, the Germans had counterattacked a third time. Again American infantry and tanks beat them off, but the small force in Strass obviously was in a bad way. In two days the infantry battalion had run through four commanders: one killed, one missing, and two wounded. About sixty casualties had accumulated and were badly in need of medical supplies. No one had food or water. Ammunition was running low. Only seven tanks remained. Though a ten-man patrol carrying a few supplies broke through to Strass during the night of 11 December, the battalion in the village needed more help than that.

To the River

On the third day of the attack, on 12 December, the two regiments at Gey and Strass renewed their efforts to clear roads into the villages and enable the 5th Armored Division to move. In the meantime, on the 83d Division's extreme left wing, more than a mile and a half northwest of Gey, a third regiment began to attack.

This was the 329th Infantry, commanded by Col. Edwin B. Crabill, which did not complete relief of 4th Division troops in its sector until 11 December. So removed from the rest of the 83d Division was this regiment at first that the corps commander contemplated attachment to the adjacent 9th Division, though later developments prompted reconsideration and instead a squadron of the 4th Cavalry Group was assigned to bridge the gap between the regiment and the rest of the division.[19] The 329th Infantry was to advance along axial Route U through Hof Hardt, northeast to the village of Guerzenich, thence east through another village, Roelsdorf, to the Roer at Dueren.

Attacking through woods toward Hof Hardt in midmorning of 12 December, troops of the 329th Infantry quickly experienced some of the difficulties of Huertgen Forest fighting: tree bursts, extensive mine fields, and problems of control. The fresh regiment nevertheless gained Hof Hardt soon after midday and by dark had secured a line of departure along the skirt of the forest for continuing the attack to Guerzenich.

On 13 December, behind an effective smoke screen, a battalion of the 329th Infantry gained Guerzenich by noon. Thereby the regiment had outpaced the adjacent 9th Division's 39th Infantry in the neighboring village of Derichsweiler. So impressed by this success was the

---

[19] 83d Div AAR, Dec 44, and G–2—G–3 Jnl, 13 Dec 44.

division commander, General Macon, that he directed the regiment to move the next day south against Birgel, a village that originally had been assigned to the 331st Infantry.

In the meantime, at Gey and Strass, the situation had taken a slow turn for the better. Behind a flail tank borrowed from the 5th Armored Division, a covey of tanks from the attached 744th Tank Battalion finally gained Gey during late afternoon of 12 December over the main road from Grosshau. Reduction of the stubborn resistance in the village now could be but a question of time. On the road to Strass, the 330th Infantry maneuvered one company after another against the bottleneck of Schafberg. Constant pressure of infantry and artillery gradually relaxed the enemy's hold.

By midafternoon of 12 December Schafberg was clear, though reinforcements still could not reach Strass because German self-propelled guns controlled a portion of the supply route where it crossed open fields south of the village. The only relief afforded the Americans in Strass during daylight was provided by artillery liaison planes from which pilots dropped medical supplies and chocolate D rations. Yet this was a minor delay; for as night cut the enemy's observation, no time was lost in sending into the village reinforcements, supplies, and evacuation vehicles for the wounded.

The condition of the battalion which had fought for Strass was indicative of another resemblance between fighting here and earlier combat deep within the Huertgen Forest. Slightly more than two reinforced rifle companies had reached Strass on 10 December; when relief arrived the night of 12 December, 150 men remained. In three days, the 83d

Division had lost almost a thousand men, primarily in two regiments. Even CCB's brief commitment on 11 December had cost 150 men. Perhaps the most surprising losses were those incurred by the 330th and 331st Infantry Regiments even before start of the attack. During five days of relatively static warfare while awaiting D Day, the two regiments had taken 472 casualties.

A road at last available through Schafberg to Strass, a second attempt to send the 5th Armored Division's CCB eastward toward the Roer now was possible. This time the armored commander, General Oliver, wanted to wait until his second combat command might attack simultaneously through Gey. During the afternoon of 13 December, he conferred with the corps commander, General Collins, and the 83d Division commander, General Macon, to co-ordinate plans for the next day.

The entire southern half of the VII Corps zone was to come alive early on 14 December with attacks by two infantry regiments and two combat commands. On the extreme left, the 329th Infantry was to continue to clear Guerzenich en route to the Roer while at the same time moving south against Birgel. The 331st Infantry was to attack northeast from Gey, cross-country in the direction of Berzbuir and Lendersdorf, which lie between Birgel and the Roer. With a battalion of the 331st Infantry attached, CCA was to move east from Gey to the village of Kufferath and eventually to Hill 211 on the west bank of the Roer. Augmented by a battalion of the 330th Infantry, CCB was to follow the original plan of attacking east from Schafberg and Strass against Hill 266, thence to Bergheim, and finally to the Hemgen Berg

(Hill 253). The average distance from lines of departure to the Roer was about two miles.

On 14 December resistance varied in intensity in relation to the nature of the terrain. On the left, the 329th Infantry had put the Huertgen Forest behind and emerged on the Roer plain. By nightfall this regiment had cleared Guerzenich and occupied much of Birgel.

At Birgel, surrender of a battalion of the *47th Volks Grenadier Division* at the first shot created for the Germans a critical situation not recognized on the American side. The capitulation severed contact between the *LXXXI* and *LXXIV Corps*, thereby endangering the so-called Dueren bridgehead at the very moment when the final shifts and assemblies for the Ardennes counteroffensive were being made. To remedy the situation, General von Zangen, commander of the *Fifteenth Army,* widened the *LXXXI Corps* sector to include Birgel and ordered the village retaken.[20]

At dusk the Germans counterattacked at Birgel with infantry supported by six assault guns. A machine gun squad leader in Company M, Sgt. Ralph G. Neppel, was largely responsible for driving off one of the assault guns and twenty accompanying infantrymen. When a round from the assault gun wounded Sergeant Neppel's entire squad and severed one of his legs below the knee, the sergeant dragged himself back to his position on his elbows, remounted his gun and killed the remaining enemy riflemen. Stripped of infantry protection, the German vehicle withdrew. Sergeant Neppel

subsequently received the Medal of Honor.

In the center of this portion of the VII Corps zone, where patches of forest still existed but where the plain was becoming more evident, the 331st Infantry and CCA found the going somewhat more tedious; nevertheless, as night came, they held a sharp rise overlooking Berzbuir and had drawn up on three sides of Kufferath. On the right, in a sector of broken and constricted terrain more nearly like the Huertgen Forest, CCB ran into serious problems.

Because of the muddy, deep-rutted road through the woods to Schafberg, CCB's tanks could not get into position during the night of 13 December for an early morning attack. Infantry alone was to strike for the first objective, Hill 266, a mile east of Schafberg. Artillery first was to fire selected concentrations before H Hour, then to create a rolling barrage. Moving before dawn, CCB's 15th Armored Infantry was to drive east from Schafberg while the attached battalion of the 330th Infantry pushed southeast from Strass. The battalions were to converge on the hill just at daylight with the specific mission of eliminating at least eight known German antitank guns.

The infantry had not long to wait before discovering that the enemy on Hill 266 was entrenched too deeply to be silenced by the artillery preparation. Further artillery concentrations, including a TOT in midmorning, were to no avail. A strafing and bombing mission in early afternoon also failed to help. Although tanks tried to get forward, they were too late to get the drive going again before nightfall.

General Oliver could not have been deeply concerned about CCB's inability to

[20] *LXXXI Corps, Befehle Gen. Kdo. an Div., vom 1.–31.12.44; Erfahrungs berichte 23.10.–30. 12.44; Befehle H. Gr. u. Armee,* order, *Fifteenth Army* to *LXXXI Corps,* 0330, 14 Dec 44.

advance, because CCA's push to Kufferath had provided an obvious opportunity to outflank the resistance from the north. This the Germans too must have noted, for on 15 December their defenses folded. Both the 5th Armored Division's combat commands encountered unexpectedly light opposition. CCA took Kufferath early and by 0830 held the high ground along the river. Its main losses were four tanks knocked out by self-propelled guns roaming near the river. On Hill 266, CCB found abandoned weapons and deserted trenches. Bergheim was in hand by dark, and the Hemgen Berg (253) fell early in the morning of 16 December.

After a flurry of concern on 16 December about possible German counterattack in conjunction with the enemy's surprising move in the Ardennes, the armor and the 83d Division the next day began a mop-up process to eliminate a few remaining pockets of resistance west of the Roer. Southeast of the 5th Armored Division's CCB, the 4th Cavalry Group lent assistance. In contrast to the collapse on 15 December, the enemy now defended most of the pockets stanchly. As had been the case farther north on the Roer plain, enemy guns on higher ground east of the Roer were a constant menace. Nevertheless, by Christmas Day, the west bank of the river, from positions of the V Corps at the eastern end of the Brandenberg–Bergstein ridge to outposts of the XIII Corps twenty-four air-line miles away at Linnich, would be free of the enemy.

Though offensive action would continue at several points in the VII Corps zone through Christmas Day, the corps— and thus, the First Army—for all practical purposes had reached the Roer by the end of 16 December. It had taken

thirty-one days to move approximately seven miles. At one time or another, seven divisions (less one combat command of armor), representing an authorized strength of approximately 100,000 men, had participated. During the course of the drive, the corps had incurred 8,550 nonbattle casualties and 15,908 battle casualties, including 2,448 killed.[21]

The casualties of the V Corps, which fought for eighteen days to gain the Roer on a limited front, were also a part of the cost of the November offensive to the First Army. The V Corps employed actively an infantry division, a ranger battalion, and an armored combat command, a force representing an authorized strength of about 20,000 men. About 2,800 of these were lost in battle, while 1,200 became nonbattle casualties. Total losses for the First Army in the drive to the Roer thus reached approximately 28,000 men.

Artillery ammunition expenditures were high, despite scarcities in supply. During the period 1–16 December, for example, when artillery pieces available to the VII Corps were less than in earlier stages of the drive, divisional and corps artillery within the VII Corps fired 258,779

---

[21] See cumulative casualty statistics in VII Corps FO and Battle Casualties file, Dec 44. Breakdown by division:

	Battle	Killed	Nonbattle
Total	15,908	2,448	8,550
1st Div	3,408	354	2,216
3d Armd Div	436	94	614
4th Div	4,149	432	1,588
5th Armd Div (—CCR)	575	70	223
9th Div	1,180	183	1,050
83d Div	1,951	589	790
104th Div*	4,209	726	2,069

* Only division of the seven to be committed actively during the entire thirty-one days.

rounds. Artillery strength was greatest during late November when the First Army employed 526 light guns, 156 mediums, and 108 heavies, a total of 790 field artillery pieces.[22]

In armor, the First Army actively employed at one time or another during the course of the Roer drive two armored divisions and six separate medium tank battalions, a total of approximately 700 tanks. Of these, 240 were listed as "losses." [23]

When the offensive had opened on 16 November, the First Army had been looking beyond the Roer to the Rhine. A month later the troops and their commanders must have been gratified to gain the Roer, which originally had been an intermediate objective. Though full realization of the meaning of the enemy's stubborn resistance was not to come until later in December when the extent of the Ardennes counteroffensive became known, this had been a German defensive victory, or, perhaps more accurately, a successful delaying action on a grand scale. If the VII Corps or any corps in this region had achieved a breakthrough, the enemy either could not have launched his counteroffensive or would have been forced to a drastic alteration in plans.

The fighting west of the Roer had not been without impact upon the counteroffensive, despite lack of a breakthrough. In prisoners alone, for example, the Germans had lost to the First Army upwards of 13,000 men.[24] Against the VII Corps they had found it necessary to commit progressively seven divisions, an impressive number even though their strengths averaged no more than about 6,000 men. Hundreds of individual replacements and numbers of small units also were involved. Before start of the attack, for example, strength of the enemy opposite the VII Corps was estimated at 13,300 men; by early December, despite battlefield attrition, the number had risen to an estimated 21,800. Though any estimate of enemy losses is hazardous, German battle and nonbattle casualties opposite the First Army during the period probably approximated those of the First Army—something like 28,000.

As the First and Ninth Armies had been nearing the Roer, plans for clearing one remaining sector of the river's west bank still were under discussion. This sector was a British responsibility, a triangle of generally marshy land between the Maas and the Roer short of the confluence of the two rivers at Roermond. Because of the tedious process of clearing the Germans from the west bank of the Maas, the British to this point had been unable to develop their intentions in the triangle.[25] Though Field Marshal Montgomery planned for the 30 Corps to begin the operation on 12 or 13 December, he saw no hope of getting started on time

---

[22] Tabulation of rounds fired made from VII Corps AAR, Dec 44; Field Artillery Firing 16–23 Nov, FUSA AAR, Nov 44.

[23] FUSA Rpt, Vol. 2, Annex 6, p. 158. Whether temporarily or permanently lost was not recorded. This figure covers the entire months of November and December, though most losses presumably occurred during the period 16 November–16 December.

[24] 12th A Gp Weekly Intell Summaries, Nov–Dec 44, 12th A Gp G–2 AAR.

[25] The intentions are evident from M–534, 21 A Gp General Operational Situation and Directive, 2 Nov 44, 12th A Gp Military Objectives, 371.3, II, and from Notes on the Operations of 21 Army Group, 6 June 1944–5 May 1945, Sec. 6, p. 41, an official British document, copy in World War II Records Division, National Archives.

unless the ground dried out considerably.[26]

Allied commanders at this point actually were less concerned about this minor operation than about renewing the push beyond the Roer to the Rhine. In a meeting attended by Eisenhower, Montgomery, and Bradley at Maastricht on 7 December, the commanders discussed a plan for continuing the main push about 1 January. The Second British Army was to drive southeastward from Nijmegen between the Maas and the Rhine while the First and Ninth Armies crossed the Roer and at least one of the two turned north to meet the British. The Third Army presumably was to be closing to the Rhine also, whereupon General Eisenhower would send two gigantic thrusts across the river: the 21 Army Group and the Ninth Army north of the Ruhr and the First and Third Armies south of the Ruhr.[27]

As the days passed and no prospect of dry ground appeared, it became increasingly evident that Montgomery might have to move the 30 Corps northward for the main drive between the Maas and the Rhine before clearing the triangle west of the Roer. It looked more and more as if the job would fall to the Ninth Army. Insisting on the need for another division, General Bradley nevertheless agreed to the assignment, though he estimated it would be 10 January before he could get around to it because of the need to take the Roer River Dams. Bradley suggested that the main attack would have to be postponed to 15 January.[28]

As events developed, the entire discussion was for the moment academic. No decision had been made when on 16 December the Germans struck in the Ardennes.

---

[26] Notes on Meeting at Maastricht on 7.12.1944, dtd 8 Dec, filed 12 Dec, SHAEF SGS 381, II.

[27] Ibid. See also, SHAEF G-3 to SHAEF

CofS, sub: SCAEF Letter to General Bradley 15 Dec 44; SHAEF G-3 to SHAEF CofS, sub: Future Operations, 12 Dec 44, both in SHAEF SGS 381, II.

[28] SHAEF G-3 to SHAEF CofS, sub: Future Operations, 12 Dec 44, SHAEF 381, II.

CHAPTER XXVI

Objective: the Roer River Dams

The Neglected Objective

While American troops were approaching the Roer in late November and early December, concern was mounting in command circles about the obstacle that remained before sizable forces might cross the river with reasonable safety. This obstacle was the neglected objective, the dams on the upper reaches of the Roer which the Germans might employ to produce flood waters to isolate any force that had crossed the Roer.

By late November, tactical air headquarters had begun to dispatch reconnaissance flights over the dams almost daily.[1] Intelligence officers pored over aerial photographs: any indication of demolitions? significant change in water level? marked increase in rate of discharge over the spillways? Message after message about the state of the dams reached headquarters at almost every echelon of command. Corps and division commanders warned their units to be prepared to evacuate low-lying portions of the Roer valley. Noting a sharp rise in the river, commanders in at least one instance feared the worst until a quick reconnaissance flight revealed that unusually heavy rainfall and not destruction of the dams was the cause.[2]

The American command had indicated the first firm appreciation of the genuine value of the Roer River Dams to the Germans when on 11 November both First and Ninth Army had directed no advance beyond the Roer "except on Army order."[3] Even at that point and not for almost a month thereafter was any scheme revealed for taking the dams by ground assault, despite the fact that the dams were a two-edged sword. If American hands had controlled the spillways, those Germans west of the Roer who subsequently made such a fight of it in the Huertgen Forest and on the Roer plain could have been denied reinforcement and supply and subjected to defeat in detail in the same manner that the Germans anticipated should American troops cross to the east bank.[4]

Perhaps the explanation for the sins of ommission that made the sobriquet "neglected objective" applicable to the dams lay in the great expectations that had accompanied start of the November offensive. Perhaps it was as chroniclers of

---

[1] See FUSA G-3 Tac Jnl and file from about 16 Nov through mid-Dec.

[2] Almost all corps and division journals for this period contain numerous references to the dams.

Note in particular FUSA G-3 Tac file, 25–26 Nov 44.

[3] On 18 December, when a six-man patrol crossed the Roer on a partially demolished bridge at Dueren, the 83d Division asked approval to reinforce the patrol, presumably to establish a bridgehead. Permission was refused. 83d Div G-2—G-3 Jnl, 18 Dec 44, and AAR.

[4] The 12th Army Group engineer hints at this possibility in Summary of the Possibilities of the Military Use of the Roer River Reservoir System, 2 Nov 44, 12th A Gp Misc Log.

the Ninth Army put it later, that the American command anticipated a rapid advance which might produce capture of the dams in the natural course of events. "The progress made by First Army . . . did not measure up to expectations, however . . . . Since the dams were not quickly overrun, . . . the possibility that the enemy would make good tactical use of the waters impounded by the dams became a matter for the most serious consideration." [5]

This explanation might well have been correct up to the point when it became obvious that the First and Ninth Armies were to achieve no rapid sweep to the Roer River. After that time, delay in launching a ground attack against the dams could be more correctly attributed to a hope that the dams might be breached from the air and the threat of controlled flooding thereby eliminated. If bombs could break the Urft Dam, upstream from the massive, earthen Schwammenauel Dam, the water level in the Schwammenauel reservoir might be raised to a point near the crest of the earthen dam, whereupon bombs might dig deep enough into the earth to get a small flow of water moving across the top of the dam. Erosion would do the rest. [6]

This kind of thinking was not without precedent. During October General Patton's Third Army had faced a similar problem with a dam which impounded waters of the Etang de Lindre near Metz. The Etang de Lindre fed the Seille River, which ran through American lines. French engineers of the seventeenth century had built the dam as a cog in the defenses of Metz. In German hands this dam could have been used in much the same manner as it was feared the Roer River Dams might be employed, that is, to flood the Seille and isolate American units east of the river. But on 20 October two squadrons of P-47's had achieved a fifteen-yard breach in the dam and removed the threat. Though the dam on the Etang de Lindre was considerably smaller than the Schwammenauel, key dam in the Roer system, it was of earth construction like the Schwammenauel. [7]

The chief proponent of the scheme to bomb the Roer River Dams was the ground commander most directly concerned with eliminating the dams, General Hodges. At least as early as 18 November, the First Army commander began studying the dams with an eye toward air bombardment and on 22 November urged General Bradley to support the plan. [8] When the G-3 for Air at 12th Army Group passed the request to SHAEF, the air officers at Eisenhower's headquarters allotted the project to the Royal Air Force, which specialized in the kind of low-level, precision bombing that would be required. The successful RAF attack on the Moehne Dam in the Ruhr in 1943, for example, came readily to mind. Yet apparently after consulting with the RAF, SHAEF air officers the next day, 23 November, reported the proposal impracticable. On the other hand, the air officers agreed that if the 12th Army Group considered breaching the dams "of paramount importance," SHAEF Air would "reconsider the matter." [9]

---

[5] NUSA Opns, IV, Pt. II, 206.
[6] *Ibid.*

[7] See Cole, *The Lorraine Campaign*, pp. 295-96.
[8] Msg, 1545, 18 Nov 44, FUSA G-3 Tac file, Nov 44; Sylvan Diary entry of 22 Nov 44.
[9] Tel Convs, G-3 Air 12th A Gp, with G-3 Air NUSA, 22 and 23 Nov 44, NUSA G-3 Jnl file, 19-25 Nov 44.

A week later, on 30 November, General Hodges learned with immense satisfaction that the RAF had finally consented to try to blow the dams,[10] but his hopes that this would solve the problem were dashed during the next few days by unfavorable weather. On 30 November and the first two days of December, planned attacks against the dams had to be canceled because of the weather,[11] while on 3 December 190 aircraft made the flight over the dams but failed to attack, presumably because of poor visibility. The next day 200 aircraft flew over the target, but only 25 Lancasters and 3 Mosquitos actually attacked. Damage to the dams was discouragingly negligible. Another attack on 5 December was canceled because of poor visibility.[12]

On 5 December SHAEF took another look at the question of breaching the dams from the air. The commander of the Royal Air Force Bomber Command, Air Chief Marshal Sir Arthur T. Harris, objected to the project on the theory that irreplaceable personnel were being wasted in an effort foredoomed to failure. Yet so impressed by now with the importance of the target was the Supreme Commander, General Eisenhower, that he ordered the attacks to be pushed over all objections.[13]

Three days later, on 8 December, 205 aircraft dropped 797 tons of bombs on the Urft and Schwammenauel Dams and on the regulating dam between the two, the Paulushof. Though two hits were registered on the Urft and 18 on the Schwammenauel, neither dam was broken. Yet for all the frustration and negligible results involved thus far, the First Army commander, General Hodges, remained firm in his belief that the dams could be broken from the air. A thousand bombers a day, Hodges believed, "should be sent over until the dam is broken." [14]

After another three-day wait occasioned by the weather, 230 Lancasters again attacked the dams. Of these, 178 concentrated against the Urft with 1,065 tons of bombs; but results again were discouraging. The bombs cut the top of the dam at the south end, allowing some water to spill through, but not enough. Although the RAF consented to two more tries, on 13 and 14 December, weather again forced cancellation. The air effort had failed.[15]

Even while the air program continued, General Hodges, for all his insistence that the dams could be breached from the air, was making plans for a ground attack. Early in December he directed General Gerow's V Corps to seize the dams. General Gerow issued his field order for the attack on 7 December.[16] The target date was 13 December.

That the V Corps should make the attack to seize the dams was in keeping both with the geographical location of the corps and with the First Army's original

[10] Sylvan Diary, entry of 30 Nov 44; Msg from CG, FUSA, 30 Nov 44, FUSA G–3 Jnl file, Nov 44.

[11] Msg, CG NUSA, to CG FUSA, 30 Nov 44, FUSA G–3 Jnl file, Nov 44; Sylvan Diary, entries of 1 and 2 Dec 44.

[12] Sylvan Diary, entries of 3–5 Dec 44; Ltr, Bradley to Montgomery, 3 Dec 44, 12th A Gp Military Objectives, 371.3, III; NUSA Opns, pp. 207–08.

[13] NUSA Opns, pp. 207–08; Eisenhower to CCS, S–69334, 3 Dec 44, SHAEF SGS 381, II.

[14] Sylvan Diary, entry of 9 Dec 44. A detailed "first phase interpretation" of results of the 8 December strike may be found in VII Corps G–2 Per Rpt, 8 Dec 44, VII Corps G–2 file, Dec 44.

[15] NUSA Opns, pp. 207–08; Sylvan Diary, entries of 11, 13, and 14 Dec 44.

[16] V Corps FO 33, 7 Dec 44, V Corps G–3 Jnl file, 8 Dec 44.

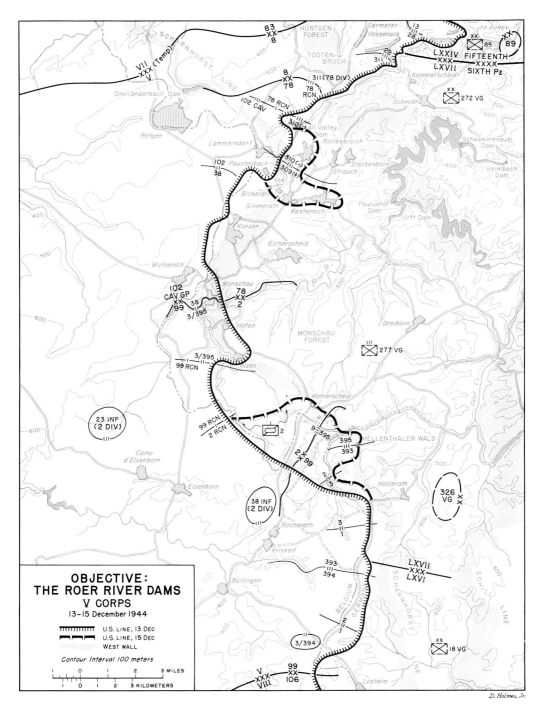

**OBJECTIVE:
THE ROER RIVER DAMS
V CORPS**
13–15 December 1944

⊥⊤⊤⊤⊤	U.S. LINE, 13 DEC
⊤⊤⊤	U.S. LINE, 15 DEC
	WEST WALL

Contour Interval 100 meters

3 MILES

3 KILOMETERS

MAP 9

D. Holmes, Jr.

broad plan for the November offensive. Holding a twenty-five-mile front from the Brandenberg–Bergstein ridge southwest, south, and southeast to a point beyond Camp d'Elsenborn, the V Corps was in a position to launch concentric attacks against the dams from three directions, from north, west, and southwest. (*Map 9*) Since General Hodges' order to the corps at the start of the November offensive had been to be prepared to drive northeast alongside the VII Corps to the Rhine at Bonn, a move to the dams would be a step in the right direction. The commitment of north-wing elements of the corps in late November to assist the VII Corps in clearing the Huertgen Forest and the Brandenberg–Bergstein ridge had in no way altered the original broad plan for the V Corps.

The terrain in front of the V Corps was as forbidding militarily as anything that had been encountered during the course of the Siegfried Line Campaign. Four good-size streams and numerous tributaries cut the sector into a complex quilt of sharply incised terrain compartments. Indeed, so precipitous are the hillsides and gorges in this region that terrain well may have been a major deterrent to earlier ground attack against the dams. A force moving against the dams from the north would have to cross the Kall River gorge and surmount the Kommerscheidt–Schmidt ridge, features already notorious as a result of the 28th Division's tragic experience in early November. Attacking from the west, troops would have to conquer two bands of pillbox defenses in the Monschau Corridor, which had stymied the overextended 9th Division in September. A force approaching the dams from the southwest would encounter another part of the West Wall secreted

within the Monschau Forest, a belt of woodland northeast of Camp d'Elsenborn, indistinguishable from the dreaded Huertgen Forest.

Strength available to General Gerow for the attack seemed more than sufficient, despite defensive responsibilities involved in his elongated front. In the north, the 8th Division, 2d Ranger Battalion, and CCR of the 5th Armored Division were putting the finishing touches to capture of the Brandenberg–Bergstein ridge and held a line southwest along the Kall River into the Huertgen Forest at Deadman's Moor (*Todten Bruch*). The 102d Cavalry Group and a regiment of the 1st Division, the latter only temporarily attached to the corps in a defensive role, faced the Monschau Corridor. From the Hoefen–Alzen ridge near Monschau southeast through the Monschau Forest to the corps right boundary, a new division, the 99th (Maj. Gen. Walter E. Lauer), held a "quiet sector" about twelve miles wide with a series of battalion and company strongpoints. Made available specifically for the attack was another new division, the 78th (Maj. Gen. Edwin P. Parker, Jr.), and the veteran 2d Division (Maj. Gen. Walter M. Robertson), which had been holding a portion of the inactive Ardennes front after having executed major assignments in Normandy and Brittany. A combat command of the inexperienced 9th Armored Division subsequently was attached as a corps reserve. Beyond normal divisional artillery, General Gerow possessed thirteen corps field artillery battalions of almost all calibers ranging as high as 8-inch and 240-mm. howitzers.[17]

---

[17] Unless otherwise noted, material at corps level is from V Corps Operations in the ETO, pp. 329–41.

In planning the corps maneuver, General Gerow decided to eschew the possibility of three concentric attacks at first in favor of a double envelopment by two divisions. The depleted condition of the 8th Division in the north, which might have formed a third prong, and the fact that the fighting for the Brandenberg–Bergstein ridge had drawn enemy strength to the north no doubt influenced this decision.

The north wing of the envelopment was to be formed by the 78th Division. Attacking through the Monschau Corridor, the 78th first was to clear the pillbox- and village-studded plateau which marks the start of the corridor, then to continue northeast along the Strauch–Schmidt highway through extremities of the Huertgen Forest to Schmidt. From Schmidt the 78th Division might come upon the Roer River Dams from the north.

In the meantime, the 2d Division, as primary component of the south wing of the envelopment, was to attack northward into the Monschau Forest from twin Belgian border villages of Krinkelt–Rocherath, southeast of Camp d'Elsenborn. The 2d Division first was to break a West Wall strongpoint at a road junction marked by a customshouse and a forester's lodge named Wahlerscheid, thence to fan out in two directions, northwest to clear resistance opposite the Hoefen–Alzen ridge between the Wahlerscheid road junction and Monschau, and northeast along a higher ridge line, the Dreiborn ridge, which leads to the Roer River Dams.[18] Perhaps in cognizance

of the tribulations exposed flanks had wrought in the Huertgen Forest, General Gerow directed that a regiment of the 99th Division make a limited objective attack within the Monschau Forest alongside the 2d Division's exposed right flank.

The German troops holding the Monschau Corridor and the Monschau Forest were part of the *LXVII Corps* (General der Infanterie Otto Hitzfeld), which had taken over the southern portion of the *LXXIV Corps* front under command of the *Sixth Panzer Army* in preparation for the Ardennes counteroffensive. The *LXVII Corps* sector covered some twenty miles from a point just south of Vossenack in the north to a point southeast of Camp d'Elsenborn in the south.[19]

The Monschau Corridor was the responsibility of the *272d Volks Grenadier Division* (commanded now by Generalleutnant Eugen Koenig). This division typified many of the problems the Germans faced in keeping units intact for the Ardennes counteroffensive. As the high command tried to do with all the new volks grenadier divisions, the *272d* had been assigned a quiet sector while awaiting the call for the counteroffensive, but the assignment could not last. When the V Corps took the Brandenberg–Bergstein ridge, thereby threatening to cross the Roer, the *272d*, then operating under the *LXXIV Corps*, had been the only unit at hand able to provide a force for counterattack. Having sent about two thirds of its infantry strength to Bergstein, the division would not get it back until 14

---

[18] In FO 33 General Gerow directed that the 2d Division first clear the sector opposite the Hoefen–Alzen ridge, then push northeast through Wahlerscheid along the Dreiborn ridge. The

plan was changed to that detailed above in a letter of instructions on 8 December (V Corps Operations in the ETO, p. 332), a logical step since seizure of Wahlerscheid would, in effect, outflank the Germans opposite the Hoefen–Alzen ridge.

[19] MSS # A–935, A–936, A–937 (Hitzfeld).

and 15 December, after heavy losses both at Bergstein and while helping deny the southwestern approaches to Dueren. As the Americans prepared to attack in the Monschau Corridor, the 272d was getting ready to regroup as the northernmost element of the *Sixth Panzer Army* and to participate in the counteroffensive.[20]

The Hoefen–Alzen ridge and the Monschau Forest were defended by the *277th Volks Grenadier Division,* which also was awaiting Ardennes action. Though the 277th had been spared active commitment in the November fighting, its regiments were overextended after having been called on at intervals to extend their boundaries northward so that the greater concentration might be achieved in the Huertgen Forest.[21]

The impending participation of both the *272d* and *277th Divisions* in the Ardennes counteroffensive was indicative of the state of flux affecting almost the entire front of the *LXVII Corps* at this stage in December. The target date for the counteroffensive was only three days away. On 13 December the *85th Infantry Division,* a depleted unit from Holland, was to begin relief of that part of the *272d Division* near Bergstein and the entire *89th Infantry Division* in the vicinity of Vossenack, so that the latter might be shored up for the counteroffensive.[22]

Like the Germans, but on a smaller scale, the V Corps took extraordinary precautions to maintain secrecy for the first blow, even to removing shoulder-patch insignia and obliterating unit ve-

---

[20] The movements of this and other divisions may be traced in Luttichau, Progressive Build-up and Operations.

[21] ETHINT–57 (Gersdorff).

[22] *Ibid.*

hicular markings. Not until the night of 11 December did the 78th Division relieve those troops which had been holding the face of the Monschau Corridor. Not until the very eve of the attack, in a blinding snowstorm, did the 2d Division arrive in assembly areas near Camp d'Elsenborn. On the assumption that secrecy had been preserved, none other than normal artillery fires were to precede the first blow.

The Second Battle of the Monschau Corridor

The leaves had been still on the trees when in September a regiment of the 9th Division first had tried to break the two bands of West Wall pillboxes in the Monschau Corridor. As the 78th Division prepared to attack across the same high plateau almost three months later, roads were icy and snow concealed many of the scars of the earlier fight. Here as much as anywhere the slow pace of the Siegfried Line Campaign was markedly evident.

In the 78th Division's first combat action, only two regiments were available, for General Gerow had directed that the third shore up the adjacent 8th Division, in poor shape after gaining the Brandenberg–Bergstein ridge. The 78th Division's commander, General Parker, ordered both remaining regiments to participate from the first. On the north, the 310th Infantry was to send a battalion from Lammersdorf east to Rollesbroich, while the 309th Infantry, close alongside, was to move two battalions southeast from Hill 554 at Paustenbach to take first the village of Bickerath, then Simmerath. These two objectives in hand, the 309th Infantry was to mount part of a third battalion on attached tanks to seize Kesternich, the next village to the east.

These four villages—Rollesbroich, Bickerath, Simmerath, and Kesternich—represented the heart of the positions remaining to the enemy on the high plateau. Once these were taken, the 309th Infantry and an attached battalion of the 310th were to turn south and southwest to sweep that part of the plateau lying between Simmerath and the upper reaches of the Roer near Monschau. In the meantime, the 310th Infantry was to prepare to renew the assault from Rollesbroich to take two more villages, Strauch and Steckenborn, which guard the main highway running northeast from the plateau to Schmidt.[23]

As men of the 78th Division moved to the attack before day on 13 December, a soupy fog aided concealment. Under radio silence and without artillery preparation, they advanced almost without sound except for low-voiced orders and the crunch of snow underfoot. The early morning darkness was bitterly cold.

One man stepped on a mine. Germans in a pillbox fired sporadically, then surrendered on the pretext that they had exhausted their ammunition. German riflemen fired at isolated points along the line, but all in all the defense was half-hearted. A battalion of the 310th Infantry (Col. Earl M. Miner) had a firm foothold soon after daylight on a steep knoll overlooking Rollesbroich. Before noon the battalion was in the village, dealing with isolated resistance while dodging increasing shellfire as the enemy came to life.

On the division's south wing, the story was much the same. Before noon one battalion of the 309th Infantry turned back the lower lip of the penetration by taking Bickerath, though mine fields and interlocking fire from pillboxes denied egress to higher ground south of the village. Despite mine fields and a stubborn strongpoint in a hamlet north of Simmerath, another battalion of the 309th Infantry gained Simmerath shortly after midday.

The first objectives in hand, the 309th Infantry commander, Col. John G. Ondrick, mounted a company of his remaining battalion on attached tanks of the 709th Tank Battalion and sent them beyond Simmerath to Kesternich. Only this time the enemy's machine gunners and mortarmen, the latter occupying defilade in deep draws beyond Kesternich, were fully alert. The tanks bogged in the soft mud while rounds from German antitank guns cut ugly black patches in the snow about them. Though the infantrymen dismounted and fought forward alone, it took them all afternoon to gain the first houses of Kesternich. Because they were but one company, they hesitated to get involved in the sprawling village after dark. The rest of this company's parent battalion either had been held up by shellfire or had become involved with pillboxes off to the flanks.

Though Kesternich remained out of reach, troops of the 78th Division on the night of 13 December could be encouraged by the results of their first day's fight. They had lost 238 men in their first day of battle,[24] yet this was hardly surprising for a first fight, particularly when they had gained all initial objectives

---

[23] 78th Div FO 1, 11 Dec 44, G–3 Jnl file, 11 Dec 44. The story of this division is based upon official unit records and an accurate unit history, titled, after the division's nickname, *Lightning* (Washington: Infantry Journal Press, 1947).

[24] 78th Div AAR, Dec 44.

and had registered advances up to a mile and a half. As expected, they had encountered the enemy's *272d Volks Grenadier Division*. Their achievement of surprise against this force had been underscored by absence of counterattack all day.

On the other hand, as the day had worn on, resistance had stiffened like a coil spring under compression. This was emphasized by the fact that in almost all instances the Americans controlled only the villages and not the pillbox-studded ground nearby, some of it commanding ground. The bulk of the two regiments would require most of the next two days for mop-up and consolidation. As others had learned from bitter experience, men of the 78th Division discovered early that the Germans were great ones for infiltrating back into captured pillboxes and villages. Not only that, the snow and cold turned the limited action into a battle for self-preservation. The insidious enemy called Trench Foot was quick to put in an appearance.

While the bulk of the two regiments consolidated, the critical fight took place at the village of Kesternich. Here the 309th Infantry commander, Colonel Ondrick, directed renewed attack on 14 December by two battalions—his 2d Battalion, which had tried to get into the village on the first day, and the 2d Battalion, 310th Infantry, attached to the 309th.

First one, then the other, of these battalions essayed the German strongpoint. Attacking from the northwest, the 2d Battalion, 309th Infantry, failed even to regain the first houses which one company had held briefly the night before. German mortars and artillery pieces in the draws beyond Kesternich were particu-

larly troublesome. Attacking from the west, the 2d Battalion, 310th Infantry, encountered much the same resistance. A platoon of accompanying tanks withdrew after antitank fire knocked out the lead vehicle. Though the infantry persisted alone and at last gained the first houses, here the Germans stood and increased their fire. Again as night came the Americans were forced to withdraw.

Apparent antidote for the German shelling was not lacking, for the 78th Division was well fixed with artillery support. In addition to normal divisional artillery and corps guns in general support, the corps commander had attached to the division two battalions of 105-mm. howitzers (one self-propelled) and the bulk of a battalion of self-propelled 155-mm. guns.[25] Nor was the artillery slothful in responding to requests for fire. At one point eight battalions of divisional and corps artillery massed their fires on the draws beyond Kesternich. Afterward, the infantry could hear screams of German wounded, but the mortars were ready to cough again when the attack was renewed.[26]

During the night artillerymen laid detailed plans for a concentrated fifteen-minute barrage against Kesternich the next morning. Guns of the 709th Tank and 893d Tank Destroyer Battalions were to add their fire, as were the infantry weapons of the 2d Battalion, 309th Infantry, northwest of the village. The assault role fell to the 2d Battalion, 310th Infantry.

At 0700 men of the 310th Infantry attacked under a noisy curtain of shellfire.

---

[25] Annex 6, 8 Dec 44, to V Corps FO 33, and Changes to Annex 6, 11 Dec 44, both in V Corps Operations in the ETO, pp. 332–33.

[26] *Lightning*, p. 51.

MEN OF THE 2D DIVISION *move through the Monschau Forest.*

For all the fire support, advance was a dogged proposition. Nevertheless, by noon, Company E had bypassed a giant pillbox to break into the objective. Hugging the buildings alongside the streets to avoid grazing fire of German machine guns, men of this company pushed quickly through the village. Mop-up they left to others who were to follow.

By 1300 Company E had gained the eastern edge of Kesternich. Hardly had the men dug in when a battalion of the *272d Division*'s *980th Regiment* counterattacked. Though Company E repulsed the enemy with timely help from supporting artillery, only a shell of the original company remained when the action subsided. In the meantime another company had dug in south of Kesternich, while a third tried to clean out the houses. Though the job was complete as night came, the condition of the 2d Battalion, 310th Infantry, left much to be desired. No rifle company could muster more than forty men.

Shortly after midnight the battalion of the *980th Regiment* came back. This time the Germans penetrated the village by exploiting gaps between the American companies. "Grey figures were all about, firing burp guns, throwing grenades." [27] Communications to the rear went out. Patrols sent from other units to reach the battalion returned with no information.

The situation in Kesternich obviously was serious. Nor was there occasion for

---

[27] *Ibid.,* p. 55.

complacency elsewhere, for in three days these two regiments of the 78th Division had lost almost a thousand men, 358 nonbattle casualties—mostly victims of trench foot—and 609 battle casualties. These losses left gaps in the line that looked more and more disturbing when after nightfall on 15 December prisoner identifications revealed the presence nearby of a new, presumably fresh German unit, the *326th Volks Grenadier Division.* This was but the first in a series of ominous developments that were to occur with increasing frequency the next day, 16 December.

Heartbreak Crossroads

If these events on the north wing of the projected double envelopment ran a minor gamut of military experience—from early success at Rollesbroich, Simmerath, and Bickerath to apparent setback at Kesternich—those on the south wing during the same three days were remarkably unvaried. Here, in the Monschau Forest approximately eight miles south and southeast of the Monschau Corridor, the 2d Division and a regiment of the 99th Division experienced three days of monotonous frustration.

Aiming first at the Wahlerscheid road junction, the West Wall strongpoint deep within the forest at the meeting point of the Hoefen–Alzen and Dreiborn ridges, the 2d Division had but one road leading to the first objective. This was a secondary highway running north through the forest into Germany from the twin Belgian villages of Krinkelt-Rocherath. Faced with this restriction, the division commander, General Robertson, had little choice of formation for the first leg of the attack other than regiments in column.

He directed the 9th Infantry (Col. Chester J. Hirschfelder) to attack astride the road, take the Wahlerscheid road junction, then swing northwest to clear those Germans opposite the Hoefen–Alzen ridge. Following in column as far as Wahlerscheid, the 38th Infantry (Col. Francis H. Boos) was to be committed northeast from the road junction along the Dreiborn ridge in the direction of the Roer River Dams. The 23d Infantry in division reserve was to remain near Camp d'Elsenborn.[28]

That part of the Monschau Forest through which the 9th Infantry first was to push was a kind of no man's land of snow-covered firs, hostile patrols, mines, and roadblocks. Though the sector belonged within the 99th Division's defensive responsibilities, that division held such an elongated front that defense of some parts had been left more to patrols than to fixed positions. Not for several miles on either side of the forest-cloaked road to Wahlerscheid were there any friendly positions in strength. The gap on the right of the road was of particular concern because the southeastward curve of the 99th Division's line left the sector open to enemy penetration from the east. Approaching along forest trails, the Germans might sever the 2d Division's lifeline, the lone highway to Wahlerscheid.

---

[28] 2d Div FO 12, 10 Dec, in 2d Div G–3 Jnl file, Bk 2, Incl 3, Dec 44. The 2d Division records are in general excellent, including a valuable G–3 message file. A unit history entitled *Combat History of the Second Infantry Division in World War II* (Baton Rouge: Army and Navy Publishing Company, 1946) is not always accurate. One of the Army's more famous regular units, the 2d Division had come ashore on D plus 1 in Normandy and fought with distinction in the push to St. Lô, then at Brest. The division's nickname of Indianhead stemmed from its shoulder patch.

This threat had been what had prompted General Gerow to order a limited objective attack by a regiment of the 99th Division close alongside the 2d Division's right flank. The assignment fell to the 395th Infantry under Col. A. J. Mackenzie. Since one of Colonel Mackenzie's battalions still was defending the Hoefen–Alzen ridge, the division commander, General Lauer, attached to the regiment a battalion of the neighboring 393d Infantry. On D Day the three battalions were to attack to occupy wooded high ground about a mile and a half southeast of Wahlerscheid around the juncture of the Wies and Olef Creeks in a portion of the forest known as the Hellenthaler Wald. General Lauer himself added to the assignment by directing another battalion of the 393d Infantry to seize a hill off the battalion's left flank which provided the enemy a choice location for enfilading fire.

Because the forested no man's land between Krinkelt–Rocherath and Wahlerscheid was some three miles deep, obtaining accurate intelligence information before the attack was difficult. About all the 2d Division knew was that the strongpoint at Wahlerscheid was held by troops of the *277th Volks Grenadier Division*'s *991st Regiment*. Any real estimate of enemy strength at Wahlerscheid or any pinpoint locations of German pillboxes and other positions were missing. This situation made it particularly difficult to plan artillery fires in support of the attack.[29] The artillery tried to solve the problem by plotting checkpoint concentrations by map, which might be shifted on call from infantry and forward observers as trouble developed. The fact that no

preparation was to precede the attack also alleviated the problem of unspecific targets.

Looking upon the 2d Division's attack as the main effort of the corps maneuver, the corps commander had provided strong fire support. Attached to the 2d Division was a battalion of 105-mm. howitzers, another of 4.5-inch rockets, a battery of 155-mm. self-propelled guns, a company of chemical mortars, the usual medium tank battalion, and two battalions of tank destroyers, one self-propelled. In addition, the 406th Field Artillery Group with four battalions of field pieces of 155-mm. caliber or larger was to reinforce the division's fires. The corps reserve—CCB, 9th Armored Division—was attached for possible exploitation of a breakthrough, so that the organic artillery of this combat command also was available. Artillery of the 99th Division was reinforced with a battery of 155-mm. guns.

The Monschau Forest was almost uncannily silent as troops of the 9th Infantry moved forward on foot in approach march formation an hour after daylight on 13 December. Because the highway was known to be mined, the men had to plow through underbrush and snow drifts on either side. When a partial thaw set in, branches of fir trees heavy with snow dumped their wet loads upon the men beneath them. In some ravines the ground was so marshy that icy water oozed over the tops of the men's overshoes. "A most taxing march," someone noted later.[30] It would have been taxing even without usual combat impedimenta, and these men were carrying more than the norm. So impressed had been their

---

[29] See 2d Div Arty AAR, Dec 44.

[30] 9th Inf AAR, Dec 44.

commanders with the misfortunes of the 28th Division when depending upon but one supply road at Schmidt that they had ordered the men to carry enough rations, ammunition, and antitank mines to last for at least twenty-four hours without resupply.

At 1240 the column neared the clearing about the Wahlerscheid road junction. "Both battalions have dropped packs," Colonel Hirschfelder reported; "contact imminent." [31] Though occasional mortar and artillery fire had struck the column en route, Colonel Hirschfelder nourished the hope that the forest had concealed the size of his force, that the Germans anticipated approach of no more than patrols. Still hoping to achieve surprise, he ordered assault against Wahlerscheid by two battalions abreast without artillery preparation.

The 9th Infantry faced a formidable position that in some respects possessed the strength of a small fortress. Grouped compactly about the road junction and sited to provide interlocking fires were machine gun and rifle positions in and about four pillboxes, six concrete bunkers, a forester's lodge, and a custom house. The forest and deep ravines formed a kind of moat around the entire position. Where trees and underbrush had encroached upon fields of fire, the Germans had cut them away. In some places rows of barbed wire entanglements stood six to ten deep. The snow hid a veritable quilt of lethal antipersonnel mines.

It took only a matter of minutes after the attack began for Colonel Hirschfelder to determine that his hope of surprise was empty. The road junction bristled with fire. Mortar and artillery shells burst in

the treetops. Exploding mines brought down man after man. One after another, eight men whose job was to clear a narrow path for the 1st Battalion were killed or seriously wounded by mines. Bangalore torpedoes set beneath the barbed wire failed to ignite because fuzes were wet. One platoon of the 2d Battalion nevertheless pressed through five aprons of barbed wire before enemy fire at last forced a halt; yet several more aprons of unbreached wire lay ahead.

As night came the weather turned colder. Drenched to the skin, the men were miserable. Their clothing froze stiff. Through the night they tried to keep warm by painfully etching some form of foxhole or slit trench in the frozen earth.

In the woods southeast of Wahlerscheid, experience of the 99th Division's 395th Infantry roughly paralleled that of the 9th Infantry. Moving northeast through the forest in a column of battalions to protect the 9th Infantry's right flank, the 395th Infantry soon after noon struck a line of log bunkers deep in the woods near the juncture of the two streams that split the high ground the regiment sought to gain. Not a dent had been made in this position when night came. Like the men at Wahlerscheid, those deep in the forest set to work trying to scoop some measure of protection from the frozen ground.[32]

When a misty, viscous daylight came at Wahlerscheid the next morning, 14 December, American artillery began a systematic effort to soften the German

---

[31] 2d Div G-3 Msg file, 13 Dec 44.

[32] 395th Inf AAR, Dec 44. See also other official 99th Division records and a unit history, Maj. Gen. Walter E. Lauer, *Battle Babies* (Baton Rouge: Military Press of Louisiana, Inc., 1951). From its shoulder patch, the 99th was known as the Checkerboard Division.

positions as a prelude to a fifteen-minute preparation for a new assault in midmorning. Although Colonel Hirschfelder asked for air attack as well, poor visibility was to deny close support from the air throughout the Wahlerscheid operation. Even assistance from the artillery was not as effective as usual because of difficulties in registration attributable to the dense forest, clinging fog, and concomitant lack of specific information on enemy positions and batteries. In at least one instance on 14 December, artillery fires fell short upon troops of the 9th Infantry.

Repeated attempts to assault and to outflank the Wahlerscheid position through the day of 14 December ended in failure. This prompted a directive from the division commander that set the tone for conduct of the next day's operation. "Base future operations," General Robertson said, "on thorough reconnaissance, infiltration, and finesse. Get deliberate picture, then act." [33]

During the afternoon, Colonel Hirschfelder pulled back his battalions several hundred yards into the forest to provide his artillery a clear field. Throughout the night, patrols probed for gaps in the mine fields and for passage through the barbed wire obstacles. The next day, big corps guns began a bombardment. An attached battery of 155-mm. self-propelled guns inched up the lone highway through the forest to pour direct fire against the concrete fortifications. Expending 287 rounds, crews of the big guns claimed penetration of three pillboxes, though later investigation revealed no material damage.[34]

As darkness fell on 15 December, the 2d Division after three days of attack

could point to no gain against the Wahlerscheid strongpoint. Though the adjacent 395th Infantry had achieved considerably more success in the pillbox belt southeast of the road junction, this was a subsidiary action geared in pace to the attack at Wahlerscheid and offered no real possibility of exploitation to assist the main attack. Both regiments had incurred heavy losses, as much from the cruel elements as from enemy action. Of 737 casualties within the 9th Infantry during these three days, almost 400 were attributable to nonbattle causes.

All might have been gloom that third night except for one thin hope which stirred one of the battalion commanders, Lt. Col. Walter M. Higgins, Jr. During the afternoon of the second day of attack, 14 December, a squad of Company G had slithered under one another of the enemy's barbed wire entanglements until all were behind. Another squad had cut the wire so that a narrow four-foot gap existed. Yet neither squad had been in communication with the company headquarters; furthermore, their company commander had been wounded and evacuated. As a result, news of the breach had not reached the battalion commander, Colonel Higgins, until long after both squads had withdrawn. When the next night came and the 9th Infantry was as far as ever from cracking the defense of Wahlerscheid, Colonel Higgins saw an outside chance to exploit the narrow gap the two squads had forged the day before.

Soon after dark on 15 December Higgins sent an eleven-man patrol equipped with sound-powered telephone to pass through the gap and report on German strength and alertness. Though wandering errantly until joined by one of the

[33] 2d Div G–3 Msg file, 14 Dec 44.
[34] Ibid., 15 Dec 44, and 9th Inf AAR.

men who had cut the wire the day before, the patrol at 2130 reported an electrifying development. We have surrounded a pillbox, the word came back. The Germans apparently were unaware that anything was afoot.

That was all Colonel Higgins was waiting for. Within a matter of minutes Company F was plodding single file through the gap in the wire. Higgins himself followed with Company E and took such an active part in the fighting that he subsequently was awarded the Distinguished Service Cross. By midnight the 2d Battalion held a substantial bridgehead within the Wahlerscheid strongpoint and another battalion was filing silently through the gap. One battalion swung northwest, the other northeast. From one position to another, the men moved swiftly, blowing the doors of pillboxes with beehive charges, killing or capturing the occupants, prodding sleepy Germans from foxholes, and capturing seventy-seven at one blow at the customshouse. Two hours after daylight on 16 December even mop-up was completed, and the 38th Infantry already was moving forward to pass through the 9th Infantry's positions and push northeastward along the Dreiborn ridge toward the Roer River Dams. The facility with which the 9th Infantry in the end had conquered Wahlerscheid was apparent from the regiment's casualty list for 16 December: 1 man killed, 1 missing, 17 wounded.

In no small way was the local success attributable to the enemy's preoccupation with his winter counteroffensive, for prior assignments in the counteroffensive had made it necessary to garrison Wahlerscheid on a catch-as-catch-can basis. The *326th Volks Grenadier Division,* scheduled to attack in the counteroffensive under juris-

diction of the *Sixth Panzer Army*'s *LXVII Corps,* had begun to relieve the *277th Volks Grenadier Division* during the night of 14 December. The *277th* then had begun to shift southward to attack under the *Sixth Panzer Army*'s *I SS Panzer Corps.*

The unit which took over at Wahlerscheid was a battalion of the *326th Division*'s *751st Regiment.* The unfamiliarity of this battalion with the defensive positions was invitation enough to loss of the strongpoint, but the Germans had compounded it during the night of 15 December even as Colonel Higgins' men were filing through the gap in the wire. So that the *751st Regiment* might move along to its assigned role in the counteroffensive, the Germans had been replacing the battalion at Wahlerscheid with the *326th Division*'s field replacement battalion. Caught in the process of relief, both units were ripe for annihilation.[35]

The Wahlerscheid road junction firmly in hand, General Robertson and others of the 2d Division now might give greater attention to other developments that, when dwelt upon, had disturbing connotations. Beginning two hours before daylight on 16 December, German artillery fire had been increasing with an ominous persistence. Counterbattery fire was particularly heavy. At 0747 the 99th Division reported a slight penetration between two companies of the 393d Infantry. There also was an attack against the 394th Infantry, "using searchlights." "The strength is unknown," the 99th Division reported. "We are out of communications."[36]

---

[35] This material from 2d Div G–2 Per Rpts, Dec 44, and Luttichau, Progressive Build-up and Operations.

[36] 2d Div G–3 Msg file, 16 Dec 44.

Something was in the air. Something disturbing. Perhaps something big. In little more than twenty-four hours after capturing the Wahlerscheid road junction, troops of the 9th Infantry would have a new name for it. They would come to know Wahlerscheid as Heartbreak Crossroads.

Something in the Air

That something was astir was apparent at several points along the V Corps front. In three places, at Wahlerscheid, in the Monschau Corridor, and on the Hoefen–Alzen ridge, identification had been made of the *326th Volks Grenadier Division*. Indeed, the attack reported in early morning "in unknown strength" against the 395th Infantry was by a battalion of the *326th Division* on the Hoefen–Alzen ridge. Though beaten back, this attack when viewed in the context of other blows along other portions of the 99th Division's elongated front prompted concern. By midmorning of 16 December the enemy had hit every regiment of the 99th Division, and in some cases the situation still was fluid. The unusual enemy tactic of using searchlights for illumination might have been construed to mean something special was in the offing.

Full portent of these developments still was not appreciated, though all division commanders began to take precautions. General Lauer of the 99th Division, who had virtually no reserves, shifted his units to provide a company here and there to reinforce threatened sectors. General Robertson of the 2d sent medium tanks to Wahlerscheid to back up his infantry in the continuing attack up the Dreiborn ridge. General Parker of the 78th re-

leased a battalion from Simmerath to go to the aid of those of his men who had been isolated the preceding night in Kesternich. Presumably at the instigation of the First Army and in light of recurring reports of serious attacks farther south against the adjacent VIII Corps, General Gerow at 1037 ordered the 9th Armored Division's CCB relieved from attachment to the 2d Division and sent south to reinforce the VIII Corps.[37]

By noon on 16 December concern about the attacks against the 99th Division was growing by the minute. In the name of the corps commander, the V Corps G–3, Colonel Hill, directed the 2d Division commander, General Robertson, to place a battalion each of tanks and infantry at the disposal of the 99th Division "if the situation . . . was such as to demand such action." Not long after, Robertson sent Lauer a battalion of his reserve regiment. General Gerow, in the meantime, attached the 2d Ranger Battalion to the 78th Division to assist in the Monschau Corridor. At 1950 Robertson gave Lauer another battalion of his reserve. "Speed is essential," General Robertson told the regimental commander, "and for God's sake get those trucks married up, and the tanks and TDs are to follow."[38]

Before daylight on 17 December, a flight of JU–52's disgorged about 200 German paratroopers in rear of the 78th Division's positions. The day was only beginning when a German armored column approached the village of Buellingen, near Krinkelt-Rocherath, where some of the 2d Division's service and engineer units had set up shop. At 0730 the 99th

---

[37] 2d Div G–3 Msg file, 16 Dec 44.
[38] *Ibid.*, and 99th Div AAR, Dec 44.

Division began moving its command post a few miles to the rear. At 0800 enemy tanks and half-tracks appeared on a ridge overlooking the 2d Division's command post and artillery installations. At 1015 General Robertson alerted his 9th and 38th Infantry Regiments near Wahlerscheid to be prepared to disengage and withdraw to Krinkelt-Rocherath. General Lauer did the same for his 395th Infantry. The integrity of these three units obviously was threatened. By seizing Buellingen, the enemy already had severed the main supply route but at a point where several secondary roads provided passage. If the twin villages of Krinkelt-Rocherath could be held and the road through the Monschau Forest maintained, then withdrawal still might be accomplished. By noon on 17 December the 9th and 38th had begun to pull back, and in late afternoon the 395th Infantry also had begun to withdraw.

The first ground attack to be aimed specifically at the Roer River Dams was over, cut short by the winter counteroffensive. By nightfall on 15 December, before first manifestations of the counteroffensive began to appear, the attack against the Roer River Dams had cost the V Corps approximately 2,500 men.[39] Almost half were nonbattle casualties. Losses of the 8th Division would raise the total figure by a thousand; for simply in mopping up and consolidating after conclusion of the fight for the Brandenberg–Bergstein ridge, the 8th Division had incurred as many losses as had either the 2d or 78th Division in their full-scale attacks.

The VIII Corps in the Ardennes–Eifel

The other part of the Allied front directly involved at the start of the counteroffensive was that held by the VIII U.S. Corps, south of the V Corps zone, in the Ardennes–Eifel region. This was the front eventually embracing eighty-eight miles which the VIII Corps had taken over from the V Corps in early October upon conclusion of the campaign in Brittany. The V Corps in turn had shifted northward in the First Army's attempt to achieve greater concentration near Aachen.

The VIII Corps front in the Ardennes was at once the nursery and the old folks' home of the American command. To this sector came new divisions to acquire their first taste of combat under relatively favorable conditions. Here too came old divisions licking their wounds from costly fighting like the Brittany peninsula and the Huertgen Forest.

The front ran from Losheim, between Camp d'Elsenborn and the northern end of the Schnee Eifel, southward generally along the Belgian and Luxembourgian borders with Germany. Eventually it stretched all the way to the southeastern corner of Luxembourg. It extended into Germany at two points: along the Schnee Eifel, where the 4th Division in September had pierced a thin sector of the West Wall, and near Uettfeld, where the 28th Division had driven a salient into the West Wall. The mission of the VIII Corps was to defend the long front in place, deceive the enemy by active patrolling, and make general plans and preparations for attacking to the Rhine.[40]

---

[39] Casualty figures from V Corps AAR, Dec 44, are for the period 8–15 Dec.

[40] VIII Corps AAR, Oct–Dec 44. This section is based primarily upon the corps and division AARs for the period.

GENERAL MIDDLETON

General Middleton's VIII Corps at first was under the Ninth Army and controlled but two divisions, the 2d and 8th. The front at this time was approximately fifty miles long, sufficient to tax the two divisions severely.[41] On 11 October the 83d Division was transferred from the Third Army to the VIII Corps but brought with it responsibility for the entire southern half of Luxembourg, thus enabling no shortening of the lines of the other divisions. The corps front then embraced about eighty-eight miles.

Arrival of the inexperienced 9th Armored Division to join the corps on 20 October did little to reduce frontages, for Middleton felt impelled to hold this force as a corps reserve. Some relief was af-

[41] An infantry battalion from each division had been left in France to guard communications lines.

forded on this date by attachment of the 14th Cavalry Group with two squadrons, the 18th and 32d. Middleton attached one squadron to the 2d Division, the other to the 83d, each to screen a gap in the line, one of which was five miles long.

Holding the line in the Ardennes was not always the cinch it might have appeared to a casual observer. It was true that the men enjoyed a few amenities usually denied in more active sectors: comparatively low casualties, more frequent visits to shower points and to division and corps rest centers, hot food for most meals, and bunker-type squad huts, dugouts, or cellars instead of foxholes to sleep in. It was also true that the Germans on the other side of the line were for the most part content to emulate the Americans in keeping the sector relatively quiescent. As soon as the panzer and SS panzer divisions which had fought here in September could be replaced, the Germans manned the line with low-rated infantry divisions as widely stretched in their defensive positions as were the American units.

Yet it was also true that some portions of the long line were perennial hot spots, and any point—even behind the lines, where German patrols often threaded their way past scattered outposts—might erupt at any time in violent little actions that were real and terrifying to the men involved in them. The 83d Division in November, for example, lost 201 men as battle casualties, including 25 killed, and 550 to nonbattle causes. The 2d Division's 23d Infantry, occupying terrain near Uettfeld where a flame-throwing half-track had awed men of the 28th Division's 110th Infantry in September, was subjected to frequent and costly shelling and several night attacks, sometimes in strength as great as two companies. There was no relief until the battalions finally blew up the West Wall pillboxes in an intricately planned and timed maneuver and withdrew on 2 November to positions of their own choosing a mile to the rear. Though the new positions contained gaps between companies sometimes greater than a mile, the withdrawal enabled General Robertson to withhold a battalion in reserve, thereby permitting gradual rotation of front-line units.

The corps commander, General Middleton, used the armored infantry of the 9th Armored Division to relieve battalions of other divisions temporarily, both to give the old units some rest and the new ones some battle experience. The bulk of the armored division's artillery backed up the 83d Division on the corps south wing.

The men were not idle. You might not have to attack, but still you had to stand watch in mud that even duckboards in the bottom of foxholes did not eliminate entirely. You had to buck the wet, cold winds of the Ardennes heights. You had to fight trench foot. You had to patrol. You also had to keep improving your defenses constantly, stringing barbed wire, laying mine fields, roofing and sandbagging foxholes and squad huts, foraging for stoves, lanterns, fuel—these and myriad other tasks.

On 20 October, the 83d Division staged simultaneous river crossing demonstrations at three points along the Sauer and Moselle Rivers, hoping to draw fire that would reveal enemy gun positions. It was partially effective. The 2d Division on the anniversary of the World War I armistice demonstrated by fire but evoked hardly a shot in return. In early December, the VIII Corps at the direction of the First Army used headquarters of the

23d Special Troops to imitate a build-up of strength in hope of drawing enemy units from the Aachen sector. Using the name, shoulder patches, and vehicular markings of the 75th Division, not yet committed to action, the special troops simulated arrival of the division by occupying billets, command posts, and assembly areas, employing vehicular sound effects, and executing fictitious radio and telephonic traffic. For a time this activity was reflected on German intelligence maps by a question mark, but the Germans soon became satisfied that no new division existed.[42]

For all the violence of the Ardennes terrain and for all the width of the division zones—sometimes as much as twenty-five miles for one division—the four divisions which made up the VIII Corps through October and much of November might have been a genuinely effective stumbling block to the counteroffensive had they still occupied the line. They were here for a long time, came to know the weak and the strong points of the terrain, organized their defenses with thoroughness and adroitness, and prepared elaborate but workable withdrawal and counterattack plans. Yet not one of the infantry divisions and only part of the armored division was on hand when the Germans struck. They had been replaced by two badly spent divisions from the Huertgen Forest and another fresh from the United States.

On 19 November the 8th Division relinquished its zone to the 28th Division, a unit needing some 3,400 replacements. The 83d Division on 7 December gave

---

[42] See H. M. Cole, The Ardennes: Battle of the Bulge, a volume in preparation for the series UNITED STATES ARMY IN WORLD WAR II.

way to the 4th, which required as many or more replacements than the 28th. On 11 December the 2d Division moved to the Roer River Dams attack, making room for the green 106th Division. A combat command of the 9th Armored Division shifted coincidentally to provide a reserve for the V Corps. This was the situation when the Germans came out of the mists on 16 December.

CHAPTER XXVII

The End of the Campaign

In the fact that the Germans and not the Allies wrote the end to the Siegfried Line Campaign rests a capsule summation of the entire campaign. Though the Germans never held the initiative, they more than the Allies had controlled the outcome. They had fought a large-scale delaying action with meager resources while at the same time building up a striking force to be used in the Ardennes. Although American patrols had crossed the border on 11 September, the deepest penetration into Germany ninety-six days later was only twenty-two miles inside the frontier. (*Map IX*)

This was not, of course, the whole story. While the First and Ninth Armies had fought in the Huertgen Forest and on the Roer plain, the Canadians had opened Antwerp, and the British, with the help of the First Allied Airborne Army, had cleared the Netherlands south and west of the Maas River. In the south the Third Army had conquered Lorraine and reached the West Wall along the Saar River, while the 6th Army Group had occupied almost all the west bank of the upper Rhine except for a big pocket hinged on the city of Colmar. The Allies had accomplished these things while fighting not only the Germans but the elements and an acute logistical crisis as well. In the process they had so occupied their adversary that Hitler's field commanders had begged their Fuehrer to scale down his grandiose scheme for a counteroffensive.

Of the German divisions in the Aachen sector scheduled to participate in the counteroffensive, only one, the *10th SS Panzer Division,* failed to make it; but this was hardly a true measure of the effect of the autumn fighting on the counteroffensive. The Siegfried Line Campaign had cost the Germans thousands of individual replacements who might have fought in the Ardennes, and it had worn out many of the divisions upon which Rundstedt was counting. In the Aachen sector alone, at least five panzer or panzer-type divisions had been reduced severely in strength and their rehabilitation dangerously delayed. One parachute and at least six volks grenadier divisions, the latter originally scheduled to have been spared active commitment before the counteroffensive, had been similarly affected. The Siegfried Line fighting also delayed use in the Ardennes of two corps headquarters and two assault gun brigades.

Although any attempt to fix German losses on a numerical basis would be little better than a guess, personnel losses obviously were high. This is evident from the fact that at least 95,000 prisoners passed through First and Ninth Army cages during the Siegfried Line Campaign.[1] German tank losses probably were considerably below American losses primarily because the Germans employed far fewer tanks. The First Army alone from 1 September to 16 December lost approximately 550 medium tanks. Entering the line in late September, the Ninth Army lost approximately a hundred.[2]

The First Army incurred 47,039 battle casualties during the Siegfried Line Campaign. This was approximately half the number of German prisoners taken.

Killed 7,024
Wounded 35,155
Missing and Captured 4,860

The Ninth Army's battle losses totaled approximately 10,000.

Killed 1,133
Wounded 6,864
Missing and Captured 2,059

American units serving under British and Canadian command during the campaign incurred approximately 11,000 casualties, bringing total American losses to approximately 68,000.[3] To this figure should be added the number of so-called nonbattle casualties—those evacuated be-

cause of fatigue, exposure, accidents, and disease. The First Army incurred 50,867 nonbattle casualties; the Ninth Army, 20,787.[4] Thus the over-all cost of the Siegfried Line Campaign in American personnel was close to 140,000.

The fact that most of these losses were incurred in the front-line units—the infantry and armor—meant that they had a particularly heavy impact on operations. The problem of replacements for the fallen, many of whom in this age of technical warfare were specialists requiring long hours of training, could never be fully solved. Contrary to experience among German artillery units, which were constantly on the defensive and thereby often subjected to direct attack, American artillery units incurred relatively few losses except among forward observer teams.[5]

Not only in these but in other aspects, the Siegfried Line Campaign was similar to the battle of Normandy. Instead of hedgerows, the Allies encountered pillboxes, dense forests, canals, urban snares, and defended villages, yet the effect on operations was much the same. It was exceedingly difficult to go very far very fast under these constricting conditions until overwhelming logistical and tactical strength could be built up or the enemy worn down by attrition. The campaign clearly had illustrated the problems that beset a military force weakened by lengthy pursuit, held in leash by taut supply lines, and confronted by an enemy that turns to fight behind strong natural and artificial barriers. The fact that the Allies approached the barriers in spread formation geared to pursuit did not help matters,

---

[1] FUSA AARs, Sep–Dec 44; *Conquer—The Story of Ninth Army*, p. 112.

[2] FUSA Rpt, Vol. 2, Annex 5; *Conquer—The Story of Ninth Army*, p. 113. FUSA's losses were almost double those of the Third Army for the same period. See Cole, *The Lorraine Campaign*, p. 592.

[3] FUSA Rpt of Opns, Annex 1; *Conquer—The Story of Ninth Army*, p. 112; 12th A Gp G–1 Daily Summaries, 25 Sep–16 Dec 44. Ninth Army figures do not include the army's defensive phase between 4 October and 16 November. Though figures for this period are available in 12th Army Group Daily Summaries, they apparently also include the latter stages of the campaign at Brest and thus are misleading. American losses under foreign command are noted above in Chapters VIII, IX, and X.

[4] 12th A Gp G–1 Daily Summaries, 11 Sep–16 Dec 44.

[5] See NUSA Opns, IV, 209.

for once deeply involved in operations it takes time to reorganize and redistribute a large tactical force and start all over again.

As in Normandy, the Americans had come up against obstacles for which they were at first ill prepared. They had had no specialized training against the hedgerows; neither were they prepared for the pillboxes. Though almost all units had undergone some training in the United States in attack against fortified positions, Normandy and the pursuit had made such inroads on trained personnel that almost all units had to learn again the hard way. Moving directly against the West Wall from the pursuit, American units had no time at first either to rehearse or to amass special assault equipment. The 28th Division's first performance against the pillboxes in mid-September, for example, was rudimentary when compared with the 30th Division's in October.

Nor was the weather of any assistance. Perhaps the most dramatic example of the deleterious effect inclement weather could exercise was the outcome of the big airborne attack, Operation MARKET-GARDEN. Yet the impact of unfavorable weather was marked elsewhere as well, particularly in the way it shackled supporting aircraft. It also added to the hardships of the front-line soldier and put muddy obstacles in the way of the men who were trying to supply him. Trench foot—the seriousness of which could be illustrated by the fact that in the first fifteen days of the Roer River offensive, trench foot cases constituted 8.2 percent of all medical admissions in the Ninth Army—was directly attributable to the wet and the cold.[6]

Inclement weather also accentuated a serious psychological situation arising from the fact that troops had to live under battle conditions for extended periods without relief. Though higher commanders were aware that prolonged exposure to combat conditions creates excessive fatigue, which in turn makes the soldier indifferent and careless, they had not sufficient troops to rotate units frequently.[7] The system of individual replacements, although it has its virtues, contributed to the problem. A man who attacks day after day and fights off the enemy night after night with no prospect of relief other than through wounds eventually becomes sluggish.

It was a tribute to the remarkable resilience of the American soldier that he could recover his morale so quickly after such an ordeal. Some of his resilience was pure resignation to the fact that a job had to be done, no matter how painful, as exemplified by the sergeant from the 4th Division who climbed from his foxhole and resumed the attack with the remark, "Well, men, we can't do a ———— thing sitting still." The soldier's mind obviously had to make tremendous adjustment from the exhilaration of the pursuit to the depression of stabilized warfare, then to the optimism of the start of the November offensive and back again to the depression of the Huertgen Forest and the muddy Roer plain. That the American could do it is illustrated by the remarks set down during November in the diary of the First Army commander's aide-de-camp. The same man who before the start of the November offensive had revealed a genuine confidence that this might be the last big push

---

[6] NUSA Opns, IV, 209.

[7] See FUSA Rpt of Opns, 1 Aug–22 Feb, Vol. 1, pp. 167–68.

of the war could, a mere week later, record the following divergent observation: "No one but the most optimistic sky-gazers expected that we would crack the line in 24 hours and dash to the Rhine in the manner of the St. Lô breakthrough. There has been nothing but the stiffest kind of fighting and opposition all along our front and the gains recorded consequently have satisfied everybody." [8]

The torpor that sometimes evidenced itself among the troops in the line, was a partial reflection of similar symptoms at the command level. Noting that a general fatigue existed at First Army headquarters, the First Army G-3 recalled after the war that General Hodges during this period "was pretty slow making the big decisions. He would study them for a long time and I often would have to press him before I got a decision." [9] If such a situation existed it could be understood in light of the fact that the Siegfried Line Campaign followed closely on a period that had been filled with momentous day-by-day decisions which taxed not only a commander's stamina but his ingenuity as well.

To some, the conduct of operations during the Siegfried Line Campaign was disconcertingly and even unnecessarily slow and conservative. The boldest and most daring plan to emerge during the period, Operation MARKET-GARDEN, was in reality an outgrowth more of the pursuit than of the Siegfried Line Campaign. Even the gigantic air support program for the November offensive was not a new solution but for all its size, a conservative copy of similar programs in Normandy. Many a student of the campaign would

question whether the reasons for failing to give responsibility for the main effort of the November offensive to the Ninth instead of the First Army were sufficient in view of the difference in terrain confronting the two armies. Surely the approach to the question of the Roer River Dams was lacking in vigor and imagination.

On the other hand, a supply situation which was not effectively alleviated until very near the close of the Siegfried Line Campaign was hardly conducive to boldness in operations. Neither was the shortage of reserve forces. Once the airborne divisions were committed to their lengthy fight in the Netherlands, even SHAEF had no real reserve. "You can't take chances without a reserve," the First Army G-3 believed. "The situation was that we had many times played our last card. All we could do was sit back and pray to God that nothing would happen." [10]

Perhaps the real difficulty lay in the fact that the First Army fought in the Aachen area in the first place. It was not, before the invasion, planned that way. The First Army originally was to have advanced south of the Ardennes in close conjunction with the Third Army. The shift had come as a compromise when Montgomery asked Eisenhower to send both the 12th and 21st Army Groups north of the Ardennes in a single powerful thrust into Germany. This Eisenhower had not agreed to, but he had shifted the First Army northward to protect Montgomery's flank for a push into Belgium to gain certain intermediate objectives, notably Antwerp. Montgomery, in turn, had oriented his forces through Holland, away from the time-honored route of the

---

[8] Sylvan Diary, entry of 21 Nov 44.
[9] Interv with Thorson, 12 Sep 56.

[10] *Ibid.*

Aachen Gap, leaving that route to the First Army in what was at first a secondary effort.

Would a more advantageous use of resources have been to send the First Army, protecting Montgomery's flank, through the Ardennes–Eifel, thus leaving the Aachen Gap to the British and thereby avoiding the pitfalls of terrain in the Netherlands? The Ardennes region—as the Germans had proved in 1914 and 1940 and were to demonstrate again in December 1944—is not the bugaboo it is commonly assumed to be. What is more, this region in September 1944 was almost devoid of Germans to defend it, perhaps the weakest-held sector along the entire Western Front. A lone U.S. armored division, the 5th, proved that point at Wallendorf, but the bulk of the First Army by that time already had been committed in the Aachen Gap.

The result was a virtual stultification of First Army maneuver within an Aachen Gap which was almost as constricted as it had been in 1914 when the Imperial German armies respected Dutch neutrality. The Peel Marshes confined the U.S. forces on the north; on the south, they were confined by a reluctance to mount a big push through the Ardennes.

Would the Siegfried Line Campaign have produced more far-reaching results —or would a slow, dogged campaign have been necessary at all—had the Ardennes–Eifel not been disregarded as a route of major advance? The question can be answered only by conjecture, but no analysis of the Siegfried Line Campaign can be complete unless it is at least considered. In a renewal of the offensive after the enemy's Ardennes attack, General Bradley's 12th Army Group turned this region to distinct advantage.

The Siegfried Line Campaign had demonstrated, as did earlier and later fighting in Europe, the basic efficacy of the American infantry-tank-artillery team. Indeed, the campaign had underscored what was fast becoming accepted fact, that the long-standing infantry-artillery relationship badly needed in almost every instance the added power of the tank. The fighting around Aachen, in particular, had shown that neither side, German or American, could make substantial progress without tank support. The airborne troops in Operation MARKET-GARDEN were at a tremendous disadvantage when the arrival of supporting armor was delayed. Those commanders in the Huertgen Forest who dared attempt a solution of the vexing problems involved in using tanks in the forest were amply repaid.

The campaign, on the other hand, had provided few examples of what exponents of armor consider true armored warfare. In general, both Germans and Americans used their tanks in an infantry support role. Germans more than Americans employed them for this purpose singly or as roving single artillery or antitank pieces; but this was attributable more to limited numbers of tanks than to any predilection for the practice.

Weapons of both sides had, in general borne up well under the rigors of the campaign. On the American side, the fighting had underscored the need for a higher velocity weapon on the M–4 Sherman tank and the U.S. tank destroyer, both in light of the enemy's heavier tanks and the excellence of his dual purpose 88-mm. gun. But the campaign had done little to answer the question of whether the U.S. Army erred in depending on a medium tank, for all its advantages in mobility, transportability, and ease of maintenance, to the virtual exclusion of a heavy tank. Though tanks more and more had assumed antitank roles, in addition to their other assignments, the self-propelled, lightly armored tank destroyer had in many instances proved its worth, despite a tendency of some commanders to misuse it as a tank. On many occasions commanders employed tank destroyers in battery to supplement divisional artillery. The destroyer clearly had shown up the general obsolescence of towed antitank pieces, particularly the 57-mm. gun, which many units by the end of the Siegfried Line Campaign were almost ready to discard. The short-barreled 105-mm. howitzer of the regimental Cannon Company also had contributed little in its normal role as artillery directly under control of the infantry regimental commander. Probably because the smooth-working relationship between the infantry regiment and divisional artillery made presence of the Cannon Company within the regiment unnecessary, many divisions shifted the company to the direct control of the divisional artillery to supplement its fires.

A distinctly encouraging aspect of the campaign was the performance of new divisions. In Normandy it had become almost routine for a division in its first action to incur severe losses and display disturbing organizational, command, and communications deficiencies for at least the first week of combat indoctrination.[11] Yet in no case was this tendency present to a similar degree among those divisions receiving their baptism of fire during the Siegfried Line Campaign. General Col-

lins might admonish the 104th Division at the Donnerberg "in no uncertain terms to get moving and get moving fast," but a division of similar experience in Normandy might have required sweeping organizational and command changes before achieving a creditable performance. In the case of the 104th, General Collins and other officers, after observing the division only a day or so longer, could pay it nothing but tribute. "General Hart [First Army artillery officer] says the whole artillery section functions beautifully according to the book and what the General [Hodges] particularly likes thus far of what he has seen of the 104th is their ability to button up tight and hold the place tight once they have taken it. There is no record yet of the 104th giving ground." [12]

New divisions, in general, entered the line during the fall of 1944 under more favorable circumstances than existed during the summer. That obviously had something to do with improved early performance. Training based on actual battle experience and reduced cannibalization of units to serve as individual replacements also may have contributed. Another factor was the caliber of the personnel. Almost all the new divisions going into action during the Siegfried Line Campaign possessed a high percentage of men transferred from the Army Specialized Training Program (ASTP), which had contained men of proved intelligence studying under army sponsorship in the nation's colleges and universities.

The amount of time consumed by and the cost of the Siegfried Line Campaign were tremendous if one looks only at the relatively small amount of territory taken

---

[11] See Blumenson, *Breakout and Pursuit,* *passim.*

[12] Sylvan Diary, entries of 16 and 26 Nov 44.

during the campaign. On the other hand, what would have happened had the Allies suspended offensive operations at the German border and waited until they could have hit harder? How successful would the counteroffensive in the Ardennes have been under those circumstances? Given several months to get ready, could the Germans have held the West Wall?

The fact is that the Siegfried Line Campaign, for all its terrible cost, paid off, not so much in real estate as in attrition of the German armies. Indeed, the Siegfried Line Campaign turned out to be primarily a battle of attrition, though it had not been intended that way. Just how effective the campaign was as a contribution to German defeat would be apparent only after the unfolding of action in the Ardennes and a renewed Allied drive toward the Rhine.

Appendix A

Table of Equivalent Ranks

U.S. Army	German Army and Air Force	German Waffen-SS
None	Reichsmarschall	None
General of the Army	Generalfeldmarschall	Reichsfuehrer-SS
General	Generaloberst	Oberstgruppenfuehrer
Lieutenant General	General der Infanterie	Obergruppenfuehrer
	Artillerie	
	Gebirgstruppen	
	Kavallerie	
	Nachrichtentruppen	
	Panzertruppen	
	Pioniere	
	Luftwaffe	
	Flieger	
	Fallschirmtruppen	
	Flakartillerie	
	Luftnachrichtentruppen	
Major General	Generalleutnant	Gruppenfuehrer
Brigadier General	Generalmajor	Brigadefuehrer
None	None	Oberfuehrer
Colonel	Oberst	Standartenfuehrer
Lieutenant Colonel	Oberstleutnant	Obersturmbannfuehrer
Major	Major	Sturmbannfuehrer
Captain	Hauptmann	Haupsturmfuehrer
Captain (Cavalry)	Rittmeister	
First Lieutenant	Oberleutnant	Obersturmfuehrer
Second Lieutenant	Leutnant	Untersturmfuehrer

Appendix B

Recipients of the Distinguished Service Cross

All who received the Medal of Honor for individual actions during operations described in this volume have been mentioned either in text or footnotes. Because of space limitations, similar mention of all who were awarded the Distinguished Service Cross could not be made. The following list of recipients of the DSC is as complete as possible in view of the fact that no single Army file listing DSC awards is maintained. Effort has been made to provide ranks as of the date of the action cited. (P) indicates a posthumous award.

Adams, Pfc. John W. (P)
Anderson, 2d Lt. Roy L. (P)
Bacle, Sgt. Peter (P)
Baum, Capt. Francis J. (P)
Berlin, 1st Lt. Walter I.
Bieber, S/Sgt. Melvin H.
Blakely, T/Sgt. Ewel (P)
Blanton, T/Sgt. Benjamin T.
Blazzard, Capt. Howard C.
Booth, Capt. Everett L.
Botts, Capt. Seth S.
Bouchlas, Capt. Michael S.
Brenner, Pvt. William E.
Brohman, Pvt. Howard E., Jr.
Bruns, T/5 Raymond E.
Bucci, Pfc. Joseph R.

Burke, 1st Lt. Robert C.
Burns, Sgt. George E.
Burton, Lt. Col. William H., Jr.
Cambron, 1st Lt. Joseph W. (P)
Castro, Pfc. Luis F.
Catanese, Pfc. Albert
Chase, Pfc. Francis T., Jr.
Chatfield, Capt. Henry H.
Chenoweth, Pfc. Charles H., Sr. (P)
Citrak, Pfc. Michael
Clark, S/Sgt. Willard D.
Clementi, T/Sgt. Vincent (P)
Clinton, T/Sgt. Weldon D.
Colombe, Pvt. David L.
Cowden, 2d Lt. Paul W.
Crabtree, S/Sgt. William H. (P)
Dew, 2d Lt. Joseph H.
Dickerson, Pfc. Harry S. (P)
Dixon, T/3 Harold M.
Dooley, 1st Lt. William E.
Drennan, Capt. Fred O. (P)
Dupas, 1st Lt. James, II (P)
Eells, 2d Lt. Calvin E.
Erbes, Capt. John
Fairchild, S/Sgt. Robert L.
Farmer, S/Sgt. Robert D. (P)
Felkins, Capt. William G., Jr. (P)
Fesmire, Pvt. Albert H.
Fiori, Pfc. Nanti J. (P)
Fitzpatrick, 1st Lt. James K. (P)
Folk, Capt. George K.

Fontes, Pvt. Eugene A. (P)
Ford, Pvt. Willis B. (P)
Foster, S/Sgt. Leslie W. (P)
Frazier, 1st Lt. Gael M.
Free, 1st Lt. Charles A.
Fretwell, Sgt. Thomas E., Jr.
Funk, Pvt. Victor P.
Gehrke, 2d Lt. Roy E. (P)
Gilbrath, Pvt. Dwight
Ginder, Col. Philip D.
Glogau, 1st Lt. Donald (P)
Golojuch, 1st Lt. Frank J.
Gomes, Lt. Col. Lloyd H.
Greene, S/Sgt. Thomas A. (P)
Greer, Maj. Howard W.
Grotelueschen, 1st Lt. Edgar W.
Hackard, Capt. Clifford T.
Hall, 1st Lt. Sanford F.
Hall, T/5 Willis B.
Hammonds, Pvt. Joseph J.
Haney, Cpl. Manning G. (P)
Harty, T/Sgt. Willard (P)
Hauschildt, 1st Sgt. Edward W.
Henley, S/Sgt. Robert M.
Herin, S/Sgt. Ralph D. (P)
Holland, Pfc. Robert H.
Holman, Capt. Grady B.
Hopes, S/Sgt. Robert D.
Howard, Pfc. Wilbur I.
Jennings, Pvt. Sheldon D.
Jett, Pfc. Arthur C.
Johnson, Pvt. Albert L.
Johnson, 1st Lt. Kenneth L. (P)
Johnson, T/5 Martin E.
Johnson, S/Sgt. Richard C.
Justice, Pvt. Clyde E.
Kalinowsky, Pfc. Henry J.
Kelleher, Lt. Col. Gerald C.
Kelley, S/Sgt. Brady O.
Kessler, 1st Lt. Albert L.
Kirk, Pfc. Owens L. (P)
Kirksey, Sgt. Earnest L.
Kudiak, Sgt. Tony
Lackner, T/Sgt. Clarence

Lanham, Col. Charles T.
Lee, 1st Lt. Robert E. (P)
Lester, 1st Lt. Vestal R.
Littleton, S/Sgt. Walter J.
Malone, Pfc. Henry A.
Mathews, Pvt. James E. (P)
McCaskey, 2d Lt. Charles I., Jr. (P)
McCully, 1st Lt. William C. (P)
McDaniel, Pvt. Doyle W. (P)
Messer, Pfc. Allen B.
Miccori, Pfc. Joseph A. (P)
Miller, Capt. Jesse R., Jr.
Mills, 2d Lt. Donald C.
Mills, Lt. Col. Herbert M. (P)
Moralez, Pfc. Frank (P)
Moses, Sgt. Albert D., Jr. (P)
Nietzel, Sgt. Alfred B. (P)
Norris, T/4 Herman W.
O'Connell, S/Sgt. Stephen W.
Olsen, 1st Lt. John
Palm, 2d Lt. Carl C.
Parrish, Capt. Edward L.
Parrow, S/Sgt. Peter J. (P)
Pece, Pfc. James T. (P)
Peebles, 1st Lt. Arthur F., Jr. (P)
Pepe, Pfc. Salvatore
Peso, 2d Lt. Frank L. (P)
Polio, Pfc. James V. (P)
Potter, Pvt. Phillip H.
Quinlan, 2d Lt. James P.
Rabreau, S/Sgt. John
Rees, Capt. Roger S.
Regan, 2d Lt. Dennis J.
Rennebaum, 1st Lt. Leon A.
Renteria, T/4 Jess T.
Rhodey, Capt. William A.
Robey, S/Sgt. Paul W., Jr.
Russell, Capt. William E.
Sawyer, T/Sgt. Phillip F. (P)
Schultz, T/5 George W., Jr.
Searles, S/Sgt. James W.
Singer, T/4 Leonard
Single, T/Sgt. James C.
Smelser, T/Sgt. Raymond B.

Speer, Pfc. Harold J.
Stevens, 1st Lt. Richard W.
Stott, Pvt. Robert H.
Swanberg, T/5 Bertol C.
Tempesta, S/Sgt. Anthony A.
Terry, Capt. John R., Jr.
Terry, S/Sgt. Joseph
Tester, 1st Lt. Perry O., Jr. (P)
Thayer, Pfc. Kenneth C.
Thomas, 2d Lt. George
Tipton, Pfc. Beverly
Tucker, T/4 William I.

Van Giesen, 1st Lt. George T. (P)
Whidden, Sgt. Adolphaus W., Jr.
Whitehouse, Sgt. Rempfer L.
Whitley, Capt. Arthur N.
Whitney, Capt. William B.
Wild, Pfc. Joseph J.
Wilson, S/Sgt. William R.
Wise, Sgt. Alvin R.
Wittkopf, Capt. Philip W.
Wohner, Maj. John H.
Wolf, Cpl. Alvin E. (P)
Worrall, 1st Lt. William T. (P)

Appendix C

First Army Staff Roster as of 11 September 1944

Commanding General
  Lt. Gen. Courtney H. Hodges

Chief of Staff
  Maj. Gen. William B. Kean

Deputy Chief of Staff, Administration
  Col. Charles F. Williams

Deputy Chief of Staff, Operations
  Col. Samuel L. Myers

Assistant Chief of Staff G–1
  Col. Joseph J. O'Hare

Assistant Chief of Staff G–2
  Col. Benjamin A. Dickson

Assistant Chief of Staff G–3
  Brig. Gen. Truman C. Thorson

Assistant Chief of Staff G–4
  Col. Robert W. Wilson

Assistant Chief of Staff G–5
  Col. Damon M. Gunn

Adjutant General
  Col. Robert S. Nourse

Antiaircraft Artillery
  Col. Charles G. Patterson

Artillery
  Brig. Gen. Charles E. Hart

Armor
  Col. Peter C. Hains 3d

Chaplain
  Col. Hamilton H. Kellogg

Chemical
  Col. Frederick W. Gerhard

Engineer
  Col. William A. Carter, Jr.

Finance
  Col. Grover A. Summa

Inspector General
  Col. Rosser L. Hunter

Judge Advocate
  Col. Ernest M. Brannon

Ordnance
  Col. John B. Medaris

Provost Marshal
  Col. William H. S. Wright

Quartermaster
  Col. Andrew T. McNamara

Signal
  Col. Grant A. Williams

Special Services
  Col. William May

Surgeon
  Brig. Gen. John A. Rogers

Secretary of the General Staff
  Maj. Earl F. Pegram

Appendix D

Ninth Army Staff Roster as of 4 October 1944

Commanding General
Lt. Gen. William H. Simpson

Chief of Staff
Maj. Gen. James E. Moore

Deputy Chief of Staff
Col. George A. Millener

Assistant Chief of Staff G–1
Col. Daniel H. Hundley

Assistant Chief of Staff G–2
Col. Charles P. Bixel

Assistant Chief of Staff G–3
Brig. Gen. Armistead D. Mead, Jr.

Assistant Chief of Staff G–4
Brig. Gen. Roy V. Rickard

Assistant Chief of Staff G–5
Col. Carl A. Kraege

Adjutant General
Col. John A. Klein

Antiaircraft Artillery
Col. John G. Murphy

Artillery
Col. Laurence H. Hanley

Armor
Col. Claude A. Black

Chaplain
Col. W. Roy Bradley

Chemical
Col. Harold Walmsley

Engineer
Brig. Gen. Richard U. Nicholas

Finance
Col. John L. Scott

Inspector General
Col. Perry L. Baldwin

Judge Advocate
Col. Stanley W. Jones

Ordnance
Col. Walter W. Warner

Provost Marshal
Col. Robert C. Andrews

Quartermaster
Col. William E. Goe

Signal
Col. Joe J. Miller

Special Services
Lt. Col. Kenneth K. Kelley

Surgeon
Col. William E. Shambora

Secretary of the General Staff
Col. Art B. Miller, Jr.

Bibliographical Note

Those who are familiar with the Army's records of World War II speak not in terms of file cabinets or linear feet but of mountains. The sheer bulk of these records and their generally high value are astounding. Yet one major element often is missing: the "why" behind a commander's decision. Indeed, it is difficult in many instances to determine even who made the decision, for the Army has a disturbing habit of speaking in the passive voice behind the anonymity of an impersonal pronoun—"it was decided," "it was ordered." Compound this practice by giving a commander a jeep and a liaison plane, not to mention an effective system of telephone and radio communications, and it is a wonder that any record of his decisions and the reasons for them survives.

From this situation has arisen perhaps the most serious research problem encountered in preparing *The Siegfried Line Campaign*. It will remain a problem to anyone who attempts further research in this period of combat operations; for the relatively static nature of the warfare gave rise to frequent informal conferences between commanders, from which a written record rarely emerged. The worst offender in this regard was the First Army. Indeed, the First Army's records are below average, a fact that is hard to reconcile with the First Army's reputation as the most meticulous and most concerned with detail of any American army in Europe during World War II.

A solution to this problem might be expected to be found in the hundreds of so-called combat interviews conducted by historians in uniform soon after most major actions; but in an attempt to fill a recognized gap at the fighting, small-unit level, the historians failed to pay sufficient attention to the command level.

Postwar interviews and comments by participants on early drafts of the manuscript thus have represented the only approach to a genuine solution of this problem. More than fifty officers who participated in the campaign either were interviewed by the author or commented on all or parts of the manuscript. These include both the First and Ninth Army commanders. The immense value of their contributions can be fully apparent only to the author. On the other hand, memories have a way of failing the most co-operative of witnesses, so that command decisions and the "why" behind them remains a lacuna of serious proportions.

This would not be the case had the Army offered more encouragement to the kind of service performed by Maj. William C. Sylvan, senior aide to the First Army commander, General Hodges. With the approval of his commander, Major Sylvan kept a day-by-day diary dealing with General Hodges' activities. He has kindly made it available to the Office of the Chief of Military History. Not in all cases was Major Sylvan, in his position as aide-de-camp, privy to the discussions and decisions at the First Army level; but in those instances where he was present or aware of the events, his diary is invaluable.

Official Records

By far the most useful documentary sources for this, as for all operational volumes, are the official records of U.S. Army units in the theater. Each headquarters, from army down through regiment and separate battalion, submitted a monthly narrative after action report, accompanied by supporting journals, periodic reports, messages, staff section reports, and overlays. Though these records vary in quantity and quality, they are essential to any detailed study of operations. Those most valuable to the historian of combat operations are housed in the historical reports files in the World War II Records Division, National Archives. Other records of organizational elements are in the Federal Records Center Annex, Kansas City, Missouri. Almost none now carry security classification.

The after action reports are in effect monthly compendiums of all the other documents, but the chance of error or the introduction of a commander's hindsight makes it imperative that these be checked carefully against the supporting documents. Where close attention was paid to preparation of journals, these are invaluable. In the manner of a ship's log, they of all the documents most nearly reflect the events and thinking in the headquarters at the time. Neither First nor Ninth Army journals, unfortunately, were prepared with care; they are virtually worthless to the historian. The same is true of almost all the corps journals for this period, with the exception of those of the XIX Corps, which sometimes include

telephone conversations. Fortunately, most of the division journals are better, particularly those of the 1st, 2d, 2d Armored, 28th, 29th, 30th, and 83d Divisions. Particularly valuable telephone journals are to be found in 30th Division records. Indeed, had all divisions kept the kind of records preserved by the 30th Division, the value of the history of World War II would be markedly increased.

Basically the same pattern of official records was followed at headquarters of the 12th Army Group, with the addition of a planning file. The file is cited in this volume as 12th Army Group, Military Objectives, 371.3, Volumes I and II.

In keeping with the theory of presenting the story of higher headquarters only as it affected tactical operations, no attempt has been made to study all SHAEF records. The basic SHAEF file used for this volume was the richest of the official SHAEF collection, that of the Secretary of the General Staff (SHAEF SGS, 381, Volumes I and II). In addition, the author has drawn on the definitive experience with the SHAEF records of Dr. Forrest C. Pogue, author of *The Supreme Command*. While preparing his volume, Dr. Pogue collected a vast amount of material, much of it transcripts or photostats of documents from General Eisenhower's wartime personal file. This material, cited as the Pogue files, is located in OCMH. Also falling under the category of SHAEF records are those of the airborne units. They are housed in World War II Records Division under the heading, SHAEF FAAA files.

Though both British and Canadian army historical sections have co-operated extensively with the UNITED STATES ARMY IN WORLD WAR II series, their official wartime files are not immediately accessible to the American historian. Those official records of their armies used in preparation of this volume are copies found in American files, notably in the SHAEF SGS records. Where American units operated under British or Canadian command, copies of Allied documents applicable to U.S. operations are usually to be found in the records of the U.S. units.

Three of the U.S. headquarters published official consolidated versions of their after action reports for limited distribution. Two of these—the 12th Army Group Report of Operations and V Corps Operations in the ETO—provide in addition to the narrative report a convenient assimilation of pertinent orders, periodic reports, and other documents. The First Army Report of Operations, 1 August 1944–22 February 1945, is more strictly narrative. In the case of the 12th Army Group and the First Army, the original after action reports should be consulted for material not included in the published versions.

The Department of the Air Force Historical Section co-operated closely with the author in his exploitation of records of U.S. air units. All air records used are located at the Research Studies Institute, Maxwell Air Force Base, Montgomery, Alabama.

Unofficial Records

Most records falling in the category of unofficial records are combat interviews conducted by teams of historical officers working under the European Theater Historical Section. In addition, there are narratives written by the field historians to accompany the interviews and occasionally field notes and important documents collected by the historical officers. In the case of units operating under the Ninth Army, combat interview material was arranged in narrative form in four mimeographed volumes. While little reason exists to question the general accuracy of these volumes, it is lamentable that the original combat interview material from which the volumes were written was destroyed. The footnotes in this volume should provide an adequate guide to the available combat interview material. The interviews and the four Ninth Army volumes are housed in the historical reports files in World War II Records Division.

Soon after the end of the war in Europe, the historians in the theater wrote a preliminary narrative history of the Siegfried Line Campaign. Though these officers did not have access to much high level material or to official German records, their work provides a convenient check on documentary sources and has helped the author of this volume considerably in organizational matters. The manuscript is filed in OCMH.

Unit Histories

Since the end of the war, almost every division and some regiments have published unofficial unit histories. In many cases, these works are heavy on the side of unit pride, but some are genuinely useful. A brief analysis of each is included in this volume in the footnote where the work is first cited. In a special class is *Conquer—The Story of Ninth Army* (Washington: Infantry Journal Press, 1947), a sober and invaluable volume.

German Sources

The account of German operations has been based primarily on the eight monographs prepared in OCMH specifically to complement this volume by Mr. Lucian Heichler, plus three monographs prepared by Mr. Charles V. P. von Luttichau to complement a forthcoming volume in the World War II series on the Ardennes campaign. These monographs were based on two principal types of material: official German records captured or seized by the U.S. Army during and immediately after the war and a series of manuscripts prepared after the war by former German commanders working under the auspices of the U.S. Army.

The contemporary German records are in the custody of World War II Records Division. There are numerous gaps attributable to wartime destruction and to the fact that many records fell into the hands of the Soviet Union. Yet enough remain to provide a remarkably clear picture of the operations, particularly when supplemented by the German officers' manuscripts.

The most important of the official records are the daily war diaries of operations, *Kriegstagebuecher* (*KTB*), maintained by the forward echelons of all commands, together with supporting documents in annexes (*Anlagen*). The most complete records to be found of any headquarters involved in the Siegfried Line Campaign are those of the *LXXXI Corps,* which fought in the Aachen area.

The German manuscripts, numbering more than two thousand, are filed in OCMH and have been adequately catalogued and indexed in *Guide to Foreign Military Studies 1945–54,* published in 1954. The quality of the manuscripts varies, reflecting the fact that almost all are based only on the memories of the writers. Yet when used with caution and when checked against the official records, these postwar accounts make a considerable contribution to knowledge of the German side of the combat.

Published Works

In addition to the previously published volumes in the series UNITED STATES ARMY IN WORLD WAR II and unofficial unit histories, those published works of particular value in preparation of this volume are as follows:

Bradley, Omar N. *A Soldier's Story.* New York: Henry Holt and Co., 1951.

Brereton, Lt. Gen. Lewis H. *The Brereton Diaries.* New York: William Morrow and Co., 1946.

de Guingand, Maj. Gen. Sir Francis. *Operation Victory.* New York: Charles Scribner's Sons, 1947.

Eisenhower, Dwight D. *Crusade in Europe.* New York: Doubleday and Co., 1948.

Montgomery, Field Marshal the Viscount of Alamein. *Normandy to the Baltic.* Boston: Houghton Mifflin, 1948.

Patton, George S. *War As I Knew It.* Boston: Houghton Mifflin Co., 1947.

Stacey, Charles P. *The Canadian Army, 1939–1945.* Ottawa: E. Cloutier, King's Printer, 1948.

———. The *Victory Campaign.* Vol. III of the "Official History of the Canadian Army in the Second World War." Ottawa: E. Cloutier, Queen's Printer, 1960.

GLOSSARY

A Gp	Army group
Abn	Airborne
ADSEC	Advance Section
Admin	Administrative
Alarmbataillon	Emergency alert battalion
Alarmeinheit	Emergency alert unit
Anlage	Appendix or annex
AW	Automatic weapons
Armd	Armored
Arty	Artillery
BAR	Browning automatic rifle
Bn	Battalion
Bomb	Bombardment
Br	British
Cav	Cavalry
CCA	Combat Command A
CCB	Combat Command B
CCR	Combat Command Reserve
CCS	Combined Chiefs of Staff
CG	Commanding general
CinC	Commander in Chief
CO	Commanding officer
Co	Company
CofS	Chief of Staff
Comdr	Commander
Conv	Conversation
Das Volk	German people
Dir	Directive
DSC	Distinguished Service Cross
Dtd	Dated
DUKW	2½-ton, 6 x 6 amphibian truck used for short runs from ship to shore
Ech	Echelon
EM	Enlisted men
Engr	Engineer
Ersatzheer	Replacement Army
ETO	European Theater of Operations
Evng	Evening
Ex	Executive

FA	Field Artillery
FAAA	First Allied Airborne Army
Feldheer	Field Army
FO	Field order
Fuesilier battalion	Separate infantry battalion performing both recon-naissance and support in German division
FUSA	First U.S. Army
GHQ	General Headquarters
Heeresgruppe	Army group
Hist	Historical; history
Hq	Headquarters
Ind	Indorsement
Instrs	Instructions
Intel	Intelligence
Interv	Interview
IPW	Interrogation of prisoner of war
Jnl	Journal
Kampfgruppe	German combat group of variable size
KTB	*Kriegstagebuch* (war diary)
Kurhaus	Thermal bath establishment
Landesschuetzen battalion	Home Guard battalion sometimes employed outside Germany
Ltr	Letter
MEW	Mobile Early Warning
Mng	Morning
Msg	Message
Mtg	Meeting
NCO	Noncommissioned officer
Nebelwerfer	Multiple rocket projector
NUSA	Ninth U.S. Army
O	Officer
OB WEST	*Oberbefehlshaber* West (Headquarters, Commander in Chief West [France, Belgium, and the Nether-lands]), highest German ground headquarters of the Western Front until May 1945
OCMH	Office of the Chief of Military History
OKH	*Oberkommando des Heeres* (Army High Command)
OKL	*Oberkommando der Luftwaffe* (Luftwaffe High Command)
OKM	*Oberkommando der Kriegsmarine* (Navy High Command)
OKW	*Oberkommando der Wehrmacht* (Armed Forces [Joint] High Command)
Opn	Operation
Organization Todt	Paramilitary construction organization of the Nazi party, auxiliary to the Wehrmacht. Named after its founder, Dr. Todt.

Ost-Bataillon	Non-German volunteer troops from east-European countries
Panzerfaust	Recoilless German antitank rocket, hand carried. A "one-shot" weapon.
Per	Periodic
Prcht	Parachute
Puppchen	A two-wheeled bazooka
PWI	Prisoner of war interrogation
RAF	Royal Air Force
Rcd	Record
Rcn	Reconnaissance
Regt	Regiment
Rpt	Report
Schuetzenpanzerwagen	Armored half-track
Schuh mine	German antipersonnel mine
S–2	Intelligence officer or section of regimental or lower staff
S–3	Operations officer or section of regimental or lower staff
SCR	Signal Corps radio
Sec	Section
SHAEF	Supreme Headquarters, Allied Expeditionary Force
Sitrep	Situation report
SP	Self-propelled
Sportplatz	Sports stadium
Sq	Squadron
SS	*Schutzstaffel* (Elite Guard)
Tac	Tactical
T/5	Technician Fifth Grade
Tel	Telephone
Topf mine	German antitank mine
TOT	Time on target, a method of timing artillery fire from various points to fall on a given target simultaneously
TUSA	Third U.S. Army
Vergeltung	Vengeance
VHF	Very high frequency
Waffen-SS	Combat arm of the SS (*Schutzstaffel,* Elite Guard); in effect a partial duplication of the German Army
Wehrkreis	German Army administrative area, for the most part inside greater Germany
Werfer	Rocket projector
WFSt	*Wehrmachtfuehrungsstab* (Armed Forces Operations Staff)

Code Names

CLIPPER   Offensive by the 30 British Corps (including 84th U.S. Infantry Division) to reduce the Geilenkirchen salient.

COMET   Plan to seize river crossings in the Netherlands near Arnhem along the projected axis of the Second British Army.

GOODWOOD   British attack in Normandy, late July 1944, preceding U.S. Operation COBRA.

MARKET-GARDEN   Combined ground-airborne operation intended to establish a bridgehead across the Rhine in the Netherlands, September 1944.

NEPTUNE   Actual operations within Operation OVERLORD. Used for security reasons after September 1943 on all OVERLORD planning papers that referred to target area and date.

OMAHA   Normandy beach assaulted by troops of U.S. V Corps, 6 June 1944.

OVERLORD   Plan for invasion of northwest Europe, spring 1944.

QUEEN   12th Army Group operation on the Roer plain, November 1944.

UTAH   Normandy beach assaulted by troops of U.S. VII Corps, 6 June 1944.

Basic Military Map Symbols*

Symbols within a rectangle indicate a military unit, within a triangle an observation post, and within a circle a supply point.

Military Units—Identification

Antiaircraft Artillery . . . .

Armored Command . . . .

Army Air Forces . . . .

Artillery, except Antiaircraft and Coast Artillery . . . .

Cavalry, Horse . . . .

Cavalry, Mechanized . . . .

Chemical Warfare Service . . . .

Coast Artillery . . . .

Engineers . . . .

Infantry . . . .

Medical Corps . . . .

Ordnance Department . . . .

Quartermaster Corps . . . .

Signal Corps . . . .

Tank Destroyer . . . .

Transportation Corps . . . .

Veterinary Corps . . . .

Airborne units are designated by combining a gull wing symbol with the arm or service symbol:

Airborne Artillery . . . .

Airborne Infantry . . . .

*For complete listing of symbols in use during the World War II period, see FM 21–30, dated October 1943, from which these are taken.

Size Symbols

The following symbols placed either in boundary lines or above the rectangle, triangle, or circle inclosing the identifying arm or service symbol indicate the size of military organization:

Squad	●
Section.	●●
Platoon	●●●
Company, troop, battery, Air Force flight	I
Battalion, cavalry squadron, or Air Force squadron	I I
Regiment or group; combat team (with abbreviation CT following identifying numeral)	I I I
Brigade, Combat Command of Armored Division, or Air Force Wing.	X
Division or Command of an Air Force.	XX
Corps or Air Force	XXX
Army.	XXXX
Group of Armies.	XXXXX

EXAMPLES

The letter or number to the left of the symbol indicates the unit designation; that to the right, the designation of the parent unit to which it belongs. Letters or numbers above or below boundary lines designate the units separated by the lines:

Company A, 137th Infantry . . . . A⊠137

8th Field Artillery Battalion. . . . . ☐8

Combat Command A, 1st Armored Division. . . . . A⬭I

Observation Post, 23d Infantry. . . . . ▲23

Command Post, 5th Infantry Division . . . . ⊠5

Boundary between 137th and 138th Infantry . . . . —|||— (137 / 138)

Weapons

Machine gun	●→
Gun.	●
Gun battery	⊔⊔⊔
Howitzer or Mortar	⟊
Tank	◇
Self-propelled gun	▣

UNITED STATES ARMY IN WORLD WAR II

The following volumes have been published or are in press:

The War Department
   Chief of Staff: Prewar Plans and Preparations
   Washington Command Post: The Operations Division
   Strategic Planning for Coalition Warfare: 1941–1942
   Strategic Planning for Coalition Warfare: 1943–1944
   Global Logistics and Strategy: 1940–1943
   Global Logistics and Strategy: 1943–1945
   The Army and Economic Mobilization
   The Army and Industrial Manpower
The Army Ground Forces
   The Organization of Ground Combat Troops
   The Procurement and Training of Ground Combat Troops
The Army Service Forces
   The Organization and Role of the Army Service Forces
The Western Hemisphere
   The Framework of Hemisphere Defense
   Guarding the United States and Its Outposts
The War in the Pacific
   The Fall of the Philippines
   Guadalcanal: The First Offensive
   Victory in Papua
   CARTWHEEL: The Reduction of Rabaul
   Seizure of the Gilberts and Marshalls
   Campaign in the Marianas
   The Approach to the Philippines
   Leyte: The Return to the Philippines
   Triumph in the Philippines
   Okinawa: The Last Battle
   Strategy and Command: The First Two Years
The Mediterranean Theater of Operations
   Northwest Africa: Seizing the Initiative in the West
   Sicily and the Surrender of Italy
   Salerno to Cassino
   Cassino to the Alps
The European Theater of Operations
   Cross-Channel Attack
   Breakout and Pursuit
   The Lorraine Campaign
   The Siegfried Line Campaign
   The Ardennes: Battle of the Bulge
   The Last Offensive
   The Supreme Command

Logistical Support of the Armies, Volume I
Logistical Support of the Armies, Volume II
The Middle East Theater
The Persian Corridor and Aid to Russia
The China-Burma-India Theater
Stilwell's Mission to China
Stilwell's Command Problems
Time Runs Out in CBI
The Technical Services
The Chemical Warfare Service: Organizing for War
The Chemical Warfare Service: From Laboratory to Field
The Chemical Warfare Service: Chemicals in Combat
The Corps of Engineers: Troops and Equipment
The Corps of Engineers: The War Against Japan
The Corps of Engineers: The War Against Germany
The Corps of Engineers: Military Construction in the United States
The Medical Department: Hospitalization and Evacuation; Zone of Interior
The Medical Department: Medical Service in the Mediterranean and Minor
    Theaters
The Medical Department: Medical Service in the European Theater of Operations
The Ordnance Department: Planning Munitions for War
The Ordnance Department: Procurement and Supply
The Ordnance Department: On Beachhead and Battlefront
The Quartermaster Corps: Organization, Supply, and Services, Volume I
The Quartermaster Corps: Organization, Supply, and Services, Volume II
The Quartermaster Corps: Operations in the War Against Japan
The Quartermaster Corps: Operations in the War Against Germany
The Signal Corps: The Emergency
The Signal Corps: The Test
The Signal Corps: The Outcome
The Transportation Corps: Responsibilities, Organization, and Operations
The Transportation Corps: Movements, Training, and Supply
The Transportation Corps: Operations Overseas
Special Studies
Chronology: 1941–1945
Military Relations Between the United States and Canada: 1939–1945
Rearming the French
Three Battles: Arnaville, Altuzzo, and Schmidt
The Women's Army Corps
Civil Affairs: Soldiers Become Governors
Buying Aircraft: Materiel Procurement for the Army Air Forces
The Employment of Negro Troops
Manhattan: The U.S. Army and the Atomic Bomb
Pictorial Record
The War Against Germany and Italy: Mediterranean and Adjacent Areas
The War Against Germany: Europe and Adjacent Areas
The War Against Japan

Index

Aa River: 131, 145, 190

Aachen: 8, 18, 28–31, 34, 36, 66, 68, 86, 129, 135n, 200, 205, 227, 231, 240–41, 251, 283n, 341, 377, 392, 402, 496, 518, 547, 619–20
  civilian evacuation: 71, 81–82, 307
  costly delay to U.S. troops: 317
  decision to bypass: 71–72
  encirclement of: 67, 77, 80–81, 90, 95–96, 112, 253, 257, 274, 277–78, 280, 281–83, 283n, 284–306, 307, 313, 319n, 498
  final assault: 304, 307–20, 340, 378, 519
  German defense of sector: 69–71, 75, 77, 81, 103, 106, 127, 201, 257–59, 279, 295, 394, 396–97, 410–11, 616
  Hitler's orders to defend: 281, 307, 314, 315
  Rundstedt's view of danger: 18, 299n
  symbol of Nazi ideology: 281, 285
  ultimatum and surrender: 289, 304, 307, 309, 316–17

Aachen Gap: 7, 9, 29, 34, 38, 66, 69, 119, 251, 620

Aachen Municipal Forest: 67, 75, 81

Aachen–Cologne autobahn: 482, 503, 580, 584

Aachen–Cologne railroad: 309

Aachen–Dueren railroad: 291, 479

Aachen–Geilenkirchen–Muenchen–Gladbach railroad: 545–46, 566

Aachen–Juelich highway: 294–95

Aachen–Juelich railroad: 485

Aachen–Laurensberg highway: 315

Aachen–Wuerselen–Linnich highway: 278, 305, 306, 313, 524

Adams, Pfc. John W.: 418n

Adams, Capt. Jonathan E. Jr.: 164

Aerial photographs: 26–27, 327, 345, 520, 596

Air bases: 13, 137, 198, 381, 412, 454

Air Defense of Great Britain: 137–38

Air forces: 5

Air landing brigades: 170–72

Air operations: 24, 64, 169n, 219, 228, 245, 381, 572, 572n. See also Air-ground cooperation; Aircraft; Eighth Air Force; Glider operations; Ninth Air Force; QUEEN; Tactical Air Commands; Troop carrier operations.
  Aachen attacks: 290–92, 296, 299, 309, 309n, 310
  air superiority: 17, 26–27, 94, 169n, 219, 318, 577
  attacks on railroads: 11, 281, 284
  battlefield isolation: 345–46, 357
  "blind bombing": 382
  bomb line marking: 405–06

Air operations—Continued
  bombing and strafing errors: 254, 260, 348, 382, 404, 405, 412–13, 424, 428
  carpet bombing: 254–55, 404, 498, 521, 525
  German: 129, 138, 153, 172, 203, 276, 382, 454. See also Luftwaffe.
  Huertgen Forest: 332, 343, 348, 360–61, 446, 449–50, 465, 490, 592
  low-level precision bombing: 597–98
  MARKET-GARDEN: 129–30, 137–39, 150, 169, 179, 196. See also Troop carrier operations.
  psychological effects: 309n, 413–14
  Roer plain: 509, 536, 538n, 576
  Roer River dams: 327, 597–98
  target bombing: 498, 517, 520–21, 525
  West Wall attack: 114, 253–55, 259–60, 260n, 261, 278–79

Air reconnaissance: 24, 26, 31, 135, 381, 596

Air Squadron, 492d: 292

Air supply: 13, 120, 129, 132, 134, 167, 172, 176, 383, 386, 563

Airborne Antiaircraft Battalion, 81st: 190

Airborne Division, 17th: 128

Airborne Division, 82d
  casualties: 159, 166–68, 176, 178, 182, 199, 199n, 206, 206n
  command and organization: 152n, 155n
  fight for the Nijmegen bridge: 174, 179–84, 247
  MARKET-GARDEN operation: 122, 128, 131–33, 138–39, 142, 154–70, 174–76, 176n, 177–78, 185, 193, 195, 199–200
  post MARKET-GARDEN fighting: 203–06

Airborne Division, 101st
  casualties: 145, 199, 199n, 206, 206n
  command and organization: 143n, 152n
  fight for Hell's Highway: 142–54, 186–95
  Operation MARKET-GARDEN: 128, 131–32, 132n, 133, 138–39, 156, 159–60, 167–68, 176n, 196, 199–200
  post MARKET-GARDEN fighting: 203–05, 573

Airborne operations: 101, 119–20, 132, 132n, 133, 136, 218, 218n, 620. See also MARKET.
  expected by Germans: 18, 120, 134–36, 240, 258
  German reaction to MARKET: 140–43

Aircraft. See also Air operations.
  A–20's: 24, 254–55
  B–17's: 137
  B–24's: 167
  B–26's: 24, 254
  bombers, heavy: 25n, 254, 403–04, 404–05n, 412–13, 498, 520
  bombers, light: 404n

Aircraft—Continued
    bombers, medium: 24–25, 254, 260, 381, 403–04, 404n, 412–13, 442, 498, 500, 520, 525
    C–47's: 129, 137
    fighter-bombers: 24, 106, 133, 240, 254–55, 260, 278, 290, 299, 302–03, 310, 332–33, 343, 381–82, 403–04, 405n, 412–13, 422, 426, 428, 433, 449, 498, 500, 508, 525, 539–40, 548, 563, 568, 572, 576
    fighters: 137–39, 404, 412–13
    Lancasters: 137, 598
    Mosquitoes: 137, 598
    night fighters: 343, 382
    P–38's: 24, 137, 254, 309, 412, 449, 525, 586
    P–47's: 24, 64, 137, 150, 196, 254, 292, 309, 332–33, 381, 418, 436, 453–54, 525, 597
    P–51's: 24, 137, 169
    P–61's: 24, 382
    Spitfires: 137, 169
    Tempests: 137
    Typhoons: 179, 196, 228
Aircraft, German: 137–38, 154, 412, 454, 611. See also Air operations.
Air-ground cooperation: 24–25, 106, 130, 227–28, 240, 287, 381–82, 403–05, 449–50, 453, 457, 459. See also Air operations; Aircraft.
Air/Sea Rescue Service: 138, 154
Albert Canal: 96, 98–103, 106–09, 115, 123–25, 134, 208–29, 219, 258, 521
Aldenhoven: 404, 498, 518, 520, 524–25, 538–39, 561
Allen, Lt. Col. Ray C.: 190
Allen, Maj. Gen. Terry de la Mesa: 222–25, 424–26, 428, 504–08, 511
Allgood, Lt. Col. James D.: 480–81
Allied Expeditionary Air Force: 218n
Alsace: 16, 395
Alsdorf: 274, 279, 283–85, 294–97, 299, 302, 305, 499
Altdorf: 509, 561, 563–64
Alzen. See Hoefen–Alzen ridge.
Ambush: 339, 361–62
Ammunition: 13, 37, 57, 68, 86, 261, 272, 275, 357, 380, 383, 545, 608. See also Shortages.
Ammunition, German: 396, 427. See also Shortages.
Amphibious operations: 221, 228–29
Amsterdam: 29
Anderson, Col. Glen N.: 58–61, 63, 445–46, 450, 459–60
Anderson, Maj. Gen. Samuel E.: 24
Antiaircraft, American: 27, 406, 454
Antiaircraft Artillery Automatic Weapons Battalion, 461st: 64n
Antiaircraft defense, German: 129–30, 132, 137–38, 145, 147n, 159–60, 170, 200, 253–54, 260, 412

Antiaircraft defense, of Antwerp: 230, 230n
Antiaircraft (ground role): 27, 63–64, 165–67, 180–81, 298, 315, 396
Antitank defenses. See Obstacles.
Antitank operations, German: 59, 67, 73, 175, 238, 242, 274–75, 295, 422–24, 426, 445–46, 450, 526–27, 530n, 533, 536, 542, 603–04
Antitank weapons: 25, 27, 45, 122, 153–54, 190, 301, 351, 514, 620–21. See also Bazooka.
Antitank weapons, German: 15, 25, 31, 45, 175, 331, 519–20, 620–21. See also Antitank operations; Artillery support; Panzerfaust.
Antwerp: 4, 6–8, 10, 19, 29, 99, 123–25, 218–20, 616, 619
    opening of the port: 121, 200, 204–05, 207–15, 222, 228–29, 241–42, 377, 383, 390–91
    V–bomb attacks: 229–30
Antwerp–Breda highway: 222–23
Antwerp–Turnhout Canal: 209, 220, 222
"Antwerp X": 230n
Apweiler: 526–27, 531–32, 540–41, 543–44, 551, 553
Ardennes: 7, 9, 28–30, 40, 379, 441n, 600, 620
Ardennes counteroffensive: 55n, 136n, 244, 346, 374, 378n, 474, 593–95, 611–12, 614–15, 620, 622
    German buildup: 393–95, 397, 410–11, 427, 431, 460, 487, 505, 539, 547, 559, 567, 583, 592, 601–02, 610, 616
Ardennes–Eifel: 29, 65, 251, 612–14, 620
Argentan–Falaise pocket: 23, 142
Armed Forces Command Netherlands: 125–27, 135, 140, 142, 171, 193, 395
Armed Forces Operations Staff: 135
Armenian troops: 220, 228n
Armor. See also Tanks.
    Allied superiority: 5, 16, 18, 94, 308
    "armor attracts armor": 518, 530–33, 539–41
    assist in Roer plain push: 482–85, 523–25, 529
    commitment in a confined bridgehead: 269–70
    defensive role: 460
    dependence on roads and bridges: 107–08, 148, 185, 238, 244, 445
    limited-objective attack: 543–44
    organization of U.S. division: 72n
    shock role: 65, 529, 534–35
    superior enemy observation: 421–24
    use in Siegfried Line campaign: 620
    use in West Wall attacks: 39–40, 46, 52, 62, 71–72, 258, 278, 285
    use in woods fighting: 333–34, 349–52, 355, 359–60, 431, 620
    West Wall campaign armored duel: 318
Armor, German: 5, 16–17, 20, 122, 143n, 156–57, 162, 168–69, 200, 394–95, 620. See also Tanks.
Armored Divisions. See also Combat Commands.

Armored Division, 2d: 23, 36
    casualties: 272, 276, 279, 279n, 530, 533, 544
    command and organization: 72n, 107n
    Roer offensive: 400, 516–18, 521–27, 529–36,
        540, 540n, 541–44, 547, 549, 551, 553, 558,
        560–61, 563–65, 572
    West Wall attack: 96, 99, 101, 107–12, 114,
        233, 236, 252–53, 257, 269–80, 285, 294, 296,
        302–03
Armored Division, 3d: 20, 23, 36, 339
    casualties: 492n, 586, 593n
    command and organization: 72, 72n
    drive to the Roer: 580–82, 584–86
    November offensive: 409, 415, 417, 422–26,
        464, 475, 480, 483–85, 492
    West Wall reconnaissance: 66–68, 72–80, 82–
        83, 86, 86n, 88–90, 286, 292, 314
Armored Division, 5th: 3, 24, 36, 383
    casualties: 65, 446, 450, 450n, 463, 493, 590–91,
        593n
    Huertgen Forest attacks: 408, 429, 438, 440–
        42, 448–55, 457–63, 471, 492–93, 600
    Monschau Corridor attack: 341–42, 370
    Roer drive: 580–82, 587–93
    West Wall attack and Wallendorf bridgehead:
        39–41, 44, 46, 52–53, 56–65, 291n, 620
Armored Division, 7th: 213, 232, 238n, 252, 400–
        403, 517, 547, 566, 568, 572n, 573
    casualties: 238, 240, 280n
    command changes: 238, 246–47
    Peel Marshes fight: 233–48, 267, 384, 392
Armored Division, 9th: 379, 600, 607, 611, 613–
        15
Armored Engineer Battalions
    17th: 533
    22d: 453
Armored Field Artillery Battalions
    56th: 462
    92d: 540
    95th: 61
    400th: 63n
Armored Infantry Battalions
    15th: 592
    46th: 473, 493
    47th: 455, 461–62
Armored Infantry Regiments
    33d: 585
    41st: 533, 560–61, 565
Armored Regiments
    66th: 533, 536, 541, 560, 565
    67th: 526–27, 540–41
Army, First: 3–4, 6, 8–9, 16, 18–19, 28–29, 34, 94,
        119, 122n, 134, 213n, 252, 377n, 379, 380.
        See also Hodges, Lt. Gen. Courtney H.   ·
    Aachen encirclement: 96, 129, 142, 201, 227,
        242, 252, 285, 294, 302–03, 314, 318

Army, First—Continued
    boundary adjustments: 232–33, 241, 251–52,
        319, 340–41, 373, 378–79, 429, 440–41, 452,
        612
    clearing west of the Maas: 231–35, 240
    command and organization: 20–24
    Huertgen Forest attacks: 248, 252, 323, 341–
        43, 347–48, 373, 431, 438–39, 464, 474, 493,
        561
    initial plans for Ruhr advance: 36–37, 203, 205,
        210–13, 215, 232–34, 240–41, 280
    November offensive: 411–15, 488, 496–98, 517–
        18, 520–21, 525, 529, 547, 578–80, 582n, 593–
        95, 611, 614, 618–19
    planning for November offensive: 341, 366, 373,
        388, 390–92, 394–409
    plans for Rhine crossing: 595
    and Roer River dams: 326–28, 342, 406, 463,
        596–600
    summary of losses: 378, 493, 593–94, 617
    summary of Siegfried Line campaign: 616–20
    supply situation: 11–13, 37, 62, 129, 230, 233,
        259, 341, 383–86, 521
    West Wall penetrations: 37–40, 42, 55–56, 62–
        63, 96, 113–15, 121, 127, 233, 252–53, 280,
        377–78
Army, First Allied Airborne: 119, 121, 127–30,
        135n, 204, 218, 616
Army, Third: 4, 6, 18, 20–21, 34, 36–40, 42,
        56, 62–63, 112, 115, 232, 251, 346, 380, 382,
        388, 399n, 597, 613, 619. See also Patton, Lt.
        Gen. George S., Jr.
    appraisal of German situation, August: 18–19
    approval to resume attack: 36
    November offensive drive from Metz: 391–92,
        402, 582, 616
    planned Rhine crossing: 595
    preparations to resume advance: 8–10, 36, 211,
        378
    supply situation: 8–13, 134, 380, 384–85
Army, Fourth: 379
Army, Seventh: 4, 381
Army, Ninth: 4, 251, 318–19, 327, 341, 388, 394,
        395, 399n, 613, 616. See also Simpson, Lt.
        Gen. William H.
    command and organization: 379–80
    final push to the Roer: 558, 577–78, 580, 584,
        594, 596–97
    November offensive: 390–92, 399–404, 406–07,
        409–12, 414, 419, 425, 428, 463, 475, 487–88,
        496–98, 516–19, 521–22, 525, 545–48
    "phantom" army: 522
    planned Rhine crossing: 595
    summary of Siegfried Line campaign: 617, 619
    supply situation: 384–86, 389, 400, 521–22, 545
    transfer to the north wing: 378–79, 378–79n

Army Group, 6th: 4, 6, 243, 380, 387–88, 391, 402, 616
Army Group, 12th: 8, 25, 121, 129, 204, 213, 231, 241, 243, 377–78, 388, 391, 394, 410, 548, 619–20. *See also* Bradley, Gen. Omar N.
  command and organization: 4
  and the Roer River dams: 327, 597
  supply situation: 12–13, 62, 259, 384–86, 389
Army Group, 21st: 6, 28, 36, 121, 129, 204, 213, 546–47. *See also* Montgomery, Field Marshal Sir Bernard L.
  command and organization: 3–4
  Maas River operations: 227, 231, 246, 248
  and opening of Antwerp: 210, 212, 214–15, 377
  and Ruhr thrust: 7–8, 112–13, 198, 205, 211–12, 215, 378, 390, 595, 619
Army Group B. *See* German Army units.
Army Group G. *See* German Army units.
Army Group H. *See* German Army units.
Army Specialized Training Program (ASTP): 621
Arnhem: 113, 120–22, 126–27, 130–32, 131n, 134, 136, 136n, 138, 140–42, 154, 166, 169–70, 174, 185–86, 188, 191, 200, 212, 241
  fight for the bridge: 164, 170–73, 179, 185–86, 195–98, 201
Arnold, General Henry H.: 119, 121
"Artificial moonlight". *See* Battlefield illumination.
Artillery. *See also* Artillery support.
  against tanks: 448, 562
  airborne: 144, 154, 167
  attacks without preparatory fire: 433, 490, 563, 568–69, 603, 607
  "blackout" and counterflak missions: 253, 255, 382, 406, 449, 524
  Cannon Company under division artillery control: 621
  casualties in units: 617
  concentrated artillery shoot: 481
  counterbattery fire: 48, 57, 224, 253, 276, 288, 524–25, 562, 572
  fire direction centers: 26
  harassing fire: 169, 562
  interdiction fire: 109, 266, 452, 481, 562
  marching fire: 550
  massed fire: 269, 276, 604
  neutralization fire: 253, 345
  prepared concentrations: 88, 291, 482, 524, 526, 543, 574, 592, 607, 609
  protective fire: 575–77
  registration difficulties: 336, 609
  rolling barrage: 254, 262, 273, 543, 555, 565, 584, 592
  "short" fires: 271, 609
  time fire: 419, 424, 504, 508, 564, 584n
  TOT: 303, 418, 442, 481, 490, 504, 561, 592

Artillery—Continued
  tree bursts: 52, 332–33, 336, 349, 420, 444, 462, 467, 476, 590, 608
  unobserved fire: 45
Artillery, American: 13, 20–22, 25–27, 620–21
Artillery fire plan: 253, 293, 524, 543, 555
Artillery, German: 15–17, 25–26, 28, 31, 620
Artillery liaison planes: 13, 26–27, 64, 443, 563, 591
Artillery support
  Aachen final assault: 77, 308–10, 312–13, 318
  assault crossing of rivers: 179–80, 226
  Donnerberg attack: 425–27
  V Corps in Roer River Dams attack: 600, 602, 604–05, 607–09
  First Army drive to the Roer: 409, 414–16, 580, 582, 592–94
  Huertgen Forest attacks: 94, 333–34, 343, 348, 355, 363, 420, 442–43, 446, 452–53, 462, 465, 467, 479, 481–82, 489–90
  MARKET–GARDEN: 178–80, 191, 194, 197
  Ninth Army and the Roer plain: 499, 502, 504, 506, 508–09, 511, 513–14, 521, 524–26, 530–532, 537–40, 543, 547–48, 550, 554, 556, 561–62, 565, 568, 572, 574, 576–77, 584
  Peel Marshes: 238–39
  West Wall and Aachen attacks: 45, 55, 57, 60–61, 89, 253–55, 258–59, 261, 270, 276, 287, 291–92, 296, 299, 301–02, 305–06
Artillery support, British: 133, 148, 197, 246, 568
Artillery support, German
  Aachen defense: 81, 283–84, 308, 318, 410
  Albert Canal: 99–100
  Huertgen Forest: 330–31, 337, 358, 361, 364–65, 368, 432, 434–38, 442–44, 452, 459, 465–66, 481, 484–85, 490–91
  MARKET–GARDEN defense: 125, 143, 165, 175–76, 180–81, 185, 189
  opposing the November offensive: 396–97, 411, 413–14, 419n, 427, 519–20
  Peel Marshes: 242–43, 245
  Roer plain: 509–10, 519–20, 526, 530, 561–62, 567, 569, 574–76, 582, 585–86
  Stohlberg Corridor: 422–24
  West Wall and Aachen encirclement: 42–43, 51, 54–55, 58, 64, 83, 87, 257, 263–64, 273–74, 276, 280, 288, 303, 305
Asch: 108
Assault boats: 101–02, 106, 174, 176, 179–81, 196–98, 224, 226–27, 229, 255
Assault guns. *See* Guns, German, SP.
Assault teams: 262, 287, 310
Asten: 191, 243–46
Asten–Meijel road: 244
Attacks. *See also* Night operations; River crossings.
  "Cannae" maneuver: 187

Attacks—Continued
  concentric: 177, 270, 359, 365, 600–01
  converging: 466
  diversionary: 266–67, 304–06, 332, 561
  double–envelopment: 573, 601, 606
  flanking maneuver: 85, 471–72, 478, 568, 584
  frontal: 71–72, 372, 493, 496, 516, 529, 568
  limited–objective: 94, 187, 253, 306, 469, 524,
    540, 567, 571, 585, 601, 607
  method used in Huertgen Forest: 430–31
  "pressure": 425–27, 503
  spoiling. See Peel Marshes.
Austrian troops: 111

Baesweiler: 278, 518, 523–24, 528–29
Baesweiler–Setterich highway: 535
Balck, General der Panzertruppen Hermann: 395
Balkans: 15
Ball, 1st Lt. James E.: 537
Ballard, Lt. Col. Robert A.: 189–90
Balloons: 406
Bane, Capt. Frank P.: 367
Bangalore torpedoes: 287, 433, 608
BAR. See Browning automatic rifle.
Bardenberg: 297–99, 300–01
Barmen: 560, 563, 565
Barrett, Lt. Col. William S.: 555
Barton, Maj. Gen. Raymond O.: 49, 51–53, 55,
    428, 430, 432–34, 436–37, 440, 464–65, 467–
    72, 474
Bass, Capt. Hubert S.: 175
Battle fatigue. See Combat exhaustion.
Battlefield illumination: 548, 550, 564, 611
Bauchem: 546, 551
Baum, Capt. Francis J.: 450
Bayonet: 88, 181, 335, 511, 562
Bazooka: 25, 148, 153, 160, 167, 226, 263–64,
    267, 299, 318, 331, 351, 356–58, 368, 419,
    486–87, 539, 541, 564, 570
Beacons: 138, 406
Beeck: 546, 549, 551, 555–56, 566–69, 571, 573
Beehive charges. See Demolition charges.
Beek: 162, 167, 176, 178, 193
Beeringen: 96, 101, 108, 124–25
Beggendorf: 256, 269, 272–73, 277–78, 518–19,
    523
Belfort Gap: 7n
Belgian troops: 208n, 232n. See also British Army
    units.
Belvedere (tower): 165
Berg en Dal (hotel): 155, 157–58, 162, 165, 167,
    174, 176–78
Bergheim: 590–91, 593
Bergrath: 506
Bergstein: 442, 453–55, 453n, 457, 459–63, 601–02
Berlin: 6, 210–11, 522
Berzbuir: 591–92

Best: 144–47, 150, 152, 187, 189, 192
Bestebreurtje, Capt. Arie D.: 184
Bettendorf: 528, 535–38
Bettingen: 59, 61
Beyer, General der Infanterie Dr. Franz: 42–43,
    56–57, 64
Bickerath: 602–03, 606
Bicycles: 15, 100, 284
Biddle, Col. William S.: 101, 103, 237
Bieber, S. Sgt. Melvin H.: 301, 301n
Biesdorf: 59–60
Billingslea, Lt. Col. Charles: 193
Bingham, Lt. Col. Sidney V., Jr.: 576
Birgel: 591–92
Birk: 297–301
Birkengang: 426–27
Birks, Col. Hammond D.: 102–03, 107, 294n
Bitburg: 40, 42, 56–57, 60–62
Bittrich, SS–Obergruppenfuehrer und General der
    Waffen–SS Willi: 127, 142, 164, 170, 182,
    185, 188, 193, 201–02
Bixel, Col. Charles P.: 379, 518, 520
Blanford, Lt. Col. William O.: 538
Blanton, Col. William L.: 44
Blaskowitz, Generaloberst Johannes: 6
Blazzard, Maj. Howard C.: 50n, 434, 472–73
Bleialf: 49
Bleialf–Pruem highway: 50, 53
"Blue Ball Express": 571
Blumentritt, General der Infanterie Guenther:
    519–20, 548, 567
Boehme, 1st Lt. William: 307, 317
Boeree, Col. Th. A.: 136n
Bogeyman Hill. See Hill 697
Bois le Duc Canal: 243
Bolling, Brig. Gen. Alexander R.: 549, 551, 553–
    56, 568, 573
Bolton, 1st Lt. Cecil H.: 226
Bombardment Division, IX: 24–25, 254, 260n, 381
Bomber Group 48th: 292
Bombs. See also Napalm bombs.
  500-pound: 292
  fragmentation: 404, 412
  tonnage dropped in Aachen: 309
  tonnage dropped in MARKET: 137
  tonnage dropped in QUEEN: 412–13
  tonnage dropped in Roer drive: 577
  tonnage dropped on Roer River Dams: 598
Bond, Lt. Col. Van H.: 85, 338–39, 586
Bonn: 37, 212, 214, 252, 399, 440, 600
Booby traps: 350, 445, 588
Boos, Col. Francis H.: 606
Bork, Generalleutnant Max: 411
Borton, 1st Lt. Don A.: 261, 263, 295
Bouchlas, Capt. Michael S.: 301
Boudinot, Brig. Gen. Truman E.: 73, 422–23
Boulogne: 204, 208–09

Bourg-Leopold: 130
Bourheim: 559–63
Bovenberg: 480–82
Bovenberger Wald: 480, 484
Boyer, Lt. Col. Howard E.: 455
Braakman (inlet): 209, 215
Brachelen: 567
Bradley, Gen. Omar N.: 4, 7–8, 13, 20–21, 23, 36–37, 40, 120, 129, 213, 369, 377n, 560, 620. *See also* Army Group, 12th.
    and boundary adjustments: 231–32, 251, 378–79
    and the November offensive: 391–92, 400–01, 403, 406, 409, 498
    relief of commanders: 246–47, 319
    and Roer River Dams: 327, 342, 597
    and Ruhr double–thrust drive: 9–10, 112–13, 211, 595
    and supply allocations: 12, 62, 259, 384–86, 388–89
    and US troops under British command: 233, 241, 378
Brand: 72, 76
Brandenberg: 451–55, 453n, 457, 459
Brandenberg–Bergstein ridge: 344–45, 349, 358, 364, 373, 440, 446, 451–60, 582–83, 592, 600–02, 612
Brandenberger, General der Panzertruppen Erich: 42, 63, 69, 87–88, 91, 93, 98, 103, 109, 273, 277, 290, 300, 330, 334, 337, 353, 359, 394–95, 460
Brandscheid: 40, 52–54
Breakthrough possibilities: 49, 51–53, 56, 86, 133, 234–35, 332, 421, 467, 475, 492, 594, 607
Breda: 224–25
Bree: 113, 231
Brereton, Lt. Gen. Lewis H.: 127–30, 128n, 132, 136–37, 154, 196, 199, 204, 218n
Breskens Pocket: 215, 218–21, 227–28
Brest: 4, 115, 232, 251, 378, 380, 441n, 606n
Bridgeheads. *See also* Meuse–Escaut Canal; River crossings; Wallendorf.
    XIX Corps in West Wall: 262–280, 496, 517–18
Bridges. *See also* Engineers; and rivers and canals (by name).
    air attack of: 346, 381, 525
    Bailey: 108, 150, 153, 187, 226
    demolished: 3, 12, 52, 57, 65, 70, 73, 75–76, 84, 101, 106, 148, 150, 152, 162, 200, 224, 436, 509, 511–12, 555
    flood effect on: 326, 522
    footbridges: 101, 148, 255, 261, 264, 266
    ground attack of: 64, 144–48, 150, 152–53, 160–61, 181–82, 187, 190, 224. *See also* Arnhem; Nijmegen.
    importance to Operation GARDEN: 131–32, 136, 154–57

Bridges—Continued
    improvised: 256–57, 265–66, 446, 533
    ponton: 525
    shortage for supply: 521–22
    treadway: 60, 103, 226, 264–66, 533
    trestle: 60
Briles, S. Sgt. Herschel F.: 480n
British Army units.
    Army, Second: 4, 11, 113–14, 120, 122n, 133–34, 135n, 157n, 196, 204–05, 207–08, 212–13, 215, 220–22, 232, 241–42, 391, 404n, 545–46, 595
    Battery, 357th Searchlight (Royal Artillery): 548, 551
    Brigade, 1st Belgian: 232–35, 232n, 237–38, 241, 246
    Brigade, 1st Polish Parachute: 128, 131–32, 172–73, 186, 195–98, 203
    Brigade, 4th Armoured: 246
    Brigade, 32nd Guards: 191
    Corps, 1st: 4, 208, 221–23, 225, 227
    Corps, 1st Airborne: 121–22, 128, 132, 136, 199, 204
    Corps, 8: 113, 120, 133, 187, 191, 195, 199n, 202, 236, 241–42, 248
    Corps, 12: 120, 133, 153, 187, 192, 202–03, 220–21, 247–48
    Corps, 30: 96, 101, 113, 120, 128, 131, 133, 148–50, 154–56, 168–70, 172, 174, 186–87, 191, 195–200, 199n, 203, 248, 403, 516, 521–22, 545–48, 551, 555–56, 566, 594–95
    Division, 1st Airborne: 128, 131n, 132–33, 138, 140, 170–74, 179, 185–87, 196–99, 201, 203
    Division, 1st Polish Armored: 224–25, 227
    Division, 3d Infantry: 242
    Division, 6th Airborne: 128n
    Division, 11th Armoured: 242
    Division, 15th Infantry: 246
    Division, 43d Infantry: 133, 185–86, 195–98, 546, 551, 556
    Division, 49th Infantry: 222, 224
    Division, 50th Infantry: 133, 195
    Division, 52d Lowland (Airportable): 128, 132, 196
    Division, 53d Infantry: 246
    Division, Guards Armoured: 133, 148–50, 157n, 174–75, 177–78, 185, 196, 208
    Drewforce: 548, 550
    Group, Coldstream Guards: 178, 185, 196
    Regiment, Dorsetshire: 197–98
    Yeomanry, 1st Fife and Forfar: 542
    Yeomanry, Sherwood Rangers: 554
British forces: 5, 617. *See also* British Army units.
    casualties in MARKET-GARDEN: 198–99, 199n
    delay in Operation GARDEN: 199–200
    role in November offensive: 401, 520, 545, 547
Brittany: 4, 8, 11, 115, 379, 522, 580, 600, 612

"Broad front" policy: 6, 199–201, 210–11
Broichweiden: 294–95, 501–02
Brooke, Field Marshal Sir Alan: 214
Brooks, Maj. Gen. Edward H.: 65, 107n
Brown, Capt. Bobbie E.: 287n
Brown, Lt. Col. John C.: 570
Browning, Lt. Gen. F. A. M.: 128, 136, 138, 157, 157n, 159, 168–69, 172, 196–97, 203
Browning automatic rifle: 25, 181
Bruges: 208–09
Bruns, Generalmajor Walter: 359, 368
Brussels: 4, 8, 29, 205, 210, 213, 218, 232n, 377, 390–91
Buellingen: 611–12
Buesbach: 76, 80
Buildings (as cover): 309n, 310–12, 333, 368, 418–19, 453, 455, 481, 484–87, 508, 511–14, 520, 520n, 532, 577, 604–05
Bulgarian troops: 15
Bulldozers: 352, 541, 555
Bunkers: 31, 35, 43, 73, 253, 255, 316, 331, 333, 372, 432, 442, 608, 613
Burp gun: 15, 27–28, 491, 605
Burt, Capt. James M.: 303n
Burton, Lt. Col. William H. Jr.: 473n

Caen: 142, 404n
Calais: 204, 208–09
Camouflage: 31, 35, 45, 259, 264, 432
Camp d'Elsenborn: 84, 251, 314, 340, 399, 600–02, 606, 612
Canadian Army units
    Army, First: 4, 204–05, 208–10, 208n, 212–15, 220–22, 227, 228n, 405n
    Corps, 2d: 220–21
    Division, 2d: 220
    Division, 3d: 221
Canadian forces: 5, 229, 617. See also Canadian Army units.
Canal de la Dérivation de la Lys: 209, 215
Cannon Company: 621
Carpenter, 1st Lt. Leonard R.: 569–70
Carr, 1st Lt. Oliver B. Jr.: 175
Carter, Col. Leslie D.: 68, 409, 582
Carter, Sgt. Noah: 577
Cassell, Lt. Col. Harold A.: 535
Cassidy, Lt. Col. Patrick F.: 146, 153, 193
Castle Hill (Burg-Berg). See Hill 400.5.
Casualties: 276, 417, 469–70, 484, 621. See also Combat exhaustion; Evacuation; Losses, summary of; Officers; Trench foot; and entries under numbered units.
    Allied forces: 4–5, 388, 388n
    British forces: 198–99, 198n, 199n
    Canadian and attached forces: 229
    caused by friendly fire: 254, 260, 348, 412–13
    German: 4–5, 14, 26, 89, 95, 152, 168, 182,

Casualties—Continued
    German—Continued
        198, 229, 293, 317, 317n, 339–40, 340n, 374, 390, 450, 488, 507, 514, 544, 578, 617
    nonbattle: 429, 438, 455–57, 474, 492, 557, 593–94, 593n, 606, 609, 612–13, 617
    specialists: 26, 617
    V-weapon attacks: 230
Cavalry Groups
    4th: 23, 36, 92, 328, 347, 590
    14th: 613
    102d: 24, 41, 600
    113th: 23, 36, 101–03, 107, 114, 232–33, 235–38, 400–02, 517, 547, 556, 566–68, 571
Cavalry Reconnaissance Squadrons
    4th: 477
    18th: 613
    32d: 613
    85th: 3
    87th: 244
Channel coast: 119, 204
Channel Islands: 5
Channel ports: 4–5, 12, 204–05, 208–09, 218, 388
Chaplains: 371
Chappuis, Lt. Col. Richard D.: 244–45
Chappuis, Lt. Col. Steve A.: 150–51
Charlemagne (Emperor): 29, 281
Charleroi: 8, 381, 384
Chartres: 36, 39, 62
Chatfield, Lt. Col. Lee W.: 84, 92–93, 333–35
Chemical Mortar Battalion, 92d: 524, 575
Cherbourg: 8, 23, 49n, 383
Chill, Generalleutnant Kurt: 124
Christiansen, General der Flieger Friedrich: 126, 135, 140, 142, 395
Churchill tanks. See Tanks.
CISCO: 260n
Civilians: 12–13, 125
    Aachen evacuation: 71, 81–82
    assistance to military forces: 102, 148, 162–64, 168–69, 184
    casualties and losses: 153, 230, 260
    Dutch reaction to airborne landings: 140, 145, 150, 160, 165, 206
    rail reconstruction work: 12, 384
    work on defense of Aachen sector: 34, 410
Clark, T. Sgt. Francis J.: 49n
CLIPPER, 546–58, 566, 568, 574
Clothing, winter: 14, 25, 383–84, 386, 444
Coal mines: 496, 510–11, 528, 536–37
Coastal "fortresses." See Channel ports.
Cochran, Col. John H.: 224, 226, 505, 507, 511, 514
Cole, Col. John T.: 61, 589
Cole, Lt. Col. Robert G.: 147, 150
Collier, Col. John H.: 108–09, 533, 541, 560, 564–65

Collins, Maj. Gen. J. Lawton: 23, 36–39, 66–68, 71, 75, 78, 86, 89–92, 95, 284, 286, 292, 313–14, 323–24, 326n, 327, 330, 342n, 364, 381, 399–400, 408–09, 421, 425–26, 474–76, 481–83, 490, 492, 498, 505, 507, 515, 580, 582, 585, 589, 591, 621. See also Corps, VII.
Colmar: 616
Cologne: 29, 37, 142, 203, 212, 232–33, 241, 252, 308, 391, 394, 399
Cologne plain: 7, 399, 496
Combat Command Hickey. See CCA, 3d Armored Division.
Combat Commands of Armored Divisions
    CCA, 2d: 108–10, 278, 279n, 523, 532–33, 541–44, 558, 560, 564–65
    CCB, 2d: 108–10, 269–278, 279n, 280, 523–24, 526–27, 530n, 532–33, 540–44, 558
    CCA, 3d: 72n, 74–77, 79–80, 88, 90, 483–84
    CCB, 3d: 72–74, 76–80, 88–91, 422–24
    CCA, 5th: 56, 65, 471–73, 591–93
    CCB, 5th: 46, 56, 60–61, 63–65, 589–93
    CCR 5th: 56–61, 63–65, 408, 429, 440, 442, 445–55, 457, 459–63, 466, 471, 493, 585–86, 600
    CCA, 7th: 238–40, 244
    CCB, 7th: 238–40, 242, 244–46
    CCR, 7th: 238, 240, 244–45
    CCB, 9th: 607, 611
Combat exhaustion: 54, 289, 346, 358, 360–61, 364, 371–72, 429, 438, 443–45, 455, 463, 467, 474, 492–93, 574, 576, 617–18
Combat indoctrination: 612–14, 621
Combined Chiefs of Staff: 3
Comet: 120, 129, 131n
Command
    in new divisions: 621
    tank-infantry command by co-ordination: 585–86
Commando operations: 228–29
Communications: 26, 293, 334. See also Radio.
    problems of: 148, 166, 169–70, 172–73, 291, 350, 491, 569–71, 605, 609–10
Communications, German: 245, 405
    problems of: 26, 34, 316, 338, 413, 459
Communications Zone: 11–13, 126, 383–85, 389
Concentration of forces: 55–56, 177, 211, 251, 273–74, 328, 378–79
Congressional Medal of Honor. See Medal of Honor.
Cook, Sgt. Ezra: 272
Cook, Maj. Julian A.: 179, 181–82
Corlett, Maj. Gen. Charles H.: 23, 96, 98, 100–01, 108, 112–15, 233, 235, 240, 252, 258–59, 269–70, 278–79, 285, 294, 302–03, 319, 319n, 320. See also Corps, XIX.
Corley, Lt. Col. John T.: 309–16, 421

Corman, Cpl. Daniel L.: 151n
Corps, V: 3, 36, 98, 251–52, 302, 314, 378, 409, 428, 430, 611–12. See also Gerow, Maj. Gen. Leonard T.
    casualties: 593, 612
    command and organization: 23–24, 107n
    November offensive: 373, 396–97, 399, 408, 438–43, 449, 451–55, 461, 464, 467, 469, 471, 561, 580–82, 587, 593, 601
    Roer Dams attack: 327, 327n, 342, 342n, 406, 463, 598–602, 615
    second attack on Schmidt: 340–43, 346, 348, 352, 366, 400
    Wallendorf bridgehead: 56–65, 114–15, 251
    West Wall reconnaissance attacks: 37–66
Corps, VII: 29–30, 252, 261, 319, 327, 327n, 340–41. See also Collins, Maj. Gen. J. Lawton.
    Aachen encirclement and assault: 96, 98, 101, 103, 107, 109, 112, 114–15, 235, 252–53, 257, 274, 277–80, 285, 291, 297, 304, 309, 318, 498
    casualties: 586, 593
    command and organization: 23, 36
    final attack to the Roer: 580–83, 585–86, 591–94, 600
    Huertgen Forest attacks: 92, 323–24, 348
    initial penetration of West Wall: 37–38, 41, 66–68, 71–72, 75, 80, 82, 86–87, 89–90, 95, 251, 283n
    November offensive: 364, 366, 373, 395, 397, 399–400, 403–04, 408–15, 421–22, 424–25, 428, 440, 442, 451, 463–64, 468, 471, 474–75, 481, 487, 498, 500, 502, 504, 507, 510–11, 515, 529, 561
Corps, VIII: 251, 373, 379, 396–97, 399, 441n, 474, 580, 611–15
Corps, XIII: 400, 400n, 401–03, 516–17, 523–24, 542–44, 546–48, 550, 554, 556, 561, 566–68, 571–72, 574, 580, 584–85, 593
Corps, XVIII (Airborne): 128
Corps, XIX: 29–30, 36–38, 95, 115, 124, 189, 212, 252. See also Corlett, Maj. Gen. Charles H.; McLain, Maj. Gen. Raymond S.
    clearing west of the Maas: 114, 231, 233–35, 237, 252
    command and organization: 23, 319–20
    final push to the Roer: 544, 558–66, 568, 572, 574, 576–77, 580, 584–85
    November offensive: 341, 378–79, 400–402, 498–500, 502–03, 507, 516–20, 522–26, 529–32, 534, 537, 545–46, 548, 550, 556
    and Roer River Dams: 327
    West Wall attacks north of Aachen: 67, 69, 72, 81, 91, 96–98, 100–01, 106, 110, 112–15, 240–41, 251–53, 257–59, 261, 266, 276–79, 283–86, 288, 290, 293–95, 298, 300, 302, 304, 313, 318, 330, 386, 519

Cota, Maj. Gen. Norman D.: 44–45, 44n, 47–48, 55, 343–44, 346–47, 350–52, 355, 358, 360, 362, 367–69, 373
Cotton, Lt. Col. Hugh W.: 302
Counterattacks, German: 274, 317, 430–31, 478. *See also* Ardennes counteroffensive.
Cox, Lt. Col. William C.: 275–78, 298, 301, 305–06
Crabill, Col. Edwin B.: 590
Craig, Maj. Gen. Louis A.: 83–84, 86, 90, 92–94, 323, 326n, 328, 331–32, 336, 338, 585
Crerar, Lt. Gen. Henry D. G.: 208, 220
Crocker, Lt. Gen. Sir John T.: 221–25, 227
Crocodile tanks. *See* Tanks.
Cross, Col. Thomas J.: 447–48
Crossroads 87: 571–73
Crucifix Hill. *See* Hill 239.
"Culverts": 256–57, 264–65
Cushman, 1st Lt. Robert P.: 262–63
Czechoslovakia: 31
Czechoslovakian troops: 208n, 229

Daddow, 1st Lt. Elwood G.: 103–04
Dahl, Sgt. Sverry: 74
Daley, Col. Edmund K.: 360, 362, 365
Daniel, Lt. Col. Derrill M.: 309–10, 314–15, 420–21, 490–91
Daser, Generalleutnant Wilhelm: 219, 228–29
Davis, Brig. Gen. George A.: 358, 361, 365, 368, 370, 372
Davison, Lt. Col. Floid A.: 47–48
Dawson, Lt. Col. Joe: 291–93, 418, 420
De Groote Barrier: 125, 133, 208
De Groote Peel: 247
De Ploeg: 163
Deadman's Ford: 59–61
Deadman's Moor: 93–94, 323, 328, 332, 600
Deception: 258, 393–95, 410, 465–66, 561, 614. *See also* Ardennes counteroffensive.
Decker, Maj. Lawrence L.: 332–33
Defense
  blocking position: 53
  in depth: 351, 364
  linear: 100, 313
  perimeter: 94, 144, 172, 186, 191, 195–96
  reverse slope: 563
  screen: 190, 195, 200
  static: 187
Defilade: 275, 452, 459, 532, 543, 603
DeLille, Lieutenant: 3n
Demolition charges: 45–47, 102, 160–61, 164, 183, 203, 255, 262–64, 275, 287, 310, 310n, 350, 359–60, 555, 596, 619. *See also* Bangalore torpedoes.
Dempsey, Lt. Gen. Miles C.: 114, 122n, 133, 196, 208, 232, 241
Denkert, Generalmajor Walter: 290–91, 410, 502

Denmark: 135
Derichsweiler: 586, 590
Deurne: 231, 237, 241–42, 244–46
Deurne Canal: 241–46
Devers, Lt. Gen. Jacob L.: 4
Devil's Hill. *See* Hill 75.9.
Dew, 2d Lt. Joseph H.: 46, 46n
Dickson, Col. Benjamin A.: 23
Diekirch: 42, 46
Dieppe: 4, 208
Diestel, Generalleutnant Erich: 220
Diekirch: 42, 46
Disney, Col. Paul A.: 272, 526–27, 531–32
Distinguished Service Cross: 46n, 50n, 53n, 63n, 64n, 279, 299n, 301n, 312n, 339n, 366n, 368n, 418n, 424n, 473n, 610
Diven, Cpl. Ralph F.: 3n
Divisions. *See* Airborne Divisions; Armored Divisions; British Army units; Canadian Army units; German Army units; Infantry Divisions.
Doan, Col. Leander LaC.; 74
Doherty, Capt. Henry R.: 361–62, 365
Dommel River: 131, 145–46, 149
Donnerberg. *See* Hill 287.
Dortmund: 28
Dowdy, Lt. Col. John: 53
Dreiborn ridge: 601, 606, 610–11
Dreiborn Dam: 325–26
Driel: 186, 195–96, 198
Driscoll, Lt. Col. Edmund F.: 416–18
Drop zones: 130, 136n, 137–39, 144–47, 159–60, 170–72, 186, 196, 200
"Drowned earth" policy: 327
Druon Antigon: 207
"Duck bills": 518
Duerboslar: 537, 539
Dueren: 30, 66–67, 78, 80, 83, 85, 258, 325, 327, 330–31, 333–34, 346, 397, 404, 408, 412–14, 428, 431, 451, 465, 469, 471–73, 488, 496, 515, 518, 520, 559, 582–83, 586–87, 590, 592, 596n, 602
Duerwiss: 505–06
Duesseldorf: 28, 113, 252, 517
Dugouts: 398, 613
Duisberg: 113
DUKW's: 196
Dummy parachute drops: 138
Dunkerque: 204, 208
"Dunkerque" operation: 219
"Dutch Panhandle": 29, 36, 96
Dutch troops: 208n. *See also* Resistance forces.
Dwyer, Col. Philip R.: 303

Eaker, Lt. Gen. Ira C.: 405
Eastern Front: 14–16
Eberding, Generalmajor Kurt: 219, 221
Eberich: 559, 561

Echternach: 40, 56–57, 59, 251
Echtz: 404, 585
Ederen: 533, 541–44, 558, 566
Eerde: 145, 189–92
Eifel: 29–30, 34, 38, 40–41, 62n, 69, 393–94, 399, 408. *See also* Ardennes-Eifel; Schnee Eifel
Eighth Air Force: 137–38, 169n, 196, 403–06, 412
Eilendorf: 76–77, 80–81, 86, 88, 284, 286, 288, 290–91, 304, 313–14
Eilendorf–Verlautenheide road: 287
Eindhoven: 113, 120, 122–23, 125, 130–31, 133–34, 137, 140, 142–44, 146, 148–50, 152–53, 168, 174, 187, 189, 199–200, 206, 231, 233, 401
Eindhoven–Grave road. *See* Hell's Highway.
Eisenhower, Gen. Dwight D.: 3, 5, 134–35, 387–88. *See also* Supreme Headquarters, Allied Expeditionary Forces (SHAEF).
  and air attack of Roer River Dams: 598
  and Berlin as ultimate goal: 210–11
  "broad-front policy": 6–7, 9–10, 36–37, 199–201, 210–11, 390–91, 619
  conferences of top commanders: 8, 10, 36, 62, 128, 205, 210–14, 231, 369, 377, 387, 390–91, 595
  and conquest of the Ruhr: 6–7, 36–37, 205, 211–12, 391, 595
  decision for the November offensive: 390–91
  and importance of opening Antwerp: 207, 209–11, 214–15, 218, 218n
  and the logistical situation: 8, 62, 207, 380, 382, 384
  and MARKET-GARDEN: 113, 119–22, 128–29, 214
  and Montgomery and the command situation: 8, 213–15, 213n, 231, 378, 619
  and release of MARKET airborne troops, 201, 204–05
  and relief of General Corlett: 319, 319–20n
  and shortage of replacements: 388–89
Ekman, Col. William E.: 158, 161–62
Elst: 195–96
Elverfeldt, General Harald Freiherr von: 244, 530
Engel, General: 410–11, 488
Engel, Col. Gerhard: 88–89, 283
Engelsdorf: 538, 558
Engineer Combat Battalions
  20th: 351–52, 360, 362, 365
  146th: 365–66
  254th: 60, 64n
  294th: 347
  298th: 328, 337–38
  1340th: 365, 367
Engineer Combat Groups
  1104th: 302
  1106th: 286–87, 309, 310n, 314–16
  1171st: 343, 360, 362, 365
Engineer support: 47, 60, 64, 74, 76, 78, 102, 108,

Engineer support—Continued
  150, 203, 226, 267, 305, 333, 347–48, 351–52, 355, 359–62, 365–67, 435–38, 445–46, 453, 455, 467, 541–42, 550, 555, 588–89
Envelopment maneuver: 85, 109, 211–12, 268–69, 275, 426
Erdmann, Generalleutnant Wolfgang: 125
Erft River: 29
Erlekom: 193
Erp: 189
Escaut River: 28
Eschweiler: 66–67, 72, 76–77, 88, 413–14, 425, 496, 503, 505
Eschweiler woods: 422, 424–28, 464, 503
Eschweiler–Weisweiler industrial triangle: 399, 403, 408, 412, 422, 424–25, 475, 480, 482, 492, 498, 580
Essen: 28
Etang de Lindre dam: 597
Euchen: 298–300, 499, 501
Eupen: 36, 67, 84, 377n, 454
Evacuation
  ordered at Aachen: 71, 81–82
  of wounded: 311, 343, 371–72, 444, 467, 591
Evans, Cpl. James L.: 147n
Evans, Lt. Col. Robert F.: 286, 421
Ewell, Lt. Col. Julian J.: 193

Farmer, S. Sgt. Robert D.: 418n
Farwick Park (Aachen): 307, 309, 311–13, 315
Fascines: 518, 526
Feldt, General der Kavallerie Kurt: 126–27
Field Artillery Battalions
  118th: 269
  258th: 259n
  991st: 332n
Field Artillery Brigade, 32d: 582n
Field Artillery Group, 406th: 607
Fighter Groups
  365th: 64, 332
  366th: 446, 453, 453n, 459
  368th: 24n, 586
  370th: 24n
  404th: 24n, 332
  474th: 24n, 449
Finnish troops: 15
Five Points: 434–35
Flail tanks. *See* Tanks, Scorpion.
Flak. *See* Antiaircraft defense, German.
Flak wagons: 166, 169
Flamethrowers: 45, 48, 221, 255, 262–63, 275, 287, 310, 613. *See also* Tanks, Crocodile.
Flanders: 7–8, 29, 131
Flank security: 84, 92, 107, 112–15, 231–32, 294–95, 339, 401, 420, 434–38, 464, 493, 553, 566–67, 566n, 601
Flares: 292, 459

Fleig, 1st Lt. Raymond E.: 355, 357–58, 360
Fleming, Pvt. Roy O.: 47
Flood, Lt. Col. Albert: 350–52, 355, 357, 368
Floods and flooding: 102, 198, 215, 227–29, 522, 597
    tactical flooding of the Roer: 326–28, 342, 406, 596–97
Flossdorf: 567, 571–73
Floverich: 526–27, 532
Flushing: 228–29
Foote, 1st Lt. Theodore: 263
Ford, Maj. James C.: 46
Ford, Col. Thomas J.: 41
Forest fighting. See Woods fighting.
Fort Eben Emael: 101–02
Fort Hof van Holland: 181
Fortifications. See also Huertgen Forest Pillboxes; Roer plain; West Wall.
    field: 260, 265, 275, 331, 350, 416–18, 432, 452, 482, 510, 520, 535–38, 550, 552, 560, 567, 572, 578, 608
Foster, Col. Robert T.: 589
Foxholes: 225, 305, 331, 336, 358, 360, 373, 398, 432, 437, 465, 476–77, 520, 577, 608, 613–14
Frankland, Lt. Col. Robert E.: 261–62, 264
Freialdenhoven: 541–44, 558
Frelenberg: 272, 278
French, Sgt. Dennis D.: 532
French forces: 4–5, 208n, 381
Frenz: 509, 513
Frenzerburg (castle): 482–87, 489, 511
Fronhoven: 558
Frost, Lt. Col. J. D.: 171–72, 179, 185–86
Frostbite: 372, 456–57
Fuehrer Reserve: 427, 488

Gangelt: 111
Garcia, Pfc. Marcario: 469, 469n
GARDEN: 120, 131, 133. See also MARKET-GARDEN.
Garlington, 1st Lt. Creswell Jr.: 569–70
Gavin, Maj. Gen. James M.: 156, 156n, 157, 157n, 158, 158n, 159, 162–63, 165, 167–69, 174, 176, 178–79, 183–84, 193, 200, 205
Gay creek: 59–61
Gehrke, 2d Lt. Roy E.: 63n
Geich: 585
Geilenkirchen: 34, 109–112, 114, 252–53, 257–58, 266, 273–74, 277–78, 315, 401–03, 414, 516–21
    clearing the salient: 545–57. See also CLIPPER.
Geilenkirchen–Aachen highway: 269–272
Geilenkirchen–Aldenhoven highway: 527, 532–33, 541–42
Geisberg. See Hill 228.
Gemert: 189
Gemuend: 324

Gereonsweiler: 516, 523, 526–27, 531–33, 540–44, 556, 558, 566, 570, 574
Gereonsweiler–Lindern highway: 568–69
Gerhardt, Maj. Gen. Charles H.: 523–24, 527–35, 535n, 537, 539, 558, 560, 563, 576
German Army
    outlook in September 1944: 14–19
    resurgence in fall 1944: 122, 377, 392–93
German Army units
    Alarm units: 42, 57–58, 127, 258, 507
    Army Groups
        B: 6, 18, 42–43, 57, 63, 87, 100, 104, 107–08, 110, 112, 125, 127, 134–35, 140–41, 197, 219, 237, 240–41, 243, 247, 277, 289–90, 304, 353, 358, 394–95, 530, 540, 545, 547, 571
        G: 6, 42, 57, 60, 243, 394–95
        H: 395, 547
        Student: 247
    Armies
        Ersatzheer (Replacement Army): 15, 393
        Feldheer (Field Army): 15
        First: 6, 42–43, 57, 60–63
        First Parachute: 6, 19, 69, 98–100, 103, 106, 108–11, 123–27, 135–36, 140–42, 146, 150, 153, 188, 193, 201–02, 219, 235–36, 247, 267, 394–95, 410
        Fifth Panzer: 6, 127, 247, 353, 394–96, 410. See also Gruppe von Manteuffel.
        Sixth Panzer: 394, 566–67, 601, 610
        Seventh: 6, 19, 43, 45, 57, 63–64, 69, 82–83, 87–88, 93, 98–99, 103–04, 108–12, 125, 127, 218, 247, 273, 283, 290, 300, 330, 334, 346, 353, 358–59, 394–96, 410, 437, 448, 460, 465, 583
        Fifteenth: 6, 8, 19, 99–100, 123, 125–27, 134, 136, 150, 193, 198, 202, 218–19, 222–23, 242, 245–47, 539, 592. See also Gruppe von Manteuffel.
        Nineteenth: 6
    Corps
        Feldt: 127, 142, 164, 166, 176–77, 193, 247
        Volks artillery: 393, 396
        I SS Panzer: 41–42, 42n, 43, 56, 61, 69, 284, 289, 300, 314, 610
        II Parachute: 142, 177, 188, 193, 202–03
        II SS Panzer: 127, 135–36, 141–42, 142n, 164, 170, 172, 185, 188, 193, 200–01
        XII SS: 201, 318n, 394, 410, 419, 519, 539, 548, 568
        XLVII Panzer: 243–45, 247, 397, 410, 518–19, 530, 540, 567, 571
        LXVII: 219–20, 601–02, 610
        LXXIV: 69, 83, 87, 91–92, 273, 330, 333, 339, 346, 353, 358, 431, 583, 592, 601
        LXXX: 42–43, 56–57, 60–61, 63–64

German Army units—Continued
  Corps—Continued
    LXXXI: 69–70, 75, 79, 83, 87, 91–93, 98, 105, 107, 110, 112, 257–59, 267, 273, 276–77, 283–84, 290, 300, 314, 318n, 330, 396, 410, 417, 419, 419n, 427, 431, 487–88, 499–500, 502, 509, 519–20, 538–39, 559, 562, 582, 592
    LXXXVI: 188, 193, 195, 235–37, 240, 247
    LXXXVIII: 123–25, 188–89, 192, 195
    388th Volks Artillery: 245, 519
    403d Volks Artillery: 488
    407th Volks Artillery: 567
  Divisions
    Panzer Lehr: 42, 59, 63–64
    Parachute Training Erdmann: 124–25, 188, 235–37
    von Tettau: 142, 171–72, 193
    Volks grenadier: 15, 393, 601, 616
    1st SS Panzer: 300n, 301, 304
    2d Panzer: 42–43, 45, 47, 61, 63, 127, 243
    2d SS Panzer: 41–43, 50–51, 53
    3d Panzer Grenadier: 284, 287, 290, 292–93, 295, 300, 304, 313–14, 396, 410, 427, 499–500, 502–03, 510, 519, 538, 562
    3d Parachute: 488–90, 492, 509–10, 514, 548, 583, 586
    5th Parachute: 42, 59, 63
    6th Parachute: 124n, 177
    7th Parachute: 125n
    9th Panzer: 18, 69–70, 75–79, 87, 91, 95, 98, 201–02, 243–44, 247, 304, 313, 397, 518, 530, 533–34, 540, 542–44, 549–54, 567, 571
    9th SS Panzer: 122, 127, 142–43, 164, 171
    10th SS Panzer: 110, 122, 127, 142–43, 164, 171, 189, 547–48, 567, 571–73, 616
    12th Infantry: 71, 79, 87–90, 92, 95, 109, 111, 258, 273–74, 277, 279, 283, 288, 295
    12th SS Panzer: 300n
    12th VG: 411, 413–14, 417, 423, 425–27, 475, 482, 484, 488, 492, 503, 507–08, 538, 583
    15th Panzer Grenadier: 243–45, 247, 396, 518, 530, 540–41, 544–45, 550, 554–56, 567
    19th VG: 60, 63
    39th Infantry: 64
    47th VG: 411, 414, 417–21, 424, 460, 475–77, 479–80, 484, 487–89, 492, 502, 508, 539, 583, 585, 592
    49th Infantry: 98–104, 107, 110–12, 253, 257–58, 266, 270, 273, 275–77, 279, 283, 295–97, 314, 318n, 500
    59th Infantry: 125, 136, 142, 146, 150, 152–53, 189, 192, 200, 219, 574
    64th Infantry: 219, 221

German Army units—Continued
  Divisions—Continued
    70th Infantry: 219–20, 227–28
    85th Infantry: 124, 583, 602
    89th Infantry: 83–85, 333, 346, 352–54, 356n, 359, 361, 367–68, 372–73, 431, 583, 602
    116th Panzer: 68–71, 75, 77, 81–82, 87, 91, 95, 98, 103, 127, 201–02, 245, 257, 283–84, 287, 289–90, 295, 300–01, 303–04, 306, 313–14, 353–54, 358–59, 362–63, 365–67, 372, 417, 419, 431, 437, 465, 538
    176th Infantry: 99–101, 106, 108–09, 111–12, 114, 124, 188, 236–37, 519–20, 548
    180th Replacement Training: 189, 236
    183d VG: 91, 109–12, 253, 257–58, 266–67, 270, 273, 277, 283, 295, 318n, 519, 530, 548, 551, 567
    245th Infantry: 125, 219
    246th VG: 91, 258, 270, 273–74, 277, 279, 283–84, 286, 288, 295–97, 301, 307–08, 314, 411, 499–500, 502, 510, 519, 537–38, 559–60, 564, 583–84
    272d VG: 352, 359, 460–62, 583, 601–02, 604
    275th Infantry: 91, 98–105, 107, 110–12, 253, 257, 273, 286, 330–31, 333, 338, 346, 352, 359, 372, 410, 431–32, 437, 442, 465
    277th VG: 602, 607, 610
    326th VG: 606, 610–11
    340th VG: 559, 561–63, 572–73, 575
    344th Infantry: 427, 439, 442, 465, 469, 583
    346th Infantry: 220, 223
    347th Infantry: 83
    353d Infantry: 70, 75–76, 87, 92–93, 330, 437, 469, 583, 588
    363d VG: 201–03, 573, 575
    406th (Landesschuetzen): 126, 142, 166, 176
    711th Infantry: 220, 223
    719th Infantry: 123–26, 219
  Brigades
    Volks-werfer: 393, 396
    102d Assault Gun: 87
    105th Panzer: 68, 70, 76
    107th Panzer: 142–43, 153, 187–89, 236, 239
    108th Panzer: 63–64, 283–84, 295–300
    280th Assault Gun: 143
    341st Assault Gun: 562
    394th Assault Gun: 70, 74–75, 81
    667th Assault Gun: 489
  Regiments
    von Fritzschen: 284, 295–97, 500
    Wegelein: 337–39, 343, 347, 353

German Army units—Continued
  Regiments—Continued
    2d Parachute: 124, 124n, 192
    5th Parachute: 489–90
    6th Parachute: 124, 124n, 125, 192–95, 221
    8th Panzer Grenadier: 291–92
    8th Parachute: 510, 514
    9th Parachute: 489
    10th Panzer Grenadier: 531, 551–52
    11th Panzer Grenadier: 531, 543
    12th Artillery: 87
    16th Panzer: 353, 356, 359, 368, 419n
    22d SS Panzer Grenadier: 573
    27th Fusilier: 87–88, 90–91, 482, 484, 488
    29th Panzer Grenadier: 290
    48th Grenadier: 87–89, 93, 417–18
    60th Panzer Grenadier: 300–01, 303–04, 354, 358, 361, 365
    89th Grenadier: 87–89, 423
    103d, 47th VG Division: 414, 480, 484, 488
    104th, 47th VG Division: 419–20, 475, 477–78, 480, 488–89
    115th Infantry: 420, 476, 479, 488
    148th Infantry: 98–99, 258, 275
    149th Infantry: 99, 258
    156th Panzer Grenadier: 306, 359, 365–66, 465
    253d Infantry: 330
    330th, 183d VG Division: 257, 530
    343d Grenadier: 273–74, 277
    352d Infantry: 284
    404th Grenadier: 273–74, 277, 284, 297, 312–13, 499–500
    689th Infantry: 284
    751st, 326th VG Division: 610
    980th, 272d VG Division: 460, 605
    983d Infantry: 330, 333, 346
    984th Infantry: 99, 330, 346
    985th Infantry: 330, 346
    991st, 277th VG Division: 607
    1055th Infantry: 85, 352-55, 359, 361, 368
    1056th Infantry: 84, 359, 368
  Kampfgruppen
    Bayer: 487, 539
    Chill: 124–25, 124n, 142, 192, 200
    Diefenthal: 300–01, 305, 312
    Eisenhuber: 484
    Engel: 488–90, 508–09, 583
    Heinke: 189
    Huber: 189–92
    von Manteuffel: 395–96, 410, 417, 488, 501, 518–19, 530, 559, 583
    Walther: 124–25, 124n, 188–92, 236, 238–39

German Army units—Continued
  Battalions
    Bucher: 305
    Jungwirth: 194
    Rink: 301, 312–13
    2d Landesschuetzen: 305
    12th Fusilier: 87, 418
    31st Machine Gun: 448
    105th Panzer Grenadier: 95
    147th Engineer: 477
    275th Fusilier: 330, 333
    301st Tank: 520, 562
    506th Tank: 283, 290, 296–97, 301, 530, 571
    559th Assault Gun: 520
  Miscellaneous
    "Ear battalions": 100, 127
    Feldjaegerkommando z. b. V.: 395
    "Fortress" battalions: 16, 75, 273, 286, 334, 372
    Garrison troops: 42
    Grenadier training units: 81, 83, 85
    Heeres units: 16
    Landesschuetzen (local security) battalions: 70, 75–77, 83, 258, 273–74, 277, 286, 330
    Military government troops: 124
    Mobile interceptor units: 135
    NCO Training School Dueren: 273–74, 277
    NCO Training School Juelich: 273–74, 277
    Ost (East) battalions: 83, 220
    Replacement units: 111, 153, 258, 330, 610
    "Security" units: 99, 258
    "Stomach" units: 83, 83n, 127, 220
    "Straggler" battalions: 258
    Werfer units: 15–16
German Navy: 15–16, 124, 126, 393, 411
Germeter: 93, 323, 331–34, 336–39, 343–45, 347, 349, 352–53, 357–58, 361, 366, 372–73, 399, 431, 438, 464–65
Germeter–Huertgen highway: 388, 347–49, 358, 428, 440, 442–47, 452, 589
Germeter–Vossenack ridge. *See* Vossenack ridge.
Gerow, Maj. Gen. Leonard T.: 23, 36–37, 39–41, 44, 46, 48–49, 51, 55–57, 59–63, 65–66, 341, 343, 347, 364, 366, 369–70, 372, 440–41, 451, 455, 461, 598–602, 607, 611. *See also* Corps, V.
Gersdorff, Col. Rudolf-Christoph Freiherr von: 110
Geul River: 105–07, 109–10
Gey: 399, 408, 412, 430, 433, 436, 469, 472–74, 580, 587–91
Ghent: 208
Gibb, Col. Frederick W.: 291–92, 418

Gibney, Col. Jesse L.: 92–94
Gillem, Maj. Gen. Alvan C., Jr.: 400, 400n, 516–17, 547, 550, 556, 566, 568, 571
Glider Field Artillery Battalion, 907th: 192, 194
Glider Infantry Regiments
  325th: 176, 193
  327th: 152, 152n, 190–91
  401st: 152n
Glider Operations: 129, 132n, 133, 137–39, 147–48, 152, 154, 159, 166–67, 170, 176, 176n, 185, 198–99, 199n
Glotzbach, Capt. Charles: 508
Goering, Reichsmarschall Hermann: 141
Gomes, Lt. Col. Lloyd H.: 550, 552
GOODWOOD: 404n
Gottberg, Obergruppenfuehrer und General der Waffen-SS Curt von: 201
Grantham: 137
Grave: 120, 131, 154, 157n, 158, 160, 174, 184, 196, 202, 206
Grave–Nijmegen highway: 158, 161
Greer, Maj. Howard: 299, 299n
Grenades: 85, 147, 151, 178, 181, 262–64, 267, 310, 315, 366, 418, 444–45, 453, 481, 486, 487, 511, 541, 564, 577
Gressenich: 72, 79–80, 89, 409, 417
Groesbeek: 155, 158, 161–62, 165, 167, 174, 177, 202
Groesbeek ridge: 155–57, 157n, 158, 161–62, 166, 174, 177
Groesbeekscheweg: 163
Grosshau: 408, 430, 432–34, 437, 450, 465–69, 471–73, 587, 589, 591
Grosshau–Gey highway: 472–73, 588, 591
Grosskampenberg: 44–45
Guerzenich: 590–92
Guingand, Maj. Gen. Sir Francis de: 211n, 212
Gulpen: 107
Gunn, Col. Damon M.: 23n
Gunn, Lt. Col. Frank L.: 337–38
Guns. See also Artillery; Howitzers; Mortar fire; Tank destroyers; Tank guns; Weapons.
  75-mm: 159
  90-mm: 27
  155-mm: 259, 287, 312–13, 316, 609
  8-inch: 481–82
Guns, German
  railroad: 64
  SP: 15–16, 50, 74, 76–77, 79, 87n, 109, 266, 272, 275, 277, 301, 313, 331, 336, 356, 438, 450, 460–61, 472, 487, 501–02, 506, 514, 520, 539–40, 543, 559, 559n, 584, 586, 591–93
  88-mm: 27–28, 50, 148–49, 175, 226, 559n, 620
Gut Hasenfeld: 574–77
Gut Merberich: 489
Gut Schwarzenbroich: 430, 432, 437, 464–65, 467–68, 477

Haaren: 288–89, 291, 309–10
Hackard, Capt. Clifford T.: 368, 368n
Half-tracks: 48, 298, 419, 450, 453, 612–13
Hall, 1st Lt. Stanford F.: 64n
Hallahan, Capt. F. J.: 514
Halsdorf: 59, 61
Hamberg, Lt. Col. William A.: 449–50, 452–54
Hamich: 404, 416–19, 421, 475–77, 479–80, 487
Hamich ridge: 399, 404, 408–09, 412, 415–18, 422–24, 464, 475–76, 479–80, 529
Hand-to-hand fighting: 180–81, 193, 437n
Hansen, Maj. Harold D.: 302
Hansen, Pvt. Henry E.: 263
Hardage, Maj. Quentin R.: 335–37, 339
Harmon, Maj. Gen. Ernest N.: 107–08, 107n, 278, 518, 522–24, 532–35, 540–42, 544, 561
Harper, Col. Joseph H.: 152, 190–91
Harris, Air Chief Marshal Sir Arthur T.: 598
Harrison, Maj. Willard E.: 161, 179, 181
Harscheidt: 352–56
Harspelt: 3n
Hart, Brig. Gen. Charles E.: 22, 621
Hasbrouck, Brig. Gen. Robert W.: 238, 244–47
Hasenfeld: 325, 345
Hasselt: 96, 98–100, 108, 124, 204, 231
Hastenrath: 404, 409, 422–24
Haswell, Pfc. James B.: 316
Hatert: 158, 161–63, 168, 174
Hatzfeld, Lt. Col. Theodore S.: 349, 358, 364–66, 368
Hauptbecken Reservoir: 325
Haviland, S. Sgt. Floyd: 577
Hazlett, Maj. Robert T.: 351, 357, 368
Heartbreak Crossroads. See Wahlerscheid.
Heckhuscheid: 46
Heerlen: 111
Heeswijk: 187
Heeze: 113
Hehlrath: 499, 503–04
Heimbach Dam: 325
Heinsberg: 30, 404, 412, 496, 498, 520, 525, 547–48, 550
Heistern: 477–79, 484
Heitrak: 244–45
Helgeson, Capt. Thomas B.: 161
Hellenthaler Wald: 607
Hellerich, S. Sgt. Harold: 89
Hell's Highway: 143–46, 148, 150, 152–54, 187–95
Helmond: 191
Hemgen Berg. See Hill 253.
Hemmeres: 3
Henbest, Lt. Col. Ross C.: 59–61, 64
Henley, S. Sgt. Robert M.: 473n
Henry, Pvt. Robert T.: 490n
Herbach: 256, 269, 275, 278
Herenthals: 208

Herlong, Lt. Col. Robert H.: 565
Herrin, Sgt. Stanley: 541
Herscheid: 54
Hertogenwald: 66, 84
Heumen: 158, 160–61, 167, 178
Heveadorp: 173, 185–86
Heydte, Lt. Col. Friedrich-August Freiherr von der: 124–25, 192–93, 221
Hickey, Brig. Gen. Doyle O.: 74, 76–77
Higgins, Brig. Gen. Gerald J.: 152
Higgins, Lt. Col. Walter M. Jr.: 609–10
Hill, Col. John G.: 611
Hill 64: 165–66
Hill 75.9: 176, 193
Hill 77.2: 158, 161, 178, 193
Hill 81.8: 161
Hill 87.9: 568, 571, 573–74
Hill 92.5: 551–53
Hill 98.1: 564–65
Hill 100.3: 564–65
Hill 101: 550–51
Hill 154: 506–08
Hill 167: 480–81, 506
Hill 187: 480–82, 506
Hill 194: 305–06, 313
Hill 203: 478–79, 484, 489
Hill 207: 478
Hill 211: 587, 591
Hill 228: 77, 79–80
Hill 231: 286–89, 295, 297, 304–06, 309, 313–14, 314n, 499
Hill 232: 416–20, 422, 424, 475–77, 481–82
Hill 239: 286–290, 287n
Hill 253: 287, 590, 592–93
Hill 266: 590–93
Hill 283: 79–80, 88, 91
Hill 287: 91, 422, 424–28, 464, 503, 529
Hill 400.5: 454, 459, 461–63
Hill 401: 448, 451–53
Hill 401.3: 450, 472–73, 473n
Hill 407: 59, 61, 63–64
Hill 520: 54
Hill 553: 46–48
Hill 554: 92, 602
Hill 559: 48
Hill 560: 47
Hill 568: 48
Hill 655: 53
Hill 697: 50
Hillyard, Lt. Col. Harry L.: 532
Himmler, Reichsfuehrer SS Heinrich: 141
Hinds, Col. Sidney R.: 272, 542
Hirschfelder, Col. Chester J.: 606, 608–09
Hirson: 383
Hitler, Adolf: 6, 218, 320, 377n, 390
    and Aachen evacuation and defense: 71, 82, 281, 307, 314–15, 320

Hitler, Adolf—Continued
    and airborne/seaborne invasion: 135–36
    and Antwerp and the Schelde: 19, 123, 215, 218, 223, 227–28
    and Ardennes counteroffensive: 136n, 393, 395, 397, 505, 559, 616
    assumption of complete military command: 16–17
    build-up of West forces: 15–16
    and the Luftwaffe: 143, 153
    order to defend Fort Eben Emael: 101
    orders to hold "to the last": 12, 18, 307, 314–15
    reaction to MARKET-GARDEN: 141, 167, 201
    and West Wall defense: 87
    and West Wall impregnability: 18, 30–31
    and withdrawal actions: 223, 505
Hitler Youth: 410
Hitzfeld, General der Infanterie Otto: 601
Hobbs, Maj. Gen. Leland S.: 101, 106–07, 109–11, 114, 253–54, 258–59, 266, 270, 279, 285, 293–305, 500–503, 561
Hodges, Lt. Gen. Courtney H.: 22–23, 379, 619. See also Army, First.
    and Aachen encirclement: 285, 302, 319n
    biography: 20–21
    and Huertgen Forest attacks: 431, 441, 451–52, 461, 493
    and November offensive: 341, 348, 399–400, 405, 411, 429, 438–39, 440, 464, 600
    and operations west of the Maas: 231–35, 240
    optimism for Rhine breakthrough: 14, 38, 233–35, 409, 421, 618–19
    postponement of West Wall assault: 115, 231
    and protection of First Army left flank: 114
    and the Roer River dams: 326, 342, 342n, 406, 597–98
    and Schmidt operation: 364, 369, 373
    and supply priorities: 36–37, 62
    and West Wall reconnaissance and attacks: 37–40, 55–56, 278
Hoefen–Alzen ridge: 84–86, 92, 328, 600–602, 606–07, 611
Hof Hardt: 474, 580, 583, 587, 590
Hoffman, Lt. John R.: 74
Hogan, Lt. Col. Samuel M.: 91
Hohe Venn: 30
Holy Roman Empire: 281
Holycross, 2d Lt. Harold L.: 275, 305, 565
Holzinger, S. Sgt. Warner W.: 3, 57
Hongen: 499–502
Honinghutje: 158, 158n, 161–62
Hontheim: 50, 52, 54
Horner, Lt. Col. Charles T. Jr.: 418–19
Horner, S. Sgt. Freeman V.: 501n
Horrocks, Lt. Gen. Brian G.: 133–34, 149, 174, 186, 191, 196–97, 200, 403, 546, 551
Horses: 15, 17, 219

Hospitals: 147, 186
Hostages: 513
Hostrup, Capt. Bruce M.: 351, 355, 359–60, 363
House-to-house fighting: 148, 175, 181, 264, 269, 310–11, 417–18, 453, 505, 508, 562–63, 565, 573, 588, 604–05
Houston, Maj. Jack A.: 326, 328
Hoven: 546, 585–86
Hoverhof: 272
Howitzers
    German: 25, 25–26n, 107
    75-mm pack: 154, 178
    105-mm: 25, 25–26n, 86, 154, 192, 261, 318, 577
    155-mm: 25, 25–26n, 481
    240-mm: 481
    8-inch: 576
Howze, Col. Robert L., Jr.: 585
Huber, Major: 189–91
Huebner, Maj. Gen. Clarence R.: 72, 81, 285–86, 288–89, 291–92, 308–09, 313–15, 408, 415–16, 475, 477, 479, 481, 494
Huecheln: 476, 481–84, 507–08
Huertgen: 90, 92, 94, 331, 337, 341, 343, 347–48, 352, 354, 370, 372, 408, 412, 414, 417, 428–29, 433, 438, 441, 443, 445–48, 450–51, 456, 464, 466–67, 587–88
Huertgen Forest: 66, 68, 87, 90, 94, 248, 252, 257, 273, 323–24, 328, 338, 341, 377, 395, 399–400, 409, 451, 474, 496, 529, 561, 583, 596, 600–602, 612 616. See also Infantry Divisions (1st; 4th; 8th; 9th; 28th; 83d).
    American method of attack: 430–31, 431n
    German impression of American troops: 334
    summary of American action: 492–93, 618, 620
    terrain and defenses: 92, 94, 330, 332–33, 345–46, 349–50, 416, 420, 432, 452, 475, 580, 583, 587
Huertgen–Kleinhau road net: 323, 331, 341, 343, 399, 448
Huissen: 164, 179
Huling, Capt. George W., Jr.: 292
Hundley, Col. Daniel H.: 380n
Hungarian troops: 15
Hunner Park: 165, 175, 181
Hurless, Col. Bernard F.: 531, 540, 543, 573
Hurley, Sgt. William: 446

IJssel River: 141, 170
IJsselmeer: 120, 131, 134, 377
Immendorf: 526–27, 531, 540, 544, 548, 550, 553
Inde River: 66, 72, 408–09, 415–16, 424–25, 475–76, 480, 482, 484, 496, 499, 506–15, 561, 564, 580, 582, 584
Inden: 499, 509–12, 515, 561, 563–64, 580, 584

"Indian" fighting: 144, 152, 154
Infantry
    airborne troops used in line: 176, 201, 204
    Huertgen Forest an infantry battle: 420
    riflemen casualties: 93–94, 302, 372, 417, 438
    shortage of: 166, 362, 365–67, 388–89, 455, 460
Infantry Battalion, 99th: 113–14, 302, 305, 313
Infantry Division, 1st: 23, 36, 68, 103, 222, 424–25, 498, 580
    Aachen encirclement and assault: 66–67, 72, 74–75, 77, 81, 90, 285–93, 299, 304, 306–18
    casualties: 293, 318, 417, 421, 478, 481, 484, 492, 492n, 593n
    Huertgen Forest attacks: 415–21, 430, 464, 468, 475–79, 490–93, 580, 586
    November offensive: 400, 408–09, 412, 414, 422, 479–90, 506–08, 511, 600
Infantry Division, 2d: 379, 600–602, 606, 606n, 607–15
    casualties: 609–10, 612
Infantry Division, 4th: 3, 24, 36, 41, 60, 341, 615, 618
    casualties: 53–55, 429, 433–35, 437–38, 464, 466, 469–74, 580, 593, 593n
    Huertgen Forest attacks: 366, 370, 373, 408, 428–40, 447, 450–51, 464–75, 477, 490, 492–93, 580, 587, 590
    Schnee Eifel attack: 44, 49–55, 612
Infantry Division, 8th: 373, 379, 614
    casualties: 443–45, 450, 450n, 463, 612
    Huertgen Forest attacks: 440–63, 493, 600–601
Infantry Division, 9th: 23, 36, 66–68, 72, 76, 82n, 294n, 326, 326n, 408, 492–93
    casualties: 93–94, 332, 334, 340, 585–86, 593n
    Huertgen Forest first fight: 90, 92–94, 115, 323, 328, 431
    Huertgen Forest second fight: 252, 285, 324, 327–28, 330–40, 345–46, 350, 353, 431
    Monschau Corridor battle: 82–86, 342–43, 600, 602
    Roer River final push: 580–87, 590
    Stolberg Corridor fight: 77–80, 82, 89
Infantry Division, 28th: 3, 3n, 24, 36, 40–41, 44n, 314, 461n, 614–15, 618
    casualties: 48, 63, 349–50, 361, 364, 372–74, 474, 493
    Eifel attack: 44–50, 52, 55, 60, 612–13
    Schmidt and the Huertgen Forest: 340–41, 342n, 343–74, 386, 397, 399–400, 406, 411, 428–29, 431, 438, 440–41, 451, 455, 474, 493, 600, 608
Infantry Division, 29th
    casualties: 539, 576
    Maas River–West Wall flank protection: 232–33, 252–53, 258, 266–67, 274, 278–79, 294, 302

Infantry Division, 29th—Continued
  Roer plain attacks: 400, 498, 503, 517–18, 523–25, 527–29, 534–40, 542, 544, 558–63, 565, 574–77
Infantry Division, 30th: 23, 36, 96, 99, 102n, 233, 320
  advance to the West Wall: 101–04, 106–112, 114–15
  casualties: 269, 271, 279, 279n, 295–96, 302, 306, 318, 500–502, 564
  encirclement of Aachen: 285, 288, 292–306, 313, 315, 317–18, 318n, 498
  November offensive: 400, 498–503, 506–07, 509, 516–17, 522–23, 529, 539, 544, 548, 558–61, 563–65
  West Wall set attack: 252–80, 618
Infantry Division, 75th: 614
Infantry Division, 78th: 600–606, 612
Infantry Division, 83d: 379, 399n, 474, 492, 580–83, 586–93, 596n, 613–15
  casualties: 590–91, 593n, 613
Infantry Division, 84th: 399n, 401–03, 499, 524
  casualties: 551, 557, 574
  final attack to Roer River: 567–74
  Geilenkirchen attack: 516–17, 545–58, 566
Infantry Division, 90th: 320, 320n, 448
Infantry Division, 94th: 388
Infantry Division, 99th: 397, 600–601, 606–12
Infantry Division, 102d: 400–402, 517, 523–24, 544, 546–47, 550, 554, 556, 566–68, 571–74
Infantry Division, 104th: 388, 392, 397, 399–401, 403, 547, 621
  casualties: 227, 227n, 426, 506–07, 510, 515, 586, 593n
  drive to the Maas: 213, 222–27
  Eschweiler-Weisweiler and Roer River drive: 408, 412, 416, 422, 424–28, 464, 475–76, 480–84, 488, 490, 498–99, 502–15, 563–64, 580–82, 584, 586
Infantry Division, 106th: 614–15
Infantry Regiments. See also Glider Infantry Regiments: Parachute Infantry Regiments.
  8th: 49, 52–53, 430, 432–33, 435–39, 464–69, 469n, 474, 477
  9th: 606–12
  12th: 49–53, 366, 370, 372–73, 428–30, 435, 438–39, 441, 447n, 466, 469, 474
  13th: 447–48, 450, 450n, 451–52, 457, 463
  16th: 67, 72, 74–75, 77, 81, 88, 286, 290–93, 304, 313, 416–21, 475, 477, 479–80, 484, 489–90, 490n, 492n
  18th: 75, 81, 95n, 286–91, 293–94, 297, 306, 309, 313, 416, 475–80, 484, 489, 492n
  22d: 3, 49–50, 52–55, 430, 432–39, 464–69, 471–74, 493
  23d: 613

Infantry Regiments—Continued
  26th: 74–75, 80–81, 91, 286, 289, 291, 307–16, 318, 416, 420–21, 430, 475–78, 490–92
  28th: 451–53, 457–59, 462–63
  38th: 606, 610, 612
  39th: 83–86, 92–94, 328, 331–34, 336–40, 586–87, 590
  47th: 76–80, 82–83, 86, 89–90, 92–93, 328, 338–40, 408–09, 415–17, 422, 424–25, 475–76, 479–89, 492–93, 506, 511
  60th: 84–86, 92–94, 323, 328, 331–37, 339–40, 350, 585–86
  109th: 3, 44–47, 49, 347–49, 352–54, 358–59, 361, 366–68, 370–73, 428–29
  110th: 3n, 44–49, 314–15, 347, 349–50, 352, 354–55, 361, 363–64, 367–68, 372, 613
  112th: 40–41, 56–57, 59–61, 63–65, 347, 349–74
  115th: 525, 527–29, 535–37, 539, 563, 576–77
  116th: 278–79, 294, 302–03, 305–06, 313, 535–36, 535n, 538, 560, 562–63, 574–77
  117th: 102–03, 106, 111, 255–56, 260–64, 266–71, 274–75, 277–79, 285, 294–97, 299, 305–06, 500–502
  119th: 101, 103, 106–07, 109, 111, 256–57, 260, 264–71, 275–79, 285, 295, 297–99, 301–02, 304–05, 500–501, 501n, 523, 541, 544, 560–61, 563–65
  120th: 102–03, 107, 110–11, 253, 258, 266, 277, 279–80, 285, 294–302, 305, 500–502, 558–59, 561, 563–64
  121st: 441–48, 450–53, 450n, 455–62
  175th: 525, 527–29, 535–39, 559–63
  309th: 602–06
  310th: 602–06
  329th: 587, 590–92
  330th: 587–92
  331st: 587–92
  333d: 549, 551, 554–57, 568, 571
  334th: 549–53, 555–57, 573–74
  335th: 548, 568–71, 573
  393d: 607, 610
  394th: 610
  395th: 607–09, 611–12
  405th: 546, 554, 556, 572–73
  406th: 523, 527, 531–32, 540, 543–44, 572–73
  407th: 572–73
  413th: 223, 225–26, 425, 503–07, 509–11
  414th: 223–24, 226–27, 425–28, 503, 505–09, 511, 515, 584
  415th: 223–26, 426–27, 503, 505–07, 511–15, 584
Infantry-tank-artillery team: 106, 537, 620
Infiltration: 358, 465, 477, 559, 589, 604, 609
Intelligence: 31, 38, 41, 61, 68, 121–22, 148, 175, 199–200, 228n, 235, 243–44, 257, 286–87, 290, 295, 328–30, 332, 337, 346, 394, 409–10, 421, 567, 582, 596

Intelligence—Continued
  from captured papers: 80, 103–04, 106, 122,
    141–42, 200, 501
  from prisoners: 46, 80, 160, 226, 327, 352,
    414, 419, 512, 556, 606
  German: 134–36, 167, 240–41, 258–59, 547–48,
    614
Irsen creek: 44–45

Jackson, Lt. Col. Langdon A., Jr.: 433
Jaegerhaus: 94, 332, 335
Jagdpanther. See Guns, German, SP.
Jedlicka, Pvt. Joseph: 180
Jeeps: 311, 362
Jenkins, Pvt. Willis: 262–63
Jennings, Pvt. Sheldon D.: 64n
Jeter, Col. John R.: 441–44, 446–47, 447n
Jodl, Generaloberst Alfred: 135
Johnson, Col. Howard R.: 145–46, 153, 188–89,
    191–92
Johnson, 1st Lt. Kenneth L.: 418n
Johnson, Col. Walter M.: 102, 106, 256, 260,
    264, 269, 275, 294–97, 500–501
Jones, Capt. Robert E.: 146–47
Juelich: 80, 88, 258, 288, 327, 397, 402, 404,
    412–13, 488, 498, 516–18, 520, 523–25, 529,
    537–38, 544, 548, 559–63, 565, 573–74, 576
Juengersdorf: 403, 408, 415–16, 420, 475–76, 489–
    90, 580
Juliana Canal: 108, 237

Kading, Pfc. Ken: 307
Kaiserslautern: 7
Kalinowsky, Pfc. Henry J.: 366n
Kall River operations: 323, 331, 336, 343–47,
    349–52, 355–72, 457, 463, 600
Kall Valley Dam: 325
Kalterherberg: 84
Kampfgruppen: 59, 69–70, 110, 112, 346, 352.
    See also German Army units.
Kappel, Capt. Carl W.: 180
Karwell, S. Sgt. Frank A.: 306
Kasteel (chateau): 145–46
Kayes, Capt. Daniel E.: 562
Kean, Maj. Gen. William G.: 23, 342
Keating, Maj. Gen. Frank A.: 566, 572
Keesee, Lt. Col. Morris J.: 447–48, 450, 457
Keizer Karel Plein: 163–64, 166
Kelley, S. Sgt. Brady O.: 473n
Kemper Steimerich Hill. *See* Hill 560.
Kennedy, Maj. Robert S.: 568
Keppler, General der Waffen-SS Georg: 41–43,
    56, 284, 300
Kerkrade: 112, 253, 266, 277, 279, 285, 295, 302
Kesfeld: 45–47
Kesternich: 603–04, 611
Kettenkreuz. *See* Hill 655.
Kettlehut, 1st Lt. Howard K.: 462

Kiekberg. *See* Hill 77.2.
Kimbacher, Col. Josef: 477–78
Kiner, Pvt. Harold G.: 264
King, Lt. Col. Roswell H.: 73, 75–76
Kinnard, Lt. Col. Harry W. O. Jr.: 145–46, 187–
    88
Kinzweiler: 499, 502–04
Kirchberg: 560–61, 563
Kleinhau: 90, 92, 408, 430, 433, 437, 439, 447–
    52, 457, 464, 466, 471–72, 587, 589
Kleinhau–Brandenberg highway: 451
Kleinsteiber, Lt. George: 453
Kleve: 30, 34, 122, 156
Kleve–Nijmegen highway: 162, 167, 176
Klundert: 224
Knobelsdorff, General der Panzertruppen Otto
    von: 42, 59–60, 63
Koblenz: 37, 39–40, 252, 399
Koechling, General der Infanterie Friedrich J.
    M.: 91, 257–59, 267, 270, 273–74, 267–77,
    284, 288, 296, 312, 487–88, 502, 520, 538–
    39, 562
Koenig, Generalleutnant Eugen: 601
Koerte, Colonel: 519
Koettnich: 409, 422
Koevering: 194–95
Kohlscheid: 305
Kommerscheidt: 343, 345, 349–52, 354–64, 367–
    72, 429
Kommerscheidt–Schmidt ridge: 345, 358, 452,
    454, 600
Kornelimuenster: 72, 75
Koslar: 560, 562–63, 576
Kossmala, Col. Eugen: 460
Krauss, Pvt. Edward: 306, 313–14
Kreider, T/4 James A.: 361–62
Krinkelt: 601, 606–07, 611–12
Kufferath: 591–93
Kunzig, Lt. Col. Henry B.: 448
Kurhaus: 309, 312–13, 315
Kyll River: 40, 52, 69

Lafley, 1st Lt. Cedric A.: 307, 317
Lamersdorf: 509, 511, 513–14
Lammerding, SS-Brigadefuehrer und Generalma-
    jor der Waffen-SS Heinz: 51
Lammersdorf: 85, 90, 92, 94, 325, 341, 602
Lammersdorf-Huertgen highway: 92–94
Lanaye: 102–03
Landau, Col. Christian: 100, 108–11, 124, 236,
    519, 548
Landing craft: 135
Landing fields: 120
Landing zones: 127, 130–31, 137, 139, 144, 146,
    148, 154, 158, 163, 165–67, 171–72, 190, 200
Lange, Generalleutnant Wolfgang: 111–12, 258–
    59, 266–67, 270, 273, 519, 548

Langerwehe: 408, 412–13, 415–16, 420, 475–79, 484–85, 489–90, 492, 510, 580
Lanham, Col. Charles T.: 49–50, 50n, 54, 430, 432, 434–36, 438–39, 464–67, 471–73
LaPrade, Maj. James L.: 147–48
Lathbury, Brig. G. W.: 171n
Latimer, Maj. Robert B.: 54
Lattre de Tassigny, Gen. Jean de: 381
Lauer, Maj. Gen. Walter E.: 600, 607, 611–12
Laufenberg (castle): 421, 475–76
Launches: 138
Laurensberg: 314–15
Le Havre: 4, 207–09, 383
Leaflets: 307, 318
Lee, Lt. Robert E.: 526
Leiffarth: 566, 568, 574
Leigh-Mallory, Air Chief Marshal Sir Trafford: 218n
Lendersdorf: 591
Leonard, Lt. Col. Henry G. Jr.: 287–88
Leonard, 1st Lt. Turney W.: 363n
Leopold Canal: 209, 215, 221
Leyherr, Lt. Col. Maximilian: 286, 307
Liaison planes. See Artillery liaison planes.
Liège: 4, 7–8, 12, 36, 81, 96, 98–99, 101–03, 119, 230, 383–84, 398, 405
Liesel: 245–46
Limburg. See "Dutch Panhandle."
Lind, Capt. Ralph E. Jr.: 367
Lindern: 566–73
Lindern-Linnich highway: 571
Lindquist, Col. Roy E.: 158, 161–63, 165–66
Lindsey, T. Sgt. Jake W.: 418, 418n
Lindsey, Pvt. Thomas G.: 148
Lines of communication: 7, 613n
Linnich: 258, 402, 404, 498, 516–20, 525, 547–48, 559, 564, 566–67, 571–73, 593
Lippe River: 135n
Locke, T/5 Coy T.: 3n
Logistics: 7–14, 62, 121, 259, 377, 380, 382–91, 521–22, 616–17, 619–20. See also Shortages; Supply.
Lohn: 506–07, 559, 561
Long, Maj. Talton W.: 177–78
Lorrach: 30
Lorraine: 7, 16, 34, 38, 42, 395, 616
Losenseifen Hill. See Hill 568.
Losheim: 52, 612
Losheim Gap: 41, 52
Losses, summary of. See also Casualties.
    Aachen battle: 317–18
    Antwerp approaches: 229
    German equipment and transport: 14–15
    Huertgen Forest: 373–74, 492–93
    Market-Garden: 138, 154, 159, 170, 198–200, 199n, 206
    November offensive: 577–78, 593–94

Losses, summary of—Continued
    Roer plain battle: 577–78
    Roer River Dams attack: 612
    Siegfried Line campaign: 616–17
    West Wall penetrations: 378
Lousberg: 309, 311–12, 314–15
Lousberg Strasse (Aachen): 316
Lovelady, Lt. Col. William B.: 73, 79
Loverich: 519, 526, 535–36
Lower Rhine. See Neder Rijn.
Luchem: 404, 485, 490, 580
Lucherberg: 510–15, 580
Luckett, Col. James S.: 49, 428–30, 441, 447n
Luerken: 499–500, 525
Luettwitz, General der Panzertruppen Heinrich Freiherr von: 45, 243–44, 397, 518
Luetzelen Castle: 511
Luftlotte 3: 6
Luftwaffe: 6, 15–16, 126, 138, 143, 153, 246, 260, 276, 299, 308, 382, 393, 454. See also Air operations.
Luftwaffe troops: 58, 70, 75, 81, 83, 100, 124, 127, 177, 286, 411
Luxembourg: 4, 28, 36, 43, 56–57, 60, 319, 328, 341, 378, 441, 474, 522, 580, 583, 612–13

M4 tanks. See Tanks, medium.
Maas River: 29, 96, 105–06, 108–09, 113–14, 120, 126, 131, 134, 154–58, 168, 198, 207, 401, 517, 519–21, 546, 548, 567. See also Meuse River.
    bridges: 155–58, 158n, 160, 162, 174, 176, 521–22
    clearing the west bank: 212–14, 220–22, 227, 231–48, 252, 346, 377, 390–92, 547, 594, 616
Maas-Scheldt. See Meuse-Escaut Canal.
Maas–Waal Canal: 131, 156–58, 160–62, 168, 176–79
Maasbracht: 546
Maashees: 231–32
Maastricht: 8, 14, 29, 36, 96, 98–100, 103–09, 113, 124–25, 231–33, 330, 379, 381, 398, 400, 522, 595
Maastricht–Aachen highway: 105
Maastricht Canal: 108–09, 113
Maastricht island: 102, 104–06, 108–09
Mabry, Maj. George L., Jr.: 437n
Macaulay, 1st Lt. J. A.: 446
McAuliffe, Brig. Gen. Anthony C.: 131n, 190–92
McCrory, Sgt. James M.: 153–54
McDaniel, Pvt. Doyle W.: 366n
McDaniel, Col. Edward H.: 529
McDowell, Lt. Col. Samuel T.: 271, 274, 296
McGraw, Pfc. Francis X.: 420–21
Machine guns: 25, 27–28, 31
Macholz, Generalleutnant Sigfrid P.: 98–99, 101, 110, 258–59, 266

Macht, 1st Lt. Walter D.: 276
McKee, Col. Richard G.: 430, 436–39, 464–67, 474
Mackenzie, Col. A. J.: 607
McLain, Maj. Gen. Raymond S.: 320, 320n, 498–500, 503, 507, 522–24, 529–30, 534, 537, 561, 563, 565–66. *See also* Corps, **XIX.**
McNeal, Pfc. George F.: 3n
Macon, Maj. Gen. Robert C.: 587–89, 591
McWaters, 1st Lt. William L.: 485–87
Maginot Line: 31
Mahogany Hill. *See* Hill 92.5.
Maintenance: 20, 132, 386, 518, 521
Mainz: 37
Malden: 158, 160–61
Malmédy: 36
Maltzahn, Major Freiherr von: 142, 153
Maness, Lt. Col. Lewis E.: 482–87
Mann, Pfc. Joe E.: 151, 151n
Mannheim: 37
Manteuffel, General der Panzertruppen Hasso von: 247, 394–95, 410, 417n
Map exercise: 353
Maps: 26, 80, 255, 336, 501
Marcum, 1st Lt. Warren E.: 54–55
Maria Plein: 165
Mariadorf: 294–97, 499–502
Mariaweiler: 404, 585–86
Marienberg: 253, 255–56, 264–69, 277
Mark IV tank. *See* Tanks, German.
Mark V tank. *See* Tanks, German.
Mark VI tank. *See* Tanks, German.
Mark River: 223–27
Marker boats: 138
Market: 120–21, 128–29, 132–33, 132n, 134–39, 200. *See also* Market-Garden.
Market-Garden:
  achievements and cost: 198–201, 211–12, 377, 618–20
  American operations: 143–95
  British operations: 170–73, 195–98. *See also* Garden.
  defense of the salient: 201–06, 213, 219–22, 231, 236, 239–41, 243
  flight from England: 136–39
  German forces opposing: 123–27, 174
  German intelligence concerning: 134–36, 136n, 140–41
  German reaction to airborne invasion: 136n, 140–43
  planning for: 113, 119–23, 127–34, 208–09, 214, 383
Marokus, Sgt. Leon: 513
Marr, Col. Richard S.: 471
Marshall, Gen. George C.: 21, 119, 214, 320n
Martin, Cpl. Russell: 263–64
Mastrobattista, Pvt. Alexander: 501

Mathews, Pvt. James E.: 339n
Maubeuge: 7–8
Mausbach: 76, 79, 88
Mead, Col. Armistead D. Jr.: 379–80
Medal of Honor: 49n, 95n, 151n, 182n, 226, 264, 287n, 299n, 303n, 314n, 363n, 418n, 421, 433n, 437n, 442n, 469n, 480n, 487n, 490n, 501n, 592
Medical aid: 357, 362, 371–72
Mediterranean Theater: 205, 380
Meerssen: 109–10
Meijel: 241, 243–48
Meijel–Deurne highway: 244–45
Meindl, General der Fallschirmtruppen Eugen: 142, 177, 188, 193, 202
Mendez, Lt. Col. Louis G., Jr.: 165–67, 178
Menkovitz, S. Sgt. Daniel: 577
Merken: 584, 584n
Merkstein: 279
Merode: 475–77, 488, 490–92, 510, 580, 583, 586, 588
Merzenhausen: 560–61, 563–65
Mettendorf: 40, 57, 59
Metz: 4, 7–8, 14, 115, 200, 238, 346, 377, 380, 384, 397, 597
Meuse River: 9–10, 28–30, 36–37, 62, 96, 101–03, 106, 119, 326. *See also* Maas River.
Meuse–Escaut Canal: 106, 113, 120, 122, 125, 133, 142, 192, 208, 236
MEW (Mobile Early Warning): 382
Michaelis, Col. John H.: 144–47, 150, 152, 187–88
Middelburg: 229
Middleton, Maj. Gen. Troy H.: 20n, 251, 613
Millener, Col. George A.: 380n
Miller, Col. Art B., Jr.: 380n
Mills, Lt. Col. Herbert N.: 76, 422–24, 424n
Mine detectors: 436, 500–501, 550, 588
Mine fields. *See* Mines, use of.
Miner, Col. Earl M.: 603
Mines
  antilifting devices: 435
  cleared by flail tanks: 548–50
  Schuh mines: 433, 500, 503
  sea mines: 212, 229
  Topf mines: 500
  use of: 89, 195, 238–39, 289, 348, 351, 356, 410, 422–24, 432, 434, 452–53, 455, 500–501, 536, 564, 575–77, 588–89
Minick, S. Sgt. John W.: 442n
"Miracle of the West": 392
Mitchell, Capt. James W.: 554
Mobilization, German: 19
Model, Generalfeldmarschall Walter: 6, 16–18, 87, 101, 105, 107–12, 125, 127, 135–36, 136n, 140–42, 164, 179, 182, 188, 193, 197 200–203

Model, Generalfeldmarschall Walter—Continued
237, 243, 245, 277, 289–90, 297, 300, 304, 353, 392, 395, 418, 420
Moehne Dam: 597
Moerdijk: 227
Mon creek: 54–55
Mons: 4, 20, 23
Monschau: 30, 66, 84–86, 90, 251, 324, 342, 601, 603
Monschau Corridor: 66, 68, 72, 76, 82–86, 90, 92, 252, 323–24, 328, 331, 341–49, 352–53, 359, 363, 370, 372, 399, 455, 460, 583, 600–606, 611
Monschau Forest: 600–602, 606–610, 612
Monschau–Huertgen–Dueren highway: 331
Montgomery, Field Marshall Sir Bernard L.: 3–4, 7–8, 246, 594–95. See also Army Group, 21st.
and Army Groups boundary: 231–33, 241
and British role in November offensive: 391–92, 401
and changes in command situation: 213–15, 213n, 378–79, 378n
and importance of capturing Ruhr: 207, 209–14, 231–32, 242, 248, 595, 619–20
and MARKET-GARDEN: 113, 120–22, 128–29, 133, 187, 196, 199–200, 204–05
"one thrust policy": 9–10, 123, 200–201, 210–11, 619–20
and opening of Antwerp: 204, 207, 209–10, 212–15, 220–21, 242, 383
and Ruhr feint: 112–13
Mook: 156, 161–62, 167, 177–78, 193
Moore, Brig. Gen. Bryant E.: 426
Moore, Brig. Gen. James E.: 379
Moore, Capt. Robert D.: 469n
Morale: 5, 230, 328, 330, 361, 441, 462, 488, 519, 618
Morris, Maj. James S.: 535–36
Mortain: 23, 269, 301
Mortar fire: 74, 144, 178, 261, 269, 287, 310, 312, 368, 416, 433, 442, 482, 485, 514, 521, 528, 530n, 531, 537–38. See also Artillery support; Nebelwerfer; Smoke.
Moselle River: 4, 30, 39, 238, 380, 614
Mud: 386, 406, 432, 435–36, 444, 467, 574, 589, 618. See also Tanks, effect of mud on.
Muellendorf: 546–49, 551, 554–56, 566–68, 574
Mueller, Generalmajor Gerhard: 75–76, 78, 87
Muenster: 135n
Muensterbusch: 90
Munich: 281
Murphy, Maj. John R.: 64n

Namur: 8
Napalm bombs: 254–55, 260, 449, 548, 577
Nazi party: 16, 71, 81–82, 125, 281, 284, 488
Nebelwerfer: 27–28

Neder Rijn: 10, 14, 29, 112, 120, 121, 130–31, 142, 157n, 164, 173, 182, 185, 197–201, 203
Nederweert: 233, 241–42, 244, 246–47
Nederweert–Wessum Canal: 233, 235–37, 241–42, 246–48
Needham, Maj. Fred E.: 224–25
Nelson, Col. Gustin M. 370–71, 370n
Neppel, Sgt. Ralph G.: 592
Netherlands: 28–29, 38, 120–22, 130–31, 198, 616
Netherlands Interior Forces: 169, 184
Newbury: 137
Nideggen: 345, 459
Niedermerz: 538–39
Niedersgegen: 59–61
Nietzel, Sgt. Alfred B.: 418n
Night operations: 129–30, 223–24, 226, 285, 287, 428, 460–61, 472, 484, 503–04, 507–09, 511–12, 554, 563–65, 568–69, 571, 575–76, 584, 613
Nijmegen: 113, 120–22, 126, 131, 134, 138, 142, 153–58, 157n, 162–69, 173–77, 179–86, 188, 191, 193, 200, 203, 205, 212, 214, 241, 247–48, 377, 391, 547, 595
Nijmegen–Arnhem highway: 181
Nijmegen–Groesbeek highway: 163
Nijmegen–Mook highway: 162
Ninth Air Force: 5, 24–25, 128, 137, 384, 404, 412, 520
Noorder Canal: 241, 243, 246–47
Normandy: 7, 11, 20, 72n, 102n, 107n, 130, 143n, 144, 155n, 177, 218, 222, 254, 383, 461, 580, 600, 606n
comparison with Siegfried Line campaign: 269, 377, 404–06, 404–05n, 411, 413, 523, 528–29, 617–19, 621
North Beveland: 229
North German Plain: 29, 120
North Wuerselen: 295, 297–301
Norwegian troops: 208n
Nothberg: 408, 476, 480–82, 506
Novak, Capt. Frank J.: 165, 175
November offensive: 390–92, 411, 619. See also Army, First; Army, Ninth.
a German defensive victory: 594
lack of large-scale British offensive: 547
optimism concerning: 522, 524, 596–97, 618
German reaction to: 392–93, 520, 547–48
Nuenen: 188
Nuetheim: 74–76
Nugent, Brig. Gen. Richard E.: 380, 498, 520
Nuremberg: 281
Nussbaumer Hardt: 57

OB WEST: 5–6, 5n, 16–18, 60, 109, 135, 141, 245, 289, 393–94, 397, 460, 505, 518, 530, 547–48. See also Rundstedt, Generalfeldmarschall Gerd von.

Ober Forstbach: 72, 74–75
Obergeich: 585–86
Oberkommando des Heeres (OKH): 16, 82, 141
Oberkommando der Wehrmacht (OKW): 16, 18,
    100, 182, 393, 488, 559
Obermaubach Dam: 325
Observation: 73, 90, 180, 345, 358, 360, 416,
    422–24, 426, 445, 454, 504, 508–09, 541, 564,
    576, 585. See also Air reconnaissance; Ar-
    tillery liaison planes.
  air and ground observers: 253, 301, 436, 438,
    617
  posts: 34, 107, 296, 478–79, 482
  restricted by terrain and weather: 55, 131, 265,
    348, 420, 442
Observatory Hill. See Lousberg.
Obstacles. See also Bridges, demolished; Mines;
    Roadblocks.
  antitank defenses: 29, 34–35, 410, 520, 533–36,
    540–41, 565, 567, 569–71
  craters: 76, 419, 445–46
  dragon's teeth: 34, 44–46, 48, 67–68, 73–75, 85
  felled trees: 332, 466, 481
  H- and I-beams: 34, 47
  wire: 34, 89, 261, 331, 350, 372, 410, 426,
    432–33, 436, 442, 452, 503, 608–10, 614
Obstfelder, General der Infanterie Hans von: 188,
    193, 195, 235–37, 247, 267
O'Connor, Lt. Gen. Sir Richard N.: 241–42, 244,
    246
Officers
  casualties: 54, 238, 272, 364, 372, 434, 435,
    438, 444, 466–67, 470–71, 474, 481, 508, 590
  German: 19, 82, 328, 337
  relief of: 47, 82, 91, 238, 246–47, 319, 319n,
    370n, 430, 444, 447, 576
O'Hare, Col. Joseph J.: 23n
Oidtweiler: 278, 518, 524, 528
Olef Creek: 607–08
Oliver, Maj. Gen. Lunsford E.: 56–57, 60–61,
    64, 431n, 589, 591–93
Olsen, 1st Lt. John J.: 512
Omer River: 409
Ondrick, Col. John G.: 603–04
"One-thrust" theory: 10, 210–11
Oosterbeek: 140–41, 170–71, 173, 185, 195–97
Oploo: 237–38
Organization Todt: 410
Ormont: 40
Ostend: 204, 208, 228
Our River: 3, 30, 40, 44, 56, 57
Overloon: 235, 238–41

Padgett, S. Sgt. Ewart M.: 316
Palast-Hotel Quellenhof: 307, 309, 312–13, 315
Palenberg: 256, 260, 264, 267, 276
Palenberg–Rimburg road: 262–63

Panel markers: 106, 405–06
Panic: 47, 50, 70–71, 81, 147, 167, 357, 364–65
Pantazopulos, Pfc. Gus: 263
Panther tanks. See Tanks, German.
Panzerfaust: 25, 46, 74, 238, 288, 311, 331, 362–
    63, 424, 445, 460, 527, 530n, 536, 565
Parachute Infantry Regiments
  501st: 145–46, 153, 187–89, 191, 193
  502d: 144–47, 150–54, 187–88, 194–95
  504th: 158, 158n, 160–61, 168, 174, 176–77,
    179–82, 184–85, 193
  505th: 158, 161–62, 165–70, 174–75, 177–78,
    181–82, 193
  506th: 143n, 144, 147–50, 152–53, 189–92, 195
  508th: 155n, 158–59, 158n, 161–68, 174, 176,
    178, 193
Paratroops, German: 611
Paris: 12–13, 20, 24, 49n, 383
Parker, Maj. Gen. Edwin P., Jr.: 600, 602, 611
Parker, Col. Hugh C.: 568, 570
Parker, 1st Lt. Warne R.: 275
Pas de Calais: 8, 208, 218
Patch, Lt. Gen. Alexander M.: 381
Pathfinders: 137, 145
Patrol actions: 146–47, 150–51, 203, 255, 609–10
Pattern: 561, 563
Patton, Lt. Gen. George S., Jr.: 9–10, 9n, 21, 23,
    36, 380, 392, 597
Paulushof Dam: 325, 598
Paustenbach: 602
Pedley, Col. Timothy A., Jr.: 554–55
Peel Marshes: 231, 233, 235–36, 238, 247, 251–
    52, 267, 280n, 377, 384, 391–92, 401–03, 517–
    19, 548, 566, 620
  German spoiling attack: 242–46, 397
Pendleton, S. Sgt. Jack J.: 299, 299n
"People's Court": 82
"People's" labor: 31
Pepe, Pvt. Salvatore: 279
Perry, Lt. Col. Collins: 226
Peterson, Lt. Col. Carl L.: 347, 349, 351, 358,
    363–64, 369, 370n
Pier: 584
Pillboxes: 27, 46, 53, 56–57, 63, 74, 112, 617–18.
    See also West Wall.
  air attacks against: 255, 260, 381
  arrangement and construction: 31, 34–35, 44,
    73, 84
  effect of artillery on: 45, 253, 259, 261–62, 272,
    609
  interlocking fire: 286, 555, 603, 608
  method of attack: 45–47, 50, 85, 92, 94, 255,
    261–65, 272, 275–76, 287–88, 294, 305, 550,
    552–55, 568, 609–10, 614, 618
Pinto, Oreste: 136n
Piron, Colonel: 232n
Plaisted, Lt. Col. Mark S.: 226

Planning. *See also* Strategy.
  for employment of airborne troops: 119–23, 127–34, 199, 619
  for January Rhine crossing: 595
  for November offensive: 390–92, 397–407
  preinvasion: 4, 4n, 6, 11, 207
Platt, Col. Washington: 235, 253, 257, 295, 520
POL (petroleum, oil, and lubricants): 13, 230. *See also* Shortages.
Pole charges. *See* Demolition charges.
Police, German: 71, 81, 308, 334
Polish troops: 5, 208n, 222. *See also* British Army units.
Poppe, Generalleutnant Walter: 125, 136, 146, 150, 152–53, 219, 574
Ports, lack of: 5, 7–8, 11–12, 207, 210–11, 383. *See also* Antwerp.
Position warfare: 90
Prisoners, Allied: 198, 276, 361, 373, 455, 508, 509, 584n, 617
Prisoners, German: 4, 152, 168, 187, 227, 229, 279, 316–17, 334–35, 338, 340, 340n, 374, 448, 450, 474n, 478, 484, 491, 501–02, 507, 514, 530, 539, 544, 578, 594, 610, 616–17 *See also* Intelligence.
Pronsfeld: 60
Propaganda: 31, 58n, 285
Provisional companies: 13
Proximity fuze: 390
Pruem: 40, 50, 54, 60
Pruem River: 40, 49, 59, 61, 63
Pruem State Forest: 49, 53, 55
Prummern: 531, 545–46, 549–56, 566
Puetzlohn: 506–10
Puffendorf: 526, 529–34, 541–44, 548
Puppchen (bazooka): 299
Purdue, Col. Branner P.: 294–95, 301, 500–501 563–64
Purnell, Col. William C.: 538
Pursuit warfare: 4, 41, 45, 106, 617, 619

QUEEN: 403–07, 409, 411–14, 412n, 416, 425, 492, 498, 517, 520–21, 524–25, 548, 580, 619
Quesada, Maj. Gen. Elwood R.: 24, 64
Quinn, Lt. Col. Daniel W.: 268

Rabenheck. See Raven's Hedge ridge.
Radio: 148, 151, 163, 172, 185–86, 191, 196, 366, 382, 406, 444, 453, 470, 485, 491, 512, 569–70, 603, 614
Radio Luxembourg: 307
Radscheid: 49
Raffelsbrand: 334–35, 343, 345, 347, 349–50, 355, 361, 372
Rafts: 196
Railroads: 11–12, 29–30, 111, 129, 167, 255, 281, 284, 381, 383–84

Ramsey, Admiral Sir Bertram H.: 212
Ranger Battalion, 2d: 455, 461–63, 493, 593, 600, 611
Ratchford, 2d Lt. William D.: 315
Rations: 13, 134, 233, 398, 569, 591, 608, 613
Ravels Hill (Ravelsberg). *See* Hill 231.
Raven's Hedge ridge: 432–35
Ray, 1st Lt. Bernard J.: 433, 433n
Reconnaissance. *See also* Air reconnaissance; Cavalry.
  in force: 37, 39, 44, 49, 55, 66–68, 75
  sea: 135
Reconnaissance Troop, 1st: 81
Red Ball Express: 12–13, 383
Red Cross: 398
Reichert, Generalleutnant Josef: 220
Reichswald: 156–58, 162, 166–69, 177–79, 200, 202
Reinhard, General der Infanterie Hans: 123–25, 188–89, 192, 195
Relief in place: 428–29, 488, 610
"Reluctant Dragon": 296
Remagen: 252
"Remote-control robot assault guns": 273, 283
Renkum: 197
Renn Weg: 436, 466–67
Rennebaum, 1st Lt. Leon A.: 63n
Replacements: 334, 336, 388, 429, 438, 455, 467, 469–71, 469n, 474, 617–18, 621
Replacements, German: 100, 126–27, 222, 258, 393, 594, 616
Reserves: 24, 89–90, 119–21, 134–35, 201, 338, 355, 397, 431, 455, 473, 475, 493, 619
Reserves, German: 6, 15–16, 31, 62n, 69, 111, 114, 121, 136, 143, 257, 273, 284, 289, 295, 334, 348, 353, 358, 393, 427, 488, 530, 547, 559
Resistance forces: 122, 154, 156, 161, 169, 183–84, 187–90, 232n
Ressen: 185–86
Rest and rehabilitation: 398, 456, 522, 612–14, 616
Rex Cinema (Antwerp): 230
Rhine River: 30, 68, 198, 215, 331–32, 496, 520, 577, 616, 619, 622. *See also* Neder Rijn.
  planned crossings: 9, 14, 37, 113, 120–21, 123, 134, 207, 210, 214, 595
  planned drive to: 115, 203, 235, 247, 251–52, 280, 324, 327, 327n, 341, 377–78, 390–91, 400, 402, 493, 517, 547, 594–95, 600, 612
Rhineland: 14, 30
Ribbentrop, Reich Foreign Minister Joachim von: 141
Richardson, Lt. Col. Walter B.: 483–85
Richelskaul: 331–38, 347, 349, 351, 353, 368
Richmond, Sgt. Leroy: 181
Rickard, Col. Roy V.: 380n
Ridgway, Maj. Gen. Matthew B.: 128

Riethorst: 155, 158, 161–62, 177–78, 193
Rifle, .30-cal. M1: 25
Rifle, 7.92-mm (Mauser): 25
Riflemen. *See* Infantry.
Rijsbergen: 224
Rimburg: 112, 114, 253, 255–57, 264, 267–68, 277
Rimburg Castle: 256–57, 264, 266, 268
Rimburg woods: 260, 265, 267–69, 271, 274–77
Ripple, Lt. Col. Richard W.: 351, 362–63, 369
Ritchie, Maj. William D.: 64n
River crossings: 120, 198
    Albert Canal: 96–98, 101–03, 107–09, 124
    demonstrations: 614
    Geul: 107, 109
    Inde: 511–15
    Leopold Canal: 221
    Maastricht Canal: 109, 113
    Mark: 224–26
    Meuse: 96–98, 101–03, 106
    Neder Rijn: 196–98
    plans for Roer River: 516–17
    Pruem: 61, 63, 255–56
    Sauer: 57, 60–61, 64–65
    Vicht: 76
    Waal: 176–77, 179–82
    Wurm: 261–62, 264–67, 269–70
Road Junction 471: 335–37, 339
Roadblocks: 89, 145, 160, 162, 167, 178, 289, 298, 313, 328, 339, 347, 432, 450, 462, 564
Roadblocks, German: 47, 52, 66–67, 75–77, 101, 108, 175, 335
Roads
    deteriorating: 386, 402, 404, 588–89
    importance of road nets: 29, 90, 92, 96, 346, 471, 496, 518, 523, 534, 586–87
    lack of: 29–30, 55, 131, 134, 200, 233, 350, 359, 416, 420, 432, 434, 436, 490, 492, 564, 606
Roads U-V-W-X-Y-Z (Huertgen Forest): 432–38, 444, 464–67, 477, 587, 590
Robertson, Maj. Gen. Walter M.: 600, 606, 609–12, 614
Robey, S. Sgt. Paul W. Jr.: 418n
Rocherath: 601, 606–07, 611–12
Rocket launcher, 2.36-inch. *See* Bazooka.
Rocket launcher, 4.5-inch: 28
Rodwell, Col. James S.: 49, 52–53
Roehe: 503–04
Roelsdorf: 590
Roer plain: 30, 283n, 328, 399, 409, 415–16, 425, 428, 469, 473, 475–77, 482, 484, 489, 515, 519, 530, 537, 562, 582, 593, 596, 616, 618
    terrain and defenses: 480, 496–98, 501–02, 504–07, 510, 517–18, 520–24, 528–29, 534, 538, 557, 564, 567, 568, 572, 574, 578, 583
Roer River: 29–30, 66–68, 80, 90, 111, 112, 253,

Roer River—Continued
    278, 285, 323–24, 341, 344–46, 369, 393, 394, 397, 399, 402, 403, 406, 408, 415–16, 428, 430, 451, 457, 459, 461, 465, 472, 482, 492, 496–98, 503, 507, 509, 510, 516–17, 522, 523–24, 525, 538, 539, 542, 544, 545, 547, 548, 556, 558, 559, 561–68, 571–74, 576, 577, 580, 582–86, 587, 590–96, 596n
Roer River Dams: 30, 324–28, 331, 342–43, 342n, 346, 374, 406–07, 410, 451, 463, 493, 517, 566, 566n, 574, 595–601, 606, 610, 612, 615, 619
Roerdorf: 571–73
Roermond: 134, 235–38, 346, 395, 520, 546, 594
Roesler, Colonel: 83, 85
Roesslershof Castle: 479–80, 484–85
Roetgen: 67, 69–70, 72, 78, 83, 325, 492, 528
Roetgen Forest: 66, 72, 78, 85, 87, 90, 94
Rogers, Col. Thomas DeF.: 286
Rollesbroich: 85, 92, 602–03, 606
Roosendaal–Breda highway: 224
Roosma, Col. John S.: 549–50, 552
Roscheid: 44–47
Rose, Maj. Gen. Maurice: 72, 72n, 80, 89, 91, 423
Rosebaum, Col. Dwight A.: 238
Rotation of troops: 398, 612, 614, 618
Roth: 52
Rothe Erde: 309
Rother Weh Creek: 331, 432–33, 436
Rott: 72–73, 76
Rotterdam: 29, 210, 210n
Roush, Pfc. Luther: 78
Rowboats: 148, 171
Royal Air Force: 137–38, 199n, 228, 404, 412, 520, 597–98
    Tactical Air Force, 2d: 5, 138, 169n, 196, 548
    Troop Carrier Group, 38: 128
    Troop Carrier Group, 46: 128
Royal Navy: 214
"Rubble pile": 455, 457
Rudder, Lt. Col. James E.: 461n
Ruhr: 6–7, 18, 28–29, 36, 113, 120–21, 134, 198, 203, 205, 208, 210–15, 231–33, 240–41, 248, 377, 391, 595, 597
Ruhrberg: 324–25
Rumors: 141, 162
Rundstedt, Generalfeldmarschall Gerd von: 5–6, 15–18, 43, 60, 63, 69, 82, 87–88, 135, 143, 201, 222–23, 243, 245–46, 273, 284, 289, 299n, 314, 397, 427, 530, 547, 567, 616. *See also OB WEST.*
Ryan, Col. John L., Jr.: 240

's Hertogenbosch: 146, 152, 221
Saar Basin: 7, 135n
Saar River: 31, 34, 616
Sabotage: 11

Saeffeler Creek: 237
St. Antonis: 195
St. Joeris: 502–03
St. Lô: 20, 384, 413, 619
St. Lô–Périers road: 254, 404–05n
St. Oedenrode: 131, 144–46, 150, 152–53, 188, 194–95, 206
St. Vith: 3, 30, 36, 41, 491, 251
Salvatorberg: 309, 311, 315
Sand tables: 255–56, 500
Satchel charges. See Demolition charges.
Sauer River: 30, 56–60, 64–65, 614
Saverne Gap: 7n
Schack, Generalleutnant Friedrich August: 69–71, 75, 77–78, 83, 87, 91, 98, 103–05, 107, 110, 112, 257
Schaefer, S. Sgt. Joseph E.: 95n
Schafberg: 587–92
Schafer, 2d Lt. Paul H.: 584n
Scharnhorst Line: 68, 72–73, 75–77, 81, 84–85
Schaufenberg: 296–97
Schelde estuary: 6, 16, 130, 207
   clearing the banks: 210, 212–22, 227–29, 377
   German control of: 99, 123, 125, 127, 150, 207, 212, 215
Scherpenseel: 404, 409, 422–24
Schevenhuette: 80, 86–89, 91–93, 328–30, 338, 340, 399, 408, 415–16, 427–28, 430–32, 464, 475, 477, 492
Schevenhuette–Langerwehe highway: 421–22
Schierwaldenrath: 267
Schijndel: 187–91
Schill Line: 68, 70, 75–78, 80, 88, 90
Schleiden: 537–38, 537n
Schlich: 586
Schmidt: 323–25, 328, 330–32, 336, 340–58, 360–61, 363–64, 367–68, 373–74, 377, 399–400, 429, 431, 440, 451, 455, 463, 588, 601, 603, 608
Schmidt, Generalleutnant Hans: 99, 101, 103, 103n, 105–07, 110–11, 330–31, 333, 337–39, 346
Schmidt–Lammersdorf road: 352
Schmidthof: 67, 72–73, 75–76
Schnee Eifel: 30, 34, 40–44, 49–55, 55n, 68–69, 341, 399, 612
Schoenberg: 52
Schoenthal: 478
Schophoven: 584
Schuetzenpanzerwagen. See Half-tracks.
Schultz, Capt. Robert H.: 47–48
Schwammenauel Dam: 30, 324–25, 325n, 328, 342, 345, 597–98
Schwarzer Mann. See Hill 697.
Schwerin, Generalleutnant Gerhard Graf von: 70–71, 75, 81–82, 91, 283, 320

Scorpion (flail) tanks. See Tanks.
SCR–300: 569
SCR–509: 569–70
SCR–536: 350, 570
SCR–584: 382
"Screeming Meemie." See Nebelwerfer.
Seaborne invasion: 135, 201
Searchlights: 138, 610–11. See also Battlefield illumination.
Sedan: 56n
Seely, Col. Theodore A.: 44, 47–48, 347, 349–50, 372
Seille River: 597
Seine River: 8, 11–13, 121
Seitz, Col. John F. R.: 309, 312–13, 420–21, 475–77, 491
Sellerich: 53–54
Setliffe, Lt. Col. Truman H.: 367
Setterich: 518, 523–26, 528–29, 534–38, 540–41, 554, 560
Sevenig: 3, 44
SHAEF. See Supreme Headquarters, Allied Expeditionary Forces.
Shea, Brig. Gen. George D.: 524
Shelters: 312, 576
Sheridan, Pfc. Carl V.: 486–87, 487n
Sheridan, 1st Lt. David: 512–13
Sherman tanks. See Tanks, medium.
Shesniek, S. Sgt. Paul: 509
Shipley, 1st Lt. John: 513
Shortages
   ammunition, 37, 45, 55–56, 68, 86, 95, 114, 172, 214, 259, 276, 341, 383, 386, 521, 562, 593
   antifreeze: 387
   food: 172, 186
   gasoline: 4, 11–13, 29, 36–37, 57, 62, 72, 96, 115
   medical supplies: 186
   replacements: 388–89
   spare parts: 385–86
   tanks: 86, 386, 521
   transport: 4, 7, 11, 13, 213, 381, 383–84
Shortages, German
   ammunition: 26, 43, 63, 150, 331, 562
   equipment: 26
   fuel: 63–64, 296
   signal equipment: 100
   small arms: 331
   transport: 100
   war industry: 392–93
   weapons: 331
Shower points: 398, 613
Shugg, Brig. Gen. R. P.: 566n
Sibbald, Capt. George H.: 306
Siegfried Line (Siegfriedstellung): 30, 30n. See also West Wall.

Siegfried Line Campaign
    a battle of attrition: 622
    comparison with Normandy: 523, 528–29, 617–19, 621
    German delaying action: 594, 616
    slow pace of: 602
    summary of gains and losses: 616–22
Siersdorf: 528, 535–38
Sievers, Generalleutnant Karl: 123, 125
Silvester, Maj. Gen. Lindsay McD.: 237–38, 240–41, 244, 246–47
Simmerath: 602–03, 606, 611
Simmons, Capt. Ross Y.: 298
Simonds, Lt. Gen. G. G.: 220, 228
Simonskall: 349–50, 352, 355, 359, 361
Simpelveld: 110
Simpson, Lt. Gen. William H.: 251, 318–19, 379, 400–403, 406, 498–99, 516, 521–23, 545, 558n. See also Army, Ninth.
Sims, Lt. Hugo, Jr.: 203
Sink, Col. Robert F.: 144, 148, 152–53, 189–90, 195
Sirokin, Pvt. Martin: 263, 267
Sittard: 108–09, 113–14, 236–37, 241, 253
Slag piles: 496, 510
Slave labor: 393
Small unit actions: 47, 146–47, 150–51, 160–61, 179–81, 261–64, 291–93, 453–54, 461–62, 471–72, 479, 481, 485–87, 490–91, 512–14, 528, 550, 564, 569–71, 576–77, 610
Smith, Col. George A., Jr.: 287–88, 291, 477–79
Smith, 1st Lt. James J.: 175
Smith, Lt. Gen. Walter B.: 122, 129
Smoke, tactical use of: 91, 179–80, 254, 260, 305, 309, 332, 336, 446, 449, 465, 473, 481, 482, 509, 526, 528, 542, 563, 570, 572, 575, 577, 584n, 586, 590
Smythe, Col. George W.: 78, 89, 480–82, 485
Snipers: 335, 350, 589
Soissons: 12
Sonnefield, Lt. Col. J. E.: 360
Sosabowski, Maj. Gen. S.: 186, 195
Sound and flash: 57, 276, 336, 443
Sound effects: 614
South Beveland: 123, 209, 215, 219–22, 227–28
Spa: 24
Special Forces teams: 184
Special Troops, 23d: 614
Spielmannsholz Hill. See Hill 559.
Sponheimer, General der Infanterie Otto: 219–20
Sportplatz: 574–77
Stalzemburg: 3, 57
Standdaarbuiten: 224–26
Steckenborn: 603
Stockem: 59, 61
Stockigt: 60–61
Stokes, Lt. Col. William M., Jr.: 113

Stolberg: 66, 72, 75–77, 80, 88–91, 98, 114, 286, 290, 295, 309, 399–400, 408, 425–26, 475, 499, 502–03, 506, 587
Stolberg Corridor: 29–30, 66, 68–69, 82, 258, 399, 408, 416
    first battle: 71–80, 90–91, 109, 111, 115, 283, 285, 330, 410
    November offensive attacks: 421–24, 475, 480, 496
Strasbourg: 391
Strass: 587–92, 587n
Strategy, Allied: 6–10. See also Planning.
Straube, General der Infanterie Erich: 69, 83, 87, 330, 333, 337, 353, 372
Strauch: 603
Strauch–Schmidt highway: 601
Street fighting. See House-to-house fighting.
Strickler, Lt. Col. Daniel B.: 347, 349, 352, 358, 366
Stroh, Maj. Gen. Donald A.: 441, 444–45, 447–48
Student, Generaloberst Kurt: 100–101, 109–10, 123–25, 135, 140–42, 146, 150, 153, 188, 193, 200–203, 235–36, 247, 395
Stumpf, Lt. Col. R. H.: 336–39
Sueggerath: 546, 551, 554–55
Summers, Lt. Col. William M.: 510
Supply: 129, 134, 199, 200, 214, 230, 233, 532, 540, 554, 571, 596. See also Air supply; Logistics; Ports; Shortages; Woods fighting.
Supreme Headquarters, Allied Expeditionary Forces (SHAEF): 6–8, 16, 119, 121–22, 214, 388, 619. See also Eisenhower, Gen. Dwight D.
    Air Priorities Board: 383
    and Roer River dams: 327, 374, 597–98
Surprise: 91, 136n, 140, 170, 243, 245, 266, 333, 362, 394, 426, 433, 466, 525–26, 531, 553, 561, 563, 584, 602–04, 608
Sussman, Pvt. Morris: 470
Sutherland, Col. Edwin M.: 101, 256–57, 264, 266, 268, 275, 279, 295, 297–99, 304–05, 500
Swanberg, Cpl. Bertol C.: 418n
Swift, Col. Ira P.: 533–34
Swimmers: 203
Swinden: 137

Tactical Air Commands
    IX: 5, 24, 24n, 254, 278, 299, 309, 332, 343, 381–82, 404, 412, 418, 446, 449, 508
    XIX: 5, 382
    XXIX: 380–81, 404, 412, 498, 500, 520, 525, 532, 539–40, 548, 572, 572n, 576–77
Tactical Reconnaissance Group, 67th: 24n
Tactics. See Night operations; Pillboxes; Small unit actions; Surprise; Tank-infantry tactics; Woods fighting.

Tank Battalions
  10th: 446, 449–50
  40th: 569–70
  70th: 472
  707th: 351, 362
  709th: 448, 453, 603–04
  743d: 279, 296, 502, 558
  744th: 237, 588, 591
  745th: 479
  747th: 536, 538, 576
  750th: 510
Tank Destroyer Battalions
  628th: 63n
  771st: 531
  893d: 360, 462, 604
  899th: 480n
Tank Destroyers: 27, 275, 287–88, 291, 293, 296, 312, 347, 359–60, 363, 368, 374, 480n, 500–501, 514, 527, 566n, 620–21. *See also* Artillery support; Tank-infantry tactics.
Tank dozers: 264
Tank guns
  75-mm: 27, 46, 436, 461, 532, 538
  76-mm: 27, 461, 532, 541
  90-mm: 27, 487
Tank-infantry tactics: 50, 85, 89, 91, 106, 175, 181–82, 195–96, 268–69, 272, 310–12, 357–38, 363, 417–18, 422–24, 436, 448, 449–50, 452–53, 455, 459, 472–73, 483–84, 487, 491, 500–501, 526–27, 536–37, 538, 540, 544, 555, 584–86, 588–90, 603–04, 620
  German: 225, 275, 290–93, 296, 298–99, 301, 353–58, 368, 419, 460–61, 514, 531–32, 539, 541, 552
  ineffective coordination: 276, 303, 466, 534–35
Tank retrievers: 446, 491, 533
Tanks. *See also* Armor; Tank guns; Tank-infantry tactics.
  captured: 63, 291
  Churchill: 223, 560
  Crocodile (flame-throwing): 542–43, 553–55, 560
  disabled: 295, 355, 359–60, 369, 446, 491, 527n, 544, 578
  effect of mud on: 257, 264–65, 288, 305, 422–23, 443, 479, 484, 510, 518, 526, 530n, 535–36, 542, 550, 555, 592, 603
  heavy: 27n, 621
  light: 434, 436, 443
  losses: 65, 65n, 67, 73–74, 77, 79, 91, 199, 239–40, 271, 272, 275, 280, 288, 336, 363, 368, 374, 422–24, 434, 450, 452, 472, 484, 485, 487, 510, 514, 526–27, 530, 530n, 532, 533, 542, 544, 560, 573, 578, 588–89, 593–94, 594n, 617
  medium: 16, 27, 620
  Scorpion (flail): 74, 548, 550, 591

Tanks—Continued
  support strength: **20–21**, **68**, **86**, **86n**, **247**, **386**, 409, 524, 540n, 594
  traction expedients: 518, 526
Tanks, German: 76, 79, 121, 153, 186, 187, 239, 242, 243n, 270, 360, 418, 438, 509, 571, 611–12
  losses: 64, 245, 296, 298–99, 301–02, 318, 318n, 357–58, 374, 419, 448, 514, 531–32, 540–41, 544, 560, 564, 617
  Mark IV: 27, 53, 59, 296, 363, 450
  Mark V (Panther): 16, 27, 73, 78, 153, 195, 357, 363, 422, 531–32, 541, 559n
  Mark VI (Tiger): 27, 290–91, 491, 530–32
  support strength: 51, 81, 87, 121, 236, 243, 283, 284, 303, 308, 397, 410–11, 519–20, 562, 567, 582
Task Forces (Combat Teams)
  1: 271–73, 526, 531–32, 541–43
  2: 272, 275, 527, 532, 542–43
  A: 533–34, 541–42
  B: 541–42
  X: 527, 531–32, 540–41, 543, 551, 566
  Biddle: 547, 566–67
  Boyer: 455, 457
  Davis: 367–68
  Doan: 74–75
  Hamberg: 449–50, 452–55, 457
  Hogan: 91, 314–15
  King: 73–76
  Lovelady: 73–74, 76, 78–79, 91, 422
  Mills: 76, 91, 422–24
  Quinn: 268–69
  Richardson: 483–85, 492n, 508
  Ripple: 362–64, 367–68
  Stokes: 113–14
Taylor, Brig. Gen. George A.: 55, 316
Taylor, Maj. Gen. Maxwell D.: 144–48, 152–54, 186–90, 192, 203, 205
Telephones: 224, 272, 570, 609, 614
Terneuzen: 221
Terrain: 19, 26, 28–30, 200, 248, 408, 409, 480, 500, 617, 619, 620
  forest barriers: 40, 53, 55, 57, 66, 72, 82–83, 90, 600, 606. *See also* Huertgen Forest.
  high ground: 131, 155–56, 170, 323
  marshes and waterways: 96, 108, 130–31, 133, 148, 187, 215, 233, 238, 244, 247
  the Roer plain: 496, 511, 517–18, 530, 545, 572, 583, 587
Tettau, Generalleutnant Hans von: 142
Teveren: 112
Thompson, Lt. John S.: 160
Thompson, Sgt. Max: 314n
Thompson, Lt. Col. Oscar H.: 85, 92–94, 333–34, 336–38
Thorson, Brig. Gen. Truman C.: 23, 400, 493

Tiefen Creek: 373, 451–53, 457
Tiger tanks. *See* Tanks, German.
Tilburg: 136, 142, 146, 150, 200, 219, 221
Toad Hill. *See* Hill 87.9.
Todt, Dr. Fritz: 31
Todten Bruch. *See* Deadman's Moor.
Touart, Col. Anthony J.: 224, 227, 425–28, 506–09, 511
Tournai: 119
Towle, Pvt. John R.: 182n
Traffic control: 134, 185, 186, 186n, 190–92, 402–03
Training: 255–56, 262, 469n, 618, 621
Traitors: 136n
Transportation: 11–13, 17, 68, 129, 383–84, 411. *See also* Shortages.
Travis, Pvt. Ben J.: 509
Trench foot: 360, 372–73, 429, 438, 455, 474, 557, 604, 606, 614, 618
Trenches. *See* Fortifications.
Trier: 14, 30, 34, 42, 57
Tripsrath: 546, 551
Troop Carrier Command, IX: 128, 199n
Troop carrier operations: 120, 128, 129–30, 132–33, 132n, 136–40, 144–45, 154, 157, 170, 172, 186, 196, 199–200, 199n. *See also* MARKET-GARDEN.
Troop strength
  Allied (September 1944): 3–5, 20, 23–24, 36
  Allied (October 1944): 378–79, 387–88, 387n
  MARKET-GARDEN: 128, 133, 139, 159, 170
  November offensive: 397, 400–403, 409, 440, 516–17, 521, 568, 580–82, 593, 600
  21st Army Group problems: 204–05, 213
Troop strength, German
  Aachen and West Wall sectors: 69–71, 75, 81, 91, 109, 111, 257–58, 273–74, 277, 283–84, 286–87, 289–90, 296, 300, 308, 314
  Albert Canal line: 98–101, 123–24
  Antwerp approaches: 218–20
  Ardennes counteroffensive buildup: 393–95, 616
  holding before the West Wall: 41–43, 51, 57, 60, 63
  Huertgen Forest: 93, 95, 330–31, 337, 346, 353–54, 359, 417–18, 431–32, 437, 465, 487–88
  Monschau Corridor: 83, 86–87, 601–02
  opposing MARKET-GARDEN: 126–27, 135–36, 142–43, 164, 170, 176–77, 188–89, 193, 201–02
  opposing November offensive: 395–97, 409–11, 499–500, 530, 559, 567, 582–83, 594
  September 1944: 5–6, 15–18
  west of the Maas: 235–37, 243, 247
Truman, President Harry: 418n
Tucker, Col. Reuben H.: 158, 160–61, 174, 176
Tufts, Lt. William C.: 225

Turner, Lt. Col. Robert G.: 113
Turnhout: 222
"Type-1944 Infantry Division": 15, 87

Uden: 188–94
Uebach: 256, 267, 269–78, 523
Uettfeld: 44–48, 612, 613
Ulmer, 1st Lt. Arthur A.: 513
Urft Dam: 30, 324–25, 326n, 327, 597–98
Urft River: 325–26
Urquhart, Maj. Gen. R. C.: 172–73, 185–86, 198
UTAH Beach: 23, 49n

"V–13": 310n
V-weapons: 8, 208, 229–30
Valburg: 195, 197
Valkenburg: 98, 107, 109
Valkenswaard: 133, 149
van Hoof, Jan: 184n
Van Houten, Col. John G.: 335
Vanderheid, Sgt. Linus: 487
Vandervoort, Lt. Col. B. H.: 174, 177, 181–82
VARSITY: 132n
Veghel: 131, 145–46, 152–53, 160, 187–92, 194–95, 201, 203, 206, 236
Venlo: 156, 238, 242, 243, 247–48, 548
Venlo–Nijmegen highway: 167
Venray: 231, 235, 238, 242, 248
Verlautenheide: 80, 88, 284, 286–91, 297, 300, 304, 309, 425, 499, 504
Versailles: 211
Verviers: 36, 66, 72, 398
Vianden: 40, 43, 56–57
Vicht: 72, 78, 80
Vicht River: 66, 72, 75, 76, 78, 90, 325
Village strongpoints. *See* Roer plain.
Visé: 99, 101, 105
Vortum: 238
Vosges Mountains: 381
Vossenack: 323, 331, 336–39, 341, 343–47, 349–51, 353–55, 357–59, 361–68, 371, 372–73, 400, 429, 438, 441, 451, 453, 455, 457, 465, 601–02
Vossenack ridge: 336–37, 344–45, 347, 349–50, 358, 361, 364–66, 370, 372–73, 455
Vught: 140

Waal River: 29, 120, 126, 131, 134, 142, 154–58, 166, 174–75, 179–82, 193, 198, 200–201, 203
Wadden Islands: 135
Waffen-SS: 15–16, 126
Wahlerscheid: 601, 606–12
Walcheren Island: 123, 209, 212, 215, 218–21, 228–29
Waldenburg, Generalmajor Siegfried von: 353–54, 359, 365, 374
Wallace, Maj. Robert W.: 568–69

Wallendorf: 43, 56–65, 115, 251, 620

Walther, Colonel: 124–25, 188–89, 191–92

Waltz, Col. Welcome P.: 223, 225, 503, 507, 509–10

War production: 12, 25

War production, German: 6, 31, 390, 392–93

Warden: 499, 502

Warren, Lt. Col. Shields, Jr.: 162–67

Warsaw: 141

Waurichen: 273, 278, 518, 523, 526

Weapons. *See also entries for various types of weapons.*
  Allied numerical superiority: 5
  comparison of U.S. and German: 25–28
  performance in Siegfried Line Campaign: 620–21
  psychological effects: 260, 262–63, 309n, 334, 413–14, 444–45, 455, 489, 575–76

Weasels (Cargo Carrier M–29): 311, 343, 351, 352, 355, 359–60, 371

Weather: 13, 19, 35, 121, 129, 210, 214, 219, 221, 364, 377, 381, 392, 400, 403, 405–07, 411–12, 475, 504, 518, 521, 522, 557, 572, 574, 578, 598, 616, 618
  effect on tactical operations: 13, 24, 52, 55, 57, 61, 86, 88, 95, 106, 115, 132, 136–37, 154, 169n, 172, 176, 186, 190, 192, 196, 224, 227, 229, 243, 257, 259–60, 270, 274, 276, 278, 288, 302, 332, 340, 344–46, 347–48, 351, 352, 357, 360, 363–64, 372, 373, 382, 402, 418, 420–22, 441–44, 453–54, 455–57, 467, 479, 492, 506, 508, 525, 532, 534, 540, 542, 555, 563, 572n, 576, 604, 607–09
  and failure of MARKET-GARDEN: 199–200, 618

Weaver, Brig. Gen. Willaim G.: 448, 451–52, 455, 457, 461–63

Weert: 231, 246

Wegelein, Colonel: 337–39, 343, 347, 353

Weh Creek: 416, 419–20, 432–33, 464, 475, 477–80, 484, 510

Wehrkreis VI: 126–27, 142, 164, 193

Wehrkreis X: 189

Weissenberg: 422

Weissenberg (hill). *See* Hill 283.

Weisser Weh: 92–93, 331–39, 347, 428–29, 432–38, 442, 444–45, 464

Weiswampach: 3

Weisweiler: 482, 484, 505–09. *See also* Eschweiler-Weisweiler industrial triangle.

Weisweiler–Langerwehe highway: 475, 480, 484–85, 489

Welz: 572

Wenau: 477–78, 480

Wenau Forest: 66, 68, 72, 75, 78–80, 87, 90, 94, 399

Werth: 409, 422

Wesel: 113, 122n, 134, 138

Wessum: 233, 235, 237, 241

West, Col. Gustavus W.: 522

West Stellung: 106

West Wall: 6, 12, 16, 18, 29, 41–43, 48, 94–95, 119–21, 208, 211, 281, 283n, 318, 332, 342, 390, 401–02, 600, 616, 618, 622
  attacks north of Aachen: 96, 107–15, 205, 231, 233, 240–41, 251–80, 283, 283n, 284–86, 293, 298, 302, 314, 319n
  construction and defenses: 30–35, 38, 40, 44–47, 50, 56–57, 66–69, 72–75, 77, 84, 95, 103, 115, 520n, 601. *See also* Pillboxes.
  defended for political reasons: 38, 41, 68
  "impregnability": 18, 31, 34–35, 51
  MARKET-GARDEN failure to turn north flank: 198, 212, 377
  race for: 41–43, 111
  reconnaissance in force penetrations: 37–41, 44–95, 283n, 287, 612

Westkapelle dike: 228–29

Westphal, General Siegfried: 62n, 143n

Wettlingen: 61, 63

White, Brig. Gen. Isaac D.: 108–09, 523, 526, 532, 540, 542–43

White phosphorus, tactical use of: 179–80, 511, 521, 584

Whitis, Pvt. Evan: 306, 313–14

Wierzbowski, Lt. Edward L.: 146–47, 150–52

Wies Creek: 607–08

Wijbosch: 189, 191–92

Wijk: 106–08

Wilck, Col. Gerhard: 283–84, 307–08, 312–16, 410, 519

Wilhelmina Canal: 131, 144–48, 150, 152–53, 187, 200

Wilhelmshoehe: 476, 479, 481–84, 507–08

Willems Canal: 131, 145, 188, 190–91

Williams, Maj. George S.: 461–63

Williams, Lt. Col. John: 287–88

Williams, Col. Laurin L.: 571

Williams, Maj. Gen. Paul L.: 128

Williamson, Lt. Col. Ellis V.: 564

Wilson, Col. Robert W.: 23n

Windmills: 528–29

Winterhilfswerk (Winter Relief Project): 316

Winterization: 383–84, 386–87

Winton, Lt. Col. Walter F., Jr.: 156, 167

Wise, Sgt. Alvin R.: 312, 312n

Withdrawal operations: 91, 166, 196–98, 225, 306, 357, 370–72, 444, 532, 612, 614

Withdrawal operations, German: 99, 104–06, 108, 112, 124, 218–19, 222–23, 505, 508, 558, 560, 563, 584

Wittkopf, 1st Lt. Phillip W.: 53, 53n

Wittscheidt: 331, 334, 336–39, 347–48

Woensdrecht: 220–21, 227

Wolfheze Station: 171

Wolpert, T. Sgt. Howard: 263
Woods fighting: 52–53, 78, 92, 94, 323, 332–34, 336, 339, 344–50, 366–68, 371, 420, 431–32, 436–37, 441–45, 465-67, 469-70, 476-77, 587, 590, 607–09. *See also* Huertgen Forest; Monschau Forest.
supply problems: 333, 335, 351, 360, 361–62, 367, 432, 434–38, 444, 465, 467, 476, 478, 588, 590–91, 608
Woodyard, Lt. Col. Thomas R.: 554
World War 1: 25, 30, 99, 323, 392
Wuerm: 546, 551, 554–55, 566–68, 574
Wuerselen: 253, 279, 284–85, 294–95, 297, 299–300, 303–06, 308, 313, 399, 402, 408, 424, 496–501, 516, 519, 522, 529, 544, 548
Wuestwezel: 222
Wurm River: 29–30, 111, 252–61, 264–71, 277–78, 295, 302–03, 304–05, 496, 516, 517, 519, 520, 523, 532, 545–56, 566

Wyler: 155, 158, 166, 176–78, 193

York, Col. Robert H.: 589
Youenes, Pvt. Brent: 262

Zangen, General der Infanterie Gustav von: 125, 193, 218–19, 223, 395, 410, 417–18, 539, 559, 592
Zeebrugge: 215, 221
Zeglien, Pvt. Harold: 263
Zon: 131, 144, 146–48, 150, 152–53, 174, 187, 189, 200, 206
Zonsche Forest: 146–48, 150, 151n, 152
Zuider Zee. *See* IJsselmeer.
Zundert: 222–24
Zweibruggen: 272
Zweifall: 72, 78, 90, 92, 94

☆ U.S. GOVERNMENT PRINTING OFFICE: 1993   333–165